PROBLEM SOLVING AND PROGRAMMING CONCEPTS

Fourth Edition

PROBLEM SOLVING AND PROGRAMMING CONCEPTS

Maureen Sprankle
College of the Redwoods

PRENTICE HALL

Upper Saddle River, New Jersey
Columbus, Ohio

Library of Congress Cataloging-in-Publication Data
Sprankle, Maureen.
Problem solving and programming concepts / Maureen Sprankle. —
4th ed.
p. cm.
Includes index.
ISBN 0-13-631805-3
1. Electronic digital computers—Programming. 2. Problem solving-
-Data processing. I. Title.
QA76.6.S684 1998
005.1—dc21 97-19415
CIP

Cover art: Marjory Dressler
Editor: Charles E. Stewart, Jr.
Production Editor: Mary M. Irvin
Design Coordinator: Julia Zonneveld Van Hook
Cover Designer: Rod Harris
Production Manager: Deidra M. Schwartz
Marketing Manager: Debbie Yarnell
Production Coordination: BookMasters

This book was set in Times Roman by BookMasters and was printed and bound by the Banta Company. The cover was printed by Phoenix Color Corp.

Printed in the United States of America

10 9 8 7 6

ISBN: 0-13-631805-3

Prentice-Hall International (UK) Limited, *London*
Prentice-Hall of Australia Pty. Limited, *Sydney*
Prentice-Hall of Canada, Inc., *Toronto*
Prentice-Hall Hispanoamericana, S. A., *Mexico*
Prentice-Hall of India Private Limited, *New Delhi*
Prentice-Hall of Japan, Inc., *Tokyo*
Simon & Schuster Asia Pte. Ltd., *Singapore*
Editora Prentice-Hall do Brasil, Ltda., *Rio de Janeiro*

To my husband, Norm, my three daughters, Bonnie, Heidi, and Tamara,
and my good friend Ann, for their continuing love, support, and understanding

Preface

A knowledge of problem solving and programming concepts is a necessity for those who work with computers, either as programmers or as users. Unfortunately, many students have greater difficulty with problem solving than they do with the syntax of computer languages or applications. Since problem-solving concepts are similar in all languages and applications, students can learn them in one preliminary course. Then, when they move on to language and application courses, both the students and the instructor can concentrate on syntax. This arrangement not only saves time but also decreases frustration for everyone involved, and it improves the success rates of the students.

Although this book is written for students who have little or no computer experience, those who have studied a computer language can benefit from the material. The book is intended for a one-semester introductory course for language or application majors. It can serve as the course textbook or as a supplement. For computer language majors, Units 1, 2, 3, 4, and 5 should be emphasized; for application majors, Units 1, 2, 5 (Chapters 13 and 16 only), and 6.

The text provides a step-by-step progression, with detailed explanations and many illustrations, from the basics of mathematical functions and operators to the design and use of such techniques as codes, indicators, control-breaks, arrays, pointers, file updates, report handling, data structures, and object oriented programming. The tools of problem solving, including structure charts, IPO charts, algorithms, and flowcharts, are demonstrated and explained. "Putting It All Together" sections illustrate the complete solution for a given problem, using the concepts previously presented. In some cases, an earlier solution is updated to incorporate more sophisticated techniques. Throughout the text, problems presented for solution are typical of the business world and provide excellent experience for the students.

DPMA/ACM Equivalents

The content of this text corresponds to parts of the ACM Computing for Information Processing Curriculum Guide (1993) and the DPMA Information Systems Model

Curriculum for the 1990s. The content of this text corresponds to the following subject areas and related knowledge units in the ACM Curriculum Guide:

- Application Generation Strategies (AG)
  - AG1: Common Productivity Software
  - AG3: Fourth Generation Development Methodology
- Programming (PR)
  - PR2: Elements of a Programming Language
  - PR3: Sequence Control
  - PR4: Data Types
  - PR5: Structured Data Types
  - PR6: Introduction to Sorting and Searching
  - PR7: Data Access
- Problem Solution Methodologies (PS)
  - PS2: Algorithm Development

The content of this text corresponds to the DPMA Information Systems Curriculum Guide's Body of Knowledge 1.2: Algorithms and Data Structures under 1.0 Computer Concepts. In referring to both models, this text contains the problem-solving strategies and general information about these subjects. It does not use any actual hands-on learning.

Organization

Unit 1, Introduction to Problem Solving and Programming, presents basic concepts of problem solving, an introduction to how problems are solved on computers, and steps in analyzing a problem and designing an appropriate solution. Unit 2, Structuring Programs for Languages and Applications, examines how and when the various types of logic structures are appropriately used. Unit 3, Data Structures, includes the use of various data structures such as arrays, stacks, linked lists, and binary trees to access and process data. Sort methods and search methods are included in this unit. Unit 4, Object Oriented Programming, includes elements of object oriented programming and scripting. Unit 5, File Processing, includes file concepts, sequential file processing, and random access file processing. Unit 6, Problem Solving for Application Software, concentrates on word processing, desktop publishing, graphics, spreadsheets, database management systems, and document processing. The appendices present formulas commonly used in business applications, sort and merge methods, ASCII and EBCDIC codes, blank forms that can be used in designing solutions, and other problem-solving tools.

Acknowledgments

I am indebted to those who reviewed the manuscript and offered suggestions and constructive comments. In particular, I thank:

- Joan Sappington—North Metro Technical Institute
- Nizar Abudiab—Jackson State Community College
- Robert Coil—Cincinnati St. Tech & Community College

In addition, I wish to thank Terri Vitale, copyeditor, for her invaluable contributions, and, at Prentice Hall, Mary Irvin, Production Editor, for her care and patience during the production process.

Short Contents

Contents

Fourth Edition

PROBLEM SOLVING AND PROGRAMMING CONCEPTS

UNIT ONE

INTRODUCTION TO PROBLEM SOLVING AND PROGRAMMING

Chapter 1

General Problem-Solving Concepts

Overview

Problem Solving in Everyday Life
Types of Problems
Problem Solving with Computers
Difficulties with Problem Solving

Objectives

When you have finished this chapter, you should be able to:

1. Describe the difference between heuristic and algorithmic solutions to problems.
2. List and describe the six problem-solving steps to solve a problem that has an algorithmic solution.

Problem Solving in Everyday Life

People make decisions every day to solve problems that affect their lives. The problems may be as unimportant as what to watch on television or as important as choosing a new profession. If a bad decision is made, time and resources are wasted, so it's important that people know how to make decisions well. There are six steps to follow to assure the best decision. These steps, the six steps in problem solving, include the following:

1. *Identify the problem.* The first step toward solving a problem is to identify the problem. In a classroom situation, most problems have been identified for you and given to you in the form of written assignments or problems out of a book. However, when you are doing problem solving outside of the classroom, you need to make sure you identify the problem before you start solving it. If you don't know what the problem is, you cannot solve it.
2. *Understand the problem.* You must understand what is involved in the problem before you can continue toward the solution. This includes understanding the

knowledge base of the person or machine for whom you are solving the problem. If you are setting up a solution for a person, then you must know what that person knows. A different set of instructions might have to be used depending on this knowledge base. For example, you would use a more detailed set of instructions to tell someone how to find a restaurant in your city if he or she has a limited knowledge of the city than if he or she knows it well. When you are working with a computer, its knowledge base is the limited instructions the computer can understand in the particular language or application you are using to solve the problem. Knowing the knowledge base is very important since you cannot use any instructions outside of this base.

3. *Identify alternative ways to solve the problem.* This list should be as complete as possible. You might want to talk to other people to find other solutions than those you have identified. Alternative solutions must be acceptable ones. You could go from Denver to Los Angeles by way of New York, but this would probably not be an acceptable solution to your travel needs.
4. *Select the best way to solve the problem from the list of alternative solutions.* In this step, you need to identify and evaluate the pros and cons of each possible solution before selecting the best one. In order to do this, you need to select criteria for the evaluation. These criteria will serve as the guidelines for evaluating each solution.
5. *List instructions that enable you to solve the problem using the selected solution.* These numbered, step-by-step instructions must fall within the knowledge base set up in step 2. No instruction can be used unless the individual or the machine can understand it. This can be very limiting, especially when working with computers.
6. *Evaluate the solution.* To evaluate or test a solution means to check its result to see if it is correct, and to see if it satisfies the needs of the person(s) with the problem. (When a person needs a piece of furniture to sleep on, buying him a cot may be a *correct* solution, but it may not be very satisfactory.) If the result is either incorrect or unsatisfactory, then the problem solver must start the process again.

If any of these six steps are not completed well, the results may be less than desired.

People solve problems daily at home, or work, or wherever they go. Problems at home include such things as what to cook for dinner, which movie to see this evening, which car to buy, or how to sell the house. At work, the problems might involve dealing with fellow employees, work policies, management, or customers. The better the decisions an employee can make, the more valuable that person will be to the company. In each case, the six steps in problem solving can be followed. Most people use them without even knowing it.

Take the problem of what to do this evening.

1. Identify the problem. How do the individuals wish to spend the evening?
2. Understand the problem. With this simple problem, also, the knowledge base of the participants must be considered. The only solutions that should be selected are ones that everyone involved would know how to do. You probably would not select as a possible solution playing a game of chess if the participants did not know how to play.
3. Identify alternatives.
   a. Watch television.
   b. Invite friends over.
   c. Play games.

   d. Go to the movies.
   e. Play miniature golf.
   f. Go to the amusement park.
   g. Go to a friend's party.

   The list is complete only when you can think of no more alternatives.
4. Select the best way to solve the problem.
   a. Weed out alternatives that are not acceptable, such as those that cost too much money or do not interest one of the individuals involved.
   b. Specify the pros and cons of each remaining alternative.
   c. Weigh the pros and cons to make the final decision. This solution will be the best alternative if all the other steps were completed well.
5. Prepare a list of steps (instructions) that will result in a fun evening.
6. Evaluate the solution. Are we having fun yet?

By going through these steps, the problem solver can be assured that he or she has arrived at the best possible solution and will achieve the desired results.

Types of Problems

Problems do not always have straightforward solutions. Some problems, such as balancing a checkbook or baking a cake, can be solved with a series of actions. These solutions are called **algorithmic solutions.** Once the alternatives have been eliminated, for example, once one has chosen the best among several methods of balancing the checkbook, the solution can be reached by completing the actions in steps. These steps are called the **algorithm.** The solutions of other problems, such as how to buy the best stock or whether to expand the company, are not so straightforward. These solutions require reasoning built on knowledge and experience, and a process of trial and error. Solutions that cannot be reached through a direct set of steps are called **heuristic solutions.**

The problem solver can use the six steps for both algorithmic and heuristic solutions. However, in step 6, evaluating the solution, the correctness and appropriateness of heuristic solutions are far less certain. It's easy to tell if your completed checkbook balance is correct and satisfactory, but it's hard to tell if you've bought the best stock. With heuristic solutions, the problem solver will often need to follow the six steps more than once, carefully evaluating each possible solution before deciding which is best. Furthermore, this same solution may not be correct and satisfactory at another time, so the problem solver may have to reevaluate and resolve the same problem later. The stock that did well in January may do poorly in June.

Most problems require a combination of the two kinds of solutions.

Problem Solving with Computers

In this book, the term **solution** means the instructions listed during step 5 of problem solving—the instructions that must be followed to produce the best results. **Results** means the outcome or the completed computer-assisted answer. **Program** means the set of instructions that make up the solution after they have been coded into a particular computer language.

Computers are built to deal with algorithmic solutions, which are often difficult or very time-consuming for humans. People are better than computers at developing heuristic solutions. Solving a complicated calculus problem or alphabetizing 10,000 names is an easy task for the computer, but the problem of how to throw a ball or how to speak English is not. The difficulty lies in the programming. How can problems such as how to throw a ball or speak English be solved in a set of steps that the computer can understand?

The field of computers that deals with heuristic types of problems is called artificial intelligence. Artificial intelligence enables a computer to do things like build its own knowledge bank and speak in a human language. As a result, the computer's problem-solving abilities are similar to those of a human being. Artificial intelligence is an expanding computer field.

Until computers can be built to think like humans, people will process most heuristic solutions and computers will process many algorithmic solutions. Therefore, this book will deal only with algorithmic solutions. Heuristic problem solving can help determine alternative solutions. However, for computer use, they must be transformed into an algorithmic format.

Difficulties with Problem Solving

People have many problems with problem solving. Some have not been taught how to solve problems. Others are afraid to make a decision for fear it will be the wrong one. Often, when people go through the problem-solving process, they complete one or more of the steps inadequately. They may not define the problem correctly or may not generate a sufficient list of alternatives. When choosing the best alternative, they may eliminate good alternatives or list the pros and cons too hastily. They may not use a logical sequence of steps in their solution, or they may focus on details before the framework for the solution is in place. Finally, they may incorrectly or haphazardly evaluate the solution.

The problem-solving process is not easy. It takes practice and time to perfect, but in the long run the process proves to be of great benefit.

When solving problems on the computer, one of the most difficult tasks for the problem solver is writing the instructions. Take the task of deciding which number is the largest from a group of three numbers. Almost anyone can immediately tell which is the largest, but many cannot explain the steps they followed to arrive at it. Most people will say, "I can't explain how I know, I just know it!" This explanation is not good enough for the computer. The computer is a tool that will perform only tasks that the user can explain.

The computer has a specific system of communication that programmers and users must learn. This system demands that no step in the solution to a problem be left unstated and that all steps be in the proper order. You must assume the computer knows nothing except what you tell it, and think of it as an ignorant but efficient aid to problem solving.

Summary

The six steps in problem solving lead to the best possible solution to a problem. They include 1) identifying the problem, 2) understanding the problem, 3) identifying alternative solutions, 4) selecting the best solution, 5) preparing a list of instructions to solve the problem by the chosen solution, and 6) evaluating the solution. Solutions to problems are classified as algorithmic or heuristic. Algorithmic solutions are reached in a series of steps. Heuristic solutions are attained through trial and error. Algorithmic solutions are easier to define for computer use than heuristic ones.

Several things can go wrong in the problem-solving process. Sometimes the problem solver does not define the problem correctly or does not complete one or more of the steps. At other times, the list of alternatives is not sufficient or the list of instructions to the computer is incorrect. Sometimes one gets lost in details and overlooks the general framework, or does not test the solution. If the problem-solving process is incomplete, the solution will not produce the desired results.

The steps in problem solving can be applied to problems in daily life as well as to problems put on computer. Good problem-solving techniques enable you to look at a problem logically and unemotionally, saving time and other resources.

New Terms

algorithm	program
algorithmic solution	results
heuristic solution	solution

Questions

1. What are the six steps of problem solving?
2. What is an algorithmic solution to a problem?
3. Name three current problems in your life that could be solved through an algorithmic process.
4. What is a heuristic solution to a problem?
5. Name three current problems in your life that might be solved through a heuristic approach.
6. Name three problems that might arise at home, at school, or in a business that could be solved more efficiently with computer assistance.

Problems

1. Complete the six problem-solving steps to solve one of the problems you listed in Question 3. Follow the form outlined as follows:
   1. Identify the problem.
   2. Understand the problem.
      a. Comments about the problem to aid in understanding it.
      b. Description of the knowledge base (this list would include what you would be expected to know to follow the solution).
   3. Identify alternative solutions.

	Solution	Pros	Cons
a.			
b.			

c.
.
.
.

4. Select the best solution.
   Why did you select this solution?
5. List a set of numbered step-by-step instructions to attain the solution.
   1.
   2.
   3.
   .
   .
   .
6. Test the solution.
   Does this solution work?
   If not, how might you change the solution so it will work?

2. For each of the following tasks, write a set of numbered, step-by-step instructions (a solution) so complete that another person could perform the task without asking questions. Define the knowledge base of this person by listing what you expect the person to know in order to follow your directions. For example, for task a. (below) make a cup of cocoa, the knowledge base might include such things as knowledge of milk or water, refrigerator, pan, spoon, cocoa, cup, range top or microwave, and so forth.
   a. Make a cup of cocoa.
   b. Sharpen a pencil.
   c. Walk from the classroom to the student lounge, your dorm, or the cafeteria.
   d. Start a car (include directions regarding what to do if the car doesn't start).
   e. Get a glass of water from your kitchen.

3. Develop the knowledge base for the following problems:
   a. balancing your checkbook
   b. driving a car
   c. repairing a car
   d. building a house
   e. calculating the cost of using your car for a month

4. Write a solution to the problem of finding the largest number out of three numbers. What are the specific steps that would enable another person to find the largest among three numbers presented?

5. This problem is about Otto the robot. Otto is not very smart; in fact, his knowledge base includes only 15 instructions. However, he can follow a set of instructions and do what he is told, as long as they are part of the 15 instructions in his knowledge base. He executes instructions in sequential order; that is, when he is finished with one instruction, he executes the next one in order. He does only what he is told to do. Otto's knowledge base includes the following instructions:

   Body instructions:
   1. Stand up.
   2. Sit down.
   3. Take a step (take one step forward—must be standing).
   4. Turn (turn right 90 degrees—must be standing).

5. Raise arms (to a forward position perpendicular to body).
6. Lower arms (to a side position).

Arithmetic instructions:
Otto has one number in his memory that he can add one to or subtract one from. This number is zero when the execution of the instruction begins.
7. Add one (adds one to a number in his memory).
8. Subtract one (subtracts one from a number in his memory).

Conditional instructions:
Otto has the ability to make three different types of tests and follow one of two sets of one or more instructions according to the yes or no results for each test. In this way, Otto can make a decision as to the course of action he will take. A test would be set up in the following way (20 is the instruction number in the numbered step-by-step solution to the problem):

Example 1:
20. Test: (the test)
    yes: set of instructions when the result of the test is yes.
    no: set of instructions when the result of the test is no.

(When there are many instructions in the conditional instructions set, it is better to use the goto instruction to transfer to where the instructions are [for yes and no].)

9. Test: Are your hands touching anything?
yes:
no:

10. Test: Are your hands touching a door?
yes:
no:

11. Test: Is the number in your memory zero?
yes:
no:

Example 2:
20 Test: (the test)
Yes: Goto 21
No: Goto 24
21 yes instruction 1
22 yes instruction 2, etc.
23 go to 26
24 no instruction 1
25 no instruction 2, etc.
26 continuation of other instructions

Repeat instruction:
12. Repeat x times [set of instructions](repeats bracketed instructions x number of times—x is a known number).

Example:
18. Repeat five times [take step].
This will instruct Otto to take five steps.

Other instructions:

13. Goto *s* (jumps to instruction step *s*—*s* is a known number—and continues to execute instructions in sequential order at *s*).

Example:
20. Goto 23
This means go to instruction 23 and execute from there.

14. Open door (door will close after Otto walks through it).

15. Stop (halts execution of instructions).

Assumptions:

a. Otto will start in a seated position.

b. Otto will end in a seated position in the same chair.

Example: Write a set of instructions to direct Otto to walk forward five steps and back five steps.
Solution:
1. Stand up.
2. Repeat five times [take step].
3. Repeat two times [turn].
4. Repeat five times [take step].
5. Repeat two times [turn].
6. Sit down.

Another solution: (combining instructions 2–5 above into new instruction 2)
1. Stand up.
2. Repeat two times: [b. repeat two times [turn]] [a. repeat five times [take step]].
3. Sit down.

Write a set of numbered, step-by-step instructions to direct Otto to perform the following tasks:

a. Direct Otto to walk in a square that is three steps on each side. All turns are to be right-hand turns.

b. Direct Otto to walk in a square that is three steps on each side. All turns are to be left-hand turns.

c. Direct Otto to walk to a wall that is any distance forward and then walk back again. Otto will be able to touch both the wall and the back of the chair when his hands are raised. The wall can be any number of whole steps in front of Otto. (*Hint:* This solution requires the use of one of the test instructions.)

d. Modify task c (above) to accommodate a change in the height of the back of the chair so that Otto's raised hands would not touch the back of the chair.

e. Write one set of instructions that will direct Otto through any maze with its entrance and exit on the same side. The maze has no dead ends and no intersections. From Otto's starting position, the entrance is two steps forward. When Otto is facing the entrance, the exit is three steps to his right. Figure 1.1 shows three example mazes for you to test your solution. Do not make separate solutions for each maze. Your solution should allow Otto to walk through any such maze as those shown in Figure 1.1 (*Hint:* Test for a wall and a door at every step.)

f. Modify the solution in task e (above) to accommodate a change in the place of the exit. Your solution should allow for the exit to be any place on the perimeter of

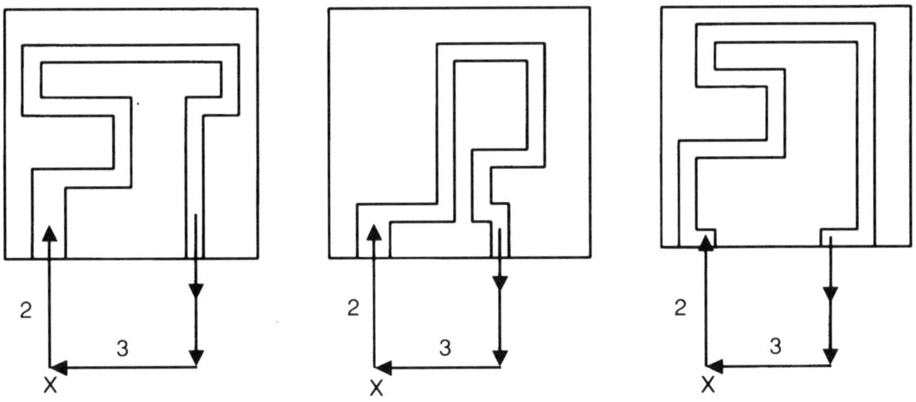

Figure 1.1 Example Mazes for Problem 5e

the maze. Figure 1.2 shows three example mazes for you to test your solution. Again, do not write separate solutions for each maze. Your solution should allow Otto to walk back to his chair from any exit, such as those in Figure 1.2.

6. How would you modify Otto's instruction set (knowledge base) so as to be able to write a solution for the following tasks?

a. Direct Otto to walk in a triangle three steps on a side.

b. Direct Otto to walk to a table and pick up a book.

c. Instruct Otto to detect an object in his path.

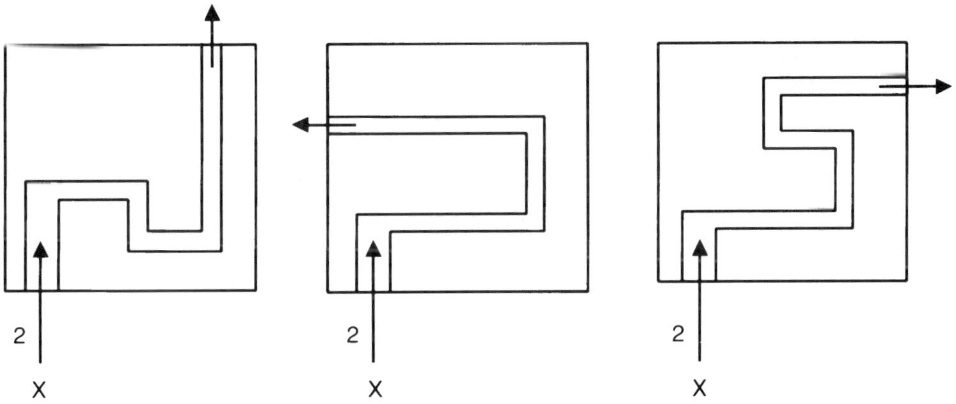

Figure 1.2 Example Mazes for Problem 5f

Chapter 2

Beginning Problem-Solving Concepts for the Computer

Overview

Constants and Variables

Data Types

Numerical Data
Character Data—Alphanumeric Data
Logical Data
Rules for Data Types
Examples of Data Types

Functions

Operators

Expressions and Equations

Objectives

When you have finished this chapter, you should be able to:

1. Differentiate between the basic data types of variables and constants, which include character, numeric, and logical data types.
2. Set up and evaluate expressions and equations using variables, constants, operators, and the hierarchy of operations.

Although problems that arise in daily life are of many types, problems that can be solved on computers generally consist of only three: 1) computational, problems involving some kind of mathematical processing; 2) logical, problems involving relational or logical processing, the kinds of processing used in decision making on the computer; and 3) repetitive, problems involving repeating a set of mathematical and/or logical instructions. This chapter explains some computer fundamentals and demonstrates ways to set up expressions and equations to solve these types of problems on the computer. End users (users of pre-written software), as well as programmers, need to know those computer fundamentals. In this chapter, both end users and programmers will be referred to as programmers.

Two of the most fundamental concepts that you will learn in this chapter are the constant and the variable. A programmer takes the data, the unorganized facts, and the information, the organized facts, relevant to a problem and defines them as constants or variables. They are the building blocks of the equations and expressions that ultimately make up solutions to computer problems. The programmer defines each constant and variable in a problem solution as a particular data type, such as numerical or character.

Other concepts that are essential to developing computer solutions to problems are operators and functions. Operators are the many signs and symbols that show relationships between the constant and variables in the expressions and equations that make up the solution. The programmer has to know all of the many operators and how to use them. The order in which operators are processed is determined by a hierarchy that programmers need to know as well.

Operators are combined with constants and variables to create expressions and equations. Expressions and equations are used in instructions that are the building blocks of the solution. Functions are sets of instructions that are so commonly used that they are built into a computer language or application, saving the programmer the trouble of writing them.

These are key concepts. Without an understanding of how the computer uses and defines data, without knowing what the operators are, and without knowing how to use these concepts to construct expressions and equations, a programmer or a user of applications software cannot effectively use the computer to solve problems.

When you study this chapter, it may help to keep these pointers in mind:

- Take each topic as it is presented, and learn the concepts pertaining to it.
- Understand the examples.
- Complete the questions and problems at the end of the chapter.
- Don't skip sections.
- Don't feel that something is too hard before you make an effort to understand it.
- Take each problem one step at a time.
- Don't skip steps.
- Don't assume anything.
- Don't be afraid to read a passage over again. Once may not be enough!

Constants and Variables

The computer uses constants and variables to solve problems. They are data used in processing. A **constant** is a value, that is, a specific alphabetical and/or numerical value, that never changes during the processing of all the instructions in a solution. Constants can be any type of data—numerical, alphabetical, or special symbols. (Data types are explained in more detail later.) Each constant is either part of the instructions in the solution or a piece of data (a datum) to be entered during processing. In some programming languages and applications, constants can be named. In this case, the constant is given a location in memory and a name. During the execution of the program, this constant is given a value and then is referred to by its name. Once the constant is given a value, it cannot be changed during the execution of the program.

In contrast, the value of a **variable** may change during processing. A programmer must give a name to each variable value used in a solution. The programmer uses a variable name as a reference name for a specific value of the variable. In turn, the computer uses the name as a reference to help it find that value in its memory. The computer sets up a specific memory location to hold the value of each variable name found in a program. Variables can be any data type, just as constants can.

Notice in Table 2.1 that when the value of a constant or a variable contains alphanumeric data—that is, numbers, and/or special symbols—it is surrounded by quotation marks. These marks indicate to the computer that the value is a datum, and not a variable name. The computer must have some way to distinguish between the two. Also notice that the variable names stand for specific data. The variable name CASH has a sum of money as its value. The variable name CITY has a city name as its value. Finally, notice that there are no blank spaces in variable names. A space indicates the end of a variable name for the computer. The programmer decides on the variable name.

In a solution that calculates payroll for a company, the name of the company would be a constant since it does not change. The employee, the hours, and the rate of pay would be variables because the values of these items change for each employee. If there were no such thing as a variable, the programmer would have to write a separate set of instructions for each employee. It is far more efficient to have one rather than a thousand programs to process payroll for 1,000 employees.

The rules for naming variables differ from language to language and application to application. However, the general rule is to name the variable as near to its meaning as

Table 2.1 Constants and Variables on the Computer

Constants	Variables
Rules: Constants cannot be changed. Examples: Value "25" Value " −1.5" Value "ARCATA" Value "95521" Named Constants Rules: A constant cannot be changed after it is initially given a value. Storage location given a name. Referred to by the given name. Example: PI "3.142857"	Rules: Storage locations are given names Values of the contents for name variable locations can be changed. Referred to by variable name in the instructions. Examples: Variable Name—AGE Value "25" Variable Name—CASH Value "83.59" Variable Name—CITY Value "EUREKA" Variable Name—ZIPCODE Value "95501"

possible: PAYRATE for the rate of pay, HOURS for the number of hours worked during the pay period, and the like. Some languages and applications have character-length limitations or other restrictions for names, so adjustments have to be made as necessary. In this book, there will be no character-length limitations for variable names.

It is important to understand the difference between the name of a variable and the value of a variable. The *name* is the label the computer uses to find the correct memory location: the *value* is the contents of the location. The computer uses the variable name to find the location; it uses the value found at the memory location to do the processing.

It is also important to be consistent in the use of variable names because the computer will go only to the location with the specified name, whether or not it is the one intended by the user. For example, if you use HOURS for hours worked, then you must use HOURS at all times in referring to hours worked. If the computer cannot find a memory location by the specified name, it will either name a new memory location and yield an incorrect result, or it will return an error message indicating there is no location as referenced and then cease execution.

Data Types

To process solutions, the computer must have data. **Data** are unorganized facts. They go into the computer as input and are processed by the program. What is returned to the user is output, or **information.** This information is printed in the form of reports. For example, when a computer calculates the balance of a checkbook, data are the checks, the deposits, and the bank charges. The information from the processing is shown on the balance sheet (see Figure 2.1).

The data the computer uses are of many different types. Computers must be told the **data type** of each variable or constant. The most common data types are numerical, character, and logical. A few languages and applications also use the date as a data type. Other languages allow the programmer to define data types.

Numerical Data

Numerical data include all types of numbers (see Table 2.2). Numerical is the only data type that can be used in calculations. The subtypes of numerical data include *integers* and *real numbers.* Integers are whole numbers, such as 5,297 or −376. They can be

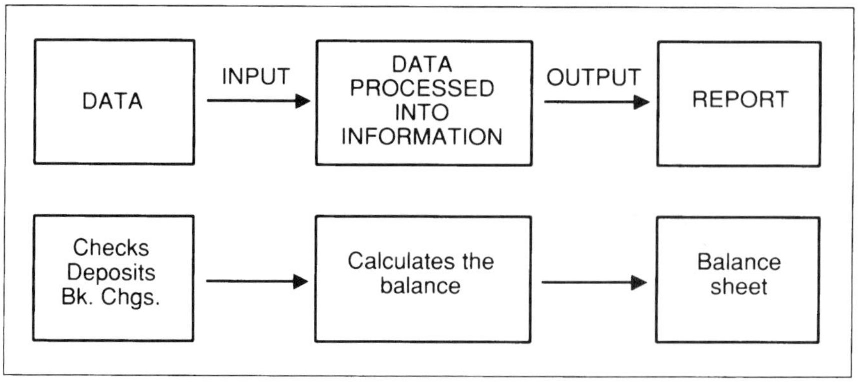

Figure 2.1 Processing Data—How a Computer Balances a Checkbook

Table 2.2 Data Types and Their Data Sets

Data Type	Data Set	Examples
Numeric: INTEGER	All whole numbers	3580 – 46
Numeric: REAL	All real numbers (whole + decimal)	3792.91 4739416.0 0.00246
CHARACTER (surrounded by quotation signs)	All letters, numbers, and special symbols	"A" "a" "M" "z" "k" "1" "5" "7" "8" "0" "+" "=" "(" "%" "$"
STRING (surrounded by quotation signs)	Combinations of more than one character	"Arcata" "95521" "707-444-5555"
LOGICAL	TRUE FALSE	TRUE FALSE

positive or negative. Real numbers, or floating point numbers, are whole numbers plus decimal parts. In problem solving on the computer, programmers use integers when there is no reason for using partial numbers, as when they are designing counters, expressions used for counting things, such as inventory items or people. A real number can be expressed in scientific notation, such as 2.3E5 or 5.4E − 3. In scientific notation, the *E* stands for *times 10 to the power of.* Therefore, 2.3E5 is the same number as 2.3×10^5, or 230,000.0, and 5.4E − 3 is the same number as 5.4×10^{-3}, or 0.0054. A number expressed in scientific notation is always considered a real data type.

Numerical data are used in business for values, such as rate of pay, salary, tax, or price, that have calculations performed on them. Numbers such as an account number or a zip code, which would not have calculations performed on them, would not be designated by the programmer as numerical data.

Each data type has a *data set,* the set of symbols necessary to specify a datum as a particular data type. The data set for the numerical data type includes all base 10 numbers, the plus sign (+), and the negative sign (−). The data set for the integers includes all whole numbers, and for the real numbers, all whole numbers with decimal parts, including zero as a whole number and zero as a decimal part.

Character Data—Alphanumeric Data

The **character data** set, sometimes called alphanumeric data set, consists of all single digit numbers, letters, and special characters available to the computer—a, A, Z, 3, #, &, and so forth—placed within quotation marks. An uppercase letter is considered a different character from a lowercase letter. The ASCII character set contains 256 characters. The first 128 comprise a standard set (see Appendix C for the ASCII and EBCDIC data codes), and the second 128 differ with each computer. Characters cannot be used for calculations even if they consist of only numbers. When more then one character is put together, the computer considers this item a *string*—derived from *a string of characters.*

Character and string data can be compared and arranged in alphabetical order in the following way. The computer gives each character a number. This numerical representation is necessary because the computer works only with numbers. The numbers are compared to see which is larger and are then arranged in ascending numerical order. Since *B* has a larger number representing it than *A, B* is placed after *A. C* would follow *B* by the same method, and so forth. String data can be tested in the same way to alphabetize names, cities, and the like. *Banana* is larger than *Apple* because *B* has a larger number representing it than *A. Joan* is larger than *James* since the letter *o* is attributed a larger number than *a.* Uppercase letters have smaller numerical representations than lowercase letters. It is important to bear this difference in mind when you are comparing letters to see if they are equal.

Character data or string data can be joined together with the + operator in an operation called **concatenation.** When two pieces of character data are joined, the concatenation results in the second being placed at the end of the first, as in "4" + "4" = "44" (not "8"). Concatenation could be used to join a first name with a last name or to join pieces of data together to make a code for an inventory item.

Most data in business—names, account numbers, addresses, cities, states, telephone numbers, zip codes—are string data. As a rule, items that would not have mathematical computations performed on them should be designated string data types. There is another reason for designating a zip code as string data. If you are using numerical data, there is no way to hold onto leading zeros, that is, the zeros at the front of a number, such as 00987. As a result, a zip code on the East Coast could not be entered correctly as a numerical datum. The leading zeros could be preserved only with string data.

Logical Data

Logical data consist of two pieces of data in the data set—the words TRUE and FALSE. (Some languages accept *yes,* T, and Y for TRUE, and *no,* F, and N for FALSE as part of the data set.) These are used in making yes-or-no decisions. For example, logical data type might be used to check someone's credit record; TRUE would mean her credit is okay, and FALSE would mean it's not okay. A home accounting system could use logical data type for check returns; TRUE would mean the check has been returned, and FALSE would mean it has not. There are many such uses for logical data. They are discussed further in later chapters.

Rules for Data Types

1. The data that define the value of a variable or a constant will most commonly be one of three data types: numerical, character (including character string), or logical.
2. The programmer designates the data type during the programming process. The computer then associates the variable name with the designated data type.
3. Data types cannot be mixed. For example, string data cannot be placed in a variable memory location that has been designated as numerical, and vice versa. When the computer expects a certain data type, the user must use that type or the computer will return an error message.
4. Each of the data types uses what is called a *data set* (see Table 2.2). The numerical data uses the set of all base 10 numbers, the plus sign (+), and the negative sign (−); the character type uses the set of all characters available to the computer; the logical data type uses the set of data consisting of the words TRUE and FALSE. The use of any data outside the data set results in an error.

5. Any numeric item that must be used in calculations resulting in a numeric result must be designated as numerical data type. All other numbers should be designated as character or character-string data types, even if the data are all numbers, as in a zip code.

Examples of Data Types

Table 2.3 illustrates some common uses for numerical, character (including character string), and logical data types. The data are drawn from everyday life and business, and are examples of the kinds of data that are commonly used in solving various types of problems on the computer. To the right of the data examples are data types and explanations of why each type is appropriate to the data.

Table 2.3 Examples of Data Types

Data	Data Type	Explanation
The price of an item: 7.39, 12.98	Numerical: real	The price of an item would be used in calculations.
An account number: "A2453," "2987"	Character string	An account number consists of alphanumeric or simply numerical data. It is not used for calculations.
A quantity: 12,389	Numerical: integer	A quantity is used for calculations. It is an integer because it normally is a whole number.
The name of a company: "Smith Corp."	Character string	A name of something is alphabetical and therefore would be character string data type.
A credit check: TRUE, FALSE	Logical	The credit check of a customer would be a choice of two answers such as *yes,* it is ok, or *no,* it is not ok. Therefore, it should be logical data.
A zip code: "95521" "76548" "00538"	Character string	A zip code would be a character string because there are no calculations to be done on a zip code, and the leading zeros need to be retained.
A date: 01/23/87 or "03/14/87"	Date or character string	If the date data type is available then it is used; if not, then it has to be a string because it is alphanumeric.
A Julian date: 187,259	Numerical: integer	A Julian calendar date is the number of days from a given date; i.e., the first of the century. It can be used for calculations.
Social Security Number "333-33-333"	Character string	A SSN is string data because it is alphanumeric and is not used for calculations.

Notice the Julian calendar date. A Julian calendar date is a numerical value equal to the number of days from a constant date, such as the first of the century. This is used when the calculation of the number of days between two dates is needed. By using the Julian calendar number, the problem of crossing from December 31 of one year to January 1 of the next year is eliminated. The date data type uses a numeric form of data in order to calculate the number of days between two dates.

Functions

Functions are small sets of instructions that perform specific tasks and return values. They are usually built into a computer language or application. Functions are used as parts of instructions in a solution. Because they are basic tasks that are used repeatedly in the problem-solving process, by using them a programmer or user can shorten the problem-solving time and improve the readability of the solution. Each language or application has a set of functions within it. This set varies with the language, the application, and the computer. Some languages allow programmers to write their own functions.

Table 2.4 lists and defines the functions that are found in many languages. Functions are unique to each language. As a programmer you need to investigate the functions used in the language in which you are writing your solution. These functions have been divided into classes.

1. *Mathematical functions.* Often used in science and business, math functions calculate such things as square root, absolute value, or a random number. Mathematical functions used primarily for scientific purposes have not been included in the table.
2. *String functions.* These are used to manipulate string variables. For example, they copy part of the string into another variable, find the length or the number of characters in the string, and so forth.
3. *Conversion functions.* These functions are used to convert data from one data type to another. For example, since character strings cannot be used in calculations, one of these functions would convert a string value to a numerical value.
4. *Statistical functions.* These functions are used to calculate things such as maximum values, minimum values, and so forth.
5. *Utility functions.* This class is very important in business programming because most reports require some use of utility functions. They access information outside the program and the language in the computer system. Examples of these include date and time functions.

Table 2.4 is only a partial list of functions. There are other functions that are not universal or not used very much. The programmer or the application user should check the particular language or software package to find any additional functions provided there.

Functions use data. These data are listed as part of the function and are called *parameters.* Functions normally do not alter the parameters. Take the square root function, SQRT(N). This function will calculate the square root of N. SQRT is the name of the function. N is the data needed to calculate the square root and, therefore, it is the parameter. Parameters are surrounded by parentheses. The maximum function, MAX(N1, N2, N3), will find which of three numbers is the largest. The name of the function is MAX. The parameters, data surrounded by parentheses and needed to do the calculation,

Table 2.4 Functions (*continued on page 22*)

Function	Definition	Example	Result
Mathematical Functions Used in Business			
SQRT(N)	Returns the square root of N.*	SQRT(4)	2
ABS(N)	Returns the absolute value of N.	ABS(−3)	3
ROUND(N, n1)	Returns the rounded value of N to the n1 place.	ROUND (3.72592)	3.73
INTEGER(N)	Returns the closest whole number less than or equal to N.	INTEGER (5.7269)	5
RANDOM	Returns a random number between 0 and 1, but not 1. This number is mathematically generated.	RANDOM	0.239768
SIGN(N)	Returns the sign of N: 1 when N is positive, 0 when N is zero, − 1 when N is negative.	SIGN(7.39)	1
String Functions			
MID(S, n1, n2)	Returns a set of characters starting at n1, n2 characters in length from S.	MID(S, 3, 2) where S = "THOMAS"	"OM"
LEFT(S, n)	Returns a set of n characters on the left side of the string S.	LEFT(S, 3) where S = "THOMAS"	"THO"
RIGHT(S, n)	Returns a set of n characters on the right side of the string S.	RIGHT (S, 3) where S = "THOMAS"	"MAS"
LENGTH(S)	Returns the number of characters in the string S.	LENGTH(S) where S = "THOMAS"	6

*Definitions of symbols:

N is a numerical value—a constant, a variable, or an expression

S is a string value—a constant, a variable, or an expression

n, n1, n2 are integer values—a constant, a variable, or an expression

are N1, N2, and N3. Not all functions need parameters. The function RANDOM generates or calculates a random number. No data are needed to do this calculation, so there are no parameters. A parameter can be a constant, a variable, or an expression. (An expression is a calculation, such as interest/100, which has not been given a permanent memory location in the computer.) The names of the functions may vary from language to language and from application to application. This book will give a generic name to each function and list the parameters in parentheses.

Table 2.4 (*continued from page 21*)

Function	Definition	Example	Result
Conversion Functions (change data type)			
VALUE(S)	Changes a string value into a numerical value.	VALUE ("57.39")	+ 57.39
STRING(N)	Changes a numerical value into a string value.	STRING (+57.39)	"57.39"
Statistical Functions			
AVERAGE(list)	Returns the average of a list of numbers.	AVERAGE (5, 3, 8, 6)	5.5
MAX(list)	Returns the maximum value from a list of numbers.	MAX (5, 3, 8, 6)	8
MIN(list)	Returns the minimum value from a list of numbers.	MIN (5, 3, 8, 6)	3
SUM(list)	Returns the sum of a list of numbers.	SUM (5, 3, 8, 6)	22
Financial Functions are listed in Chapter 19.			
Utility Functions			
DATE	Returns the current date from the system. The date may be in various forms: mm/dd/yy, day only, month only, year only, or julian calendar.	DATE	09/15/98
TIME	Returns the current time from the system, The time may be in various forms: hh:mm:ss, seconds from midnight, or minutes from midnight.	TIME	9:22:38
ERROR	Returns control to the program when a systems error occurs.		

Operators

The computer has to be told how to process data. This task is accomplished through the use of operators. **Operators** are the data connectors within expressions and equations. They tell the computer how to process the data. They also tell the computer what type of processing (mathematical, logical, or whatever) needs to be done. The types of operators used in calculations and problem solving include mathematical, relational, and logical operators. Without these operators very little processing can be done.

The *operand* and the *resultant* are two concepts related to the operator. Operands are the data that the operator connects and processes. The resultant is the answer that results when the operation is completed. For example, in the expression 5 + 7, the + is the operator, 5 and 7 are the operands, and 12 is the resultant. Operands can be constants or variables. The data type of the operands and the resultant depends on the operator.

Mathematical operators include addition, subtraction, multiplication, division, integer division, modulo division, powers, and functions. The computer has a symbol for each of them (see Table 2.5). You are probably familiar with addition, subtraction, multiplication, division, and powers. However, you may not be familiar with integer and modulo division.

These two operations are related. In integer division, the resultant is the whole number in the quotient. In modulo division, the resultant is the whole number remainder. These two types of division are used in business to find the hours and minutes someone has worked given the total number of minutes, or the days and weeks worked given the total number of days. For example, if Jane Smith has worked 19 days during the month, then, assuming a 5-day work week, she has worked 19/5 = 3 weeks and 19 MOD 5 = 4 days. Therefore, she has worked 3 weeks and 4 days.

Relational operators include the following: equal to, less than, greater than, less than or equal to, greater than or equal to, and not equal to. A programmer uses relational operators to program decisions. The resultant of a relational operation is logical data type

Table 2.5 Operators and Their Computer Symbols

Operator	Computer Symbol	Example	
Mathematical		Operation	Resultant
Addition	+	3.0 + 5.2	8.2
Subtraction	−	7.5 − 4.0	3.5
Multiplication	*	8.0 * 5.0	40.0
Division	/	9.0/4.0	2.25
Integer division	\	9\4	2
Modulo division	MOD	9 MOD 4	1
Power	^	3 ^ 2	9
Relational			
Equal to	=	5 = 7	FALSE
Less than	<	5 < 7	TRUE
Greater than	>	5 > 7	FALSE
Less than or equal to	< = (two key strokes)	5 < = 7	TRUE
Greater than or equal to	> = (two key strokes)	5 > = 7	FALSE
Not equal to	< > (two key strokes)	5 < > 7	TRUE
Logical			
Not	NOT	NOT TRUE	FALSE
And	AND	TRUE AND TRUE	TRUE
Or	OR	TRUE OR FALSE	TRUE

TRUE or FALSE. The programmer designs one action or set of actions that will follow when a relational expression is TRUE, and another action or set of actions that will follow when the expression is FALSE. The use of relational operators is the only way for the computer to make decisions.

For example, when a credit card customer's balance is *less than 500* (TRUE), then the customer can charge another purchase. When the balance is *not less than $500* (FALSE), then he cannot charge another purchase. The expression would be set up as BALANCE < 500. The operands are BALANCE and 500; the operator is < ; the resultant is either TRUE or FALSE depending on the value of the balance. The programmer would use this expression in what is called a *decision instruction.*

Relational operators are also used to control repetitive instructions called *loops.* A set of instructions to enter data for a client, which would be repeated until the data are entered for every client, is one example of a loop. When the computer processes this type of instruction, the loop repeats until the resultant changes from TRUE to FALSE, or vice versa. In the example, the resultant would change when the computer can find no more client data to enter.

Logical operators are the third type of operator (see Table 2.6). Logical operators are used to connect relational expressions (decision-making expressions) and to perform operations on logical data. For example, a store might require a driver's license or a check-cashing card on file for a customer to cash a check. When the customer has a dri-

Table 2.6 Definitions of the Logical Operators

NOT

A	Not A	When A is		The Resultant is
T	F	NOT TRUE	IS	FALSE
F	T	NOT FALSE	IS	TRUE

AND

A	B	A AND B	When A is		When B is		The Resultant is
T	T	T	TRUE	OR	TRUE	IS	TRUE
T	F	F	TRUE	OR	FALSE	IS	FALSE
F	T	F	FALSE	OR	TRUE	IS	FALSE
F	F	F	FALSE	OR	FALSE	IS	FALSE

OR

A	B	A OR B	When A is		When B is		The Resultant is
T	T	T	TRUE	OR	TRUE	IS	TRUE
T	F	T	TRUE	OR	FALSE	IS	TRUE
F	T	T	FALSE	OR	TRUE	IS	TRUE
F	F	F	FALSE	OR	FALSE	IS	FALSE

ver's license, the check can be cashed. When he or she has a check-cashing card, the check can be cashed. The expression is written as LICENSE OR CARD. LICENSE and CARD are the operands. They are logical data; that is, the value of each is TRUE or FALSE. The operator is OR. The resultant is TRUE or FALSE depending on the values of the operands. When one or both of the operands is TRUE, then the resultant is TRUE. When both of the operands are FALSE, then the resultant is FALSE.

The OR operator is one of three logical operators. The others are AND and NOT. When the AND operator is used, the resultant is TRUE only when both of the operands are TRUE. When either or both of the operands are FALSE, the resultant is FALSE. A programmer uses AND when two requirements must be TRUE in order for an action or set of actions to take place, such as when a store requires a customer to have *both* a driver's license *and* a check-cashing card to cash a check. The NOT operator is the only logical operator that requires only one operand. The resultant of the NOT operator changes in an operand from TRUE to FALSE, or from FALSE to TRUE. A programmer uses the NOT operator to change an operand to the opposite value. This operation is sometimes called *reversing* the value of the operand.

These mathematical, relational, and logical operators have a **hierarchy,** or precedence, an order in which their operations take place (see Table 2.7). To reorder the normal processing sequence, the programmer uses parentheses. The processing of the operands (as directed by the operators) always starts with the innermost parentheses and

Table 2.7 Hierarchy of Operations

Order of Operations	Operand Data Type	Resultant Data Type
( ) Reorders the hierarchy; all operations are completed within the parentheses using the same hierarchy.		
1. Functions		
Mathematical Operators		
2. Power	Numerical	Numerical
3. \, MOD	Numerical	Numerical
4. *, /	Numerical	Numerical
5. +, -	Numerical	Numerical
Relational Operators		
6. =, <, >, <=, >=, <>	Numerical or string or character	Logical
Logical Operators		
7. NOT	Logical	Logical
8. AND	Logical	Logical
9. OR	Logical	Logical

works outward, and processes from left to right. Each level of operators within a set of parentheses requires that the computer make another pass through the parentheses, until all levels have been cleared. This hierarchy is important to the programmer because the order of the operations determines the result of the expression. If the operations are not completed in the correct order, the result of the expression may be incorrect. For example, assuming a 40-hour work week and overtime pay at 1.5 times regular pay, the expression to calculate overtime pay would subtract 40 from the hours worked and multiply the result by the regular wage times 1.5. The expression would be written as,

(HOURS − 40) * WAGE * 1.5

As you can see from the hierarchy chart, multiplication is processed before subtraction, so parentheses must be added to tell the computer to do the subtraction first, before the multiplication. If the parentheses are not added, the result will be incorrect.

Each type of operator requires a certain data type for operands and determines the data type of the resultant. Mathematical operators require numerical data as the operands and have numerical resultants. When any of the relational or logical operators are used (whether or not they are used in conjunction with mathematical operators), the resultant is logical data. Relational operators use numerical, character, or string data types as the operands; however, the data type of the operands of an operator must be the same. The logical operators require logical data for operands.

Expressions and Equations

A knowledge of constants and variables, of the three data types, and of operators, operands, and resultants is not very valuable until you can use these concepts to create expressions and equations. The problem you are trying to solve may be calculating pay, including tax, Social Security, and medical deductions. It may be an inventory problem with reorder quantities and cash values. It may be a problem of calculating interest or payments on a loan, or of putting a mailing list in order. These tasks all require the use of different operators, and would be written as expressions and equations in order for the computer to process the data and arrive at a result. There are very few computer problems that do not use expressions and equations in their solutions.

Expressions and equations make up part of the instructions in the solution to a computer problem. An **expression** processes data, the operands, through the use of operators. For example, to find the number of square feet in a room you would multiply the length of the room by the width in the expression,

LENGTH * WIDTH

An **equation** stores the resultant of an expression in a memory location in the computer through the equals (=) sign. The expression above would be used as part of an instruction in the equation

AREA = LENGTH * WIDTH

The resultant of the expression LENGTH * WIDTH would then be stored in a memory location called AREA.

As you can see in Table 2.8, expressions use no equals sign and are used as part of an instruction, such as part of an equation. The resultant of an expression is not stored and, therefore, is not available for use at another time. An expression can use numerical, string, character, or logical data types.

Table 2.8 Expressions and Equations

Expressions	Equations
A + B A and B are numerical. The resultant is not stored; the resultant is numerical.	C = A + B C, A, and B are numerical. The resultant is stored in C.
A < B A and B are numerical, character, or string. The resultant is logical and is not stored.	C = A < B A and B are numerical, character, or string. The resultant is stored in C; C is logical.
A OR B A and B are logical. The resultant is logical and is not stored.	C = A OR B C, A, and B are logical. The resultant is stored in C.

Equations are often called *assignment statements* because the variable on the left-hand side of the equals sign is assigned the value of the expression on the right-hand side. The equals sign does not mean *equals;* instead, it means *replaced by* or *is assigned the value of.* This distinction is important because it is possible to have equations on the computer that are not allowed in a mathematics class, such as N = N + 1 (one is added to the old value of N to get a new value of N). This equation is the way the computer counts. There is only one variable on the left-hand side of the equals sign. On the right-hand side of the equals sign is an expression. The right-hand side is processed before the assignment is made (see Table 2.8 and the examples that follow).

For the beginning programmer, a big part of learning to solve problems on the computer is learning how to write and evaluate expressions and equations. (Recall that to *evaluate* means to test for correctness using actual data.) The following examples illustrate how to use the concepts you've learned in this chapter to write and evaluate expressions and equations.

Example 1: Setting Up a Numerical Expression

A programmer will often be given an expression to use in solving a problem. Assume the programmer has to modify the following mathematical expression for computer use:

$$X(3Y + 4) - \frac{4Y}{X + 6}$$

The appropriate computer expression would be the following:

$$X * (3 * Y + 4) - 4 * Y/(X + 6)$$

All variables, constants, and operators have to be on the same line. There must be an operator between variables and/or constants. For the computer, there are no assumed multiplication signs. Parentheses are added when the hierarchy has to be reordered or when parentheses would improve readability.

Example 2: Setting up a Mathematical Equation

A mathematical equation might be given to the programmer in the following form:

$$Y + 3 = X(Z + 5)$$

The programmer has to modify the equation so that it is in the form of an assignment instruction:

$$Y = X * (Z + 5) - 3$$

Notice that there is only one variable (and no calculations) on the left side and an expression on the right side of the equals sign.

Example 3: Setting up a Relational Expression

A relational expression is used to make decisions. Given the expression,

$$X \text{ is less than } Y + 5$$

the programmer would change its form to the following:

$$X < Y + 5$$

Because this is a relational expression, either a variable or a mathematical expression is on either side of the operator. X and Y would be the same data type, in this case, a numerical data type. The resultant would be a logical data type—TRUE or FALSE, depending on the values of X and Y.

Example 4: Setting up a Logical Expression

Often a computer decision is based on more than one TRUE or FALSE operand. For example, in order to cash a check a customer must have a driver's license (A) or a check-cashing card (B) on file at the store. As is the case with all logical expressions, this case would require a logical operator, A OR B. The operands, A and B, are logical data type; it is either TRUE or FALSE that the customer has a driver's license, and TRUE or FALSE that she has a check-cashing card. The resultant is also a logical type: The customer can cash a check (TRUE or FALSE).

Example 5: Evaluating a Mathematical Expression

To find out if proposed solutions are correct, it is important for the programmer to evaluate, or test, all expressions and equations. Assume the programmer has written the expression,

$$5 * (X + Y) - 4 * Y/(Z + 6)$$

The programmer uses the following values to evaluate the expression:

$$X = 2 \qquad Y = 3 \qquad Z = 6$$

Notice the structure of the evaluation that follows. A dashed line leading to a circle indicates the operator. The solid lines indicate the operands. Following the illustration of the equation is a list of the operations and the resultant of each operation. The number of circles should equal the number of operators.

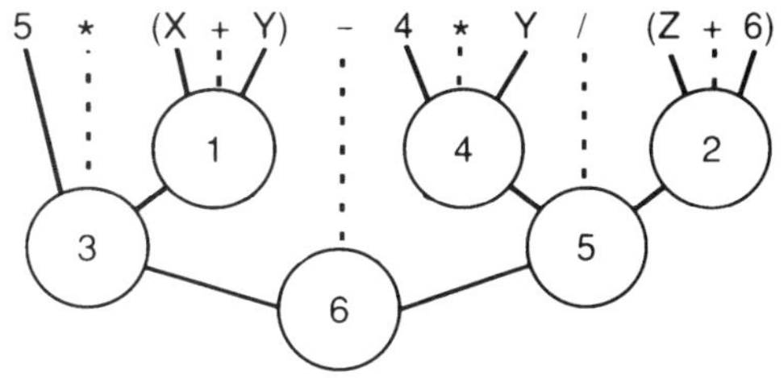

Operation	*Resultant*
1. X + Y	5
2. Z + 6	12
3. 5 * resultant of 1	25
4. 4 * Y	12
5. Resultant of 4 / resultant of 2	1
6. Resultant of 3 − resultant of 5	24

Illustrating the structure of the expression and listing the operations and results in this way simplifies the evaluation process for the programmer. The evaluation must be completed according to the hierarchy of operations. The operations within the parentheses would be completed first, moving from left to right—so X + Y would be completed first, and Z + 6 second. According to the hierarchy, the programmer would then complete the multiplications and the divisions from left to right. The division would be completed after the multiplications in this expression only because it is to their right. The final operation to be completed would be addition followed by subtraction (outside of parentheses).

This evaluation shows how to test a computer expression to see if it matches an equivalent mathematical expression. It gives the programmer a correct result that can be compared to the results manually calculated by the client, or by whoever requested the computer solution to the problem, so one can be sure that the solution is correct.

Example 6: Evaluating a Relational Expression

Assume the programmer has written the expression,

$$A - 2 > B$$

The programmer uses the following values to evaluate the expression:

$$A = 6 \qquad B = 8$$

The following illustration shows the structure of the evaluation:

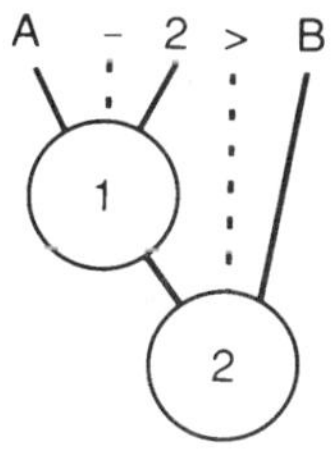

Operation	*Resultant*
1. A − 2	4
2. Resultant of 1 > B	FALSE

According to the hierarchy of operations, the mathematical operation is completed first.

Example 7: Evaluating a Logical Expression

Assume the programmer has written the expression:

A AND B OR C AND A

The programmer uses the following values to evaluate the expression:

A = TRUE B = FALSE C = TRUE

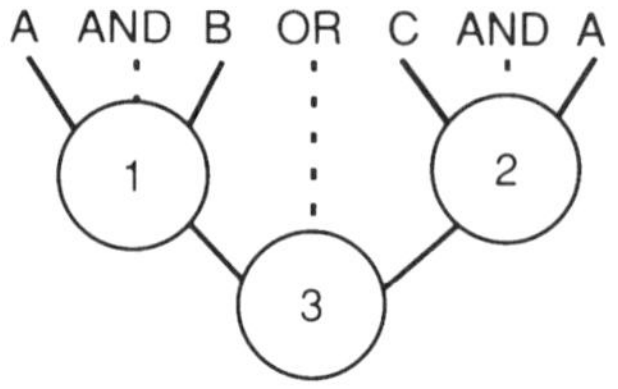

Operation	*Resultant*
1. A AND B	FALSE
2. C AND A	TRUE
3. Resultant of 1 OR resultant of 2	TRUE

Example 8: Evaluating an Equation That Uses Both Relational and Logical Operators

Assume the programmer has written the following equation:

F = NOT (A < B) AND (C OR D)

The programmer uses the following values to evaluate the equation:

A = 4 B = 2 C = TRUE D = FALSE

The operations are completed in hierarchical order from left to right, as illustrated in the figure.

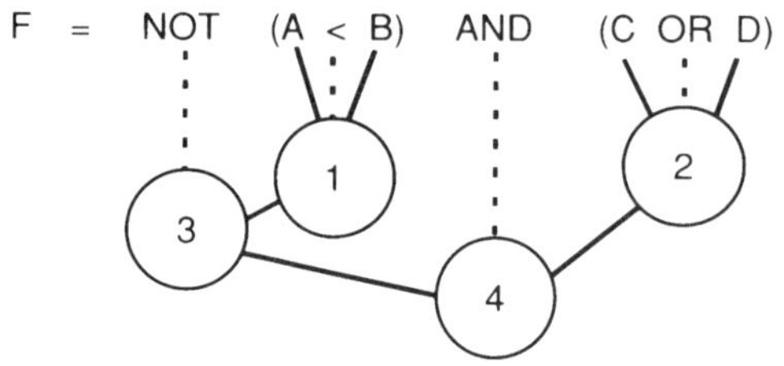

Operation	*Resultant*
1. A < B	FALSE
2. C OR D	TRUE
3. NOT the resultant of 1	TRUE
4. Resultant of 3 AND resultant of 2	TRUE
5. Store the resultant of 4 in the memory location called F.	

Example 9: Developing a Table of All Possible Resultants of a Logical Expression

It is often valuable for a programmer to figure out the resultants for all of the possible combinations of values of the variables in an expression. To create a table of all possible combinations, double the number of combinations from a table with one less unknown. For example:

- One unknown—A. Two combinations: A can be either T or F.

A
T
F

- Two unknowns—A and B. Four combinations: B can be either T or F for each value of A.

A
T
F

A	B
T	T
T	F
F	T
F	F

- Three unknowns—A, B, and C. Eight combinations.

A	B
T	T
T	F
F	T
F	F

A	B	C
T	T	T
T	T	F
T	F	T
T	F	F
F	T	T
F	T	F
F	F	T
F	F	F

Given the expression,

NOT A OR B

the following table gives the resultants for all combinations of the values of A and B. The equation to find the number of combinations is 2^n, where n is the number of variables. For example, with two variables, A and B, there are four combinations; and with three variables, A, B, and C, there are eight combinations.

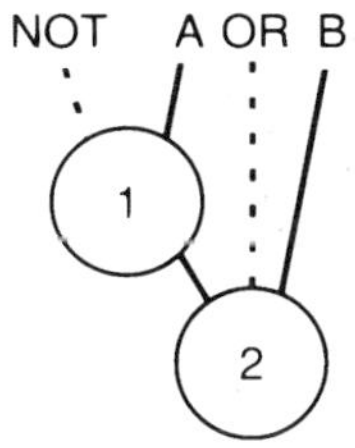

A	B	NOT A OR B
T	T	T
T	F	F
F	T	T
F	F	T

Example 10: Developing a Logical Expression from a Given Problem

Many times a programmer will be given the policies of a company and then be required to set up a logical expression from those policies. To do this, the programmer first needs to list the items on which the condition is dependent. Then the logical expression can be developed from this list.

> Problem: A large department store has its own charge card. The policy for a customer to charge an item is that the customer must have a valid charge card and either a balance of less than $500 or a charge of less than $50.

1. The first step is to list the items the charge is dependent on and their data types:
   a. the charge card (logical data type)
   b. the balance (numerical data type)
   c. the charge amount (numerical data type)
2. The second step is to write down these items as variables along with the conditions on each. Put them on one line, leaving space between, so that the logical operator can be added next. The resultant or the data type of each expression must be logical. Remember that the operators must match the data types of the operands (see Table 2.7). Do not put the logical operators in as of yet.

   CHARGE_CARD   BALANCE < 500   AMOUNT < 50

3. The third step is to put in the logical operators and parentheses:

   CHARGE_CARD AND (BALANCE < 500 or AMOUNT < 50)

   Because the condition between the balance and the amount is one or the other, the OR operator is needed. The condition between the charge card and the other two items is both; this calls for the AND operator. Since the AND has precedence over the OR, the parentheses are added around the OR operation.
4. You have now created the logical expression. This expression can be used in various ways:
   a. In an assignment statement:

      OKTOCHG = CHARGE_CARD AND (BALANCE < 500 OR
      AMOUNT < 50)

   b. In a decision statement (this will be explained in Chapter 6, Problem Solving with Decisions):

      IF CHARGE_CARD AND (BALANCE < 500 or AMOUNT < 50)
      THEN PRINT "OKAY TO CHARGE"
      ELSE PRINT "NOT OKAY TO CHARGE"

Summary

This chapter explains fundamental concepts for solving problems on the computer, including constants, variables, data types, common functions, operators, expressions, and equations. It also shows the beginning programmer how to set up computer expressions and equations.

Constants are values that never change during processing, even if they are named constants; variables are values that do change. Constants and variables are assigned data types and are used in expressions and equations. The most common data types include numerical, character, and logical.

Expressions and equations use functions to process standard tasks. Most functions are part of the computer language. Expressions and equations use operators to process the data. These operators are of three types: mathematical, relational, and logical. By using operators and the hierarchy of operations, a programmer can design calculations and decisions, which are the key to solving problems on the computer.

New Terms

character data
concatenation
constant
data
data type
equation
expression
function
hierarchy
information
logical data
logical operator
mathematical operator
numerical data
operator
relational operator
variable

Questions

1. What is a constant? What is a variable?
2. Fill in the following table with the data needed to solve an inventory problem for White Auto Supplies. Give each data item a name and specify its data type.

Data Item	Variable Name	Data Type
a. Name of the company		
b. Inventory item name		
c. Inventory number		
d. Quantity		
e. Price		
f. Address of company		
g. Vendor name (company from which inventory item is ordered)		
h. Reorder quantity		
i. Obsolete item (yes/no)		

3. Name the data type for each of the following constants. Explain your answer.
   a. 5.38
   b. "87654"
   c. TRUE
   d. "A"
   e. "707-434-5555"
   f. "New York"
   g. − 389
   h. 2.45E6
   i. 48976.0
   i. FALSE
4. What is a function?
5. Why are functions used?
6. What is the difference between the operators /, \, and MOD?
7. Find the result of the following operations:
   a. 5 + 4
   b. 10/2
   c. TRUE OR FALSE
   d. 20 MOD 3
   e. 5 < 8
   f. 25 MOD 70
   g. "A" > "H"
   h. NOT TRUE
   i. 25/70
   j. FALSE AND TRUE
   k. 20 * .5
   l. 35 < = 35
   m. 35/7
   n. FALSE OR FALSE
   o. TRUE AND TRUE
   p. 50 MOD 5
   q. − 35 < 67
   r. 4.0 ^ 3
   s. 60\9
   t. 35 < 35
   u. TRUE AND FALSE
8. Using the hierarchy chart (Table 2.7), list the order in which the following operations would be processed. (Remember: operations are processed left to right within a level in the hierarchy table.)
   a. + , − , *
   b. /, \, =
   c. OR, *, <
   d. NOT, AND, *
   e. NOT, > , +
   f. AND, OR, NOT
   g. < , AND, > , +
   h. *, ^ , +
   i. NOT, + , \
   j. MOD, \, <

9. Name the data type of the operands and the resultant of each of the following expressions or equations.

	Data type	
	Operands	Resultant
a. A * B		
b. D > R		
c. NOT C		
d. B AND F		
e. G = B		

10. What is the difference between an expression and an equation?

11. What does the equals sign mean in an equation? Is the meaning of the equals sign as a relational operator different from that in an assignment statement?

Problems

1. Evaluate the following equations, given the values A = 12, B = 3, C = 6, D = 2.

a. F = A + B/C − D ^ 2
b. F = (A + B)/C − D ^ 2
c. F = A + B/(C   D ^ 2)
d. F = (A + B)MOD C
e. F = (A + B)\D ^ 2

2. Write the following equations in computer form.

a. $X = Y + 3Z - \frac{Z + Y}{Z - 3}$

b. $X = 5Y + \frac{3Z - 1}{4(3Z + 1) - Y}$

c. $X = (X - Y)^2$

3. An employee came in to work and clocked in at MORNING_IN, clocked out at NOON_OUT for lunch, clocked back in at NOON_IN, and clocked out to go home at NIGHT_OUT (all in minutes since midnight). Set up equations to calculate the number of hours and the number of minutes the employee worked for the day. (You will develop two equations.)

4. Steve Thompson bought and charged an electric saw on DATE1 and made the first payment on DATE2. Write an equation to calculate how many days (DAYS) elapsed between the two dates.

DAYS =

5. Eureka Lumber Company gives a 2% discount if the remaining balance is paid within 10 days of purchase. Write a logical expression to verify whether or not a customer qualifies for this discount. Use the following variable names:

BUYING_DATE: date the customer purchased the merchandise

PAID_DATE: date the customer made the final payment

6. A part-time employee worked 20 hours in the first week and 15 hours in the second week of a two-week pay period. He is paid a weekly salary based on a 40-hour week. What is his full-time equivalent for the two weeks based on a 40-hour week? What is his full-time equivalent for the two weeks (i.e., what percentage of full time did he work)? Write a general equation that could be used to express and store the full-time equivalent of any hours worked per week.

FULL_TIME =

7. Evaluate the following equations, given A = FALSE, B = TRUE, C = FALSE, D = TRUE. (Include the structure of the order of processing—see page 30 for example.)
   - **a.** R = A AND B OR C AND D
   - **b.** R = NOT (A AND B) OR NOT (D AND C)
   - **c.** R = (A OR B) AND (D OR C)
   - **d.** R = NOT (A AND B OR C) AND (A OR B AND D)
   - **e.** R = C OR NOT (A AND D) AND (A OR B) OR NOT (A OR C)
8. Make a table that gives all possible answers for the following logical equations. (Include the structure of the order of processing—see page 30 for example.) Make clear how you set up the table.
   - **a.** R = A OR B
   - **b.** R = NOT A OR B
   - **c.** R = A AND B AND (B OR C)
   - **d.** R = NOT (A OR B) AND NOT (B OR C)
   - **e.** R = B AND NOT (A OR C) OR NOT (B AND C)
9. Evaluate the following for the values A = 5, B = 2, C = TRUE, D = FALSE. (Include the structure of the order of processing.)
   - **a.** R = A + 3 > B − 1 AND C OR D
   - **b.** R = NOT C OR D OR A − 3 < = B
10. Set up a logical expression for the following conditions. A company gives a bonus at the end of each fiscal year. For an employee to get a bonus, the following must be true:
    - **a.** The employee has been working at the company for more than six months with no negative reports.
    - **b.** The employee has earned more than $5,000 during the fiscal year.
11. Set up a logical expression for the following conditions. A retail store has this check-cashing policy:
    - **a.** The customer must have a driver's license.
    - **b.** When the check is for more than $50, the customer must have a check-cashing card on file.

Chapter 3

Programming Concepts

Overview

Objectives

When you have finished this chapter, you should be able to:

1. Differentiate between fields, records, files, and databases.
2. List and describe the five basic tools used in this book to aid in the development of a program. These tools include the program analysis chart, the structure chart, the IPO chart, algorithms, and flowcharts.
3. Describe the importance of internal and external documentation.

Computers are only as good as their hardware, their software, and the people using them. Assuming the hardware has been engineered to accomplish a given job, the efficiency of the computer relies on the effectiveness of the programmer.

The computer must be told what to do. It needs a set of instructions, the solution, in order to process data in the correct sequence and reach the desired results. For greatest efficiency, the programmer or the user has to be able to easily read and interpret the solution. The solution will be most effective if the programmer follows certain steps and rules, described in this chapter, which have been developed over the years. The solution becomes a **program** when it is coded into a computer language during the final stages of programming.

Early computers were much less useful and efficient than they are today. Programmers worked alone, and only when they left a company did their programs go to others. Since computers were slow and had small memories, conservation of computer time and memory was of utmost importance. For these reasons and the fact that the profession was new, programs were often hard to read and maintain. Over the years, both computers and programming methods have changed. Because programs are larger and more complex, and need to be completed in less time than ever before, today many programmers work together on the same program. As a result, readability is now what's most important. Since computers are much faster with much more memory, programmers may sacrifice these resources somewhat in favor of improved readability. Cost effectiveness, decrease in programmer frustration, and increase in programmer satisfaction are the rewards.

The type of problem the computer can solve best is one that can be solved algorithmically—that is, the problem can be solved with a single sequence of instructions. These instructions must be written in a way the computer can understand, and the computer executes them in the order presented in the program. If the instructions are written according to the appropriate rules and they correctly follow the syntax of the computer language, then the computer will complete the task. While this scrupulous adherence to the instructions is usually what the programmer wants, it is also, believe it or not, the most frustrating thing about the computer. If the instructions make sense to the computer, it will complete them. If the programmer has made an error in the instructions, the results are not likely to be what was intended. The computer does not reason, nor does it read minds; it only follows instructions.

How the Computer Stores Data

The computer stores data internally in memory locations. These data are found by the variable names used by a program. Each variable name is given a memory location, and each memory location can hold one and only one value at a time. When a user enters a new value into the variable location, the previous value is destroyed.

Data and instructions are temporarily stored in the computer's internal memory during the processing. These data and instructions are destroyed when they are replaced by more data or by another program. When data, information, or programs have to be kept for future use, they are stored externally on an auxiliary storage medium such as a hard disk or a floppy diskette in storage areas called **files.** There are basically two types of files: program files and data files. Program files contain the instructions to tell the computer what to do. This book helps the programming student create programs that will be saved on the auxiliary storage device as program files. Data files contain the data required to execute the program files. A data file consists of all the data pertaining to a subject, such as a payroll or a mailing list. Within each file are **records,** which contain all the data pertaining to one entity of the file, such as one employee's payroll data or one vendor's data. Within each record are **fields,** which contain one piece of data, such as a name, an address, or a pay rate. A database contains two or more interrelated files, such as a payroll file and a personnel file.

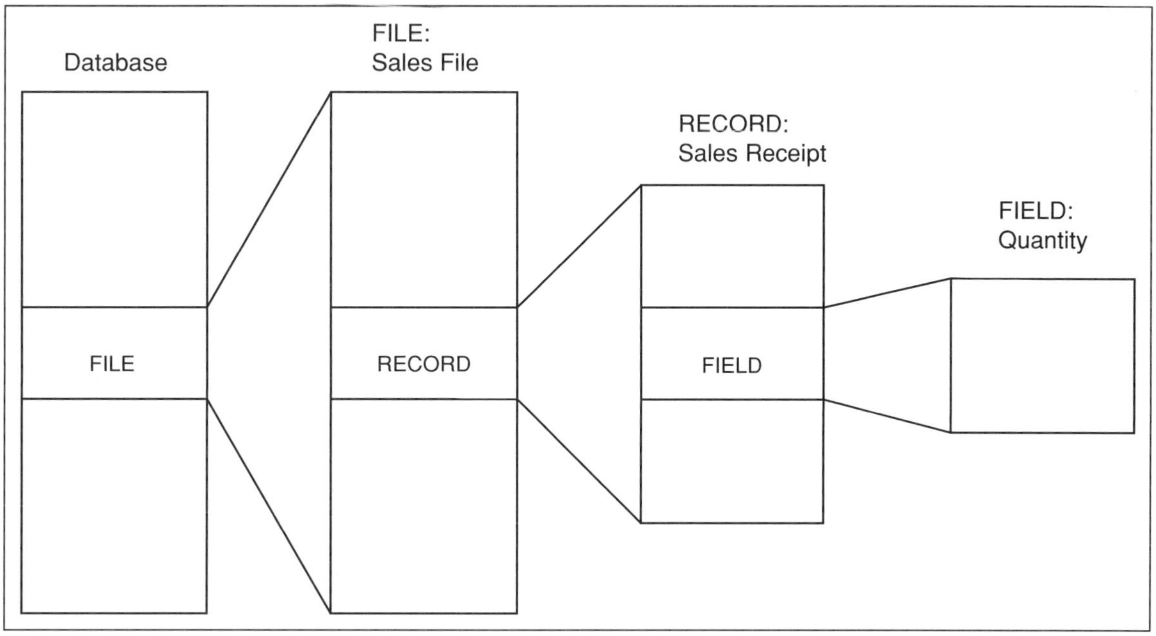

Figure 3.1 Files, Records, and Fields

A good analogy for the way a computer stores data externally is a filing cabinet. One drawer holding all the data on a company's employees is like a file on the computer. Each employee's folder in the file is a record. A field is one piece of data about the employee. For example, assume that the sales file for a company contains all the data needed to process orders for the week. Each record contains all the data from one sales receipt including quantity, item, price, name, and so forth. Each field contains one piece of the data from the sales receipt (Figure 3.1.) A database would be analogous to multiple file drawers in a filing cabinet.

Before a file can be used, the operating system, which is the manager of the computer, must open the files, preparing the computer to receive data from and send data to the auxiliary storage device. One of the tasks the operating system completes at this time is to set up a small temporary memory called a **buffer.** The data are transferred between the internal memory in the computer and the external memory on disk through the buffer. Normally one record or a group of records, called a *block* of records, is copied from memory location (internal or external) into the buffer and then copied to the other. The use of buffers makes both external memory and input/output devices more efficient. At the conclusion of the program, the operating system also executes certain closing instructions when the user tells it to CLOSE the file. The user must OPEN and CLOSE every file or an error can occur. More about file processing is presented in Chapters 13, 14, 15, and 16.

Communicating with the Computer

Since the computer does not speak English as you do, you have to learn its system of communication. For the computer to "understand" a message, its system of communication requires instructions governed by specific rules. If the instructions you write are incorrect, the computer will give an error message, the wrong answer, or no answer at all. If the instructions are not properly sequenced, the computer will, nevertheless, execute them in the order given, and the result will be wrong.

The meaning of an instruction is essentially the same in any computer language or application. The differences between instructions from one language or application and another are in how they are set up. **Syntax** refers to the rules governing the computer operating system, the language, and the application. An error is called a **bug.** A bug must be found and corrected, a process called **debugging.** Many bugs are a result of syntax errors, but some are logic errors. You can find and correct most logic errors during the problem-solving process. You will find and correct syntax errors when you enter your program into the computer. All syntax errors must be corrected before you execute and test your program.

Although a set of instructions must be in a correct order to lead to the correct result, there may be several "correct" orders, just as there are several routes leading from New York to San Francisco. Whether or not the routes are equally efficient doesn't affect the result. When efficiency is important, then and only then should each route be examined and kept or discarded. People employ different logic and different ways of thinking. Two programmers may develop equally good solutions to a problem, but the solutions may look entirely different. There is nothing wrong with this. Computers are exact machines, but the people working with them are not.

Organizing the Problem

Certain organizational tools will help you learn to solve problems on the computer. The tools used in this book and illustrated in this chapter include the **problem analysis chart,** which shows a beginning analysis of the problem; the **structure chart,** which shows the overall layout or structure of the solution; the **IPO chart,** which shows the input, the processing, and the output; the **algorithms,** which show the sequence of instructions comprising the solution; and the **flowcharts,** which are graphic representations of the algorithms. To analyze a problem and set up the most efficient solution, a programmer organizes the solution by using all or some of these tools. When the programmer does not use these tools during the problem-solving process, the solution takes longer to program, and the final program is less efficient, lacks readability, and increases programmer frustration.

Analyzing the Problem

To organize a solution, the programmer first has to understand and analyze the requirements of the problem. A good way to analyze a problem is to separate it into four parts, shown in the problem analysis chart (PAC) in Figure 3.2:

1. the given data
2. the required results
3. the processing that is required in the problem
4. a list of solution alternatives

(A blank problem analysis chart for student use appears in Appendix D, Figure D.1.) As a problem unfolds (in a textbook or in the real world), the programmer can use this form to sort it out. The PAC allows the problem solver to eliminate the words and glean only

Given Data	Required Results
Section 1: Data given in the problem or provided by the user. These can be known values or general names for data, such as price, quantity, and so forth.	Section 2: Requirements for the output reports. This includes the information needed and the format required.
Processing Required	**Solution Alternatives**
Section 3: List of processing required. This includes equations or other types of processing, such as sorting, searching, and so forth.	Section 4: List of ideas for the solution of the problem.

Figure 3.2 Problem Analysis Chart

the facts from the problem. Data would be entered in the Given Data section. These data are the input. Requirements for the output reports would be entered under Required Results. Any equations or other processing requirements would be listed in the Processing Required section. Finally, the programmer would write any other ideas that spring to mind concerning the solution in the Solution Alternatives section.

The following problem illustrates the use of the problem-solving tools. Calculate the gross pay of an employee. The formula to be used is:

$$\text{GROSSPAY} = \text{HOURS} * \text{PAYRATE}$$

Figure 3.3 shows how the problem solver would fill in the PAC for this problem. The hours worked and the pay rate are the data given and are put into the Given Data box. The gross pay is what needs to be calculated and given to the user; therefore it is put into the Required Results box. The formula used is

$$\text{GROSSPAY} = \text{HOURS} * \text{PAYRATE}$$

It is put into the Required Processing box. The Solution Alternatives are:

1. Define the hours worked and the pay rate as constants.
2. Define the hours worked and the pay rate as input values.

The second alternative will be used, as signified by the asterisk in the figure, since the program will not need to be changed in order to calculate the gross pay for another employee.

The problem analysis chart is an aid to clear thinking because it helps the problem solver to identify the essential data and information in a problem and to disregard the

Given Data	Required Results
Hours Pay Rate	Gross Pay
Processing Required	**Solution Alternatives**
GROSS PAY = HOURS * PAYRATE	1. Define the hours worked and pay rate as constants. *2. Define the hours worked and pay rate as input values.

Figure 3.3 Problem Analysis Chart for the Payroll Problem

nonessentials. Most problems programmers work with are word problems. This is true whether they are working in a classroom situation or out on the job. The PAC helps to pare down the words.

Developing the Structure Chart

Developing the structure chart is the second step in organizing a problem for the computer. In a structure chart, you divide the problem into subtasks called **modules.** In many cases you will break down these modules even further into smaller subtasks. This breakdown enables you to view a complex problem in simpler parts and to program smaller, simpler programs rather than one large, complex one. In developing the structure chart, use a top-down solution method. The top-down method simply means that as you divide the problem into subtasks, you illustrate them in the order in which they will be processed from the top to the bottom of the chart. When using the top-down method, the module that encompasses the complete solution becomes what is called the *Control Module* because it controls the processing of all the data. The subtasks of this module are then located below it in the structure chart. The structure chart shows what will happen, not how it will happen.

As you can see in Figure 3.4, the structure chart shows the relationships of the parts of a problem to each other and to the whole. Notice that the programmer numbers the rectangles in a logical order from top to bottom and from left to right. This arrangement illustrates the order of processing. The programmer labels the top rectangle on the chart (the Control Module) with the lowest number (0000). The next level of rectangles starts with the number 1000 and increases from left to right by increments of 1000. The other sublevels increase by numbers that are one magnitude less than the numbers above them. That is, if the higher level of rectangles increases by increments of 1000, then the programmer would label the next level by increasing increments of 100, as in 2100, 2200, 2300, in the third row in Figure 3.4. The levels below that, if there are any, would increase by 10s, and so forth. The programmer marks any duplicate modules by darkening

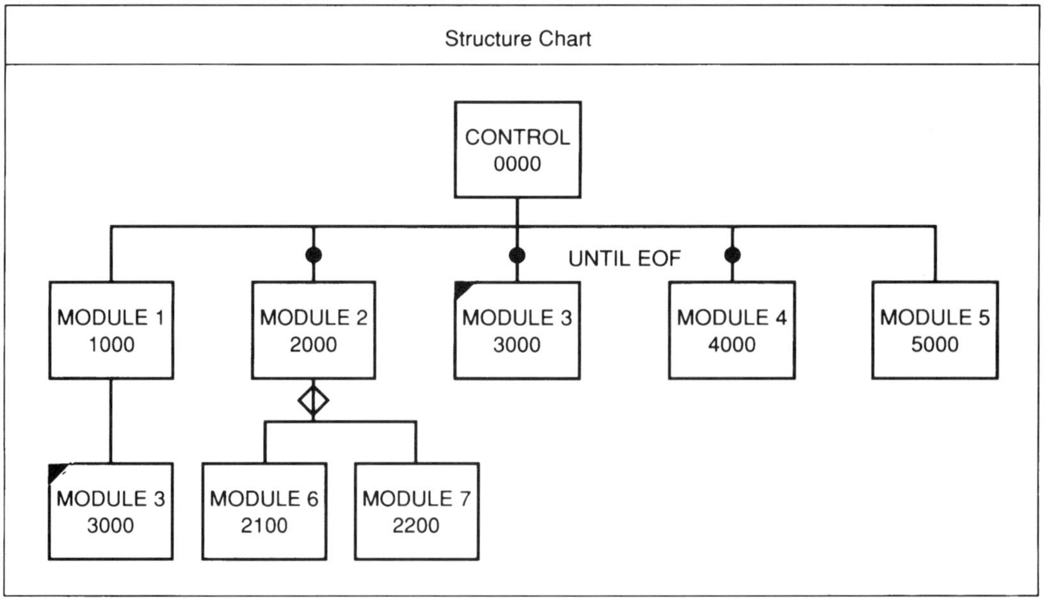

Figure 3.4 The Structure Chart

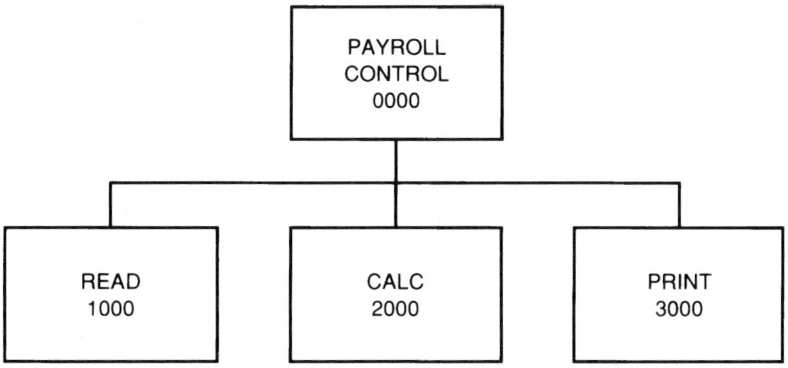

Figure 3.5 The Structure Chart for the Payroll Problem

the upper left-hand corner and writes the name of the module inside the rectangle, giving the same name to identical tasks.

Notice in Figure 3.4 that Module 3 is found in two places, indicating that it is processed at two different points in the solution. Since it is the same module in both places, it carries the same name and number. The number is that of its top-most position in the structure chart. If both Module 3s are on the same level, the number should be that of its left-most position.

A module processes only those tasks below it and directly connected to it by a network of horizontal and vertical lines. In Figure 3.4, the Control Module processes Module 1, Module 2, Module 3, Module 4, and Module 5. The darkened circles indicate that the module is part of a set of modules that are processed many times—those in a loop. At the level below the Control Module, Module 1 processes Module 3, and Module 2 processes Module 6 and Module 7. However, only one of these modules will be processed since they are part of a decision. That is, the instructions in Module 2 and the appropriate data would lead the computer to choose one of the two modules. The diamond on the vertical line above the box indicates which modules are involved in a decision. Annotation may be placed beside the circle or diamond to indicate the condition. (Appendix D, Figure D.2 is a structure chart for student use.)

Figure 3.5 shows the structure chart for the payroll problem. The top rectangle is the Control Module, which processes the READ, the CALC, and the PRINT Modules.

Developing the IPO Chart

The IPO (Input-Processing-Output) chart extends and organizes the information in the problem analysis chart. It shows in more detail what data items are input, what processing takes place on that data, and what information will be the end result, the output (see Figure 3.6). The IPO chart also shows where in the solution the processing takes place.

Input	Processing	Module Reference Number	Output
All input data (from Section 1 of problem analysis chart)	All processing in steps (from Sections 3 and 4 of the problem analysis chart)	Module reference number from the structure chart	All output requirements (from Sections 1 and 2 of the problem analysis chart)

Figure 3.6 The IPO Chart

Input	Processing	Module Reference Number	Output
Hours Worked Pay Rate	1. Enter hours worked 2. Enter Pay Rate 3. Calculate Pay 4. Print pay 5. End	1000 1000 2000 3000 0000	Gross pay

Figure 3.7 The IPO Chart for the Payroll Problem

The output is the first to be completed in an IPO chart. The next is the input, and the last is the processing. This may sound backwards, but it is really very logical. An analogy to completing an IPO chart would be planning a trip. The first thing you need to know is the destination—San Francisco, Paris, New York. This information is the output. Then you can plan what to pack, your means of transportation, and all the other essentials for starting out—the input. Finally, you plan the route—the processing. How can you know what to pack or what route to follow if you don't know where you're going?

The IPO chart has four sections: the Input, the Processing, the Module Reference Number, and the Output. The Input section contains all input data from the problem analysis chart. The input includes all given data from Section 1 on the problem analysis chart. The Processing section contains all processing, evident and implied, from Sections 3 and 4 of the problem analysis chart. The Module Reference Number section contains the number from the structure chart of the module in which each step in the processing is to be completed. The Output section includes all required output as designated by the problem and/or the user; it comes from Section 2, along with the needed input items from Section 1, of the problem analysis chart. (An IPO chart for student use appears in Appendix D, Figure D.3.)

To illustrate how to use an IPO chart, Figure 3.7 shows one for the payroll problem. The input, the processing, and the output are taken from Figure 3.3, the problem analysis chart for the payroll problem. The module reference numbers are taken from Figure 3.5, the structure chart for this problem. They show which module will perform each step in the processing. Notice also that these steps are numbered in the order to be processed.

Writing the Algorithms

After using the structure chart and the IPO chart, the next step in organizing a solution is for the programmer to develop sets of instructions for the computer, called algorithms (see Figure 3.8). **Pseudocode** may replace the algorithm in the development of a program when working in industry. Pseudocode is close to the actual language the programmer

```
Control Module       Name of Module
1. INSTRUCTION       1. INSTRUCTION
2. INSTRUCTION       2. INSTRUCTION
3. ..                3. ..
4. ..                4. ..
   ..                   ..
—. end               —. exit
```

Figure 3.8 The Form of an Algorithm

will be using. The algorithms we develop in this text are generic, and therefore we will not be able to use pseudocode. By using pseudocode, the programmer can start to write the actual code while finishing the final steps in the development of the program. Algorithms and pseudocode serve the same purpose.

To complete all of the algorithms needed to solve a problem, the programmer writes a separate set of instructions for each module in the structure chart. To be understood by the computer, the instructions have to be written according to certain rules that will be explained in future chapters throughout this book. Setting up the algorithms is probably the hardest part of problem solving on the computer. *The instructions cannot assume anything, cannot skip steps, must be executable one step at a time, and must be complete.* The modules are taken from the structure chart, and the processing is taken from the IPO chart. The number of instructions in an algorithm is determined by the way the programmer chooses to solve the problem. The algorithms pull the structure chart and the IPO chart together to give a logical step-by-step solution. Note in Figure 3.8, the control module uses an END since this is the end of the processing. The other modules use EXIT since the processing continues.

There are four algorithms and flowcharts for the payroll problem because there are four different modules in the structure chart. Figure 3.9 shows how the flowcharts and algorithms correspond for the payroll problem. Figure 3.10 shows the order of processing from module to module.

Drawing the Flowcharts

From the algorithms the programmer develops the flowcharts, graphic representations of the algorithms. The algorithms and the flowcharts are the final steps in organizing a solution. Using them, the programmer can test the solution for bugs and go on to code the problem into a computer language for entry into the computer. A flowchart will show errors in logic not readily visible in the other charts. Also, a set of data can be tested easily using a flowchart.

There are flowchart symbols for use with various types of processing. Figure 3.10 shows and explains some general flowchart symbols. There are many specific symbols, such as printer output, monitor output, and so forth, which are used in systems flowcharts. These are discussed later in this book in Chapters 13, 14, 15, and 16.

A flowchart shows the flow of the processing from the beginning to the end of a solution. Each block in a flowchart represents one instruction from an algorithm. *Flowlines* indicate the direction of the data flow. Most blocks have one or more *entrances,* flowlines directing the flow of the data into the block. Most blocks have only one *exit,* flowlines directing the data out of the block, since, in most cases, data can flow to only one other block. The exception to this rule is a block representing a *decision instruction,* an instruction that enables the computer to make one of two choices. A decision block has two exits, one for each choice.

Besides the decision instructions, Figure 3.11 refers to another type of instruction that you will learn to use later, but that deserves a brief explanation here. A *loop* enables the computer to perform a task repeatedly during the processing of a solution. An *automatic counter loop* is a type of loop that enables the computer to count in increments of a given value; the increment can be 1, 2, 5, or whatever. That given value is the *incrementor* referred to in Figure 3.11.

Figure 3.12 shows a flowchart illustrating Otto the Robot walking to a wall and back again. Notice the use of the different flowchart symbols.

The following are some of the rules for drawing flowcharts:

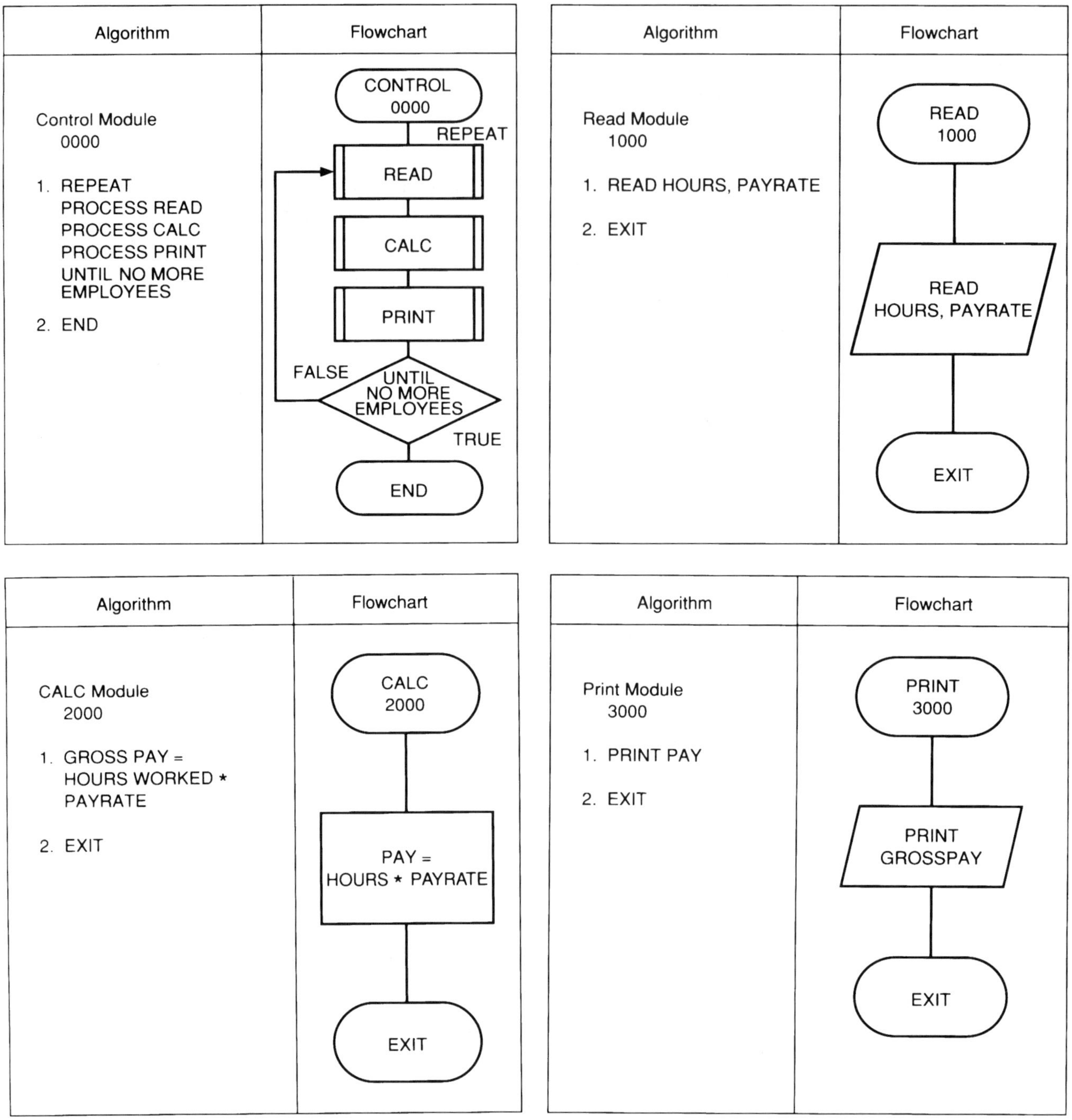

Figure 3.9 The Algorithms and Flowcharts for the Payroll Problem

1. You should write the instructions inside the blocks.
2. If there is something you need to remember, you can write a note beside a block. Test values of variables also can be placed beside flowchart blocks. This makes the flowchart an **annotated flowchart.**
3. A flowchart always starts at the top of the page and flows to the bottom. If you need more than one page for a flowchart, start another column on the same page or go on to another page. On- and off-page connectors are used to connect parts

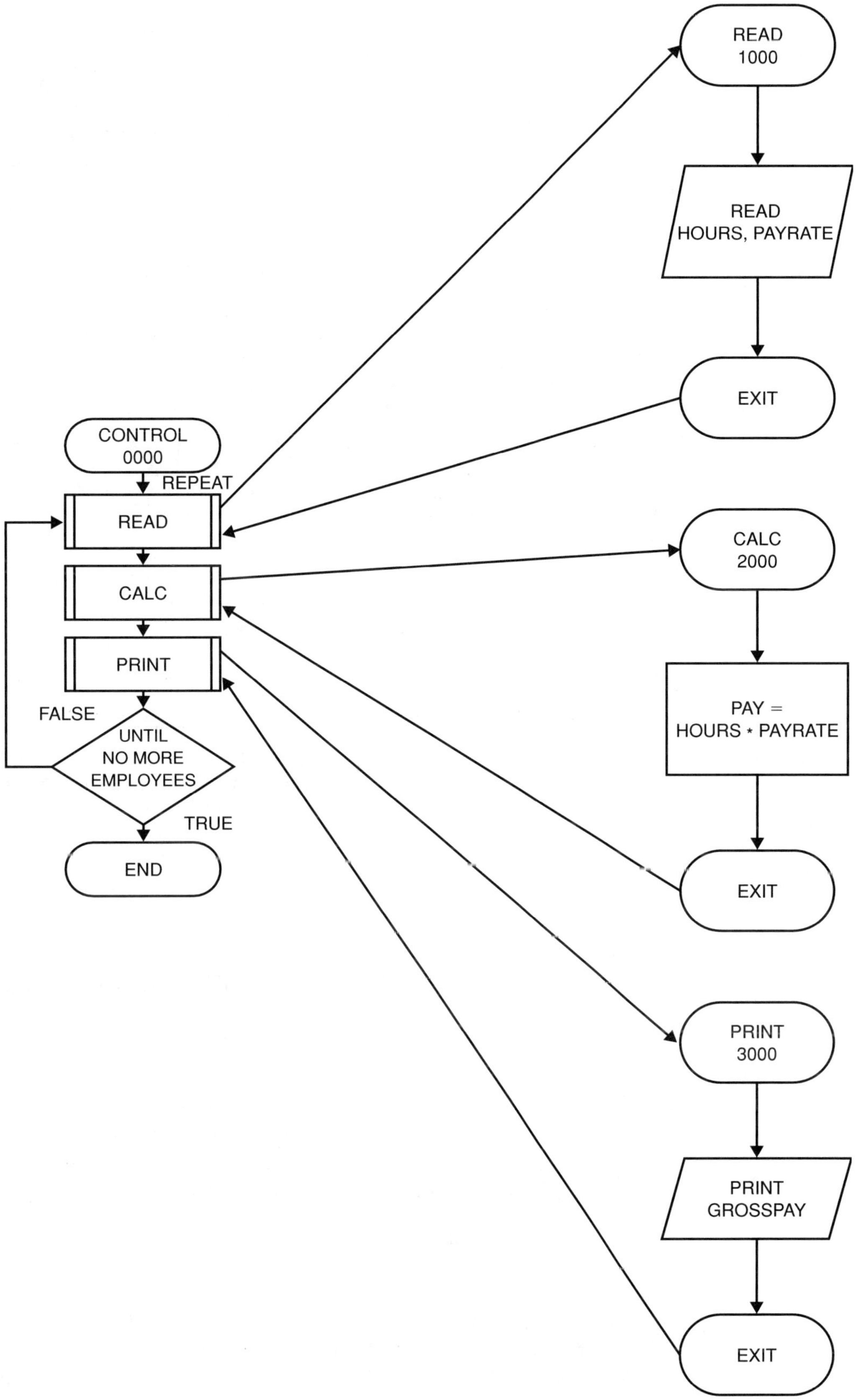

Figure 3.10 Order of execution of instructions

Flowchart Symbol	Explanation
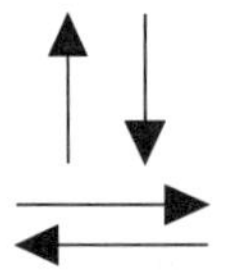 Flowlines	Flowlines are indicated by straight lines with optional arrows to show the direction of data flow. The arrowhead is necessary when the flow direction might be in doubt. Flowlines are used to connect blocks by exiting from one and entering another.
 Start 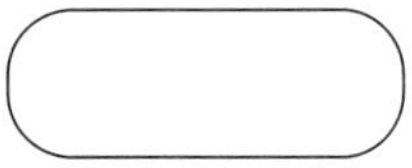 End/Stop/Exit	Flattened ellipses indicate the start and the end of a module. An ellipse uses the name of the module at the start. The end is indicated by the word *end* or *stop* for the top or Control Module and the word *exit* for all other modules. A start has no flowlines entering it and only one exiting it; an end or exit has one flowline entering it but none exiting it.
 Processing	The rectangle indicates a processing block, for such things as calculations, opening and closing files, and so forth. A processing block has one entrance and one exit.
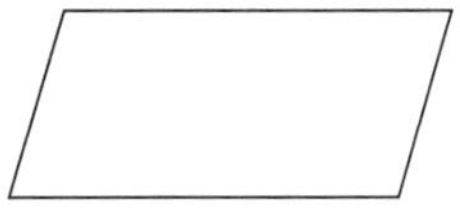 I/O	The parallelogram indicates input to and output from the computer memory. An I/O block has one entrance and only one exit.

Figure 3.11 Flowchart Symbols (*continued on page 49*)

of the flowchart. A flowchart should not flow up, or sideways, or all over the page (see Figure 3.12).

4. Use a flowchart template to draw the symbols and a straight edge to draw the flowlines. When you use a template, the symbols are the same size and your flowchart will be neater and easier to read.
5. Make the blocks big enough to write instructions so they can be easily read.
6. Put the module number and name from the structure chart in the upper right-hand corner of the page for quick reference to the correct module.
7. Have plenty of paper on hand since the final copy of the flowchart normally will not be the first draft.
8. Use a pencil with a larger eraser.

It is helpful to keep the algorithm and the flowchart of a module on the same page. Figure 3.13 shows a form (also in Appendix D, Figure D.4) you can use to develop your algorithms and flowcharts. Notice that there are four sections on page 2 of the form. The first is the Annotation section. Here you put notes about the algorithms and the flowcharts including test data, information about variables, things to remember, and so forth.

Flowchart Symbol	Explanation
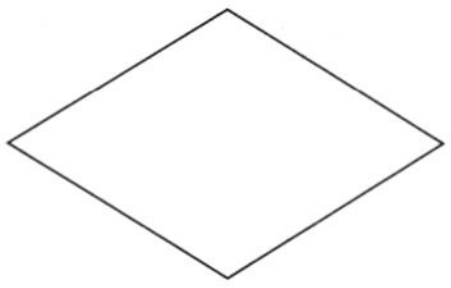 Decision	The diamond indicates a decision. It has one entrance and two and only two exits from the block. One exit is the action when the resultant is TRUE and the other exit is the action when the resultant is FALSE.
 Process Module	Rectangles with lines down each side represent tasks that are processed in a different place in the program. These are called modules. They have one entrance and only one exit.
 Automatic Counter Loop	The polygon indicates a loop with a counter. The counter starts with A (the beginning value), is incremented by S (the incrementor value) until the counter is greater than B (the ending value).
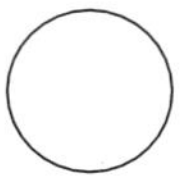 On-Page Connectors*  Off-Page Connectors*	Flowchart sections can be connected with two different symbols. The circle connects sections on the same page, and the home base plate connects flowcharts from page to page. Inside these two symbols the programmer writes letters or numbers. The on-page connector uses letters inside the circle to indicate where the adjoining connector is located. An A connects to an A, a B to a B, etc. The off-page connectors use the page number where the next part or the previous part of the flowchart is located. This allows the reader to easily follow the flowchart. On- and off-page connectors will have either an entrance or an exit.

* These connectors should be used as little as possible. They should be used to enhance readability. Overuse decreases readability and produces a cluttered effect.

Figure 3.11 (*continued from page 48*)

The Test section is used to test the solution with sample data. The other two sections, Internal Documentation and External Documentation, are for notes to refer to later when you are completing the internal and external documentation. The sections on the second page of Figure 3.13 are optional but helpful in many cases.

Internal and External Documentation

Internal documentation consists of remarks written with the instructions to explain what is being done in the program. **External documentation** is made up of the manuals written about the solution. Documentation of your program is very important.

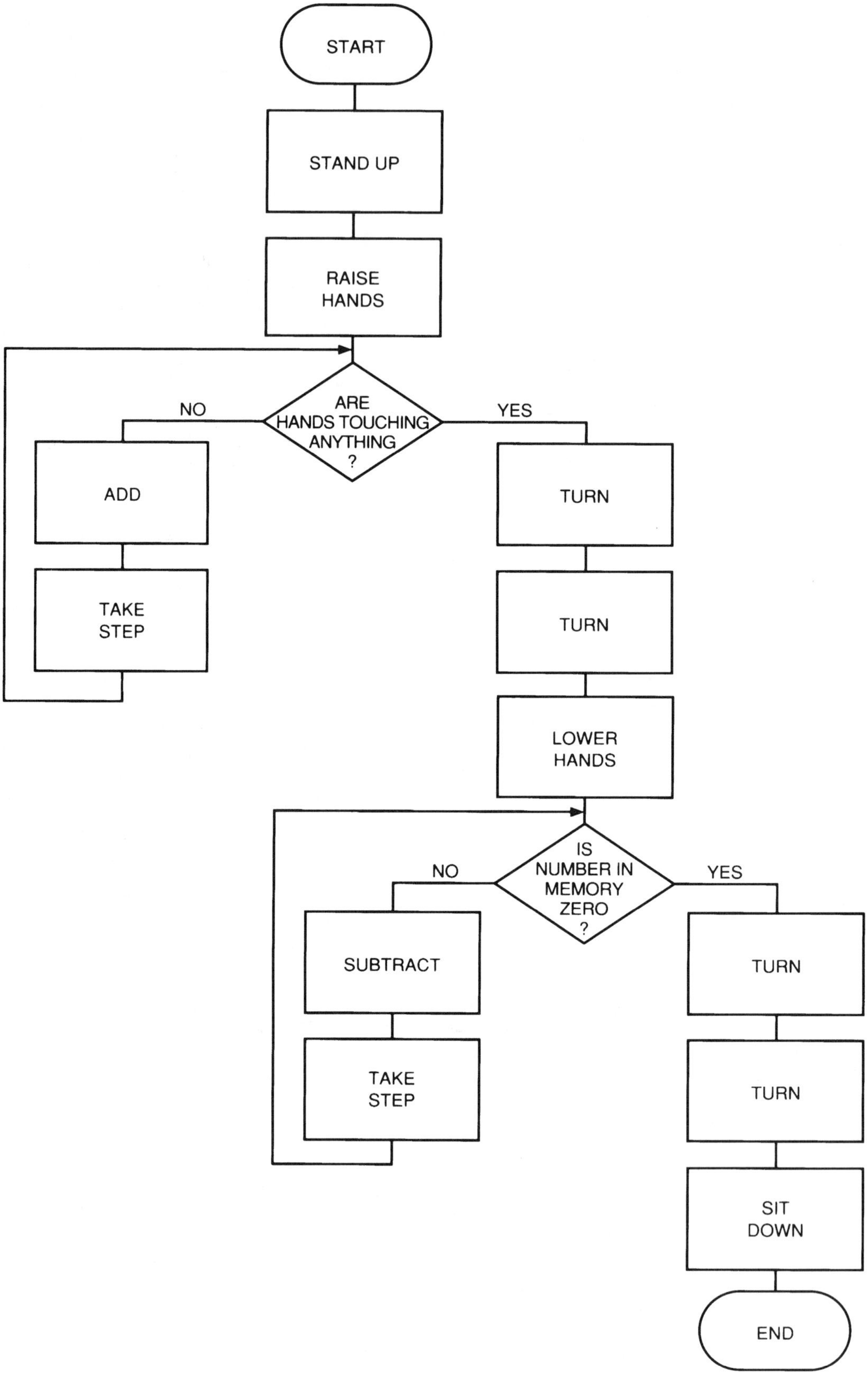

Figure 3.12 A Flowchart for Otto the Robot

Algorithm	Flowchart

Figure 3.13 Algorithm and Flowchart Form (*continued on page 52*)

Annotation	Test	Internal Documentation	External Documentation

Figure 3.13 (*continued from page 51*)

Good programming techniques require a program to be easily read by another programmer. The majority of the time, a program is passed from one programmer to another programmer. Proper internal documentation ensures that the new programmer will be able to learn about the program in the least amount of time. Internal documentation should include such things as people who have worked on the program, an abstract of the program, variable usage, notes about the development of the program, and anything else that will enable the new programmer to understand this program in the least amount of time. Internal documentation is written as the program is coded.

External documentation is for the user of the program. The end user will use the program to help solve problems. Proper external documentation ensures that the end user will have good instructions in order to learn to use this program in the least amount of time. External documentation should also allow the end user to find answers to questions arising while using the program. Good external documentation increases productivity for the end user. External documentation should include such things as tutorials, input definitions, usage instructions, installation instructions, command explanations, and anything else that will allow the end user to learn to use this program in the least amount of time.

Using the Tools

The problem-solving tools used in this book are the problem analysis chart, the structure chart, the IPO chart, the algorithm, and the flowchart. There is much duplication in these tools. Because of this duplication, you will find that after the first few weeks you will drop the use of some of these tools. However, for the first few problems, you should use all of the tools. In this way you will know which ones help you the most. You should end up using at least three of the five tools:

1. the PAC or the IPO chart
2. the structure chart
3. the algorithm or the flowchart

Other tools are presented in Appendix E.

Testing the Solution

When a solution is complete, it is important to test it to make sure it meets the requirements of the user, and to check for errors in logic or in the setup of the expressions and equations. To test a solution, the programmer selects test data, a set of values for the input data, and works them through every step in the solution. It is important to select test data carefully, so the correctness of the results can be checked with as much accuracy as possible. The values of the input data should be capable of checking logic and calculations thoroughly. For example, to test the expression X/Y, the test data should be numbers other than 1. Since 1/1 is 1, and 1 * 1 is also 1, this set of data would not accurately test the expression.

A solution should never be assumed correct. If a bug is detected, the solution has to be modified to correct it, and then the testing process started again at the beginning. Logic errors, such as incorrect loop conditions or wrong conditions in a decision statement, are the hardest to find and correct. It takes only a few logic errors to produce a program that is unreadable and a programmer who is frustrated. It is far easier to correct the solution in the problem-solving stages of program development than after the program is put into the computer.

Coding the Program

Once you have completed the steps described so far, you have finished analyzing the problem and organizing the solution. This book stops with testing the solution. The next step is writing the solution of the problem into a computer language—that is, *coding* the solution. You will learn to code solutions when you take language and applications courses.

If the programmer follows the proper steps in developing the solution, there should be few logic errors in the program, and the testing and coding should go quickly. Most bugs will be syntax errors or will stem from a misunderstanding of the original problem. Often the process will appear shorter and easier if you skip these problem-solving steps and code directly into the computer. The experienced programmer knows the fallacy of this shortsighted reasoning; this approach is almost always more time-consuming, and the resulting program less readable and less efficient.

Summary

The efficiency of the computer relies on the effectiveness of the programmer or the user. The programmer must write solutions that are clear, organized, and correct. A solution is a sequence of instructions for solving a problem. A program is a solution after it has been coded into a computer language. Data are stored internally in memory locations according to variable names and externally on a magnetic disk. External data are stored in sections called files, which are divided into records, which are further divided into fields. The file must be opened before accessing the data and closed when the user has finished with it.

The steps in organizing the solution to a problem start with problem analysis, a process whereby you separate a problem into four parts, including given data, required results, processing needs of the problem, and solution alternatives. The problem analysis chart is an aid to completing this first step. Second, the structure chart is developed, showing the breakdown of the whole problem into subtasks called modules. The IPO chart is the third step; it shows the input, the processing, and the output. The algorithms are developed fourth, showing in detail the sequence of instructions in the solution. Finally, from the algorithms the programmer draws the flowcharts, showing graphic representations of the algorithms. After completing these steps, the programmer can test, code, and implement the solution.

New Terms

algorithm
annotated flowchart
buffer
bug
debugging
external documentation
field
file

flowchart
internal documentation
IPO chart
module
problem analysis chart
program
pseudocode
record
structure chart
syntax

Questions

1. What is a program?
2. Why is problem analysis important?
3. Define a database, a file, a record, and a field. Give an example of each.
4. What happens when a programmer opens or closes a file?
5. Would each of the following be classified as a file, a record, or a field? Explain your answer.
   - **a.** a pay rate
   - **b.** all student data at a university
   - **c** one salesperson's data
   - **d.** a telephone number
   - **e.** a quantity
   - **f.** an employee's personnel data
   - **g.** an inventory item number
   - **h.** a price
   - **i.** information on one class
   - **j.** a sales receipt
6. What are the tools of problem solving described in this chapter?
7. What are the relationships of the problem-solving tools to each other?
8. How would each of the flowchart symbols be used? Include an example in your explanation.

Unit One

Supplementary Exercises

1. Write a set of numbered step-by-step instructions to plan a trip to San Francisco. Be sure to take into account the knowledge base of those who are going.
2. Design your own robot.
   - **a.** What can he do?
   - **b.** What is his knowledge base? (List the instructions that your robot will understand.)
   - **c.** List three problems that your robot could solve.
   - **d.** List the solution for one of these problems.
3. Evaluate, if A = 6, B = 4, and C = 2.
   - **a.** F = A ^ 2/3 * B
   - **b.** F = 3 * B/A ^ 2
   - **c.** F = A * C\(A + C)
   - **d.** F = (A + 7 − C) MOD B
   - **e.** F = (C * (B + 3 * A) + 5 * A)/C
4. **a.** Joe Brown's Shoe Store expects to increase its sales by 5% during the next year. Write an equation to calculate the projected sales at the end of the year. *Hint:* The standard expression to increase a number by a percentage is

   NUMBER * (1 + PERCENTAGE)

   b. However, inflation will decrease his profit increase. Expected inflation is 4½%, and 50% of Joe's expenses are directly affected by inflation. Joe's expenses are equal to 80% of his sales. Modify the equation in Exercise 4a to calculate the projected profit, taking into consideration inflation.
5. Evaluate (A = TRUE, B = TRUE, C = FALSE, D = FALSE):
   - **a.** R = (A OR B) AND C
   - **b.** R = A AND B OR C
   - **c.** R = B AND C OR A
   - **d.** R = NOT C AND NOT D OR A
   - **e.** R = NOT C OR NOT D AND A

6. Set up a logical expression for the following policy on using a company credit card. The card may be used if:
   a. balance plus sales amount is less than maximum allowable amount
   b. last payment was less than 45 days ago
   c. credit card has not expired
7. Set up a logical expression to check data using the following criteria. The data are assumed correct when:
   a. number is < 1000
   b. number is positive
   c. number is divisible by 2
8. Complete a flowchart for problem 4e in Chapter 1.

Unit 1: Find the Errors

The following problems have errors in them. Find the error, explain what is wrong and correct the error.

1. Set up the following equations for the computer:

Mathematical Equation	Computer Equation
a. $A + B = 5D$	**a.** D = A + B/5
b. $\frac{X + Y}{4} = Z$	**b.** (X + Y) / 4 = Z
c. $5X - 3Y = Z$	**c.** Z = 5X − 3Y

2. What is the order of processing of the following equations:

Computer Equation	Order of Processing
a. D = A + B/5	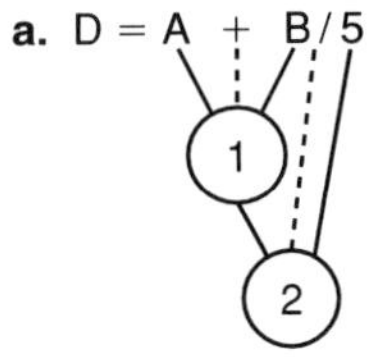
b. S = 5/D + 6* (C + B) / E	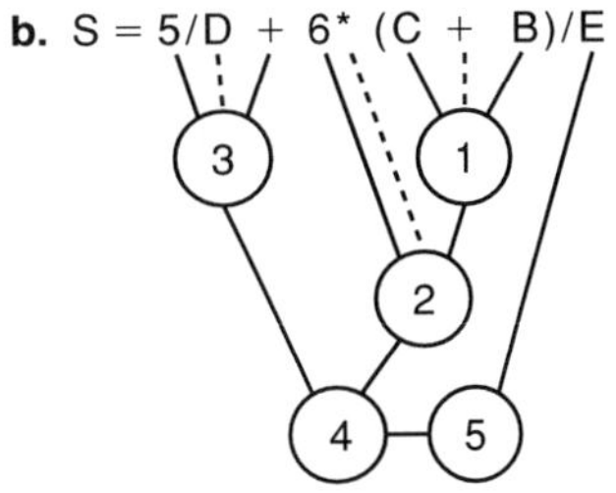
c. R = A < B AND C * F > G + 3	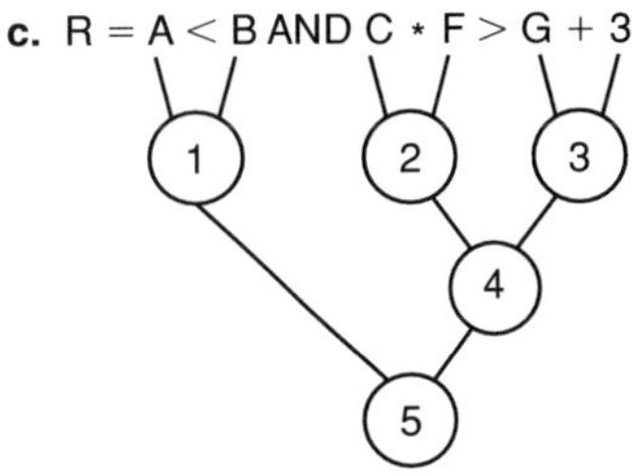

3. Write a truth table for the following equation:
R = A AND B OR NOT C

R = A AND B OR NOT C

A	B	C	R
0	0	0	0
1	1	1	1
0	0	1	0
1	0	1	1
1	0	0	0
0	1	1	0

UNIT TWO

STRUCTURING PROGRAMS FOR LANGUAGES AND APPLICATIONS

Chapter 4

An Introduction to Programming Structure

Overview

Objectives

When you have finished this chapter, you should be able to:

1. Explain the need for structured programming.
2. Explain how to design a module, in terms of cohesion, coupling, and function.
3. Explain the difference between local and global variables.
4. List and describe the four logic structures: sequential, decision, loops, and case.

The tools described in Chapter 3 help programmers organize programs as they arise in the business world or in a textbook. The techniques explained in Chapters 4 through 8 of Unit 2 provide ways to structure solutions so the computer can efficiently read and process the finished programs. That is, the techniques explained in these chapters help you write the several types of instructions that make up algorithms.

Pointers for Structuring a Program

The computer should be a tool to help people find solutions to their problems and to increase their productivity. The solutions must be developed according to methods that accomplish these goals. You can develop efficient computer solutions to problems if you heed the following pointers:

1. Use modules—break the whole into parts, each part having a particular function.
2. Use the four logic structures to assure that the solution flows smoothly from one instruction to the next, rather than jumping from one point in the solution to another.
   a. The **sequential structure** executes instructions one after another in a sequence.
   b. The **decision structure** branches to execute one of two possible sets of instructions.
   c. The **loop structure** executes a set of instructions many times.
   d. The **case structure** executes one set of instructions out of several sets. (This is a special case of the decision structure. Many textbooks include the case structure with the decision structure; however, because of the unique uses of the case structure, it has been placed in a separate chapter in this text.)
3. Eliminate the rewriting of identical processes by using modules.
4. Use techniques to improve readability, including the four logic structures, proper naming of variables, internal documentation, and proper indentation.

You can structure programs more easily if you build a library of techniques that have been perfected by the experts over the years. One of the rules for programming a computer is don't reinvent the wheel. Experienced programmers are productive because, among other reasons, they have learned good programming techniques.

In addition to techniques for structuring programs, the beginning programmer needs to learn the techniques of working with data structures. Techniques used with data structures teach the student how to store data in order to access and process it as efficiently as possible. These include techniques for processing arrays, linked lists, and trees. Beginning students also need to learn techniques for programming in a graphical user interface computer world where instructions are not necessarily executed in a procedural manner. This is called object oriented programming. These techniques are discussed in units 3 and 4 in this textbook.

Cohesion and Coupling

One of the most difficult tasks in the development of a solution to a problem is to divide the solution into modules. The question arises as to what should be included in each module. Modules should be functionally independent and perform a single task. However, modules will need to be connected, primarily through the data needed to complete the specified task within the modules. These opposing concepts are called **cohesion** and **coupling.** The concepts describe conflicting principles that lead to program design compromise.

Cohesion relates to the functional independence of the module and to the performance of a single "task" within the module. The overall objective is to separate the problem into parts such that each part becomes a module that will be designed to complete an independent task, such as entering data, printing data, initializing data, and the like. Each module is independent of each other module, with a single entrance and a single exit.

Coupling allows modules to be connected by an interface, which enables the programmer to transfer data from one module to another. Three coupling techniques are parameters used in functions, function names, and data that all modules can access. Coupling allows for communication between modules.

Cohesion and coupling are especially important concepts to the modern programmer, who in all probability will be working with many other programmers on the same problem. Cohesion allows a programmer to write a module of a larger program and test it independently. This module can then become a "black box" in a large program. Coupling allows all programmers to use necessary variable names without losing the cohesion of the module. For example, if Module 1 performs task 1 successfully, it may be required to provide data to Module 2. Cohesion results from having separate modules; coupling results when data are passed from Module 1 to Module 2. Another example of cohesion and coupling would be the use of the square root function. The square root function is a set of instructions to calculate the value of the square root of a number. The independence of these instructions is *cohesion.* The function is basically a black box. The programmer really doesn't worry about what the instructions are as long as a correct value is returned. However, in order to calculate the square root, the function needs a value to calculate the square root, and a value to return to the programmer. These data links, the number and the square root of the number, are what connects or *couples* the function to the rest of the program. This is *coupling.*

The Modules and Their Functions

Just as an author would not sit down and write without thinking about the structure of the book, neither should a programmer write without thinking about the structure of the program. First, an author thinks about the subject. A programmer studies the problem. Next, the author breaks the subject matter into chapters. The programmer breaks the problem into modules, each with a specific function. Once the chapters are in the correct order then the author starts to write them, one by one. Once the modules are in the correct processing order in the structure chart, then the programmer writes the algorithm for each module, one by one. A good programmer tests the algorithm for each module for correctness, as thoroughly as possible, before writing the next one. It is much easier to write and test many small modules than a single large one. Not only that, but when the program needs to be modified, it is much easier to test and change small modules.

Follow these rules for designing modules when you design your own solutions:

1. Each module is an entity in itself. There is one entrance and one exit. That is, the processing starts at the top and ends at the bottom of the module. Processing does not jump out of the middle of a module to another module, nor does it jump into the middle of a module.
2. Each module has a single function, such as printing, calculating, or entering data.
3. Each module is short enough to be easily read and modified.
4. The length of a module is governed by its function and the number of instructions to be executed to perform that function.

The types of modules needed for the solutions to most problems in this unit are the following:

1. **Control Module**—This module shows the overall flow of the data through the program. All other modules are subordinate to it.
2. **Init Module**—The **Initialization Module**, sometimes called the Preparation Module, processes instructions that are executed only once during the program, and only at the beginning. These instructions include opening files, setting the beginning values of variables used in the processing, and printing report headings.
3. **Process Data Modules**—These modules may be processed only once, or they may be part of a loop, which is processed more than once during the solution. There are several kinds of Process Data Modules:
   a. **Calculation Modules,** which do arithmetic calculations, accumulating (summing to calculate totals), counting, or manipulating numerical data in some other way, such as putting numbers in numerical order. Sometimes Calculation Modules manipulate string data to perform tasks such as putting a list of values in alphabetical order.
   b. **Print Modules,** which print output lines (the results of the processing, line by line), including headings and summaries.
   c. **Read** and **Data Validation Modules,** which read or input the data into the internal memory of the computer, validate data (check the accuracy of the data), enter data from the keyboard, and so forth. Validation Modules are usually separate from Read Modules.
4. **Wrap-up Module**—This module processes all instructions that are executed only once during the program and only at the end. These instructions include closing files and printing totals, among others.

Different types of modules are often combined in one solution. A module can be broken into several smaller modules to make the parts of a program more manageable. One module performing a specific function can be used by one or more other modules in which that same function is needed. Other types of modules are introduced in later chapters. The above types are the most frequently used.

Local and Global Variables

The concept of local and global variables is important in many languages. Programmers use the concept of local and global variables to allow cohesion and coupling to occur. Both local and global variables are defined in modules; however, the difference between the two is in the **scope** of the variables. The scope of the variables designates where the value of the variable can be used.

Local variables may be used only by the module itself. Other modules have no knowledge of these variables. This allows cohesion to take place. Through the use of local variables the programmer does not have to worry about variable name duplication in modules created by other programmers. If other modules need to use the value of variable, the modules must be coupled through the use of parameters or return values.

All modules have knowledge of **global variables.** They are global to the program as they can be seen by all modules. The use of global variables defeats one of the purposes of cohesion, that is to allow for the duplication of variable names in different modules. While global variables allow data coupling through the entire program, they should be used with caution. Only those variables which will be used in all modules should be designated as global variables. The programmer must be careful not to use the same variable name for a local variable and a global variable, since the hierarchy of use is to search the local variable list first, the parameter list second, and the global variable list last. The use of parameters and return values are not necessary since global variables couple the data from module to module.

Figure 4.1 shows a typical small structure chart. Figure 4.2 shows the scope of the variables found in this program. The variable, A, B, and C are global. All modules can use and change the values of these variables. All other variables are local. Only the Control Module can see the values of X, Y, and Z. The values of D, E, and F can only be seen by Module1. Module2 can see G, H, and I. Module3 can see only X, J, and K. Notice the duplication of the variable name X. In this case, there are two memory locations named X, one which can be used by the Control Module and the other which can be used by Module3. The computer will not get confused by this duplicity, since each X is linked to its own module.

Parameters

Parameters are data that are passed from one module to another. Parameters are another way of facilitating coupling. Parameters allow communication of data between modules. They are placed after the module name and within parentheses: READ (A, B, C). The formal parameter listing is the list as it appears in the declaration of the module. The actual parameter listing is the list as it appears in the calling module. The names of the parameters in the formal listing do not have to have the same names as those found in the actual listing. The values are passed according to the position in the listing. In Figure 4.3, 2 is the formal listing and 1 is the actual listing. The value of X becomes the value of A, and the value of Y becomes the value of B, and the value of Z becomes the value of C.

There are two kinds of parameters. First is the *call-by-value parameter.* This is an input value only. The value is transferred to the module, but the value of the variable will remain the same in the calling module, even though it may be changed in the receiving module. The second type of parameter is the *call-by-reference parameter.* This is an input and output parameter. The value is transferred to the receiving module and then may be changed. The changed value is then passed back to the calling

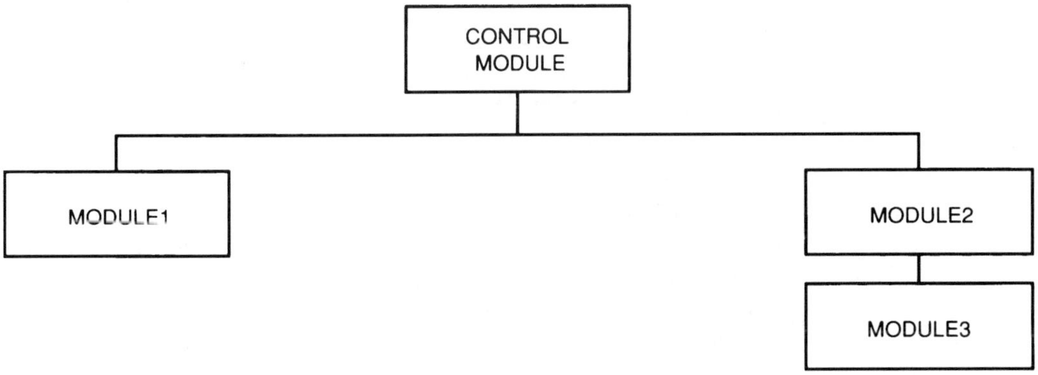

Figure 4.1 Structure Chart

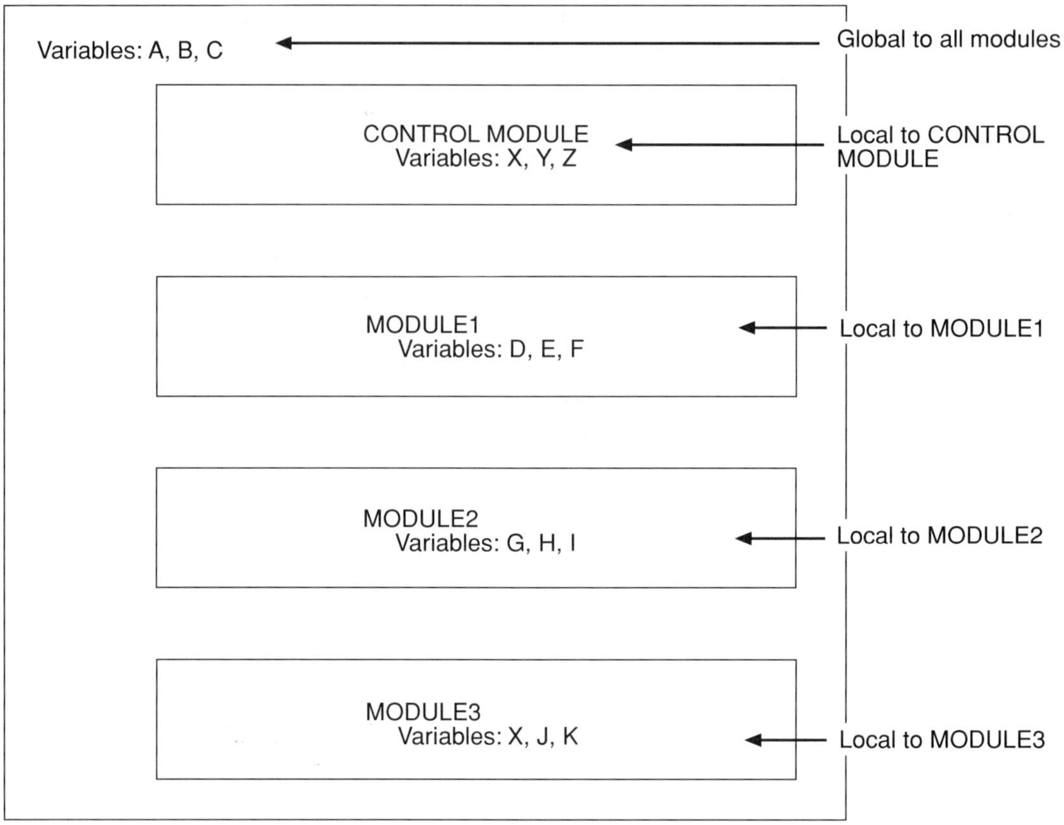

Figure 4.2 Scope of Local and Global Variables

module (see Figure 4.3). In Figure 4.3, the calling module is Module1 and the receiving module is Module2.

Figure 4.4 shows the *coupling diagram* for Figure 4.3. A coupling diagram indicates how data couple modules together. A coupling diagram has a rectangle for each module and a line connecting the modules for each datum passed from one module to another. In this case, there is a rectangle for Module1 and another one for Module2. Notice the connecting lines. There is one for A→X, another for B→Y, and another for C→Z. The names of the variables are added beside the lines. The names that Module1 uses are directly below the Module1 rectangle. The names that Module 2 uses are directly above the Module2 rectangle. This shows that the value of A becomes the value of X, the value of B becomes the value of Y, and the value of C becomes the value of Z. The arrowhead indicates the type of parameter. A single-headed arrow shows that the datum is passed into Module2, but not out. Therefore, a single-headed arrow indicates a *call-by-value* parameter. A double-headed arrow shows that the datum is passed into Module2, can be changed, and then the changed value is passed out of Module2. Therefore, a double-headed arrow indicates a *call-by-reference* parameter.

Parameters are one of the best methods of coupling modules. The programmer does not have to worry about variable name duplication in modules that other programmers are developing. Parameters in the formal parameter listing are not local or global variables and therefore should not be declared as local or global variables. In the event of variable name duplication, the local variable has precedence over the parameter name, and the parameter name has precedence over the global variable name. When the program is looking for a variable name, it first looks at the local variable list, second at the

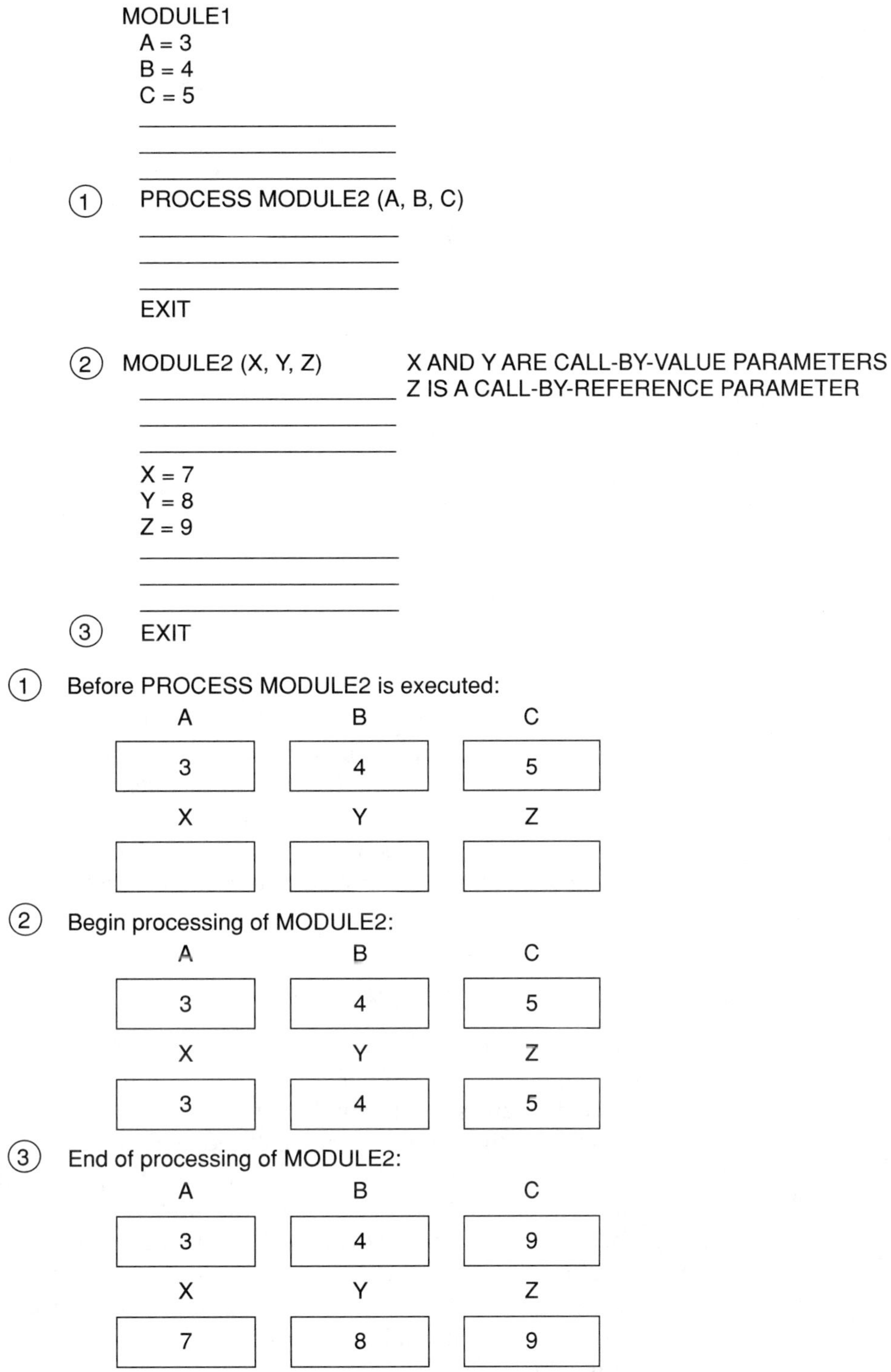

Figure 4.3 Parameters

formal parameter list, and last at the global variable list. If it is not found at any of the three, an error occurs.

The three ways to couple modules are through the use of global variables, parameters, and the module name. As we learned in Chapter 2, each function has a return value. This return value is the result of the function. This is accomplished through the

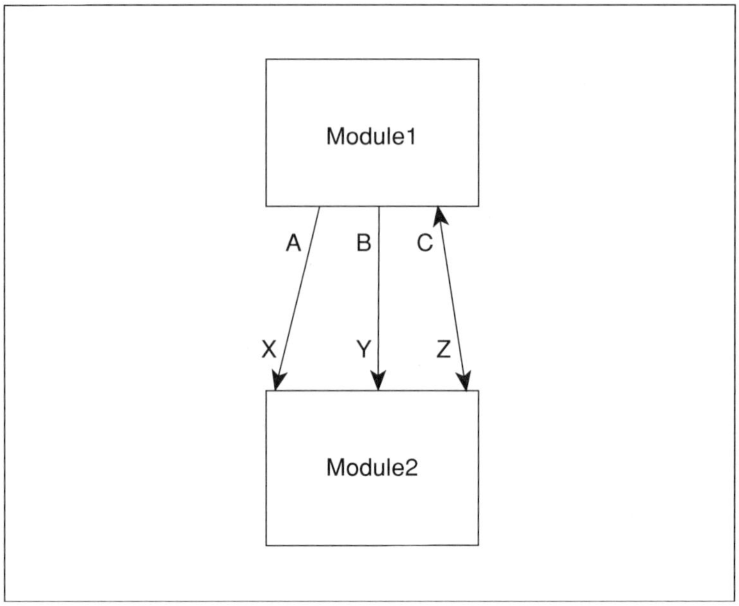

Figure 4.4 Coupling Diagram

name of the function. At the conclusion of the execution of the function, the result is placed temporarily in the name. The function must be used as part of another instruction. The value of the name of the function is no longer available once the instruction has been executed. Some languages allow the programmers to use this technique to couple their modules. In this case the value is only passed out of the second module into the first module. In a coupling diagram the arrowhead would be a single-headed arrow, but pointing to the first module.

Variable Names and the Data Dictionary

Variables must be named according to what they represent. If they represent *hours* then the variable name should be HOURS. When the variables are all local or used as parameters, variable names must be unique to the module in which they are defined. If variables are global, they must be unique to the total program. When you name a variable, that name must be used whenever you are referring to that item. You cannot use HOURS in one place and HRS in another place in one module, or again, if the variable is global, throughout the whole program. The computer references values by their names. Therefore if you change the name the computer assumes the new name represents a new item. A data dictionary is a great help to keep track of the variable usage in your program. It contains a list of all items, their variable names, their data types, the module in which they are found, pseudonyms and the module in which the pseudonym is found, and any error check that needs to be made on the variable. Figure D.5 in Appendix D is a form to use for your data dictionary. Figure 4.5 shows an example of a data dictionary. If you are using different names in different modules, you must also show the coupling diagram. In this text, the variable names will be consistent throughout the program, and therefore will not include a coupling diagram nor a data dictionary in most of the examples in the book. However, many of the assignments will require either or both.

Data Dictionary

Item	Variable Name	Data Type	Module(s)	Scope	Pseudonyms/Module	Error Checks
Hours worked	HOURS	Numeric—real	Read	Local	None	Hours < 0
Hours worked	HOURS	Numeric—real	Calc	Local	None	None
Payrate	PAYRATE	Numeric—real	Read	Local	None	Payrate < 4.00
Payrate	PAYRATE	Numeric—real	Calc	Local	None	None
Net pay	NETPAY	Numeric—real	Calc	Local	None	None
Net pay	NETPAY	Numeric—real	Print	Local	None	None

Figure 4.5 Example of a Data Dictionary

The Four Logic Structures

Up to now, this book has discussed the structure of the *problem,* that is, how to break a problem into parts, or modules, and arrange them so the data flow in a solution is logical. There are other types of structures used to design the modules themselves. These structures are called **logic structures,** and they control the logic of the data flow though the module. The instructions that make up the algorithms and the flowcharts are combinations of the four logic structures.

Chapters 5, 6, 7, and 8 in this unit are devoted to the four basic logic structures:

1. The sequential logic structure
2. The decision logic structure
3. The loop logic structure
4. The case logic structure

A brief explanation of each of these logic structures follows.

The sequential logic structure processes data one instruction after another. This logic structure is the most widely used, and it is normally used in conjunction with others. The programmer uses the decision logic structure to program the computer to make choices. The programmer uses calculations that use relational or logical operators to design these choices. The third logic structure is the loop, which enables the computer to repeat tasks. The last logic structure, the case logic structure, enables the programmer to request that the computer pick one of a set of tasks through a code or through an option using a number, a letter, or a string. When a problem is broken down in modules, the appropriate logic structures can be applied to each module. Effective use of the four logic structures results in efficient and readable solutions.

Summary

Unit 2 consists of several chapters on how to structure solutions for particular computer languages and applications. You will learn four logic structures for designing programs for problem solving—plus additional techniques for record processing. These techniques are extremely important because they can greatly increase productivity. They help you effectively organize the instructions in each of the algorithms that make up your solution. As a result, the computer can read the solution easily and process your program efficiently.

Cohesion is designing a module to be as independent of the rest of the modules as possible. Coupling refers to how data couple the modules. The three ways to couple modules are through the use of global variables, parameters and module names. Global variables are those variables known to other modules. Local variables are those variables known to only one module. The computer searches for variables first in the local variable list, then the parameter list, and finally the global list.

To make a computer problem manageable, break your solution into modules. For Unit 2, the types of modules you'll need include Control, Init, Process Data, and Wrap-up. There are several kinds of Process Data Modules, including Calculation Modules, various Print Modules, Read Modules, and File Maintenance Modules.

New Terms

- cohesion
- coupling
- global variables
- local variables
- logic structures:
  - sequential structure
  - decision structure
  - loop structure
  - case structure
- parameters
- scope
- types of modules:
  - Control
  - Initialization
  - Process Data
    - Calculation
    - Print
    - Read
    - Data Validation
  - Wrap-up

Questions

1. Name the four logic structures.
2. What is a module? How is it used?
3. Name the major types of modules and explain their functions.

4. List the kinds of Process Data Modules.
5. What is meant by the cohesion of a module?
6. What is meant by coupling modules?
7. Why are cohesion and coupling important to programmers?
8. How are modules coupled?
9. What does a coupling diagram show?
10. Define the two types of parameters. How do they differ? Under what circumstances would you use each type?

Chapter 5

Problem Solving with the Sequential Logic Structure

Overview

Objective

When you have finished this chapter, you should be able to:

> Develop problems for the computer using the five program developmental tools and the sequential logic structure.

Algorithm Instructions and Flowchart Symbols

The computer's system of communication dictates how the programmer designs algorithms and flowcharts. Recall that an algorithm is a set of instructions telling the computer how to process a module in a solution. You'll write an algorithm for each module in a program. A flowchart is a visual illustration of an algorithm. You'll draw a flowchart to accompany each algorithm. This chapter begins with only a few of the specific algorithm instructions and flowchart symbols you'll use as a trained programmer, those required to solve problems using the sequential structure. They are found in Table 5.1 and include the instructions to start and stop each module, to enter data, to output data, to process modules, and to perform calculations.

You write an instruction in two parts: a general instruction followed by specifications regarding what is to be processed. In Table 5.1 the general instruction is the first word in the Algorithm Instruction column, that is, START, ENTER, VARIABLE =, and so forth. The specifications—a specific module name, a list of variable names, a specific expression, and so forth—follow the instruction. They are data and ways of processing drawn from the problem and collected for the problem, and information from the structure chart and the other charts you completed prior to the algorithms.

Table 5.1 Algorithm Instructions and Flowchart Symbols

Algorithm Instruction	Flowchart Symbol	Definition (What the instruction tells the computer)
START [module name] [module number]	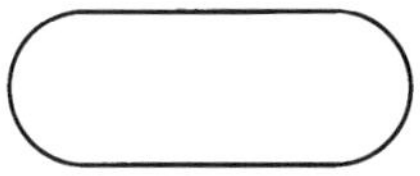	Start processing a module. The word START is optional and is not used in this text.
ENTER [list of variable names]		Enter data from a data block or from the keyboard into the following variable memory locations.
Variable = [expression]	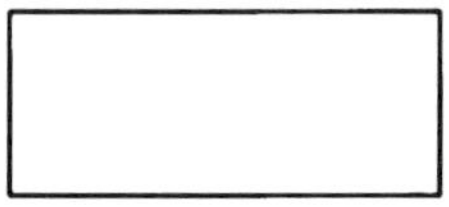	Assign the value of the following expression to a variable location. Called the *assignment instruction.*
WRITE [list of variable names]	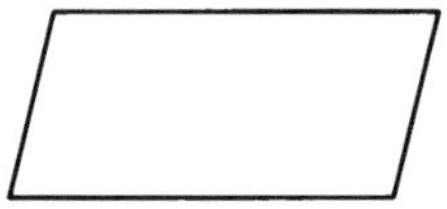	Write to the printer the values represented by the following variable names.
PRINT [list of variable names]	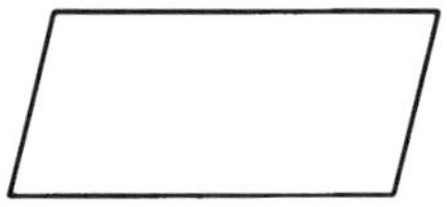	Print on the screen the values represented by the following variable names.
PROCESS [module name]	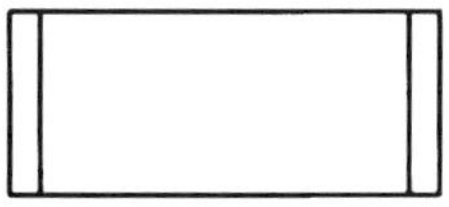	Execute the instructions in the named module, and then return to execute the next instruction.
END/EXIT	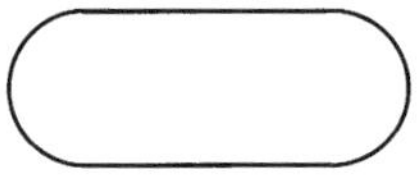	Stop the processing of the module. Processing ceases with the End; with the Exit, processing continues with the next instruction after the PROCESS.

The START instruction is always understood, if not stated, at the beginning of an algorithm and flowchart and indicates where the module begins. The oval is the flowchart symbol for the START instruction. The instruction includes the name and number of the module. For example,

Init (1000)

or

Print (4000)

The name and number of the module also may be written at the beginning of the algorithm, which is the case throughout this text.

The ENTER instruction enables the user to enter data into memory locations with variable names. The list of variable names follows the ENTER instruction. For example,

ENTER NAME, AGE

Data are entered from the keyboard or from a set of data called a *data block,* specified in the program. Variable = (commonly called the *assignment instruction*) enables a user to instruct the computer to store a constant, a variable, or an expression in a named variable memory location. The order of the instruction is the variable name followed by the equals sign followed by a constant, a variable name, or an expression as in

PAY = HOURS * WAGE

The WRITE instruction outputs values to the printer. The list of information to be printed follows the WRITE, as in

WRITE NAME, AGE

The PRINT instruction is similar to the WRITE instruction except that the output is directed to the screen rather than the printer. The PROCESS instruction tells the computer to process the instructions of a named module before continuing. The name of the module to be processed follows the PROCESS instruction, as in

PROCESS Init

or

PROCESS Calc

The END or EXIT instruction specifies the completion of a module. END is used to end the Control Module and indicates that the processing of the solution is complete. EXIT is used to end a subordinate module and indicates that the processing will continue in another module, the module where the PROCESS instruction originated. The programmer writes each instruction in its entirety within the appropriate flowchart symbol.

The list of instructions in Table 5.1 will be expanded in future chapters.

The Sequential Logic Structure

The most commonly used and the simplest logic structure is the sequential structure. All problems use the sequential structure, and most problems use it in conjunction with one or more of the other logic structures. To illustrate how to use this structure, this chapter develops a sample problem solution demonstrating each of the computer problem-solving steps explained in Chapter 3.

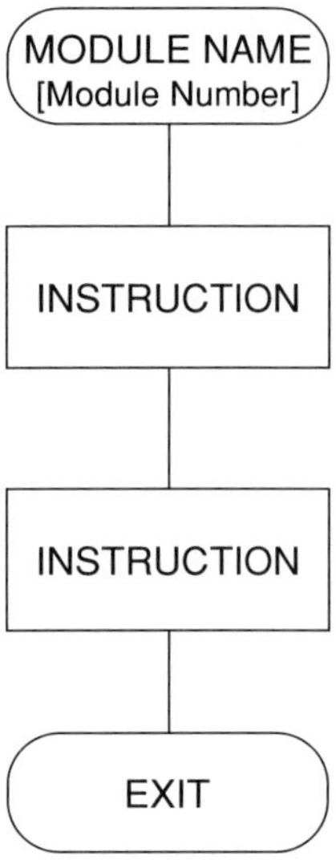

Figure 5.1 Flowchart Diagram for the Sequential Structure

A programmer who uses the sequential logic structure is asking the computer to process a set of instructions in sequence from the top to the bottom of an algorithm. In general, the form of the algorithm looks like this:

MODULE NAME [Module Number]
1. INSTRUCTION
2. INSTRUCTION
3. . . .
. . .
XX.END or EXIT

The algorithm begins with the START instruction represented by the name and number of the module. The numbered instructions following the START might be any of the instructions other than START and END/EXIT, depending on the problem. The form of the flowchart corresponds to the form of the algorithm (see Figure 5.1). The first block is the START block. Other instruction blocks follow. These blocks can be of any type other than the flattened ellipse, which indicates START or END/EXIT. The final block is the END or EXIT block. See Figure 5.2 for an example of the algorithm and the flowchart for a solution that enters a name and an age into the computer and prints them to the screen.

Solution Development

In Chapter 3, the tools for organizing problems were introduced. Now you will use them to solve problems from the business world. These organizing tools are used in the first five steps of developing a solution.

1. The problem analysis chart—helps you define and understand the problem, develop ideas for the solution, and select the best solution
2. The structure chart—breaks the solution to the problem into parts
3. The IPO chart—helps define the input, the output, and the processing steps

Algorithm	Flowchart
NAMEAGE (0000) 1. START 2. ENTER NAME, AGE 3. PRINT NAME, AGE 4. END	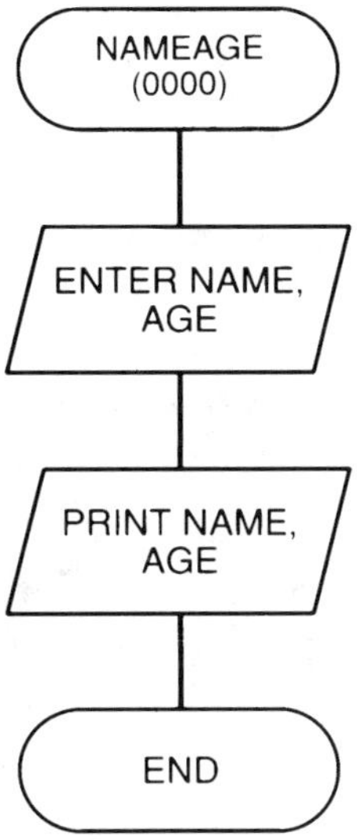

Figure 5.2 Algorithm and Flowchart to Enter and Print Two Variables

4. The algorithms
5. The flowcharts

The sixth step in solving the problem is to test the solution to catch any errors in logic or calculation. Remember, the charts are aids to the efficient development of a well-written program. They will not be perfect the first time around, and will often need several revisions.

As you follow the solution to the sample sequential-structure problem that follows, take the time to think through each step. Photocopy the forms in Appendix D to complete the six steps. The solution to the following problem will be developed.

> Mary Smith is looking for the bank that will give the most return on her money over the next five years. She has $2,000 to put into a savings account. The standard equation to calculate principal plus interest at the end of a period of time is

$$AMOUNT = P * (1 + I/M)\text{^}(N * M)$$

where P = PRINCIPAL (amount of money to invest, in this case $2,000)
I = INTEREST (percentage rate the bank pays to the investor)
N = NUMBER OF YEARS (time for which the principal is invested)
M = COMPOUND INTERVAL (the number of times per year the interest is calculated and added to the principal)

(Refer to Table 2.5 to review the meanings of the operators used here.)

Problem Analysis

The first step in analyzing the problem is to understand what is needed and what is given, and to separate them from all of the unessential information in the problem.

Write down the input and the output. Record the processing that the problem demands in the section of the problem analysis chart headed Required Processing. Finally, write possible solutions for the problem and any ideas related to the solution in the Solution Alternatives section. Generate solution ideas through brainstorming and creative thinking. When you are first learning problem-solving skills, brainstorming is best accomplished in groups of two to three people. The more ideas, the easier it is to develop a good solution.

In Figure 5.3, the problem analysis chart has been filled in for the interest problem given in the previous section. The given data are the PRINCIPAL ($2,000), the INTEREST (variable), the NUMBER OF YEARS the PRINCIPAL is to be invested (5), and the COMPOUND INTERVAL (variable). The required result is the AMOUNT of PRINCIPAL plus INTEREST at the end of the time period. The required processing is the equation for the AMOUNT. Solution ideas include the following:

1. Enter all input data as variables.
2. Enter the principal and interest as constants, and the other values as variables.
3. Enter the data for one bank per run.
4. Enter the data for all banks per run.

Figure out the best solution involves weighing the ideas and alternatives in the Solution Alternatives section of the problem analysis chart. Since a solution should be as flexible as possible, it would be better to enter all the data as variables. Variables provide flexibility because their values can be changed whereas the values of constants cannot. It is best to use variables wherever there is a possibility that the data might change, and constants only if it is known that the data won't change. Furthermore, since the user probably will not have all data from all banks at once, entering one bank per run would be the best for this solution.

Given Data	Required Results
PRINCIPAL–$2,000 INTEREST NUMBER OF YEARS–5 COMPOUND INTERVAL (#/year)	PRINCIPAL plus INTEREST at the end of the time period

Required Processing
AMOUNT = P * (1 + I / M)^(N * M)

Solution Alternatives
*1. Enter all data as variables. 2. Enter principal and interest as constants and the other data as variables. *3. Process one bank in one run. 4. Process all banks in one run. *Processes selected for the best solution.

Figure 5.3 Problem Analysis Chart—Interest Problem

The Structure Chart

At this point, you can develop the structure chart. To complete the structure chart you have to answer the question, How can I divide this problem into smaller, more manageable parts? In Figure 5.4, the interest problem is broken into four modules—the Interest Control Module, which controls the solution; the Read Module, which enters the data; the Calc Module, which calculates the amount; and the Print Module, which prints the result. The structure chart shows that the Interest Control Module processes the other three modules in the following order—the Read, Calc, and Print Modules, respectively. These four modules are the only ones in this solution. There is no Init Module since there is nothing to be initialized (no files to open, no headings to print, or the like), nor is there a Wrapup Module since there is nothing to be done at the conclusion of the processing (no files to close, no totals to print, or the like). The solution requires only that data be entered, that a calculation be performed, and that the results be printed. Each box represents a module. Each module has a function and represents one or more instructions.

The IPO Chart

Now the IPO chart can be developed from the problem analysis chart and the structure chart. To complete the IPO chart you have to answer the question, How can the input be processed to achieve the required output? You'll provide general instructions for the solution on the IPO chart. You will not write the specific instructions to the computer until you complete the algorithms and the flowcharts.

In Figure 5.5, the output is the amount of the PRINCIPAL plus INTEREST after five years. The input required to produce this result includes the beginning PRINCIPAL, the INTEREST RATE (changed to hundredths after it is input), the NUMBER OF YEARS INVESTED, and the COMPOUNDED TIME INTERVAL. The processing includes entering the data (found in module 1000, the Read Module), calculating the amount (found in the module 2000, the Calc Module), and printing the amount (found in module 3000, the Print Module). This information is found in the Processing and the Module Reference Number columns.

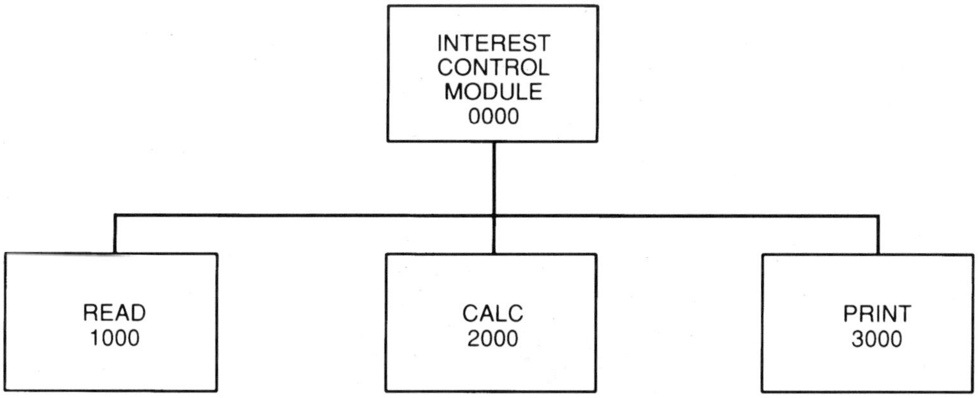

Figure 5.4 The Structure Chart—Interest Problem

Input	Processing	Module Reference Number	Output
1. BEGINNING PRINCIPAL 2. INTEREST RATE 3. NUMBER OF YEARS 4. NUMBER OF TIMES INTEREST IS COMPOUNDED YEARLY	1. Enter data (Change interest rate to hundredths)	1000	1. Ending PRINCIPAL plus INTEREST 2. All input data
	2. Calculate ending PRINCIPAL and INTEREST AMOUNT = PRINCIPAL*(1 + INTEREST / TIME)^(YEARS*TIME)	2000	
	3. Print required results	3000	

Figure 5.5 The IPO Chart—Interest Problem

Coupling Diagram and Data Dictionary

Figure 5.6, the Coupling Diagram, and Figure 5.7, the Data Dictionary, are interrelated. The coupling diagram shows which variables are passed from one module to another. The data dictionary shows which modules use each variable and the scope of each variable (whether the variable is local or global.) In this problem, all variables are local, therefore, all coupling will be done through parameters. The variables which couple the Interest Control Module and the Read Module are the Principal, the Interest, the Number of Years, and the Compounding Time. These are all call-by-reference parameters since the variables sent to the Read Module must have values assigned to them. The new values are then passed back to the Interest Control Module. The same four are call-by-value parameters when coupling the Interest Control Module to the Calc Module. This

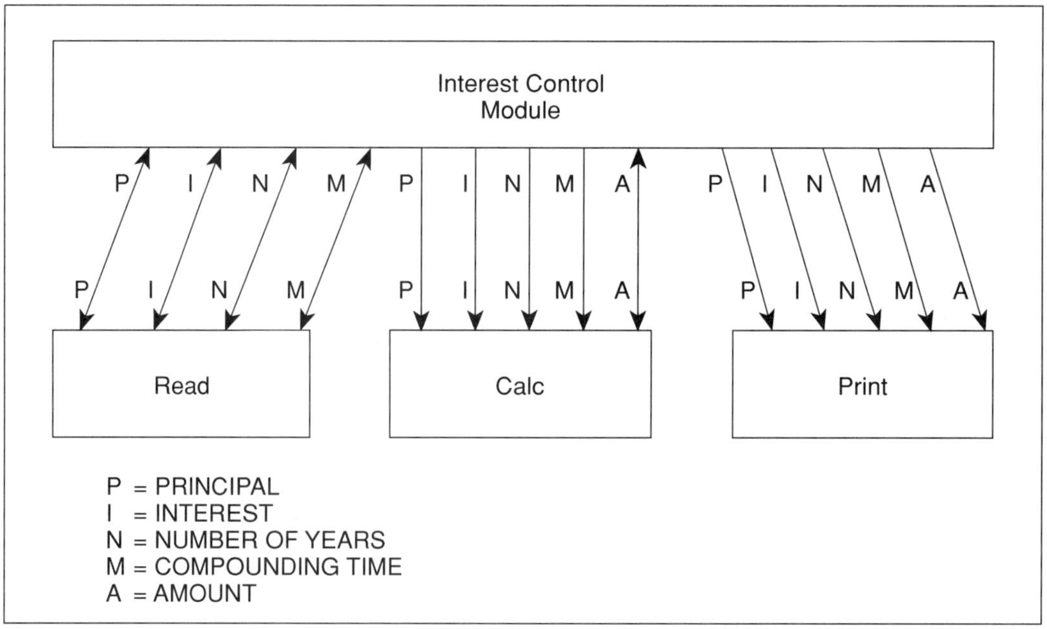

Figure 5.6 Coupling Diagram

Data Dictionary

Item	Variable Name	Data Type	Module(s)	Scope	Pseudonyms/ Module	Error Checks
Principal	PRINCIPAL	Numeric—real	Interest Control/Read/ Calc/Print	Local	None	None
Interest	INTEREST	Numeric—real	Interest Control/Read/ Calc/Print	Local	None	None
Number of years	YEARS	Numeric—real	Interest Control/Read/ Calc/Print	Local	None	None
Compounding time	TIME	Numeric—real	Interest Control/Read/ Calc/Print	Local	None	None
Amount	AMOUNT	Numeric—real	Interest Control/ Calc/Print	Local	None	None

Figure 5.7 Data Dictionary

is because they will not be changed, only used, in the Calc Module. The amount, however, needs to be a call-by-reference parameter since the value of the Amount will be calculated in the Calc Module and then sent back to the Interest Control Module. All five variables couple the Interest Control Module to the Print Module. They are call-by-value parameters since the Print Module only needs to use them. The four variables will not be changed in the Print Module. To determine which variables are call-by-reference parameters and which are call-by value parameters, the programmer needs to see which variables will be changed in the called module. If the variable is changed, then it needs to be a call-by-reference parameter. If the called module is only going to use the value of the variable, then it needs to be a call-by-value parameter.

Internal and External Documentation

Documentation is useful to everyone involved with the program, so it is important that the programmer or the user of the application package write down important details about the program. The programmer's colleagues need to know what was done, how it was done, and where, in order to finish and maintain the program. The user needs to know what has been done and how, in order to use the program or application effectively, and, further, to make sure the processing is correct. Internal documentation involves noting within the instruction set what the instructions do. This is accomplished through the use of remark or comment statements. These statements appear only in the listing of the statements and nowhere else. They are for the use of the programmer only. The end user never sees them. External documentation involves writing manuals with detailed explanations of the program and how to use it.

You take notes for internal and external documentation during problem solving because it is easy to forget the details that you need later when you are writing the documentation. There is an Annotation section for these notes on page 457 of Figure

D.4—Algorithm and Flowchart, Appendix D. You write the notes for the documentation as you develop the algorithms and the flowcharts, including any important information that is not already part of the algorithms and flowcharts. In the Interest Control Module in Figure 5.8a-d, the exact task of each of the Process Modules (the Read, the Calc, and the Print Modules) is not specified. The remarks in the Annotation section specify those tasks. For example, the Read Module enters all data from the keyboard. The Annotation section is the only place you can explain such things in any depth. Only after the module has been developed completely can you sell all that belongs in the documentation, so it is best not to finish the notes on each module until then. The Annotation and Documentation sections of the Algorithm and Flowchart form are optional, but are often useful later.

The Algorithms and Flowcharts

Once the structure chart and the IPO chart are completed, you can proceed with the algorithms and the flowcharts. To complete an algorithm, you have to answer the question, How can this module complete its function? To draw the flowchart you answer the ques-

Algorithm	Flowchart	Annotation	Test
Interest Control Module (0000) 1. PROCESS READ 2. PROCESS CALC 3. PROCESS PRINT 4. END	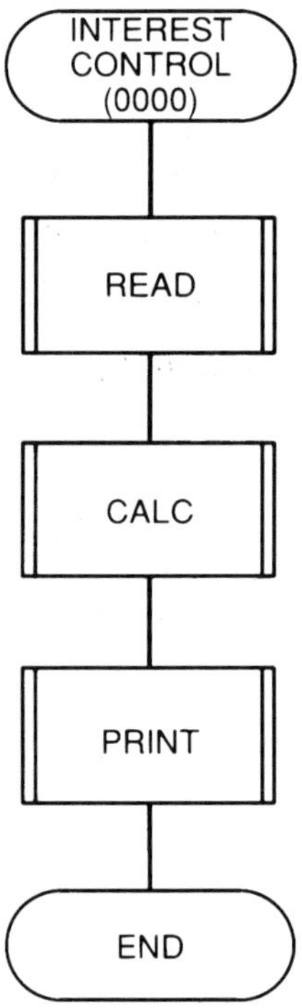	Enters all data from keyboard Calculates amount Prints data and amount	1. Start 2. Transfer to Read 3. Transfer to Calc 4. Transfer to Print

Internal Documentation	External Documentation
1. Remark at top: Calculates principal and interest given beginning principal, interest rate, number of years, and compounded time interval 2. Include annotations	1. Same as 1 in Internal Documentation

Figure 5.8a Algorithm and Flowchart for INTEREST CONTROL Module

Algorithm	Flowchart	Annotation	Test
Read Module (1000) 1. ENTER PRINCIPAL, INTEREST, YEARS, TIME 2. INTEREST = INTEREST / 100 3. EXIT	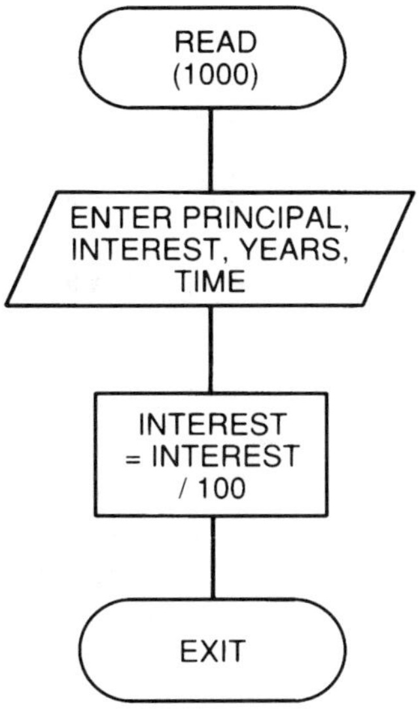	1. Interest is Rate 2. Time is number of times interest is compounded yearly	Principal 2000 Interest 5% Years 5 Time 2

Internal Documentation	External Documentation
1. Remark at top: Module to enter all data and to convert interest rate	1. Explain input data

Figure 5.8b Algorithm and Flowchart for READ Module

Algorithm	Flowchart	Annotation	Test
Calc Module (2000) 1. AMOUNT = PRINCIPAL * (1 + INTEREST/TIME) ^ (YEARS * TIME) 2. EXIT	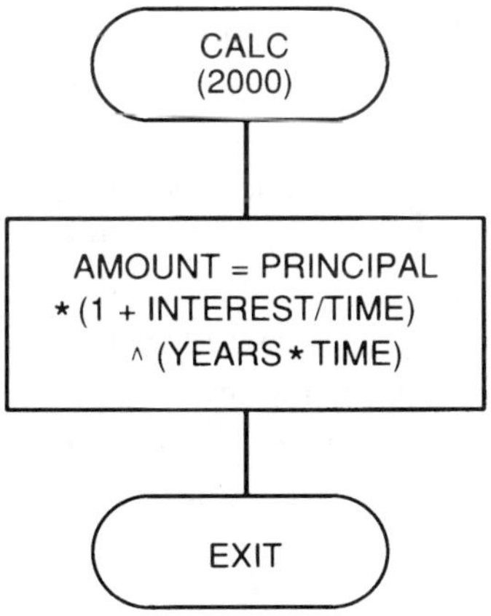	None	Amount = 2000 * (1 + .05 / 2) ^ (5 * 2) Amount = 2000 * (1 + .025) ^ 10 Amount = 2560

Internal Documentation	External Documentation
1. Remark at top: Module to calculate principal and interest	1. Specify equation

Figure 5.8c Algorithm and Flowchart for CALC Module

Algorithm	Flowchart	Annotation	Test
Print Module (3000) 1. PRINT AMOUNT, PRINCIPAL, INTEREST, YEARS, TIME 2. EXIT	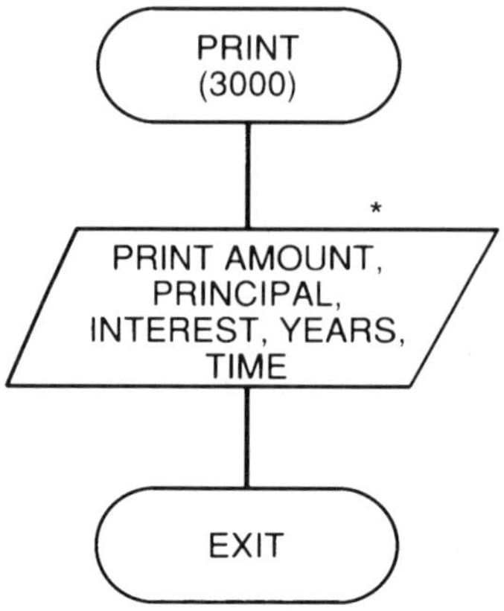	1. Print each variable on a separate line with a label*	Prints what is required

Internal Documentation	External Documentation
1. Remark at top: Module to print required output	1. Specify output

*Specify only what and when the information is printed, not how it is printed.

Figure 5.8d Algorithm and Flowchart for PRINT Module

tion, How does the algorithm look graphically? By using the completed algorithms and the flowcharts, you can find and correct logic errors.

Figure 5.8a-d shows the four algorithms, one for each module in the structure chart, and their corresponding flowcharts. The Interest Control Module uses a sequential structure to execute the instructions, as do each of the other modules. Notice how the instructions simply flow in order from the top to the bottom of each algorithm. The Annotation and Documentation sections of this figure have been completed to show how to use these sections in the Algorithm and Flowchart form.

The next step in developing the solution is to take a set of test data and work it through the algorithm instructions on a piece of paper or in the section provided on the Algorithm and Flowchart form. Do not skip any steps. It is important to process the data as you have instructed the computer to do it, starting at the beginning of the Interest Control Module and working a set of data through the instructions in the algorithms for each module, one by one. As you process each module, write down the results. The solution is correct if the output matches the desired results. In this problem, the output should match the hand-calculated value of the amount. If the correct output is produced, then the analysis is complete. If not, you need to make corrections in the algorithm until you reach the correct output. At that point the analysis will be complete and coding into a language or application can begin. Coding is done in a language or applications course.

Summary

The instructions in every algorithm must use particular logic structures in order to increase readability for the programmer or user. The first logic structure is the sequential structure, in which the processing flows from one instruction to the next from start to end. The particular instructions used with the sequential structure include START, STOP, ENTER data, PRINT and WRITE data, assign a value to a variable (variable =), PROCESS another module, and END/EXIT.

A solution to a problem is developed in six steps:

1. Analyze the problem.
2. Develop the structure chart.
3. Develop the IPO chart.
4. Develop the algorithms.
5. Develop the flowcharts.
6. Test the solution.

These steps will help you develop a solution that is efficient and easy to understand, code, and maintain.

After preparing the structure chart and the IPO chart, and while developing the algorithms and flowcharts, the programmer takes notes for the internal and external documentation that will be completed later. The internal documentation will be written within the program. The external documentation will be written in the form of manuals explaining the program.

Questions

1. What is the sequential logic structure?

2. Which flowchart symbols are used for the sequential logic structure?

3. Why is documentation important?

Problems

Complete the six steps of solution development and a data dictionary for the following problems:

1. A painter wants to know the amount of paint needed to paint only the walls and the interior side of the door in a room. The chosen paint covers 100 square feet per gallon. There are two windows. Test the problem with the following data:

The room is 12 feet long, 10 feet wide, and 8 feet tall.

The two windows are 5 by 3 feet, and 6 by 2 feet, respectively.

2. One of the jobs that Joe Roberts has been given at work is to order special paper for a report for a board meeting. The paper comes in reams of 500 sheets. He always makes 5 more copies than the number of people that will be there. Joe wants to know how many reams of paper he needs for a meeting. He can order only whole, not partial, reams. Test your solution with the following data:

The report is 140 pages long.

There will be 25 people at the meeting.

3. An instructor calculates grades by dropping the lowest homework score and the lowest test score, and adding the remaining scores together. He then calculates the final points as a percentage of the total points possible. The instructor needs to know the final points for a given student. (*Hint:* Use the minimum function, that is, the function that returns the minimum value in a list of values.) Test your solution with the following data:

Total points possible—500 points

Tom Johnson

Homework scores—45, 46, 41, 31, 44

Test scores—95, 84, 75, 98

4 a. Develop a solution that would return the fewest coins in change from a purchase of under one dollar. (Include pennies, nickels, dimes, quarters, and half dollars.)

Example:	purchase	63¢
	change	37¢
	coins	1 quarter
		1 dime
		2 pennies

b. Develop a solution that would return the fewest bills and coins for a purchase under $50.

5. Mary Williams needs to change a Fahrenheit temperature to Celsius. Use the Fahrenheit temperature of 80 degrees to test your solution.

6. Write a solution to print the number of months (use 30 days to a month) and remaining days given the number of days between two dates.

Chapter 6

Problem Solving with Decisions

Overview

The Decision Logic Structure
Multiple IF/THEN/ELSE Instructions
Using Straight-through Logic
Using Positive Logic
Using Negative Logic
Logic Conversion
Which Decision Logic?
Decision Tables

Objectives

When you have finished this chapter, you should be able to:

1. Develop problems for the computer using the five program developmental tools, the sequential logic structure, and the decision logic structure.
2. Use nested decision instructions to develop a problem solution.
3. Develop decision tables given a set of policies.

The logic structures will almost always be used in some combination with each other in a program. In this chapter you'll learn how to use a second logic structure, the decision structure, as a way to design instructions. The decision structure is one of the most powerful because it is the only way that the computer can choose between two or more sets of actions. Without decisions, the computer would be nothing more than a fast calculator.

The decision logic structure is relatively easy to understand since it works much like the way humans think. Because of the complexity of some of the decisions a programmer has to design, however, it is often one of the most difficult structures to implement. The difficulty goes back to the fact that people make decisions without understanding the reasoning involved. Also, a decision can be written in many different ways, which can add to the confusion.

The Decision Logic Structure

The decision logic structure uses the **IF/THEN/ELSE instruction**. It tells the computer that IF a condition is true, THEN execute a set of instructions, or ELSE execute another set of instructions. The following algorithm instruction for the decision structure (the decision instruction) should be added to the list in Table 5.1. Notice the brackets and the indentation in the illustration of the algorithm of the decision instruction. Programmers use these features when they are writing instructions in the decision structure because they improve readability.

```
    ┌────────IF <condition(s)>
    ├────────── THEN
T   │              <TRUE instruction(s)>
    ├────────── ELSE
F   │              <FALSE instruction(s)>
    └────────
```

The TRUE instructions are processed when the resultant of the condition is TRUE, and the FALSE instructions are processed when the resultant of the condition is FALSE. A condition can be one of four things: a logical expression, that is, an expression that uses logical operators (AND, OR, and NOT); an expression using relational operators (greater than, less than, greater than or equal to, less than or equal to, equal to, and not equal to); a variable of the logical data type (TRUE or FALSE); or a combination of logical, relational, and mathematical operators.

Some examples of conditional expressions are:

1. $A < B$ (A and B are the same data type—either numeric, character, or string)
2. $X + 5 > = Z$ (X and Z are numeric data)
3. $E < 5$ or $F > 10$ (E and F are numeric data)
4. DATAOK (DATAOK is a logical datum)

Logical operators are used to link more than one condition together. For example, consider a store policy requiring that to cash a check, a customer must have a driver's license, AND the check must be under $50. Two conditions are linked by the logical operator AND. (See Tables 2.5, 2.6, and 2.7 for the definitions and the hierarchy of all the operators).

The programmer can set up the conditions for a decision through the use of operands and various operators. These conditions can be used alone or linked with other conditions for use in the instruction. The programmer derives the information needed to set up the condition(s) for a decision from the problem itself during problem analysis.

Figure 6.1 shows a simple flowchart illustrating the decision structure. In the figure, the resultant of the condition(s) can be TRUE or FALSE depending on the data. From the decision block (the diamond), there will be a flowline, a branch for each set of instructions: one branch for the instructions to be executed if the resultant is TRUE, and another branch for the instructions to be executed if the resultant is FALSE. There can never be more than two flowlines coming from a decision block since there are only two possibilities for the resultant of the condition(s). The TRUE branch and the FALSE branch can come from any of the lower three points of the diamond. It is best to be as consistent as possible in choosing the points of the diamond on which these branches are placed. The convention is to draw the TRUE branch on the right and the FALSE branch on the left or bottom, although it depends on the decisions to be made. This book follows that convention whenever possible. The processing flow from both

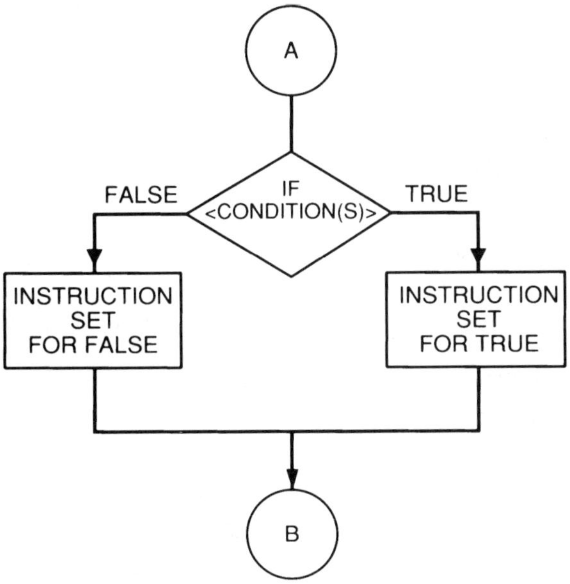

Figure 6.1 Flowchart Diagram of the Decision Structure

the TRUE branch and the FALSE branch must connect to the rest of the processing somewhere before exiting the module. There can be no dangling flowchart blocks—blocks with no flowlines leading to another block. The processing must flow somewhere. Each module can have only one entrance and one exit. The only way to get to another module is through a PROCESS instruction, that is, by telling the computer to process the instructions in another module and then return to continue processing in the current module.

A simple decision with only one condition and one action or set of actions (one instruction or set of instructions) for TRUE and another for FALSE is relatively simple. For example, assume you are calculating pay at an hourly rate, and overtime pay (over 40 hours) at 1.5 times the hourly rate. The decision to calculate pay would be stated in the following way: IF the hours are greater than 40, THEN the pay is calculated for overtime, or ELSE the pay is calculated in the usual way (see Figure 6.2).

Decisions in which you have *multiple* conditions that lead to one action or set of actions for TRUE and another action or set of actions for FALSE are slightly more complicated than those with single conditions. In these decisions you will use logical operators to connect the conditions. As with decisions based on a single condition, the resultant will determine whether the TRUE or the FALSE actions are taken.

The decision structure becomes more complicated as the number of conditions and/or the number of actions for a TRUE or FALSE resultant increases.

Multiple IF/THEN/ELSE Instructions

There are three types of decision logic you will use to write algorithms for solutions consisting of more than one decision. These types of decision logic include straight-through logic, positive logic, and negative logic.

Straight-through logic means that all of the decisions are processed sequentially, one after the other. There is no ELSE part of the instructions; the FALSE branch always

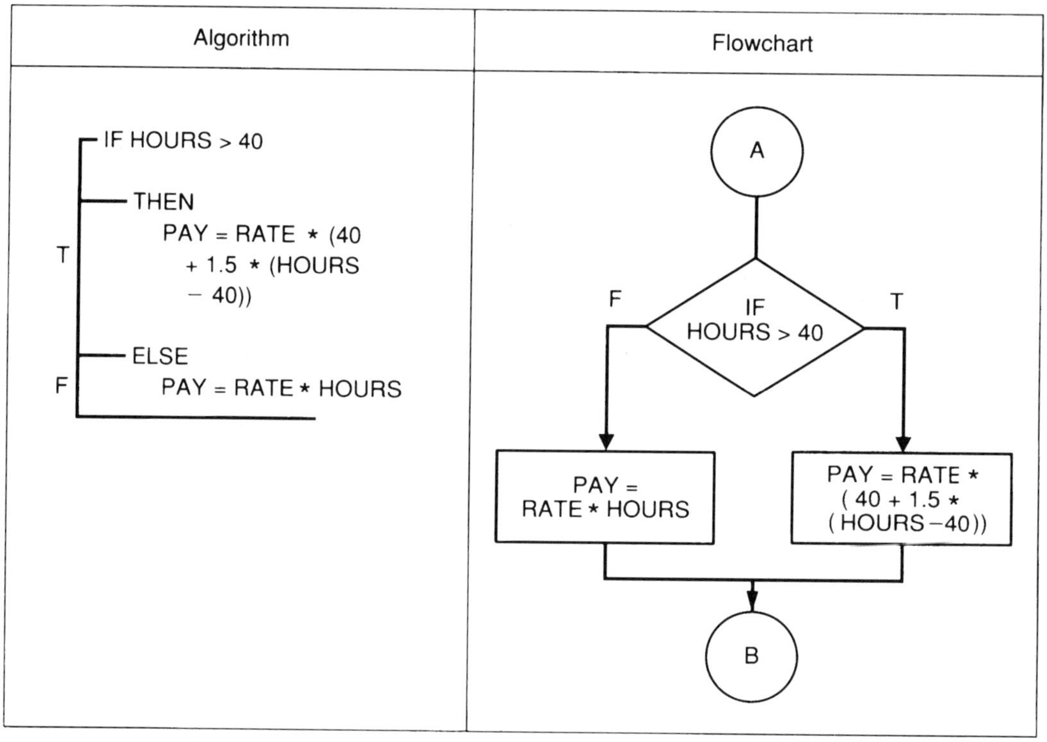

Figure 6.2 Single Condition—Two Possible Actions or Sets of Actions. Note: For all flowcharts with decision blocks, T = TRUE and F = FALSE

goes to the next decision, and the TRUE branch goes to the next decision after the instructions for the TRUE branch have been processed.

On the other hand, with positive logic not all of the instructions are processed. **Positive logic** allows the flow of the processing to continue through the module instead of processing succeeding decisions, once the resultant of a decision is TRUE. Whenever the resultant is FALSE (the ELSE part of the decision), another decision in the sequence is processed until the resultant is TRUE, or there are no more decisions to process. At that time, the FALSE branch processes the remaining instructions.

Negative logic is similar to positive logic except that the flow of the processing continues through the module when the resultant of a decision is FALSE. Whenever the resultant is TRUE, another decision is processed until the resultant is FALSE, or there are no more decisions to process. At that time, the TRUE branch processes the remaining instructions. Negative logic is the hardest to use and understand.

Some series of decisions will require a combination of two or more of these logic types. The use of each decision logic type will be further explained and illustrated later in this chapter.

In algorithms containing multiple decisions, you may have to write **nested IF/THEN/ELSE instructions.** Decisions using positive and negative logic use nested IF/THEN/ELSE instructions. Decisions using straight-through logic do not. Nested IF/THEN/ELSE instructions are sets of instructions in which each level of a decision is embedded in a level before it; like nesting baskets, one goes inside the next. You use the nested IF/THEN/ELSE structure only when one of several possible actions or sets of actions are to be processed (see Figure 6.3). In composing an IF/THEN/ELSE instruction, draw a large bracket around each IF/THEN/ELSE in the algorithm to ensure that each instruction is in the proper place. The top part of the bracket indicates the con-

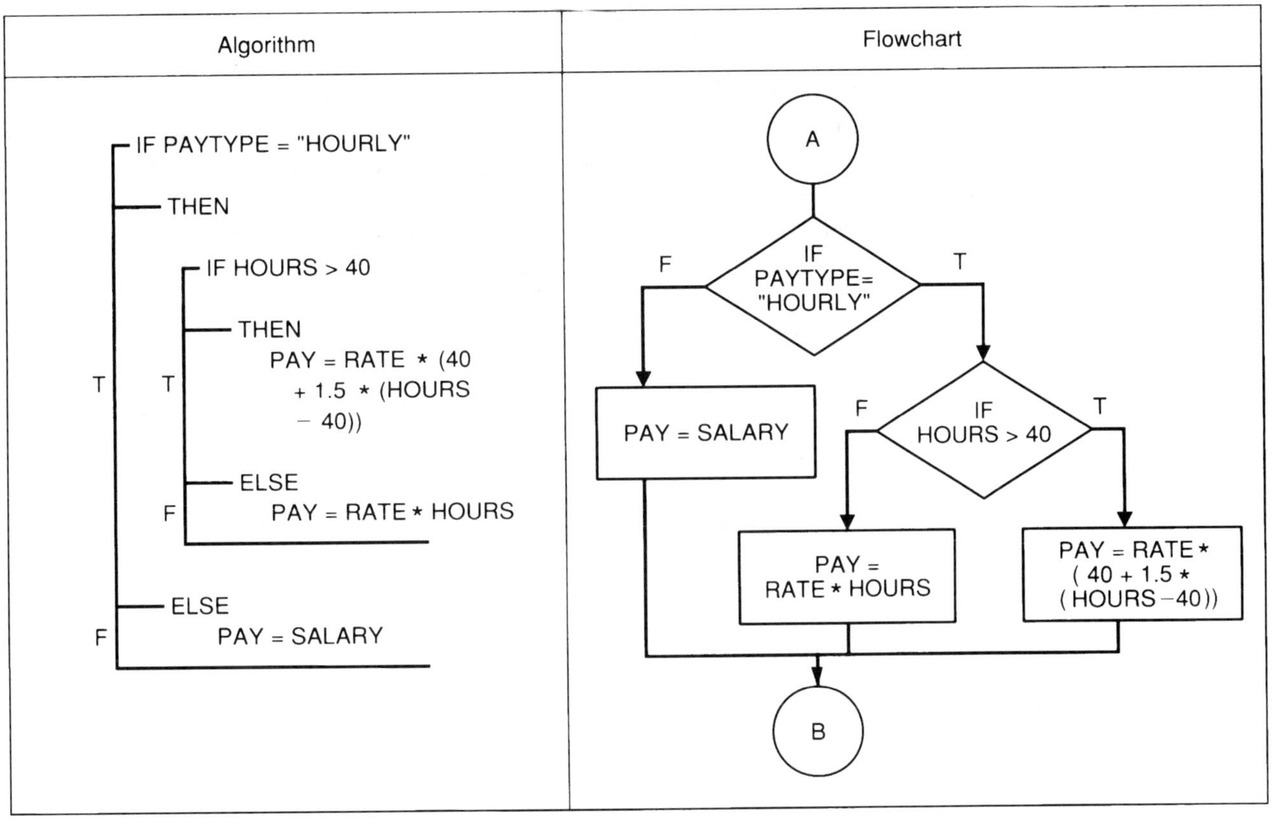

Figure 6.3 Nested IF/THEN/ELSE Instructions

dition. The middle section of the bracket indicates the TRUE branch, or the THEN part of the decision. The bottom part of the bracket indicates the FALSE branch, or the ELSE part of the decision.

In Figure 6.3, the decision is IF PAYTYPE = "HOURLY". The decision says, Is PAYTYPE equal to the string constant "HOURLY"? If the two are equal, then the resultant is TRUE and the instruction set for the TRUE is processed. If the resultant is FALSE, the instruction set for the FALSE branch is processed. The TRUE branch uses a nested IF/THEN/ELSE instruction; the decision is embedded in the TRUE branch of the first decision. This decision says, Are the hours worked greater than 40? If the answer is "yes," the resultant is TRUE, and the pay is processed at the overtime rate. When the resultant is FALSE, that is, when the hours the hours are not greater than 40, the pay is processed at the normal rate. When the resultant of the first decision is FALSE, that is, when the PAYTYPE is not equal to "HOURLY", then the pay is processed at the salary rate. (Notice that when the PAYTYPE is not equal to "HOURLY", the embedded decision on the TRUE branch cannot be processed—an example of negative logic.) A good programmer thoroughly tests algorithms that use decision logic with many sets of test data. Every path in every algorithm is checked, and a separate set of data is used for each path. It is important to test each path so errors will be eliminated.

Using Straight-through Logic

With decisions following straight-through logic, all conditions are tested. To test a condition means to process a condition to get a TRUE or FALSE resultant. Straight-through logic is the least efficient of all types of decision logic because all the decisions must be processed. However, you must use it to solve certain problems, those that require two or more unrelated decisions, and those in which all decisions must be processed. It is often used in conjunction with the other two logic types and in data validation (checking data to make sure it is correct). It is also used with languages that have limited features in their decision instruction.

The problem illustrated in Figure 6.4 is to find the amount to charge people of varying ages for a concert ticket. When the person is under 16, the charge is $7; when

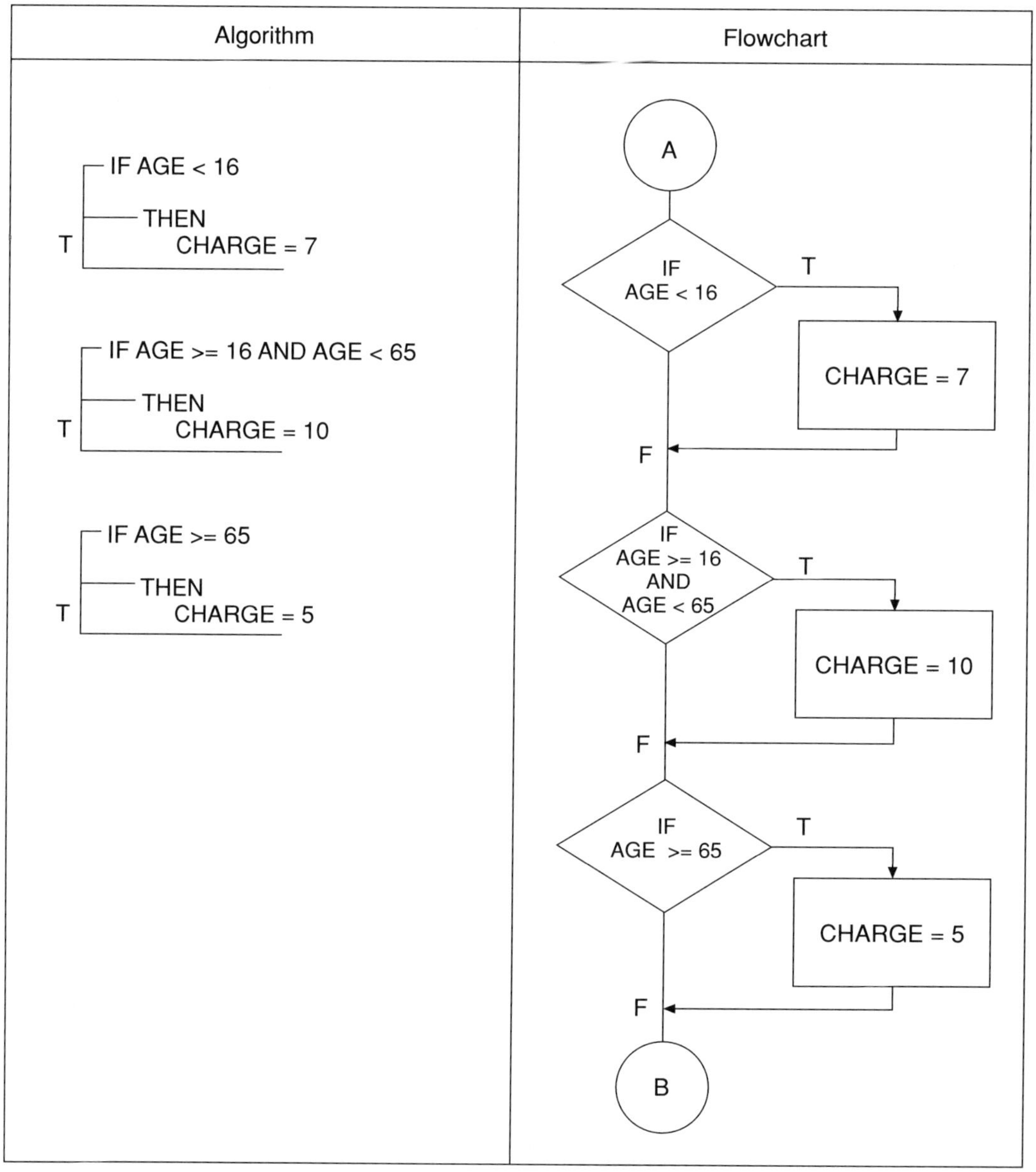

Figure 6.4 Straight-through Logic—Example 1

the person is 65 or over, the charge is $5; all others are charged $10. The conditions are the following:

AGE	CHARGE
AGE < 16	7
AGE > = 16 and AGE < 65	10
AGE > = 65	5

Notice in Figure 6.4 that even when the age is less than 16, the other decisions must be processed.

In the algorithm and flowchart in Figure 6.4, notice that there is no ELSE in straight-through logic. If the resultant of the condition is FALSE, then the processing flow drops to the next instruction. There is no need for the ELSE since there are no instructions for the FALSE branch. If the resultant of the condition is TRUE, then the set of instructions for the TRUE part is processed, and the processing flow then drops to the next instruction. The set of conditions in Figure 6.4 is more efficiently executed by using either of the other types of logic since only one condition has to be met in order to execute the correct set of instructions.

The problem found in Figure 6.5 is to change the value of X to 0 when X becomes greater than 100, and to change the value of Y to 0 when Y becomes greater than 250. Each decision is independent of the other. The conditions are

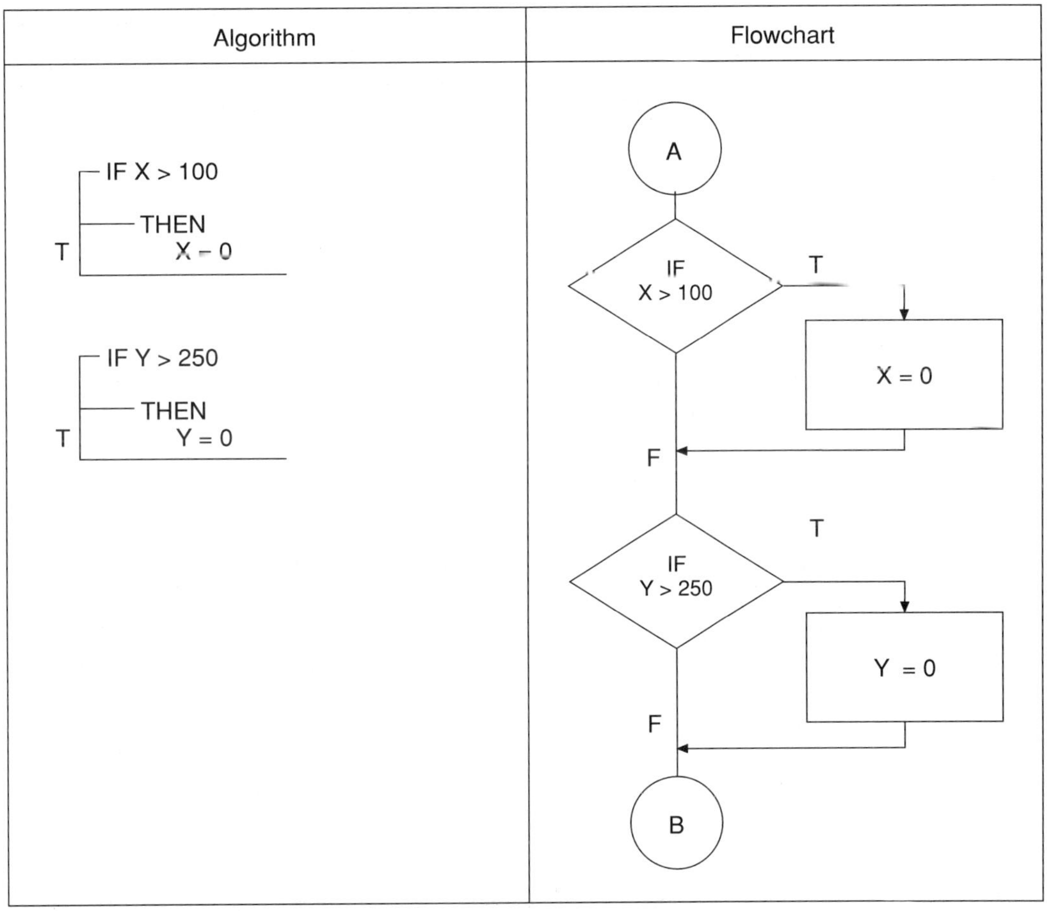

Figure 6.5 Another Example of Straight-through Logic—Example 2

X > 100   X becomes 0

Y > 250   Y becomes 0

Straight-through logic is required when all the decisions have to be processed, and when they are independent of each other. Based on these criteria, the only appropriate logic type for the decision in Figure 6.5 would be straight-through logic.

The following example is a similar problem, but with two sets of actions rather than one. When the age of a person is greater than 18, the person can vote; when the age is greater than 21, the person can have alcoholic beverages. Both decisions are contingent on the age of the person; however, the two actions take place at different ages. At the age of 20, a person can vote, but cannot be served alcoholic beverages. In this case, straight-through logic is required because all the decisions have to be processed, and because they are independent of each other.

Using Positive Logic

Positive logic is the easiest type for most people to use and understand because it is the way we think. Positive logic always uses nested IF/THEN/ELSE instructions. In general, when you use positive logic, you are telling the computer to follow a set of instructions and continue processing if the condition is TRUE; if the condition is not TRUE, then the computer processes another decision. When you use this logic, no more decisions are processed once the resultant of a condition is TRUE. Taking the same problem, and therefore, the same set of conditions as in Figure 6.4, Figure 6.6 shows how the algorithm

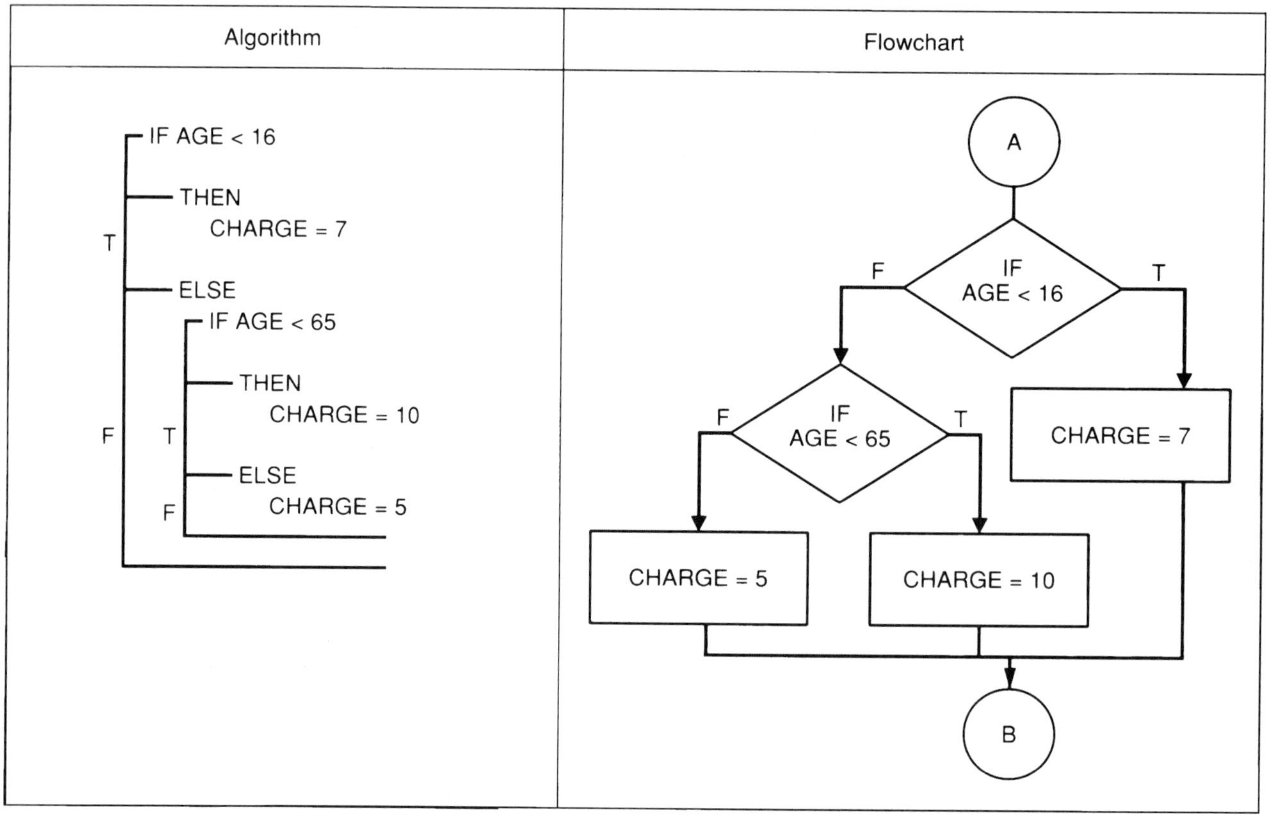

Figure 6.6 Positive Logic—Example 1

would be structured using positive logic. Notice that there are fewer decisions processed than in Figure 6.4—two compared to three—even if all the decisions are processed. There is no need to process the third decision because the resultant of the third condition statement has to be TRUE once you have processed the second statement and found it FALSE. That is, when the age is NOT less than 16, it has to be greater than or equal to 16. Therefore, this test can be eliminated if nested IF/THEN/ELSE instructions are used. Likewise, if the age is NOT less than 65, it must be greater than or equal to 65. Therefore, the third decision in the set of conditions is not necessary.

Figure 6.7 illustrates another set of conditions using positive logic and a nested IF/THEN/ELSE structure. The problem illustrated in this figure is to calculate the commission rate for a salesperson, given the amount of sales. When the salesperson has sold less than or equal to $2,000 worth of goods, the commission is 2%. When the sales total is more than $2,000 and less than or equal to $4,000, the commission is 4%. When sales total is more than $4,000 and less than or equal to $6,000, the commission is 7%. When the person has sold more than $6,000, the commission is 10%. The conditions are the following:

SALES	COMMISSION
< = 2000	.02
2001—4000	.04
4001—6000	.07
>6000	.10

Notice that in Figure 6.7 there are only three decisions. The fourth decision is not necessary; when the sales are NOT < = 6000 they have to be >6000.

Figure 6.7 is easy to read and understand because of the structure of the algorithm: Brackets and indentation are used with positive logic to show the nested levels of the decision structure. These features are important to readability.

To test positive logic for correctness, choose data to test every path. In the Test section of the algorithm and flowchart in Figure 6.7, there are four separate sets of data tested, one for each commission. You should arrive at the correct commission (hand calculated) by working each piece of test data through the flowchart. Notice that when SALES = 1500, there is only one decision to be processed; the resultant is TRUE, the COMMISSION is replaced by .02, and the processing continues at on-page connector B. When the SALES is equal to 3,500, two decisions are processed before the resultant of one of them is found to be TRUE.

There are times when it is more efficient to start an algorithm with one condition rather than another. The general rule is that the condition that will have a resultant of TRUE most of the time should be the first. This way you will have to process the fewest decisions. See Figure 6.8 for another way to set up a solution or the conditions found in the sales commission problem illustrated in Figure 6.7. Notice the changes in the operators and in the order of the decisions. If you are unable to judge the condition that is most likely to be TRUE, then it really does not matter how the logic starts.

Using Negative Logic

Negative logic is the hardest for most people to comprehend because they do not think in negative terms. In general, when you use negative logic you are telling the computer to process another decision when the resultant of the condition is TRUE; if the resultant

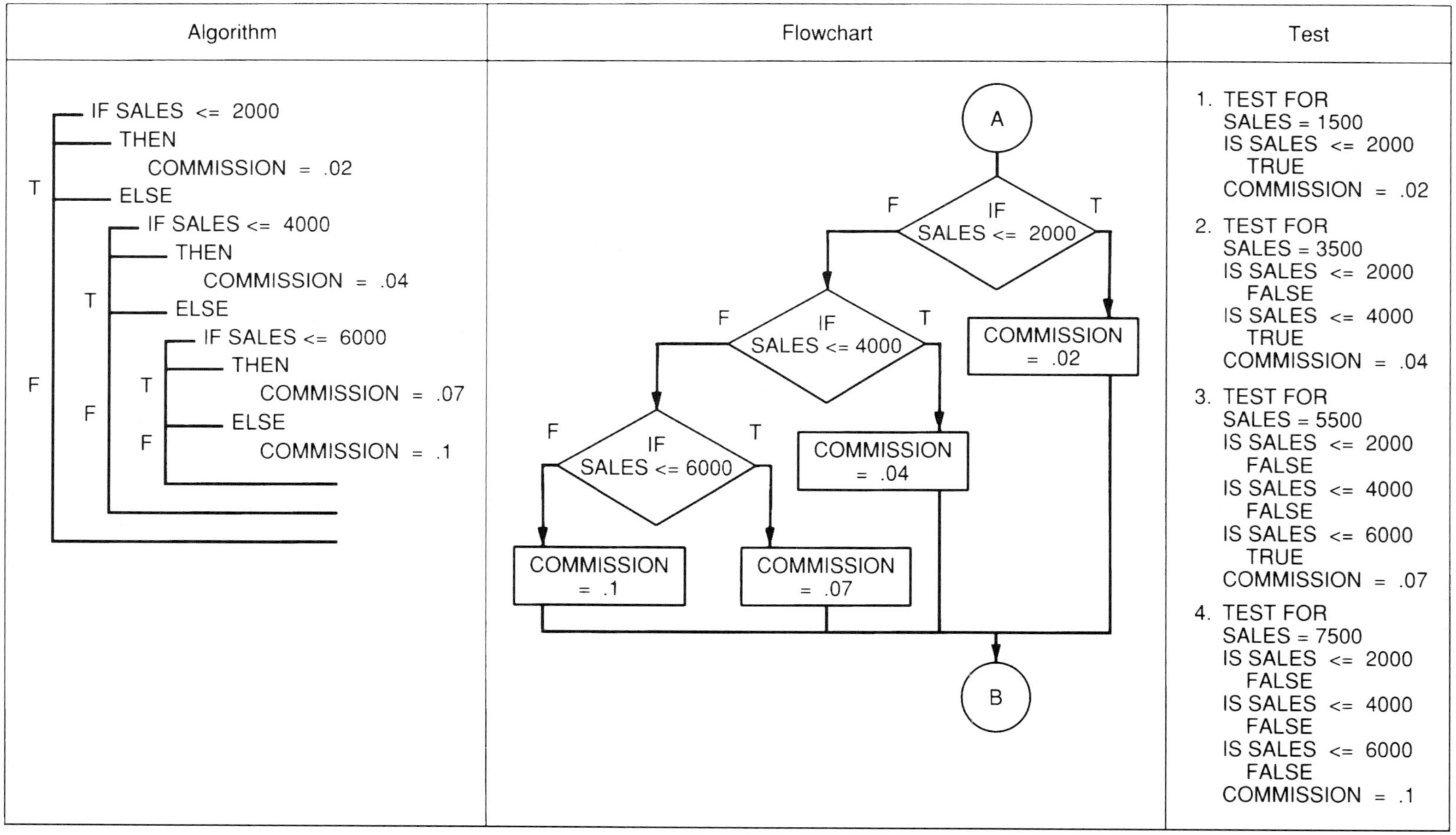

Figure 6.7 Positive Logic—Example 2

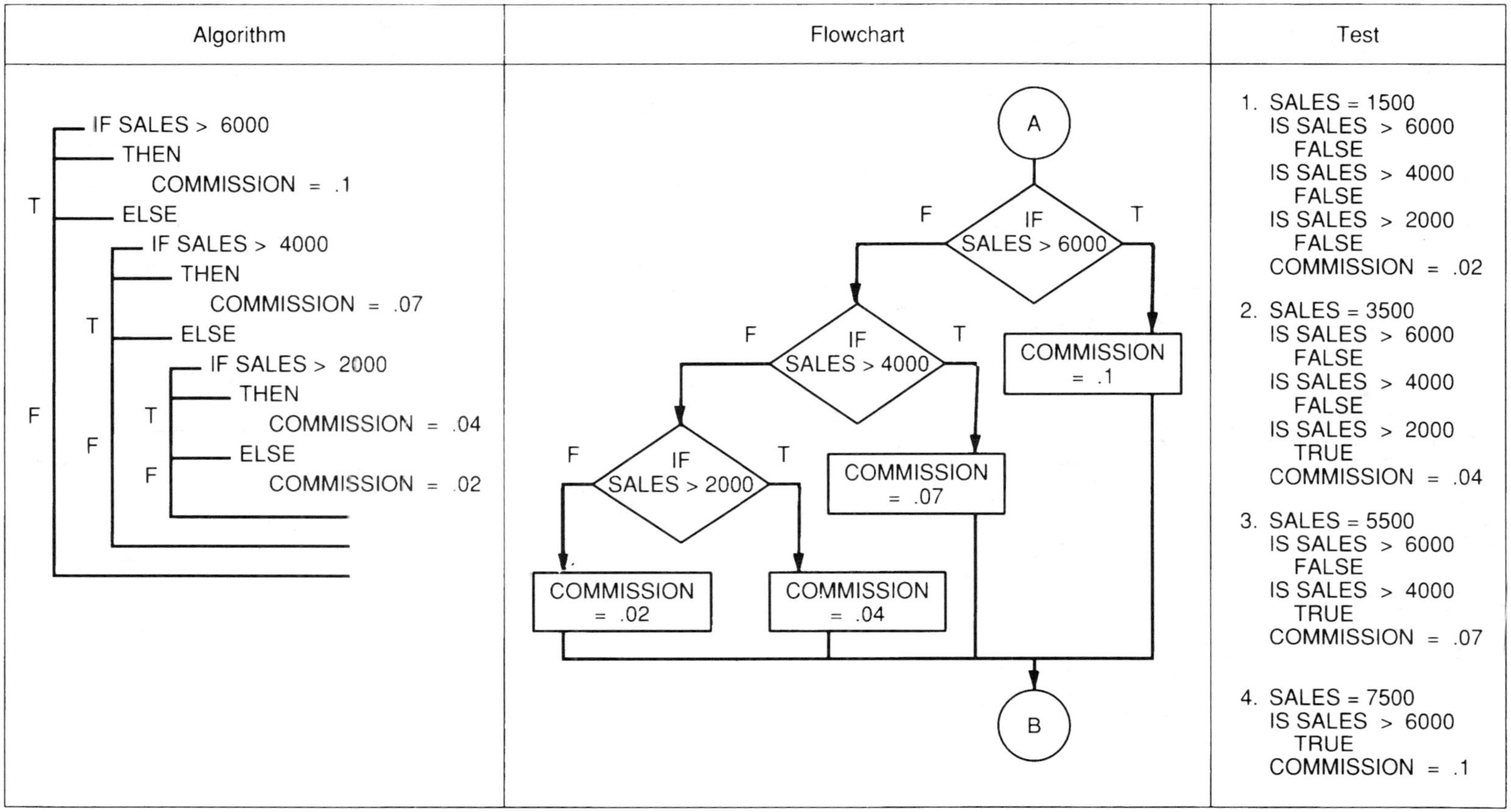

Figure 6.8 The Figure 6.7 Conditions Set Up in a Different Way

is FALSE, then the computer processes a consequent set of instructions and then continues processing the module. It is often advantageous to use negative logic to decrease the number of tests or to improve the readability of a program.

In Figure 6.9, negative logic is used with the same set of conditions as in Figure 6.4. Notice that the actions take place on the FALSE part of the instruction unless there are no more tests. Again, the algorithm uses brackets and indentation for readability. With the indentations the algorithm makes a sideways V. If a nested IF/THEN/ELSE instruction using negative logic does not form a sideways V, then either the indentation is wrong, or some of the instructions for each TRUE or FALSE are set up incorrectly. The top section of each bracket indicates a condition or conditions. The middle section indicates the instructions processed when the resultant of the condition(s) is TRUE. This section is much larger when a decision uses negative logic than when the decision uses positive logic. The bottom section indicates the instructions to process when the resultant of the condition(s) is FALSE. This section is much smaller when a decision uses negative logic than when the decision uses positive logic. The brackets make the nested IF/THEN/ELSE instruction easier to read by partitioning the conditions, the TRUE section, and the FALSE section.

For example, in the algorithm and the flowchart in Figure 6.9, when the resultant of the first condition (AGE > = 16) is TRUE, another decision is processed (AGE > = 65). When the resultant of the first condition is FALSE, the charge of the ticket is $7; after this decision the processing continues through the rest of the module. When the resultant of the second condition is TRUE the charge is $5; when FALSE, the charge is $10.

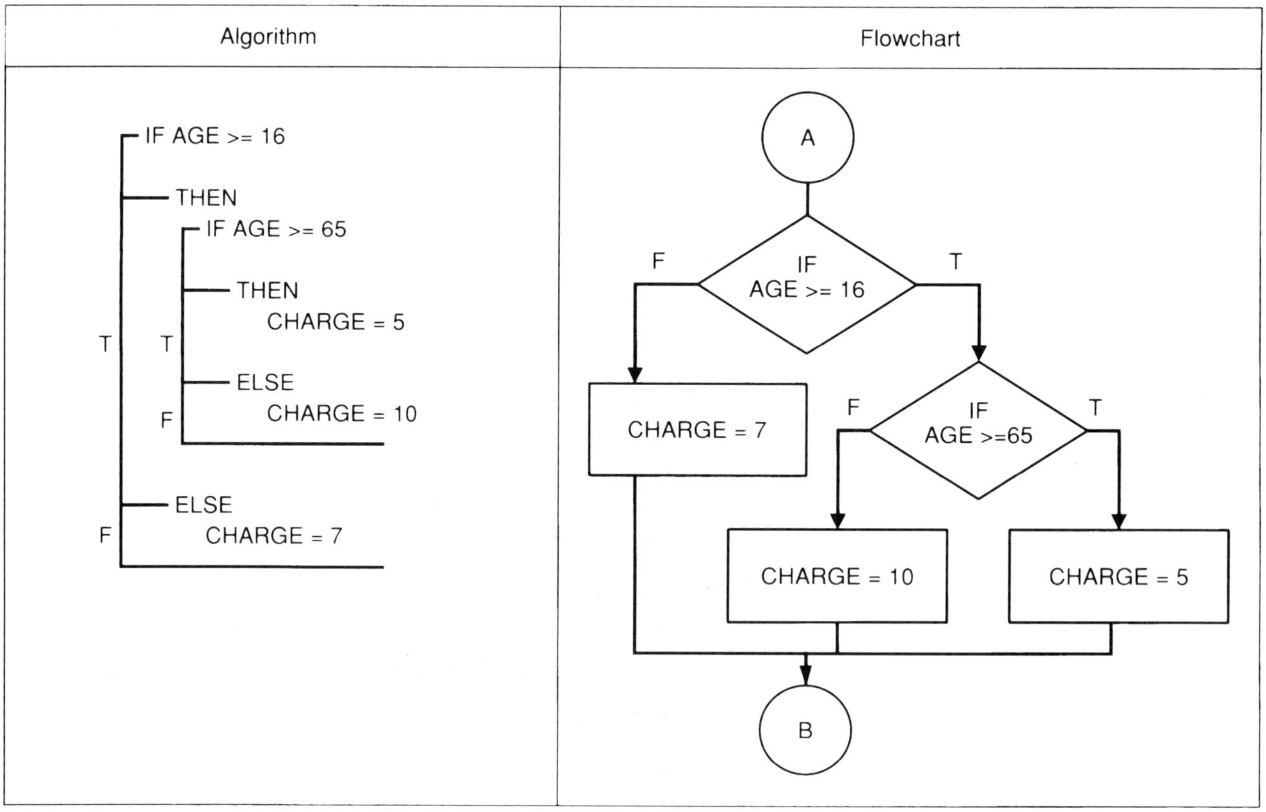

Figure 6.9 Negative Logic—Example 1

Figure 6.10 shows the solution from the positive logic illustration in Figure 6.7 if we were to use negative logic. The conditions are the following:

SALES	COMMISSION
< = 2000	.02
2001—4000	.04
4001—6000	.07
>6000	.10

Notice how the testing takes place. Without proper testing, the problem-solving process is useless. Testing the algorithm or the flowchart reveals errors in logic, so corrections can be made before proceeding. It is far easier to make corrections during problem solving than after the coding has been done.

Figure 6.11 shows another way to organize the set of conditions in Figure 6.10 using negative logic. Here again, the rule is to have the computer make as few tests as possible.

Logic Conversion

There are times when it is necessary to change the logic from positive to negative or vice versa in order to improve the efficiency or readability of a solution. Sometimes the structure of a solution simply does not lend itself to the logic type that you've used, either because of the number and nature of the instructions to be processed, or because there are no instructions to be processed. In a decision, there must always be instructions for a TRUE section, but not always for a FALSE section. If there are no instructions for the TRUE section of a decision instruction, then it is better to convert the logic type.

To convert from positive logic to negative logic or vice versa, do the following:

1. Change all < to >=.
2. Change all <= to >.
3. Change all > to <=.
4. Change all >= to <.
5. Change all = to <>.
6. Change all <> to =.
7. Interchange all of the THEN set of instructions with the corresponding ELSE set of instructions.

If you are using the convention to keep all TRUES to the right and all FALSES to the left in the flowchart, then reverse flowchart sections (see Figure 6.12). Figure 6.12 revisits the problem regarding the charge for a concert ticket based on age, illustrated in Figure 6.6. Notice that first, the relational operators are changed in the conditions. Second, the TRUE sections of the algorithms and flowcharts are exchanged with the FALSE sections.

Which Decision Logic?

How do you decide which type of decision logic to use? The general rule is to evaluate all three types for each solution and choose the one that is most readable, requires the fewest tests, and is easiest to maintain. It is easy to fall into the trap of always using the

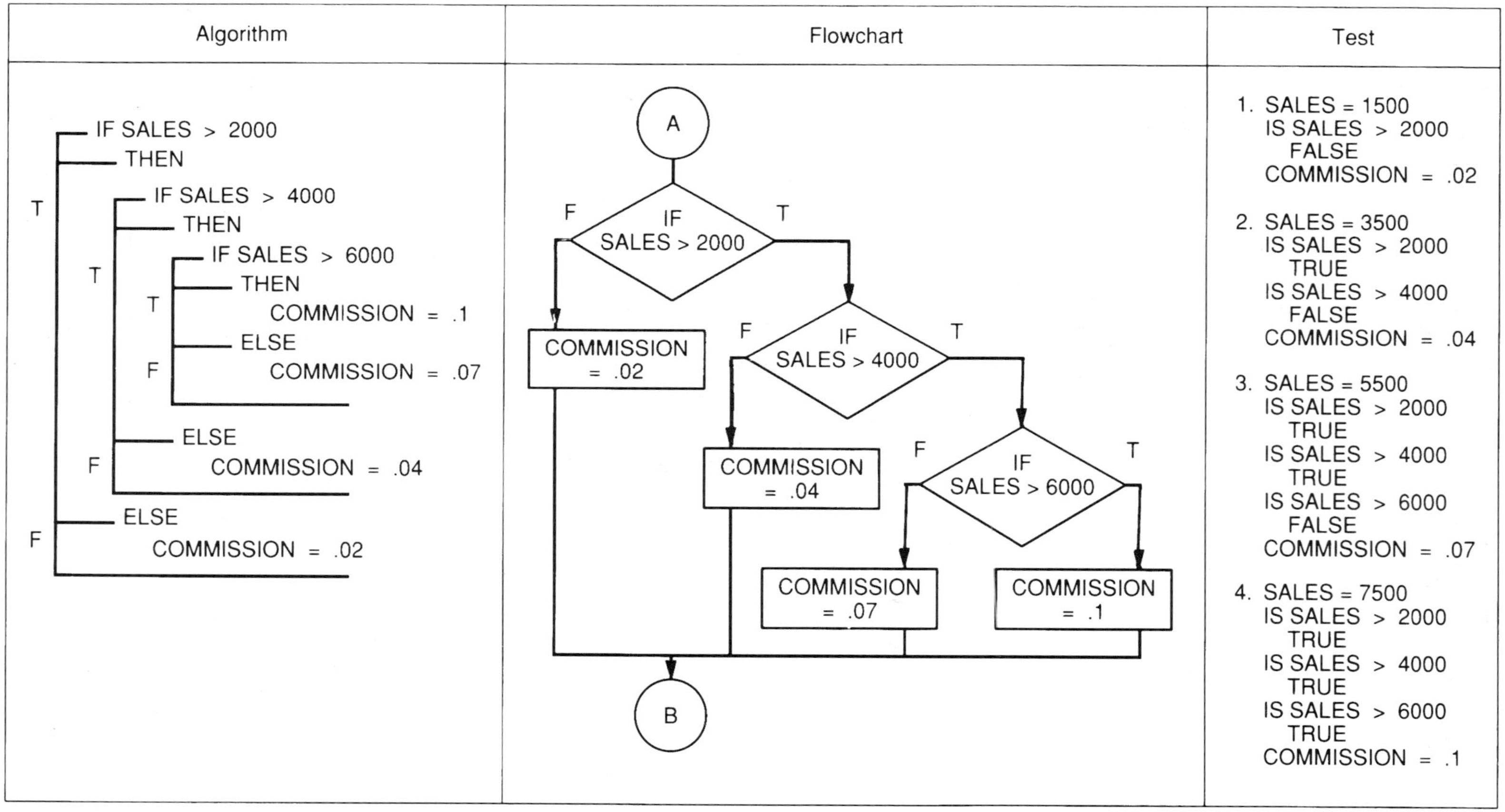

Figure 6.10 Negative Logic—Example 2

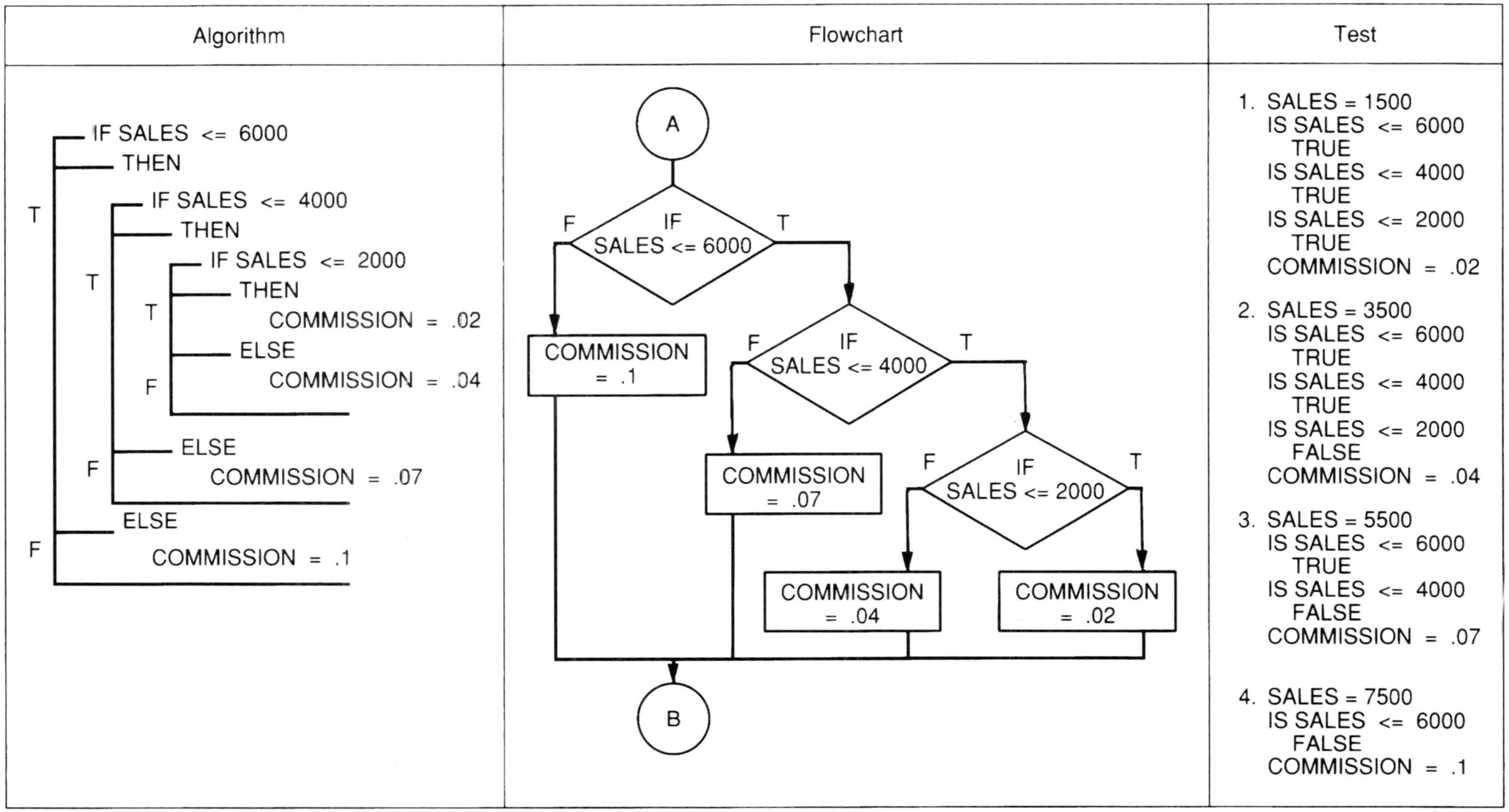

Figure 6.11 The Figure 6.10 Conditions Set Up in a Different Way

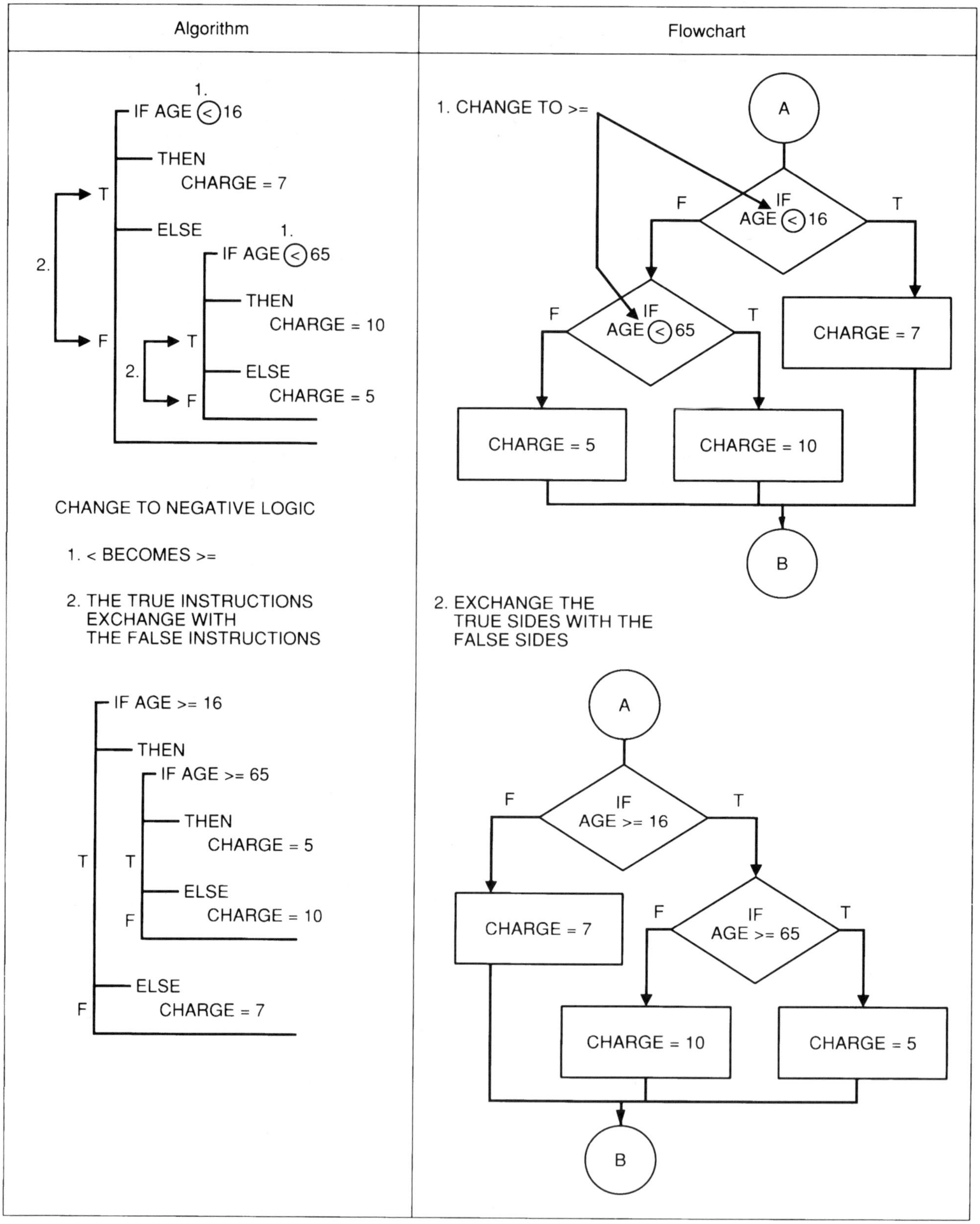

Figure 6.12 Conversion from Positive Logic to Negative Logic

same logic type. It is also easy to fall into the habit of accepting and using a set of conditions exactly as the customer has given them. Such habits are not the most efficient ways of solving problems.

Figure 6.13 contains flowcharts showing four ways to set up the same conditions. The problem is to calculate a pay bonus given the set of conditions in the figure. From the data given, which logic type is the most efficient? Since the first and second solutions, the examples of positive logic, are easy to read, and the second solution requires the fewest tests, the second solution would be the best.

To analyze which type of decision logic would be most efficient for a particular solution, answer the following questions:

1. Which type would make the solution most readable?
2. Which type would make the solution the easiest to maintain or change?
3. Which would require the fewest tests when you don't know anything about the data?
4. Which would require the fewest tests when you're given some data?

If you find at the end of the analysis that more than one of the logic types could be equally effective, then simply choose one.

Decision Tables

You may have a problem with multiple conditions and multiple consequent actions. In such a case discovering all of the actions that correspond to particular conditions—and discovering which combination of conditions, if any, leads to meaningful actions—can be complicated. A good way to simplify this process is to draw a decision table. You would draw a decision table during problem analysis. It is an excellent tool to use as a communication vehicle with a customer or with the person for whom you are solving the problem. You can also use it to test the algorithm and the flowchart.

A **decision table** consists of four parts:

1. the conditions
2. the actions
3. the combinations of TRUE and FALSE for the conditions
4. the action to be taken or the consequences for each combination of conditions

Draw a decision table in the form of a rectangle divided into the four major sections. Each section is divided into smaller sections, as needed, according to the number of possible combinations of TRUE and FALSE (see Table 6.1). The total number of possible combinations of TRUE and FALSE for the conditions is two to the power of the number of conditions. That is, if there are two conditions, then there are 2 ^ 2, or 4 possible combinations of TRUE and FALSE. If there are three conditions, then there are 2 ^ 3, or 8 possible combinations. If there are four conditions then there are 2 ^ 4, or 16 possible combinations.

A flowchart must then be developed from the decision table. Figure 6.14a-c shows the flowchart development from the decision table in Table 6.1. The first step in the development of the flowchart is to draw in all decisions. Figure 6.14a shows the starting flowchart. Notice that the first decision is the first condition. The second decision is the second condition and is repeated on the true side and the false side of the first decision. The third decision is the third condition. This decision is repeated four times, once for each true and false for the second decision. This will allow all combinations of true and false values. Step two is to look at both sides of each decision, starting with decision one.

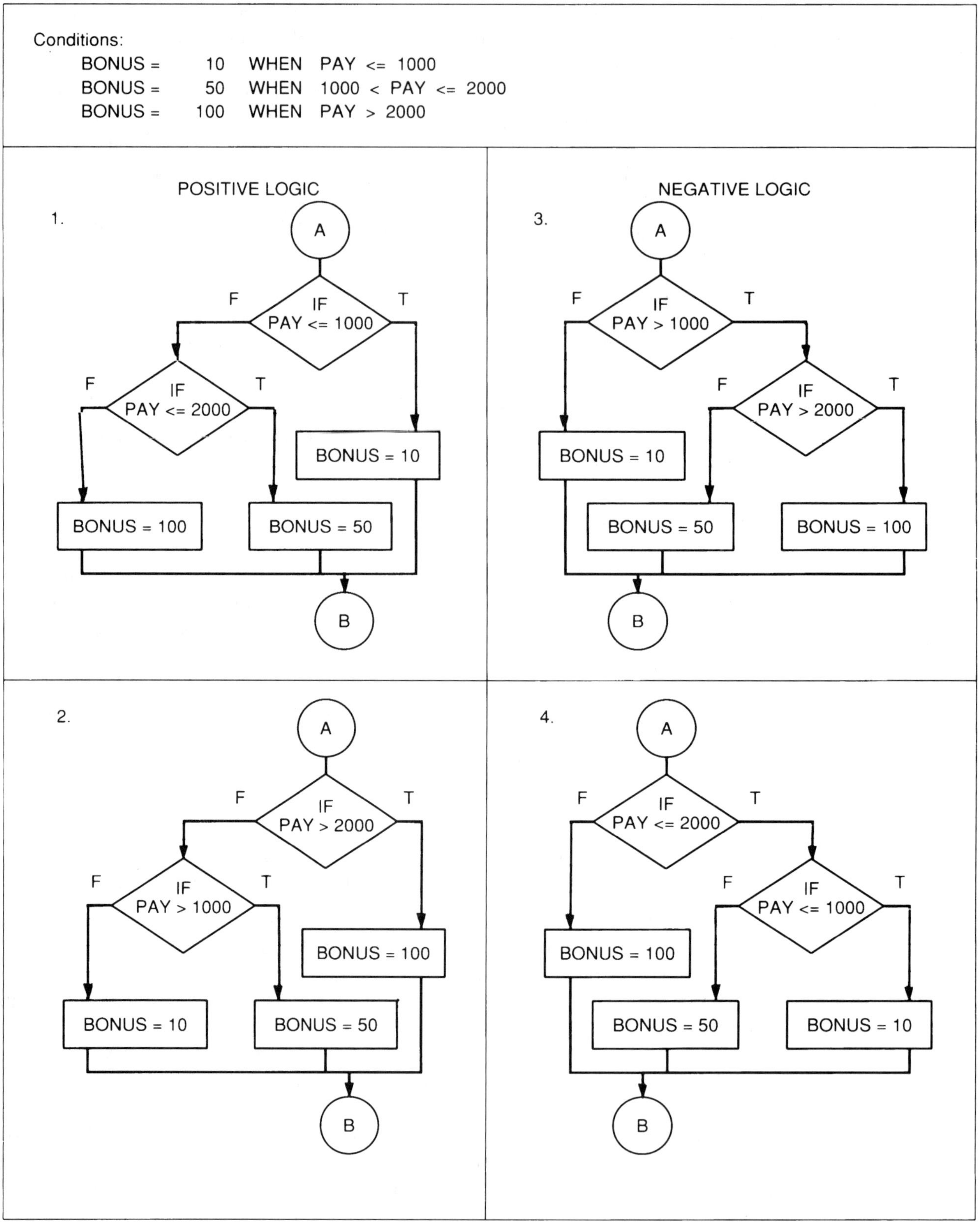

Figure 6.13 Four Ways to Design a Set of Conditions

Table 6.1 Decision Table Format

List of Conditions	CONDITION 1	T	T	T	T	F	F	F	F	All Possible Combinations of T & F
	CONDITION 2	T	T	F	F	T	T	F	F	
	CONDITION 3	T	F	T	F	T	F	T	F	
List of Actions	ACTION 1		X				X			Consequences
	ACTION 2	X			X	X			X	
	ACTION 3			X				X		

Figure 6.14b shows the comparison of sides. If both sides are the same the decision is not needed. Notice that the true side of decision one is exactly the same as the false side. Therefore, this decision is not needed. The decision and the false side can be eliminated. The true side and the false side of the second decision are different and therefore, they need to stay. The same is true for the third decision. Figure 6.14c shows the final algorithm and flowchart. The four steps to develop a flowchart from the decision table are:

1. Draw all decisions in flowchart form.
2. Compare the true and false sides of each decision, starting with the first one.
3. Eliminate any decisions which have the same instructions on both the true and false sides.
4. Redraw the flowchart.

The decision table is a graphical way of stating a policy for a company, such as a policy for cashing a check or for giving a bonus. Only the manager of the company can instruct the programmer regarding the company policy, so the programmer must work with the manager to complete the decision table. The manager tells the programmer the conditions and the actions, or consequences, of the decisions. The only part the programmer fills in is the upper right-hand section showing the possible combinations of TRUE and FALSE. It is important for the programmer to work with the customer to make sure all combinations have the correct set of actions. From the decision table, the programmer proceeds to write the algorithm and the flowchart to solve the problem. The major difficulty in designing the algorithm is to make decision structure as efficient as possible by weeding out all unnecessary tests and putting the conditions in the best possible order. It often takes several experiments to come up with the best structure.

Table 6.2 shows a decision table for a store policy for charging a purchase. There are three conditions:

1. The purchase is less than $100.
2. The last payment to the account was made in the last 30 days.
3. The balance of the account is less than $1,000.

Each of these three conditions could be TRUE or FALSE depending on the customer. The following actions could be taken:

1. Credit is OK, and the customer can charge the item.
2. Refer the customer to the credit department.
3. Credit is denied and the customer cannot charge the item.

These conditions and actions are supplied by the manager of the credit department. The manager also states when each of the actions will take place. The policy illustrated in Table 6.2 specifies that a customer can charge an item when all three conditions are

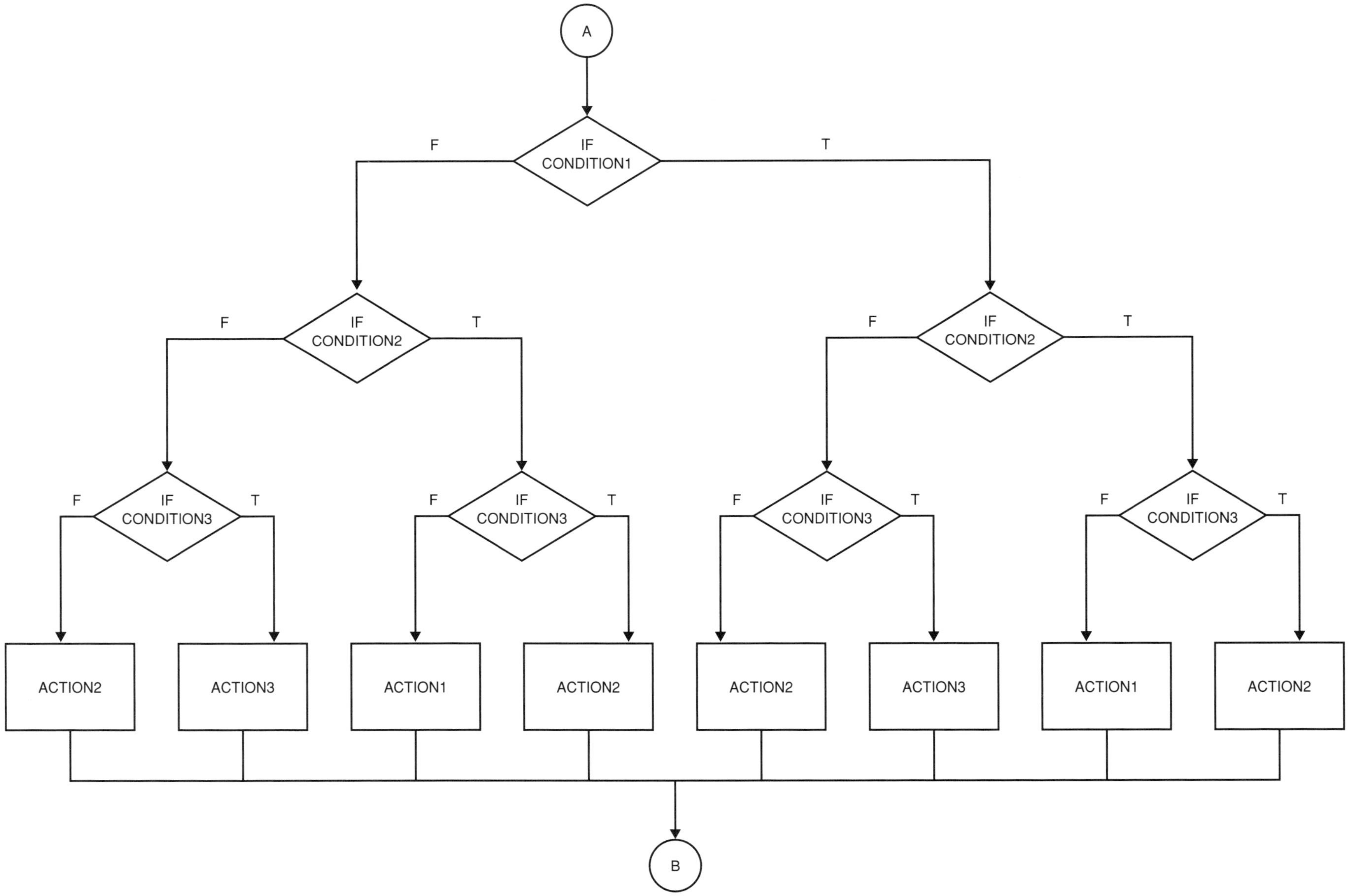

Figure 6.14a Starting Flowchart from table 6.1

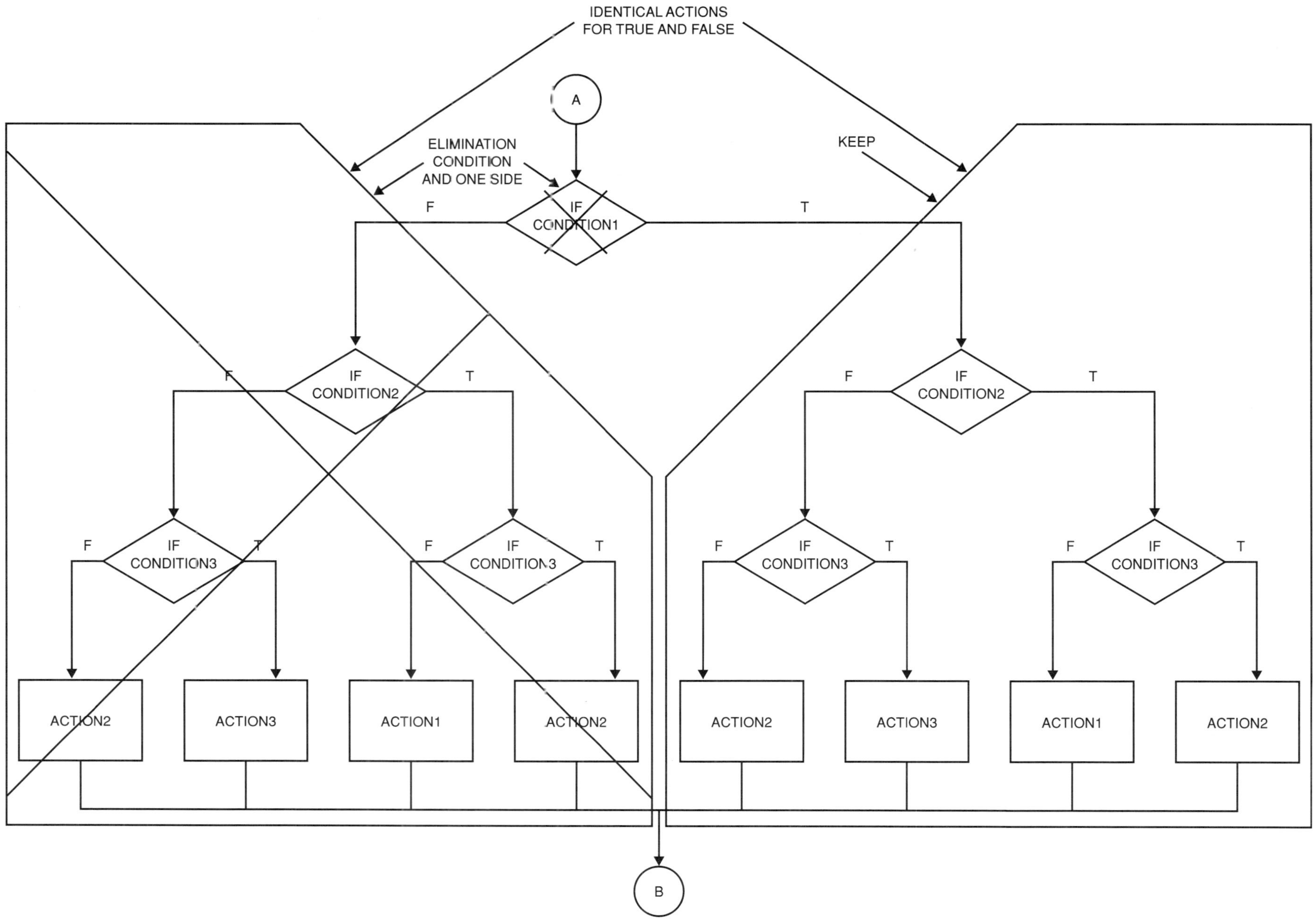

Figure 6.14b Elimination of Conditions

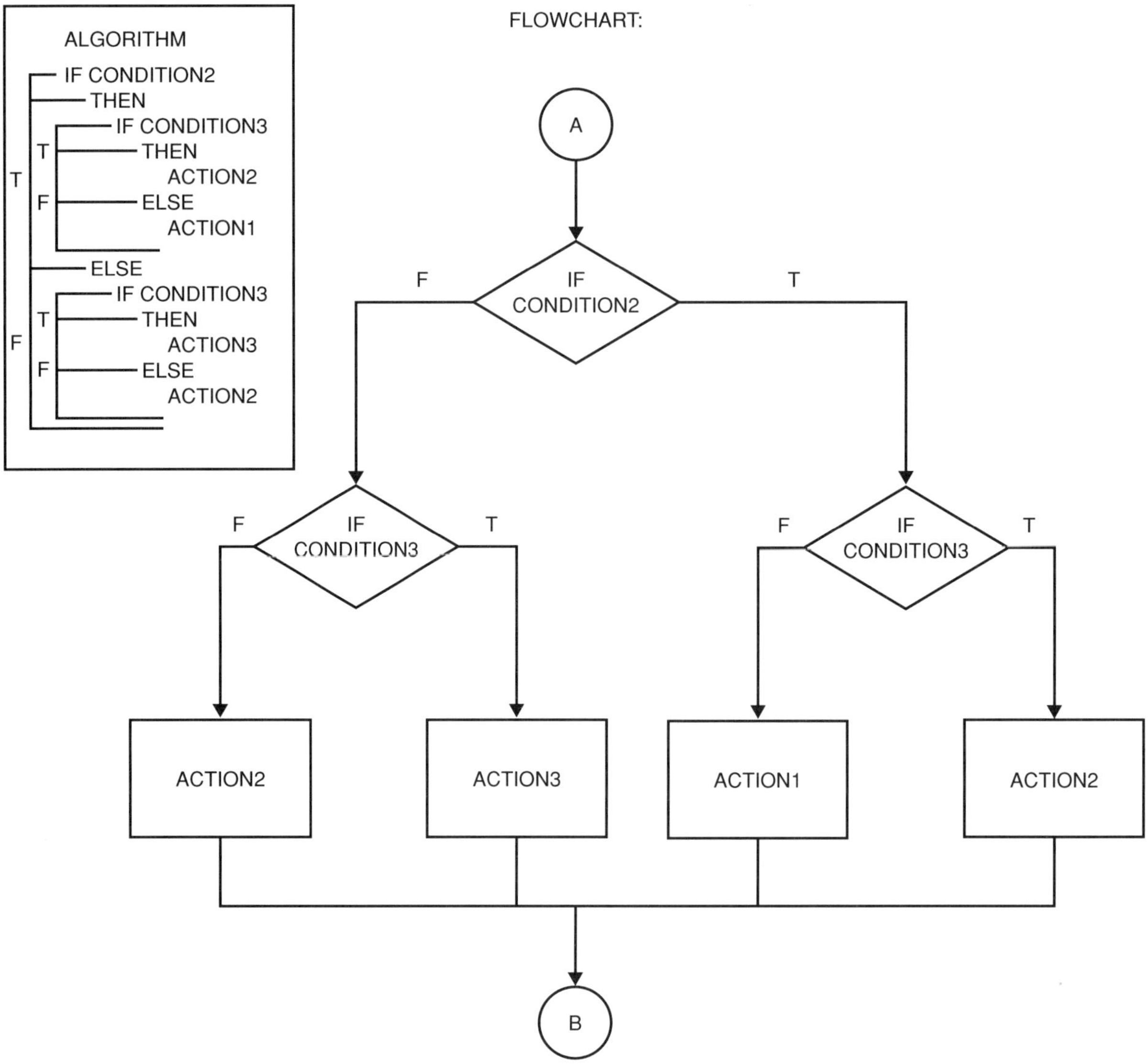

Figure 6.14c Final Flowchart

Table 6.2 Decision Table

List of Conditions	1	PURCHASE < $100	T	T	T	T	F	F	F	F
	2	LAST PAYMENT WITHIN 30 DAYS	T	T	F	F	T	T	F	F
	3	BALANCE < $1000	T	F	T	F	T	F	T	F
List of Actions	1	CREDIT OK	X		X					
	2	REFER TO CREDIT DEPARTMENT		X			X		X	
	3	CREDIT DENIED				X		X		X

TRUE, or when the first and third conditions are TRUE and the second one is false. The customer is referred to the credit department in the following cases: when conditions 1 and 2 are TRUE and 3 is FALSE; when 2 and 3 are TRUE and 1 is FALSE; and when 1 and 2 are FALSE and 3 is TRUE. Credit is denied in these cases: when conditions 2 and 3 are FALSE and 1 is TRUE; when 1 and 3 are FALSE and 2 is TRUE; and when all three are FALSE.

Figure 6.15 shows the development of the flowchart from Table 6.2. Figure 6.15a shows the complete flowchart with all decisions. The condition Purchase < \$100 is the first decision. Last Payment within 30 Days is the second condition and is repeated twice, once each for the true and false in the first decision. The third decision is Balance < \$1000. This decision is repeated 4 times, once for each true and false in decision two. This will give the actions for all combinations of true and false. Figure 6.15b shows the decisions which have the same true and false actions. Notice that the second decision on the false side of the first decision has identical actions on the true side and the false side. This indicates that this decision is not necessary and can be eliminated. After all, if the same action takes place whether the decision is true or false, the decision is not needed. Figure 6.15c shows the redrawn flowchart and the associated algorithm.

Putting It All Together

The Putting It All Together (PIAT) sections in this book are designed to show students how to pull together and use the concepts from a previous section or sections. The following PIAT demonstrates how to use the six steps of problem solving on the computer to develop a solution that uses the sequential and the decision logic structures. The problem is the following:

The Fantastic Floral Company sells to wholesale and retail buyers. The wholesale buyer needs a resale number in order to buy at no tax and to receive discounts. The retail buyer pays 6% tax. The following are the discounts to the wholesale buyer:

AMOUNT < \$100	DISCOUNT = 2%
AMOUNT >= \$100 and < \$500	DISCOUNT = 5%
AMOUNT >= \$500	DISCOUNT = 10%

Given an amount of purchase, how much will the customer owe the company? (See Figure 6.16a-g.)

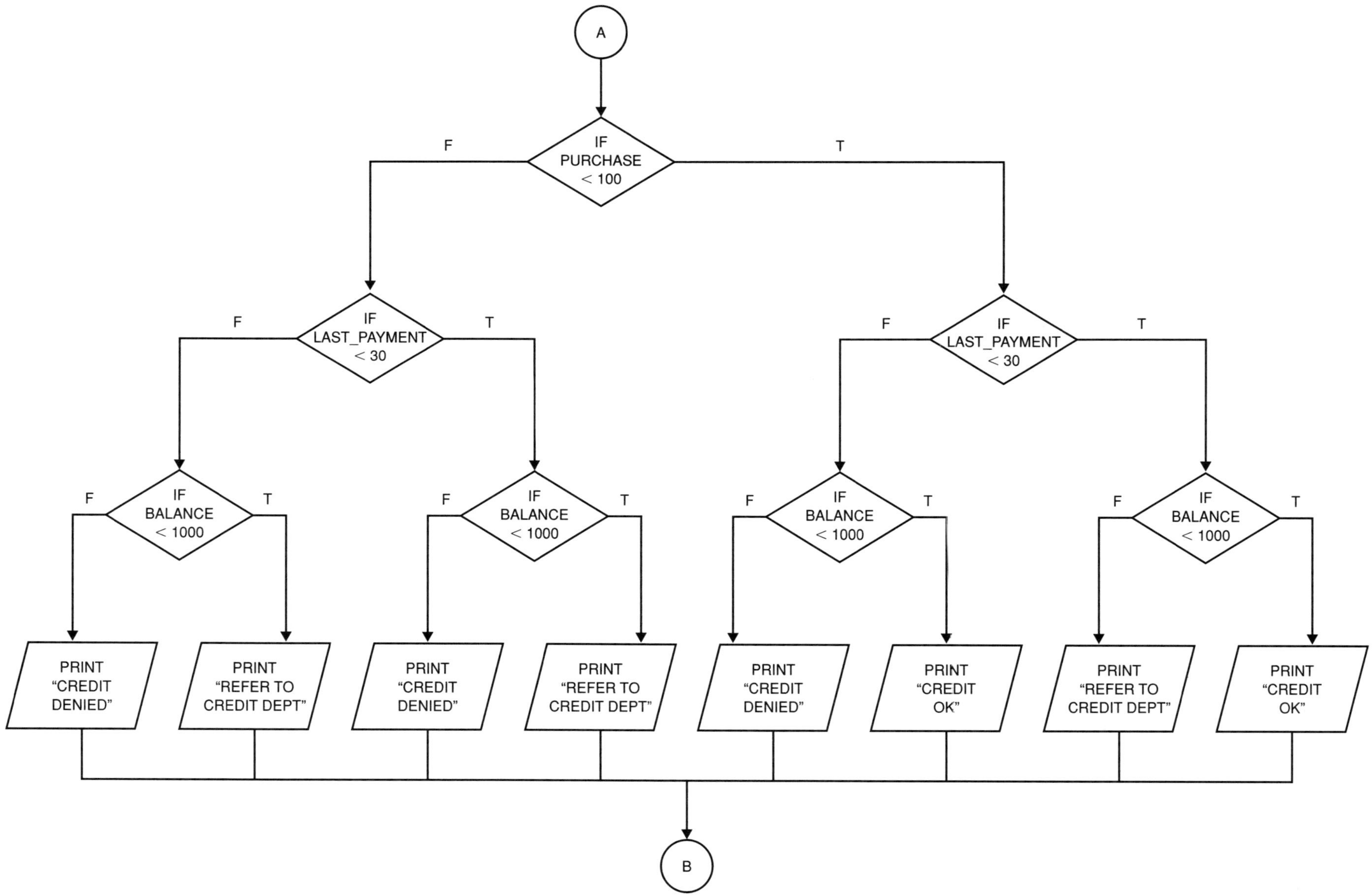

Figure 6.15a Starting Flowchart from Table 6.2

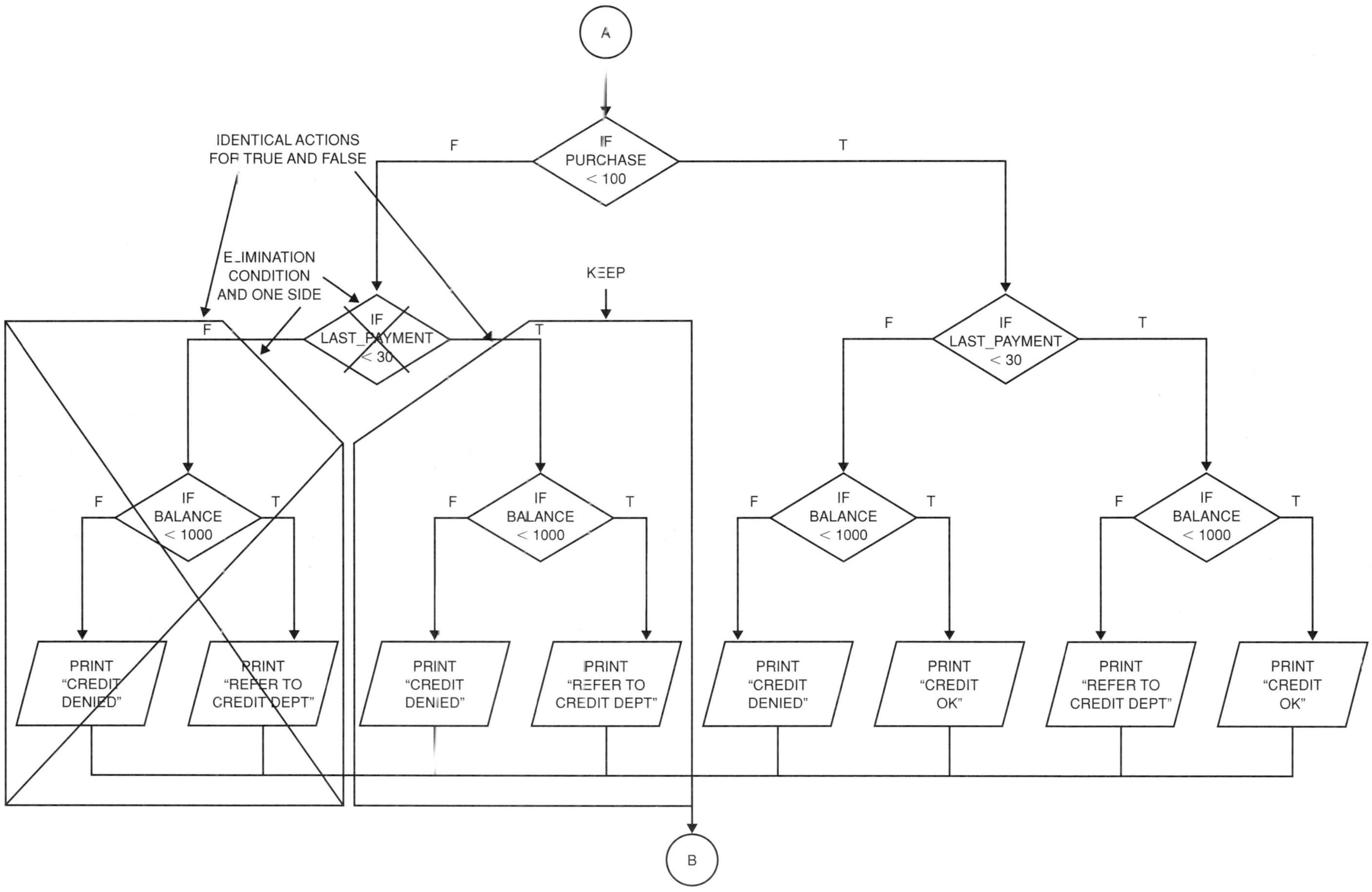

Figure 6.15b Elimination of Conditions

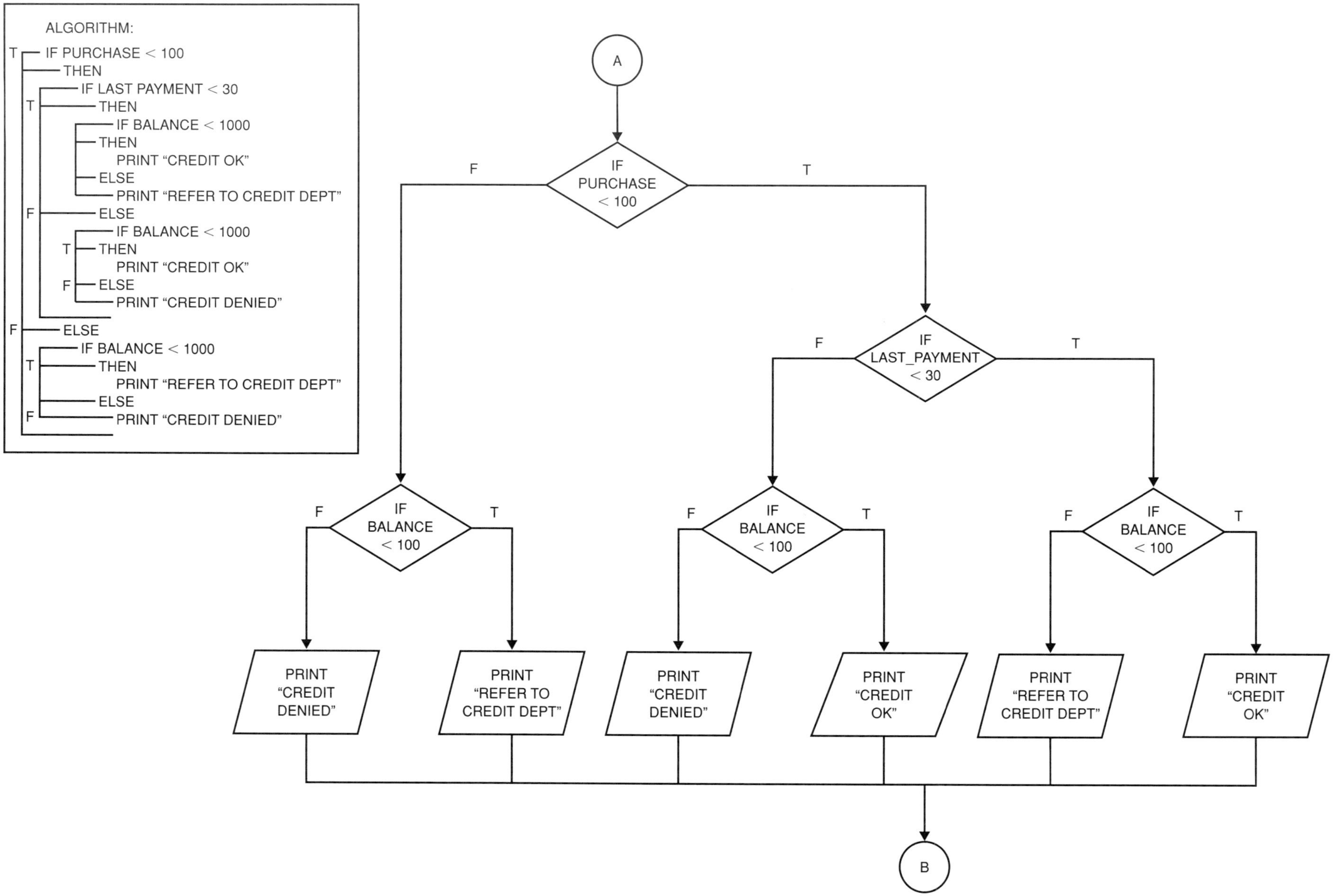

Figure 6.15c Final Flowchart

Given Data	Required Results
Wholesale buyers: • Must have resale no. • Amount of purchase — discount < 100 — 2% >= 100 & < 500 — 5% >= 500 — 10% Retail buyers: • No discount Amount of purchase (AP) 6% Tax	Amount owed
Processing Required	**Solution Alternatives**
Retail = 1 * AP Wholesale = (1–D) * AP	*• Use positive logic for discount • Use negative logic for discount • Use straight-through logic for discount *This solution was chosen because it results in the fewest number of tests and it is easily read.

Figure 6.16a Fantastic Floral Company—Problem Analysis Chart

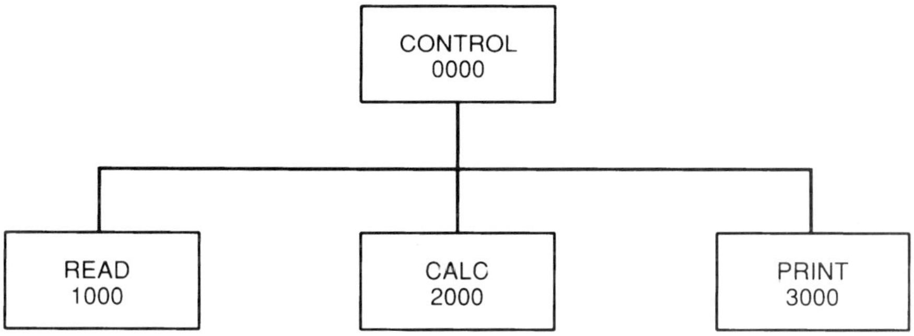

Figure 6.16b Fantastic Floral Company—Structure Chart

Input	Processing	Module Reference Number	Output
1. Amount of purchase 2. Resale number (If 0 then a retail customer)	1. ENTER input data 2. CALC discount 3. CALC amount owed 4. PRINT output information	1000 2000 2000 3000	1. Amount of purchase 2. Resale # 3. Amount owed

Figure 6.16c Fantastic Floral Company—IPO Chart

Algorithm	Flowchart	Annotation	Test
Control Module (0000) 1. PROCESS READ 2. PROCESS CALC 3. PROCESS PRINT 4. END	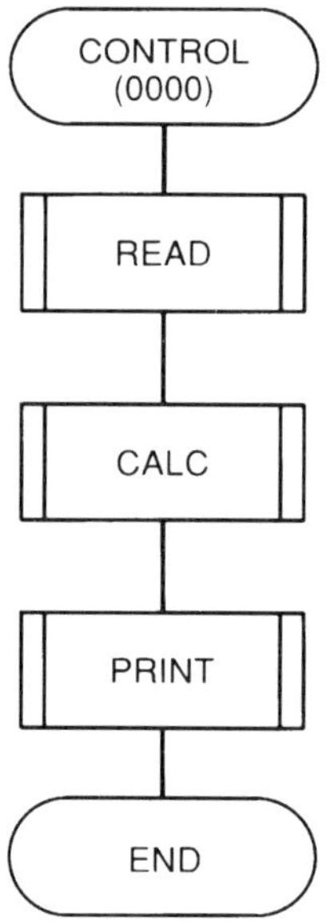	 Enters data Calculates amount owed Prints output	 GO TO READ MODULE GO TO CALC MODULE GO TO PRINT MODULE STOP

Internal Documentation	External Documentation
1. Title: calculates amount owed given amount of sale and resale #	1. Same as internal documentation 2. Explain problem

Figure 6.16d The Algorithms and Flowcharts—CONTROL Module

Algorithm	Flowchart	Annotation	Test
Read Module (1000) 1. ENTER PURCHAMT 2. ENTER RESALENO 3. EXIT	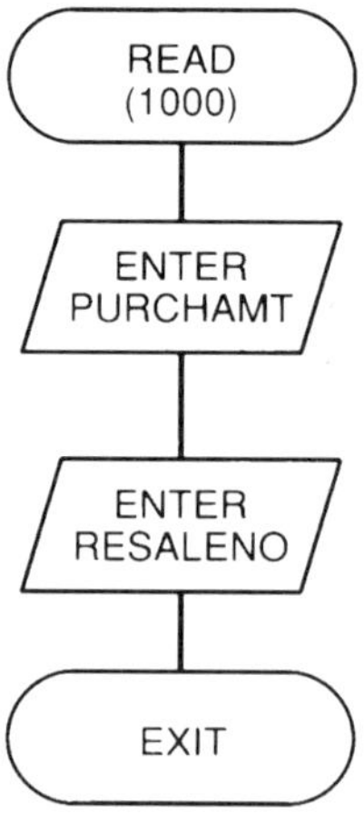	Purchamt = amount of purchase Resaleno = resale number (0 means retail purchase)	PURCHAMT 300 RESALENO 27505 Return

Internal Documentation	External Documentation
1. Title: Enters data from keyboard 2. See annotations	1. Same as internal documentation

Figure 6.16e The Algorithms and Flowcharts—READ Module

Algorithm

```
Calc Module
  (2000)
1. IF RESALENO = 0
   THEN
      AMTOWED = PURCHAMT * 1.06
   ELSE
      IF PURCHAMT < 100
      THEN
         AMTOWED = PURCHAMT * .98
      ELSE
         IF PURCHAMT < 500
         THEN
            AMTOWED = PURCHAMT
                          * .95
         ELSE
            AMTOWED = PURCHAMT
                          * .9
2. EXIT
```

Flowchart

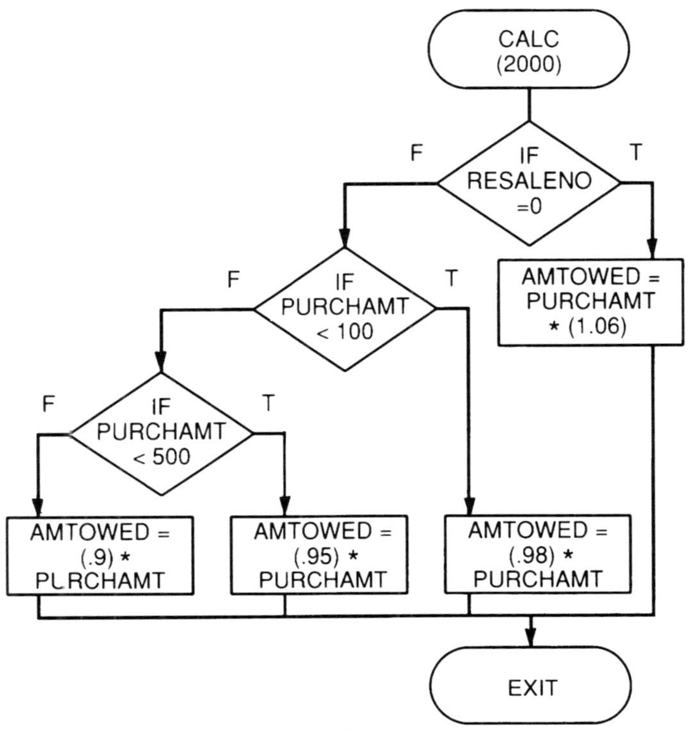

Annotation

Resaleno = 0
(retail customer)

Test

AMTOWED

285

RETURN

Internal Documentation	External Documentation
1. Title: Calculates amount owed 2. See annotation	1. Same as Internal Documentation

Figure 6.16f The Algorithms and Flowcharts—CALC Module

Algorithm	Flowchart	Annotation	Test
Print Module (3000) 1. PRINT PURCHAMT, RESALENO, AMTOWED 2. EXIT	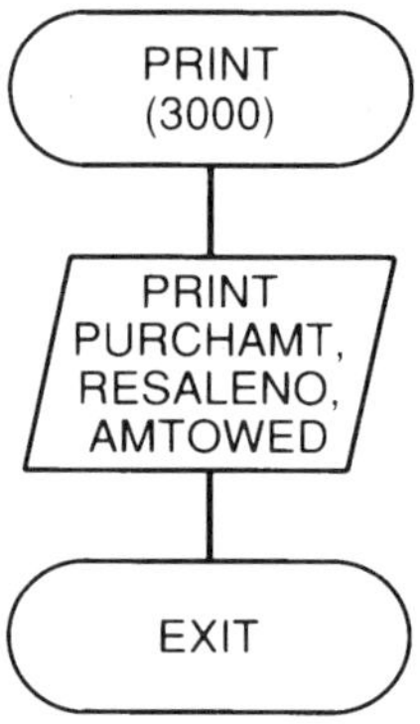	None	PRINTS OUTPUT RETURN

Internal Documentation	External Documentation
1. Title: prints output data	1. Same as internal documentation

Figure 6.16g The Algorithms and Flowcharts—PRINT Module

Summary

The decision logic structure is the second basic logic structure used to design algorithms, the first being the sequential logic structure. You now know the following types of instructions for communicating with the computer:

- START
- STOP
- PRINT
- assignment
- IF/THEN/ELSE
- PROCESS module

The instruction added in this chapter was IF/THEN/ELSE, the decision instruction. This instruction is powerful because it enables the computer to make decisions. It is an instruction that is easy to understand but more difficult to put to work.

There are three decision logic types: straight-through, positive, and negative logic. The programmer evaluates the conditions that arise in the problem to decide which logic type to use.

When you are using the decision structure, a decision table is a tool to help you develop the best set of decision instructions. You can use it to find the consequences following from every condition in a decision, so you can design the most efficient algorithms to solve the problem.

New Terms

decision table	nested IF/THEN/ELSE instruction
IF/THEN/ELSE instruction	positive logic
negative logic	straight-through logic

Questions

1. What is the decision logic structure?
2. What are the three types of decision logic?
3. Without specific data, outline an algorithm and a flowchart for each of the three types of decision logic.
4. What factors should determine which decision logic type to use for a specific problem?
5. How do you use a decision table?
6. **a.** Is the following nested IF/THEN/ELSE statement valid? Why or why not?

```
IF X < Y
 THEN
     IF Y < Z
       THEN
            X = X + 1
ELSE
       Y = Y + 1
```

   b. Which IF does the ELSE go with? Explain your answer.
   c. How would you change the statement to clarify the statement?
   d. Discuss your answer with your classmates and your instructor.

Problems

1. Set up four different algorithms and flowcharts for calculating a student's letter grade given the following (do not use straight-through logic):

   90 – 100 = A
   80 – 89 = B
   70 – 79 = C
   60 – 69 = D
   below 60 = F

2. Which of the four solutions from problem 1 would be the best? Justify your answer.
3. Using first positive and then negative logic, write the algorithms and draw the flowcharts for the following set of conditions:

   R = 50 for S <= 1000
   R = 100 for S = 1001—4000
   R = 250 for S = 4001—8000
   R = 75 for S >8000

4. Change the positive logic algorithm and flowchart from Problem 3 to reflect the following:

R = 100 for S = 1000—4000

R = 250 for S = 4001—8000

otherwise R = 75

5. **a.** Write the Calculation Module to choose the largest number from a set of three numbers, A, B, and C. Write the algorithm and draw the flowchart.
   b. Modify the logic in the calculation module to put A, B, and C in the correct order.
6. Complete the six problem-solving steps for the following problem. Include a data dictionary with your solution.

   Eureka Water Company charges the homeowner one of the following:

   a. A flat rate of $15.00 for usage up to and including 1,000 cubic feet.
   b. $.0175 per cubic foot for usage over 1,000 cubic feet and up to and including 2,000 cubic feet.
   c. $.02 per cubic foot for usage over 2,000 cubic feet and up to and including 3,000 cubic feet.
   d. A flat rate of $70 for usage over 3,000 cubic feet.
   Test your flowchart with actual data.
7. A company that issues check-cashing cards uses an algorithm to create card numbers. The algorithm adds the digits of a four-digit number, and then adds a fifth digit of 0 or 1 to make the sum of the digits even. The last digit in the number is called the *check digit.* Complete the six problem-solving steps to develop a solution which accepts a four-digit number into one variable, adds the check digit, and prints the original number and the new number. Include a data dictionary with your solution. Test your flowchart with the following data: Original number = 4737 (47371) and 4631 (46310). *Hint:* You may use any or all of the functions:

   INTEGER (X)—Integer function

   STRING (X)—Numeric to string

   VALUE (A)—String to numeric

   and the principle of concatenation of strings.

   [*Note:* The INTEGER (X) gives the whole number value of the real number X. When X is 546.43, the INTEGER (X) is 546, when X is 23.899 the INTEGER (X) is 23. The STRING (X) and VALUE (A) are conversion functions. The resultant of the function STRING (X) is the string value of the numerical X. The resultant of VALUE (A) is the numerical value of the string A. Concatenation is the combining of strings by placing the first string in front of the second one. For example, the resultant of "4" + "5" would be "45".]
8. Create a decision table for Problem 11 in Chapter 2.

Chapter 7

Problem Solving with Loops

Overview

The Loop Logic Structure
Incrementing
Accumulating
WHILE/WHILE-END
REPEAT/UNTIL
Automatic-Counter Loop
Nested Loops
Indicators
Algorithm Instructions and Flowchart Symbols
Recursion

Objectives

When you have finished this chapter, you should be able to:

1. Develop problem solutions for the computer using the five program developmental tools, the sequential logic structure, the decision logic structure, and the loop logic structure.
2. Use the three types of loop instructions in problem solutions.
3. Use nested loops in problem solutions.

The Loop Logic Structure

A third logic structure for designing decisions is the loop structure. The loop logic structure is the repeating structure. Most problems in business involve doing the same task over and over for different sets of data, so this structure is extremely important. Through the loop structure, a program can process many payroll records or inventory items, or put a mailing list in alphabetical or zip code order. This structure is harder to understand than the decision structure, but easier to use. The main difficulty in using it as part of a solution is identifying what instructions should be repeated. Besides being used to repeat instructions in a solution, the loop structure is also used to return the processing to an earlier point in the solution. When it is used in this way, it is a replacement for the GOTO statement. (The GOTO is an instruction that tells the computer to transfer to another instruction in the solution instead of processing the next instruction in sequence.) Replacing the GOTO statement in this way increases the readability of the program.

There are three types of loop structures, and each of them can be written in another way as a set of instructions using the IF/THEN/ELSE structure and the GOTO instruction. However, the IF/THEN/ELSE is a decision logic structure and generally should not be used to facilitate a loop. The loop structure is easier to read and to maintain than the IF/THEN/ELSE and GOTO combination. Since you already understand the decision logic structure, the decision equivalence to each loop structure will be illustrated to aid your understanding of loops.

The first type of loop structure is the WHILE/WHILE-END loop, which repeats instructions while a condition is TRUE and stops repeating when a condition arises that is not TRUE. The second type is the REPEAT/UNTIL loop, which repeats instructions while a condition is false or until a condition is TRUE. The third is the automatic-counter loop in which a variable is set equal to a given number and increases in equal increments until it is greater than an ending number. Each of the three loop structures has a specific use according to the language and/or the problem.

The algorithm and the flowchart differ with each type of loop structure. It is extremely important to indent the instructions in algorithms using the loop structure—as it is with the decision structure—to improve readability. Also, nested loops are common, and in these solutions indentation with brackets allows you to easily identify each loop.

Several standard types of tasks are accomplished through the use of the loop structure. Two of these are counting (also called incrementing and decrementing), and accumulating (also called calculating a sum or a total). In both tasks a number is added or subtracted from a variable and the result is stored back into the same variable. The basic difference between counting and accumulating is in the value that is added or subtracted. When counting, the value is a constant; when accumulating, the value is a variable. In each case the resultant variable is assigned the value of zero before starting the loop. This is called *initializing* the variable.

Incrementing

The task of **incrementing,** or counting, as we said, is done by adding a constant, such as 1 or 2, to the value of a variable. To write the instruction to increment a variable, you use an assignment statement. For example,

$$\text{COUNTER} = \text{COUNTER} + 1 \text{ OR } (\text{C} = \text{C} + 1)$$

when counting by one's. An assignment statement allows the variable on the left side of the equal sign to be assigned the value of, or to be replaced by, the resultant of the expression on the right side of the equal sign. The counter or incrementor instruction is a special version of the assignment instruction. This instruction enables the programmer to count the number of items, people, temperatures, and so on, as part of the solution to a problem.

Notice the structure of the assignment instruction for incrementing. The same variable name is on both sides of the equal sign; the amount the variable is to be incremented follows the plus sign. This instruction takes the value of the counter, adds one to it, and then replaces the old value of the counter with the new. The increment can be one, two, or any other constant, including negative numbers if you want to decrement rather than increment. In this example COUNTER or C must be initialized to zero before starting the loop.

Accumulating

Another task that a program must often perform is **accumulating,** or summing, a group of numbers. The process of accumulating is similar to incrementing, except a variable instead of a constant is added to another variable, which holds the value of the sum or total. The instruction for accumulating is the following:

SUM = SUM + VARIABLE or (S = S + V)

For example, the instruction to find total sales would be

TOTALSALES = TOTALSALES + SALES

Like the instruction to increment, the instruction to accumulate is a special version of the assignment instruction. As in incrementing, the same variable name appears on both sides of the equal sign (TOTALSALES) but in accumulating, a variable rather than a constant is on the right-hand side of the plus sign (SALES in this case). In other words, with an accumulator you are adding a variable (the item you are accumulating) to the value of another variable, which holds the sum or total. In these examples SUM and TOTALSALES must be initialized to zero before starting the loop.

WHILE/WHILE-END

The first of the three types of loop structures is the **WHILE/WHILE-END** structure. This type of loop tells the computer that while the condition is TRUE, repeat all instructions between the WHILE and the WHILE-END. The form of the algorithm is the following:

```
┌─ WHILE<CONDITION(S)>
│     INSTRUCTION
│     INSTRUCTION
│        .
│        .
└─ WHILE-END
```

When you design WHILE/WHILE-END loops, use brackets and indentation to improve the readability of the algorithms. In the illustration, notice how the bracket connects the beginning (WHILE) and the end (WHILE END) of the loop, and how the instructions are indented within the brackets to make the algorithm easily readable. The general form of the WHILE/WHILE-END flowchart is shown in Figure 7.1.

The symbol used for the WHILE part of the instruction is the diamond, the symbol for a decision. Since this flowchart shows only part of an algorithm, on-page connectors are used. The completed algorithm would have one part that would connect to A and another part that would connect to B.

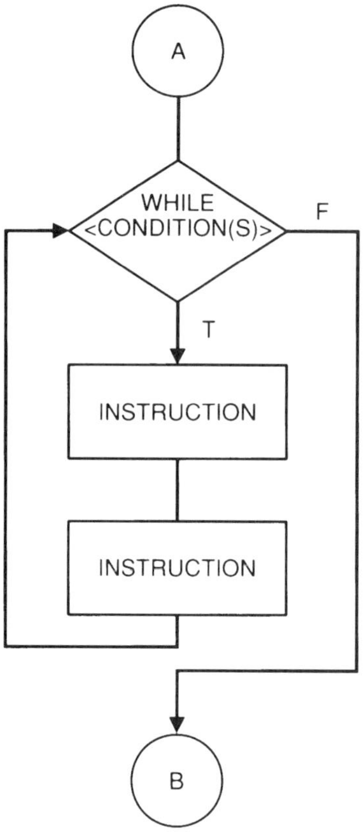

Figure 7.1 Flowchart Diagram of WHILE/WHILE-END

At the beginning of the WHILE/WHILE-END loop, the program processes the condition in order to decide whether or not to execute the loop instructions, as illustrated in the diamond at the top of the flowchart. When the resultant of the condition is FALSE at the start, the instructions within the loop will not be executed. When the resultant of the condition is TRUE, the complete set of instructions will be executed, and then the computer will go back to the beginning of the loop and process the condition again. The loop will repeat until the resultant of the condition is FALSE, at which time the processing will continue with the instruction following the WHILE-END.

Figure 7.2 shows the decision-structure equivalent to the WHILE/WHILE-END loop structure. Notice that the decision structure requires a separate GOTO instruction to return to the top of the loop. Also notice that when the condition is FALSE, the line of execution transfers to the instruction after the loop instructions.

Use the WHILE/WHILE-END structure when you do not know the number of times the instructions will be repeated, or if there are cases when the instructions in the loop should not be processed. In those cases, the resultant of the condition is FALSE at the start of the loop, so the loop is not processed. Examples of such cases are when you are entering information on clients and you don't know the number of clients; when you are finding the total amount of sales for the day and you don't know the number of sales; or when you are calculating test averages for each student in a class. In the case of calculating test averages, the loop instructions should not be executed for students who for some reason have no test grades. To calculate the average you would accumulate and count the test scores and then divide the total score by the number of tests. Since the number of grades would be zero for the student who didn't take any tests, the computer would

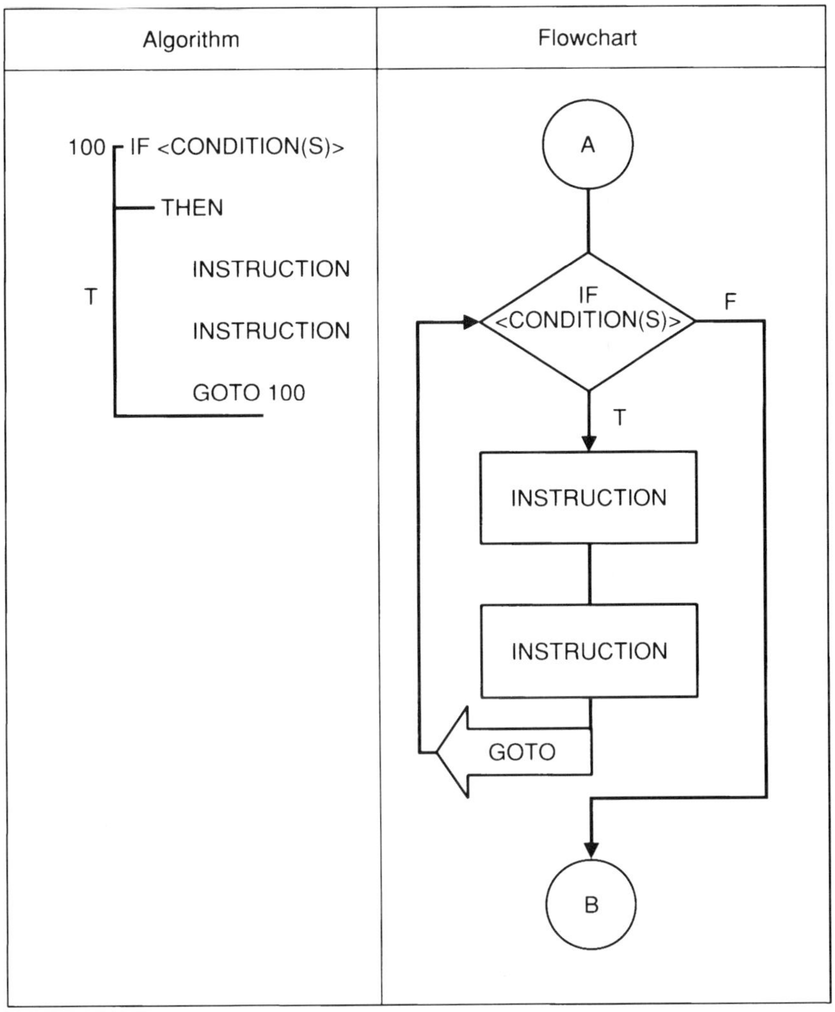

Figure 7.2 Decision Equivalent to WHILE/WHILE-END

try to divide by zero, and an error would result. The WHILE/WHILE-END loop would enable the processing to pass over the student and go on to the next student.

Putting It All Together

> Problem: Create the algorithm and the flowchart to find the average age of all the students in a class.

Figure 7.3 demonstrates the use of a WHILE/WHILE-END structure to calculate the average age of a group of people. The first instruction initializes the value of the SUM (the total of all ages) to zero. The second instruction initializes the value of the counter variable to zero. Next the first age is entered. An age must be entered before the loop so that the condition has data to use to get a resultant. The WHILE begins the loop and processes the condition AGE $< >$ 0. When the resultant is TRUE, the instructions in the loop are processed; when the resultant is FALSE, the processing continues with the calculation of the average. The first loop instruction accumulates the ages by adding each age to the total, followed by an instruction that counts the people by adding one

Algorithm	Flowchart

AVERAGE AGE
(0000)

```
1.  SUM = 0

2.  COUNTER = 0

3.  ENTER AGE

4. ┌ WHILE AGE <> 0
   │    SUM = SUM + AGE
   │    COUNTER = COUNTER + 1
   │    ENTER AGE
   └ WHILE-END

5.  AVERAGE = SUM/COUNTER

6.  PRINT AVERAGE

7.  END
```

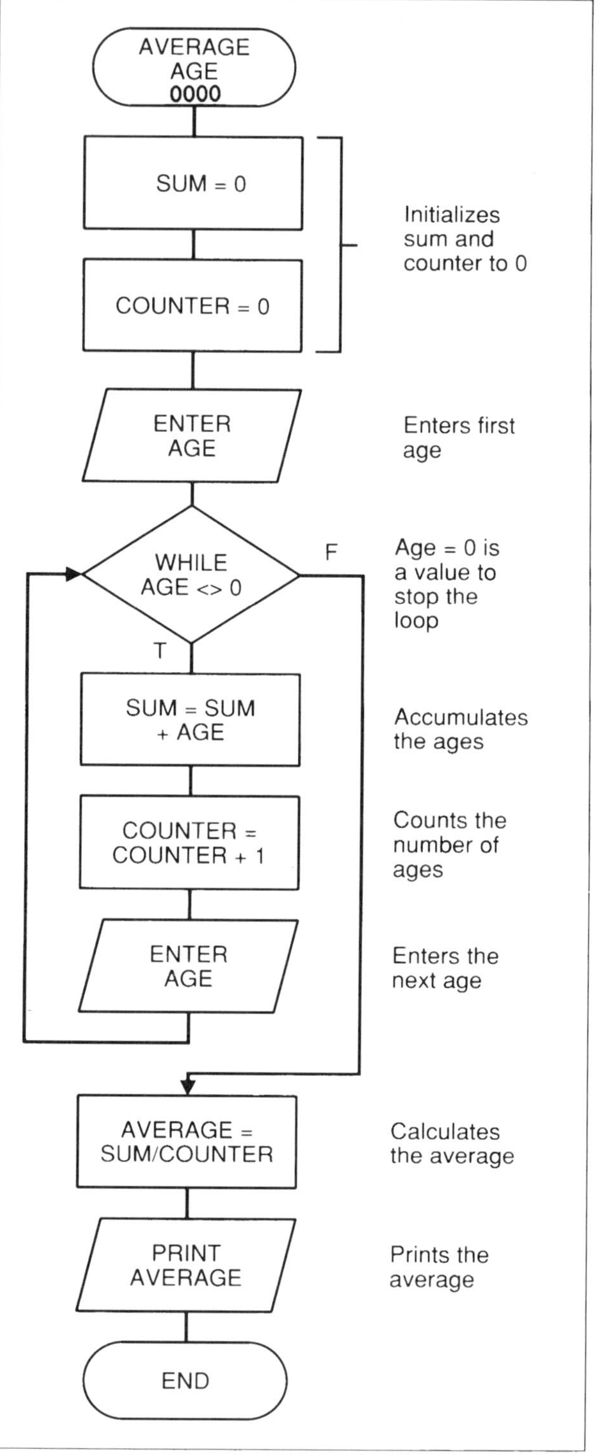

Figure 7.3 Average Age of a Class-WHILE/WHILE-END

to the counter variable. The final instruction in the loop enters the next age. The processing then returns to process another condition. The last age should be zero. This zero is called a *trip value,* or a *flag*. It allows the value of AGE to control when to stop the looping process and continue with the rest of the solution. When the looping process stops, the processing continues at the calculation of the average age, and finally, the printing of the average age.

The data for this problem can be entered from the keyboard; the user enters a 0 when there are no more ages to enter.

REPEAT/UNTIL

The second type of loop structure is the **REPEAT/UNTIL** structure. This type of loop tells the computer to repeat the set of instructions between the REPEAT and the UNTIL, until a condition is TRUE. There are two major differences between this instruction and the WHILE/WHILE-END. First, in the WHILE/WHILE-END loop, the program continues to loop as long as the resultant of the condition is TRUE; in the REPEAT/UNTIL loop, the program stops the loop process when the resultant of the condition is TRUE. Second, in the WHILE/WHILE-END loop, the condition is processed at the beginning; in the REPEAT/UNTIL loop, the condition is processed at the end. When the condition is processed at the end, the instructions in the loop are processed entirely at least once, whether it's necessary or not.

It is important that you be able to distinguish between the loop structures so you can use them appropriately. Both the setup and the uses for the two loop structures are different. When you are using the WHILE/WHILE-END, you must initialize the data so that the resultant of the condition is TRUE the first time through the loop. Otherwise, the loop instructions will never be processed. With the REPEAT/UNTIL, you can set the operands of the conditions anywhere within the loop since the condition is processed at the end. If there is any reason that the loop instructions should not be processed the first time, then the WHILE/WHILE-END must be used because the REPEAT/UNTIL always processes the instructions at least once.

The format of the REPEAT/UNTIL algorithm is the following:

```
┌─ REPEAT
│    INSTRUCTION
│    INSTRUCTION
│       .
│       .
└─ UNTIL<CONDITION(S)>
```

Here again, use brackets and indentation to improve readability. Figure 7.4 shows the form of the flowchart. When you are designing a REPEAT/UNTIL flowchart, write the word REPEAT above the first instruction of the loop.

Figure 7.5 shows the equivalent decision structure. Unlike the WHILE/WHILE-END decision equivalent, in which the processing of the condition is always at the beginning of the instructions to be repeated, with the REPEAT/UNTIL decision equivalence, the processing of the condition always takes place at the end of the instructions to be repeated. Also notice that there is no evidence of a loop until the condition is reached. The loop structure provides a solution that is easier to read and understand.

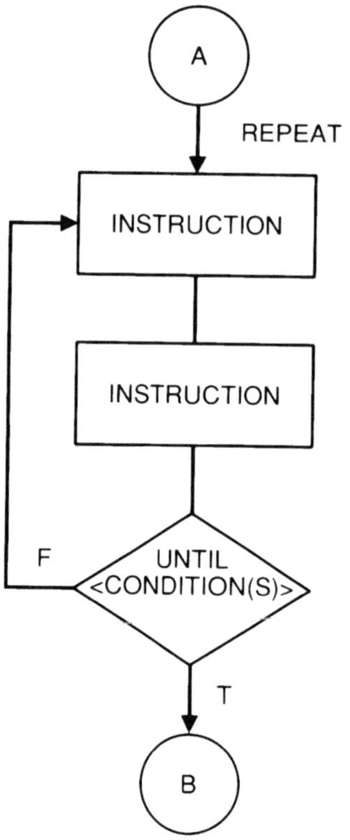

Figure 7.4 Flowchart Diagram of REPEAT/UNTIL

Use the REPEAT/UNTIL structure when you do not know the number of times the instructions will be executed, when you know they will be executed at least once, or when you do not know the condition for repeating until after the instructions in the loop are processed. Usually, the problem will dictate which loop to use.

Putting It All Together

Using the REPEAT/UNTIL loop structure, this section illustrates the same problem as in the "Putting It All Together" section for the WHILE/WHILE-END loop.

Figure 7.6 demonstrates the use of the REPEAT/UNTIL structure to calculate the average age of a group of people. The first instruction initializes the value of the SUM (the total of all ages) to zero. The second instruction initializes the value of the counter variable to zero. Next the first age is entered. An age must be entered so that there is a value for AGE to use in the calculations the first time through. The data must be entered just before processing the condition, or the trip values will be used in the last calculations in the solution. This is called a *primer read.* However, unlike the WHILE/WHILE-END loop structure, when a zero is entered at this place in the processing, the instructions within the loop will be executed at least once, depending on what is entered at the second ENTER instruction. For this reason, the WHILE/WHILE-END loop structure is often the preferred choice. The REPEAT begins the loop. The first instruction in the loop accumulates the ages by adding each age to the total, followed by an instruction that counts the people by adding 1 to the counter variable. The last instruction in the loop enters the next age. The next instruction is the loop-end in-

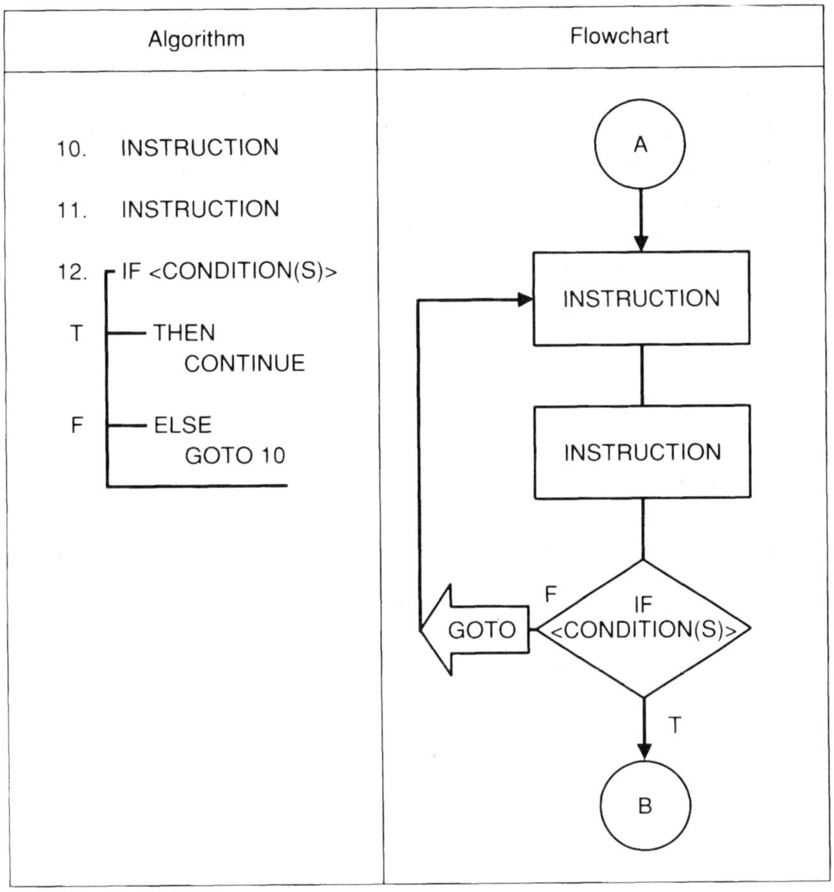

Figure 7.5 Decision Equivalent to REPEAT/UNTIL

struction. This instruction processes the condition AGE = 0. When the resultant is FALSE the instructions in the loop are processed; when the resultant is TRUE the processing continues with the calculation of the average. The last age is a zero, the trip value or dummy value. It allows the value of AGE to control when to stop the loop process and continue with the rest of the solution. When the looping process stops, the processing continues at the calculation of the average age, and finally, the printing of the average age.

The programmer or the language dictates which loop structure to use. Sometimes the WHILE/WHILE-END and the REPEAT/UNTIL could be used with equal efficiency. The choice is then a matter of the preference of the programmer.

Automatic-Counter Loop

The third type of loop structure is the **automatic-counter loop.** This type of loop increments or decrements a variable each time the loop is repeated. To design an automatic-counter loop, the programmer uses a variable as a counter that starts counting at a specified number and increments the variable each time the loop is processed. The amount to be incremented is specified by the instruction. The set of instructions within the loop repeats until the counter is greater than an ending number. The beginning value,

Algorithm	Flowchart
AVERAGE AGE (0000) 1. SUM = 0 2. COUNTER = 0 3. ENTER AGE 4. REPEAT SUM = SUM + AGE COUNTER = COUNTER + 1 ENTER AGE UNTIL AGE = 0 5. AVERAGE = SUM/COUNTER 6. PRINT AVERAGE 7. END	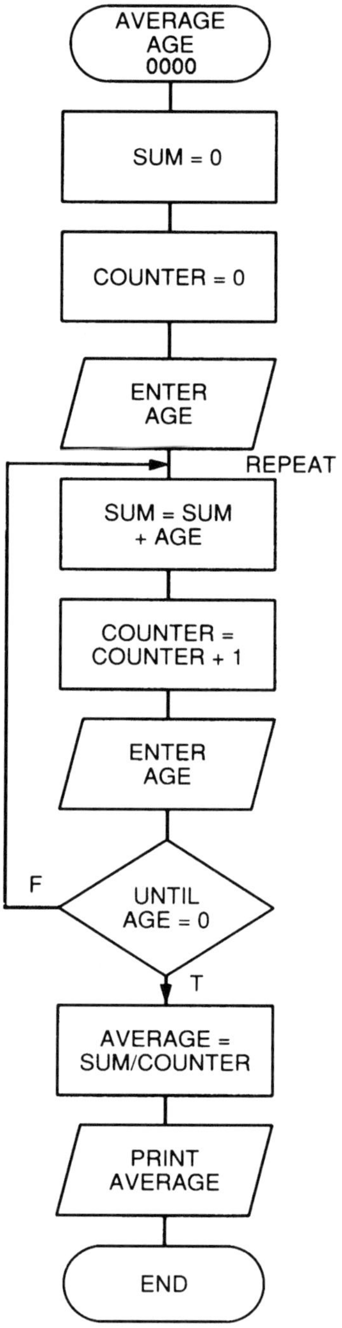

Figure 7.6 Average Age of a Class—REPEAT/UNTIL

the ending value, and the increment value may be constants, variables, or expressions (calculations). They should not be changed during the processing of the instructions in the loop. They may be changed after the loop is completed. The test for whether or not to process the loop instructions in an automatic-counter loop will be found at the beginning or at the end of the loop depending on the language or the version of the language.

The form of the algorithm for the automatic-counter loop is the following:

```
┌── LOOP: COUNTER = BEGIN TO END STEP S
│    INSTRUCTION
│    INSTRUCTION
│    .
│    .
│    .
└── LOOP-END: COUNTER
```

Here again, a bracket connects the beginning (LOOP) and the end (LOOP-END) of the algorithm, and the instructions are intended to improve readability, just as in the other loop structures.

The flowchart in Figure 7.7 shows the automatic-counter loop structure. C is the variable used for the counter, BEGIN is the beginning value, END is the ending value, and STEP is the value by which the counter is to be incremented.

Figure 7.8 shows the decision equivalents to the automatic-counter loop structure. There are two solutions illustrated since there are two places the decision can be processed: at the beginning of the loop or at the end of the loop. Which decision equivalent would be used depends on the language or the version of the language. You will not find both versions in the same language or language version.

There are rules that the computer follows when processing the automatic-counter loop. The rules are simple, and it is important that the user understands and follows them when testing a solution.

1. When the computer executes the LOOP instruction, it sets the counter equal to the beginning number (see a, a_1, and a_2 in Figures 7.7 and 7.8).
2. When the computer executes the LOOP-END, it increments the counter. Since the counter is usually incremented before the condition is processed, this book assumes the incrementing of the counter at LOOP-END (see b, b_1, and b_2 in Figures 7.7 and 7.8).
3. When the counter is less than or equal to the ending number, the processing continues at the instruction that follows the LOOP instruction. When the counter is greater than the ending number, the processing continues at the instruction that follows the LOOP-END instruction (see c, c_1, and c_2 in Figures 7.7 and 7.8).

It is important to understand these rules in order to use this structure correctly.

Use the automatic-counter loop structure when you know from the start the number of times the loop will be executed, for example, when you know the exact number of people in the group for the average age problem. Do not use a decision to exit from this loop. A decision cannot be used to exit a loop since to do so would require a GOTO instruction. GOTO instructions tend to decrease readability, so they are used as little as possible in structured programming. If a decision instruction is necessary, then consider using one of the other types of loop structures for your solution. Counter loops are overused because they are easy to code. A good programmer is careful not to fall into this trap. It is important to choose the best loop structure for the problem.

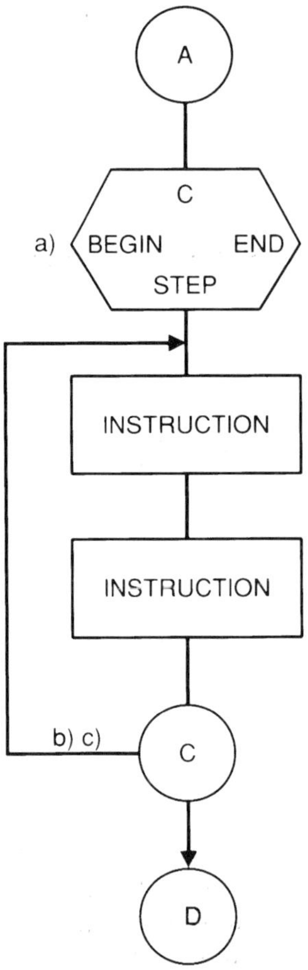

Figure 7.7 Flowchart of Automatic-Counter Loop

Putting It All Together

This section illustrates the same problem, using the automatic-counter structure, that the previous two Putting It All Together sections did, using the other two types of loop instructions. The solution calculates the average age of a group of people. The programmer would use the automatic-counter loop structure for this solution only if the number of students in the class—in this case, 12—is known.

In the automatic-counter loop in Figure 7.9, as in the other two loop structures, the first two instructions initialize the variables SUM and COUNTER. The next instruction begins the loop. The A is the counter variable. The counter begins at 1 and is incremented by 1 until the counter is greater than 12, so the loop will be repeated 12 times. Notice that there is no increment value. When the increment value is left out, the computer assumes the value to be 1. When the counter increases to a value greater than 12, the average age is calculated and printed. Whenever the number of items to be counted is known, the automatic-counter loop is preferred. If that number is not known, then one of the other loop structures is preferred.

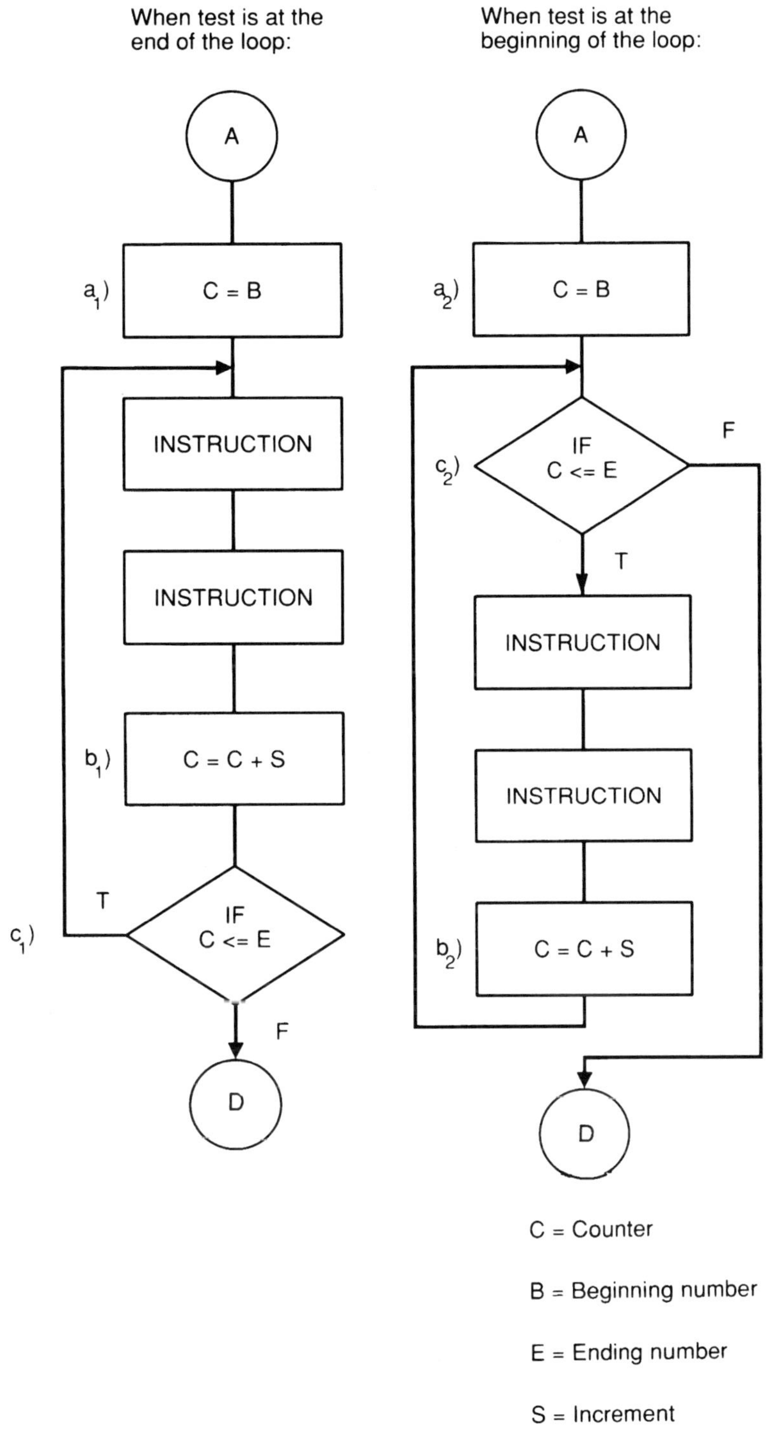

Figure 7.8 Decision Equivalents to Automatic-Counter Loop

Nested Loops

Loops can be nested like decisions can. Each loop must be nested inside the loop just outside it. The general rules regarding loops, such as where the condition is processed and how indentation and brackets are used, hold true for nested loops as well as single

Algorithm	Flowchart
AVERAGE AGE 1. SUM = 0 2. COUNTER = 0 3. LOOP: J = 1 TO 12 SUM = SUM + AGE COUNTER = COUNTER + 1 LOOP-END: J 4. AVERAGE = SUM/COUNTER 5. PRINT COUNTER, AVERAGE 6. END	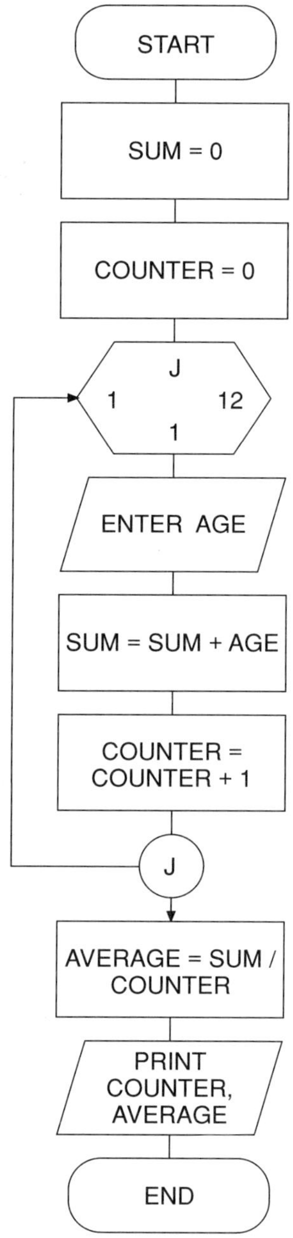

Figure 7.9 Example of an Algorithm and Flowchart for a Problem Using an Automatic-Counter Loop

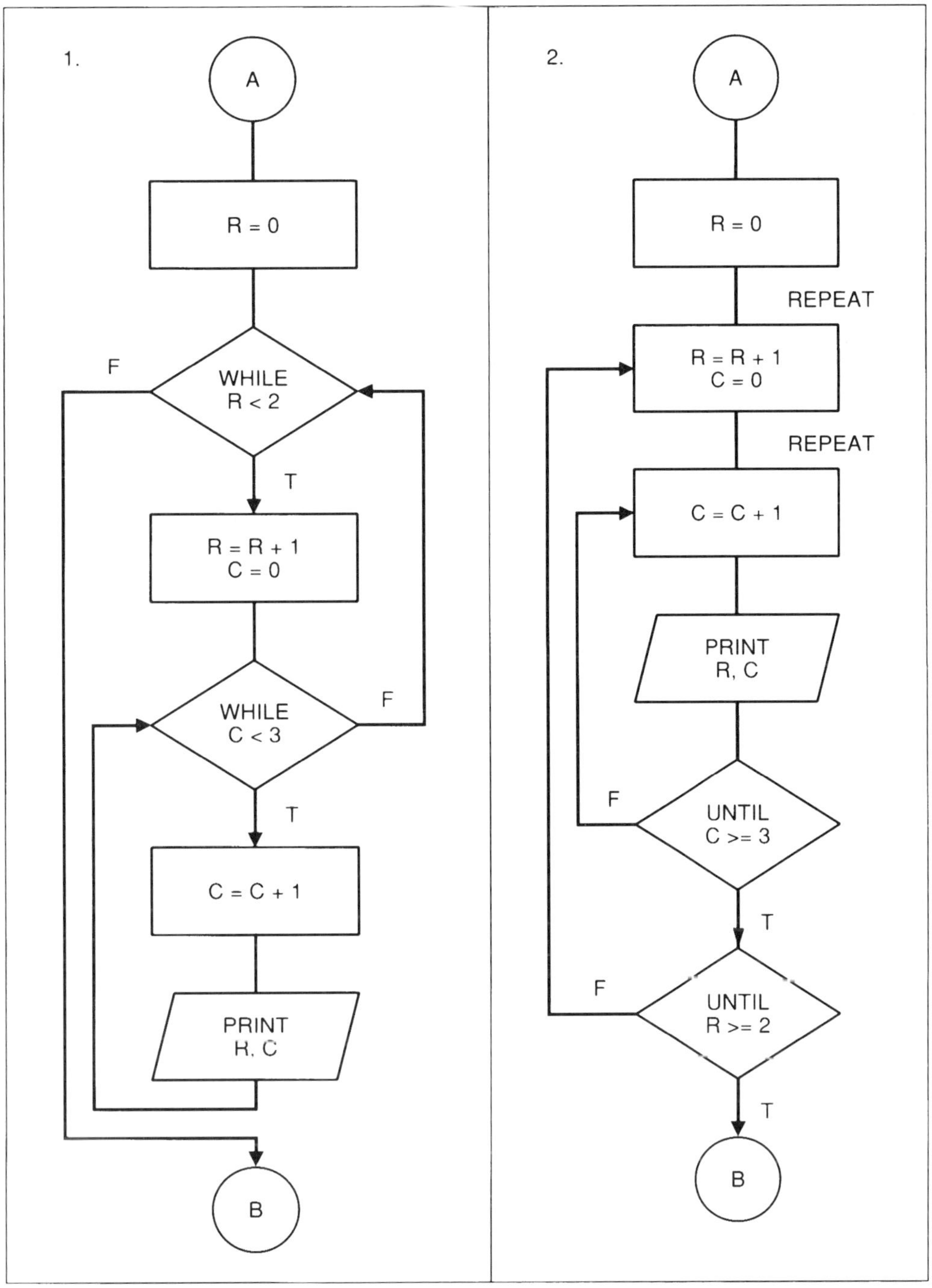

Figure 7.10 Nested Loops (*continued on page 136*)

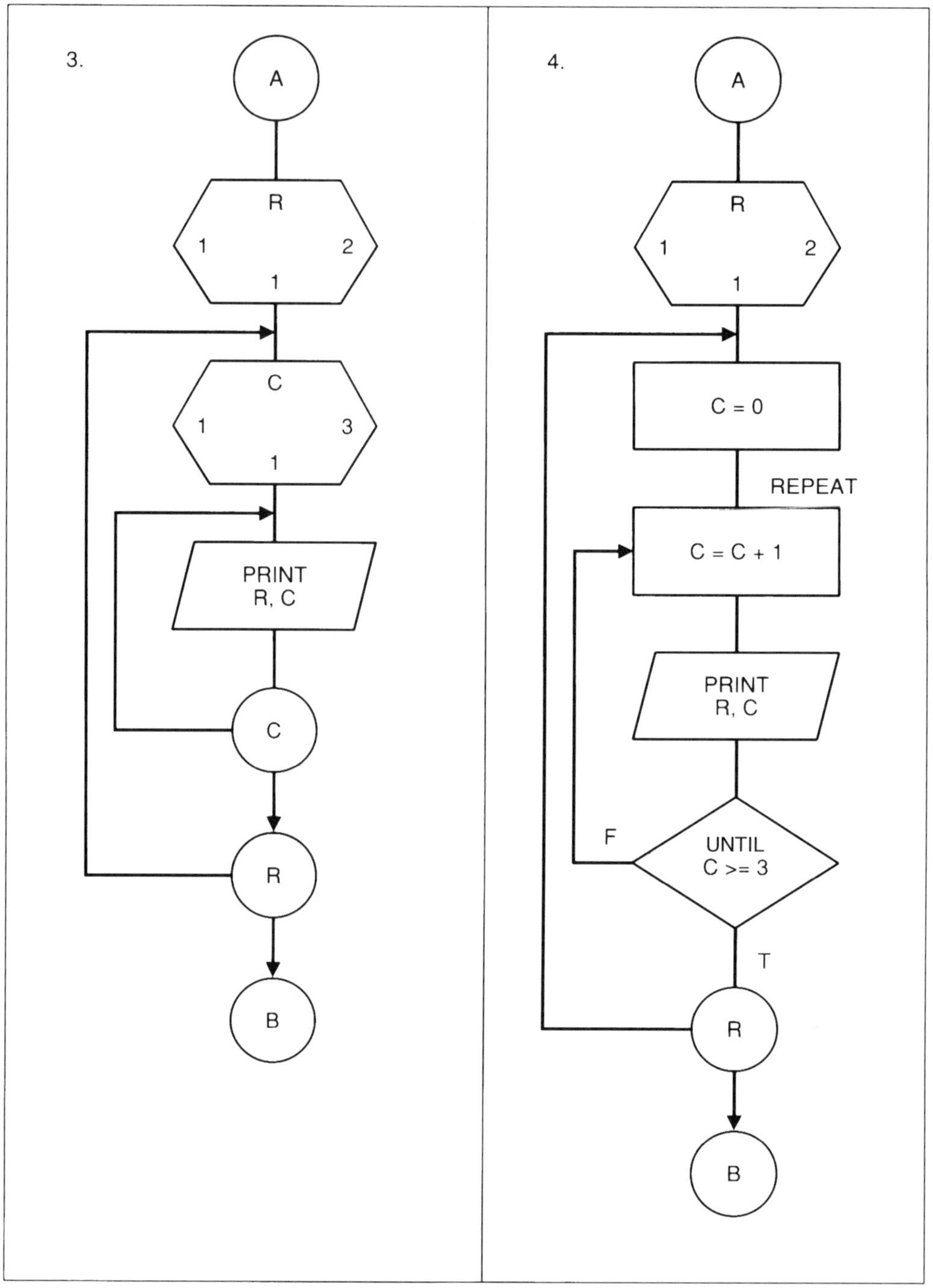

Figure 7.10 *(continued from page 135)*

loops. The inner loops do not have to be the same types of loop structures as the outer loops; that is, a WHILE/WHILE-END may be nested inside a REPEAT/UNTIL loop, or vice versa.

Examples of nested loops are found in Figure 7.10 Notice that the nested loop in each flowchart results in the same output. The output for all four nested loops is

R *(outer loop counter)*	C *(inner loop counter)*
1	1
1	2
1	3
2	1
2	2
2	3

In the first flowchart in Figure 7.10, the nested loops are both WHILE/WHILE-END structures. The inner loop will be processed as long as the value of C is less than 3. The inner loop increments C and, later, prints the values of R and C. During the processing of the inner loop the value of R does not change. When C becomes equal to 3, the inner loop has completed the processing, and the processing continues with the outer loop. The outer loop increments R, sets C equal to 0, and then processes the inner loop. When R becomes equal to 2, processing continues at B. This whole process is essentially what happens in the other three examples of nested loops. The outer loop increments R, sets C equal to 0 or 1, and processes the inner C loop. The inner loop increments C and prints the values of R and C.

Indicators

Indicators are logical variables that a programmer sets within a program to change the processing path or to control when the processing of a loop should end. They are sometimes called *flags, switches,* or *trip values.* The user has no knowledge of these indicators during processing. These indicators are used to detect changes in the output line, in the processing of data, and so forth. An error indicator designates that an error has occurred in the input or the output. An end-of-data indicator designates that there are no more data to be entered.

The main thing to remember about indicators is that they are set internally to change the processing. An indicator was used in the average-age problem in Figures 7.3 and 7.6 (the zero value of AGE) to stop the looping when there were no more ages to be entered. An indicator can be a variable of logical data type or a value that the variable can never equal. For example, an indicator for AGE might be 0 or 500 or −300. An indicator for an error could be a variable with the value TRUE when an error has occurred, and FALSE when there have been no errors.

Algorithm Instructions and Flowchart Symbols

Table 7.1 is an update of the Algorithm Instructions and Flowchart Symbols table, last seen in Chapter 5. The new instructions and logic structures for combinations of instructions shown on page 139 have been added to this table.

Table 7.1 Algorithm Instructions and Flowchart Symbols (*continued on page 139*)

Algorithm Instruction	Flowchart Symbol	Definition (What the instruction tells the computer)
START [module name] [module number]	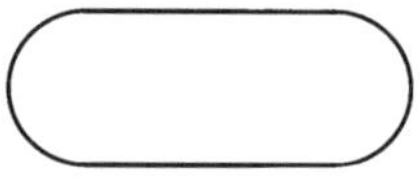	Start processing a module.
ENTER [list of variable names]	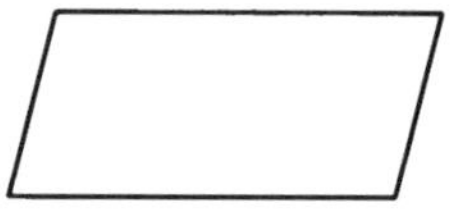	Enter data from a data block or from the keyboard into the following variable memory locations.
variable = [expression]	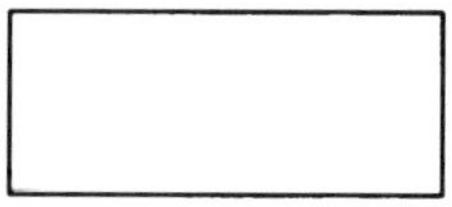	Assign the value of the following expression to a variable location. Called the *assignment instruction.*
WRITE [list of variable names]	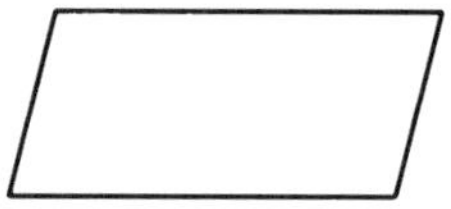	Write to the printer the values represented by the following variable names.
PRINT [list of variable names]	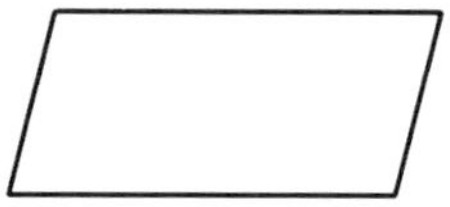	Print on the screen the values represented by the following variable names.
PROCESS [module name]		Execute the instructions in the named module, and then return to execute the next instruction.
END/EXIT	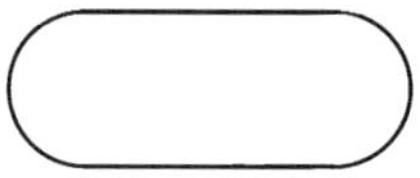	Stop the processing of the module. Processing ceases with the End; with the Exit, processing continues with the next instruction after the PROCESS.
IF/THEN/ELSE	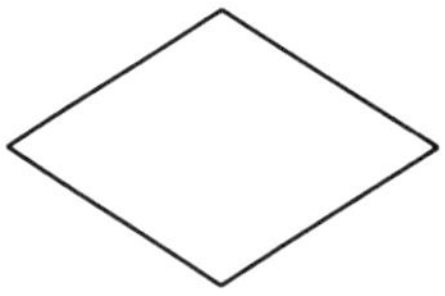	When the condition is TRUE, use one set of instructions; when the condition is FALSE, use another set of instructions.

Table 7.1 *(continued from p. 138)*

Algorithm Instruction	Flowchart Symbol	Definition (What the instruction tells the computer)
COUNTER = COUNTER + 1 (C = C + 1)		Increments the counter C.
SUM = SUM + VARIABLE (S = S + V)		Accumulates the values of the variable V.
WHILE/WHILE-END	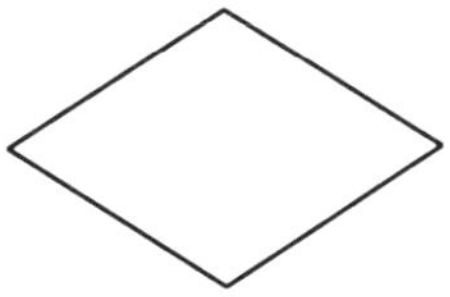	Repeat a set of instructions as long as a condition is TRUE.
REPEAT/UNTIL	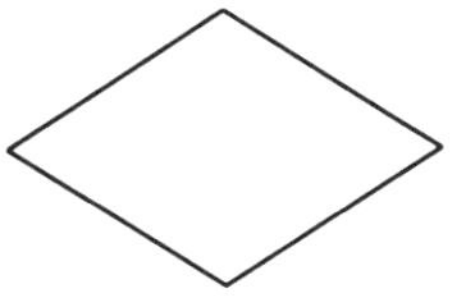	Repeat a set of instructions as long as a condition is FALSE.
LOOP: C = BEGIN TO END STEP S LOOP-END: C	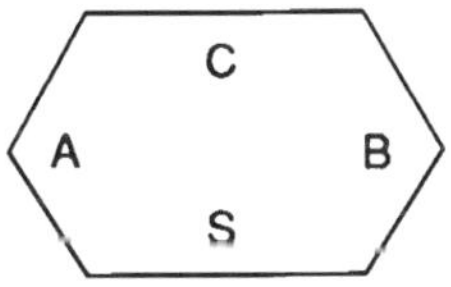	**Repeat a set of instructions using a counter C which starts at A(BEGIN) and increments by S(STEP) until C is greater than B(END).**

- Decision Logic Structure — IF/THEN/ELSE
- Instructions
  - Incrementing — COUNTER = COUNTER + 1 (C = C + 1)
  - Accumulating — SUM = SUM + VARIABLE (S = S + V)
- Loop Logic Structures — WHILE/WHILE-END
  REPEAT/UNTIL
  LOOP: COUNTER = BEGIN TO END
  STEP S
  LOOP-END: COUNTER

Recursion

Another type of loop structure is **recursion.** Recursion occurs when a module or a function calls itself. The condition that ends the loop must be within the module. Pascal and C are the main languages that use recursion. Recursive procedures can be replaced by conventional loop structures; however, recursive procedures are usually faster. Figure 7.11 is

Algorithm	Flowchart
CONTROL MODULE 0000 1. ENTER N 2. NFACTORIAL = FACTORIAL (N)* 3. PRINT NFACTORIAL 4. END * FACTORIAL (N) is a user-defined function	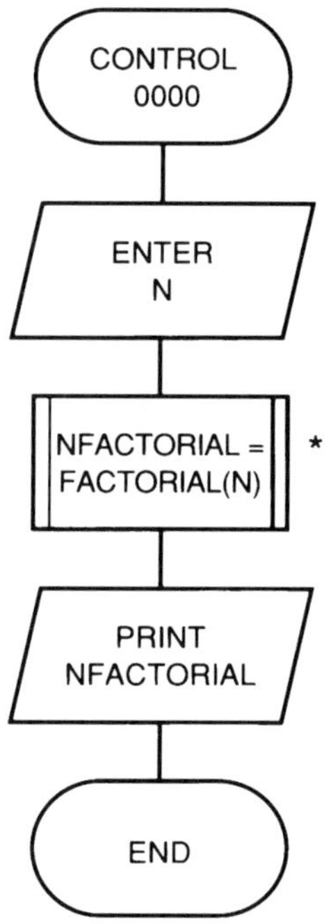
FACTORIAL (N) 1000 1. IF N > 1 THEN FACTORIAL = N * FACTORIAL (N - 1) ELSE FACTORIAL = 1 2. EXIT	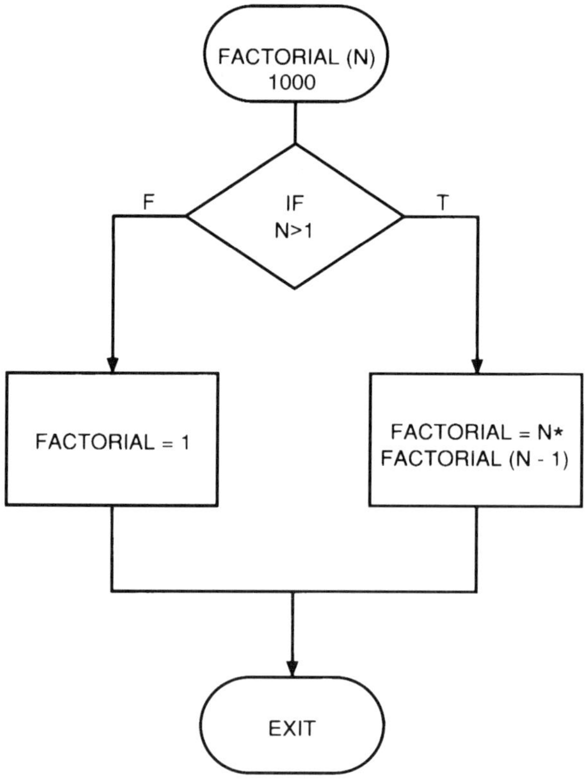

Figure 7.11 Recursion

an example of a recursive function that calculates a factorial number such as 5! (5! = 5 * 4 * 3 * 2 * 1).

Summary

The third basic logic structure is the loop logic structure. By using this structure a programmer can design solutions that repeat processes.

There are three common tasks associated with the loop logic structure. The first is counting, or incrementing, to determine a total number of items. The second is summing, or accumulating, to find totals. The third is processing arrays, which are presented in Chapter 10.

The loop logic structure includes three types of loops. The WHILE/WHILE-END loop repeats a set of instructions as long as the resultant of a condition is TRUE. The condition is processed before the first instruction of the loop. The second type of loop structure is the REPEAT/UNTIL loop. This loop repeats the instructions until a condition is TRUE. The condition in this case is processed after the last instruction in the loop. The third loop structure is the automatic-counter loop. In this case the instructions are repeated a given number of times, directed by a loop counter, which starts at a beginning number and is increased by a given increment until the counter is greater than an ending number. The condition can be processed at the beginning or the end of an automatic-counter loop depending on the language. For a programmer, the type of loop to use is determined by the problem and the language or application.

Indicators are used with loop structures to change the course of processing and to control the ending of a loop. Indicators are written in the instructions within the solution and normally are not entered externally by the user.

New Terms

accumulating
automatic-counter loop
incrementing
indicators
recursion
REPEAT/UNTIL
WHILE/WHILE-END

Questions

1. Write the instruction to increment a variable by one.
2. Write the instruction to accumulate a variable A.
3. Name the three types of loop structures.
4. State the major differences in the three types of loop structures.

Problems

Complete the six steps of solution development and a data dictionary for the following problems.

1. The Last Stop Boutique is having a five-day sale. Each day, starting on Monday, the price will drop 10% of the previous day's price. For example, if the original price of a product is $20.00, the sale price on Monday would be $18.00 (10% less than the original price). On Tuesday the sale price would be $16.20 (10% less than Monday). On Wednesday the sale price would be $14.58; on Thursday the sale price would be $13.12; and on Friday the sale price would be $11.81. Develop a solution that will calculate the price of an item for each of the five days, given the original price. Test the solution for an item costing $10.00.
2. Make changes in the solution to Problem 1 to *set* the price at wholesale when the sale price drops below the wholesale price. Test the solution with the following prices:

Retail Prices:	$20.00, $25.00
Wholesale Prices:	$10.00, $20.00

Develop a solution that will calculate the average temperature, given a set of temperatures. The number of temperatures may differ from time to time. (Use a trip value to stop the processing of the loop.) Test the solution with the following 10 temperatures:

78°	90°
85°	80°
87°	83°
75°	90°
86°	70°

4. Mr. Brown has given a test to his class. He would like to have the average score for the class, and the highest and lowest scores. Develop a solution to calculate and print out these values. (Use a trip value to stop the processing of the loop.)
5. Mary Smith, a student, has borrowed $3,000 to help pay her college expenses. After setting up a budget, $85 was the maximum monthly payment she could afford to make on the loan. Develop a solution to calculate and print the interest, the principal, and the balance on the loan per month. Other information she would like to know is the number of years and months it will take to pay the loan back and the total interest she will pay during that period. The interest rate is 1% per month on the unpaid balance. Keep in mind these formulas:

$$\text{interest} = \text{balance} * \text{interest rate}$$
$$\text{payment} = \text{balance} - \text{interest}$$
$$\text{new balance} = \text{balance} - \text{payment}$$

6. Develop a solution to flip a coin a given amount of times and then print the number of heads and the number of tails. The equation to toss the coin is:

$$\text{COIN} = \text{INT(RANDOM} * 2) - 1$$

When COIN = 0 the toss is heads, and when COIN = 1 the toss is tails. RANDOM returns a number between 0 and 1, including 0 but not 1. Therefore, when RANDOM is less than or equal to .5, COIN will equal 0: and when RANDOM is greater than .5 and less than 1, COIN will equal 1.

7. Develop a solution to calculate a student's grade average for one semester. The letter grades should be entered and the grade average printed out. An A is equivalent to 4 grade points, a B is 3 grade points; a C is 2 grade points, a D is 1 grade point, and an F is zero grade points.

Chapter 8

Problem Solving with the Case Logic Structure

Overview

The Case Logic Structure
Codes
Menus

Objectives

When you have finished this chapter, you should be able to:

1. Develop problem solutions using the five program developmental tools and the four logic structures.
2. Develop a menu-driven solution for a problem.

Sometimes a solution to a problem requires the computer to choose one action from a set of actions. This kind of solution can be designed through the decision logic structure, but the case logic structure is more efficient for this purpose. The case logic structure is a special variation of the decision structure, although it is different enough to present here separately. This structure is used in many business-related problems, such as those dealing with types of accounts in a bank or types of insurance available to an employee. The case logic structure is also used in solutions that involve menu-driven programs.

The Case Logic Structure

The case logic structure is made up of several or many sets of instructions, only one of which will be selected by the user and executed by the computer. Through the use of the case logic structure, a programmer can enable a user to enter the value of a variable from the keyboard or from a file to select one of several options in a list. Then the instruction following the END-OF-CASE instruction is executed. (The END-OF-CASE instruction is the last instruction in the case logic structure.) The case logic structure does not enable the program to loop back to select another option. If the solution requires looping back, then the programmer has to use the loop logic structure. The form of the case logic structure is the following:

```
CASE OF VARIABLE
          = constant1:
             actions for VARIABLE = constant 1
          = constant2:
             actions for VARIABLE = constant 2
          = constant3:
             actions for VARIABLE = constant 3
             .
             .
          OTHERWISE:
             actions for VARIABLE = anything else
END-OF-CASE
```

Notice how the indentation improves the readability of the algorithm.

When the case logic structure is processed, the computer compares the value of the variable against each of the constants. When it finds a constant that is equal to the value of the variable, it executes the corresponding set of instructions. Then the computer skips to the instruction after the END-OF-CASE. The variable must be an integer or a character. For example, take an inventory problem in which the name of the vendor for each item is entered as a variable in the computer in the form of a code (S = Small's Auto Parts, W = Wilson's Water Pumps, J = Johnson's Ignition Systems, and so on). The computer selects the vendor's name, when the user enters, as the value of the variable, the value of the code (S, W, J, and so on). The variable with the value of the vendor code would be used in the CASE OF VARIABLE part of the logic structure. S, W, J, and so on, would be the constants. Under each constant would be the instruction to be executed once the vendor is selected. The last section is the OTHERWISE section of the structure. This section has the set of instructions executed when the variable has a value of anything but the named constants in the list of options. Inclusion of the OTHERWISE option will allow for all possible responses and may be used as a response for validation of data; however, it is optional. The END-OF-CASE tells the computer where the case logic structure ends.

Other examples of the appropriate use of the case logic structure would be a solution for the computer to choose the deduction for medical insurance or to choose the retirement plan for an employee when there are several different plans. The values of the constants, the codes for the insurance or retirement plans, and the set of instructions corresponding to each constant would be part of the input data and processing given in the problem.

The number of possible options, or sets of instructions, in the case logic structure is limited only by the language or the application package in use. The options may be in any order, but it is best to arrange them according to how frequently they're used starting with the most frequently used option. For a given problem, the programmer would rely on the customer to find out which options would be used most often. When the options are ordered this way, the computer will have to check all possible options fewer times before it finds the one selected by the user. If no one knows which options would

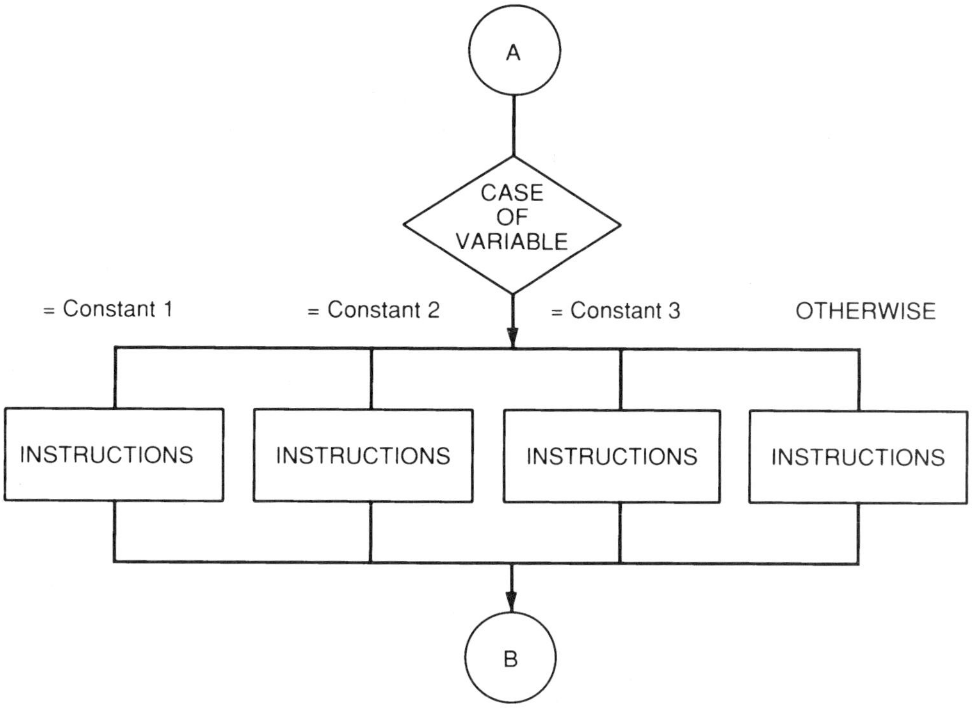

Figure 8.1 Flowchart Diagram for the Case Logic Structure

be used more often, then the options are arranged in the most logical order. That arrangement might be alphabetical, numerical, the order given by the customer, or some other order. The OTHERWISE section is always last.

Figure 8.1 shows the flowchart of the case structure. The decision equivalent would be a set of nested IF/THEN/ELSE instructions using positive logic (see Figure 8.2). In the case logic structure, the relative operator is always *equals* (=). The case logic structure is really a special form of the decision logic structure; it allows the computer to select one set of instructions from many sets through the use of the relative operator, equals. Compare Figures 8.1 and 8.2 to see how much easier it is to design a solution requiring the computer to choose one option out of many by using the case logic structure rather than the decision logic structure.

Codes

Codes are characters, character strings, numbers, or some combination of these types of data that a programmer uses to name the options, the constants, in a case structure. They are abbreviations for each of the options. They direct the processing path just as indicators do by specifying the choice that the user prefers—and, therefore, that the computer will make, such as a particular employee medical plan out of many plans: B for Best Medical Insurance Company, D for Direct Medical Insurance Company, and the like.

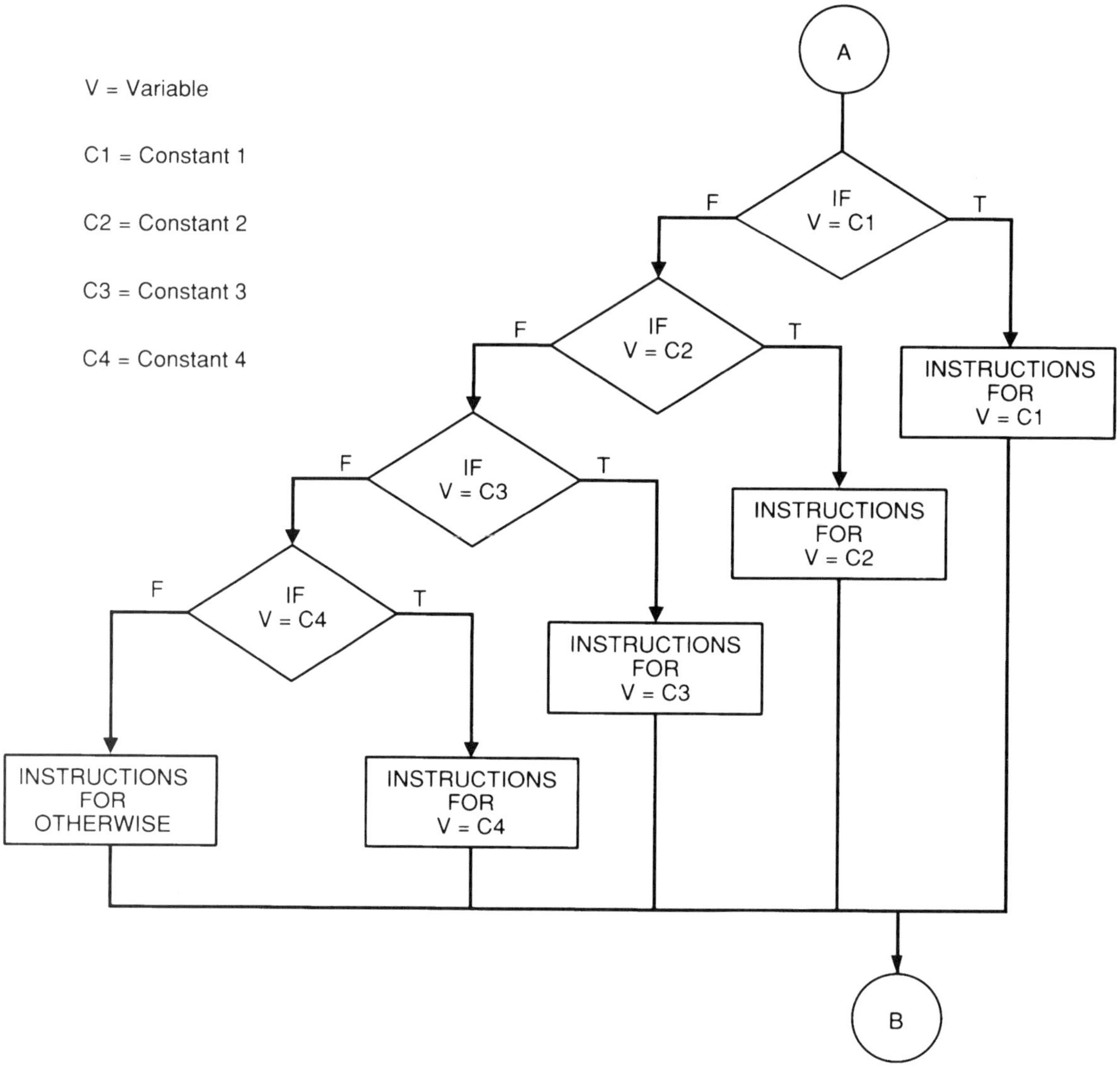

Figure 8.2 Decision-Structure Equivalent to the Case Logic Structure

The major differences between indicators and codes are the following:

1. Codes are data to be entered by the user. Indicators are internal signals to change the processing path.
2. A code can have a value of many different types. The value of an indicator can be logical data, TRUE or FALSE, or it can have an implausible value for the variable it represents in the solution.

A code is used to indicate choices such as the type of insurance an employee is buying, the sex of an individual, or the vendor in an inventory problem. When using codes the OTHERWISE option indicates an error. Without the use of codes, solutions requiring a choice from among several options would be longer, harder to read, and more difficult to maintain.

Putting It All Together

This PIAT illustrates the use of codes in a solution using the case logic structure.

> Problem: A company has four different medical plans. The programmer has given each plan a code corresponding to the beginning initial of the company: Plan 1 = F, Plan 2 = B, Plan 3 = K, Plan 4 = E.
>
> The company pays for all of Plan 1. The individual has to pay for part of the others. The payroll deduction for Plan 2 = 4.65, for Plan 3 = 7.85, and for Plan 4 = 5.50. Any other codes are considered in error. Write the algorithm and draw the flowchart for a module to determine the payroll deduction.

Figure 8.3 shows the module to calculate the insurance deduction. The variable name for the medical plan code is MEDCODE. MEDCODE can have only the value of F, B, K, or E. Any other value is unacceptable, and therefore, an error. When MEDCODE has the value of F, then MEDDEDUCTION, the medical deduction, is 0; when it has the value of B, MEDDEDUCTION is 4.65; when it has the value of K, MEDDEDUCTION is 7.85; when it has the value of E, MEDDEDUCTION is 5.50. If MEDCODE has any other value, then an error module is processed. An error module is simply the module that prints out an error message.

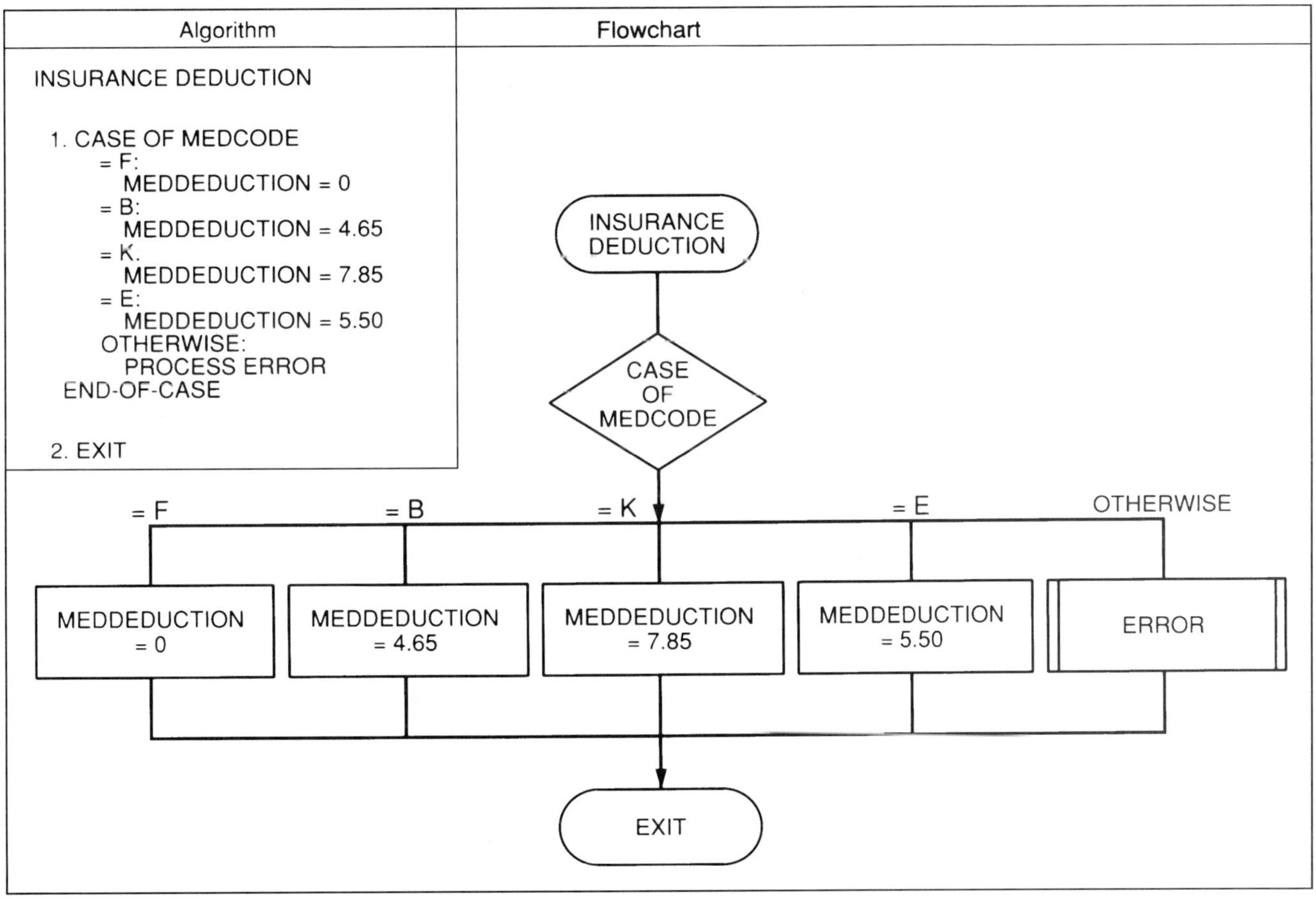

Figure 8.3 Using Codes—Medical Insurance Problem

Menus

A **menu** is a list of the options that a program based on the case logic structure can perform. The list might be calculations, such as average grade, standard deviation, or mean grade for a test; types of reports; processes to be completed on a file, such as adding, deleting, or changing data, printing a report, and the like. Programs that use a menu are called **menu-driven programs.** The user chooses a process through the use of a code, such as A for *add data,* D for *delete data,* and so on.

Menu-driven programs or applications are popular with the novice user of computers. Menus make solutions user-friendly since all choices are visible on the screen. If programmers set up menus correctly, the user will not often need to refer to the external documentation.

The major problem with menu-driven solutions is that they are not flexible. The user can do only what is allowed in the menu. Many experienced users find this frustrating. Also, menu-driven solutions tend to run slower because the computer has to execute more instructions, and the computer is continually waiting for the user to enter data. However, if the solution is for a client who will be doing data entry only, and who wants to be able to choose among several alternatives, then the best solution is a menu.

The programmer who designs a menu-driven program includes in the solution a module to print the menu and to enter the desired option code. The program begins by printing the coded choices, and then the user enters a choice, thereby selecting the desired process. The programmer should include instructions to check the entered option code to be sure it is within the allowed list of codes for the options (see Figure 8.4). If the code is not within the allowed options, the user must reenter the option code. Also, the programmer adds the sets of the desired actions to the Control Module. These actions were added through the use of a case logic structure. There is a set of actions or instructions for every item in the menu, except for the *quit* option. The number of items in the menu depends on the problem. Notice that in the menu module in Figure 8.4 the list of menu choices is written at the side of the flowchart to make the flowchart more readable. Menus are always directed to the screen and never to the printer because they require interaction with the user. To remove any previous print, the screen is cleared before the menu is printed. A REPEAT/UNTIL loop is used to make sure the option code the user enters is within the scope of the menu. If the REPEAT/UNTIL loop is not available in the language you are using, then the WHILE/WHILE-END loop can be used. Figure 8.4 shows the use of both loop types. Notice that when using the WHILE/WHILE-END loop type to check the value of the option code, the programmer has to set the menu option code to a value that will make the resultant of the condition TRUE in order for the instructions in the loop to be processed the first time.

Putting It All Together

This PIAT illustrates a menu-driven program. By way of review, all six of the problem-solving steps have been illustrated for the solution (Figure 8.5).

Algorithm	Flowchart

CONTROL MODULE
0000
1. PROCESS INIT
2. PROCESS MENU
3. WHILE CHOICE <> 0
  1. CASE OF CHOICE
    =1:
      PROCESS TASK 1
    =2:
      PROCESS TASK 2
    =3:
      PROCESS TASK 3
    END-OF-CASE
  2. PROCESS PRINT
  3. PROCESS MENU
WHILE-END
4. END
	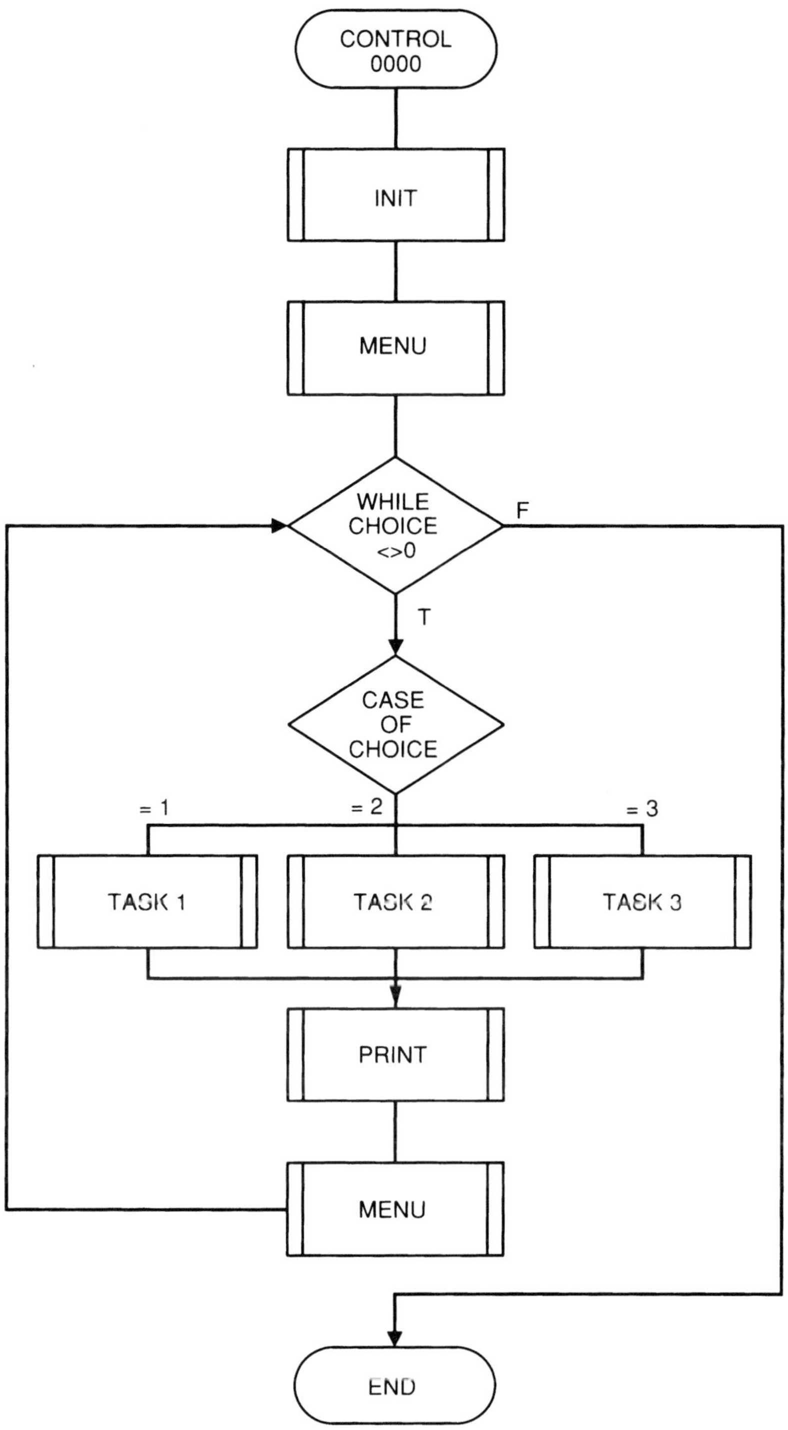

Figure 8.4 Structure of a Menu-driven Solution (*continued on page 150*)

Algorithm	Flowchart
MENU MODULE (3000)0) (REPEAT/UNTIL STRUCTURE) 1. CLEAR SCREEN 2. PRINT MENU 3. REPEAT [1. ENTER CHOICE UNTIL CHOICE < 4 AND CHOICE > -1 4. EXIT (WHILE/WHILE-END STRUCTURE) 1. CLEAR SCREEN 2. PRINT MENU 3. CHOICE = -1 4. WHILE CHOICE < 0 OR CHOICE > 3 [ENTER CHOICE WHILE-END 5. EXIT	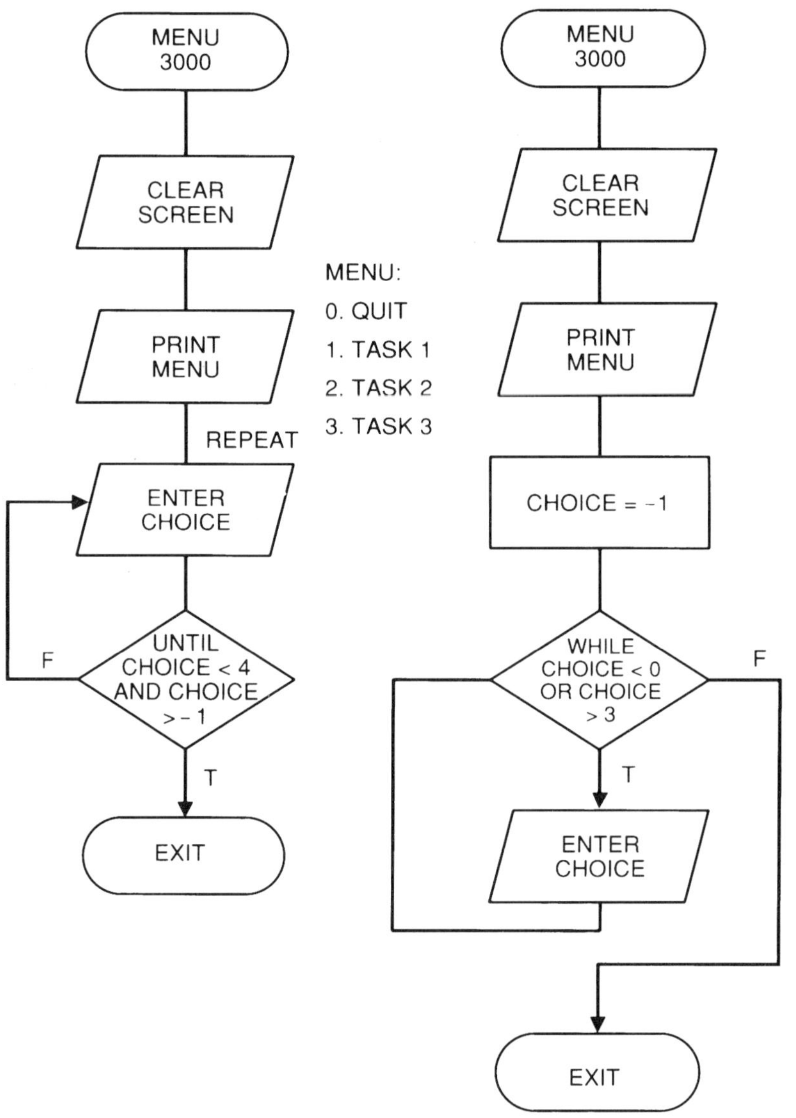

Figure 8.4 *(continued from page 149)*

Problem: A contractor needs four types of information to build each of the rooms in a building: the floor area, the wall area, the volume of the room, and the total area of the floor, walls, and ceiling. The contractor would like to be able to calculate any one of the four types of information at any one time.

Given Data	Required Results
Length Width Height	Need one of following: Floor area Wall area Volume Total (wall + ceiling + floor) area
Processing Required	**Solution Alternatives**
Floor area = L * W Wall area = 2 * H * (L + W) Volume = L * W * H Total area = 2 * (L * W + H * (L + W)	*1. Menu-driven case structure 2. Calculate all four results for all cases 3. Use IF/THEN/ELSE structure *Solution

Figure 8.5a Problem Analysis Chart

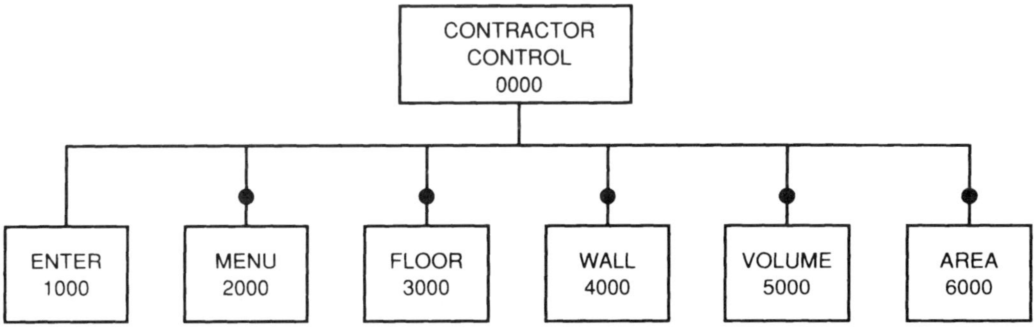

Figure 8.5b Structure Chart

Input	Processing	Module Reference Number	Output
1. Length of room	1. Enter data	1000	1. Calculated value
2. Width of room	2. Enter choice	2000	
3. Height of room	3. Choice = 1 Floor Area = L * W	3000	
4. Choice of calculation	Choice = 2 Wall Area = 2 * H * (L + W)	4000	
	Choice = 3 Volume = L * W * H	5000	
	Choice = 4 Total Area = 2 * (L * W + H (L + W))	6000	
	4. Print output	3000-6000	

Figure 8.5c IPO Chart

Algorithm	Flowchart	Annotation	Test
CONTROL MODULE (0000)			
1. PROCESS ENTER			GOTO ENTER
2. PROCESS MENU			GOTO MENU
3. WHILE OPTION <> Q			
CASE OF OPTION			
= F: PROCESS FLOOR	See next page	See next page	
= W: PROCESS WALL			OPTION = W TRUE GOTO WALL
= V: PROCESS VOLUME			
= A: PROCESS AREA			
OTHERWISE: PRINT ERROR MESSAGE			
END-OF-CASE			
PROCESS MENU			GOTO MENU
WHILE-END			
4. END			QUIT

Internal Documentation	External Documentation
1. Title: Calculates values needed by a contractor — area, volume, wall area, total area 2. Annotation	1. Same as internal documentation 2. Explain formulas used

Figure 8.5d Algorithms and Flowcharts—CONTROL Module

Flowchart	Annotation
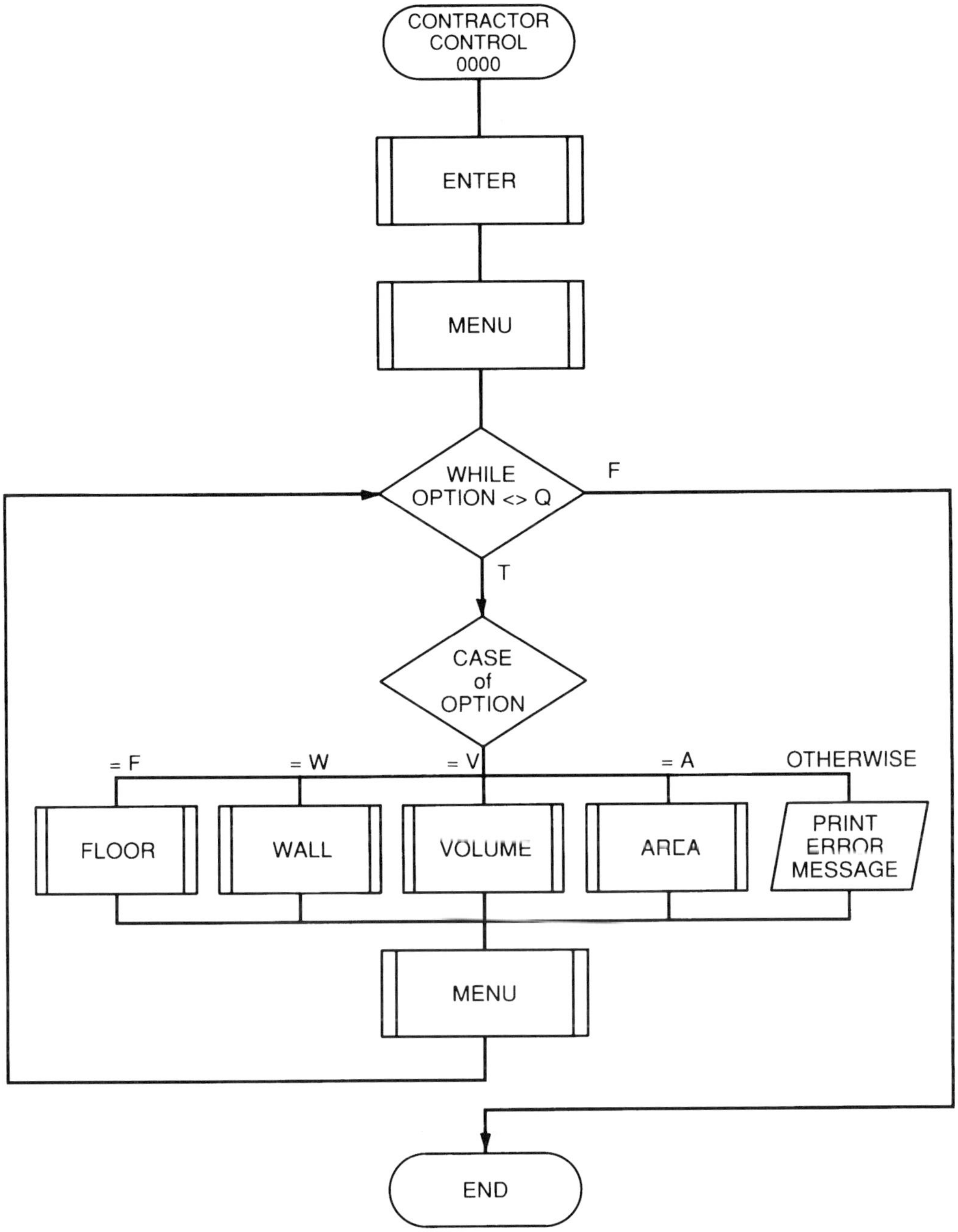	Enter data Print menu and enter option Loop as long as option <> Q Choose one according to value of option Print menu and enter option End

Figure 8.5e Annotation and Flowchart—CONTROL Module

Algorithm	Flowchart	Annotation	Test
ENTER MODULE (1000) 1. ENTER LENGTH, WIDTH, HEIGHT 2. WRITE LENGTH, WIDTH, HEIGHT 3. EXIT	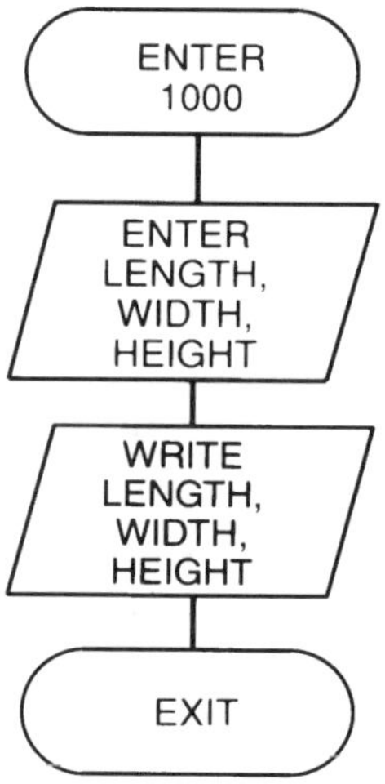	Must be in feet Prints input data to printer	LENGTH: 12 WIDTH: 10 HEIGHT: 8

Internal Documentation	External Documentation
1. Title: Enters length, width, and height 2. Annotation	1. Same as internal documentation

Figure 8.5f Algorithms and Flowcharts—ENTER Module

Algorithm	Flowchart	Annotation	Test
MENU MODULE (2000) 1. PRINT MENU 2. ENTER OPTION 3. EXIT	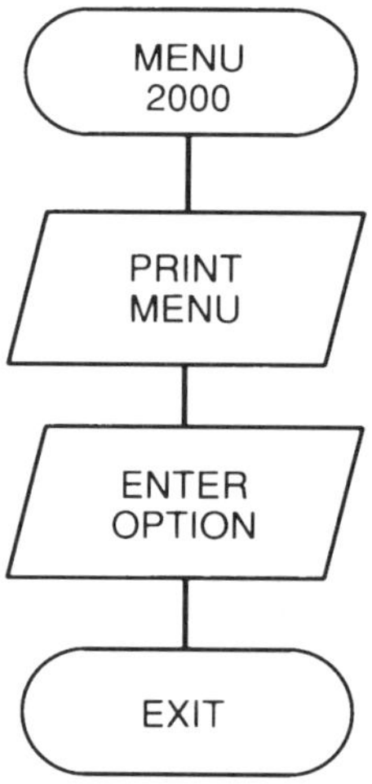	Menu: F = floor area W = wall area V = volume of room A = total area Q = quit Enter one of the above with option	OPTION: W

Internal Documentation	External Documentation
1. Title: Prints menu and enters option	1. Same as internal documentation 2. Annotation

Figure 8.5g Algorithms and Flowcharts—MENU Module

Algorithm	Flowchart	Annotation	Test
FLOOR MODULE (3000) 1. AREA = LENGTH * WIDTH 2. PRINT AREA 3. EXIT	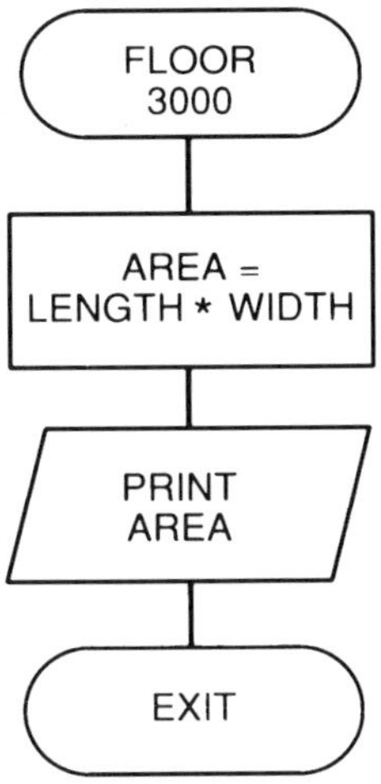	None	If option = F then: AREA 120

Internal Documentation	External Documentation
1. Title: Calculates floor area	1. Same as internal documentation 2. Specify formula

Figure 8.5h Algorithms and Flowcharts—FLOOR Module

Algorithm	Flowchart	Annotation	Test
WALL MODULE (4000) 1. WALL AREA = 2* HEIGHT * (LENGTH + WIDTH) 2. PRINT WALL AREA 3. EXIT	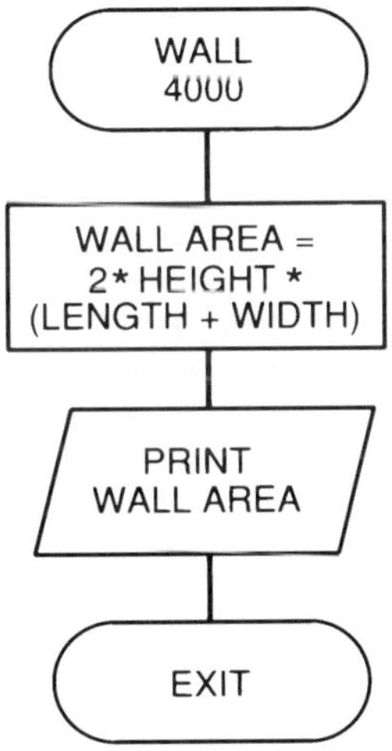	None	If option = W then: WALL 352

Internal Documentation	External Documentation
1. Title: Calculates wall area	1. Same as internal documentation 2. Specify formula

Figure 8.5i Algorithms and Flowcharts—WALL Module

Algorithm	Flowchart	Annotation	Test
VOLUME MODULE (5000) 1. VOLUME = HEIGHT * WIDTH * LENGTH 2. PRINT VOLUME 3. EXIT	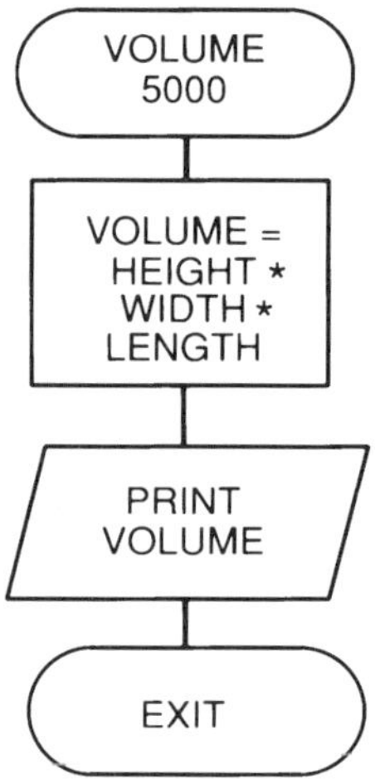	None	If option = V then : VOLUME 960

Internal Documentation	External Documentation
1. Title: Calculates volume	1. Same as internal documentation 2. Specify equation

Figure 8.5j Algorithms and Flowcharts—VOLUME Module

Algorithm	Flowchart	Annotation	Test
AREA MODULE (6000) 1. TOTALAREA = 2*(LENGTH* WIDTH + HEIGHT *(LENGTH + WIDTH)) 2. PRINT TOTALAREA 3. EXIT	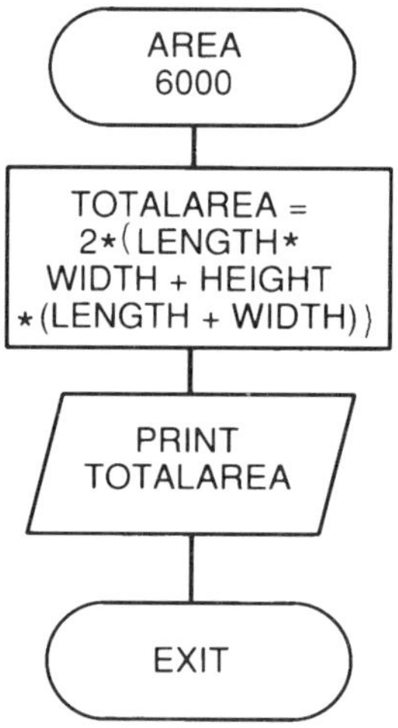	None	If option = A then : TOTALAREA 592

Internal Documentation	External Documentation
1. Title: Calculates total area of walls, ceiling, and floor	1. Same as internal documentation 2. Specify formula

Figure 8.5k Algorithms and Flowcharts—AREA Module

Summary

The case logic structure is the fourth basic logic structure. It enables the computer to select one set of actions from many by selecting an integer or a character from a list of coded choices designed by a programmer. Codes are one of the tools of the case logic structure. A menu-driven solution is one of its uses. The case structure replaces a multiple nested IF/THEN/ELSE instruction that uses positive logic and the relative operator *equals*. By using the case structure rather than the nested IF/THEN/ELSE alternative, a programmer can improve the readability and reduce the complexity of the program.

New Terms

codes
menu
menu-driven program

Questions

1. Why would the case logic structure be used instead of the decision structure?
2. What are the differences between an indicator and a code?
3. What is a menu?
4. What advantages does a menu-driven program have over other types of programs?
5. How does the case structure aid in developing a menu-driven program?
6. What disadvantages does a menu-driven program have over other types of programs?

Problems

1. Develop the algorithm and the flowchart for the calculation module that calculates pay according to the following pay-type code:

H = hourly	pay = rate * hours
P = piece	pay = rate * number of pieces
C = commission	pay = commission * sales
S = salary	pay = salary

2. Develop the algorithm and flowchart for a module that calculates the retirement deduction rate according to the following codes:

R = 10%
P = 8%
G = 5%

3. Develop a solution to change Roman numerals into their decimal equivalents. Consider all possibilities of Roman numerals—no letters, only one letter, two letters, and so forth. Assume that the Roman numerals are in correct order. One

Roman numeral character is entered at a time. The Roman numeral is entered from left to right.

4. A student wants to know his grade average for the semester. The grades are given in letter grades with numerical equivalents. Develop a solution to calculate a grade average given the letter grades. (Remember, the grade average is figured per unit of credit, not per course). An A = 4.0, B = 3.0, C = 2.0, D = 1.0, F = 0.0. Test the solution with the following data:

History	B	3 units
Economics	A	3 units
P.E.	A	1 unit
Chemistry	C	4 units
Art	B	3 units

(Use a trip value to stop the processing of the loop and a case structure to find the grade points.)

5. A bank has five different types of savings accounts. The interest rates on these accounts change often. The bank manager would like to have the computer print out information about the account type of her choice. Develop a solution to solve the manager's problems.

6. Develop a solution that enables a user to choose one of the following types of calculations to perform on an input number:
   - **a.** Calculate the square of the number.
   - **b.** Calculate the cube of the number.
   - **c.** Round the number to two decimal places.
   - **d.** Calculate the square root of the number.

7. Develop a solution that enables a user to choose one of the following types of calculations to perform on a list of numbers. The quantity of numbers in the list is unknown. The user will enter the list of numbers one at a time and will not save them.
   - **a.** Count the number of entries.
   - **b.** Calculate the average.
   - **c.** Determine the highest number.
   - **d.** Determine the lowest number.

UNIT TWO

SUPPLEMENTARY EXERCISES

Develop a complete solution and develop a data dictionary for the following problems:

1. Draw a solid diamond on the screen using a single character. The size of the diamond should be entered from the keyboard:
   Example: Size = 5 CHARACTER = "*"

```
  *
 ***
*****
 ***
  *
```

2. Draw the same diamond except make it hollow:
   Example: SIZE = 5 CHARACTER = "*"

```
  *
 * *
*   *
 * *
  *
```

3. Modify Problem 4 in Chapter 5 so that the program stops when the remaining change becomes zero.
4. Reverse the digits of a number such that 1234 becomes 4321.
5. Calculate the ending balance of your checking account, given the beginning balance, the checks written, the deposits made, and the bank charges.
6. Create your own dice game. Print directions and rules. Have the user play against the computer.
7. Print all prime factors of a number entered from the keyboard.

UNIT THREE

Data Structures

Chapter 9

Processing Arrays

Overview

Objectives:

When you have finished this chapter, you should be able to:

1. Develop problem solutions for the computer using one-dimensional and two-dimensional arrays.
2. Develop problem solutions requiring table look-ups, sequential and binary searches, frequency distributions, and cross-tabulations.

Arrays

Data are stored in the computer in a logical way in order to find values as fast as possible. The way data are stored is called the structure of the data, hence the term *data structures.* The only data structure you have used so far in this text is the single variable. Using this data structure a single value is stored in a single named location. This is the simplest of all data structures. Another type of data structure is the array.

It is often advantageous for a user to store several values for the same variable in the internal memory of the computer because it decreases processing time. This multiple storage means there has to be more than one memory location in the computer for each variable name. When more than one memory location is designated for a single variable, it is called an **array.** Sometimes these variables are called *subscripted variables.* This term comes from mathematics, where subscripts are used to designate multiple values. Arrays are also called *tables,* a term from business, where data are often put into tables. For the purposes of this book, *array* will be used because it is universal and is becoming the most common term. The other two terms may be used in other sources.

Arrays are used in the problem-solving process. A programmer who has many values of data of the same kind—many ages, temperatures, names, or the like—can store them in the computer in the form of an array, which makes them easier to read and use. The programmer can also use the values in one array to point to values in another array. This is the way the computer tallies the number of times a value appears in an array. Without arrays this task would be very difficult.

A programmer uses arrays when more than one value of a variable is used in the solution—for example, when calculating the percentage of each store's sales out of the total company's sales or when calculating each student's test grade based on the highest and lowest score. The store sales or the student grade would be the variable with more than one value—a value for each store or for each student. If the user does not need to use the data more than once in the solution, then there is no need for the programmer to use arrays. Their overuse is a common mistake for beginning programmers.

The programmer tells the computer how many memory locations to save for an array through a special instruction or within the definitions of the data types. In many languages this is called *dimensioning the variable.* The number of memory locations to be saved is equal to or greater than the number of locations used in the solution. If it is less than the number of locations used, an error will result. For problem-solving purposes, this number is part of the annotation of the flowchart.

Most languages use **static arrays.** This means that once the computer is told how many locations to save, that number cannot be changed unless the instruction is changed. In most languages, the number in the instruction is a constant. However, some languages allow the number to be a named constant, which is set once, and only once, during the execution of the solution. In this case, the number of memory locations saved for an array can change from execution to execution, but it cannot change during an execution. This type of array is still considered static.

Some languages allow **dynamic arrays.** When using dynamic arrays, the programmer designates the number of array locations as a variable, which can be expanded or contracted during the execution of the solution. Dynamic arrays are more flexible and use less memory space than static arrays, but are usually more time-consuming during processing.

If the number of the designated memory locations is a constant, then the programmer has to know how big the array will be, at its largest, while writing the solution. When that number is a variable but cannot be changed during execution, then the size of the array is part of the input data. This kind of static array allows more flexibility in the solution and in the use of memory than the static array in which the number of memory locations is a constant. The most flexible arrays are dynamic. The solution itself determines the size of a dynamic array, and thus, the programmer does not have to predict the size of the array.

Each array memory location is called an *element* and is given a number or numbers corresponding to the position of the location in the array. This number is a reference number relative to the location of the first value of the array. The name of the element has two parts. The first part is the variable name; the second part is the reference number, also called the *index number,* an *element number* or subscript in parentheses.

Because computers are zero-based, for counting purposes, many programming languages are also zero-based. This means that the first array element is numbered *zero,* and not *one.* In this way, the computer adds the element number to the memory location number of the beginning box to locate the needed value. If the language uses base one, then to identify a specific data memory location, add the element number minus one to the beginning number (see Figure 9.1). Base one is easier for the programmer to understand since the first element is the first box, the second element is the second box, and so on. When using zero-based arrays, the zero element is the first box, the first element is the second box, and so on. Often programmers will avoid zero elements in an array because they make it more difficult to keep track of element numbers. In this chapter, base one will be assumed.

You do not have to use an array in any special order. The data used as the actual values of the elements must have the same data type as you have identified for the variable name of the array. By using the assignment instruction, you can assign the value of a constant, a variable, or an expression to an element.

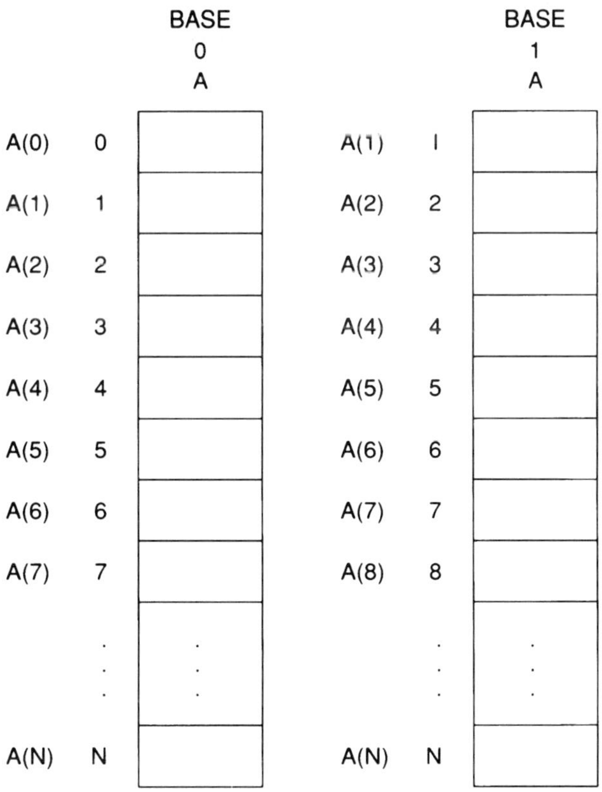

Figure 9.1 Base-Zero versus Base-One Arrays

One-Dimensional Arrays

The simplest array structure is the **one-dimensional array.** This array consists of one column of memory locations. In Figure 9.2, there is a one-dimensional array named AGE. In mathematics, the reference name for each of the equation elements would be age_1, age_2, age_3, and so forth. Array elements are given similar reference names. Since the computer has trouble with subscripts (because it is hard to roll the screen up a little to print subscripts), the reference names are written as AGE(1), AGE(2), AGE(3), and so forth. The number in the parentheses is a reference number only and can be a constant, a variable, or an expression. AGE(5) would be the fifth element of the AGE array. In most languages the reference numbers must be of the integer data type, although a few computer languages allow any data type for the index or reference value. Since this practice is not common, and since the use of each of the data types is very similar to the use of integers as element numbers, this book will use only integers for the index.

Parallel arrays are two or more arrays in which values in the same elements relate to each other. For example, in Figure 9.3 there are three arrays: Thc first array contains area numbers, the second array contains temperatures for day 1, and the third, temperatures for day 2. The data in the first elements in the second and third arrays pertain to the area in the first array; the data in the second elements in the second and third arrays pertain to the area in the second element of the first array, and so forth. They are called parallel arrays because the same element number in all arrays has data pertaining to the same subject.

Entering Data into an Array

When you enter data into an array, or *load an array,* you use a loop. If you know the number of elements, then use the automatic-counter loop. If you do not know the number of elements, then use an indicator code with the REPEAT/UNTIL or the WHILE/WHILE-END loop. Use a counter to keep track of how many elements are entered into the array.

	Array AGE	Variable Reference Name	
1	32	AGE(1)	The number in the parentheses refers to the box number in the array, the element number.
2	54	AGE(2)	
3	25	AGE(3)	
4	36	AGE(4)	
5	45	AGE(5)	
6	20	AGE(6)	
7	28	AGE(7)	
8	50	AGE(8)	
9	42	AGE(9)	

Figure 9.2 One-Dimensional Array

Figure 9.4 shows the loop process for entering the data into an array. In Figure 9.4a, the number of elements in the array is known to be the value of N. The counter (R) of the loop allows the computer to increase the element number by 1 each time a piece of

	AREANO	DAY1	DAY2
1	5	82	80
2	9	75	72
3	15	80	82
4	35	90	87
5	50	95	92
6	73	78	80
7	88	85	83

Figure 9.3 Parallel Arrays

Algorithm

LOOP: R = 1 TO N STEP 1

[ENTER A(R)

LOOP-END: R

R = Counter

N = Number of elements in the array

A(R) = Element R in the A array

Flowchart

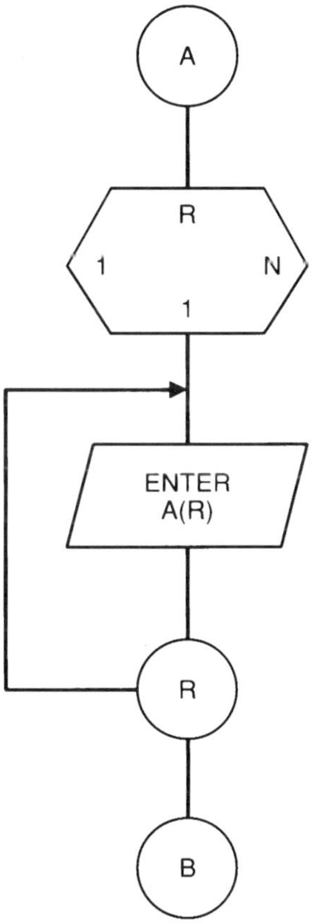

Figure 9.4a Loading an Array Using the Automatic-Counter Loop

data is entered into a memory location. The computer can find a particular memory location for an element in the array by first finding the set of locations for the array A, and then using the reference number, which has the value of R. Figure 9.4b shows the use of the REPEAT/UNTIL loop structure. Here, the elements are counted to find the total number of elements (N) in the array. The number N is then used for the number of elements through the rest of the solution. Figure 9.4c shows the use of the WHILE/WHILE-END loop structure. Here again, the elements are counted to find the total number of elements.

Algorithm	Flowchart

1. R = 0
2. REPEAT
    [R = R + 1
    [ENTER A(R)
    UNTIL A(R) = − 1
*3. N = R − 1
	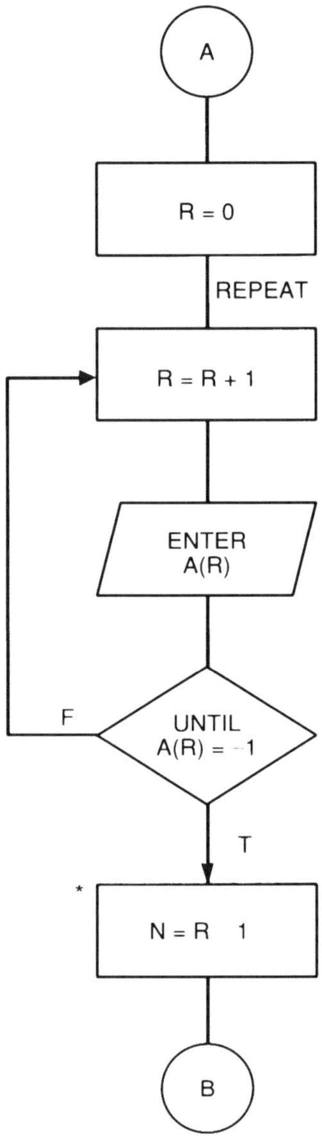

*The number of elements in the array should not include the trip value of -1.

Figure 9.4b Loading an Array Using the REPEAT/UNTIL Loop

Algorithm	Flowchart

1. R = 1
2. ENTER A(R)
3. WHILE A(R) <> −1
    [R = R + 1
    [ENTER A(R)
    WHILE - END
* 4. N = R − 1
	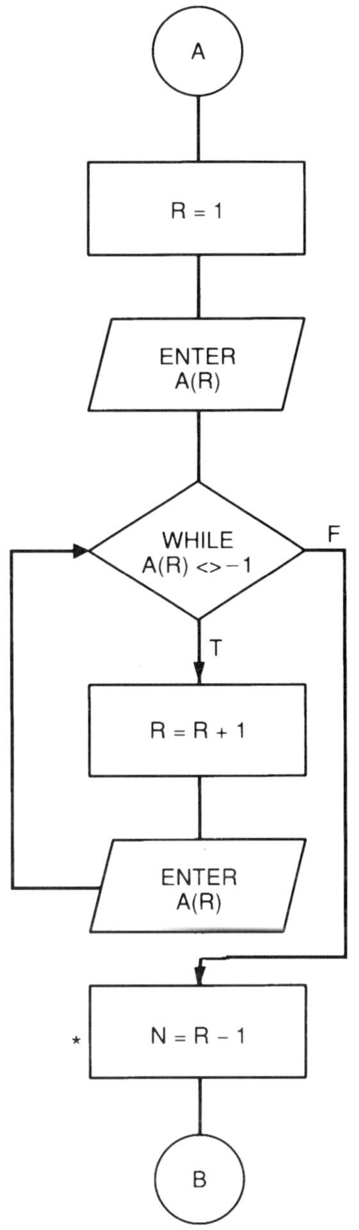

*The number of elements in the array should not include the trip value of -1.

Figure 9.4c Loading an Array Using the WHILE/WHILE-END Loop

Notice that in the REPEAT/UNTIL and the WHILE/WHILE-END loops, the indicator element number (indicating the end of the array) is not included in the total number of elements since it is not needed. The number of elements is known and, therefore, the indicator is not needed to signal the end of the array.

Algorithm	Flowchart
LOOP: R = 1 TO N STEP 1 [PRINT A(R) LOOP-END: R R = Element number N = Total number of elements A(R) = Rth element of the A array	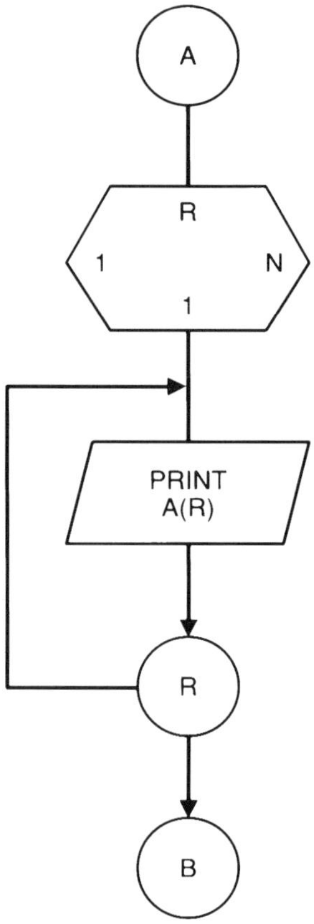

Figure 9.5 Printing a One-Dimensional Array

Printing an Array

After the array is loaded, it can be used in other calculations or printed. You write the algorithm to print an array by using the automatic-counter loop since the number of elements in the array is now known (see Figure 9.5). The array will be printed one element at a time down the page. To print the array across the page, you must use the WRITE or PRINT instruction without a carriage-return. With parallel arrays, the corresponding elements will be printed in columns on the same line. The headings to the columns have to be printed before the processing starts into the automatic-counter loop.

Accumulating the Elements of an Array

Often you need the sum of the elements in an array. Use the accumulation instruction to total the sum (see Figure 9.6). Initially, set the variable containing the value of the sum to zero. The accumulation instruction (SUM = SUM + A(R)) tells the computer to add the value of the element A(R) to the old value of the sum (SUM) and to store the result in the sum memory location (SUM). The value of the element number R changes as the loop counter progresses from one element to the other during summing.

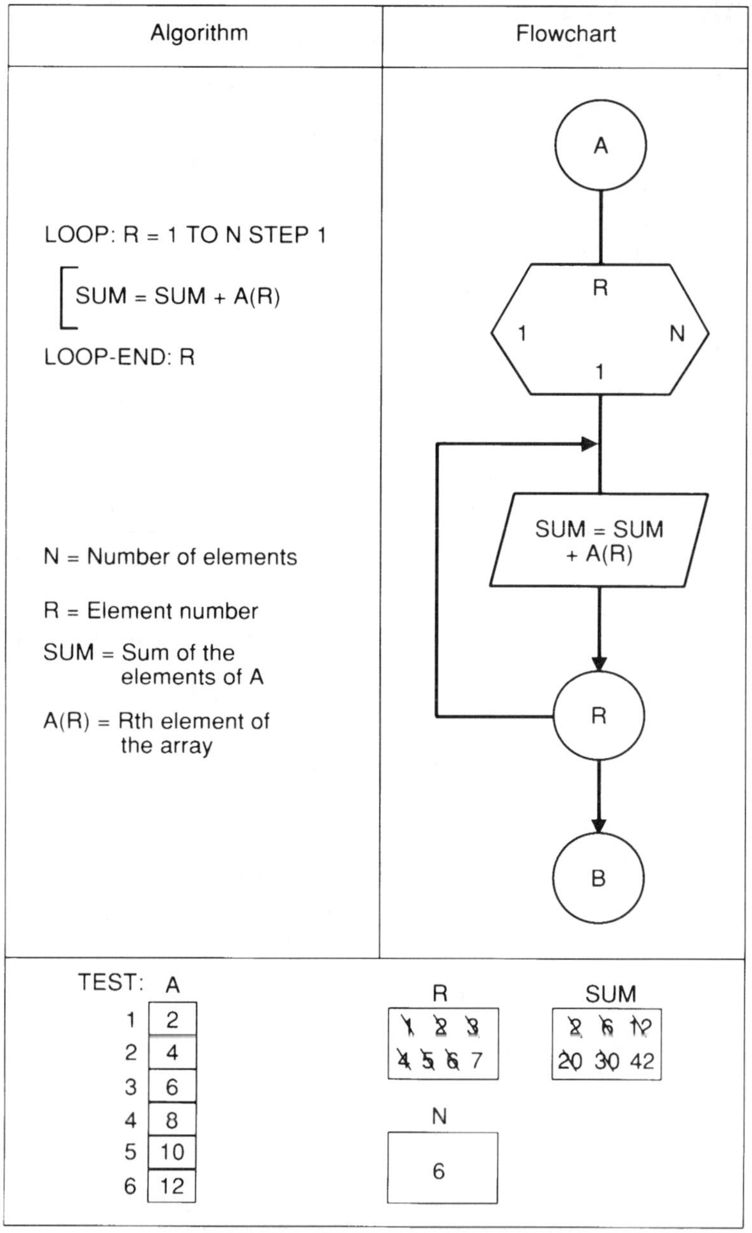

Figure 9.6 Accumulating the Elements of a One-Dimensional Array

Observe the testing of the flowchart in Figure 9.6 through the use of the various variable memory locations. The first time the loop is processed, the value of R is 1, and the value of A(R), or A(1), is 2. This value is added to the previous value of the SUM, which is zero since the value of SUM is zero at the start. The resultant is 2, which is placed into the SUM memory location. The second time the loop is processed, R is incremented to 2 and the value of A(R), or A(2), is 4. This value is added to the previous value of SUM, which is 2, and placed into the SUM memory location. SUM now has the value of 6. The third time the loop is processed, R is incremented to 3, and A(R), which has the value of 6, is added to SUM and placed into the SUM memory location. The value of SUM is now 12. This sequence is repeated each time the loop is processed until the value of R has increased to a number greater than the value of N. The final value of SUM is 42.

Putting It All Together

This PIAT illustrates how to enter, use, and print one-dimensional arrays.

Problem: The president of the Too Little Variety Stores would like to know each store's percentage of the total sales of the corporation. There are 15 stores altogether.

Figure 9.7 shows the complete solution to this problem. Parts c-f show the algorithms and flowcharts for each module. The Control Module processes each of the modules, Init, Read, Calc, and Print. The SUM is set equal to zero in the Init Module. The Read Module enters the values of the sales per store into the SALES array. The value of R becomes the store number. In the Calc Module, the sum of the sales for all 15 stores is

Given Data	Required Results
1. 15 stores 2. Sales per store	Percent of total sales per store
Processing Required	**Solution Alternatives**
Percent (store) = sales (store)/total sales	Must use arrays

Figure 9.7a Problem Analysis Chart

Structure Chart

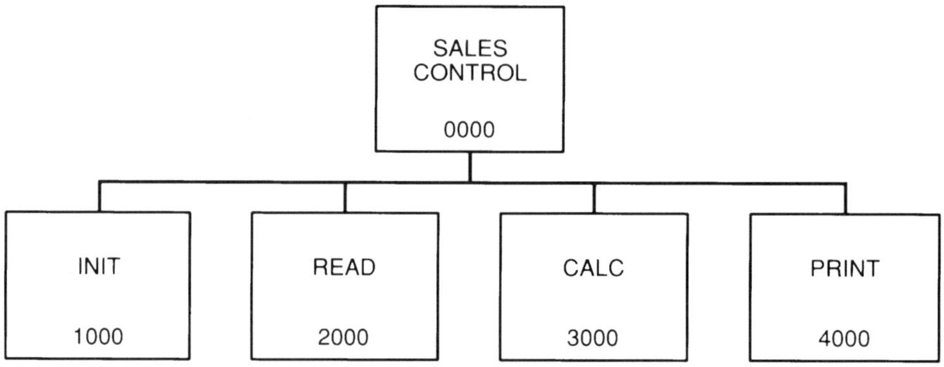

IPO Chart

Input	Processing	Module Reference Number	Output
1. Sales per store	1. Enter data 2. Set sum to 0 3. Accumulate sales 4. Calculate percent 5. Print output	2000 1000 3000 3000 4000	For each store: 1. Store number 2. Sales 3. % of total sales

Figure 9.7b Structure Chart and IPO Chart

Algorithm	Flowchart	Testing
CONTROL MODULE (0000) 1. PROCESS INIT 2. PROCESS READ 3. PROCESS CALC 4. PROCESS PRINT 5. END	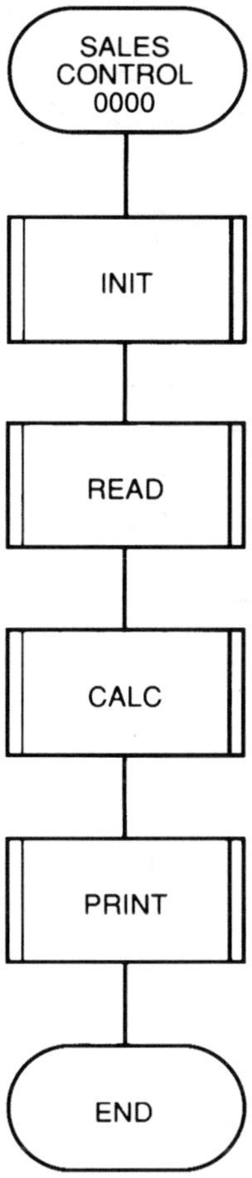	
INIT MODULE (1000) 1. SUM = 0 2. EXIT	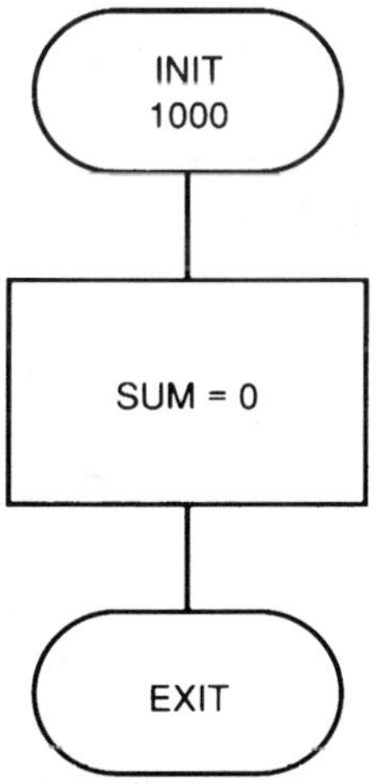	SUM 0

Figure 9.7c Algorithms and Flowcharts for the CONTROL and INIT Modules

Algorithm	Flowchart	Testing

Algorithm

READ MODULE
(2000)

1. LOOP: R = 1 TO 15

   ENTER SALES(R)

   LOOP-END: R

2. END

Flowchart

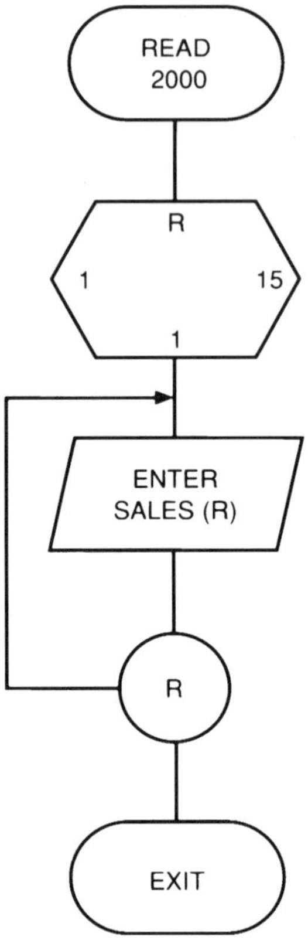

Testing

R

1 2 3 4 5 6 7
8 9 10 11 12 13
14 15

	SALES
1	200
2	300
3	150
4	400
5	275
6	125
7	175
8	450
9	475
10	350
11	375
12	100
13	325
14	225
15	500

Figure 9.7d Algorithm and Flowchart for the READ Module

calculated through the use of a loop and the accumulation instruction. The next loop calculates the value of the percentage for each store and places that value in the PERCENT array. The SALES array and the PERCENT array are parallel arrays since each element corresponds to the same store. The values of the store number, the SALES, and the PERCENT, are printed, element by element, in the Print Module.

Two-Dimensional Arrays

A **two-dimensional array** is a block of memory locations associated with a single memory variable name and designated by row and column numbers. Each element number is written as A (Row #, Column #). The row number is always first, and the column number, second. As in one-dimensional arrays, the row and column numbers can be constants, variables, or expressions, and they are of the integer data type. Whatever processing takes place, the row and column numbers always remain in the same positions in the parentheses. As with one-dimensional arrays, you can change the values in a two-dimensional array by using the assignment instruction.

Two-dimensional arrays are used for tables of values. They can replace parallel arrays if the data are of the same data type in all of the arrays. In Figure 9.8, the

Algorithm	Flowchart	Testing

Algorithm

CALC MODULE
(3000)

1. LOOP: R = 1 TO 15

   SUM = SUM
   +SALES(R)

   LOOP-END:R

2. LOOP: R = 1 TO 15

   PERCENT(R) =
   SALES(R)
   /SUM*100

   LOOP-END:R

3. EXIT

Flowchart

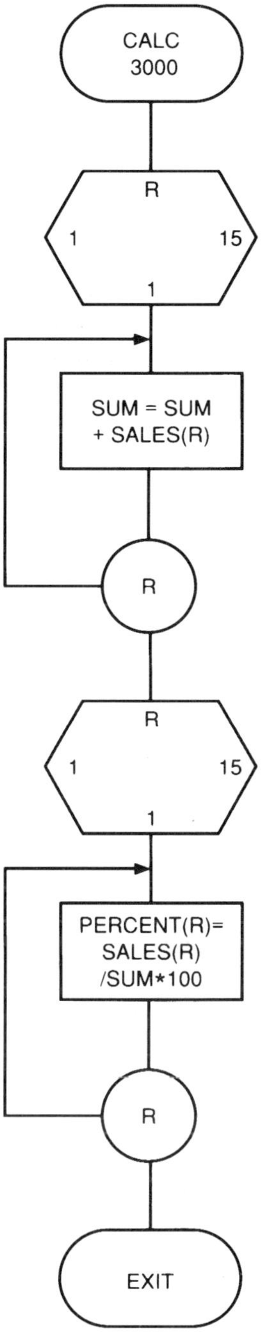

Testing

R

~~1~~ 2 ~~3~~ ~~4~~ ~~5~~ ~~6~~ ~~7~~
~~8~~ ~~9~~ ~~10~~ ~~11~~ ~~12~~ ~~13~~
~~14~~ 15

SUM

~~0~~ ~~200~~ ~~500~~
~~650~~ ~~1050~~
~~1325~~ ~~1450~~
~~1625~~ ~~2075~~
~~2550~~ ~~2900~~
~~3275~~ ~~3375~~
~~3700~~ ~~3925~~
4425

	PERCENT
1	4.5
2	6.8
3	3.4
4	9.0
5	6.2
6	2.8
7	4.0
8	10.2
9	10.7
10	7.9
11	8.5
12	2.3
13	7.3
14	5.1
15	11.3

Figure 9.7e Algorithm and Flowchart for the CALC Module

Algorithm	Flowchart	Testing

Algorithm

PRINT MODULE
(4000)

1. PRINT HEADINGS
2. LOOP: R = 1 TO 15
   - PRINT R, SALES(R), PERCENT(R)

   LOOP-END: R
3. EXIT

Flowchart

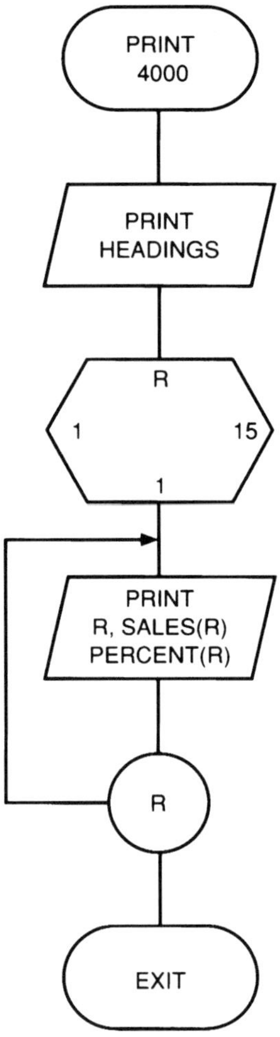

Testing

#	SALES	PERCENT
1	200	4.5
2	300	6.8
3	150	3.4
4	400	9.0
5	275	6.2
6	125	2.8
7	175	4.0
8	450	10.2
9	475	10.7
10	350	7.9
11	375	8.5
12	100	2.3
13	325	7.3
14	225	5.1
15	500	11.3

Figure 9.7f Algorithm and Flowchart for the PRINT Module

two-dimensional array *A* is shown. This figure shows the general form of a two-dimensional array, and of reference names (including the variable name and the row and column numbers), for each location. For example, A(3,2) is found at the intersection of row 3 and column 2.

Loading a Two-Dimensional Array

You load a two-dimensional array with nested loops (see Figure 9.9). The data are normally loaded row by row. When you load the data row by row, the outer loop represents the row, and the inner loop represents the column. This order of the loops allows the row number to remain constant while the column number varies. In Figure 9.9, compare the data block to the array block. In the flowchart, notice that the first four numbers in the data block are read into the first row of the array, the second four into the second row, and the last four into the third row. The array is now loaded with the numbers 1 to 12.

A

ROW \ COLUMN →	1	2	3	4	. . .	C
1	A(1,1)	A(1,2)	A(1,3)	A(1,4)	. . .	A(1,C)
2	A(2,1)	A(2,2)	A(2,3)	A(2,4)	. . .	A(2,C)
3	A(3,1)	A(3,2)	A(3,3)	A(3,4)	. . .	A(3,C)
. . .	. . .	. . .	. . .	. . .	. . .	. . .
R	A(R,1)	A(R,2)	A(R,3)	A(R,4)	. . .	A(R,C)

Figure 9.8 General Form of a Two-Dimensional Array

Printing a Two-Dimensional Array

After the array is loaded, it can be used in calculations or it can be printed. As in loading, use nested loops to print a two-dimensional array. Normally, the array is printed row by row. For example, in Figure 9.10 the outer loop (R loop) is the row loop and the inner loop (C loop) is the column loop. Notice that the flowchart is designed so that the element is printed without a carriage-return. The carriage-return is executed after a row is printed, that is, after the end of the column loop. Place the CARRIAGE-RETURN instruction between the two LOOP-END instructions. The column headings are printed before either loop is executed. Each row heading is printed between the two begin loop instructions.

Follow the execution of the loop in Figure 9.10 to see how the array is printed. Notice that the column headings are printed first. Then the row loop (R loop) prints row 1 and continues to print through row NR, the total number of rows. Within each row, the row heading must be printed first. Then, through the use of the C loop, each element of the row, designated by the column number (C), is printed without a cursor or carriage-return. Once the elements of the row are printed, the cursor or carriage has to be returned before the next row can be printed.

Accumulating the Rows and Columns of a Two-Dimensional Array

In many solutions you need a total of rows, columns, and the grand total of all elements in a two-dimensional array, and as in the one-dimensional array, you use the assignment statement to do so. In the solution, you can use a row following the last row of the array for the sums of the columns, and a column to the right of the last column for the sums of the rows (see Figure 9.11). For the grand total, use the intersection of the last row and the last column. This placement of row, column, and grand totals facilitates printing them in the printout of the array.

In the array in Figure 9.11, the fourth row is used for the sum of each column, and the fifth column is used for the sum of each row. The element in the lower right-hand

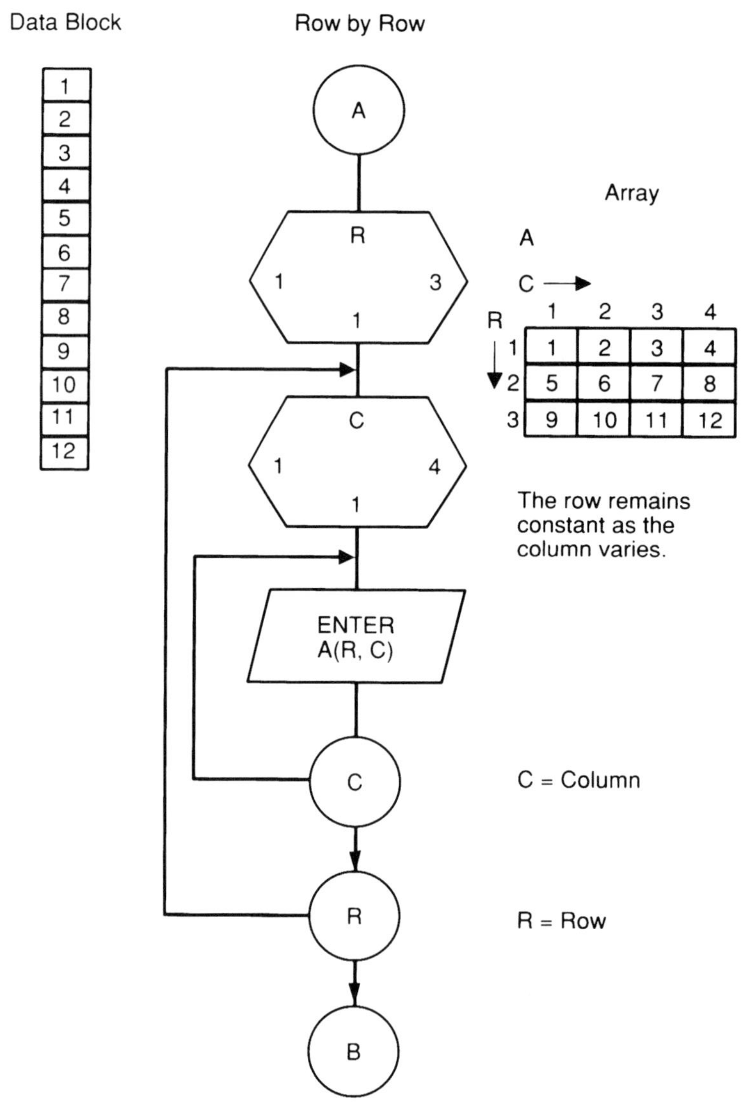

Figure 9.9 Loading a Two-Dimensional Array, Row by Row and Column by Column

corner (A(4,5)) holds the grand total. In the solution, the sum of both the rows and columns can be done in the same nested loop. It does not make any difference if the sum of a single row is completed before the start of the sum of the next row, or if the sums of all rows are done at the same time, column by column. Notice in Figure 9.11 that the final sum is the same if you accumulate a whole row at one time or all of the rows at the same time. Either way, the sum of the first row is 10, the sum of the second row is 26, and the sum of the third row is 42. The same is true of the columns.

In Figure 9.12, the algorithm and the flowchart are shown for summing the rows and columns of the array in Figure 9.11. Notice the differences between the assignment instructions for summing the rows, the columns, and the grand total. The only difference is in the reference numbers of the array elements containing the sums. The grand total is the sum of the last column since the sum of the rows is complete at the end of the inner loop.

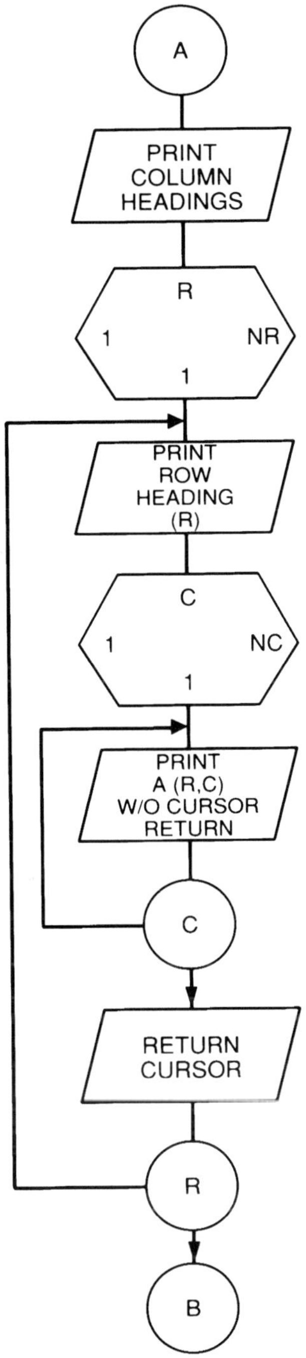

R = Row

NR = Number of rows

C = Column

NC = Number of columns

Figure 9.10 Printing a Two-Dimensional Array

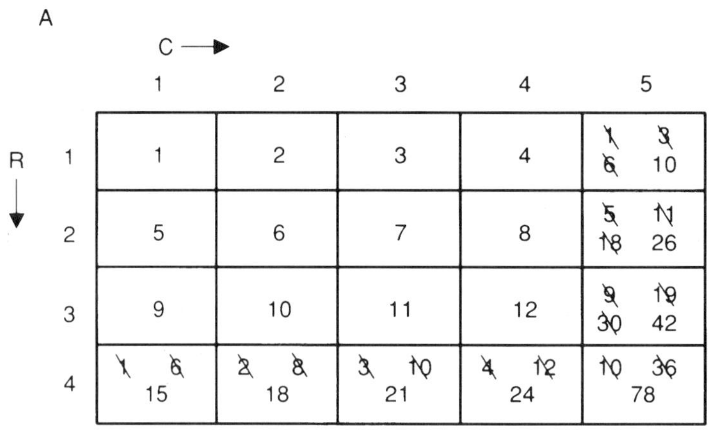

- Column 5 holds the sum of each of the rows.
- Row 4 holds the sum of each of the columns.
- A(4,5) holds the grand total.

Figure 9.11 Accumulating a Two-Dimensional Array

In the instruction to sum the rows in Figure 9.12, the element numbers are represented by the variable R for the row number, and the expression NC + 1 for the column number containing the sum of the rows. In the instruction to sum the columns, the element numbers are represented by the expression NR + 1 for the row containing the sum of the columns, and the variable C for the column number. The element numbers of the box containing the grand total, at the intersection of the sums of the rows and the columns, are NR + 1 and NC + 1. When the rows are summed in the outer loop, they are summed one row at a time; the columns are summed when all the rows have been processed. The summation of the grand total is placed between the two LOOP-ENDs because it is the summation of the sums of the rows. The elements to be accumulated for the grand total are the row sums in A(R,NC + 1).

Putting It All Together

This PIAT illustrates how to enter, use, and print a two-dimensional array.

> Problem: The president of the Too Little Variety Stores has collected sales data on the 15 stores in the corporation for seven days. He would like to know the total sales for each store for the week, the total sales for the company for each of the seven days, and the total sales for the company for the week (see Figure 9.13).

In this problem the data can be stored in a two-dimensional sales array; the sum of the store sales per week can be stored in a one-dimensional array; the sum of the store sales per day can be stored in another one-dimensional array; and the grand total for the week can be stored in a single variable. An alternative way to store the data would be to place the totals in an additional row and column in the two-dimensional sales array. The latter would be the better alternative since there is only one array to keep track of and to print. This makes the processing easier and more readable.

Algorithm	Flowchart

```
LOOP: R = 1 TO NR STEP 1
  LOOP: C = 1 TO NC STEP 1
    A(R,NC + 1) = A(R,NC + 1)
        + A(R,C)
    A(NR + 1,C) = A(NR + 1,C)
        + A(R,C)
  LOOP-END: C
  A(NR + 1,NC + 1) =
      A(NR + 1,NC + 1)
          + A(R,NC + 1)
LOOP-END: R
```

R = Row

NR = Number of rows

C - Column

NC = Number of columns

A = Array

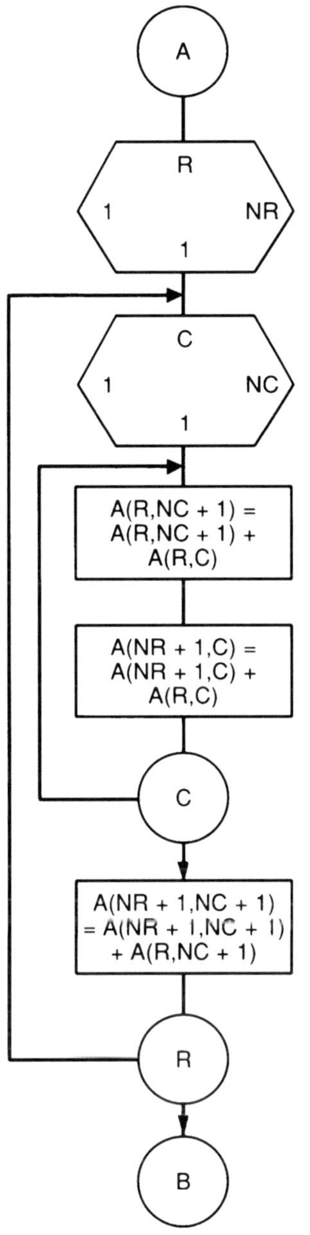

Figure 9.12 Algorithm and Flowchart for Column and Row Summation

The problem is divided into five modules: the Control, Init, Read, Calc, and Print Modules. The Control Module uses the sequential logic structure to process the modules. The Init Module sets the elements of the array to zero. The Read Module enters the sales data into the SALES array, row by row. The Calc Module sums the rows to give the totals for each store, the columns to give the totals for each day, and the grand total for the total sales for the company for the week. The Print Module prints the SALES array including the totals.

Given Data	Required Results
1. 15 stores 2. Sales for all stores for seven days	1. Total sales for each store for the week 2. Total sales for the company for each day 3. Total sales for the company for the week
Processing Required	**Solution Alternatives**
1. Summing store sales 2. Summing day's sales 3. Summing all sales	1. Use two-dimensional array for data, one-dimensional arrays for store totals and day's totals, and a single variable for grand total *2. Use a two-dimensional array to store all values

Figure 9.13a Problem Analysis Chart for Array Problem

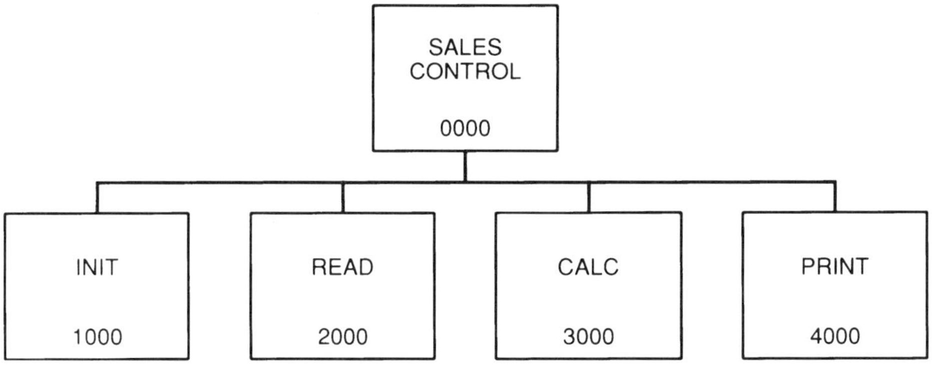

Figure 9.13b Structure Chart

Input	Processing	Module Reference Number	Output
1. Sales/day/store 2. 15 stores	1. Enter data 2. Set array = 0 3. Calculate totals 4. Print output	2000 1000 3000 4000	1. Total sales for each store for the week 2. Total sales for each day for company 3. Total sales for week for company

Figure 9.13c IPO Chart for Array Problem

Algorithm	Flowchart
CONTROL MODULE (0000) 1. PROCESS INIT 2. PROCESS READ 3. PROCESS CALC 4. PROCESS PRINT 5. END	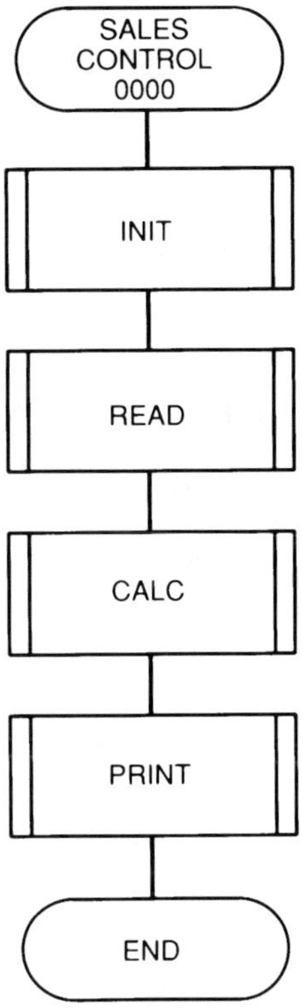

Figure 9.13d Algorithms and Flowcharts for Array Problem

Algorithm	Flowchart

INIT MODULE
(1000)
 	
1. LOOP: R = 1 TO 16
    LOOP: C = 1 TO 8
        SALES(R,C) = 0
    LOOP-END: C
LOOP-END: R
 	
2. EXIT
	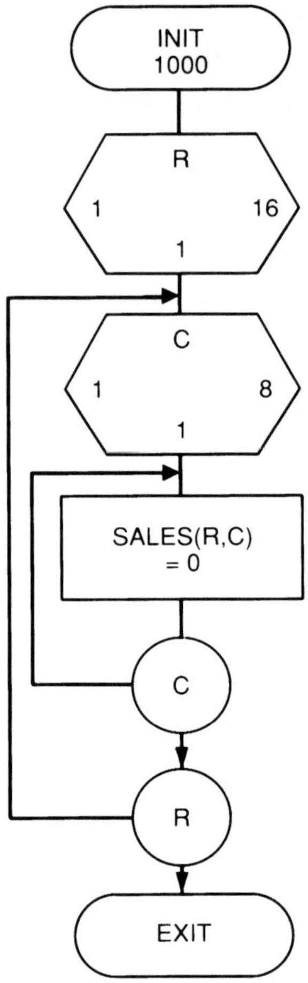

Figure 9.13e Algorithms and Flowcharts for Array Problem

Algorithm	Flowchart
READ MODULE (2000) 1. LOOP: R = 1 TO 15 LOOP: C = 1 TO 7 ENTER SALES(R,C) LOOP-END: C LOOP-END: R 2. EXIT	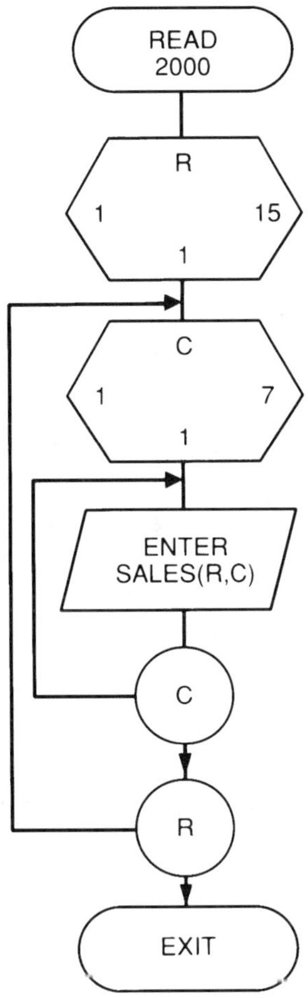

Figure 9.13f Algorithms and Flowcharts for Array Problem

Algorithm	Flowchart	Annotation

Algorithm

```
CALC MODULE
  (3000)

1. LOOP: R = 1 TO 15
   ┌ LOOP: C = 1 TO 7
   │  ┌ SALES(R,8) = SALES(R,8)
   │  │     + SALES(R,C)
   │  │
   │  │ SALES(16,C) = SALES(16,C)
   │  └     + SALES(R,C)
   │  LOOP-END:C
   │
   │  SALES(16,8) = SALES(16,8)
   └        + SALES(R,8)
   LOOP-END:R

2. EXIT
```

Flowchart

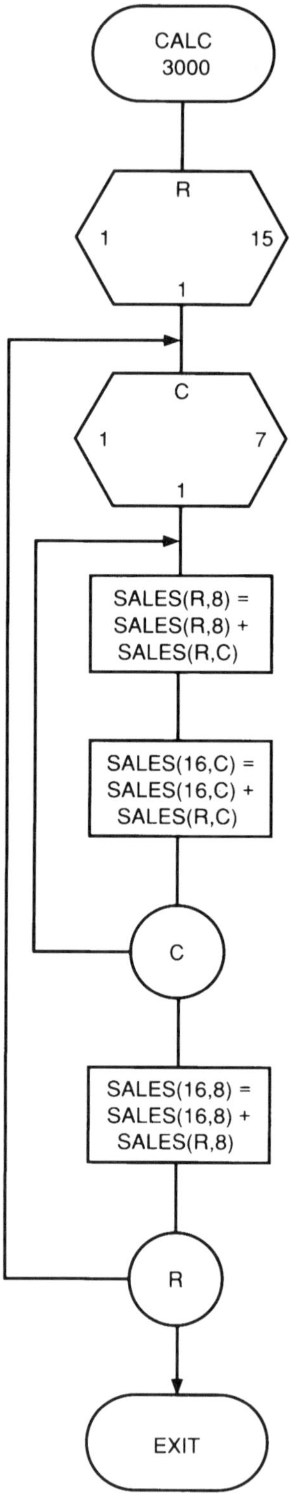

Annotation

- Row loop
- Column loop
- Sum of each row*
- Sum of each column**
- Grand total of all elements

*Column 8 contains the sum of each of the rows.
**Row 16 contains the sum of each of the columns.
Element row 16, column 8, contains the grand total.

Figure 9.13g Algorithms and Flowcharts for Array Problem

Algorithm	Flowchart
PRINT MODULE (4000) 1. PRINT COLUMN HEADINGS 2. LOOP: R = 1 TO 16 PRINT ROW HEADINGS(R) W/O {CR} LOOP: C = 1 TO 8 PRINT SALES(R,C) W/O {CR} LOOP-END: C PRINT {CR} LOOP-END: R 3. EXIT	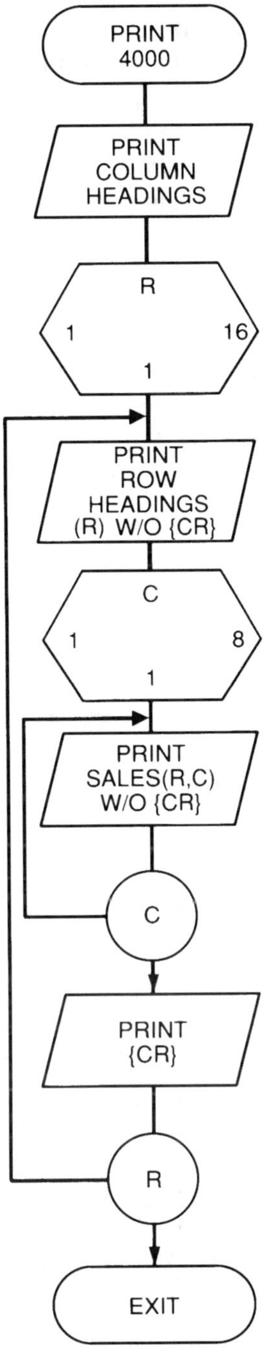

Figure 9.13h Algorithms and Flowcharts for Array Problem

Multidimensional Arrays

In some cases there is a need for arrays with a third or even a fourth dimension. These arrays are called **multidimensional arrays.** You will use these multidimensional arrays relatively infrequently. They can facilitate an understanding of the data, improve the readability of algorithms, and facilitate processing since the data can be processed through the use of three or more nested loops. For example, with input data on temperatures referenced by day, city, county, and state, *day* would be the first dimension, *city* would be the second dimension, *county* would be the third dimension, and *state* would be the fourth dimension of the array. In any case, any temperature could be found as long as the day, the city, the county, and the state are known. A multidimensional array allows the programmer to use one array for all the data.

Figure 9.14 shows a block of memory locations and their reference names for a three-dimensional array. The recommended variable names for the indexes of a three-dimensional array are R or ROW for row, C or COLUMN for column, and D or DEPTH for depth. For a fourth dimension, V or VOLUME for volume is used. These arrays are processed much like two-dimensional arrays, and, therefore, are not discussed further.

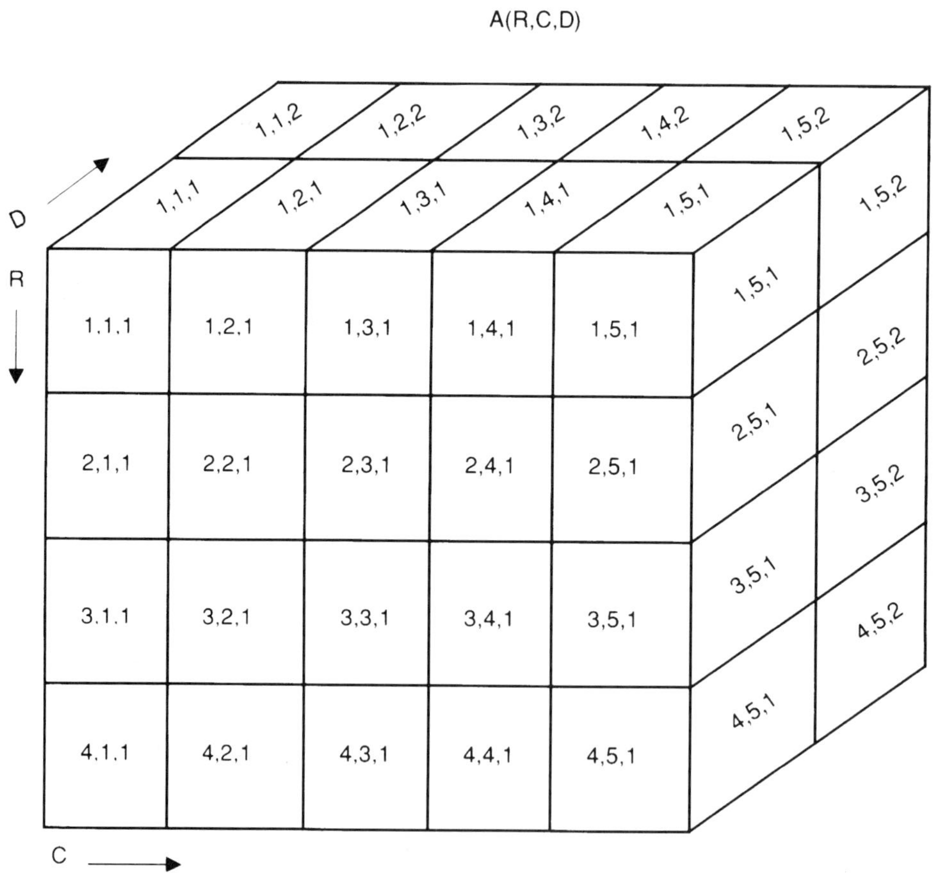

Figure 9.14 Three-Dimensional Array

Table Look-up Technique

A common application for arrays is using a value to look up another value in a table. A one-dimensional array would be used if the element number can be utilized as the given value (see Figure 9.15) A two-dimensional array with two columns would be used if the element number cannot be utilized. In this case the first column would contain the values to compare with the given value, and the second column would contain the values to be located. Figure 9.15 illustrates a one-dimensional array and the algorithm and flowchart for a table look-up problem. In this problem we need to find the number of days in a month given the month number. In this case we can utilize the element number as the month number. For example, given month number 3, the number of days in the month would be 31.

element	DAYS
1	31
2	28
3	31
4	30
5	31
6	30
7	31
8	31
9	30
10	31
11	30
12	31

ALGORITHM:

1. ENTER MONTH
2. DAYS__OF__MONTH = DAYS(MONTH)
3. PRINT DAYS__OF__MONTH
4. END

FLOWCHART:

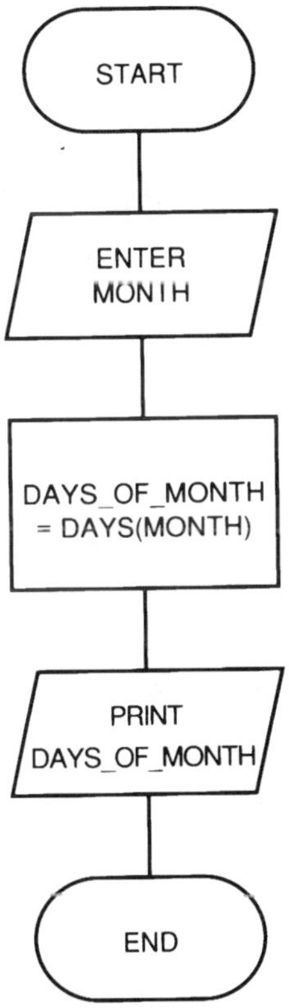

Figure 9.15 Table Look-up Technique

Sequential Search

There are instances when you do not know the element number, but you do know the value of the element. In this case a search must be made on the array to find the correct element. The easiest way to search an array is called a **sequential search.** Figure 9.16 shows the algorithm and the flowchart of a sequential search. The methodology is simple. Given the search value of the element you want to find, element number one is tested to see if it matches the search variable. If it does, the flow of the program drops out of the loop with the desired element number. If it doesn't match, the element number is incremented and loops back to test again.

Algorithm	Flowchart

```
1.  R = 1

2.  WHILE SEARCHNAME <> ARRAY(R)
      AND R < = N

      R = R + 1

    WHILE-END


3.  IF R > N

      THEN
        PRINT "ELEMENT
          NOT FOUND"

      ELSE
        PRINT ARRAY(R)
```

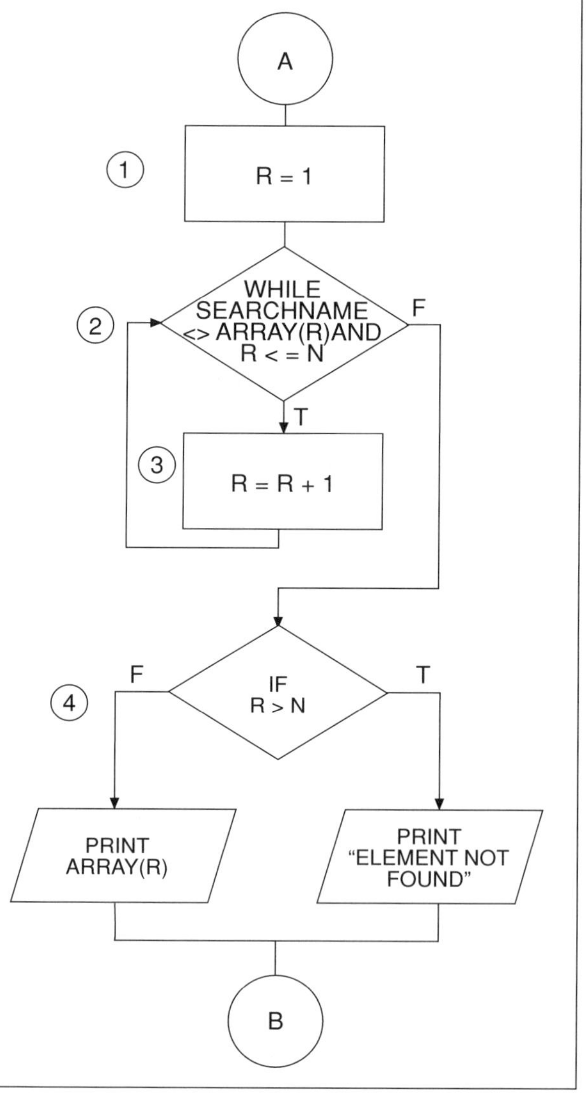

Figure 9.16 Search Algorithm and Flowchart

Notes on Figure 9.16

The numbers of the notes correspond to the circled numbers in Figure 9.16.

1. The element number is set to 1.
2. A loop is set up to test the search value against the value of the present element of the array. This test also includes a test to make sure the element number is less than or equal to the number of elements in the array. If the element number is greater than the number of elements, then the value was not found.
3. The element number is incremented.
4. A test is made on the element number. If the element number is greater than the number of elements in the array, an error message is printed; if not, the value of the element is printed.

Binary Search

A faster method of finding the desired element of an array is the **binary search.** Figure 9.17 shows the algorithm and flowchart of the binary search. The binary search technique involves comparing the mid-element of all or part of the array. If it compares, the flow of the program drops out of the loop with the desired element number. If it does not compare, the program checks to see if the value is lower or higher than the middle value. The boundaries are then reset to select a new section of the array in which the search value should be found. The midpoint of this new section is then checked. The program continues to divide the remaining elements by half until the desired element is found. At that time the program drops out of the loop with the element number of the desired element. Even with 1,000 elements, this method will take less than 10 comparisons.

Notes on Figure 9.17

The numbers of the notes correspond to the circled numbers in Figure 9.17.

1. The lower boundary is set at 1 (lowest element number).
2. The upper boundary is set at the maximum number of elements in the array.
3. The flag is set at zero. This flag is set at 1 when the element is found and 2 when the element could not be found. The flag is zero until one of the two preceding conditions is met.
4. The loop is started and will continue as long as FLAG = 0.
5. The mid-element number is calculated. This always rounds down because the INT function is used.
6. This is the test to see if the mid-element is equal to the value of the desired element. If it is, FLAG is set equal to 1, and the flow goes back to the WHILE statement. The condition at the WHILE statement is now false so the flow drops out of the loop. If the mid-element is not equal to the desired value, then the flow of the program will need to loop again to test another element against the search value.
7. The next test is made so the upper or lower boundaries can be reset. This will designate the new section of the array. This is accomplished by testing the value of the element against the search value. If the search value is greater than

Algorithm

Binary Search

LB = Lower bound
UB = Upper bound
N = # IN LIST
R = Current record position
S = Search value

```
1. LB = 1

2. UB = N

3. FLAG = 0

4. WHILE FLAG = 0
      R = INT((LB + UB) / 2)
      IF A(R) = S
        THEN
          FLAG = 1
        ELSE
          IF S > A(R)
            THEN
              LB = R + 1
            ELSE
              UB = R- 1
          IF LB > UB
            THEN
              FLAG = 2
   WHILE-END

5. IF FLAG = 2
     THEN
       PRINT "RECORD
        NOT FOUND"
     ELSE
       PRINT
        RECORD R

6. EXIT
```

Flowchart

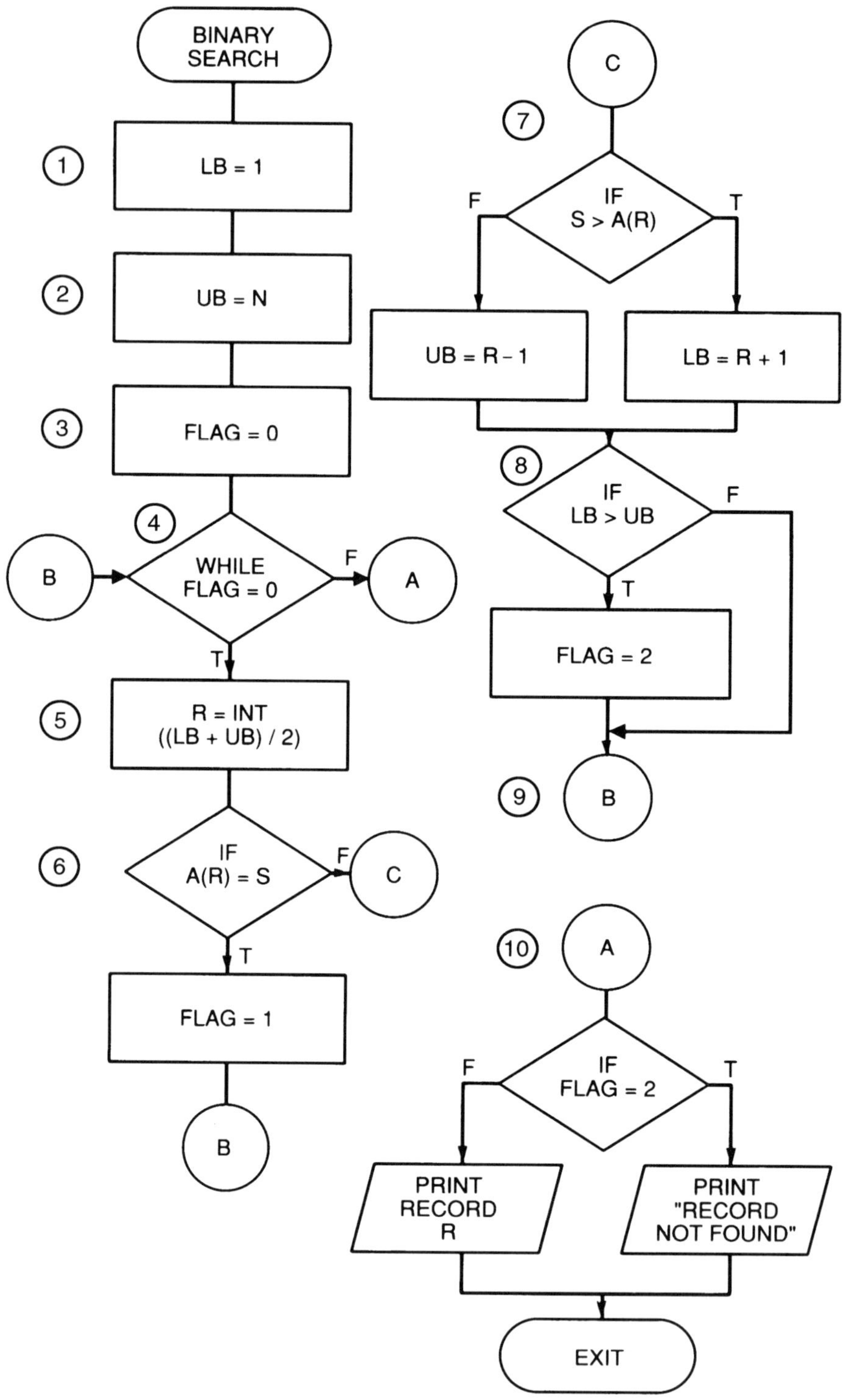

Figure 9.17 The Binary Search

the value of the mid-element number, then the lower boundary is set to one more than the midpoint. This means that the desired element is in the upper half of this section. If not, the upper boundary is set to one less than the midpoint. This means the desired element is in the lower half of the section.

8. This test is to make sure there are still elements in the section to be tested. If the lower boundary is less than the upper boundary, the flag is set to 2, indicating that the element could not be found.
9. The flow then returns to the WHILE statement and continues or drops out of the loop according to the value of FLAG.
10. After the flow of the program drops out of the loop, the flag is checked. When the FLAG is 1, the element (or elements if using parallel arrays or multidimensional arrays) information is printed. If FLAG is equal to 2, an error message is printed.

The Pointer Technique

Another way to use arrays is to specify the value of an element in one array as the element number in another array. This use of array is called the **pointer technique** because the value of the element in the first array points to the element in the second. The pointer technique is used in frequency distributions. A *frequency distribution* is a tally of one type of value in an array, such as how many students in a school are in each class or how many of a company's customers live in each zip code area. The result of a frequency distribution is a one-dimensional array that contains the tally for the value of each element number. The pointer technique is also used for calculating statistics from a questionnaire by cross-tabulating items, such as how many students are in each major and each class. The result of this cross-tabulation is a two-dimensional array containing the tally for the combination of the majors and the classes; the majors would be the rows and the classes would be the columns.

Frequency Distribution

In the development of the solution for a frequency distribution, the arrays must be defined. First, you define the array from which the frequency distributions is to be calculated. This array contains data that are coded using the numbers from 1 to the number of different values in the array. For example, when doing a frequency distribution on grades in a class, the grades must be coded numerically, such as, 1 = A, 2 = B, 3 = C, 4 = D, 5 = F. Or if the frequency distribution deals with the number of freshmen, sophomores, juniors, seniors, and graduate students in a college, each class would be given a number from 1 to 5. The number of values of the code then becomes the number of elements in the frequency distribution array.

Figure 9.18 illustrates the solution to the following problem: Using a grading scale of 1 to 10, design a solution to find the number of students out of a class of 30 who received each grade (1 through 10) on a test. The GRADE array contains 30 elements, one element for each student, which have the values of 1, 2, 3, 4, 5, 6, 7, 8, 9, or 10

Algorithm	Flowchart
FREQ. DIST. CONTROL (0000) 1. PROCESS INIT 2. PROCESS READ 3. PROCESS CALC 4. PROCESS PRINT 5. END	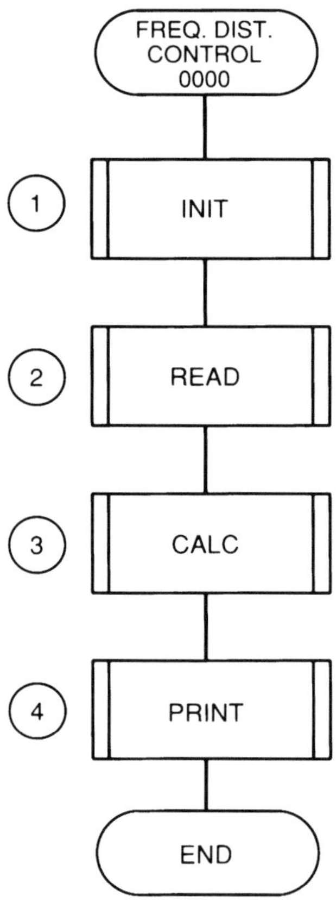

Figure 9.18a Algorithms and Flowcharts for a Frequency Distribution

depending on the student's grade. The F (frequency distribution) array contains 10 elements, one for each different grade: The first element contains the number of students who received a 1, the second element contains the number of students who received a 2, the third element contains the number of students who received a 3, and so forth.

Figure 9.18 demonstrates the use of pointers for a frequency distribution. Notice in the Calc Module that the value of the GRADE array element is the element number of the frequency distribution array. The GRADE array element value points to the location of the element in the frequency distribution array that needs to be incremented, an example of the pointer technique. Follow the notes for Figure 9.18 for an explanation of each major step in the solution to the frequency distribution problem.

Algorithm	Flowchart
INIT MODULE (1000) 1. LOOP: R = 1 TO 10 [F(R) = 0 LOOP-END: R 2. EXIT	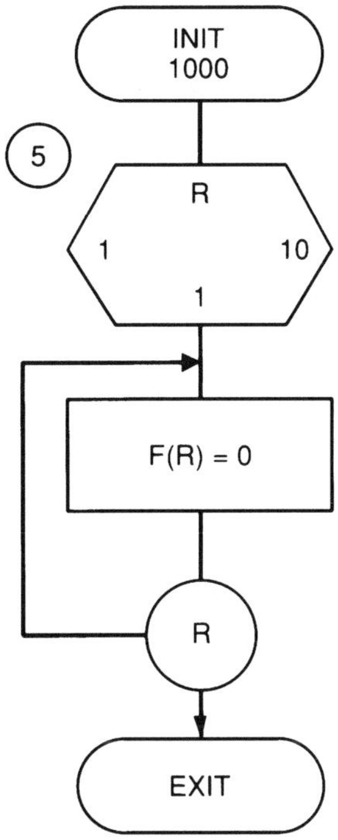
READ MODULE (2000) 1. LOOP: R = 1 TO 30 [ENTER GRADE(R) LOOP-END: R 2. EXIT	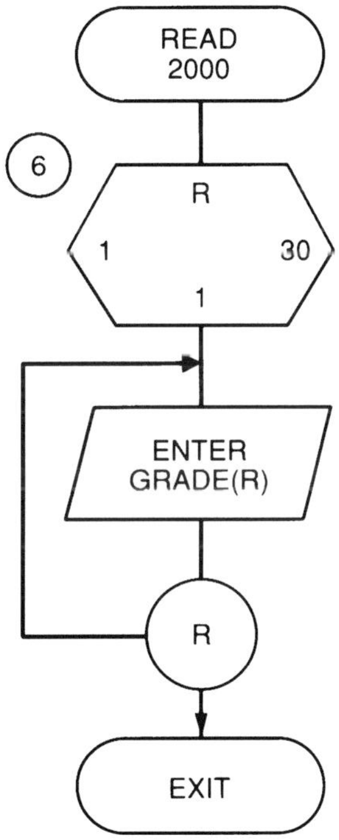

Figure 9.18b Algorithms and Flowcharts for a Frequency Distribution

Algorithm	Flowchart
CALC MODULE (3000) 1. LOOP: R = 1 TO 30 [P = GRADE(R) F(P) = F(P) + 1] LOOP-END: R 2. EXIT	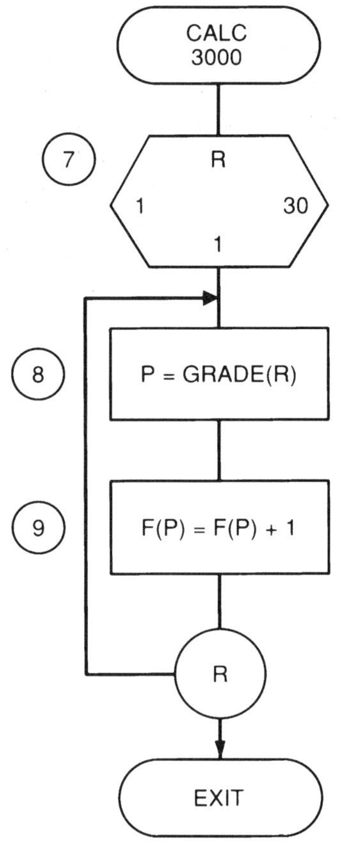
PRINT MODULE (4000) 1. LOOP: R = 1 TO 10 [PRINT R, F(R)] LOOP-END: R 2. EXIT	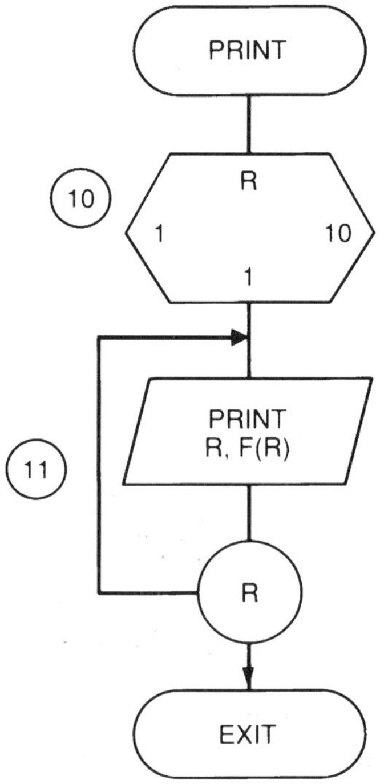

Figure 9.18c Algorithms and Flowcharts for a Frequency Distribution

Notes for Figure 9.18

The following notes explain the flowcharts for a frequency distribution. The numbers of the notes correspond to the circled numbers in Figure 9.18.

1. The Init Module initializes the variables to zero.
2. The Read Module enters the data.
3. The Calc Module calculates the frequency distribution.
4. The Print Module prints the frequency distribution.
5. The frequency distribution array (F) is 10 elements long since there are 10 grades. Each element in this array is set to zero since each element is a counter.
6. There are 30 elements in the GRADE array since there are 30 students. This loop enters the grades into the GRADE array. There is one element per student.
7. In this loop the ending number is the number of students, since that will determine the frequency distribution.
8. Through the pointer technique, the value of the GRADE(R) points to the element number of the frequency distribution array to indicate which element will be incremented. The P variable is the pointer variable. It has the same value as the grade of student number R.
9. The P element of the frequency array is incremented. At the conclusion of the loop, the frequency array will contain the values of the number of students receiving each of the 10 grades.
10. This loop executes 10 times since there are 10 elements in the frequency array.
11. This loop prints the number of the element (R), which is equal to the grade and the value of the R element of the frequency array (F), which is the number of students receiving the grade (R).

Cross-Tabulation

Figure 9.19 demonstrates the use of pointers for a cross-tabulation. Notice that in this case, one value points to the row and another value points to the column in the cross-tabulation array. The data for cross-tabulation problems come from questionnaires. A cross-tabulation shows the number of people who gave the same answers to two questions from the questionnaire. A frequency distribution shows the number of people who gave the same answer to one question.

Figure 9.19 shows the algorithms and flowcharts for a cross-tabulation for the following problem: A questionnaire has been sent out by a company that conducts polls. The company needs a program to calculate the cross-tabulation for any two items on the questionnaire. The questionnaire has five items. Items 1 and 2 are *age* and *education* (5 possible answers). Items 3 through 5 are *yes* or *no* questions. There were 150 questionnaires returned.

Notes to Figure 9.19

The following notes explain the flowcharts in Figure 9.19. The numbers of the notes correspond to the circled numbers in Figure 9.19.

1. The Init Module initializes the variables.
2. The Enter Data Module enters the questionnaire data.
3. The Choose Options Module chooses the two items for the cross-tabulation.

Algorithm	Flowchart

CROSSTAB CONTROL
(0000)

1. PROCESS INIT
2. PROCESS ENTERDATA
3. PROCESS CHOOSEOPTIONS
4. WHILE C1 > 0
    - PROCESS CALC
    - PROCESS PRINT
    - PROCESS INIT
    - PROCESS CHOOSEOPTIONS

   WHILE-END
5. END

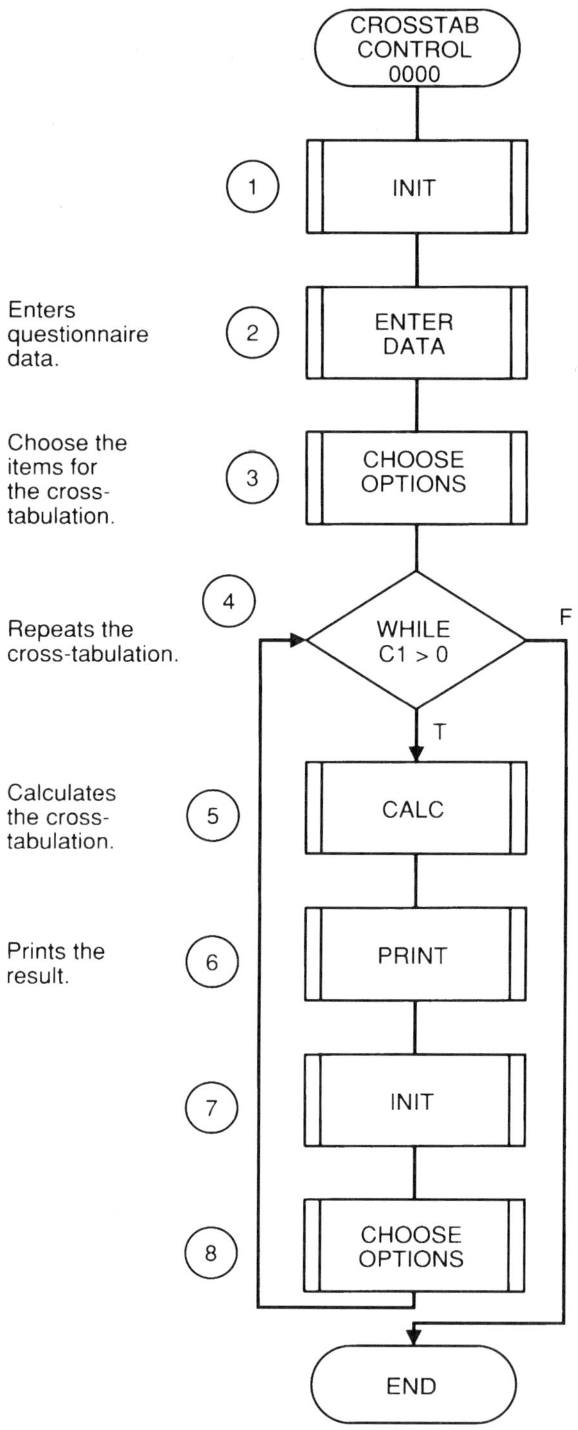

Figure 9.19a Algorithms and Flowcharts for Cross-Tabulation Solution

Algorithm	Flowchart
INIT MODULE (1000) 1. LOOP: R = 1 TO 5 LOOP: C = 1 TO 5 CT(R,C) = 0 LOOP-END: C LOOP-END: R 2. EXIT	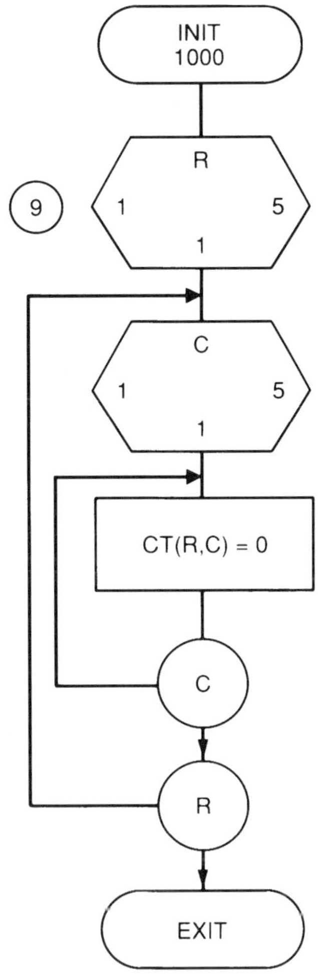

Figure 9.19b Algorithms and Flowcharts for Cross-Tabulation Solution

4. This loop repeats the cross-tabulation until no more cross-tabulations are desired by the user.
5. The Calc Module calculates the cross-tabulation.
6. The Print Module prints the results of the cross tabulation.
7. The Init Module, processed at this point, reinitializes the variables for another cross tabulation on the same data.
8. This Choose Options Module chooses the two items for the next cross-tabulation.
9. This nested automatic-counter loop sets the elements of the cross-tabulation array to zero.

Algorithm	Flowchart

Algorithm

```
ENTER DATA MODULE
    (2000)
1. LOOP: R = 1 TO 150
      LOOP: C = 1 TO 5
         ENTER TDATA(R,C)
         IF C = 1
            THEN
               IF TDATA(R,1) < 21
                  THEN
                     TDATA(R,1) = 1
                  ELSE
                     IF TDATA(R,1) < 40
                        THEN
                           TDATA(R,1) = 2
                        ELSE
                           TDATA(R,1) = 3
      LOOP-END: C
   LOOP-END: R
2. EXIT
```

Flowchart

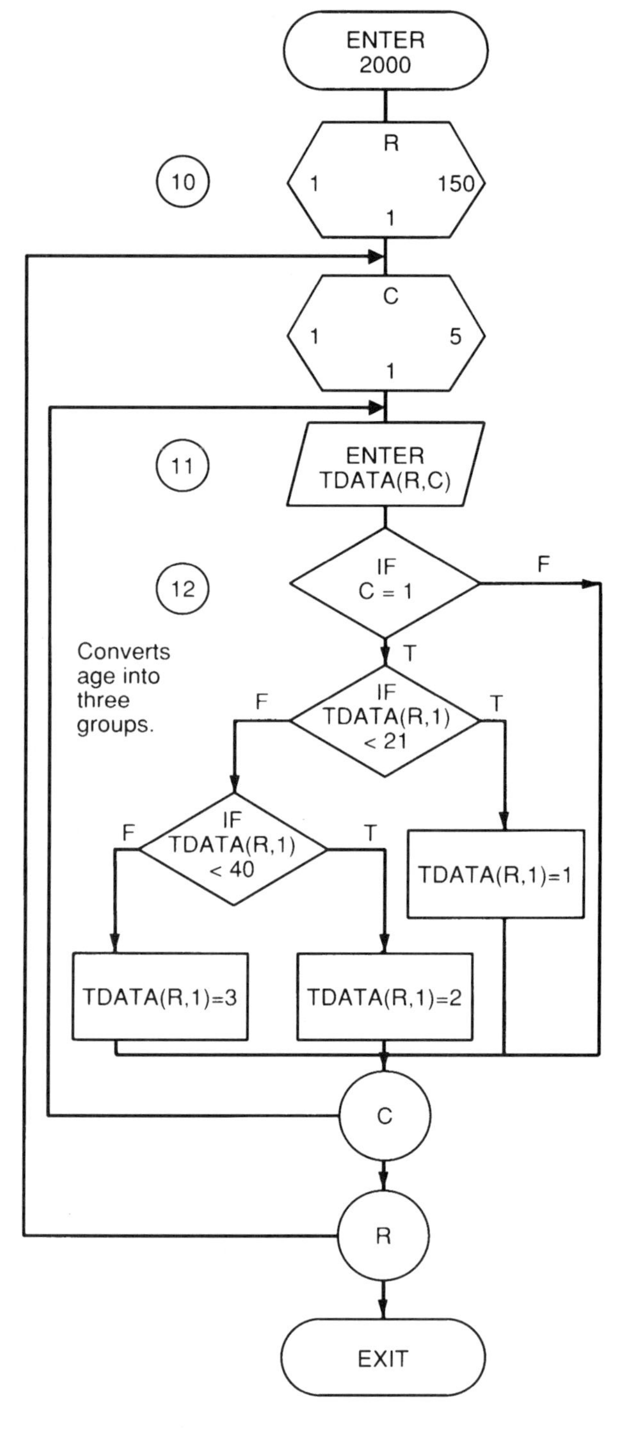

Figure 9.19c Algorithms and Flowcharts for Cross-Tabulation Solution

Algorithm	Flowchart
CHOOSE OPTIONS MODULE (3000) 1. CLEAR SCREEN 2. PRINT MENU 3. REPEAT: [ENTER OPTION1 UNTIL OPTION1 > -1 AND OPTION1 < 5 4. OPTION2 = OPTION1 5. WHILE OPTION1 <> 0 AND (OPTION1 = OPTION2 OR OPTION2 < 0 OR OPTION2 > 4) [ENTER OPTION2 WHILE-END 6. EXIT	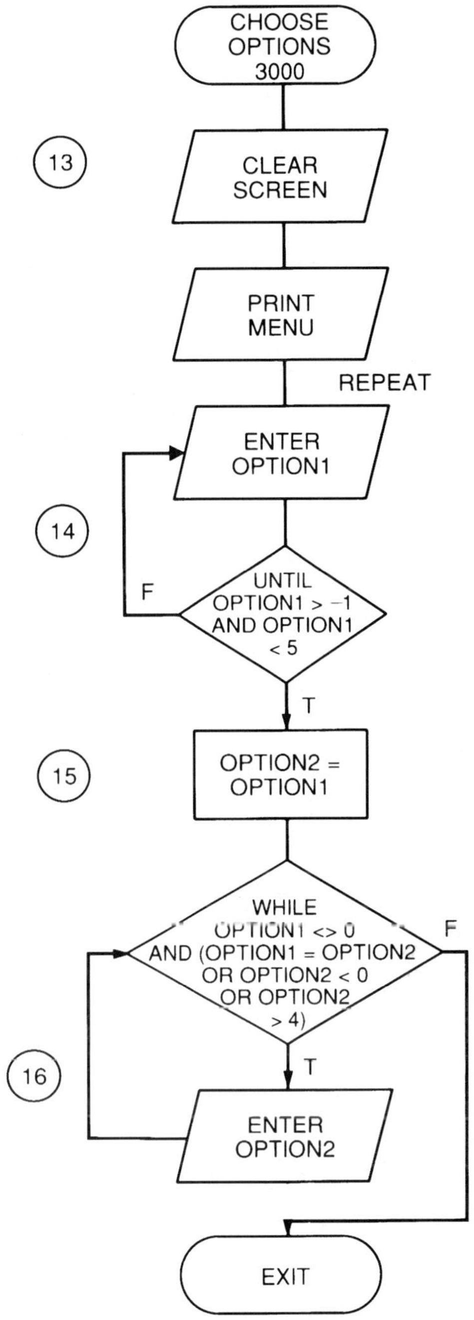

Figure 9.19d Algorithms and Flowcharts for Cross-Tabulation Solution

Algorithm

```
CALC MODULE
  (4000)

1. RMAX = 0

2. CMAX = 0

3. LOOP: Q = 1 TO 150
   ┌ R = TDATA(Q,OPTION1)
   │
   │ C = TDATA(Q,OPTION2)
   │
   │ CT(R,C) = CT(R,C) + 1
   │
   │┌ IF R > RMAX
   ││
   │├── THEN
   ││
   ││     RMAX = R
   │└─────
   │┌ IF C > CMAX
   ││
   │├── THEN
   ││
   ││     CMAX = C
   │└─────
   └─
   LOOP-END: Q

4. EXIT
```

Flowchart

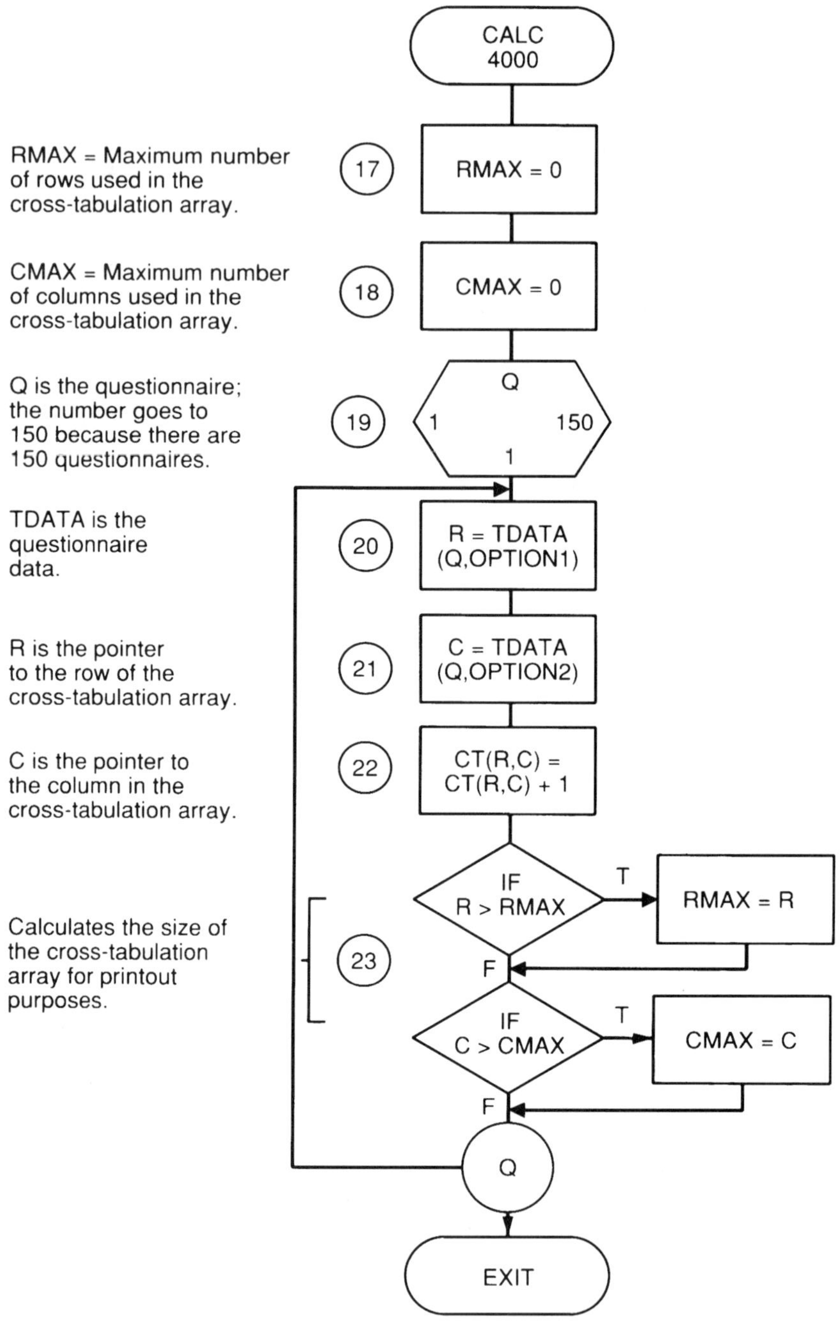

Figure 9.19e Algorithms and Flowcharts for Cross-Tabulation Solution

Algorithm	Flowchart

PRINT MODULE
(5000)

1. PRINT COLUMN HEADINGS
2. LOOP: R = 1 TO RMAX

    PRINT ROW HEADING

        LOOP: C = 1 TO CMAX

            PRINT CT(R,C) W/O {CR}

        LOOP-END: C

    PRINT {CR}

   LOOP-END: R

3. EXIT

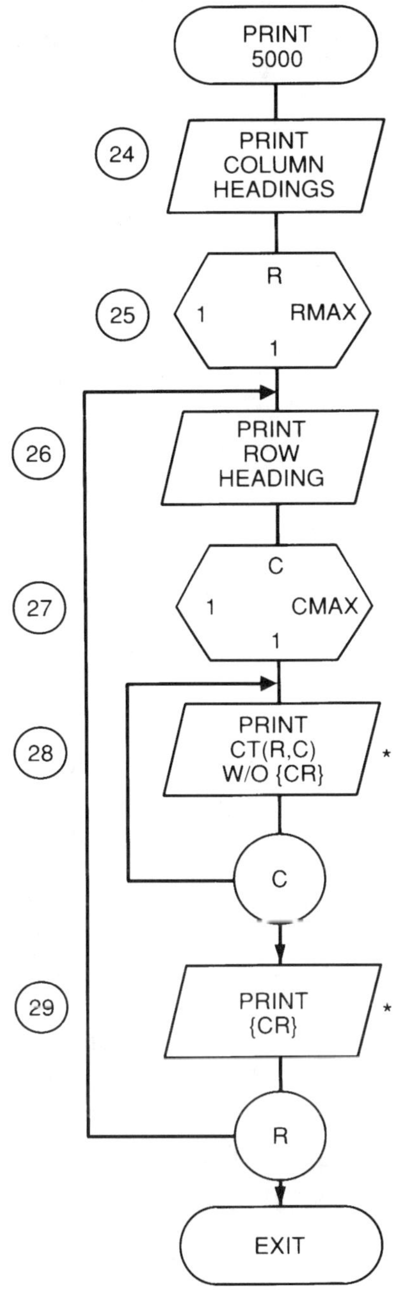

* {CR} = Cursor return for monitor or carriage return for printer.

Figure 9.19f Algorithms and Flowcharts for Cross-Tabulation Solution

10. These loops are set so that the rows (R) are the questionnaires (1 to 150) and the columns (C) are the items (1 to 5).
11. This instruction enters the questionnaire data, one element at a time.
12. This decision instruction checks to see if the column number is one; if it is, then the instruction changes the ages to age groups: 1 = under 21, 2 = between 21 and 40, 3 = over 40.
13. These instructions clear the screen and print the menu of the questionnaire items.
14. This loop enters the first item number (OPTION1) for the cross-tabulation option. It repeats until the number entered is within the limits of the options of the menu (0 to 5).
15. This instruction initializes OPTION2 to prepare for the next loop.
16. This loop enters the second item number (OPTION2) and repeats until the answer is within the limitations of the number of items (1 to 5) and is not equal to OPTION1.
17. RMAX is the maximum number of rows used in the cross-tabulation. It is set to zero since the maximum number of rows has to be greater than zero.
18. CMAX is the maximum number of columns used in the cross-tabulation. It is set to zero since the maximum number of columns has to be greater than zero.
19. This loop is set up for the number of questionnaires (150).
20. R is the pointer to the row of the cross-tabulation array. The value comes from the value in the OPTION1 column for that questionnaire. OPTION1 is the first item number entered by the user.
21. C is the pointer to the column of the cross-tabulation array. The value comes from the value in the OPTION2 column for that questionnaire. OPTION2 is the second item number entered by the user.
22. This instruction increments the element in the cross-tabulation array specified by the pointers R and C.
23. These decisions calculate the maximum row number and the maximum column number for printing.
24. This instruction prints column headings.
25. This loop specifies the number of rows to print, determined by RMAX.
26. This instruction prints the row heading each time through the loop.
27. This loop specifies the number of columns to print, determined by CMAX.
28. This instruction prints an element without a carriage-return, as specified by R and C.
29. This instruction returns the carriage after a row is printed.

Putting It All Together

This PIAT illustrates the use of arrays in the solution to a cross-tabulation problem.

> Problem: A company has data on the number of days each employee was absent during the previous year. The data also include sex (1 = female, 2 = male), pay-type (1 = salary, 2 = hourly wage, 3 = commission), education (1 = no diploma or degree, 2 = high school diploma, 3 = associate degree, 4 = bachelor's degree, 5 = graduate degree), and age group (1 = below 30, 2 = 30-50, 3 = over 50). The personnel manager would like a cross-tabulation on these data giving the average number of days absent. The company has 55 employees (see Figure 9.20).

	Sex	Pay-Type	Education	Age Group	# of Days Absent
Employee 1					
2					
3					
⋮	⋮	⋮	⋮	⋮	⋮
55					

Figure 9.20a Cross-Tabulation Problem

Given Data	Required Results
Per employee: Sex (1 = F, 2 = M) Pay-type (1 = S, 2 = H, 3 = C) Education (1 = N, 2 = HS, 3 = C, 4 = B, 5 = G) Age group (1 - < 30, 3 - 30 to 50, 3 - > 50) # of days absent	Cross tabulate for average number of days absent
Processing Required	
Calculation of average using cross-tabulation technique	
Solution Alternatives	
Must use cross-tabulation pointer technique	

Figure 9.20b Problem Analysis Chart

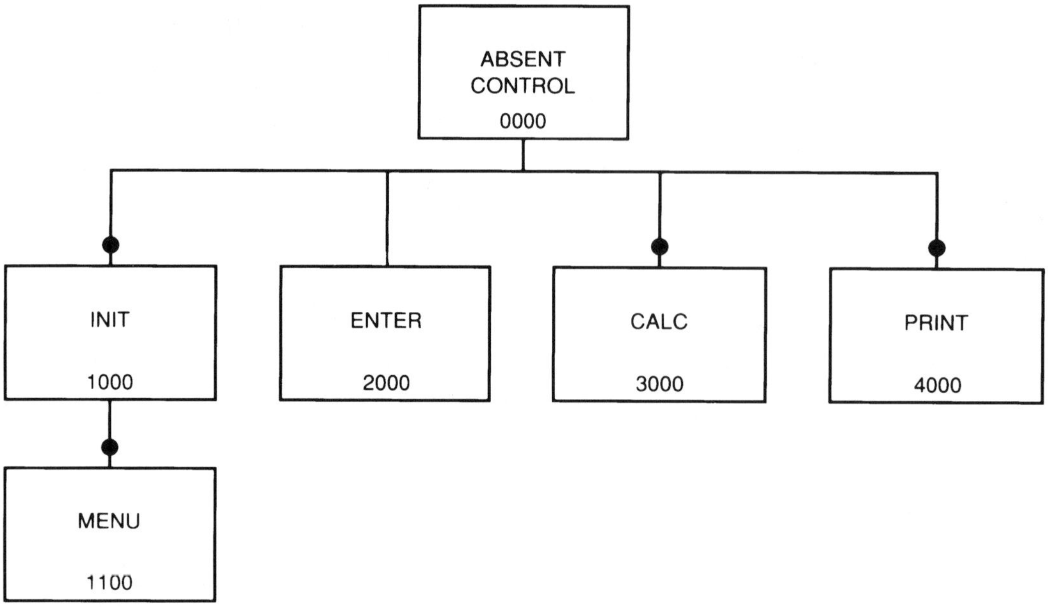

IPO Chart

Input	Processing	Modular Reference Number	Output
For each employee	1. Set cross-tab array and counter array = 0	1000	Average # of days absent for any two: (Cross-tabulation)
1. Sex			
	2. Enter data	2000	1. Sex
2. Pay-type	3. Print menu	1100	2. Pay-type
3. Education	4. Choose options	1100	3. Education
4. Age group	5. Calculate cross-tabulation	3000	4. Age
5. # of days absent			
	6. Print cross-tab array	4000	
	7. Repeat 3 - 7 until option1 = 0		

Figure 9.20c Structure Chart and IPO Chart

Algorithm	Flowchart

CONTROL MODULE
(0000)
 	
1. PROCESS INIT
 	
2. PROCESS ENTER
 	
3. WHILE OPTION1 > 0
    PROCESS CALC
    PROCESS PRINT
    PROCESS INIT
  WHILE-END
 	
4. END
	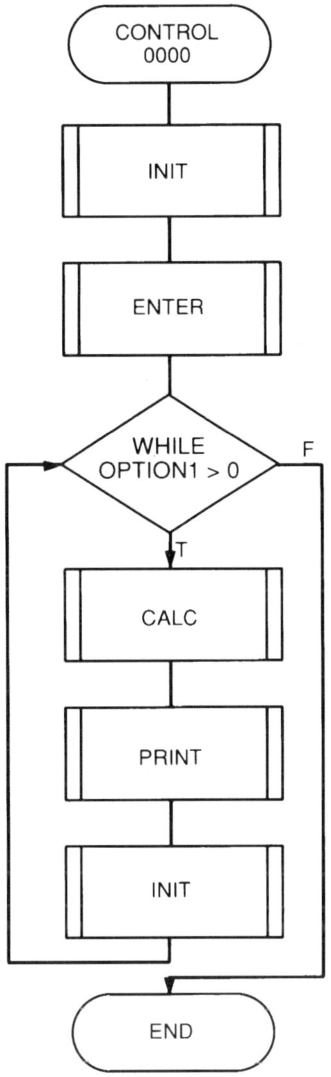

Figure 9.20d Algorithms and Flowcharts

Algorithm	Flowchart

INIT MODULE (1000)
1. LOOP: R = 1 TO 5
  LOOP: C = 1 TO 5
    CT(R,C) = 0
    N(R,C) = 0
  LOOP-END: C
LOOP-END: R
2. PROCESS MENU
3. RMAX = 0
4. CMAX = 0
5. EXIT
	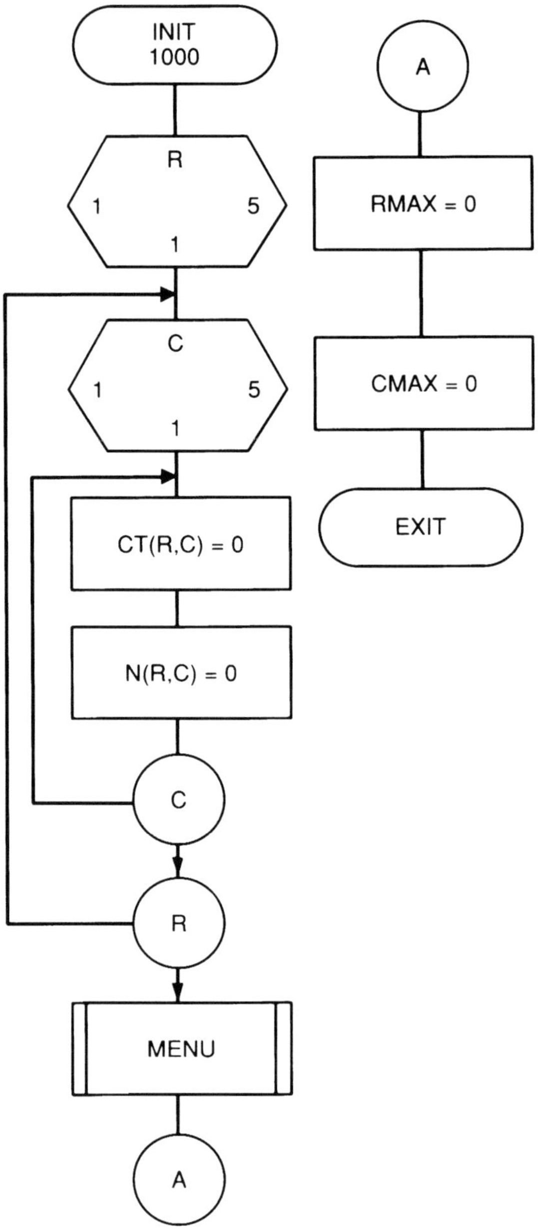

Figure 9.20e Algorithms and Flowcharts

Algorithm	Flowchart
MENU MODULE (1100) 1. CLEAR SCREEN 2. PRINT MENU 3. REPEAT [ENTER OPTION1 UNTIL OPTION1 > -1 AND OPTION1 < 5 4. OPTION2 = OPTION1 5. WHILE OPTION1 <> 0 AND (OPTION1 = OPTION2 OR OPTION2 > 4 OR OPTION2 < 0) [ENTER OPTION2 WHILE - END 6. EXIT	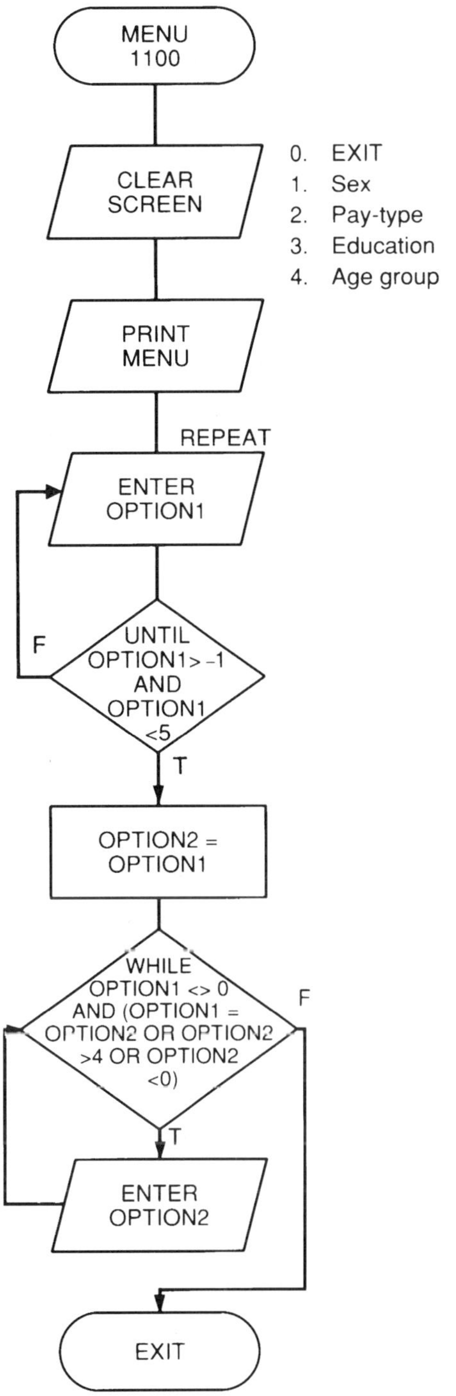

Figure 9.20f Algorithms and Flowcharts

Algorithm	Flowchart
ENTER MODULE (2000) 1. LOOP: R = 1 TO 55 LOOP: C = 1 TO 5 ENTER A(R,C) LOOP-END: C LOOP-END: R 2. EXIT	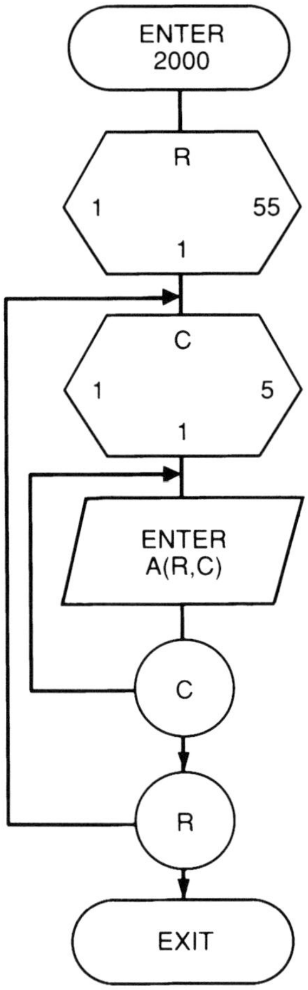

Figure 9.20g Algorithms and Flowcharts

Algorithm	Flowchart
see below	see below

Algorithm

```
CALC MODULE
      (3000)

1.  LOOP: R = 1 TO 55
        ROW = A(R,OPTION1)
        COL = A(R,OPTION2)
        CT(ROW,COL) =
           CT(ROW,COL)
           + A(R,5)
        N(ROW,COL) =
           N(ROW,COL) + 1

        IF ROW > RMAX
           THEN
              RMAX = ROW

        IF COL > CMAX
           THEN
              CMAX = COL
    LOOP-END: R

2.  LOOP: R = 1 TO RMAX
       LOOP: C = 1 TO CMAX
          IF CT(R,C) > 0
             THEN
                CT(R,C) =
                   CT(R,C)/
                   N(R,C)
       LOOP-END: C
    LOOP-END: R

3.  EXIT
```

Flowchart

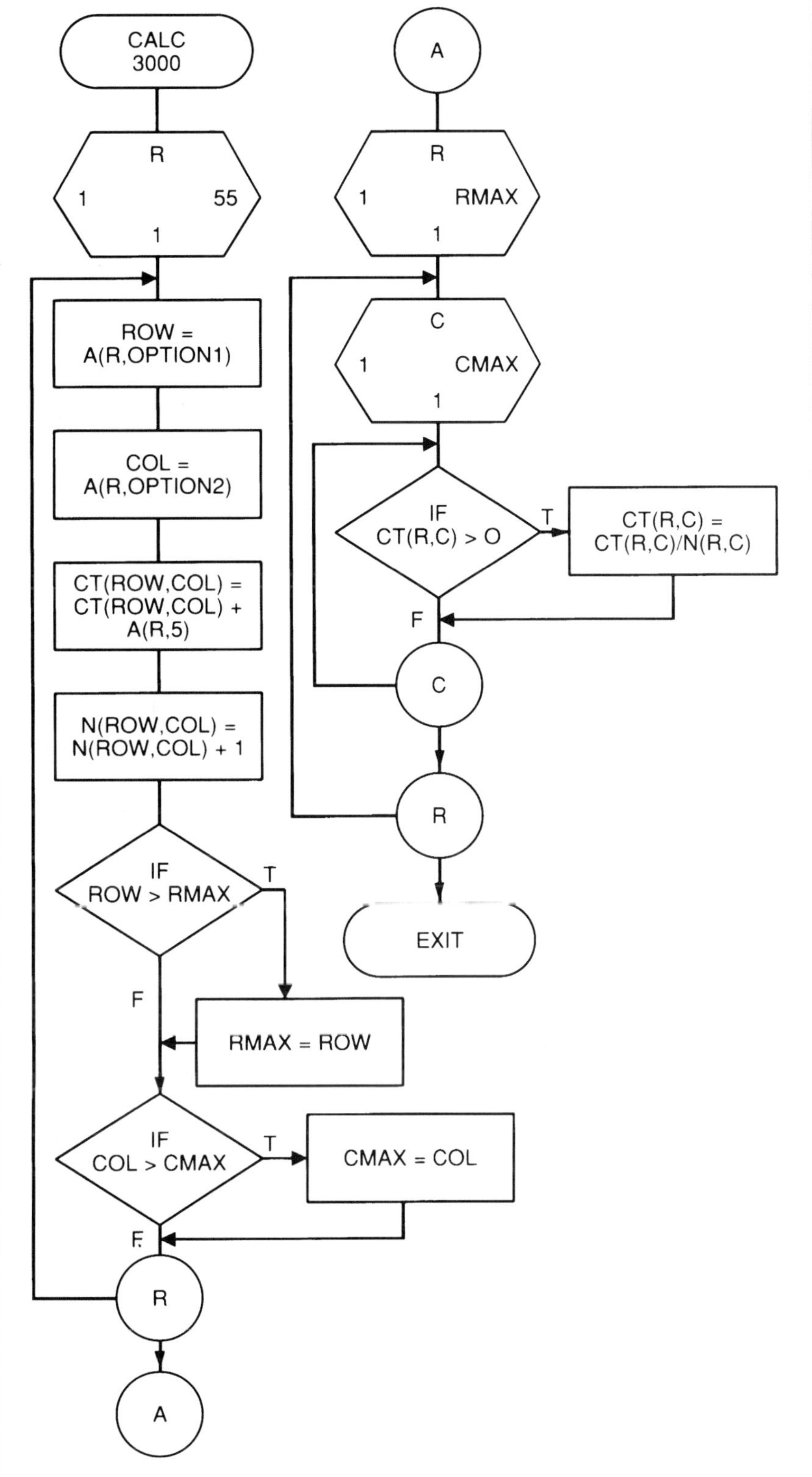

Figure 9.20h Algorithms and Flowcharts

Algorithm	Flowchart
PRINT MODULE (4000) 1. WRITE COLUMN HEADINGS 2. LOOP: R = 1 TO RMAX WRITE ROW HEADINGS LOOP: C = 1 TO CMAX WRITE CT(R,C) W/O {CR} LOOP-END: C WRITE {CR} LOOP-END: R 3. EXIT	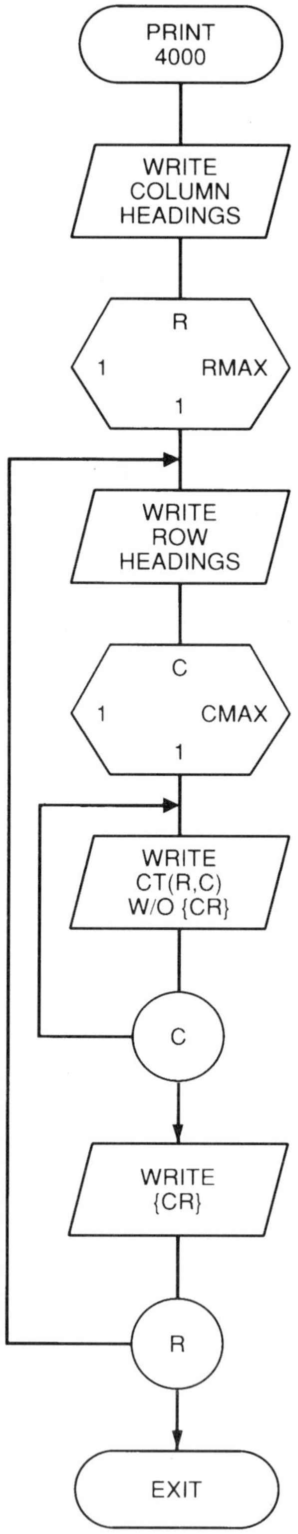

Figure 9.20i Algorithms and Flowcharts

Summary

Arrays facilitate the processing of data that is needed more than once in the processing of a solution. Even though arrays are not difficult to learn, they are difficult to use well. Therefore, it is important that a student of programming learn how to use them in a solution. To use arrays, the student needs to learn to enter or load data into an array, to print an array, to sum the elements of an array, and to use an array to store data needed at a later point in the solution. There are three types of arrays: one-dimensional, two-dimensional, and multidimensional.

A technique that is important to the use of arrays is the pointer technique, wherein you use the value of an element in one array to point to the number of the element in another. It is used in frequency distributions and cross-tabulations.

New Terms

array
binary search
dynamic arrays
multidimensional array
one-dimensional array
parallel arrays
pointer technique
sequential search
static array
two-dimensional array

Questions

1. Draw and name a one-dimensional array that would hold 10 temperatures. Number the elements.
2. Draw and name four parallel arrays that would hold the following data:

Store	*Sales*	*Customers*	*Region*
A24	5000	500	A
A26	3000	200	A
C30	6000	550	C
B44	4000	560	B

3. Draw and name a two-dimensional array that would hold the data for 10 homework scores for 15 students. Number the rows and the columns.
4. Can all of the data in Question 2 be put into a two-dimensional array? Explain.
5. What is the pointer technique for finding data? Why is it used?
6. What are the problem requirements for using the pointer technique?

Problems

Complete the six steps of solution development and a data dictionary for the following problems.

1. Mr. Jones always gives True/False tests to his class. His tests always have 20 questions. The maximum class size is 35. He needs a program that will calculate the students' grades based on the best score.

   Grade

   A will range from the best score, to the best score minus 2.

   B will range from the best score minus 3, to the best score minus 4.

   C will range from the best score minus 5, to the best score minus 6.

   D will range from the best score minus 7, to the best score minus 8.

   F will be anything below the best score minus 8.

   Each student's ID and test answers will be entered. The output will be each student's ID, number correct, and grade, along with the single highest score for the class. Develop a solution for Mr. Jones' problem. Use four one-dimensional arrays—one for the correct scores and the other three for the needed output.
2. A restaurant manager wants to know how many employees are needed at the restaurant each hour of the day. The minimum number of employees needed at any hour is 3. After that, one additional employee is required for each 20 customers. The restaurant is open 24 hours a day. The manager has counted the number of customers each hour for 14 days. The manager will use the average number of customers for each hour over the 14 days to calculate the needed number of employees for each hour. Develop a solution to output the needed number of employees per hour. (There is no such thing as a partial employee.)
3. A company has 10 salespeople. The manager needs to know the average dollar amount of sales for each salesperson for a week, and the total dollar amount of sales for the store for each day and for the week. The store is open 7 days a week, and each salesperson gets 2 days off. The data are entered into a two-dimensional array with the days of the week as the columns and the salespeople as the rows. Develop a solution to output the needed information.
4. An instructor has 30 students in his class. Each student is identified by a number from 1 to 30. Grades are stored in a one-dimensional array. The instructor would like to enter a student number and have the student's test score printed on the monitor. Develop a solution to output the needed information.
5. An instructor has a class of 25 students. Each student is identified by a number from 1 to 25. All tests are stored in a two-dimensional array, with each column containing the grades for each test. The instructor would like to enter the student number and the test number and have the grade for that test printed on the monitor. Develop a solution to output the needed information.
6. The instructor in Problem 5 would like to enter the last name of the student instead of the student number. Modify your solution to allow the instructor to enter the student name instead of the student number.
7. A university has four undergraduate class levels and a graduate school. There are 7 majors, although not all students have chosen a major. There are 1,200 students attending the university. The administration would like to know how many students are in each level, and how many students have each major. They also would like to know how many of each class level have declared each major. Develop a solution to output the needed information.

8. A questionnaire was sent to a random selection of the alumni of a college. In all, 95 questionnaires were returned. The questionnaire requested the following items:

age

sex

marital status

college major

salary

The administration would like to know the average salary, given any two sets of items. Develop a solution to cross-tabulate the items and output the needed information. (Remember, the computer cannot divide by zero.)

9. a. The student names and the grades for four tests for Mr. Smith's class have been placed in parallel arrays. Mr. Smith would like to have one student's name and test scores printed. Develop a solution that will enter the student's name, search for the name in the same array, and then print the name and test scores. Use the sequential-search method.

b. What would have to change in the solution in 9a if we were to use the binary search instead of the sequential-search method?

c. Modify the solution in 9a to use the binary search instead of the sequential search.

Chapter 10

Data Structures

Overview

Sorting Techniques
Stacks
Linked Lists
Binary Trees

Objectives

When you have finished this chapter, you should be able to:

1. Explain the different types of data structures used in a computer.
2. Use several sorting techniques.
3. Use stacks in a solution.
4. Develop a solution to a problem using a linked list technique.
5. Develop a solution to a problem using linked lists to access data.
6. Explain how a binary tree is set up.
7. Develop a solution to a problem using a binary tree to search for data.

Data are stored in the computer in one of many logical ways in order to find needed values as fast as possible. The way data are stored is called the structure of the data, hence the term data structures. You have already used several types of data structures in developing solutions for problems in this text. The simplest data structure is the single variable. This data structure was the first one you used. The single variable data structure includes single values of the data types presented in Chapter 2. Other data structures include strings, arrays, and records. The string is a type of array because it is a group of characters. An array consists of multiple values for one variable name. The data can be stored in one-dimensional, two-dimensional, or multidimensional arrays. The single variable and the array are types of data structures which are used as methods of storing data in the internal memory during the processing of the data. Data often need to be saved from one processing time to the next. Also, with large amounts of data, it is impractical or impossible to store all of the data internally during processing. Therefore, data need to be stored in files on an external storage device. Files used records as the data structure. A record is an entity in a file that is designed to store data about that item. All records in a file have the same layout or structure. This chapter emphasizes methods of accessing data in a file, including linked lists and binary trees. Sorting techniques, and a brief description of other data structures, such as stacks, queues, and hashing are also included in this chapter.

Sorting Techniques

Most accessing techniques require data to be sorted. **Sorting** is the process of putting data in alphabetical or numerical order using one key field or a concatenation of two or more fields. Data are sorted according to the primary key first and then can be sorted by secondary keys within the primary key. An example would be a mail list that needs to be sorted in zip code order, with the names in alphabetical order within each zip code. The zip-code is the primary key and the name is the secondary key. Once data are in order, it can be accessed by various means, including the sequential search and the binary search. These techniques were presented in Chapter 9.

There are many different techniques of sorting. Appendix B provides the algorithm and flowchart for three techniques, including the selection exchange sort, the bubble sort, and the shell sort. In this chapter we explain how these three techniques work, along with showing the algorithm and the flowchart. Other popular sorting techniques include the quick sort and the heap sort. The best sorting method is determined by how large the array or file is and how close the file is to being in order. Ultimately the best sorting method is determined by the number of comparisons and switches that need to take place.

All sorting techniques require a comparison of two data items with a possibility of a switch. If the sort is in ascending order, the comparison would be to see if the primary key of data 1 is larger than the primary key of data 2. If it is, then data 1 is switched with data 2, and if not, they are left in the same position. The comparisons take place until data are in the required order. If the secondary key is required, the concatenation of the primary key and the secondary key is used as the sort key.

The first technique is the *selection exchange sort.* Figure 10.1 shows the switches made during each pass. The theory is to find the smallest value of the remaining values

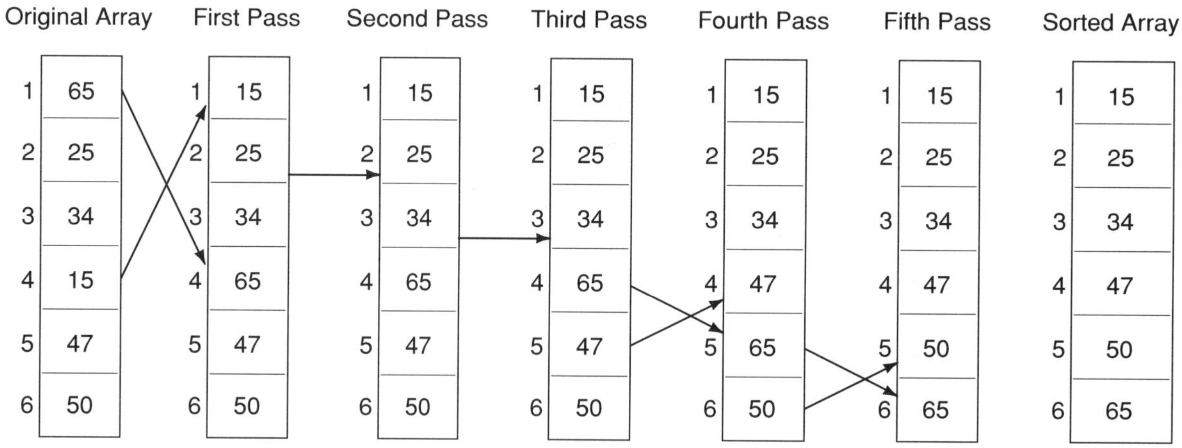

Figure 10.1 Selection Exchange Sort Technique

and switch with the value found in the first position of the remaining elements. During the first pass (first time through the outer loop) the smallest value (15) is switched with the first element (65). During the second pass the smallest of the remaining values (25) remained as the second element (25). During the third pass through the smallest of the remaining values (34) remains as the third element since there was no element found that is smaller. This continues until the last position is in the right order. See Figure 10.1 for all passes. Figure 10.2 shows the algorithm and the flowchart for the selection exchange sort.

Notes on Figure 10.2

The following are notes explaining the circled numbers on the flowchart of Figure 10.2.

1. This loop is set up to start with the first element and continue to the second-to-last element. The last element will be in the correct order when the second-to-last element is in order, because there is nowhere else for the last element to be placed.
2. The initial start value for the minimum value is the value of the lowest element number of the unordered elements.
3. This is the comparison test. It tests to see if this value is less than the previously saved minimum value. If it is, then the element number of the minimum value is set equal to the present element number. If not, then the flow continues to loop back either to make another comparison or to drop out of the loop.
4. This test is to see if the minimum value is in an element other than the smallest element of this segment. If it is, then the two values are swapped; if not, then the elements remain the same.
5. The end of this loop increments the element number.

The next sorting technique we discuss is the *bubble sort.* Figure 10.03 shows the switches made in each pass using the bubble sort. The theory of the bubble sort is to compare each element with the next element. If the element is larger than the next element, the elements are switched. If not, they remain the same. After the first pass, the largest element has "bubbled" its way to the bottom. On the next pass elements 1 through $n - 1$ are considered, because the nth element is the largest. The elements are again compared and the largest is bubbled down to the $n - 1$ element. A flag is set during each pass. If a switch has been made, another pass is made; if a switch has not been made, then data are in order and no more passes are made. In Figure 10.3, 65 is compared to each element and switches are made for each element, since 65 began at the top and needs to be at the bottom. All other elements are bubbled up to make room for 65 in the sixth element. During the second pass, only 15 and 34 need to be switched. All others are either in order or nearly in order. During the third pass 15 and 25 are switched. The value 15 now has bubbled to the top. During the fourth pass there are no switches; the flag has not been set, which indicates that the data are in order and no more passes need to be made. Figure 10.4 shows the algorithm and the flowchart for the bubble sort.

Notes on Figure 10.4

The following are notes explaining the circled numbers on the flowchart of Figure 10.4.

1. The flag is set equal to 1. This primes the loop so the test will pass the first time through.

Algorithm	Flowchart

Selection/Exchange Sort

```
LOOP: I = 1 TO N – 1
    MIN = I
    LOOP: J = I + 1 TO N
        IF A(MIN) > A(J)
        THEN
            MIN = J
    LOOP-END: J
    IF I < MIN
        THEN
            R = A(I)
            A(I) = A(MIN)
            A(MIN) = R
LOOP-END: I
```

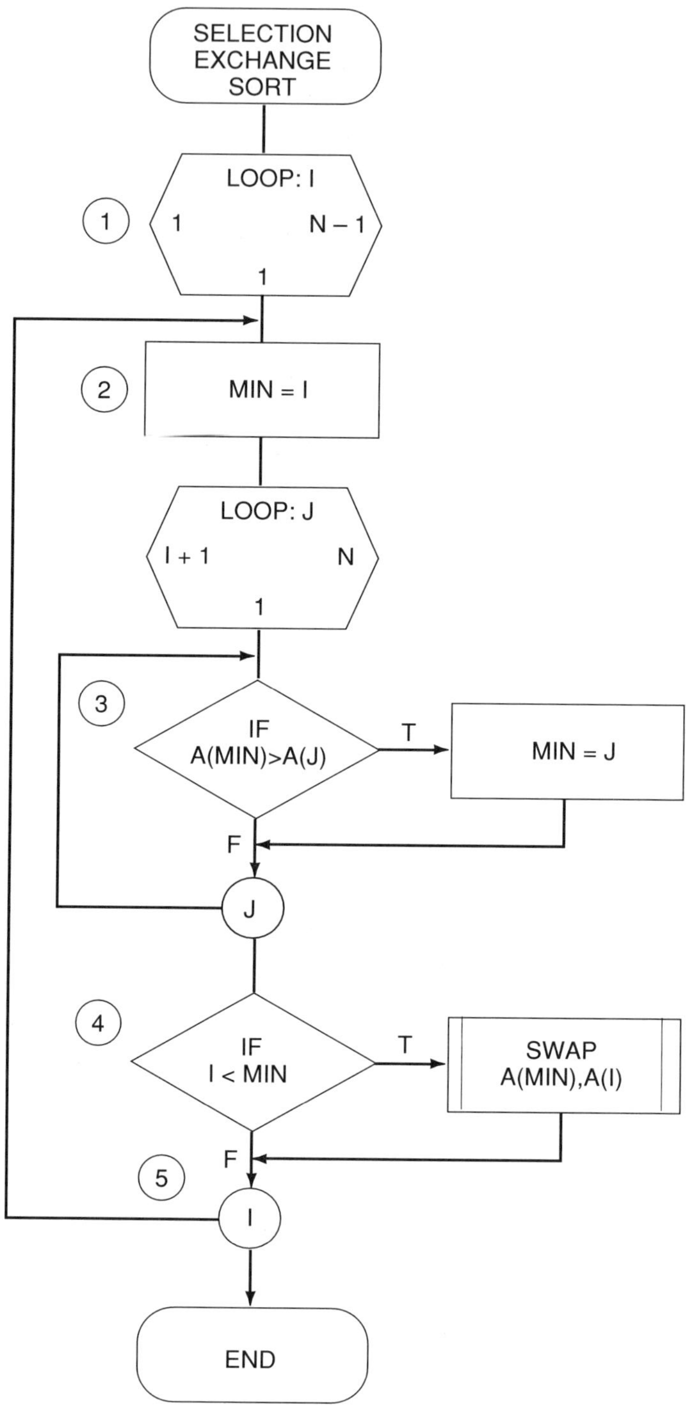

Figure 10.2 The Selection Exchange Sort

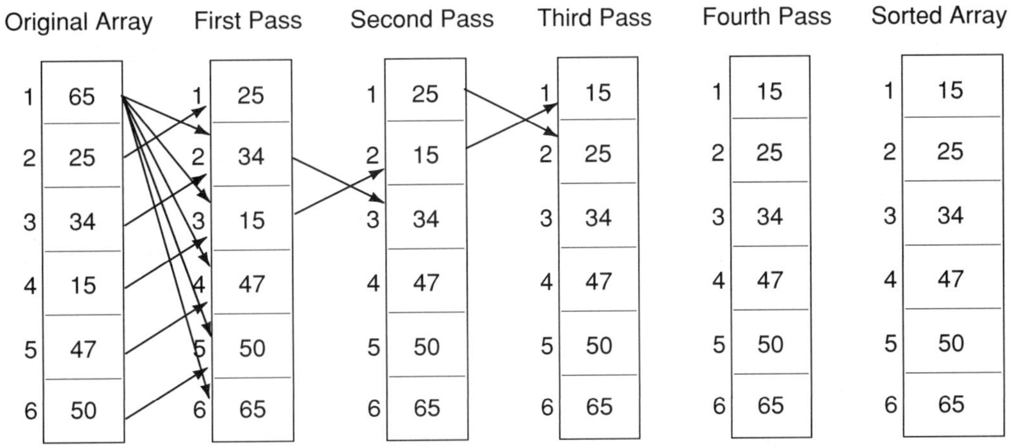

Figure 10.3 Bubble Sort

2. The number of elements being compared is set equal to the number of elements minus 1. Since the comparison is always with one element and the next element, the last element does not need to be tested.
3. The loop is set to continue as long as the flag is set equal to 1. This indicates that data are not in order.
4. The flag is set equal to 0. This says that data are in order until a switch is made and the flag is set equal to 1.
5. A loop is set up to compare the elements.
6. The comparison of the elements is made. When the present element is greater than the next element, the elements are switched and the flag is set equal to 1, indicating the data may not be in order as of yet.
7. The counter is incremented and the loop continues with the next element. If the elements have all been compared, the flow of the program drops out of the loop.
8. The number of elements to be compared is decreased by 1 since the last element of each loop is in the correct order.

The last sort technique to be presented is the *shell sort.* Figure 10.5 shows the switches that have been made in each pass using the shell sort technique. The theory of the shell sort is to compare each element with another element in the data set using a gap to separate the elements. The gap during the first pass is the number of elements divided by 2. The truncated value is used. In Figure 10.5 the gap is 3 for the first pass since there are 6 elements. In the succeeding passes, the new gap is the old gap divided by 2. Again, the truncated value is used. In the second pass, the gap is 1 since the previous gap was 3. When two elements need to be switched, and there are elements a gap above the present element, then elements are compared upward until elements are reached that do not need switching. During the first pass the following comparisons are made:

1. *element 1 to element 4*—a switch is made (there are no elements a gap above element 1 so the next comparison is in order)
2. *element 2 to element 5*—no switches
3. *element 3 to element 6*—no switches

During the second pass the following comparisons are made:

1. *element 1 to element 2*—no switches
2. *element 2 to element 3*—no switches

Algorithm	Flowchart

Algorithm

```
Bubble Sort
1. FLAG = 1
2. E = N – 1
3. ┌ WHILE FLAG = 1
   │  FLAG = 0
   │ ┌ LOOP: J = 1 TO E
   │ │ ┌ IF A(J) > A(J + 1)
   │ │ ├── THEN
   │ │ │    SWAP A(J),A(J + 1)
   │ │ │    FLAG = 1
   │ │ └────
   │ └ LOOP-END: J
   │  E = E – 1
   └ WHILE-END
   EXIT
```

Flowchart

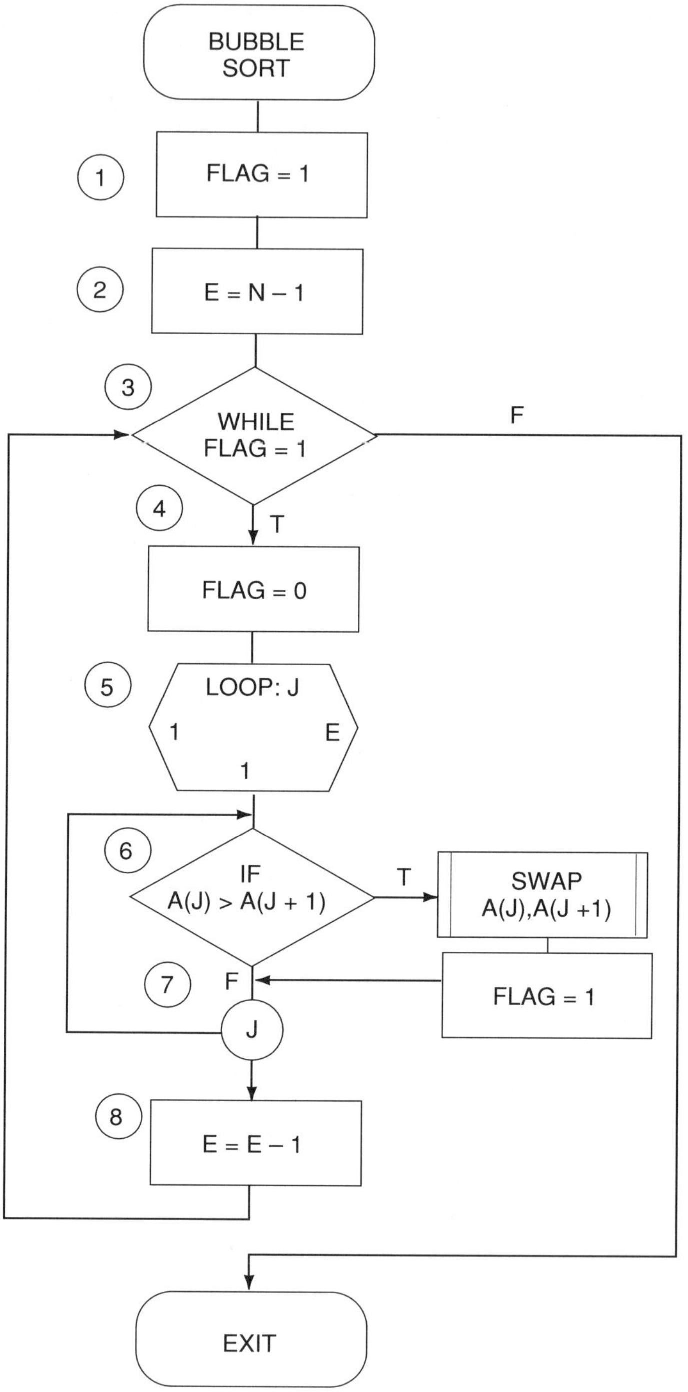

Figure 10.4 The Bubble Sort

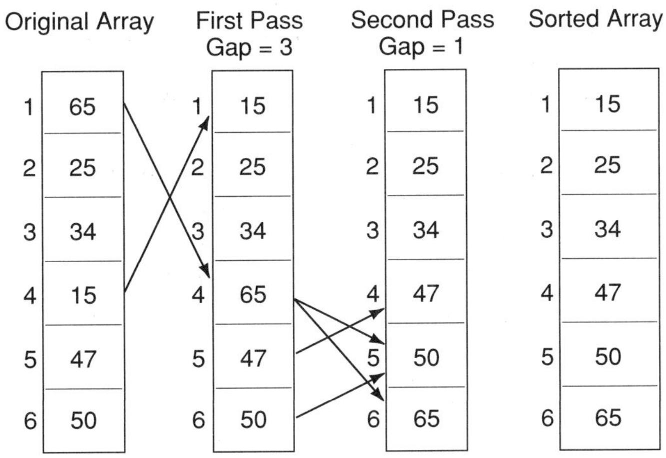

Figure 10.5 Shell Sort

3. *element 3 to element 4*—no switches
4. *element 4 to element 5*—A switch is made and, because there are elements a gap above, the following elements are compared: the new value of element 4 to element 3—no switches; since no switch took place, the elements above the fourth element are assumed to be in order and the comparison continues in order.
5. *element 5 to element 6*—A switch is made, and other comparisons are made as above in 4.

At this time the data are in order. Figure 10.6 shows the algorithm and the flowchart for the shell sort.

Notes on Figure 10.6

The following are notes explaining the circled numbers on the flowchart of Figure 10.6.

1. The gap is set to the truncated value of the number of elements divided by 2.
2. A loop is set up to continue while the gap is greater than zero.
3. The number of elements to be compared with another element is set equal to the number of elements minus the gap.
4. A loop is set up to start at the first element and continue to the element number set in note 3.
5. The comparison is made. If the element is greater than the element a gap below, then a switch needs to take place; if not, then the flow continues to the end of the loop.
6. The element number is incremented and the flow returns to the loop set up in note 4.
7. The gap is set equal to the truncated value of the last gap divided by 2. The flow then returns to the loop set in note 2.
8. L is set equal to the element number. This allows the comparisons with elements above the present element.
9. The FLAG is set equal to TRUE to prime the loop so flow will continue through the loop at least once.

Algorithm	Flowchart

Shell Sort

```
1.   G = INT(N/2)
2.   WHILE G > 0
       M = N - G
       LOOP: J = 1 TO M
         IF A(J) > A(J + G)
         THEN
           L = J
           FLAG = TRUE
           WHILE FLAG
             SWAP A(L), A(L + G)
             L = L - G
             IF L > = 1
               THEN
                 IF A(L) < = A(L + G)
                   THEN
                     FLAG = FALSE
                   ELSE
                     CONTINUE
               ELSE
                 FLAG = FALSE
           WHILE-END
       LOOPEND: J
       G = INT(G/2)
     WHILE-END
3.   EXIT
```

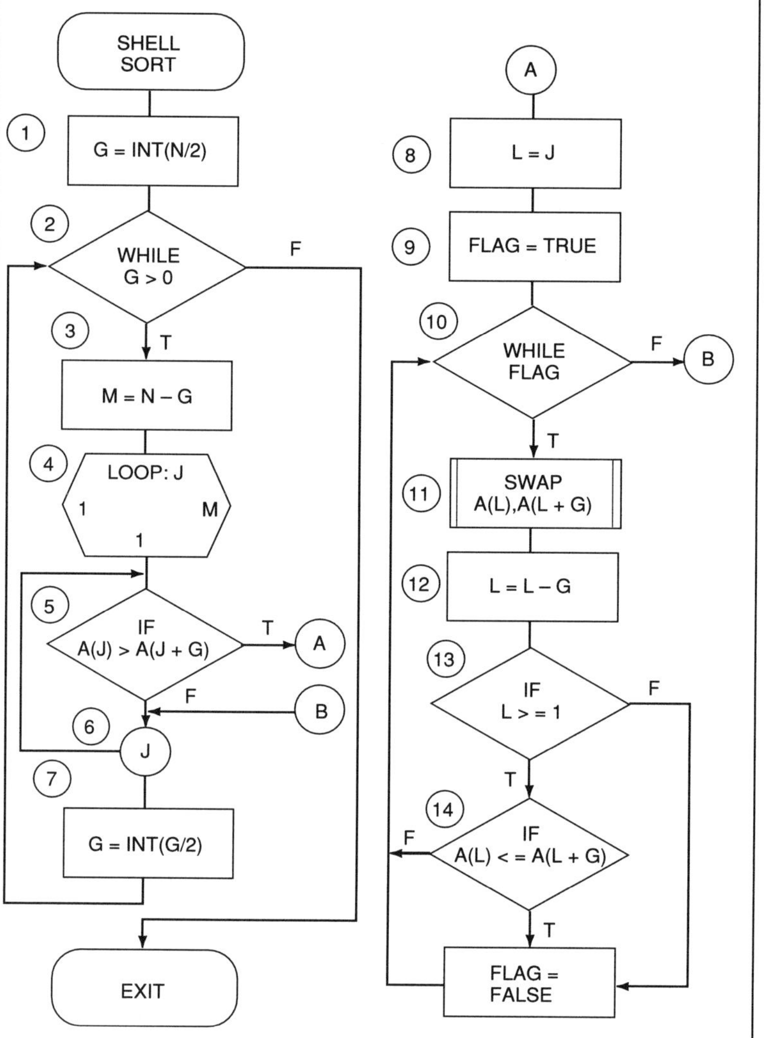

Figure 10.6 The Shell Sort

10. A loop is set up to continue as long as FLAG is TRUE. FLAG will be set equal to false when a switch is not necessary.
11. The switch is made.
12. L is set equal to the previous value of L minus the gap. This allows the checking to be made with elements above the present element.
13. This checks to see if there are any more elements to be compared.
14. If the elements need to be switched, the flow continues through the loop. If not, the FLAG is set to FALSE to stop the loop.

Stacks

A **stack** is a list of numbers, such as an array of numbers, to which all additions are at one end and all deletions are at the same end. This is a last-in, first-out procedure. A stack is like a stack of plates, the last one added on the top is the first one to be used. When a value (X) is added to the stack it is called **pushing the stack.** When a value (X) is used from the stack it is called **popping the stack.** Once a number is used, it cannot be used again. The stack has a number, called the *stack pointer,* which points to the last value pushed and the next value to be popped. When the stack is pushed, the pointer is incremented and the value (X) being pushed is placed in the stack at the element number in the pointer. When the stack is popped, the value in the stack at the element number of the pointer is placed in X, and the pointer is decremented. Figure 10.7 shows a stack to which the following procedures have been implemented:

PUSH 3
PUSH 4
PUSH 7
POP X
POP X
PUSH 6

Notes on Figure 10.8

Figure 10.8 shows the algorithm and flowchart to PUSH the stack and to POP the stack. The following are notes explaining the circled numbers on the two flowcharts:

1. The ERROR flag is set to 0.
2. When the pointer is equal to the maximum number of elements in the stack, no more values can be pushed. An error message is printed, and the ERROR flag is set equal to 1.
3. When the pointer is not equal to the maximum number of elements, the pointer is incremented, and X is placed in the stack at the element number that is equal to the pointer.

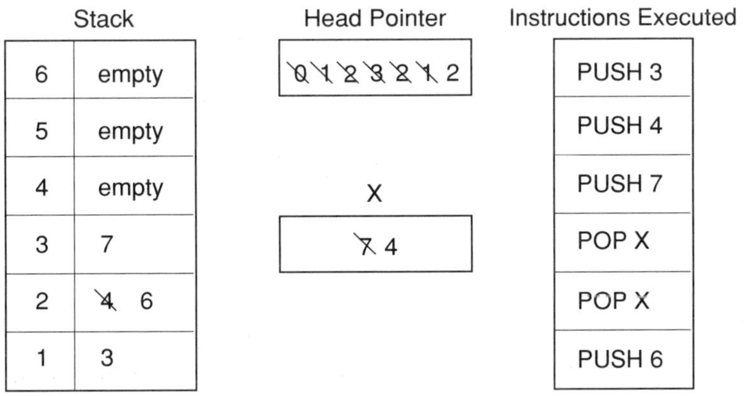

Figure 10.7 Example of a Stack that Has Been Pushed and Popped

Algorithm	Flowchart

```
PUSH (X)
1. ERROR = 0
2. IF POINTER = MAX
   THEN
      PRINT "ERROR: STACK FULL"
      ERROR = 1
   ELSE
      POINTER = POINTER + 1
      STACK(POINTER) = X
3. EXIT
```

DEFINITIONS:
MAX = Maximum elements in stack
POINTER = Pointer to last element to be pushed or next element to be popped
STACK = Stack array
X = Value to be PUSHED or POPPED

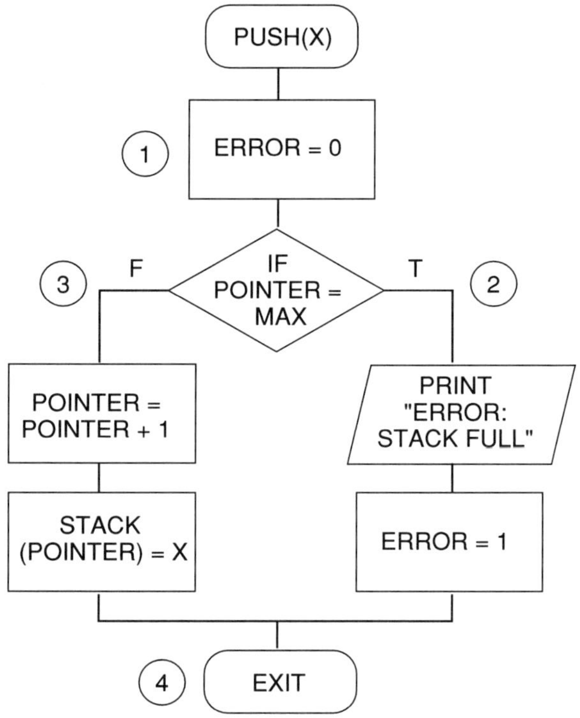


```
POP (X)
1. ERROR = 0
2. IF POINTER = 0
   THEN
      PRINT "ERROR: EMPTY STACK"
      ERROR = 2
   ELSE
      X = STACK (POINTER)
      POINTER = POINTER –1
3. EXIT
```

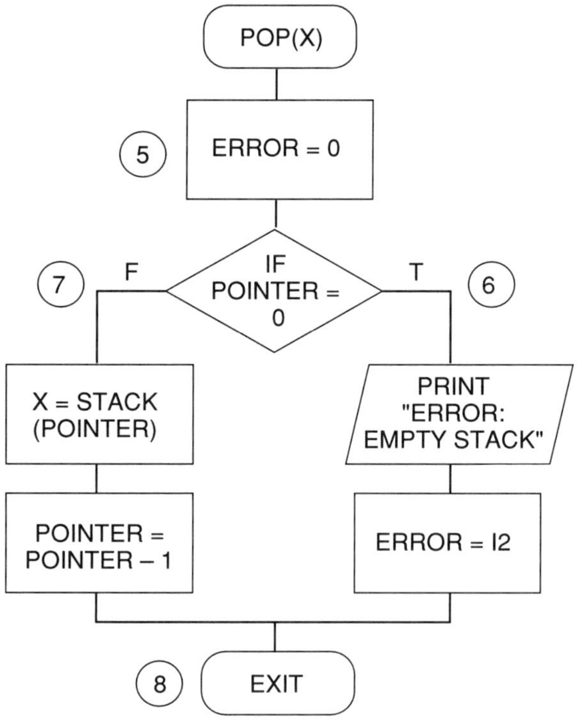

Figure 10.8 Algorithm and Flowchart to PUSH and POP a Stack

4. The module is exited.
5. The ERROR flag is set to 0.
6. When the pointer is equal to 0, there are no values in the stack to be popped. An error message is printed, and the ERROR flag is set equal to 2.
7. When the pointer is greater than 0, X is set equal to the value of the element of the stack that has the element number of the pointer. The pointer is then decremented.
8. The module is exited.

Linked Lists

A **linked list** is a file in which each record points to its successor, except for the last record, which has an end-of-list indicator. The method of pointing to the next record is a field, which contains the record number of the next record in order. This is called the *linking field,* since the value in this field links the records in proper order. Figure 10.9 shows a file that is a linked list. The file must contain a key field along with a corresponding link field. Notice that the link field of the first record points to the second record, which is the next to be processed. The link field of the second record points to the third record, which is the third record to be processed. The linking continues through the last record. The last record contains a 0, which indicates the last record in order.

The advantage of a linked list is in the addition and deletion process. A file does not have to be physically rewritten to add and delete records. When a record is deleted, it is put into an empty list. The additions are placed in the records that have been deleted or at the end if there are no empty records. An empty records linked list is kept in the link field to locate the records that are available in which to place the additions.

If there are no empty records, the addition is placed at the bottom of the file. Figure 10.10 shows a file that has had additions and deletions. Notice the two linked lists—the data linked list is processed in the following order: 2, 1, 3, 7, 8, 6. The empty list is as follows: 4, 5. The data list starts at 2, which is designated by the LISTPOINTER. The empty list starts at 4, which is designated by the empty pointer. The 0 indicates the end of the list. Notice there is a 0 in the link field for the end of each list.

Record No.	Key	Other Data	Link
1	5		2
2	10		3
3	17		4
4	25		5
5	30		6
6	35		0

LISTPOINTER: 1

EMPTYPOINTER: 0

0 indicates end of list.

Figure 10.9 Example of an Initially Created Linked List

Record No.	Key	Other Data	Link
1	15		3
2	3		1
3	17		7
4	14		5
5	30		0
6	35		0
7	25		8
8	28		6

LISTPOINTER: 2

EMPTYPOINTER: 4

0 indicates end of list.

Figure 10.10 Example of a Linked List After Multiple Adds and Deletions

Notes on Figure 10.11

Figure 10.11 shows the algorithm and flowchart to create a linked list. The following are notes explaining the circled numbers for this figure.

1. Process a READ module, which opens the data file, enters all records for the file, and counts the number of records (N). The file must have a key and an extra field for the link field.
2. The file is sorted in key order.
3. The HEADPOINTER is set to 1, since the first record would be the first record in order.
4. A loop is set up to process all records in order to add the correct link number in the link field. The loop starts with the first record and continues to the next to the last record, since the last record must have a 0 to indicate the end of the list.
5. A record is read. The LINK field is set equal to the record + 1, which would be the next record in order. The record is written to the file. The next record is then processed.
6. The last record is read. The LINK field is set equal to 0. The record is written to the file.
7. The POINTER file is opened. The HEADPOINTER, EMPTYPOINTER, and the number of records (N) is written to this file. ALL files are then closed.
8. The Create module is completed.

Notes on Figure 10.12

Figure 10.12a–k shows the structure chart, the algorithms, and the flowcharts for a program that processes and updates a file using a linked list technique. Figure 10.12a shows the structure chart for this program. The following are the notes explaining the circled numbers in Figure 10.12b–k.

1. The control module for the LINKED LIST program.
2. Process the INIT module.
3. This instruction primes the loop so the condition will be true the first time through the loop.

Algorithm	Flowchart

CREATE
1. PROCESS READ
2. PROCESS SORT
3. HEADPOINTER = 1
4. EMPTYPOINTER = 0
5. LOOP: R = 1 TO N – 1
   READ 1, RECORD (R)
   LINK = R + 1
   WRITE 1, RECORD (R)
   LOOP-END
6. READ 1, RECORD (N)
7. LINK = 0
8. WRITE 1, RECORD (N)
9. OPEN 2, POINTERS
10. WRITE 2, HEADPOINTER,
    EMPTYPOINTER, N
11. CLOSE ALL FILES
12. EXIT

DEFINITIONS:

HEADPOINTER = Record number of first record in ordered list
R = Current record
Link = Linked field

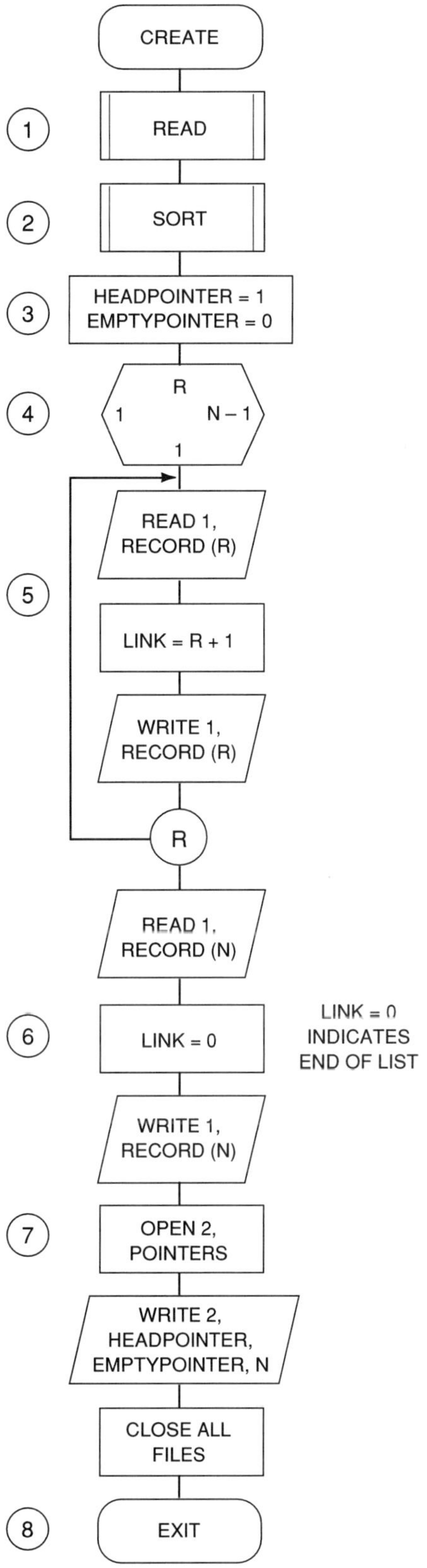

Figure 10.11 Algorithm and Flowchart to Create a Linked List

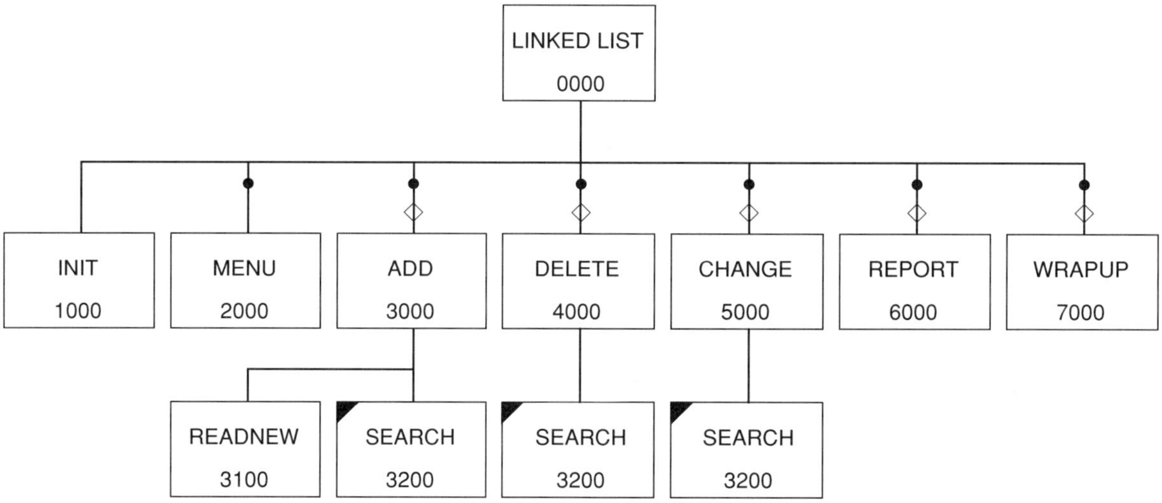

Figure 10.12a Structure Chart for Processing and Updating a Linked List

4. A loop is set up to continue to process or update the file until Q is entered for the choice in the MENU module.
5. The MENU module is processed, which prints the menu and allows the user to enter a value for CHOICE.
6. One of the modules is processed, according to the value of CHOICE.
7. The program is completed.
8. The INIT module initializes values for the program.
9. The files are opened.
10. The values of HEADPOINTER, EMPTYPOINTER, and N are read.
11. The POINTER file is closed, which ends the INIT module.
12. The MENU module prints the menu and allows the user to enter a value for CHOICE.
13. The screen is cleared and the menu is printed on the screen.
14. A loop is set up to make sure a correct value is entered for CHOICE. When a correct value is entered the MENU module is completed.
15. The ADD module allows the user to add a record to the linked list.
16. The new record number (NR) is set equal to the empty pointer. The data for a new record is entered through processing the READNEW module.
17. The search for the records that precede and succeed the new record is executed.
18. A test is made to see if there is a duplicate record. If there is, a message is printed and the ADD module is exited.
19. If there is no duplicate record, a test is made to see if there is an empty record in which to place the new record. If there is no empty record, a record is appended to the end of the file. The number of records is incremented by 1 and the new record number (NR) is set equal to the last record number, which is the total number of records.
20. If there is an empty record, the empty record is read and the EMPTYPOINTER is set equal to the LINK field value.
21. A test is made to see if the new record should be placed before the first record in order. If so, the LINK field is set equal to the HEADPOINTER, the HEADPOINTER is set equal to the new record number (NR), and the record is written to the file.

Algorithm	Flowchart

```
LINKED LIST
  1. PROCESS INIT
  2. CHOICE = "A"
  3. WHILE CHOICE < > "Q"
     PROCESS MENU
     CASE OF CHOICE
     "A": PROCESS ADD
     "D": PROCESS DELETE
     "C": PROCESS CHANGE
     "R": PROCESS REPORT
     "Q": PROCESS QUIT
     CASE-END
     WHILE-END
  4. END
```

DEFINITIONS:
R = Present record
HEADPOINTER = First ordered record
EMPTYPOINTER = First empty record
CHOICE = Menu selection
S = Error flag
  = 1: Record found
  = 2: Record not found
LINK = Value of link field
KEY = Value of key field
SKEY = Search key
PR = Previous record

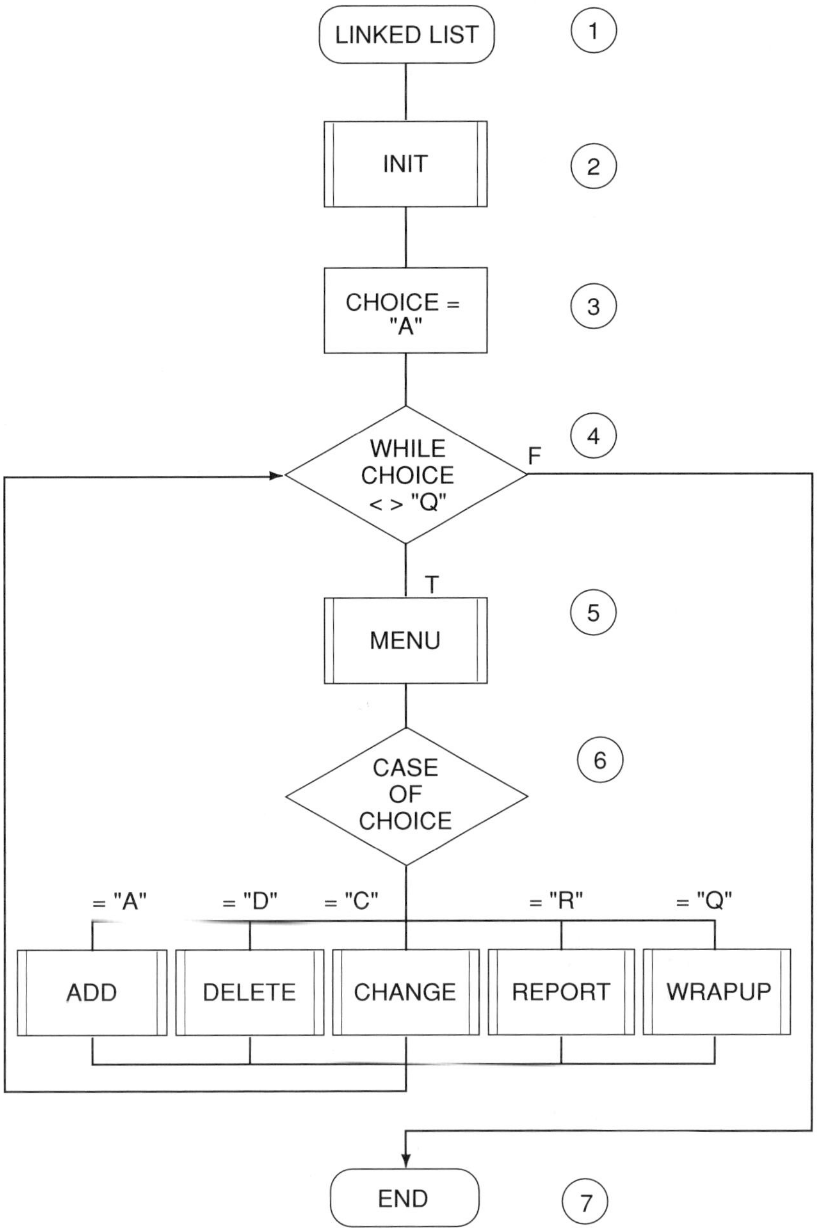

Figure 10.12b Algorithm and Flowchart for Processing and Updating a Linked List

22. If not, the link field of the previous record and the new record need to be updated. To do this, the new record is written to the file and the previous record is read. The LINK field value is saved and the LINK field is set equal to the new record number (NR). The previous record is then written to the file and the new record is read. The LINK field of the new record is set equal to the saved link value from the previous record and the new record is written to the file. This completes the ADD module.

Algorithm	Flowchart
INIT 1. OPEN 1, DATAFILE 2. OPEN 2, POINTERFILE 3. READ HEADPOINTER 4. READ EMPTYPOINTER 5. CLOSE 2 6. EXIT	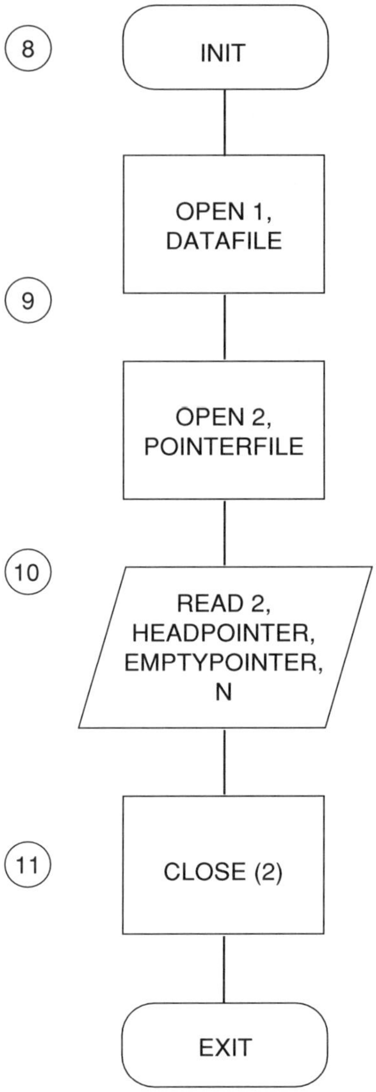

Figure 10.12c

Algorithm	Flowchart
MENU 1. CLEAR SCREEN 2. PRINT MENU 3. CHOICE = "Z" 4. WHILE CHOICE < > "A" OR CHOICE < > "D" OR CHOICE < > "R" OR CHOICE < > "C" OR CHOICE < > "Q" ENTER CHOICE WHILE-END 5. EXIT	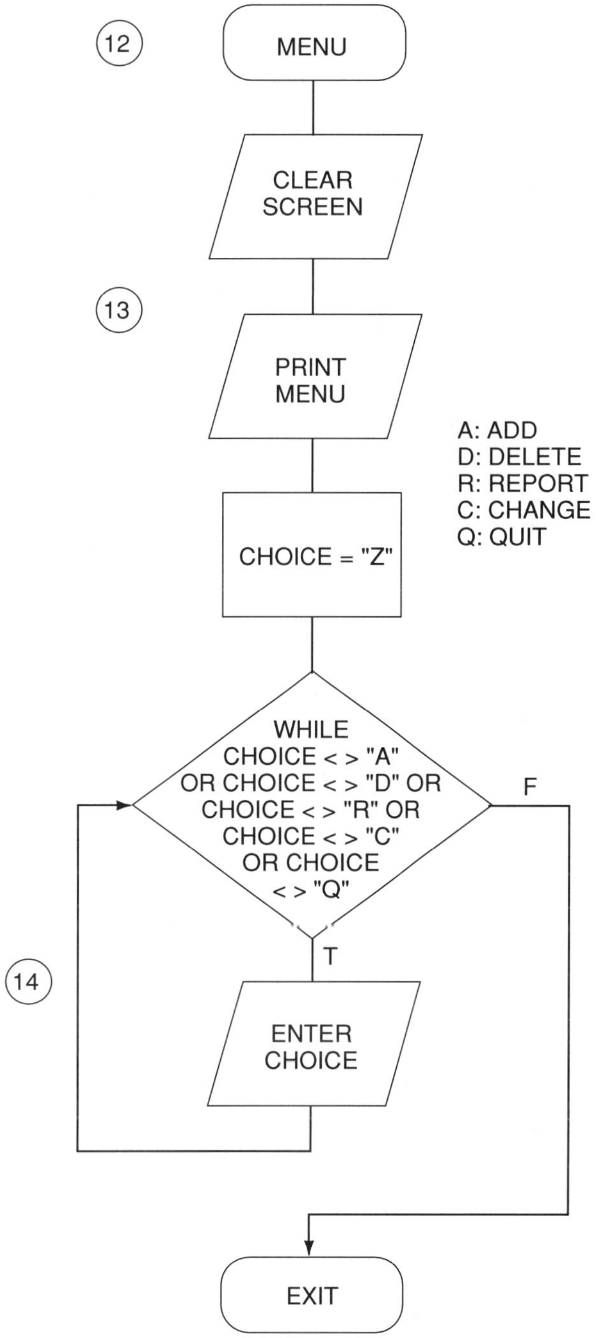

Figure 10.12d

Algorithm	Flowchart
see below	see below

Algorithm

```
ADD
 1.  NR = EMPTYPOINTER
 2.  PROCESS READNEW
 3.  PROCESS SEARCH
 4.┌─ IF S = 1
  ├─ THEN
  │    PRINT "DUPLICATE RECORD"
  ├─ ELSE
  │ ┌IF NR = 0
  │ ├── THEN
  │ │     APPEND RECORD
  │ │     N = N + 1
  │ │     NR = N
  │ ├── ELSE
  │ └──── READ 1, RECORD (NR)
  │       EMPTYPOINTER = LINK
  │┌IF PR = 0
  │├──── THEN
  ││      LINK = HEADPOINTER
  ││      HEADPOINTER = NR
  ││      WRITE 1,  RECORD (NR)
  │├──── ELSE
  ││      WRITE 1,  RECORD (NR)
  ││      READ 1,  RECORD (PR)
  ││      SAVELINK = LINK
  ││      LINK = NR
  ││      WRITE 1,  RECORD (PR)
  ││      READ 1,  RECORD (NR)
  ││      LINK = SAVELINK
  │└────  WRITE 1,  RECORD (NR)
  └──────────
 5.  EXIT
```

Flowchart

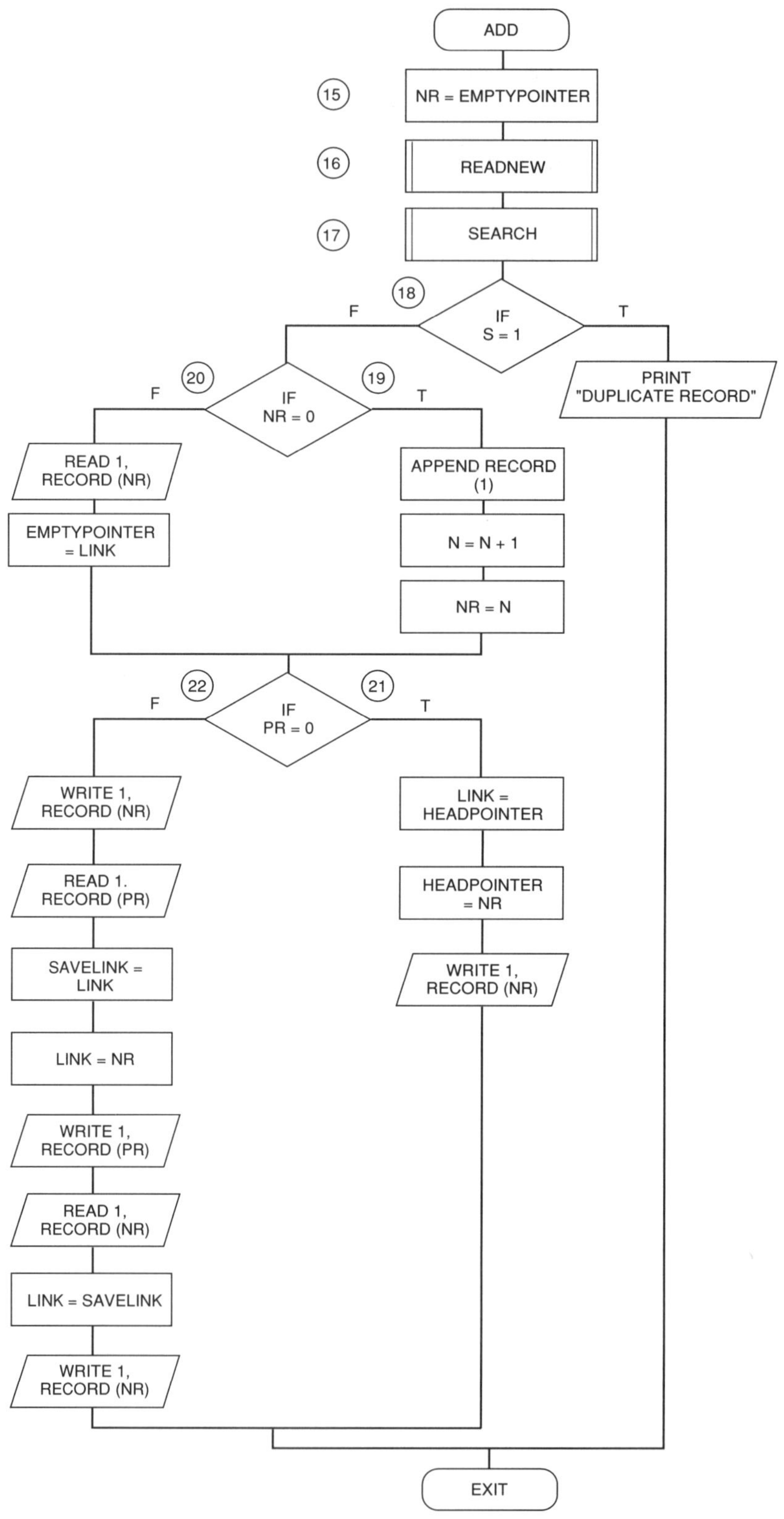

Figure 10.12e

Algorithm	Flowchart
READNEW 1. READ NEW RECORD DATA 2. SKEY = NRKEY 3. EXIT	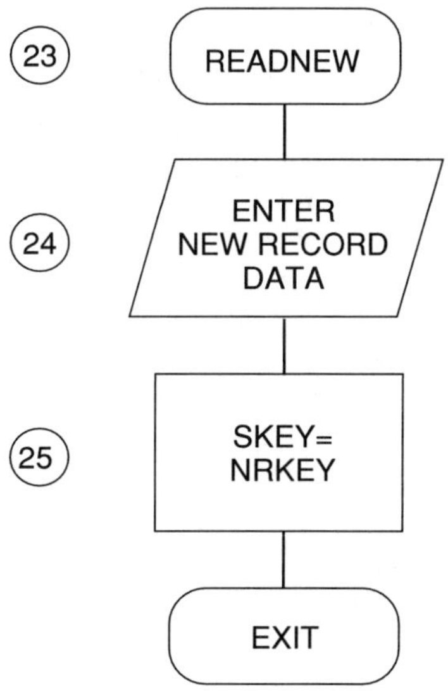

Figure 10.12f

Algorithm	Flowchart
See algorithm below	See flowchart below

Algorithm

```
SEARCH
  1. R = HEADPOINTER
  2. S = 0
  3. PR = 0
  4. WHILE S = 0
       READ 1, RECORD(R)
       IF KEY = SKEY
         THEN
           S = 1
         ELSE
           IF KEY <SKEY
             THEN
               PR = R
               IF LINK = 0
                 THEN
                   R = 0
                   S = 2
                 ELSE
                   R = LINK
             ELSE
               S = 2
  5. EXIT
```

Flowchart

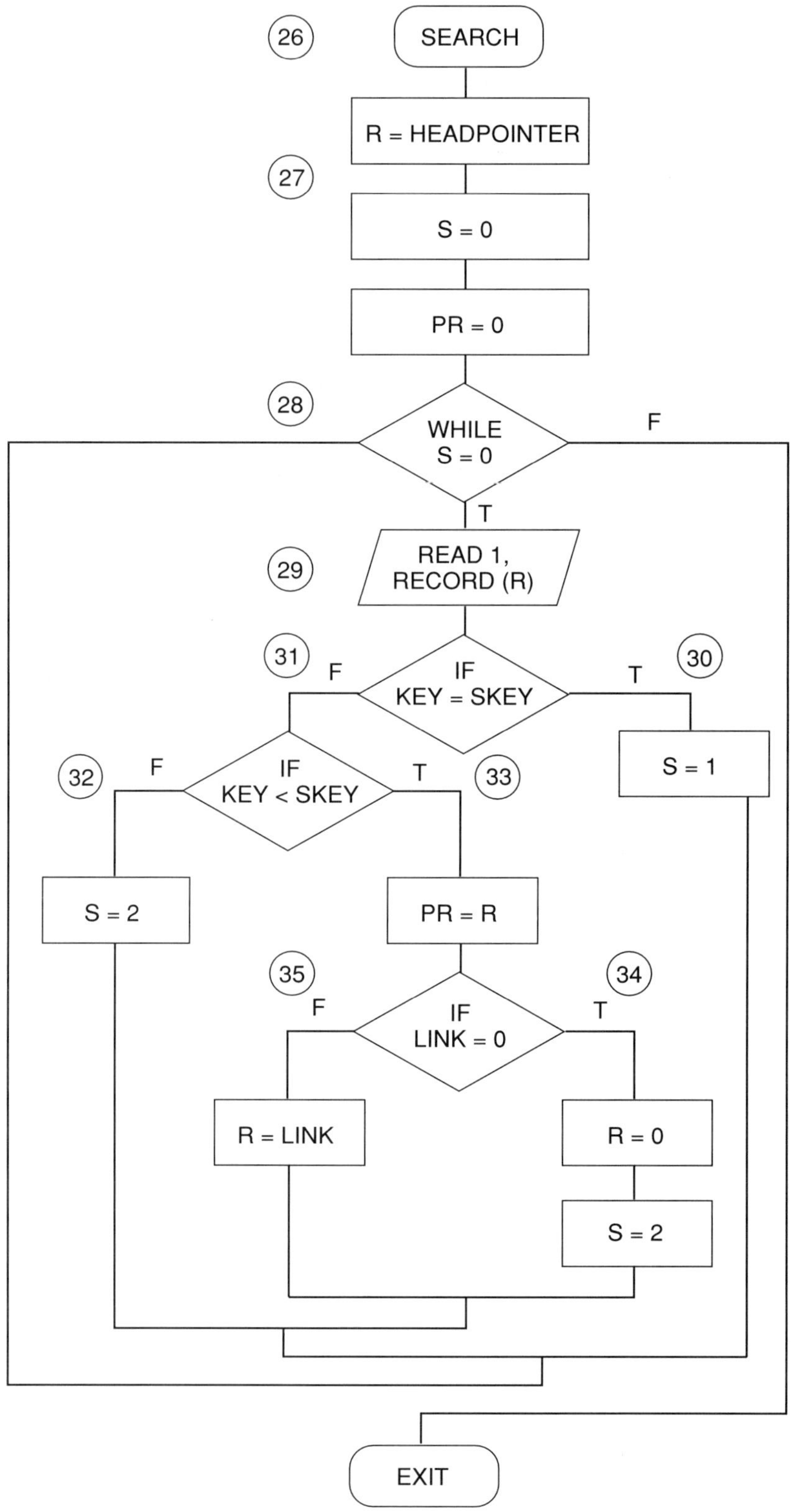

Figure 10.12g

Algorithm	Flowchart

Algorithm

```
DELETE
 1. ENTER SKEY
 2. PROCESS SEARCH
 3.── IF S = 2
   ── THEN
       PRINT "RECORD NOT FOUND"
   ── ELSE
     ─ IF PR = 0
       ─ THEN
           HEADPOINTER = LINK
       ─ ELSE
           SAVELINK = LINK
           READ 1, RECORD (PR)
           LINK = SAVELINK
           WRITE 1, RECORD (PR)
           READ 1, RECORD (R)

     ─ IF EMPTYPOINTER = 0
       ── THEN
           EMPTYPOINTER = R
           LINK = 0
       ── ELSE
           READ 1, RECORD
             (EMPTYPOINTER)
           SAVELINK = LINK
           LINK = R
           WRITE 1, RECORD
             (EMPTYPOINTER)
           READ 1, RECORD (R)
           LINK = SAVELINK
 4. EXIT
```

Flowchart

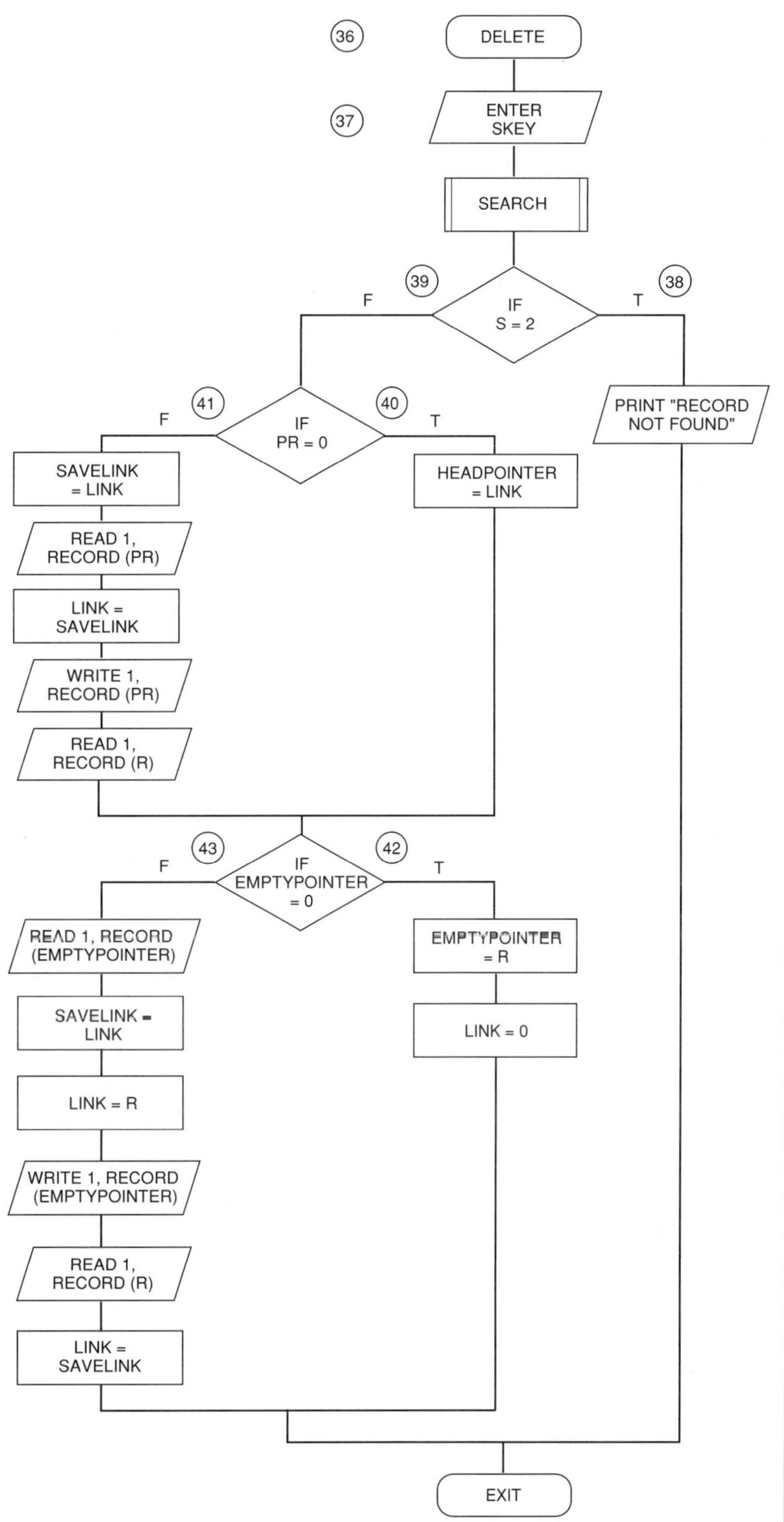

Figure 10.12h

Algorithm	Flowchart

Algorithm

```
CHANGE
1.  ENTER SKEY
2.  PROCESS SEARCH
3.┌─IF S = 2
  ├── THEN
  │      PRINT "RECORD NOT FOUND"
  ├── ELSE
  │      CHANGE RECORD (R) DATA
  │      WRITE 1, RECORD (R)
  └──────
4.  EXIT
```

Flowchart

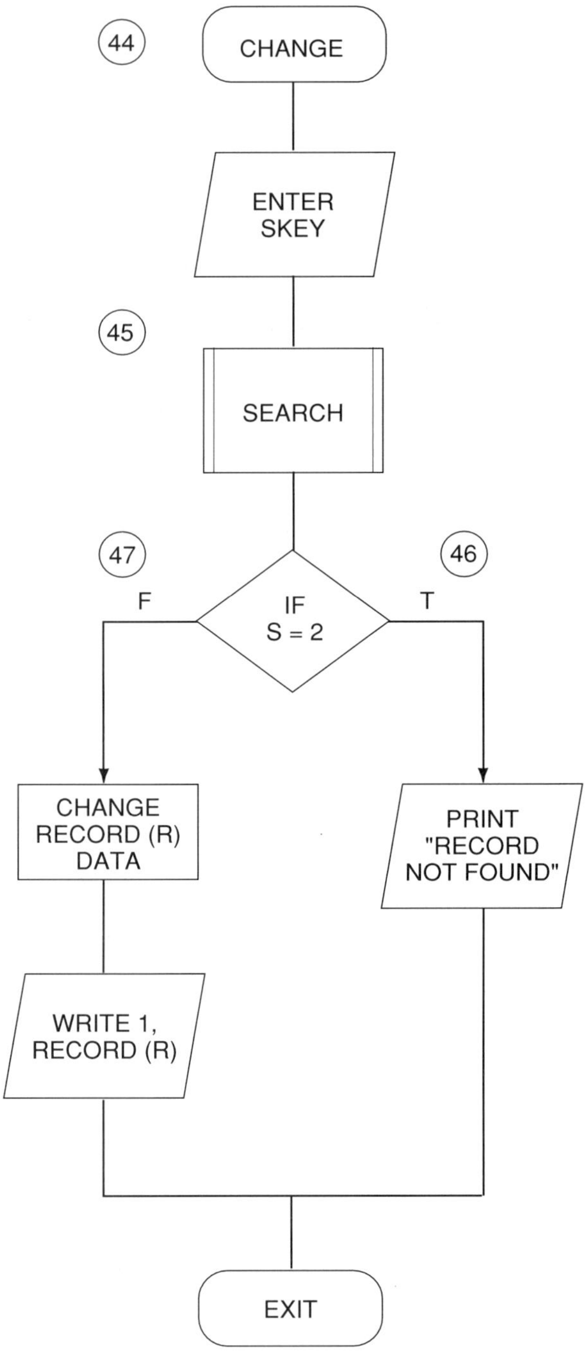

Figure 10.12i

Algorithm	Flowchart
REPORT 1. R = HEADPOINTER 2. WHILE R < > 0 READ 1, RECORD(R) PRINT RECORD(R) R = LINK WHILE-END 3. EXIT	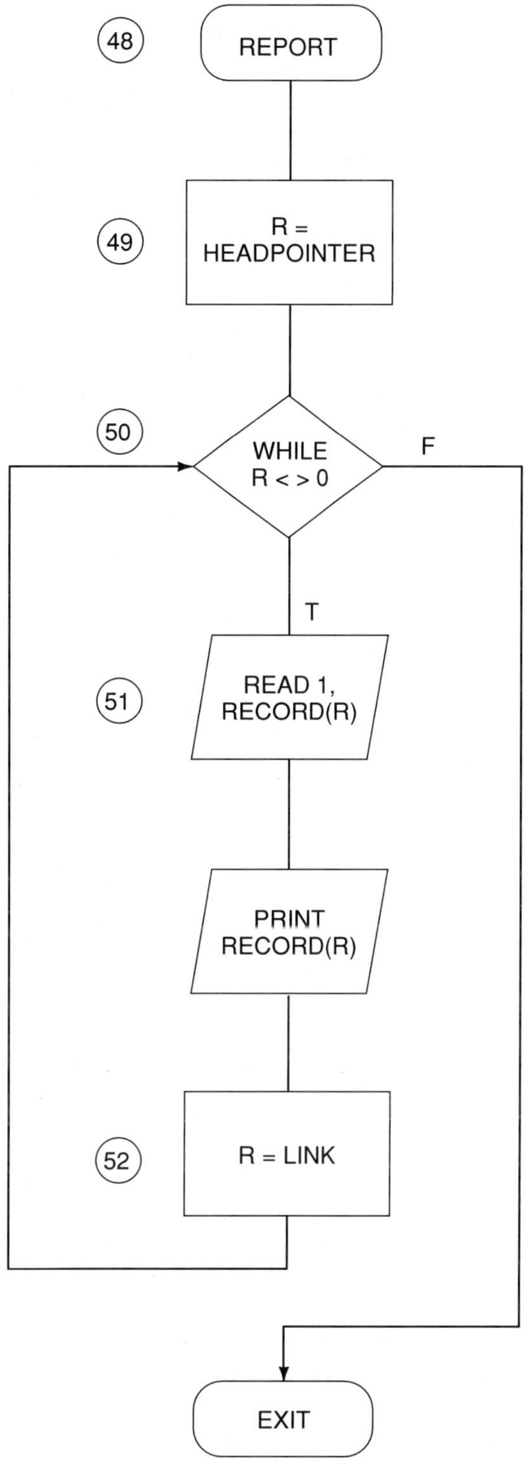

Figure 10.12j

Algorithm

WRAPUP
1. OPEN 2, POINTERS
2. WRITE 2, HEADPOINTER, EMPTYPOINTER, N
3. CLOSE ALL FILES
4. PRINT "RUN COMPLETE"
5. EXIT

Flowchart

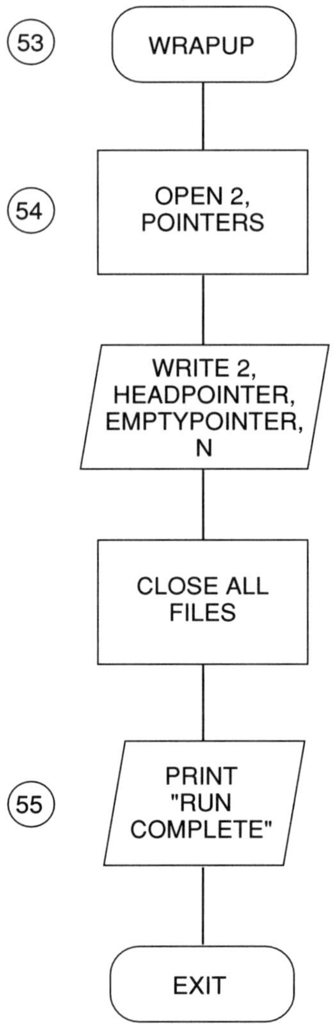

Figure 10.12k

23. The READNEW module enters data for the new record.
24. The new data are entered.
25. The search key (SKEY) is set equal to the new record key. The READNEW module is completed.
26. The SEARCH module searches for a record using a search key value (SKEY).
27. The record number is set equal to the HEADPOINTER. The error flag (S) is set equal to 0, and the previous record number (PR) is set equal to 0.
28. A loop is set up to process the file until a record is found (S=1), or the key of the record is less than the search key (S=2), or the end of the list occurs (S=2).
29. The current record is read.
30. A test is made to see if the record has been found; if it has, S is set equal to 1 and the module is exited.
31. If the record has not been found, a test is made to see if the record key is less than the search key.
32. If it is not, S is set equal to 2 and the module is exited.
33. If it is, the record has not been found yet. The previous record (PR) is set equal to the present record number (R), and the end of the link is checked.
34. If the present record is at the end of the list, S is set equal to 2, R is set equal to 0, and the module is exited.
35. If present record is not at the end of the list, then the present record number (R) is set equal to the LINK field value and the loop continues.
36. The DELETE module allows the user to delete a record.
37. The search key of the record to be deleted is entered and the SEARCH module is processed to find the correct record.
38. A test is made to see if the record was found. If it was not, an error message is printed, and the module is exited.
39. If a record was found, the link fields need to be updated. A test is made to see if the deleted record is the first record in the ordered list.
40. If it is, the HEADPOINTER is set equal to the LINK field value.
41. If not, the LINK field value is saved. The previous record is read. The LINK field value is set equal to the saved link value. The previous record is written to the file, and the record to be deleted is read.
42. Next the empty linked list needs to be updated. A test is made to see if the EMPTYPOINTER is equal to 0. If it is, the EMPTYPOINTER is set equal to the record number to be deleted and the LINK field is set equal to 0.
43. If the EMPTYPOINTER is not equal to 0, the EMPTYPOINTER record is read. The LINK field value is saved. The LINK field is set equal to R. The EMPTYPOINTER record is written to the file. The record to be deleted is read and the LINK field is set equal to the saved link. The record to be deleted is written to the file. The module is exited.
44. The CHANGE module allows the user to change data in a record.
45. A search key of the record to be deleted is entered and the SEARCH module is processed to find the correct record.
46. A test is made to see if the record was found. If it was not, an error message is printed, and the module is exited.
47. If the record was found, the data are changed, and the record is written to the file. The module is then exited.
48. The REPORT module processes a linked list in order.
49. The current record number is set equal to the HEADPOINTER.
50. A loop is set up to continue until the next record to be processed is 0.

51. The record is read, processed, and printed.
52. The current record is set equal to the LINK field value and the loop continues until the value of the link field is 0.
53. The WRAPUP module completes the program.
54. The POINTER file is opened. The values of the HEADPOINTER, EMPTYPOINTER, and N are written to the POINTER file. All files are closed.
55. A message telling the user that the program run is complete is printed to the monitor. The module is exited.

The theory of linked lists can be expanded to include circularly linked lists, doubly linked lists, and multilinked lists. Circularly linked lists have no end. The last record is linked to the first record. This allows a search to continue from the last search, without starting at the first ordered record again. A doubly linked list has two linked fields. One is in ascending order, and the other is in descending order. Multilinked lists have multiple link fields, one for each way the file needs to be ordered.

Binary Trees

A tree structure uses a top down or hierarchical structure for the data. The tree structure looks like an upside down tree found in nature, with the root on top, the branches growing down and the leaves at the bottom. A genealogy chart is an example of a tree structure. Each record is called a node. The top position is called the root. In Figure 10.13, the node with the key value of "G" is the root node. A node at a higher level in the tree is called the *parent.* Referring again to Figure 10.13, the node with the key value of "D" is the parent of the nodes with the key values of "B" and "F". The nodes with the key values of "B" and "F" are called *children* since they are on a lower level in the tree. They are the children of "D". The bottom nodes are called leaf nodes. A branch consists of the chain of nodes from the leaf to the root. A subtree consists of the chain of nodes from a node to the leaves.

A **binary tree** is a tree in which each node has at the most two children. Each record of the file has all of the regular data, including a key, plus two other fields. One holds the pointer to the left child node (called the *left node*) and the other holds the pointer to the right child node (called the *right node*). Figure 10.14 shows the data file that accompanies the tree diagram in Figure 10.13. Note that the root is midpoint at record 7. The left pointer for the root node is 4, and the right pointer is 11. These are shown as the children

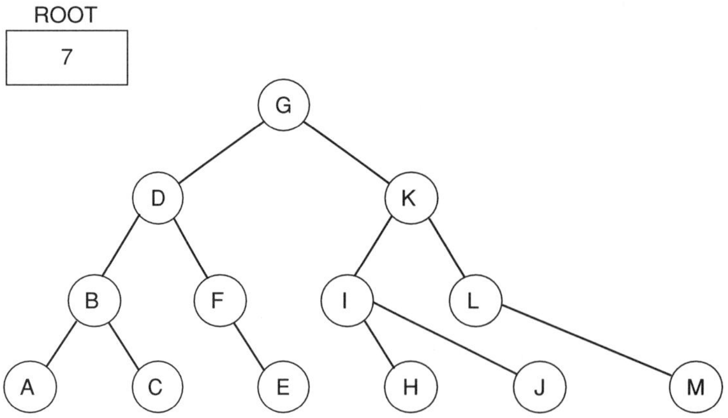

Figure 10.13 An Example of a Binary Tree

Record	Key	Data	Left Pointer	Right Pointer
1	A		*	*
2	B		1	3
3	C		*	*
4	D		2	6
5	E		*	*
6	F		5	*
7	G		4	11
8	H		*	*
9	I		8	10
10	J		*	*
11	K		9	12
12	L		*	13
13	M		*	*

Figure 10.14 File for Binary Tree in Figure 14.13

nodes of the root node in the tree diagram. The binary tree is in order when the left node is less than the current node and the right node is greater than the current node. Note on Figure 10.13 that this is always true.

Notes on Figure 10.15

Figure 10.15 shows the algorithm and the flowchart to create a binary tree. The following are the notes explaining the circled numbers on the flowchart for this procedure.

1. The CREATE module **creates** a data file with two pointer fields—the left pointer (pointer to the left node) and the right pointer (pointer to the right node).
2. Read the data for the file and count the number of records. Sort the file according to the key field.
3. Set the initial value of the lower bound (LB) to 1 and the upper bound (UB) to the number of records in the file (N).
4. Set the current node (CNODE) to the whole number average of the lower bound and the upper bound. This is an integer division and therefore always rounds down.
5. The root node (ROOT) is set to the current node.
6. The node counter (C) is set equal to 0.
7. A loop is set up to continue to process the nodes as long as the node counter is less than the total records in the file.
8. The node counter is incremented.
9. The current node is read.
10. A test is made to see if the current node has a left child. If it does, the left pointer is set equal to the integer average of the lower bound and the current node minus 1. If it does not, the left pointer is set equal to 0, which indicates there are no more left nodes.

Algorithm	Flowchart

```
CREATE
  1. PROCESS READ
  2. PROCESS SORT
  3. LB = 1
  4. UB = N
  5. CNODE = (LB + UB)\ 2
  6. ROOT = CNODE
  7. C = 0
  8. WHILE C < N
       C = C + 1
       READ 1,  RECORD (CNODE)
     IF LB < = CNODE – 1
       THEN
         LPTR = RND((LB + CNODE –1)/2)
       ELSE
         LPTR = 0
     IF UB > = CNODE + 1
       THEN
         RPTR = RND((CNODE + 1 + UB)/2)
       ELSE
         RPTR = 0
     WRITE 1,  RECORD (CNODE)
     IF LPTR < > 0
       THEN
         IF RPTR = 0
           THEN
             CONTINUE
           ELSE
             PUSH RPTR
             PUSH CNODE + 1
             PUSH UB
         UB = CNODE –1
         CNODE = LPTR
     ELSE
         IF RPTR < > 0
           THEN
             LB = CNODE + 1
             CNODE = RPTR
       ELSE
         IF POINTER = 0
           THEN
             C = N
           ELSE
             POP UB
             POP LB
             POP CNODE
   WHILE-END
 9. OPEN 2, ROOT
10. WRITE 2, ROOT
11. CLOSE FILES
12. EXIT
```

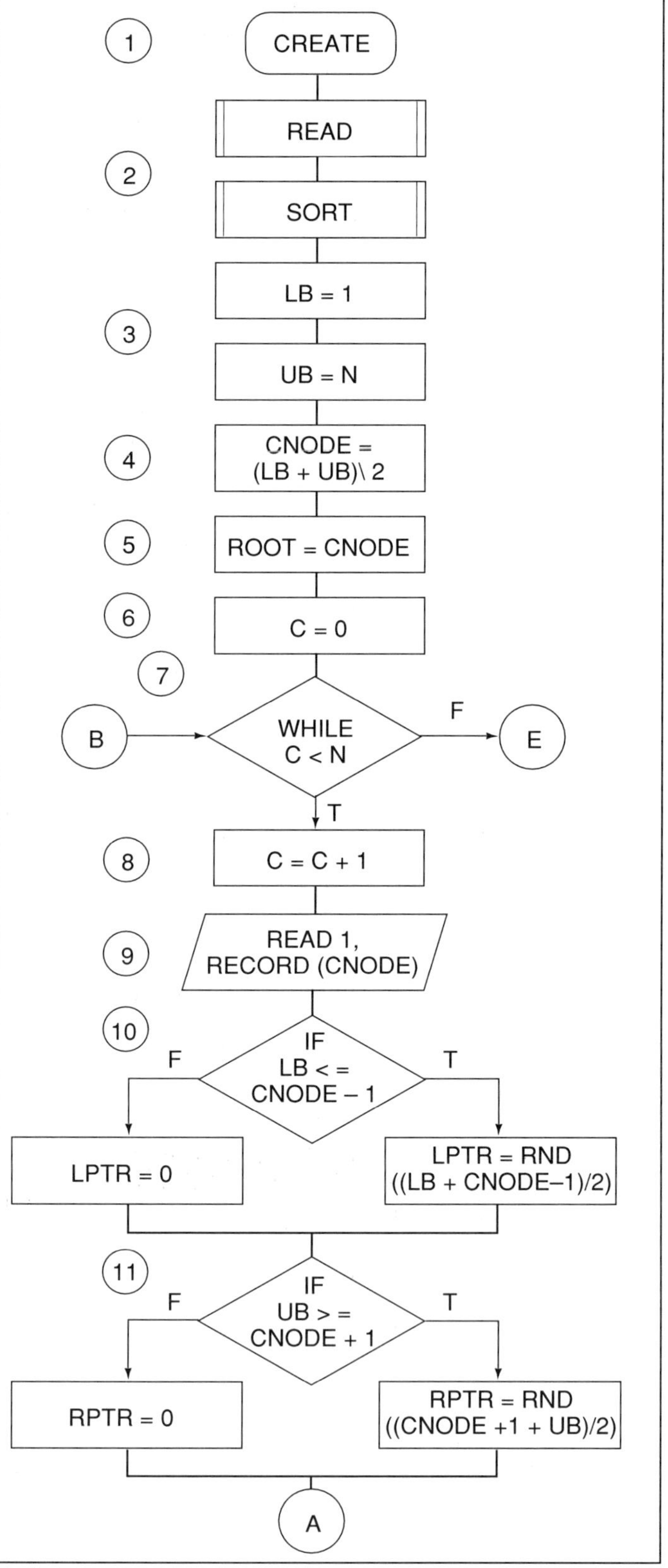

Figure 10.15 Algorithm and Flowchart to Create a Binary Tree (*continued on page 245*)

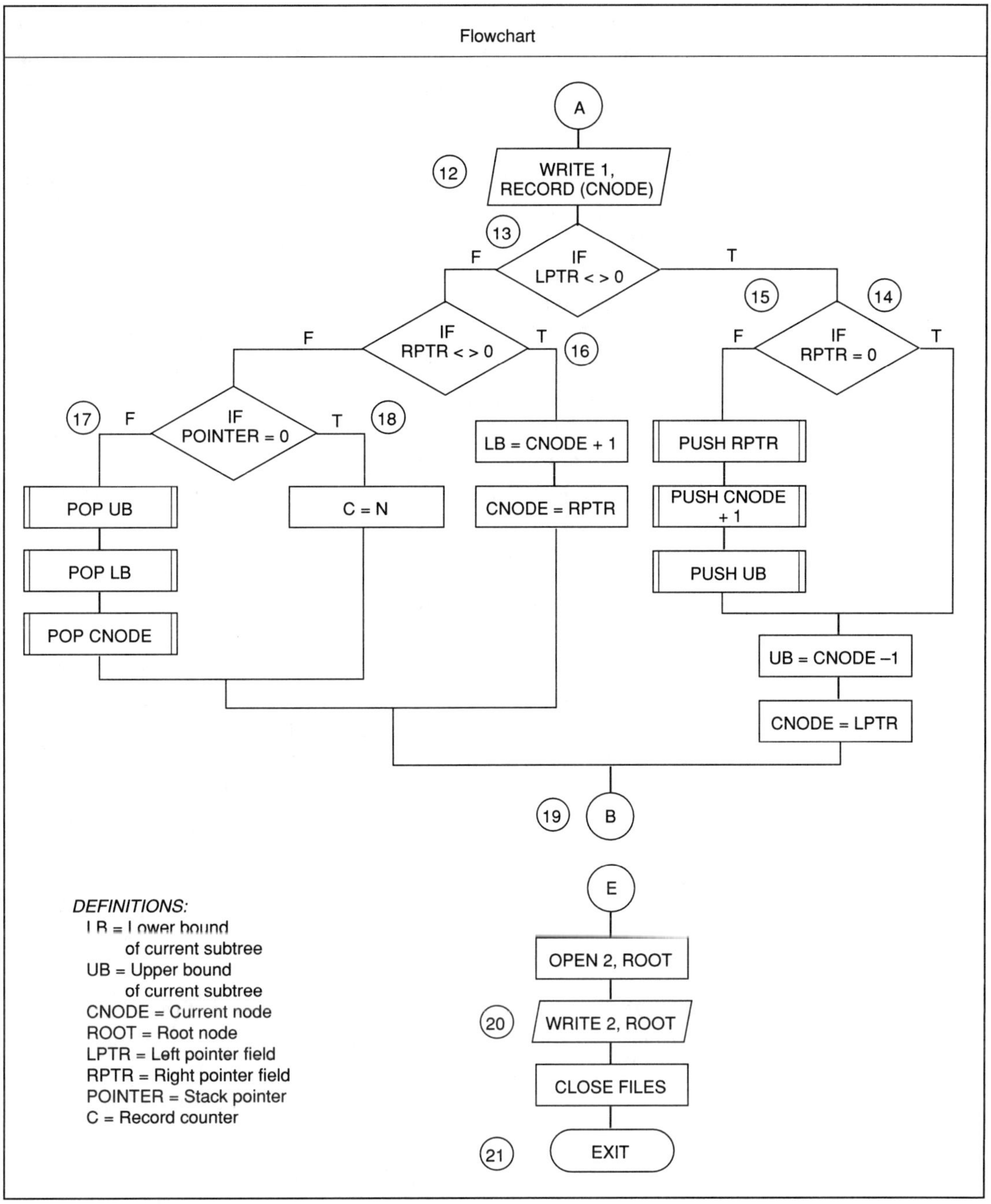

Figure 10.15 *(continued from page 244)*

11. A test is made to see if the current node has a right child. If it does, the right pointer is set equal to the integer average of the upper bound and the current node plus 1. If it does not, the right pointer is set equal to 0, which indicates there are no more right nodes.
12. The pointers have values, and the record can now be written to the file.
13. The next node needs to be found.
14. When the left pointer is not equal to 0 and the right pointer is not equal to 0, the new upper boundary is set equal to the current node minus one and the current node is set equal to the left pointer.

15. When the left pointer is not equal to 0 and the right pointer is equal to 0, the values of the right pointer, the current node plus one, and the upper bound need to be saved by pushing the stack. The new upper boundary is equal to the current node minus one and the current node is set equal to the left pointer.
16. When the left pointer is equal to 0 and the right pointer is not equal to 0, the lower bound needs to be set equal to the current node plus one and the current node is set equal to the right pointer.
17. When the left pointer is equal to 0 and the right pointer is equal to 0 and the stack pointer is equal to 0, all of the records in the file have been processed and the node counter is set equal to the total number of records in the file.
18. When the left pointer is equal to 0 and the right pointer is equal to 0 and the stack pointer is not equal to 0, the values of the upper bound, the lower bound, and the current node are popped from the stack.
19. The loop continues until the value of the node counter is greater than or equal to the number of records in the file.
20. The ROOT file is opened and the root record number is saved. All of the files are then closed.
21. The module is exited.

Figure 10.16 shows the tree diagram for the file found in Figure 10.17, which was created from the procedure in Figure 10.15.

One advantage of a tree structure is the **search** technique. Since all of the keys on the left of a node are less than the current node, and all of the keys on the right of a node are greater than the current node, the search can proceed down a branch, moving to the left or right according to the key. Using the file in Figure 10.17, the order of comparisons to find 30 would be 35, 15, 25, and 30. This would take four comparisons instead of six in a sequential search. To find the number 45, the order of comparisons would be 35, 55, and 45. This would take three comparisons instead of nine in a sequential search. As soon as the key value of the node equals the search key the procedure stops.

Notes on Figure 10.18

Figure 10.18 shows the algorithm and the flowchart of the search module for a binary tree. The following are notes explaining the circled numbers in the flowchart of Figure 10.18.

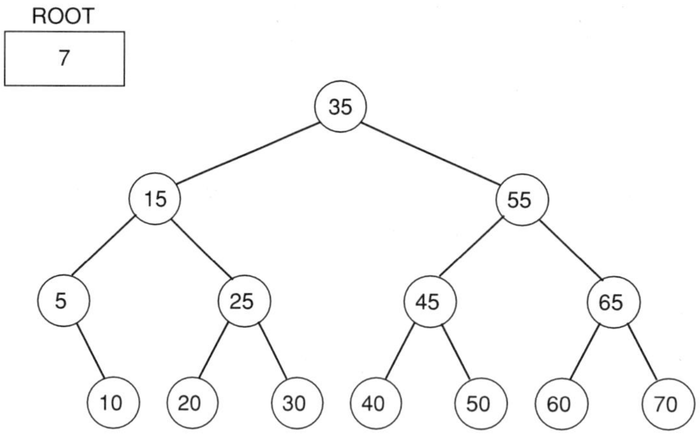

Figure 10.16 Binary Tree Created Using the Flowchart in Figure 10.15

Record	Key	Data	Left Pointer	Right Pointer
1	5		0	2
2	10		0	0
3	15		1	5
4	20		0	0
5	25		4	6
6	30		0	0
7	35		3	11
8	40		0	0
9	45		8	10
10	50		0	0
11	55		9	13
12	60		0	0
13	65		12	14
14	70		0	0

Figure 10.17 File for Binary Tree in Figure 14.16

1. The SEARCH module searches for a record given a search key.
2. The current node (CNODE) is set equal to the root node (ROOT).
3. The parent node (PN) is initialized to 0.
4. The search flag (S) is initialized to 0.
5. A loop is set up to process the file as long as the search flag is equal to 0.
6. The current node record is read.
7. If the key of the current node is equal to the search key, the record has been found. The search flag is set equal to 1, indicating that the record has been found.
8. If the key of the current node is not equal to the search key, the parent node is set equal to the current node and a new current node is located. (The value of the parent node is required if you are adding or deleting records.)
9. If the key of the current node is less than the search key, then the next node to be compared is found at the left pointer.
10. If the key of the current node is greater than the search key, then the next node to be compared is found at the right pointer.
11. If the new current node is equal to zero, the record could not be found. The search flag is set equal to 2, indicating that the record could not be found.
12. If the search flag is 1, the record data are printed; if not, a message is printed stating that the record could not be found.
13. The module is exited.

Records in a file need to be processed. If a report is needed, this processing will most likely need to be in order. However, a binary tree can be processed in any of several orders. The processing of each node once in an orderly manner is called tree **traversal.** Every **traversal** algorithm faces three choices at each node:

Algorithm

```
SEARCH
 1.  CNODE = ROOT
 2.  PN = 0
 3.  S = 0
 4.┌ WHILE S = 0
 │    READ 1, RECORD (CNODE)
 │   ┌IF KEY = SKEY
 │   ├── THEN
 │   │      S = 1
 │   ├── ELSE
 │   │     ┌IF KEY < SKEY
 │   │     ├─THEN
 │   │     │   CNODE = LPTR
 │   │     ├─ELSE
 │   │     └  CNODE = RPTR
 │   │     ┌IF CNODE = 0
 │   │     ├─THEN
 │   │     │   S = 2
 │   │     ├─ELSE
 │   │     └   CONTINUE
 │   └─────────
 │    WHILE–END
 └
5. IF S = 1
   THEN
      PRINT RECORD DATA
   ELSE
      PRINT "RECORD NOT FOUND"

6. EXIT
```

DEFINITIONS:
CNODE = CURRENT NODE
PN = PARENT NODE
S = SEARCH FLAG
1 = RECORD FOUND
2 = RECORD NOT FOUND
KEY = KEY OF CURRENT RECORD
SKEY = SEARCH KEY
RPTR = POINTER TO RIGHT NODE

Flowchart

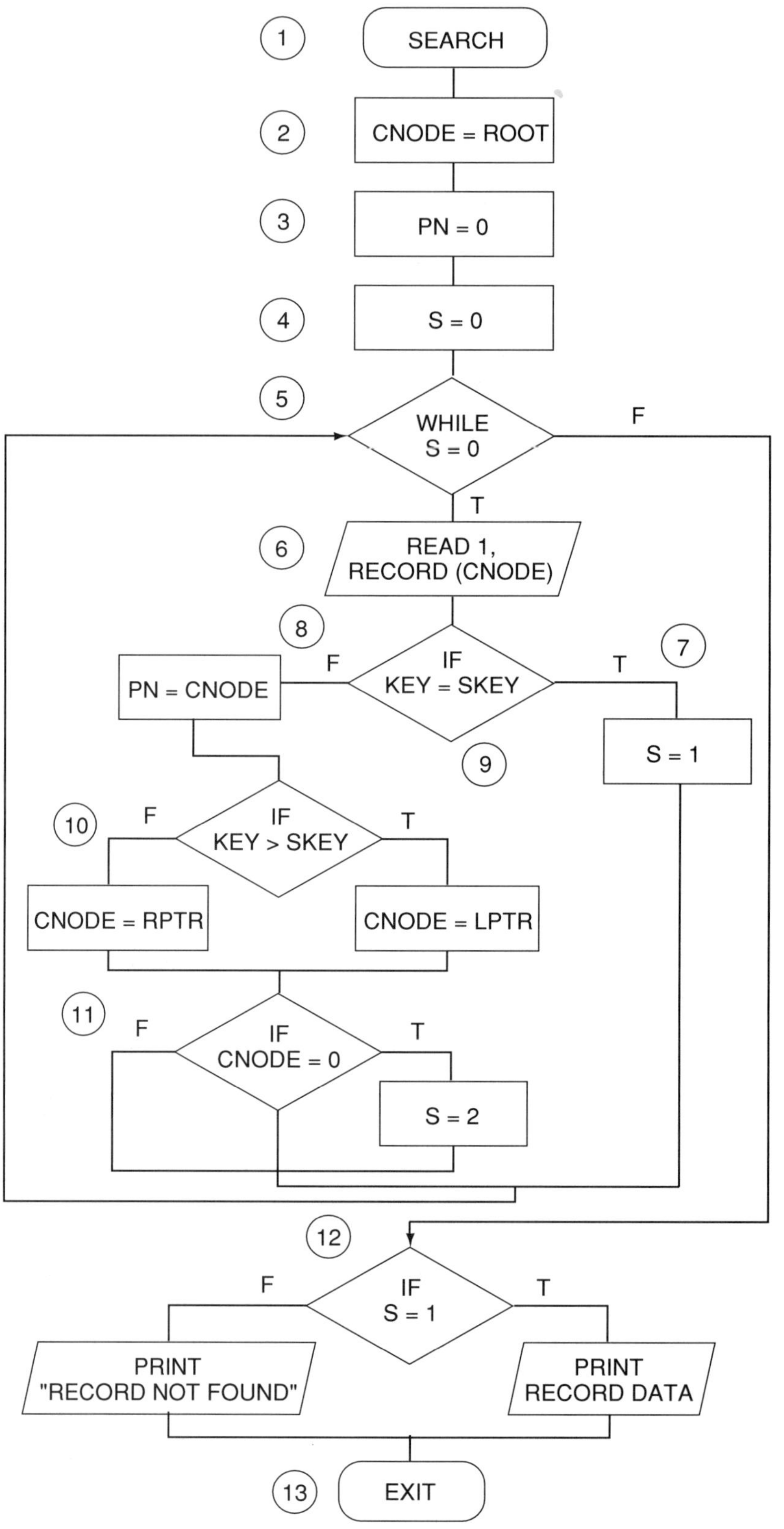

Figure 10.18 Algorithm and Flowchart to Search a Binary Tree

1. Process the node.
2. Follow the left branch (follow the left node).
3. Follow the right branch (follow the right node).

Whatever of these three choices is taken, the other two must be completed at a later time. It is the order of these choices that specifies the traversal method. Three traversal methods are as follows:

1. *Preorder:* The node is processed first, then the left branch, and then the right branch. This is abbreviated as NLR and represents the choices in 1, 2, 3 order.
2. *Inorder:* The left branch is processed first, then the node, and finally the right branch. This is abbreviated as LNR and represents the choices in 2, 1, 3 order.
3. *Postorder:* The left branch is processed first, then the right branch, and finally the node. This is abbreviated as LRN and represents the choices in 3, 2, 1 order.

The following list shows the order of the binary tree in Figure 10.13 when it is processed in each of the three methods:

1. *Preorder* (NLR): GDBACFEKIHJLM
2. *Inorder* (LNR): ABCDEFGHIJKLM
3. *Postorder:* (LRN): ACBEFDGHJIMLK

Notes on Figure 10.19

Figure 10.19 shows the algorithm and the flowchart to process an inorder traversal of a binary tree. The following are notes for Figure 10.19:

1. The REPORT module processes the binary tree using an inorder traversal method.
2. The stack is initialized to 0.
3. The current node (CNODE) is set equal to the root node.
4. The process flag is set equal to 0.
5. A loop is set up to process the file as long as the process flag is 0.
6. The current node is pushed into the stack. This is to keep track of where to return since the current node is the middle choice and needs to be processed.
7. If the left pointer is not zero, the current node is set equal to the left pointer.
8. If the left pointer is 0, either the end of the file is found, or a node is found that needs to be processed. A process branch flag is set equal to 0.
9. A loop is set up to process the nodes in the stack.
10. If the stack pointer is 0, all of the records have been processed. The process stack nodes flag (FLAG) is set equal to 1 as is the process stack flag (S).
11. If the stack pointer is not zero, then a node needs to be processed.
12. The stack is popped with the current node. The current node data are read and the data are printed.
13. If the right pointer of the current node is 0, the next node to be processed is in the stack. If not, the right node needs to be processed. The process stack nodes flag is set equal to 1, and the current node is set equal to the right pointer.
14. The REPORT module is exited.

The binary tree of Figure 10.19 is balanced since there is no more than one node difference between the number of nodes on the right from the number of nodes on the left. When nodes are added and deleted, the tree tends to become unbalanced. The more the imbalance, the less effective the tree becomes. Therefore, the tree either needs to be

Algorithm	Flowchart

```
REPORT
 1.  PROCESS INIT STACK
 2.  CNODE = ROOT
 3.  S = 0
 4.  WHILE S = 0
      PUSH CNODE
      IF LPTR = 0
        THEN
          FLAG = 0
          WHILE FLAG = 0
            IF POINTER = 0
            THEN
              FLAG = 1
              S = 1
            ELSE
              POP CNODE
              READ 1, RECORD (CNODE)
              PRINT RECORD DATA
            IF RPTR = 0
              THEN
                CONTINUE
              ELSE
                FLAG = 1
                CNODE = RPTR
        ELSE
          CNODE = LPTR
 5.  EXIT
```

DEFINITIONS:

CNODE = Current node
ROOT = Root node
S = Process flag
    0 = CONTINUE
    1 = STOP
LPTR = Pointer to left nude
RPTR = Pointer to right node
FLAG = Process subtree flag
POINTER = Stack pointer

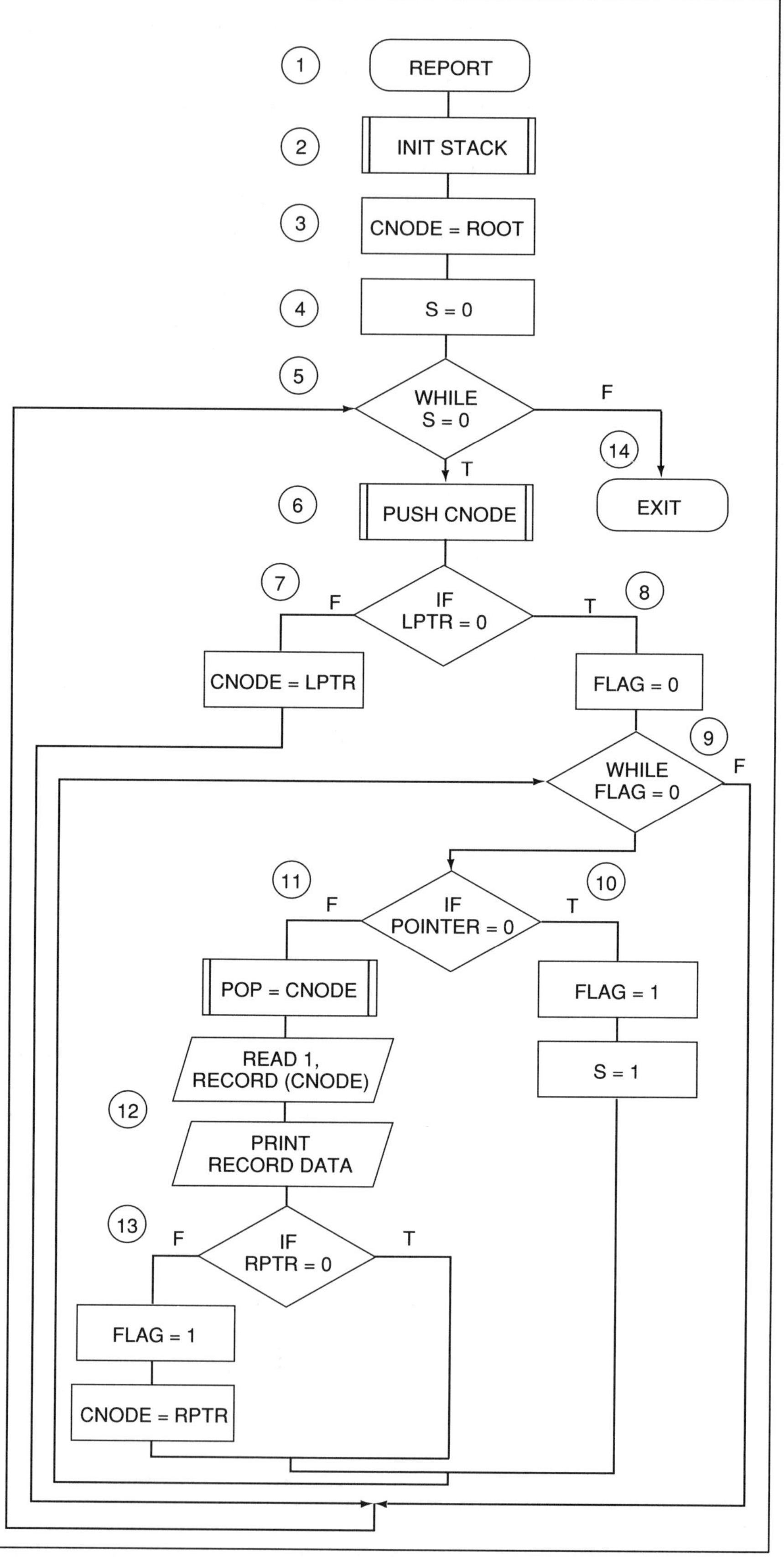

Figure 10.19 Algorithm and Flowchart to Process a Binary Tree in Order

balanced as the nodes are added or deleted, or the tree needs to be balanced periodically. There are standard techniques for these processes. Because of the complexities of balancing a binary tree, this text does not present the algorithms and flowcharts to update a binary tree.

More complex trees use multilinked tree structure techniques. In a multilinked tree structure, one node can have many children. This fact adds much complexity to the techniques of processing and updating these files.

Other structures are also used with different types of lists. Included are **queues** and hashing techniques. A queue is a list that is added to at one end and used from the other end. That is, the first datum in is the first datum used. An example of a queue is waiting in line at the grocery store. The first person in the line is the first person out.

Another technique is **hashing.** An algorithm for a formula is devised to find the correct record to retrieve. The major problem with this method is that of creating an algorithm that produces a unique record number, since two records cannot have the same record number.

Summary

Many data structures are used in programming today. Among those covered in this text include a single variable, arrays, and records in a file, which can be accessed sequentially or randomly. Sorting techniques are discussed in this chapter, since many of these data structures required ordering at one time or another. The techniques presented here include the exchange sort, the bubble sort and the shell sort. Other data structures include stacks, linked lists, binary trees, etc. Stacks are lists of values that are entered at one end and used from the other end. A linked list is a file that has one or more fields which link the records in order. A binary tree file has two fields, one of which points to the left node and the other to the right node. The method of tree traversal is determined by how the nodes need to be processed. Other data structure techniques include multilinked trees, queues, and hashing.

New Terms

binary tree
create
hashing
linked list
queue
pushing the stack
popping the stack
sorting
stack
traversal

Questions

1. What is a stack?
2. How does a stack differ from a queue?
3. What is a linked list?
4. Does a linked list have to be in order? Explain your answer.

5. How does a circularly linked list differ from a singly linked list?
6. What is a binary tree?
7. Does a binary tree have to be in order? Explain your answer.
8. Under what circumstances would you use a stack?
9. Under what circumstances would you use a linked list?
10. Under what circumstances would you use a binary tree?

Problems

1. Identify the comparisons and the exchanges made to sort the following array using the selection exchange sort technique.

Number
23
45
13
5
56
74
10
30
65
40

2. Identify the comparisons and the exchanges made to sort the array found in Problem 1 using the bubble sort technique.
3. Identify the comparisons and the exchanges made to sort the array found in Problem 1 using the shell sort technique.
4. What would be the values found in a stack and the value of the stack pointer after the following executions:

PUSH 34

PUSH 54

PUSH 32

POP X

POP X

PUSH 10

PUSH 11

POP X

5. Using the master file found in Figure 13.1 in Chapter 13, develop a link field. Do not sort first.
6. Show the following updates on the file from Problem 5:

Add:	Peterson	55
Delete:	Black	
Delete:	Adams	
Delete:	Stone	
Add:	Hudson	255
Add:	Neill	167

7. List the records that were compared when searching for Green. Use the file as updated in Problem 6.
8. Using the master file found in Figure 13.1 in Chapter 13, develop the two pointer fields for a binary tree. Draw the tree diagram for this file.
9. List the records that were compared when searching for Green. (Use the tree developed in Problem 8.)

UNIT THREE

SUPPLEMENTARY EXERCISES

Develop a complete solution, including a data dictionary, to the following problems:

1. Have the computer deal four hands of 13 cards each. The deck should be randomly set up. Check to make sure there are no duplicate cards in the deck. You will need to use the random number generator and arrays.
2. Given a two-dimensional table, look up a value given a number corresponding to the first row and a number corresponding to the first column. Accept only values that are equal to the values found in the table (see Chapter 9—table look-up).

   Example: ROW_NUMBER = 25 COL_NUMBER = 100

   TABLE:

0	10	50	100	200	400
5	65	78	98	67	54
10	99	54	36	77	65
15	55	66	75	87	43
25	34	44	53	32	75
50	54	65	76	87	34

   THE ANSWER WOULD BE: 53

3. Modify the solution in Problem 2 to accept values of ROW_NUMBER and COL_NUMBER that are not exactly equal to one of the values found in the table.
4. The president of a college would like to know the age distribution of the students. Complete a solution using the frequency distribution technique to output the needed results.
5. Create a linked list of the following data. The data will be in ascending order of the temperature.

Day	Temperature
Nov. 28	33
Nov. 29	38
Nov. 30	30

Dec. 1	43
Dec. 2	48
Dec. 3	42
Dec. 4	40

Delete all November readings and add:

Dec. 5	35
Dec. 6	33
Dec 7	40

6. Create a binary tree using all data found in question #5.

UNIT FOUR

OBJECT ORIENTED PROGRAMMING

Chapter 11

Concepts of Object Oriented Programming

Overview

Objected Oriented Languages Such as C++

Classes
Instance of a Class or an Object
Inheritance
Interaction Between Classes

GUI

Event-Driven Object Oriented Programming

Events
Interactivity

Objectives

When you have finished this chapter, you should be able to:

1. Determine the difference between a procedural solution and an object oriented solution.
2. Use object oriented concepts in the design of a solution to a problem.

Computer hardware and software are becoming more and more complex as time goes by. The faster a computer runs and the more data a computer can process, the more people want a computer to accomplish. Because of this increasing complexity, new strategies in programming design have been implemented. **Object oriented programming** is one of these strategies. **Object oriented programming (OOP)** is a different way of thinking about a problem. Instead of thinking about the processes or the procedures of how to solve the problem, we look at the parts of the problem in terms of data, its properties, its responsibilities, and how it interacts with other parts. We will still work with modules; however, the modules will be related to the data parts and not the procedural parts of the solution. The result is a non-procedural solution to a problem.

This chapter will introduce the many new concepts and terms used in object oriented programming. The chapter is broken down into two parts. The first part will present concepts and terms used in object oriented languages such as C++. The second part will present concepts and terms used in event-driven objected oriented languages such as Visual Basic and Lingo.

Objected Oriented Languages Such as C++

Program design using object oriented programming languages such as C++ allows the programmer to look at the solution in terms of parts instead of procedures. Lets look at a library book check out system. In a procedural program you would design the program with the procedures in mind:

- Menu driven program
- Input of the data—book name, book number, date, client, etc.
- Check out of the book
- Check in of the book
- Print out of all outstanding books
- Print out of all books

In an object oriented program you would design the program with the parts in mind:

- Items to be checked out: books, magazines, tapes, etc.
- Client
- Check in/out device
- Printer

Each part then would be assigned responsibilities:

- Items to be checked out:
  - know id code
  - check self out
  - check self in
  - know location of self
- Client:
  - know client id code
  - keep list of items checked out
  - update client id data
- Check in/out/ device:
  - check out items
  - check in items
  - know location of items
  - add and delete items
  - add, delete, and change client data
  - query client data
- Printer
  - print book list
  - print outstanding book list

There may be other parts and other responsibilities, but you should be able to see the difference in the strategy of the solution. In order to complete the responsibilities, each part needs to interact with other parts. Now lets put some common names to the ideas we have just discussed.

Classes

A **class** is the name of a part of the solution. In our library problem, the classes would be item class, client class, device class, and printer class. Associated with the class is a set of properties, structures, or behaviors. A class models the characteristics of one part of the solution. Item class would have the properties of an id code, location in the library, abstract, be able to check in and out, etc. The client class would have the properties of client name, client address, client id code, etc. Classes are made up of instances of objects. Superclasses can be created in which all sub-classes have inherited characteristics. Each sub-class adds characteristics and therefore becomes more specific. Each sub-class of mammals has certain characteristics. Humans are a sub-class of mammals and have inherited all the characteristics of the class mammals, but have also added more characteristics which distinguish humans from other mammals. In our example from above, the book class, tape class, and magazine class would be subclasses of the item class.

Instance of a Class or an Object

An **instance of a class** is also called an **object.** In the preceding example, each type of book, magazine, and tape would be a specific object. The object is the variable of the class. An object has inherited the characteristics or attributes of the class. Programmers work with objects.

Inheritance

A sub-class or object inherits the characteristics or attributes of the class of which it is a member. Items will have attributes of id number, location, check in, check out, etc. The magazine sub-class will have all of the attributes of the item class plus some attributes which are specific to magazines, such as the date of publication. Programmers need to be sure the attributes are in the correct class or sub-class.

Interaction Between Classes

A class needs to interact with other classes in order to perform its responsibilities. A programmer needs to designate the nature of the interaction. This **interaction** may be in the form of requesting data or performing some other function. Each class is a cohesive module. Interaction provides coupling of the classes. Interaction takes place through the use of messages sent between classes. The method of executing the responsibilities of the classes uses the logic structures described in Chapters 4–8.

GUI

A **graphics user interface (GUI)** is a computer screen designed for easy interaction between the user and the computer. Each item on the screen is an object with related responsibilities. A GUI can be designed using a language such as C++ or an event-driven language such as Visual Basic or Lingo. Chapter 12 presents information on interface design. Most applications today are driven by a graphics user interface because of the change in attitudes toward computers. Computers are becoming more graphic oriented and people are demanding that the computer be user friendly. The solution from the software industry is the use of the GUI.

Event-Driven Object Oriented Programming

Event-driven object oriented programming uses actions or events to trigger the execution of a set of instructions called a script. The GUI is designed so that each item on the screen is an object with assigned properties. There are no classes in this form of programming. The objects may be in the form of a button, a graphic, a user input box, an output box, a pull down menu, a text box, a video clip, a sound clip or anything else on the screen. The properties of these objects may be such things as location on the screen, the name of the object, color, text formats, color palette used, designation of editable text, size, speed of video or sound, etc. A script may be attached to each object. There is an overall program script which designates any actions which refer to the entire application, such as initializations, beeps of the mouse, designating global variables (called public variables), etc. Once the application starts, the user has complete control over the order of processing through the use of events.

Events

An **event** is a happening in the computer. Some typical events are:

- on mousedown
- on mouseup
- on keydown
- on keyup

Each language has its own set of events. The only time the script for an event is executed is when the event happens. When a button is clicked, instructions are executed when the mouse goes down, or a different set of instructions are executed when the mouse comes up. When a key is depressed or released another set of instructions is executed. In this case, the computer saves the value of the key. The programmer may use this information in the script. The program is executed through the use of events, many of which are directed by the user.

Interactivity

When using event driven languages, interactivity is between screens and/or between the user and the computer. Each screen becomes an entity to be designed and programmed. Interaction takes the user to either a new or a modified screen. This interaction produces a non-linear application. For example, lets look at a problem to calculate the interest of an amount of money over several years. The user has to input the amount, the interest, and the number of years. In a procedural solution, the order in which the user enters the data is specified by the program and changes may or may not be allowed. In an event-driven object oriented solution, there would be three user input boxes on the screen. The user may input the data in any order and change any of the data as necessary. The calculation does not take place until the user requests the answer through the use of a button—an event.

Interactivity requires that navigational tools be built into the program. These tools include hot spots, hot objects, time, and different types of buttons such as a back button, a forward button, a jump button, a menu button, a quit button, etc. It is very important to plan navigation carefully. The user needs to navigate through the program with ease and with as little frustration as possible.

Summary

Object oriented programming requires a different approach to the development of a solution to a problem. The programmer must look at the parts of the problem and not the processes of the problem. New terminology is used with object oriented programming. A class is one of the parts of the solution and has its own properties. An object is an instance of the class. Sub classes and objects inherit the properties of the class of which it is a member. Classes must interact with each other to obtain needed data or functions required to complete the responsibilities of the class. Event-driven object oriented programming uses screen objects which are assigned properties and scripts. Interaction between screens is accomplished by events which happen when the program is executed.

New Terms

class
event
event-driven object oriented programming
graphics user interface (GUI)
instance of a class
interaction
object
object oriented programming (OOP)

Questions

1. What is the relationship between a class and an object in object oriented programming?
2. What is the difference between a procedural solution and an object oriented solution to a problem?
3. What is a GUI?
4. Why is a GUI important to the development of solutions to problems today?
5. What is an example of an event?

Problems

1. What would be considered the classes in a solution to each of the following problems:
   a. A restaurant would like to have a scheduling system for its employees. The software will allow the restaurant owner to schedule each employee for up to 40 hours in a seven-day week. The restaurant is open from 6:00 AM to 10:00 PM. The system should include a check in and a check out system for the employees, a print out of employees' work hours, and the ability to change hours as needed.
   b. A college computer lab manager would like to have a system of check in and check out of the students using the lab. The system would include the ability to check the student in and out of the lab, to check in and out lab materials, to keep track of students' hours, and to track all materials which are checked out. The system would also have the ability to check to see if a computer is open before allowing the student to check in.

Chapter 12

Object Oriented Program Design

Overview

Steps in Designing an Object Oriented Application
Interface Design
Steps in Designing an Event-Driven Object Oriented Application

Objectives

When you have finished this chapter, you should be able to:

1. Determine the classes, responsibilities, and interaction for an object oriented solution.
2. Design a user friendly, functional user interface.
3. Design the storyboards for an event-driven object oriented solution.
4. Determine the objects and the scripts needed for an event-driven object oriented solution.

Designing object oriented applications requires different tools and problem-solving strategies. Modules take on a different meaning as does interactivity within the application. New tools need to be explored. These tools have not been standardized as have the procedural tools presented in the beginning of this text. The tools presented in this chapter include the class responsibility and interactivity chart, two interactivity charts, the storyboard, and the object dictionary.

Steps in Designing an Object Oriented Application

When working with an object oriented language such as C++, there are certain steps you need to take in the basic design of the application. These are:

1. Define the classes.
2. Define the responsibilities for each class.

3. Determine the interactivity between the classes.
4. Determine the instructions to accomplish each responsibility.

Step 1: Define the Classes

The first thing that has to take place in the design of the solution of the problem is to break the total problem into components or classes. A programmer needs to ask "What are the component parts of this problem?" Typical classes might be a client class, a source document class, an input/output class, etc. Figure 12.1 shows a chart to be used to define the classes, its responsibilities, and the needed coupling or interaction with other modules. The boxes in the first column are used to list each class as defined by the developer. Each box should contain one class name. The boxes in the second column are used to list the responsibilities of each class in the first column. There will be one or more responsibilities for each class. If a class has no responsibility, then the class can be deleted. The third column is used to list the other classes it needs to interact with in order to obtain data. This column describes the coupling between classes. Figure 12.2 illustrates the chart in use for the problem described in Chapter 11.

Step 2: Define the Responsibilities for Each Class

The next step is to define the responsibilities of each class. Boxes in the middle column of the chart are used to accomplish this task. A programmer needs to define what each class should be able to do and what each class should know. These are the responsibilities and are listed on the chart. If a class has no responsibilities, the class is not necessary and must be deleted.

Step 3: Determine the Interactivity between the Classes

Some of the data needed to accomplish the responsibilities of the class are found in other classes. These classes need to be listed in the third column. This provides the coupling between classes. One type of interactivity diagram is found in Figure 12.3. It shows the interactivity from class to class. An irregular circle is drawn for each class. The name of the class is entered inside the circle. Lines with directional arrows are drawn between the circles indicating where the class is asking for information. Figure 12.4 presents the interactivity diagram for our example.

Step 4: Determine the Instructions to Accomplish Each Responsibility

Determining instructions to accomplish each responsibility is the last step in the design of an object oriented application. These instructions are similar to the instructions presented in Units 1 and 2 of this text. Each language may have some specialized instructions, but the use of the four logic structures is consistent with this part of the design. Programmers need to be careful about using coupling devices such as global variables, local variables, parameters, etc., just as with the procedural approach to program design.

Class	Responsibilities	Interaction with Other Classes

Figure 12.1 Class, Responsibilities, and Interaction Chart

Class	Responsibilities	Interaction with Other Classes
Item	know id code check self out check self in know location of self	
Client	know client id code keep list of items checked out update client id data	Item
Check in/out device	check out items check in items know location of items add and delete items add, delete, and change client data query client data	Client Item Printer
Printer	print book list print outstanding book list	Item Client

Figure 12.2 Example of a Class, Responsibilities, and Interaction Chart

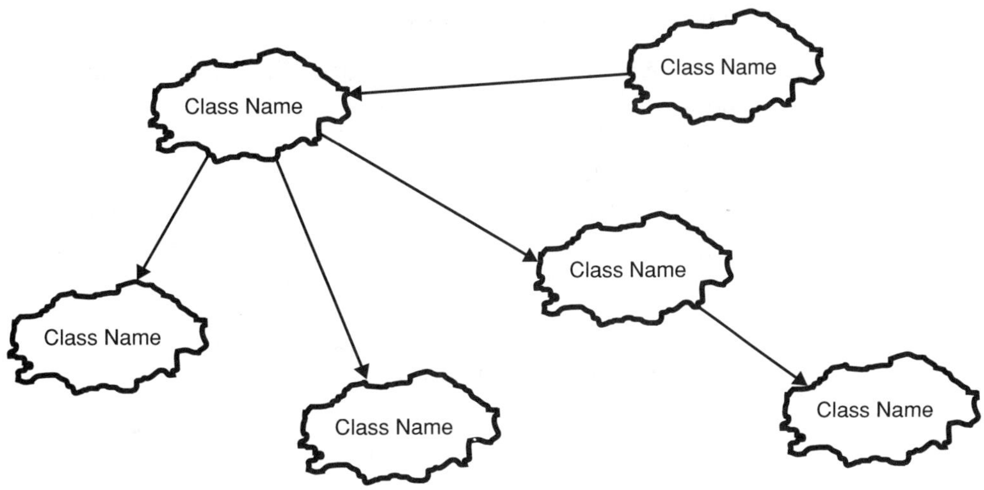

Figure 12.3 Class Interactivity Chart

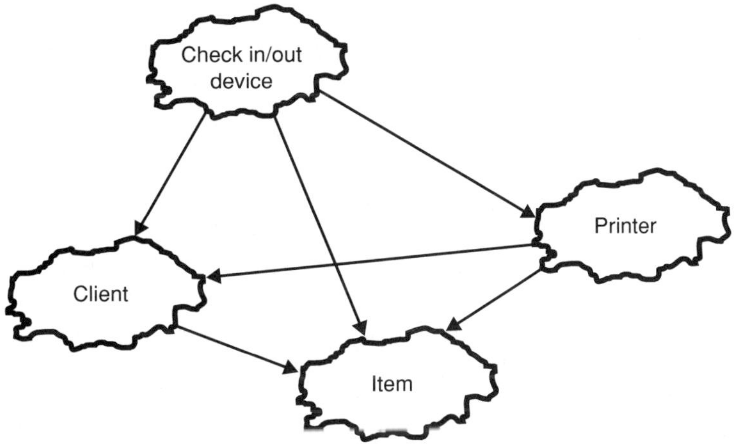

Figure 12.4 Example of a Class Interactivity Chart

Interface Design

A graphics user interface (GUI) is usually developed when using a language such as C++, and it must be developed when using an event-driven object oriented language such as Visual Basic or Lingo. The success of an application many times depends on the GUI design. There are four very basic rules you must follow.

Rule Number 1: Never Lose Sight of the Purpose or the Message

The problem should have a purpose. Never lose sight of that purpose. Interface **screens** should be designed with this purpose in mind. The use of appropriate art work, video clips and sound clips assures the enhancement of the message. If an appropriate object cannot be found, leave it out. If you are designing an interface which introduces Alaska and you can only find palm trees, leave the trees out. Consider finding something else that is appropriate, such as a bear or a seal.

Rule Number 2: Keep it Simple

With so much clip art, photoclips, video clips, and other art work available, it is easy to overdo the amount of material on the screen. The message is always the key to a successful application. If the message is lost in the glitz of other material on the screen the application is a failure. Text should be kept to a minimum. People will not read a lot of text on a screen, even in a scroll bar text box. To increase readability, spread the text over several screens, instead of cramming everything on one screen. In our complex world, many times simplicity is a welcome format.

Rule Number 3: Be Consistent

Consistent does not mean constant. Screens should have the same look and feel throughout the application, but should not be boring. Subtle changes can be very attractive and eye catching. The different screens should use the same or look-alike fonts. A font is the typeface of the text. Fonts vary greatly in looks. There are formal fonts, informal fonts, text fonts, title fonts, etc. You want to choose your font carefully in conjunction with the purpose of the application. You would not want to use a different set of fonts on each screen. The user will get frustrated. Be consistent with colors. Develop a color scheme and use it throughout the application. Change only when the change enhances the message.

Rule Number 4: Understand When You Can Break the Rules

Rules can be broken, but only for good reasons. If you break one of the first three rules, make sure the message has been enhanced and interest in the topic has been increased.

These rules allow the designer to create a user friendly, functional interface. This is important, as a user will be more satisfied with a well-designed interface.

The application should have a visual style which is consistent with the purpose of the project. If the project is formal the style should be formal. The fonts should be traditional fonts, the artwork should be serious and in conjunction with the theme of the project. If the project is informal, then more fun fonts can be used and the art work can include some cartoons. However, even in the most formal project, a moment of levity is often appreciated.

Each screen needs to be designed using the following elements: backgrounds, windows, navigational tools such as buttons, hot spots, etc., input and output boxes, graphics, text, video, sound, and animation. The background of each screen should be similar to all other screens. Again, subtle changes add interest. Navigational tools should be placed in the same place on the screen. Navigational tools do not need to be buttons. Leaves on a tree, fish in a pond, rocks on the beach, and houses on a street can all be navigational tools. Buttons tend to be boring. Try to create new types of navigational tools. User input needs to be large enough for the user to see and in a convenient and logical place on the screen to enter the data. The same holds true for the output. Text should be limited to a few lines per screen or placed in a scrolled text box with a contrasting background for easy reading. Graphics, video, and sound should be added with caution and only to enhance the message or purpose of the screen. These items should add interest or information to data already presented.

A well-designed interface is pleasant to look at, functional, and provides easy access to all of the functions of the program. A well-designed interface allows the user to navigate through the program in a non-linear mode, including the ability to quit the program at any time.

Steps in Designing an Event-Driven Object Oriented Application

The steps to follow in creating an event-driven object oriented project are as follows:

Step 1. Define the audience and the environment.
Step 2. Create the storyboards.
Step 3. Define all objects.
Step 4. Define the interactivity between screens.
Step 5. Define the scripts.

Step 1. Define the Audience and the Environment

In addition to the problem definition as part of the problem-solving steps as described in Chapter 1, the audience and the environment in which the project will be viewed must also be defined. The audience needs to be defined in terms of size, age, and knowledge. In general, the larger the audience the fewer objects on the screen. More text and more objects can be placed on the screen if the viewer is sitting in front of the monitor versus someone who is part of a 500-person audience. Terminology and graphics differ according to age and knowledge of the subject. Buzz words may be used if the audience is knowledgeable, but should not be used for an audience with no subject knowledge. The environment in which the project will be viewed is also important to analyze. Questions which need to be answered include: what hardware and software will be used, what type of equipment will be required, and what the viewing area will be. Audience and environment analysis can make the difference between a successful project and one which is unsuccessful.

Step 2. Create the Storyboards

Storyboards define what is placed on the screens and the order of development of the screens. Figure 12.5 presents a storyboard. Figure D.12 in the Appendix presents a form with multiple storyboards on one page. In the box, the developer sketches the objects to be placed on the screen. Fine detail is not necessary, but all objects should be placed in enough detail so the programmer can use this document as a plan to start the

Figure 12.5 A Storyboard

computerization of the application. The lines allow for notes on the screen such as interactivity guidelines, object sources, animation effects, etc. Each storyboard should have a reference number. Storyboards allow the developer to organize data, objects, and ideas.

Step 3. Define all Objects

Screens are made up of objects. These objects may be developed in the software package or they may be imported from another source. Just as we needed a data dictionary when using a procedural language, we need an object dictionary for object-oriented languages. Figure 12.6 (also found in Appendix D.13) shows an object dictionary. The data needed in this form include the name of the object, the source and/or filename, the file type and extension, the screens in which it appears, whether the object is a hyperobject, an input object, or an output object, and whether or not there is a script attached to it. The name of the object identifies it as an object which can later be referred to by its name. This is a little like naming constants. The source and/or filename column identifies where the object was created or obtained. The object may be created within the program, or it may be obtained from a CD-ROM, created in another package such as a paint package or an animation package, or obtained from a digital camera, an audio tape, or one of many other sources. The name of the file is necessary so the file can be located. The file type and extension column define the type of object such as a background, a window, a button, a hot object, a graphic, text, video, sound, animation, etc. The file extension defines the format of the file. The next column lists the storyboards or screens in which the object is found. The last two columns are check columns. The first indicates if this object is a hyperobject, an input object, or an output object, indicated by H, I, or O. The last column indicates whether or not there is a script attached to the object. A check mark indicates a script. The programmer can refer to this list when creating the screens on the computer. This will save time in trying to locate objects.

Step 4: Define the Interactivity between Screens

The next step is to design the interactivity between the screens. Figure 12.7 shows an interactivity diagram. Each screen is indicated by a box with the screen number or name in the middle. The main menu screen box is placed in the middle with all other screens surrounding it. The screens are then hooked together by arrows to show the interaction between screens. The arrow indicates the navigational direction. Notice there are some short lines which cross the arrow with a return arrow. This indicates that input values must be entered before the navigation is complete. The number of lines indicates the number of input values needed before the interactivity can take place. This is accomplished through scripting.

Step 5. Define the Scripts

Scripts are short sets of instructions attached to objects or to the entire solution. These individual instruction sets are procedural in nature. However, the only time the instruction sets are executed is when an event happens. The logic structures presented in the earlier chapters in this text hold true for these scripts. Variables are made public (global) or they are kept as local variables. If the data is needed in another script, the variables must be public. There is no other way of coupling scripts.

Object oriented programming allows easier handling of solutions for complex projects. It is a different way of approaching a solution to a problem. Object oriented programming has grown in popularity and will continue to grow. However, procedural

Object Name	Source/Filename	File Type/Extension	Screen Number(s)	H/I/O*	Script

*H = Hyper, I = Input, O = Output

Figure 12.6 Object Dictionary

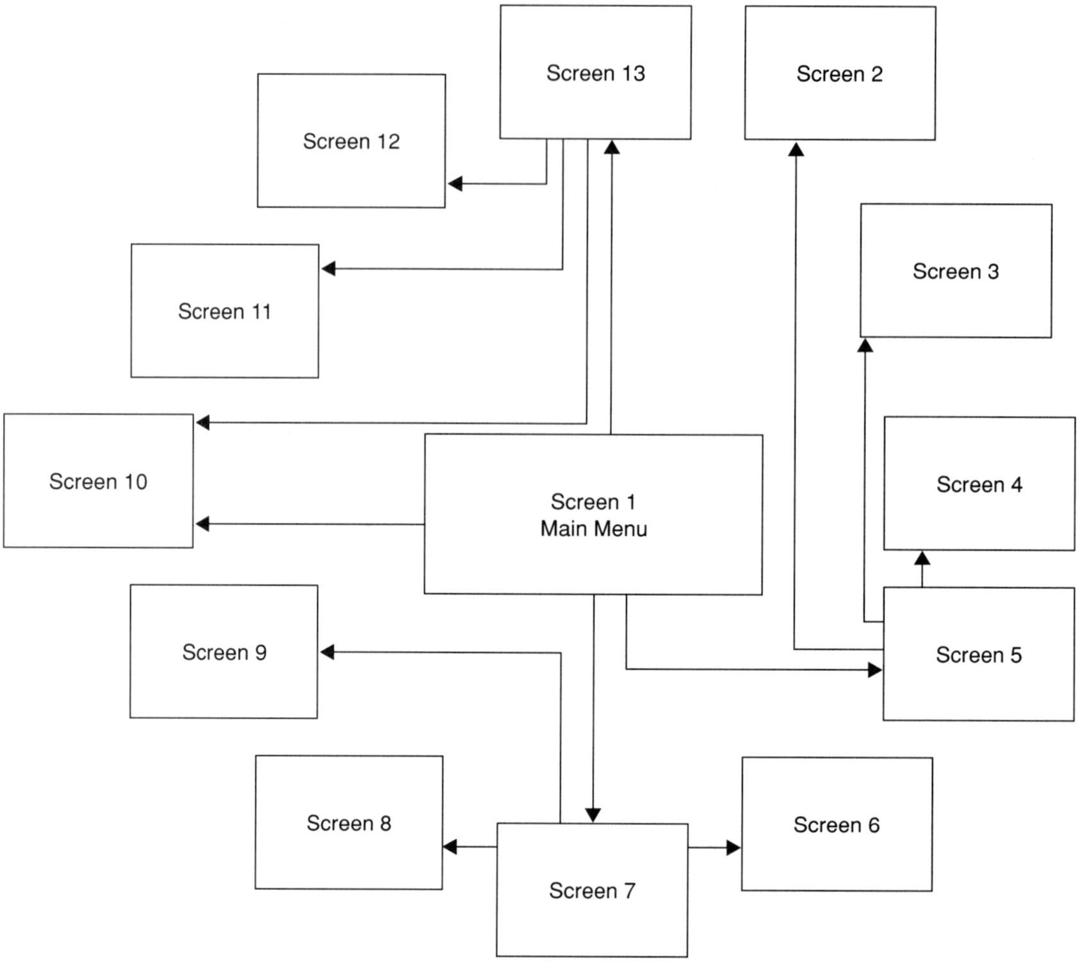

Figure 12.7 Interactivity Diagram

programming design is still prevalent in many industries. Students should learn to use both techniques and evaluate which is the best technique for the problem at hand.

Summary

There are several steps a programmer should follow when designing an object oriented program. They include:

1. Define the classes.
2. Define the responsibilities for each class.
3. Determine the interactivity between the classes.
4. Determine the instructions to accomplish each responsibility.

Most programs today use a graphics user interface so the user can easily guide the program. A user interface needs to be functional, nice to look at, and easy to use. When designing an event-driven object oriented program, other steps are necessary to follow:

Step 1. Define the audience and the environment.
Step 2. Create the storyboards.

Step 3. Define all objects.
Step 4. Define the interactivity between screens.
Step 5. Define the scripts.

Tools introduced in this chapter include the class-responsibility chart, two interactivity charts, the storyboard, and an object dictionary. A well-designed program allows for better efficiency in programming and maintenance.

New Terms

screen
script
storyboard

Questions

1. What is the purpose of the following charts:
   a. class-responsibility chart
   b. interactivity chart
   c. storyboard
   d. object dictionary
2. What are the steps to design an object oriented solution to a problem?
3. What are the steps to design an event-driven object oriented solution to a problem?
4. What are the rules to design a user interface?

Problems

1. Design a solution to the following problems using the four steps to the design of an object oriented solution.
   a. A restaurant would like to have a scheduling system for its employees. The software will allow the restaurant owner to schedule employees for up to 40 hours in a seven-day week. The restaurant is open from 6:00 AM to 10:00 PM. The system should include a check in and a check out system for the employees, a print out of employees' work hours, the ability to change hours if needed.
   b. A college computer lab manager would like to have a system of check in and check out of the students using the lab. The system would include the ability to check students in and out of the lab, to check in and out lab materials, to keep track of students' hours, and to track all materials which are checked out. The system would also have the ability to check to see if a computer is open before allowing the students to check in.
2. Design a solution to the problems found in Problem 1 using the five steps to the design of an event-driven object oriented solution.

UNIT FOUR

SUPPLEMENTAL EXERCISES

1. Design a solution to the following problems using the four steps to the design of an object oriented solution.
   a. A retail store would like an inventory system to track inventory in and out of the warehouse. The system should allow inventory to come into and out of the warehouse from outside the store and from within the store. It should allow a numbering system and have the ability to reorder items as needed.
   b. A catalog company would like to have a customer ordering system. This system should allow clients to phone in an order, have the computer process the order, update the inventory, and print out an order form which is also electronically sent to the warehouse.
2. Design a solution to the problems found in Problem 1 using the five steps to the design of an event-driven object oriented solution.

UNIT FIVE

FILE PROCESSING

Chapter 13

File Concepts

Overview

Objectives

When you have finished this chapter, you should be able to:

1. Explain the concepts of files including sequential files, random-access files records, fields, and the primer Read.
2. Develop a systems flowchart.
3. Design an input record.

Most large business solutions require record processing of some kind. One type of record processing is sequential access, designed so the computer can access records one after another in a sequence. Payroll, inventory, sales analysis, and other kinds of problems require sequential access to data. Another type of record processing is random-access or indexed sequential-access. Random-access processing is used in query situations, which require that one record out of many be accessed without going through all of the records before it. This type of access is used to find information about a single record, such as the balance in an account, information on one sales receipt, or information on one inventory item.

This chapter presents file concepts for both sequential-access and random-access files. Chapter 14 presents techniques of using sequential files. Chapter 15 presents techniques of updating these files. Chapter 16 presents techniques of processing and updating random-access files.

Sequential-Access Files

To process **sequential-access files,** the programmer arranges the files in the order in which they are to be processed. Putting data in order is called **sorting.** Data can be sorted in a variety of ways. The most common sort modes are alphabetical order and ascending numerical order, sorting on one field. Another way to sort data includes ordering on two or more fields—one a major or primary field, the others, minor or secondary fields. For example, a mailing list usually needs to be alphabetical within the zip code. In this case the zip code would be the major field, and the last name (of persons on the list) would be the minor field. There are many processing methods of sorting. Appendix B presents several standard techniques for sorting, both for internally stored data (within the computer's internal memory) and also for externally stored data (on an auxiliary memory device). This chapter does not deal with sorting. We assume that the file is in the order to be processed. The file is usually sorted during the update process. The processing order of the data should be included in the internal documentation.

Random-Access Files

Random-access files are used for interactive and on-line processing. Random-access files enable the user to interact with the computer in order to retrieve the most current information in answer to specific inquiries as they arise in the workplace.

Random-access files can be updated interactively, or sequentially using transaction files, as with sequential files. If it is important for the data to be current at all times, then the update program must be interactive. Applications such as airline reservations and sales at ticket agencies must be interactive; the user must continually update the files with information about how many and which seats have been sold. Other applications, such as bank accounts, need to have the data available to the users at all times, but the files can be updated periodically. In these cases, the files need to be accessed interactively but can be updated either sequentially (through the use of a transaction file) or interactively (through random-access update techniques, presented in this chapter). Random files on microcomputers are normally updated interactively.

Buffers

All input and output operations work through buffers. Records are read from an auxiliary storage device into a buffer. Input can be used from a buffer or read from a buffer into the internal memory of the computer according to the designated language. Output is moved first to a buffer and then to the screen or printer. To save time, many languages are able to direct the computer to retrieve values straight from the buffer. Changes to records are made in a buffer. This often involves extra or special *language-specific* instructions, which you will learn when you learn the syntax of particular languages. For problem solving, it is only necessary to realize how input and output instructions work.

Primary and Secondary Keys

A **key** is a value that is used in the solution either to arrange the file in order or to search through the file for a specific record. Each file has one or more key fields. A *key field* is the field in the record that is designated for the key. For example, the key field for a client file might be the field designated for the client number.

The **primary key** is the main key. This key is required to find a record in a random-access file. It should be unique so the computer can find an individual record. If there were two or more records with the same value for the key field, the computer would not know which record in that file the user wanted. Many times a field that is part of the data for the record will be unique, such as the client number for a client file. In this case, the programmer can designate this field as the key field. In other cases, such as a mailing list file, there are no fields that are unique. If no fields are unique a primary key can be made up of a combination of all or parts of two or more fields. In a mailing list file, for example, none of the fields are necessarily unique. However, a combination of parts of the zip code, the last name, and possibly the first name would make the key unique, such as 95521SPRM. The programmer would use concatenation to combine these fields.

Sometimes a record is accessed by a key other than the primary key. These other keys are called **secondary keys.** They may or may not be unique. In the case of the mailing list, a user may need a list of people living in a particular zip-code area. In this case, the zip code would be a secondary key.

In designing a record for a random-access file, it is important for the user to designate the primary key and secondary keys. The keys, both primary and secondary, are usually designed by the application and the needed output requirements of the problem. The keys are designated within the solution through the use of the fields; they do not have any special designation in the file. For example, the output requirements of a client-tracking problem might be, first, to search for one individual client; second, to output an alphabetical list of clients; and, third, to print out address labels in zip-code order. The primary key would be the client number, since this is unique and would be used to search for an individual client. The secondary keys would be the name and the zip code, since they give the order in which the two output lists are to be arranged. In this case, the secondary keys probably would not be unique since more than one client may have the same name, and certainly more than one client would have the same zip code.

Algorithm Instructions and Flowchart Symbols

Several algorithm instructions and flowchart symbols have been covered so far in the text. In this chapter three more instructions will be added.

1. The OPEN LFN filename instruction tells the computer that the data in the file called *filename* is to be used, starting at the first record. LFN stands for **logical file number,** a reference number to be used in the solution. It is used in the

READ instruction and the CLOSE instruction and refers to the filename in the OPEN instruction, which has the same logical file number. The LFN is used since there can be more than one file open at one time and the computer has to know which file to read from and which file to close. It is easier to use the LFN than to write the name of the file each time you want to reference it.

2. READ (LFN) RECORD copies the next record into the internal memory or into a small holding memory called a *buffer memory.* The use of the buffer memory speeds up the input processing.
3. CLOSE LFN tells the computer that the file will not be used anymore. If a file is not closed, the data in the files may be lost. Once closed, the file may not be used again until it is reopened.

Table 13.1 includes all of the instructions and flowchart symbols covered so far.

Systems Flowcharts

A **systems flowchart** indicates the flow of data throughout the entire computer system. This includes where the data are coming from (keyboard, disk drive, etc.), the name of the program to be processed, and where the information is to go (disk drive, tape drive, printer, etc.). Figure 13.1 includes some of the more common systems flowchart symbols. These include the keyboard, a disk drive, a tape drive, a printer, a program, and a monitor. Most of these symbols can be found on a flowchart template. Figure 13.2 shows an example of a systems flowchart. This chart shows that the data are read from the disk drive and processed by the report program. The results are printed on a printer and also written to the disk drive.

Designing Records

Recall that a file is composed of records. A record contains all of the data on a given subject, such as all of the employment and benefit information for one employee. Records are composed of individual items, called *fields*—for example, one employee's withholding status for income tax.

A programmer beginning to design a solution to a problem must first identify the data to be put in the files. It is important to design the record carefully to make sure all of the necessary data are included and the lengths of the fields are correct. The length of a field is measured by the number of character spaces an item in the field occupies when it is entered in the computer. For example, the length of the field for the field name, ZIPCODE_IN (*in* for *input*), would be 10 characters long, allowing space in the field for a nine-digit zip code plus the underscore. The order of the fields is also important. When you fill out the Given Data section of the problem analysis chart, you will identify all of the data needed to process the file. Use the Record Data Dictionary and Record Layout (Appendix D, Figure D.6) to identify the name, length, data type, and so forth of each data field, and to design the record. These fields will become the record. Figure 13.3 shows the Record Data Dictionary and the design of a record, the record layout, for a mailing list file. All records in a file will have the number of fields identified in the record data dictionary, so you design only one record.

When you are designing a record, there are many items to consider: the number of fields and their order, names, data types and lengths, and the total record length.

Table 13.1 Algorithm Instructions and Flowchart Symbols (*continued on page 284*)

Algorithm Instruction	Flowchart Symbol	Definition (What the instruction tells the computer)
START [module name] [module number]		Start processing a module.
ENTER [list of variable names]		Enter data from a data block or from the keyboard into the following variable memory locations.
variable = [expression]		Assign the value of the following expression to a variable location. Called the *assignment instruction.*
WRITE [list of variable names]		Write to the printer the values represented by the following variable names.
PRINT [list of variable names]		Print on the screen the values represented by the following variable names.
PROCESS [module name]		Execute the instructions in the named module, and then return to execute the next instruction.
END/EXIT		Stop the processing of the module. Processing ceases with the End; with the Exit, processing continues with the next instruction after the PROCESS.
IF/THEN/ELSE	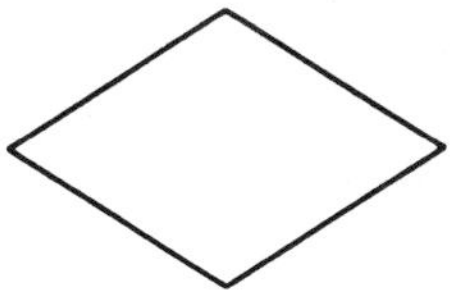	When the condition is TRUE, use one set of instructions; when the condition is FALSE, use another set of instructions.
COUNTER = COUNTER + 1 (C = C + 1)		Increments the counter C.

Table 13.1 *(continued from page 283)*

Algorithm Instruction	Flowchart Symbol	Definition
SUM = SUM + VARIABLE (S = S + V)	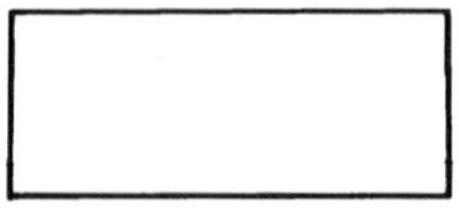	Accumulates the values of the variable V.
WHILE/WHILE-END	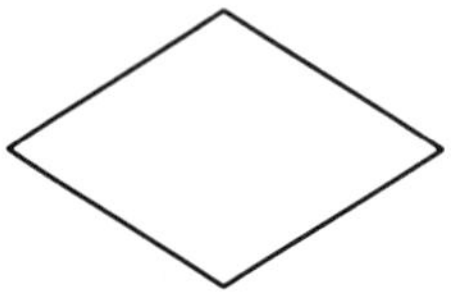	Repeat a set of instructions as long as a condition is TRUE.
REPEAT/UNTIL	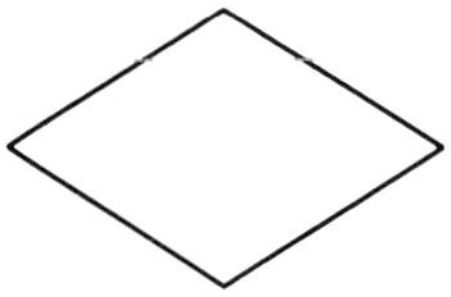	Repeat a set of instructions as long as a condition is FALSE.
LOOP: C = BEGIN TO END STEP S LOOP-END: C	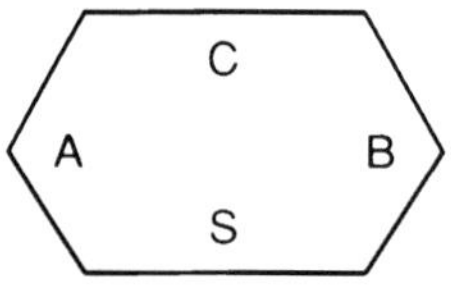	Repeat a set of instructions using a counter C which starts at A(BEGIN) and increments by S(STEP) until C is greater than B(END).
CASE OF variable END-OF-CASE	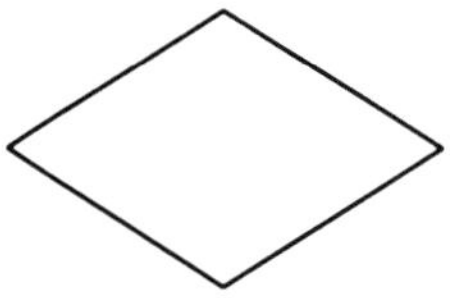	Select a set of instructions to execute according to the value of the variable.
OPEN LFN, FN	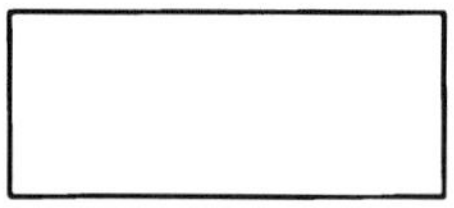	Tells the computer the data in the file named FN is needed starting with the first record. (FN is given a reference number called the LFN)
READ (LFN) RECORD		Copy the next record into the internal memory from the opened file LFN.
CLOSE LFN	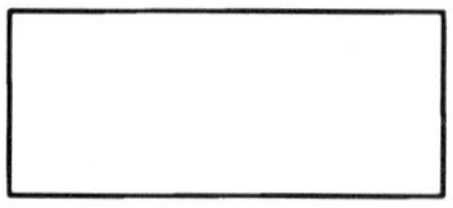	Tells the computer that the file corresponding to the LFN will not be used again.

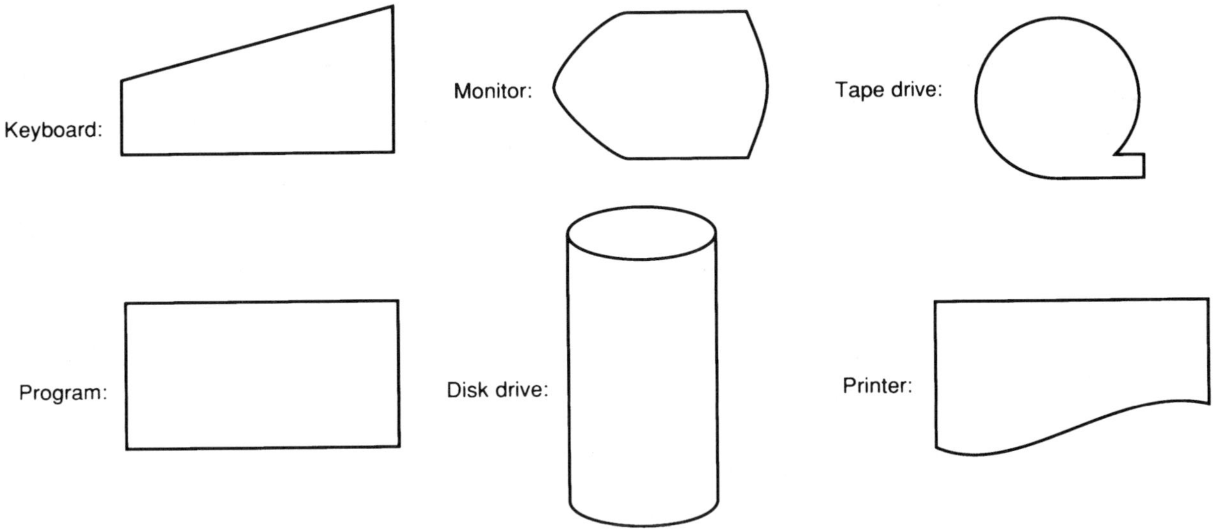

Figure 13.1 Systems Flowchart Symbols

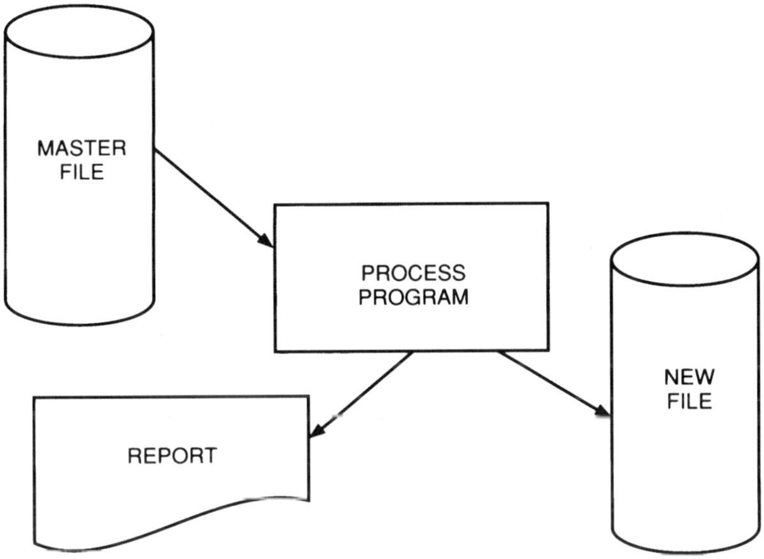

Figure 13.2 Example of a Systems Flowchart

1. The number of fields is the number of items you listed under the heading *Item Description* in the Record Data Dictionary.
2. The order of the fields is determined by the order of importance of the data. Normally, the identifying fields will be first—those fields that will determine the order of the file, or the field that will be used to search for a specific record. Fields are also generally in the order of data entry, although this is not as important since the data-entry screen can be reordered.

   The problem will dictate the field used to order the file. If it is a mailing list, the field for ordering the file will be the zip code or the last name. The zip-code field would be arranged numerically; the last-name field, alphabetically. Also, the problem will dictate which fields will be used for a search. If the name of an individual is used to find the record, then the last name would be the search field. The fields used to order the file and the search fields are usually at the

Record Data Dictionary

File Name: Mailing List

Field Number	Item Description	Field Name	Field Length	Data Type	# of Decimals	Comments
1	Last Name	LNAME_IN	15	C		
2	First Name	FNAME_IN	10	C		
3	Street Address	STADDRESS_IN	20	C		
4	City	CITY_IN	20	C		
5	State	STATE_IN	2	C		
6	Zip Code	ZIPCODE_IN	10	C		
7	Telephone Number	TELENO_IN	12	C		

Record Layout

1 — 15 LNAME_IN	16 — 25 FNAME_IN	26 — 45 STADDRESS_IN	46 — 65 CITY_IN	66 — 67 STATE_IN

68 — 77 ZIPCODE_IN	78 — 89 TELENO_IN	

Figure 13.3 Record Data Dictionary and Record Layout for a Mailing List File

beginning of the record. The order of data entry would then be considered for the remaining fields.

3. The names of the fields should correspond to the item descriptions of the data. Part of the name should also indicate that it is input. The total hours worked might be written as HOURS_IN, or the rate of pay as PAYRATE_IN. The field name is up to the programmer. Any name is acceptable as long as it is an understandable name and can be read and interpreted easily by another programmer. The field name is used as a variable name in the solution.
4. The data type of each field is determined by the requirements of the solution. If the data type is numerical, then specify the number of decimal places. Field data types include numerical (numbers), character string (alphanumeric), and logical (TRUE and FALSE).
5. The length of the field is largely determined by the number of characters in the field. When the field is string character data, the length is determined by the

longest piece of data that would be entered. For example, the length of the field *Salesperson name* would be at least as long as the longest name that would be entered into that field—such as Gullickson or Stanislovsky, at 10 and 12 characters long, respectively. String data are normally left justified in the field with the remainder of the field on the right filled in with blanks. If the programmer did not design enough space in the field and the data are longer than the field, then the computer will truncate the data on the right.

When the data type is numerical, the length of the field must be large enough to accept the number of digits in the largest number that might be placed in the field. The length must include spaces for the decimal point and a negative sign. If the field is not large enough for the number, the computer will either return an error or truncate the number on the left. If the number is to be in scientific notation, four spaces must be included for the magnitude of the number, which is E + nn. The letter E stands for *times ten to the power of.* It is followed by a plus or minus sign and a two-digit number indicating the power of ten. Numbers are normally right justified in the field.

When the data type is logical, normally the field length is one character—for T or F. If the date data type is used, the field length is predetermined, normally in the form of MM/DD/YY.

6. Records are normally stored in external memory in blocks or sections of a specific length. Normally the length of a block is 256 characters, but systems may differ. It is more efficient to transfer sections of data or blocks of data at one time than to transfer a character at a time from external memory to internal memory. The length of a block is determined by the operating system of the computer system you are using, and therefore, the programmer has little or no control over this number. The total record length should be equal to or less than the number of characters in a block or else multiples of this number. That is, the total length of a record or block of records should be less than or equal to 256 or some multiple of 256. Planning record length this way saves space on the disk drive. If the length of a record is 260, for example, then each record will take two blocks of memory for storage. If the fields can be modified so the total length of the record is 256, which is only 4 characters less, the file will take half the space on the auxiliary storage device.

The following problem is used in many of the figures in this chapter and in Chapter 14 to illustrate record-processing techniques.

Problem: The vice president in charge of sales for a company needs to know the company's total sales during the last period. The sales are made by individual sales people. The output needed is a list of all individual sales and the total sales for the company. Figure 13.4 illustrates the Record Data Dictionary and the Record Layout for this problem:

Processing Sequential-Access Files

To process the records in a file by sequential access, either the WHILE/WHILE-END or the REPEAT/UNTIL loop is used. The processing is very similar with both of these loop structures. The WHILE/WHILE-END loop logic structure will be used throughout this chapter and Chapter 14.

File Name: Sales

Record Data Dictionary

Field Number	Item Description	Field Name	Field Length	Data Type	# of Decimals	Comments
1	Sales Date	DATE	8	STRING		MM/DD/YY
2	Salesperson #	SN	3	STRING		
3	District #	DN	3	STRING		
4	Region #	RN	3	STRING		
5	Salesperson Name	SNAME	20	STRING		Last name first
6	Customer Name	CNAME	20	STRING		Last name first
7	Customer Street	CSTREET	10	STRING		
8	Customer City	CCITY	8	STRING		
9	Customer State	CSTATE	2	STRING		
10	Customer Zip Code	CZIPCODE	10	STRING		
11	Customer Phone	CPHONE	14	STRING		(xxx)-xxx-xxxx
12	Sales Amount	SALES	10	REAL	2	
			111			

Record Layout

1 8	9 11	12 14	15 17	18 37	38 57
1 DATE	2 SN	3 DN	4 RN	5 SNAME	6 CNAME

58 67	68 75	76 77	78 87	88 101	102 111
7 CSTREET	8 CCITY	9 CSTATE	10 CZIPCODE	11 CPHONE	12 SALES

Figure 13.4 Record Data Dictionary and Record Layout

When the user enters file data, a whole record is copied either into the computer's working memory or into a buffer memory. In sequential-access record processing, after a record is read into memory, it is processed and then the next record is read. This sequence continues until the computer encounters the **END-OF-FILE (EOF)** marker, at which time the processing stops. The EOF marker is a signal to the computer indicating that there are no more records in the file. When the END-OF-FILE marker is encountered, a status flag, or indicator, is set internally in the computer. This indicator is then tested as a logical data type function. The function name is EOF(LFN). The value of the EOF(LFN) function is FALSE until the END-OF-FILE marker is encountered. At this time the value of the EOF(LFN) becomes TRUE. When the EOF(LFN) function has a value of TRUE, all processing of records must stop. The END-OF-FILE is encountered during the READ instruction. The user should not do any processing after the EOF because there are no more records to be processed. If the EOF marker is processed as a record, the computer will either return an error, or the last record will be processed twice since no new data replaced the old. Therefore, within the loop, the Read cannot be the first module to be processed. It must be processed just before the processing of the condition of the EOF(LFN); therefore, it has to be the last module processed in the loop. This is the case when the READ statement actually sets the EOF status flag at the time of the execution of the READ. However, some languages look ahead for the EOF. In this case, during the execution of the READ, the last record to be processed would be read and the status flag set at the same time. When the language uses the look ahead method of finding the EOF, the primer Read is not used, and the READ statement is the first statement in the loop. This book will present file processing using the primer Read.

The Primer Read

Since the Read must be the last module processed, the computer needs data to process the first time through the loop. Therefore, there has to be a Read before the loop begins. This Read is called the **primer Read.** It primes the loop with data just as a pump is primed with water. Without this primer Read there would be no data to process the first time through the loop. If the READ were at the beginning of the loop, the EOF(LFN) would be processed as a record.

Figure 13.5 shows the Control Module algorithm and flowchart for record processing. Notice the primer Read just before the loop. Also, notice the use of the logical EOF function. The condition to be processed is NOT EOF(LFN). The resultant of this condition is TRUE when the value of the function EOF(LFN) is FALSE, or when the end of flag has not been encountered. This is because NOT FALSE is TRUE. When the END-OF-FILE marker is encountered, the value of the function is TRUE. The resultant of the condition, therefore, is FALSE since NOT TRUE is FALSE. The loop condition is read as WHILE NOT END-OF-FILE. The three modules processed in the loop are the Calc, the Print, and the Read Modules. An alternative method is to incorporate these three modules into one module called the Proc Module. The Proc Module would then process these three modules. In some languages this method is preferred because of the syntax of the loop structure.

Processing Random-Access Files

Random-access files are usually updated and processed (producing output reports through calculation and printing of data from each record) in the same program. Entire books have been written about how to store data in order to find it again in the shortest possible time. The method presented in this book is that of using index files. Other methods include:

1. *Linked lists.* The records are linked through an extra field in the record. This field points to the next record to be processed. A header number specifies the

Algorithm

SALES CONTROL MODULE
(0000)

1. PROCESS INIT
*2. PROCESS READ
3. WHILE NOT EOF(1)
   1. PROCESS CALC
   2. PROCESS PRINT
   3. PROCESS READ

   WHILE-END
4. PROCESS WRAPUP
5. END

*Usually the primer READ is part of the Init Module, however it is put in the Control Module here only to show the sequence of actions.

Flowchart

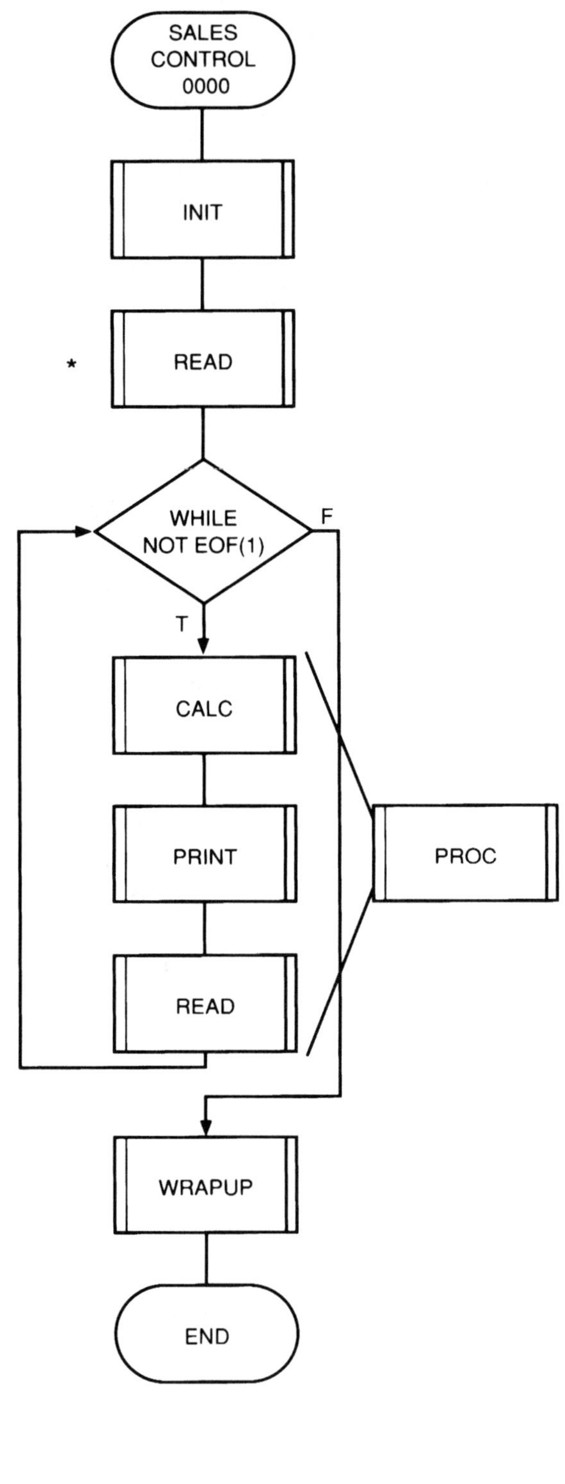

Figure 13.5 The Control Module Showing the Primer Read

first record to be processed. The last record to be processed either has an end marker or points back to the first record again.

2. *Directories.* The file is subdivided into parts. Another file, which consists of two fields, holds the values of the record number of the first record in each subdivision and the key value of the last record in the division. Within the subdivisions the records are processed sequentially.
3. *Hashing.* Hashing methods require an algorithm using one or more of the fields of the record to calculate the record number.

These concepts are discussed in Chapter 10.

Summary

Record processing is a very important aspect of business applications on the computer. Record processing of sequential files embodies basic problem-solving concepts for the business programmer. The concepts of record processing are used in both the programming and the applications areas. When designing a record for a sequential-access file, there are many items to consider: the number of fields, the order of the fields, the names of the fields, the data type of each field, the length of each field, and the total record length.

Random-access files are becoming more and more important as business demands more up-to-date information. Random-access files are used any time data might be needed at a moment's notice or when data must be kept as current as possible. The program must be interactive because the user needs to "converse" regularly with the computer through the keyboard and monitor.

For the business user of computers, concepts of sequential-access file processing and random-access file processing are vital if the computer is to be used as a productivity tool.

New Terms

END-OF-FILE (EOF)
key
logical file number (LFN)
primary key
primer Read
random-access file
secondary key
sequential-access file
sorting
systems flowchart

Questions

1. What is primer Read?
2. What is sorting?
3. What is the difference between a random-access file and a sequential-access file?
4. What is the LFN? Why is it used?
5. What is an EOF?
6. Can you efficiently process a sequential-access file randomly? Explain.
7. Can you process a random-access file sequentially? Explain.

8. Define a buffer and explain why it is used.
9. Define a key and explain why it is used.

Problems

The following problems will be presented again in Chapters 14 and 16. You are to design the input records and system flowcharts to be used in Chapters 11 and 13.

1. Eureka Lumber Company would like to calculate the gross pay for its employees. The input records should include the following: name, address, social security number, pay type (H = hourly, S = Salary), pay rate, and hours worked.
2. A sales manager wants a program that lists all of the company's customers according to the salesperson assigned to each. The input file contains the following data: the customer's name, address, and telephone number, and the salesperson's name.
3. The UP-TO-DATE Department Store needs to convert its inventory from a manual system to a computerized system. The input record should include the following: the inventory number, the department number, the store number, the item description, the quantity, the wholesale price, the markup percentage, and the vendor.
4. A sales manager would like to be able to track the clients of each of his salespeople. He would like to know when each customer was last contacted, the outcome of the contact (not interested, sale made, call back later, no contact made), the sale amount if a sale was made, and the name and number of the salesperson.
5. Design the input record for a video/sound inventory for a TV or radio station. (LP records, cassettes, CDs, and VCRs are all used by the station.) How would this file be ordered?

Chapter 14

Sequential-Access File Applications

Overview

Designing Output Reports
Headings and Line Counters
Control-Breaks
Multiple Control-Breaks
Using Indicators for Program Control
Error Handling
Null Files

Objectives

When you have finished this chapter, you should be able to:

1. Design an output report.
2. Develop a computer program to process a sequential-access file, which includes headings, multiple control-breaks, indicators, and error handling.

Most business computer applications require some type of file processing. In many such cases reports are generated for managers. These reports greatly aid the company's managers in making decisions for the present and future well-being of the company. Therefore the design of these reports should be well thought out. Some rules for good report design are presented in this chapter. Chapter 13 introduced the concept of sequential files. This chapter presents techniques of processing sequential files for business applications. Such techniques include page breaks, page headings, control-breaks, multiple control-breaks, indicators, error handling, and null files.

The problem to be used throughout this chapter was introduced in Chapter 13. The problem as presented in Chapter 13 is:

> The vice president in charge of sales for a company needs to know the company's total sales during the last period. The sales are made by individual

salespeople. The output needed is a list of all individual sales and the total sales for the company. Each new record-processing technique covered in this chapter will be added to the previously developed solution.

Designing Output Reports

Output reports should be designed with the user in mind. When you are working on a problem solution, you record the information needed on the report in the Required Results Section of the problem analysis chart. Where to place specific information within a report depends on the user's needs. The report should be designed so that the user can glean all the information needed in a matter of minutes. The basic rule for developing good reports is to plan to print only the information relevant to the person using the report. Any very important information should be highlighted in some way, so it is easily spotted. Time is valuable, and the computer is a productivity tool. The report should increase the productivity of the person for whom it was designed.

Within the report there are different types of lines. Heading lines are found at the top of the report or at the top of each page. The information found in these lines includes such items as company name, date and time of the execution of the program, programmer name, column headings, page number, manager's name, and the like. Detail lines print the specific information for each record in the file. Summary lines print information about groups of like records; summary lines are printed during a control-break and at the end of the report. Exception lines indicate an error in the data of the record. Exception lines can be either printed as part of the report or as a separate report called an *exception report.*

Report headings can also include relevant information about the company, such as its address, the division, the department and so on; the name of the report; the date; and any other pertinent information, such as the name of the person who will be using the report, the programmer, and so on, which is listed only once on the report. Print this report heading either on a page by itself or on the top of the first page. On the first page, as on all succeeding pages, print the column headings. Number all pages at the top, except for the first page with report headings. Using the Screen Design and Printer Design Forms (Figures D.7 and D.8 in Appendix D), you can design output reports. The design of reports should be accomplished with the help and approval of the user.

The computer screen has 80 columns and from 24 to 26 rows. All of it can be used for input and output and for communication with the user. The screen design form can be used to design whatever has to be placed on the screen. Generally, the input and all inquiries and communication with the user are printed on the screen. All reports are generally written to the printer. Printers use paper that is normally 66 lines long and anywhere from 80 to 144 characters wide, although other paper sizes can be used. The printer form can be used to design the output reports.

Headings and Line Counters

To implement the report design, the programmer designs a few new modules. One is the Report Heading Module, which writes the report heading. Another module writes the column headings. A third processes what needs to be done when one page is full and another page is to begin. This module is called a **page-break,** since there is a break in the processing in order to change the page.

The first thing to do is to incorporate each of these modules into the structure chart. The Report Heading and the primer Read are processed by the Init Module. The Page-break Module is executed by the Print Module since it is part of the printing process (see Figure 14.1).

In the Init Module, the page number needs to be initialized to one and the report headings processed. In Figure 14.2b is the algorithm and the flowchart of the Init Module. The sales file is opened first. Then the total sales is set equal to zero, the maximum line count (the number of lines to the bottom margin) is set equal to 60, and the page number is set equal to 1. Next, the primer Read is processed, and finally, the report headings are written to the printer.

In the Print Module, the line count has to be tested to see if the end of the page is encountered. If it is, then the Page-break Module is executed. Figure 14.2e shows the algorithm and the flowchart of the Print Module. Every time a line is written to the printer, it is counted in the line counter (LINECT). In the Print Module, before anything can be written to the printer, the line count must be compared to the maximum line count. When the line count is greater than or equal to the maximum line count, then the page-break must be processed before the record is written to the printer. If it is not, the record is written to the printer and one is added to the line count.

Each of the additional modules—the Report Heading, the Page Heading, the Column Heading, and the Page-break—must be developed. The Report Heading Module gets the data from the system, prints the lines of the report heading, including the column headings, and initializes the line counter to the number of lines already used by the Report Heading. See Figure 14.2c to see the order of processing. Notice that the report headings are written first, and then the system date is retrieved and printed, the line count is initialized to 6, and the column headings are written to the printer.

The page-break adds one to the page counter, prints the lines of the page headings, and reinitializes the line counter to the number of lines used by the page headings. The Page-break Module also ejects the page, writes the Page Heading, and processes the Column Heading Module. The Page-break Module is shown in Figure 14.2f. Notice that the page is ejected first. Next, the page number is incremented, and then the page headings, which include the page number, are written. The line count is set to the number of lines used by the page headings. Finally, the column headings are written.

The Column Headings Module prints the column headings and increments the line counter by the number of lines the column headings use (see Figure 14.2d). Be sure to include the spacer lines in the total line count. Spacer lines are lines in which nothing is printed. These lines allow extra white space for readability.

Keep in mind the function of each module as you analyze what is processed in it. Figure 14.2 shows all the algorithms and flowcharts for the sales problem, including the headings and the page-breaks.

Control-Breaks

Control-breaks are used to give subtotals for a group of similar records. For example, the requirements for a report might be to list all sales, with totals for each salesperson and a grand total for the company. The processing must temporarily break and write each salesperson's total to the printer before proceeding to the next salesperson.

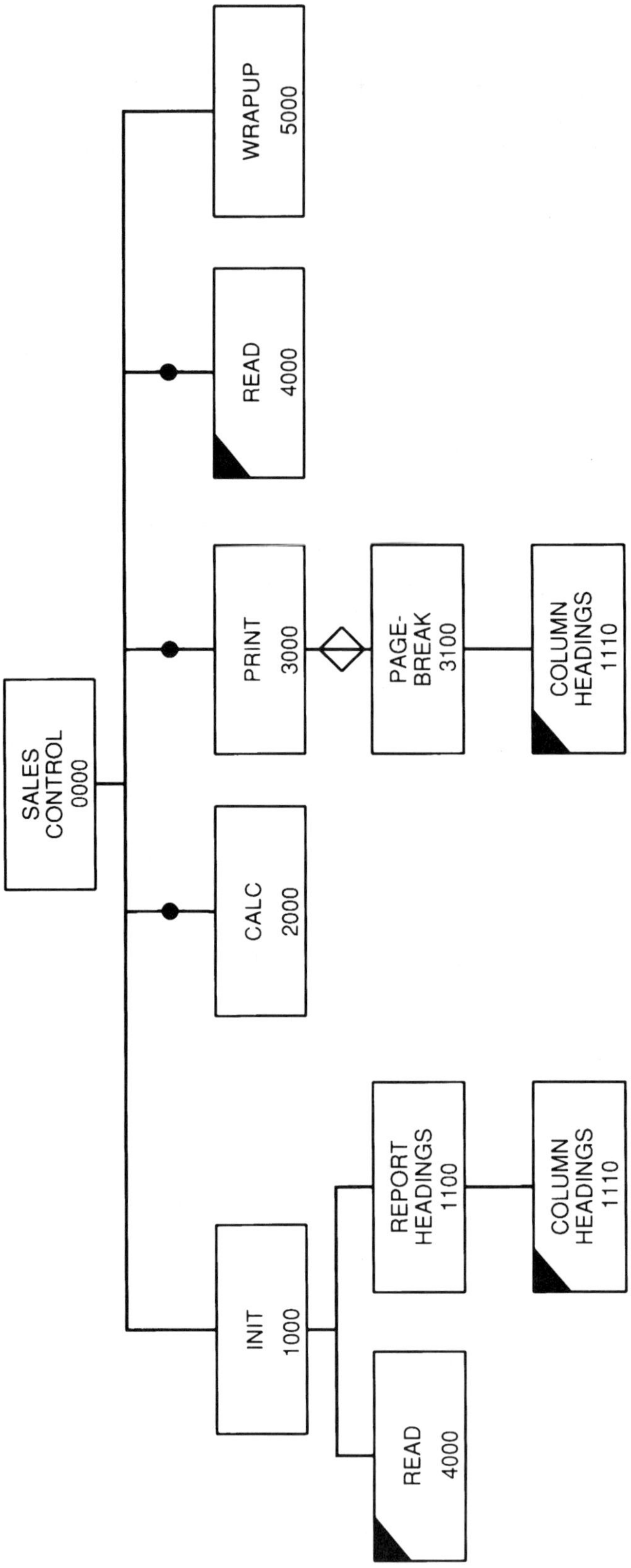

Figure 14.1 Structure Chart for Sales Problem

Algorithm	Flowchart

CONTROL MODULE
(0000)
 	
1. PROCESS INIT
 	
2. WHILE NOT EOF(1)
  1. PROCESS CALC
  2. PROCESS PRINT
  3. PROCESS READ
WHILE-END
 	
3. PROCESS WRAPUP
 	
4. END
	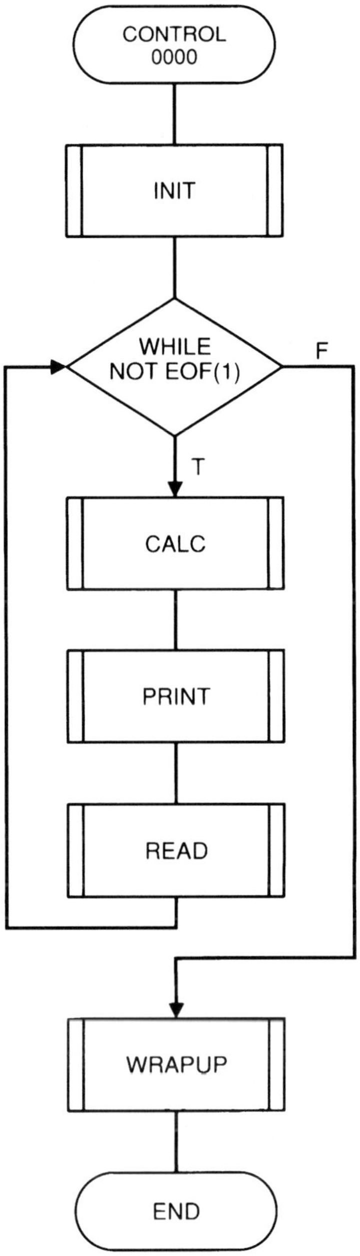

Figure 14.2a Algorithms and Flowcharts for Sales Problems

Algorithm	Flowchart
INIT MODULE (1000) 1. OPEN 1, SALESFILE 2. SALESTOTAL = 0 3. MAXLINECT = 60 4. PAGENO = 1 5. PROCESS READ 6. PROCESS REPORT HEADINGS 7. EXIT	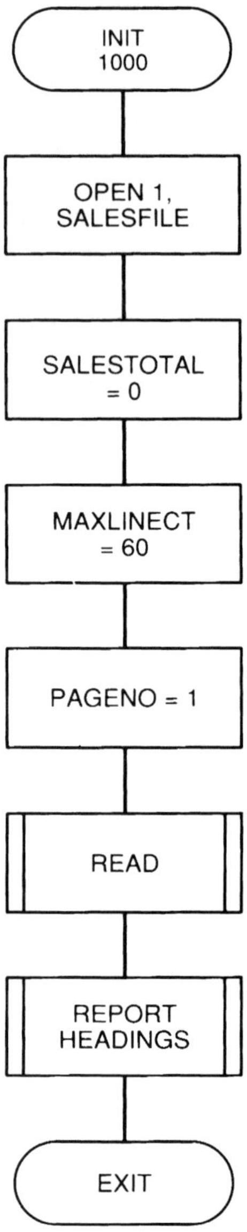

Figure 14.2b Algorithms and Flowcharts for Sales Problems

Algorithm	Flowchart
READ MODULE (4000) 1. READ RECORD 2. EXIT	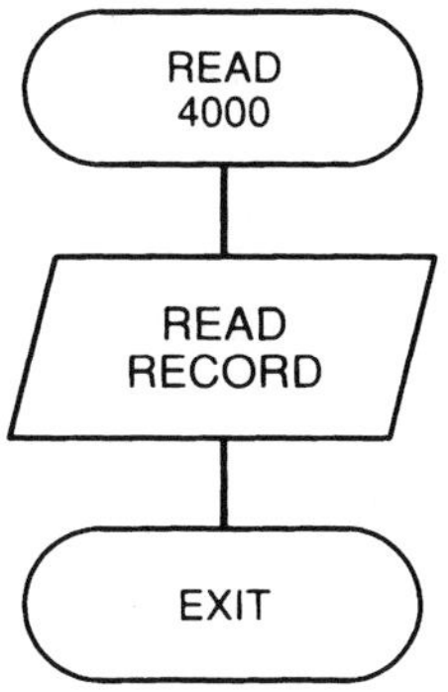
REPORT HEADINGS (1100) 1. WRITE REPORT HEADINGS 2. GET DATE FROM SYSTEM 3. WRITE DATE 4. LINECT = 6 5. PROCESS COLUMN HEADINGS 6. EXIT	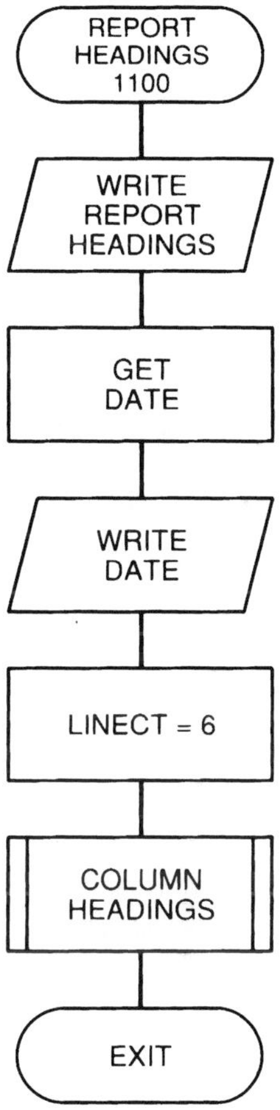

Figure 14.2c Algorithms and Flowcharts for Sales Problems

Algorithm	Flowchart
COLUMN HEADINGS (1110) 1. WRITE COLUMN HEADINGS (Including line space before and after) 2. LINECT = LINECT + 3 3. EXIT	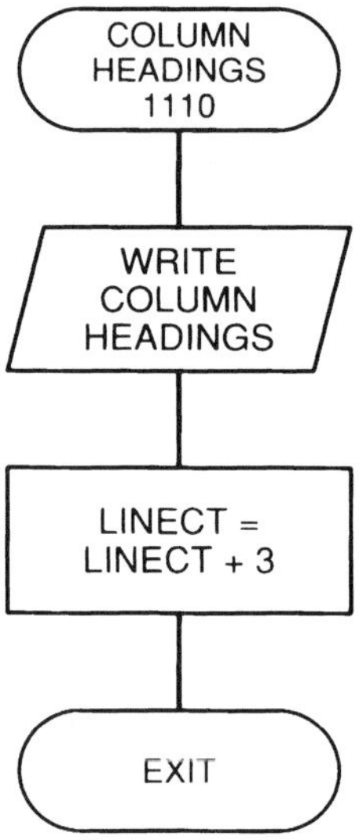
CALC (2000) 1. SALESTOTAL = SALESTOTAL + SALES 2. EXIT	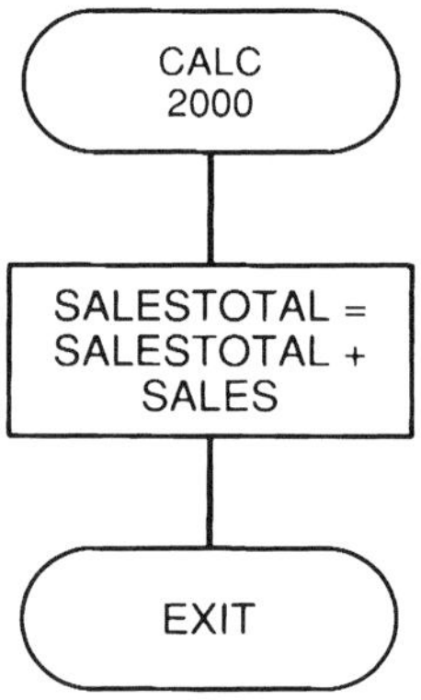

Figure 14.2d Algorithms and Flowcharts for Sales Problems

Algorithm	Flowchart
PRINT MODULE (3000) 1. IF LINECT >= MAXLINECT THEN PROCESS PAGE-BREAK 2. WRITE RECORD INFORMATION 3. LINECT = LINECT + 1 4. EXIT	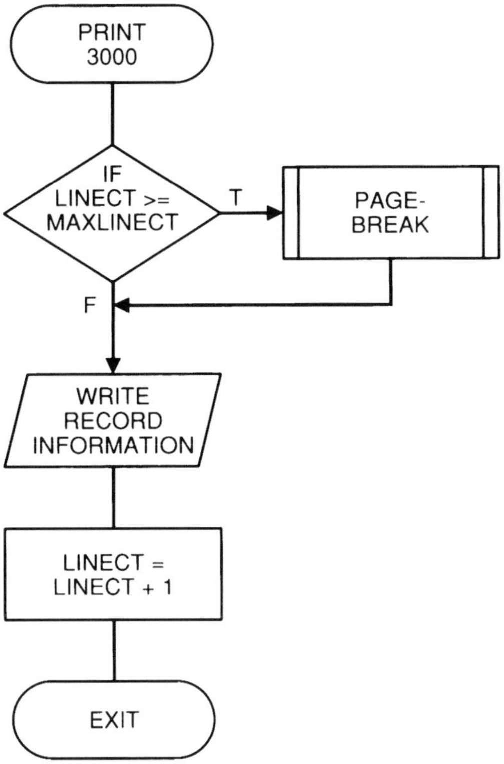

Figure 14.2e Algorithms and Flowcharts for Sales Problems

Algorithm	Flowchart
PAGE BREAK (3100) 1. EJECT PAGE 2. PAGENO = PAGENO + 1 3. WRITE PAGE HEADINGS (INCLUDING LINE SPACING) 4. LINECT = 3 5. PROCESS COLUMN HEADINGS 6. EXIT	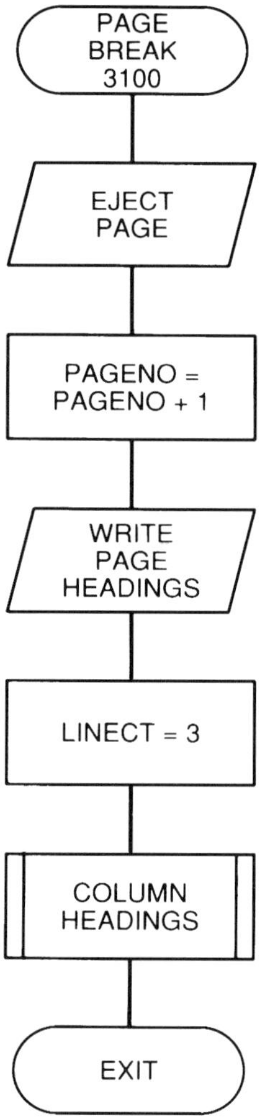

Figure 14.2f Algorithms and Flowcharts for Sales Problems

Algorithm	Flowchart
WRAPUP MODULE (5000) 1. WRITE SALESTOTAL 2. CLOSE 1 3. PRINT "RUN COMPLETED" 4. EXIT	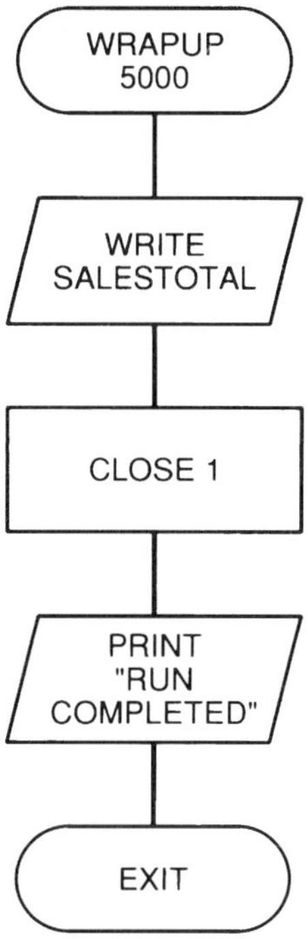

Figure 14.2g Algorithms and Flowcharts for Sales Problems

In order to design a program that processes control-breaks, designate one field, such as salesperson's number, as the control field. The file must be previously sorted using this field. The file must be in order of the salesperson's number so that each salesperson's records will be together in the file. If the file has not been sorted by salesperson's number, then the control-break cannot work; that is, the program will not process totals for each salesperson, much less compile the necessary information for each.

Keep the value of the control field of the first record, or the first record after the control-break occurs, in a holding variable memory location. This holding variable contains the first value of the control field of each group of records. In the example in Figure 14.3, the holding variable would be where the initial value of each salesperson's number is kept. The variable name used in the example is SNHOLD meaning *salesperson number hold value.* The value of the field is the same for all records for a salesperson; therefore, only the first value has to be kept. The salesperson's number does not change until a new salesperson is encountered. At that time the control-break is processed and the hold value is assigned a new value. The value of the control field of each record is compared to the hold value, and when they are no longer equal, the control-break occurs.

The Control-break Module processes all instructions that the computer has to follow each time the value of the control field changes. The instructions for the sales example stated previously in this chapter would include the following: Print the subtotals, add the subtotals to the total for the company, set each subtotal to zero, and set the hold value to the value of the new control field. In Figure 14.3 the control-break

Algorithm	Flowchart

INIT MODULE
(1000)

1. OPEN 1, SALES
2. SALESTOTAL = 0
* 3. SALESMANTOTAL = 0
4. MAXLINECT = 60
5. PAGENO = 1
6. PROCESS READ
* 7. SNHOLD = SN
8. PROCESS HEADINGS
9. EXIT

* Additions to solution

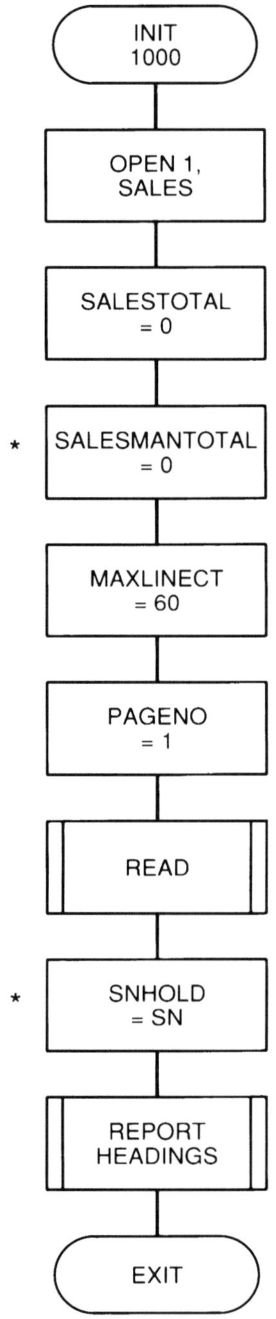

Figure 14.3a New and Revised Modules for Control-break

Algorithm	Flowchart

```
CALC MODULE
        (2000)

 *  1. ┌ IF SNHOLD <> SN
       ├─ THEN
       │     PROCESS
       │        SALESMAN
       │        CONTROL-BREAK
       └──────

**  2. SALESMANTOTAL =
       SALESMANTOTAL
       + SALES

    3. EXIT
```

* Additions to solution

** Changes to solution

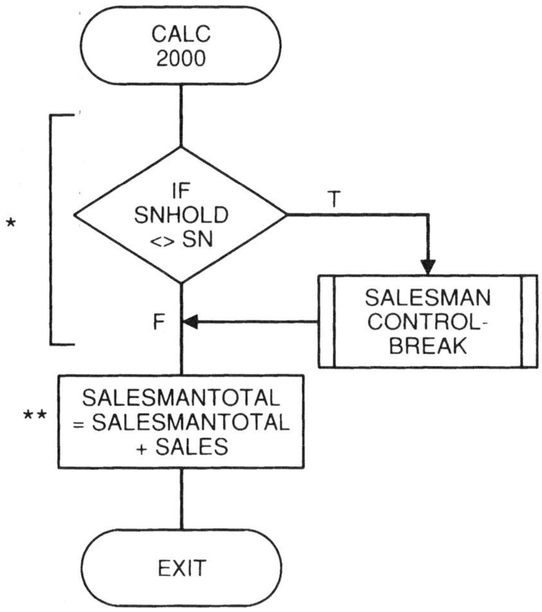

Figure 14.3b New and Revised Modules for Control-break

Algorithm	Flowchart
SALESMAN CONTROL-BREAK (2300) 1. WRITE SALESMANTOTAL 2. LINECT = LINECT + 4 3. SALESTOTAL = SALESTOTAL + SALESMANTOTAL 4. SALESMANTOTAL = 0 5. SNHOLD = SN 6. EXIT	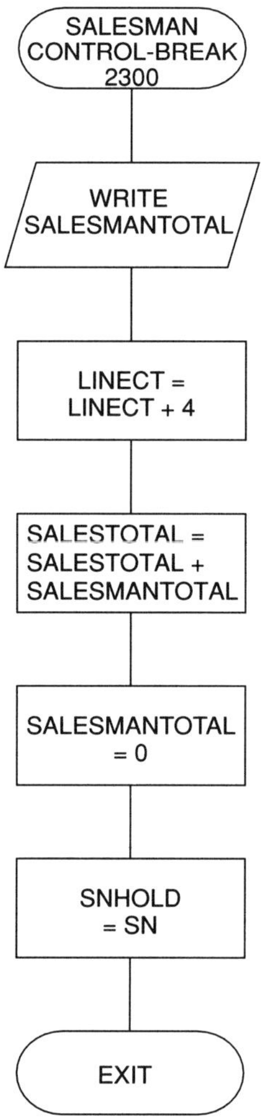

Figure 14.3c New and Revised Modules for Control-break

is illustrated. The salesperson's total is written to the printer. Next, the line count is incremented by the number of lines it took to write the totals, including the spacer lines. Next, the salesperson's total is added to the company total. Finally, the salesperson's total is set back to zero, and the salesperson's hold value (SNHOLD) is set equal to the new salesperson's number.

The Control-break is the only new module required to process control-breaks. However, you must make changes in other modules. In the Init Module, set the totals to zero and the hold value to the value of the control field for the first record. In the Calc Module, test for the Control-break. That is, test the present value of the control field against its hold value. When the two values are not equal, the Control-break Module will be processed. In the Wrapup Module, the control-break will be executed to process the totals for the last value of the control field.

Algorithm	Flowchart
WRAPUP (5000) 1. PROCESS SALESMAN CONTROL-BREAK 2. WRITE SALESTOTAL 3. CLOSE 1 4. PRINT "RUN COMPLETED" 5. EXIT * Additions to solution	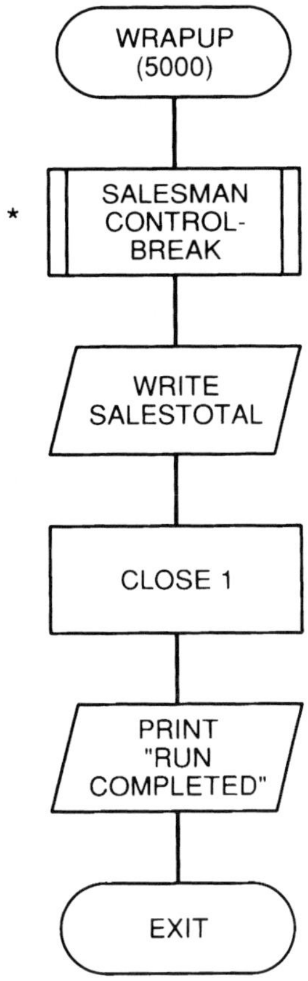

Figure 14.3d New and Revised Modules for Control-break

Notice in Figure 14.3a the two changes in the Init Module are to set the salesperson's total to zero, and the salesperson's hold value (SNHOLD) to the first person's number. In the Calc Module (Figure 14.3b) the hold value is compared to the current salesperson number. When they are not equal, the record is the first record for the next salesperson and, therefore, the control-break has to be processed. The other change in the Calc Module is that the salesperson's total is accumulated instead of the company's total. The company's total is accumulated in the Control-break Module using the salesperson's total. The last change is in the Wrapup Module in Figure 14.3d. The last salesperson's total must be written to the printer, and the company total must be updated before the completion of the processing; therefore, the control-break must be processed as the first instruction in the Wrapup Module.

Figure 14.3 shows all of the changes needed in the solution to the sales problem in order to include the subtotal for each salesperson. A single asterisk indicates where additional instructions were placed. The double asterisk indicates instructions that were changed.

Multiple Control-Breaks

Multiple control-breaks involve subtotals on more than one field. For example, the requirements of a problem might be to find the total sales for each region, for each district within each region, and for each salesperson within each district. In this case there would be three control fields—region, district, and salesperson. The file must be sorted using a concatenation of the fields on which there will be a control-break, starting with the field that encompasses the largest grouping, and ending with the field that encompasses the smallest grouping. This file would be sorted the following way: regions in order within the company; districts in order within each region; salespersons in order within each district. The programmer would sort the file on the concatenation (the combining of strings by placing the first in front of the second) of the three fields, with the largest area of sales first, the second largest second, and the smallest third. In this case, the file would be ordered by region + district + salesperson.

All instructions processed in a single control-break also would be executed in each of the control-breaks in a multiple control-break. In the Init Module, the programmer initializes all three totals to zero, and sets the hold values for all three control fields to the value of the first control field. In the Calc Module, all control fields are tested, moving from largest to smallest. The programmer designs a Control-break Module for each control field, with the first instruction a process block for the next smaller group.

Again, using the sales file as an example, whenever the region changes, the district and the salesperson fields also must change. This sweeping change occurs because there is no overlap of districts between regions, or of salespersons between districts. The programmer sets up the solution so that the largest group is processed, which then processes the next largest group, and so forth, until the smallest group has been processed. Figure 14.4 shows the structure chart of the multiple control-break for the sales file discussed in this section.

Figure 14.5 shows the algorithms and flowcharts of a multiple control-break for the sales problem illustrated throughout this chapter. SNHOLD, DNHOLD, and RNHOLD are the hold values for the salesperson, the district, and the region, respectively.

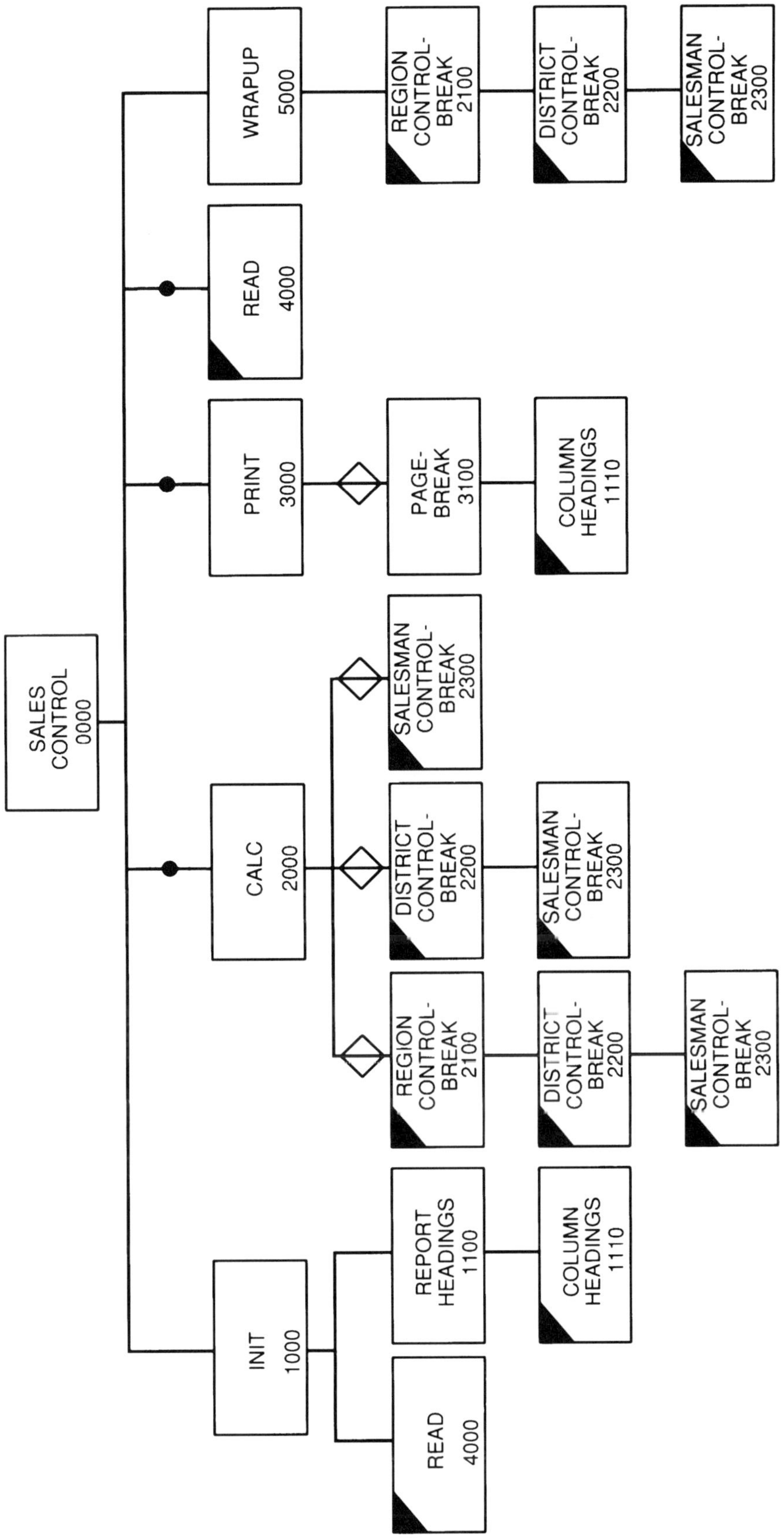

Figure 14.4 Structure Chart for Multiple Control-breaks

Algorithm

INIT MODULE
(1000)

1. OPEN 1, SALES
2. SALESTOTAL = 0
3. SALESMANTOTAL = 0
* 4. DISTRICTTOTAL = 0
* 5. REGIONTOTAL = 0
6. MAXLINECT = 60
7. PAGENO = 1
8. PROCESS READ
9. SNHOLD = SN
* 10. DNHOLD = DN
* 11. RNHOLD = RN
12. PROCESS REPORT HEADINGS
13. EXIT

* Additions to solution

Flowchart

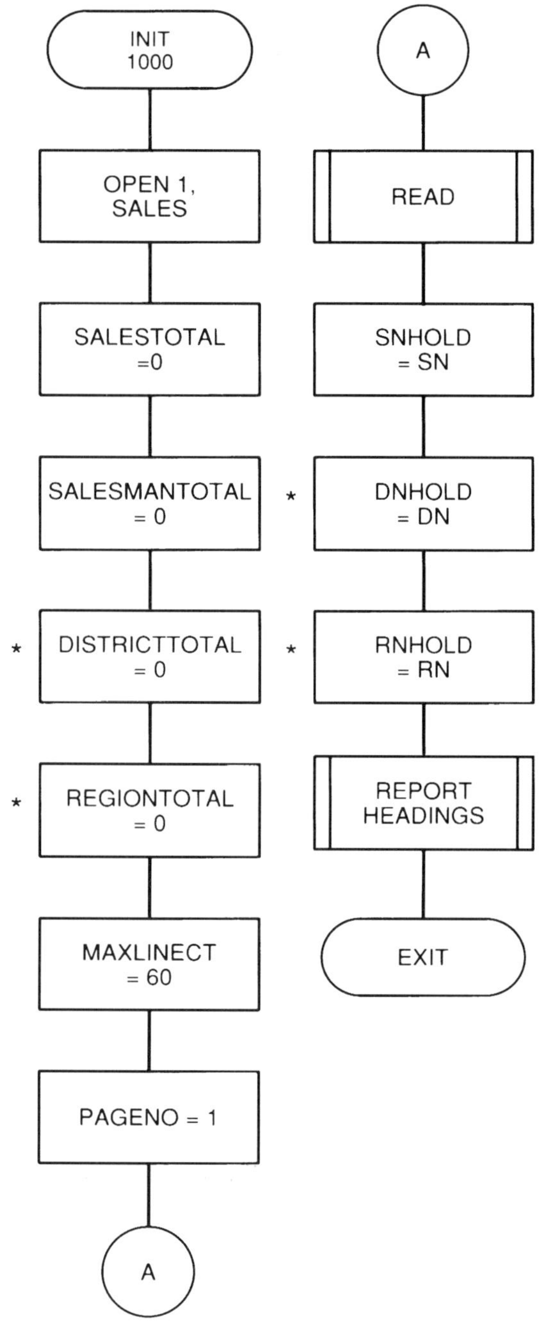

Figure 14.5a New and Revised Modules for Multiple Control-breaks

Algorithm	Flowchart

```
CALC MODULE
      (2000)

   1. IF RNHOLD <> RN
        THEN
           PROCESS REGION
              CONTROL-BREAK
        ELSE
           IF DNHOLD <> DN
              THEN
                 PROCESS
                    DISTRICT CONTROL-
                    BREAK
*             ELSE
                 IF SNHOLD <> SN
                    THEN
                       PROCESS
                          SALESMAN
                          CONTROL-BREAK
                    ELSE
                       CONTINUE

   2. SALESMANTOTAL = SALESMANTOTAL
      + SALES

   3. EXIT
```

* Additions to solution

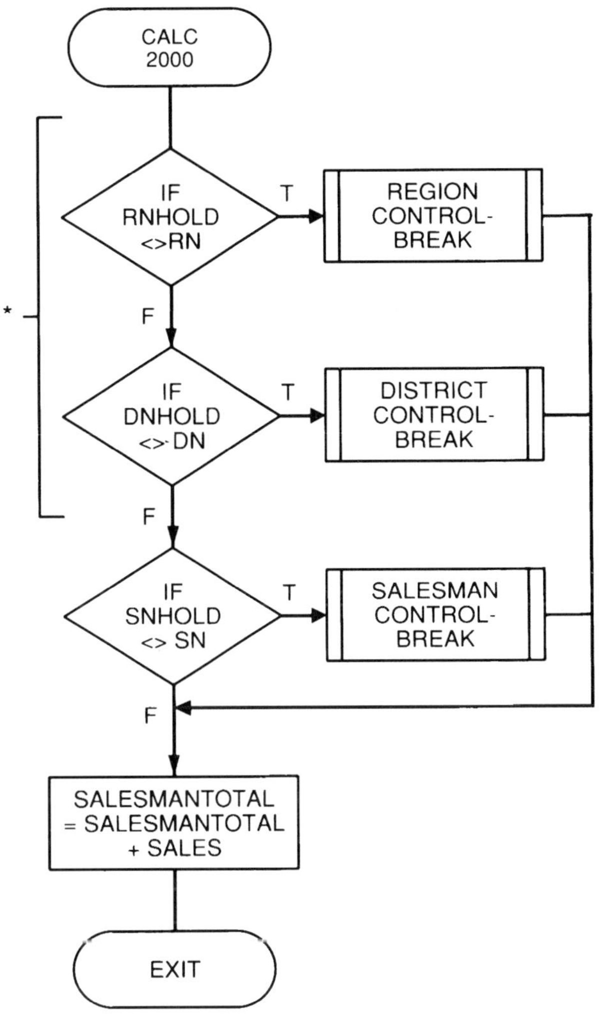

Figure 14.5b New and Revised Modules for Multiple Control-breaks

Algorithm	Flowchart
REGION CONTROL-BREAK MODULE (2100) 1. PROCESS DISTRICT CONTROL-BREAK 2. WRITE REGIONTOTAL 3. LINECT = LINECT + 4 4. SALESTOTAL = SALESTOTAL + REGIONTOTAL 5. REGIONTOTAL = 0 6. RNHOLD = RN 7. EXIT * New module * * Salesman Control-Break Module number is now 2300 instead of 2100	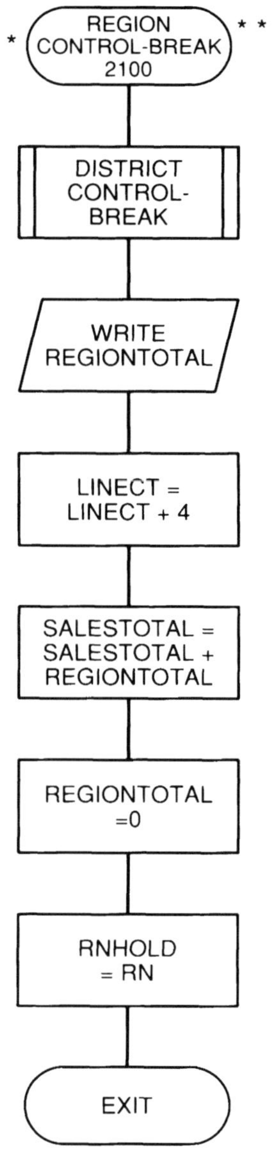

Figure 14.5c New and Revised Modules for Multiple Control-breaks

Algorithm	Flowchart
* DISTRICT CONTROL-BREAK (2200) 1. PROCESS SALESMAN CONTROL-BREAK 2. WRITE DISTRICTTOTAL 3. LINECT = LINECT + 4 4. REGIONTOTAL = REGIONTOTAL + DISTRICTTOTAL 5. DISTRICTTOTAL = 0 6. DNHOLD = DN 7. EXIT * New module ** The Salesman Control-Break now accumulates the district total instead of the company total.	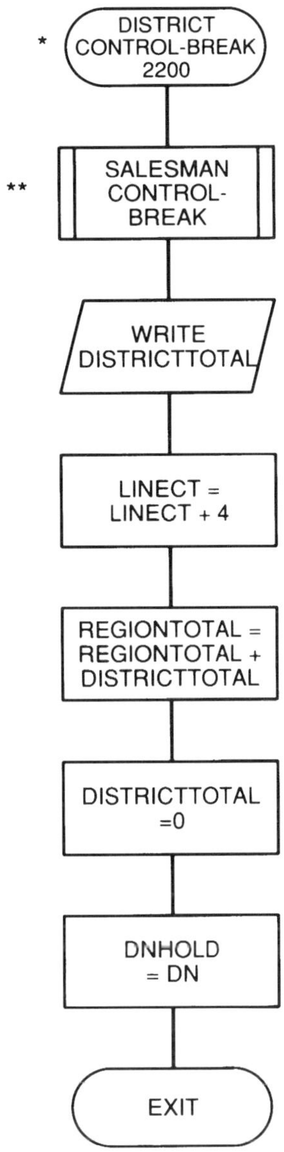

Figure 14.5d New and Revised Modules for Multiple Control-breaks

Algorithm	Flowchart
SALESMAN CONTROL-BREAK (2300) 1. WRITE SALESMANTOTAL 2. LINECT = LINECT + 4 3. DISTRICTTOTAL = DISTRICTTOTAL + SALESMANTOTAL 4. SALESMANTOTAL = 0 5. SNHOLD = SN 6. EXIT * This module is new	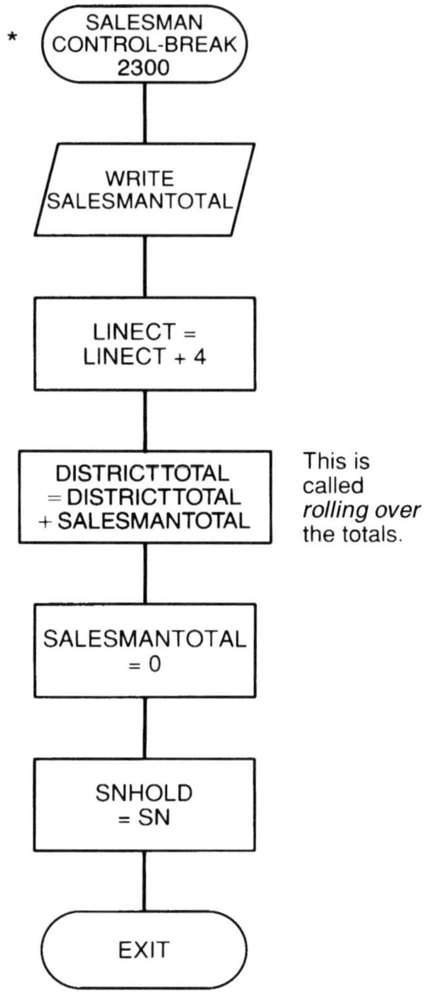

Figure 14.5e New and Revised Modules for Multiple Control-breaks

Algorithm	Flowchart
WRAPUP MODULE (5000) 1. PROCESS REGION CONTROL-BREAK 2. WRITE SALESTOTAL 3. CLOSE 1 4. PRINT "RUN COMPLETED" 5. EXIT ** Changes to solution	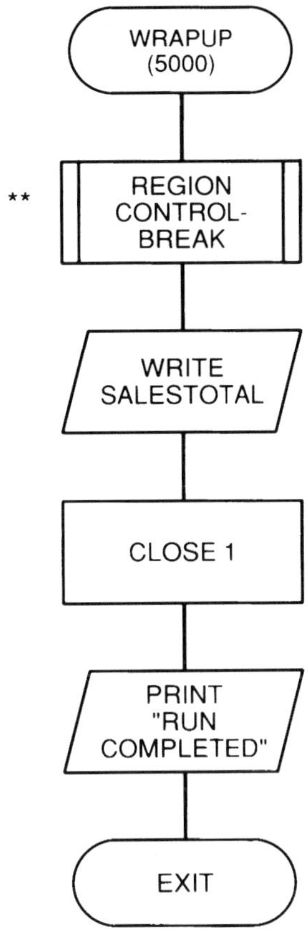

Figure 14.5f New and Revised Modules for Multiple Control-breaks

SN, DN, and RN are the current values of the salesperson's number, the district number, and the region number, respectively. Here again, the single asterisk indicates where additional instructions were placed. The double asterisk indicates instructions that were changed.

Using Indicators for Program Control

As in other types of processing, programmers can use indicators in record processing to change the normal course of processing. A printed date of purchase or sales may be required at the beginning of each page of a report and each time the date changes, but not with every record. The value of the control field may be printed only when it changes and at the start of a new page. Indicators are used to signal the computer regarding when to print the date or the value of the control field. Indicators also are used in data validation. Data validation is done by checking the data to see that it is correct or within proper range limits. When the computer finds an error, an indicator is set to TRUE to indicate that there has been an error. A programmer can then use this error indicator to signal the computer not to process the record that contains an error.

The sales example can be modified to show how a programmer can use an indicator to print the date of sales at the top of each page, as well as when the date of sales changes. The programmer sets an indicator to TRUE in both the Page-break Module and the Read Module to indicate when the date is to be printed. In the Print Module, the indicator is tested; when it is on, the date of sales is printed. When it is off, the date of sales is not printed. Figure 14.6 illustrates the use of indicators in the sales problem used throughout this chapter.

Error Handling

For data validation (finding errors in the data records), you need a new module to be processed from the Read Module. Data validation is accomplished through the decision structure. Usually, straight-through logic is used because all data error conditions have to be processed in order for the computer to find all errors in the record. The conditions for data validation are provided to the programmer by the problem. When the computer finds an error while processing the Error Validation Module, a message is written to an error report, the error indicator is set equal to TRUE, and the processing of the Data Validation Module or Error Module is continued. If any errors are found, the record with errors is not processed, and the next record is read. This results in two reports—the regular report, which excludes the records with errors, and the error report (sometimes called an exceptions report), which includes them. For example, a Data Validation or Error Module might check to see that the amount of a check is less than a given amount, or that an account number is all numbers, or that a name is all letters.

After the computer reads the record in the Read Module, it should process the Error Module. In the programming, use a loop structure to read until a good record or an END-OF-FILE is found. Examples of the Read Module and the Error Module for the sales problem are found in Figure 14.7.

Algorithm	Flowchart

INIT MODULE
(1000)

1. OPEN 1, SALES
2. SALESTOTAL = 0
3. SALESMANTOTAL = 0
4. DISTRICTTOTAL = 0
5. REGIONTOTAL = 0
6. MAXLINECT = 60
7. PAGENO = 1
8. * DATEHOLD = " "
9. PROCESS READ
10. SNHOLD = SN
11. DNHOLD = DN
12. RNHOLD = RN
13. PROCESS REPORT HEADINGS
14. EXIT

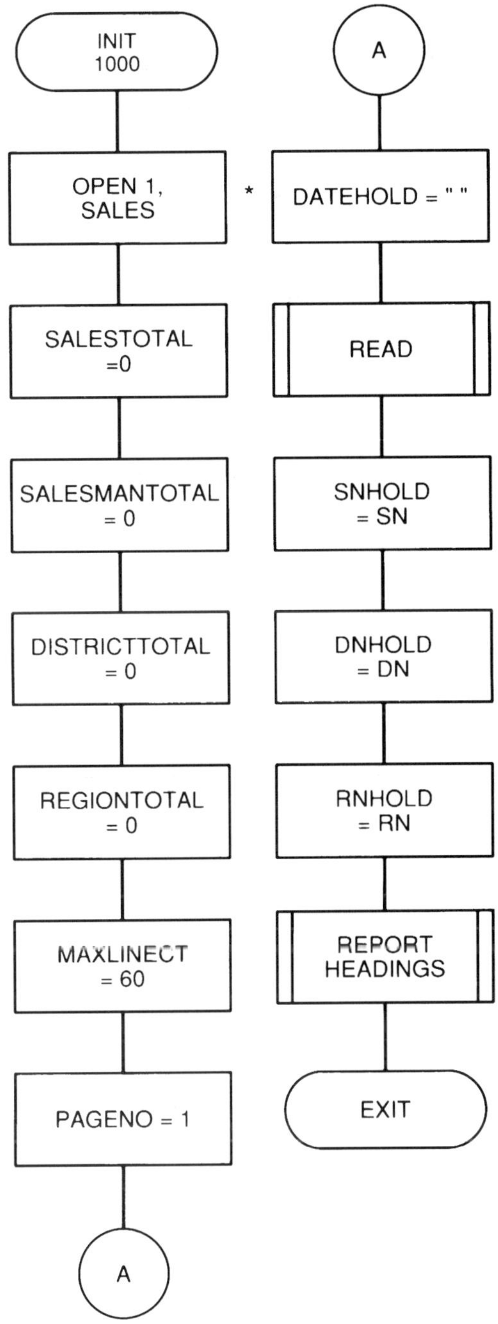

* Additions to solution

Figure 14.6a Use of Indicator

Algorithm	Flowchart
READ MODULE (4000) 1. READ RECORD * 2. IF DATEHOLD <> DATE AND NOT EOF(1) — THEN DATEINDICATOR = TRUE DATEHOLD = DATE — ELSE CONTINUE 3. EXIT * Additions to solution	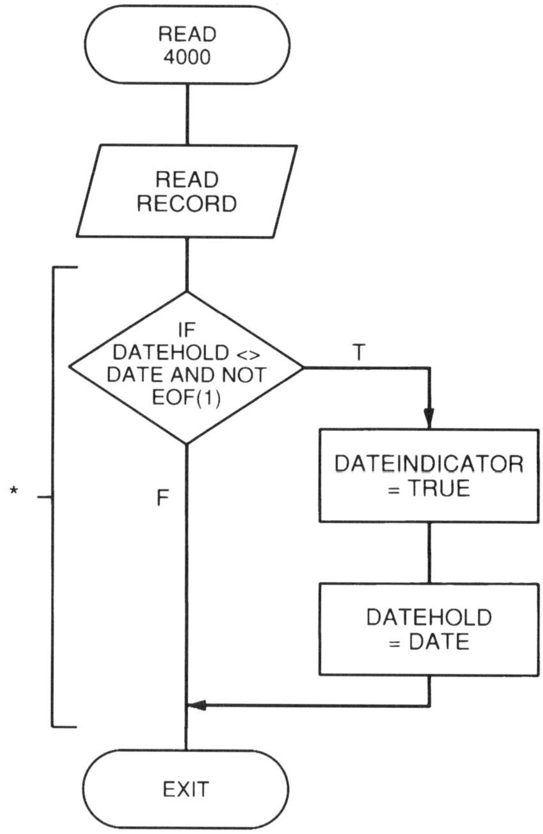

Figure 14.6b Use of Indicator

Algorithm	Flowchart
PRINT MODULE (3000) 1. IF LINECT >= MAXLINECT — THEN PROCESS PAGE-BREAK * 2. IF DATE INDICATOR — THEN WRITE DATE W/O {CR} DATEINDICATOR = FALSE 3. WRITE RECORD INFORMATION 4. LINECT = LINECT + 1 5. EXIT * Additions to solution	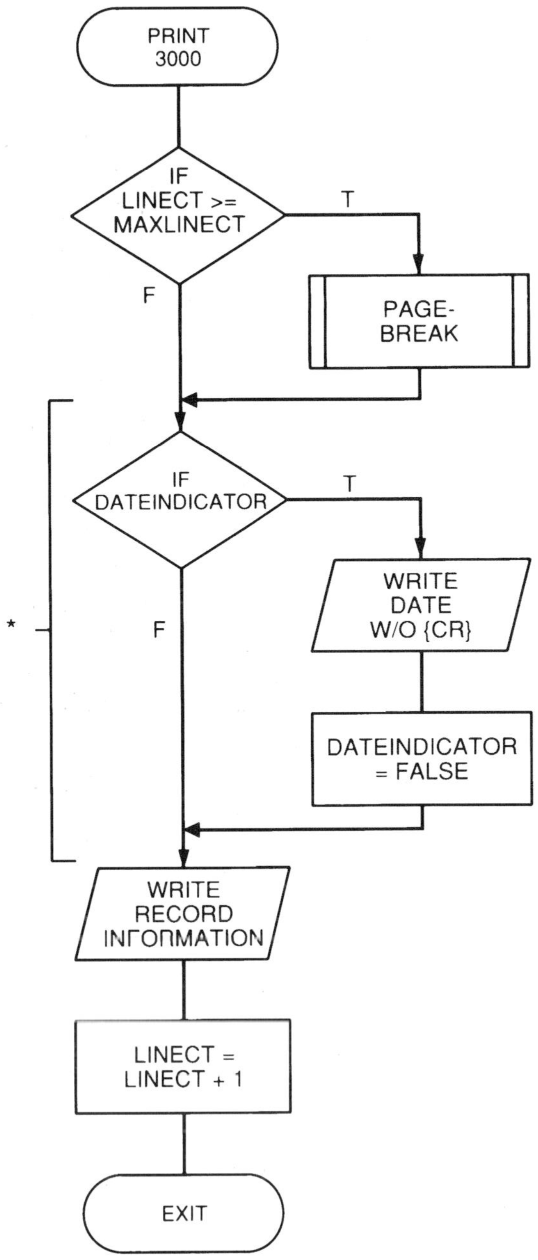

Figure 14.6c Use of Indicator

Algorithm	Flowchart

PAGE-BREAK MODULE
(3100)

1. EJECT PAGE
2. PAGENO = PAGENO + 1
3. WRITE PAGE HEADINGS
4. LINECT = 3
* 5. DATEINDICATOR = TRUE
6. PROCESS COLUMN HEADINGS
7. EXIT

* Additions to solution

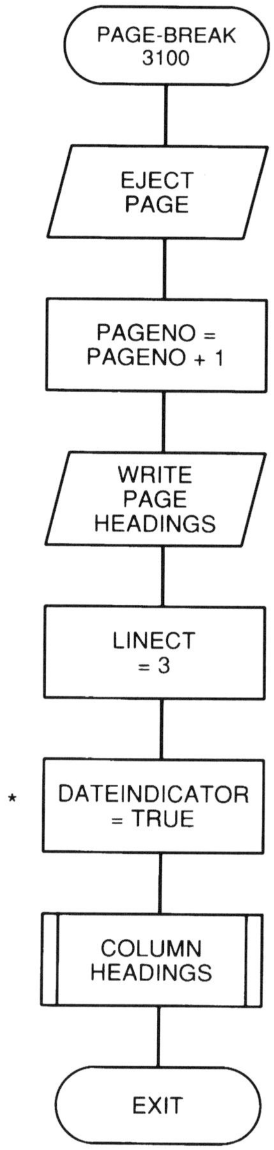

Figure 14.6d Use of Indicator

Algorithm	Flowchart
READ MODULE (4000) 1. REPEAT READ RECORD ERRORINDICATOR = FALSE PROCESS ERROR UNTIL ERROR INDICATOR = FALSE OR EOF(1) 2. IF NOT EOF(1) AND DATEHOLD <> DATE THEN DATEINDICATOR = TRUE DATEHOLD = DATE 3. EXIT	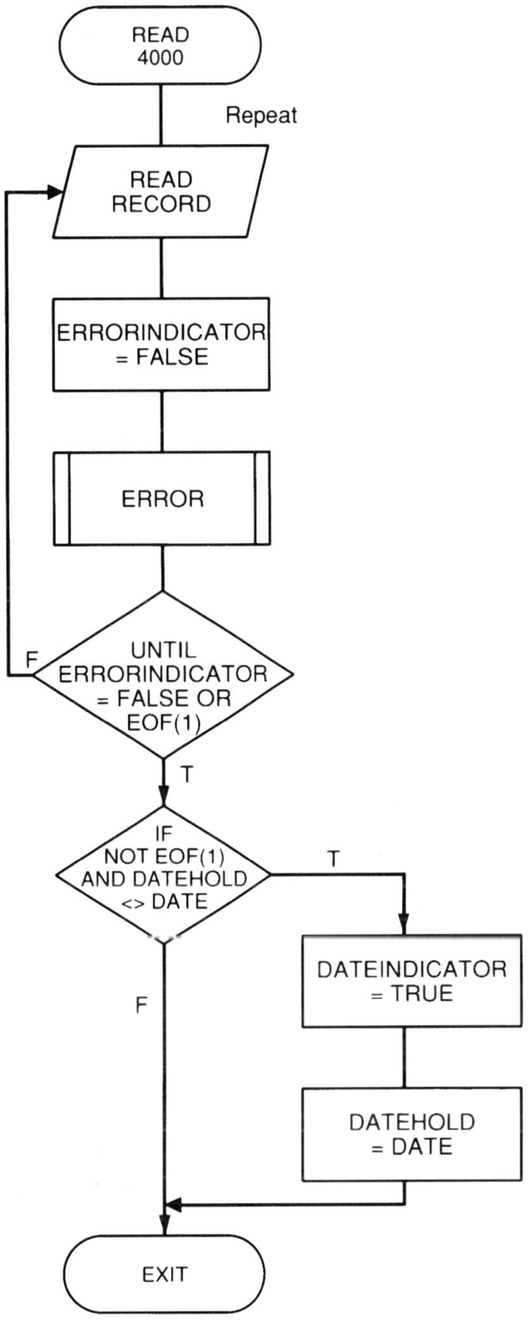

Figure 14.7 Data Error Handling (*continued on page 322*)

Algorithm	Flowchart

```
ERROR MODULE
     (4100)

1. ┌ IF NOT EOF(1)
   │
   ├── THEN
   │    ┌ IF <DATA> INVALID
   │    │
   │    ├── THEN
 * │    │       ERRORINDICATOR
   │    │          = TRUE
   │    │       WRITE ERROR
   │    │          MESSAGE
   │    └────────────────
   └─────────────────────

2.  EXIT
```

* Repeat for each error check

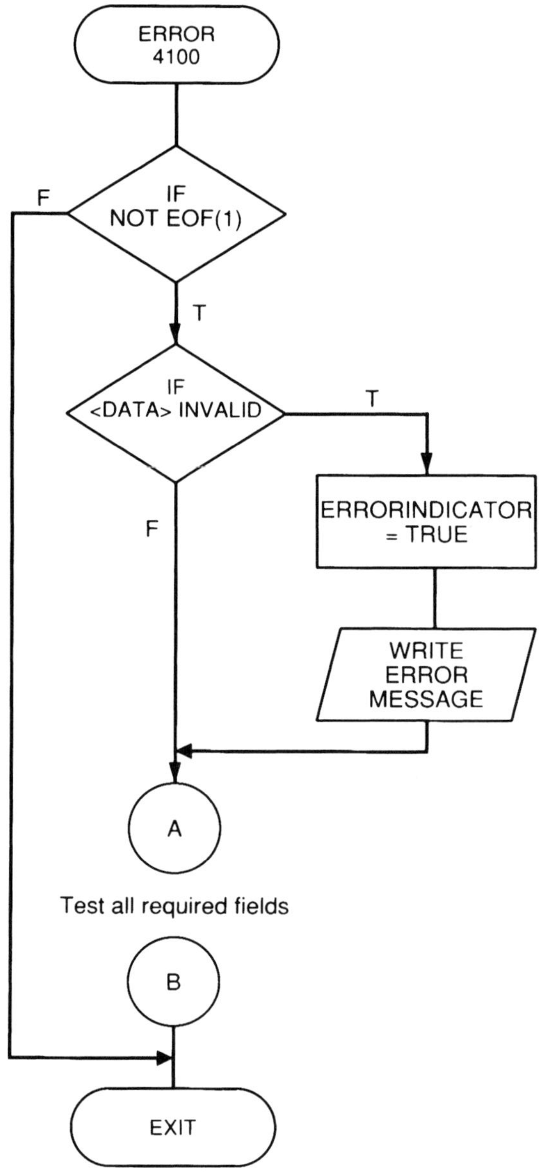

Figure 14.7 *(continued from page 321)*

Algorithm	Flowchart

INIT MODULE
(1000)

1. OPEN 1, SALES
2. SALESTOTAL = 0
3. SALESMANTOTAL = 0
4. DISTRICTTOTAL = 0
5. REGIONTOTAL= 0
6. MAXLINECT = 60
7. PAGENO = 1
8. DATEHOLD = " "
9. PROCESS READ
10. IF EOF(1)
    THEN
        PRINT ERROR MESSAGE
        NULLINDICATOR = TRUE
    ELSE
        SNHOLD = SN
        DNHOLD = DN
        RNHOLD = RN
        PROCESS REPORT HEADINGS
11. EXIT

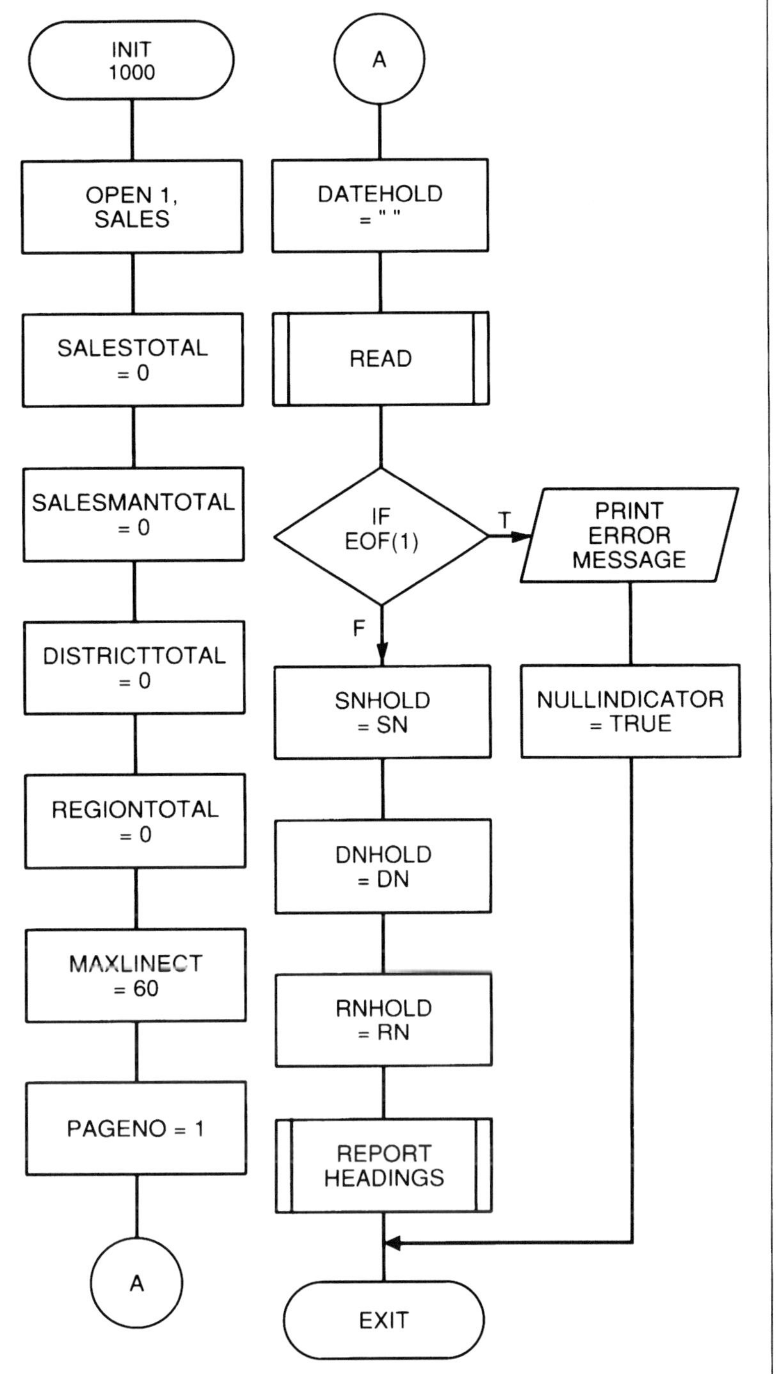

Figure 14.8 The Null File (*continued on page 324*)

Algorithm	Flowchart
WRAPUP MODULE (5000) 1. IF NOT NULLINDICATOR THEN PROCESS REGION CONTROL-BREAK WRITE SALESTOTAL 2. CLOSE 1 3. PRINT "RUN COMPLETED" 4. EXIT	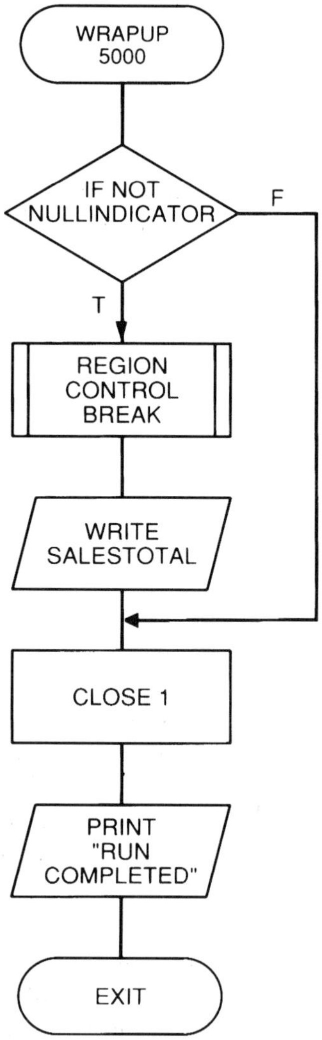

Figure 14.8 (*continued from page 323*)

Often a large portion of the processing of a record is data validation. It is an important part of record processing because it helps eliminate problematical and costly errors.

Null Files

Another problem that arises when you are working with files is how to deal with the **null file,** or empty file. If a file is empty the computer prints an error message on the screen and processing halts. See Figure 14.8 to see the changes a programmer makes in the Init and the Wrapup Modules to accommodate a null file. The Init Module is designed so a null file indicator is set to TRUE, an error message is printed, and all processing is skipped, except to close the files in the Wrapup Module if an END-OF-FILE is encountered after the primer Read.

Summary

The concepts of record processing, including control-breaks, indicators, and data validation, are important to both programming and applications. Control-breaks are important because many business reports call for subtotals or other intermediate results, such as the number of customers a salesperson contacted or the number of items in an inventory.

A good programmer designs output reports with the user in mind. Report headings, data placement, and general organization are very important.

A programmer handles data errors, null files, or changes in processing with the use of indicators. A finished solution should be as correct and as foolproof as possible. Data-entry errors are made often. Even if 99% of entry records are correct, that means there is still one error in every one hundred entries. With thousands of pieces of data entered daily, there are many errors. Indicators are used any time the programmer needs to indicate to the computer that another set of instructions is to be used.

For computer users in business, sequential-access processing techniques such as those covered in this chapter are keys to productivity.

New Terms

control-break
multiple control-break
null file
page-break

Questions

1. Name the items to consider when designing a record. Explain each.
2. What is a page-break?
3. What are control-breaks?
4. What is a null file?
5. Why is it important to consider a null file when processing files?

Problems

Using the input records and systems flowcharts developed in Chapter 13, develop a solution for the following problems. Your solution should include a Problem Analysis chart, an IPO chart, a data dictionary, a structure chart, algorithms and flowcharts for each module, and an output report design.

1. Develop a solution to calculate the gross pay for the employees of a company. The input records should include the following: name, address, social security number, pay type (H = hourly, S = salary), rate of pay, and hours worked. The output report should include all input data plus the gross pay.
2. A sales manager wants a program that lists all of the company's customers according to the salesperson assigned to each. She would also like the number of the salesperson's customers to be totaled at the end of the list. The name of the salesperson should be printed only at the top of the page or when the processing encounters a new salesperson. The input file contains the following data: the customer's name, address, and telephone number, and the salesperson's name.
3. Develop a solution for an inventory problem. The input record should include the following: the inventory number, the department number, the store number, the item description, the quantity, the wholesale price, the markup percentage, and the vendor. The output report should include the input data, plus the retail price, the total value of the item in stock (quantity * price), and the total wholesale and retail values of the stock for each department and for each store. The company totals should be printed at the end of the report.
4. A sales manager would like to be able to track the clients of each of her salespeople. She would like to know when each customer was last contacted, the outcome of the contact (not interested, sale made, call back later, no contact made), the sale amount if a sale was made, and the name and number of the salesperson. She would like the list of clients to be in chronological order according to the last contact time by salesperson. She would also like a total of sales per day per salesperson. Develop the solution to the manager's problem. In what order should the file be sorted?

   What would you have to do if the manager also wanted a client list in alphabetical order?

Chapter 15

Sequential-Access File Updating

Overview

Creating Files
The Master File
Transaction Files
Activity Files
Backup Files
Updating the Master File Using a Transaction File
A Useful Alternative Method

Objectives

When you have finished this chapter, you should be able to:

1. Design a computer program to update sequential files.
2. List and explain the different types of files including the master file, the transaction file, the activity file, and the backup file.

Businesses are dynamic, and so are their data-processing requirements. Therefore, the data files used in business must be easily updated. Chapter 14 explained how to process a sequential-access file, including data validation, but it did not explain how to update one. This chapter explains and illustrates the technique for updating a sequential file using a transaction file.

Updating a file means adding, deleting, or changing records to keep the information in the file current.

1. *Adding records.* When new data are generated, new records have to be added to a file. When a new employee starts work, data about that person must be added to the personnel file; when a sale has been made, the data from the sales receipt must be added to the sale file, and so on.
2. *Deleting records.* There must be a way to delete obsolete data from a file. When a record is deleted, the user chooses one of several options about what to do with it. These options include:
   a. the record may be discarded, never to be seen again;

   b. the record may be placed in an archival file, so that the information can be retrieved at a later date, if needed;
   c. the record may be placed in an activity file to show when it was deleted.
3. *Changing records.* Data in a record must be changed from time to time for a variety of reasons. The data may be incorrect, or they may have changed. When data have changed, the date and the changes themselves can go into an activity file for future inquiries.

Files can be processed in two ways. The first method is **batch processing,** in which data collected over a period of time are processed all at once without human intervention. This is the most efficient for the computer because it doesn't have to wait for a person to respond. However, it is not as efficient for people since they have to wait until a batch-run is made. Because of the relatively long batch turnaround time, data that are currently being used are frequently not up-to-date. The more efficient type of processing for people is **interactive processing,** in which data are entered and updated at the same time. In this case, the data in the file are as current as the data being entered at any given time. The person communicating with the computer is interacting with it through commands or menus. The use of commands and menus to update files is discussed in Chapter 16.

Since sequential files are processed in order, it is inefficient to update them interactively. Therefore, sequential files are best updated by batch processing. All of the changes are put into a transaction file, which is a separate file that is periodically used to update all the files at one time. This update may be done daily, weekly, or as often as company policies require.

Creating Files

You have to create a file before you can use it. That is, you have to design the structure of the file and communicate it to the computer. This structure includes the layout of the record and the kind of file—sequential or random-access. The files discussed in this chapter, as well as all other files, are designed by the methods described in Chapter 13. Use the record data dictionary and layout form (Appendix D, Figure D.6) to design the structure of the record. When you create a file, you designate the fields of each record and specify the attributes of each field, such as the name of the field, the length of the field, the data type, and the number of decimals of numeric. All records have different data but the same attributes. Then you put together the record layout to specify the way the record will look.

When you create a new file from an old one, all previous data in the file are destroyed. Therefore, create a new file over an old one only when it is necessary, and when you wish to delete the information in the old file.

The Master File

The **master data file** is the file in which all the data needed for processing are kept current. Common types of master files include inventory files, payroll files, and mailing list files. The files used in the sequential-access solutions in Chapter 14 are master data files. The data are arranged in order of processing, and they are kept in the same order during processing and after the updates are completed. In this chapter, the terminology *old mas-*

ter file and *new master file* are used. The former means the master file before the update, and the latter expression refers to the master file after the update.

Transaction Files

Transaction files contain all the data needed to update the master file. You construct a transaction file by entering records that contain new data for the master file. The entries are made as new data arise and then are sorted according to the requirements of the master file. The records in the transaction file must be in the same order as that in the master file since they will be used to update the master file records sequentially. That is, if the master file is sorted in account number order, then the transaction file must be sorted in account number order. Or if the master file is sorted according to the last name, then the transaction file must be sorted accordingly.

Activity Files

All completed file updates are listed in an **activity file** (audit trail file). Each time a user executes the update program, he or she will append the activity file (add new entries to the end of the file) to show what has happened to the master file. The activity file is the only file in a company from which the records are never deleted. It is important because it is the only file that can tell auditors what has happened to any particular record.

Backup Files

Backup files contain the records as they were before the last file update. It is important to keep backup files in case something happens to the current master file. Machine or human errors that destroy part or all of a file are fairly common occurrences. If the current master file is destroyed, the user can copy the backup file into the old master file, rerun the update program with the last transaction file, and then start the processing again. There are two ways to make a backup file: one is to rename the old master file (containing the data that existed before the most recent update) as a backup; the other is to copy a file—old, new, master, transaction, or activity—onto another auxiliary storage medium, either disk or tape.

Updating the Master File Using a Transaction File

Figure 15.1 shows a generalized systems flowchart to update a sequential-access file. Figure 15.2a–d shows a specific solution for updating a file. You design an update solution by using the loop structure and the decision structure. Be cautious to avoid common programming errors, such as allowing the addition of a record with a key field that already exists. The key field, remember, is the field that has a unique piece of data that is

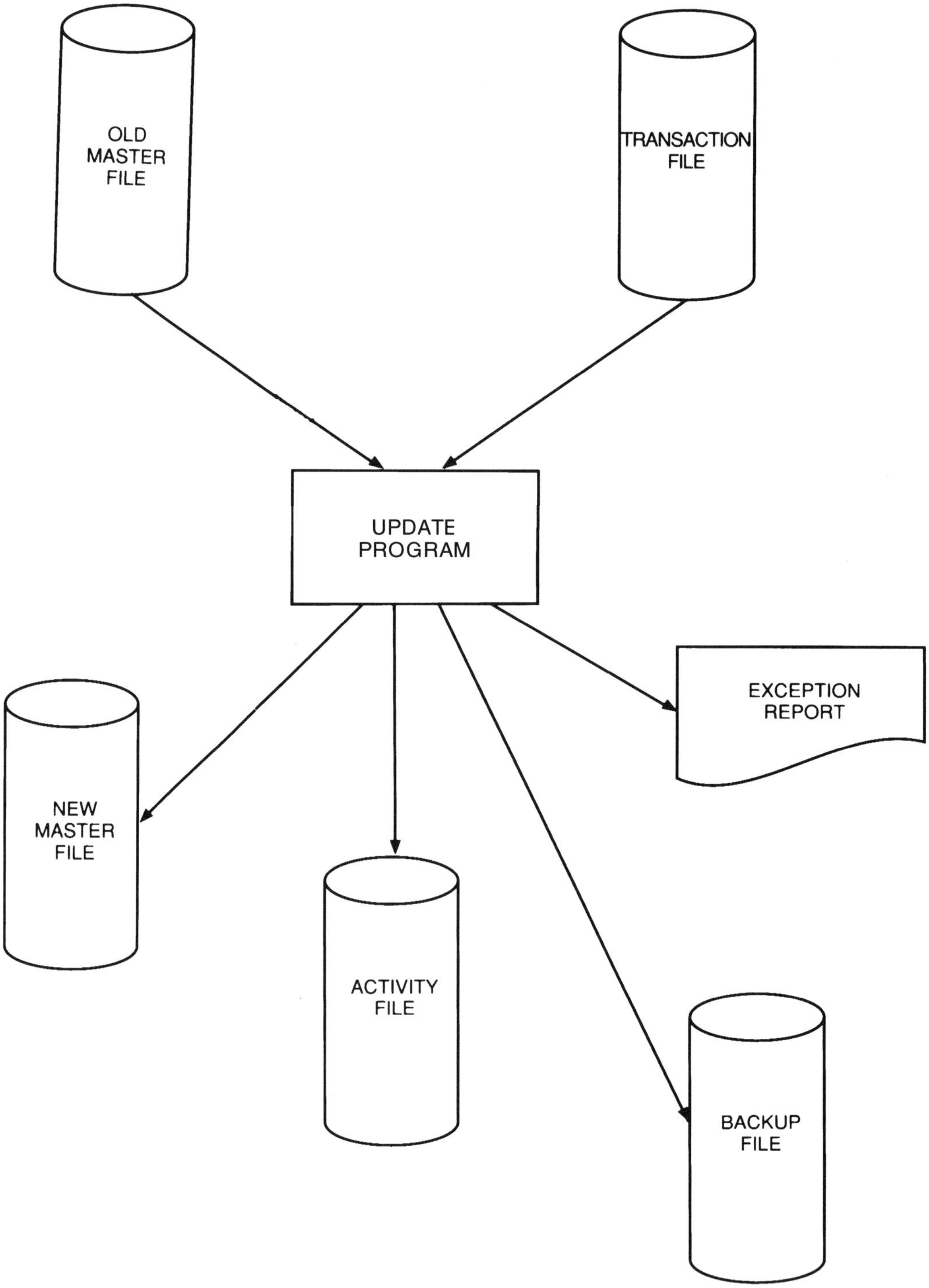

Figure 15.1 Systems Flowchart to Update a Sequential-Access File

UPDATE FILE MODULE

```
1. WHILE NOT EOF(MF) AND NOT EOF(TF)
     IF MFKEY = TFKEY
       THEN
         IF TCODE = "D"
           THEN
             WRITE AF RECORD
             READ MF RECORD
             READ TF RECORD
           ELSE
             IF TCODE = "C"
               THEN
                 WRITE AF RECORD
                 PROCESS CHANGE
                 READ TF RECORD
                 IF MFKEY <> TFKEY
                   THEN
                     WRITE MF RECORD TO HF
                     READ MF RECORD
               ELSE
                 ERROR CODE = 2
                 PROCESS ERROR
                 READ TF RECORD
       ELSE
         IF MFKEY < TFKEY
           THEN
             WRITE MF RECORD TO HF
             READ MF RECORD
           ELSE
             IF TCODE = "A"
               THEN
                 WRITE AF RECORD
                 WRITE TF RECORD TO HF
                 READ TF RECORD
               ELSE
                 ERROR CODE = 1
                 PROCESS ERROR
                 READ TF RECORD
   WHILE-END
```

Figure 15.2a Sequential-File Updating Through a Transaction File—Algorithm

```
2.   ┌ IF EOF(MF)
     ├──── THEN
     │        ┌ WHILE NOT EOF(TF)
     │        │    ┌ IF TCODE = "A"
     │        │    ├──── THEN
     │        │    │          WRITE AF RECORD
     │        │    │          WRITE TF RECORD TO HF
     │        │    ├──── ELSE
     │        │    │          ERROR CODE = 2
     │        │    └───────── PROCESS ERROR
     │        │      READ TF RECORD
     │        └ WHILE-END
     ├──── ELSE
     │        ┌ WHILE NOT EOF(MF)
     │        │      WRITE MF RECORD TO HF
     │        │      READ MF RECORD
     │        └ WHILE-END
     └──────────

3.      CLOSE FILES (MF, TF, HF, AF)

4.      REPLACE BACKUP FILE WITH MF

5.      REPLACE MF WITH HF

6.      EXIT
```

Figure 15.2b Sequential-File Updating Through a Transaction File—Algorithm

used to order the master file and the transaction file. This error can be caused by incorrectly entering a key in the transaction file. Entering an incorrect key can cause another error: trying to delete or change a nonexistent record. Therefore, part of the solution should contain checks so that any transaction records containing such errors are not used to update the master file but instead are written to an error output report. Check data for errors by using an IF/THEN/ELSE instruction. When an error is found, that transaction record will not be processed but will be written to the error output record. See Chapter 14 for more information about error checks.

[An alternative solution to the problem of updating a sequential file is presented in the final section of this chapter and illustrated in Figure 15.4a–d (pp. 348–351). See the discussion there.]

After the data in a transaction record have been used to update the file, a new transaction record is read into internal memory. Likewise, after a master file record has been updated, or found to have no changes, a new master file record is read into internal memory. Through the use of transaction codes—codes that indicate to the computer what type of transaction is to take place, whether adding the record, deleting the record, or changing the record—and the comparison of the transaction record to the master file record, the file is updated record by record.

Flowchart

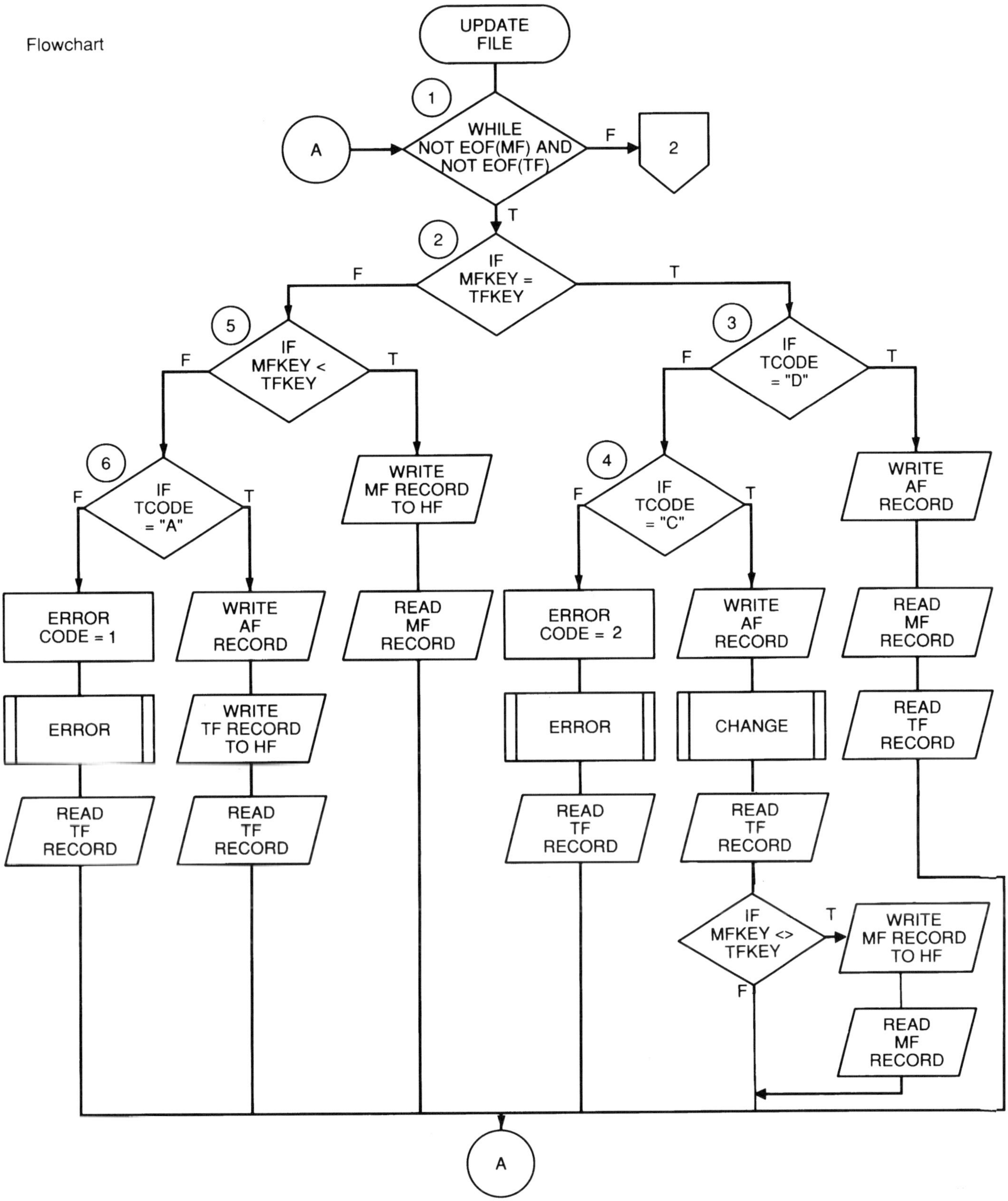

Figure 15.2c Sequential-File Updating Through a Transaction File—Flowchart

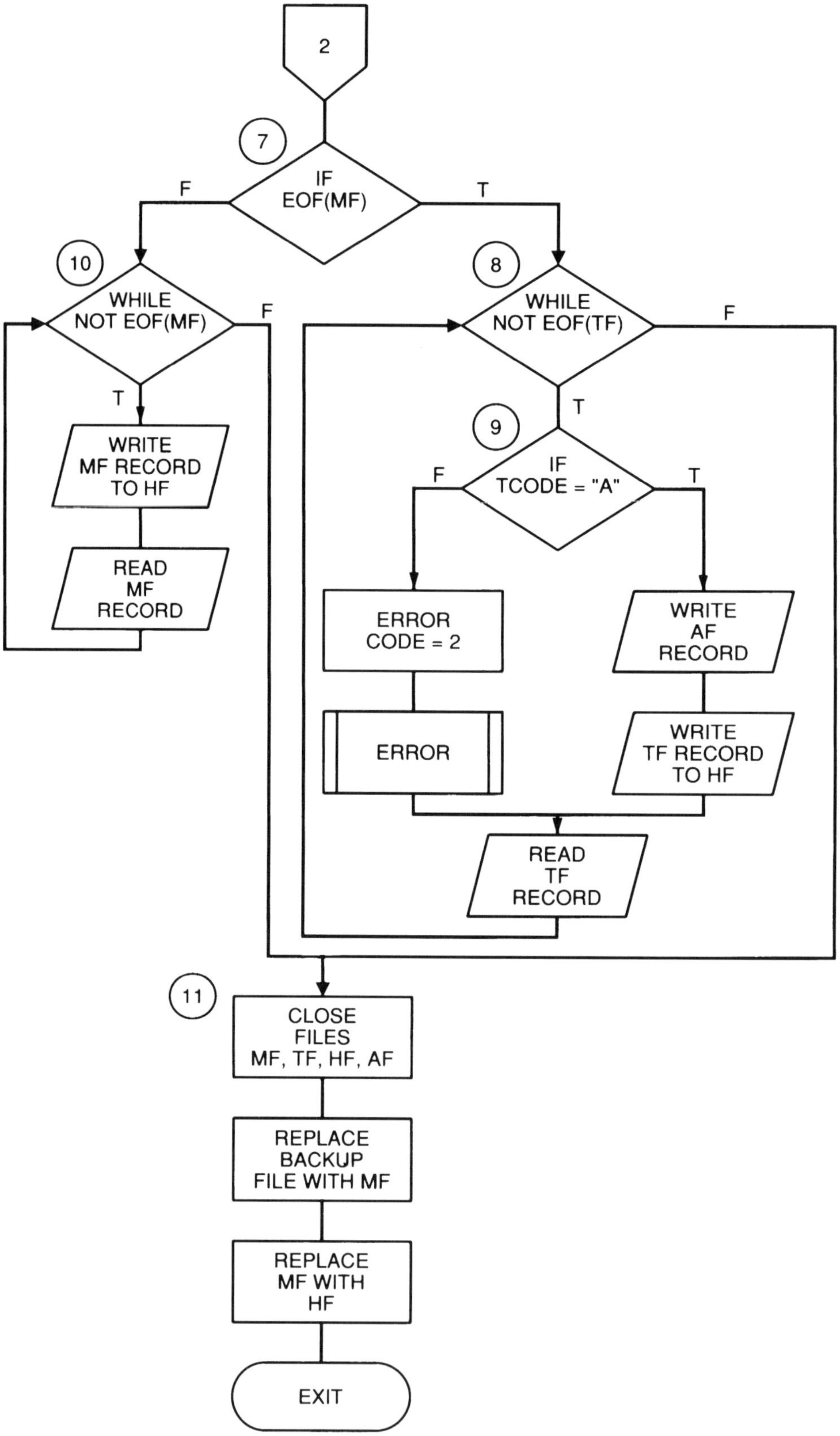

Figure 15.2d Sequential-File Updating Through a Transaction File—Flowchart

The master file might contain payroll data, inventory data, or sales data. The technique of updating is the same for all sequential files and does not depend on the type of data in a given file. The example in Figure 15.2, therefore, indicates the type of files to be read in and used rather than using specific data. The following notes explain each of the steps in Figure 15.2.

Notes For Figure 15.2

Definitions

- MF—old master file
- TF—transaction file
- AF—activity file
- HF—new master file
- TCODE—transaction code (a field in the transaction record)
  "A"—add a record
  "D"—delete a record
  "C"—change a record
- MFKEY—master file key field
- TFKEY—transaction key field
- ERRORCODE—code that indicates an error has been found: a 1 indicates an attempt to change to delete a nonexistent record; a 2 indicates that a record with a duplicate key is being added.

The numbers of the notes correspond to the circled numbers in the flowchart.

1. This loop continues as long as there are records in both the old master file and the transaction file. When the END-OF-FILE (EOF) of either file is reached, the processing continues at 7.
2. When the old master file key field is equal to the transaction file key field, the only two processes that occur are changing or deleting records. When the two fields are not equal, either the old master file record is to remain the same, or the transaction file record is added to the master file. There may be many records that will not have any updates made to them.
3. When the transaction code is equal to "D", then the information is written to the activity file, and another master file record and another transaction file record are read. Since the record was not written to the new master file, it has been deleted.
4. When the transaction code is equal to "C", then the information is written to the activity file, the master record is changed internally in the computer's memory (not in external memory), and then the changed master file record is written to the new master file. Another transaction file record is then read. This transaction file key is checked against the current master file key. If they are equal, processing continues without reading in another master file record. If they are not equal, then no more updating needs to be done to the current master file record, and another one is read.

   If the transaction file and master file keys are equal and the transaction code does not equal either "D" or "C", then there is an error in the transaction record. When an error occurs, an error message is written to an error report, and another transaction record is read.

5. When the master file key is less than the transaction file key, then nothing has to be done to that record. The master file record is written to the new master file, and another master file record is read.
6. When the master file key is greater than the transaction file key, then the transaction file should be added to the master file. When the transaction code is equal to an "A", then the information is written to the activity file, the transaction record is written to the new master file, and another transaction record is read. If the master file key is greater than the transaction file key and the transaction code does not equal "A", then there is an error in the transaction record. An error message is then written to the error report, and another transaction record is read.
7. When an EOF occurs in either the old master file or the transaction file, the preceding loop stops, and the program processes the remaining records on the file that has not encountered an EOF. That is, if the EOF is encountered on the old master file, then the remaining transaction file records are processed; if the EOF is encountered on the transaction file, then the remaining old master file records are processed.
8. The transaction file records are processed until the EOF on the transaction file has been reached.
9. The remaining records on the transaction file must be records to be added to the master file. When the transaction code is equal to "A", then the information is written to the activity file, the transaction record is written to the new master file, and another transaction file record is read. If the transaction code is not equal to "A", then there is an error in the transaction file record. When an error occurs, an error message is written to the error report, and another transaction file record is read.
10. The master file records are processed until the EOF on the old master file is encountered. Since there are no more transactions to be done on the master file, these records are simply written to the new master file and a new record is read.
11. After the EOF has been encountered on both the old master file and the transaction file, all files are closed. Then the data in the backup file are replaced with the data in the old master file, and the data in the old master file are replaced with the data in the new master file. It is then ready to be used for the next update processing.

Putting It All Together

Figure 15.3 demonstrates a complete solution for an update to an inventory file. The Control Module (Figure 15.3b) is very simple: the INIT is processed, then the UPDATE module, and finally the WRAPUP module. The INIT module of Figure 15.3c opens the four files and reads the first record in the old master file (the inventory file) and the transaction file.

The UPDATE module (Figure 15.3d) contains three loops. The first loop continues as long as there are records in both files. Either the second or third loop completes the process of updating the inventory file. In the first loop, one module (EQUAL) is processed when the transaction file key (TINVNO) is equal to the master file key

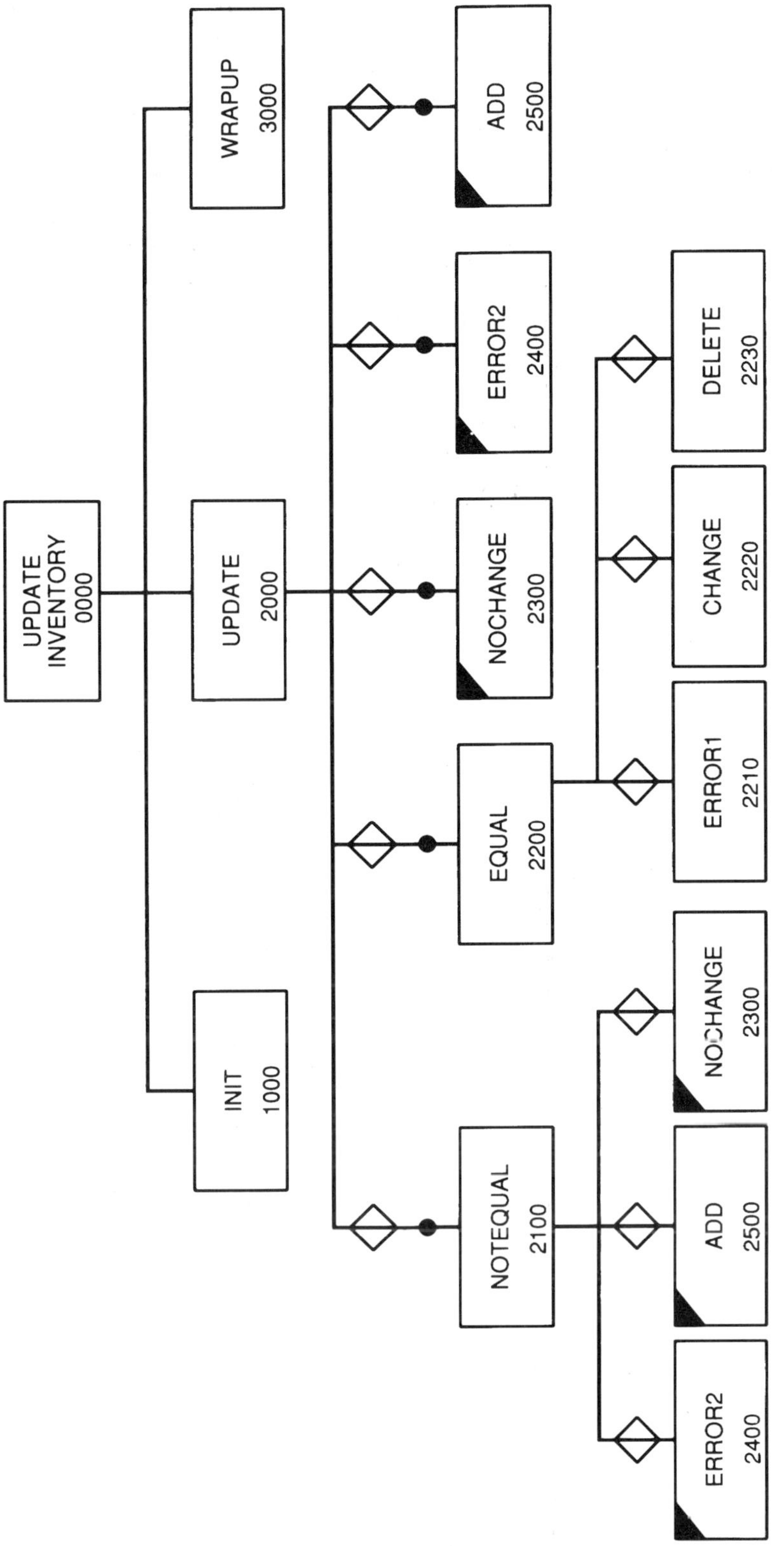

Figure 15.3a Structure Chart for Inventory Problem

Algorithm	Flowchart
UPDATE INVENTORY CONTROL 0000 1. PROCESS INIT 2. PROCESS UPDATE 3. PROCESS WRAPUP 4. END	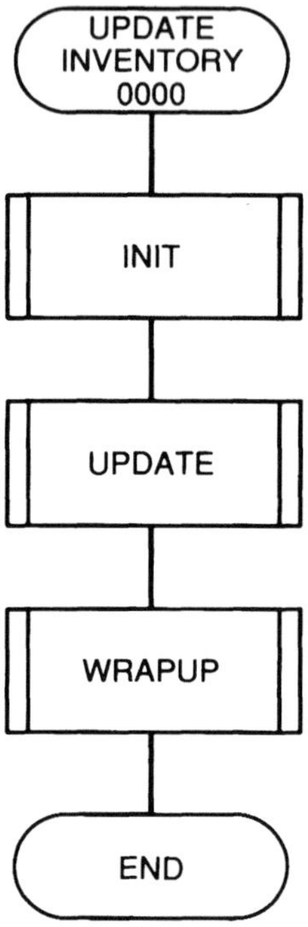

Figure 15.3b Algorithm and Flowchart for CONTROL Module

Algorithm	Flowchart
INIT MODULE 1000 1. OPEN 1, INVENTORY FOR INPUT 2. OPEN 2, TRANSACTION FOR INPUT 3. OPEN 3, ACTIVITY FOR APPEND 4. OPEN 4, TEMPORARY FOR OUTPUT 5. READ (1) RECORD 6. READ (2) RECORD 7. EXIT	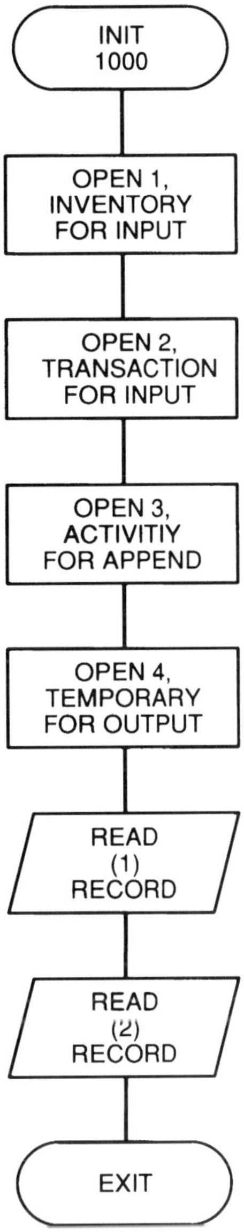

Figure 15.3c Algorithm and Flowchart for INIT Module

Algorithm

```
UPDATE MODULE
    2000

1. ┌ WHILE NOT EOF(1) AND
   │     NOT EOF(2)
   │
   │   ┌ IF TINVNO = INVNO
   │   │
   │   ├── THEN
   │   │       PROCESS EQUAL
   │   │
   │   ├── ELSE
   │   └──     PROCESS NOTEQUAL
   │
   └ WHILE-END

2. ┌ IF EOF(1)
   │
   ├── THEN
   │
   │     ┌ WHILE NOT EOF(2)
   │     │
   │     │   ┌ IF TCODE = "A"
   │     │   │
   │     │   ├── THEN
   │     │   │       PROCESS ADD
   │     │   │
   │     │   ├── ELSE
   │     │   │       PROCESS ERROR2
   │     │   └──────
   │     └ WHILE-END
   │
   ├── ELSE
   │
   │     ┌ WHILE NOT EOF(1)
   │     │   PROCESS NOCHANGE
   │     └ WHILE-END
   └──────

3. EXIT
```

Flowchart

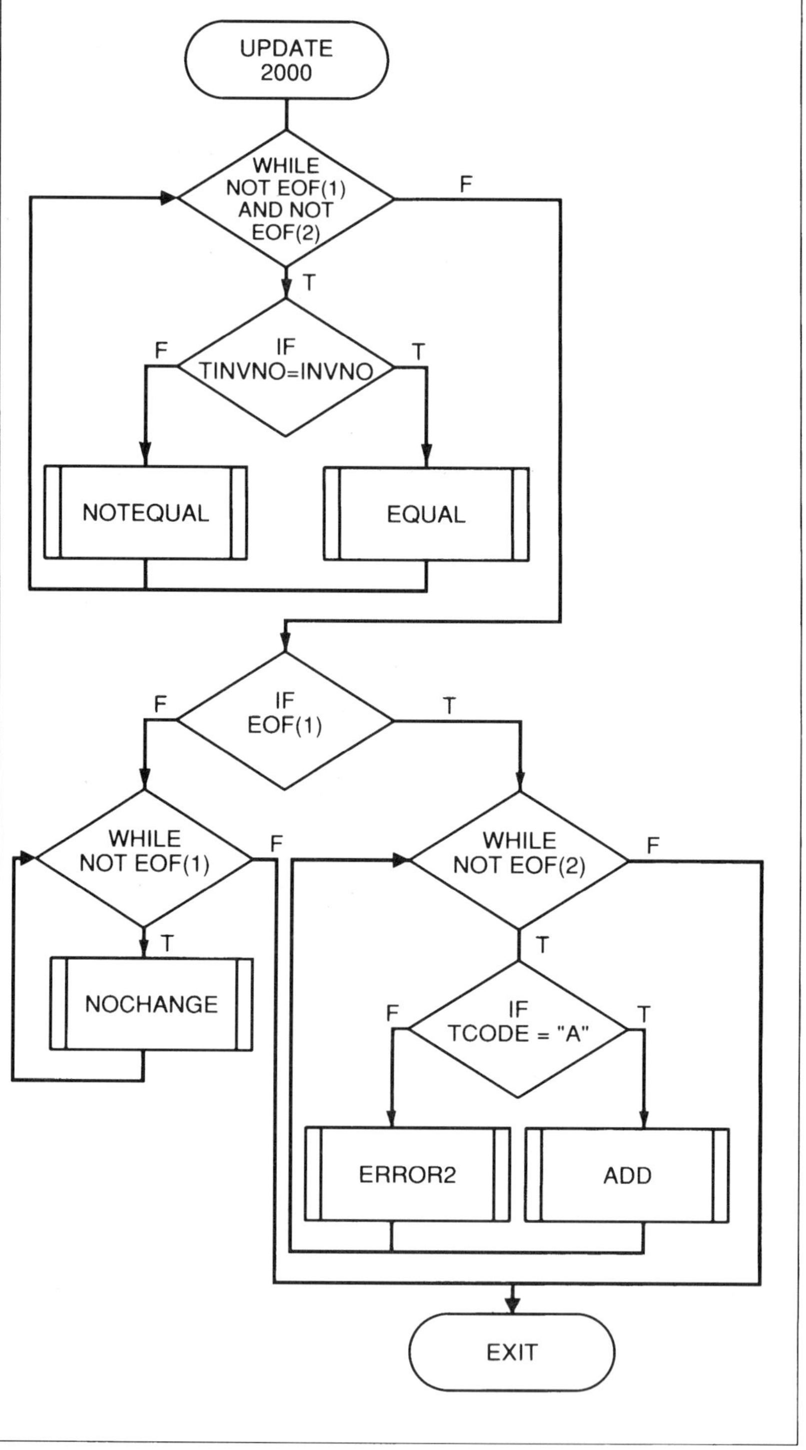

Figure 15.3d Algorithm and Flowchart for UPDATE Module

Algorithm	Flowchart

```
EQUAL MODULE
    2200

1. ┌ IF TCODE = "D"
   │
   ├─ THEN
   │     PROCESS DELETE
   │
   ├─ ELSE
   │
   │     ┌ IF TCODE = "C"
   │     │
   │     ├─ THEN
   │     │     PROCESS CHANGE
   │     │
   │     ├─ ELSE
   │     │     PROCESS ERROR1
   │     └──────────
   └──────────

2.  EXIT
```

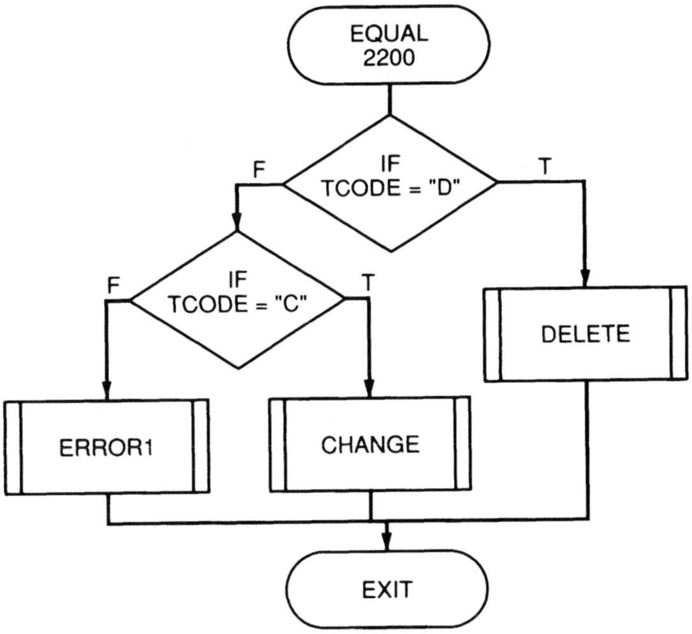


```
NOTEQUAL MODULE
    2100

1. ┌ IF INVNO < TINVNO
   │
   ├─ THEN
   │     PROCESS NOCHANGE
   │
   ├─ ELSE
   │
   │     ┌ IF TCODE = "A"
   │     │
   │     ├─ THEN
   │     │     PROCESS ADD
   │     │
   │     ├─ ELSE
   │     │     PROCESS ERROR2
   │     └──────────
   └──────────

2.  EXIT
```

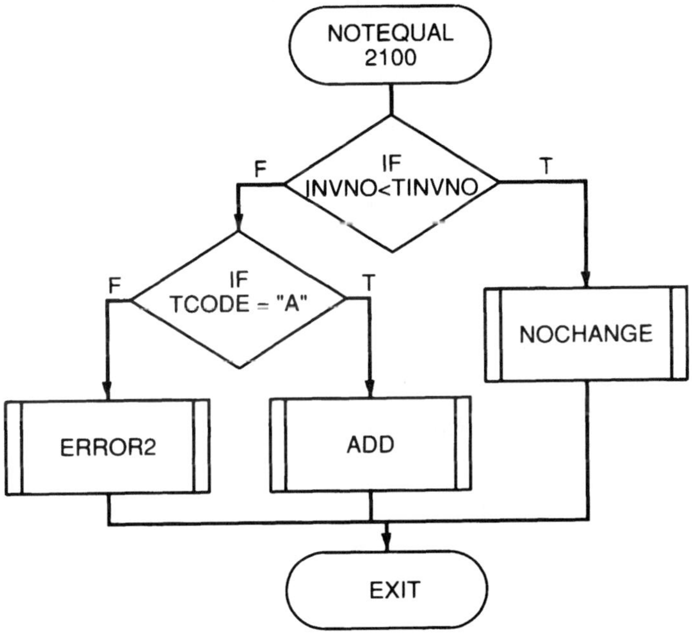

Figure 15.3e Algorithm and Flowchart for EQUAL and NOTEQUAL Modules

Algorithm	Flowchart
NOCHANGE MODULE 2300 1. WRITE (4) RECORD 2. READ (1) RECORD 3. EXIT	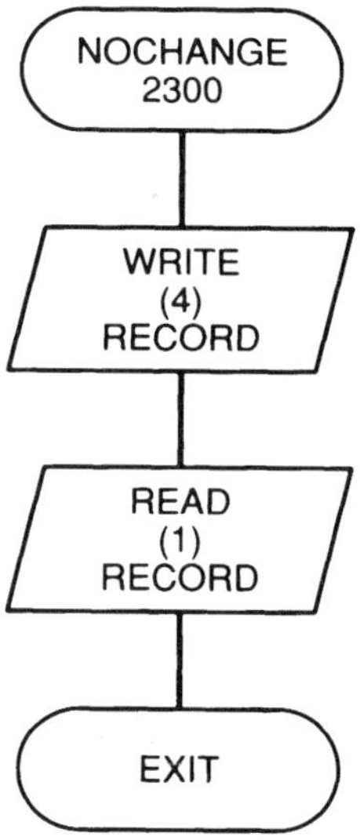
ADD MODULE 2500 1. WRITE (3) RECORD 2. WRITE (4) RECORD 3. READ (2) RECORD 4. EXIT	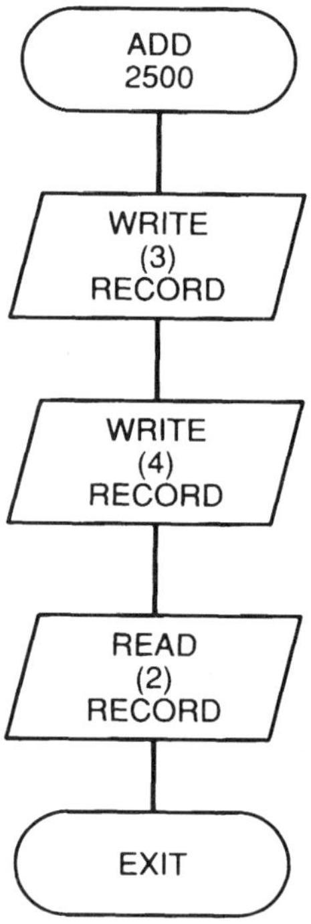

Figure 15.3f Algorithm and Flowchart for NOCHANGE and ADD Modules

Algorithm

ERROR2 MODULE
2400

1. WRITE ERROR MESSAGE (NONEXISTENT INVNO)
2. READ (2) RECORD
3. EXIT

Flowchart

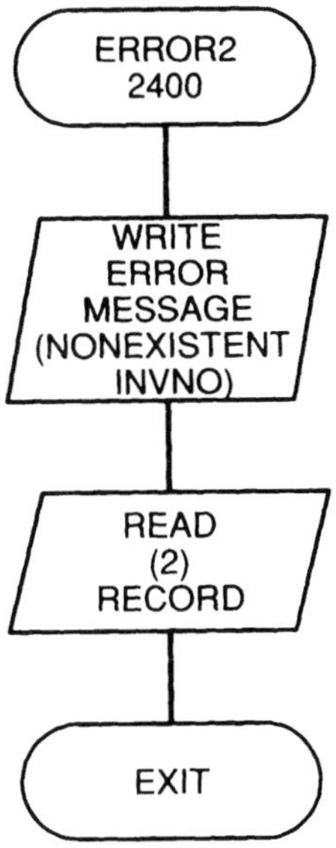

Figure 15.3g Algorithm and Flowchart for ERROR2 Module

Algorithm	Flowchart
DELETE MODULE 2230 1. WRITE (3) RECORD 2. READ (1) RECORD 3. READ (2) RECORD 4. EXIT	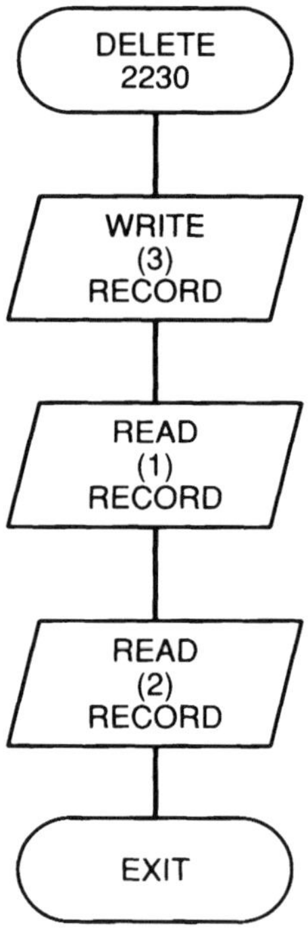
ERROR1 MODULE 2210 1. WRITE ERROR MESSAGE (DUPLICATE INVNO) 2. READ (2) RECORD 3. EXIT	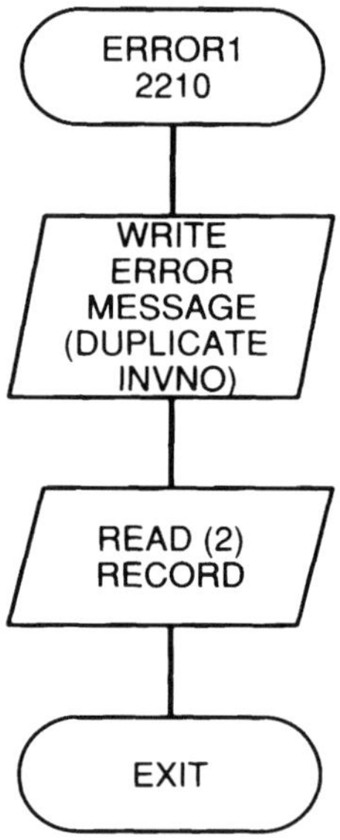

Figure 15.3h Algorithm and Flowchart for DELETE and ERROR1 Modules

Algorithm	Flowchart
CHANGE MODULE 2220 1. WRITE (3) RECORD 2. IF TQUANTITY <>- 1 QUANTITY = TQUANTITY 3. IF TPRICE <>- 1 PRICE = TPRICE * 4. IF TVENDOR <> "" VENDOR = TVENDOR 5. IF TMARKUP <> - 1 MARKUP = TMARKUP 6. READ (2) RECORD 7. IF TINVNO <> INVNO WRITE (4) RECORD READ (1) RECORD EXIT * " " indicates a null field, which is a field with nothing in it.	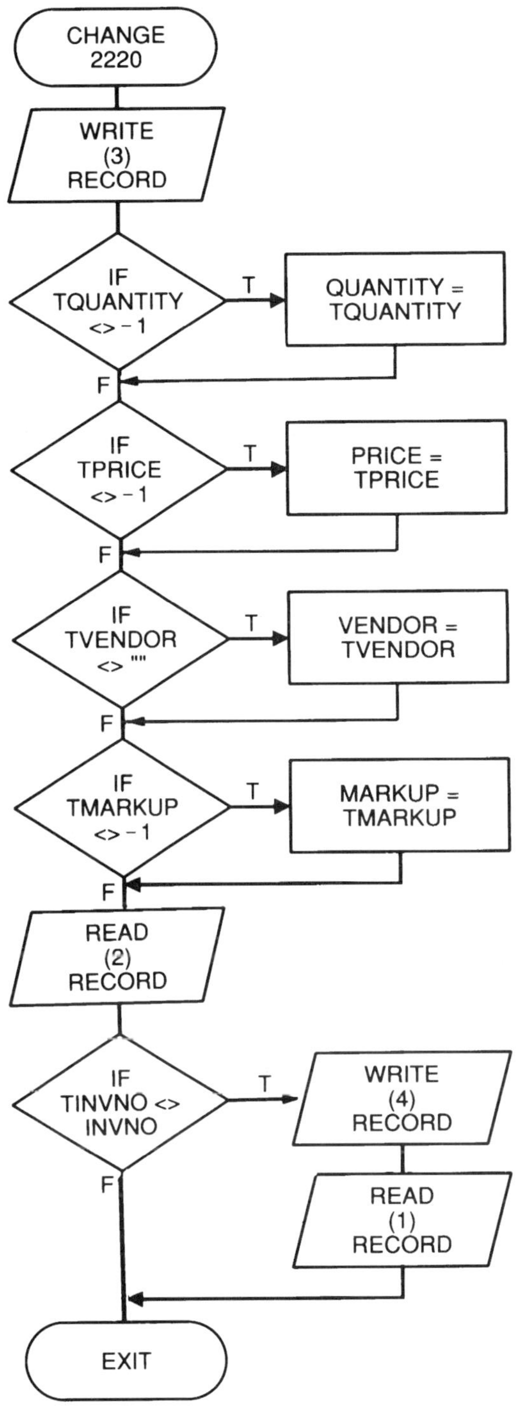

Figure 15.3i Algorithm and Flowchart for CHANGE Module

Algorithm	Flowchart
WRAPUP MODULE 3000 1. CLOSE 1 2. CLOSE 2 3. CLOSE 3 4. CLOSE 4 5. RENAME INVENTORY FILE TO BACKUP FILE 6. RENAME TEMPORARY FILE TO INVENTORY FILE 7. PRINT "RUN COMPLETED" 8. EXIT	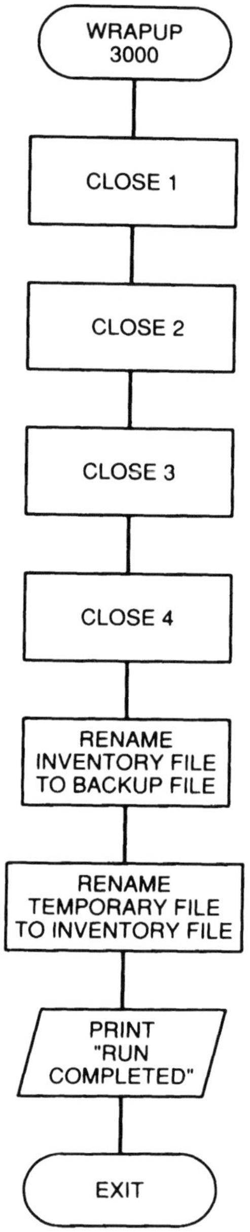

Figure 15.3j Algorithm and Flowchart for WRAPUP Module

(INVNO) for the current record; another module (NOTEQUAL) is processed when they are not equal. In the second loop, when the end-of-file has been reached for the old master file, the remaining transaction records should all be add records and are added in the ADD module. If the transaction code is not equal to "A", then the ERROR module is processed. In the third loop, the end-of-file for the transaction file has been reached and there are no more updates to the master file. The remaining master file records are copied to the new master file in the NOCHANGE module. Either the second or third loop is processed, not both.

In the EQUAL module (Figure 15.3e), the processes that can take place are to change the record (transaction code = "C") or to delete the record (transaction code = "D"). If the transaction code equals anything else, it is an error and the ERROR1 module is processed. In the NOTEQUAL module, when the master file key is less than the transaction file key, there are no updates to that master file record. When it is not less than the transaction file key, then the transaction code should be an "A" and the transaction record is added to the master file. If it is not an "A", then there is an error and the ERROR2 module is processed.

The NOCHANGE module (Figure 15.3f) writes the data to the new master file and reads the next record from the old master file. The ADD module writes the transaction record to the activity file and the new master file and then reads the next record from the transaction file.

The ERROR2 module (Figure 15.3g) writes an error message to the output error report and reads the next transaction file record. If there is an error in the transaction file, that record should not be processed. The DELETE module (Figure 15.3h) writes the transaction file record to the activity file and reads the next record from the old master file and the transaction file. The ERROR1 module writes an error message to the output error report and reads the next transaction file record.

The CHANGE module (Figure 15.3i) is the most involved in that each field must be checked to see if the data in that field need to be changed. In this solution, −1 or "" (a null field—a field with nothing in it) indicates there is to be no change in that field. First, the transaction record is written to the activity file. Then the master file record is changed. The updated master file record is written to the new master file. The next transaction file record is read and checked to see if it is still equal to the master file record. If it is equal, there are more changes to be made to the master file record; if not, the next master file record is read.

In the WRAPUP module (Figure 15.3j), the files are closed, the old master file is renamed as the backup file, the new master file is renamed as the inventory file, and a message is printed to the screen that the run is completed.

A Useful Alternative Method

Figure 15.4a–d shows an alternative solution to the sequential file update problem. The main difference between the alternative solutions is how the update is driven. In the other examples in this chapter, the update is driven by the key. All updates, including adding records, changing records, and deleting records, are completed at the same time in key order. In the alternate method, the update is driven by the type of update; that is, all adds are completed at one time, as are the deletions and changes. When using the alternative method the transaction file must be sorted using the transaction code as the primary key and the primary key of the master file as the secondary key.

```
Algorithm:
1. OPEN TF, AF
2. READ TF RECORD
3. HCODE = TCODE
4. WHILE NOT EOF(TF)
   OPEN MF, HF
   READ MF RECORD
   WHILE NOT EOF(MF) AND NOT EOF(TF) AND TCODE = HCODE
     IF TCODE = "A"
       THEN
         IF MKEY = TFKEY
           THEN
             PROCESS ERROR 1
             READ TF RECORD
           ELSE
             IF MFKEY < TFKEY
               THEN
                 WRITE MF RECORD TO HF
                 READ MF RECORD
               ELSE
                 WRITE AF RECORD
                 WRITE TF RECORD TO HF
                 READ TF RECORD
     ELSE
         IF TCODE = "D"
           THEN
             IF MFKEY = TFKEY
               THEN
                 WRITE AF RECORD
                 READ MF RECORD
                 READ TF RECORD
               ELSE
                 IF MFKEY < TFKEY
                   THEN
                     WRITE MF RECORD TO HF
                     READ MF RECORD
                   ELSE
                     PROCESS ERROR 2
                     READ TF RECORD
           ELSE
             IF MFKEY = TFKEY
               THEN
                 WRITE AF RECORD
                 PROCESS CHANGE
                 WRITE MF RECORD TO HF
                 READ TF RECORD
                 IF MFKEY <> TFKEY
                   THEN
                     READ MF RECORD
                   ELSE
                     CONTINUE
               ELSE
             IF MFKEY < TFKEY
               THEN
                 WRITE MF RECORD TO HF
                 READ MF RECORD
               ELSE
                 PROCESS ERRORS
                 READ TF RECORD
   WHILE-END
   WHILE NOT EOF(MF)
     WRITE MF RECORD TO HF
     READ MF RECORD
   WHILE-END
   CLOSE FILE (MF, HF)
   REPLACE BACKUP FILE WITH MF
   REPLACE MF WITH HF
   WHILE-END
5. CLOSE FILE (TF, AF)
6. EXIT
```

Figure 15.4a Algorithm for an Alternative Method of Sequential File Update

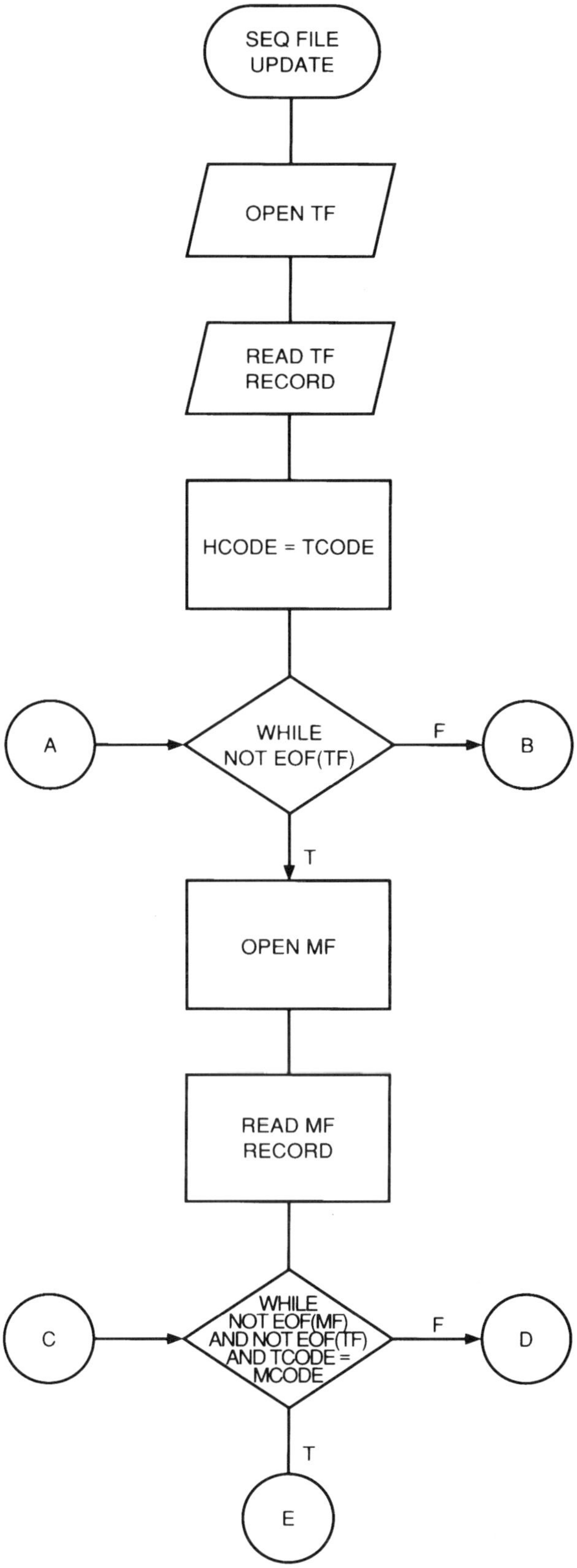

Figure 15.4b Flowchart for Alternative Method of Sequential-Access File Update

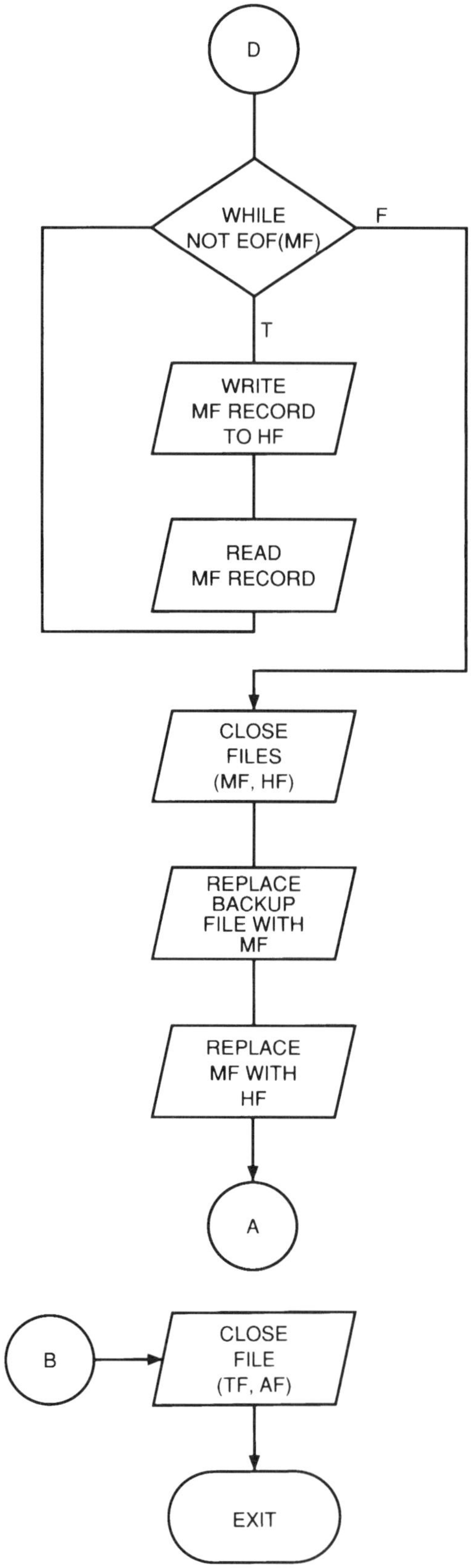

Figure 15.4c Flowchart for Alternative Method of Sequential-Access File Update

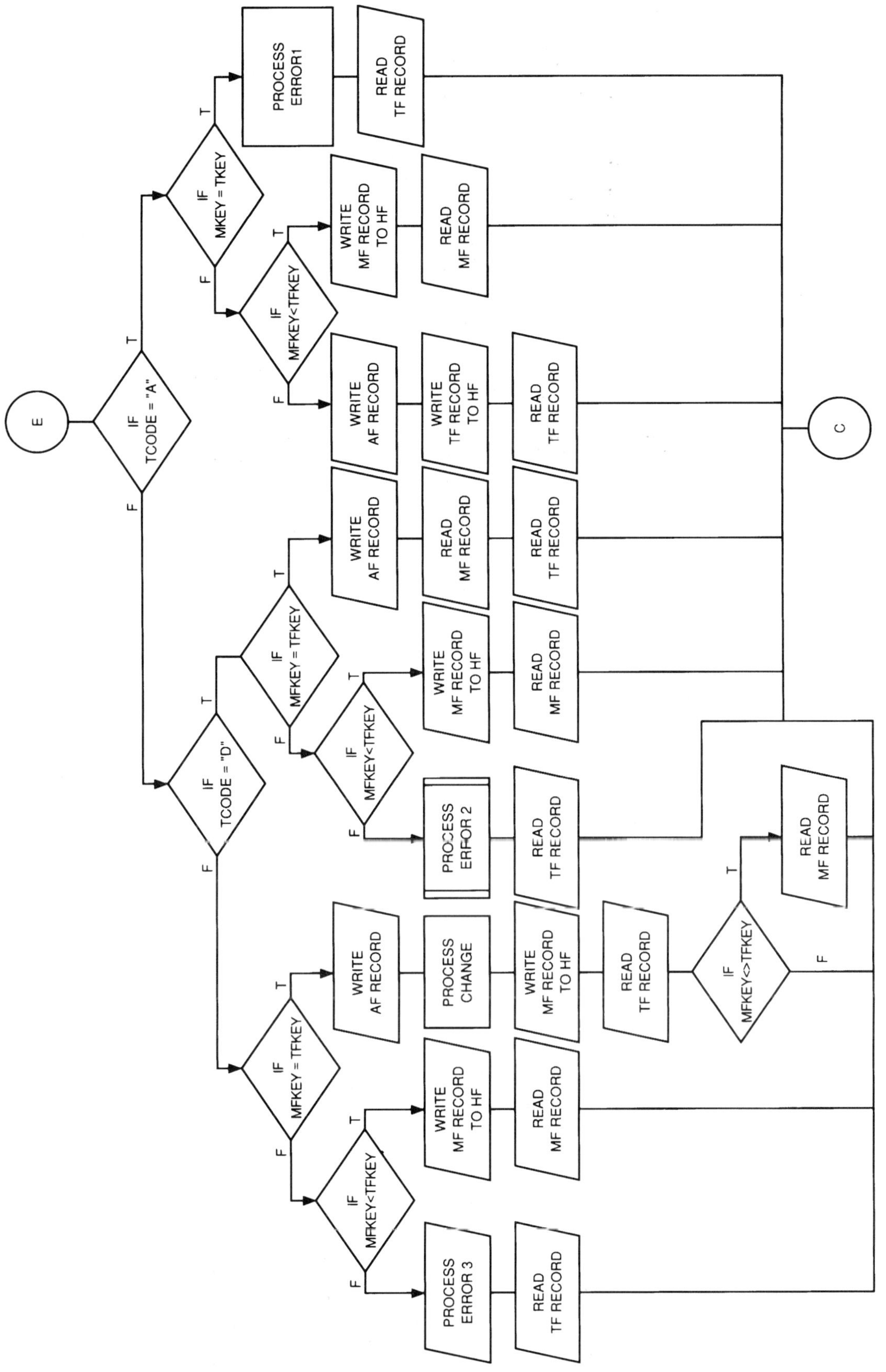

Figure 15.4d Flowchart for Alternative Method of Sequential-Access File Update

Summary

File updating is an essential part of working with files. The process of updating files includes adding, deleting, and changing records. Computer users use batch processing to update sequential files since random processing of sequential records is time-consuming on the computer. Updating a sequential file involves the following files: a transaction file, which contains all the updates; an activity file, which contains a record of all processes completed on the file; a backup file, which is the master file before the last update; a new master file, the updated master file; and, of course, the old master file, which contains the records to be updated. Sequential file updating involves updating the master file with the additions, deletions, and changes listed in the transaction file. After an update is completed, a new transaction file is created, and after a period of time, the user processes the master and the transaction files together again.

New Terms

activity file
backup file
batch processing
updating a file
interactive processing
master file
transaction file

Questions

1. What processes are included in updating a file?
2. State the functions of the following files:
   a. old master file
   b. transaction file
   c. activity file
   d. new master file
   e. backup file

Problems

1. Develop a solution and data dictionary to update a client file given the following master and transaction file records: (The master file is in client number order.)

Master File Record

client #	name	telephone	address	city-state	zip code	last call	amount of last order

Transaction File Record

client #	tcode	name	telephone	address	city-state	zip code	last call	amount of last order

2. Develop a solution and data dictionary to update a book file for a library. After each update is complete, the librarian would like a copy of all new listings. Design the master file record and the transaction file record. The data in the master file record should include:

  a. reference number
  b. author
  c. title
  d. publisher
  e. ISBN
  f. copyright date
  g. number of copies
  h. subject

3. Develop a solution to update the file used in Problem 1 in Chapter 14, on page 326.

4. Develop a solution to update the file used in Problem 3 in Chapter 14, on page 326.

Chapter 16

Random-Access File Processing and Updating

Overview

Index Files
Updating Random-Access Files Using an Interactive Process

Objectives

When you have finished this chapter, you should be able to:

1. Explain the concept of index files.
2. Design a computer program that requires updating of random-access files through the use of interactive processing.

Many computer applications require that the user be able to inquire about specific data in a file at any time or require that the data be current at all times. Random-access files enable the user to retrieve the most current information available on the computer. Chapter 13 discussed the different ways that random-access files could be updated, either interactively or sequentially, as the need required.

Menu-driven programs for random-access files allow the user to update, make an inquiry, or print a report. A record is accessed by giving the record number to the computer, which then retrieves it from the auxiliary storage device. The major problems with this type of retrieval are that the user normally does not know the record number and that the records normally are not physically in the required order but, instead, are in the order in which they were originally entered. Therefore, the programmer must use some method to permit accessing the desired record using the proper key. There are many ways to access the desired record as fast as possible and in some type of order. As mentioned in Chapter 13, the method taught in this text is that which uses index files.

Index Files

When using indexed files, there are one or more index files for each master file. An **index file** consists of two fields: The first is the key and the second is the corresponding record number. The index file is small enough to fit into the internal memory of the computer in order to speed up the retrieval of a random-access record. The index file is then sorted using the key field. This file is used to process the master file.

Figure 16.1 demonstrates the use of index files. The master file that contains all the data needed for a client file is stored on an external-storage device. To develop an index file, such as the NAMEINDEX file, the file is first created with two fields. The first field is the name field, and the second is the record number of that name. This NAMEINDEX file is then sorted by one of many sorting techniques. The file is then used to process the MASTERFILE in alphabetical order of the names. Within the solution, the first record number in the MASTERFILE to be used is the value of the RECORDNO field in the NAMEINDEX file, which is 7. Therefore, the seventh record

MASTER FILE

RECORD NO.	NAME	NUMBER	OTHER DATA
1	DUNLAP	210	
2	JOHNSON	100	
3	WHITE	125	
4	BENNET	275	
5	GREEN	225	
6	SMITH	200	
7	ADAMS	25	
8	BLACK	400	
9	COOPER	50	
10	OLSON	350	
11	WILLIAMS	75	
12	NELSON	175	
13	HOLDING	335	
14	LITTLE	150	
15	GREY	250	
16	BROWN	325	
17	STONE	300	
18	SMART	40	

INDEX ON NAME
NAMEINDEX FILE

	NAME	RECORDNO
1	ADAMS	7
2	BENNET	4
3	BLACK	8
4	BROWN	16
5	COOPER	9
6	DUNLAP	1
7	GREEN	5
8	GREY	15
9	HOLDING	13
10	JOHNSON	2
11	LITTLE	14
12	NELSON	12
13	OLSON	10
14	SMART	18
15	SMITH	6
16	STONE	17
17	WHITE	3
18	WILLIAMS	11

INDEX ON NUMBER
NUMBERINDEX FILE

NUMBER	RECORDNO
25	7
40	18
50	9
75	11
100	2
125	3
150	14
175	12
200	6
210	1
225	5
250	15
275	4
300	17
325	16
335	13
350	10
400	8

Figure 16.1 Index Files

is the first to be used, because it is the first record in alphabetical order. The second record to be used in the NAMEINDEX file is the fourth record in the MASTERFILE; the third is the eighth record; and so on. If at another time the MASTERFILE is to be accessed by NUMBER, then the NUMBERINDEX is used in a similar manner. Thus, by creating the NAMEINDEX and NUMBERINDEX files, the MASTERFILE does not have to be sorted again every time the requirements of the problem demand that the file be used in a different order.

Another use for the index file is to find a single record. This is done through either a **sequential search** of the file or through another search method, such as the **binary search**. (The method for a binary search is illustrated in Chapter 9). The sequential search is the easiest, but it is usually the most time-consuming; the key field of the index file is checked, record by record, until the correct record is found. Then the record is retrieved from the master file by using its record number from the index file. Figure 16.2 demonstrates the sequential method of searching for a record. In Figure 16.2, the NAMEINDEX file has been read into two parallel arrays called NAME and RECNO. The search takes place by checking the SEARCHNAME against the NAME array element by element until they match. After the loop has concluded, the element number of the array is checked to see if it is greater than the number of records in the MASTERFILE. If it is, then the record was not found. If the element number is less than or equal to the number of records in the MASTERFILE, then the record is retrieved from the MASTERFILE by using the corresponding record number in the RECNO array to find the correct record in the MASTERFILE.

Updating Random-Access Files Using an Interactive Process

A menu-driven program is often used to update and process random files. The control menu lists the options for the user. The options usually include the following:

1. add records
2. delete records
3. change records
4. query
5. print records
6. quit

The processing always loops back to the control menu after completing one of the tasks such as adding a record. The only way out of the processing is for the user to use the quit option. There may be submenus within any of the listed options. For example, the report module may have a submenu of various types of reports so that the user can select the type desired. In the add, delete, and change-a-record modules, processing continues until there are no more records to be processed. Then the program returns the user to the main menu. The program uses an index file to search for a particular record in the file.

The sections of Figure 16.3 show the development of a random-file update and processing problem for a mailing list. A company needs a program to maintain a mailing list for advertising purposes. The company collects data for the list from the mail and from people who request advertising material. The company needs a program to update the list and to print labels and a directory.

ARRAYS FOR
INDEX FILE
FROM FIGURE 13.1

R	NAME	RECNO
1	ADAMS	7
2	BENNET	4
3	BLACK	8
4	BROWN	16
5	COOPER	9
6	DUNLAP	1
7	GREEN	5
8	GREY	15
9	HOLDING	13
10	JOHNSON	2
11	LITTLE	14
12	NELSON	12
13	OLSON	10
14	SMART	18
15	SMITH	6
16	STONE	17
17	WHITE	3
18	WILLIAMS	11

R: ELEMENT NUMBER OF THE NAME ARRAY

SEQUENTIAL SEARCH

ALGORITHM

```
R = 1
WHILE NAME(R) <> SEARCHNAME AND R <= N
    R = R + 1
WHILE-END
IF R > N
    THEN
        PRINT "RECORD NOT FOUND"
    ELSE
        READ (1)RECORD RECNO(R)
```

FLOWCHART:

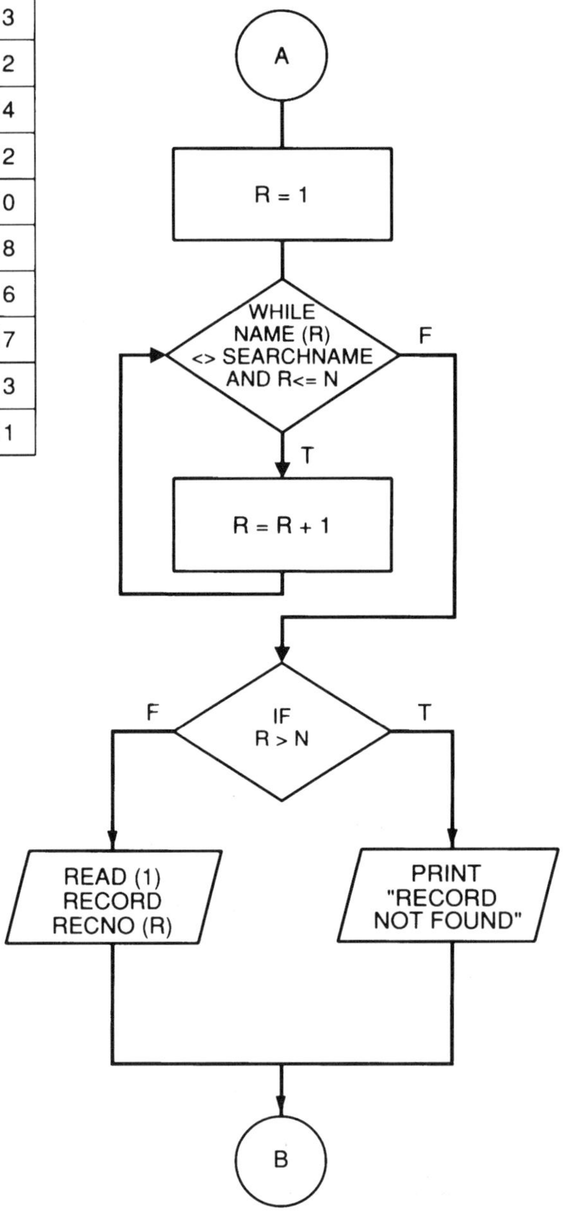

Test:

SEARCHNAME

GREEN

NAME (R)

~~ADAMS~~ ~~BENNET~~ ~~BLACK~~ ~~BROWN~~ ~~COOPER~~ ~~DUNLAP~~ GREEN

R

~~1~~ ~~2~~ ~~3~~ ~~4~~ ~~5~~ ~~6~~ 7

RECNO (R)

~~7~~ ~~4~~ ~~8~~ ~~16~~ ~~9~~ ~~1~~ 5

The record number for Green in the masterfile is 5.

Figure 16.2 Sequential Method of Searching for a Record

(1)

Record Data Dictionary

File Name: MAILLIST

Field Number	Item Description	Field Name	Field Length	Data Type	# of Decimals	Comments
1	Last Name	LNAME	15	C		Indexed on this field
2	First Name	FNAME	15	C		
3	Address	ADDRESS	20	C		
4	City	CITY	18	C		
5	State	STATE	2	C		
6	Zip Code	ZIPCODE	10	C		Will be used as a Secondary Key

Record Layout

1 15	16 30	31 50	51 68	69 70	71 80
LNAME	FNAME	ADDRESS	CITY	STATE	ZIPCODE

Figure 16.3a Menu-Driven Random-Access File Update and Reports Program

Notes on Figure 16.3

The following notes explain the solution to the mailing list problem illustrated in Figure 16.3. Items 1 and 2, which describe the field data and the layouts of the two records necessary to the solution, are illustrated in Figures 16.3a and 16.3b. The items numbered 3 through 51 correspond to the circled numbers in Figures 16.3d through 16.3m.

1. This is the MAILLIST file field data dictionary and record layout. The key field is the last name. There are 80 characters per record.
2. This is the INDEXFILE file record layout. There are 19 characters per record.
3. This setup module for the program is equivalent to the Init module. This is the first module that is executed since these are the first tasks that need to be completed. Once the program executes these instructions, it never returns to this module.
4. This instruction prints instructions for the user.
5. These instructions open both files.
6. These instructions copy the index file into parallel arrays. The index file is then closed since it will not be used again until the Wrapup module.
7. This instruction clears the screen.
8. This instruction prints the main menu.
9. This loop enters the user's choice from the main menu. It loops until the entered number is within the range of choices on the menu.

(2)

Record Data Dictionary

File Name: INDEXFILE

Field Number	Item Description	Field Name	Field Length	Data Type	# of Decimals	Comments
1	Last Name	NAME	15	C		Ordered on this field
2	Record Number	RECNO	4	I		

Record Layout

1 — 15	16 — 19	
NAME	RECNO	

Figure 16.3b Record Data Dictionary and Record Layout

10. This CASE OF instruction, along with the user's choice from the menu, chains one of the modules.
11. This module adds a record.
12. This instruction enters the last name of the first record to be added to the file.
13. This instruction loops as long as the last name is not equal to "Q". This allows multiple records to be added at the same time without going through the menu in the driver each time.
14. This instruction enters the remaining data for each record.
15. This instruction appends the record to the file (adds the record to the end of the file).
16. This instruction searches to find the place in the index file to insert the key and the record number.
17. When FALSE, this decision indicates the new record should be appended to the end of the index file.
18. This loop moves all records down one record in the file to leave room for the new record to be inserted.
19. These two instructions insert the values of the key field and the record number of the new record into the parallel arrays (the index arrays).
20. This counter increases the number of records by one.

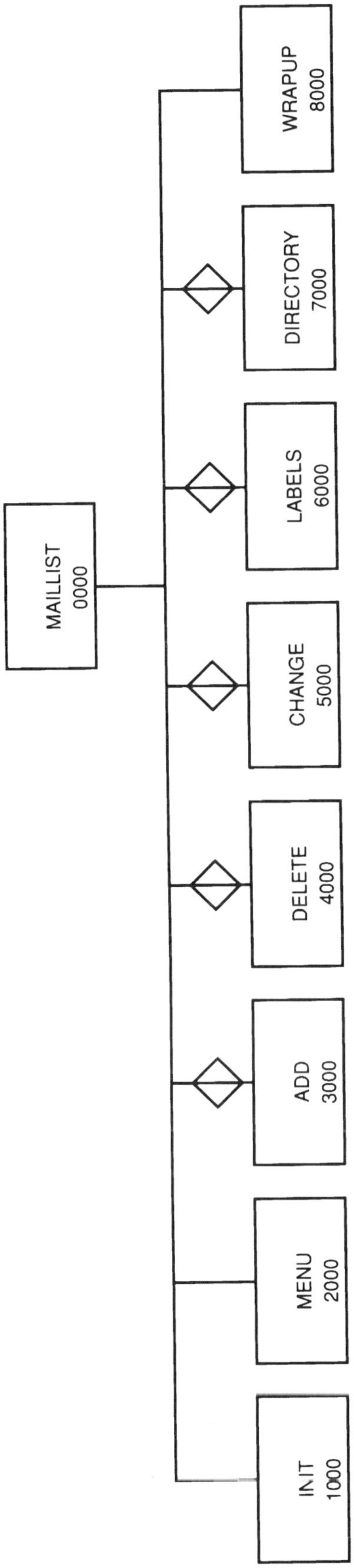

Figure 16.3c Structure Chart

Algorithm	Flowchart

```
CONTROL MODULE
    0000

1.  PROCESS INIT

2.  PROCESS MENU

3.  WHILE CHOICE <> 6

        CASE OF CHOICE

          =1: PROCESS ADD

          =2: PROCESS DELETE

          =3: PROCESS CHANGE

          =4: PROCESS LABELS

          =5: PROCESS DIRECTORY

        END-OF-CASE

        PROCESS MENU

      WHILE-END

4.  PROCESS WRAPUP

5.  END
```

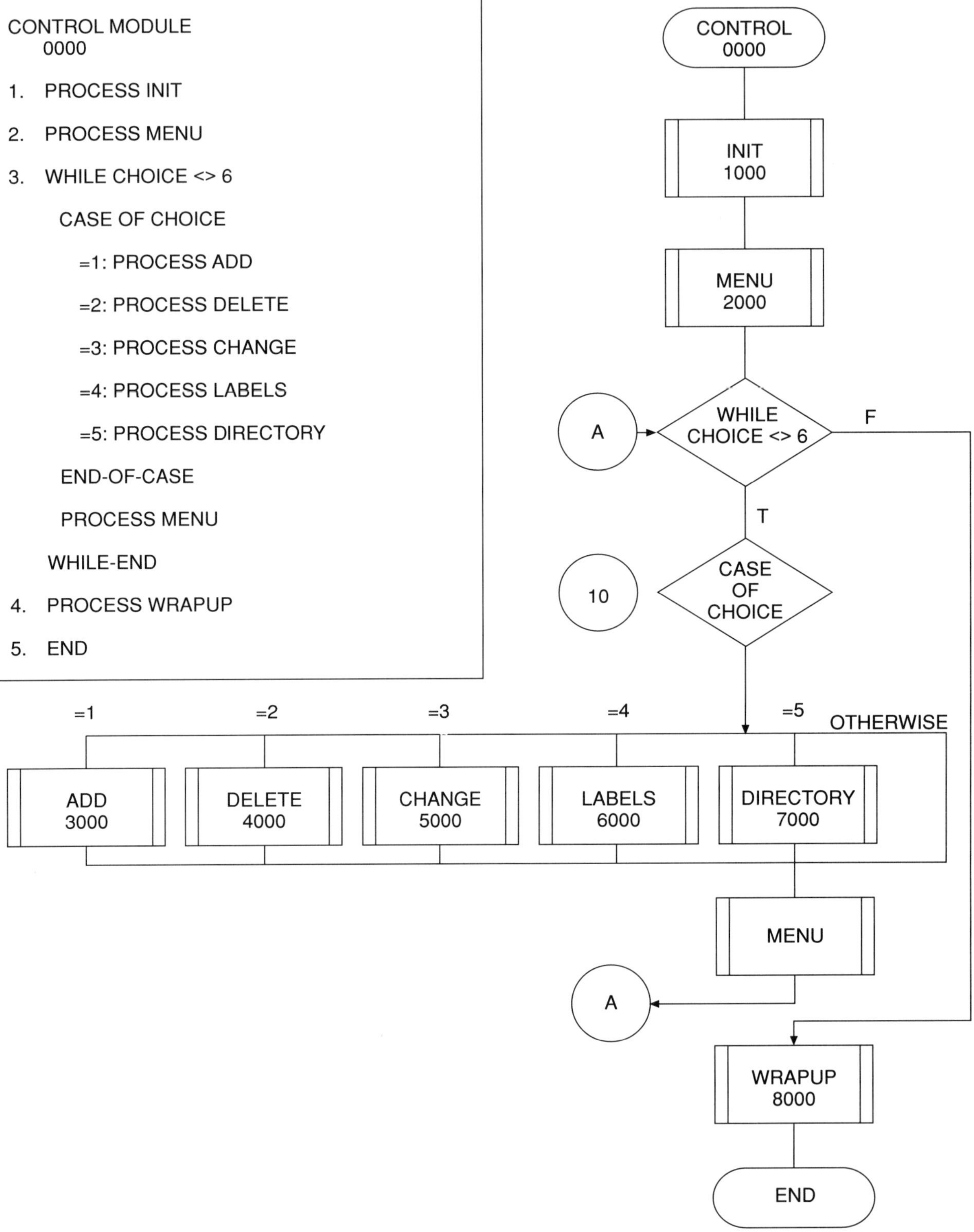

Figure 16.3d Algorithm and Flowchart for CONTROL Module

Algorithm

INIT MODULE
1000

1. PRINT INSTRUCTIONS
2. OPEN 1, MAILLIST
3. OPEN 2, INDEXFILE
4. READ (2), NAME (1), RECNO (1)
5. N = 1
6. WHILE NOT EOF(2)

    N = N + 1

    READ (2), NAME (N) RECNO (N)

   WHILE-END
7. CLOSE 2
8. EXIT

NAME = Name array

RECNO = Array of record numbers

N = Number of records in the data file and index file

Flowchart

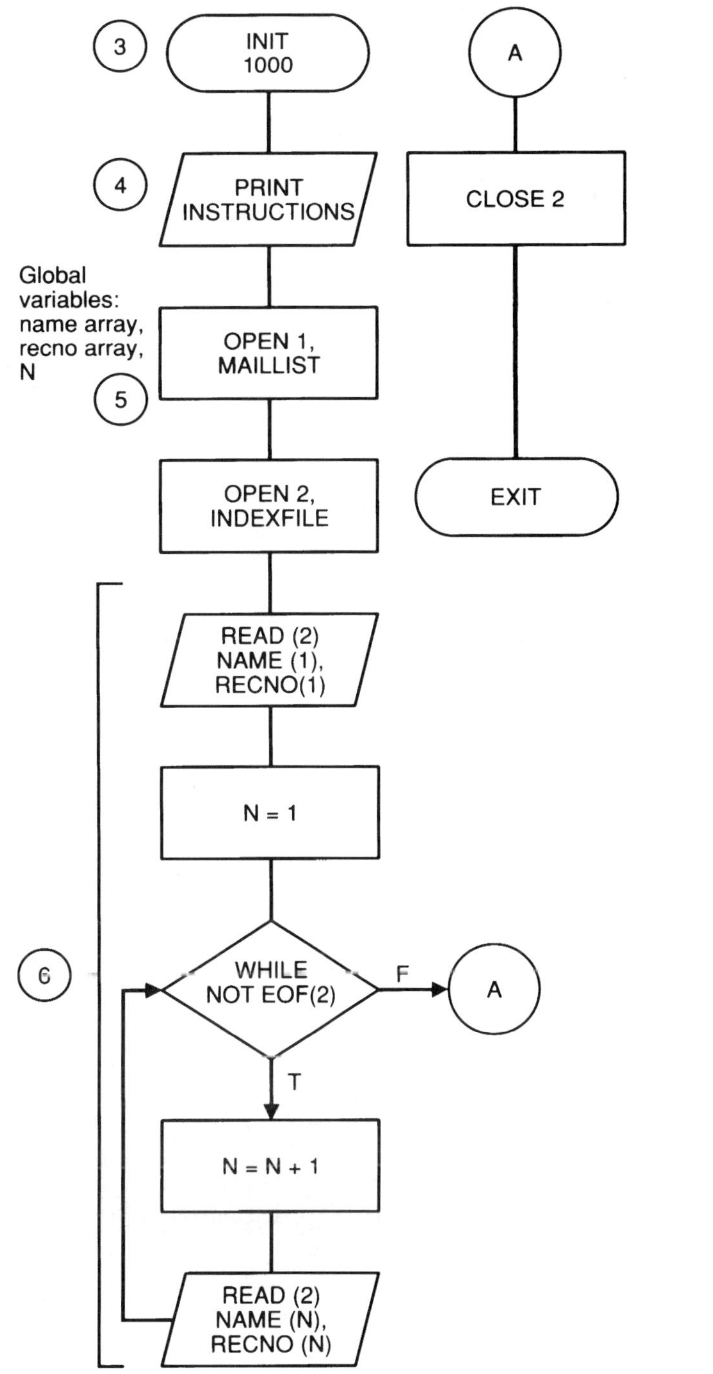

Figure 16.3e Algorithm and Flowchart for MAILLIST Module

Algorithm	Flowchart
MENU MODULE 2000 1. CLEAR SCREEN 2. PRINT MENU 3. REPEAT ENTER CHOICE UNTIL CHOICE>0 AND CHOICE<7 4. EXIT	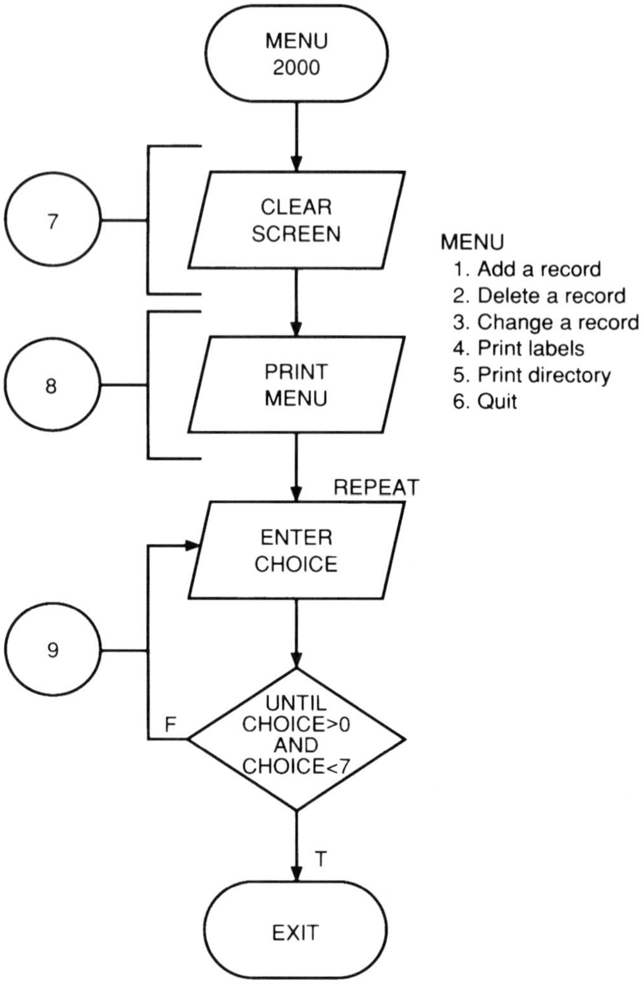

Figure 16.3f Algorithm and Flowchart for MENU Module

21. This instruction allows the user to enter the last name of the next record to be added to the file. The user enters a Q when there are no more records to be added.
22. This is the module to delete a record.
23. This instruction loops until there are no more records to be deleted.
24. This loop searches to find the record to be deleted.
25. When this condition is TRUE, the record could not be found. The processing then continues at the end of the loop by entering another name.
26. These instructions read and print the record and then ask the user whether it is the correct record. If it is not, then the processing continues at the end of the loop by entering a new name.
27. This loop moves the records up. In doing so the requested record is deleted.
28. This loop moves the elements up in the index arrays.
29. This counter decreases the number of records by one.

Algorithm

```
ADD MODULE
    3000

1.  ENTER LNAME

2. ┌ WHILE LNAME <> "Q"
   │
   │     ENTER FNAME, ADDRESS,
   │        CITYSTATE, ZIPCODE
   │
   │     WRITE (1) RECORD N + 1
   │
   │     R = 1
   │
   │    ┌ WHILE NAME(R) < LNAME
   │    │    AND R <= N
   │    │
   │    │    R = R + 1
   │    │
   │    └ WHILE-END
   │
   │    ┌ IF R <= N
   │    │
   │    ├── THEN
   │    │    ┌ LOOP: I = N to R
   │    │    │        STEP -1
   │    │    │
   │    │    │     NAME (I + 1) =
   │    │    │        NAME (I)
   │    │    │     RECNO (I + 1) =
   │    │    │        RECNO (I)
   │    │    │
   │    │    └ LOOPEND: I
   │    │
   │    ├── ELSE
   │    │
   │    │    R = R + 1
   │    └──────────────
   │     NAME(R) = LNAME
   │     RECNO(R) = N + 1
   │     N = N + 1
   │     ENTER LNAME
   │
   └ WHILE-END

3.  EXIT
```

Flowchart

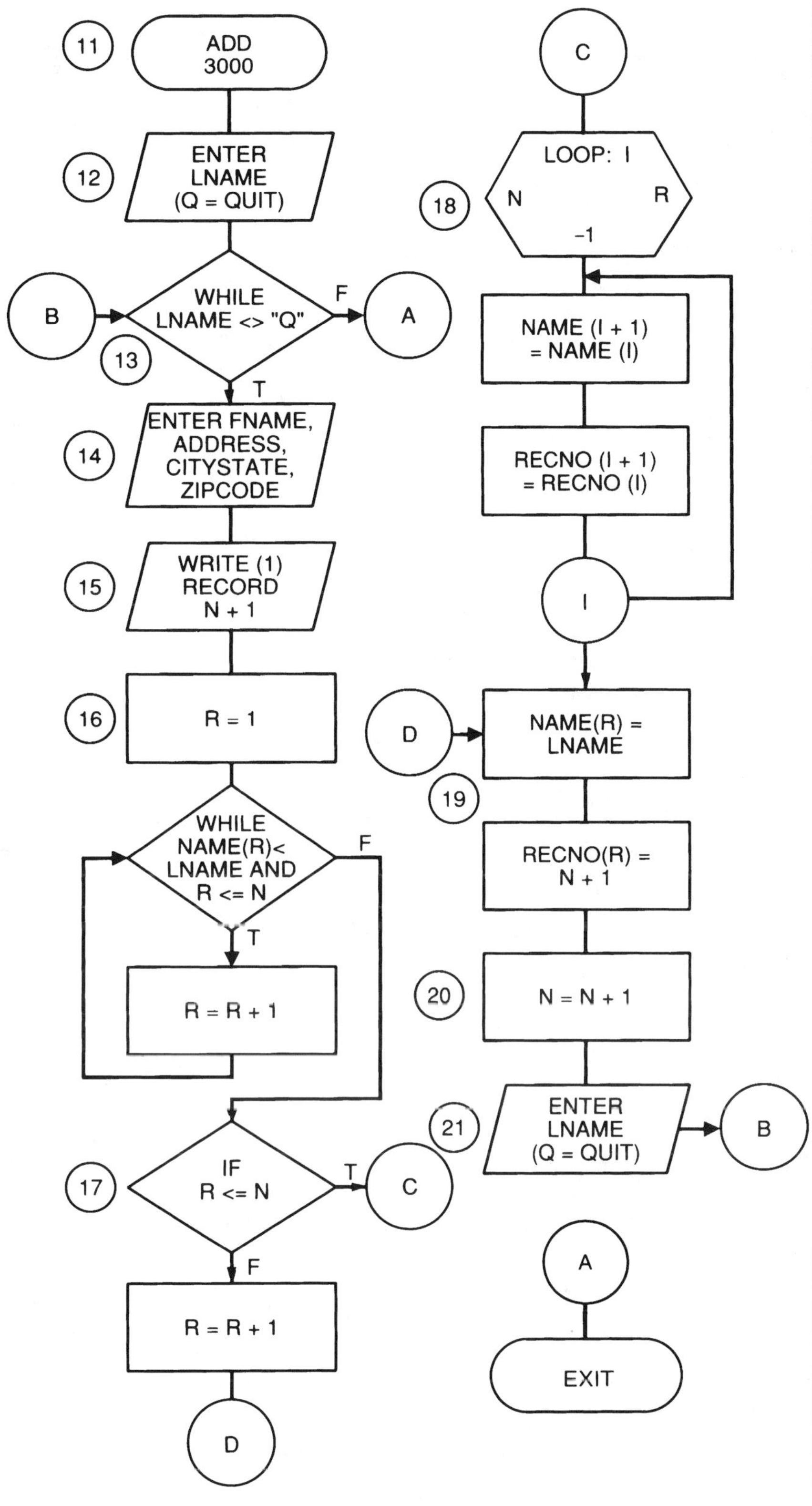

Figure 16.3g Algorithm and Flowchart for ADD Module

Algorithm	Flowchart

```
DELETE MODULE
      4000

1.  ENTER LNAME

2. ┌ WHILE LNAME <> "Q"
   │   R = 1
   │  ┌ WHILE NAME (R) <> LNAME
   │  │        AND R <= N
   │  │     R = R + 1
   │  └ WHILE-END
   │  ┌ IF R > N
   │  │
   │  ├── THEN
   │  │      PRINT "RECORD NOT
   │  │         FOUND"
   │  │
   │  ├── ELSE
   │  │      READ (1) RECORD R
   │  │      PRINT RECORD R
   │  │      ENTER "CORRECT
   │  │         RECORD?" ANS
   │  │   ┌ IF ANS = "Y"
   │  │   │
   │  │   │     THEN
   │  │   │      ┌ LOOP:  J =
   │  │   │      │    RECNO (R) TO N
   │  │   │      │
   │  │   │      │    READ (1) RECORD J
   │  │   │      │
   │  │   │      │    WRITE (1) RECORD J - 1
   │  │   │      │
   │  │   │      └ LOOPEND:  J
   │  │   │      ┌ LOOP:  J = R TO N
   │  │   │      │
   │  │   │      │    NAME (J) = NAME (J+1)
   │  │   │      │
   │  │   │      │    RECNO (J) = RECNO (J+1)
   │  │   │      │
   │  │   │      └ LOOPEND:  J
   │  │   │        N = N - 1
   │  │   └──────────────
   │  └──────────────────
   │   ENTER LNAME
   └ WHILE-END

3.  EXIT
```

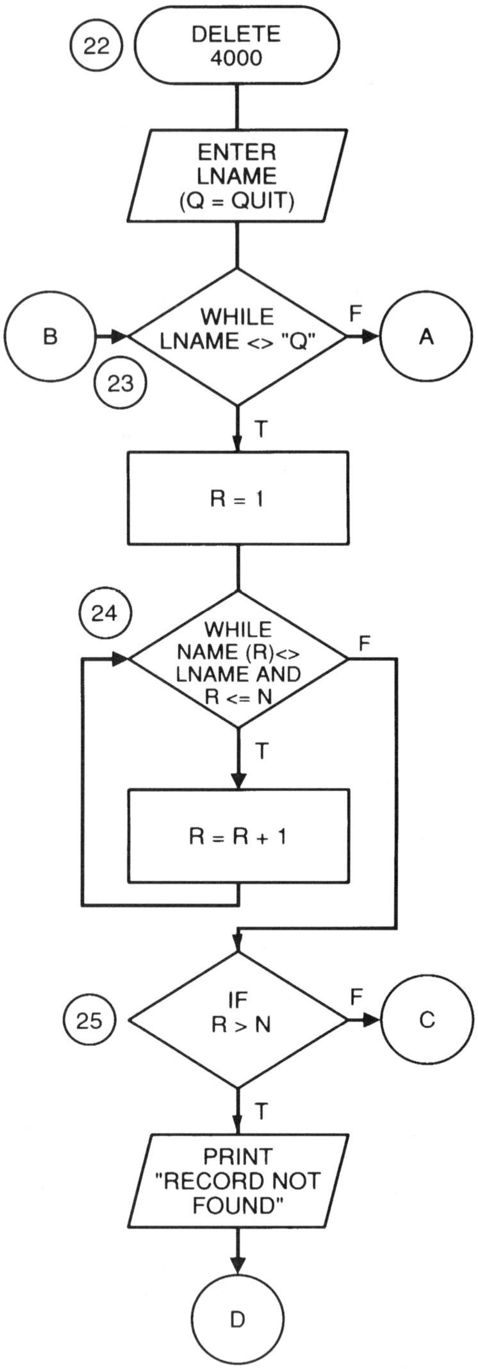

Figure 16.3h Algorithm and Flowchart for DELETE Module

Flowchart

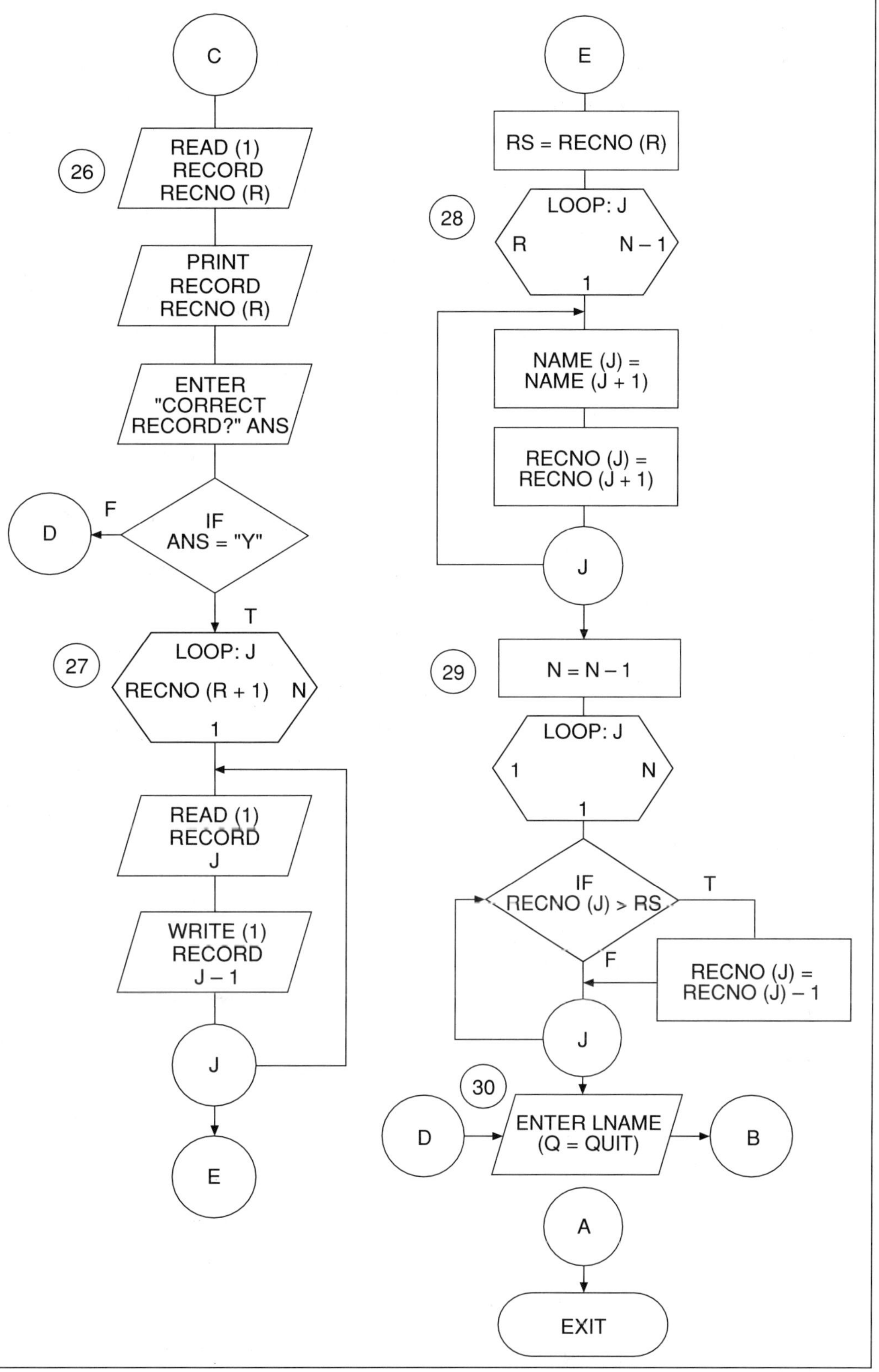

Figure 16.3i Algorithm and Flowchart for DELETE Module

Algorithm	Flowchart

```
CHANGE MODULE
     5000

1.  ENTER LNAME

2. ┌ WHILE LNAME <> "Q"
   │
   │   R = 1
   │
   │ ┌ WHILE NAME (R) <> LNAME
   │ │        AND R <= N
   │ │
   │ │    R = R + 1
   │ │
   │ └ WHILE-END
   │
   │ ┌ IF R > N
   │ │
   │ ├─── THEN
   │ │       PRINT "RECORD NOT
   │ │          FOUND"
   │ │
   │ ├─── ELSE
   │ │       READ (1) RECORD R
   │ │
   │ │       PRINT RECORD R
   │ │
   │ │       ENTER "CORRECT
   │ │          RECORD" ANS
   │ │
   │ │     ┌ IF ANS = "Y"
   │ │     │
   │ │     ├─── THEN
   │ │     │       ENTER FNAME,
   │ │     │          ADDRESS,
   │ │     │          CITYSTATE,
   │ │     │          ZIPCODE
   │ │     │       WRITE (1)
   │ │     │          RECORD R
   │ └─────┴────────────
   │
   │   ENTER LNAME
   │
   └ WHILE-END

3.  EXIT
```

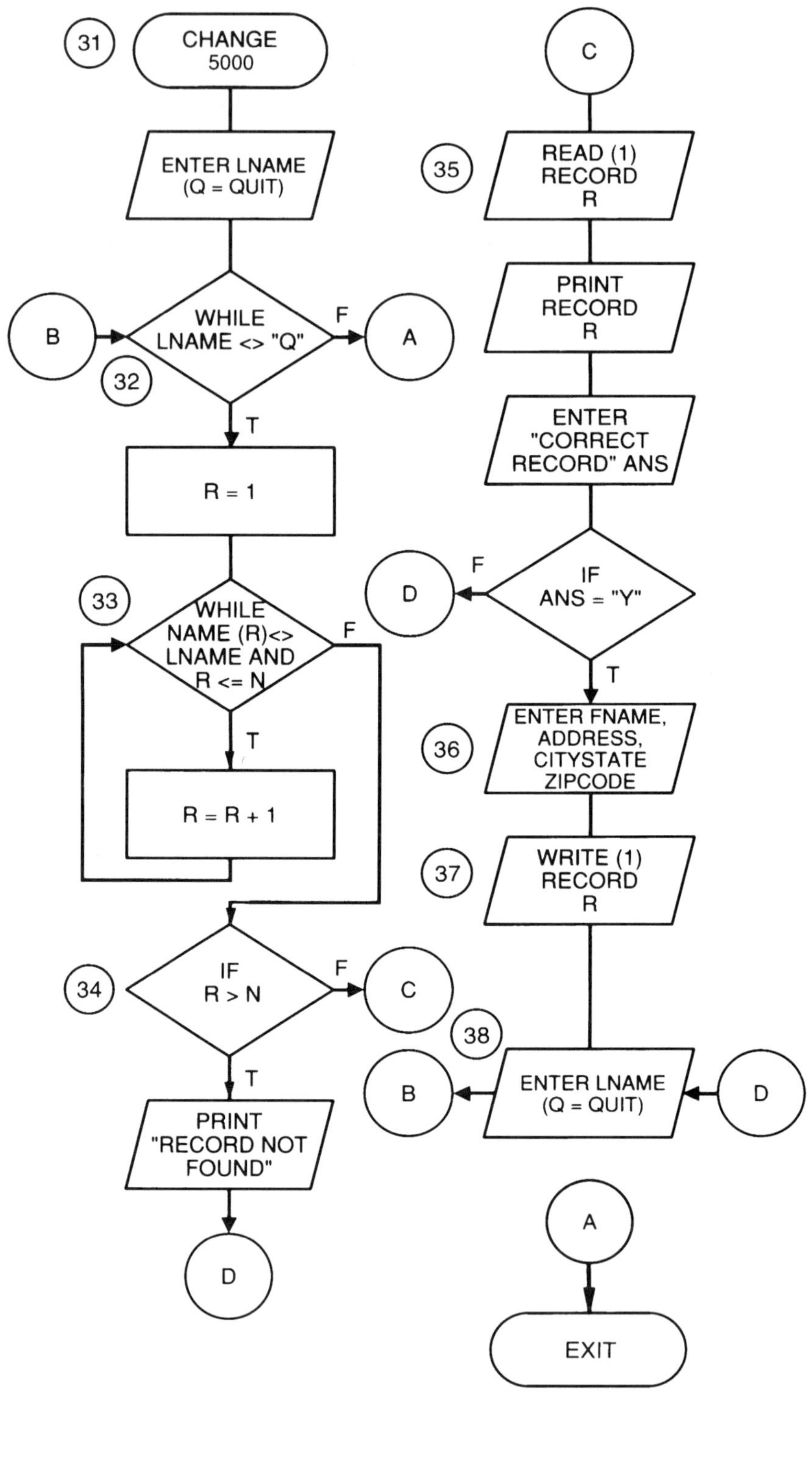

Figure 16.3j Algorithm and Flowchart for CHANGE Module

Algorithm	Flowchart
LABELS MODULE 6000 1. ┌ LOOP: R = 1 TO N │ J = RECNO (R) │ READ (1) RECORD J │ PRINT LABEL RECORD J └ LOOP-END: R 2. EXIT	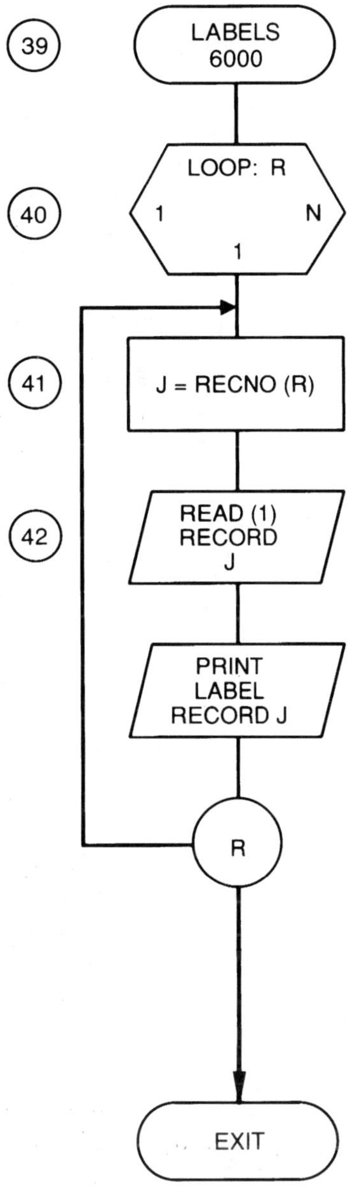

Figure 16.3k Algorithm and Flowchart for LABELS Module

Algorithm	Flowchart
DIRECTORY MODULE 7000 1. ┌ LOOP: R = 1 TO N │ J = RECNO (R) │ READ (1) RECORD J │ PRINT RECORD J └ LOOP-END: R 2. EXIT	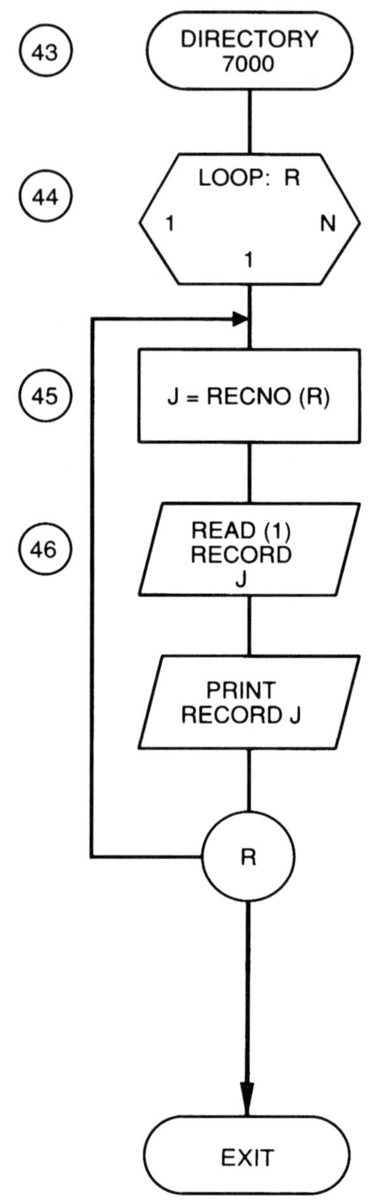

Figure 16.3l Algorithm and Flowchart for DIRECTORY Module

Algorithm

WRAPUP MODULE
8000

1. CLOSE 1
2. OPEN 2, INDEX FILE
3. LOOP: R = 1 TO N

   WRITE (2), RECORD R

   LOOPEND: R
4. CLOSE 2
5. PRINT "RUN COMPLETED"
6. EXIT

Flowchart

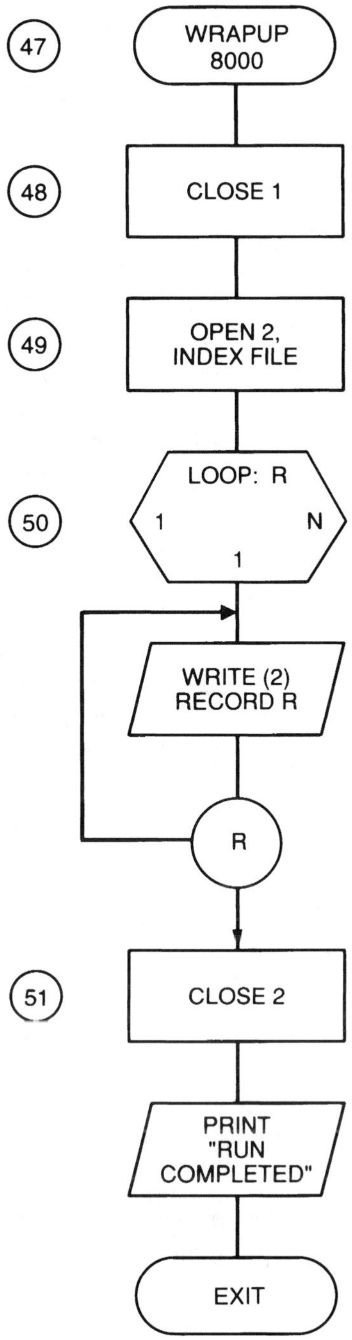

Figure 16.3m Algorithm and Flowchart for WRAPUP Module

30. This instruction allows the user to enter the next record to be deleted. If there are no more records to be deleted, the user enters a Q.
31. This is the module to change data in a record.
32. This instruction loops until there are no more records to change.
33. This loop searches for the record to change.
34. If this condition is TRUE, the record could not be found. Processing then continues at the end of the loop by entering a new name.
35. These instructions read and print the record and then ask the user whether it is the correct record. If it is not, then the processing continues at the end of the loop by entering a new name.
36. This instruction enters the changed data.
37. This instruction writes the record back to its original location in the file.
38. This instruction allows the user to enter the name of the next record to be changed. If there are no more records to be changed, the user enters a Q.
39. This is the module to print labels.
40. This loop prints the labels for all records.
41. J is the pointer that points to the next record to be processed. RECNO(R) is the corresponding record number in the index arrays.
42. These instructions read the record to be processed and print the label of the record in the memory.
43. This is the module to print the directory.
44. This loop prints the information for all records.
45. J is the pointer that points to the next record to be processed. RECNO(R) is the corresponding record number in the index arrays.
46. These instructions read the record to be processed and print the data on the record for the directory.
47. This module processes all the necessary tasks after the files have been updated and processed.
48. This instruction closes the MAILLIST data file.
49. This instruction opens the INDEXFILE.
50. This loop copies the data in the index arrays to the INDEXFILE.
51. This instruction closes the INDEXFILE.

Summary

Random-access files are becoming more and more important as businesses demand more up-to-date information. Random-access files are used any time data might be needed at a moment's notice and/or when data must be as current as possible. The program must be interactive because the user needs to converse regularly with the computer through the keyboard and monitor.

The student programmer has to learn some specialized techniques and concepts to work with random-access files.

Many random-access programs allow the user to both update and process files through the use of a menu. The menu usually consists of options to add, delete, and change a record, make a query, print reports, and quit. The program loops until the user is ready to quit.

New Terms

binary search
index file
sequential search

Questions

1. What is the difference between a random-access file and a sequential-access file?
2. Can you efficiently process a sequential-access file randomly? Explain.
3. Can you process a random-access file sequentially? Explain.
4. Define *index*. What is the purpose of an index?

Problems

Using the input records developed in Problems 5–7 in Chapter 13, develop solutions for the following problems. Your solution should include a problem analysis chart, an IPO chart, a structure chart, a data dictionary, output report designs, and the algorithms and flowcharts for all modules.

1. **a.** Use the random-access file developed in Problem 5 in Chapter 13 for a stereo system for a TV or radio station. (LP records, cassettes, CDs, and VCRs are all used by the station.) How would this file be ordered? Which field(s) would be used for searching? Which fields might need to be updated? What reports would be needed?
   b. Develop a solution to update and print the records for the file in Problem 1a.
2. Complete Problems 1a and 1b for the following:
   a. a book inventory
   b. the students and their grades for a course
   c. a checking account for an individual
3. An airline has information on all of its flights from departure to arrival time. The company needs to update information constantly about the number of seats sold, the number of seats remaining, the time of departure, the estimated time of arrival, the departure airport, and the destination airport. The file must be updated whenever a reservation is made or canceled, or when a flight begins or ends. The airline has to be able to inquire about a particular flight and about all flights to one particular airport within a certain time frame. The company also needs a report on all completed flights. Develop the solution to this problem.

UNIT FIVE

SUPPLEMENTARY EXERCISES

Develop a complete solution, including a data dictionary, to the following problems:

1. The financial director of a private school would like a tracking system for the students at the school.

   a. Design the file. The information on the student includes: name, home address and telephone, age, sex, class status, parent's name (one parent), dormitory room, tuition, room fees, board fees, book fees, computer fees, miscellaneous fees, date of payment on each charge.

   b. Design the reports needed:
   Student directory
   Charges
   Outstanding fees
   List of students by dormitory
   List of students by class

   c. Develop a solution using sequential access files to output the needed reports.

   d. Develop an update program.

2. Develop Problem 1 using random-access files.

UNIT SIX

PROBLEM SOLVING FOR APPLICATION SOFTWARE

Chapter 17

Introduction to Application Software

Overview

Types of Horizontal Software
Steps to Learning a New Software Package
Software Compatibility Problems

Objectives

When you have finished this chapter, you should be able to:

1. List and define the major types of horizontal software.
2. List and explain the steps needed to learn a new application software package.
3. List and explain some of the compatibility problems associated with applications software.

Microcomputers started a revolution in the computer industry during the late 1970s. Until that time, computers were used only by large businesses because of the initial and operating costs of a computer. Microcomputers made computers affordable for almost anyone, but many people who were interested in using them were not interested in programming them.

The microcomputer industry responded to this new consumer need by developing software programs for the general public. The first software was **vertical software.** Vertical software is purpose specific; that is, it is for dental accounting, retail inventory, recreation games, education programs, and so forth. In the early 1980s the software industry started to sell **horizontal software.** Horizontal software is broader in purpose and capable of solving many kinds of problems.

Types of Horizontal Software

The five main types of horizontal software in use today are word processing, graphics, desktop publishing, data-management, and spreadsheet programs. Word processing enables the user to edit text electronically without the erasing and retyping involved when conventional typewriters are used.

The use of graphics with all productivity packages is increasing. Graphics can be obtained from a variety of sources, including buying clip art, photo clips, and drawing your own. There are also packages which allow you to create animation and capture sound and video. These are part of multimedia. The use of multimedia in applications is also increasing in use. Multimedia is defined as combining text, graphics, video, animation, and sound in developing an interactive application. Chapters 11 and 12 present topics on the design and development of graphics user interfaces for use in the development of multimedia applications. The following chapters will not include these topics. They will, however, include the use of still graphics in connection with word processing, desktop publishing, and spreadsheets.

Desktop publishing is the combination of word processing and computer graphic arts. This type of software at the present, is usually a page layout program; however, the trend is to combine word processing and desktop publishing into one package. Data management allows the user to easily enter and organize data and to create reports. Spreadsheets enable a user to calculate worksheets with a computer instead of a calculator and to recalculate easily whenever the data change. These tasks are performed in business every day. Just as a person does not have to be a jeweler to use a watch or a mechanic to drive a car, users no longer need to know how to program, in the traditional sense, to perform these tasks on a computer. However, computer users do still need to know how to operate the computer and how to use the software. The end user can use all productivity packages without knowing anything about programming. However, many horizontal productivity software packages have built-in programming languages. The word *programming* may not be used, but that is really what the end user is doing. Word processors and spreadsheets have macros the end user can write. A macro is a short set of instructions or keystrokes that can be saved for use whenever needed. Database management systems have a more extensive built-in language. So, the end users must have some knowledge of programming if they are going to use the software package to the extend it is intended. Chapters 18, 19, and 20 will explain the types of languages used for each type of application.

Computers and horizontal software packages are designed to help the user make better decisions and to increase productivity, efficiency, and accuracy. For this reason, horizontal software packages are called **productivity packages.** If after learning to use a horizontal software package your productivity has not increased, then you are not using the package correctly, you are not using the correct package, or you should not be using a computer for that particular application. It is very important to choose the correct tool to complete the job.

Steps to Learning a New Software Package

A software package contains the following parts:

1. One or more diskettes or a CD-ROM containing the programs, computer-based tutorials, and any other files necessary to use the package.

2. One or more manuals. These manuals provide instructions for the use of the software, manual-based tutorials for learning the package, installation instructions, and other information for the end user.

It is advisable to be systematic when you are learning a new software package. Here are some recommended steps to learning new software.

1. Look through the manuals to get an overview of the sections for future reference.
2. Find the section in one of the manuals on how to install the program *for your computer.* Computer systems vary. Software packages, however, are universal, so they have to be adapted to a specific computer. When you **install a software package,** you match it to the type of printer, the type of monitor, and the type of disk drive in your computer setup. Follow the directions in the manual very closely. If the program comes on diskettes, the first step usually is to copy all of the diskettes onto other diskettes and to put the originals away for safekeeping. The second step is to run an install program—a program that helps the user install the software package. Most installation programs are very user-friendly. If new hardware is bought, then software to be used on the new hardware may need to be reinstalled.
3. Run the computer-based **tutorials.** Tutorials consist of demonstrations and instructions for the productivity packages. Start the tutorial and work through the lessons. Do not try to remember everything the first time, but try to get an understanding of the capabilities of the package.
4. Examine the manuals and get a general idea of their contents. Find all the indexes. Often there will be more than one index in a manual. You can find an answer to most questions by using the indexes and the table of contents.
5. Look through any tutorials in the manuals. Complete the tutorial exercises as needed. After each tutorial, complete the same task with other data. Run the computer-based tutorial as often as you need to.
6. Complete one of the types of tasks for which the package was designed, just to get a feel for the package. When problems occur, read the manual to find a solution. Use the on-line help as much as possible. Today's applications packages often have almost the complete manual available for use under the help menus. Some software packages offer on-line tutorials for the end user to use without exiting the package. These are extensive and provide timely reminders of how to accomplish something. Keep a notebook of solutions to problems, and repeat the steps that caused the problem, to better understand what happened. If there is a problem that you cannot solve, ask other users about it or call the company hotline. Most of the larger software houses offer help to those who register software with them.
7. Add several features every time you use the package for a new problem. Do not be content with using only a few features of a full-featured package.

Productivity packages are designed to help. They can be frustrating at first because they are complex. However, it doesn't take too long to become familiar with them. Once you are comfortable with them, the capabilities and speed of the packages will amaze you. Once you overcome initial fears and frustrations, the programs are fun and exciting.

Software Compatibility Problems

Depending on the computer system and software packages you are using, you may have compatibility problems when you try to import files (transfer data files from another program to the one you are using) or to export files (transfer data files from the program you are using to another program). An example of compatibility would be to create a graphic in a paint package and import it to a desktop publishing package. The saved file may or may not be compatible with the software package doing the importing. If it is not, then you have to use a utility to convert the data from the format in which it is saved to a format that is acceptable to the importing software package.

Most word-processing packages import and export ASCII files without any problem. However, ASCII files are saved without any of the special print features produced in the word-processing package. Many application software packages have lists of formats that the package will accept on opening a document. Likewise, there are many formats in which the end user can save a document. This includes other versions of the same package. Most manufacturers of software make sure their new versions are **upward compatible.** This means that documents produced in previous versions of the software are compatible with the new version. The term **downward compatible** means that a document produced by a new version is compatible in a previous version of the software.

Integrated software combines multiple types of full-featured horizontal software into one package. The advantage of using integrated software is the ease of importing and exporting data from one type to another type of software. The disadvantage is the decrease in the number of features of each package.

Summary

With the advent of the microcomputer came the need for software. Part of this need has been met through the development of such productivity packages as word processing for text editing, graphic packages, desktop-publishing packages for combining word-processing and graphics capabilities, data-management systems for data organization, and spreadsheets for automatic calculation of worksheets. These packages require the user to learn how to use a computer and to learn how to enter instructions to solve problems, but they do not require any programming in the traditional sense. Problem solving for applications requires different skills than for languages.

The steps to learning a new package include installing the software for a particular computer, using the tutorials, examining the manuals, and using the package for practice problems.

New Terms

downward compatible
horizontal software
install a software package
productivity package
tutorials
upward compatible
vertical software

Questions

1. Define the term *productivity package.*
2. Name at least three types of productivity packages.
3. State the steps to learning a new productivity package.
4. What is meant by "installing your software"?
5. What is meant by *upward compatibility?*
6. What is meant by *downward compatibility?*
7. Why are upward and downward compatibility important to the end user?

Chapter 18

Problem Solving for Word Processing and Desktop Publishing

Overview

Word Processing
Graphics
Desktop Publishing
Some Design Concepts
Word-Processing and Desktop-Publishing Planning
Types of Documents

Objectives

When you have finished this chapter, you should be able to:

1. Define the concepts of a well-designed document.
2. List and describe the types of documents produced by a word processor and a desktop publisher.
3. Develop a planning guide for the page layout of a document.

Word processing and desktop publishing are discussed here, in a problem-solving text, because some problem solving is involved when a user designs and produces a document. A **document** is the text and graphics placed in one file. **Word processing** software enables the user to design, edit, and view a document before it is printed. A **desktop publisher** is a page layout program. It will take text from a word processor and graphics from a graphics program and combine them into a professional quality document. Some word processors have limited desktop-publishing capabilities, and some desktop publishers have limited word-processing capabilities; if at all possible, you should use the software best designed for your particular needs.

Word processing is the most widely used productivity application. Word processing is coming very close to replacing the typewriter both at home and in the office. It is usually the first package implemented when a computer system is purchased. Most people learn to use a word processor in a relatively short time, but it takes longer to use it efficiently. With a word processor, text no longer has to be typed and retyped every time there is a correction or revision. The text is stored electronically on a separate file and is accessed through the word-processing program. The extent of what a word-processing package can do depends on the functions provided in the package.

Word Processing

The primary goal of a word processor is to increase productivity by editing text electronically. Editing is accomplished through such basic functions as cursor control for moving around in the document, formatting pages, correcting text, copying and moving text from one place to another, checking spelling, style, and grammar, enhancing characters, and merging and separating documents. The functions found in a package vary from few to many, depending on the package. Some functions are automatically performed by the computer; others are performed manually by the user. The user executes functions through commands given directly to the computer, by choosing the desired functions from a menu, or by the click of a mouse button.

Graphics

Graphics to be used with word processors or with a desktop publisher enhance the aesthetics and clarify the meaning of the information presented in the document. There are several sources of graphics. One of the easiest sources of artwork is **clip art.** Clip art packages contain pictures that can be imported into the document on which you are working. Photo collections and clip art collections can be found on disk or CD-ROM. Another means of importing artwork is through the use of a scanner. A scanner allows you to take a paper picture and digitize it into the computer. A further source of art is to draw it yourself through the use of a paint or draw package. Any of these methods is an appropriate means of producing artwork for your document. In this chapter, we will not be concerned about where the art came from but how to use it. The only problem with importing artwork is compatibility. Certain graphics packages are not compatible with many word processors and the desktop-publishing packages on the market. If the packages are not compatible, then you will need to go through the process of converting to a compatible format. Directions for doing so are found in the manuals for the software.

Desktop Publishing

Desktop-publishing application software packages are page layout software packages. They are designed to take text from a word processor and graphics and easily place them on a page to be aesthetically pleasing. The text from the word processor is unformatted. The formatting is accomplished in the desktop publisher. The graphic images come from clip art, photo art, a scanner, or original art. Some text can be entered using the desktop publisher; however, a desktop publisher is not designed to be as efficient as a word processor at entering text. Some artwork can be accomplished in the desktop publisher, but it is very limited. Again, the desktop publisher is not a draw or a paint program. Desktop publishers allow the user to flow text easily around graphics, to use guidelines to place text and graphics accurately on the page, to allow the user to set up a master page, and to allow placement of lines, circles, and boxes on a page along with many other things. If there is plain text only on a page, then a word processor is probably the best tool. If there are graphics to be placed on the page; lines, circles, or boxes to be used; or fancy headings, fonts, etc., to be used; then the best tool is a desktop publisher. We will not be concerned with the specific package in this text; instead we are concerned with the plan of the document.

Some Design Concepts

A word-processing program and a desktop publisher considerably simplify planning the appearance of the text of a document, the first step in its production. Planning includes **formatting** the pages, paragraphs, lines, and words, that is, designing page length, margins, paragraph indentation, line spacing, and so forth. A document planning guide—a form that shows the layout of a document page with margins, footers, and headers—can help in planning the format of the page. However, a sketch showing the format is just as helpful. Figure 18.1 presents an example of a page planning guide (also Figure D.9, Appendix D). The planner makes notes on the guide to use later when actually creating the document.

Although preplanning may seem like a waste of time, a few minutes spent doing it saves many minutes of shaping the document by trial and error on the computer. Certainly, there will be changes to the document in the final stages, but if the document is well planned, the changes will be minimal.

Planning a well-designed document requires a knowledge of page design concepts. These include the placement of graphics; the use of white space; the use of lines, boxes, and circles; the placement and alignment of text; the use of effective fonts and point sizes; and the understanding of the movement of the eye on the page. It is also important to consider the purpose of the document. After all, a memo should have a different design from an advertising flyer.

One of the most important considerations in designing a document is to understand how the eye naturally scans a page without any redirection. The eye naturally falls in the upper right-hand part of the page, then follows the page in an S-shaped path. Therefore, it starts at the right, moves to the upper left of the page, then to the bottom right and finally to the bottom left. If another part of the page is to be seen first, then part of the design needs to redirect the eye to the specified part. This can be done with graphics, lines, circles, color, or any other eye-catching mechanism. When redirecting the eye, though, make sure you provide redirection to stay on the page. The use of an arrow is a good tool; however, it can redirect the eye right off the edge of the page. Hence, we offer *Rule Number One:* Keep the eye on the page through the use of redirection methods until you want the reader's eye to go to another page.

The use of fonts and point sizes can increase the aesthetics and readability of a document unless too many are used. Font refers to how the characters look. There are many font styles. Points refer to the size of the characters. Point sizes generally go from 9 points (smallest) to 128 points (largest), although this is also determined by the software package. Generally, there should be no more than two different fonts and four different point sizes, although there are always exceptions. *Rule Number Two:* Use no more than two fonts and four point sizes on a page. When more are used, the document becomes cluttered, confusing, and unreadable.

Header: ______________________________

Left Margin: ______________ Top Margin: ______________ Right Margin: ______________

Tabs:

Bottom Margin: ______________

Footer: ______________________________

Paper Size: ______________

Page Orientation: ______________

Justification: ______________

Other Information

Graphics To Be Used:

Reminders:

Mark Guidelines

Mark Page Number Placement

Figure 18.1 Page Planning Guide for Word Processing

Lines, boxes, and circles should also be used in moderation. The use of a box surrounding the document can pull the information together. However, sometimes it makes the document very confining. Use boxes, lines, and circles to emphasize elements that are very important, or to confine a graphic or an idea to a particular area. Too many boxes, lines, and circles will only confuse the ideas you intended to emphasize. Boxes should be aligned with the text. Alignment provides an invisible line connecting the elements together; therefore, alignment is very important. When elements are aligned, the document looks neater and better. *Rule Number Three:* Use properly aligned boxes, lines, and circles sparingly.

The placement of graphics on the page should enhance the attractiveness of the document. The graphics should pertain to the document. You should not use clip art of a boat when the article is talking about the desert, nor would you place a palm tree on a memo. The graphic should be relevant or it should not be there. Do not clutter the page with graphics. Use them sparingly. You should keep your document as simple as possible, while still getting the idea across to your readers. You should use prepackaged photo art or clip art whenever possible. It is easy to overestimate the time it takes to make your own artwork or to take your own photos. As with boxes, alignment is very important. A graphic should be aligned with text and other graphics on the page. *Rule Number Four:* Use relatively few graphics to enhance the aesthetics of the document, and increase communication of the document.

The use of white space increases readability. Still, do not put too much white space on a page. Leading is the space between the lines. There should be enough space to increase the readability, but not so much that the eye does not flow naturally. On a flyer or a brochure, or on a business card, use white space to attract the eye. When you are creating a flyer, there should be as little text as possible, without sacrificing pertinent information. White space should enhance the attractiveness of the flyer. *Rule Number Five:* Be conscious of the use of white space, using enough to enhance readability but not so much as to lose continuity.

The placement of the text is a very important aspect of designing the document. After all, the reason the document is being created is so that it can be read. The placement of the text should make it as readable as possible. It should flow around the graphics in a way that will increase interest in the subject. Consider the justification (alignment of the text). There are four different types of justification: aligned left, aligned right, justified right and left, and aligned center (ragged outside). Text should be aligned with the graphics on the page. This adds continuity to the document along with good eye flow. Kerning can add to the aesthetics of the document. Be careful of hyphenation. Do not hyphenate over a graphic or to another page, unless absolutely necessary. *Rule Number Six:* Carefully place the text to increase readability, interest, and aesthetics.

Consider the type of document you are creating. Be aware of the purpose of the document. A flyer needs, first, to attract attention, and, second, to easily read. A memo should be very simple in format. A newsletter should have more graphics intermixed with the text than a poem. *Rule Number Seven:* Design the document with its purpose in mind.

Color is expensive to add to your document, although it does add to the attractiveness of the page. Color should be added to enhance and attract the eyes of the reader to pertinent information. Many times color is added to a document, but the color does not allow the reader's eye to flow to the rest of the page. Using colored paper is a way to cut the cost and yet add some color. *Rule Number Eight:* Use color to enhance the elements of a document and to attract the eye to the document.

All documents should communicate a message. When your document is finished, test its effectiveness by answering the question: Does this document communicate the intended message? If it doesn't, you need to modify the document until the message is clearly communicated. *Rule Number Nine:* Make sure the document is effective in communicating the message.

1. Keep the reader's eye on the page through the use of redirection methods until you want it to go to another page.
2. Use no more than two fonts and four point sizes on a page.
3. Use boxes, lines, and circles sparingly.
4. Use relatively few graphics to enhance the aesthetics of the document and those relevant.
5. Be conscious of the use of white space, using enough to add readability, but not so much as to lose continuity.
6. Carefully place the text to increase readability, interest, and aesthetics.
7. Design the document with its purpose in mind.
8. Use color to enhance the elements of a document and to attract the eye to the document.
9. Make sure the document is effective in communicating the message.

Above all, use common sense and good judgment to see if you like to look at the document. If it is pleasing to your eye (please be honest), then it probably will be pleasing to others.

Word-Processing and Desktop-Publishing Planning

Planning a document is important. Just as in all other applications on the computer, there are certain steps you should complete in planning your document. The following section lists the steps to accomplish a well-designed document. No matter what the purpose of the document, it should be done well and in the least amount of time. Remember the rules of good design in every step of the planning process. Use the page planning guide shown in Figure 18.1 to help in the planning of your document. This guide is also found in Appendix D in Figure D.9.

Step 1: Determine your audience. This is important since the design will differ from audience to audience. The audience determines the terminology used, the form of the document, and the overall appearance. An advertisement would be designed differently to advertise a party for the office staff versus advertising for a public band concert.

Step 2: Determine the purpose of the document. You need to know why this document is being developed before you can design it. A memo will have a different design than a report.

Step 3: Determine the page setup. The page setup includes margins, headers, footers, page numbering, justification, size of paper, and orientation of paper. The margins include the top, bottom, left, and right margins. If the document is to be bound, the margin needs to be wider on the left or if the pages are to be copied back to back, then you will need to have a right page and a left page. In this case, if this is to be a bound document, there will be inside margins and outside margins, the inside margins being larger than the outside margins. A header is one line of text placed in the top margin and printed on every page. This might include the name of the chapter, the name of the book, the page numbers, or the date. A footer is basically the same as the header except that it is in the bottom margin. The page numbers are normally placed as part of the header or the footer, depending on the desired placement. Justified is the alignment of the text. Left justification means the text is aligned on the left, right justification means the text is aligned on the right, justified means the text is aligned on both the left and right, and center justification means the text is centered. The size of paper includes letter size, legal size, envelope size, or any custom paper size. The orientation of the paper includes portrait (tall) or landscape (wide). Portrait is printed on the page so the left and right margins are on the long sides of the paper. Landscape is printed on the page so the left and right margins are on the narrow sides of the paper.

Step 4: Determine where the guidelines are to be placed. There are three types of guides. The first type is margins. Included are the top, bottom, right, left, header, and footer margins. See step three for more information about margins. The second is column guides. These designate the separation between columns on a page. The third type of guides is ruler guides or blue line guides. These are lines used to align text and graphics on the page. They can be horizontal or vertical. All guides are visible on the monitor only and are not printed.

Step 5: Determine the type and placement of all graphics. This will include artwork, pictures, clip art, scanned images, photo images, mastheads for newsletters, and the captions that accompany the graphics.

Step 6: Determine the placement of the text and what the text will include. The text needs to be written and the placement of the text on the page needs to be determined. The format of tables and columns of data is determined at this time. This would include any mathematical formulas that need to be entered and the determination of tabs. There are five types of tabs: right tab—text is aligned to the right of the column, left tab—text is aligned to the left of the column, center tab—text is centered in the column, decimal tab—a right-aligned tab with the decimal points aligned, and tab leader—a right tab that includes a dotted line placed between the last text character on the left and the beginning character of the text in the column. See Figure 18.2. Also, at this time, determine any

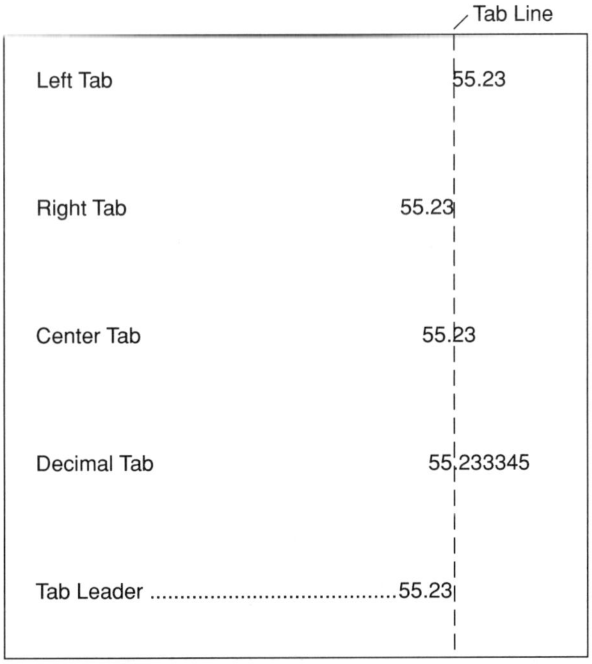

Figure 18.2 Types of Tabs

files that need to be inserted from other applications such as a report from a spreadsheet program or a report from a database management system.

Step 7: Determine the type styles of all text. Figure 18.3 shows some of the different type styles available. The font and size are the first to be determined. The font should be chosen with the audience and purpose in mind. You probably would not use a cursive font for a very formal report. Many fonts are available on the market today. Check to see what fonts are provided for your use. It is very useful to have the fonts and the sizes printed out and kept in your notebooks. Some words need to be emphasized. To do this, you would boldface the characters or italicize them. Characters used in mastheads of newsletters many times need to be emphasized by outlining the characters or putting a shadow on them. In a document that is being revised, the characters that are being deleted are often struck out instead of being deleted. In this case you would use the strike-through type style. Some characters need to be raised or lowered as superscripts or subscripts. Others need to be placed one character on another character as in the case of an accent over a letter. You also need to determine whether or not you want words to be hyphenated.

Step 8: Determine any other special needs of the document. These special needs might include development of an index or a table of contents; special enhancement using boxes, circles, or lines; added color; or anything else you would like to place on this document.

Types of Documents

A word processor can be used to create various types of documents. It can be used by a writer to compose a book, by a secretary to type and polish a letter or memo, by a teacher to create assignments or tests, or by a student to finish a paper or report. Different people bring different needs to a word processor.

Bold type Style
Italic type style
Outline type style
Shadow type style
~~Strike through type style~~
Underline type style
Examples of fonts:
- *Font*
- Font
- Font
- Font
- **Font**

Examples of sizes:
- 10 point
- 12 point
- 18 point
- 24 point

Figure 18.3 Examples of Type Styles, Fonts, and Sizes

A report, an article, or a book is a lengthy textual document that needs very few enhancements, such as boldface or underlining. It is usually composed on the computer, edited, and then printed in its final form. The planning required for this type of document is an outline and page formatting.

A word processor increases productivity with this type of document simply because it enables the user to design, edit, and print the document electronically. The user can simplify footnoting by placing footnotes immediately following the paragraph in which they appear, and then after the document is completed, moving them to the bottom of the correct page. The footnotes should initially be typed exactly as they will appear. When you footnote in this manner, the footnotes at first take up space in the body of the report. During typing, the writer can edit and move paragraphs without having to keep track of the footnotes—they move with the paragraphs—or without having to guess how many lines to leave at the bottom of the page. Some word processing packages have a footnote feature.

The memo is a document intended for distribution. The form is generally standard. A memo can be distributed in print or as a message sent on E-mail. The memo is stored electronically and can be easily updated later for redistribution. This type of document is short, and the enhancements are few. They might include boldface, underlining, and indentation. With the word processor, increased productivity again lies in the speed of editing and printing.

Templates, or boilerplates, are empty forms or shells that can be used repeatedly with different data. Templates include forms for letters, schedules, or any other forms needed in the workplace. A newsletter can be set up as a template. Figure 18.3 shows an example of a newsletter template. The template for a newsletter should include the masthead, guidelines, and any other elements included in every newsletter. The example in Figure 18.4 includes the masthead, the box around the news, and the place for the editor's column.

Increase in productivity lies with the use of the completed template. The template will be completed once and then used many times. For example, a form for a schedule can be completed in just a few minutes. The form is then saved in a file of its own. When the user needs to fill it in, she or he copies the form into a new file. The Search or the Search-and-Replace function can help the user find the data needed to fill in the form. When using a word processor, there are two modes of correcting text. One is the replacement mode, which enables the user to replace characters that need changing. The other mode is the insert mode, which allows the user to insert characters that have been left out. When characters are inserted, all of the remaining characters are moved to the right. Therefore, in order to keep the shape of the form when filling in data, the user should turn off the insert mode, or else the vertical lines and structure of the form will be destroyed. The final filled-in form is then saved and printed. In the planning stages, only the blank form is designed.

An instructor can create lesson plans, assignments, and tests for one term and then easily modify them for the next term. Although the word processor does not significantly increase productivity for the instructor the first semester, it does each time the course is offered thereafter. In addition, word processing improves an instructor's productivity by helping in the production of all of the types of documents mentioned earlier.

Advertising employs many types of documents. A flyer is a one-page sheet advertising an event. A brochure is more elaborate and more costly. It is usually six to twelve pages and is folded for sending in the mail. Some desktop publishers have page templates set up for brochures, so all you have to do is to add text and graphics.

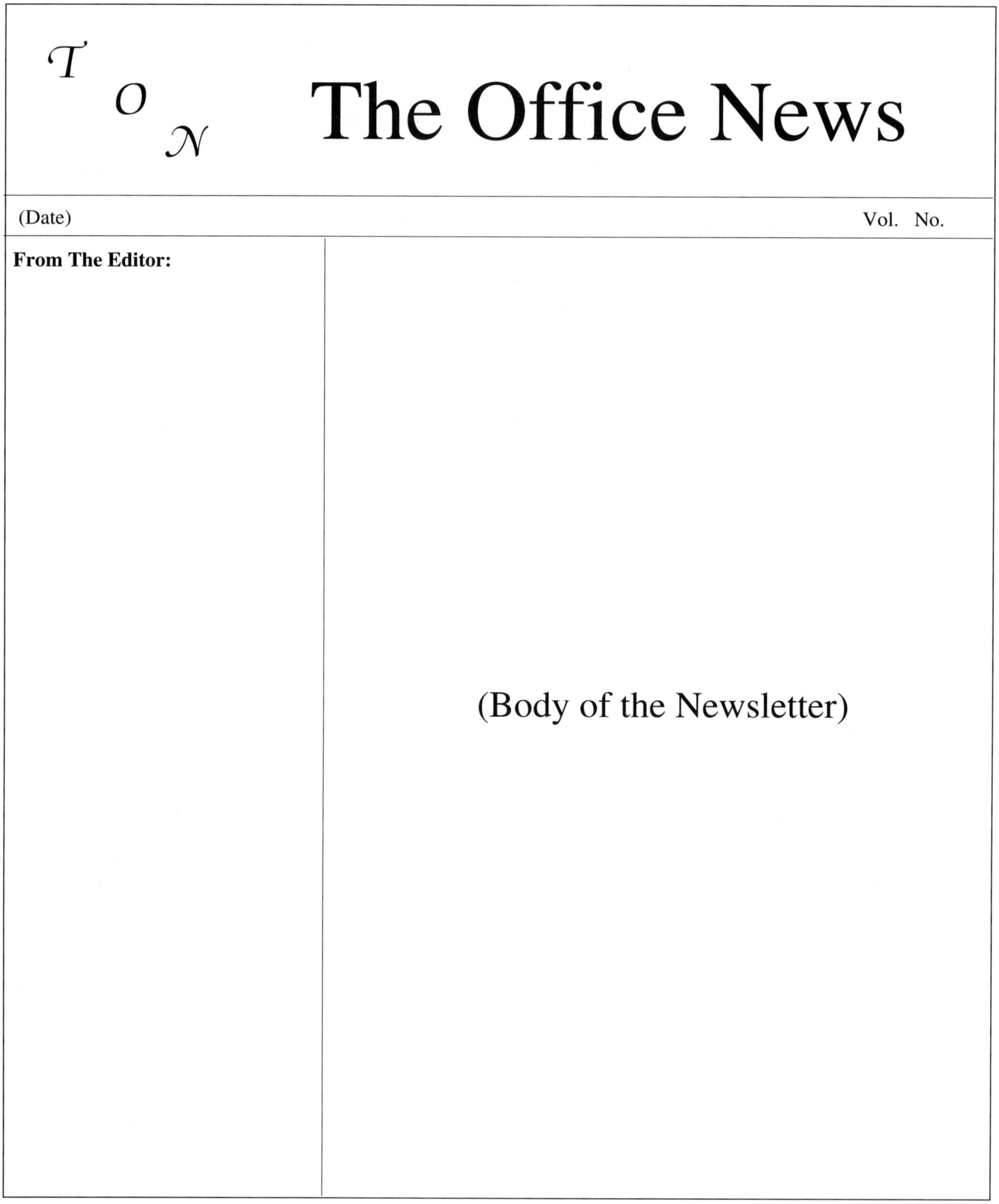

Figure 18.4 Example of a Newsletter Template

Business cards can be designed. Stationery, signs, and all kinds of forms can be designed for businesses.

Resumes are another type of document that can be designed for use with a word processor or desktop publisher. Figure 18.5 shows one form of a resume. You would need to fill in the information. The main sections of the document include your name, address, and phone number; objectives of employment; education; experience; other information; and references. The section headings should be enhanced. The information under each heading should be indented. The information should be as concise as possible without leaving out any pertinent information. The resume should be no longer than two pages. Productivity is increased by the use of electronic editing and the ease of modification of the resume.

Manuals can be created very easily through the use of the master page setup. A master page has elements that are found on all pages, including margins, guidelines, headers, footers, page numbers, etc. The text is written in a word processor, and then can be placed on the pages at a relatively rapid speed. The manual can then be modified without a great deal of difficulty when revisions are necessary.

Documents that require file merging can be accomplished on a word processor. There are two types of merges. The first involves merging two or more documents into the same file. The user will find it faster to develop small files and then merge them in another file later than to create the large document in one file. As a text gets larger, the computer takes longer to transfer from one part of the document to another. Therefore, this type of merge saves time for the user and the computer.

The second type of merge is merging data with text. In this type, often used for form letters, the document is in one file called the shell or the primary file with variables placed wherever a word or words will differ from one printed copy to another. A second file called the data file or secondary file contains the data that will be entered as the values of the variables. One record from the data file contains the information for one printed copy of the completed document. When merging the two files, the computer matches the data in the data file to the variable name in the text file to print the copy of the document. Therefore, it is important that the two files be developed

Name
Street Address
City, State Zip code
Telephone

Objectives:

(Short narrative about your employment objectives.)

Education:

(List all schools you have attended and the degrees you hold.)

Experience:

(List all employment experience.)

References:

(List all references or state "Available upon request.")

Figure 18.5 Example of a Resume Template

Primary File: Fields will be indicated by an F followed by the field number

F1
F2
F3, F4

Dear F5:

I am writing to inquire about an entry level programming job with your company.

Having just graduated from University of the North Coast, in Computer Information Systems, I am eager to begin my career. Attached is my resume. I have summarized my qualifications and my experience in my resume. I believe I could be a valuable asset to your company.

I can be reached at 707-545-4321. I would welcome a chance to discuss employment possibilities with you. Please let me know if there is a job opening.

I am looking forward to hearing from you.

Sincerely,

John Johnson
5555 H Street
Arcata, CA 95521

Enclosure: Resume

Figure 18.6a Mail Merge—Primary File

Field: 1	2	3	4		5
Dr. John Smith	545 Wood St.	New Town	CA	95367	Dr. Smith
Mr. Roy Jones	764 Tree St.	Old City	WA	98700	Mr. Jones
Ms. Jane Brown	888 Oak St.	Middle Town	OR	96787	Ms. Brown

Figure 18.6b Mail Merge—Secondary File

together. Once the files have been developed, the merge function can be executed, and, assuming the two files have been set up correctly, the printed document will differ for each record in the data file. See Figures 18.6a and b for a sample of the primary and secondary files. Productivity is increased since one form letter and one data file can produce many individualized letters.

There are many other types of documents, ranging from poems to books with many graphics that can be desktop published. In doing these, and all other documents, you need to be aware of the capabilities of your software and hardware. There are limitations with all packages, and you need to create your documents with the limitations, as well as the special features of your package, in mind.

Many word processors have the ability to create macros. Macros are short sets of keystrokes and/or instructions to accomplish tasks. These macros are then saved with the document to be used whenever the document is used. An example of a macro would be the keystrokes to type a name that is used many times throughout the document. This improves productivity by using one keystroke to execute many keystrokes.

Summary

Word processing is one of the four major productivity packages available to the computer user. It allows text to be edited electronically. The features of word-processing packages vary greatly, so a user should choose one that is best for the types of documents to be created.

Desktop publishing is a composition program, which merges text and graphics onto one page. Follow the rules for good page design when designing any type of document.

The steps to produce a well-designed document are:

- *Step 1:* Determine your audience.
- *Step 2:* Determine the purpose of the document.
- *Step 3:* Determine the page setup.
- *Step 4:* Determine where the guidelines are to be placed.
- *Step 5:* Determine the type and placement of any graphics.
- *Step 6:* Determine the placement of the text and what the text will include.
- *Step 7:* Determine the type styles of all text.
- *Step 8:* Determine any other special needs of the document.
- *Step 9:* Make sure the document is effective in communicating the message.

Many types of documents can be produced by a word processor and a desktop publisher, including reports, newsletters, form letters, manuals, flyers, etc.

New Terms

clip art
desktop publishing
document
format
templates
word processing

Questions

1. What is word processing?
2. What is a document?
3. What are some of the functions of a word processor?
4. What are some of the types of documents?
5. Why use a word processor?
6. In what ways are problem-solving techniques important in word processing?
7. Describe how the six steps of problem solving described in Chapter 1 would be used in word processing.
8. What is the difference between a word processor and a desktop publisher?

Problems

Develop a document plan using the document planning guide, rules for good design, and the eight steps to produce a well-designed document for the following problems:

1. Select a poem and develop a plan to put it on a word processor, or a desktop publisher.
2. Develop an hourly schedule for a week for yourself. Then, using a planning guide, develop the design of that document that would use the fewest possible keystrokes. Never retype the same line twice; that is what the copy function is for. Remember, there are 66 lines per page and 80 characters per line.
3. Develop a letter that has at least seven variables at different locations in the text, and develop the data file for the letter. Specify at least three records of data.
4. Answer the following questions about a flyer you received in the mail, in the newspaper, or at a store (answer the questions with the eight rules of document design in mind):
   - **a.** What do you see first on the page? Why?
   - **b.** What do you see next? Why?
   - **c.** Is there anything on the page that you missed at first glance?
   - **d.** How many fonts were used?
   - **e.** How many different point sizes were used?
   - **f.** How many colors were used?
   - **g.** How much text was used?
   - **h.** Did you know what the flyer was advertising at first glance?
   - **i.** How effective do you think this flyer is? How would you change the flyer to make it more effective?
5. Design your own flyer to advertise a product or service that interests you.
6. When designing a page for a report, or a flyer, how can you accomplish the following?:
   - **a.** keeping the eye on the page
   - **b.** an uncluttered look
   - **c.** an aesthetically attractive format (one that is pleasing to the eye)
7. Design a brochure advertising an interesting new product.
8. Analyze a brochure you received. Answer the same questions as in Problem 4.

Chapter 19

Problem Solving for Spreadsheets

Overview

Spreadsheet Basics
Design of a Spreadsheet
Macros
Graphs and Presentation Graphics

Objectives

When you have finished this chapter, you should be able to:

1. Explain the basic principles of a spreadsheet.
2. List and explain the steps to design a spreadsheet.
3. Develop a planning guide for a spreadsheet that will be entered into the computer at a later date.

A **spreadsheet** package allows the user to design a worksheet so that the computer will do the calculations and continually display the results in matrix form. The package simplifies accounting, cost analysis, forecasting, grades, and many other tasks that require mathematical calculations. Spreadsheets increase productivity because the computer does the calculation and recalculation of the data.

The time a worker saves by using a spreadsheet does not necessarily lie in the initial calculation but in the recalculations. The **worksheet** is a display on the monitor of answers to the calculations, along with the data to use in the calculations and the labels that tell the user what the numbers on the screen represent. It takes time to initially set up the worksheet and to test it to make sure the answers are correct. The testing is important because the chance of serious error is greater with a spreadsheet program than with any of the other productivity packages. If there is an error in a word-processing document or in a piece of data in a database management system, the impact on the results is usually minimal. However, if there is an error in an equation or in assumed data in a spreadsheet, the results could be catastrophic. Once the initial calculations are completed on the worksheet, it's quick and easy to recalculate any of the figures.

Spreadsheet Basics

A spreadsheet package consists of several parts. The first part is the worksheet itself. On the monitor, all or part of the worksheet appears as a grid of boxes arranged in rows and columns. Worksheet boxes, called **cells,** are designated by row and column identifiers. A **cell** is where the row meets the column. A cell may contain one or more characters. Cursor movement in the worksheet is from cell to cell rather than from character to character. The worksheet displays mathematical information and results in a form similar to manual worksheets.

A second part of a spreadsheet package, also found on the screen, is the Control Panel and **status line.** This area is located above the worksheet. There are three standard lines in the status area. The first is the menu bar. The second is the tool bars. These are icon substitutions for menu items. The third is the input line, where the computer communicates with the user. The status line is an information line and is found at the bottom of the screen. It displays such information as whether the computer is calculating, what type of data is in the cell where the cursor is, and whether there is an error.

Another part of a spreadsheet package is the contents of the cells. For each displayed worksheet cell, another cell in the computer memory contains user-established instructions to the computer regarding how and what to put into the worksheet cell for display on the screen. Displayed worksheet cells show only the results of instructions, not the instructions themselves. The contents of the cell in which the cursor is presently found are shown on the status line in the status area. The type of data making up the contents of the cell is shown on the information line in the status area. The contents of a cell can be one of two data types. The first is a label, which is character or string data type. Labels allow the user to identify rows and columns. The second type is a value, which is a numeric data type. Calculations, called formulas, and constants are considered values in a spreadsheet.

A fourth part of the spreadsheet package is the **commands.** Commands help the user set up and use the spreadsheet. This is accomplished through the use of menus and tool bars. Pull-down menus allow the user to choose the needed command. Some spreadsheet software packages have tool bars. The click of the mouse on an icon in the tool bar will accomplish a task normally found in one of the menus. Many of the commands have keyboard equivalents. Some of the commands include cut and paste, save and retrieve, assigning cell attributes, graph, data query, and many more. Many of the commands require the use of a **range** or **block of cells.** A range or a block of cells consists of a single cell, a consecutive group of vertical cells, a consecutive group of horizontal cells, or a rectangular block of cells. In reference to Figure 19.1, A1 would be a single cell range, A1 to A3 would be a vertical range of cells, A1 to D1 would be a horizontal range of cells, and A1 to D3 would be a block range of cells. The number and types of commands depend on the spreadsheet package.

The cell is the central part of the spreadsheet package. Each cell is designated by column letter and a row number (see Figure 19.1). Rows are numbered in order, starting at the top of the spreadsheet with number one. Columns are designated with letters starting with A on the left-hand side of the spreadsheet. The name of the cell is the column letter followed by the row number; for example, the cell found in Column C and row

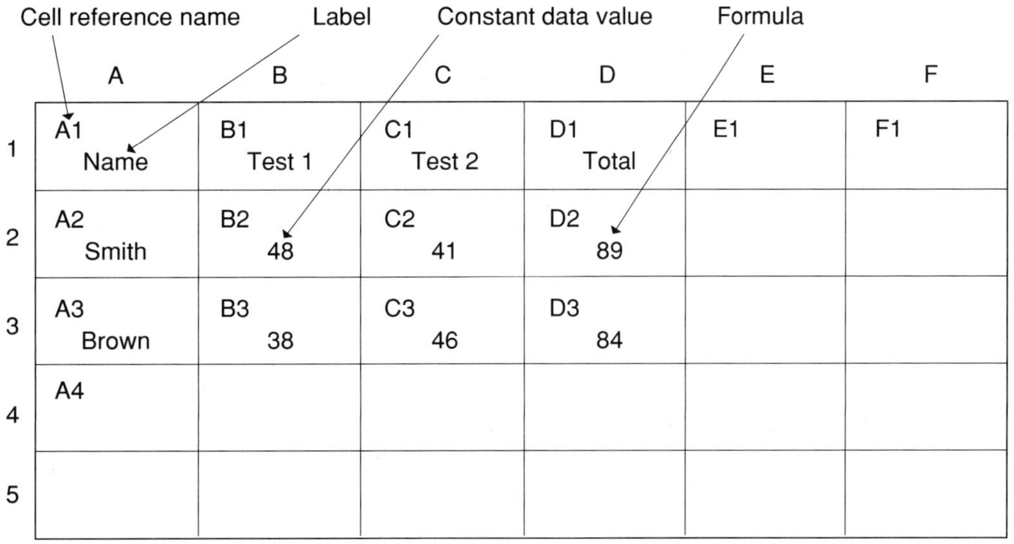

CELL CONTENTS

A1: Name	C1: Test 2
A2: Smith	C2: 41
A3: Brown	C3: 46
B1: Test 1	D1: Total
B2: 48	D2: +B2+C2
B3: 38	D3: +B3+C3

Figure 19.1 A Worksheet and the Cell Contents

5 is called C5. Some spreadsheet programs have three-dimensional spreadsheets. Pages are designated by letters or names. A cell found in page B, column C, row 5 would be called B:C5. Pages, cells, and blocks of cells can be named relevant names through the use of a command.

Many options are available to the user to specify how the data in a cell will be displayed. The first option is what is to be entered into the cell. Three things can be entered: labels, which are string data; values, which are numerical; and formulas, which are mathematical expressions. Another option is the width of the cells in one column (the number of characters in each cell). The width can be specified as something other than the default value. (A **default value** is a value that is built into the program; the computer uses this value unless the user specifies otherwise.) When a cell contains values or formulas and the width of the cell is insufficient, the program will tell the user that there is an error. When the content of a cell is a label, and the column is not wide enough, it will spill over into the next cell. The cell width must be the same for all cells in a column. The command to change the default value for width allows the user to change the width of the column but not of an individual cell.

A third option is that the user can specify the format of the cell. The various formats include right or left justification or centering of labels, as well as value formats for fixed decimals, scientific notation, currency that includes the dollar sign ($), percentages that include the percent sign (%), and the insertion of commas and other symbols for values and formulas.

The user can change cell contents through an editing process. Contents can be erased, moved to another cell, or copied to another cell or cells. When a user copies the contents of one cell to other cells, the cell names in the formulas change. These are designated relative cell references. A formula in cell D2 designated as B2 + C2 will copy to cell D3 as B3 + C3. If one of the cells in the formula should not change, then it must be designated an absolute cell reference. This designation is usually accomplished by the insertion of a $ before the column letter and row number.

A variety of other features are available to users of spreadsheets. Some commands can be executed either globally or through a range of values, such as changing column widths or formatting cells. Other commands are designated as either global or range, but not both. **Global commands** address the entire worksheet; *range commands* address only a designated part, such as a single cell, part of a row of cells, part of a column of cells, or a block of cells. Other commands address particular tasks to be accomplished.

Cell protection is a feature of many spreadsheets. It guards against the accidental destruction of a cell's contents by blocking the cursor out of the cell, which means the user is locked out. Also, a row or a column can be hidden from view. This guards against someone seeing sensitive information. In either case, the user has to specify the cells to be protected and/or hidden.

Recalculation, another spreadsheet feature, can be done in several ways. *Manual* recalculation means that it will be done only when the user specifies it. *Automatic* recalculation means that the worksheet will be recalculated every time a value or a formula in a cell is changed. *Natural* recalculation is done in a natural order, similar to the way a person would do it. This means that the computer decides which cells should be calculated first according to the cells the formulas use. *Row* recalculation is completed row by row, beginning with the upper-left cell, working across the row, and then moving down the spreadsheet to the next row. *Column* recalculation occurs column by column, beginning with the upper-left cell and moving down the column, and then moving across the spreadsheet to the next column. When the spreadsheet is large, it saves time to recalculate manually so the recalculation is done only periodically rather than every time any cell is filled or changed. With a small spreadsheet, the time for recalculation is relatively short, but on a larger spreadsheet the time can be considerable.

Sometimes the user has to insert or delete a row or a column. Often the user makes insertions or deletions to improve the appearance of a worksheet. The spreadsheet automatically updates any cells that reference the altered cells.

The row labels in the left-hand column and the column labels in the top row usually define the row and the columns. When the user scrolls the worksheet down or to the right, these labels disappear to the top or to the left. They can be fixed to make them stay on the screen so the user can see them at all times.

The window feature on some spreadsheets enables the user to view and derive information from two sections of the worksheet at the same time.

All or part of a worksheet and/or the cell contents can be printed. Depending on the package, other options are available, such as headers, footers, variations on margins, and scaling.

File operations are an important part of the commands of a spreadsheet package. The user can save a worksheet to an auxiliary storage device under many different names if desired. The program saves only the cell contents; when the file is retrieved, the worksheet on the screen is recalculated. Through other file operations, files can be combined, parts of worksheets saved, directory listings printed on the screen, and data disk drives changed.

Some spreadsheet packages include the ability to graph the data and create interactive slide shows. Also, some packages include data management features, such as finding a piece of data, sorting a range of cells, and easily filling in tables.

Many different spreadsheet packages are available. The more features a package has, the more flexible it is, but also the harder it is to learn. Even though packages with fewer features may be easier to learn, they are less flexible and can become frustrating because they lack certain useful features.

Design of a Spreadsheet

A spreadsheet is an electronic calculator. Since a spreadsheet is primarily a mathematical tool, many people have problems with the mathematics end of working with a spreadsheet. It is important to be able to glean the facts out of a problem, whether you are solving a textbook problem or a real-life problem. The PAC (problem analysis chart) introduced in Chapter 3 will help. Word problems are a problem to some people. However, if you can eliminate the words while keeping the facts, you no longer have a word problem. The PAC will help you do this. Use the PAC to separate the given data, the required results, and the needed formulas from the problem. This is the first step in the problem-solving stage of designing a spreadsheet.

Steps to Design a Spreadsheet

Just as in all other aspects of computer work, it is important to plan what you are going to do before sitting down to start work on the computer. The following are the steps you should follow to complete your planning of a spreadsheet. Remember as you plan that this is just a starting point. You will modify this plan as you test out your solution.

Step 1: Use the PAC to glean the given data, the required results, and the needed formulas. As you are reading through the problem, write down all facts in the appropriate box. You will use this to develop the cell contents in later steps.

Step 2: Create the overall design of the spreadsheet. Figure 19.2 shows a general design of most spreadsheets used for business analysis. The headings are at the top. The

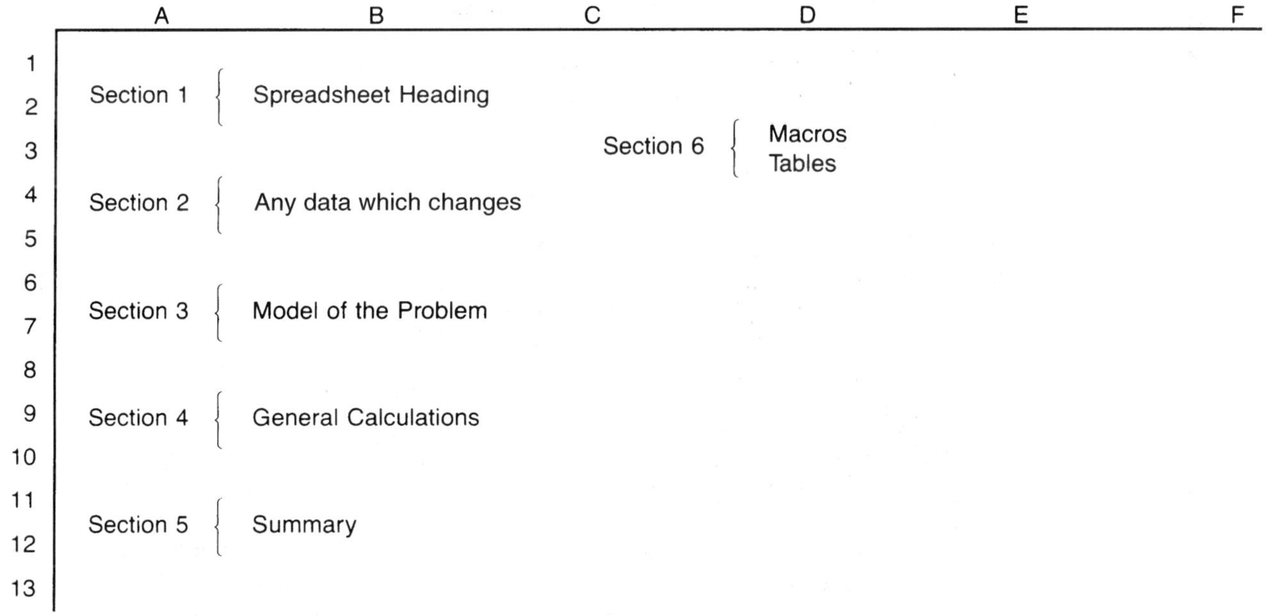

Figure 19.2 General Design of Most Spreadsheets

headings include such things as the company name, the title of the spreadsheet, the date, the time, and any other pertinent information about the spreadsheet. The second section includes all changes that are made from calculation to calculation. This would include such things as percentage increase or decrease, inflation rates, and the like. This third section is the model. This would include such things as number of employees, salaries, number of students, and so forth. The next section is where the general calculations take place. This would include such things as costs, revenues, or grade calculations. The next section is the summary section. This would include such things as the gross profit, tax, net profit, or average test scores. The last section is placed out of the area of the other sections. This section includes the macros and any tables required for the general calculations, such as tax tables.

Step 3: Place the labels on the worksheet. Using a piece of paper, or the form found in Appendix D, draw horizontal and vertical lines to simulate a worksheet. Next label the columns with letters (A, B, C, . . .) and rows (1, 2, 3 . . .). Next designate the column widths. Check with the default values since you may want to use these column widths. Now is the time to start designating the cell contents. Starting with the first section of your overall plan, fill in the labels in the proper cells. The labels will designate the overall worksheet heading, the column headings, the row headings, plus any other general labels that need to be entered. You should designate the format of each cell (right, left, or center justified).

Step 4: Enter the constant data, which are any data that will not change often. This includes data such as quantity, wholesale price, names, base salaries, deductions, and scores. You should designate the format for each cell (fixed, currency, percent, date, etc.).

Step 5: Enter the formulas (the mathematical expressions). Formulas are used to calculate the displayed value of a cell. Cells are referenced by the row and column in which they are found. The contents of cells that contain formulas are expressions, whereas the value of the expression is found in the worksheet cell on the screen. This value can be used in any other cell by using the cell reference name. Mathematical operators are used to perform the calculations. In some spreadsheet programs, the user can name a cell or a group of cells by giving it a variable name. This is called a **range name.** This chapter will not use range names.

Formulas use mathematical operators in the calculations. They also can use functions. Many functions are specific to spreadsheets. The following are some of the functions you might find in a spreadsheet package:

Mathematical Functions:

INT(*x*)	Returns the integer part of *x*
MOD(*x, y*)	Returns the remainder of *x*/*y*
ROUND(*x, n*)	Returns the number *x* rounded to *n* decimal places
SQRT(*x*)	Returns the square root of *x*

Other Functions:

IF(condition, *x, y*)	Returns *x* if condition is true, *y* if false
CHOOSE(*x, v*0, *v*1, *v*2, *v*3, . . .)	Returns the *x*th value in the list $v_0 - v_n$
VLOOKUP(*x, range, column*)	Looks up the value *x* in the table at *range* (range where the table is located) and then returns the value found in *column* (column number in the table starting with the left-most column as zero)

DATE(*year, month, day*)	The julian calendar date of *year, month, day*
NOW	The julian calendar date of today

Financial Functions:

CTERM(*int, fv, pv*)	Returns the number of periods for the investment of *pv* to grow to *fv,* earning the rate of *int*
DDB(*cost, salvage, life, period*)	Returns the double-declining depreciation of an asset, during *period,* given *cost, salvage value,* and the *life* of the asset
FV(*pmt, int, term*)	Returns the future value of *term* number of payments, earning *int* rate
IRR(*guess, range*)	Returns the internal rate of return of the cash flows in *range,* with a guess needed for calculating purposes
NPV(*int, range*)	Returns the net present value of a series of cash flows in *range,* discounted at *int* rate
PMT(*prin, int, term*)	Returns the payment needed to pay off the loan of *prin,* at the *int* interest rate, over *term* number of periods
PV(*pmt, int, term*)	Returns the present value of *term* number of *pmt* payments, discounted at the *int* interest rate
RATE(*fv, pv, term*)	Returns the rate needed for *pv* to grow to *fv* over *term* number of periods
SLN(*cost, salvage, life*)	Returns the straight-line depreciation of an asset, given *cost, salvage value,* and the *life* of the asset
SYD(*cost, salvage, life, period*)	Returns the sum-of-the-years digits depreciation of an asset, during *period,* given *cost, salvage value,* and the *life* of the asset
TERM(*pmt, int, fv*)	Returns the term needed for periodic payments of *pmt* to grow to *fv* with an interest rate of *int*

Statistical Functions:

AVG(*range*)	Returns the average of the values in *range*
COUNT(*range*)	Returns the number of values in *range*
COUNTIF(*range, x*)	Returns the number of *x* values in the range
MAX(*range*)	Returns the highest value in *range*
MIN(*range*)	Returns the lowest value in *range*
STD(*range*)	Returns the standard deviation of the values in *range*
SUM(*range*)	Returns the summation of the values in *range*
VAR(*range*)	Returns the variance of the values in *range*

A function is used in an expression to specify how to find the value of a specific cell. Formulas are used whenever possible to reduce the amount of data that has to be entered into the cells. For example, when several cells have the same constant value, the first cell will be given the constant, and the other cells will reference the first cell. In this way, when the value changes, the user has to change the value in only one cell instead of all the cells. Figure 19.3 presents some expressions that might be used in cells.

Mark any cells that need to be copied. Productivity increases when formulas can be copied. Copying cell formulas decreases data entry time and reliability of data entry. Two rules to increase productivity with spreadsheets are as follows: 1) reference as many cells as possible and 2) copy as many formulas as possible. Make sure you specify absolute cell references before copying the formula.

```
To add 2 cells together:
    +A5+A6

To sum a range of values (cells C3 through C19):
      SUM(C3..C19)                .. indicates all cells
                                  between the first cell
                                  and the second cell

To average the same range of values:
      AVG(C3..C19)

To find the payment for a loan:   where
      PMT(E1,E2/E4,E3*E4)         E1 = Cell where the amount of loan is
                                  E2 = Cell where the interest is
                                  E3 = Cell where the number of years is
                                  E4 = Cell where the compound period (12/year, 24/year, etc.) is

To find % of a sum:
    +E5/@SUM(E1..E10)*100
                                  E5 is what % of the sum of E1 through E10

To make a decision:
      IF(E1<E7,0,E7)              when E1<E7 the cell value = 0
                                  otherwise the cell value = E7

To increase a number by a percentage:
    A10*(1+A4)                    A10 = number to be increased
                                  A4 = % (in decimal form) increase (to decrease a number
                                  this A4 would have to be negative)

To perform a table lookup:

      VLQOKUP(3,A4..C7,1) = 14.42
      VLOOKUP(A1,A4..C7,B1) = 14.42
      VLOOKUP(2,A4..C7,2) = 3.85
      VLOOKUP(A2,A4..C7,B2) = 3.85
```

	A	B	C
1	3	1	
2	2	2	
3			
4	1	12.92	1.75
5	2	13.67	3.85
6	3	14.42	5.95
7	4	15.17	8.05

Figure 19.3 Sample Cell Contents of Formulas

Step 6: Enter any tables required in the formulas.
Step 7: Develop any macros needed for use with the problem.
Step 8: Test your formulas as much as possible.

Putting It All Together

Figure 19.4 shows the development of a program for the amortization of a loan. Notice that the only cells containing data are the cells containing the values of the loan amount, the interest, and the time. All other cells are referenced to these three. Also notice the number of cells that are copied. Cells that have the same formula are typed only once and copied into the other cells. This can result in a big increase in productivity.

Macros

Some spreadsheet packages allow the user to develop macros. **Macros** are small sets of instructions that facilitate the use of the spreadsheet. In reality, they are short programs. To use the capabilities of macros, the user must specify the set of commands to accomplish the desired tasks. This set of commands and/or instructions is placed in a section of the worksheet that is out of the range of the labels, values, and formulas of the problem. The user names the macro and tells the computer where to find it. From then on, the user implements the macro by its name. Macros increase productivity; however, some users avoid them because they do not understand or are afraid of them.

Figure 19.5 shows some examples of macros. Macro 1 writes a name in cell A1. Macro 2 allows the user to enter a number into D2. The steps to create a macro are:

1. Develop and write down the keystrokes or instructions for the macro.
2. Choose an out-of-the-way place or a different page on which to place the macro.
3. Enter the macro into one or more consecutive vertical cells with the last cell remaining empty. This signals the computer to stop executing the macro.
4. Label the macro so you will not forget what you named it.
5. Name the macro—the name is usually a "\" followed by one letter.
6. Execute the macro with either the control key or the alternate key (depends on the package) and the letter you named the macro.
7. Debug your macro using the debugging command built into your package or by stepping through the macro yourself.

Keystroke macros replace a series of keystrokes that complete a task. For example, a user could develop a keystroke macro that would replace the keystrokes to set column width, to print the cell contents, or to erase the contents of a cell. Keystroke macros speed up the development of a worksheet by reducing the number of keystrokes. A keystroke macro template also can be developed, saved, and used later to prepare all new templates or worksheets. Any new macros that are developed are added to the macro template. The template holds all macros you use on a regular basis.

The second type of macro involves a combination of keystrokes and special instructions built into the package. These macros are harder to develop, but they save time on tasks that have to be repeated.

Another use for templates is as a structure for doing calculations for a user who knows little or nothing about spreadsheets and wants only the results. A macro can be

ROW ↓ / COL. →		12 A		12 B		12 C		12 D		12 E	F	G	H
1					L	Principal		=	C	$1,500			
2						Interest		=	P	15%			
3						Years		=		1.			
4						PMT		=	C	PMT(E1, E2/12,12*E3)			
5		Period		Beg. Bal.		Interest		App. Prin.		E. Bal.			
6		1	C	E1	C	B6 * (E2)	C	(E4) – C6	C	B6 – D6			
7		2		E6		Copy		Copy		Copy			
8		3		Copy									
9		4											
10		5											
11		6											
12		7											
13		8											
14		9											
15		10											
16		11											
17		12											
18													
19													
20													

Figure 19.4 Worksheet Planning Guide for a Loan Amortization (circled cells are absolute)

A	A	B	C	D	E
1	John Smith			Age	
2				25	
3					
4	W	{GOTO} A1~		|	{GETNUMBER Enter an age, D2} ~
5		John Smith ~			

Figure 19.5 Examples of Macros

written to enable the user to enter any data needed for calculations and then let the spreadsheet do the calculations. The template would be developed for problems that recur in an organization.

Macros are absolute. The user must be careful when inserting rows and columns after a macro has been developed. Any references to other cells will not be changed when the cells are moved. This can lead to serious errors. The best solution to this problem is planning. A well-planned solution involving macros should not require the insertion of new rows or columns.

Steps to Complete the Spreadsheet on the Computer

After the planning stage is completed on paper, it is time to go to the computer. These are the steps to follow at this time:

Step 1: Start with your macro template.

Step 2: Enter the cell contents you developed on your planning sheet. Copy as many formulas as possible. Be sure to designate all absolute references.

Step 3: Develop your template. A template is a worksheet that contains all labels, formulas, and values that do not change often; it contains everything except the data that change with each recalculation. A template is stored under a separate name from the worksheets containing the data. When the user needs to enter new values into the worksheet, he or she retrieves the template from storage and enters the new values. The worksheet is then recalculated and saved under a different name. It is never wise to save the completed worksheet under the same name as the template, or the template will not be available next time it is needed.

Templates make it easy to use a worksheet over and over again. A template can be very complicated or it can be simple. The aim of any user of a spreadsheet program should be to develop templates that will be reused later for similar problems.

Step 4: Test your answers. This is a very important step. If the answers in a spreadsheet are wrong, the results can be disastrous. Figure 19.6 shows the worksheet and the cell contents that result from the loan amortization problem in Figure 19.4.

Step 5: Recalculate and print for all different values of the data that change with each recalculation.

Step 6: Develop macros pertaining to this spreadsheet, graphs, and other types of analysis aids to help with the postanalysis.

Step 7: Analyze the results of the spreadsheet problem—this is the postanalysis. Problem solving for designing spreadsheets is important before, during, and after the

	A	B	C	D	E
1			Principal	=	$1,500.00
2			Interest	=	15.00%
3			Years	=	1
4			Payment	=	$135.39
5	Period	Beg. Bal.	Interest	App. Prin.	End. Bal.
6	1	$1,500.00	$18.75	$116.64	$1,383.36
7	2	$1,383.36	$17.29	$118.10	$1,265.27
8	3	$1,265.27	$15.82	$119.57	$1,145.70
9	4	$1,145.70	$14.32	$121.07	$1,024.63
10	5	$1,024.63	$12.81	$122.58	$902.05
11	6	$902.05	$11.28	$124.11	$777.94
12	7	$777.94	$9.72	$125.66	$652.27
13	8	$652.27	$8.15	$127.23	$525.04
14	9	$525.04	$6.56	$128.82	$396.22
15	10	$396.22	$4.95	$130.43	$265.78
16	11	$265.78	$3.32	$132.07	$133.72
17	12	$133.72	$1.67	$133.72	($0.00)

```
C1:  'Principal
D1:  ^=
E1:  (C2)  1500
C2:  'Interest
D2:  ^=
E2:  (P2)  0.15
C3:  (C2)  'Years
D3:  (C2)  ^=
E3:  (FO)  1
C4:  (C2)  'Payment
D4:  (C2)  ^=
E4:  (C2)  PMT (E1,E2/12,E3*12) ——▶ Calculation of payment
A5:  "Period
B5:  "Beg. Bal.
C5:  (C2)  ^Interest
D5:  (C2)  ^App. Prin.
E5:  (C2)  ^End. Bal.
A6:  1
B6:  (C2)  +E1
C6:  (C2)  +B6*$E$2/12 ————————▶ Interest / month -- E2 must be absolute
D6:  (C2)  +$E$4-C6 ————————▶ Applied Interest -- E4 must be absolute
E6:  (C2)  +B6-D6 ————————▶ Ending Balance
A7:  2
B7:  (C2)  +E6
C7:  (C2)  +B7*$E$2/12
D7:  (C2)  +$E$4-C7
E7:  (C2)  +B7-D7
A8:  3
B8:  (C2)  +E7
C8:  (C2)  +B8*$E$2/12
D8:  (C2)  +$E$4-C8
E8:  (C2)  +B8-D8
A9:  4
B9:  (C2)  +E8
C9:  (C2)  +B9*$E$2/12
D9:  (C2)  +$E$4-C9
E9:  (C2)  +B9-D9
A10:  5
B10:  (C2)  +E9
C10:  (C2)  +B10*$E$2/12
D10:  (C2)  +$E$4-C10
E10:  (C2)  +B10-D10
A11:  6
B11:  (C2)  +E10
C11:  (C2)  +B11*$E$2/12
D11:  (C2)  +$E$4-C11
E11:  (C2)  +B11-D11
A12:  7
B12:  (C2)  +E11
C12:  (C2)  +B12*$E$2/12
D12:  (C2)  +$E$4-C12
E12:  (C2)  +B12-D12
A13:  8
B13:  (C2)  +E12
C13:  (C2)  +B13*$E$2/12
D13:  (C2)  +$E$4-C13
E13:  (C2)  +B13-D13
A14:  9
B14:  (C2)  +E13
C14:  (C2)  +B14*$E$2/12
D14:  (C2)  +$E$4-C14
E14:  (C2)  +B14-D14
A15:  10
B15:  (C2)  +E14
C15:  (C2)  +B15*$E$2/12
D15:  (C2)  +$E$4-C15
E15:  (C2)  +B15-D15
A16:  11
B16:  (C2)  +E15
C16:  (C2)  +B16*$E$2/12
D16:  (C2)  +$E$4-C16
E16:  (C2)  +B16-D16
A17:  12
B17:  (C2)  +E16
C17:  (C2)  +B17*$E$2/12
D17:  (C2)  +$E$4-C17
E17:  (C2)  +B17-D17
```

Figure 19.6 Worksheet and Cell Contents for Loan Amortization user develops the worksheet. After completing the check of the worksheet, the user does a postanalysis, entering sample key values and recalculating the worksheet several times. Each result is evaluated and analyzed. This is the "what if" part of spreadsheets. Problems to determine the best bank for a loan or what investment to make are types of problems that require several worksheet calculations and analysis of each of the results.

The postanalysis should answer questions such as:

- What happens to the profit when inflation increases and demand for our product also increases? (when completing a business analysis)
- How can we increase our savings? (using a budget analysis)
- Should we buy another business?
- Should we expand our store to include more square footage?
- How should we finance our car?
- How much profit can I project during the upcoming sale?
- How should we expand our product line?

Postanalysis is what spreadsheets are all about. Once the numbers are correct, they need to be analyzed to determine the outcome of the spreadsheet numbers. Postanalysis is a report summarizing the outcome along with recommendations resulting from the analysis. This analysis is difficult, and it requires practice to know what to look for and how to interpret the numbers. Graphs and summary sheets help in this analysis. Data modeling also helps. Data modeling is available only in the high-end spreadsheet package. Data modeling allows the user to set up and cross reference the data in multiple ways. Again this is a tool to help in the final analysis.

Graphs and Presentation Graphics

Most spreadsheets have a means to graph the results. These graphs have two functions. First, they are useful for analyzing results. It is much easier to analyze information in graph form than in numeric form. The second use of these graphs is for presentations. Many spreadsheet packages include the capability to make presentation-quality graphs and to incorporate these graphs in a slideshow. Presentation quality graphs are attractive because of the use of special fonts, clip art, character enhancement, multidimensional graphs, and color. Stand alone presentation graphics packages allow the user to import spreadsheet data to create slides and interactive slideshows which include text slides as well as graph slides. Presentation graphics is an expanding field. Using a multimedia notebook computer and a take along projection system, a person can use an electronic slideshow to give a professional quality presentation.

There are several types of graphs. The most common graphs are the line graph, the bar graph, and the pie graph. The line graph shows movement, usually over a period of time. An example would be profit over the last five years. The bar graph show comparisons, such as comparing the amount of corn produced in three states. The pie graph show percentage of the whole. Pie graphs are usually used with budgets. Other types include a donut graph, a scatter graph, and three-dimensional graphs of the above. It is important to choose the graph type which best represents the data. It is easy to become influenced by all of the fancy graph types; however, many times a simple graph portrays the data the best. Remember the graph should enhance communication of the data.

Putting It All Together

Figure 19.7a, b is an example of the development of a spreadsheet. The spreadsheet is a budget. A budget is a very good problem to solve using a spreadsheet. The spreadsheet is set up in three sections:

1. spreadsheet headings
2. income
3. expenditures

A	A	B	C	D	E	F	G
1	**My Budget**						
2							
3	Income (after deductions)						
4		January	February	March	Total	% of income	
5	Ron's Salary	1400	+B5	Ⓒ→	SUM(B5..D5)	+E5/$E$8	
6	Ann's Salary	1400	+B6	Ⓒ→	Ⓒ↓	Ⓒ↓	
7	Interest	100	+B7	Ⓒ→	↓	↓	
8	Total Income	@SUM (B5..B7)	Ⓒ→	→	↓	↓	
9							
10	Expenditures						
11		January	February	March	Total	% of income	% of Exp.
12	Rent	600	+B12	Ⓒ→	SUM(B12..D12)	+E12/$E$8	+E12/$E$25
13	Gas/Electricity	100	+B13	Ⓒ→	Ⓒ↓	Ⓒ↓	Ⓒ↓
14	Telephone	75	+B14	Ⓒ→	↓	↓	↓
15	Gasoline	100	+B15	Ⓒ→	↓	↓	↓
16	Car Payment	250	+B16	Ⓒ→	↓	↓	↓
17	Food	250	+B17	Ⓒ→	↓	↓	↓
18	Entertainment	200	+B18	Ⓒ→	↓	↓	↓
19	Clothes	100	+B19	Ⓒ→	↓	↓	↓
20	Vacation Fund	300	+B20	Ⓒ→	↓	↓	↓
21	Insurance	300	+B21	Ⓒ→	↓	↓	↓
22	Car Expenses	150	+B22	Ⓒ→	↓	↓	↓
23	Miscellaneous	300	+B23	Ⓒ→	↓	↓	↓
24	Savings	+B8–SUM(B12..B23)	Ⓒ→	→	↓	↓	↓
25	Total Expenses	SUM(B12..B24)	Ⓒ→	→	↓	↓	↓

Figure 19.7a Example of a Planning Guide and Report for a Budget

My Budget

Income (after deductions)

	January	February	March	Total	% of income
Ron's Salary	1400	1400	1400	4200	48.28%
Ann's Salary	1400	1400	1400	4200	48.28%
Interest	100	100	100	300	3.45%
Total Income	2900	2900	2900	8700	100.00%

Expenditures

	January	February	March	Total	% of income	% of Exp.
Rent	600	600	600	1800	20.69%	20.69%
Gas/Electricity	100	100	100	300	3.45%	3.45%
Telephone	75	75	75	225	2.59%	2.59%
Gasoline	100	100	100	300	3.45%	3.45%
Car Payment	250	250	250	750	8.62%	8.62%
Food	250	250	250	750	8.62%	8.62%
Entertainment	200	200	200	600	6.90%	6.90%
Clothes	100	100	100	300	3.45%	3.45%
Vacation Fund	300	300	300	900	10.34%	10.34%
Insurance	300	300	300	900	10.34%	10.34%
Car Expenses	150	150	150	450	5.17%	5.17%
Miscellaneous	300	300	300	900	10.34%	10.34%
Savings	175	175	175	525	6.03%	6.03%
Total Expenses	2900	2900	2900	8700	100.00%	100.00%

Figure 19.7b Example of a Planning Guide and Report for a Budget

The finished planning guide in Figure 19.7a includes:

1. the labels, including the spreadsheet heading and the row and column headings
2. the values for January
3. the formulas for the totals, the percentages, and the references from January
4. the cells where the formulas will be copied

Figure 19.7b shows results of the planning guide after the spreadsheet has been entered into the computer.

Summary

Spreadsheet packages allow the user to develop a worksheet of labels, values, and formulas for the computer to calculate. The spreadsheet is used when a problem requires a matrix of numbers and formulas. Spreadsheets increase productivity by allowing the computer to calculate and recalculate the worksheet. Once a worksheet is developed, the user can be assured that the results will be correct time and time again because the computer is very accurate.

A spreadsheet consists of the worksheet seen on the screen, the status area (also on the screen), the cell contents, and the commands. The worksheet is made up of rows and columns. The place where a row and column meet is called a cell. The cell name is designated by the column letter followed by the row number. The cell can contain a label, a value, or a formula. Labels are strings that tell the user what is in a cell, a row, or a column. A value is a numerical constant. A formula is an expression. The resultant of the expression becomes the value of the cell as seen on the screen. Formulas contain constants, cell names, arithmetic operators, and functions.

Templates and macros increase productivity. A template contains the spreadsheet labels, the values that do not change, and the formulas. A template is saved and can be retrieved to enter new data time and time again. A macro saves keystrokes by setting up an instruction set so that it takes only one keystroke instead of many to perform a task. A problem that is solved with a spreadsheet must be well planned to be efficient. The steps to design a spreadsheet are:

Step 1: Use the PAC to glean the given data, the required results, and the needed formulas.
Step 2: Create the overall design of the spreadsheet.
Step 3: Place the labels on the worksheet.
Step 4: Enter the constant data.
Step 5: Enter the formulas.
Step 6: Enter any tables required in the formulas.
Step 7: Develop any macros you will be using for the problem.
Step 8: Test your formulas as much as possible.

The steps to finish your spreadsheet on the computer are:

Step 1: Start with your macro template.
Step 2: Enter the cell contents you developed on your planning sheet.
Step 3: Develop your template.
Step 4: Test your answers.
Step 5: Recalculate and print for all different values of the data that change with each recalculation.
Step 6: Develop macros pertaining to this spreadsheet, graphs, and other types of analysis aids to help with the postanalysis.
Step 7: Analyze the results of the spreadsheet problem—the postanalysis.

New Terms

cell
cell protection
command
default value
global command
macros
range name
range of cells
spreadsheet
status line
worksheet

Questions

1. What is the difference between a spreadsheet and a worksheet?
2. Define the term *cell.* Name three things that can go into a cell.
3. Name the parts of the status area.
4. Name six features of a spreadsheet.

5. Define *template.*
6. Define *macro.*
7. How is a cell named?

Problems

1. A student has to take out a loan to cover school expenses. He has gone to five banks, and each has a slightly different policy for student loans. The differences are in the areas of interest rate, payback period, and due date for the first payment. Design a template that will help the student choose the best bank for the loan.
2. **a.** Design a template for a budget for three months so that the amount of each variable category is a percent of the total amount brought in each month. Any money left over would go into savings.
   b. Modify Problem 2a to ensure having a minimum balance of $200 each month. When the balance is less than $200, borrow enough to bring the balance up to $200. When the balance is greater than $200, repay the loan.
3. A new father wants to save money for his child's college education. In 18 years he would like to have $20,000. He can get 8% interest for 18 years compounded monthly. Write the formula you would enter into a cell to find the amount of money the father has to deposit monthly in the account.
4. Evaluate the following formulas using the following data:

A1: 100	B1: 7	C1: 15	D1: 250
A2: 200	B2: 10	C2: 15	
A3: 500	B3: 6	C3: 12	
A4: TOTAL			

   a. IF(A1< A2,B1,B2)
   b. SUM(A1 . . . C1)
   c. VLOOKUP(D1,A1 . . . C3,1)
   d. COUNT(A1 . . . A4)
   e. IF(C1< C2,B1,B2)
5. Dave's Bookstore is going to have a five-day sale on book bags. At present, the price of these bags is $12.00. The bookstore paid $7.00 for the bags, which means they make a profit of $5.00 on each bag they sell. The manager wants to see what the profits will be for the five-day sale, under the following assumptions:
   a. Each day of the sale, the price should be reduced by 10% of the previous day's price.
   b. The sale price should never fall below $7.00.
   c. They expect the sales to be as follows:

Monday	12 bags
Tuesday	15 bags
Wednesday	19 bags
Thursday	25 bags
Friday	40 bags

   Follow the steps to design a worksheet for this problem.

6. Design a spreadsheet to calculate your grade point average for all of the classes you have taken so far in college.
7. Design a spreadsheet to calculate the number of square feet that needs to be painted per room in a house and the amount of paint needed per room. The number of square feet per gallon of paint will be a variable number. There are no more than three windows per room in the house. Also include the total number of square feet and the total number of gallons of paint needed.
8. Design a spreadsheet to calculate the charges to customers of the Good Taste Water Company. The total charges should be calculated also. The charges are as follows:
   a. A flat rate of $15.00 for usage up to and including 1,000 cubic feet.
   b. $0.0175 per cubit foot for usage over 1,000 cubic feet and up to and including 2,000 cubic feet.
   c. $0.02 per cubic foot for usage over 2,000 cubic feet and up to and including 3,000 cubic feet.
   d. A flat rate of $70 over 3,000 cubic feet.

Chapter 20

Problem Solving for Relational Database Management Systems

Overview

Database Management Systems Versus Record Management Systems

Design of a Database Management System

Objectives:

When you have finished this chapter, you should be able to:

1. List and explain the steps needed to design a problem solution using a database management system.
2. Develop a problem solution using a database management system.
3. Develop queries for selecting records.

A **database management system (DBMS)** is a productivity package designed to store data in files that can be easily edited, so as to organize the data and to retrieve the data in the form of reports. Database management systems use random-access files in a random or sequential manner. Although there are different ways of accessing DBMS files, some of the relevant concepts are the same as those presented in earlier chapters. Chapters 13 and 16 should be read before approaching this chapter. The major concepts from those chapters that apply here are:

- random-access files
- designing records
- keys
- designing output reports
- index files

Database management systems increase productivity because they allow the user to design files for data and use them to access information easily. The process of setting up and using a database is much easier than writing a program to do the same thing in a programming language. The major problem with a DBMS is that the user has to design the problem around the limits of the DBMS to be used. Other disadvantages include the complexity of the software package, greater impact of a failure, and more difficult recoveries. Advantages include consistency and integrity of data, data independence, increased productivity, and increased data security. A DBMS is often inflexible, not allowing the user to do everything that is required. Many database systems contain very high-level languages that can be programmed to store a series of instructions. In all cases, a DBMS cannot be learned in a few hours, and in some cases, mastering the package requires several weeks. Database management systems are probably the most difficult of all productivity packages to master.

Database management systems work with various types of files. These files include data files, which hold the data; report files (sometimes called report forms), which hold the designs of the reports; index files, which hold the data needed to process the data files in the correct order; query files, which hold selection methods; and table files, which hold selected records from the database. Table files may be viewed in list view or form view. The list view lists all records in a spreadsheet format. The form view allows the user to see one record on the screen at a time, with each field labeled much as you would see on an index card. Other files specialized to a particular software package include special output and screen layout files. In this chapter, only the data file, the report file, the index file and the query file are discussed in depth.

Database Management Systems Versus Record Management Systems

Many data management systems are actually **record management systems.** The major difference between the two types of systems is that a record management system uses only one file, and a DBMS interrelates two or more files. Database systems relate one file to another through a common field. The number of data entry errors for the DBMS is lower because the amount of data in one file is less then in a record management system. Figure 20.1 shows an inventory file in a record management system. In Figure 20.2 the same file appears as two files in a DBMS system. Notice how data are duplicated in the record management file. All of the vendor's data have to be in every record. In the DBMS, all of the vendor's data are in a separate file, referenced through one field (referred to as a relational field) in the inventory file. This interaction of files in a DBMS increases productivity and accuracy in several ways. First, less data must be entered into the inventory file. Second, since data are entered into the vendor's file only once, the chance of error is greatly diminished. Third, it is easier to date data for each vendor since data must be changed in only one place in the DBMS, instead of in every record in the record management system.

A record management system is usually easier to learn and use than a DBMS, so the user should consider a record management system if the advantages of a DBMS are not required. A record management system should be used when the data require only one file and can fit into the limits of the chosen system. When the problem requires large files or multiple files, the user should choose a DBMS. If the user projects that a DBMS will be needed sometime in the future, then the choice should be a DBMS. This chapter presents problem-solving techniques only for a DBMS. Because problem solving for record management systems is similar, it is not discussed in depth.

REC NO.	INV. NO.	ITEM DESC.	QTY	PRICE	VNAME	VADDRESS	VPHONE
1	5320	DESK	22	350.00	JONES	572 H ST	4435522
2	7372	CHAIR	35	65.00	JONES	572 H ST	4435522
3	8992	LAMP	21	30.00	WHITE	729 MAIN	4455555
4	5331	TABLE	10	120.00	JONES	572 H ST	4435522
5	2891	PAPER	300	5.00	WHITE	729 MAIN	4455555
6	5731	ENVELOPES	300	25.00	WHITE	729 MAIN	4455555
.	.	.	.	.	.	.	.
.	.	.	.	.	.	.	.
.	.	.	.	.	.	.	.

Figure 20.1 Record Management File—Inventory Problem

Design of a Database Management System

A DBMS software package helps the user design a database management system for a specific problem. The database management system contains all the files and instructions to create, organize, and output data in the files. The user must design the database management system for a specific problem. That is, the user needs to design the data files, the output reports, how the data are to be organized, and the processing needed to obtain the necessary reports.

As in all other aspects of working with a computer, certain steps should be followed to develop the system on paper before you go to the computer with the problem. These are the basic steps to design a database management system:

1. Decide on the output reports that are needed, such as a directory and labels for a mailing system.
2. List all data needed to produce the output reports.
3. Divide the data into interrelated files, if necessary.
4. Develop the **schema** of the system. The schema is the interrelationship between files.
5. Develop the data dictionary and record layouts for all files.
6. Plan all reports.
7. Decide on which fields the files will be ordered.
8. Develop any specialized report programs. These are sometimes called custom reports.
9. Develop query files.

Inventory file

REC. NO.	INV. NO.	ITEM DESCRIPTION	QTY.	PRICE	VENDOR CODE
1	5320	DESK	22	350.00	J
2	7372	CHAIR	35	65.00	J
3	8992	LAMP	21	30.00	W
4	5331	TABLE	10	120.00	J
5	2891	PAPER	300	5.00	W
6	5731	ENVELOPES	300	25.00	W
⋮	⋮	⋮	⋮	⋮	⋮

Relational Field

Vendor file

REC. NO.	VCODE	VNAME	VADDRESS	VPHONE
1	J	JONES	572 H ST	4435522
2	W	WHITE	729 MAIN	4455555
⋮	⋮	⋮	⋮	⋮

Figure 20.2 DBMS Files—Inventory Problem

After the design is completed, the problem is entered into the computer. The files are created, and data are entered. The reports are created. The index files are created. The files are printed. The program files are created and tested.

After everything is tested, the files need to be maintained. All database files require maintenance. This includes appending records (adding records), deleting records, and editing records. One of the main problems with DBMS is in the maintenance of the data. People do not take time to maintain the files; hence, the integrity of the data is lost.

The problem developed throughout this chapter is a mailing list problem. An individual needs to put the addresses of his friends on the computer. The steps just listed will be used to create a solution to this problem.

Step 1: Decide on the output reports that are needed.

1. directory to printer
    - □ all records/all fields
    - □ selected entries as desired

2. labels to printer
   - □ all records
   - □ selected entries

Step 2: List all data needed to produce the output reports.

1. last name
2. first name
3. spouse
4. title for mailing (Mr., Mrs., Ms., etc.)
5. company name (if any)
6. street address
7. city
8. state
9. zip code
10. telephone

Step 3: Divide the data into interrelated files, if necessary. A mail list application does not require multiple files since there is no duplicate data; therefore, there is only one file to develop (MAILLIST). It includes

1. last name
2. first name
3. spouse
4. title for mailing
5. company name (if any)
6. street address
7. city
8. state
9. zip code
10. telephone

Step 4: Develop the schema of the system. The schema is a diagram of the interrelationship between files. It is produced by drawing circles around the file names and, if there is more than one file, adding lines connecting the circles. The name of the relation field is then placed on the line. Figure 20.3 shows the schema of the mail list files, which consists of only one circle since there is only one file.

Step 5: Plan the record data dictionary and record layouts for all files. Figure 20.4 shows the record data dictionary and record layouts for the MAILLIST file. In the record data dictionary, the attributes of the fields are specified. The following attributes should be specified:

Figure 20.3 Schema for Mail List Files

Record Data Dictionary

FILE: MAILLIST

Field Number	Item Description	Field Name	Field Length	Data Type	# of Decimals	Comments
* 1	Last Name	LASTNAME	12	C		
2	First Name	FIRSTNAME	12	C		
3	Spouse's Name	SPOUSE	12	C		
4	Mailing Title	TITLE	10	C		Mr., Mrs., Ms., etc.
5	Company Name	CONAME	15	C		
6	Street Address	STREET	15	C		
7	City	CITY	12	C		
8	State	STATE	3	C		
* 9	Zip Code	ZIPCODE	10	C		
10	Telephone	TELEPHONE	13	C		

Record Layout

1 12	13 24	25 36	37 46	47 61	62 76
1 LASTNAME	2 FIRSTNAME	3 SPOUSE	4 TITLE	5 CONAME	6 STREET

77 88	89 91	92 101	102 87	88 101	102 114
7 CITY	8 STATE	9 ZIPCODE	10 TELEPHONE		

*Index Fields

Figure 20.4 MAILLIST Record Data Dictionary and Record Layout

1. field number
2. field name—which can be up to 32 characters in length, but should be as short as possible, while remaining long enough to identify the field
3. field length—which should be long enough to hold any piece of data that might be entered into the field
4. field data type—normally including numeric, character, logical, data, and memo
5. number of decimals, if the data type is numeric

Other items on the record data dictionary are informational items, such as the field description or any comments about the field. The record layouts show the relationship of all of the fields in the record and the total length of the record.

Step 6: Plan all reports. Figure 20.5a, b shows the layout of the reports using an 80-column printer. The considerations for report design include:

1. report headings
2. column headings
3. column contents—which field(s) will be placed in the column
4. column width—usually the field width or the column heading width, whichever is longer
5. paper size
6. totals and subtotals
7. groupings—control breaks
8. justification of character data
9. selection of records

Step 7: Decide on which fields the files will be ordered. An important consideration is the ordering of your files. Files are ordered using a field or a combination of fields. A mail list file might be ordered on the last name field so the printout will be in alphabetical order. However, if a mailing is to be bulk mail, then the labels must be in zip-code

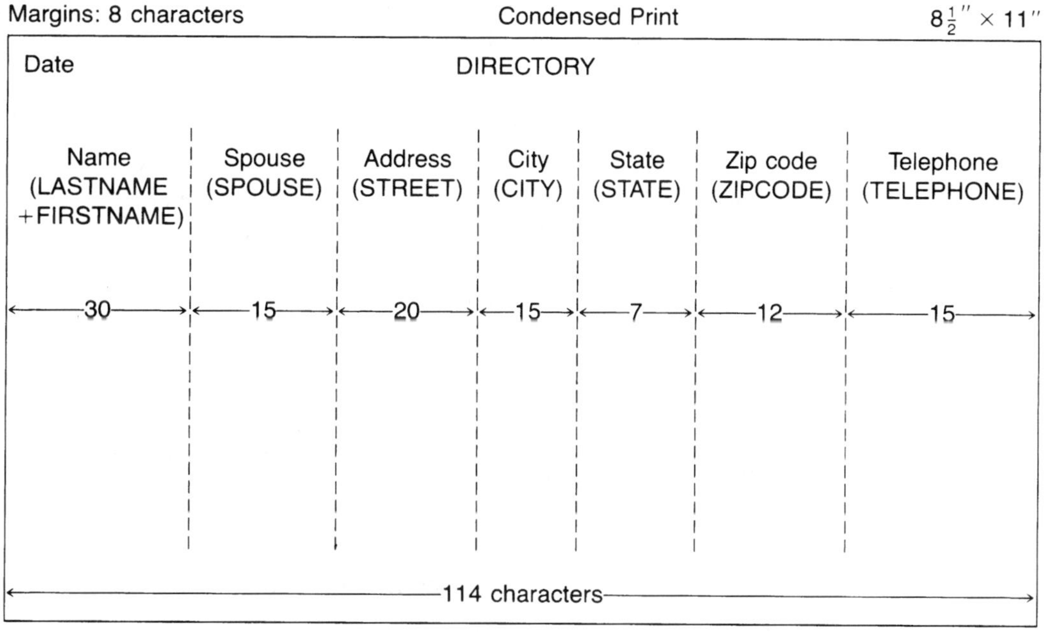

Figure 20.5a Directory Report

(TITLE + FIRSTNAME + LASTNAME)
(CONAME)
(STREET)
(CITY + "," + STATE + ZIPCODE)

Figure 20.5b Label Report

order. Therefore, the file must be in zip-code order. Using a combination of zip code concatenated with the last name would print the file in alphabetical order within each zip code, with the whole file in zip-code order. To put the file in order, index files are built. See Chapter 13 for information on index files. The MAILLIST file would be indexed on the last name field and also the zip-code field.

Step 8: Develop any specialized report programs.
All of the reports required for this application can be done using the quick reports.

Step 9: Develop query files. Queries are logical expressions which allow the user to select records. Through the use of a query file the DBMS searches the database and develops a table which holds the selected records. Queries are logical expressions, with a TRUE or FALSE resultant. The DBMS looks at each record, performs the logical expression on that individual record, and places the record in the table if the result is TRUE. If the result is FALSE the record is ignored. The following are some possible queries for the MAILLIST file:

1. ZIPCODE = "95521" This expression would develop a table of all records with a zip code of 95521.
2. LASTNAME < "M" AND STATE = "CA" This expression would develop a table of all records of people who live in California with a last name which starts with a letter from A to L.
3. COMPANY = "XYZ CORPORATION" This expression would develop a table of all records of people working for XYZ Corporation.

There are some pitfalls people can fall into. The most problematic area is in the use of the *AND* and the *OR.* Lets say you would like to have a list of people who work for one of two companies, XYZ Corporation and Johnson Lumber Yard. The use of the AND would result in no one in the table, since there is no one in the database who works for both XYZ Corporation *AND* the Johnson Lumber Yard. Since we are looking at a single record at a time, the use of OR is required. A person works for either XYZ Corporation *OR* Johnson Lumber Yard. It is necessary to write the expression as if you were looking at a single record, not the entire file. Once the table is developed, a report file is used to print the records.

Putting It All Together

Problem: Dave's Rental needs to keep information on its customers, its equipment, and rental of equipment. The reports that Dave needs are:

1. customer report (customer identification number, customer name, and amount due)
2. equipment report (equipment number, equipment description, and rental rate)
3. equipment rental report (equipment number, customer number, date checked out, and date checked in)
4. equipment checked out report (customer name, equipment description, and date checked out)

Complete the first eight steps in the nine problem-solving steps for a DBMS.

Step 1: Decide on the output reports that are needed. The output reports needed are:

1. customer report
2. equipment report

3. equipment rental report
4. equipment checked out report

Step 2: List all data needed to produce the output reports.

1. customer identification number
2. customer name
3. amount due from customer
4. equipment number
5. equipment description
6. rental rate
7. date checked out
8. date checked in

Step 3: Divide the data into interrelated files.

Customer File:
1. customer identification number
2. customer name
3. amount due from customer

Equipment File:
1. equipment number
2. equipment description
3. rental rate

Rental File:
1. customer identification number
2. equipment number
3. date checked out
4. date checked in

Step 4: Develop the schema of the system. Figure 20.6 shows the schema for this problem. Note that the customer identification number and the equipment number are the relational fields.

Step 5: Develop the data dictionary and record layouts for all files. Figure 20.7 shows the record data dictionary and record layouts for the three files.

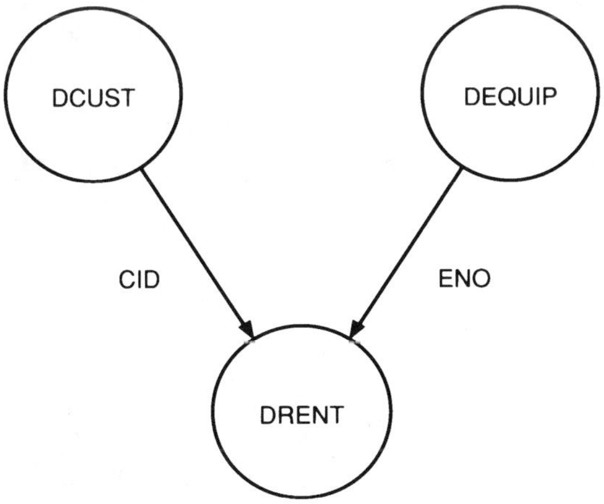

Figure 20.6 Schema for Dave's Rental

File: DCUST

Field	Field Name	Type	Width	Dec
1	CID	Character	4	
2	NAME	Character	10	
3	DUE	Numeric	6	2

Data:

Record #	CID	NAME	DUE
1	1111	Joe	0.00
2	2222	Sue	0.00
3	3333	Dave	300.00

File: DEQUIP

Field	Field Name	Type	Width	Dec
1	ENO	Character	3	
2	EDESC	Character	10	
3	RATE	Numeric	6	2

Data:

Record #	ENO	EDESC	RATE
1	A11	Loader	120.00
2	A22	Loader	125.00
3	B11	Compressor	45.00
4	C11	Dishes	25.00
5	D11	Chain Saw	12.50
6	D22	Chain Saw	22.50

File: DRENT

Field	Field Name	Type	Width	Dec
1	ENO	Character	3	
2	CID	Character	4	
3	DATE_OUT	Date	8	
4	DATE_IN	Date	8	

Data:

Record #	ENO	CID	DATE_OUT	DATE_IN
1	A11	2222	09/10/90	09/12/90
2	B11	1111	10/10/90	10/12/90
3	D11	3333	10/15/90	10/23/90
4	D22	1111	10/25/90	10/26/90
5	C11	1111	11/05/90	/ /
6	A22	3333	11/15/90	/ /
7	A11	1111	11/30/90	/ /
8	D11	3333	12/01/90	12/03/90

Figure 20.7 Structure and Data

Step 6: Plan all reports. Figure 20.8 shows the report layout for each report for Dave's Rental.

Step 7: Decide on which fields the files will be ordered. The customer file should be in customer identification number order and in name order. The equipment file should be in equipment number order and equipment description order. The rental file should be in date checked out order.

Step 8: Develop any specialized report programs. Reports 1, 2, and 3 can be produced through the use of a quick report. Report 4 must be a custom report and must use all three files.

Step 9: Develop the query files. The following logical expressions might be some desired tables from this application:

1. DATE.IN = "" This would create a table of all equipment which is out.
2. DUE > 0.0 This would create a table of all outstanding moneys.
3. RATE > 100.00 This would create a table of all expensive equipment.

1. Customer Report
   Margins: 8 characters — $8\frac{1}{2}'' \times 11''$

Date

DAVE'S RENTAL
CUSTOMER REPORT

Customer ID (CID)	Name (NAME)	Amount Due (DUE)
20	24	20

64 characters

2. Equipment Report
   Margins: 8 characters — $8\frac{1}{2}'' \times 11''$

Date

DAVE'S RENTAL
EQUIPMENT REPORT

Equipment No. (ENO)	Description (DESC)	Rate (RATE)
20	24	20

64 characters

3. Equipment Rental Report
   Margins: 10 characters — $8\frac{1}{2}'' \times 11''$

Date

DAVE'S RENTAL
EQUIPMENT RENTAL REPORT

Equipment No. (ENO)	Customer ID (CID)	Date_Out (DATE_OUT)	Date_In (DATE_IN)
15	15	15	15

60 characters

4. Equipment Checked Out Report
   Margins: 8 characters — $8\frac{1}{2}'' \times 11''$

Date

DAVE'S RENTAL
EQUIPMENT CHECKED OUT REPORT

Customer Name (NAME)	Equipment (DESC)	Date Checked Out (DATE-OUT)
20	24	20

64 characters

Figure 20.8 Report Layout for Dave's Rental

Summary

Data management systems allow users to easily set up data files and access, update, and produce reports using the data in those files. There are two different types of systems. A record management system is limited to the use of only one data file. A database management system can interrelate two or more data files.

The steps to develop a database include the following:

1. Decide on the output reports that are needed.
2. List all data needed to produce the output reports.
3. Divide the data into interrelated files, if necessary.
4. Develop the schema of the system.
5. Develop the data dictionary and record layouts for all files.
6. Plan all reports.
7. Decide on which fields the files will be ordered.
8. Develop any specialized report files (custom reports).
9. Develop Query files.

The user should follow these steps to decrease frustration and increase productivity.

New Terms

database management system (DBMS)

record management system

schema

Questions

1. What is a DBMS?

2. How does a record management system differ from a DBMS?

3. List the steps in using a DBMS.

4. Why is problem solving important when you are using a DBMS?

5. Name four applications for a DBMS at home. For each application, state whether a record management system or a DBMS would be better.

6. Name four applications for a DBMS in a business. For each application, state whether a record management system or a DBMS would be better.

Problems

1. Design the data files and reports for a personal mailing list. Include more items than those presented in this chapter, such as spouse's name, birthday, correspondence (Christmas cards, birthday cards, etc.). What is the criteria you will use to select records? Complete steps 1–9 for developing a database as needed.

2. Design a DBMS for your checking account. Include accounts for various expenditures and income. Include as one of the reports a bank reconciliation report. Develop the nine steps to design a DBMS for this problem.
3. Dan's Auto Supply Company needs its inventory set up on a DBMS. The company wants to be able to access an individual inventory item from the screen, print a complete list of data on all inventory items in inventory-number order, print a complete list of data on all vendors, print a list of inventory items ordered from each vendor, and print order forms for each vendor of items that need to be reordered. The data items needed are inventory item number, item description, quantity, wholesale price, percent markup, reorder number, reorder quantity, vendor name, vendor address, vendor city, vendor state, vendor zip code, and vendor telephone number. Complete the nine steps to design a DBMS for this application.
4. Get Smart College needs a system to track students, classes, teachers, and class rosters. The schema would look like this:

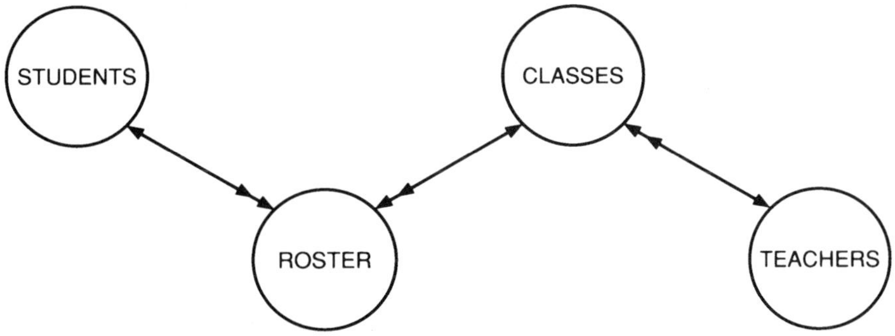

   The reports the administration needs are as follows: student information report, class schedule, class lists for the teachers, and a teacher information report. Complete the nine steps to design a DBMS for this application.
5. Take one of the applications you listed in Question 5 and design a DBMS for it. Develop a solution that would be used with a DBMS for the application. Include the order in which the data files should be accessed.
6. Take one of the applications you listed in Question 6 and design a DBMS for it. Develop a solution that would be used with a DBMS for the application. Include the order in which the data files should be accessed.
7. The Ever-So-Green Christmas Tree Company is developing a new marketing strategy. Instead of relying on their customers to come to their place of business, the company has hired a salesperson to contact local businesses and take preorders. The company needs a database to keep track of the customers and their orders. The data on the trees include type of tree, size, grade of tree, flocked or not, flameproofed or not, and if a tree stand needs to be included. The date of delivery needs to be included with the customer data. The company needs a report of the customers, the quantity of each type of tree, and the trees to be delivered by date. Develop a database that will give the company the needed reports.
8. An on-campus club needs to keep track of their members, the committees on which each member serves, and any offices they hold. Develop a database that will produce reports on the committee members, the club members, and the officers. Also, include an optional dues status in the club membership report.

Chapter 21

Document Processing

Overview

The Six Elements of a Computer System
Sharing Data
Linking Data

Objectives

When you have finished this chapter, you should be able to:

1. Identify and explain the six components of a computer system.
2. Explain how cross-integration and object linking and embedding help to process the required data to produce a needed document.

Individual software packages improve productivity by electronically accomplishing a job that would otherwise be done manually. The types of software packages presented in this text include word processing, graphics, spreadsheets, and database management systems. The word processor allows us to electronically edit text. The graphics package allows us to paint on an electronic canvas. The spreadsheet package allows us to complete calculations electronically. The database management system allows us to organize data electronically and easily produce electronic reports on the data. However, many times the finished document requires the use of a combination of these packages. This requires sharing data. There are times when the same data needs to be entered in two or more packages. This takes extra time and is a source of error. To eliminate this double entry system, the files need to be linked. This chapter discusses document processing that requires file sharing and linking.

The Six Elements of a Computer System

An understanding of a complete computer information system is important to see the complete picture of computing. The definition of a computer system includes *all components required to complete a task.* A **computer information system** consists of six components.

The first component is the hardware, which is the physical components of the computer. A computer system must have all the hardware parts needed to complete the tasks required of the business or home. This would include the system unit, input devices such as a keyboard and a mouse, output devices such as a monitor and a printer, secondary storage devices such as a hard disk drive and a floppy disk drive, and communications devices such as a modem. The second component is software. A system includes the software products required to complete the activities of the system. The third component is data. A system needs data to use with the hardware and the software. The fourth component is people. A system needs people to use the other components in the system. The fifth component is procedures. Procedures include how to use the software and the hardware (manuals and tutorials). The sixth component is facilities. The system must be placed somewhere. Furniture and square footage are required for every system. If any one of these six components is missing the computer information system is not complete.

The Johnson Lumber Yard will be used as an example throughout this chapter. Along with the regular applications such as using a database management system for inventory, using a word processor to write letters and prepare reports, using a spreadsheet for costing a project, and using an accounting package for all of the general accounting, Mr. Johnson would like to be able to write a letter to a customer. This letter would include a list of everything the customer ordered along with a price and the total cost. Mr. Johnson would like this to be done by the computer without re-entering data.

The computer system for the Johnson Lumber Yard would include the six components. The hardware would include three system units networked together, each with a keyboard, a mouse, a monitor, a hard disk drive, and a floppy disk drive. A printer would be included as part of the network. Software would include a word processor, a spreadsheet package, a graphics package, a database management system, and an accounting package. The data would be supplied from inventory lists, sales receipts, customer order forms, and other source documents. The people using the system would include the office staff and Mr. Johnson. Procedures would include the manuals that came with the hardware and software and the written procedures for the users. The facilities include the main office and Mr. Johnson's office, and the sales desk.

Document processing uses all components of the computer information system. This is an important concept. Document processing uses data from source documents created by hand and entered into the computer system using one of many software packages. Hardware and software are used to enter data, process data, store data, retrieve data, and create the final document. People complete the entry of the data and create the process of how to create the final document. People need manuals to learn how to use the software and the hardware. People need a place to put the hardware components, and a place to work, hence the need for facilities.

Sharing Data

Mr. Johnson would like to develop a letter that includes the total cost of a project. He would like this to be done by the computer without re-entering data. This requires data sharing. Data sharing is accomplished by importing and exporting data. **Importing data** is using data from another application. **Exporting data** is preparing data to be used by another application. Data are usually format specific for each application and for each brand of the same application. Therefore, when you want data developed in software package A to be used in software package B, the data must be saved from software package A in a format that can be received by software package B. One way to save text data (different from graphics data) is to save it as an **ASCII data file.** This is a generic file and usually can be read by other applications or other brands of the same software. An ASCII file is saved as an unformatted file. Software packages also have options to convert formatted data from other software package formats when the data are imported or exported. These software packages have built-in **filters** that accomplish the conversions.

Another way to transfer data—text or graphics—from one package to another is through the clipboard. The clipboard temporarily stores one section of selected text or a selected graphic. It is important to note that it only saves it until the computer is turned off. A scrapbook allows you to save several selected text sections and selected graphics. You cut or copy the selected item to the clipboard in one package and paste it in another package. It is usually better to copy it to the clipboard since the selected section will remain in the original package in case you need to copy it again. Any time you cut or copy, the selection goes to the clipboard.

Software today is packaged in **suites.** A software suite contains several stand-alone software packages that allow cross-application integration and have a common look and feel. Two or more of these stand-alone packages can be open at the same time in windows on the monitor. They have the capability to drag and drop data across applications. This allows the transfer of data from one package to another without going to the clipboard, or importing and exporting the data. This increases productivity by decreasing the number of steps needed to transfer the data.

The use of multiple packages, along with other components of a computer information system, to produce one document is called **document processing.** Figure 21.1 shows the flow of data from one package to another to produce the required document

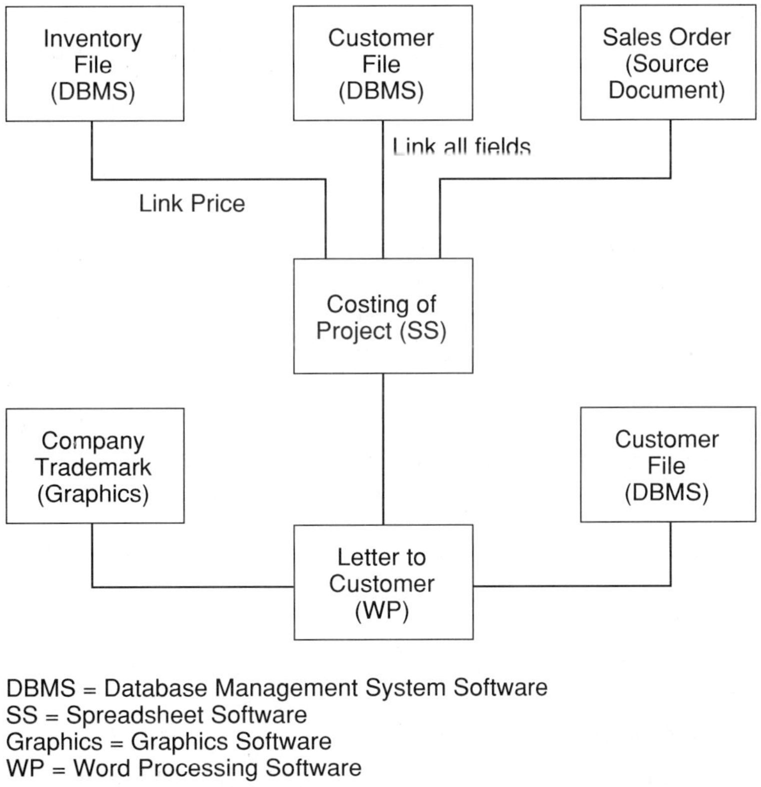

Figure 21.1 Data Flow to Produce Customer Letter

for the Johnson Lumber Company. The inventory file contains the product prices needed to develop the cost of the project. The customer file contains all customer information. These two files are developed through the use of a database management system. The sales document is the source document; it contains the project information. The data from these two files are imported into a spreadsheet along with keying the data from the source document. A report on the total cost of the project is completed in the spreadsheet package. A letter is produced in a word processor by bringing in the company trademark as a letterhead (produced by a graphics package), the customer information from the customer file, and the cost of the components of the project along with the totals from the spreadsheet. This is document processing. There is no re-entering of data.

Linking Data

Many times the same data are found in two or more places in the complete system. If this is true, then the data need to be entered in multiple places. Using traditional software procedures, these data would be entered multiple times. A solution to this time-consuming and error-inducing problem is to link files, so when a number is changed or added in one file it will be automatically changed or added in another file. This is called **object linking and embedding (OLE).** Back to the Johnson Lumber Yard. The costing of the project has been accomplished in the spreadsheet. However, before the letter is written the price is changed for one of the components of the project. It would be very easy to make the change in the inventory file and either forget to make the changes in the project files or inadvertently not realize the change has been made. However, if the price in the inventory file could be linked to the price in the project file, then when the price changes in the inventory file, the price in the project file would automatically be changed also. This eliminates costly errors along with labor costs. Productivity and accuracy have now been improved.

Summary

Many times a document requires the acquisition of data from other packages. This requires importing and exporting of data. The transfer of data from one package to another may be accomplished through the use of ASCII files, built-in filters, or drag and drop through the use of cross-application integration.

Duplicate data found in multiple places may be linked. Linking allows the user to change the data in one place and have all other places updated at the same time. OLE is the term for object linking and embedding. A computer information system includes six components: hardware, software, data, people, procedures, and facilities.

New Terms

ASCII data file
computer information system
document processing
exporting data
filters
importing data
object linking and embedding (OLE)
suite

Questions

1. What are the components of a computer information system?
2. Why is the ability to share data important to the user?
3. What is an ASCII file?
4. What is a filter? Why is it important?
5. Why is cross-application integration important?
6. What are the advantages of a software suite?
7. What is OLE and why is it an important concept?

Problems

1. The Exceptional Consultant Company has just finished a marketing survey for one of their clients. They would like to produce a letter to the client that will include a summary report of the results, a statistical analysis of the results, and two charts of the results. How would the data be set up in files? How would the document be processed to obtain the required results? How would cross-application integration and OLE be used in the application?
2. John Green is head of sales at the Best Computer Company. He needs to make a presentation to the board of directors on the sales of the past year along with projections for the future. John uses a database for all of the statistics on sales and his salespeople. He uses a spreadsheet to calculate needed figures from the database, along with calculations to project the figures into the next year. He uses a word processor to create the outline of his talk. He would like to use a presentation graphics package to create a slide show for his presentation, using data from these other packages along with clip art and scanned images. How would the slide show document be processed to obtain the required results? How would cross-applicatiton integration and OLE be used in the application? Create a diagram to show how the data would be processed.

UNIT SIX:

SUPPLEMENTARY EXERCISES

Develop a complete solution to the following problems:

1. Design a flyer to advertise the class you are taking.
2. Design a page for a training manual. The requirements are:
   - page numbers in upper outside corners
   - header with the name of the chapter
   - footer with the name of the training manual
   - a margin large enough to make notes
   - a line separating the outside margin from the text
3. **a.** Design a form letter to use with the mail merge function of a word processor to send to friends inviting them to a party. Include graphics as necessary.
   b. Design the data file that would accompany the letter in Exercise 3a.
4. You are going to buy a car and need to borrow $10,000 for five years. Design a spreadsheet template that will calculate the following for four different lending sources:
   - monthly payment
   - total amount paid
   - total interest
5. Develop a spreadsheet template that will calculate your grade average. (Use the @IF function to find the grade points.)
6. The Buycheap Department Store is going to have a five-day sale. Each day the price will drop 10%. Develop the template to solve this problem. The columns should include the item number, name, wholesale price, retail price, and sale price for each day. The sale price should not drop below the wholesale price.
7. Evaluate the following formulas:
   a. + A1 + B1 where A1:7
   B1:10
   b. @IF(A1 < B1, B1 − 7, B1 + 7) where A1:25
   B1:15

c. @VLOOKUP(C10, A50 . . C54,1)

where:

	A	B	C
50	0	.1	300
51	5	.7	200
52	15	.2	100
53	27	.6	0
54	35	.9	200

where: 1. C10: 25
2. C10: 27

8. Design a database system to track your computer diskettes.
  a. Design the file(s).
  b. List and design the reports you would need.
  c. Develop a menu-driven program to help update and print reports.

9. Design a database system to track your audiotapes or CDs.
  a. Design the file(s).
  b. List and design the reports you need.
  c. Develop a menu-driven program to help update and print reports.

10. Imagine yourself as a microcomputer specialist for a small business in a field of your choosing.
  a. How would you use word processor, spreadsheet, and database application packages to best serve your company? List and explain specific uses for each package.
  b. List and explain several situations in which the packages could be used in combination.

11. You are planning to buy a new computer and would like to compare four different brands. Find four advertisements for computers to complete this problem.
  a. Using a word processor create a document which would compare the four systems.
  b. Using a spreadsheet create a spreadsheet which would compare the four systems.
  c. Using a DBMS create a database and a report to compare the four systems.
  d. Which of the applications packages was the best one to use for this problem? Justify your answer.
  e. You would like to write a letter to your bank to obtain a loan for your computer system. How would you use a word processor, a spreadsheet, and a DBMS in combination to accomplish this task. What pieces of data would you designate as linked data?

Appendix A

Formulas Commonly Used in Business Applications

The formulas found in Appendix A are commonly used in business applications. It is not necessary for the programmer or the user to know how to develop the formulas; however, it is very important to know how to use each of them. Almost every application will use one or more of these formulas. Included are the formulas to calculate principal and interest, commission, discount price, mark-up price, percent of a sum, economic order quantity, depreciation, break-even analysis, present value, future value, net present value, internal rate of return, average, payment, and others.

Equation	Explanation
$A = P\left(1 + \frac{I}{T}\right)^{NT}$	**Interest (A)** A = Amount of Principal + Interest P = Principal I = Interest rate N = Number of years T = Number of payments per year
$C = R\,S$	**Commission (C)** R = Rate S = Sales
$D = P - PR$	**Discount Price (D)** P = Price R = Percent discount
$C = P + PR$	**Mark-up Price (C)** P = Wholesale price R = Mark-up price
$\% = \left(\frac{P}{T}\right)100$	**Percent of a sum (%)** P = Item T = Total of all items
$E = \sqrt{\frac{2DC}{PH}}$	**Economic Order Quantity (E)** D = Average weekly demand C = Cost of placing an order P = Unit purchase price H = % cost of purchase price for inventory overhead
$D = \frac{P - S}{N}$	**Straight-Line Depreciation (D)** D = Depreciation P = Purchase cost S = Salvage value N = Useful life in years
$B = \frac{F}{S - V}$	**Break-Even Analysis (B)** B = Break-even point F = Fixed costs V = Variable costs S = Expected sales
Spreadsheet Function	**Present Value (PV)** This is the present value of known amount of money in the future.

Figure A.1 Commonly Used Business Equations (*continued on page 439*)

Equation	Explanation
Spreadsheet Function	**Future Value (FV)** This is the future value of a known amount of money today.
Spreadsheet Function	**Net Present Value (NPV)** This is the net return on an investment. It is the present value of cash inflows minus the present value of cash outflows.
Spreadsheet Function	**Internal Rate of Return (IRR)** Percentage of return on an investment.
$A = \frac{S}{N}$	**Average (A)** S = Sum of the items N = Number of items
Spreadsheet Function	**Payment (P)** Given an amount of a loan, the interest rate, and the number of years to payback, will calculate the payment. L = Amount of loan R = Monthly Interest N = Number of payments
$P = \frac{N}{S}$	**Profit Margin (P)** N = Net profit after tax S = Sales
$ROA = \frac{N}{A}$	**Return on Assets (ROA)** N = Net profit after tax A = Total assets
$R = \frac{A}{L}$	**Current Ratio (R)** A = Current assets L = Current liabilities
$C = \frac{A}{S}$	**Average Collection Period (C)** A = Accounts receivable S = Sales per day

Figure A.1 (*continued from page 438*)

Appendix B

Sort, Merge, and Search Methods

Appendix B contains the algorithms and the flowcharts of popular methods of sorting data, merging files, and searching for a single record.

- Selection/exchange sort (Figure B.1)
- Bubble sort (Figure B.2)
- Shell sort (Figure B.3)
- Merge of two lists (Figure B.4)

Definitions:

N = Number of elements in list
I, J, K = Index values of arrays, counters
Min = Minimum value
A(I) = Element I of List A

Algorithm	Flowchart

Selection/Exchange Sort

```
LOOP: I = 1 TO N- 1
    MIN = I
    LOOP: J = I + 1 TO N
        IF A(MIN) > A(J)
            THEN
                MIN = J
    LOOP-END: J
    IF I < MIN
        THEN
            R = A(I)
            A(I) = A(MIN)
            A(MIN) = R
LOOP-END: I
```

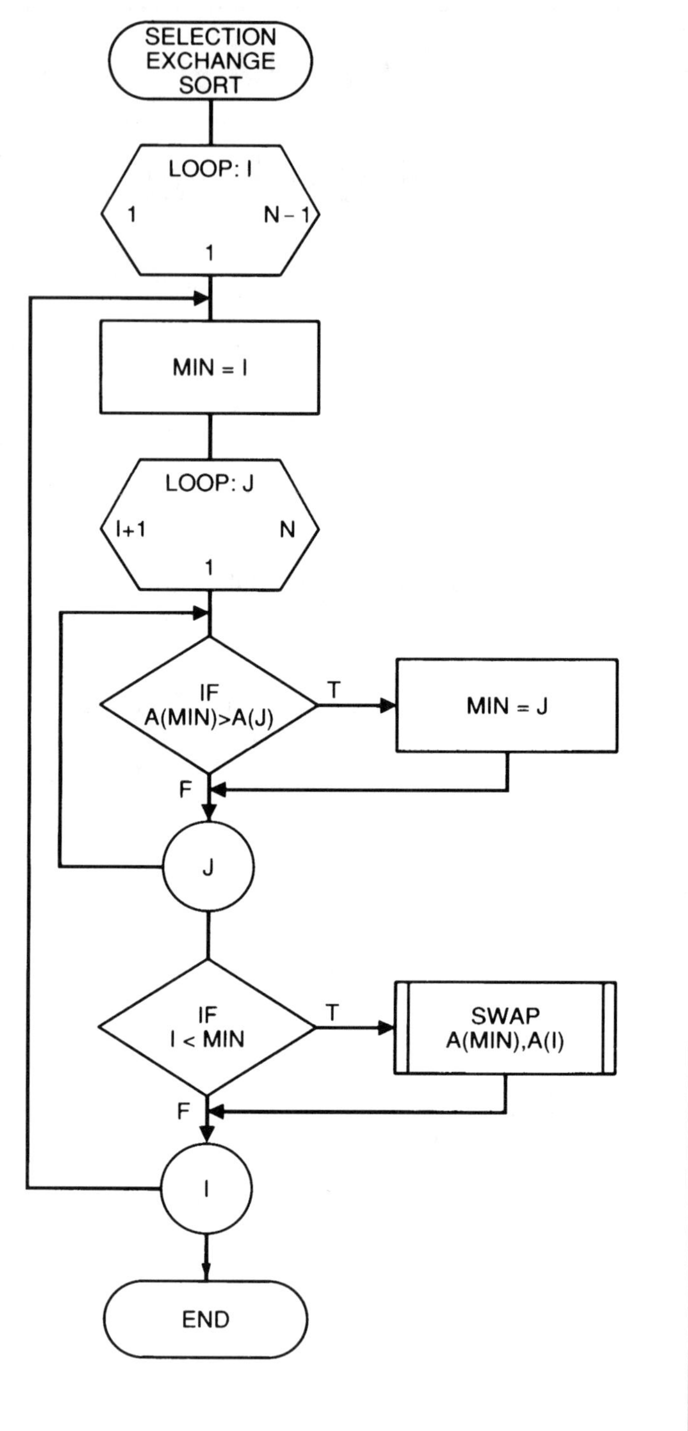

Figure B.1 The Selection/Exchange Sort

Algorithm	Flowchart

Bubble Sort

```
1. FLAG = 1
2. E = N - 1
3. WHILE FLAG = 1
     FLAG = 0
     LOOP: J = 1 TO E
       IF A(J) > A(J + 1)
       THEN
            SWAP A(J),A(J + 1)
            FLAG = 1
     LOOP-END: J
     E = E - 1
   WHILE-END
   EXIT
```

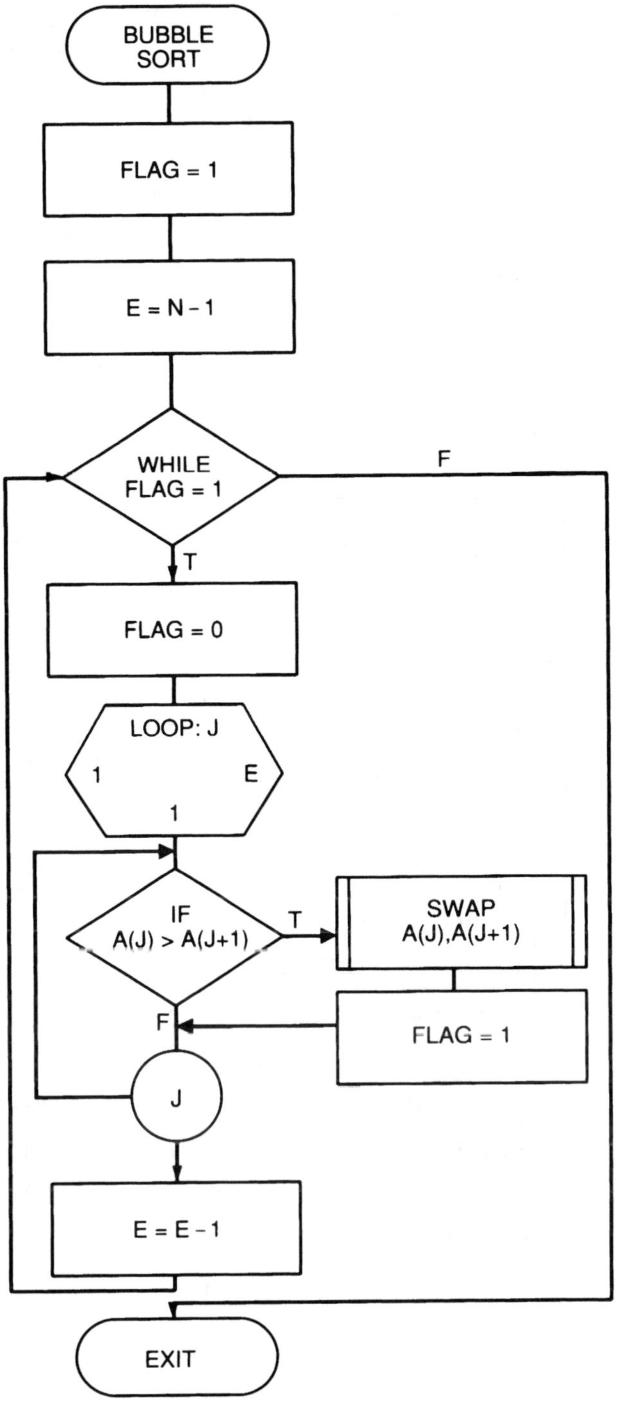

Figure B.2 The Bubble Sort

Algorithm	Flowchart
See algorithm below	See flowchart below

Algorithm

Shell Sort

```
1. G = INT(N/2)
2. WHILE G > 0
     M = N - G
     LOOP: J = 1 TO M
       IF A(J) > A(J+G)
       THEN
         L = J
         FLAG = TRUE
         WHILE FLAG
           SWAP A(L), A(L+G)
           L = L - G
           IF L >= 1
             THEN
               IF A(L) <= A(L+G)
                 THEN
                   FLAG = FALSE
                 ELSE
                   CONTINUE
             ELSE
               FLAG = FALSE
         WHILE-END
     LOOPEND: J
     G = INT(G / 2)
   WHILE-END
3. EXIT
```

Flowchart

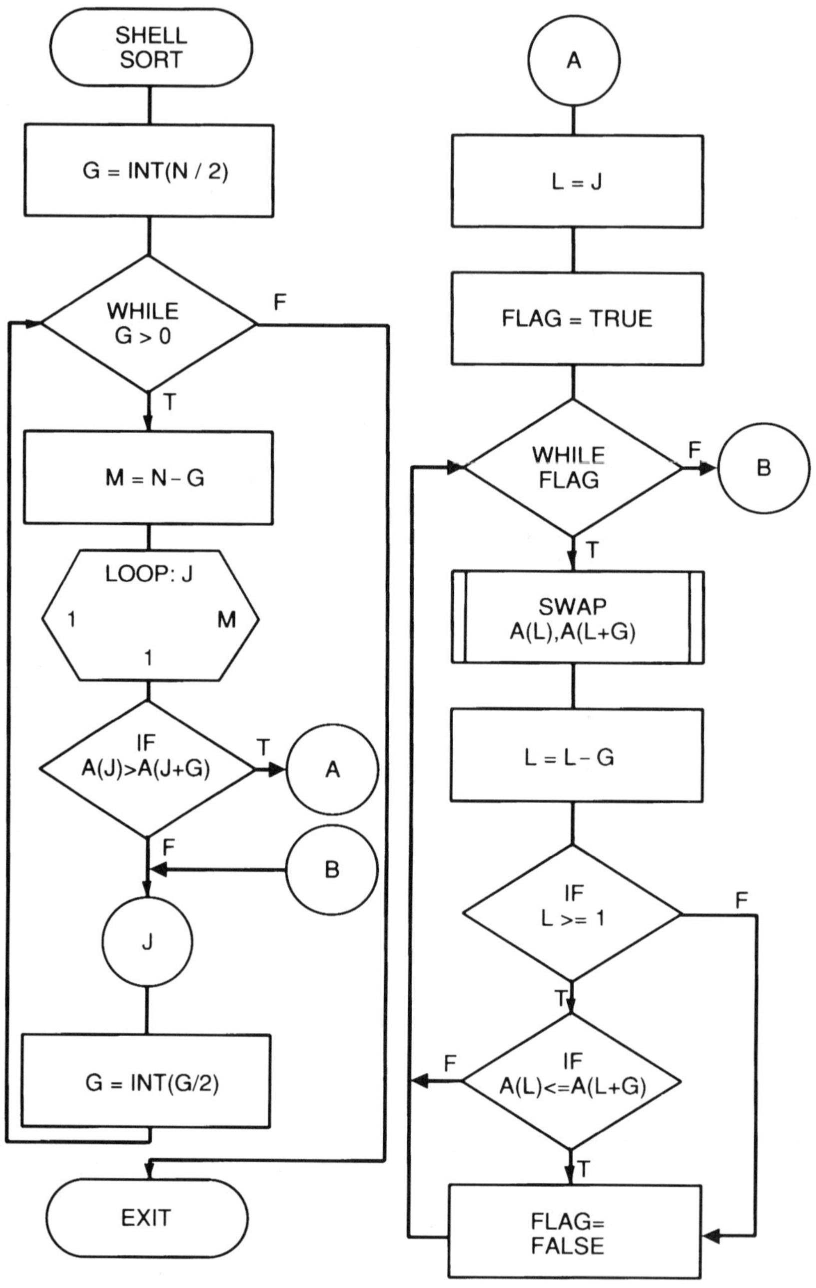

Figure B.3 The Shell Sort

Algorithm	Flowchart

Algorithm

```
1.   I = 1

2.   J = 1

3.   K = 1

4. ┌ WHILE I <= M AND J <= N
   │  ┌ IF X(I) < Y(J)
   │  ├── THEN
   │  │       MERGE (K) = X(I)
   │  │         I = I + 1
   │  ├── ELSE
   │  │       MERGE (K) = Y(J)
   │  │         J = J + 1
   │  └──────────
   │   K = K + 1
   └ WHILE-END

5. ┌ IF I > M
   ├── THEN
   │    ┌ LOOP: L = J TO N
   │    │   MERGE (K) = Y(L)
   │    │     K = K + 1
   │    └ LOOPEND: L
   ├── ELSE
   │    ┌ LOOP: L = I TO M
   │    │   MERGE (K) = X(L)
   │    │     K = K + 1
   │    └ LOOPEND: L
   └──────────

6.   EXIT
```

Flowchart

M = # in X array

N = # in Y array

I = X array index

J = Y array index

K = Merge array index

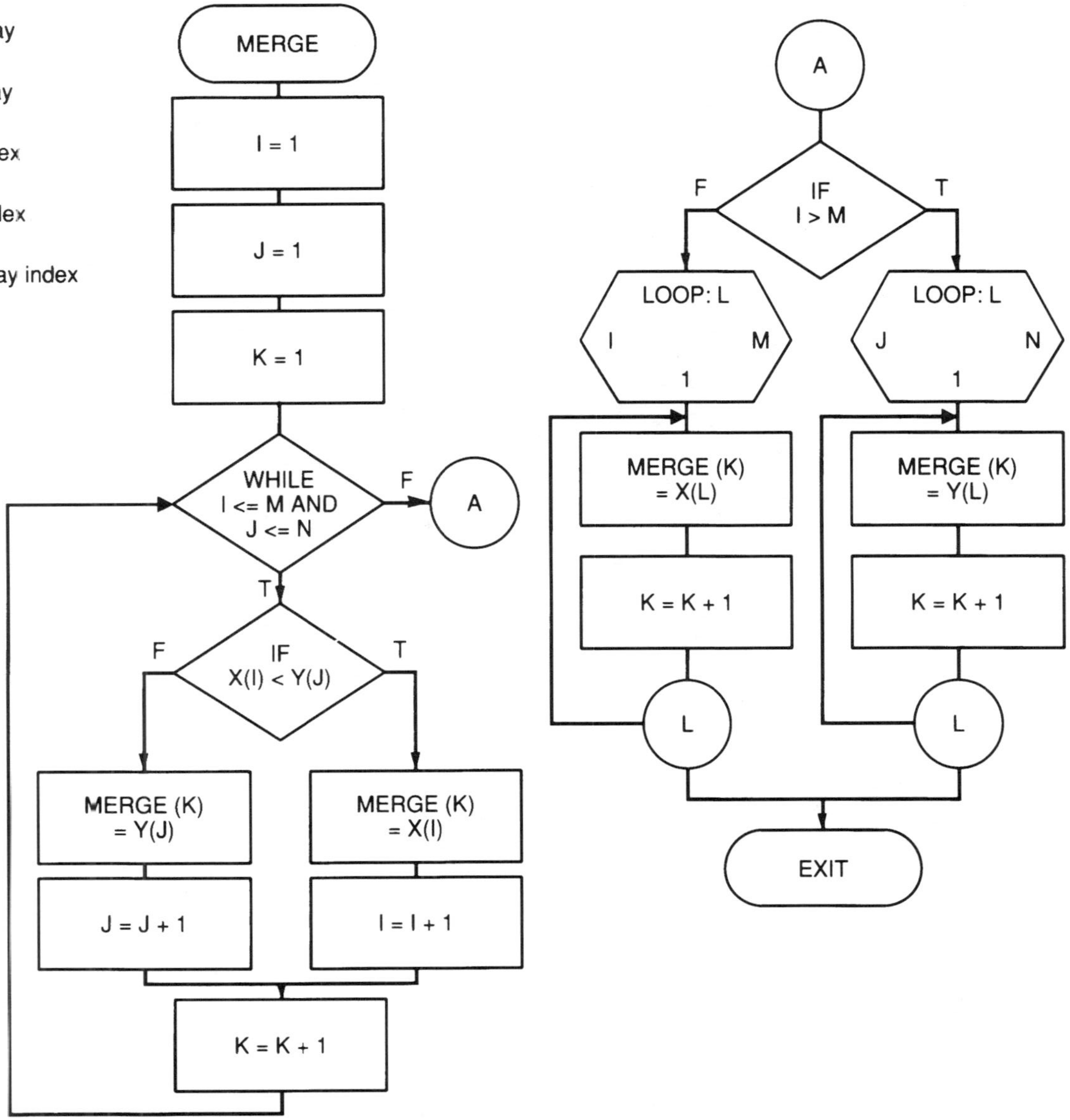

Figure B.4 Merge of Two Lists

Appendix C

ASCII and EBCDIC Codes for Data Representation

Character	EBCDIC Code Binary Code	EBCDIC Code Decimal Value
0	1111 0000	240
1	1111 0001	241
2	1111 0010	242
3	1111 0011	243
4	1111 0100	244
5	1111 0101	245
6	1111 0110	246
7	1111 0111	247
8	1111 1000	248
9	1111 1001	249
Space	0100 0000	64
.	0100 1011	75
<	0100 1100	76
(	0100 1101	77
+	0100 1110	78
&	0101 0000	80
!	0101 1010	90
$	0101 1011	91
*	0101 1100	92
)	0101 1101	93
;	0101 1110	94
,	0110 1011	107
%	0110 1100	108
-	0110 1101	109
>	0110 1110	110
?	0110 1111	111
:	0111 1010	122
#	0111 1011	123
@	0111 1100	124
'	0111 1101	125
=	0111 1110	126
"	0111 1111	127

Character	EBCDIC Code Binary Code	EBCDIC Code Decimal Value
A	1100 0001	193
B	1100 0010	194
C	1100 0011	195
D	1100 0100	196
E	1100 0101	197
F	1100 0110	198
G	1100 0111	199
H	1100 1000	200
I	1100 1001	201
J	1101 0001	209
K	1101 0010	210
L	1101 0011	211
M	1101 0100	212
N	1101 0101	213
O	1101 0110	214
P	1101 0111	215
Q	1101 1000	216
R	1101 1001	217
S	1110 0010	226
T	1110 0011	227
U	1110 0100	228
V	1110 0101	229
W	1110 0110	230
X	1110 0111	231
Y	1110 1000	232
Z	1110 1001	233
a	1000 0001	129
b	1000 0010	130
c	1000 0011	131
d	1000 0100	132
e	1000 0101	133
f	1000 0110	134
g	1000 0111	135
h	1000 1000	136
i	1000 1001	137
j	1001 0001	145
k	1001 0010	146
l	1001 0011	147
m	1001 0100	148
n	1001 0101	149
o	1001 0110	150
p	1001 0111	151
q	1001 1000	152
r	1001 1001	153
s	1010 0010	162
t	1010 0011	163
u	1010 0100	164
v	1010 0101	165
w	1010 0110	166
x	1010 0111	167
y	1010 1000	168
z	1010 1001	169

Figure C.1 EBCDIC Codes

ASCII in Mnemonic	Binary Code	Decimal Code	Octal Code	Hex Code	Remark
NUL	00 00 00 00	0	000	00	Null, tape feed.
SOH	00 00 00 01	1	001	01	Start of heading; also SOM, start of message.
STX	00 00 00 10	2	002	02	Start of text; also EOA, end of address.
ETX	00 00 00 11	3	003	03	End of text; also EOM, end of message.
EOT	00 00 01 00	4	004	04	End of transmission (End); shuts off TWX machines.
ENQ	00 00 01 01	5	005	05	Inquiry (Inqry); also WRU.
ACK	00 00 01 10	6	006	06	Acknowledge; also RU.
BEL	00 00 01 11	7	007	07	Ring the bell.
BS	00 00 10 00	8	010	08	Backspace; also FEO format effector.
HT	00 00 10 01	9	011	09	Horizontal tab.
LF	00 00 10 10	10	012	0A	Line feed or line space (New line); advance paper to next line.
VT	00 00 10 11	11	013	0B	Vertical tab (VTAB).
FF	00 00 11 00	12	014	0C	Form feed to top of next page (Page).
CR	00 00 11 01	13	015	0D	Carriage-return to beginning line.
SO	00 00 11 10	14	016	0E	Shift out; changes ribbon color to red.
SI	00 00 11 11	15	017	0F	Shift in; changes ribbon color to black.
DLE	00 01 00 00	16	020	10	Data line escape.
DC1	00 01 00 01	17	021	11	Device control 1; turns transmitter (reader) on.
DC2	00 01 00 10	18	022	12	Device control 2; turns punch or auxiliary on.
DC3	00 01 00 11	19	023	13	Device control 3; turns transmitter (reader) off.
DC4	00 01 01 00	20	024	14	Device control 4; turns punch or auxiliary off.
NAK	00 01 01 01	21	025	15	Negative acknowledge; also ERR, error.
SYN	00 01 01 10	22	026	16	Synchronous file (SYNC).
ETB	00 01 01 11	23	027	17	End of transmission block; also LEM, logical end of medium.
CAN	00 01 10 00	24	030	18	Cancel (Cancl).
EM	00 01 10 01	25	031	19	End of medium.
SUB	00 01 10 10	26	032	1A	Substitute.
ESC	00 01 10 11	27	033	1B	Escape.
FS	00 01 11 00	28	034	1C	File separator.
GS	00 01 11 01	29	035	1D	Group separator.
RS	00 01 11 10	30	036	1E	Record separator.
US	00 01 11 11	31	037	1F	Unit separator.
Space	00 10 00 00	32	040	20	
!	00 10 00 01	33	041	21	
"	00 10 00 10	34	042	22	
#	00 10 00 11	35	043	23	
$	00 10 01 00	36	044	24	
%	00 10 01 01	37	045	25	
&	00 10 01 10	38	046	26	
'	00 10 01 11	39	047	27	Apostrophe
(	00 10 10 00	40	050	28	
)	00 10 10 01	41	051	29	
*	00 10 10 10	42	052	2A	
+	00 10 10 11	43	053	2B	
,	00 10 11 00	44	054	2C	
-	00 10 11 01	45	055	2D	Hyphen
.	00 10 11 10	46	056	2E	
/	00 10 11 11	47	057	2F	

Figure C.2 ASCII code (*continued on pages 450–451*)

ASCII in Mnemonic	Binary Code	Decimal Code	Octal Code	Hex Code	Remark
0	00 11 00 00	48	060	30	
1	00 11 00 01	49	061	31	
2	00 11 00 10	50	062	32	
3	00 11 00 11	51	063	33	
4	00 11 01 00	52	064	34	
5	00 11 01 01	53	065	35	
6	00 11 01 10	54	066	36	
7	00 11 01 11	55	067	37	
8	00 11 10 00	56	070	38	
9	00 11 10 01	57	071	39	
:	00 11 10 10	58	072	3A	
;	00 11 10 11	59	073	3B	
<	00 11 11 00	60	074	3C	
=	00 11 11 01	61	075	3D	
>	00 11 11 10	62	076	3E	
?	00 11 11 11	63	077	3F	
@	01 00 00 00	64	100	40	
A	01 00 00 01	65	101	41	
B	01 00 00 10	66	102	42	
C	01 00 00 11	67	103	43	
D	01 00 01 00	68	104	44	
E	01 00 01 01	69	105	45	
F	01 00 01 10	70	106	46	
G	01 00 01 11	71	107	47	
H	01 00 10 00	72	110	48	
I	01 00 10 01	73	111	49	
J	01 00 10 10	74	112	4A	
K	01 00 10 11	75	113	4B	
L	01 00 11 00	76	114	4C	
M	01 00 11 01	77	115	4D	
N	01 00 11 10	78	116	4E	
O	01 00 11 11	79	117	4F	
P	01 01 00 00	80	120	50	
Q	01 01 00 01	81	121	51	
R	01 01 00 10	82	122	52	
S	01 01 00 11	83	123	53	
T	01 01 01 00	84	124	54	
U	01 01 01 01	85	125	55	
V	01 01 01 10	86	126	56	
W	01 01 01 11	87	127	57	
X	01 01 10 00	88	130	58	
Y	01 01 10 01	89	131	59	
Z	01 01 10 10	90	132	5A	
[	01 01 10 11	91	133	5B	
]	01 01 11 00	92	134	5C	
]	01 01 11 01	93	135	5D	
ˆ or	01 01 11 10	94	136	5E	
_ or	01 01 11 11	95	137	5F	Underline

Figure C.2 (*continued from page 449*)

ASCII in Mnemonic	Binary Code	Decimal Code	Octal Code	Hex Code	Remark
‘	01 10 00 00	96	140	60	Accent grave
a	01 10 00 01	97	141	61	
b	01 10 00 10	98	142	62	
c	01 10 00 11	99	143	63	
d	01 10 01 00	100	144	64	
e	01 10 01 01	101	145	65	
f	01 10 01 10	102	146	66	
g	01 10 01 11	103	147	67	
h	01 10 10 00	104	150	68	
i	01 10 10 01	105	151	69	
j	01 10 10 10	106	152	6A	
k	01 10 10 11	107	153	6B	
l	01 10 11 00	108	154	6C	
m	01 10 11 01	109	155	6D	
n	01 10 11 10	110	156	6E	
o	01 10 11 11	111	157	6F	
p	01 11 00 00	112	160	70	
q	01 11 00 01	113	161	71	
r	01 11 00 10	114	162	72	
s	01 11 00 11	115	163	73	
t	01 11 01 00	116	164	74	
u	01 11 01 01	117	165	75	
v	01 11 01 10	118	166	76	
w	01 11 01 11	119	167	77	
x	01 11 10 00	120	170	78	
y	01 11 10 01	121	171	79	
z	01 11 10 10	122	172	7A	
{	01 11 10 11	123	173	7B	
|	01 11 11 00	124	174	7C	Alt mode
}	01 11 11 01	125	175	7D	
~	01 11 11 10	126	176	7E	
DEL	01 11 11 11	127	177	7F	Delete, rub out

Figure C.2 (*continued from page 450*)

Appendix D

Forms to Use in Problem Solving

Given Data	Required Results
Required Processing	**Solution Alternatives**

Figure D.1 Problem Analysis Chart

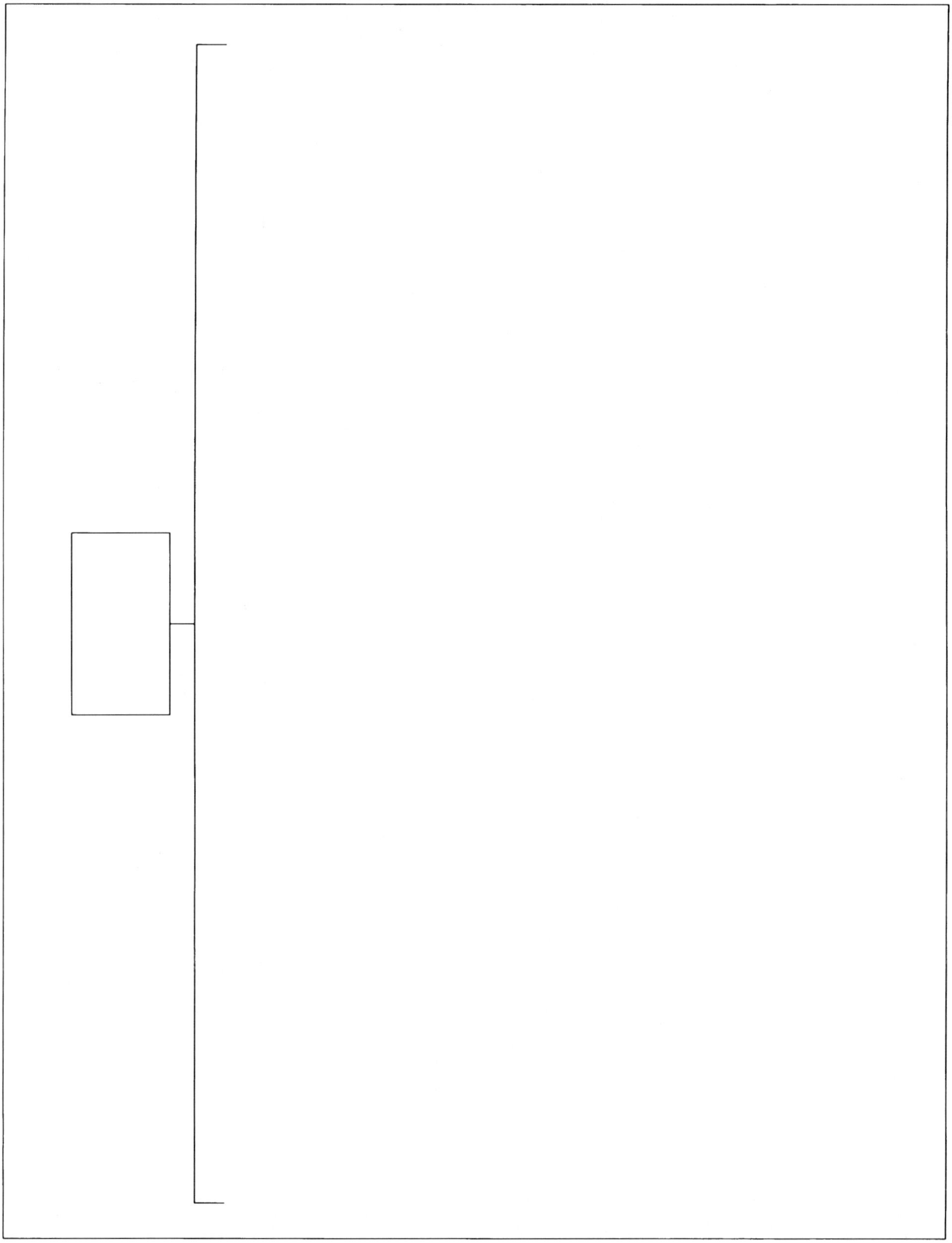

Figure D.2 The Structure Chart

Input	Processing	Module Reference Number	Output

Figure D.3 The IPO Chart

Algorithm	Flowchart

Figure D.4 Algorithm and Flowchart (*continued on page 458*)

Annotation	Test	Internal Documentation	External Documentation

Figure D.4 *(continued from page 457)*

Item	Variable Name	Data Type	Module	Pseudonyms/Module	Error Checks

Figure D.5 Data Dictionary

Record Data Dictionary

Field	Item Description	Field Name	Field Length	Data Type	# of Decimals	Comments

Record Layout

Figure D.6 Record Data Dictionary and Record Layout

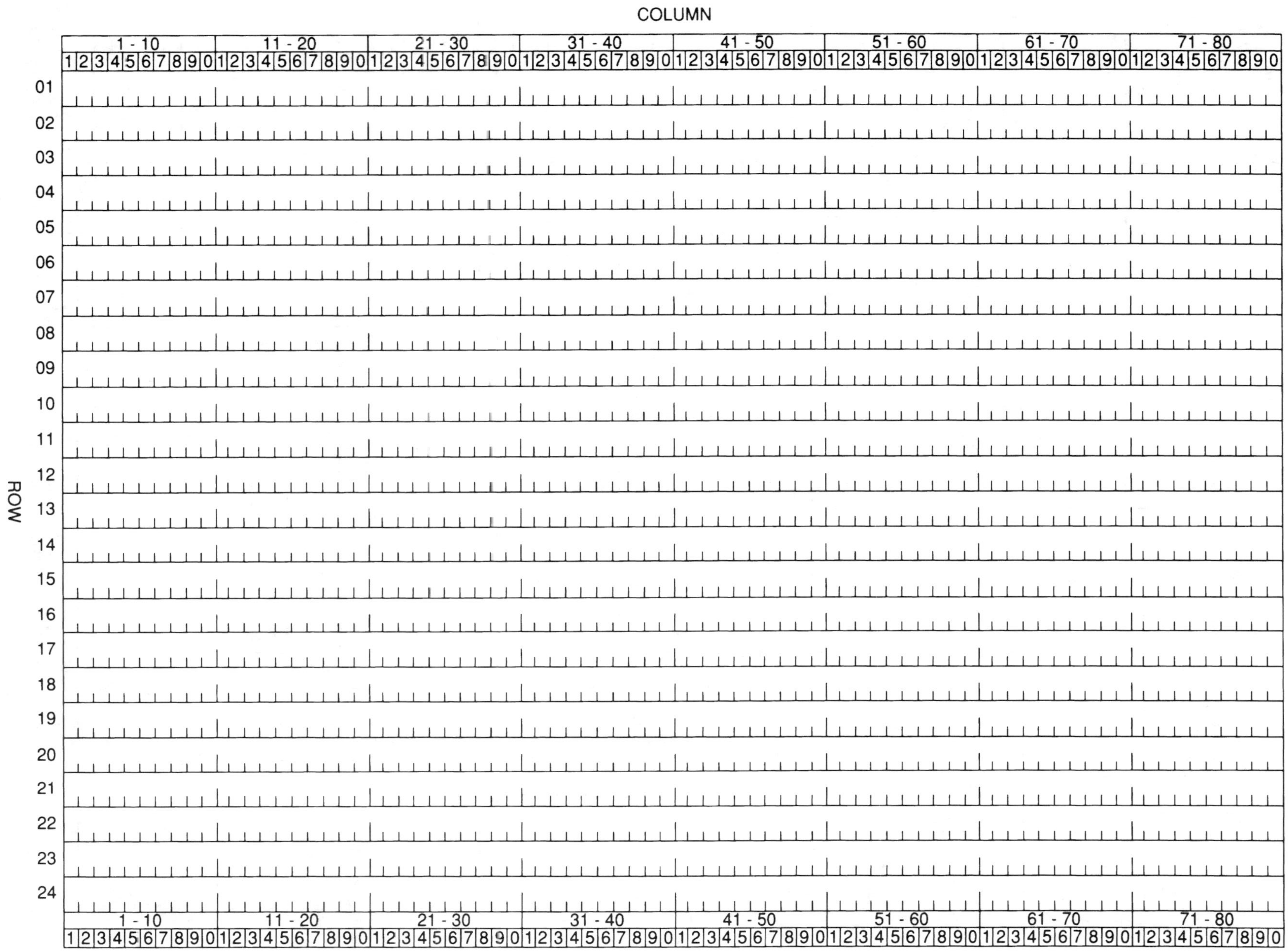

Figure D.7 Screen Design

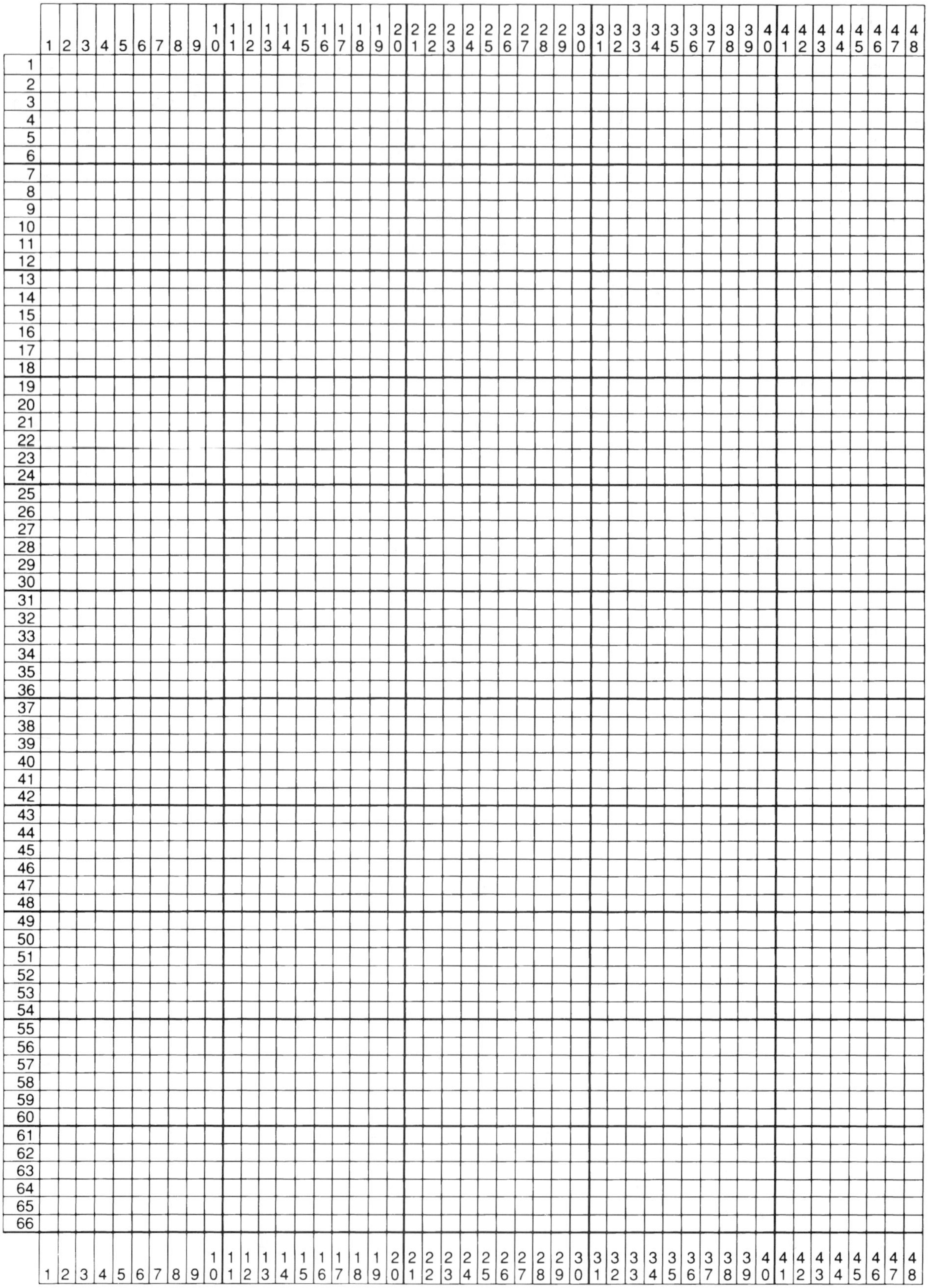

Figure D.8 The Print Chart (*continued on pages 463–464*)

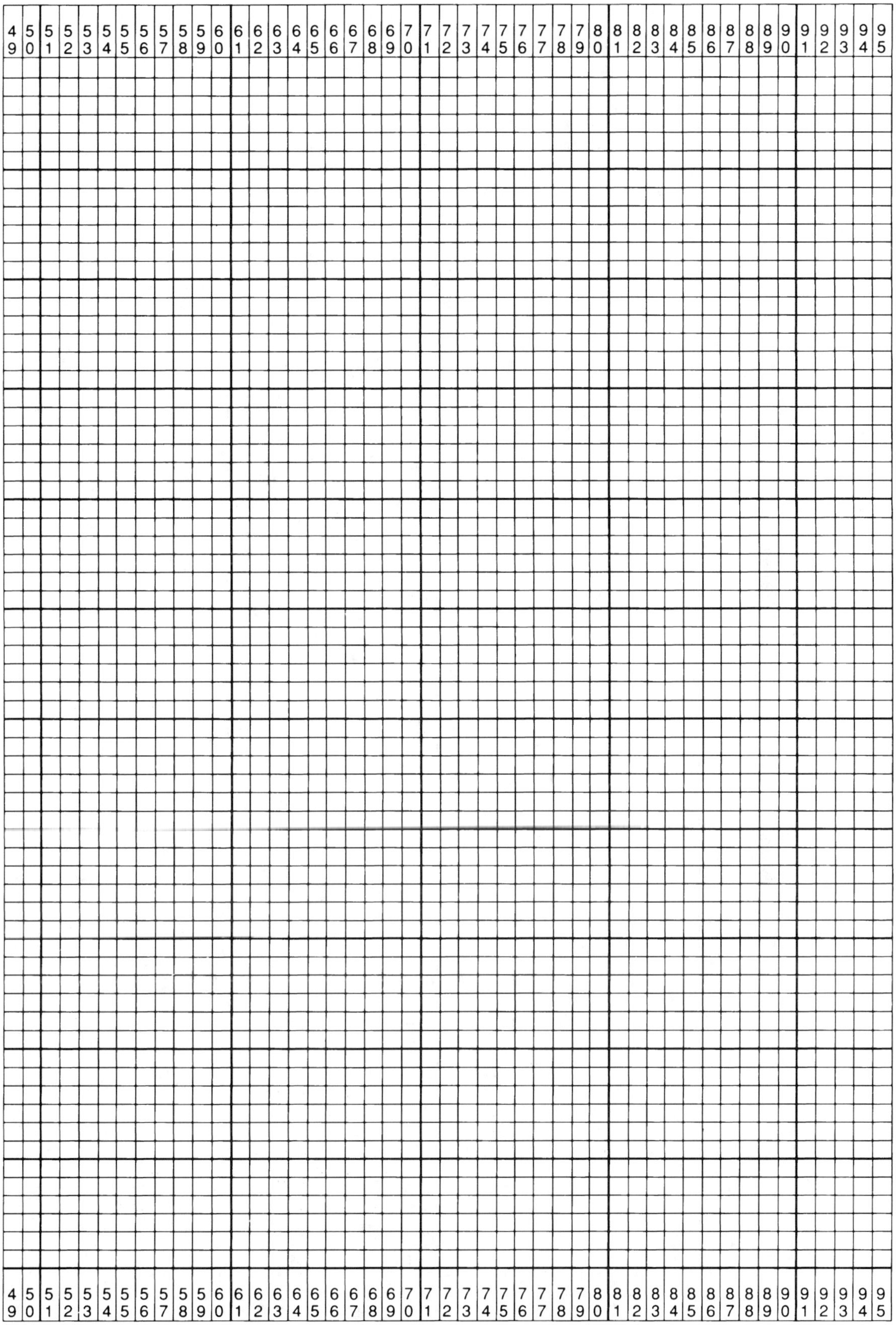

Figure D.8 *(continued from page 462)*

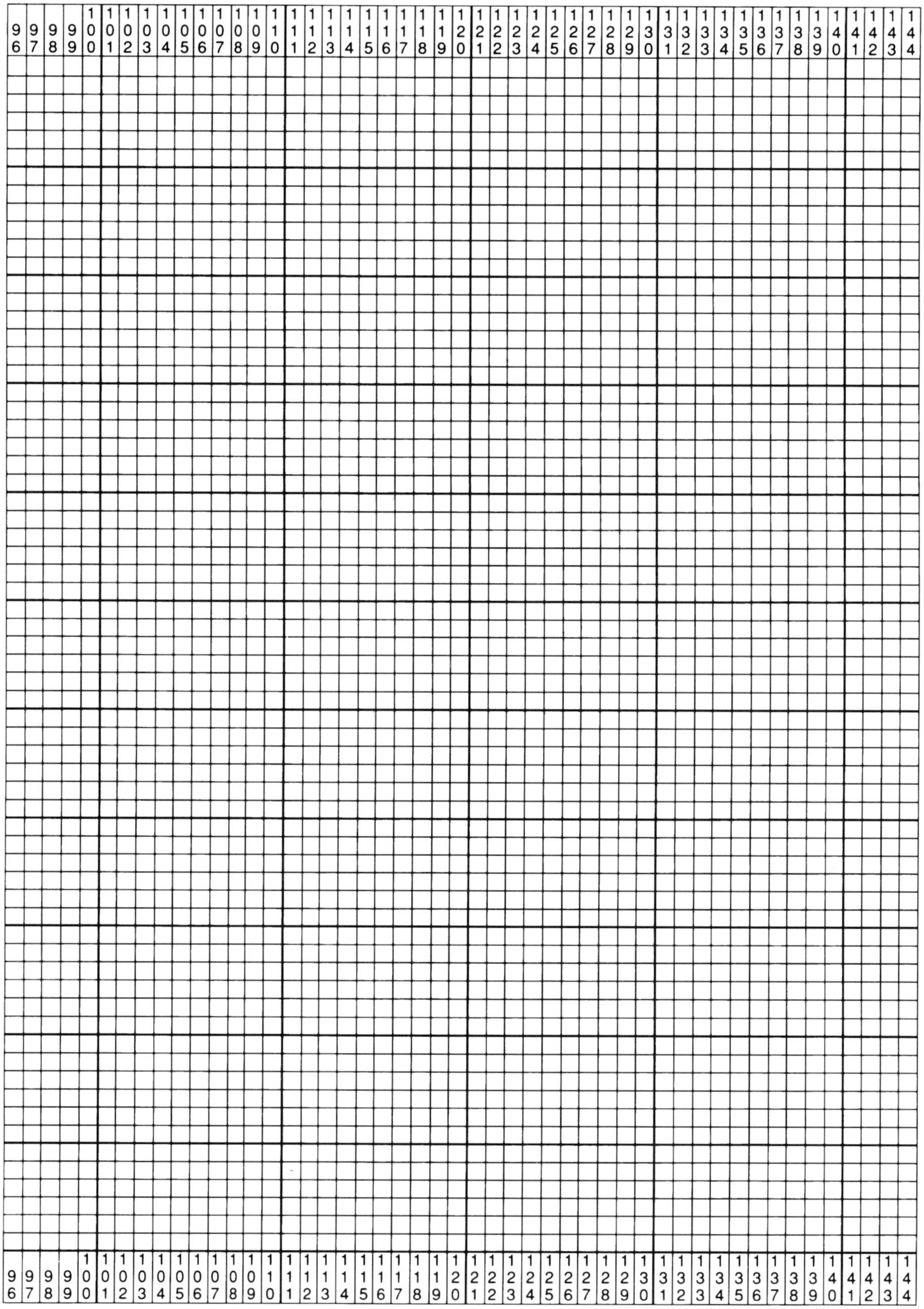

Figure D.8 (*continued from page 463*)

Header: ______________________________

Left Margin: ______________ Top Margin: ______________ Right Margin: ______________

Tabs:

Bottom Margin: ______________

Footer: ______________________________

Paper Size: ______________

Page Orientation: ______________

Justification: ______________

Other Information

Graphics To Be Used:

Reminders:

Mark Guidelines

Mark Page Number Placement

Figure D.9 Page Planning Guide for Word Processing

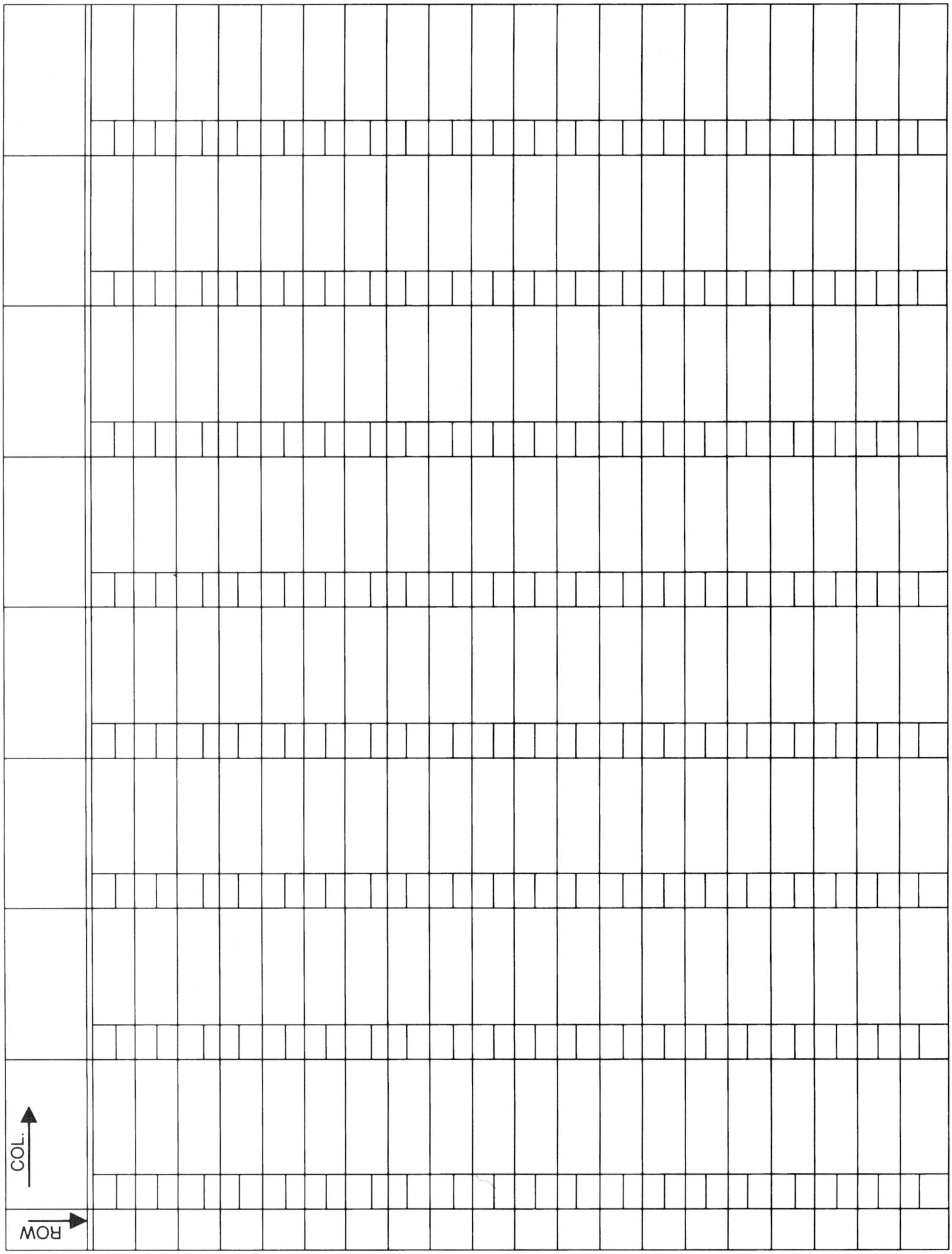

Figure D.10 Spreadsheet Planning Guide

Class	Responsibilities	Interaction with Other Classes

Figure D.11 Class, Responsibilities, and Interaction Chart

Figure D.12 Storyboard

Object Dictionary

Object Name	Source/Filename	File Type/Extension	Screen Number(s)	H/I/O*	Script

*H = Hyper, I = Input, O = Output

Figure D.13 Object Dictionary

Appendix E

Other Problem-Solving Tools

Problem-solving techniques using five basic tools have been presented throughout this book. There are other tools for problem solving that have not been presented. Among these tools are Nassi-Schneiderman charts and Warnier-Orr diagrams. Since these tools are replacement tools for the algorithm and flowcharts, they were not presented earlier in this text.

Both Nassi-Schneiderman charts (N-S) and Warnier-Orr diagrams are used to create structured solutions. Many people prefer one of these tools to flowcharts. Whichever tool is chosen, the use is the same. You should plan the solution, complete the problem-solving process, and end with a solution that is well done.

Nassi-Schnciderman Charts

Nassi-Schneiderman charts are sometimes called structured flowcharts. They are also referred to as N-S charts. These charts consist of a stack of rectangles one on top of the other and put together without flowlines. Processing flow always runs from the top to the bottom of the stack of rectangles. Figure E.1 shows the four logic structures as they would appear in an N-S chart. Note the similarity to algorithms as presented in this book. Figure E.3 shows an example problem and as compared to an algorithm, a flowchart, and a Warnier-Orr diagram. N-S charts fit better on one page. However, since there is no means to continue to the next page and there is no way to indicate a GOTO, the modules are required to be short and cohesive.

Warnier-Orr Diagrams

The theory behind Warnier-Orr diagrams is similar to a structure chart. The differences are:

1. The Warnier-Orr diagrams are sideways.
2. There are no rectangles.
3. They use a pseudocode for the instructions.

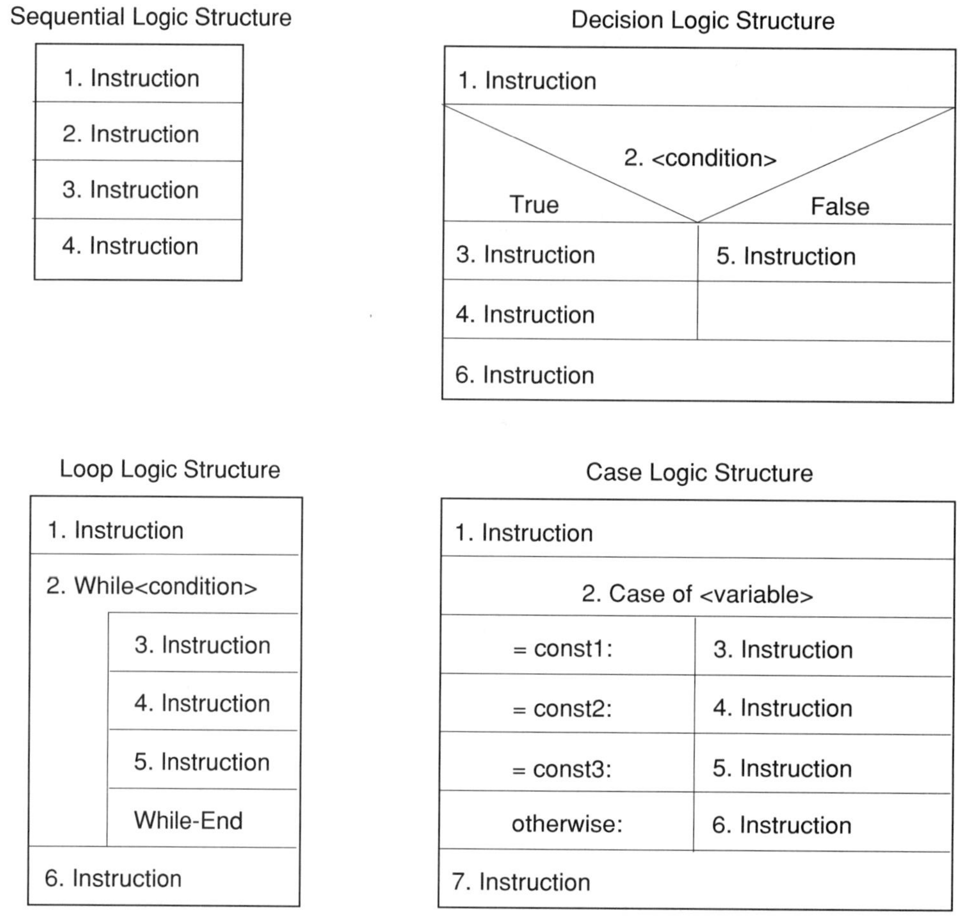

Figure E.1 The Four Structures Using Nassi-Schneiderman Charts

A Warnier-Orr diagram consists of a series of left braces, pseudocode-like instructions, and a few special symbols. The symbols include:

{	The brace is used to enclose a zero logically related set of instructions.
(0,1)	A set of instructions is executed zero or one times. This is the notation for the decision and the case structure.
(0,*n*) or *n*	A set of instructions is executed zero to *n* times. This is the notation for the WHILE/WHILE-END loop structure.
(1,*n*)	A set of instructions is executed one to *n* times. This is the notation for REPEAT/UNTIL structure.
Blank or 1	A set of instructions is executed one time.
+	Exclusive OR. This is used with the (0,1) notation to show a selection.

Figure E.2 shows the four structures as written with Warnier-Orr diagrams. Notice the processes are broken up into modules just as in the structure chart. Most flowcharting templates have the Warnier-Orr bracket on one side. Figure E.3 shows the same problem developed using a Warnier-Orr diagram and a Nassi-Schneiderman chart.

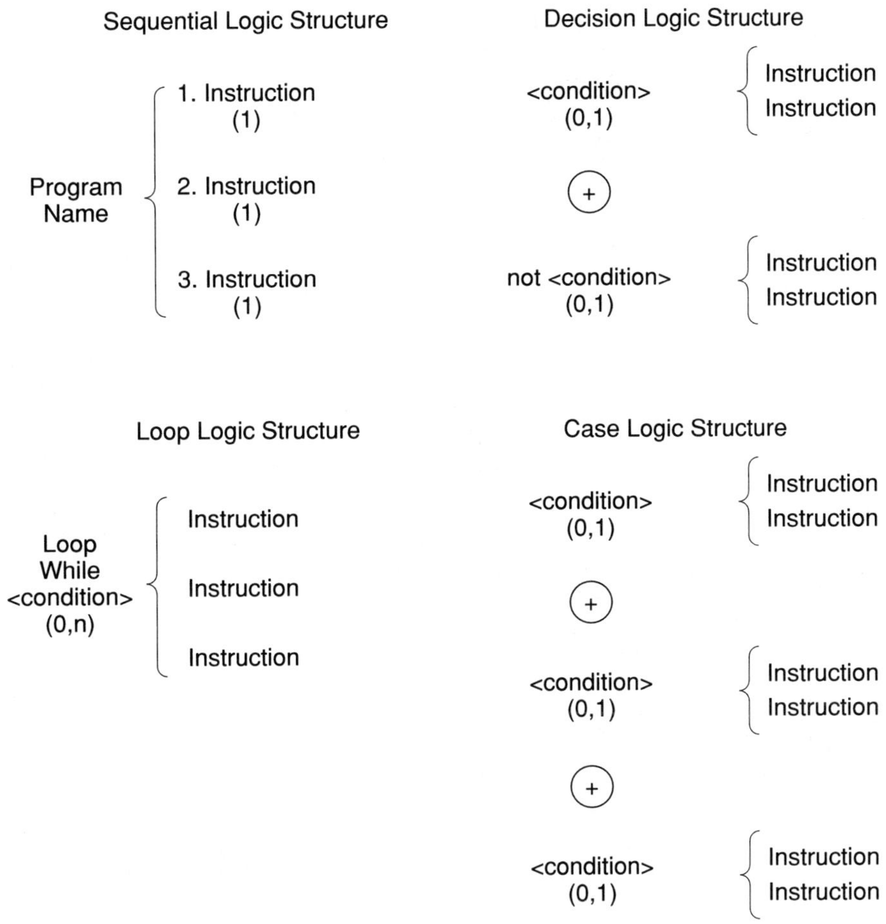

Figure E.2 The Four Structures Using Warnier-Orr Diagrams

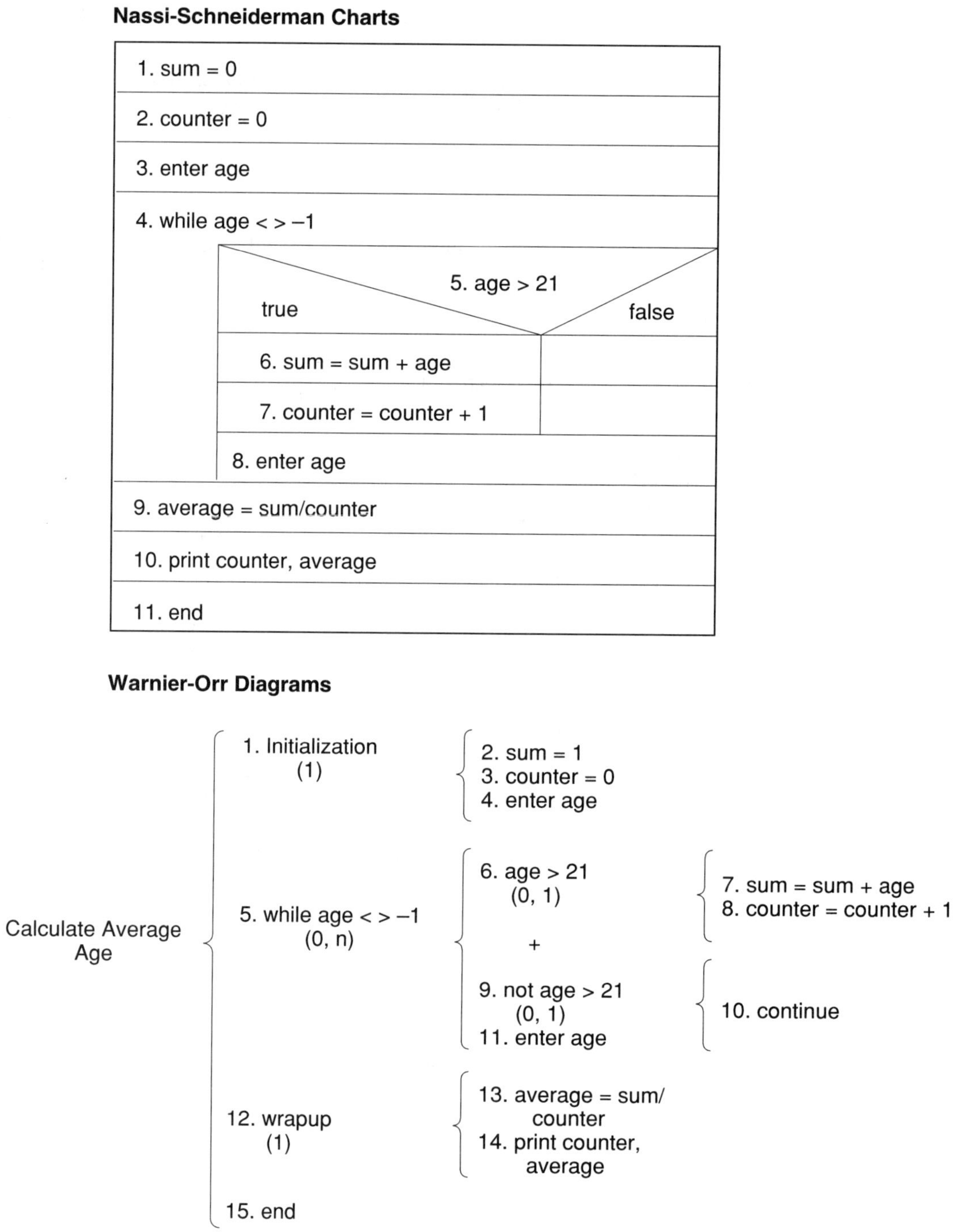

Figure E.3 Comparison of a Nassi-Schneiderman Chart and a Warnier-Orr Diagram

Glossary

Accumulating Keeping a running total by adding a current value in the form of a variable to a previous sum to find the current total. The instruction for accumulating is SUM = SUM + VARIABLE.

Activity file A file containing all of the updates to a master file.

Algorithm A sequence of instructions to solve a problem. A computer programmer writes a solution in the form of an algorithm before coding it into a computer language.

Algorithmic solution A solution to a problem that can be solved through a sequence of instructions.

Annotated flowchart A flowchart with explanations written beside the symbols.

Array Sometimes called a subscripted variable; a block of memory locations in the internal memory that is assigned to one variable name. Arrays may be one-dimensional, two-dimensional, or multidimensional.

ASCII file A file that contains the ASCII values of text. This is an unformatted file.

Automatic-counter loop One of three types of loop instructions. The automatic-counter loop enables the computer to repeat a set of instructions by using a variable as a counter that starts at a beginning number that is incremented by a given number each time the program executes the set of instructions. The loop stops when the counter is larger than a given ending number.

Backup file A file containing a master file as it was before the last update.

Base one system A computer system in which array element numbers begin with one rather than zero.

Base zero system A computer system in which element numbers begin with zero rather than one.

Batch processing Running successive sets of data through a program all at one time without human intervention.

Binary operator An operator that requires two operands.

Binary tree A list that has been created to have two linked fields—one to the right and one to the left to form a tree structure.

Buffer A small internal memory that is used to help process input and output operations.

Bug An error in a computer program.

Calculation module A process data module that does arithmetic calculations and accumulates, counts, or manipulates numerical data in some way.

Case logic structure One of the four logic structures for organizing the instructions to the computer that make up a program. The case structure allows the computer to select one set of instructions from among many, through data given by the user or calculated in the solution.

Cell protection A command used with spreadsheet packages to prevent the movement of the cursor into a cell.

Character data The data set of the character data type; it includes all symbols available on a computer.

Class A class is part of a solution of an object oriented solution to a problem. A class models the properties or characteristics of a set of objects.

Codes Character data input by a user to direct the flow of processing, such as in the coded options in a record.

Command An instruction to the computer in a productivity package or an operating system. Normally, a command is not part of a program.

Computer information system All components required to complete the tasks required to complete a job. These components include hardware, software, data, people, procedures, and facilities.

Concatenation Adding one piece of string data to another by placing the second piece immediately after the first.

Constant A value in a program that cannot change during processing.

Control-break A break in processing to print subtotals, or number of items, controlled by one field in a file.

Control module The module controlling the processing of all of the subtasks in a solution.

Data Unorganized facts.

Database management system (DBMS) A productivity software package that enables the user to easily set up, access, update, and report on data in files.

Data type The kind of data of a variable or a constant. The three basic data types are numerical, character, and logical.

Debugging The process of correcting errors in a computer program.

Decision logic structure One of the four logic structures for organizing the instructions to the computer that make up a program. The decision structure selects one of two sets of instructions according to the resultant of a condition.

Decision table A programming aid to writing decision instructions for the computer; it consists of a rectangular grid divided into four parts, which specifies all possible actions the computer could take for each possible set of conditions.

Default value A value of a variable that is built into a program and that the computer automatically uses unless the value is changed by the user.

Document Text that is formatted and stored in a file.

Document processing The use of multiple software packages, along with the other components of a computer information system, to process a document.

Dynamic array An array in which the maximum number of elements can change during processing.

END-OF-FILE (EOF) The marker in a computer solution indicating that there are no more records to be processed.

Equation A variable that is assigned the value of an expression, another variable, or a constant, as in A = 5 + B, A = B (where B is a variable), or A = 5, respectively.

Event a happening in the computer, such as mouse down, key down, mouse up, or key up

Event-driven object oriented programming a solution to a problem in which the processing is controlled through events in the computer

Exporting data The saving of a document in a format to be received by another software package.

Expression An operation or series of operations performed on variables or constants, as in 5 + B.

External documentation Instructions to the user in the form of manuals or other written documents.

Field One piece of data.

File A collection of related records.

File maintenance module A process data module that updates the master file.

File updating Adding, deleting, or changing data in records in a file to keep the records current.

Flowchart A graphic illustration of an algorithm.

Format In word processing, the size, shape, and appearance of a document, involving such factors as margins, indentations, line spacing, and type styles. In a spreadsheet, the way the contents of the cell will look on the screen.

Function A small set of instructions built into a computer language or applications that enables the user to complete a frequently repeated task with fewer keystrokes than would be required without the function.

GUI Graphic User Interface. an interactive screen in which the user controls what happens in a program

Global variable A variable that can be accessed by all modules below and in line (in the structure chart) with the module that declared the variable.

Hard carriage return A carriage return inserted by the user of a word-processing software package. The computer cannot move this carriage return. A paragraph is defined by a word processor as the text from one hard carriage return to another.

Heuristic solution A solution to a problem that cannot be solved through a single sequence of instructions.

Hierarchy The order in which operations are performed for mathematical, relational, and logical operations.

Horizontal software Multipurpose software, such as word-processing programs, database management systems, and spreadsheets.

IF/THEN/ELSE instruction The instruction to the computer that implements the decision logic structure.

Importing data Using documents created in another software package.

Incrementing The process of counting on the computer by adding a number to a previous number. The instruction for incrementing by one is COUNTER = COUNTER + 1.

Index file A file containing the key field and corresponding record number for all records in the master file. The file is in order of the key.

Indicator A value built into a solution by the programmer to redirect the flow of processing.

Information Organized facts.

Inheritance a set of properties which have been passed down from a class

Initialization module The module containing all of the processing that has to be completed only once and at the beginning of the solution.

Installing software Setting up a software package so that it can be used on the computer for which it was bought.

Instance of a class an object

Interactive processing Processing that involves user intervention to enter new data as needed, usually at a keyboard.

Interactivity the interaction between classes or between screens

Internal documentation Remarks within a computer solution to explain the processing.

IPO chart Input-processing-output chart; describes the input, the output, and the processing needed to solve a problem on the computer.

Key The field of the records that is used to order a file or search for a record.

Linked list A list that has one field that contains the record number of the next record to be processed.

Local variable A variable accessed by the module that declared the variable. A single variable can be both local and global (see Chapter 4).

Logical file number (LFN) In record processing, a number used to reference a file.

Logical operator An operator within an expression that uses logical data as operands and produces logical data as the resultant. The logical operators include NOT, AND, and OR.

Logic structure A structure for organizing the instructions to the computer that make up a program. There are four logic structures: the sequential structure, the decision structure, the loop structure, and the case structure.

Loop logic structure One of the four logic structures for organizing the instructions to the computer that make up a program. The loop structure enables the computer to process the same set of instructions repeatedly.

Macro A small set of instructions to the computer executed by a single command.

Master file The file in which all of the data needed for processing are kept current.

Mathematical operator An operator that uses numerical data as its operands and produces numerical data as the resultant. The mathematical operators include − (subtraction), + (addition), * (multiplication, / (division), \ (integer division). MOD (modulo division), and ^ (power).

Menu A list of user options in a menu-driven program.

Menu-driven program A solution that uses a list of user options to control the processing.

Merging files The process of combining two files.

Module A subtask of the larger task the computer performs to complete a whole solution. The modules include the Control, Initialization, Process, and Wrapup modules.

Multidimensional array A multidimensional block of elements with a single variable name. Each element is designated by element numbers representing row, column, page, and so on.

Multiple control-break A control-break on more than one field.

Navigation the method of traversing a program; the control mechanism the user uses to continue from screen to screen in an interactive solution to a problem.

Negative logic A type of decision logic in which the action the computer is to perform follows from the FALSE side of the instruction.

Nested IF/THEN/ELSE A type of decision structure that nests one IF/THEN/ELSE instruction within another.

Nested loop A type of loop structure that nests one loop instruction within another.

Null file A file containing no records.

Object an item, or an instance of a class; an item on the screen when using an event-driven object oriented programming language

Object oriented programming a language which supports object oriented principles; a strategy of program design in which the data parts are the principal items, instead of the process

OLE Object linking and embedding. OLE allows a piece of data to be automatically changed in one package when changed in another.

One-dimensional array One column of elements with a single variable name. Each element is designated by an element number.

Operator A sign or symbol in an expression or equation telling the computer how to process the data. The three types of operators are mathematical, relational, and logical.

Ordinal value The place value of one value of the data set for a data type.

Page-break A break in the process of printing to finish one page and begin another.

Parallel arrays Two or more arrays where the data in the same element numbers are related to each other.

Parameter A variable passed from one module to another module through the calling sequence of the module or function. There are two types of parameters, call-by-value parameters and call-by-reference. Call-by-value parameters cannot be changed in the module. Call-by-reference parameters can be changed and the changed value will be passed back to the calling module.

Pointer technique A programming technique that uses the value in one array to point to an element in another array.

Positive logic A type of decision logic in which the action the computer is to perform follows from the TRUE side of the instruction.

Primary key A unique key that is the major key for ordering a file or searching for a record.

Primer Read The first record that is read into the internal memory before starting a processing loop, in order to have values to process the first time through the loop.

Print module A process data module that prints the results of processing.

Process data modules The modules that process the data. They include Calculation, Print, Read, and File maintenance modules.

PROCESS instruction An instruction that tells the computer to execute a module and then return to the instruction following the PROCESS instruction.

Productivity package Software designed to help the user solve problems, make better decisions, and increase productivity, efficiency, and accuracy. The most common types of productivity packages are word processing, database management, and spreadsheets.

Program A computer solution to a problem; a set of instructions in a given computer language that solves the problem.

Pseudocode A set of step-by-step instructions with working similar to that found in the programming language to be used.

Pushing and popping the stack Adding (pushing) and taking from (popping) a stack.

Queue A list where the next value used was the first one to be added. Data are added and used in a first-in, first-out basis.

Range name The name of a group or range of cells in a spreadsheet.

Range of cells A rectangular group of one or more cells in a spreadsheet.

Read module A process data module that enters data into the computer.

Record The set of data for one entity in a file.

Record management system A productivity package that performs many of the same functions as a database management system but which uses only one file rather than two or more.

Recursion Recursion occurs when a module or a function calls itself.

Relational operator An operator within an expression or equation that uses numerical or string data as operands and produces logical data as the resultant. The relational operators include: = (equal to), < (less than), > (greater than), < = (less than or equal to), > = (greater than or equal to), and < > (not equal to).

REPEAT/UNTIL One of three types of loop instructions; this loop logic structure tests at the end of each loop to see if it should repeat; it repeats the instructions in the loop until the condition is TRUE.

Results The required answers to or output from a problem.

Schema The files and their relationships in a database.

Screen the image on the monitor in one instance

Script a set of instructions attached to an object or a solution

Secondary key A key, which may or may not be unique, that is used to order a file or to search for one or more records in a file. A secondary key is considered a minor key.

Sequential logic structure One of the four logic structures for organizing the instructions to the computer that make up a solution. The sequential structure processes the instructions one after another in a sequence.

Sequential search A method for locating a record in a file in which the computer starts at the first record and continues through the file, record by record, until the needed record is found.

Soft carriage return A carriage return that the computer puts into the text to mark the end of a line and that can be moved by the computer as needed to adjust the text after editing.

Solution The set of instructions to the computer that will output the results; a computer program before it is coded into a computer language.

Sorting Arranging data in order; the order may be numerical or alphabetical.

Spreadsheet package A productivity program that allows the user to set up, calculate, change, and recalculate a worksheet.

Stack A list where the value to be added and the value to be used are on the same end of the list. Data are added and used in a last-in, first-out basis.

Static array An array in which the maximum number of elements cannot change during processing.

Storyboard a design tool used to create screens

Straight-through logic A type of decision logic that processes all decisions sequentially, one after another.

Structure chart A chart showing all of the subtasks, or modules, in a program.

Structured techniques Programming techniques, including the use of modules and structured instructions, indentation, variable names that relate to the data, and the avoidance of GOTO instructions, that lead to a readable and efficient program.

Suite A group of standalone software packages designed to work together. They have the same look and feel, as well as the ability to share and link data easily.

Syntax The rules of setting up instructions and commands in an operating system, a programming language, or an application program.

System flowchart Shows the overall flow of data throughout the entire computer system, including all peripheral equipment.

Template A shell, or structure, of a document or worksheet that can be reused repeatedly with new data.

Transaction file A file containing all of the updates that need to be made to a master file.

Traversal of a binary tree The order in which a tree is processed.

Tutorial A program provided with a software package to help the user learn how to use the package.

Two-dimensional array A block of elements with one variable name. Each element is designated by element numbers designating the row and column.

Unary operator An operator that uses one operand.

Variable A named memory location in the computer that is given a value that can be changed at any time during the processing.

Vertical software Software with a single purpose, such as dental accounting software, real estate management software, and the like.

WHILE/WHILE-END One of the three types of loop instructions; the loop logic structure that tests at the beginning of the loop and repeats as long as a condition is TRUE.

Word processing Editing text electronically through the use of a horizontal software package.

Worksheet The contents of the cells as seen on the screen when using a spreadsheet.

Wrapup module The module containing all of the processing that has to be completed only once and at the end of the processing.

Index

E

F

G

H

I

J

K

L

T

U

V

W

QBASIC™

With an Introduction to Visual Basic™

Fourth Edition

David I. Schneider
University of Maryland

Prentice Hall, Upper Saddle River, New Jersey 07458

Library of Congress Cataloging-in-Publication Data

Schneider, David I.
QBASIC: with an introduction to Visual Basic / David I. Schneider. — 4th ed.
p. cm.
Includes bibliographical references and index.
ISBN 0–13–973876–2
1. Qbasic (Computer program language) 2. Microsoft Visual BASIC. I. Title
QA76.73.Q33S37 1998
005.26′2—dc21 98-27509
CIP

Acquisitions editor: **Laura Steele**
Production editor: **Rhodora Penaranda**
Managing editor: **Eileen Clark**
Editor-in-chief: **Marcia Horton**
Vice-president and director of manufacturing and production: **David W. Riccardi**
Copy editor: **Bob Lentz**
Cover director: **Heather Scott**
Cover designer: **Joe Sengotta**
Manufacturing buyer: **Donna Sullivan**
Editorial assistant: **Kate Kaibni**
Compositor: **Rebecca Evans & Associates**

Simon & Schuster / A Viacom Company
Upper Saddle River, NJ 07458

Printed in the United States of America

10 9 8 7 6 5 4 3 2 1

ISBN 0-13-973876-2

Prentice-Hall International (UK) Limited, London
Prentice-Hall of Australia Pty. Limited, Sydney
Prentice-Hall Canada Inc., Toronto
Prentice-Hall Hispanoamericana, S.A., Mexico
Prentice-Hall of India Private Limited, New Delhi
Prentice-Hall of Japan, Inc., Tokyo
Simon & Schuster Asia Pte. Ltd., Singapore
Editora Prentice-Hall do Brasil, Ltda., Rio de Janeiro

Contents

Preface

This text presents the fundamentals of programming in Microsoft® QBasic™ on IBM PC compatible computers and an introduction to Microsoft® Visual Basic™.

My objectives when writing this text were as follows:

1. To develop focused chapters. Rather than covering many topics superficially, I concentrate on important subjects and cover them thoroughly.
2. To use examples and exercises with which students can relate and feel comfortable. I frequently use real data. Examples do not have so many embellishments that students are distracted from the programming techniques illustrated.
3. To produce compactly written text that students will find both readable and informative. The main points of each topic are discussed first and then the peripheral details are presented as comments.
4. To teach good programming practices that are in step with modern programming methodology. Problem solving techniques and structured programming are discussed early and used throughout the book.
5. To provide insights into the major applications of computers.

Unique and Distinguishing Features

Exercises for Most Sections. Each section that teaches programming has an exercise set. The exercises both reinforce the understanding of the key ideas of the section and challenge the student to explore applications. Most of the exercise sets require the student to trace programs, find errors, and write programs. The answers to all the odd-numbered exercises in Chapters 2 through 8 and selected odd-numbered exercises from Chapters 9 through 12 are given at the end of the text.

Practice Problems. Practice problems are carefully selected exercises located at the end of a section, just before the exercise set. Complete solutions are given following the exercise set. The practice problems often focus on points that are potentially confusing or are best appreciated after the student has worked on them. The reader should seriously attempt the practice problems and study their solutions before moving on to the exercises.

Programming Projects. Beginning with Chapter 3, every chapter contains programming projects. The programming projects not only reflect the variety of ways that computers are used in the business and engineering communities, but also present some games and general-interest topics. The large number and range of difficulty of the programming projects allow adapting the course to the students' interests and abilities. Some programming projects in Chapters 7 through 12 can be assigned as end-of-the-semester projects.

Comments. Extensions and fine points of new topics are deferred to the "Comments" portion at the end of each section so that they will not interfere with the flow of the presentation.

Case Studies. Each of the five case studies focuses on an important programming application. The problems are analyzed and the programs are developed with top-down charts and pseudocode. The programs can be found in the EXAMPLES directory of the enclosed CD.

Chapter Summaries. In Chapters 3 through 12 the key results are stated and the important terms are highlighted.

Strings Used Throughout Text. The introduction of strings in Chapter 3 and their regular use from then on prepare the student for substantial string-handling programs.

Procedures. The early introduction of procedures in Chapter 4 allows structured programming to be used in simple situations before being applied to complex problems. However, the text is written so that the presentation of procedures can easily be postponed until decision and repetition structures have been presented. In Chapters 5 and 6 (and Sections 7.1 and 7.2) all programs using procedures appear at the ends of sections and can be deferred or omitted.

Arrays. Arrays are introduced gently in two sections. The first section presents the basic definitions and avoids procedures. The second section presents the techniques for manipulating arrays and shows how to pass arrays to procedures.

Visual Basic. Chapter 12 provides an introduction to Visual Basic, the programming language most used on PCs. Since Visual Basic uses essentially the same programming constructs as QBasic, students can leverage their knowledge of QBasic and make themselves more marketable. (Why more marketable? Because its extraordinary combination of power and ease of use has made Visual Basic the tool of choice for developing user-friendly applications in the business world. In addition, Microsoft has made Visual Basic the language used to take full control of its best-selling Windows application, Microsoft Office.)

Another good point of Visual Basic is—it's fun! Learning Visual Basic was very exciting to me—most students have similar reactions when they see how easy it is to build powerful visual interfaces using it.

The chapter on Visual Basic can be used in several ways.

(a) The chapter can be covered in detail.
(b) The instructor can give a survey of the language in one or two lectures.
(c) The chapter can be assigned as an optional enrichment topic.

Whether or not the chapter is covered in class, I encourage all students to learn about Visual Basic.

Appendix on Debugging. Placing the discussion of QBasic's sophisticated debugger in an appendix allows the instructor flexibility in deciding when to cover this topic.

Reference Appendices. Appendices serve as a compact reference manual for the environments and statements of both QBasic and Visual Basic.

Instructors Manual. A diskette containing the solution to every exercise and programming project, and a test-item file for each chapter, is available for the instructor.

Examples, Case Studies, and Visual Basic CD. Each book contains a CD holding all the examples and case studies from this text and also a copy of the Control Creation Edition of Visual Basic 5.0.

What's New in the Fourth Edition

1. Suggestions from students and reviewers of the book have been incorporated as much as possible.
2. The real-life data in the examples and exercises have been updated and revised.
3. Chapter 10 has been modified to refer primarily to VGA monitors. Information on capturing the graphics screen from Windows has been added.
4. The version of Visual Basic has been upgraded to Visual Basic 5.0. The CD packaged with the text contains the Control Creation Edition of VB 5.0. This version has most of the features of the other versions of VB 5.0. The main differences are that the Control Creation Edition does not allow compilation to an EXE file and does not contain the Data control which is used to access databases. Because VB 5.0 requires Windows 95 or Windows 98, these versions of Windows are discussed in Appendix H.

Acknowledgments

Many talented instructors, students, and programmers provided helpful comments and thoughtful suggestions at each stage in the preparation of this text. I extend my gratitude for their contributions to the quality of the book to Shakil Akhtar, Central Michigan University; William A. Bailey, Jr., University of North Carolina at Charlotte; Abdel Fatah Bashir, Moorhead State University; Curtis Bring, Moorhead State University; John Caldwell, College of Lake County; Gene B. Chase, Messiah College; Curtis Childress, Rancho Santiago College; Michael Cooper, University of California at Berkeley; Noel Dahlen, Rancho Santiago College; Louise Darcy, Texas A&M University; Mark Ellis, MIT; Richard Fedder, Grand Valley State University; Ronald D. Ferguson, San Antonio College; W. Fred Fry, Rancho Santiago College; Kevin Gorman, University of North Carolina at Charlotte; Samuel Graff, John Jay College of Criminal Justice; Bill Higgins, Messiah College; Bill Hoffman, Cogswell Polytech College; Milo Johnson, College of the Redwoods; Monte Johnson, St. Cloud State University; Dee Joseph, San Antonio College; James P. Kelsh, Central Michigan University; Suban Krishnamoorthy, Framingham State College; Shelly Langman; Norman Lindquist, W. Washington University; Jackie Lou, Montgomery College; Lewis D. Miller, Canada College; Calvin Mittman, St. John's University; Barry Parris, University of South Carolina at Spartanburg; Juanita J. Peterson, College of Alameda; James T. Ramey, Jr., Francis Marion College; John Repede, University of North Carolina at Charlotte; Peter Rosenbaum, Framingham State College; R. Waldo Roth, Tulsa Research Center; Barbara Saxton, Lehigh County Community College; Sandra M. Schleiffers, Colorado State University; Y. Sitaraman, Kentucky Wesleyan College; Phil Steitz, Beloit College; Brooke Stephens, University of Maryland; Bill Strausbaugh, Messiah College; Brian Turnquist, University of Maryland; Michael Willis, Montgomery College; Charles M. Williams, Georgia State University; Sheryl Barricklow, Grand Valley State University; Joseph Farrelly, Palomar College; Raymond Fadous, University of Michigan at Flint; Francis A. Greene, Essex Community College; Patricia A. Joseph, Slippery Rock University of Pennsylvania; Andy Lau, Pennsylvania State at Harrisburg; Glen Lobo, Ferris State University; Robert Spear, Prince George's Community College; William A. Moy, University of Wisconsin-Parkside; Andrew McConnell, Napa Valley College; Rita Mudd, Inver Hills Community College; Ernst Rilki, Harper College; Ronald W. Surprenant, Suffolk County Community College; Thomas P. Wiggen, University of North Dakota

Rebecca Evans & Associates used state-of-the-art technology to compose the text. Donna Sullivan of Prentice Hall did a fantastic job of keeping the book on schedule.

My editor, Laura Steele, not only capably handled the many details needed to bring the book to production, but nurtured me with her ideas and enthusiasm during the preparation of this revision.

Last, but not least, I am grateful to the Microsoft Corporation for their commitment to producing outstanding programming languages and for their permission to include a copy of the Control Creation Edition of Visual Basic with each book.

1

An Introduction to Computers and QBasic

1.1 AN INTRODUCTION TO COMPUTERS

QBasic with an Introduction to Visual Basic is a book about problem solving with computers. The programming languages used are QBasic and Visual Basic, but the principles taught apply to many modern structured programming languages. The examples and exercises present a sampling of the ways that computers are used in society.

Computers are so common today that you certainly have seen them in use and heard some of the terminology applied to them. Here are some of the questions that you might have about computers and programming.

Question: What is meant by *personal computer*?

Answer: The word *personal* does not mean that the computer is intended for personal, as opposed to business, purposes. Rather, it indicates that the machine is operated by one person at a time instead of by many people.

Question: What are the main components of a personal computer?

Answer: The visible components are shown in Figure 1.1. Instructions are entered into the computer by typing them on the **keyboard** or by reading them from a **diskette** in a **diskette drive** or from a **hard disk**. Characters normally appear on the **monitor** as they are typed. Information processed by the computer can be displayed on the monitor, printed on the **printer**, or recorded on a diskette or a hard drive. Hidden from view inside the **system unit** are the microprocessor and the memory of the computer. The **microprocessor**, which can be thought of as the brain of the computer, carries out all computations. The **memory** stores the instructions and data that are processed by the computer.

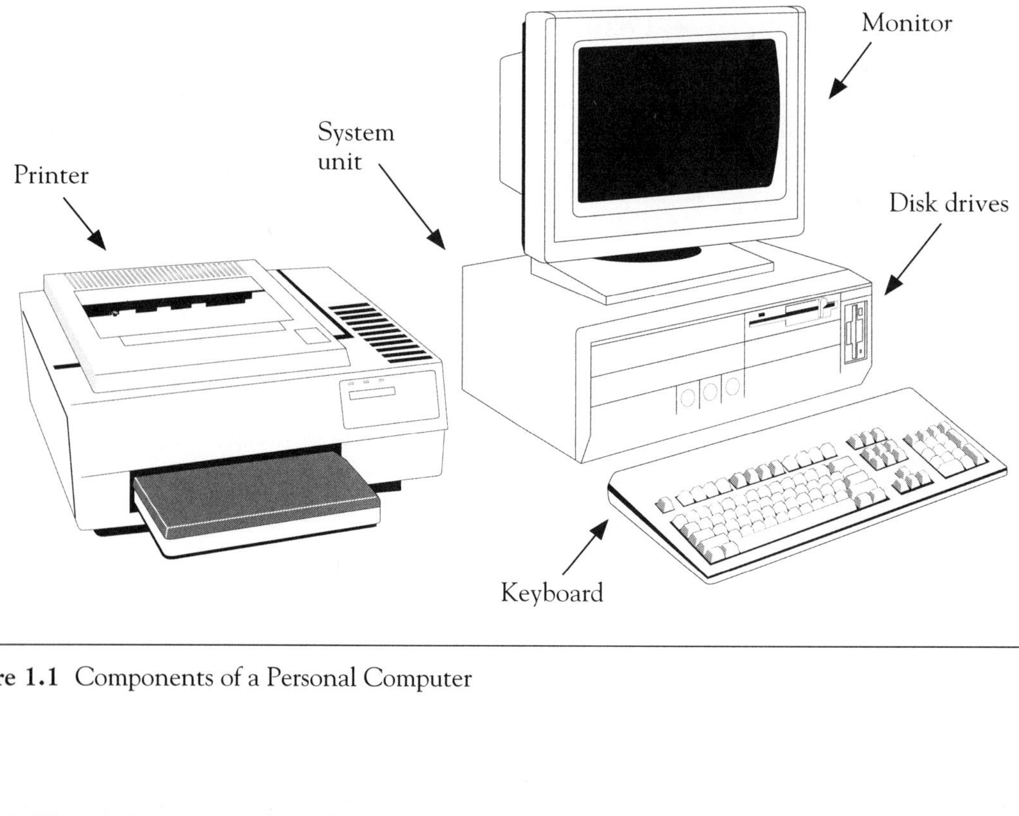

Figure 1.1 Components of a Personal Computer

Question: What are some uses of computers in our society?

Answer: Whenever we make a phone call, a computer determines how to route the call and calculates the cost of the call. Banks store all customer transactions on computers and process these data to revise the balance for each customer. Airlines record all reservations into computers. This information, which is said to form a database, can be accessed to determine the status of any flight. NASA uses computers to calculate the trajectories of satellites. Business analysts use computers to create pie and bar charts that give visual impact to data.

Question: What are some topics covered in this text that students can use immediately?

Answer: Computer files can be created to hold lists of names, addresses, and phone numbers, which can be alphabetized and printed in entirety or selectively. Line graphs or attractive tables can be created to enhance the data in a term paper. Mathematical computations can be carried out for science, business, and engineering courses. Personal financial transactions, such as bank deposits and loans, can be recorded, organized, and analyzed.

Question: How do we communicate with the computer?

Answer: Many languages are used to communicate with the computer. At the lowest level there is *machine language*, which is understood directly by the microprocessor but is awkward for humans. QBasic is an example of a higher-level language. It consists of instructions to which people can relate, such as PRINT, LET, and DO. The QBasic software translates QBasic programs into machine-language programs.

Question: How do we get computers to perform complicated tasks?

Answer: Tasks are broken down into a sequence of instructions that can be expressed in a computer language. (This text uses the language QBasic.) The sequence of instructions is called a **program**. Programs range in size from two or three instructions to tens of thousands. Instructions are typed on the keyboard and stored in the computer's memory. (They can also be stored permanently on a diskette or hard disk.) The process of executing the instructions is called **running the program**.

Question: Are there certain features that all programs have in common?

Answer: Most programs do three things: take in data, manipulate it, and give desired information. These operations are referred to as **input**, **processing**, and **output**. The input data might be held in a portion of the program, reside on a diskette or hard disk, or be provided by the computer operator in response to requests made by the computer while the program is running. The processing of the input data takes place inside the computer and can take from a fraction of a second to many hours. The output data are either displayed on the screen, printed on the printer, or recorded onto a disk. As a simple example, consider a program that computes sales tax. An item of input data is the cost of the thing purchased. The processing consists of multiplying the cost by a certain percentage. An item of output data is the resulting product, the amount of sales tax to be paid.

Question: What are the meanings of the terms *hardware* and *software*?

Answer: The term **hardware** refers to the physical components of the computer, including all peripherals, data terminals, disk drives, and all mechanical and electrical devices. Programs are referred to as **software**.

Question: What are the meanings of the terms *programmer* and *user*?

Answer: A **programmer** is a person who solves problems by writing programs on a computer. After analyzing the problem and developing a plan for solving it, he or she writes and tests the program that instructs the computer how to carry out the plan. The program might be run many times, either by the programmer or by others. A **user** is any person who uses a program. While working through this text, you will function both as a programmer and as a user.

Question: What is meant by *problem solving?*

Answer: Problems are solved by carefully reading them to determine what data are given and what output is requested. Then a step-by-step procedure is devised to process the given data and produce the requested output. This procedure is called an **algorithm**. Finally, a computer program is written to carry out the algorithm. Algorithms are discussed in Section 2.2.

Question: What types of problems are solved in this text?

Answer: Carrying out business computations, creating and maintaining records, alphabetizing lists, simulating games, and drawing line graphs are some of the types of problems we will solve.

Question: What is the difference between *standard BASIC* and *QBasic?*

Answer: In the early 1960s two mathematics professors at Dartmouth College developed BASIC to provide their students with an easily learned language that could tackle complicated programming projects. As the popularity of BASIC grew, other languages were introduced that included so-called *structured programming* (discussed in Chapter 2), which increases the reliability of programs. QBasic is a version of BASIC that was written by the Microsoft Corporation to incorporate structured programming into BASIC and to take advantage of other capabilities of modern personal computers. QBasic has most of the features of standard BASIC, as well as many enhancements.

1.2 GETTING STARTED

The QBasic language is supplied with DOS 5.0 (and later versions of DOS) and all versions of Windows. (DOS stands for Disk Operating System.) If you are using Windows 95, or a later version of Windows, most likely QBasic has not been installed on your hard drive. See Comment 12 for the details of copying QBasic from the Windows 95 CD. If you are using a computer in a computer lab where the computer is connected to a network, consult a lab assistant about invoking QBasic.

1. Turn on the computer.
2. There will be a delay after which your computer starts either DOS or Windows. If your computer starts up in Windows, perform Step 3 to invoke DOS. Otherwise, go to Step 4.
3. With Windows 95 or later version, click the Start button, point to Programs, and click on the "MS-DOS Prompt." If the DOS window does not fill the screen, hold down the Alt key and press the Enter key to enlarge the window.

   With Windows 3.1, from the Program Manager, click on Window in the menu bar, click on Main in the menu that drops down, and double-click on the MS-DOS Prompt icon.
4. A DOS prompt will appear. The first letter identifies the drive for the hard disk. Type

   ```
   QBASIC
   ```

   and press the Enter key to start QBasic. If this is not successful, see Comment 11.
5. When the welcome message appears, press the **Esc key** to obtain the QBasic screen shown in Figure 1.2. (Most of the information in the Survival Guide referred to on the opening screen will be covered in this section.)

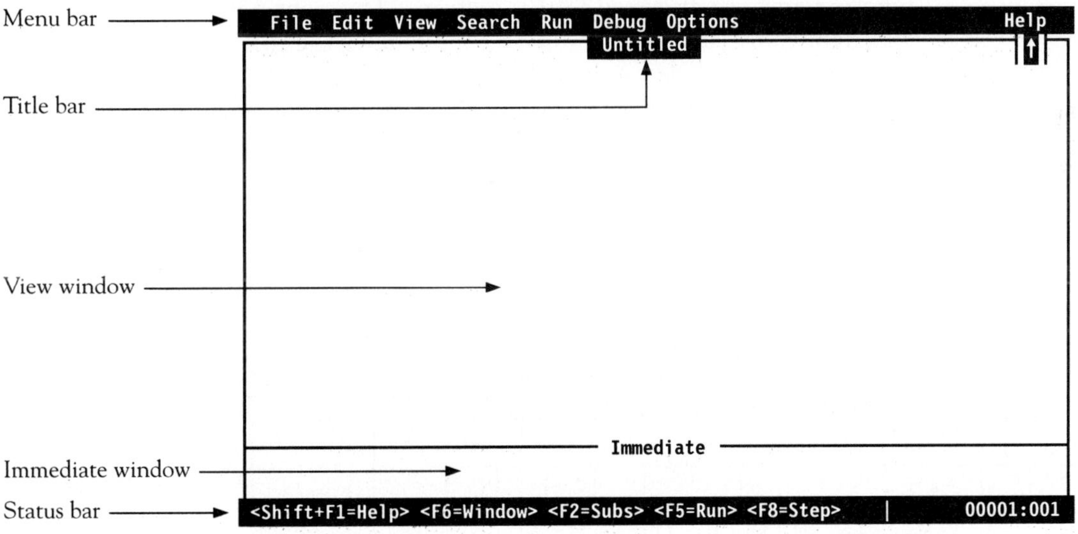

Figure 1.2 Screen after QBasic Is Invoked

The blinking dash is called the **cursor**. Each letter you type will appear at the cursor. The QBasic screen is divided into five parts. The part containing the cursor is called the **View window**. It is the largest and most important part of the screen, since programs are typed into this window.

The **Menu bar** at the top of the screen is used to call up menus, or lists of tasks. Several of these tasks are described in this section. All the tasks are discussed in Appendix F.

The small **Title bar** just below the Menu bar holds the name of the program currently being written. Until the program is given a name, the program is called "Untitled."

The narrow **Immediate window** is used to execute QBasic statements directly, instead of in a program. The Immediate window is discussed in detail in Appendix D—QBasic Debugging Tools.

The bottom line of the screen contains the **Status bar**. The information displayed in the bar will vary during the entering and execution of the program. In Figure 1.2, the display 00001:001 informs us that the cursor is located on the first line and in the first column of that line.

Programs are created from the keyboard in much the same way they would be written with a typewriter. In computerese, writing a program is referred to as **editing** the program; therefore, the part of QBasic used to create and alter programs is called the **editor**. Before discussing the editor, we must first examine the workings of the keyboard.

There are several different styles of keyboards. Figure 1.3 shows a typical one. The keyboard is divided into several parts. The largest portion looks and functions like an ordinary typewriter keyboard. Above this portion are twelve keys labeled from F1 through F12, called the **function keys**. (On many keyboards the function keys also are located on the left side. Older keyboards have only ten function keys.) Function keys are used to perform certain tasks with a single keystroke. For instance, holding down a Shift key and pressing the function key F1 causes a help screen to appear. (The commands associated with some of the function keys are discussed in this section.) The right portion of the keyboard, called the **numeric keypad**, is used either to move the cursor or to enter numbers. Press the **Num Lock key** a few times and notice the letter N appearing and disappearing in the right part of the Status bar. When the letter N is present, the numeric keypad produces numbers; otherwise, it moves the cursor. The Num Lock key is called a **toggle key**, since it "toggles" between two states. When the numeric keypad is in the cursor-moving state, the four arrow keys each move the cursor one space.

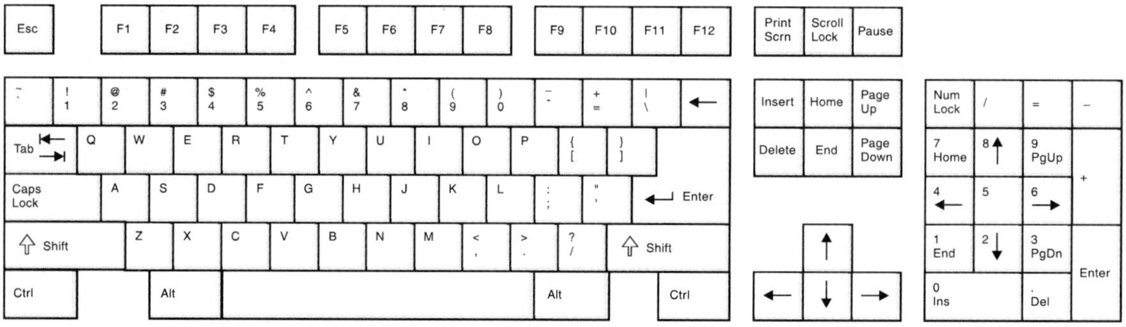

Figure 1.3 IBM PC Keyboard

Two very important keys may not have names printed on them. The **Enter key** is the key with the hooked arrow (and/or the word Enter). It is used to execute commands or to start a new line of a program. The Enter key corresponds to the carriage return on a typewriter. The **Backspace key** is the gray key with the left-pointing arrow located above the Enter key. It moves the cursor one space to the left and erases any character in that location.

After QBasic has been invoked, the following routine will introduce you to the keyboard.

1. Use the right and left cursor-moving keys on the numeric keypad to move the cursor. Notice that the cursor-position number at the lower right corner of the screen changes each time one of these keys is pressed.

2. Press the **Home key** to move the cursor back to the beginning of the line. In general, the Home key moves the cursor to the beginning of the line on which it currently is located.

3. Type some letters using the central typewriter portion of the keyboard. The two **Shift keys** are used to obtain uppercase letters or the upper character of keys showing two characters.

4. Press the **Caps Lock key** and then type some letters. The letters will appear in uppercase. We say the computer is in uppercase mode. To toggle back to lowercase mode, press the Caps Lock key again. Only alphabetic keys are affected by Caps Lock. ***Note:*** When the editor is in the uppercase state, the letter C appears in the right part of the Status bar.

5. Hold down the **Ctrl key** (Ctrl stands for "Control") and press the **Y key**. This combination erases the line containing the cursor. We describe this combination as **Ctrl+Y**. (The plus sign indicates that the Ctrl key is to be held down while pressing the Y key.) There are many useful key combinations like this. You can find a complete list at the beginning of Appendix E.

6. Type some letters and then press the Backspace key a few times. It will erase letters one at a time. Another method of deleting a letter is to move the cursor to that letter and press the **Del key** (Del stands for "Delete"). The backspace key erases the character to the left of the cursor, and the Del key erases the character at the cursor.

7. Type a few letters and use the appropriate cursor-moving key to move the cursor under one of the letters. Now type any letter and notice that it is inserted at the cursor position and that the letters following it move to the right. This is because **insert mode** is active. The **overwrite mode**, in which a typed letter overwrites the letter located at the cursor position, is invoked by pressing the **Ins key** (Ins stands for "Insert"). Pressing this toggle key again reinstates insert mode. The cursor size indicates the active mode; a large cursor means overwrite mode.

8. Type some letters and move the cursor left a few spaces. Now press the **End key** (on the numeric keypad). The cursor will move to the end of the line.

9. The key to the left of the Q key is called the **Tab key**. It is marked with a pair of arrows, the upper one pointing to the left and the lower one pointing to the right. At the beginning of the line, pressing the Tab key indents the cursor several spaces.

10. Type more characters than can fit on one line of the screen. Notice that the leftmost characters scroll off the screen to make room for the new characters. Up to 255 characters can be typed on a line.

11. The Enter key is used to begin a new line on the screen in much the same way the carriage return lever is used on a manual typewriter. However, pressing the Enter key also causes QBasic to examine the contents of the line. If the line is not a proper QBasic program line, this fact is conveyed in a message that points out the error. If the line is a proper QBasic program line, then certain spacings and capitalizations will be carried out to make the line conform to standard conventions.

12. The **Alt key** activates the Menu bar. Then, pressing one of the highlighted letters, such as F, E, or V, selects a menu. (A menu can also be selected by pressing the right-arrow key to highlight the name and then pressing the Enter key.) As shown in Figure 1.4, after opening a menu, each option has one letter highlighted. Pressing the highlighted letter selects the option. For instance, pressing A from the file menu selects the option "Save As." Selections also can be made with the cursor-moving keys and the Enter key.

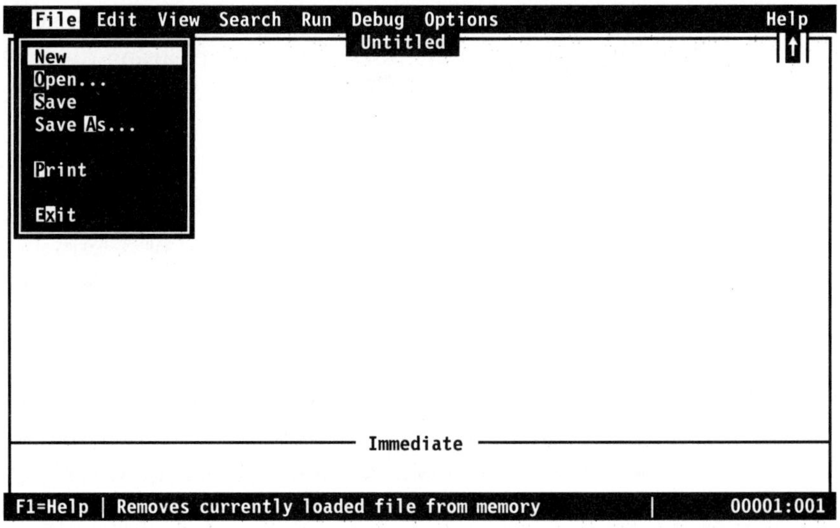

Figure 1.4 A Menu and Its Options

13. The **Esc key** (Esc stands for "Escape") is used to return to the View window.

A Programming Walkthrough

The following walkthrough is designed to introduce you to the mechanics of creating and running a program. Just follow the directions and observe the results. The QBasic statements used here will be explained later in the text.

1. Use the cursor-moving keys and the combination Ctrl+Y to clear the View window, and then move the cursor to the top of the screen.

2. Type the word

```
cls
```

in lowercase letters and then press the Enter key. Notice that the word was automatically capitalized by QBasic. CLS is an example of what is called a **keyword** or **reserved word**. Keywords have special meanings to QBasic. (See Appendix C at the end of this book for a complete list of QBasic's reserved words.) When the statement CLS is executed, the screen will be cleared. There are about 200 keywords that QBasic understands. A **statement** (or instruction) consists of one of these keywords and possibly some parameters. Each statement is written on a separate line and tells the computer to perform a specific task. A program consists of a collection of statements.

3. On the second line of the View window, type

```
FOR i=1 TO
```

and press the Enter key. (The number 1 in the line above is typed by pressing the "one" key, the key just above and left of the Q key, not the L key.) The box shown in Figure 1.5 will appear on the screen to inform you that this is not a proper QBasic line. Press the Esc key and then continue typing on the same line to obtain

```
FOR i=1 TO 100
```

Now press the Enter key and notice that a space is added before and after the equals sign to make the line more legible. ***Note:*** The box that appeared is called a **dialog box**. Dialog boxes appear at various times to point out errors or to offer assistance. The Tab key is used to move to different parts of a dialog box and the Esc key is used to remove a dialog box.

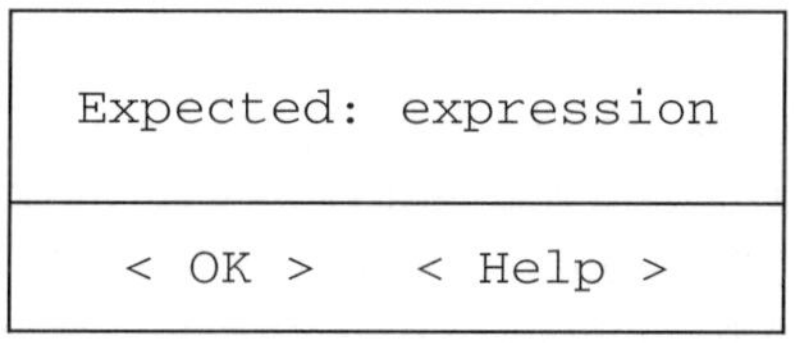

Figure 1.5 A Dialog Box

4. Type additional lines to create the display shown below. This is our first example of a QBasic program. It consists of a sequence of lines that instruct the computer to perform certain tasks. This program causes the word "Hello" to be displayed 100 times. Like every program in this text, it begins with a CLS statement and finishes with an END statement. The computer is said to **execute** or **run** the program when it carries out the instructions.

```
CLS
FOR i = 1 TO 100
PRINT "Hello",
NEXT i
END
```

5. To execute the program, hold down the Shift key and press the F5 key (abbreviated Shift+F5). The screen you are now viewing is called the **Output screen**. ***Note:*** Pressing the key combination Shift+F5 is denoted later in the book by the term **[run]**.

6. As stated at the bottom of the screen, press any key to return to the View window.

7. Press F4 to see the Output screen again. This key toggles between the View window and Output screen. Press F4 again to return to the View window.

8. Press Shift+F5 to run the program again if you so desire.

9. Sometimes errors are found in the program after pressing Shift+F5. To see an example of this, move the cursor to the fourth line of the program and delete the letter X from the word NEXT. Now, upon running the program, a dialog box with the message "Syntax error" appears and the offending line of the program is highlighted. The dialog box can be removed by pressing either the Esc key or the Enter key. The cursor will then appear on the line to be corrected. After the correction is made, the cursor-moving keys can be used to move the cursor off the corrected line.

10. Modify the program by inserting the line

```
PRINT i;
```

    before the third line. To create space for the line, move the cursor to the end of the second line and press the Enter key. (Alternatively, move the cursor to the beginning of the third line, press the Enter key, and move the cursor up one line.) Now type the new line. Moving the cursor off the line will cause QBasic to check for certain types of errors, to capitalize keywords, and to adjust the spacing.

11. Run the new program. Now each of the *Hellos* will be numbered.

12. Press any key to return to the View window.

13. You can store the program as a file on a diskette or hard disk so you can run it later without having to retype it. To save the program, press and release Alt, then press and release F, and then press A. (This key combination is abbreviated Alt/**F**ile/Save **A**s or Alt/**F**/**A**.) A dialog box will appear and ask you to give a file name to the program. Type a drive letter, a colon, and a name containing at most eight letters and digits (no spaces), and then press the Enter key. For instance, you might type A:MYPROG1. The program will then be stored on drive A. This process is called **saving** the program. QBasic automatically adds a period and the suffix BAS to the name. Therefore, the complete file name is MYPROG1.BAS on the diskette or hard disk and in the Title bar.

14. Suppose you want to write a new program. To clear MYPROG1.BAS from the View window, press the key combination Alt/**F**ile/**N**ew—that is, press and release Alt, then press and release F, and then press N. ***Note:*** If you pressed Alt/F/N before saving the previous program, a dialog box will appear to give you another chance to save it before it is removed. You can use the Tab key to move around inside the dialog box and then press the Enter key to select the highlighted item.

15. At any time, you can restore MYPROG1.BAS as the program in the View window by pressing Alt/**F**ile/**O**pen, typing MYPROG1 (possibly preceded by a drive letter and a colon, such as A:) at the cursor position, and then pressing the Enter key. Alternately, instead of typing and entering MYPROG1, you can enter the appropriate drive letter and a colon, press the Tab key, press the cursor-down key until MYPROG1 is highlighted, and press the Enter key.

Note: The inside front cover of this book lists the key combinations used in this walkthrough.

A Walkthrough of Menus

1. Press the Alt key to activate the Menu bar.

2. Press F to "pull down" the File menu. Notice that the task "New Program" is highlighted and that the Status bar contains a sentence describing the task.

3. Press the cursor-down key to highlight other items in the file menu. At each item, read the description of the task in the Status bar.

4. Press the cursor-right key to examine the other menus.

5. Use the cursor-down key to examine each of the tasks in the menus.

6. Press the Esc key to return to the View window.

Comments:

1. The key sequences discussed in this section have the form key1+key2 or key1/key2. The plus sign (+) instructs you to hold down key1 and then press key2. The slash symbol (/) tells you to release key1 before pressing key2.

2. QBasic has various Help screens that can be called upon for assistance. Press Shift+F1 to obtain information on using QBasic help. The first item of that Help screen states that if the cursor is placed on a keyword and F1 is pressed, an explanation of the use of that keyword will appear on the screen. Press the Esc key to remove the Help screen.

3. Press Alt/**H**elp/**C**ontents to see a listing of several topics for which help is available. Press the Tab key five times and then press the Enter key to obtain a list of editing keys. The PgDn and PgUp keys can be used to scroll the list down and up. Some useful key combinations from this list that we have not discussed yet are:

(a) Ctrl+Home: moves the cursor to the beginning of the program
(b) Ctrl+End: moves the cursor to the end of the program
(c) Alt/F/P/Enter: prints a copy of the current program on the printer
(d) Alt/F/X: exits QBasic and returns to DOS

4. Both Shift+F5 and F5 alone can be used to run a program. The difference between them is that Shift+F5 *always* starts at the beginning of the program whereas F5 doesn't. If the program has been stopped in the middle, F5 will continue execution at that point, while Shift+F5 will rerun the program from the beginning.

5. When the View window is completely filled with program lines, the program scrolls upward to accommodate additional lines. The lines that have scrolled off the top can be viewed again by pressing PgUp. The PgDn key moves farther down the program.

6. There are two methods to clear the View window. You can either erase the lines one at a time with Ctrl+Y or erase all lines simultaneously and begin a new program with Alt/F/N. With the second method, a dialog box may query you about saving the current program. In this case, use Tab to select the desired option and press the Enter key. The program name in the Title bar might change to Untitled.

7. The term **enter a line** means to type in a line of a program and then either press the Enter key with the cursor at the end of the line or use a cursor-moving key to move the cursor off the line. When a line is entered, the editor checks for certain types of errors, capitalizes keywords, and formats the line. For these reasons, the QBasic editor is called a **smart editor**.

8. The QBasic editor can perform many of the tasks of word processors, such as search and block operations. However, these features needn't concern us presently. They are discussed in Appendix G, under "HOW TO: Use the Editor," and in Appendix E.

9. There are many uses of dialog boxes. For instance, they pop up to report errors in a program and to allow us to name a program. In general, the Tab key is used to move around inside a dialog box and the Enter key makes a selection. Although dialog boxes often have a cancel rectangle, the Esc key also can be used to remove the dialog box from the screen.

10. You can perform many QBasic tasks, such as accessing the Menu bar, with a mouse. See Appendix B for details.

11. For most computers, QBasic is invoked by typing QBASIC at the DOS prompt and pressing the Enter key. If this does not work, type DIR \QBASIC.EXE/S at the DOS prompt and press the Enter key. After a few seconds, the screen will display information beginning with four lines that should appear something like this:

```
 Volume in drive C is HARDDISK
 Volume Serial Number is 1234-6789

Directory of C:\DOS

QBASIC   EXE    194309 07-11-95   9:50a
```

The third line identifies the place (directory) where the QBASIC program resides. (In the display above, this is the \DOS directory on drive C.) To invoke QBasic, type CD *nameOfDirectory*, press the Enter key, type QBASIC, and press the Enter key. (In the display above, CD *nameOfDirectory* would be CD \DOS.)

If the fourth line of the displayed information above reads "File not found," then your computer does not have QBasic installed. Consult your lab assistant or instructor.

12. If you are using Windows 95, follow these steps to install QBasic on your hard drive.

    (a) Insert your Windows 95 CD into your CD-ROM drive.
    (b) Wait about ten seconds. If a window titled "Windows 95 CD-ROM" appears, hold down the Alt key and press F4 to remove the window.
    (c) Click the Start button, point to Programs, and click on MS-DOS prompt.
    (d) A prompt (such as C:\WINDOWS) will appear. The first letter is your current hard-drive letter. In step (g) we use the letter C. [If a different first letter appears, use that letter instead of C in step (g).]
    (e) Type the letter of your CD-ROM drive, followed by a colon, and then press the Enter key.
    (f) Type CD\OTHER\OLDMSDOS and press the Enter key.
    (g) Type COPY QBASIC.* C:\WINDOWS\COMMAND and press the Enter key.

PRACTICE PROBLEMS 1.2

(Solutions to Practice Problems always follow the exercises.)

1. What QBasic statement appears as the last statement of the program in the walkthrough?

2. What should you do if no messages appear immediately after you turn on the computer?

EXERCISES 1.2

1. What is the name of the window in which a program is written?

2. What information is given by the two numbers on the right side of the Status bar?

3. What does DOS stand for?

4. What command clears the screen?

5. By what name is a program known before it is named as part of being saved on disk?

6. What is the small blinking dash called, and what is its purpose?

7. What is a toggle key?

8. Name three toggle keys.

Figure 1.6 shows many of the special keys on the keyboard. In Exercises 9 through 38 select the key (or key combination) that performs the task.

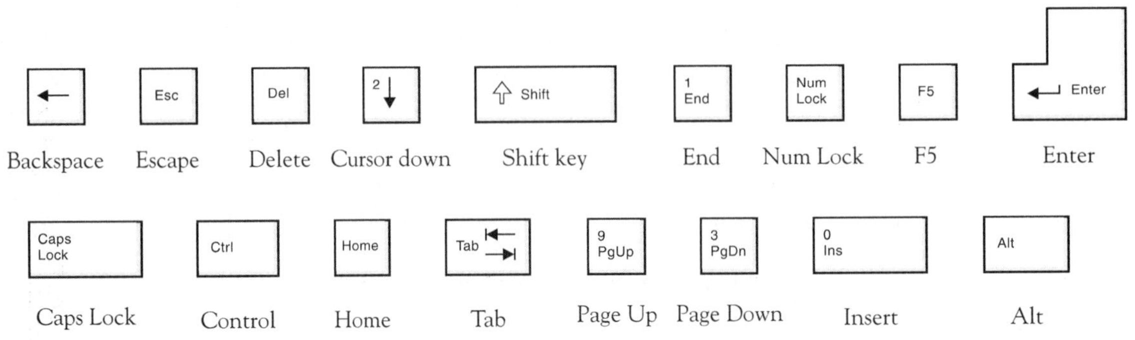

Figure 1.6 Some Special Keys

9. Erase the line containing the cursor.
10. Toggle from insert mode to overwrite mode.
11. Erase the character to the left of the cursor.
12. Toggle the Numeric keypad between states.
13. Erase the character at the cursor.
14. Toggle the case for alphabetic characters.
15. Move the cursor to the beginning of the line containing the cursor.
16. Move the cursor to the end of the line containing the cursor.
17. Run the current program.
18. Cause the upper character of a double-character key to be displayed.
19. Move the cursor down to the next row of the screen.
20. Print a copy of the current program on the printer.
21. Exit QBasic and return to DOS.
22. Move the cursor to the beginning of the program.
23. Move the cursor to the end of the program.
24. Move the cursor from the View window to the Menu bar.
25. Cancel a dialog box.
26. Move from the Menu bar to the View window.
27. Move from one option rectangle of a dialog box to another rectangle.
28. Save the current program on a diskette.
29. Clear the current program from the View window and start a new program.
30. Create a blank line in the middle of a program.
31. With the cursor at the end of a line, begin a new line.
32. Remove a pull-down menu from the screen.

33. Obtain information about the keyword located at the cursor.

34. Look at the Output screen.

35. Scroll the program to view a higher part.

36. Scroll the program to view a lower part.

37. Obtain a listing of topics for which help is available.

38. Obtain information on using QBasic help.

Exercises 39 through 42 require several tasks from the QBasic environment.

39. Enter, run, and save the following program. (Give the program the name HAPPY.BAS when saving it.)

```
CLS
PLAY "CCDCFE"
PRINT "Happy Birthday"
END
```

40. Add the following line to the program in Exercise 39 just before the END statement. What three changes occur when the cursor is moved off the line?

```
print "to ";"you.
```

41. Remove any previously written program from the View window and then enter and run the following program. Then save the program with the name HAPPY.BAS.

```
CLS
FOR i = 1 TO 65
  LOCATE 12, i
  PRINT " Happy Birthday"
NEXT i
END
```

42. Use the Open command from the File window to load the program written during the walkthrough.

SOLUTIONS TO PRACTICE PROBLEMS 1.2

1. The END statement. Although this statement is optional, good programming style requires its use.

2. Wait 15 to 20 seconds. The computer uses this time to perform diagnostic tests and check its memory locations.

1.3 USING DISKETTES AND DOS

Note: This section can be skipped for the time being and referred to as needed.

We assume your computer has a hard disk and at least one diskette drive. The hard disk is permanently housed in a drive inside the computer. Figure 1.7 shows the most common type of diskette.

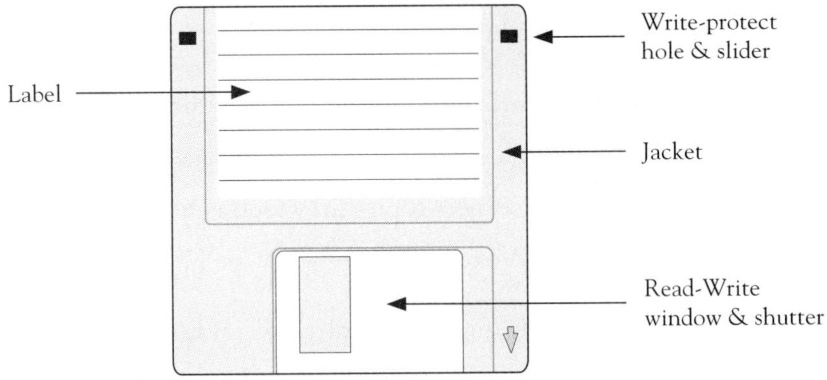

Figure 1.7 3½″ Diskette

The 3½″ diskette in Figure 1.7 has a plastic jacket. When the diskette is inserted into the drive, the shutter slides to the right and exposes the read-write window. The diskette drive records and reads data through the read-write window. The write-protect hole is normally covered. When the write-protect hole is uncovered by sliding the slider on the back of the diskette, nothing can be erased from or recorded on the diskette. To insert a diskette, hold the diskette with the label facing up and the read/write window pointing toward the diskette drive. You insert the diskette by pushing it into the drive until you hear a click. You remove it by pressing the button on the drive.

When handling a diskette, be careful not to touch the exposed surface in the read-write window. Also, do not remove a diskette from a diskette drive while the little light on the diskette drive is lit.

We use the word **disk** to refer to either the hard disk, a diskette, or a CD. Each disk drive is identified by a letter. Often a hard drive is identified by C, the diskette drive by A, and the CD drive by D or E.

Each computer comes with a set of DOS (Disk Operating System) programs on the hard disk. The DOS programs carry out disk operations. After DOS has been invoked, we say that the computer is in the DOS environment. After QBasic has been invoked, we say that the computer is in the QBasic environment. To return to DOS from QBasic, execute the Exit command from the File menu by pressing Alt/F/X.

At any time, one of the drives, called the **current drive** or **default drive**, is given preferential treatment. When DOS is first invoked, normally the prompt C:\> appears and the C drive is the default drive. To change the default drive to A, enter A:. The prompt will change to A:\>.

Files and Directories

Disks hold not only programs but also collections of data stored in **data files**. The term **file** refers to either a program or a data file. In Section 1.2 we created a program file. Chapters 8 and 9 are devoted to data files. Each file has a name consisting of a **base name** of at most eight characters followed by an optional **extension** consisting of a period and at most three characters. Letters, digits, and a few other assorted characters (see Comment 1) can be used in either the base name or the extension. Blank spaces are not allowed. Some examples of file names are INCOME.94, CUSTOMER.DAT, and FORT500.

Since a disk is capable of storing thousands of files, locating a specific file can be quite time consuming. Therefore, DOS allows related files to be grouped into directories.

Think of a disk as a large envelope, called the root envelope, which contains several smaller envelopes, each with its own name. (The naming of envelopes follows the same rule as the naming of files.) Each of these smaller envelopes can contain yet other named envelopes. Each envelope is identified by listing it preceded by the successively larger envelopes that contain it, with each envelope name preceded by a backslash. Such a sequence is called a **path**. For instance, the path \SALES\NY.90\JULY identifies the envelope JULY, contained in the envelope NY.90, which in turn is contained in the envelope SALES.

Think of a file name as written on a slip of paper that can be placed into either the root envelope or any of the smaller envelopes. At any time, we can select one of the envelopes. The selected envelope is called the **current** envelope. All commands to place a slip of paper into an envelope or list the contents of an envelope refer to the current envelope unless a path leading to another envelope is specified. In the language of directories, the root envelope is the **root directory**, the other envelopes are **subdirectories**, and the current envelope is the **current directory**.

When DOS is first invoked, the root directory of the current drive is the current directory. The command

```
CD pathName
```

tells DOS to change the current directory to the directory at the end of the named path. The command

```
CD \
```

makes the root directory the current directory.

The command

```
MD directoryName
```

tells DOS to create a new subdirectory with the specified name in the current directory of the current drive.

The command

```
RD directoryName
```

tells DOS to remove the specified subdirectory from the current directory of the current drive. A subdirectory can be removed only if it has no files or subdirectories. The current directory cannot be removed.

The combination of a drive letter followed by a colon, a path, and a file name is called a **filespec**, an abbreviation of "file specification." Some examples of filespecs are C:\DOS\QBASIC.EXE and A:\PERSONAL\INCOME94.DAT. If the drive (along with the colon) or the path is omitted, then the file is assumed to reside in the current drive or the current directory, respectively.

Other DOS Commands

Some other commands that can be executed in DOS are FORMAT, DIR, COPY, ERASE, and RENAME.

FORMAT

The first time a blank diskette is used, it must be formatted for the computer. The formatting process is analogous to preparing graph paper by drawing grid lines. Let's assume the unformatted diskette is in the A drive, and the current drive is C. To format the diskette, enter

```
FORMAT A:
```

and then follow the directions displayed on the screen. While the formatting is taking place, the light on the A drive will be on, the blank diskette will spin, and the percentage of the diskette formatted will be displayed. After about one minute, the message "Format complete" will appear on the screen, and you will be prompted for a volume label. A volume label is a name (consisting of 1 to 11 characters) for your diskette. You can decline to specify a volume label by pressing the Enter key. You will be informed of the amount of space on the diskette, and the statement "Format another (Y/N)?" will be displayed. Answer the question by pressing either the Y or N key and then the Enter key. If the answer is N, the DOS prompt will appear and await your next command. If the answer is Y, the steps above will be repeated.

Caution: Formatting any disk destroys all its existing files. The hard disk is formatted when the computer is first readied for use, so never enter FORMAT C:.

DIR

The command

```
DIR
```

displays the names of the files and subdirectories in the current directory. (Periods are omitted and the base names are separated from the extensions.)

If the disk has more than a screenful of files, enter the command

```
DIR /P
```

which makes the computer display just a screenful of files at a time.

The command

```
DIR *.BAS
```

displays only files with the extension BAS. To generalize, the command

```
DIR *.ext
```

displays only files with the specified extension and the command

```
DIR baseName.*
```

displays only files with the specified base name.

COPY

The command COPY is used to make a second copy of a file. The command

```
COPY filespec A:
```

copies the specified file to the current directory of the diskette in drive A. In general, the command

```
COPY filespec path:
```

copies the specified file to the location specified by the path.

ERASE

The command

```
ERASE filespec
```

removes the specified file from the disk. For instance, the command ERASE A:\ACCOUNTS.BAS deletes the file ACCOUNTS.BAS from the root directory of the diskette in drive A.

RENAME

The command

```
RENAME filename1 filename2
```

changes the name of the file identified as *filename1* to the new name *filename2*. The new name must be different from the name of any file in the current directory.

Comments:

1. File names can consist of digits, letters of the alphabet, and the characters & ! _ @ ' ' ~ ( ) { } – # % $. Spaces are not allowed in file names.
2. Neither DOS nor QBasic distinguishes between upper- and lowercase letters in file names. For instance, the names COSTS89.BAS, Costs89.Bas, and costs89.bas are equivalent. DOS always displays file names with uppercase characters.
3. The asterisk used with the DIR command is called a **wildcard character**. It also can be used with COPY or ERASE to apply the command to many files at once. For instance, COPY *.BAS A: copies files with extension .BAS to the A drive, ERASE TEMP.* erases files with base name TEMP, and COPY *.* B: copies all files in the current directory of the current drive to drive B.
4. The QBasic command NAME can be used in a program to change the file name of any file on any disk. The statement

   ```
   NAME "filename1" AS "filename2"
   ```

   has the same effect as the corresponding DOS command RENAME. Note that with the NAME command, *filename1* and *filename2* must each be surrounded by quotation marks.

5. The QBasic command

```
KILL "filespec"
```

can be used in a program and has the same effect as the DOS command ERASE. Note that with the KILL command, *filespec* must be surrounded by quotation marks.

6. If the name of a QBasic program is not given an extension when saved, QBasic automatically gives it the extension .BAS. This extension can be omitted when opening the program with Alt/F/O but must be used when deleting or renaming the program.

7. The QBasic environment provides a list of the programs on a disk at appropriate times. For instance, pressing Alt/F/O to open a program produces a dialog box similar to the one in Figure 1.9. The file to be retrieved from the disk can either be typed into the narrow rectangle at the top or selected from the list of QBasic programs in the lower rectangle. To make a selection from the listed programs, press Tab to move to the lower rectangle, use the cursor-moving keys to highlight the desired program, and then press the Enter key. With a mouse, you can select a program by double-clicking on it.

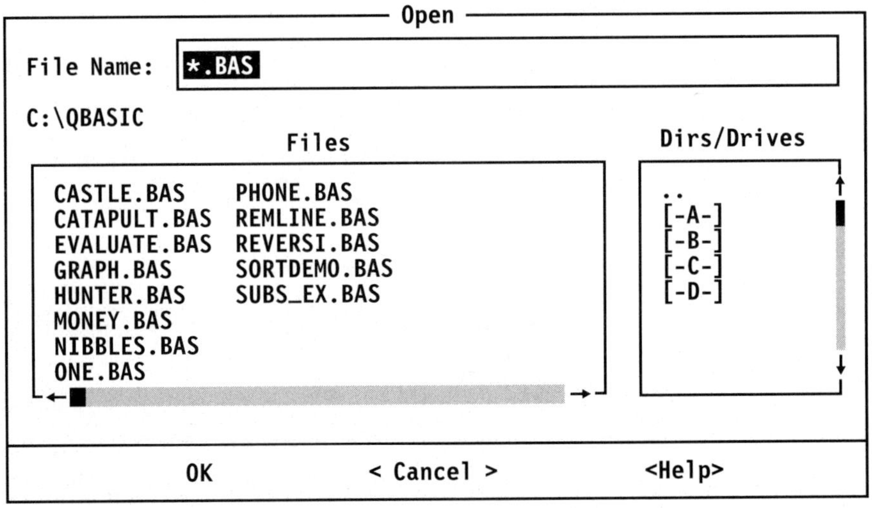

Figure 1.9 Dialog Box for Opening a File

PRACTICE PROBLEMS 1.3

1. The commands KILL "OPUS.1" and ERASE OPUS.1 both remove the file named OPUS.1 from a disk. What is the criterion for deciding when a file name must be enclosed by quotes?

2. Suppose you have saved a QBasic program with the name MYPROG on drive A and you now want to erase the program from the disk. You execute the command KILL "A:MYPROG" from a QBasic program and receive the error message "File not found." What happened?

EXERCISES 1.3

In Exercises 1 through 9, give the DOS command that accomplishes the stated task.

1. Reproduce a file on another disk.
2. Delete a file from a disk.
3. Change the name of a file.
4. Prepare a new diskette for use.
5. List the files in the current directory.
6. Change the current disk drive to drive B.
7. Create a new subdirectory of the current directory.
8. Change the current directory.
9. Remove a subdirectory of the current directory.

In Exercises 10 and 11, give the QBasic command that accomplishes the stated task.

10. Delete a program from a disk.
11. Change the name of a program.
12. Suppose your computer has just one diskette drive. How could you use the commands discussed in this section to copy all the files in the root directory of a diskette onto another diskette?

SOLUTIONS TO PRACTICE PROBLEMS 1.3

1. The criterion is the "environment" that the user is in. File names used in QBasic programs must always be enclosed in quotes. File names used in DOS are never enclosed in quotes.
2. Since an extension was not specified when the program was saved, QBasic added the extension BAS. The proper command to erase the program is KILL "A:MYPROG.BAS".

1.4 BIOGRAPHICAL HISTORY OF COMPUTING

The following people made important contributions to the evolution of the computer and the principles of programming.

1800s

George Boole: a self-taught British mathematician; devised an algebra of logic that later became a key tool in computer design. The logical operators presented in Section 5.1 are also known as Boolean operators.

Charles Babbage: a British mathematician and engineer; regarded as the father of the computer. Although the mechanical "analytical engine" that he conceived was never built, it influenced the design of modern computers. It had units for input, output, memory, arithmetic, logic, and control. Algorithms were intended to be communicated to the computer via punched cards, and numbers were to be stored on toothed wheels.

Augusta Ada Byron: a mathematician and colleague of Charles Babbage; regarded as the first computer programmer. She encouraged Babbage to modify the design based on programming considerations. Together they developed the concepts of decision structures, loops, and a library of procedures. Decision structures, loops, and procedures are presented in Chapters 5, 6, and 4 of this text respectively.

Herman Hollerith: the founder of a company that was later to become IBM; at the age of 20 he devised a computer that made it possible to process the data for the U.S. Census of 1890 in one-third the time required for the 1880 census. His electromagnetic "tabulating machine" passed metal pins through holes in punched cards and into mercury-filled cups to complete an electronic circuit. Each location of a hole corresponded to a characteristic of the population.

1930s

Alan Turing: a gifted and far-sighted British mathematician; made fundamental contributions to the theory of computer science, assisted in the construction of some of the early large computers, and proposed a test for detecting intelligence within a machine. His theoretical "Turing machine" laid the foundation for the development of general-purpose programmable computers. He changed the course of the Second World War by breaking the German "Enigma" code, thereby making secret German messages comprehensible to the Allies.

John V. Atanasoff: a mathematician and physicist at Iowa State University; declared by a federal court in Minnesota to be the inventor of the first electronic digital special-purpose computer. Designed with the assistance of his graduate assistant, Clifford Berry, this computer used vacuum tubes (instead of the less efficient relays) for storage and arithmetic functions.

1940s

Howard Aiken: a professor at Harvard University; built the Mark I, a large-scale digital computer functionally similar to the "analytical engine" proposed by Babbage. This computer, which took five years to build and used relays for storage and computations, was technologically obsolete before it was completed.

Grace M. Hopper: retired in 1986 at the age of 79 as a rear admiral in the United States Navy; wrote the first major subroutine (a procedure used to calculate sin *x* on the Mark I computer) and one of the first assembly languages. In 1945 she found that a moth fused into a wire of the Mark I was causing the computer to malfunction, thus the origin of the term "debugging" for finding errors. As an administrator at Remington Rand in the 1950s, Dr. Hopper pioneered the development and use of COBOL, a programming language for the business community written in English-like notation.

John Mauchley and J. Presper Eckert: electrical engineers working at the University of Pennsylvania; built the first large-scale electronic digital general-purpose computer to be put into full operation. The ENIAC used 18,000 vacuum tubes for storage and arithmetic computations, weighed 30 tons, and occupied 1500 square feet. It could perform 300 multiplications of 2 10-digit numbers per second, whereas the Mark I required 3 seconds to perform a single multiplication. Later they designed and developed the UNIVAC I, the first commercial electronic computer.

John von Neumann: a mathematical genius and member of the Institute of Advanced Studies in Princeton, New Jersey; developed the stored program concept used in all modern computers. Prior to this development, instructions were programmed into computers by manually rewiring connections. Along with Hermann H. Goldstein, he wrote the first paper on the use of flowcharts.

Stanislaw Ulam: American research mathematician and educator; pioneered the application of random numbers and computers to the solution of problems in mathematics and physics. His techniques, known as Monte Carlo methods or computer simulation, are used in Chapter 11 to determine the likelihoods of various outcomes of games of chance and to analyze business operations.

Maurice V. Wilkes: an electrical engineer at Cambridge University in England and student of von Neumann; built the EDSAC, the first computer to use the stored-program concept. Along with D.J. Wheeler and S. Gill, he wrote the first computer programming text, *The Preparation of Programs for an Electronic Digital Computer* (Addison-Wesley, 1951), which dealt in depth with the use and construction of a versatile subroutine library.

John Bardeen, ***Walter Brattain***, and ***William Shockley:*** physicists at Bell Labs; developed the transistor, a miniature device that replaced the vacuum tube and revolutionized computer design. It was smaller, lighter, more reliable, and cooler than the vacuum tube.

1950s

John Backus: a programmer for IBM; in 1953 headed a small group of programmers who wrote the most extensively used early interpretive computer system, the IBM 701 Speedcoding System. An interpreter translates a high-level language program into machine language one statement at a time as the program is executed. In 1957, Backus and his team produced the compiled language Fortran, which soon became the primary academic and scientific language. A compiler translates an entire program into efficient machine language *before* the program is executed. QBasic combines the best of both worlds. It has the power and speed of a compiled language and the ease of use of an interpreted language.

Donald L. Shell: in 1959, the year that he received his Ph.D. in mathematics from the University of Cincinnati, published an efficient algorithm for ordering (or sorting) lists of data. Sorting has been estimated to consume nearly one-quarter of the running time of computers. The Shell sort is presented in Chapter 7 of this text.

1960s

John G. Kemeny and Thomas E. Kurtz: professors of mathematics at Dartmouth College and the inventors of BASIC; led Dartmouth to national leadership in the educational uses of computing. Kemeny's distinguished career included serving as an assistant to both John von Neumann and Albert Einstein, serving as president of Dartmouth College, and chairing the commission to investigate the Three Mile Island accident. In recent years, Kemeny and Kurtz have devoted considerable energy to the promotion of structured BASIC.

Corrado Bohm and Guiseppe Jacopini: two European mathematicians; proved that any program can be written with the three structures discussed in Section 2.2: sequences, decisions, and loops. This result led to the systematic methods of modern program design known as structured programming.

Edsger W. Dijkstra: professor of computer science at the Technological University at Eindhoven, The Netherlands; stimulated the move to structured programming with the publication of a widely read article, "Go To Statement Considered Harmful." In that article he proposes that GOTO statements be abolished from all high-level languages such as BASIC. The modern programming structures available in QBasic do away with the need for GOTO statements.

Harlan B. Mills: IBM Fellow and Professor of Computer Science at the University of Maryland; has long advocated the use of structured programming. In 1969, Mills was asked to write a program creating an information database for the *New York Times*, a project that was estimated to require thirty man-years with traditional programming techniques. Using structured programming techniques, Mills single-handedly completed the project in six months. The methods of structured programming are used throughout this text.

Donald E. Knuth: Professor of Computer Science at Stanford University; is generally regarded as the preeminent scholar of computer science in the world. He is best known for his monumental series of books, *The Art of Computer Programming,* the definitive work on algorithms. The algorithm presented in Exercise 27 of Section 11.1 of this text is an example of the programming gems appearing in Knuth's books.

Ted Hoff, Stan Mazer, Robert Noyce, and Federico Faggin: engineers at the Intel Corporation; developed the first microprocessor chip. Such chips, which serve as the central processing units for microcomputers, are responsible for the extraordinary reduction in the size of computers. A computer with greater power than the ENIAC can now be held in the palm of the hand.

1970s

Paul Allen and Bill Gates: cofounders of Microsoft Corporation; developed languages and the operating system for the IBM PC. The operating system, known as MS-DOS, is a collection of programs that manage the operation of the computer. In 1974, Gates dropped out of Harvard after one year, and Allen left a programming job with Honeywell to write software together. Their initial project was a version of BASIC for the Altair, the first microcomputer. Microsoft is one of the most highly respected software companies in the United States and a leader in the development of programming languages.

Stephen Wozniak and Stephen Jobs: cofounders of Apple Computer Inc.; started the microcomputer revolution. The two had met as teenagers while working summers at Hewlett-Packard. Another summer, Jobs worked in an orchard, a job that inspired the names of their computers. Wozniak designed the Apple computer in Jobs' parents' garage and Jobs promoted it so successfully that the company was worth hundreds of millions of dollars when it went public. Both men resigned from the company in 1985. Jobs returned in 1997.

Dan Bricklin and Dan Fylstra: cofounders of Software Arts; wrote VisiCalc, the first electronic spreadsheet program. An electronic spreadsheet is a worksheet divided into rows and columns, which analysts use to construct budgets and estimate costs. A change made in one number results in the updating of all numbers derived from it. For instance, changing a person's housing expenses will immediately produce a change in his total expenses. Bricklin got the idea for an electronic spreadsheet after watching one of his professors at the Harvard Business School struggle while updating a spreadsheet at the blackboard. VisiCalc became so popular that many people bought personal computers just so they could run the program. A simplified spreadsheet is developed as a case study in Section 7.5 of this text.

Robert Barnaby: a dedicated programmer; best known for writing WordStar, one of the most popular word processors. Word processing programs account for 30% of all software sold in the United States. The QBasic editor uses WordStar-like commands.

1980s

William L. Sydnes: manager of the IBM Entry Systems Boca engineering group; headed the design team for the IBM Personal Computer. Shortly after its introduction in 1981, the IBM PC dominated the microcomputer field. QBasic runs on all IBM Personal Computers and compatibles.

Mitchell D. Kapor: cofounder of Lotus Corporation; wrote the business software program 1-2-3, one of the most successful piece of software for personal computers. Lotus 1-2-3 is an integrated program consisting of a spreadsheet, a database manager, and a graphics package. Databases are studied in Chapters 8 and 9 of this text and graphics in Chapter 10.

Tom Button: group product manager for applications programmability at Microsoft; headed the team that developed QuickBasic, QBasic, and Visual Basic. These modern, easy-to-use languages have greatly increased the productivity of programmers.

Alan Cooper: director of applications software for Coactive Computing Corporation; is considered the father of Visual Basic. In 1987 he wrote a program called "Ruby" that delivered visual programming to the average user. A few years later, Ruby was combined with QuickBasic to produce Visual Basic, the remarkably successful language that allows Windows programs to be written from within Windows easily and efficiently.

Tim Berners-Lee: British computer scientist, proposed the World Wide Web project in 1989 while working in Switzerland. His brainchild has grown into a global phenomenon.

1990s

Mark Andreessen: while a graduate student at the University of Illinois, led a small band of fellow students to develop Mosaic, a program that allowed the user to move around the World Wide Web by clicking on words and symbols. Andreessen went on to cofound Netscape Communications Corporation; today Netscape is the world's leading Web browser. Visual Basic can be used to build a simplified Web browser.

2

Problem Solving

2.1 PROGRAM DEVELOPMENT CYCLE

We learned in the first chapter that hardware refers to the machinery in a computer system (such as the monitor, keyboard, and CPU) and software refers to a collection of instructions, called a program, that directs the hardware. Programs are written to solve problems or perform tasks on a computer. Programmers translate the solutions or tasks into a language the computer can understand. As we write programs, we must keep in mind that the computer will only do what we instruct it to do. Because of this, we must be very careful and thorough with our instructions.

Designing a Computer Program

The first step in designing a program is to determine what the **output** of the program should be—that is, exactly what the program should produce. The second step is to identify the data, or **input**, necessary to obtain the output. The last step is to determine how to **process** the input to obtain the desired output, that is, to determine what formulas or ways of doing things can be used to obtain the output.

This problem-solving approach is the same as that used to solve word problems in an algebra class. For example, consider the following algebra problem:

How fast is a car traveling if it goes 50 miles in 2 hours?

The first step is to determine the type of answer requested. The answer should be a number giving the rate of speed in miles per hour (the output). The information needed to obtain the answer is the distance and time the car has traveled (the input). The formula

$$\text{rate} = \text{distance} / \text{time}$$

is used to process the distance traveled and the time elapsed in order to determine the rate of speed. That is,

$$\begin{aligned} \text{rate} &= 50 \text{ miles} / 2 \text{ hours} \\ &= 25 \text{ miles} / \text{hour} \end{aligned}$$

A pictorial representation of this problem-solving process is

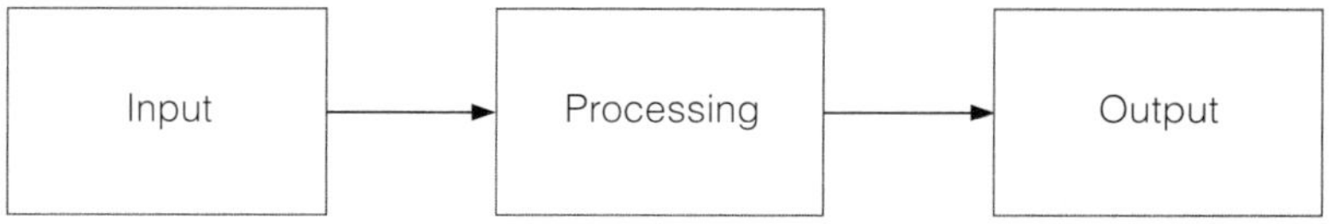

We determine what we want as output, get the needed input, and process the input to produce the desired output. In the following chapters we discuss how to write programs to carry out the above operations. But first we look at the general process of writing programs.

Program Planning

A recipe provides a good example of a plan. The ingredients and the amounts are determined by what is to be baked. That is, the *output* determines the *input* and the *processing*. The recipe, or plan, reduces the number of mistakes you might make if you tried to bake with no plan at all. While it's difficult to imagine an architect building a bridge or a factory without a detailed plan, many programmers (particularly students in their first programming course) frequently try to write programs without first making a careful plan. The more complicated the problem, the more complex the plan must be. You will spend much less time working on a program if you devise a carefully thought out step-by-step plan and test it before actually writing the program.

Many programmers plan their programs using a sequence of steps, referred to as the **program development cycle**. The following step-by-step process will enable you to use your time efficiently and help you design error-free programs that produce the desired output.

1. ***Analysis:*** Define the problem.

   Be sure you understand what the program should do—that is, what the output should be. Have a clear idea of what data (or inputs) are given and the relationship between the input and the desired output.

2. ***Design:*** Plan the solution to the problem.

   Find a logical sequence of precise steps that solve the problem. Such a sequence of steps is called an **algorithm**. Every detail, including obvious steps, should appear in the algorithm. In the next section we discuss three popular methods used to develop the logic plan: flowcharts, pseudocode, and top-down charts. These tools help the programmer break a problem into a sequence of small tasks the computer can perform to solve the problem.

   Planning also involves using representative data to test the logic of the algorithm by hand to ensure that it is correct.

3. ***Coding:*** Translate the algorithm into a programming language.

   Coding is the technical word for writing the program. During this stage, the program is written in QBasic and entered into the computer. The programmer uses the algorithm devised in step 2 along with a knowledge of QBasic.

4. ***Testing and debugging:*** Locate and remove any errors in the program.

   Testing is the process of finding errors in a program and **debugging** is the process of correcting errors that are found. (An error in a program is called a **bug.**) As the program is typed into the View window, QBasic's smart editor points out certain types of program errors. Other types of errors will be detected by QBasic when the program is executed; however, many errors due to typing mistakes, flaws in the algorithm, or incorrect usages of the QBasic language rules can only be uncovered and corrected by careful detective work. An example of such an error would be using addition when multiplication was the proper operation.

5. ***Completing the documentation:*** Organize all the material that describes the program.

   Documentation is intended to allow another person, or the programmer at a later date, to understand the program. Internal documentation consists of statements in the program that are not executed but point out the purposes of various parts of the program. Documentation might also consist of a detailed description of what the program does and how to use the program (for instance, what type of input is expected). For commercial programs, documentation includes an instruction manual. Other types of documentation are the flowchart, pseudocode, and top-down chart that were used to construct the program. Although documentation is listed as the last step in the program development cycle, it should take place as the program is being coded.

2.2 PROGRAMMING TOOLS

This section discusses some specific algorithms and develops three tools used to convert algorithms into computer programs: flowcharts, pseudocode, and top-down charts.

You use algorithms every day to make decisions and perform tasks. For instance, whenever you mail a letter, you must decide how much postage to put on the envelope. One rule of thumb is to use one stamp for every five sheets of paper or fraction thereof. Suppose a friend asks you to determine the number of stamps to place on an envelope. The following algorithm will accomplish the task.

1. Request the number of sheets of paper, call it Sheets. *(input)*
2. Divide Sheets by 5. *(processing)*
3. Round the quotient up to the next highest whole number, call it Stamps. *(processing)*
4. Reply with the number Stamps. *(output)*

The algorithm above takes the number of sheets (Sheets) as input, processes the data, and produces the number of stamps needed (Stamps) as output. We can test the algorithm for a letter with 16 sheets of paper.

1. Request the number of sheets of paper, Sheets = 16.
2. Dividing 5 into 16 gives 3.2.
3. Rounding 3.2 up to 4 gives Stamps = 4.
4. Reply with the answer, 4 stamps.

This problem-solving example can be pictured by

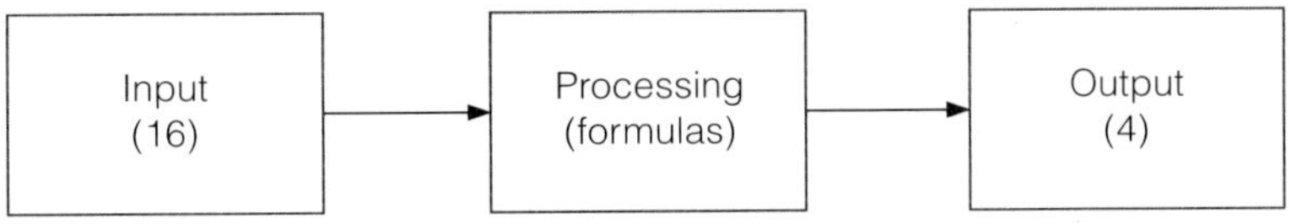

Of the program design tools available, the three most popular are the following:

Flowcharts: Graphically depict the logical steps of the program and show how the steps relate to each other.

Pseudocode: Uses English-like phrases with some QBasic terms to outline the program.

Top-down charts: Show how the different parts of a program relate to each other.

Flowcharts

A flowchart consists of special geometric symbols connected by arrows. Within each symbol is a phrase presenting the activity at that step. The shape of the symbol indicates the type of operation that is to take place. For instance, the parallelogram denotes input or output. The arrows connecting the symbols, called **flowlines**, show the progression in which the steps take place. Flowcharts should "flow" from the top of the page to the bottom. Although the symbols used in flowcharts are standardized, no standards exist for the amount of detail required within each symbol.

Below is a table of the flowchart symbols adopted by the American National Standards Institute (ANSI). Figure 2.1 shows the flowchart for the Postage Stamp problem.

Symbol	Name	Meaning
	Flowline	Used to connect symbols and indicate the flow of logic.
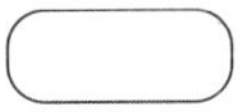	*Terminal*	Used to represent the beginning (Start) or the end (End) of a program.
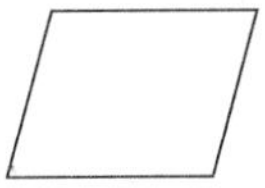	*Input/Output*	Used for input and output operations, such as reading and printing. The data to be read or printed are described inside.
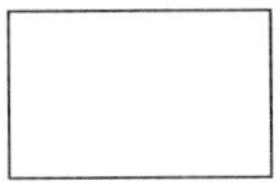	*Processing*	Used for arithmetic and data-manipulation operations. The instructions are listed inside the symbol.
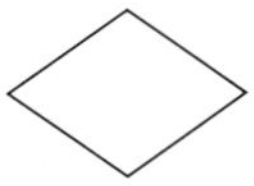	*Decision*	Used for any logic or comparison operations. Unlike the input/output and processing symbols, which have one entry and one exit flowline, the decision symbol has one entry and two exit paths. The path chosen depends on whether the answer to a question is "yes" or "no."

	**Connector**	Used to join different flowlines.
	**Offpage Connector**	Used to indicate that the flowchart continues to a second page.
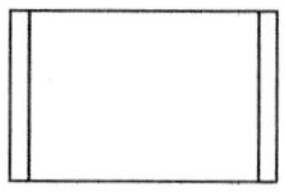	**Predefined Process**	Used to represent a group of statements that perform one processing task.
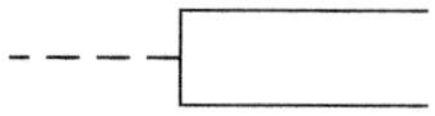	**Annotation**	Used to provide additional information about another flowchart symbol.

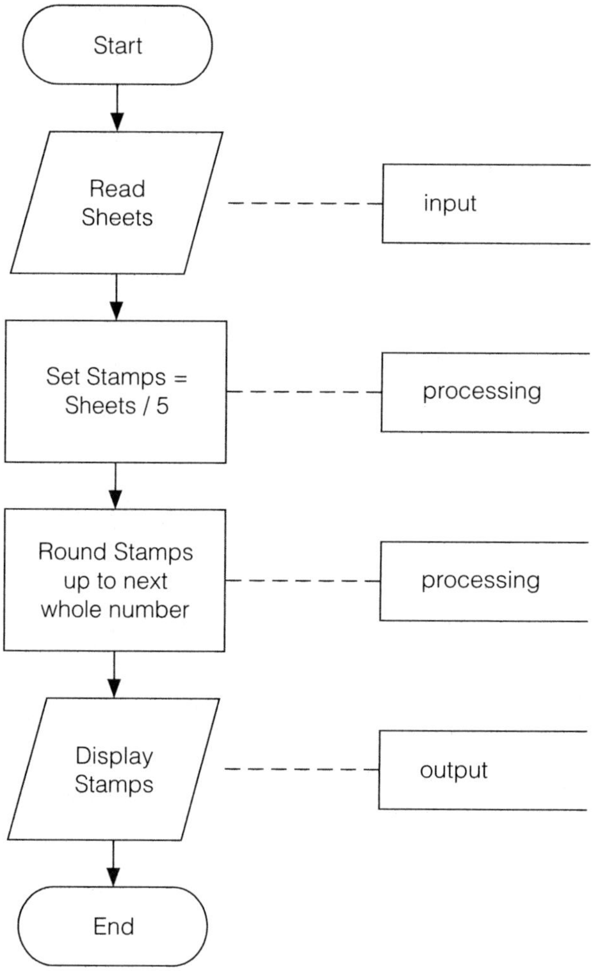

Figure 2.1 Flowchart for the Postage Stamp Problem

The main advantage of using a flowchart to plan a program is that it provides a pictorial representation of the program, which makes the program logic easier to follow. We can clearly see every step of the program and how each step is connected to the next. The major disadvantage with flowcharts is that when a program is very large, the flowcharts may continue for many pages, making them hard to follow and modify.

Pseudocode

Pseudocode is an abbreviated version of actual computer code (hence, *pseudocode*). The geometric symbols used in flowcharts are replaced by English-like statements that outline the program. As a result, pseudocode looks more like a program than does a flowchart. Pseudocode allows the programmer to focus on the steps required to solve a problem rather than on how to use the computer language. The programmer can describe the algorithm in QBasic-like form without being restricted by the rules of QBasic. When the pseudocode is completed, it can be easily translated into the QBasic language.

The following is pseudocode for the Postage Stamp problem:

```
Program: Determine the proper number of stamps for a letter
Read Sheets                                                   (input)
Set the number of stamps to Sheets / 5                        (processing)
Round the number of stamps up to the next whole number        (processing)
Display the number of stamps                                  (output)
```

Pseudocode has several advantages. It is compact and probably will not extend for many pages as flowcharts commonly do. Also, the plan looks like the code to be written and so is preferred by many programmers.

Top-Down Chart

The last programming tool we'll discuss is the top-down chart, which shows the overall program structure. Top-down charts are also called hierarchy charts, HIPO (Hierarchy plus Input-Process-Output) charts, structure charts, or VTOC (Visual Table of Contents) charts. All these names refer to planning diagrams that are similar to a company's organization chart. Top-down charts depict the organization of a program but omit the specific processing logic. They describe what each part, or **module**, of the program does and they show how the modules relate to each other. The details on how the modules work, however, are omitted. The chart is read from top to bottom and from left to right. Each module may be subdivided into a succession of submodules that branch out under it. Typically, after the activities in the succession of submodules are carried out, the module to the right of the original module is considered. A quick glance at the top-down chart reveals each task performed in the program and where it is performed. Figure 2.2 shows a top-down chart for the Postage Stamp problem.

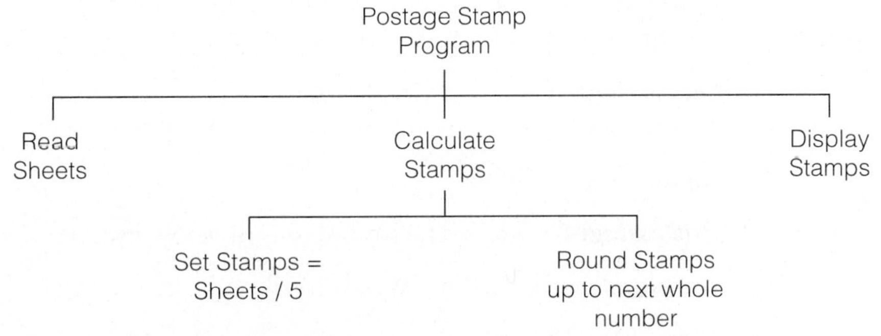

Figure 2.2 Top-Down Chart for the Postage Stamp Problem

The main benefit of top-down charts is in the initial planning of a program. We break down the major parts of a program so we can see what must be done in general. From this point, we can then refine each module into more detailed plans using flowcharts or pseudocode. This process is called the **divide-and-conquer** method.

The Postage Stamp problem was solved by a series of instructions to read data, perform calculations, and display results. Each step was in a sequence; that is, we moved from one line to the next without skipping over any lines. This kind of structure is called a **sequence structure**. Many problems, however, require a decision to determine whether a series of instructions should be executed. If the answer to a question is "Yes," then one group of instructions is executed. If the answer is "No," then another is executed. This structure is called a **decision structure**. Figure 2.3 contains the pseudocode and flowchart for a decision structure.

```
IF condition is true THEN
    Process step(s) 1
  ELSE
    Process step(s) 2
END IF
```

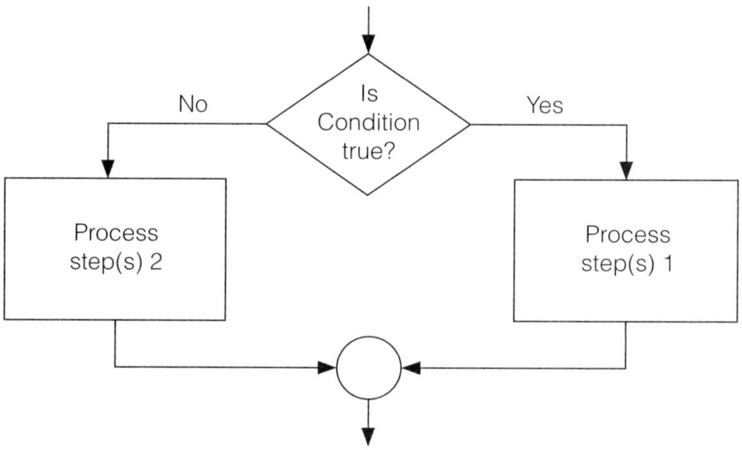

Figure 2.3 Pseudocode and Flowchart for a Decision Structure

The sequence and decision structures are both used to solve the following problem.

Direction of Numbered New York Streets Algorithm

Problem: Given a street number of a one-way street in New York City, decide the direction of the street, either eastbound or westbound.

Discussion: There is a simple rule to tell the direction of a one-way street in New York City: Even-numbered streets run eastbound.

Input: Street number

Processing: Decide if street number is divisible by 2.

Output: "Eastbound" or "Westbound"

Figures 2.4 through 2.6 show the flowchart, pseudocode, and top-down chart for the New York City Numbered Streets problem.

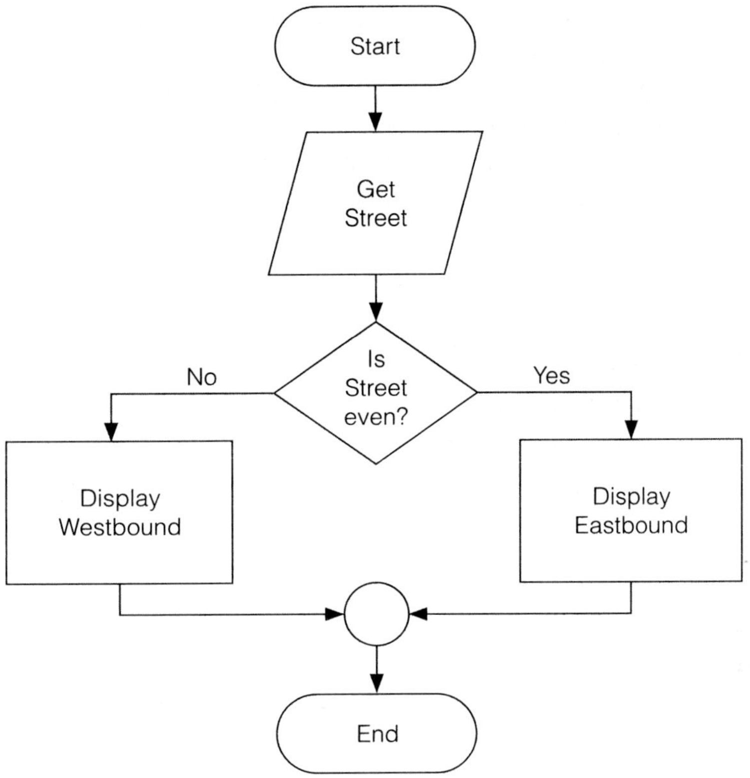

Figure 2.4 Flowchart for the New York City Numbered Streets Problem.

```
Program: Determine the direction of a numbered NYC street
Get Street
IF Street is even THEN
   Display Eastbound
 ELSE
   Display Westbound
END IF
```

Figure 2.5 Pseudocode for the New York City Numbered Streets Problem

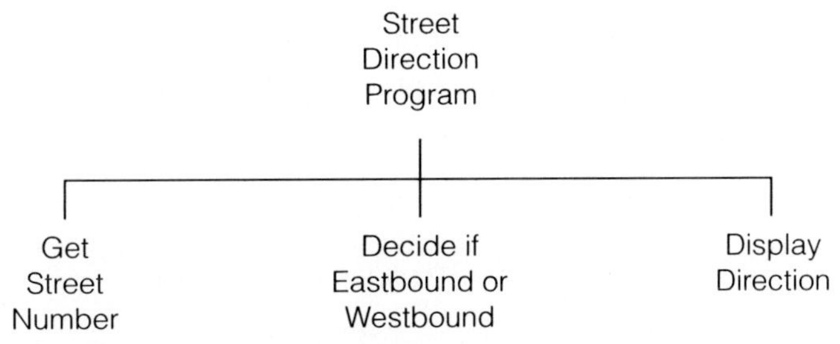

Figure 2.6 Top-Down Chart for the New York City Numbered Streets Problem

The solution to the next problem requires the repetition of a series of instructions. A programming structure that executes instructions many times is called a **loop structure**.

We need a test (or decision) to tell when the loop should end. Without an exit condition, the loop would repeat endlessly (an infinite loop). One way to control the number of times a loop repeats (often referred to as the number of passes or iterations) is to check a condition before each pass through the loop and continue executing the loop so long as the condition is true.

```
DO WHILE condition is true
  Process step(s)
LOOP
```

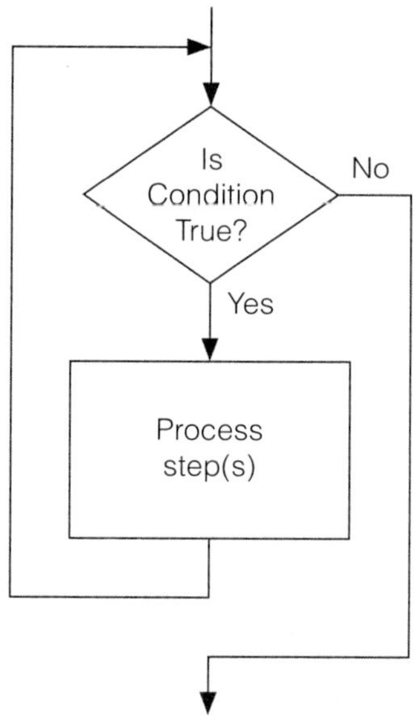

Figure 2.7 Pseudocode and Flowchart for a Loop

Class Average Algorithm

Problem: Calculate and report the grade-point average for a class.

Discussion: The average grade equals the sum of all grades divided by the number of students. We need a loop to read and then add (accumulate) the grades for each student in the class. Inside the loop we also need to total (count) the number of students in the class. See Figures 2.8 through 2.10.

Input: Student grades.

Processing: Find the sum of the grades; count the number of students; calculate average grade = sum of grades / number of students.

Output: Average grade.

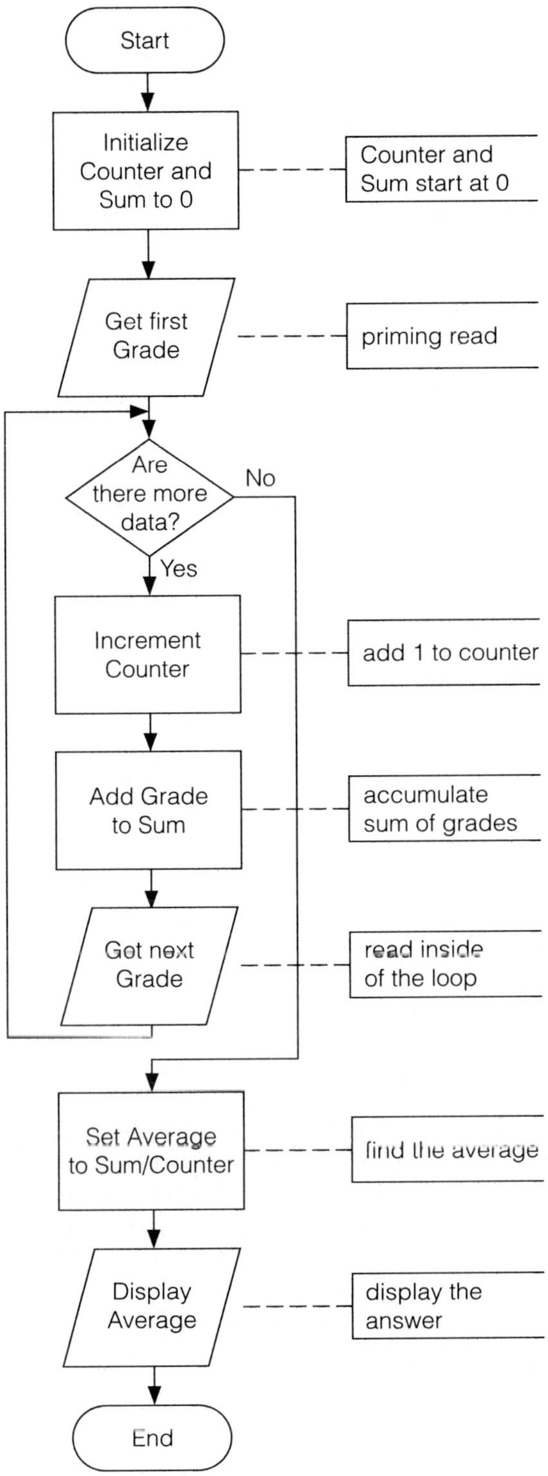

Figure 2.8 Flowchart for the Class Average Problem

```
Program: Determine the average grade of a class
Initialize Counter and Sum to 0
Get the first Grade
DO WHILE there are more data
    Add the Grade to the Sum
    Increment the Counter
    Get the next Grade
LOOP
Compute Average = Sum / Counter
Display Average
```

Figure 2.9 Pseudocode for the Class Average Problem

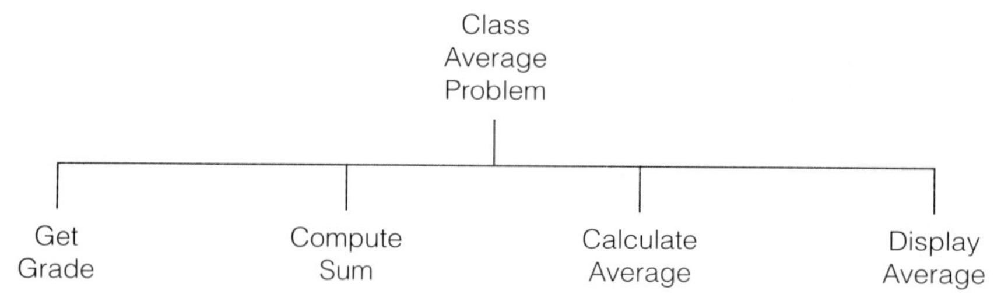

Figure 2.10 Top-Down Chart for the Class Average Problem

Comments:

1. Tracing a flowchart is like playing a board game. We begin at the Start symbol and proceed from symbol to symbol until we reach the End symbol. At any time we will be at just one symbol. In a board game, the path taken depends on the result of spinning a spinner or rolling a pair of dice. The path taken through a flowchart depends on the input.

2. The algorithm should be tested at the flowchart stage before being coded into a program. Different data should be used as input and the output checked. This process is known as **desk checking**. The test data should include nonstandard data as well as typical data.

3. Flowcharts, pseudocode, and top-down charts are universal problem-solving tools. They can be used to construct programs in any computer language, not just QBasic.

4. Flowcharts are used throughout this text to provide a visualization of the flow of certain programming tasks and QBasic control structures. Major examples of pseudocode and top-down charts appear in the case studies.

5. There are four primary logical programming constructs: sequence, decision, loop, and unconditional branch. Unconditional branch, which appears in some languages as GOTO statements, involves jumping from one place in a program to another. Structured programming uses the first three constructs but forbids the fourth. One advantage of pseudocode over flowcharts is that pseudocode has no provision for unconditional branching and thus forces the programmer to write structured programs.

6. Flowcharts are time consuming to write and update. For this reason, professional programmers are more likely to favor pseudocode and top-down charts. Since flowcharts so clearly illustrate the logical flow of programming techniques, however, they are a valuable tool in the education of programmers.

7. There are many styles of pseudocode. Some programmers use an outline form, whereas others use a form that looks almost like a programming language. The pseudocode appearing in the case studies of this text focuses on the primary tasks to be performed by the program and leaves many of the routine details to be completed during the coding process. Several QBasic keywords, such as READ, PRINT, IF, DO, and WHILE, are used extensively in the pseudocode appearing in this text.

8. Many people draw rectangles around each item in a top-down chart. In this text, rectangles are omitted to encourage the use of top-down charts by making them easier to draw.

3

Fundamentals of QBasic

3.1 NUMBERS

Much of the data processed by computers consist of numbers. In "computerese," numbers are often called **numeric constants**. This section discusses the operations that are performed with numbers and the ways numbers are displayed.

Arithmetic Operations

The five arithmetic operations are addition, subtraction, multiplication, division, and exponentiation. (Since exponentiation is not as familiar as the others, it is reviewed in detail in Comment 12.) Addition, subtraction, and division are denoted in QBasic by the standard symbols +, –, and /. However, the notations for multiplication and exponentiation differ from the customary mathematical notations.

Mathematical Notation	QBasic Notation
$a \cdot b$ or $a \times b$	$a * b$
a^r	a ^ r

(The asterisk [*] is the upper character of the 8 key on the top row of the keyboard. The caret [^] is the upper character of the 6 key on that row.) ***Note:*** In this book, the proportional font used for text differs from the monospaced font used for programs. In the program font, the asterisk appears as *.

If *n* is any number, then the statement

```
PRINT n
```

displays the number *n* on the screen. If the PRINT statement is followed by a combination of numbers and arithmetic operations, it carries out the operations and displays the result.

EXAMPLE 1 The following program applies each of the five arithmetic operations to the numbers 3 and 2. Notice that 3 / 2 is displayed in decimal form. QBasic never displays numbers as common fractions. ***Note 1:*** The star in the fourth and seventh lines is the computer-font version of the asterisk. ***Note 2:*** The notation [run] indicates that Shift+F5 is pressed to execute the program.

```
CLS
PRINT 3 + 2
PRINT 3 - 2
PRINT 3 * 2
PRINT 3 / 2
PRINT 3 ^ 2
PRINT 2 * (3 + 4)
END

[run]
 5
 1
 6
 1.5
 9
 14
```

Scientific Notation

Let us review powers of 10 and scientific notation. Our method of decimal notation is based on a systematic use of exponents.

$$
\begin{array}{ll}
10^1 = 10 & 10^{-1} = 1/10 = .1 \\
10^2 = 100 & 10^{-2} = .01 \\
10^3 = 1000 & 10^{-3} = .001 \\
\cdot & \cdot \\
\cdot & \cdot \\
10^n = \underbrace{1000\ldots0}_{n \text{ zeros}} & 10^{-n} = \underbrace{.000\ldots01}_{n \text{ digits}}
\end{array}
$$

Scientific notation provides a convenient way of writing numbers by using powers of 10 to stand for zeros. Numbers are written in the form $b \cdot 10^r$, where b is a number from 1 up to (but not including) 10, and r is an integer. For example, it is much more convenient to write the diameter of the sun (1,400,000,000 meters) in scientific notation: $1.4 \cdot 10^9$ meters. Similarly, rather than write .0000003 meters for the diameter of a bacterium, it is simpler to write $3 \cdot 10^{-7}$ meters.

Any acceptable number can be entered into the computer in either standard or scientific notation. The form in which QBasic displays a number depends on many factors, with size being an important consideration. In QBasic, $b \cdot 10^r$ is usually written as *bEr*. (The letter E is an abbreviation for *exponent*.) The following forms of the numbers mentioned above are equivalent.

1.4 * 10^9	1.4E+09	1.4E+9	1.4E9	1400000000
3 * 10^–7	3E–07	3E–7	.0000003	

The computer displays r as a two-digit number, preceded by a plus sign if r is positive and a minus sign if r is negative.

EXAMPLE 2 The following program illustrates scientific notation. The computer's decision on whether to display a number in scientific or standard form depends on the magnitude of the number.

```
CLS
PRINT 1.2 * 10 ^ 34
PRINT 1.2 * 10 ^ 8
PRINT 1.2 * 10 ^ 3
PRINT 10 ^ -20
PRINT 10 ^ -2
END

[run]
 1.2E+34
 1.2E+08
 1200
 1E-20
 .01
```

Numeric Variables

In applied mathematics problems, quantities are referred to by names. For instance, consider the following high school algebra problem. "If a car travels at 50 miles per hour, how far will it travel in 14 hours? Also, how many hours are required to travel 410 miles?" The solution to this problem uses the well-known formula

$$\text{distance} = \text{rate} \times \text{time}$$

Here's how this problem would be solved with a computer program.

```
CLS
LET rate = 50
LET time = 14
LET distance = rate * time
PRINT distance
LET distance = 410
LET time = distance / rate
PRINT time
END

[run]
 700
 8.2
```

The second line sets the rate to 50 and the third line sets the time to 14. The fourth line multiplies the value for rate by the value for time and sets distance to this product. The next line displays the answer to the first question. The last three lines before the END statement answer the second question in a similar manner.

The names *rate*, *time*, and *distance*, which hold numbers, are referred to as **variables**. Consider the variable *time*. In the third line its value was set to 14. In the seventh line its value was changed as the result of a computation. On the other hand, the variable *rate* had the same value, 50, throughout the program.

In general, a variable is a name that is used to refer to an item of data. The value assigned to the variable may change during the execution of the program. In QBasic, variable names can be up to 40 characters long, must begin with a letter, and can consist only of letters, digits, and periods. (The shortest variable names consist of a single letter.) QBasic does not distinguish between upper- and lowercase letters used in variable names. Some examples of variable names are *total*, *numberOfCars*, *taxRate.1998*, and *n*. As a convention, we will keep variable names in lowercase letters except for the first letters of additional words (as in *numberOfCars*). LET statements are used to assign values to variables and PRINT statements are used to display the values of variables.

If *var* is a numeric variable and *num* is a numeric constant, then the statement

```
LET var = num
```

assigns the number *num* to the variable *var*. Actually, the computer sets aside a location in memory with the name *var* and places the number *num* in it. The statement

```
PRINT var
```

looks into this memory location for the value of the variable and displays the value on the screen.

A combination of constants, variables, and arithmetic operations that can be evaluated to yield a number is called a **numeric expression**. Expressions are evaluated by replacing each variable by its value and carrying out the arithmetic. Some examples of expressions are 2 * time + 7, *n* + 1, and (*a* + *b*) / 3.

EXAMPLE 3 The following program displays the value of an expression.

```
CLS
LET a = 5
LET b = 4
PRINT a * (2 + b)
END

[run]
 30
```

If *var* is a variable, then the statement

```
LET var = expression
```

first evaluates the expression on the right and *then* assigns its value to the variable. For instance, the program in Example 3 can be written as

```
CLS
LET a = 5
LET b = 4
LET c = a * (2 + b)
PRINT c
END
```

The expression *a* * (2 + *b*) is evaluated to 30 and then this value is assigned to the variable *c*.

Since the expression in a LET statement is evaluated before an assignment is made, a statement such as

```
LET t = t + 1
```

is meaningful. It first evaluates the expression on the right (that is, it adds 1 to the original value of the variable *t*) and then assigns this sum to the variable t. The effect is to increase the value of the variable *t* by 1. In terms of memory locations, the statement retrieves the value of *t* from *t*'s memory location, uses it to compute *t* + 1, and then places the sum in *t*'s memory location.

PRINT Statement

Consider the following program.

```
CLS
PRINT 3
PRINT -3
END

[run]
 3
-3
```

Notice that the negative number –3 begins directly at the left margin, whereas the positive number 3 begins one space to the right. The PRINT statement always displays nonnegative numbers with a leading space. The PRINT statement also displays a trailing space after every number. Although the trailing spaces are not apparent here, we will soon see evidence of their presence.

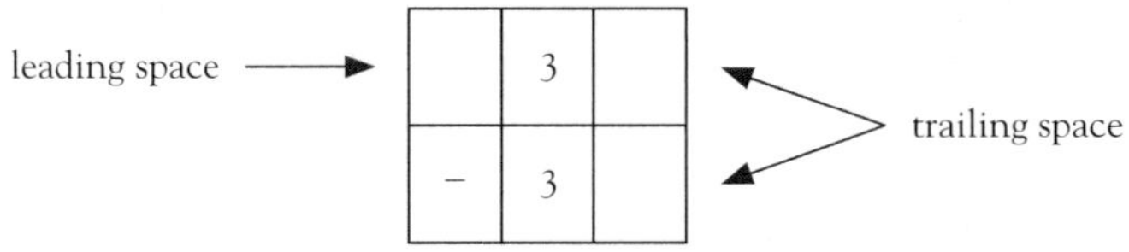

The PRINT statements considered so far display only one number per line. After displaying a number, the cursor moves to the leftmost position and down a line for the next display. Borrowing some typewriter terminology, we say that the computer performs a carriage return and a line feed after each number is displayed. The carriage return and line feed, however, can be suppressed by placing a semicolon at the end of the PRINT statement.

EXAMPLE 4 The following program illustrates the use of semicolons in PRINT statements. The output reveals the presence of the space trailing each number. For instance, the space trailing –3 combines with the leading space of 99 to produce two spaces between the numbers.

```
CLS
PRINT 3;
PRINT -3;
PRINT 99;
PRINT 100
END

[run]
 3 -3  99  100
```

Semicolons can be used to display several numbers with one PRINT statement. If *m*, *n*, and *r* are numbers, a statement of the form

```
PRINT m; n; r;
```

or

```
PRINT m; n; r
```

displays the three numbers, one after another, separated only by their leading and trailing spaces. For instance, the PRINT statements in Example 4 above can be replaced by the single line

```
PRINT 3; -3; 99; 100
```

Comments:

1. Numbers must not contain commas, dollar signs, or percent signs. Also, mixed numbers, such as $8\frac{1}{2}$, are not allowed.

2. In this text we use lowercase letters for variable names. For names such as *interestRate*, however, we capitalize the first letter of the second word to improve readability. QBasic allows any type of capitalization you like and helps you to be consistent with the use of uppercase letters in a variable name. For instance, if you use the variable name *interestRate* in a program and later enter a line using *InterestRate*, the appearance of the first variable name will automatically be changed to *InterestRate* by QBasic.

3. Some people think of the equals sign (=) in a LET statement as an arrow pointing to the left. This stresses the fact that the value on the right is assigned to the variable on the left.

4. Parentheses should be used when necessary to clarify the meaning of an expression. When there are no parentheses, the arithmetic operations are performed in the following order: (1) exponentiations; (2) multiplications and divisions; (3) additions and subtractions. In the event of ties, the leftmost operation is carried out first.

   Level of Precedence for Arithmetic Operations

( )	Inner to outer, left to right
^	Left to right in expression
* /	Left to right in expression
+ –	Left to right in expression

5. QBasic statements and certain other words that have a specific meaning in the QBasic language cannot be used as names of variables. For instance, the statements LET print = 99 and LET end = 99 are not valid. These words are called **keywords** (or **reserved words**). Some keywords that are most likely to be used inadvertently are COLOR, ERROR, INT, KEY, POS, SELECT, VAL, and WIDTH. To view the list of keywords, press Alt/H/I and then use the PgDn and PgUp keys to scroll through the list. Every capitalized word in the listing is a keyword.

6. Grammatical errors, such as misspellings or incorrect punctuations, are called **syntax errors**. Certain types of syntax errors are spotted by the smart editor when they are entered, whereas others are not detected until the program is executed. When QBasic spots an error, it displays a dialog box. Some incorrect statements and their errors are given below.

Statement	**Reason for Error**
PRIMT 3	Misspelling of keyword
PRINT 2 +	No number follows the plus sign
LET 9W = 5	9W is not a valid variable name

7. Numeric variables that have not been assigned values by LET statements have the value 0. We say that the **default value** is 0.

```
CLS
LET a = 5
PRINT a + b; b
END

[run]
 5  0
```

8. When a variable is first assigned a value, we say that the variable is **initialized**. The failure to initialize variables can cause some programs to malfunction. Uninitialized numeric variables have the value 0.

9. The statement LPRINT produces an output on the printer identical to the display on the screen produced by PRINT.

10. The omission of the asterisk to denote multiplication is a common error. For instance, the expression $a(b + c)$ is not valid. It should read $a * (b + c)$.

11. The largest number the numeric variables considered in this text can represent is 3.402823E+38. Attempting to generate larger values produces the message "Overflow." The numbers generated by the programs in this text usually have a maximum of seven digits.

12. *A Review of Exponents*. The expression 2^3 means $2 \cdot 2 \cdot 2$, the product of three 2's. The number 3 is called the **exponent**, and the number 2 is called the **base**. In general, if r is a positive integer and a is a number, then a^r is defined as follows:

$$a^r = \underbrace{a \cdot a \ldots a}_{r \text{ factors}}.$$

The process of calculating a^r is called *raising a to the rth power*. Some other types of exponents are:

$a^{1/2} = \sqrt{a}$		$9^{1/2} = 3$
$a^{1/n} = \sqrt[n]{a}$	n positive integer	$16^{1/4} = 2$
$a^{m/n} = (\sqrt[n]{a})^m$	m, n positive integers	$8^{2/3} = (\sqrt[3]{8})^2 = 4$
$a^{-r} = 1/a^r$	$a \neq 0$	$10^{-2} = .01$

13. More than one statement can be placed on a single line of a program, provided the statements are separated by colons. For instance, the program in Example 3 can be written as

```
CLS: LET a = 5: LET b = 4: PRINT a * (2 + b)
END
```

In general, though, programs are much easier to follow if just one statement appears on each line. In this text we almost always use single-statement lines.

PRACTICE PROBLEMS 3.1

1. Evaluate 2 + 3 * 4.

2. Complete the table by filling in the value of each variable after each line of the program is executed.

Program	a	b	c
`LET a = 3`	3	0	0
`LET b = 4`	3	4	0
`LET c = a + b`			
`LET a = c * a`			
`PRINT a - b`			
`LET b = b * b`			
`END`			

EXERCISES 3.1

In Exercises 1 through 6, evaluate the numeric expression.

1. 3 * 4
2. 7 ^ 2
3. 1 / (2 ^ 5)
4. 3 + (4 * 5)
5. (5 – 3) * 4
6. 3 * ((–2) ^ 5)

In Exercises 7 through 10, write the number in scientific notation as it might be displayed by the computer.

7. 3 billion
8. 12,300,000
9. 4 / (10 ^ 8)
10. 32 * (10 ^ 20)

In Exercises 11 through 16, determine whether or not the name is a valid variable name.

11. balance
12. room&Board
13. fOrM.1040
14. 1040B
15. expenses?
16. INCOME 1987

In Exercises 17 through 22, evaluate the numeric expression where a = 2, b = 3, and c = 4.

17. (a * b) + c
18. a * (b + c)
19. (1 + b) * c
20. a ^ c
21. b ^ (c – a)
22. (c – a) ^ b

In Exercises 23 through 28, write a QBasic program to calculate the value of the expression.

23. $7 \cdot 8 + 5$

24. $(1 + 2 \cdot 9)^3$

25. 5.5% of 20

26. $15 - 3(2 + 3^4)$

27. 17 (3 + 162)

28. $4\frac{1}{2} - 3\frac{5}{8}$

In Exercises 29 and 30, complete the table by filling in the value of each variable after each line of the program is executed.

29.

Program	x	y
`LET x = 2`		
`LET y = 3 * x`		
`LET x = y + 5`		
`PRINT x + 4`		
`LET y = y + 1`		
`END`		

30.

Program	bal	inter	withDr
`LET bal = 100`			
`LET inter = .05`			
`LET withDr = 25`			
`LET bal = bal + inter * bal`			
`LET bal = bal - withDr`			
`END`			

In Exercises 31 through 38, determine the output of the program.

31.
```
LET amount = 10
PRINT amount - 4
END
```

32.
```
LET a = 4
LET b = 5 * a
PRINT a + b; b - a
END
```

33.
```
PRINT 1; 2;
PRINT 3; 4
PRINT 5 + 6
END
```

34.
```
LET number = 5
LET number = 2 * number
PRINT number
END
```

35.
```
PRINT a
LET a = 4
LET b = a ^ 2
PRINT a * b
END
```

36.
```
LET tax = 200
LET tax = 25 + tax
PRINT tax
END
```

37.
```
LET x = 3
PRINT x ^ x; x + 3 * x
END
```

38.
```
LET n = 2
PRINT 3 * n
LET n = n + n
PRINT n + n
END
```

In Exercises 39 through 42, identify the errors.

39.
```
LET a = 2
LET b = 3
LET a + b = c
PRINT c
END
```

40.
```
LET a = 2
LET b = 3
LET c = d = 4
PRINT 5((a + b) / (c + d)
END
```

41.
```
LET balance = 1,234
LET deposit = $100
PRINT balance + deposit
END
```

42.
```
LET .05 = interest
LET balance = 800
PRINT interest * balance
END
```

In Exercises 43 and 44, rewrite the program with fewer statements.

43.
```
PRINT 1;
PRINT 2;
PRINT 1 + 2
END
```

44.
```
LET a = 1
LET b = a + 2
PRINT b
END
```

In Exercises 45 through 52, write a program beginning with a CLS statement, ending with an END statement, and having one line for each step.

45. The following steps calculate a company's profit.

(a) Assign the value 98456 to the variable *revenue*.
(b) Assign the value 45000 to the variable *costs*.
(c) Assign to the variable *profit* the difference between the variables *revenue* and *costs*.
(d) Display the value of the variable *profit*.

46. The following steps calculate the amount of a stock purchase.

(a) Assign the value 25.625 to the variable *costPerShare*.
(b) Assign the value 400 to the variable *numberOfShares*.
(c) Assign the product of *costPerShare* and *numberOfShares* to the variable *amount*.
(d) Display the value of the variable *amount*.

47. The following steps calculate the price of an item after a 30% reduction.

(a) Assign the value 19.95 to the variable *price*.
(b) Assign the value 30 to the variable *discountPercent*.
(c) Assign the value of *discountPercent* divided by 100 times *price* to the variable *markDown*.
(d) Decrease price by *markDown*.
(e) Display the value of *price*.

48. The following steps calculate a company's break-even point, the number of units of goods the company must manufacture and sell in order to break even.

(a) Assign the value 5000 to the variable *fixedCosts*.
(b) Assign the value 8 to the variable *pricePerUnit*.
(c) Assign the value 6 to the variable *costPerUnit*.
(d) Assign the value *fixedCosts* divided by the difference of *pricePerUnit* and *costPerUnit* to the variable *breakEvenPoint*.
(e) Display the value of the variable *breakEvenPoint*.

49. The following steps calculate the balance after three years when $100 is deposited in a savings account at 5% interest compounded annually.

(a) Assign the value 100 to the variable *balance*.
(b) Increase the variable *balance* by 5% of its value.
(c) Increase the variable *balance* by 5% of its value.
(d) Increase the variable *balance* by 5% of its value.
(e) Display the value of the variable *balance*.

50. The following steps calculate the balance after three years when $100 is deposited at the beginning of each year in a savings account at 5% interest compounded annually.

(a) Assign the value 100 to the variable *balance*.
(b) Increase the variable *balance* by 5% of its value and add 100.
(c) Increase the variable *balance* by 5% of its value and add 100.
(d) Increase the variable *balance* by 5% of its value and add 100.
(e) Display the value of the variable *balance*.

51. The following steps calculate the balance after ten years when $100 is deposited in a savings account at 5% interest compounded annually.

(a) Assign the value 100 to the variable *balance*.
(b) Multiply the variable *balance* by 1.05 raised to the 10th power.
(c) Display the value of the variable *balance*.

52. The following steps calculate the percentage profit from the sale of a stock.

(a) Assign the value 10 to the variable *purchasePrice*.
(b) Assign the value 15 to the variable *sellingPrice*.
(c) Assign to the variable *percentProfit* 100 times the value of the difference between *sellingPrice* and *purchasePrice* divided by *purchasePrice*.
(d) Display the value of the variable *percentProfit*.

In Exercises 53 through 58, write a program to solve the problem. The program should use variables for each of the quantities.

53. Suppose each acre of farmland produces 18 tons of corn. How many tons of corn can be produced on a 30-acre farm?

54. Suppose a ball is thrown straight up in the air with an initial velocity of 50 feet per second and an initial height of 5 feet. How high will the ball be after 3 seconds? **Note:** The height after t seconds is given by the expression $-16t^2 + v_0t + h_0$, where v_0 is the initial velocity and h_0 is the initial height.

55. If a car left Washington, D.C., at two o'clock and arrived in New York at seven o'clock, what was its average speed? **Note:** New York is 233 miles from Washington.

56. A motorist wants to determine her gas mileage. At 23,340 miles (on the odometer) the tank is filled. At 23,695 miles the tank is filled with 14.1 gallons. How many miles per gallon did the car average between the two fillings?

57. A U.S. geological survey showed that Americans use an average of 1600 gallons of water per person per day, including industrial use. How many gallons of water are used each year in the United States? **Note:** The current population of the United States is about 260 million people.

58. According to FHA specifications, each room in a house should have a window area equal to at least 10% of the floor area of the room. What is the minimum window area for a 14-ft by 16-ft room?

SOLUTIONS TO PRACTICE PROBLEMS 3.1

1. 14. Multiplications are performed before additions. If the intent is for the addition to be performed first, the expression should be written (2 + 3) * 4.

2.

Program	a	b	c
`LET a = 3`	3	0	0
`LET b = 4`	3	4	0
`LET c = a + b`	3	4	7
`LET a = c * a`	21	4	7
`PRINT a - b`	21	4	7
`LET b = b * b`	21	16	7
`END`	21	16	7

Each time a LET statement is executed, only one variable has its value changed (the variable to the left of the equals sign).

3.2 STRINGS

Two types of data can be processed by QBasic: numbers and strings. Sentences, phrases, words, letters of the alphabet, names, phone numbers, addresses, and dates are all examples of strings. Formally, a **string constant** is a sequence of characters that is treated as a single item. Strings can be assigned names with LET statements, can be displayed with PRINT statements, and can be combined by an operation called concatenation (denoted by +).

String Variables

A **string variable** is a name used to refer to a string. The allowable names of string variables are identical to those of numeric variables with one modification: each string variable name must be followed by a dollar sign ($). The value of a string variable is assigned or altered with LET statements and displayed with PRINT statements just like the value of a numeric variable.

EXAMPLE 1 The following program shows how LET and PRINT statements are used with strings. The string variable *today$* is assigned a value by the third line and this value is displayed by the fourth line. The quotation marks surrounding each string constant are not part of the constant and are not displayed by the PRINT statements.

```
CLS
PRINT "hello"
LET today$ = "9/17/98"
PRINT today$
END

[run]
hello
9/17/98
```

If *x*, *y*, . . ., *z* are characters and *var$* is a string variable, then the statement

```
LET var$ = "xy...z"
```

assigns the string constant *xy...z* to the variable, and the statement

```
PRINT "xy...z"
```

or

```
PRINT var$
```

displays the string *xy...z* on the screen. If *var2$* is another string variable, then the statement

```
LET var2$ = var$
```

assigns the value of the variable *var$* to the variable *var2$*. (The value of *var$* will remain the same.) String constants used in LET or PRINT statements must be surrounded by quotation marks, but string variables are never surrounded by quotation marks.

As with numbers, semicolons can be used with strings in PRINT statements to suppress carriage returns and line feeds. However, PRINT statements do not display leading or trailing spaces along with strings.

EXAMPLE 2 The following program illustrates the use of the LET and PRINT statements.

```
CLS
LET phrase$ = "win or lose that counts."
PRINT "It's not whether you "; phrase$
PRINT "It's whether I "; phrase$
END

[run]
It's not whether you win or lose that counts.
It's whether I win or lose that counts.
```

Concatenation

Two strings can be combined to form a new string consisting of the strings joined together. The joining operation is called **concatenation** and is represented by a plus sign (+). For instance, "good" + "bye" is "goodbye". A combination of strings and plus signs that can be evaluated to form a string is called a **string expression**. The LET and PRINT statements evaluate expressions before assigning them to variables or displaying them.

EXAMPLE 3 The following program illustrates concatenation.

```
CLS
LET quote1$ = "The ballgame isn't over, "
LET quote2$ = "until it's over."
LET quote$ = quote1$ + quote2$
PRINT quote$ + "   Yogi Berra"
END

[run]
The ballgame isn't over, until it's over.   Yogi Berra
```

EXAMPLE 4 The following program has strings and numbers occurring together in a PRINT statement.

```
CLS
LET interestRate = .0655
LET principal = 100
PRINT "The balance after a year is"; (1 + interestRate) * principal
END

[run]
The balance after a year is 106.55
```

ASCII Table

Each of the 47 keys in the center typewriter portion of the keyboard can produce two characters, for a total of 94 characters. Adding 1 for the space character produced by the space bar makes 95 characters. Many more characters can be displayed.

Appendix A shows the complete table of characters, numbered 0 to 255, that the computer recognizes. (The number assigned to each character is called its **ASCII value**.) The keyboard characters appear with numbers 32 to 126. Figures 3.1 to 3.4 show some different types of characters. The box-drawing characters in Figure 3.3 have been grouped to show how they fit together. The characters in these figures are referred to by their ASCII values. If *n* is a number between 0 and 255, then

```
CHR$(n)
```

is the string consisting of the single character with ASCII value *n*. For instance, CHR$(227) is the string constant consisting of the Greek letter *pi*.

Ç ü é â ä à å ç ê ë è ï î ì
Ä Å É æ Æ ô ö ò û ù ÿ Ö Ü ¢
£ ¥ P *f* á í ó ú ñ Ñ ª º ¿

Figure 3.1 Foreign Language Characters (128 to 168)

α β Γ π Σ σ µ τ Φ θ Ω δ ∞ φ ∈ ∩
≡ ± ≥ ≤ ⌠ ⌡ ÷ ≈ ° • · √ n 2 ■

Figure 3.2 Greek Letters and Mathematical Symbols (224 to 254)

╔ ╦ ╗ ═   ╒ ╤ ╕ ═   ┌ ┬ ┐ ─
╠ ╬ ╣   ╞ ╪ ╡   ├ ┼ ┤
╚ ╩ ╝ ║   ╘ ╧ ╛ │   └ ┴ ┘ │

Figure 3.3 Some of the Box-Drawing Characters (179 to 218)

☺ ☻ ♥ ♦ ♣ ♠ ◘ ♫ ☼ ► ◄ ↕ ‼ ¶ §
↨ ↑ ↓ → ← ∟ ¬ ½ ¼ ¡ « » ░ ▒ ▓

Figure 3.4 Miscellaneous Characters

EXAMPLE 5 The following program illustrates the use of CHR$ to produce strings.

```
CLS
PRINT CHR$(227)
LET queenOfHearts$ = "Q" + CHR$(3)
PRINT queenOfHearts$
LET a$ = CHR$(227) + CHR$(114) + CHR$(253)
PRINT "The area of a circle of radius r is "; a$
END

[run]
π
Q♥
The area of a circle of radius r is πr²
```

Comments:

1. The string "", which contains no characters, is called the **null string** or the **empty string**. It is different from " " and CHR$(0). String variables that have not been assigned values by LET statements initially have "" as their default values.

2. The characters in the ASCII table can be displayed on the screen by using the Alt key and the numeric keypad. If you hold down the Alt key, press 227 on the numeric keypad, and then release the Alt key, the Greek letter *pi* will appear on the screen. Most of the ASCII characters can be displayed in this manner. (The exceptions are character 127 and some of the characters with ASCII values less than 32.) This technique is used to place characters not found on the keyboard into strings. (*Caution:* With this procedure, the numbers *must* be typed from the numeric keypad, not from the standard number keys in the center part of the keyboard.)

```
CLS
LET a$ = "π"
PRINT a$
END

[run]
π
```

3. Characters numbered 7, 9 through 13, and 28 through 31 in the ASCII table are called **control characters**. For these numbers, the statement PRINT CHR$(*n*) produces the stated effect. For instance, the statement PRINT CHR$(28) moves the cursor right one space. The character with ASCII value 12 can be used with LPRINT to advance the paper to the top of the next sheet.

4. CHR$ gives the ASCII character associated with a number. The reverse of this information can be found with ASC. If *c* is a character, then the value of ASC("c") is the ASCII number of the character *c*. For instance, ASC("A") is 65.

5. The statement PRINT, with no string, simply skips a line on the screen.

6. Assigning string constants to numeric variables and assigning numeric constants to string variables are common errors.

Valid	**Not Valid**
`LET n = 5`	`LET n = "5"`
`LET x$ = "5"`	`LET x$ = 5`

The string "5" is different than the number 5. It is displayed without any leading or trailing spaces and cannot be used in arithmetic calculations.

7. In QBasic, the maximum allowable number of characters in a string is 32,767.

8. Names of string variables in which the parts preceding the dollar signs are keywords, such as name$ and print$, are valid in QBasic. Actual keywords, however, such as date$, input$, mid$, str$, time$, and ucase$, are not acceptable names. **Note:** Standard BASIC does not permit the use of variable names such as name$ and print$.

9. To display the ASCII table on the screen, press Alt/H/C, use the cursor-moving keys to position the cursor under the phrase "ASCII Character Codes," and then press Enter. PgDn and PgUp can be used to scroll through the table.

10. The quotation mark character (") can be placed into a string constant by using CHR$(34). For example,

```
CLS
PRINT "Thomas J. " + CHR$(34) + "Stonewall" + CHR$(34) + " Jackson"
END

[run]
Thomas J. "Stonewall" Jackson
```

11. Information about a keyword can be obtained either by placing the cursor on the word and pressing F1 or by using the Help index. To use the index to obtain information about the keyword LET, first press Alt/H/I to invoke the index. Press the L key to move to the keywords beginning with L, move the cursor to "LET statement," and press the Enter key. The bracket around the word LET in the discussion indicates that the word LET is optional. An explanation of the conventions used in the description of keywords is found in the Contents section of the Help menu under "Syntax Conventions."

PRACTICE PROBLEMS 3.2

1. Compare the string of text in the fourth line of the program in Example 4 with the string of text in the sixth line of the program in Example 5.

```
PRINT "The balance after a year is"; (1 + interestRate) * principal
PRINT "The area of a circle of radius r is "; a$
```

Why is a trailing space necessary for the string in the second PRINT statement but not for the string in the first PRINT statement?

2. Modify the program in Example 3 to display the following output (that is, the output should actually show the quotation marks).

```
"The ballgame isn't over, until it's over."    Yogi Berra
```

EXERCISES 3.2

In Exercises 1 through 10, determine the output of the program.

1.
```
PRINT "Hello"
PRINT "12" + "34"
END
```

2.
```
PRINT "Welcome; my friend."
PRINT "Welcome"; "my friend."
END
```

3.
```
PRINT "12"; 12; "TWELVE"
END
```

4.
```
PRINT CHR$(104) + CHR$(105)
END
```

5.
```
LET r$ = "A ROSE"
LET b$ = " IS "
PRINT r$; b$; r$; b$; r$
END
```

6.
```
LET n = 5
LET x$ = "5"
PRINT n
PRINT x$
END
```

7.
```
LET houseNumber = 1234
LET street$ = "Main Street"
PRINT houseNumber; street$
END
```

8.
```
LET p$ = "f"
LET word$ = "lute"
PRINT p$ + word$
END
```

9.
```
LET quote$ = "We're all in this alone."
LET person$ = "Lily Tomlin"
LET qMark$ = CHR$(34)
PRINT qMark$ + quote$ + qMark$ + "   " + person$
END
```

10.
```
LET a$ = "D"
PRINT a$; " is the"; ASC(a$) - ASC("A") + 1;
PRINT "th letter of the alphabet."
END
```

In Exercises 11 through 15, identify the errors.

11.
```
LET phone = "234-5678"
PRINT "My phone number is "; phone
END
```

12.
```
LET x$ = "2"
LET y = 3
PRINT x$ + y
END
```

13.
```
LET quote$ = I came to Casablanca for the waters.
PRINT quote$; "  "; "Bogart"
END
```

14.
```
LET hi-Yo$ = "Silver"
PRINT "Hi-Yo "; hi-Yo
END
```

15.
```
LET mid$ = "Ira"
PRINT "My middle name is "; mid$
END
```

In Exercises 16 and 17, write the given string in the form CHR$(m) + CHR$(n) + ...

16. Happy Day!

17. 4th: "Babe" Ruth

In Exercises 18 through 21, write a program beginning with a CLS statement, ending with an END statement, and having one line for each step. Lines that display data should use the given variable names.

18. (a) Assign "Thomas" to the variable *firstName$*.
    (b) Assign "Alva" to the variable *middleName$*.
    (c) Assign "Edison" to the variable *lastName$*.
    (d) Assign 1847 to the variable *yearOfBirth*.
    (e) Display the inventor's full name followed by a comma and his year of birth.

19. (a) Assign "ketchup" to the variable *item$*.
    (b) Assign 1.80 to the variable *regularPrice*.
    (c) Assign .27 to the variable *discount*.
    (d) Display the phrase "1.53 is the sale price of ketchup"

20. (a) Assign "New York" to the variable *state$*.
    (b) Display the phrase "I ♥ New York."

21. (a) Assign "Fore" to the variable *prefix$*.
    (b) Display the phrase "Forewarned is Forearmed."

In Exercises 22 through 26, write a program to solve the problem. The program should use variables for each of the quantities and display the outcome with a complete explanation, as in Example 4.

22. If a company's annual revenue is $550,000 and its expenses are $410,000, what is its net income (revenue minus expenses)?

23. If the price of a 17-ounce can of corn is 68 cents, what is the price per ounce?

24. If a company earns $5.25 per share for the year and the price of one share of stock is $68.25, what is the company's price-to-earnings ratio (that is, price/earnings)?

25. If the radius of the earth is 6170 kilometers, what is the volume of the earth? **Note:** The volume of a sphere of radius r is (4/3) * (3.14159) * r^3.

26. How many pounds of grass seed are needed to seed a lawn 40 feet by 75 feet if 40 ounces are recommended for 2000 square feet? **Note:** There are 16 ounces in a pound.

27. Write a program to draw a rectangle on the screen.

28. A store manager needs three shelf signs. Write a program to produce the output shown below. The words "SALE! Everything on this shelf" and "% off!" should appear only once in the program.

```
SALE! Everything on this shelf 10% off!
SALE! Everything on this shelf 30% off!
SALE! Everything on this shelf 50% off!
```

SOLUTIONS TO PRACTICE PROBLEMS 3.2

1. In the first PRINT statement, the item following the phrase is a positive number, which is displayed with a leading space. Since the corresponding item in the second PRINT statement is a string, which is *not* displayed with a leading space, a space had to be included at the end of the phrase.

2. Change the fifth line to

```
PRINT CHR$(34) + quote$ + CHR$(34) + "   Yogi Berra"
```

3.3 DATA INPUT

So far we have relied on the LET statement to assign values to variables. Data can also be stored in DATA statements and accessed through READ statements, or data can be supplied by the user in response to a request by an INPUT statement.

READ and DATA Statements

DATA statements store values to be assigned to variables by READ statements during the execution of a program. If a DATA statement contains more than one item of data, the items are separated by commas. Examples of DATA statements are

```
DATA "Mike Jones", 7.35, 35
DATA "John Smith", 6.75, 33
```

These six items of data could have been placed in one DATA statement or in six different DATA statements. The items of data will be assigned to variables one at a time in the order they appear in the DATA statements. That is, "Mike Jones" will be the first value assigned to a variable. After all the items from the first DATA statement have been assigned to variables, subsequent requests for values will be read from the next DATA statement. Although DATA statements can appear anywhere in a program, they are usually placed at the end, just before the END statement. This makes them easy to find and modify. If *var* is a variable, then the statement

```
READ var
```

causes the program to look in the DATA statements for the next available item of data and assign it to the variable *var*.

EXAMPLE 1 Write a program that uses READ and DATA statements for data assignment and produces the same output as the program below.

```
CLS
LET address = 1600
LET street$ = "Pennsylvania Ave."
PRINT "The White House is located at"; address; street$
END

[run]
The White House is located at 1600 Pennsylvania Ave.
```

SOLUTION In the following program, the second line looks for the first item of data, 1600, and assigns it to the numeric variable address. (QBasic records that this piece of data has been used.) The third line looks for the next available item of data, "Pennsylvania Ave.", and assigns it to the string variable *street$*.

```
CLS
READ address
READ street$
PRINT "The White House is located at"; address; street$
DATA 1600, "Pennsylvania Ave."
END
```

A single READ statement can assign values to several different variables. For instance, the two READ statements in the solution of Example 1 can be replaced by the single statement

```
READ address, street$
```

In general, a statement of the form

```
READ var1, var2, ..., varn
```

has the same effect as the sequence of statements

```
READ var1
READ var2
 .
 .
 .
READ varn
```

EXAMPLE 2 The following program computes weekly pay. Each DATA statement holds a person's name, hourly wage, and number of hours worked. Notice that the variables in the READ statement are the same types (string, numeric, numeric) as the constants in the DATA statements.

```
CLS
READ name$, wage, hrs
PRINT name$; hrs * wage
READ name$, wage, hrs
PRINT name$; hrs * wage
DATA "Mike Jones", 7.35, 35
DATA "John Smith", 6.75, 33
END

[run]
Mike Jones 257.25
John Smith 222.75
```

RESTORE Statement

In certain situations, we must read the data in the DATA statements more than once. The RESTORE statement allows us to do this. After the statement

```
RESTORE
```

is executed, the program will return to the first item of the first DATA statement when assigning values to variables in future READ statements.

EXAMPLE 3 The following program takes the average annual amounts of money spent by single person households for several categories and converts these amounts to percentages. The data are read once to compute the total amount of money spent and then read again to calculate the percentage for each category. The purpose of the second line is to initialize the numeric variable total, which keeps a running total of the amounts. ***Note:*** These figures were compiled for the year 1995 by the Bureau of Labor Statistics.

```
CLS
LET total = 0
READ category$, amount
LET total = total + amount
READ category$, amount
LET total = total + amount
READ category$, amount
LET total = total + amount
READ category$, amount
LET total = total + amount
RESTORE
READ category$, amount
PRINT category$; amount / total
READ category$, amount
PRINT category$; amount / total
READ category$, amount
PRINT category$; amount / total
READ category$, amount
PRINT category$; amount / total
DATA "Transportation", 3887
DATA "Housing", 7643
DATA "Food", 3017
DATA "Other", 7804
END

[run]
Transportation .1739072
Housing .3419534
Food .1349828
Other .3491566
```

INPUT Statement

The person executing a program is called the **user**. QBasic has the capability for interactive programming in which the user supplies information in response to a request by the program. The statement

```
INPUT var
```

causes a question mark (and a space) to be displayed and the execution of the program to pause until the user types in a value and presses the Enter key. The entered value is then assigned to the variable *var*.

EXAMPLE 4 The Social Security or FICA tax has two components—the Social Security benefits tax and the Medicare tax. The following program computes Medicare taxes. The response, 300, is entered by the user after the question mark appears. The user's response is underlined. ***Note:*** In 1998, the Medicare tax rate was 1.45 percent.

```
CLS
PRINT "Enter taxable earnings."
INPUT earnings
PRINT "Your Medicare tax is"; .0145 * earnings
END

[run]
Enter taxable earnings.
? 300
Your Medicare tax is 4.35
```

The prompting string in the first PRINT statement told the user what type of response was requested. Without the PRINT statement, the program would have paused and the user wouldn't have the foggiest idea what to do. Actually, a prompt string can be included in an INPUT statement. The statement

```
INPUT prompt string; var
```

displays the prompt string followed by a question mark (and a space) and proceeds as before.

EXAMPLE 5 Rewrite the solution to Example 4 with a prompt string in the INPUT statement.

SOLUTION

```
CLS
INPUT "What are your taxable earnings"; earnings
PRINT "Your Medicare tax is"; .0145 * earnings
END

[run]
What are your taxable earnings? 300
Your Medicare tax is 4.35
```

If the prompt string of an INPUT statement is followed by a comma instead of a semicolon, then the question mark and the space will be suppressed.

EXAMPLE 6 Rewrite the solution to Example 4 with a prompt string in the INPUT statement followed by a comma.

SOLUTION

```
CLS
INPUT "Enter taxable earnings: ", earnings
PRINT "Your Medicare tax is"; .0145 * earnings
END

[run]
Enter taxable earnings: 300
Your Medicare tax is 4.35
```

A single INPUT statement can request values for several variables. In such a case, the variables must be separated by commas in both the INPUT statement and the user's response.

EXAMPLE 7 Write a program to request an employee's name, hourly wage, and number of hours worked, and then report his or her wages.

SOLUTION Since the three pieces of data supplied will be a string constant and two numeric constants, the three variables in the INPUT statement must be of these types.

```
CLS
INPUT "Enter name, hourly wage, hrs worked: ", name$, wage, hrs
PRINT name$; hrs * wage
END

[run]
Enter name, hourly wage, hrs worked: "Mike Jones", 7.35, 35
Mike Jones 257.25
```

REM Statement

Now that we have the capability to write more complicated programs, we must concern ourselves with program documentation. **Program documentation** is the inclusion of comments that specify the intent of the program, the purpose of the variables, the nature of the data in the DATA statements, and the tasks performed by individual portions of the program. If *text* is any information whatsoever, then the statement

```
REM text
```

is completely ignored when the program is executed. Program documentation appears whenever the program is displayed or printed. Also, a line can be documented by adding

```
'text
```

to the end of the line.

EXAMPLE 8 Document the program in Example 2.

SOLUTION In the following program, the first REM statement describes the entire program, the text following the apostrophe gives the meanings of the variables, and the second REM statement tells the nature of the items in the DATA statements.

```
REM Compute weekly wages
CLS
READ name$, wage, hrs     'Name, hourly wage, hours worked
PRINT name$; hrs * wage
READ name$, wage, hrs
PRINT name$; hrs * wage
REM -- Data: name, hourly wage, hours worked
DATA "Mike Jones", 7.35, 35
DATA "John Smith", 6.75, 33
END

[run]
Mike Jones 257.25
John Smith 222.75
```

Some of the benefits of documentation are:

1. Other people can easily comprehend the program.
2. The program can be understood when read later.
3. Long programs are easier to read, since the purposes of individual pieces can be determined at a glance.

Comments:

1. The INPUT statement provides a whole new dimension to the capabilities of a program. The user, rather than the programmer, can provide the data to be processed. Also, as we will see in Chapter 5, INPUT allows the user to select from a menu the tasks to be performed.
2. A string used in a DATA statement or as a response to an INPUT statement does not have to be enclosed by quotation marks. The only exceptions are strings containing commas, colons, or leading and trailing spaces. Therefore, the quotation marks used in this section were unnecessary. From now on, quotation marks will be omitted unless they are absolutely necessary.
3. If a READ statement looks for a string and finds a number, it will treat the number as a string.

```
CLS
READ a$, b$
PRINT a$ + b$
DATA 2, 3
END

[run]
23
```

If a READ statement looks for a number and finds a string, the program will terminate and the message "Syntax error" will be displayed.

```
CLS
READ n
PRINT n * n
DATA ten
END

[run]
{Syntax error}
```

4. If all the DATA have been read and another item is requested by a READ statement, then the program will terminate with the error message "Out of DATA".

```
CLS
READ a, b
PRINT a + b
DATA 5
END

[run]
{Out of DATA}
```

5. There is no limit to the number of items in a single DATA statement, provided the total number of characters (including spaces and commas) does not exceed 255.

6. Any item appearing in a DATA statement or used in response to an INPUT request must be a constant. It *cannot* be a variable or an expression. For instance, 1 / 2 or 2 + 3 are not acceptable numeric responses to an INPUT statement.

7. An incorrect response to an INPUT statement (such as the wrong number or type of items) causes the message "Redo from start" and a new request to be displayed.

```
CLS
INPUT "Name, Phone number "; name$, phone$
PRINT name$
END

[run]
Name, Phone number? John Doe

Redo from start
Name, Phone number? John Doe,123-4567
John Doe
```

8. The INPUT statement can be used to pause a program until the user is ready to continue. For example, suppose a program displays many screens full of text. If the computer reaches the lines

```
INPUT "Press the Enter key to continue.", n$
CLS
```

after 20 or so lines are displayed on the screen, then the user can read the first block of text at leisure. After the Enter key is pressed, the CLS statement clears the screen and the next block of text can be displayed. The string variable *n$* is a *throwaway* or *dummy* variable that is never used in the program.

9. The programs in this text are documented in the following ways:

   (a) The first line of each program is a REM statement that describes the purpose of the program.

   (b) Blocks of DATA statements are preceded by a statement of the form

   ```
   REM -- Data: description1, description2
   ```

   (c) Each variable either has a descriptive name or is followed by a descriptive comment (using an apostrophe) the first time it is assigned a value.

10. Large programs, or programs to be submitted to a supervisor or instructor, should include documentation at the top of the program that identifies the author and variables. For instance, the program in Example 8 might begin with the lines shown below. The reader can refer to this block of REM statements at any time to determine the meaning of a variable.

```
REM Compute weekly wages
REM
REM John Doe
REM CS 111
REM September 14, 1998
REM
REM        Variables
REM name$  Name of employee
REM wage   Hourly wage
REM hrs    Number of hours worked during week
REM
```

PRACTICE PROBLEMS 3.3

1. Find the error in the following program and make the correction.

```
CLS
READ tme$
PRINT "The world record for the mile is "; tme$
DATA 3:34.41
END
```

2. Why was the "Redo from start" message produced by the following program?

```
CLS
INPUT "Enter weight of item in pounds: ", wp
PRINT "The weight in ounces is"; 16 * wp
END

[run]
Enter weight of item in pounds: 1/2

Redo from start
Enter weight of item in pounds: _
```

EXERCISES 3.3

In Exercises 1 through 9, determine the output of the program.

1.
```
READ n
PRINT n * n
DATA 4
END
```

2.
```
READ m, n, r
PRINT (m + n) * r
DATA 3, 4, 5
END
```

3.
```
READ a$
PRINT "un" + a$
DATA speakable
END
```

4.
```
READ a, b$
READ c$, d
RESTORE
PRINT d
READ d
PRINT d
DATA 8, MI, Wolverine, 23
END
```

5.
```
READ b$, r     'Building, number of rooms
PRINT "The "; b$; " has"; r; "rooms."
REM -- Data: building, number of rooms
DATA White House, 132
END
```

6.
```
READ n$, g1, g2          'Name, grade on exam 1, grade on exam 2
LET gs = (g1 + g2) / 2   'Semester grade
PRINT n$; " ======> "; gs
READ n$, g1, g2
LET gs = (g1 + g2) / 2
PRINT n$; " ======> "; gs
REM -- Data: name, score (exam 1), score (exam 2)
DATA Al Adams, 72, 88
DATA Betty Brown, 76, 82
END
```

7.
```
READ college$, yrFounded
INPUT "What is the current year"; yr
PRINT college$; " is"; yr - yrFounded; "years old."
REM -- Data: school, year founded
DATA Harvard University, 1636
END
```

(Assume the response is *1998*.)

8.
```
INPUT "What is the percent interest rate"; rate
PRINT "At that rate, your money will double in"; 72 / rate; "years."
END
```

(Assume the response is 6.)

9.
```
REM Demonstrate use of INPUT without a prompt
INPUT "Enter your favorite color: ", hue$
PRINT "How many "; hue$ ; " sweaters do you have";
INPUT quantity
PRINT "You have"; quantity; hue$; " sweaters."
END
```

(The user's responses are *red* and *2*.)

In Exercises 10 through 14, identify the errors.

10.
```
READ a$, b$
PRINT "Hello "; a$
DATA John Smith
END
```

11.
```
READ a
READ b
PRINT a - b
DATA 5, a + 2
END
```

12.
```
READ name$, neck    'Name, neck size
PRINT name$; " had a size"; neck; "neck."
DATA John Wayne, 14"
END
```

13.
```
READ b$, h              'Building, height in feet
PRINT b$, h
READ b$, h
PRINT b$, h
REM -- Data: building, height, number of stories
DATA World Trade Center, 1350, 110
DATA Sears Tower, 1454, 110
END
```

14.
```
READ rem           'Reminder
PRINT "Don't forget to remember the number"; rem
DATA 4
END
```

15. Fill in the table with the value of each variable after each line of the program is executed.

Program	t	c$	p
`LET t = 0`			
`READ c$, p`			
`LET t = t + p`			
`READ c$, p`			
`LET t = t + p`			
`PRINT t`			
`DATA phone, 35.25`			
`DATA postage, 14.75`			
`END`			

16. Fill in the table with the value of each variable after each line of the program is executed.

Program	a	b	c
`READ a, b, c`			
`LET a = b + c`			
`RESTORE`			
`READ a, c`			
`LET c = c + 1`			
`DATA 2, 3, 5`			
`END`			

In Exercises 17 through 20, write a program beginning with REM and CLS statements and having one line for each step. Lines that display data should use the given variable names.

17. The following steps display the increase in the percentages of college freshmen planning to major in two fields. The information is stored in DATA statements.

    (a) Use a READ statement to assign values to the variables *major*, *percent1990*, and *percent1997*.

(b) Display a sentence giving the percentage change in enrollment from 1990 to 1997.
(c) Repeat the first two steps.
(d) Place the information "Biological Sciences", 4,7 in a DATA statement.
(e) Place the information "Computer Science", 2, 3 in a DATA statement.

18. The following steps display information about Americans' eating habits. The information is stored in DATA statements.

(a) Use a READ statement to assign values to the variables *food*, *units*, and *quantityPerDay*.
(b) Display a sentence giving the quantity of a food item consumed by Americans in one day.
(c) Place the information "soft drinks", "million gallons", 23 in a DATA statement.

19. The following steps calculate the percent increase in a typical grocery basket of goods.

(a) Assign 200 to the variable *begOfYearPrice*.
(b) Request the price at the end of the year and assign it to the variable *endOfYearPrice*.
(c) Assign 100 * (*endOfYearPrice* – *begOfYearPrice*) / *begOfYearPrice* to the variable *percentIncrease*.
(d) Display a sentence giving the percent increase for the year.
(Test the program with a $215 end-of-year price.)

20. The following steps calculate the amount of money earned in a walk-a-thon.

(a) Request the amount pledged per mile and assign it to the variable *pledge*.
(b) Request the number of miles walked and assign it to the variable *miles*.
(c) Display a sentence giving the amount to be paid.
(Test the program with a pledge of $2.00 and a 15-mile walk.)

21. Table 3.1 summarizes the month's activity of three checking accounts. Write a program that displays the account number and the end-of-month balance for each account and then displays the total amount of money in the three accounts. The data should be stored in DATA statements.

Account Number	Beginning-of-Month Balance	Deposits	Withdrawals
AB4057	1234.56	345.67	100.00
XY4321	789.00	120.00	350.00
GH2222	321.45	143.65	0.00

Table 3.1 Checking-Account Activity

22. Table 3.2 contains a list of colleges with their student enrollments and faculty sizes. Write a program to display the names of the colleges, their student/faculty ratios, and the ratio for the total collection of students and faculty. The data for the colleges should be stored in DATA statements.

	Enrollment	Faculty
Ohio State	48352	2518
Univ. of MD, College Park	31475	1849
Princeton	6340	890

Table 3.2 Colleges (*Source:* World Almanac, 1998)

23. Write a program to compute semester averages. Each DATA statement should contain a student's Social Security number and the grades for three hourly exams and the final exam. (The final exam counts as two hourly exams.) The program should display each student's Social Security number and semester average, and then the class average. Use the data in Table 3.3.

Soc. Sec. No.	Exam 1	Exam 2	Exam 3	Final Exam
123-45-6789	67	85	90	88
111-11-1111	93	76	82	80
123-32-1234	85	82	89	84

Table 3.3 Student Grades

24. Table 3.4 gives the 1997 populations of three New England states. Write a program that calculates the average population and then displays the name of each state and the difference between its population and the average population. The states and their populations should be stored in DATA statements.

Maine	1243
Massachusetts	6092
Connecticut	3274

Table 3.4 Population (in thousands) of New England States

25. If n is the number of seconds between lightning and thunder, then the storm is $n/5$ miles away. Write a program that requests the number of seconds between lightning and thunder and reports the distance of the storm. (Test the program for the case where there are one and a quarter seconds between the lightning and thunder.)

26. Write a program to request as input the name of a baseball team, the number of games won, and the number of games lost. Then display the percentage of games won. (Execute the program with the input *Atlanta, 102, 61.*)

27. The numbers of calories burned per hour by bicycling, jogging, and swimming are 200, 475, and 275, respectively. A person loses one pound of weight for each 3500 calories burned. Write a program that allows the user to input the number of hours spent at each activity and then calculates the number of pounds worked off. (Test the program for a triathalon participant who bicycles 2 hours, jogs 3 hours, and swims 1 hour.)

28. The American College of Sports Medicine recommends that you maintain your *training heart rate* during an aerobic workout. Your training heart rate is computed as .7 * (220 – *a*) +.3 * *r* where *a* is your age and *r* is your resting heart rate (your pulse when you first awaken). Write a program to request a person's age and resting heart rate and then calculate the training heart rate. (Test the program with an age of 20 and a resting heart rate of 70. Then determine your training heart rate.)

In Exercises 29 and 30, write a program from the given flowchart.

29.

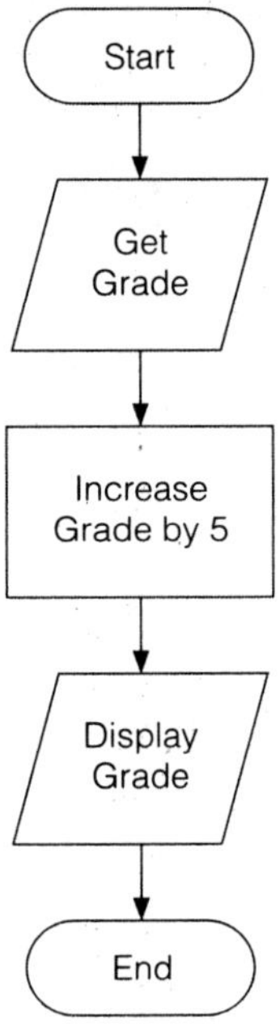

30.

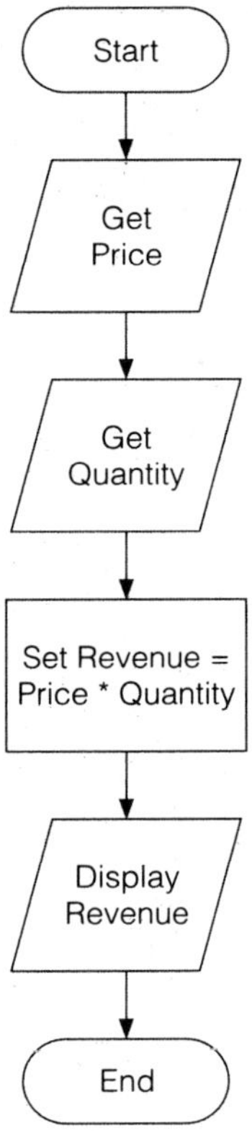

SOLUTIONS TO PRACTICE PROBLEMS 3.3

1. The colon is used to place two or more statements on the same line. Therefore, the fourth line is interpreted as the statement DATA 3 followed by the improper statement 34.41. The program can be corrected by placing quotation marks around the time in the fourth line.

2. The response, ½, was an expression. The correct response should have been the constant .5.

3.4 BUILT-IN FUNCTIONS

QBasic has a number of built-in functions that greatly extend its capability. These functions perform such varied tasks as taking the square root of a number, counting the number of characters in a string, and capitalizing letters. Functions associate with one or more values, called the *input*, a single value called the *output*. The function is said to **return** the output value. The two functions considered below have numeric input and output.

Numeric Functions: SQR, INT

The function SQR calculates the square root of a number. The function INT finds the greatest integer less than or equal to a number. Therefore, INT discards the decimal part of positive numbers. Some examples are:

```
SQR(9) is 3.              INT(2.7) is 2.
SQR(0) is 0.              INT(3) is 3.
SQR(2) is 1.414214.       INT(-2.7) is -3.
```

The terms inside the parentheses can be either numbers (as above), variables, or expressions. Expressions are evaluated first to produce the input.

EXAMPLE 1 The following program evaluates each of the functions for a specific input given by the value of the variable *n*.

```
REM Evaluate functions at a variable
CLS
LET n = 6.25
PRINT SQR(n); INT(n)
END

[run]
 2.5  6
```

EXAMPLE 2 The following program evaluates each of the functions above at an expression.

```
REM Evaluate functions at expressions
CLS
LET a = 2
LET b = 3
PRINT SQR(5 * b + 1); INT(a ^ b)
END

[run]
 4  8
```

EXAMPLE 3 The following program shows an application of the SQR function.

```
REM  Find the length of the hypotenuse of a right triangle
CLS
INPUT "Length of one leg"; leg1
INPUT "Length of other leg"; leg2
LET hyp = SQR(leg1 ^ 2 + leg2 ^ 2)
PRINT "The length of the hypotenuse is"; hyp
END

[run]
Length of one leg? 3
Length of other leg? 4
The length of the hypotenuse is 5
```

EXAMPLE 4 The following program rounds a positive number to the nearest integer.

```
REM Round positive number to nearest integer
CLS
INPUT "Number to be rounded: ", n
LET r = INT(n + .5)
PRINT "The rounded value of"; n; "is"; r
END

[run]
Number to be rounded: 2.6
The rounded value of 2.6 is 3

[run]
Number to be rounded: 2.4
The rounded value of 2.4 is 2
```

The idea in Example 4 can be extended to round a number to two decimal places, an essential task for financial applications. Just replace the fourth line by

```
LET r = INT(100 * n + .5) / 100
```

Then, substitute some different values for *n* and carry out the computation to check that the formula works.

EXAMPLE 5 The following program shows how INT is used to carry out long division. When the integer *m* is divided into the integer *n* with long division, the result is a quotient and a remainder. (See Figure 3.5.)

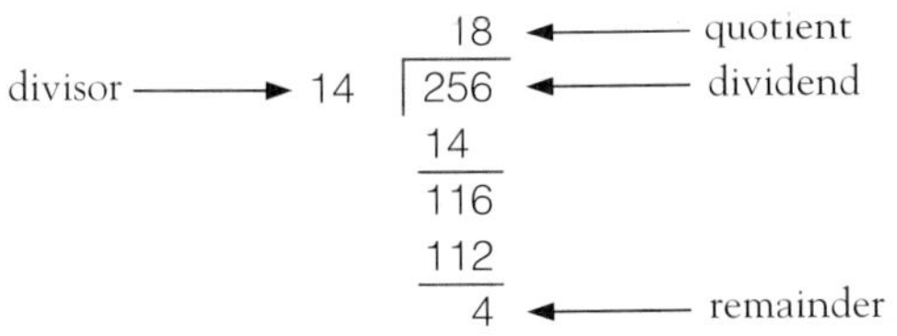

Figure 3.5 Long Division

```
REM Long division
CLS
INPUT "Divisor"; divisor
INPUT "Dividend"; dividend
PRINT "The quotient is"; INT(dividend / divisor)
PRINT "The remainder is"; dividend - INT(dividend / divisor) * divisor
END

[run]
Divisor? 14
Dividend? 256
```

```
The quotient is 18
The remainder is 4
```

String Functions: LEFT$, MID$, RIGHT$, UCASE$

The functions LEFT$, MID$, and RIGHT$ are used to extract characters from the left end, middle, and right end of a string. Suppose *a$* is a string and *m* and *n* are positive integers. Then LEFT$(*a$*, *n*) is the string consisting of the first *n* characters of *a$* and RIGHT$(*a$*, *n*) is the string consisting of the last *n* characters of *a$*. MID$(*a$*, *m*, *n*) is the string consisting of *n* characters of *a$*, beginning with the *m*th character. UCASE$(*a$*) is the string *a$* with all of its lowercase letters capitalized. Some examples are:

```
LEFT$("fanatic", 3) is "fan".         RIGHT$("fanatic", 3) is "tic".
LEFT$("12/15/93", 2) is "12".         RIGHT$("12/15/93", 2) is "93".
MID$("fanatic", 5, 1) is "t".         MID$("12/15/93", 4, 2) is "15".
UCASE$("Disk") is "DISK".             UCASE$("12three") is "12THREE".
```

The strings produced by LEFT$, MID$, and RIGHT$ are referred to as **substrings** of the strings from which they were formed. For instance, "fan" and "t" are substrings of "fanatic". The substring "fan" is said to begin at position 1 of "fanatic" and the substring "t" is said to begin at position 5.

Like the numeric functions discussed above, LEFT$, MID$, RIGHT$, and UCASE$ also can be evaluated at variables and expressions.

EXAMPLE 6 The following program evaluates the functions above at variables and expressions. Note that spaces are counted as characters.

```
REM Evaluate functions at variables and expressions.
CLS
LET a$ = "Quick as "
LET b$ = "a wink"
PRINT LEFT$(a$, 7)
PRINT MID$(a$ + b$, 7, 6)
PRINT UCASE$(a$ + b$)
PRINT "The average "; RIGHT$(b$, 4); " lasts .1 second."
END

[run]
Quick a
as a w
QUICK AS A WINK
The average wink lasts .1 second.
```

String-Related Numeric Functions: LEN, INSTR

The functions LEN and INSTR operate on strings but produce numbers. The function LEN gives the number of characters in a string. The function INSTR searches for the first occurrence of one string in another and gives the position at which the string is found. Suppose *a$* and *b$* are strings. The value of LEN(*a$*) is the number of characters in *a$*. The value of INSTR(*a$*, *b$*) is 0 if *b$* is not a substring of *a$*. Otherwise, its value is the first position of *b$* in *a$*. Some examples of LEN and INSTR are

```
LEN("Shenandoah") is 10.        INSTR("Shenandoah", "nand") is 4.
LEN("Just a moment") is 13.     INSTR("Just a moment", " ") is 5.
LEN(" ") is 1.                  INSTR("Croissant", "ist") is 0.
```

EXAMPLE 7 The following program evaluates functions at variables and expressions. The fourth line locates the position of the space separating the two names. The first name will end one position to the left of this position and the last name will consist of all but the first *n* characters of the full name.

```
REM Evaluate functions at variables and expressions.
CLS
INPUT "Name (first and last names only)"; name$
LET n = INSTR(name$, " ")
LET first$ = LEFT$(name$, n - 1)
LET last$ = RIGHT$(name$, LEN(name$) - n)
PRINT "Your first name is "; first$
PRINT "Your last name has"; LEN(last$); "letters."
END

[run]
Name (first and last names only)? John Doe
Your first name is John
Your last name has 3 letters.
```

Converting Strings to Numbers and Numbers to Strings: VAL, STR$

A string containing numerical information can be converted to a number with the function VAL. For instance, VAL("123") is the number 123.

EXAMPLE 8 The following program requests the users' date of birth and returns their age at their first birthday in the next century. Many forms of the date of birth are acceptable. Some possibilities are: 4–6–1976, 04/06/1976, and April 6, 1976

```
REM Determine a person's age in the year 2000
CLS
INPUT "Enter your date of birth: ", dob$
LET year = VAL(RIGHT$(dob$, 4))
PRINT "On your birthday in the year 2000, your age will be"; 2000 - year
END

[run]
Enter your date of birth: 4-6-1976
On your birthday in the year 2000, your age will be 24
```

A number can be converted to a string representation with the function STR$. For instance, STR$(–5) is "–5" and STR$(5) is " 5". When a nonnegative number is converted to a string, its first character is a blank space.

EXAMPLE 9 The following program finds the sum of the digits of a number.

```
REM Find the sum of the digits of a two-digit number
CLS
INPUT "Enter a two-digit number: ", num
LET num$ = STR$(num)
LET m = VAL(MID$(num$, 2, 1))
LET n = VAL(RIGHT$(num$, 1))
PRINT "The sum of the digits is"; m + n
END

[run]
Enter a two-digit number: 35
The sum of the digits is 8
```

Comments:

1. Requesting the square root of a negative number terminates the execution of the program and gives the error message "Illegal function call."

2. If *n* is greater than the length of *a$*, then the value of LEFT$(*a$*, *n*) will be the entire string *a$*. A similar result holds for MID$ and RIGHT$.

```
CLS
PRINT LEFT$("USA", 5); "*****"
END

[run]
USA*****
```

3. VAL can be applied to strings containing nonnumeric characters. If the beginning of the string *a$* represents a number, then VAL(*a$*) is that number; otherwise, it is 0. For instance, VAL("123Blastoff") is 123, and VAL("abc") is 0.

4. QBasic has a function called LCASE$ that is analogous to UCASE$. LCASE$ converts all uppercase letters in a string to lowercase letters.

5. The names of the functions LEFT$, MID$, RIGHT$, UCASE$, and STR$ are followed by dollar signs since their values are strings. They are referred to as **string-valued functions**.

6. MID$ is an important function. It will be used several times in this book to examine each letter of a string.

7. The INSTR function has a useful extension. The value of INSTR(*n*, *a$*, *b$*) is the position of the first occurrence of *b$* in *a$* in position *n* or greater. For instance, INSTR(5, "Mississippi", "ss") is 6.

8. In Example 5, we found that 4 is the remainder when 256 is divided by 14. Mathematicians say "4 = 256 modulo 14." QBasic has an operation, MOD, that performs this calculation directly. If *m* and *n* are positive integers, then *n* MOD *m* is the remainder when *n* is divided by *m*. QBasic also has an operation called **integer division**, denoted by \, which gives the quotient portion of a long-division problem.

9. Recall that the function MID$ has the form MID$(*a$*, *m*, *n*) and returns the substring of *a$* starting with position *m* and having length *n*. QBasic does its best to please for unexpected values of *m* and *n*. If *m* is greater than the length of the string or *n* is 0, then the empty string is returned. If *m* + *n* is greater than the length of the string, then MID$(*a$*, *m*, *n*) is the right part of the string beginning with the *m*th character. For instance, the value of MID$("abcdef", 3, 9) is "cdef".

PRACTICE PROBLEMS 3.4

1. What is the value of INSTR("Computer", "E")?
2. What is the value of SQR(12 * LEN("WIN"))?
3. Suppose n is greater than or equal to 0 and less than 1. What are the possible values of INT(6 * n) + 1?
4. When will INT(n / 2) be the same as n / 2?

EXERCISES 3.4

In Exercises 1 through 20, find the value of the given function.

1. `UCASE$("McD's")`
2. `SQR(64)`
3. `INT(10.75)`
4. `LEFT$("harp", 2)`
5. `SQR(3 * 12)`
6. `INT(9 - 2)`
7. `LEFT$("ABCD", 2)`
8. `MID$("ABCDE", 2, 3)`
9. `MID$("shoe", 4, 1)`
10. `UCASE$("2$ bill")`
11. `LEN("shoe")`
12. `INSTR("shoe", "h")`
13. `INSTR("shoe", "f")`
14. `LEN("s" + LEFT$("help", 2))`
15. `RIGHT$("snow", 3)`
16. `VAL("$16.00")`
17. `STR$(17)`
18. `RIGHT$("123", 1)`
19. `VAL("2B")`
20. `STR$(-20)`

In Exercises 21 through 39, find the value of the given function where a = 5, b = 3, c$ = "Lullaby", and d$ = "lab".

21. `LEN(d$)`
22. `SQR(4 + a)`
23. `INT(-a / 2)`
24. `UCASE$(d$)`
25. `SQR(a - 5)`
26. `INT(b * .5)`
27. `LEFT$(c$, LEN(d$))`
28. `MID$(c$, a, 3)`
29. `MID$(c$, a - b, 2 * a)`
30. `LEFT$(d$, b - 2)`

31. `UCASE$(c$)`

32. `INSTR(c$, d$)`

33. `INSTR(c$, "r")`

34. `LEN(c$ + LEFT$(d$, 2))`

35. `RIGHT$(c$, 2)`

36. `STR$(a + b)`

37. `VAL(STR$(a))`

38. `STR$(4 - a)`

39. `RIGHT$("Sky" + d$, 5)`

In Exercises 40 through 48, determine the output of the program.

40.
```
READ m, n
PRINT INT(10 * m + .5) / 10;
PRINT INT(10 * n + .5) / 10
DATA 3.67, 7.345
END
```

41.
```
LET day$ = "SunMonTueWedThuFriSat"
INPUT "Day of week (1 to 7)"; n
PRINT "Today is "; MID$(day$, 3 * n - 2, 3)
END
```

(Assume the response is 5.)

42.
```
INPUT "Date (mm/dd/yy)"; d$
PRINT "The year is 19" + MID$(d$, 7, 2)
END
```

(Assume the response is *08/23/95*.)

43.
```
INPUT "Word"; w$
PRINT MID$(w$, LEN(w$), 1)
END
```

(Assume the response is *Hello*.)

44.
```
INPUT "First and second names"; n$
PRINT LEFT$(n$, 1) + MID$(n$, INSTR(n$, " ") + 1, 1)
END
```

(Assume the response *James Cash*.)

45.
```
INPUT "Do you like jazz (yes or no)"; a$
LET n = INT(INSTR("YyNn", LEFT$(a$, 1)) / 2 + .5)
LET a$ = MID$("yesno ", 3 * n - 2, 3)
PRINT "I guess your answer is "; a$
END
```

(Assume the response is *yup* or *Yeah*.)

46.
```
LET n = 3567
LET m = LEN(STR$(n))
PRINT "The number of digits in 3567 is"; m - 1
END
```

47.
```
LET address$ = "1600 Pennsylvania Avenue"
PRINT "Bill, your house number is"; VAL(address$)
END
```

48.
```
LET n = 123
LET a$ = STR$(n)
PRINT RIGHT$(a$, LEN(a$) - 1)
END
```

In Exercises 49 through 54, determine the errors.

49.
```
LET a$ = "Thank you"
PRINT INSTR(a$, k)
END
```

50.
```
INPUT "Year of birth"; y
PRINT MID$(y, 3, 2)
END
```

51.
```
READ first$
PRINT "Your first name is "; first$
DATA LEFT$("John Doe", 4)
END
```

52.
```
READ m, n
PRINT SQR(m - 2 * n)
DATA 7, 5
END
```

53.
```
LET numString = 123
PRINT 2 * VAL(numString)
END
```

54.
```
LET a$ = STR$(23Skidoo)
PRINT a$
END
```

55. Write a program that requests a positive number with at most 7 digits as input and then displays the units digit of the number.

56. Write a program that requests a (complete) phone number as input and then displays the area code.

57. The formula $s = \sqrt{24d}$ gives an estimate of the speed of a car in miles per hour that skidded d feet on dry concrete when the brakes were applied. Write a program that requests the distance skidded and then displays the estimated speed of the car. (Try the program for a car that skids 54 feet.)

58. A college graduation is to be held in an auditorium with 2000 seats available for the friends and relatives of the graduates. Write a program that requests the number of graduates as input and displays the number of tickets to be distributed to each graduate. Assume each graduate receives the same number of tickets. (Try the program for 325 graduates.)

59. Suppose you decide to give 3 pieces of Halloween candy to each trick-or-treater. Write a program that requests the number of pieces of candy you have and displays the number of children you can treat. (Try the program for 101 pieces of candy.)

60. The optimal inventory size for a specific item is given by the formula $s = \sqrt{2qh/c}$, where q is the quantity to be sold each year, h is the cost of placing an order, and c is the annual cost of stocking one unit of the item. Write a program that requests the quantity, ordering cost, and storage cost as input and displays the optimum inventory size. (Use the program to compute the optimal inventory size for an item selling 3025 units during the year, where placing an order costs $50 and stocking a unit for one year costs $25.)

61. Write a program that requests a whole number of inches and converts it to feet and inches. (Try the program with 72, 53, and 8 inches.)

62. Write a program that requests a number and the number of decimal places to which the number should be rounded, and then displays the rounded number.

63. Write a program that requests a letter, converts it to uppercase, and gives its first position in the sentence "THE QUICK BROWN FOX JUMPS OVER A LAZY DOG." A sample output is

```
[run]
Letter? b
B first occurs in position 11
```

64. Write a program that requests an amount of money between 1 and 99 cents and gives the number of quarters to be used when making that amount of change. (Try each of the amounts 85, 43, and 15 as input.)

65. Write a program that requests a day of the week (Sunday, Monday, . . . , Saturday) and gives the numerical position of that day in the week. A sample outcome is

```
[run]
Day of week? Wednesday
Wednesday is day number 4
```

66. On the nautical clock, hours of the day are numbered from 0 to 23, beginning at midnight. Write a program to convert nautical hours to standard hours. A sample outcome is

```
[run]
Nautical hour (0 to 23)? 17
The standard hour is 5
```

67. Write a program that requests a sentence, a word in the sentence, and another word, and then displays the sentence with the first word replaced by the second. A sample outcome is

```
[run]
Sentence? What you don't know won't hurt you.
Word to find? know
Replace with? owe
What you don't owe won't hurt you.
```

68. Write a program that requests a positive number containing a decimal point as input, and then displays the number of digits to the left of the decimal point and the number of digits to the right of the decimal point.

SOLUTIONS TO PRACTICE PROBLEMS 3.4

1. 0. There is no uppercase letter E in the string "Computer". INSTR distinguishes between upper and lower case.

2. 6. LEN("WIN") is 3, 12 * 3 is 36, and SQR(36) is 6. This expression is an example of function composition. The inner function will be evaluated first.

3. 1, 2, 3, 4, 5, or 6. Since $0 \le n < 1$, then $0 \le 6 * n < 6$, and therefore INT(6 * n) is 0, 1, 2, 3, 4, or 5. Adding 1 gives the stated result. (This process will be used in Chapter 11 to simulate the roll of a die.)

4. When n / 2 is an integer—that is, when n is an even number. (This idea will be used later in the text to determine whether an integer is even.)

3.5 SCREEN PLACEMENT AND FORMATTING

The PRINT statement, with a little help from the functions LOCATE and TAB, can put data at specific places on the screen. A variation of the PRINT statement, PRINT USING, is custom designed to display data in an orderly and familiar form.

PRINT Zones

The screen can hold 25 rows of text, with each row consisting of at most 80 characters. Each row can be thought of as being subdivided into five zones, as shown in Figure 3.6. The first four zones contain 14 positions each and the fifth zone contains 24 positions.

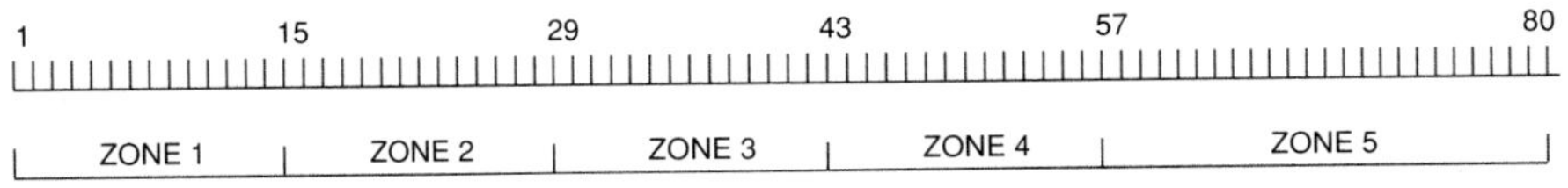

Figure 3.6 PRINT Zones

We have seen that when a PRINT statement is followed by several items separated by semicolons, the items are displayed one after another. When commas are used instead of semicolons, the items are displayed in consecutive zones.

EXAMPLE 1 Display the motto of the state of Alaska with each word in a separate print zone.

SOLUTION The first program displays the motto directly, whereas the second program uses variables. Actually, any combination of constants and variables can be used.

```
REM Motto of the state of Alaska
CLS
PRINT "North", "to", "the", "future."
END

[run]
North         to            the           future.
```

```
REM Motto of the state of Alaska
CLS
LET a$ = "North"
LET b$ = "to"
LET c$ = "the"
LET d$ = "future."
PRINT a$, b$, c$, d$
END

[run]
North         to            the           future.
```

EXAMPLE 2 The following program uses PRINT zones to organize expenses for public and private schools into columns.

```
REM Average college expenses of commuter students (1995-96)
CLS
PRINT " ", "Pb 2-yr", "Pr 2-yr", "Pb 4-yr", "Pr 4-yr"
PRINT
PRINT "Tuit & Fees", 1387, 6350, 2860, 12432
PRINT "Bks & Suppl", 577, 567, 591, 601
PRINT "Board", 1752, 1796, 1721, 1845
PRINT "Other Exp", 1142, 1220, 1348, 1169
PRINT "Trans", 894, 902, 929, 863
PRINT " ", "------", "------", "------", "------"
PRINT "Total", 5752, 10835, 7449, 16910
END
```

```
[run]
              Pb 2-yr       Pr 2-yr       Pb 4-yr       Pr 4-yr

Tuit & Fees    1387          6350          2860          12432
Bks & Suppl    577           567           591           601
Board          1752          1796          1721          1845
Other Exp      894           902           929           863
Trans          1142          1220          1348          1169
              ------        ------        ------        ------
Total          5752          10835         7449          16910
```

TAB Function

If an item appearing in a PRINT statement is preceded by

`TAB(n);`

where *n* is an integer from 1 to 80, then that item will be displayed (if possible) beginning at the *n*th position of the line. (Exceptions are discussed in Comments 4 and 5.)

EXAMPLE 3 The following program uses the TAB function to organize data into columns. (*Source:* National Center of Educational Statistics.)

```
REM Bachelor's degrees conferred (in units of 1000)
CLS
PRINT TAB(10); "1970-71"; TAB(20); "1980-81"; TAB(30); "1990-91"
PRINT
PRINT "Male"; TAB(10); 476; TAB(20); 470; TAB(30); 490
PRINT "Female"; TAB(10); 364; TAB(20); 465; TAB(30); 560
PRINT "Total"; TAB(10); 840; TAB(20); 935; TAB(30); 1050
END
```

```
[run]
         1970-71   1980-81   1990-91

Male      476       470       490
Female    364       465       560
Total     840       935       1050
```

LOCATE Statement

The LOCATE statement is used together with the PRINT statement to place text exactly where we want it. Each position on the screen can be identified by giving its row (an integer from 1 to 25) and its column (an integer from 1 to 80.) The statement

```
LOCATE r, c
```

moves the cursor to the *r*th row and *c*th column of the screen. The next PRINT statement will display items beginning at that position.

EXAMPLE 4 The following program places the title of the national anthem beginning at the 5th position of the 2nd row of the screen.

```
REM Display name of national anthem
CLS
LOCATE 2, 5
PRINT "The Star-Spangled Banner"
END
```

```
[run]

    The Star-Spangled Banner
```

PRINT USING Statement

The PRINT USING statement is used to display numeric data in a familiar form (with commas, an appropriate number of decimal spaces, and possibly preceded by a dollar sign) and to coordinate the combined display of string and numeric data. Figure 3.7, a portion of an accountant's ledger, shows some different ways of filling the spaces. Six spaces are reserved for the whole-number part of each number (and possibly a comma or dollar sign), one space for the decimal point, and two spaces for the decimal part of each number. The space reserved for each number is referred to as a **field** of length 9. Such formats can be obtained in QBasic with the PRINT USING statement.

		1	2	3	4	.	5	6
	1	,	2	3	4	.	5	6
$	1	,	2	3	4	.	5	6
				1	2	.	3	4
			$	1	2	.	3	4

Figure 3.7 Accountant's Ledger

PRINT USING statements use a string to specify the format for a number. A typical **format string** is "##,###.##". The **field** of the statement consists of the positions reserved for the display of the digits, comma, and decimal point. The length of the field equals the number of symbols in the format string. If *n* is a number less than 100,000, then the statement

```
PRINT USING "##,###.##"; n
```

displays the number in a nine-character field. The displayed number will be rounded to two decimal places, contain a comma as appropriate, and be right-justified in the field. The statement above also can be written with the format string specified by a variable, as shown in the next example.

EXAMPLE 5 The following program illustrates the use of PRINT USING.

```
REM Demonstration of PRINT USING
CLS
LET a$ = "##,###.##"
PRINT USING a$; 12345.67
PRINT USING a$; 123
PRINT USING a$; 12.3456
END

[run]
12,345.67
   123.00
    12.35
```

One comma in a format string is sufficient to produce commas separating each triple of digits as appropriate. For example, the statement PRINT USING "#######,###."; 1234567 results in the output 1,234,567.

The field for a PRINT USING statement can contain anywhere from 1 to 24 # signs. Decimal points and commas are optional. If a number fed into a numeric format string has too many digits to the left of the decimal point for the field, the number will be displayed preceded by a percent sign. Excess digits to the right of the decimal point are rounded.

EXAMPLE 6 In the following program, the field is too small to accommodate the number.

```
CLS
PRINT USING "##.#"; 123.47
END

[run]
%123.5
```

Numbers also can be displayed with dollar signs. The statement

```
PRINT USING "$##,###.##"; n
```

will display the number as before in a ten-character field with a dollar sign as the leftmost character. The statement

```
PRINT USING "$$#,###.##"; n
```

will do the same, but with a single dollar sign immediately to the left of the number.

EXAMPLE 7 The following program illustrates the placing of dollar signs with PRINT USING.

```
REM Include dollar signs with amounts
CLS
PRINT USING "$##,###.##"; 123.45
PRINT USING "$$#,###.##"; 123.45
END

[run]
$    123.45
   $123.45
```

PRINT USING statements can combine text with numbers in several ways. One method is for the format string to contain the text along with the special numeric formatting characters. The text will be displayed as it appears, and the number will conform to the rules of its formatting characters.

EXAMPLE 8 The following program combines text and numbers.

```
REM Text and numbers combined in a format string
CLS
LET a$ = "Tuition   $$##,###.##"
INPUT "Tuition"; t
PRINT USING a$; t
END

[run]
Tuition? 2137
Tuition    $2,137.00
```

The backslash character (\) can be used to format text in a format string. The string "\   \" reserves a block of *n* positions to hold the text, where *n* is the length of "\   \". The statement

```
PRINT USING "\          \"; c$
```

places the string *c$* in this reserved block. If *c$* has less than *n* characters, spaces are added to fill out the block. If *c$* has more than *n* characters, only the first *n* are displayed.

A single format string can consist of several format strings strung together. The PRINT USING statement will consist of such a format string followed by a semicolon and then a sequence of numbers and strings separated by semicolons. The items in the sequence are considered one at a time. The first item is formatted by the first format string, the second by the second format string, and so on.

EXAMPLE 9 The following program formats both text and numbers. The backslash string in *a$* has length 10.

```
REM  Text and numbers formatted in same string
CLS
LET a$ = "\          \    $#,###.##"
INPUT "Category"; c$
INPUT "Amount"; amt
PRINT USING a$; c$; amt
END

[run]
Category? Transportation
Amount? 742
Transporta    $  742.00
```

EXAMPLE 10 The following program produces the same table as the program in Example 2. However, PRINT USING is used to gain complete control of the layout. The format string *a$*, specified in the fifth line, will process one string and four numbers. In each of the PRINT USING lines these items are supplied in the proper order.

```
REM Average expenses of commuter students (1995-96)
CLS
PRINT "                    Pb 2-yr   Pr 2-yr   Pb 4-yr   Pr 4-yr"
PRINT
LET a$ = "\                 \ ##,###     ##,###     ##,###     ##,###"
PRINT USING a$; "Tuition & Fees"; 1387; 6350; 2860; 12432
PRINT USING a$; "Books & Supplies"; 577; 567; 591; 601
PRINT USING a$; "Board"; 1752; 1796; 1721; 1845
PRINT USING a$; "Transportation"; 894; 902; 929; 863
PRINT USING a$; "Other Expenses"; 1142; 1220; 1348; 1169
PRINT TAB(19); "------    -------    ------    -------"
LET b$ = "\                 \$$#,###   $$#,###   $$#,###   $$#,###"
PRINT USING b$; "Total"; 5752; 10835; 7449; 16910
END

[run]
                    Pb 2-yr   Pr 2-yr   Pb 4-yr   Pr 4-yr

Tuition & Fees       1,387     6,350     2,860    12,432
Books & Supplies       577       567       591       601
Board                1,752     1,796     1,721     1,845
Transportation         894       902       929       863
Other Expenses       1,142     1,220     1,348     1,169
                    ------   -------    ------   -------
Total               $5,752   $10,835    $7,449   $16,910
```

Output to the Printer

There are two ways to obtain a printed copy of the output of a program. (Make sure the printer has paper, is turned on, and is set to ON LINE before trying these methods.)

1. After a program has executed, pressing the key combination Shift+Print Screen causes the contents of the screen to be printed on the printer.

2. When the word PRINT is replaced with the word LPRINT, the output of the statement is sent to the printer instead of displayed on the screen. For instance, the statement LPRINT "Hello" causes the printer to print the word *Hello*. PRINT zones, TAB, and PRINT USING format strings also apply to printer output.

Comments:

1. To skip a PRINT zone, just include two consecutive commas.

```
PRINT "one",,"two"
END

[run]
one                         two
```

2. If a PRINT statement ends with a comma, then the next PRINT statement will normally display its data beginning in the next PRINT zone.

3. Consider a statement of the form PRINT *a$*, *b$* where *a$* and *b$* are strings. If *a$* fills one of the zones or extends into the next zone, then one or more zones will be skipped before *b$* is displayed. When commas are used to place strings, there is always at least one space between the strings.

```
CLS
PRINT "The Star-Spangled", "Banner"
END

[run]
The Star-Spangled           Banner
```

4. The TAB function cannot be used to move the cursor to the left. If the position specified in a TAB function is to the left of the current cursor position, the cursor will move to that position on the next line.

```
CLS
PRINT "hello"; TAB(3); "goodbye"
END

[run]
hello
  goodbye
```

5. When there is insufficient space remaining on a line to accommodate an item in the position specified by a PRINT statement, the item will be placed on the next line.

```
CLS
PRINT TAB(75); "good morning"
END

[run]

good morning
```

6. Numeric variables or expressions can be used in TAB and LOCATE statements. Some possibilities are `TAB(2 * a)` or `LOCATE r, c`.

7. PRINT USING is a rich statement with many enhancements. However, the variations of PRINT USING discussed in this section are sufficient for all the examples and exercises in this text. If you would like to explore further variations, read the discussion of PRINT USING in Appendix C.

8. In addition to $, #, and \, the characters *, &, ^, and ! serve special purposes in the format strings of PRINT USING statements. However, if one of these special characters is preceded by an underscore character, it will be treated as an ordinary character.

```
CLS
PRINT USING "We are _##"; 1
END

[run]
We are #1
```

PRACTICE PROBLEMS 3.5

1. The following two programs produce identical output on the screen. However, there is an important difference between them. What is it?

```
LET n = 123.458
LET n = INT(100 * n + .5) / 100
PRINT n
END
```

```
LET n = 123.458
LET f$ = "###.##"
PRINT USING f$; n
END
```

2. What is the output of the following program?

```
CLS
READ a$, b$, c$
PRINT TAB(11 - LEN(a$)); a$
PRINT TAB(11 - LEN(b$)); b$
PRINT TAB(11 - LEN(c$)); c$
REM -- Data: presidents
DATA Washington, Adams, Jefferson
END
```

EXERCISES 3.5

In Exercises 1 through 12, determine the output of the program.

1.
```
PRINT 1; "one", "won"
END
```

2.
```
PRINT TAB(10); "hello", "goodbye"
END
```

3.
```
PRINT "1234567890"
PRINT TAB(4); 5
END
```

4.
```
PRINT "one",
PRINT "two"
END
```

5.
```
LOCATE 20, 1
PRINT "hello"
END
```

6.
```
PRINT "1234567890"
LET n = 890.1234
PRINT USING "######.##"; n
END
```

7.
```
CLS
LET row = 3
LET col = 2
LOCATE row, col
PRINT "hello"
END
```

8.
```
REM Major rivers
READ r$, length       'River, length
PRINT TAB(12 - LEN(r$)); r$; length
READ r$, length
PRINT TAB(12 - LEN(r$)); r$; length
READ r$, length
REM -- Data: river, length
DATA Amazon, 4000
DATA Mississippi, 2348
DATA Nile, 4160
END
```

9.
```
PRINT "1234567890"
LET a$ = "ABC \ \"
PRINT USING a$; "abcdefg"
END
```

10.
```
PRINT "1234567890"
LET a$ = "\     \ ## #"
PRINT USING a$; "goodbye", 1, 2
END
```

11.
```
PRINT "1234567890"
LET a$ = "#####"
PRINT USING a$; 123456
END
```

12.
```
LET a$ = "\       \"
LET b$ = "$$###.##"
PRINT USING a$ + b$; "Cab", 8.75
END
```

In Exercises 13 through 16, determine the error.

13.
```
LOCATE 26, 26
PRINT "hello"
END
```

14.
```
LOCATE 1; 2
PRINT "hello", 56
END
```

15.
```
PRINT USING "##", 12
END
```

16.
```
PRINT USING "###"; "123"
END
```

In Exercises 17 through 20, what will be displayed by the statement PRINT USING a$; n?

17. a$ = "###.##", n = 3 * 100

18. a$ = "$$###.##", n = 123.4

19. a$ = "$#,###.##", n = 98.76

20. a$ = "Cost is $##.##", n = 25

In Exercises 21 and 22, what will be displayed by the statement PRINT USING a$; c$; n?

21.
```
LET a$ = "The median \ \ in the U.S. is ##.#"
LET c$ = "age"
LET n = 31.34
```

Note: There is 1 space between the backslashes in *a$*.

22.
```
LET a$ = "\               \ has #,### counties."
LET c$ = "The United States of America"
LET n = 3070
```

Note: There are 15 spaces between the backslashes in *a$*.

In Exercises 23 through 26, complete the LET statements.

23.
```
PRINT "1234567890"
LET a$ =
PRINT USING a$; 456.785
END

[run]
1234567890
$   456.79
```

24.
```
PRINT "1234567890"
LET n =
PRINT TAB(n); 76
END

[run]
1234567890
     76
```

25.
```
CLS
PRINT "1234567890"
LET r =
LET c =
LOCATE r, c
PRINT "hello"
END

[run]
1234567890
     hello
```

26.
```
LET a$ =
PRINT USING a$; 1.06 * 1.05
END

[run]
The balance is $1.11
```

27. Write a program to produce Table 3.5. (The amounts are given in millions of dollars.) For each person, the name, sport, salary or winnings, and endorsements should be contained in a data file. The totals should be computed by the program.

Athlete	Sport	Salary or Winnings	Endorsements	Total
M. Jordan	basketball	29.3	193.2	222.5
E. Holyfield	boxing	110.3	7.5	117.8
A. Agassi	tennis	11.3	63.5	74.8
W. Gretski	hockey	36.8	31.5	68.3

Table 3.5 1990-96 Earnings (in millions) of Athletes

28. Write a program to generate a rent receipt. The program should request the person's name, amount received, month for which rent was paid, and the current date as input and produce an output of the type shown below.

```
[run]
Name? Jane Smith
Amount? 675
Month? August
Current date? July 28, 1998

Received from Jane Smith the sum of $675.00
as rent for August.

          Signed _ _ _ _ _ _ _ _ _ _ _ _ _ _ _ _ _ _ _ _ _ _ _
          July 28, 1998
```

29. Write a program that requests a string with an INPUT statement and displays the string centered in a line of the screen. (Run the program with the string "My Favorite Program" as input.)

30. Write a program to produce Table 3.6. (The population is for 1992, the area is given in square miles, and the density is in people per square mile.) For each state, the name, capital, population, and area should be contained in a DATA statement. The densities should be computed by the program.

State	Capital	Population	Area	Density
Alaska	Juneau	607,000	570,374	1.06
New York	Albany	18,185,000	47,224	385.08
Texas	Austin	19,128,000	261,914	73.03

Table 3.6 State Data
Source: Statistical Abstract of the United States, 1997

31. Write a program to compute the balance in a savings account after one year. The program should request the principal and interest rate and then produce the display shown in the sample output below. (Assume the interest is compounded once during the year.)

```
[run]
Principal? 980.00
Interest rate (percent)? 5.5

                 Earned              New
 Principal     Interest          Balance

$    980.00       53.90        $1,033.90
```

32. Table 3.7 provides approximate information about certain occupations and projects the percent change in job openings from 1990 to 2005. Write a program to produce this table. Place the data in DATA statements and use the functions presented in this section as much as possible. Notice that the names of the occupations are right-justified.

Occupation	Number of Jobs in 1990	% Change	Weekly Median Earning
Computer Programmer	565,000	63	$653
Teacher, Secondary School	1,280,000	45	$648
Physician	580,000	41	$2,996

Table 3.7 Job Openings to 2005 and 1990 Earnings
Source: Bureau of Labor Statistics

33. Write a program that requests a positive number and a row of the screen as input and then displays the number flush left in the row. (***Hint:*** Use STR$ and RIGHT$ to strip away the space that would otherwise be displayed to the left of the number.)

SOLUTIONS TO PRACTICE PROBLEMS 3.5

1. In the first two lines on the left, the value of *n* is changed to its rounded value. In the lines on the right, the value of *n* remains the same but is displayed in its rounded form. The difference would be seen if the line PRINT *n* were added to the program segment on the right.

2.
```
Washington
     Adams
 Jefferson
```

The names are displayed right-justified—that is, lined up on the right. The TAB function can be used in a similar way to center a string on a line.

Chapter 3 Summary

1. Two types of *constants* can be stored and processed by computers, *numbers* and *strings*.

2. A *variable* is a name used to refer to data. String-variable names end with a dollar sign to distinguish them from numeric variables.

3. *Functions* can be thought of as accepting numbers or strings as input and returning numbers or strings as output.

Function	Input	Output
ASC	string	number
CHR$	number	string
INSTR	string, string	number
INT	number	number
LEFT$	string, number	string
LEN	string	number
MID$	string, number, number	string
RIGHT$	string, number	string
SQR	number	number
STR$	number	string
UCASE$	string	string
VAL	string	number

4. The arithmetic *operations* are +, –, *, /, and ^. The only string operation is +, concatenation. An *expression* is a combination of constants, variables, functions, and operations that can be evaluated.

5. Values are assigned to variables by LET, READ, and INPUT statements. The values assigned by LET statements can be constants, variables, or expressions. READ statements look to DATA statements for constants, and INPUT statements request the user to type in a constant. String constants used in LET statements must be surrounded by quotation marks, whereas quotation marks are optional for string constants input with READ or INPUT.

6. The PRINT statement displays information on the screen. *Semicolons*, *commas*, and TAB control the placement of the items on a particular line. LOCATE allows items to be placed anywhere on the screen.

7. The PRINT USING statement is ideal for displaying data in tables. Numbers can be made to line up uniformly and be displayed with dollar signs, commas, and a specified number of decimal places.

Chapter 3 Programming Projects

1. Figure 3.8 shows a simplified bill for long-distance phone calls. (The items in the third and fourth columns are the rates for the first minute and each additional minute.) Write a program to produce this bill. The data for the date, destination, the two rates, and the number of minutes should be stored in DATA statements. The program should compute the amounts and the total. ***Note:*** [amount] = [rate for first min] + [rate for each additional min] * ([number of min] – 1).

```
Date     To            1st Min   Addl. Min    Mins   Amount

JUN 16   BOSTON         .4698     .3740         17     6.45
JUN 23   SAN FRANCI     .5330     .4158          5     2.20
                                          Total       $8.65
```

Figure 3.8 Bill for Long-Distance Calls

2. Suppose automobile repair customers are billed at the rate of $35 per hour for labor. Also, costs for parts and supplies are subject to a 5% sales tax. Write a program to print out a simplified bill. The customer's name, the number of hours of labor, and the cost of parts and supplies should be entered into the program in response to INPUT statements. The computer should display the customer's name (indented) and the three costs shown in the sample run below.

```
[run]
Customer? John Doe
Hours of labor? 3.5
Cost of parts (and supplies)? 23.55

    John Doe
Labor cost    $122.50
Parts cost     $24.73
Total cost    $147.23
```

3. Write a program to generate the personalized form letter shown below. The person's name and address should be entered in response to INPUT statements.

```
Mr. John Jones
123 Main Street
Juneau, Alaska  99803

Dear Mr. Jones,

     The Jones family has been selected as the
first family on Main Street to have the opportunity
to purchase an Apex solar-powered flashlight. Due to limited
supply, only 1000 of these amazing inventions will be available
in the entire state of Alaska. Don't delay. Order today.

                              Sincerely,
                              Cuthbert J. Twillie
```

4. At the end of each month, a credit card company constructs the table in Figure 3.9 to summarize the status of the accounts. Write a program to produce this table. The first four pieces of information for each account should be stored in DATA statements. The program should compute the finance charges (1.5% of the unpaid past due amount) and the current amount due.

Account Number	Past Due Amount	Payments	Purchases	Finance Charges	Current Amt Due
123-AB	123.45	10.00	934.00	1.70	$1,049.15
456-CD	134.56	134.56	300.00	0.00	$300.00

Figure 3.9 Status of Credit Card Accounts

5. Table 3.7 gives the distribution of the U.S. population (in thousands) by age group and sex. Write a program to produce the table that is partially shown in Figure 3.10. For each age group, the column labeled %Males gives the percentage of the people in that age group that are male, and similarly for the column labeled %Females. The last column gives the percentage of the total population in each age group. (***Note:*** Store the information in Table 3.8 in DATA statements. For instance, the first row should be stored as DATA Under 20, 39168, 37202.)

Age Group	Males	Females
Under 20	39,168.00	37,202.00
20 – 64	76,761.00	78,291.00
Over 64	13,881.00	19,980.00

Table 3.7 U.S. Resident Population (1996)

U.S. Population (in thousands)

Age Group	Males	Females	%Males	%Females	%Total
Under 20	39,168.00	37,202.00	51.3%	48.7%	33.0%
20 - 64	76,761.00	78,291.00			
Over 64	13,881.00	19,980.00			

Figure 3.10 Partial Output of Programming Project 5

6. Write a program to convert a U.S. Customary System length in miles, yards, feet, and inches to a Metric System length in kilometers, meters, and centimeters. After the numbers of miles, yards, feet, and inches are requested as input, the length should be converted entirely to inches and then divided by 39.37 to obtain the value in meters. The INT function should be used to break the total number of meters into a whole number of kilometers and meters. The number of centimeters should be displayed to one decimal place. Some of the needed formulas are

   total inches = 63360 * miles + 36 * yards + 12 * feet + inches
   total meters = total inches / 39.37
   kilometers = INT(meters / 1000)

```
[sample run] Miles: 5
Yards: 20
Feet: 2
Inches: 4
Kilometers: 8
Meters: 65
Centimeters; 73.5
```

4

Procedures

4.1 SUBPROGRAMS, PART I

Structured program design requires that large problems be broken into smaller problems to be solved one at a time. QBasic has two devices, subprograms and functions, that are used to break problems into manageable chunks. Subprograms and functions are known as **procedures**. Procedures also eliminate repetitive code, can be reused in other programs, and allow a team of programmers to work on a single program.

In this section we show how subprograms are defined and used. The programs in this section are designed to demonstrate the use of subprograms rather than to accomplish sophisticated programming tasks. Later chapters of the book use procedures for more substantial programming efforts.

A **subprogram** is a part of a program that performs one or more related tasks, has its own name, is written as a separate part of the program, and is accessed via a CALL statement. The simplest type of subprogram has the form

```
SUB SubprogramName
  statement(s)
END SUB
```

Consider the following program that calculates the sum of two numbers. This program will be revised to incorporate subprograms.

```
REM Display the sum of two numbers
CLS
PRINT "This program displays a sentence"
PRINT "identifying two numbers and their sum."
PRINT
LET a = 2
LET b = 3
PRINT "The sum of"; a; "and"; b; "is"; a + b
END

[run]
This program displays a sentence
identifying two numbers and their sum.

The sum of 2 and 3 is 5
```

The tasks performed by this program can be summarized as follows:

Explain purpose of program.
Display numbers and their sum.

Subprograms allow us to write and read the program in such a way that we first focus on the tasks and later on how to accomplish each task.

EXAMPLE 1 The following program uses a subprogram to accomplish the first task of the program above. When the statement CALL ExplainPurpose is reached, execution jumps to the SUB statement. The lines between SUB and END SUB are executed, and then execution continues with the line following the CALL statement. ***Note:*** Do not type this program into the computer until you have read the two paragraphs following the example.

```
REM Display the sum of two numbers
CLS
CALL ExplainPurpose
PRINT
LET a = 2
LET b = 3
PRINT "The sum of"; a; "and"; b; "is"; a + b
END

SUB ExplainPurpose
  REM Explain the task performed by the program
  PRINT "This program displays a sentence"
  PRINT "identifying two numbers and their sum."
END SUB
```

The portion of the program preceding the END statement is called the **main body** of the program. In a certain sense, subprograms are self-contained programs accessed by the main body.

Subprograms are not typed into the View window. Instead, a separate window is created to hold each subprogram. The steps for creating a subprogram are as follows.

1. Move the cursor to a new line.
2. If *SubName* is the name of the subprogram, then type SUB *SubName* and press the Enter key.
3. After the Enter key is pressed, a special window is set up for the subprogram. The line SUB *SubName* appears at the top of the screen, and the cursor appears just above the words END SUB.
4. Type the subprogram into this window.
5. To return to the main body of the program, press Shift+F2 (that is, hold down Shift and press F2). Pressing Shift+F2 again displays the subprogram. (In general, successively pressing Shift+F2 cycles through the main body and procedures of the program.)

The second task performed by the addition program can also be handled by a subprogram. The values of the two numbers, however, must be transmitted to the subprogram. This transmission is called **passing**.

EXAMPLE 2 The following revision of the program in Example 1 uses a subprogram to accomplish the second task. The statement `CALL Add(2, 3)` causes execution to jump to the `SUB Add (a, b)` statement, which assigns the number 2 to *a* and the number 3 to *b*.

```
CALL Add(2, 3)
          ↓  ↓
SUB Add (a, b)
```

After the lines between SUB and END SUB are executed, execution continues with the line following `CALL Add(2, 3)`, namely the `END` statement. ***Note:*** When you create the subprogram Add, you can type in (a, b) either before or after pressing the Enter key. Notice that the subprograms are listed in alphabetical order.

```
REM Display the sum of two numbers
CLS
CALL ExplainPurpose
PRINT
CALL Add(2, 3)
END

SUB Add (a, b)
  REM Display numbers and their sum
  PRINT "The sum of"; a; "and"; b; "is"; a + b
END SUB

SUB ExplainPurpose
  REM Explain the task performed by the program
  PRINT "This program displays a sentence"
  PRINT "identifying two numbers and their sum."
END SUB
```

Subprograms make the program above easy to read, modify, and debug. The main body gives an unencumbered description of what the program does and the subprograms fill in the details. Another benefit of subprograms is that they can be called several times during the execution of the program. This feature is especially useful when there are many statements in the subprogram.

EXAMPLE 3 The following extension of the program in Example 2 displays several sums.

```
REM Display the sums of several pairs of numbers
CLS
CALL ExplainPurpose
PRINT
CALL Add(2, 3)
CALL Add(4, 6)
CALL Add(7, 8)
END

SUB Add (a, b)
  REM Display numbers and their sum
  PRINT "The sum of"; a; "and"; b; "is"; a + b
END SUB

SUB ExplainPurpose
  REM Explain the task performed by the program
  PRINT "This program displays sentences"
  PRINT "identifying pairs of numbers and their sums."
END SUB
```

```
[run]
This program displays sentences
identifying pairs of numbers and their sums.

The sum of 2 and 3 is 5
The sum of 4 and 6 is 10
The sum of 7 and 8 is 15
```

The variables *a* and *b* appearing in the subprogram Add are called **parameters**. They are merely temporary placeholders for the numbers passed to the subprogram; their names are not important. The only essentials are their type, quantity, and order. In the Add subprogram, the parameters must be numeric variables and there must be two of them. For instance, the subprogram could have been written

```
SUB Add (num1, num2)
  REM Display numbers and their sum
  PRINT "The sum of"; num1; "and"; num2; "is"; num1 + num2
END SUB
```

A string also can be passed to a subprogram. In this case, the receiving parameter in the subprogram must have the tag $.

EXAMPLE 4 The following program passes a string and two numbers to a subprogram. When the subprogram is first called, the parameter *state$* is assigned the string constant "Hawaii", and the numeric parameters *pop* and *area* are assigned the numeric constants 1184000 and 6471, respectively. The subprogram then uses these parameters to carry out the task of producing the population density of Hawaii. The second CALL statement assigns different values to the parameters.

```
REM Calculate the population density of a state
CLS
CALL ProduceDensity("Hawaii", 1184000, 6471)
CALL ProduceDensity("Alaska", 607000, 591000)
END

SUB ProduceDensity (state$, pop, area)
  REM The density (number of people per square mile)
  REM will be rounded to a whole number
  LET rawDensity = pop / area
  LET density = INT(rawDensity + .5)
  PRINT "The density of "; state$; " is"; density;
  PRINT "people per square mile."
END SUB

[run]
The density of Hawaii is 183 people per square mile.
The density of Alaska is 1 people per square mile.
```

The parameters in the density program can have any names, as with the parameters in the addition program of Example 3. The only restriction is that the first parameter be a string variable and the last two parameters be numeric variables. For instance, the subprogram could have been written

```
SUB ProduceDensity (x$, y, z)
  REM The density (number of people per square mile)
  REM will be rounded to a whole number
  LET rawDensity = y / z
  LET density = INT(rawDensity + .5)
  PRINT "The density of "; x$; " is"; density;
  PRINT "people per square mile."
END SUB
```

When nondescriptive names are used, the subprogram should contain REM statements giving the meanings of the variables. Possible REM statements for the program above are

```
REM x$    name of the state
REM y     population of the state
REM z     area of the state
```

Variables and Expressions as Arguments

The items appearing in the parentheses of a CALL statement are called **arguments**. These should not be confused with parameters, which appear in the heading of a procedure. In Example 3, the arguments of the CALL Add statements were constants. These arguments also could have been variables or expressions. For instance, the main body of the program could have been written as follows. (See Figure 4.1.)

```
REM Display the sum of two numbers
CLS
CALL ExplainPurpose
PRINT
LET x = 2
LET y = 3
CALL Add(x, y)
CALL Add(x + 2, 2 * y)
LET z = 7
CALL Add(z, z + 1)
END
```

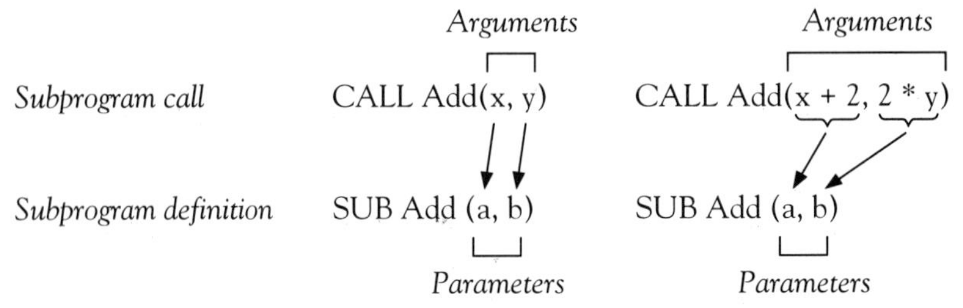

Figure 4.1 Passing Arguments to Parameters

This feature allows values obtained from INPUT statements to be passed to a subprogram.

EXAMPLE 5 The following variation of the addition program requests the two numbers as input from the user. Notice that the names of the arguments, *x* and *y*, are different from the names of the parameters. The names of the arguments and parameters may be the same or different; what matters is that the order, number, and types of the arguments and parameters match.

```
REM Display the sum of two numbers
CLS
REM "This program requests two numbers and"
REM "displays the two numbers and their sum."
INPUT "Enter two numbers separated by a comma: ", x, y
PRINT
CALL Add(x, y)
END

SUB Add (a, b)
  REM Display numbers and their sum
  PRINT "The sum of"; a; "and"; b; "is"; a + b
END SUB

[run]
Enter two numbers separated by a comma: 2, 3

The sum of 2 and 3 is 5
```

EXAMPLE 6 The following variation of Example 4 obtains its input from DATA statements. The second CALL statement uses different variable names for the arguments to show that using the same argument names is not necessary. (See Figure 4.2.)

```
REM Calculate the population density of a state
CLS
READ state$, pop, area
CALL ProduceDensity(state$, pop, area)
READ s$, p, a
CALL ProduceDensity(s$, p, a)
DATA Hawaii, 1184000, 6471
DATA Alaska, 607000, 591000
END

SUB ProduceDensity (state$, pop, area)
  REM The density (number of people per square mile)
  REM will be rounded to a whole number
  LET rawDensity = pop / area
  LET density = INT(rawDensity + .5)
  PRINT "The density of "; state$; " is"; density;
  PRINT "people per square mile."
END SUB
```

```
[run]
The density of Hawaii is 175 people per square mile.
The density of Alaska is 1 people per square mile.
```

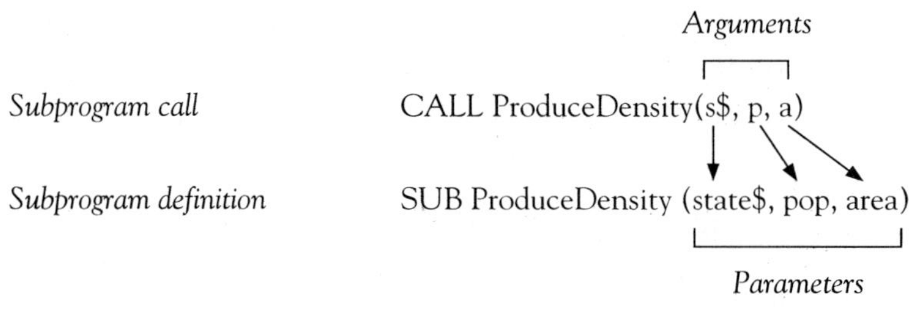

Figure 4.2 Passing Arguments to Parameters in Example 6

Arguments and parameters also can be used to pass values from subprograms back to the main body of the program. This important property of subprograms is explored in detail in the next section.

Comments:

1. READ statements can appear inside a subprogram, but not DATA statements. The DATA statements must be part of the main body.

2. In this text, subprogram names begin with uppercase letters in order to distinguish them from variable names. Like variable names, however, they can be written with any combination of upper- and lowercase letters. To improve readability, the QBasic editor will automatically ensure that the capitalization of a subprogram name is consistent throughout a program. For instance, if you type `CALL SUBPROGRAMNAME` and later type `CALL SubprogramName`, the first name will be changed to match the second. ***Note:*** Parameters appearing in a SUB statement are not part of the subprogram name.

3. The rules for naming subprograms are identical to the rules for naming numeric variables. The name chosen for a subprogram should describe the task it performs.

4. Subprograms allow programmers to focus on the main flow of the program and defer the details of implementation. Modern programs use subprograms liberally. The main body of the program acts as a supervisor, delegating tasks to the subprograms. This method of program construction is known as **modular** or **top-down** design.

5. As a general rule, a subprogram should perform only one task, or several closely related tasks, and should be kept relatively small.

6. Pressing the F2 key produces a list of all subprograms in the current program. The subprograms are listed in alphabetical order, not in the order they were created or in the order they are called. They can be selected by name from this list as an alternative to cycling through them with Shift+F2.

7. To delete a subprogram, press F2, select the subprogram to be removed, press the Tab key four times to reach the Delete box, and press the Enter key.

8. In this text, the first line inside a subprogram is often a REM statement describing the task performed by the subprogram. If necessary, several REM statements are used for this purpose. Conventional programming practice also recommends all variables used by the subprogram be listed in REM statements with their meanings. In this text, we give several examples of this practice but only adhere to it when the variables are especially numerous or lack descriptive names.

9. Although both constants and expressions can be used as arguments in CALL statements, only variables can be used as parameters in SUB statements.

10. When a program containing subprograms is saved, QBasic adds DECLARE statements to the beginning of the program that identify all the subprograms and their parameters. For instance, the program in Example 6 would begin with the line

```
DECLARE SUB ProduceDensity (state$, pop!, area!)
```

(Don't be concerned about the exclamation marks following the numeric variables.) DECLARE statements also can be entered by the programmer at the top of a program. So doing will allow QBasic to check that each CALL statement has the proper number and types of arguments. Although optional, many people regard the inclusion of DECLARE statements as good programming practice. It should definitely be done in large programs, especially when subprograms are written by different people. When DECLARE statements are typed into the top of a program by the programmer, there is no need for the parameters used to have the same names as the parameters in the corresponding SUB statement. They need only match in number, type, and order.

11. A subprogram can call another subprogram. If so, after the END SUB of the called subprogram is reached, execution continues with the statement in the calling subprogram that follows the CALL statement.

12. An alternate method of creating subprograms is to press Alt/E/S. When the dialog box appears, type the name of the subprogram and press the Enter key.

PRACTICE PROBLEMS 4.1

1. What is the output of the following program?

```
REM Demonstrate subprograms calling other subprograms
CALL First
PRINT 4;
END

SUB First
  PRINT 1;
  CALL Second
  PRINT 3;
END SUB

SUB Second
  PRINT 2;
END SUB
```

2. What is wrong with the following program?

```
INPUT "What is your complete phone number"; phone$
CALL AreaCode(phone$)
END

SUB AreaCode
  PRINT "Your area code is "; LEFT$(phone$, 3)
END SUB
```

EXERCISES 4.1

In Exercises 1 through 34, determine the output of the program.

1.
```
REM Quote from Kermit
CALL Quotation
PRINT "          Kermit the frog"
END

SUB Quotation
  REM Display a quotation
  PRINT "It isn't easy being green."
END SUB
```

2.
```
PRINT "Today ";
CALL Day
PRINT "of the rest of your life."
END

SUB Day
  PRINT "is the first day ";
END SUB
```

3.
```
CALL Question
CALL Answer
END

SUB Answer
  PRINT "Because they were invented in the northern"
  PRINT "hemisphere where sundials move clockwise."
END SUB

SUB Question
  PRINT "Why do clocks run clockwise?"
END SUB
```

4.
```
CALL FirstName
PRINT "How are you today?"
END

SUB FirstName
  INPUT "What is your first name"; name$
  PRINT "Hello " + UCASE$(name$)
END SUB
```

(Assume the response is *Bill*.)

5.
```
REM The fates of Henry the Eighth's six wives
CALL CommonFates
PRINT "died;"
CALL CommonFates
PRINT "survived."
END

SUB CommonFates
  REM The most common fates
  PRINT "Divorced, beheaded, ";
END SUB
```

6.
```
PRINT "A rose";
CALL Rose
CALL Rose
PRINT "."
END

SUB Rose
  PRINT ", is a rose";
END SUB
```

7.
```
REM Good advice to follow
CALL Advice
END

SUB Advice
  PRINT "Keep cool, but don't freeze."
  CALL Source
END SUB

SUB Source
  PRINT "Source: A jar of mayonnaise."
END SUB
```

8.
```
CALL Answer
CALL Question
END

SUB Answer
  PRINT "The answer is 9W."
  PRINT "What is the question?"
END SUB

SUB Question
  REM Note: "Wagner" is pronounced "Vagner"
  PRINT
  PRINT "Do you spell your name with a V, Mr. Wagner?"
END SUB
```

9.
```
CALL Piano(88)
END

SUB Piano(num)
  PRINT num; "keys on a piano"
END SUB
```

10.
```
REM Opening line of Moby Dick
CALL FirstLine("Ishmael")
END

SUB FirstLine (name$)
  REM Display first line
  PRINT "Call me "; name$
END SUB
```

11.
```
REM Opening of Tale of Two Cities
CALL Times("best")
CALL Times("worst")
END

SUB Times (word$)
  REM Display line
  PRINT "It was the "; word$; " of times."
END SUB
```

12.
```
CALL Potato(1)
CALL Potato(2)
CALL Potato(3)
PRINT 4
END

SUB Potato (quantity)
  PRINT quantity; "potato,";
END SUB
```

13.
```
REM Analyze a name
LET name$ = "Gabriel"
CALL AnalyzeName(name$)
END

SUB AnalyzeName (name$)
  REM Display length and first letter
  PRINT "Your name has"; LEN(name$); "letters."
  PRINT "The first letter is "; LEFT$(name$, 1)
END SUB
```

14.
```
INPUT "What is your favorite color"; color$
CALL Flattery(color$)
END

SUB Flattery (color$)
  PRINT "You look dashing in "; color$
END SUB
```

(Assume the response is *blue*.)

15.
```
INPUT "Enter a number from 1 to 26: ", num
CALL Alphabet(num)
END
```

```
SUB Alphabet (num)
  LET n = num
  PRINT LEFT$("abcdefghijklmnopqrstuvwxyz", n)
END SUB
```

(Assume the response is *5*.)

16.
```
LET size = 435
CALL House(size)
PRINT "of Representatives"
END

SUB House (size)
  PRINT size; "members in the House ";
END SUB
```

17.
```
LET num = 144
CALL Gross(num)
END

SUB Gross (amount)
  PRINT amount; "items in a gross"
END SUB
```

18.
```
LET a$ = "mile"
CALL Acres(a$)
END

SUB Acres (len$)
  PRINT "640 acres in a square "; len$
END SUB
```

19.
```
LET candy$ = "M&M's Plain Chocolate Candies"
CALL Brown(candy$)
END

SUB Brown (item$)
  PRINT "30% of "; item$; " are brown."
END SUB
```

20.
```
LET annualRate = .08
CALL Balance(annualRate)
END

SUB Balance (r)
  INPUT "What is the principal"; p
  PRINT "The balance after 1 year is"; (1 + r) * p
END SUB
```

(Assume the response is *100*.)

21.
```
LET hours = 24
CALL Minutes(60 * hours)
END

SUB Minutes (num)
  PRINT num; "minutes in a day"
END SUB
```

22.
```
LET a$ = "United States"
LET b$ = "acorn"
CALL Display(LEFT$(a$, 3) + MID$(b$, 2, 4))
END

SUB Display (word$)
  PRINT word$
END SUB
```

23.
```
INPUT "Enter a word: ", word$
CALL T(INSTR(word$, "t"))
END

SUB T (num)
  PRINT "t is the"; num; "th letter of the word."
END SUB
```

(Assume the response is *computer*.)

24.
```
LET states = 50
LET senators = 2
CALL Senate(states * senators)
END

SUB Senate (num)
  PRINT "The number of members of the U.S. Senate is"; num
END SUB
```

25.
```
CALL DisplaySource
CALL Language("BASIC", 22)
CALL Language("Assembler", 16)
CALL Language("C", 15)
CALL Language("Pascal", 13)
END

SUB DisplaySource
  PRINT "According to a poll in the May 31, 1988 issue of PC Magazine,"
  PRINT "75% of the people polled write programs for their companies."
  PRINT "The four most popular languages used are as follows."
END SUB

SUB Language(name$, users)
  PRINT users; "percent of the respondents use "; name$
END SUB
```

26.
```
REM Sentence using number, thing, and place
CALL Sentence(168, "hour", "a week")
CALL Sentence(76, "trombone", "the big parade")
END

SUB Sentence (num, thing$, where$)
  PRINT num; thing$; "s in "; where$
END SUB
```

27.
```
READ pres$, college$
CALL PresAlmaMater(pres$, college$)
READ pres$, college$
CALL PresAlmaMater(pres$, college$)
```

```
REM --- Data: president, college attended
DATA Bush, Yale University
DATA Clinton, Georgetown University
END

SUB PresAlmaMater (pres$, college$)
  PRINT "President "; pres$; " is a graduate of "; college$
END SUB
```

28.
```
INPUT "Name"; name$
INPUT "Year of birth"; yob
CALL AgeIn2000(name$, yob)
END

SUB AgeIn2000 (name$, yob)
  PRINT name$; ", in the year 2000 your age will be"; 2000 - yob
END SUB
```

(Assume the responses are *Gabriel* and *1980*.)

29.
```
READ word$, num
CALL FirstPart(word$, num)
DATA QBasic, 2
END

SUB FirstPart (term$, digit)
  PRINT "The first"; digit; "letters are"; LEFT$(term$, digit)
END SUB
```

30.
```
READ object$, tons
CALL HowHeavy(object$, tons)
DATA The Statue of Liberty, 250
END

SUB HowHeavy (what$, weight)
  PRINT what$; " weighs"; weight; "tons"
END SUB
```

31.
```
LET word$ = "worldly"
CALL Negative("un" + word$, word$)
END

SUB Negative (neg$, word$)
  PRINT "The negative of "; word$; " is "; neg$
END SUB
```

32.
```
INPUT "How old are you"; age
INPUT "In how many years will you graduate"; years
INPUT "What type of major do you have (Arts or Sciences)"; major$
CALL Graduation(age + years, LEFT$(major$, 1))
END

SUB Graduation (num, letter$)
  PRINT "You will receive a B"; letter$; " degree at age"; num
END SUB
```

(Assume the responses are *19*, *3*, and *Arts*.)

33.
```
CALL HowMany(24)
PRINT "a pie."
END

SUB HowMany (num)
  CALL What(num)
  PRINT " baked in ";
END SUB

SUB What (num)
  PRINT num; "blackbirds";
END SUB
```

34.
```
PRINT "All's";
CALL PrintWell
CALL PrintWords(" that ends")
PRINT "."
END

SUB PrintWell
  PRINT " well";
END SUB

SUB PrintWords (words$)
  PRINT words$;
  CALL PrintWell
END SUB
```

In Exercises 35 through 38, find the errors.

35.
```
LET n = 5
CALL Alphabet
END

SUB Alphabet (n)
  PRINT LEFT$("abcdefghijklmnopqrstuvwxyz", n)
END SUB
```

36.
```
LET word$ = "seven"
LET number = 7
CALL Display(word$, number)
END

SUB Display (num, term$)
  PRINT num; term$
END SUB
```

37.
```
INPUT "Name"; name$
CALL Print(name$)
END

SUB Print (handle$)
  PRINT "Your name is "; handle$
END SUB
```

38.
```
LET num = 2
CALL Tea(num)
END

SUB Tea
  PRINT "Tea for"; num
END SUB
```

In Exercises 39 through 42, rewrite the program so the output is performed by CALLs to a subprogram.

39.
```
REM Display a lucky number
CLS
LET num = 7
PRINT num; "is a lucky number."
END
```

40.
```
REM Greet a friend
CLS
LET name$ = "Jack"
PRINT "Hi, "; name$
END
```

41.
```
REM Information about trees
CLS
READ tree$, height
PRINT "The tallest "; tree$; " in the U.S. is"; height; "feet."
```

```
READ tree$, height
PRINT "The tallest "; tree$; " in the U.S. is"; height; "feet."
REM --- Data: tree, height
DATA redwood, 362, pine, 223
END
```

42.
```
REM Average starting salaries
CLS
READ major$, salary
PRINT "In 1997-98, the average starting salary for ";
PRINT major$; " majors "; "was ";
PRINT USING "$$#,###."; salary
READ major$, salary
PRINT "In 1997-98, the average starting salary for ";
PRINT major$; " majors "; "was ";
PRINT USING "$$#,###."; salary
DATA General Business Administration, 30373
DATA Computer Science, 38741
END
```

43. Write a program that requests a number as input and displays three times the number. The output should be produced by a call to a subprogram named Triple.

44. Write a program that requests a word as input and displays the word followed by the number of letters in the word. The output should be produced by a call to a subprogram named Length.

45. Write a program that requests a word and a column number from 1 through 10 as input and displays the word tabbed over to the column number. The output should be produced by a call to a subprogram named PlaceNShow.

46. Write a program that requests three numbers as input and displays the average of the three numbers. The output should be produced by a call to a subprogram named Average.

In Exercises 47 through 50, write a program to produce the output shown. The last two lines of the output should be displayed by one or more subprograms using data passed by variables from the main body.

47. [run]
```
According to a 1997 survey of college freshmen
taken by the Higher Educational Research Institute:

 16 percent said they intend to major in business
 3 percent said they intend to major in computer science
```

48. [run] (Assume the current date is 12/31/1998.)
```
What is your year of birth? 1979
You are now 19 years old.
You have lived for more than 6935 days.
```

49. [run]
```
What is your favorite number? 7
The sum of your favorite number with itself is 14
The product of your favorite number with itself is 49
```

50. [run]

```
In the year 1994,
 3.2 million public high school students took a course in Spanish
 1.1 million public high school students took a course in French
```

51. Write a program to display four verses of *Old McDonald Had a Farm*. The primary verse, with variables substituted for the animals and sounds, should be contained in a subprogram. The main body of the program should use the DATA statement

```
DATA lamb, baa, firefly, blink, chainsaw, brraap, computer, beep
```

The first verse of the output should be

```
Old McDonald had a farm. Eyi eyi oh.
And on his farm he had a lamb. Eyi eyi oh.
With a baa baa here, and a baa baa there.
Here a baa, there a baa, everywhere a baa baa.
Old McDonald had a farm. Eyi eyi oh.
```

52. Write a program that displays the word WOW vertically in large letters. Each letter should be drawn in a subprogram. For instance, the subprogram for the letter W is shown below.

```
SUB DrawW
  REM Draw the letter W
  PRINT "**          **"
  PRINT " **        **"
  PRINT "  **  **  **"
  PRINT "   **    **"
  PRINT
END SUB
```

53. Write a program to display the data from Table 4.1. The occupations and numbers of people for 1994 and 2005 should be contained in DATA statements. A subprogram, to be called four times, should read the three pieces of data for an occupation, calculate the percent change from 1994 to 2005, and display the four items. **Note:** The percent change is calculated as 100 * (2005 value – 1994 value) / (1994 value).

Occupation	1994	2005	Percent Change
Personal home care aides	179	391	118%
Home health aides	420	848	102%
System analysts	483	928	92%
Computer engineers	195	372	90%

Table 4.1 Occupations Projected to Experience Fastest Job Growth, 1994–2005 (numbers in thousands)
Source: U.S. Bureau of the Census, Statistical Abstract of the U.S., 1996

54. Write a program to compute tips for services rendered. The program should request the person's occupation, the amount of the bill, and the percentage tip as input and pass this information to a subprogram to display the person and the tip. A sample output is:

```
[run]
Enter the person's occupation: waitperson
Enter the amount of the bill: 20.00
Enter the percentage tip: 15
Tip the waitperson  $3.00
```

SOLUTIONS TO PRACTICE PROBLEMS 4.1

1. 1 2 3 4

   After the subprogram Second is called, execution continues with the remaining statements in the subroutine First before returning to the main body.

2. The statement SUB AreaCode must be replaced by SUB AreaCode (phone$). Whenever an argument is passed to a subprogram, the SUB statement must provide a parameter to receive the variable.

4.2 SUBPROGRAMS, PART II

The previous section introduced the concept of a subprogram but left some questions unanswered. Why can't the value of a variable be passed from the main body to a subprogram by just using the variable in the subprogram? How do subprograms pass values back to the main body? The answers to these questions provide a deeper understanding of the workings of subprograms and reveal their full capabilities.

Passing Values from Subprograms to the Main Body

Suppose a variable, call it *arg*, appears as an argument in a CALL statement, and its corresponding parameter in the SUB statement is *par*. After the subprogram is executed, *arg* will have whatever value *par* had in the subprogram. Hence, not only is the value of *arg* passed to *par*, but the value of *par* is passed back to *arg*.

EXAMPLE 1 The following program illustrates the transfer of the value of a parameter to its calling argument.

```
REM Illustrate effect of value of parameter on value of argument
CLS
LET amt = 2
PRINT amt;
CALL Triple(amt)
PRINT amt
END

SUB Triple (num)
  REM Triple a number
  PRINT num;
  LET num = 3 * num
  PRINT num;
END SUB
```

```
[run]
 2  2  6  6
```

Although this feature may be surprising at first glance, it provides a vehicle for passing values from a subprogram back to the main body of the program. Different names may be used for an argument and its corresponding parameter, but only one memory location is involved. Initially, the main body allocates a memory location to hold the value of *amt* (Figure 4.3(a)). When the subprogram is called, the parameter *num* becomes the subprogram's name for this memory location (Figure 4.3(b)). When the value of *num* is tripled, the value in the memory location becomes 6 (Figure 4.3(c)). After the completion of the procedure, the parameter name *num* is forgotten; however, its value lives on in *amt* (Figure 4.3(d)). The variable *amt* is said to be **passed by reference**.

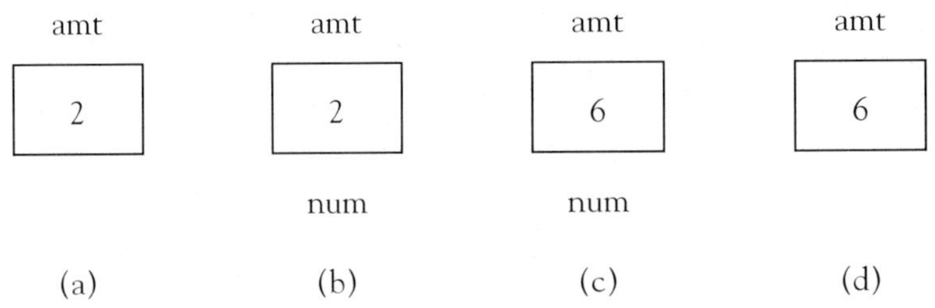

Figure 4.3 Passing a Variable by Reference to a Subprogram

Passing by reference has a wide variety of uses. In the next example, it is used as a vehicle to transport a value from a subprogram back to the main body of the program.

EXAMPLE 2 The following variation of the addition program from the previous section uses a subprogram to acquire the input. The variables *x* and *y* are not assigned values prior to the execution of the first CALL statement. Therefore, before the CALL statement is executed, they have the value 0. After the CALL statement is executed, however, they have the values 2 and 3. These values then are passed by the second CALL statement to the subprogram Add.

```
REM Display the sum of two numbers
CLS
PRINT "This program requests two numbers and"
PRINT "displays the two numbers and their sum."
PRINT
CALL InputNumbers(x, y)
PRINT
CALL Add(x, y)
END

SUB Add (num1, num2)
  REM Display numbers and their sum
  PRINT "The sum of"; num1; "and"; num2; "is"; num1 + num2
END SUB
```

```
SUB InputNumbers (num1, num2)
  REM Request two numbers as input from the user
  INPUT "Enter two numbers: ", num1, num2
END SUB

[run]
This program requests two numbers and
displays the two numbers and their sum.

Enter two numbers: 2, 3

The sum of 2 and 3 is 5
```

In most situations, a variable with no preassigned value is used as an argument of a CALL statement for the sole purpose of carrying back a value from the subprogram.

EXAMPLE 3 The following variation of Example 2 allows the main body of the program to be written in the input-process-output style.

```
REM Display the sum of two numbers
CLS
PRINT "This program requests two numbers and"
PRINT "displays the two numbers and their sum."
PRINT
CALL InputNumbers(x, y)
CALL CalculateSum(x, y, s)
CALL DisplayResult(x, y, s)
END

SUB CalculateSum (num1, num2, sum)
  REM Add the values of num1 and num2
  REM and assign the value to sum
  LET sum = num1 + num2
END SUB

SUB DisplayResult (num1, num2, sum)
  REM Display a sentence giving the two numbers and their sum
  PRINT
  PRINT "The sum of"; num1; "and"; num2; "is"; sum
END SUB

SUB InputNumbers (num1, num2)
  REM Request two numbers as input from the user
  INPUT "Enter two numbers: ", num1, num2
END SUB
```

Local Variables

When the same variable name appears in two different subprograms or in a subprogram and the main body, QBasic gives the variables separate identities and treats them as two different variables. A value assigned to a variable in one part of the program will not affect the value of the like-named variable in the other part of the program, unless, of course, the values are passed by a CALL statement. Also, each time a subprogram is called, all variables that are not parameters assume their default values, either zero or the empty string. The variables in a subprogram are said to be **local** to the subprogram in which they reside.

EXAMPLE 4 The following program illustrates the fact that each time a subprogram is called, its variables are set to their default values; that is, numerical variables are set to 0 and string variables are set to the empty string.

```
REM Demonstrate that variables in a subprogram do
REM not retain their values in subsequent calls
CLS
CALL Three
CALL Three
END

SUB Three
  REM Display the value of num and assign it the value 3
  PRINT num;
  LET num = 3
END SUB

[run]
 0  0
```

EXAMPLE 5 The following program illustrates the fact that variables are local to the part of the program in which they reside. The variable *x* in the main body and the variable *x* in the subprogram are treated as different variables. QBasic handles them as if their names were separate, such as *x.MainBody* and *x.Trivial.* Also, each time the subprogram is called, the value of variable *x* inside the subprogram is reset to 0.

```
REM Demonstrate the local nature of variables
CLS
LET x = 2
PRINT x;
CALL Trivial
PRINT x;
CALL Trivial
PRINT x;
END

SUB Trivial
  REM Do something trivial
  PRINT x;
  LET x = 3
  PRINT x;
END SUB

[run]
 2  0  3  2  0  3  2
```

Comments:

1. In addition to the reasons presented earlier, some other reasons for using subprograms are

   (a) Programs with subprograms are easier to debug. Each subprogram can be checked individually before being placed into the program.
   (b) The task performed by a subprogram might be needed in another program. The subprogram can be reused with no changes. Programmers refer to the collection of their most universal subprograms as a **library** of subprograms. (The fact that variables appearing in subprograms are local to the subprograms is quite helpful when reusing subprograms in other programs. There is no need to worry if a variable in the subprogram is used for a different purpose in another part of the program.)
   (c) Often, programs are written by a team of programmers. After a problem has been broken into distinct and manageable tasks, each programmer is assigned a single subprogram to write.
   (d) Subprograms make large programs easier to understand. Some programming standards insist the main body of the program not exceed two pages. Similarly, each subprogram should be at most two pages long.
   (e) Subprograms permit the following program design, which provides a built-in outline of the program. A reader can focus on the main flow of the program first, and then go into the specifics of accomplishing the secondary tasks.

   ```
   REM A program written entirely as subprograms
   CALL FirstSubprogram      'Perform first task
   CALL SecondSubprogram     'Perform second task
   CALL ThirdSubprogram      'Perform third task
   END
   ```

2. Subprograms can call other subprograms. In such cases, the calling subprogram plays the role of the main body with respect to the called subprogram. Complex problems are thereby broken into simpler tasks, which are then broken into still more elementary tasks. This approach to problem solving is called **top-down design**.

3. In Appendix D, the section "Stepping Through a Program Containing a Procedure: Chapter 4" uses the QBasic debugger to trace the flow through a program and observe the interplay between arguments and parameters.

PRACTICE PROBLEMS 4.2

1. What is the output of the following program?

   ```
   LET b = 1
   LET c = 2
   CALL Rhyme
   PRINT b; c
   END
   ```

```
SUB Rhyme
  PRINT b; c; "buckle my shoe."
  LET b = 3
END SUB
```

2. When a variable appears as a parameter in a SUB statement, how do we know if its role is to receive a value from the main body or to pass a value back to the main body, or both?

EXERCISES 4.2

In Exercises 1 through 18, determine the output of the program.

1.
```
LET num = 7
CALL AddTwo(num)
PRINT num
END

SUB AddTwo (num)
  LET num = num + 2
END SUB
```

2.
```
LET term$ = "Fall"
CALL Plural(term$)
PRINT term$
END

SUB Plural (term$)
  LET term$ = term$ + "s"
END SUB
```

3.
```
LET dance$ = "Can "
CALL Twice(dance$)
PRINT dance$
END

SUB Twice (dance$)
  LET dance$ = dance$ + dance$
END SUB
```

4.
```
INPUT "Enter a number: ", num
CALL Format(formatString$)
PRINT "The number is ";
PRINT USING formatString$; num
END

SUB Format (formatString$)
  PRINT "Enter a PRINT USING format string suitable for"
  INPUT "displaying the number: ", formatString$
END SUB
```

(Assume the responses are *1234.567* and "##,###.##".)

5.
```
LET a = 5
CALL Square(a)
PRINT a
END

SUB Square (num)
  LET num = num * num
END SUB
```

6.
```
LET state$ = "NEBRASKA"
CALL Abbreviate(state$)
PRINT state$
END

SUB Abbreviate (a$)
  LET a$ = LEFT$(a$, 2)
END SUB
```

7.
```
CALL GetWord(word$)
PRINT "Less is "; word$
END

SUB GetWord (w$)
  LET w$ = "more"
END SUB
```

8.
```
LET hourlyWage = 10
CALL CalculateAnnualWage(hourlyWage, annualWage)
PRINT "Approximate Annual Wage:"; annualWage
END

SUB CalculateAnnualWage (hWage, aWage)
  LET aWage = 2000 * hWage
END SUB
```

9.
```
CALL InputVita(name$, yob)
PRINT name$; " was born in the year"; yob
END

SUB InputVita (name$, yob)
  INPUT "Enter your name: ", name$
  INPUT "Enter your year of birth: ", yob
END SUB
```

(Assume the responses are *Gabriel* and *1980*.)

10.
```
LET word1$ = "fail"
LET word2$ = "plan"
PRINT "If you ";
CALL Sentence(word1$, word2$)
CALL Exchange(word1$, word2$)
PRINT " then you ";
CALL Sentence(word1$, word2$)
END

SUB Exchange (word1$, word2$)
  LET temp$ = word1$
  LET word1$ = word2$
  LET word2$ = temp$
END SUB

SUB Sentence (word1$, word2$)
  PRINT word1$; " to "; word2$;
END SUB
```

11.
```
LET state$ = "Ohio"
CALL Team
END

SUB Team
  PRINT state$;
  PRINT "Buckeyes"
END SUB
```

12.
```
LET a = 5
CALL Multiply(7)
PRINT a * 7
END

SUB Multiply (num)
  LET a = 11
  PRINT a * num
END SUB
```

13.
```
LET a = 5
CALL Multiply(7)
END

SUB Multiply (num)
  PRINT a * num
END SUB
```

14.
```
LET name$ = "Ray"
CALL Hello(name$)
PRINT n$; " and "; name$
END

SUB Hello (name$)
  LET n$ = name$
  LET name$ = "Bob"
  PRINT "Hello "; n$; " and "; name$
END SUB
```

15.
```
LET num = 1
CALL Amount(num)
CALL Amount(num)
END

SUB Amount (num)
  LET total = total + num
  PRINT total;
END SUB
```

16.
```
LET river$ = "Wabash"
CALL Another
PRINT river$
CALL Another
END

SUB Another
  PRINT river$;
  LET river$ = "Yukon"
END SUB
```

17.
```
LET explorer$ = "de Leon"
CALL Place(explorer$)
END

SUB Place (name$)
  PRINT explorer$; " discovered Florida"
END SUB
```

18.
```
LET tax = .05
CALL InputPrice("bicycle", price)
CALL ProcessItem(price, tax, total)
CALL DisplayResult(total)
END

SUB DisplayResult (total)
  PRINT "With tax, the price is ";
  PRINT USING "###.##"; total
END SUB

SUB InputPrice (item$, price)
  PRINT "What is the price of a "; item$;
  INPUT price
END SUB

SUB ProcessItem (price, tax, total)
  LET total = (1 + tax) * price
END SUB
```

(Assume the cost of the bicycle is $200.)

In Exercises 19 and 20, find the errors.

19.
```
LET a = 1
LET b = 2
CALL Sum(a, b, c)
PRINT "The sum is"; c
END

SUB Sum (x, y)
  LET c = x + y
END SUB
```

20.
```
CALL GetWord(word$)
PRINT word$
CALL GetWord(meaning$)
PRINT meaning$
END

SUB GetWord (word$)
  READ word$
  DATA one, two
END SUB
```

In Exercises 21 through 24, rewrite the program so input, processing, and output are each performed by CALLs to subprograms.

21.
```
REM Calculate sales tax
CLS
INPUT "Enter the price of the item: ", price
LET tax = .05 * price
LET cost = price + tax
PRINT "Price: "; price
PRINT "Tax: "; tax
PRINT "-----------"
PRINT "Cost: "; cost
END
```

22.
```
REM Letter of acceptance
CLS
INPUT "What is your full name"; name$
LET n = INSTR(name$, " ")
LET firstName$ = LEFT$(name$, n - 1)
PRINT "Dear "; firstName$; ","
PRINT "We are proud to accept you to Gotham College."
END
```

23.
```
REM Determine the area of a rectangle
CLS
READ length, wdth
LET area = length * wdth
PRINT "The area of the rectangle is"; area
REM --- Data: length, width
DATA 4, 5
END
```

24.
```
REM Convert feet and inches to centimeters
CLS
PRINT "Give the length in feet and inches."
INPUT "Number of feet"; feet
INPUT "Number of inches"; inches
LET totalInches = 12 * feet + inches
LET centimeters = 2.54 * totalInches
PRINT "The length in centimeters is"; centimeters
END
```

In Exercises 25 through 30, write a program to perform the stated task. The input, processing, and output should be performed by calls to subprograms.

25. Request a person's first name and last name as input and display the corresponding initials.

26. Request the amount of a restaurant bill as input and display the amount, the tip (15%), and the total amount.

27. Request the cost and selling price of an item of merchandise as input and display the percentage markup. Test the program with a cost of $4 and a selling price of $6. ***Note:*** The percentage markup is 100 * ((selling price – cost) / cost).

28. Read the number of students in public colleges (10.8 million) and private colleges (3.1 million) from a DATA statement, and display the percentage of college students attending public colleges.

29. Read a baseball player's name (Sheffield), times at bat (557), and hits (184) from a DATA statement and display his name and batting average. ***Note:*** Batting average is calculated as (hits)/(times at bat) and is given to three decimal places.

30. Request three numbers as input and then calculate and display the average of the three numbers.

31. The Hat Rack is considering locating its new branch store in one of three malls. The DATA statements below give the monthly rent per square foot and the total square feet available at each of the three locations. Write a program to display a table exhibiting this information along with the total monthly rent for each mall.

```
REM --- name of mall, rent per square foot, square feet available
DATA Green Mall, 6.50, 583
DATA Red Mall, 7.25, 426
DATA Blue Mall, 5.00, 823
```

32. Write a program that uses the DATA statements below to display the end-of-month credit card balances of three people. The end-of-month balance is calculated as [finance charges] + [beginning-of-month balance] + [purchases] – [payment], where the finance charge is 1.5% of the beginning-of-month balance.

```
REM --- person, beginning balance, purchases during month, payment
DATA John Adams, 125.00, 60.00, 110.00
DATA Sue Jones, 0, 117.25, 117.25
DATA John Smith, 350.00, 200.50, 300.00
```

SOLUTIONS TO PRACTICE PROBLEMS 4.2

1. [run]

```
0  0 buckle my shoe.
1  2
```

This program illustrates the local nature of the variables in a subprogram. Notice that the variables b and c appearing in the subprogram have no relationship whatsoever to the variables of the same name in the main body. In a certain sense, the variables inside the subprogram can be thought of as having alternate names, such as *b.Rhyme* and *c.Rhyme*.

2. You cannot determine this by simply looking at the arguments and the parameters. The code of the subprogram must be examined.

4.3 FUNCTIONS

QBasic has many built-in functions. In one respect, functions are like miniature programs. They use input, they process the input, and they have output. Some functions we encountered earlier are listed in Table 4.2.

Function	Example	Input	Output
INT	INT(2.6) is 2	number	number
CHR$	CHR$(65) is "A"	number	string
LEN	LEN("perhaps") is 7	string	number
MID$	MID$("perhaps",4,2) is "ha"	string,number,number	string
INSTR	INSTR("to be"," ") is 3	string,string	number

Table 4.2 Some QBasic Built-In Functions

Although the input can involve several values, the output always consists of a single value. The items inside the parentheses can be constants (as above), variables, or expressions. The type of output can be determined by looking at the name of the function. If the name is followed by a dollar sign, then the output is a string.

In addition to using built-in functions, we can define functions of our own. These new functions, called **user-defined functions**, are defined in much the same way as subprograms and are used in the same way as built-in functions. Like built-in functions, user-defined functions have a single output which is either string or numeric. User-defined functions can be used in expressions in exactly the same way as built-in functions. Programs refer to them as if they were constants, variables, or expressions. They reside outside the main body and are defined by function blocks of the form

```
FUNCTION FunctionName (var1, var2, ...)
  statement(s)
  FunctionName = expression
END FUNCTION
```

The variables in the top line are called **parameters**, and variables inside the function block that are not parameters are local. Function names should be suggestive of the role performed and must conform to the rules for naming variables. The name of the function must be followed by a dollar sign if the output is a string. Two examples of functions are:

```
FUNCTION Round (x)
  REM Round the number x to two decimal places
  Round = INT(100 * x + .5) / 100
END FUNCTION

FUNCTION FirstName$ (name$)
  REM Extract the first name from the full name name$
  LET firstSpace = INSTR(name$, " ")
  FirstName$ = LEFT$(name$, firstSpace - 1)
END FUNCTION
```

The value of each of the preceding functions is assigned by a statement of the form *FunctionName* = *expression*. (Such a statement can also be written as LET *FunctionName* = *expression*.) The variables *x* and *name$* appearing in the functions above are parameters. They can be replaced with any variable of the same type without affecting the function definition. For instance, the function Round could have been defined as

```
FUNCTION Round (num)
  REM Round the number num to two decimal places
  Round = INT(100 * num + .5) / 100
END FUNCTION
```

Like subprograms, functions are created in separate windows. The only difference is that FUNCTION *FunctionName* should be entered on the blank line. After the Enter key is pressed, the lines FUNCTION *FunctionName* and END FUNCTION will automatically be placed in the function window.

EXAMPLE 1 The following program uses the function ROUND.

```
REM Divide an amount of money by six
CLS
INPUT "Positive amount of money"; money
PRINT "One-sixth of"; money; "is $"; Round(money / 6)
END

FUNCTION Round (x)
  REM Round the number x to two decimal places
  Round = INT(100 * x + .5) / 100
END FUNCTION

[run]
Positive amount of money? 123.46
One-sixth of 123.45 is $ 20.58
```

EXAMPLE 2 The following program uses the function FirstName$.

```
REM Determine a person's first name
CLS
INPUT "Person's name"; name$
```

```
PRINT "The person's first name is "; FirstName$(name$)
END

FUNCTION FirstName$ (name$)
  REM Extract the first name from a full name
  LET firstSpace = INSTR(name$, " ")
  FirstName$ = LEFT$(name$, firstSpace - 1)
END FUNCTION

[run]
Person's name? Thomas Woodrow Wilson
The person's first name is Thomas
```

The input to a user-defined function can consist of one or more values. Two examples of functions with several parameters are shown below. One-letter variable names have been used so the mathematical formulas will look familiar and be readable. Since the names are not descriptive, the meanings of these variables are carefully stated in REM statements.

```
FUNCTION Hypotenuse (a, b)
  REM Calculate the hypotenuse of right triangle
  REM having sides of lengths a and b
  Hypotenuse = SQR(a ^ 2 + b ^ 2)
END FUNCTION

FUNCTION FutureValue (p, r, c, n)
  REM Find the future value of a bank savings account
  REM p  principal, the amount deposited
  REM r  annual rate of interest
  REM c  number of times interest is compounded per year
  REM n  number of years
  REM i  interest per period
  REM m  total number of times interest is compounded
  LET i = r / c
  LET m = c * n
  FutureValue = p * (1 + i) ^ m
END FUNCTION
```

EXAMPLE 3 The following program uses the Hypotenuse function.

```
REM Calculate the length of the hypotenuse of a right triangle
CLS
INPUT "Enter lengths of two sides of a right triangle: ", a, b
PRINT "The hypotenuse has length"; Hypotenuse(a, b)
END

FUNCTION Hypotenuse (a, b)
  REM Calculate the hypotenuse of right triangle
  REM having sides of lengths a and b
  Hypotenuse = SQR(a ^ 2 + b ^ 2)
END FUNCTION
```

```
[run]
Enter lengths of two sides of a right triangle: 3, 4
The hypotenuse has length 5
```

EXAMPLE 4 The following program uses the future-value function. With the responses shown, the program computes the balance in a savings account when $100 is deposited for 5 years at 4% interest compounded quarterly. Interest is earned 4 times per year at the rate of 1% per interest period. There will be 4 * 5 or 20 interest periods.

```
REM Find the future value of a bank deposit
CLS
CALL InputData(p, r, c, n)
CALL DisplayResult(p, r, c, n)
END

SUB DisplayResult (p, r, c, n)
  PRINT "Balance: $"; FutureValue(p, r, c, n)
END SUB

FUNCTION FutureValue (p, r, c, n)
  REM Find the future value of a bank savings account
  REM p  principal, the amount deposited
  REM r  annual rate of interest
  REM c  number of times interest is compounded per year
  REM n  number of years
  REM i  interest per period
  REM m  total number of times interest is compounded
  LET i = r / c
  LET m = c * n
  FutureValue = p * ((1 + i) ^ m)
END FUNCTION

SUB InputData (p, r, c, n)
  INPUT "Amount of bank deposit"; p
  INPUT "Annual rate of interest"; r
  INPUT "Number of times interest is compounded per year"; c
  INPUT "Number of years"; n
END SUB

[run]
Amount of bank deposit? 100
Annual rate of interest? .04
Number of times interest is compounded per year? 4
Number of years? 5
Balance: $ 122.019
```

Note: The balance can be displayed in dollars and cents by adding the function Round to the program and changing the PRINT statement to

```
PRINT "Balance: $"; Round(FutureValue(p, r, c, n))
```

EXAMPLE 5 Some computer languages have a useful built-in function called CEIL that is similar to the function INT, except that it rounds noninteger numbers up to the next integer. For instance, CEIL(3.2) is 4 and CEIL(–1.6) is –1. The following program creates CEIL in QBasic as a user-defined function.

```
REM Demonstrate the CEIL function
CLS
INPUT "Enter a number: ", num
PRINT "CEIL of the number is"; Ceil(num)
INPUT "Enter a number: ", num
PRINT "CEIL of the number is"; Ceil(num)
END

FUNCTION Ceil (x)
  REM Round nonintegers up
  Ceil = -INT(-x)
END FUNCTION

[run]
Enter a number: 4.3
CEIL of the number is 5
Enter a number: 4
CEIL of the number is 4
```

There are many reasons for employing user-defined functions.

1. User-defined functions are consistent with the modular approach to program design. Once we realize a particular function is needed, we can give it a name but save the task of figuring out the computational details until later.
2. Sometimes a single formula must be used several times in a program. Specifying the formula as a function saves repeated typing of the same formula, improves readability, and simplifies debugging.
3. Functions written for one program can be used in other programs. Programmers maintain a collection, or library, of functions that might be needed.

Comments:

1. The word **procedure** refers to either a function or a subprogram.
2. Functions can perform the same tasks as subprograms. For instance, they can request input and display text; however, they are primarily used to calculate a single value. Normally, subprograms are used to carry out other tasks.
3. Functions differ from subprograms in the way they are accessed. Subprograms are invoked with CALL statements, whereas functions are invoked by placing them where you would otherwise expect to find a constant, variable, or expression.
4. Functions can invoke other functions or subprograms.
5. Functions, like subprograms, need not have any parameters. The following program uses a "parameterless" function.

```
REM Request and display a saying
CLS
PRINT Saying$
END

FUNCTION Saying$
  REM Retrieve a saying from the user
  INPUT "What is your favorite saying"; response$
  Saying$ = response$
END FUNCTION

[run]
What is your favorite saying? Less is more.
Less is more.
```

6. An alternate method of creating functions is to press Alt/E/F. When the dialog box appears, type the name of the function and press the Enter key.

7. QBasic provides another type of user-defined function that is defined in the main body of the program with a statement of the form DEF FN*FunctionName* (*var1*, *var2*, ...) = *expression*. Such functions are not used in this text, since the block functions can do everything DEF FN functions do and much more. However, because of the provision for DEF FN functions in QBasic, the names of block functions and variables must not begin with the letters FN.

PRACTICE PROBLEMS 4.3

1. Suppose a program contains the line

```
PRINT a$(n, x$)
```

What types of inputs and output (numeric or string) does the function a$ have?

2. What is the output of the following program, if the first response is 3 and the second response is 9?

```
REM How many gallons of apple cider can we make?
CALL InputData(gallonsPerBushel, apples)
CALL DisplayNumOfGallons(gallonsPerBushel, apples)
END

FUNCTION Cider (g, x)
  Cider = g * x
END FUNCTION

SUB DisplayNumOfGallons (galPerBu, apples)
  PRINT "You can make"; Cider(galPerBu, apples); "gallons of cider."
END SUB

SUB InputData (gallonsPerBushel, apples)
  PRINT "How many gallons of cider will 1 bushel"
  INPUT "of apples make"; gallonsPerBushel
  INPUT "How many bushels of apples do you have"; apples
END SUB
```

EXERCISES 4.3

In Exercises 1 through 10, determine the output of the program.

1.
```
REM Convert Fahrenheit to Celsius
READ temp
PRINT FtoC(temp)
DATA 95
END

FUNCTION FtoC (t)
  FtoC = (5 / 9) * (t - 32)
END FUNCTION
```

2.
```
INPUT "How many acres is your parking lot"; a
PRINT "You can park about"; Cars(a); "cars."
END

FUNCTION Cars (x)
  REM Parking cars
  Cars = 100 * x
END FUNCTION
```

(Assume the response is 5.)

3.
```
REM Rule of 72
INPUT "Population growth as a percent"; p
PRINT "The population will double in"; DoublingTime(p); "years."
END

FUNCTION DoublingTime (x)
  REM Estimate time required for a population to double
  REM at a growth rate of x percent
  DoublingTime = 72 / x
END FUNCTION
```

(Assume the response is 3.)

4.
```
REM Calculate max. ht. of a ball thrown straight up in the air
READ initVel, initHt      'Initial velocity and height of ball
PRINT MaximumHeight(initVel, initHt)
REM --- Data: initial velocity, initial height
DATA 96, 256
END

FUNCTION MaximumHeight (v, h)
  MaximumHeight = h + v ^ 2 / 64
END FUNCTION
```

5.
```
REM Compute volume of a cylinder
READ r, h
CALL DisplayVolume(r, h)
READ r, h
CALL DisplayVolume(r, h)
REM --- Data: radius, height
DATA 1, 2, 3, 4
END
```

```
FUNCTION Area (r)
  Area = 3.14159 * r ^ 2
END FUNCTION

SUB DisplayVolume (r, h)
   PRINT "Volume of cylinder having base area"; Area(r);
   PRINT "and height"; h; "is"; h * Area(r)
END SUB
```

6.
```
REM Determine the day of the week from its number
LET days$ = "SunMonTueWedThuFriSat"
INPUT "Enter the number of the day"; num
PRINT "The day is "; DayOfWeek$(days$, num)
END

FUNCTION DayOfWeek$ (x$, n)
  REM x$  string containing 3-letter abbreviations of days of the week
  REM n   the number of the day
  LET position = 3 * n - 2
  DayOfWeek$ = MID$(x$, position, 3)
END FUNCTION
```

(Assume the response is 4.)

7.
```
REM Demonstrate local variables
LET a$ = "Choo "
PRINT TypeOfTrain$
END

FUNCTION TypeOfTrain$
  LET a$ = a$ + a$
  TypeOfTrain$ = a$ + "train"
END FUNCTION
```

8.
```
REM Triple a number
LET num = 5
PRINT Triple(num);
PRINT num
END

FUNCTION Triple (x)
  LET num = 3
  Triple = num * x
END FUNCTION
```

9.
```
READ word$
CALL Negative(word$)
READ word$
CALL Negative(word$)
DATA moral, political
END

FUNCTION AddA$ (word$)
  AddA$ = "a" + word$
END FUNCTION

SUB Negative(word$)
  PRINT word$; " has the negative "; AddA$(word$)
END SUB
```

10.
```
READ city$, pop, shrinks
CALL DisplayData(city$, pop, shrinks)
READ city$, pop, shrinks
CALL DisplayData(city$, pop, shrinks)
REM --- Data: city, population, number of psychiatrists
DATA Boston, 2824000, 8602
DATA Denver, 1633000, 3217
END
```

```
SUB DisplayData (city$, pop, shrinks)
  PRINT city$; " has"; ShrinkDensity(pop, shrinks);
  PRINT "psychiatrists per 100,000 people."
END SUB

FUNCTION ShrinkDensity (pop, shrinks)
  ShrinkDensity = 100000 * (shrinks / pop)
END FUNCTION
```

In Exercises 11 and 12, identify the errors.

11.
```
REM Select a greeting
INPUT "Enter 1 or 2: ", answer
PRINT Greeting$(answer)
END

FUNCTION Greeting (x)
  Greeting$ = MID$("hellohi ya", 5 * x - 4, 5)
END FUNCTION
```

12.
```
INPUT "What is your favorite word"; word$
PRINT "When the word is written twice,";
PRINT Twice$(word$); "letters are used."
END

FUNCTION Twice$ (w$)
  REM Compute twice the length of a string
  Twice$(w$) = 2 * LEN(w$)
END FUNCTION
```

In Exercises 13 through 21, construct user-defined functions to carry out the primary task(s) of the program.

13. To convert temperatures from centigrade to Fahrenheit, multiply the Celsius temperature by (9/5) and add 32. Write a program that requests a temperature in Celsius as input and gives the corresponding temperature in Fahrenheit.

14. According to Plato, a man should marry a woman whose age is half his age plus seven years. Write a program that requests a man's age as input and gives the ideal age of his wife.

15. Write a program that accepts a number (m) and a small positive integer (n) as input and rounds m to n decimal places.

16. In order for exercise to be beneficial to the cardiovascular system, the heart rate (number of heart beats per minute) must exceed a value called the training heart rate, THR. A person's THR can be calculated from their age and resting heart rate (pulse when first awakening) as follows:

(a) Calculate the maximum heart rate as 220 – age.
(b) Subtract the resting heart rate from the maximum heart rate.
(c) Multiply the result in step (b) by 60% and then add the resting heart rate.

Write a program to request a person's age and resting heart rate as input and display their THR. (Test the program with an age of 20 and a resting heart rate of 70, then determine *your* training heart rate.)

17. The three ingredients for a serving of popcorn at a movie theater are popcorn, butter substitute, and a bucket. Write a program that requests the cost of these three items and the price of the serving as input and then displays the profit. (Test the program where popcorn costs 5 cents, butter substitute costs 2 cents, the bucket costs 25 cents, and the selling price is $2.)

18. Rewrite the population-density program from Example 4 of Section 4.1 using a function to calculate the population density.

19. The original cost of airmail letters was 5 cents for the first ounce and 10 cents for each additional ounce. Write a program to compute the cost of a letter whose weight is entered using an INPUT statement. ***Hint:*** Use the function Ceil discussed in Example 5. (Test the program with the weights 4, 1, 2.5, and .5 ounces.)

20. Suppose a fixed amount of money is deposited at the beginning of each month into a savings account paying 6% interest compounded monthly. After each deposit is made, [new balance] = 1.005*[previous balance one month ago] + [fixed amount]. Write a program that requests the fixed amount of the deposits as input and displays the balance after each of the first four deposits. A sample outcome is:

```
[run]
Enter the amount to be deposited each month: 800

Month 1     800.00
Month 2    1604.00
Month 3    2412.02
Month 4    3224.08
```

21. Write a program to request the name of a United States senator as input and display the address and greeting for a letter to the senator. Assume the name has two parts and use a function to determine the senator's last name. A sample output is:

```
[run]
Enter the senator's name: William Smith

The Honorable William Smith
United States Senate
Washington, DC 20001

Dear Senator Smith,
```

SOLUTIONS TO PRACTICE PROBLEMS 4.3

1. Since the name of the function is followed by a dollar sign, the output will be a string. The first argument, n, takes numeric values and the second argument, x$, takes string values; therefore, the input consists of a number and a string.

2. You can make 27 gallons of cider. In this program, the function was used by a subprogram rather than by the main body.

4.4 MODULAR DESIGN

Top-Down Design

Large problems usually require large programs. One method programmers use to make a large problem more understandable is to divide it into smaller, less complex subproblems. Repeatedly using a "divide-and-conquer" approach to break up a large problem into smaller subproblems is called **stepwise refinement**. Stepwise refinement is part of a larger methodology of writing programs known as **top-down design**. The term top-down refers to the fact that the more general tasks occur near the top of the design and tasks representing their refinement occur below. Top-down design and structured programming emerged as techniques to enhance programming productivity. Their use leads to programs that are easier to read and maintain. They also produce programs containing fewer initial errors, with these errors being easier to find and correct. When such programs are later modified, there is a much smaller likelihood of introducing new errors.

The goal of top-down design is to break a problem into individual tasks, or modules, that can easily be transcribed into pseudocode, flowcharts, or a program. First, a problem is restated as several simpler problems depicted as modules. Any modules that remain too complex are broken down further. The process of refining modules continues until the smallest modules can be coded directly. Each stage of refinement adds a more complete specification of what tasks must be performed. The main idea in top-down design is to go from the general to the specific. This process of dividing and organizing a problem into tasks can be pictured using a top-down chart showing a hierarchy of the modules. When using top-down design, certain criteria should be met:

1. The design should be easily readable and emphasize small module size.
2. Modules proceed from general to specific as you read down the chart.
3. The modules, as much as possible, should be single-minded. That is, they should only perform a single well-defined task.
4. Modules should be as independent of each other as possible, and any relationships among modules should be specified.

This process is illustrated with the following example.

EXAMPLE 1 Write a top-down chart for a program that gives certain information about a car loan. The amount of the loan, the duration (in years), and the interest rate should be input. The output should consist of the monthly payment and the amount of interest paid during the first month.

SOLUTION In the broadest sense, the program calls for obtaining the input, making calculations, and displaying the output. Figure 4.4 shows these tasks as the first row of a top-down chart.

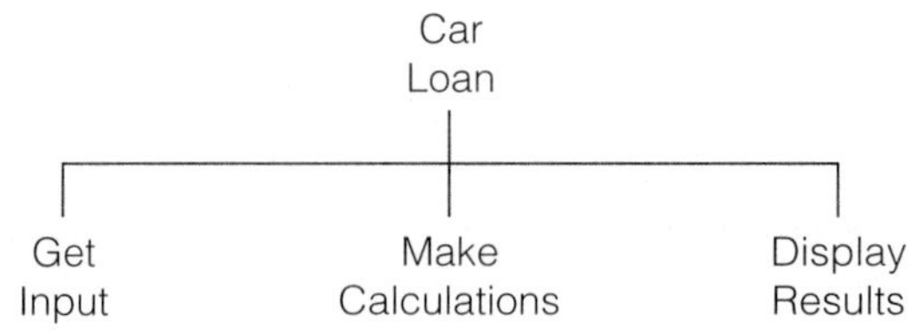

Figure 4.4 Beginning of a Top-Down Chart for the Car Loan Program

Each of these tasks can be refined into more specific subtasks. (See Figure 4.5 for the final top-down chart). Most of the subtasks in the second row are straightforward and so do not require further refinement. For instance, the first month's interest is computed by multiplying the amount of the loan by one-twelfth of the annual rate of interest. The most complicated subtask, the computation of the monthly payment, has been broken down further. This task is carried out by applying a standard formula found in finance books; however, the formula requires the number of payments.

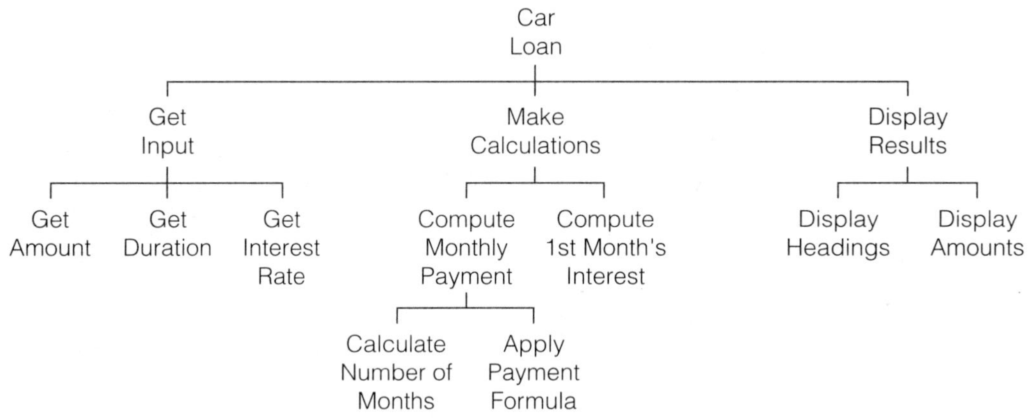

Figure 4.5 Top-Down Chart for the Car Loan Program

It is clear from the top-down chart that the top modules manipulate the modules beneath them. While the higher-level modules control the flow of the program, the lower-level modules do the actual work. By designing the top modules first, specific processing decisions can be delayed.

Structured Programming

A program is said to be **structured** if it meets modern standards of program design. Although there is no formal definition of the term **structured program**, computer scientists are in uniform agreement that such programs should have modular design and use only the three types of logical structures discussed in Chapter 2: sequences, decisions, and loops.

Sequences: Statements are executed one after another.

Decisions: One of two blocks of program code is executed based on a test for some condition.

Loops (iteration): One or more statements are executed repeatedly as long as a specified condition is true.

Chapters 5 and 6 are devoted to decisions and loops, respectively.

One major shortcoming of the earliest programming languages was their reliance on the GOTO statement. This statement was used to branch (that is, jump) from one line of a program to another. It was common for a program to be composed of a convoluted tangle of branchings that produced confusing code referred to as *spaghetti code*. At the heart of structured programming is the assertion of E. W. Dijkstra that GOTO statements should be eliminated entirely since they lead to complex and confusing programs. Two Italians, C. Bohm and G. Jacopini, were able to prove that GOTO statements are not needed and that any program can be written using only the three types of logic structures discussed above.

Structured programming requires that all programs be written using sequences, decisions, and loops. Nesting of such statements is allowed. All other logical constructs, such as GOTOs, are not allowed. The logic of a structured program can be pictured using a flowchart that flows smoothly from the top to the bottom without unstructured branching (GOTOs). The portion of a flowchart shown in Figure 4.6(a) contains the equivalent of a GOTO statement and, therefore, is not structured. A correctly structured version of the flowchart in which the logic flows from the top to the bottom appears in Figure 4.6(b).

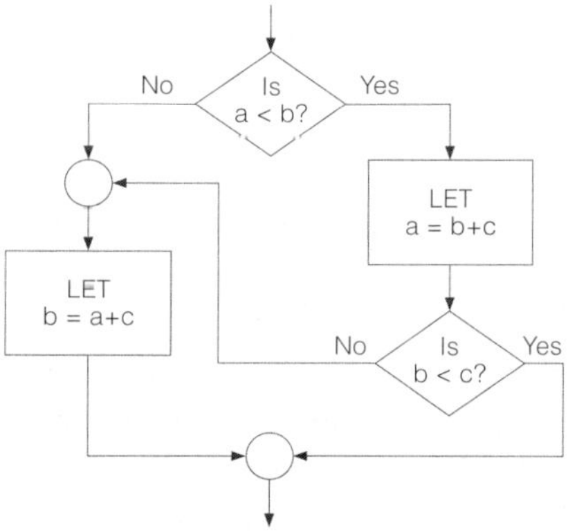

(a)

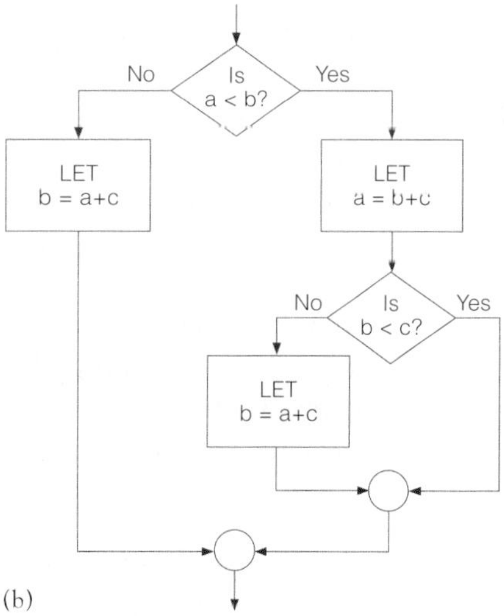

(b)

Figure 4.6 Flowcharts Illustrating the Removal of a GOTO Statement

Advantages of Structured Programming

The goal of structured programming is to create correct programs that are easy to write, understand, and change. Let us now take a closer look at the way modular design, along with a limited number of logical structures, contributes to attaining these goals.

1. *Easy to write.*

   Modular design increases the programmer's productivity by allowing him or her to look at the big picture first and focus on the details later. During the actual coding, the programmer works with a manageable chunk of the program and does not have to think about an entire complex program.

   Several programmers can work on a single large program, each taking responsibility for a specific module.

   Studies have shown structured programs require significantly less time to write than standard programs.

   Often, procedures written for one program can be reused in other programs requiring the same task. Not only is time saved in writing a program, but reliability is enhanced, because reused procedures will already be tested and debugged. A procedure that can be used in many programs is said to be **reusable**.

2. *Easy to debug.*

   Since each procedure is specialized to perform just one task, a procedure can be checked individually to determine its reliability. A dummy program, called a **driver**, is set up to test the procedure. The driver contains the minimum definitions needed to call the procedure to be tested. For instance, if the procedure to be tested is a function, the driver program assigns diverse values to the arguments and then examines the corresponding function value. The arguments should contain both typical and special-case values.

   The main body can be tested and debugged as it is being designed with a technique known as **stub programming**. In this technique, the main body and perhaps some of the smaller modules are coded first. Dummy modules, or stubs, are written for the remaining modules. Initially, a stub procedure might consist of a PRINT statement to indicate the procedure has been called, and thereby confirm that the procedure was called at the right time. Later, a stub might simply display values passed to it in order to confirm not only that the procedure was called, but also that it received the correct values from the calling procedure. A stub also can assign new values to one or more of its parameters to simulate either input statements or computations. This provides greater control of the conditions being tested. The stub procedure is always simpler than the actual procedure it represents. Although the stub program is only a skeleton of the final program, the program's structure can still be debugged and tested. (The stub program consists of the main body, some coded procedures, and the stub procedures.)

   Old-fashioned unstructured programs consist of a sequence of instructions that are not grouped for specific tasks. The logic of such a program is cluttered with details and therefore difficult to follow. Needed tasks are easily left out and crucial details easily neglected. Tricky parts of the program cannot be isolated and examined. Bugs are difficult to locate, since they might be present in any part of the program.

3. *Easy to understand.*

   The interconnections of the procedures reveal the modular design of the program.

   The meaningful procedure names, along with relevant comments, identify the tasks performed by the modules.

   The meaningful variable names help the programmer to recall the purpose of each variable.

4. *Easy to change.*

   Since a structured program is self-documenting, it can easily be deciphered by another programmer.

   Modifying a structured program often amounts to inserting or altering a few procedures rather than revising an entire complex program. The programmer does not even have to look at most of the program. This is in sharp contrast to the situation with unstructured programs that require an understanding of the entire logic of the program before any changes can be made with confidence.

Chapter 4 Summary

1. A *procedure* is a portion of a program that resides outside of the main body and is accessed by the main body or another procedure. The two types of procedures are *subprograms* and *user-defined functions*.
2. Subprograms are defined in blocks beginning with SUB statements and ending with END SUB statements. They are accessed by CALL statements.
3. User-defined functions are defined in blocks beginning with FUNCTION statements and ending with END FUNCTION statements. A function is activated by a reference in an expression and returns a value.
4. In any procedure, the arguments appearing in the calling statement must match the parameters of the SUB or FUNCTION statement in number, type, and order. They need not match in name.
5. A variable appearing inside a procedure is *local* to the procedure if it does not appear in the parameter list. The values of these variables are reinitialized each time the procedure is called. A variable with the same name appearing in another part of the program is treated as a different variable.
6. Structured programming uses modular design to refine large problems into smaller subproblems. Programs are coded using the three logical structures of sequences, decisions, and loops.

Chapter 4
Programming Projects

1. The numbers of calories per gram of carbohydrate, fat, and protein are 4, 9, and 4, respectively. Write a program that requests the nutritional content of a 1-ounce serving of food and displays the number of calories in the serving. The input and output should be handled by subprograms and the calories computed by a function. The following output corresponds to a typical breakfast cereal.

```
[run]
Enter grams of carbohydrate: 24
Enter grams of fat: 1
Enter grams of protein: 1

The serving contains 109 calories.
```

2. About seven million notebook computers were sold in 1997. Table 4.3 gives the market share for the four largest vendors. Write a program that displays the number of computers sold by each of the Big Four. The input and output should be handled by subprograms and the number of computers calculated by a function.

Company	Market Share
Toshiba	20%
IBM	11%
Compaq	9%
Dell	6%

Table 4.3 1997 Market Shares of the Top Notebook Vendors
Source: PC Magazine, January 20, 1998

3. Table 4.4 gives the advertising expenditures (in millions of dollars) for the four most advertised soft-drink brands during the first nine months of 1995 and 1996. Write a program that displays the percentage change in advertising for each brand. Subprograms should be used for input and output, and the percentage change should be computed with a function. **Note:** The percentage change is 100 * ([1996 expenditure] – [1995 expenditure]) / [1995 expenditure].

Brand	1995 Expenditure	1996 Expenditure
Coca-Cola Classic	60.7	121.6
Pepsi-Cola	94.8	83.0
Diet Coke	43.7	70.0
Dr. Pepper	46.3	51.8

Table 4.4 Most Advertised Soft Drinks
Source: Beverage World, March 1997

4. A fast-food vendor sells pizza slices ($1.25), fries ($1.00), and soft drinks ($.75). Write a program to compute a customer's bill. The program should request the quantity of each item ordered in a subprogram, calculate the total cost with a function, and use a subprogram to display an itemized bill. A sample output is shown in Figure 4.7.

```
[run]
How many pizza slices? 3
How many fries? 4
How many soft drinks? 5

Item           Quantity       Price

pizza slices   3              $ 3.75
fries          4              $ 4.00
soft drinks    5              $ 3.75

Total                         $11.50
```

Figure 4.7 Sample Output of Programming Project 4

5. Write a program to generate a Business Travel Expense attachment for an income tax return. The program should request as input the name of the organization visited, the date and location of the visit, and the expenses for meals and entertainment, airplane fare, lodging, and taxi fares. (Only 50% of the expenses for meals and entertainment are deductible.) The program should display an output similar to the one below. Subprograms should be used for the input and output.

```
[run]
Enter organization visited: Association for Computing Machinery
Enter date: February 25-28
Enter location: Atlanta
Enter expenses for meals and entertainment: 190.10
Enter airline fare: 210.15
Enter expenses for lodging: 475.35
Enter taxi fares: 35.00
```

{The following report is printed on the printer.}

```
Business Travel Expense

Trip to attend meeting of
Association for Computing Machinery
February 25-28 in Atlanta

Meals and entertainment     $190.10
Airplane fare               $210.15
Lodging                     $475.35
Taxi fares                  $ 35.00

Total other than Meals and Entertainment: $720.50

50% of Meals and Entertainment: $95.05
```

5

Decisions

5.1 RELATIONAL AND LOGICAL OPERATORS

A **condition** is an expression involving relational operators (such as < and =) that is either true or false when evaluated. Conditions also may incorporate logical operators (such as AND, OR, and NOT).

The relational operator *less than* (<) can be applied to both numbers and strings. The number a is said to be less than the number b if a lies to the left of b on the number line. For instance, $2 < 5$, $-5 < -2$, and $0 < 3.5$.

The string *a$* is said to be less than the string *b$* if *a$* precedes *b$* alphabetically when using the ASCII table to alphabetize their values. For instance, "cat" < "dog", "cart" < "cat", and "cat" < "catalog". Digits precede uppercase letters, which precede lowercase letters. Two strings are compared working from left to right, character by character, to determine which one should precede the other. Therefore, "9W" < "bat", "Dog" < "cat", and "Sales-89" < "Sales-retail".

Table 5.1 shows the different mathematical relational operators, their representations in QBasic, and their meanings.

Mathematical Notation	QBasic Notation	Numeric Meaning	String Meaning
$=$	=	equal to	identical to
$\neq$	<>	unequal to	different from
$<$	<	less than	precedes alphabetically
$>$	>	greater than	follows alphabetically
$\leq$	<=	less than or equal to	precedes alphabetically or is identical to
$\geq$	>=	greater than or equal to	follows alphabetically or is identical to

Table 5.1 Relational Operators

EXAMPLE 1 Determine whether each of the following conditions is true or false.

(a) 1 <= 1
(b) 1 < 1
(c) "car" < "cat"
(d) "Dog" < "dog"

SOLUTION

(a) True. The notation <= means "less than *or* equal to." That is, the condition is true provided either of the two circumstances holds. The second one (equal to) holds.
(b) False. The notation < means "strictly less than" and no number can be strictly less than itself.
(c) True. The characters of the strings are compared one at a time working from left to right. Since the first two match, the third character decides the order.
(d) True. Since uppercase letters precede lowercase letters in the ASCII table, the first character of "Dog" precedes the first character of "dog."

Conditions also can involve variables, numeric operators, and functions. To determine whether a condition is true or false, first compute the numeric or string values and then decide if the resulting assertion is true or false.

EXAMPLE 2 Suppose the values of a, b, c$, and d$ are 4, 3, "hello", and "bye", respectively. Are the following conditions true or false?

(a) (a + b) < 2 * a
(b) (LEN(c$) – b) = (a / 2)
(c) c$ < ("good" + d$)

SOLUTION

(a) The value of a + b is 7 and the value of 2 * a is 8. Since 7 < 8, the condition is true.
(b) True, since the value of LEN(c$) – b is 2, the same as (a / 2).
(c) The condition "hello" < "goodbye" is false, since "h" follows "g" in the ASCII table.

Logical Operators

Programming situations often require more complex conditions than those considered so far. For instance, suppose we would like to state that the value of a numeric variable, n, is strictly between 2 and 5. The proper QBasic condition is:

(2 < n) AND (n < 5)

The condition (2 < n) AND (n < 5) is a combination of the two conditions 2 < n and n < 5 with the logical operator AND.

The three main logical operators are AND, OR, and NOT. If *cond1* and *cond2* are conditions, then the condition

```
cond1 AND cond2
```

is true if both *cond1* and *cond2* are true. Otherwise, it is false. The condition

```
cond1 OR cond2
```

is true if either *cond1* or *cond2* (or both) is true. Otherwise, it is false. The condition

```
NOT cond1
```

is true if *cond1* is false, and is false if *cond1* is true.

EXAMPLE 3 Suppose n has value 4 and an$ has value "Y". Determine whether each of the following conditions is true or false.

(a) (2 < n) AND (n < 6)
(b) (2 < n) OR (n = 6)
(c) NOT (n < 6)
(d) (an$ = "Y") OR (an$ = "y")
(e) (an$ = "Y") AND (an$ = "y")
(f) NOT (an$ = "y")
(g) ((2 < n) AND (n = 5 + 1)) OR (an$ = "No")
(h) ((n = 2) AND (n = 7)) OR (an$ = "Y")
(i) (n = 2) AND ((n = 7) OR (an$ = "Y"))

SOLUTION

(a) True, since the conditions (2 < 4) and (4 < 6) are both true.

(b) True, since the condition (2 < 4) is true. The fact that the condition (4 = 6) is false does not affect the conclusion. The only requirement is that at least one of the two conditions be true.

(c) False, since (4 < 6) is true.

(d) True, since the first condition becomes ("Y" = "Y") when the value of an$ is substituted for an$.

(e) False, since the second condition is false. Actually, this compound condition is false for every value of an$.

(f) True, since ("Y" = "y") is false.

(g) False. In this logical expression, the compound condition ((2 < n) AND (n = 5 + 1)) and the simple condition (an$ = "No") are joined by the logical operator OR. Since both of these conditions are false, the total condition is false.

(h) True, because the second OR clause is true.

(i) False. Comparing (h) and (i) shows the necessity of using parentheses to specify the intended grouping.

The use of parentheses with logical operators improves readability; however, they can be omitted sometimes. QBasic has an operator hierarchy for deciding how to evaluate logical expressions without parentheses. First, all arithmetic operations are carried out, and then all expressions involving >, <, and = are evaluated to true or false. The logical operators are next applied, in the order NOT, then AND, and finally OR. For instance, the logical expression in part (g) of Example 3 could have been written 2 < n AND n = 5 + 1 OR an$ = "No". In the event of a tie, the leftmost operator is applied first.

EXAMPLE 4 Place parentheses in the following condition to show how it would be evaluated by QBasic.

a < b + c OR d < e AND NOT f = g

SOLUTION ((a <(b + c)) OR ((d < e) AND (NOT (f = g))))

The step-by-step analysis of the order of operations is

a < (b + c)	OR	d < e	AND	NOT f = g		arithmetic operation
(a < (b + c))	OR	(d < e)	AND	NOT (f = g)		relational expressions
(a < (b + c))	OR	(d < e)	AND	(NOT (f = g))		NOT
(a < (b + c))	OR	((d < e)	AND	(NOT (f = g)))		AND
((a < (b + c))	OR	((d < e)	AND	(NOT (f = g))))		OR

Comments:

1. A condition involving numeric variables is different from an algebraic truth. The assertion (a + b) < 2 * a, considered in Example 2, is not a valid algebraic truth since it isn't true for all values of a and b. When encountered in a QBasic program, however, it will be considered true if it is correct for the current values of the variables.

2. Conditions evaluate to either true or false. These two values often are called the possible **truth values** of the condition.

3. A condition such as 2 < n < 5 should never be used, since QBasic will not evaluate it as intended. The correct condition is (2 < n) AND (n < 5).

4. A common error is to replace condition NOT (2 < 3) by condition (3 > 2). The correct condition is (3 >= 2).

PRACTICE PROBLEMS 5.1

1. Is the condition "Hello " = "Hello" true or false?

2. Complete Table 5.2.

cond1	cond2	cond1 AND cond2	cond1 OR cond2	NOT cond2
true	true	true		
true	false		true	
false	true			false
false	false			

Table 5.2 Truth Values of Logical Operators

EXERCISES 5.1

In Exercises 1 through 12, determine whether the condition is true or false. Assume a = 2 and b = 3.

1. 3 * a = 2 * b
2. (5 – a) * b < 7
3. b <= 3
4. a ^ b = b ^ a
5. a ^ (5 – 2) > 7
6. 3E–02 < .01 * a
7. (a < b) OR (b < a)
8. (a * a < b) OR NOT (a * a < a)
9. NOT ((a < b) AND (a < (b + a)))
10. NOT (a < b) OR NOT (a < (b + a))
11. ((a = b) AND (a * a < b * b)) OR ((b < a) AND (2 * a < b))
12. ((a = b) OR NOT (b < a)) AND ((a < b) OR (b = a + 1))

In Exercises 13 through 24, determine whether the condition is true or false.

13. "9W" <> "9w"
14. "Inspector" < "gadget"
15. "Car" < "Train"
16. "J" >= "J"
17. "99" > "ninety-nine"
18. "B" > "?"
19. ("Duck" < "pig") AND ("pig" < "big")
20. "Duck" < "Duck" + "Duck"
21. NOT (("B" = "b") OR ("Big" < "big"))
22. NOT ("B" = "b") AND NOT ("Big" < "big")

23. (("Ant" < "hill") AND ("mole" > "hill")) OR NOT (NOT ("Ant" < "hill") OR NOT ("Mole" > "hill"))

24. (7 < 34) AND ("7" > "34")

In Exercises 25 through 34, determine whether or not the two conditions are equivalent—that is, whether they will be true or false for exactly the same values of the variables appearing in them.

25. a <= b; (a < b) OR (a = b)

26. NOT (a < b); a > b

27. (a$ = b$) AND (a$ < b$); a$ <> b$

28. NOT ((a = b) OR (a = c)); (a <> b) AND (a <> c)

29. (a < b) AND ((a > d) OR (a > e));
((a < b) AND (a > d)) OR ((a < b) AND (a > e))

30. NOT ((a$ = b$ + c$) OR (a$ = b$)); (a$ <> b$) OR (a$ <> b$ + c$)

31. (a < b + c) OR (a = b + c); NOT ((a > b) OR (a > c))

32. NOT (a >= b); (a <= b) OR NOT (a = b)

33. NOT (a >= b); (a <= b) AND NOT (a = b)

34. (a = b) AND ((b = c) OR (a = c));
(a = b) OR ((b = c) AND (a = c))

In Exercises 35 through 39, write a condition equivalent to the negation of the given condition. (For example, a <> b is equivalent to the negation of a = b.)

35. a > b

36. (a = b) OR (a = d)

37. (a < b) AND (c <> d)

38. NOT ((a$ = b$) OR (a$ > b$))

39. (a$ <> "") AND (a$ < b$) AND (LEN(a$) < 5)

SOLUTIONS TO PRACTICE PROBLEMS 5.1

1. False. The first string has six characters, whereas the second has five. Two strings must be 100% identical to be called equal.

2.

cond1	cond2	cond1 AND cond2	cond1 OR cond2	NOT cond2
true	true	true	true	false
true	false	false	true	true
false	true	false	true	false
false	false	false	false	true

5.2 IF BLOCKS

An IF block allows a program to decide on a course of action based on whether a certain condition is true or false. A block of the form

```
IF condition THEN
    action1
  ELSE
    action2
END IF
```

causes the program to take *action1* if *condition* is true and *action2* if *condition* is false. Each action consists of one or more QBasic statements. After an action is taken, execution continues with the line after the IF block. Figure 5.1 contains the pseudocode and flowchart for an IF block.

```
IF condition is true THEN
    Processing step(s) 1
  ELSE
    Processing step(s) 2
END IF
```

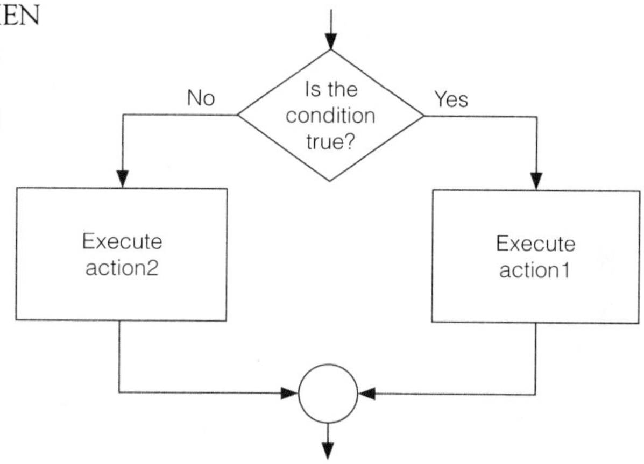

Figure 5.1 Pseudocode and Flowchart for an IF Block

EXAMPLE 1 Write a program to find the larger of two numbers input by the user.

SOLUTION In the following program, the condition is firstNum > secondNum, and each action consists of a single LET statement. With the input 3 and 7, the condition is false and so the second action is taken.

```
REM Find the larger of two numbers
CLS
INPUT "First number"; firstNum
INPUT "Second number"; secondNum
IF firstNum > secondNum THEN
    LET largerNum = firstNum
  ELSE
    LET largerNum = secondNum
END IF
PRINT "The larger number is"; largerNum
END

[run]
First number? 3
Second number? 7
The larger number is 7
```

EXAMPLE 2 Write a program that requests the costs and revenue for a company and displays the message "Break even" if the costs and revenue are equal or otherwise displays the profit or loss.

SOLUTION In the following program, action2 is another IF block.

```
REM Analyze costs versus revenue
CLS
INPUT "Enter costs, revenue: ", costs, revenue
IF costs = revenue THEN
    PRINT "Break even"
  ELSE
    IF costs < revenue THEN
        PRINT "Profit is"; revenue - costs
      ELSE
        PRINT "Loss is"; costs - revenue
    END IF
END IF
END

[run]
Enter costs, revenue: 9500, 8000
Loss is 1500
```

EXAMPLE 3 The IF block in the following program has a logical operator in its condition.

```
REM Quiz
CLS
INPUT "How many gallons does a ten-gallon hat hold"; answer
IF (.5 <= answer) AND (answer <= 1) THEN
    PRINT "Good, ";
  ELSE
    PRINT "No, ";
END IF
PRINT "it holds about 3/4 of a gallon."
END

[run]
How many gallons does a ten-gallon hat hold? 1
Good, it holds about 3/4 of a gallon.
```

The ELSE part of an IF block can be omitted. In its absence, a false condition causes execution to continue with the statement after the IF block. This important type of IF block appears in the next example.

EXAMPLE 4 The following program offers assistance to the user before presenting a quotation.

```
REM Display a quotation with a possible preceding explanation
CLS
INPUT "Before we proceed, do you know what 'skittles' is (Y/N)"; answer$
IF answer$ = "N" THEN
    PRINT "Skittles is an old form of bowling in which a wooden"
    PRINT "disk is used to knock down nine pins arranged in a square."
END IF
```

```
PRINT "Life ain't all beer and skittles. - Du Maurier (1894)"
END

[run]
Before we proceed, do you know what 'skittles' is (Y/N)? Y
Life ain't all beer and skittles. - Du Maurier (1894)
```

An extension of the IF block allows for more than two possible alternatives with the inclusion of ELSEIF clauses. A typical block of this type is

```
IF condition1 THEN
    action1
  ELSEIF condition2 THEN
    action2
  ELSEIF condition3 THEN
    action3
  ELSE
    action4
END IF
```

This block searches for the first true condition, carries out its action, and then skips to the statement following END IF. If none of the conditions are true, then ELSE's action is carried out. Execution then continues with the statement following the block. In general, an IF block can contain any number of ELSEIF clauses. As before, the ELSE clause is optional.

EXAMPLE 5 Redo Example 1 so that if the two numbers are equal, the program so reports.

SOLUTION

```
REM Find the larger of two numbers
CLS
INPUT "First number"; firstNum
INPUT "Second number"; secondNum
IF firstNum > secondNum THEN
    PRINT "The larger number is"; firstNum
  ELSEIF secondNum > firstNum THEN
    PRINT "The larger number is"; secondNum
  ELSE
    PRINT "The two numbers are equal."
END IF
END

[run]
First number? 7
Second number? 7
The two numbers are equal.
```

IF blocks allow us to define functions whose values are not determined by a simple formula. The function in Example 6 uses an IF block.

EXAMPLE 6 The Social Security or FICA tax has two components—the Social Security benefits tax, which in 1998 is 6.2% on the first $68,400 of earnings for the year, and the Medicare tax, which is 1.45% of earnings. Write a program to calculate an employee's FICA tax for a specific paycheck.

SOLUTION

```
REM Calculate FICA tax
CLS
CALL GetWageInfo(yearToDateEarnings, currentEarnings)
PRINT "Your FICA taxes for the current pay period are";
PRINT USING "$$#,###.##"; FICA(yearToDateEarnings, currentEarnings)
END

FUNCTION FICA (yearToDateEarnings, currentEarnings)
  REM Calculate Social Security benefits tax and Medicare tax for a single
  REM pay period
  LET socialSecurityBenTax = 0
  IF (yearToDateEarnings + currentEarnings) <= 68400 THEN
      LET socialSecurityBenTax = .062 * currentEarnings
    ELSEIF yearToDateEarnings < 68400 THEN
      LET socialSecurityBenTax = .062 * (68400 - yearToDateEarnings)
  END IF
  LET medicare = .0145 * currentEarnings
  FICA = socialSecurityBenTax + medicare
END FUNCTION

SUB GetWageInfo (yearToDateEarnings, currentEarnings)
  REM Input two pieces of data needed to calculate FICA tax
  PRINT "Enter this year's total earnings prior";
  INPUT " to the current pay period: ", yearToDateEarnings
  INPUT "Enter your earnings for the current pay period: ", currentEarnings
END SUB

[run]
Enter this year's total earnings prior to the current pay period: 12345.67
Enter your earnings for the current pay period: 543.21
Your FICA taxes for the current pay period are    $41.56
```

Comments:

1. The actions of an IF block and the words ELSE and ELSEIF do not have to be indented. For instance, the IF block of Example 1 can be written

```
IF firstNum > secondNum THEN
LET largerNum = firstNum
ELSE
LET largerNum = secondNum
END IF
```

However, since indenting improves the readability of the block, it is regarded as good programming style. As soon as you see the word IF, your eyes can easily scan down the program to find the matching END IF and the enclosed ELSE and ELSEIF clauses. You then immediately have a good idea of the size and complexity of the block.

2. Constructs in which an IF block is contained inside another IF block are referred to as **nested** IF blocks.

3. Care should be taken to make IF blocks easy to understand. For instance, in Figure 5.2, the block on the left is difficult to follow and should be replaced by the clearer block on the right.

```
IF cond1 THEN                 IF cond1 AND cond2 THEN
    IF cond2 THEN                 action
        action                END IF
    END IF
END IF
```

Figure 5.2 A Confusing IF Block and an Improvement

4. Some programs call for selecting among many possibilities. Although such tasks can be accomplished with complicated nested IF blocks, the SELECT CASE block (discussed in the next section) is often a better alternative.

5. In Appendix D, the section "Stepping Through Programs Containing Selection Structures: Chapter 5" uses the QBasic debugging tools to trace the flow through an IF block.

6. QBasic also has a single-line IF statement of the form

   ```
   IF condition THEN action1 ELSE action2
   ```

   which is a holdover from earlier, unstructured versions of BASIC; it is not used in this text.

7. Another holdover from unstructured versions of BASIC is the controversial GOTO statement which is commonly used along with IF. Although this statement is not needed in structured versions of BASIC, there are some rare situations in which it provides the clearest way to handle a task. QBasic has a device called a label, which is a name (of the same type as a variable name) followed by a colon, that is placed on its own line preceding a line of a program. The statement GOTO *label* causes execution to jump to the line following *label*. As an alternative to a label, a line of a program can be preceded by a positive integer, called a **line number**. In this case, the statement GOTO *lineNumber* causes that line to be the next line executed. The GOTO statement is not used in this text.

PRACTICE PROBLEMS 5.2

1. Fill in the IF block so the program below either will display the message "Number can't be negative" or will display the square root of the number.

   ```
   REM Check reasonableness of data
   CLS
   INPUT "Number to take square root of"; num
   IF

   END IF
   END
   ```

2. Improve the block

```
IF a < b THEN
    IF c < 5 THEN
        PRINT "hello"
    END IF
END IF
```

EXERCISES 5.2

In Exercises 1 through 12, determine the output of the program.

1.
```
LET i = 4
IF i <= 9 THEN
    PRINT "Less than ten"
  ELSE
    IF i = 4 THEN
        PRINT "Equal to four"
    END IF
END IF
END
```

2.
```
READ gpa
IF gpa >= 3.5 THEN
    PRINT "Honors ";
END IF
PRINT "Student"
REM --- Data: grade point average
DATA 3.49
END
```

3.
```
LET a = 5
IF 3 * a - 4 < 9 THEN
    PRINT "Remember, "
END IF
PRINT "Tomorrow is another day."
END
```

4.
```
READ change                         'Amount of change in cents
IF change >= 100 THEN
    PRINT "Your change contains"; INT(change / 100); "dollars."
  ELSE
    PRINT "Your change contains no dollars."
END IF
REM --- Data: amount of change from a purchase (stated in cents)
DATA 356
END
```

5.
```
LET a = 2
LET b = 3
LET c = 5
IF a * b < c THEN
    LET b = 7
  ELSE
    LET b = c * a
END IF
PRINT b
END
```

6.
```
INPUT a, b
IF a > b THEN
    LET a = a + 1
  ELSE
    LET b = b + 1
END IF
PRINT a; b
END
```

(Assume the response is *7, 11*.)

7.
```
REM Cost of phone call from NY to LA
CALL InputLength(length)
CALL DisplayCost(length)
END

FUNCTION Cost (length)
  IF length < 1 THEN
      Cost = .46
    ELSE
      Cost = .46 + (length - 1) * .36
  END IF
END FUNCTION

SUB DisplayCost (length)
  REM Display the cost of a call
  LET a$ = "The cost of the call is $$#.##"
  PRINT USING a$; Cost(length)
END SUB

SUB InputLength (length)
  REM Request the length of a phone call
  INPUT "What is the duration of the call in minutes"; length
END SUB
```

(Assume the response is *31*.)

8.
```
INPUT "Enter A, B, or C: ", letter$
IF letter$ = "A" THEN
    CALL DisplayAmessage
  ELSEIF letter$ = "B" THEN
    CALL DisplayBmessage
  ELSEIF letter$ = "C" THEN
    CALL DisplayCmessage
  ELSE
    PRINT "Not a valid letter"
END IF
END

SUB DisplayAmessage
  PRINT "A, my name is Alice."
END SUB
```

```
SUB DisplayBmessage
  PRINT "To be or not to be."
END SUB

SUB DisplayCmessage
  PRINT "Oh, say can you see."
END SUB
```

(Assume the response is *B*.)

9.
```
LET vowels = 0    'Number of vowels
CALL ExamineLetter(vowels)
CALL ExamineLetter(vowels)
CALL ExamineLetter(vowels)
PRINT "The number of vowels is"; vowels
REM --- Data: letters
DATA U, B, A
END

SUB ExamineLetter (vowels)
  READ a$       'Letter
  IF a$="A" OR a$="E" OR a$="I" OR a$="O" OR a$="U" THEN
      LET vowels = vowels + 1
  END IF
END SUB
```

10.
```
LET a = 5
IF (a > 2) AND (a = 3 OR a < 7) THEN
    PRINT "Hi"
END IF
END
```

11.
```
LET num = 5
IF num < 0 THEN
    PRINT "neg"
  ELSE
    IF num = 0 THEN
        PRINT "zero"
      ELSE
        PRINT "positive"
    END IF
END IF
END
```

12.
```
LET m$ = "You are eligible to vote"
INPUT "Enter your age"; age
IF age >= 18 THEN
    PRINT m$
  ELSE
    PRINT m$ + " in"; 18 - age; "years"
END IF
END
```

(Assume the response is *16*.)

In Exercises 13 through 20, identify the errors.

13.
```
LET num = 2
IF 1 < num < 3 THEN
    PRINT "Number is between 1 and 3."
END IF
END
```

14.
```
LET num = 6
IF num > 5 AND < 9 THEN
    PRINT "Yes"
  ELSE
    PRINT "No"
END IF
END
```

15.
```
IF 2 <> 3
    PRINT "Numbers are not equal"
END IF
END
```

16.
```
IF major$ = "Business" OR "Computer Science" THEN
    PRINT "Yes"
END IF
END
```

17.
```
LET n$ = "Seven"
READ num
IF num < n$ THEN
    PRINT "Less than"
  ELSE
    PRINT "Greater than"
END IF
REM --- Data: number
DATA 6
END
```

18.
```
REM Change switch$ from "on" to "off", or from "off" to "on"
INPUT switch$
IF switch$ = "off" THEN
    LET switch$ = "on"
END IF
IF switch$ = "on" THEN
    LET switch$ = "off"
END IF
END
```

19.
```
REM Display "OK" if either j or k equals 4
LET j = 2
LET k = 3
IF j OR k = 4 THEN
    PRINT "OK"
END IF
END
```

20.
```
REM Is your program correct?
PRINT "Are you certain everything in your program is correct?";
INPUT answer1$
IF answer1$ = "N" THEN
    PRINT "Don't patch bad code, rewrite it."
  ELSE
    INPUT "Does your program run correctly"; answer2$
    IF answer2$ = "Y" THEN
        PRINT "Congratulations"
      ELSE
        PRINT "One of the things you are certain about is wrong."
    END IF
END
```

In Exercises 21 through 26, simplify the code.

21.
```
IF a = 2 THEN
    LET a = 3 + a
  ELSE
    LET a = 5
END IF
```

22.
```
IF NOT (answer$ <> "y") THEN
    PRINT "YES"
  ELSE
    IF (answer$ = "y") OR (answer$ = "Y") THEN
        PRINT "YES"
    END IF
END IF
```

23.
```
IF j = 7 THEN
    LET b = 1
  ELSE
    IF j <> 7 THEN
        LET b = 2
    END IF
END IF
```

24.
```
IF a < b THEN
    IF b < c THEN
        PRINT b; "is between"; a; "and"; c
    END IF
END IF
```

25.
```
INPUT "Is Alaska bigger than Texas and California combined"; answer$
IF LEFT$(answer$, 1) = "Y" THEN
    LET answer$ = "YES"
END IF
IF LEFT$(answer$, 1) = "y" THEN
    LET answer$ = "YES"
END IF
IF answer$ = "YES" THEN
    PRINT "Correct"
  ELSE
    PRINT "Wrong"
END IF
END
```

26.
```
INPUT "How tall (in ft.) is the Statue of Liberty"; feet
IF feet <= 141 THEN
    PRINT "Nope"
END IF
IF feet > 141 THEN
    IF feet < 161 THEN
        PRINT "Close"
      ELSE
        PRINT "Nope"
    END IF
END IF
PRINT "The Statue of Liberty is 151.08 ft from base to torch."
END
```

27. Write a program to determine how much to tip the waiter in a fine restaurant. The tip should be 15% of the check with a minimum of $1.

28. Write a quiz program to ask "Who was the first Ronald McDonald?" The program should display "Correct" if the answer is Willard Scott and otherwise should display "Nice try."

29. A computer store sells diskettes at 50 cents each for small orders or at 30 cents each for orders of 25 diskettes or more. Write a program that requests the number of diskettes ordered and displays the total cost. (Test the program for purchases of 5, 25, and 35 diskettes.)

30. A copying center charges 5 cents per copy for the first 100 copies and 3 cents per copy for each additional copy. Write a program that requests the number of copies as input and displays the total cost. (Test the program with the quantities 25 and 125.)

31. Write a program to handle a savings-account withdrawal. The program should request the current balance and the amount of the withdrawal as input and then display the new balance. If the withdrawal is greater than the original balance, the program should display "Withdrawal denied." If the new balance is less than $150, the message "Balance below $150" should be displayed.

32. Write a program that requests three scores as input and displays the average of the two highest scores. The input and output should be handled by subprograms and the average should be determined by a function.

33. A lottery drawing produces three digits. Write a program that requests the three digits as input and then displays "Lucky seven" if two or more of the digits are 7.

34. Federal law requires hourly employees be paid "time-and-a-half" for work in excess of 40 hours in a week. For example, if a person's hourly wage is $8 and he works 60 hours in a week, his gross pay should be

$$(40 \times 8) + (1.5 \times 8 \times (60 - 40)) = \$560.$$

Write a program that requests as input the number of hours a person works in a given week and his hourly wage, and then displays his gross pay.

35. Write a program that requests a word (with lowercase letters) as input and translates the word into pig latin. The rules for translating a word into pig latin are:

(a) If the word begins with a consonant, move the first letter to the end of the word and add *ay*. For instance, *chip* becomes *hipcay*.
(b) If the word begins with a vowel, add *way* to the end of the word. For instance, *else* becomes *elseway*.

36. The current calendar, called the Gregorian calendar, was introduced in 1582. Every year divisible by 4 was declared to be a leap year with the exception of the years ending in 00 (that is, those divisible by 100) and not divisible by 400. For instance, the years 1600 and 2000 are leap years, but 1700, 1800, and 1900 are not. Write a program that requests a year as input and states whether or not it is a leap year. (Test the program on the years 1994, 1995, 1900, and 2000.)

37. The flowchart in Figure 5.3 calculates New Jersey state income tax. Write a program corresponding to the flowchart. (Test the program with taxable incomes of $15,000, $30,000, and $60,000.)

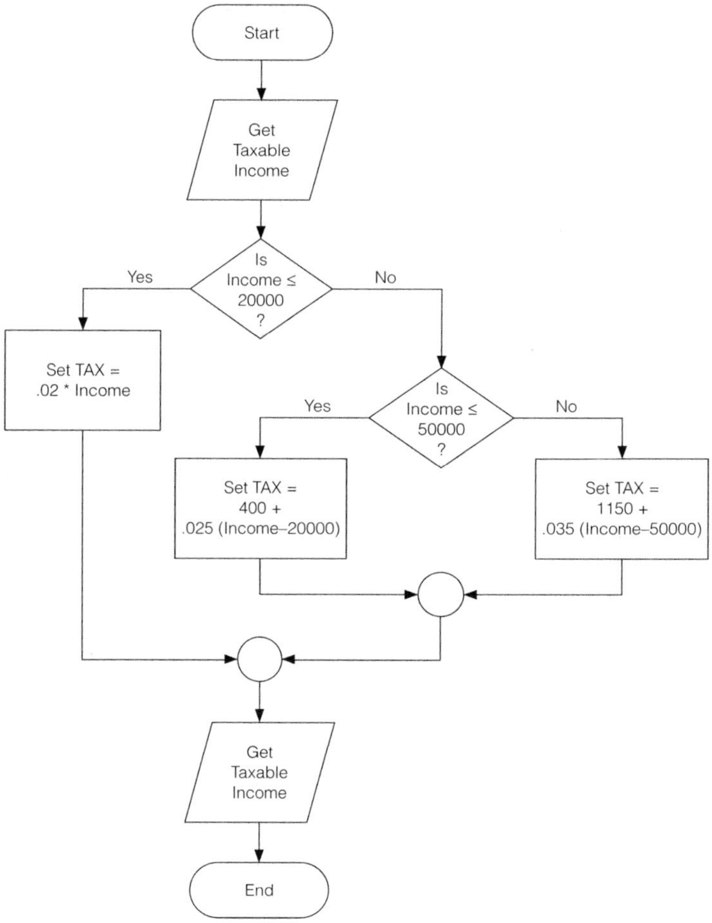

Figure 5.3 Flowchart for New Jersey State Income Tax Program

SOLUTIONS TO PRACTICE PROBLEMS 5.2

1.
```
IF num < 0 THEN
    PRINT "Number can't be negative."
  ELSE
    PRINT SQR(num)
END IF
```

2. The PRINT statement will be executed when $a < b$ is true and $c < 5$ is also true. That is, it will be executed when both of these two conditions are true. The clearest way to write the block is

```
IF (a < b) AND (c < 5) THEN
    PRINT "hello"
END IF
```

5.3 SELECT CASE BLOCKS

A SELECT CASE block is an efficient decision-making structure that simplifies choosing among several actions. It avoids complex nested IF constructs. IF blocks make decisions based on the truth value of a condition; SELECT CASE choices are determined by the value of an expression called a **selector**. Each of the possible actions is preceded by a statement of the form

```
CASE valueList
```

where *valueList* itemizes the values of the selector for which the action should be taken.

EXAMPLE 1 The following program converts the finishing position in a horse race into a descriptive phrase. After the variable *position* is assigned a value by the INPUT statement, the computer searches for the first CASE statement whose value list contains that value and executes the succeeding statement. If the value of *position* is greater than 5, then the statement following CASE ELSE is executed.

```
REM Describe finishing positions in a horse race
CLS
INPUT "Enter finishing position (1, 2, 3, etc.): ", position
SELECT CASE position
  CASE 4, 5
    PRINT "You almost placed in the money."
  CASE 3
    PRINT "Show"
  CASE 2
    PRINT "Place"
  CASE 1
    PRINT "Win"
  CASE ELSE
    PRINT "Out of the money."
END SELECT
END
```

```
[run]
Enter finishing position (1, 2, 3, etc.): 2
Place

[run]
Enter finishing position (1, 2, 3, etc.): 5
You almost placed in the money.
```

EXAMPLE 2 In the following program, the value lists specify ranges of values. The first value list provides another way to specify the numbers 1, 2, and 3. The second value list covers all numbers from 4 on.

```
REM Describe finishing positions in a horse race
CLS
INPUT "Enter finishing position (1, 2, 3, etc.): ", position
SELECT CASE position
  CASE 1 TO 3
    PRINT "In the money"
    PRINT "Congratulations"
  CASE IS > 3
    PRINT "Not in the money."
END SELECT
END

[run]
Enter finishing position (1, 2, 3, etc.): 4
Not in the money.
```

The general form of the SELECT CASE block is

```
SELECT CASE selector
  CASE valueList1
    action1
  CASE valueList2
    action2
   .
   .
  CASE ELSE
    action of last resort
END SELECT
```

where CASE ELSE (and its action) is optional, and each value list contains one or more of the following types of items separated by commas:

1. a constant
2. a variable
3. an expression
4. an inequality sign preceded by IS and followed by a constant, variable, or expression
5. a range expressed in the form *a* TO *b*, where *a* and *b* are either constants, variables, or expressions.

Different items appearing in the same list must be separated by commas. Each action consists of one or more statements. After the selector is evaluated, the computer looks for the first value-list item containing the value of the selector and carries out its associated action. Figure 5.4 contains the flowchart for a SELECT CASE block. The pseudocode for a SELECT CASE block is the same as for the equivalent IF block.

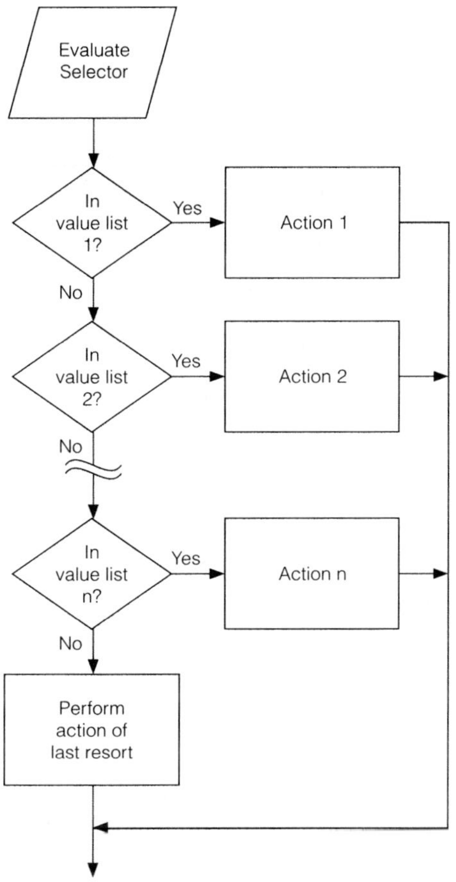

Figure 5.4 Flowchart for a SELECT CASE Block

EXAMPLE 3 The following program illustrates several different types of value lists. With the response shown, the first action was selected because the value of $y - x$ is 1.

```
REM One, Two, Buckle My Shoe
CLS
LET x = 2
LET y = 3
INPUT "Enter a number from 1 to 10: ", num
SELECT CASE num
  CASE y - x, x
    PRINT "Buckle my shoe"
  CASE IS <= 4
    PRINT "Shut the door"
```

```
  CASE x + y TO x * y
    PRINT "Pick up sticks"
  CASE 7, 8
    PRINT "Lay them straight"
  CASE ELSE
    PRINT "Start all over again"
END SELECT
END

[run]
Enter a number from 1 to 10: 1
Buckle my shoe
```

In each of the three preceding examples the selector was a numeric variable; however, the selector also can be a string variable or an expression.

EXAMPLE 4 The following program has the string variable *name$* as a selector.

```
REM Quiz
CLS
INPUT "What was President Wilson's first name"; name$
SELECT CASE name$
  CASE "Thomas"
    PRINT "Correct"
  CASE "Woodrow"
    PRINT "Sorry, his full name was Thomas Woodrow Wilson."
  CASE "President"
    PRINT "Are you for real?"
  CASE ELSE
    PRINT "Nice try, but no cigar."
END SELECT
END

[run]
What was President Wilson's first name? Woody
Nice try, but no cigar.
```

EXAMPLE 5 The following program has the selector LEFT$(*anyString$*, 1), a string expression. In the sample run, only the first action was carried out, even though the value of the selector was in both of the first two value lists. The computer stops looking as soon as it finds the value of the selector.

```
REM Analyze the first character of a string
CLS
INPUT "Enter any string: ", anyString$
LET anyString$ = UCASE$(anyString$)
SELECT CASE LEFT$(anyString$, 1)
  CASE "S", "Z"
    PRINT "The string begins with a sibilant."
  CASE "A" TO "Z"
    PRINT "The string begins with a nonsibilant."
  CASE "0" TO "9"
    PRINT "The string begins with a digit."
```

```
  CASE IS < "0"
    PRINT "The string begins with a character having ASCII"
    PRINT "value less than 48 (e.g. +, &, #, or %)."
END SELECT
END

[run]
Enter any string: Sunday
The string begins with a sibilant.
```

EXAMPLE 6 The color of the beacon light atop Boston's John Hancock Building forecasts the weather according to the rhyme below. Write a program that requests a color (blue or red) and a mode (steady or flashing) as INPUT and displays the weather forecast. The program should contain a SELECT CASE block with a string variable as selector.

Steady blue, clear view.
Flashing blue, clouds due.
Steady red, rain ahead.
Flashing red, snow instead.

SOLUTION

```
REM Interpret a weather beacon
CLS
INPUT "Enter color of the light: ", color$
INPUT "Enter the mode (S or F): ", mode$
SELECT CASE UCASE$(mode$) + LCASE$(color$)
  CASE "Sblue"
    PRINT "Clear view"
  CASE "Fblue"
    PRINT "Clouds due"
  CASE "Sred"
    PRINT "Rain ahead"
  CASE "Fred"
    PRINT "Snow ahead"
END SELECT
END

[run]
Enter color of the light: red
Enter the mode (S or F): S
Rain ahead
```

EXAMPLE 7 SELECT CASE is useful in defining functions that are not determined by a formula. The following program assumes the current year is not a leap year.

```
REM Determine the number of days in a season
CLS
INPUT "Enter a season: ", season$
PRINT season$; " has"; NumDays(season$); "days."
END
```

```
FUNCTION NumDays (season$)
  REM Look up the number of days in a given season
  SELECT CASE UCASE$(season$)
    CASE "WINTER"
      NumDays = 87
    CASE "SPRING"
      NumDays = 92
    CASE "SUMMER", "AUTUMN", "FALL"
      NumDays = 93
  END SELECT
END FUNCTION

[run]
Enter a season: Autumn
Autumn has 93 days.
```

Comments:

1. Some programming languages do not allow a value to appear in two different value lists; QBasic does. If a value appears in two different value lists, the action after the first value list will be carried out.
2. In QBasic, if the value of the selector does not appear in any of the value lists and there is no CASE ELSE clause, then execution of the program will continue with the statement following the SELECT CASE block.
3. The CASE statements and their actions do not have to be indented; however, since indenting improves the readability of the block, it is regarded as good programming style. As soon as you see the words SELECT CASE, your eyes can easily scan down the block to find the matching END SELECT statement. You then immediately know the number of different cases under consideration.
4. The items in the value list must evaluate to a constant of the same type, string or numeric, as the selector. For instance, if the selector evaluates to a string value, then the clause

   ```
   CASE LEN(a$)
   ```

   produces the run-time error message "Type mismatch."
5. If the word IS, which should precede an inequality sign in a value list, is accidentally omitted, the smart editor will automatically insert it upon checking the line.
6. A CASE clause of the form CASE *b* TO *c* selects values from *b* to *c inclusive*. However, the extreme values can be excluded by placing the action inside an IF block beginning with IF (*selector* <> *b*) AND (*selector* <> *c*) THEN.
7. The value of *b* must be less than or equal to the value of *c* in a CASE clause of the form CASE *b* TO *c*.
8. Every SELECT CASE block can be replaced by an IF block. SELECT CASE is preferable to an IF block when the possible choices have more or less the same importance.
9. In Appendix D, the section "Stepping Through Programs Containing Selection Structures: Chapter 5" uses the QBasic debugging tools to trace the flow through a SELECT CASE block.

PRACTICE PROBLEMS 5.3

1. Suppose the selector of a SELECT CASE block is the numeric variable num. Determine whether each of the following CASE clauses is valid.

   (a) CASE 1, 4, IS < 10
   (b) CASE IS < 5, IS >= 5
   (c) CASE "2"

2. Do the two programs below always produce the same output for a whole-number grade from 0 to 100?

```
INPUT "Enter a grade: ", g
SELECT CASE g
  CASE IS >= 90
    PRINT "A"
  CASE IS >= 60
    PRINT "Pass"
  CASE ELSE
    PRINT "Fail"
END SELECT
```

```
INPUT "Enter a grade: ", g
SELECT CASE g
  CASE IS >= 90
    PRINT "A"
  CASE 60 TO 89
    PRINT "Pass"
  CASE 0 TO 59
    PRINT "Fail"
END SELECT
```

EXERCISES 5.3

In Exercises 1 through 8, determine the output of the program for each of the responses shown in the parentheses.

1.
```
INPUT age
SELECT CASE age
  CASE IS < 6
    LET price = 0
  CASE 6 TO 17
    LET price = 3.75
  CASE IS > 17
    LET price = 5.00
END SELECT
PRINT price
END
```
(8.5, 17)

2.
```
INPUT n
SELECT CASE n
  CASE 5
    PRINT "case 1"
  CASE 5 TO 7
    PRINT "case 2"
  CASE 7 TO 12
    PRINT "case 3"
END SELECT
END
```
(7, 5, 11.2)

3.
```
INPUT "Enter age (in millions of years): "; age
SELECT CASE age
  CASE IS < 70
    PRINT "Cenozoic Era"
  CASE IS < 225
    PRINT "Mesozoic Era"
  CASE IS <= 600
    PRINT "Paleozoic Era"
  CASE ELSE
    PRINT "?"
END SELECT
END
```
(100, 600, 700)

4.
```
CALL AskQuestion(year)
CALL ProcessAnswer(year)
END

SUB AskQuestion (year)
  REM Ask question and obtain answer
  INPUT "In what year was the ENIAC computer completed"; year
END SUB

SUB ProcessAnswer (year)
  REM Respond to answer
  SELECT CASE year
    CASE 1945
      PRINT "Correct"
    CASE 1943 TO 1947
      PRINT "Close, 1945."
    CASE IS < 1943
      PRINT "Sorry, 1945. Work on the ENIAC began in June 1943."
    CASE IS > 1947
      PRINT "No, 1945. By then IBM had built a stored program computer."
  END SELECT
END SUB
```

(1940, 1945, 1950)

5.
```
INPUT "Who developed the stored program concept"; name$
SELECT CASE UCASE$(name$)
  CASE "JOHN VON NEUMANN", "VON NEUMANN"
    PRINT "Correct"
  CASE "JOHN MAUCHLY", "MAUCHLY", "J. PRESPER ECKERT", "ECKERT"
    PRINT "He worked with the developer, von Neumann, on the ENIAC."
  CASE ELSE
    PRINT "Nope"
END SELECT
END
```

(Grace Hopper, Eckert, John von Neumann)

6.
```
PRINT "Enter the value of the coefficients for the "
PRINT "quadratic equation A*X^2 + B*X + C = 0"
INPUT "A, B, C"; a, b, c
SELECT CASE b * b - 4 * a * c
  CASE < 0
    PRINT "The equation has no real solutions."
  CASE 0
    PRINT "The equation has exactly one solution."
  CASE > 0
    PRINT "The equation has two solutions."
END SELECT
END
```

(1,2,3; 1,5,1; 1,2,1)

7.
```
REM State a quotation
LET a = 3
LET a$ = "hello"
INPUT b
SELECT CASE 2 * b - 1
  CASE a * a
    PRINT "Less is more."
  CASE IS > LEN(a$)
    PRINT "Time keeps everything from happening at once."
  CASE ELSE
    PRINT "The less things change, the more they remain the same."
END SELECT
END
```

(2, 5, 6)

8.
```
INPUT whatever
SELECT CASE whatever
  CASE ELSE
    PRINT "Hi"
END SELECT
END
```

(7, –1)

In Exercises 9 through 16, identify the errors.

9.
```
LET num = 2
SELECT CASE num
  PRINT "Two"
END SELECT
END
```

10.
```
LET num = 5
LET a = 7
SELECT CASE num
  CASE 3 <= num <= 10
    PRINT "Between 3 and 10"
  CASE a TO 5; 4
    PRINT "Near 5"
END SELECT
END
```

11.
```
LET a$ = "12BMS"
SELECT CASE a$
  CASE 0 TO 9
    PRINT "Begins with a digit"
  CASE ELSE
END SELECT
END
```

12.
```
LET word$ = "hello"
SELECT CASE LEFT$(word$, 1)
  CASE h
    PRINT "Begins with h"
END SELECT
END
```

13.
```
INPUT "Enter a word from the United States motto: ", word$
SELECT CASE word$
  CASE "E"
    PRINT "This is the first word of the motto."
  CASE LEFT$(word$, 1) = "P"
    PRINT "The second word is PLURIBUS."
  CASE ELSE
    PRINT "The third word is UNUM."
END SELECT
END
```

14.
```
LET num = 5
SELECT CASE num
  CASE 5, IS <> 5
    PRINT "Five"
  CASE IS > 5
    PRINT "Greater than 5"
END
```

15.
```
LET a = 3
SELECT CASE a * a < 9
  CASE "true"
    PRINT "true"
  CASE "false"
    PRINT "false"
END SELECT
END
```

16.
```
SELECT CASE purchase
  CASE IS < 10000
    PRINT "Five dollars per item."
  CASE IS 10000 TO 30000
    PRINT "Four dollars per item."
  CASE IS > 30000
    PRINT "Three dollars per item."
END SELECT
END
```

In Exercises 17 through 22, suppose the selector of a SELECT CASE block, a$, evaluates to a string value. Determine whether the CASE clause is valid.

17. CASE "un" + a$

18. CASE "hello", IS < "goodbye"

19. CASE 0 TO 9

20. CASE a$ <> "No"

21. CASE LEFT$("abc", 1)

22. CASE hello

In Exercises 23 through 26, rewrite the code using a SELECT CASE block.

23.
```
IF a = 1 THEN
    PRINT "one"
  ELSE
    IF a > 5 THEN
        PRINT "two"
    END IF
END IF
```

24.
```
IF a = 1 THEN
    PRINT "lambs"
END IF
IF a <= 3 AND a < 4 THEN
    PRINT "eat"
END IF
IF a = 5 OR a > 7 THEN
    PRINT "ivy"
END IF
```

25.
```
IF a < 5 THEN
    IF a = 2 THEN
        PRINT "yes"
      ELSE
        PRINT "no"
    END IF
  ELSE
    IF a = 2 THEN
        PRINT "maybe"
    END IF
END IF
```

26.
```
IF a = 3 THEN
    LET a = 1
END IF
IF a = 2 THEN
    LET a = 3
END IF
IF a = 1 THEN
    LET a = 2
END IF
```

27. Table 5.3 gives the terms used by the National Weather Service to describe the degree of cloudiness. Write a program that requests the percentage of cloud cover as input and then displays the appropriate descriptor.

Percentage of Cloud Cover	Descriptor
0–30	clear
31–70	partly cloudy
71–99	cloudy
100	overcast

Table 5.3 Cloudiness Descriptors

28. Table 5.4 shows the location of books in the library stacks according to their call numbers. Write a program that requests the call number of a book as input and displays the location of the book.

Call Numbers	Location
100 to 199	basement
200 to 500 and over 900	main floor
501 to 900 except 700 to 750	upper floor
700 to 750	archives

Table 5.4 Location of Library Books

29. Write an interactive program that requests a month of the year and then gives the number of days in the month. If the response is February, the user should be asked whether or not the current year is a leap year. The first request should be made in a subprogram, and the computation should be carried out in a function.

30. Figure 5.5 shows some geometric shapes and formulas for their areas. Write a menu-driven program that requests the user to select one of the shapes, requests the appropriate lengths, and then gives the area of the figure. Input and output should be handled by subprograms, and the areas should be computed by functions.

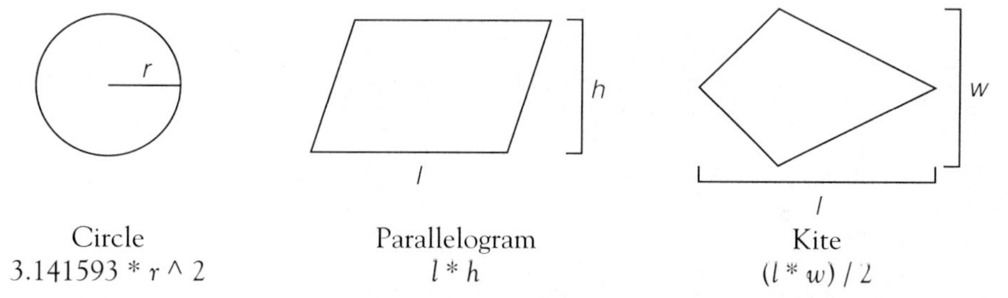

Figure 5.5 Areas of Geometric Shapes

31. Write an interactive program that requests an exam score and assigns a letter grade with the scale 90–100 (A), 80–89 (B), 70–79 (C), 60–69 (D), 0–59 (F). The input should be accomplished by a subprogram and the computation carried out in a function. (Test the program with the grades 84, 100, and 57.)

32. *Computerized quiz show.* Write a program that asks the contestant to select one of the numbers 1, 2, or 3 and then calls a subprogram that asks the question. Another subprogram should then request the answer as input and tell the contestant if the answer is correct. Use the following three questions:

    (a) Who was the only living artist to have his work displayed in the Grand Gallery of the Louvre?
    (b) Who said "Computers are useless. They can only give you answers."?
    (c) By what name is Pablo Blasio better known?

    Note: These questions have the same answer, *Pablo Picasso*.

33. IRS informants are paid cash awards based on the value of the money recovered. If the information was specific enough to lead to a recovery, the informant receives 10% of the first $75,000, 5% of the next $25,000, and 1% of the remainder, up to a maximum award of $50,000. Write a program that requests the amount of the recovery as input and displays the award. (Test the program on the amounts $10,000, $125,000, and $10,000,000.) **Note:** The source of this formula is *The Book of Inside Information*; Boardroom Books, 1993.

34. Table 5.5 contains information on several states. Write a program that requests a state and category (flower, motto, and nickname) as input and displays the requested information. If the state or category requested is not in the table, the program should so inform the user.

State	Flower	Nickname	Motto
California	Golden poppy	Golden State	Eureka
Indiana	Peony	Hoosier State	Crossroads of America
Mississippi	Magnolia	Magnolia State	By valor and arms
New York	Rose	Empire State	Ever upward

Table 5.5 State Flowers, Nicknames, and Mottos

SOLUTIONS TO PRACTICE PROBLEMS 5.3

1. (a) Valid. These items are redundant, since 1 and 4 are just special cases of IS < 10. However, this makes no difference in QBasic.
   (b) Valid. These items are contradictory. However, QBasic looks at them one at a time until it finds an item containing the value of the selector. The action following this CASE clause will always be carried out.
   (c) Not valid. "2" is a string and the selector has numeric type.
2. Yes. However, the program on the right is clearer and therefore preferable.

5.4 A CASE STUDY: WEEKLY PAYROLL

This case study processes a weekly payroll using the 1998 Employer's Tax Guide. Table 5.6 shows typical data used by a company's payroll office. These data are processed to produce the information in Table 5.7 that is supplied to each employee along with his or her paycheck. The program should request the data from Table 5.6 for an individual as input and produce output similar to that in Table 5.7.

The items in Table 5.7 should be calculated as follows:

Current Earnings: Hourly wage times hours worked (with time and a half after 40 hours)

Year-to-Date Earnings: Previous year-to-date earnings plus current earnings

FICA Tax: Sum of 6.2% of first $68,400 of earnings (Social Security benefits tax) and 1.45% of total wages (Medicare tax)

Federal Income Tax Withheld: Subtract $51.92 from the current earnings for each withholding exemption and use Table 5.8 or Table 5.9, depending on marital status

Check Amount: [Current earnings] – [FICA taxes] – [Income tax withheld]

Name	Hourly Wage	Hours Worked	Withholding Exemptions	Marital Status	Previous Year-to-Date Earnings
Al Johnson	26.25	38	4	Married	$68,100.00
Ann Jones	14.00	35	3	Married	$21,840.50
Sue Williams	27.50	43	2	Single	$41,890.50

Table 5.6 Employee Data

Name	Current Earnings	Yr. to Date Earnings	FICA Taxes	Income Tax Wh.	Check Amount
Al Johnson	997.50	69,097.50	33.06	99.87	864.56

Table 5.7 Payroll Information

Adjusted Weekly Income	Income Tax Withheld
$0 to $51	0
Over $51 to $517	15% of amount over $51
Over $517 to $1,105	$69.90 + 28% of amount over $517
Over $1,105 to $2,493	$234.54 + 31% of amount over $1,105
Over $2,493 to $5,385	$664.82 + 36% of amount over $2,493
Over $5,385	$1,705.94 + 39.6% of amount over $5,385

Table 5.8 1998 Federal Income Tax Withheld for a Single Person Paid Weekly

Adjusted Weekly Income	Income Tax Withheld
$0 to $124	0
Over $124 to $899	15% of amount over $124
Over $899 to $1,855	$116.25 + 28% of amount over $899
Over $1,855 to $3,084	$383.93 + 31% of amount over $1,855
Over $3.084 to $5,439	$764.92 + 36% of amount over $3,084
Over $5,439	$1,612.72 + 39.6% of amount over $5,439

Table 5.9 1998 Federal Income Tax Withheld for a Married Person Paid Weekly

Designing the Weekly Payroll Program

After the data for an employee have been requested as input, the program must compute the five items appearing in Table 5.7 and then display the payroll information. The five computations form the basic tasks of the program.

1. Compute current earnings.
2. Compute year-to-date earnings.
3. Compute FICA tax.
4. Compute federal income tax withheld.
5. Compute paycheck amount (that is, take-home pay).

Tasks 1, 2, 3, and 5 are fairly simple. Each involves applying a formula to given data. (For instance, if hours worked is at most 40, then Current Earnings = Hourly Wage times Hours Worked.) Thus, we won't break down these tasks any further. Task 4 is more complicated, so we continue to divide it into smaller subtasks.

4. *Compute Federal Income Tax Withheld.* First the employee's pay is adjusted for exemptions, and then the amount of income tax to be withheld is computed. The computation of the income tax withheld differs for married and single individuals. Task 4 is, therefore, divided into the following subtasks:

   4.1 Compute pay adjusted by exemptions.
   4.2 Compute income tax withheld for single employee.
   4.3 Compute income tax withheld for married employee.

The top-down chart in Figure 5.6 shows the stepwise refinement of the problem.

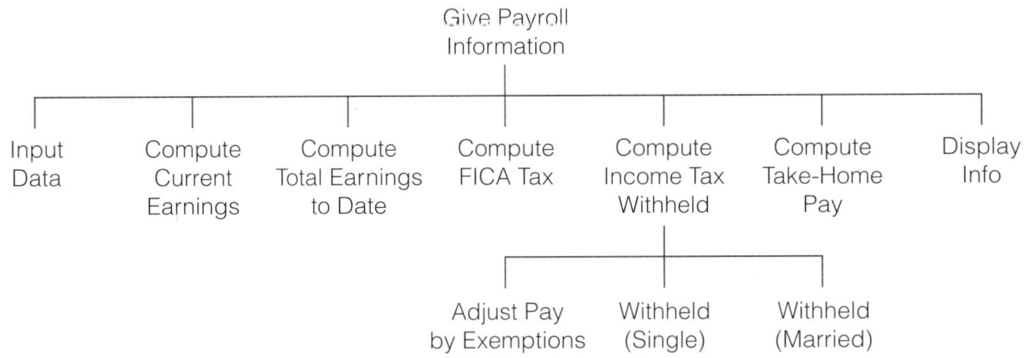

Figure 5.6 Top-Down Chart for the Weekly Payroll Program

Pseudocode for the Weekly Payroll Program

```
INPUT employee data (Subprogram InputData)
COMPUTE CURRENT GROSS PAY (Function ComputePay)
COMPUTE TOTAL EARNINGS TO DATE (Function ComputeTotalPay)
COMPUTE FICA TAX (Function ComputeFICATax)
COMPUTE FEDERAL TAX (Function ComputeFedTax)
  Adjust pay for exemptions
  IF employee is single THEN
      COMPUTE INCOME TAX WITHHELD from adjusted pay using tax
      brackets for single taxpayers (Function TaxSingle)
    ELSE
      COMPUTE INCOME TAX WITHHELD from adjusted pay using tax
      brackets for married taxpayers (Function TaxMarried)
  END IF
COMPUTE CHECK (Function ComputeCheck)
Display payroll information (Subprogram ShowInformation)
```

Writing the Weekly Payroll Program

The main body of the program calls a sequence of seven subprograms. Table 5.10 shows the tasks and the procedures that perform the tasks.

Task	Procedure
0. Input employee data.	InputData
1. Compute current earnings.	ComputePay
2. Compute year-to-date earnings.	ComputeTotalPay
3. Compute FICA tax.	ComputeFICATax
4. Compute Federal Income Tax withheld.	ComputeFedTax
4.1 Compute adjusted pay.	ComputeFedTax
4.2 Compute amount withheld for single employee.	TaxSingle
4.3 Compute amount withheld for married employee.	TaxMarried
5. Compute paycheck amounts.	ComputeCheck
6. Display payroll information.	ShowInformation

Table 5.10 Tasks and Their Procedures

```
REM Program to compute employees' weekly payroll
REM
REM ***********************************************************
REM *         Variable Table                                  *
REM *                                                         *
REM *  a$            Formatting string for PRINT USING        *
REM *  exemptions    Number of exemptions for employee        *
REM *  fedTax        Federal income tax withheld this week    *
REM *  ficaTax       FICA taxes for this week                 *
REM *  hrsWorked     Hours worked this week                   *
REM *  hrWage        Hourly wage                              *
REM *  medicare      Medicare tax for this week               *
REM *  mStatus$      Marital status (SINGLE or MARRIED)       *
REM *  name$         Name of employee                         *
REM *  pay           This week's pay before taxes             *
REM *  check         Paycheck this week (take-home pay)       *
REM *  prevPay       Total pay for year excluding this week   *
```

```
REM *  socialSecurity  Social Security tax for this week       *
REM *  totalPay        Total pay for year including this week  *
REM ***********************************************************
CLS
CALL InputData(name$, hrWage, hrsWorked, exemptions, mStatus$, prevPay)
LET pay = ComputePay(hrWage, hrsWorked)
LET totalPay = ComputeTotalPay(prevPay, pay)
LET ficaTax = ComputeFICATax(pay, prevPay, totalPay)
LET fedTax = ComputeFedTax(pay, exemptions, mStatus$)
LET check = ComputeCheck(pay, ficaTax, fedTax)
CALL ShowInformation(name$, pay, totalPay, ficaTax, fedTax, check)
END

FUNCTION ComputeCheck (pay, ficaTax, fedTax)
  REM Compute amount of money given to employee
  ComputeCheck = pay - ficaTax - fedTax
END FUNCTION

FUNCTION ComputeFedTax (pay, exemptions, mStatus$)
  REM Compute federal tax
  LET adjPay = pay - (47.12 * exemptions)
  IF adjPay < 0 THEN
      LET adjPay = 0
  END IF
  IF UCASE$(mStatus$) = "SINGLE" THEN
      ComputeFedTax = TaxSingle(adjPay)
    ELSE
      ComputeFedTax = TaxMarried(adjPay)
  END IF
END FUNCTION

FUNCTION ComputeFICATax (pay, prevPay, totalPay)
  REM Compute Social Security and Medicare tax
  LET socialSecurity = 0
  IF totalPay <= 60600 THEN
      LET socialSecurity = .062 * pay
    ELSEIF prevPay < 60600 THEN
      LET socialSecurity = .062 * (60600 - prevPay)
  END IF
  LET medicare = .0145 * pay
  ComputeFICATax = socialSecurity + medicare
END FUNCTION

FUNCTION ComputePay (hrWage, hrsWorked)
  REM Compute weekly pay before taxes
  IF hrsWorked <= 40 THEN
      ComputePay = hrsWorked * hrWage
    ELSE
      ComputePay = 40 * hrWage + (hrsWorked - 40) * 1.5 * hrWage
  END IF
END FUNCTION

FUNCTION ComputeTotalPay (prevPay, pay)
  REM Compute total pay before taxes
  ComputeTotalPay = prevPay + pay
END FUNCTION
```

```
SUB InputData (name$, hrWage, hrsWorked, exemptions, mStatus$, prevPay)
  REM Get payroll data for employee
  INPUT "Name: ", name$
  INPUT "Hourly wage: ", hrWage
  INPUT "Number of hours worked: ", hrsWorked
  INPUT "Number of exemptions: ", exemptions
  INPUT "Marital status SINGLE/MARRIED: ", mStatus$
  INPUT "Total pay prior to this week: ", prevPay
END SUB

SUB ShowInformation (name$, pay, totalPay, ficaTax, fedTax, check)
  REM Display headings and information for paycheck
  PRINT "              Current  Yr. to date  FICA    Income   Check"
  PRINT "Name          Earnings Earnings     Taxes   Tax Wh.  Amount"
  PRINT
  LET a$ = "\           \ ####.##    ##,###.##  ###.##   ###.##  ####.##"
  PRINT USING a$; name$; pay; totalPay; ficaTax; fedTax; check
END SUB

FUNCTION TaxMarried (adjPay)
  REM Compute federal tax for married person based on adjusted pay
  SELECT CASE adjPay
    CASE 0 TO 124
      TaxMarried = 0
    CASE 124 TO 899
      TaxMarried = .15 * (adjPay - 124)
    CASE 899 TO 1855
      TaxMarried = 116.25 + .28 * (adjPay - 899)
    CASE 1855 TO 3084
      TaxMarried = 383.93 + .31 * (adjPay - 1855)
    CASE 3084 TO 5439
      TaxMarried = 764.92 + .36 * (adjPay - 3084)
    CASE IS > 5439
      TaxMarried = 1612.72 + .396 * (adjPay - 5439)
  END SELECT
END FUNCTION

FUNCTION TaxSingle (adjPay)
  REM Compute federal tax for single person based on adjusted pay
  SELECT CASE adjPay
    CASE 0 TO 51
      TaxSingle = 0
    CASE 51 TO 517
      TaxSingle = .15 * (adjPay - 51)
    CASE 517 TO 1105
      TaxSingle = 69.9 + .28 * (adjPay - 517)
    CASE 1105 TO 2493
      TaxSingle = 234.54 + .31 * (adjPay - 1105)
    CASE 2493 TO 5385
      TaxSingle = 664.82 + .36 * (adjPay - 2493)
    CASE IS > 5385
      TaxSingle = 1705.94 + .396 * (adjPay - 5385)
  END SELECT
END FUNCTION
```

Comments:

1. In ComputeFICATax, care has been taken to avoid computing Social Security benefits tax on income in excess of $68,400 per year. The logic of the program makes sure an employee whose income crosses the $68,400 threshold during a given week is taxed only on the difference between $68,400 and his previous year-to-date income.

2. The two functions TaxMarried and TaxSingle use SELECT CASE to incorporate the tax brackets given in Tables 5.8 and 5.9 for the amount of federal income tax withheld. The upper limit of each CASE clause is the same as the lower limit of the next CASE clause. This ensured fractional values for adjPay, such as 51.50 in the TaxSingle function, would be properly treated as part of the higher salary range.

Chapter 5 Summary

1. The *relational operators* are <, >, =, <>, <=, and >=.

2. The principal *logical operators* are AND, OR, and NOT.

3. A *condition* is an expression involving constants, variables, functions, and operators (arithmetic, relational, and/or logical) that can be evaluated to either true or false.

4. An IF block decides what action to take depending upon the truth values of one or more conditions. To allow several courses of action, the IF and ELSE parts of an IF statement can contain other IF statements.

5. A SELECT CASE block selects one of several actions depending on the value of an expression, called the *selector*. The entries in the *value lists* must have the same type (string or numeric) as the selector.

Chapter 5 Programming Projects

1. Table 5.11 gives the price schedule for Eddie's Equipment Rental. Full-day rentals cost one-and-a-half times half-day rentals. Write a program to display Table 5.11, ask the customer to select an item and time period, and then display a bill. The bill should include a $30.00 deposit.

Piece of Equipment	Half-Day	Full-Day
1. Rug cleaner	$16.00	$24.00
2. Lawn mower	$12.00	$18.00
3. Paint sprayer	$20.00	$30.00

Table 5.11 Price Schedule for Eddie's Equipment Rental

A sample output after the display of the table is:

```
Select an item (1, 2, or 3): 2
Select a duration (H or F): F

Receipt from Eddie's Equipment Rental

Lawn mower     18.00 (Full day rental)
Deposit        30.00

Total         $48.00
```

2. The American Heart Association suggests that at most 30% of the calories in our diet come from fat. Whereas food labels give the number of calories and amount of fat per serving, they often do not give the percentage of calories from fat. This percentage can be calculated by multiplying the number of grams of fat in one serving by 9, dividing that number by the total number of calories per serving, and multiplying the result by 100. Write a program that requests the name, number of calories per serving, and the grams of fat per serving as input, and tells us whether the food meets the American Heart Association recommendation. A sample output is as follows:

```
[run]
Enter name of food: Lowfat milk
Enter number of calories per serving: 120
Enter grams of fat per serving: 5

Lowfat milk contains 37.5% calories from fat.
Lowfat milk exceeds the AHA recommendation.
```

3. Table 5.12 gives the 1998 federal income tax rate schedule for single taxpayers. Write a program that requests the taxable income and calculates the federal income tax. Use a subprogram for the input and a function to calculate the tax.

Taxable Income Over–	But Not Over–	Your Tax Is–	Of Amount Over–
$0	$25,350	15%	$0
$25,350	$61,400	$ 3,802.50 + 28%	$25,350
$61,400	$128,100	$13,896.50 + 31%	$61,400
$128,100	$278,450	$34,573.50 + 36%	$128,100
$278,450		$86,699.50 + 39.6%	$278,450

Table 5.12 1998 Federal Income Tax Rates for Single Taxpayers

4. Write a program to determine the real roots of the quadratic equation $ax^2 + bx + c = 0$ (where $a \neq 0$) after requesting the values of a, b, and c. Use a subprogram to insure that a is nonzero. **Note:** The equation has 2, 1, or 0 solutions depending upon whether the value of b^2 – 4 * a * c is positive, zero, or negative. In the first two cases the solutions are given by the quadratic formula (–b ± SQR(b^2 – 4 * a * c)) / (2 * a).

5. Table 5.13 contains seven proverbs and their truth values. Write a program that presents these proverbs one at a time and asks the user to evaluate them as true or false. The program should then tell the user how many questions were answered correctly and display one of the following evaluations: Perfect (all correct), Excellent (5 or 6 correct), You might consider taking Psychology 101 (less than 5 correct).

Proverb	Truth Value
The squeaky wheel gets the grease.	True
Cry and you cry alone.	True
Opposites attract.	False
Spare the rod and spoil the child.	False
Actions speak louder than words.	True
Familiarity breeds contempt.	False
Marry in haste, repent at leisure.	True

Table 5.13 Seven Proverbs
Source: "You Know What They Say . . . ," by Alfie Kohn, *Psychology Today*, April 1988.

6. Write a program to find the day of the week for any date after 1582, the year our current calendar was introduced. The program should:
   (a) Request the year and the number of the month as input.
   (b) Determine the number of days in the month. **Note:** All years divisible by 4 are leap years, with the exception of those years divisible by 100 and not by 400. For instance, 1600 and 2000 are leap years, but 1700, 1800, and 1900 are not.
   (c) Request the number of the day as input. The prompt should list the possible range for the number.
   (d) Determine the day of the week with the following algorithm.
      (1) Treat January as the 13th month and February as the 14th month of the previous year. For example 1/23/1986 should be converted to 13/23/1985 and 2/6/1987 should be converted to 14/6/1986.
      (2) Denote the number of the day, month, and year by d, m, and y. Compute

$$w = d + 2*m + \text{INT}(.6 * (m+1)) + y + \text{INT}(y/4) - \text{INT}(y/100) + \text{INT}(y/400) + 2$$

      (3) The remainder when w is divided by 7 is the day of the week of the given date, with Saturday as the zeroth day of the week, Sunday the first day of the week, Monday the second, and so on.

Some sample outputs of the program are:

```
[run]
Year (xxxx)? 1776
Month (1 - 12)? 7
Day of Month (1 - 31)? 4
The day of the week was Thu

[run]
Year (xxxx)? 1987
Month (1 - 12)? 2
Day of Month (1 - 28 )? 28
The day of the week was Sat
```

Test the program with the following memorable dates in the history of the U.S. space program.

On Tuesday, February 20, 1962, John Glenn became the first American to orbit the earth.

On Sunday, July 20, 1969, Neil Armstrong became the first person to set foot on the moon.

On Saturday, June 18, 1983, Sally Ride became the first American woman to travel in space.

6

Repetition

6.1 DO LOOPS

A **loop**, one of the most important structures in QBasic, is used to repeat a sequence of statements a number of times. At each repetition, or **pass**, the statements act upon variables whose values are changing.

The DO loop is one of the most important structures in QBasic. It repeats a sequence of statements either as long as or until a certain condition is true. A DO statement precedes the sequence of statements and a LOOP statement follows the sequence of statements. The condition, along with either the word WHILE or UNTIL, follows the word DO or the word LOOP. When QBasic executes a DO loop of the form

```
DO WHILE condition
  statement(s)
LOOP
```

it first checks the truth value of *condition*. If *condition* is false, then the statements inside the loop are not executed and the program continues with the line after the LOOP statement. If *condition* is true, then the statements inside the loop are executed. When the statement LOOP is encountered, the entire process is repeated, beginning with the testing *condition* in the DO WHILE statement. In other words, the statements inside the loop are repeatedly executed as long as the condition is true. Figure 6.1 contains the pseudocode and flowchart for this loop.

DO WHILE condition is true
  Processing step(s)
LOOP

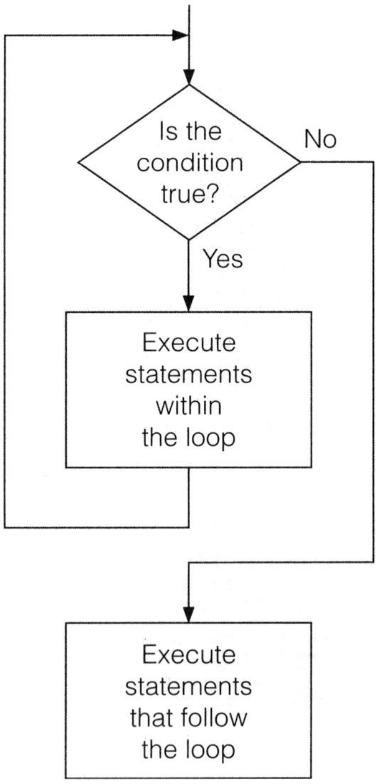

Figure 6.1 Pseudocode and Flowchart for a DO Loop

EXAMPLE 1 Write a program that displays the numbers from 1 through 10.

SOLUTION The condition in the DO loop is num <= 10.

```
REM Display the numbers from 1 to 10
CLS
LET num = 1
DO WHILE num <= 10
  PRINT num;
  LET num = num + 1
LOOP
END

[run]
 1  2  3  4  5  6  7  8  9  10
```

DO loops are commonly used to insure that a proper response is received by an INPUT statement.

EXAMPLE 2 The following program requires the user to give an acceptable response.

```
REM Request and check for proper phone number
CLS
INPUT "Enter your phone number (xxx-xxx-xxxx): ", phoneNum$
DO WHILE LEN(phoneNum$) <> 12
  PRINT "Don't forget your area code."
  INPUT "Enter your phone number (xxx-xxx-xxxx): ", phoneNum$
LOOP
PRINT "Your phone number is "; phoneNum$
END

[run]
Enter your phone number (xxx-xxx-xxxx): 123-4567
Don't forget your area code.
Enter your phone number (xxx-xxx-xxxx): 888-123-4567
Your phone number is 888-123-4567
```

Note: If a valid response is given at the first request, the statements inside the loop are not executed.

In Examples 1 and 2 the condition was checked at the top of the loop—that is, before the statements were executed. Alternately, the condition can be checked at the bottom of the loop when the statement LOOP is reached. When QBasic encounters a DO loop of the form

```
DO
  statement(s)
LOOP UNTIL condition
```

it executes the statements inside the loop and then checks the truth value of *condition*. If *condition* is true, then the program continues with the line after the LOOP statement. If *condition* is false, then the entire process is repeated beginning with the DO statement. In other words, the statements inside the loop are executed at least once and then are repeatedly executed until the condition is true. Figure 6.2 shows the pseudocode and flowchart for this type of DO loop.

DO
  statement(s)
LOOP UNTIL condition is true

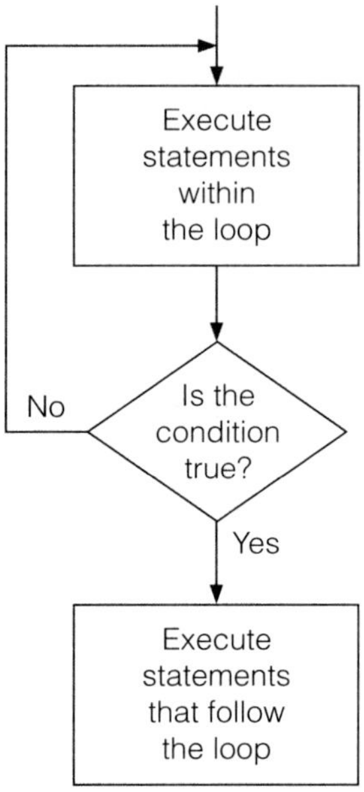

Figure 6.2 Pseudocode and Flowchart for a DO Loop with Condition Tested at the Bottom

EXAMPLE 3 The following program uses a DO loop to repeat a question until the correct answer is given.

```
REM Pose a multiple-choice question
CLS
REM Show question and possible responses
PRINT "What is the last line of the movie Gone with the Wind?"
PRINT
PRINT "1. Oh, Auntie Em, there's no place like home."
PRINT "2. It wasn't the airplanes, it was beauty killed the beast."
PRINT "3. Th-that's all folks!"
PRINT "4. After all, tomorrow is another day."
PRINT
REM Process the response
DO
  INPUT "Enter a number from 1 to 4: ", num
  IF num <> 4 THEN
      PRINT "No, try again."
  END IF
LOOP UNTIL num = 4
PRINT "Correct"
END

[run]
What is the last line of the movie Gone with the Wind?
```

```
1. Oh, Auntie Em, there's no place like home.
2. It wasn't the airplanes, it was beauty killed the beast.
3. Th-that's all folks!
4. After all, tomorrow is another day.

Enter a number from 1 to 4: 2
No, try again.
Enter a number from 1 to 4: 4
Correct
```

DO loops allow us to calculate useful quantities for which we might not know a simple formula.

EXAMPLE 4 Suppose you deposit $100 into a savings account and let it accumulate at 7% interest compounded annually. The following program determines when you will be a millionaire.

```
REM Compute years required to become a millionaire
CLS
LET balance = 100
LET numYears = 0
DO WHILE balance < 1000000
  LET balance = balance + .07 * balance
  LET numYears = numYears + 1
LOOP
PRINT "In"; numYears; "years you will have a million dollars."
END

[run]
In 137 years you will have a million dollars.
```

Accessing menus is one of the fundamental tasks in interactive programming. The user makes choices until he or she decides to quit. The general form of a menu-driven program is as follows.

```
REM Generic menu-driven program
DO
  CALL DisplayMenu
  CALL GetChoice(num)
  SELECT CASE num
    CASE 1
      CALL Task1
    CASE 2
      CALL Task2
    CASE 3
      CALL Task3
    CASE 4
      Quit
    CASE ELSE
      PRINT "Invalid choice"
  END SELECT
LOOP UNTIL num = 4
END
```

EXAMPLE 5 The following elementary menu-driven program illustrates this important use of DO loops.

```
REM Display a word
CLS
INPUT "Enter a word: ", word$
DO
  CALL DisplayMenu(word$)
  CALL GetChoice(choice)
  SELECT CASE choice
    CASE 1
      PRINT TAB(80 - LEN(word$)); word$
    CASE 2
      PRINT TAB(40 - LEN(word$) / 2); word$
    CASE 3
      INPUT "Enter new word: ", word$
    CASE 4
      PRINT "Goodbye. Have a nice day."
    CASE ELSE
      PRINT "Invalid choice."
  END SELECT
LOOP UNTIL choice = 4
END

SUB DisplayMenu (word$)
  PRINT
  PRINT "The current word is "; word$
  PRINT "  1. Right-justify word."
  PRINT "  2. Center word."
  PRINT "  3. Change word."
  PRINT "  4. Quit."
END SUB

SUB GetChoice (choice)
  INPUT "Enter a number from 1 through 4: ", choice
END SUB

[run]
Enter a word: Happy

The current word is Happy
  1. Right-justify word.
  2. Center word.
  3. Change word.
  4. Quit.
Enter a number from 1 through 4: 2
                                     Happy

The current word is Happy
  1. Right-justify word.
  2. Center word.
  3. Change word.
  4. Quit.
Enter a number from 1 through 4: 3
Enter a new word: Birthday
```

```
The current word is Birthday
  1. Right-justify word.
  2. Center word.
  3. Change word.
  4. Quit.
Enter a number from 1 through 4: 4
Goodbye. Have a nice day.
```

Comments:

1. Be careful to avoid infinite loops—that is, loops that are never exited. The following loop is infinite, since the condition *num* <> 0 will always be true. **Note:** The program can be terminated by pressing Ctrl+Break.

```
REM An infinite loop
LET num = 7
DO WHILE num <> 0
  LET num = num - 2
LOOP
END
```

   Notice that this slip-up can be avoided by changing the condition to *num* >= 0.

2. The statements between DO and LOOP do not have to be indented. However, since indenting improves the readability of the program, it is regarded as good programming style. As soon as you see the word DO, your eyes can easily scan down the program to find the matching LOOP statement. You then know immediately the size of the loop.

3. QBasic allows the use of the words WHILE and UNTIL either at the top or bottom of a DO loop. In this text, the usage of these words is restricted for the following reasons.

   (a) Since any WHILE statement can easily be converted to an UNTIL statement and vice versa, the restriction produces no loss of capabilities and the programmer has one less matter to think about.
   (b) Restricting the use simplifies reading the program. The word WHILE proclaims testing at the top and the word UNTIL proclaims testing at the bottom.
   (c) Certain other major structured languages, such as Pascal, only allow WHILE at the top and UNTIL at the bottom of a loop. Therefore, following this convention will make life easier for people already familiar with Pascal or planning to learn it.
   (d) Standard pseudocode uses the word WHILE to denote testing a loop at the top and the word UNTIL to denote testing at the bottom.

4. Good programming practice requires that all variables appearing in a DO loop be assigned values before the loop is entered, rather than relying on default values. For instance, the code on the left below should be replaced with the code on the right below.

```
REM Add 1 through 10
DO WHILE num < 10
  LET num = num + 1
  LET sum = sum + num
LOOP
```

```
REM Add 1 through 10
LET num = 0
LET sum = 0
DO WHILE num < 10
  LET num = num + 1
  LET sum = sum + num
LOOP
```

PRACTICE PROBLEMS 6.1

1. How do you decide whether a condition should be checked at the top of a loop or at the bottom?

2. Change the following loop so it will be executed at least once.

```
DO WHILE continue$ = "Yes"
  INPUT "Do you want to continue (Y or N)"; answer$
  IF answer$ = "Y" THEN
      LET continue$ = "Yes"
    ELSE
      LET continue$ = "No"
  END IF
LOOP
```

EXERCISES 6.1

In Exercises 1 through 6, determine the output of the program.

1.
```
LET q = 3
DO WHILE q < 15
  LET q = 2 * q - 1
LOOP
PRINT q
END
```

2.
```
LET balance = 1000
LET interest = .1
LET n = 0                    'Number of years
DO
  PRINT n; balance
  LET balance = (1 + interest) * balance
  LET n = n + 1
LOOP UNTIL balance > 1200
PRINT n
END
```

3.
```
REM Display a message
LET num = 4
DO
  SELECT CASE num
    CASE 1
      LET mes$ = "upe"
      LET num = 3
    CASE 2
      LET mes$ = "mmer!"
      LET num = -1
    CASE 3
      LET mes$ = "r pr"
      LET num = 8 - num
    CASE 4
      LET mes$ = "Yo"
      LET num = 16 - 2.5 * num
```

```
    CASE 5
      LET mes$ = "ogra"
      LET num = 2
    CASE 6
      LET mes$ = "u ar"
      LET num = 1 + num
    CASE 7
      LET mes$ = "e a s"
      LET num = (6 - num) * (4 - num) - 2
  END SELECT
  PRINT mes$;
LOOP UNTIL num = -1
END
```

4.
```
REM Computer-assisted instruction
DO
  INPUT "In what year was the IBM PC first produced"; year
  SELECT CASE year
    CASE 1981
      PRINT "Correct. The computer was an instant success. By the end"
      PRINT "of 1981, there was such a backlog of orders that"
      PRINT "customers had a three-month waiting period."
    CASE IS < 1981
      PRINT "Later than that. The Apple II computer, which"
      PRINT "preceded the IBM PC, appeared in 1977."
    CASE IS > 1981
      PRINT "Earlier than that. The first successful IBM PC clone,"
      PRINT "the Compaq Portable, appeared in 1983."
  END SELECT
  PRINT
LOOP UNTIL year = 1981
END
```

(Assume the first response is *1980* and the second response is *1981*.)

5.
```
REM Calculate the remainder in long division
PRINT Remainder(3, 17)
END

FUNCTION Remainder (divisor, dividend)
  LET sum = 0
  DO WHILE sum <= dividend
    LET sum = sum + divisor
  LOOP
  Remainder = dividend - sum + divisor
END FUNCTION
```

6.
```
REM Simulate INSTR, search for the letter t
LET a$ = "Potato"
LET counter = 0
LET letter$ = ""
DO WHILE (letter$ <> "t") AND (counter <= LEN(a$))
  LET counter = counter + 1
  LET letter$ = MID$(a$, counter, 1)
  IF letter$ = "t" THEN
      PRINT counter
  END IF
```

```
LOOP
IF letter$ <> "t" THEN
    PRINT 0
END IF
END
```

In Exercises 7 through 10, identify the errors.

7.
```
LET q = 1
DO WHILE q > 0
  LET q = 3 * q - 1
  PRINT q;
LOOP
END
```

8.
```
REM Display the numbers from 1 to 5
DO WHILE num <> 5
  LET num = 1
  PRINT num;
  LET num = num + 1
LOOP
END
```

9.
```
REM Repeat until a yes response is given
LOOP
  INPUT "Did you chop down the cherry tree (Y/N)"; answer$
DO UNTIL answer$ = "Y"
END
```

10.
```
REM Repeat as long as desired
DO
  LET n = n + 1
  PRINT n
  INPUT "Do you want to continue (Y/N)"; answer$
UNTIL answer$ = "Y"
END
```

In Exercises 11 through 20, replace each phrase containing UNTIL with an equivalent phrase containing WHILE, and vice versa. For instance, the phrase UNTIL sum = 100 would be replaced by WHILE sum <> 100.

11. UNTIL num < 7
12. UNTIL name$ = "Bob"
13. WHILE response$ = "Y"
14. WHILE total = 10
15. WHILE name$ <> ""
16. UNTIL balance >= 100
17. WHILE (a > 1) AND (a < 3)
18. UNTIL (a$ = "") OR (n = 0)
19. UNTIL NOT (n = 0)
20. WHILE (a$ = "Y") AND (n < 7)

In Exercises 21 and 22, write a simpler and clearer program that performs the same task as the given program.

21.
```
INPUT num
PRINT num
INPUT num
PRINT num
INPUT num
PRINT num
END
```

22.
```
LET loopNum = 0
DO
  IF loopNum >= 1 THEN
      INPUT "Do you want to continue (Y/N)"; answer$
    ELSE
      LET answer$ = "Y"
  END IF
  IF (answer$ = "Y") OR (loopNum = 0) THEN
      LET loopNum = loopNum + 1
      PRINT loopNum
  END IF
LOOP UNTIL answer$ <> "Y"
END
```

23. Write a program that requests a temperature between 0 and 100 degrees Celsius and converts the temperature to Fahrenheit. If the response is not between 0 and 100, the request should be repeated until a proper response is given. **Note:** The formula $f = (9 / 5) * c + 32$ converts Celsius to Fahrenheit.

24. Write a program that repeats the question "D'you know the capital of Alaska?" until the correct answer is given. When an incorrect answer is given, the program should display the statement, "It rhymes with D'you know." **Note:** The capital of Alaska is Juneau.

25. Write a program to forecast the weather in Oregon. The program should request input with the prompt "Can you see the mountains (Y/N)?" The program should display "It is going to rain" or "It is raining," depending upon whether the first letter of the response is Y (or y) or N (or n), respectively. If the first letter of the response is not Y, y, N, or n, the request should be repeated until a proper response is given.

26. A car's computer can determine the number of gallons of gasoline in the tank and sense whether the driver's seatbelt is fastened and the doors are closed. The computer will not allow the car to be shifted out of "Park" if either the driver's seatbelt is not fastened or any door is open. If the tank contains less than two gallons of gasoline, the message "Get gas" is displayed. Write a program to simulate the operation of the computer. A sample output is:

```
[run]
Is the driver's seatbelt fastened (Y or N)? N
Are all doors closed (Y or N)? Y

Please fasten your seatbelt.
```

```
Is the driver's seatbelt fastened (Y or N)? Y
How many gallons of gas are in the tank? 1

You may proceed.
Get gas.
```

27. Write a program that asks the user to enter positive numbers into the computer until the product of the numbers exceeds 400. The program should then display the highest number.

28. Write a program to display all the numbers between 1 and 100 that are perfect squares (a perfect square is an integer that is the square of another integer; 1, 4, and 16 are examples of perfect squares).

29. The population of Mexico City is currently 14 million people and growing at the rate of 3% each year. Write a program to determine when the population will reach 20 million.

30. Write a program to solve the equation $a * x + b = c$, where the numbers a, b, and c are supplied via INPUT statements. Allow for the case where a is 0. In this case, either there will be no solution or every number will be a solution. After solving each equation, ask the user if he wants another equation solved.

31. Write a program that requests a word containing the two letters r and n as input and determines which of the two letters appears first. If the word does not contain both of the letters, the program should keep requesting words until one does. (Test the program with the words *colonel* and *merriment*.)

32. The coefficient of restitution of a ball, a number between 0 and 1, specifies how much energy is conserved when a ball hits a rigid surface. A coefficient of .9, for instance, means a bouncing ball will rise to 90% of its initial height after each bounce. Write a program to input a coefficient of restitution and a height in meters and report how many times a ball bounces before it rises to a height of less than 10 centimeters. Also report the total distance traveled by the ball before this point. The coefficients of restitution of a tennis ball, basketball, super ball, and softball are .7, .75, .9, and .3, respectively.

In Exercises 33 through 36, write a program to solve the stated problem.

33. *Savings Account.* $15,000 is deposited into a savings account paying 5% interest and $1000 is withdrawn from the account at the end of each year. Approximately how many years are required for the savings account to be depleted?

34. Rework Exercise 33 for the case where the amount of money deposited initially is input by the user and the program computes the number of years required to deplete the account. **Note:** Be careful to avoid infinite loops.

35. $1000 is deposited into a savings account, and an additional $1000 is deposited at the end of each year. If the money earns interest at the rate of 5%, how long will it take before the account contains at least $1 million?

36. A person born in 1980 can claim "I will be *x* years old in the year *x* squared." Write a program to determine the value of *x*.

In Exercises 37 and 38, write a program corresponding to the flowchart.

37. The flowchart in Figure 6.3 requests an integer greater than 1 as input and factors it into a product of prime numbers. (***Note:*** A number is prime if its only factors are 1 and itself. Test the program with the numbers 660 and 139.)

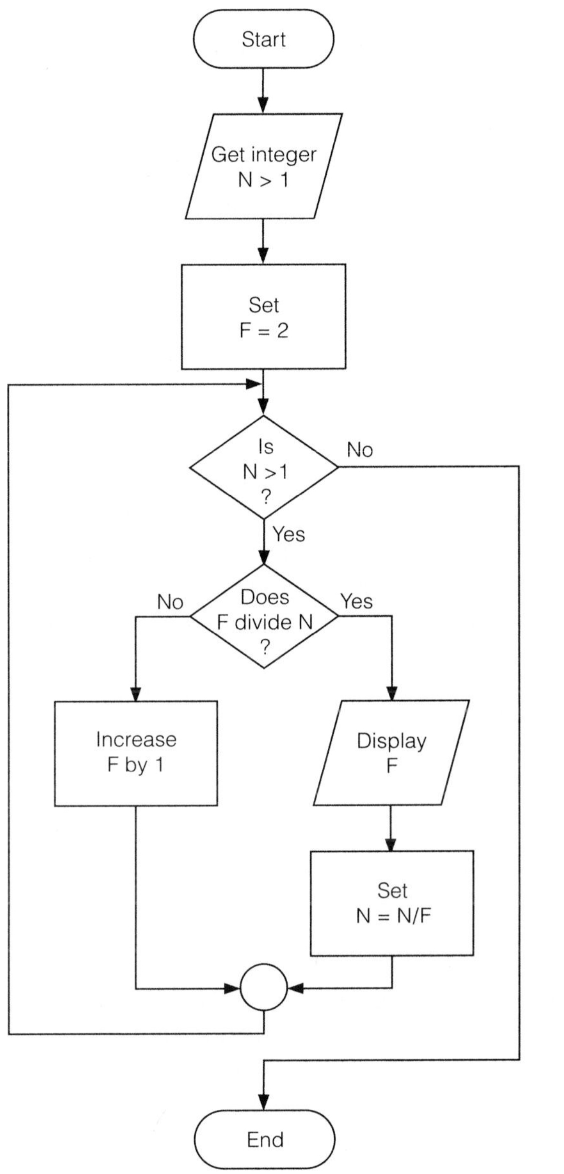

Figure 6.3 Prime Factors

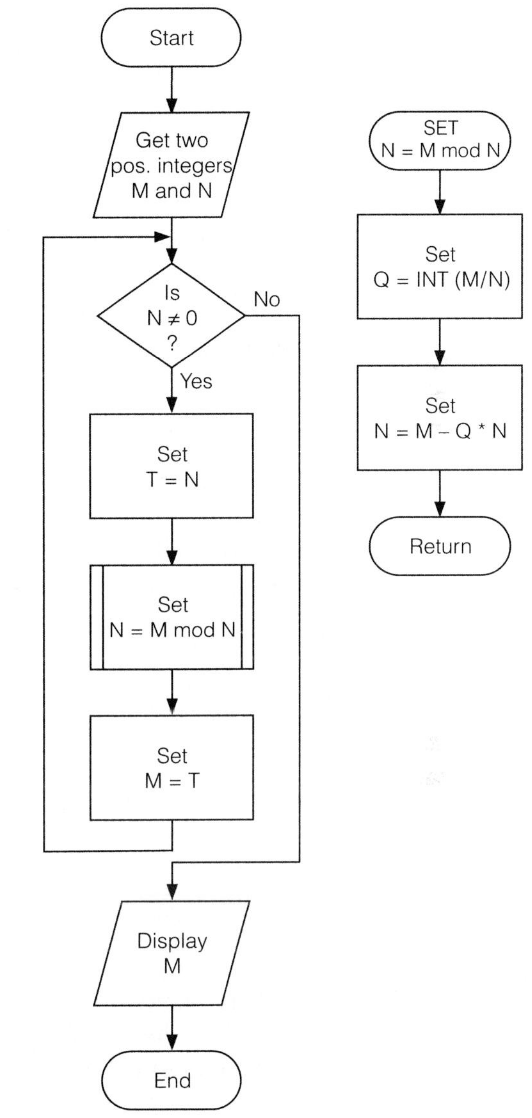

Figure 6.4 Greatest Common Divisor

38. The flowchart in Figure 6.4 finds the greatest common divisor (the largest integer that divides both) of two positive integers input by the user. Write a program that corresponds to the flowchart.

SOLUTIONS TO PRACTICE PROBLEMS 6.1

1. As a rule of thumb, the condition is checked at the bottom if the loop should be executed at least once.

2. Either precede the loop with the statement LET *continue$* = "Yes" or change the first line to DO and replace the LOOP statement with LOOP UNTIL *continue$* <> "Yes".

6.2 PROCESSING LISTS OF DATA WITH DO LOOPS

One of the main applications of programming is the processing of lists of data. DO loops are used to display all or selected items from lists, search lists for specific items, and perform calculations on the numerical entries of a list. This section introduces several devices that facilitate working with lists. **Counters** calculate the number of elements in lists, **accumulators** sum numerical values in lists, **flags** record whether certain events have occurred, and **trailer values** indicate the ends of lists. **Nested loops** add yet another dimension to repetition.

Trailer Values

The data to be processed are retrieved by a DO loop either from DATA statements or from the user with INPUT statements. In order for the loop to know when all the data have been read, special data called **trailer values** or **sentinels** are added to the end of the list. Commonly used trailer values are –1 and EOD, which stands for "End of Data." Trailer values should not be possible responses for processing. For instance, if a loop calculates a bowling score, 0 is not a good trailer value since the user might enter 0 to represent a gutter ball.

One of the first programs I wrote when I got my computer stored a list of names and phone numbers and printed a phone directory. I first had the program display the directory on the screen and later changed the PRINT statements to LPRINT statements to produce a printed copy. I stored the names in DATA statements so I could easily add, change, or delete entries.

EXAMPLE 1 The following program displays the contents of a telephone directory. The names and phone numbers are contained in DATA statements. The first trailer value is EOD. The loop will repeat until EOD is read. The second trailer value, *, provides something to assign to *phoneNum$* on the last execution of READ.

```
REM Telephone directory
CLS
READ name$, phoneNum$
DO WHILE name$ <> "EOD"
  PRINT name$, phoneNum$
  READ name$, phoneNum$
LOOP
REM --- Data: name, phone number
DATA Bert, 123-4567
DATA Ernie, 987-6543
DATA Grover, 246-8321
```

```
DATA Oscar, 135-7900
DATA EOD, *
END

[run]
Bert          123-4567
Ernie         987-6543
Grover        246-8321
Oscar         135-7900
```

The program in Example 1 illustrates the proper way to process a list of data having a trailer value. The DO loop should be tested at the top. The first item of data should be obtained before the DO statement and used to determine whether the loop should be entered. The loop begins by processing the data and then requests the next piece of data just before the LOOP statement. This method of processing a list guarantees that the trailer value will not be processed. Figure 6.5 contains the pseudocode and flowchart for this technique.

```
Get first item
DO WHILE item is not the trailer value
    Process the item
    Get the next item
LOOP
```

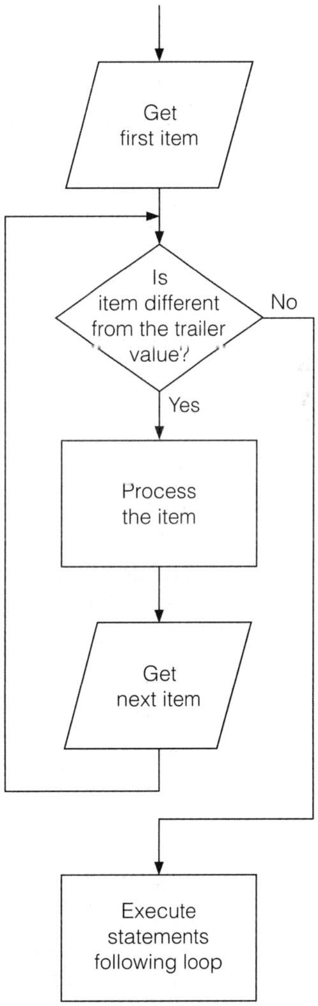

Figure 6.5 Pseudocode and Flowchart for Processing a List with Trailer Value

EXAMPLE 2 Modify the program in Example 1 to search the telephone directory for a name specified by the user. If the name does not appear in the directory, so notify the user.

SOLUTION For starters, we should begin with an INPUT statement to request the sought name. We want to keep searching as long as there is no match *and* we have not reached the end of the list. Therefore, the condition for the DO WHILE statement is a compound logical expression with the operator AND. After the last pass through the loop, we will know whether the name was found and be able to display the requested information.

```
REM Look for a specific telephone number
CLS
INPUT "Name"; searchName$                'Name to search for in list
READ name$, phoneNum$                    'Name, phone number
DO WHILE (name$ <> searchName$) AND (name$ <> "EOD")
  READ name$, phoneNum$
LOOP
IF name$ = "EOD" THEN
    PRINT "Name not found."
  ELSE
    PRINT name$, phoneNum$
END IF
REM --- Data: names, phone numbers
DATA Bert, 123-4567, Ernie, 987-6543
DATA Grover, 246-8321, Oscar, 135-7900, EOD, *
END

[run]
Name? Ernie
Ernie          987-6543

[run]
Name? Kermit
Name not found.
```

EXAMPLE 3 Consider the list of three names Al, Carl, and Fred. Write a program that asks the user for an additional name and then displays the four names in alphabetical order.

SOLUTION

```
REM Merge a new name into an ordered list of names
CLS
INPUT "Enter a name: ", searchName$
READ name$
DO WHILE (name$ <= searchName$) AND (name$ <> "EOD")
  PRINT name$,
  READ name$
LOOP
PRINT searchName$,
DO WHILE name$ <> "EOD"
  PRINT name$,
  READ name$
LOOP
```

```
REM --- Data: names
DATA Al, Carl, Fred, EOD
END

[run]  Enter a name: Bob
Al            Bob           Carl          Fred

[run]
Enter a name: Ken
Al            Carl          Fred          Ken
```

Nested Loops

The statements inside of a DO loop can consist of another DO loop. Such a configuration is referred to as a **nested loop** and is useful in repeating a single data processing routine several times.

EXAMPLE 4 Modify the program in Example 2 to allow the user to look up as many names as desired.

SOLUTION The statements inside the DO WHILE loop will be used to look up names as before. At least one pass through the outer DO loop is guaranteed, and passes will continue as long as the user responds "Y".

```
REM Look up a specific telephone number
CLS
DO
  RESTORE
  INPUT "Name"; searchName$          'Name to search for in list
  READ name$, phoneNum$              'Name, phone number
  DO WHILE (name$ <> searchName$) AND (name$ <> "EOD")
    READ name$, phoneNum$
  LOOP
  IF name$ = "EOD" THEN
      PRINT "Name not found."
    ELSE
      PRINT name$, phoneNum$
  END IF
  INPUT "Do you want to look up another number (Y/N)"; response$
LOOP UNTIL response$ <> "Y"
REM --- Data: name, phone number
DATA Bert, 123-4567, Ernie, 987-6543
DATA Grover, 246-8321, Oscar, 135-7900, EOD, *
END

[run]
Name? Oscar
Oscar         135-7900
Do you want to look up another number (Y or N)? Y
Name? Bert
Bert          123-4567
Do you want to look up another number (Y or N)? N
```

Counters and Accumulators

A **counter** is a numeric variable that keeps track of the number of items processed. An **accumulator** is a numeric variable that totals numbers.

EXAMPLE 5 Write a program to count and find the value of coins listed in a DATA statement.

SOLUTION

```
REM How much change do you have?
CLS
LET numCoins = 0
LET sum = 0
READ num
DO WHILE num <> -1
  LET numCoins = numCoins + 1
  LET sum = sum + num
  READ num
LOOP
PRINT "The value of the"; numCoins; "coins is"; sum; "cents."
REM --- Data: coin
DATA 1, 1, 5, 10, 10, 25, -1
END

[run]
The value of the 6 coins is 52 cents.
```

The value of the counter, *numCoins*, was initially 0 and changed on each execution of the loop to 1, 2, 3, 4, 5, and finally 6. The accumulator, *sum*, initially had the value 0 and increased with each execution of the loop to 1, 2, 7, 17, 27, and finally 52.

Flags

A **flag** is a variable that keeps track of whether a certain event has occurred. Typically, it is initialized with the value 0 and then assigned a nonzero value when the event occurs. It is used within a loop to provide information that will be taken into consideration after the loop has terminated. The flag also provides an alternate method of terminating a loop.

EXAMPLE 6 The following program counts the number of words in the DATA statements and then reports whether the words are in alphabetical order. In each execution of the loop, a word is compared to the next word in the list. The flag variable, called *orderFlag*, is initially assigned the value 0 and is set to 1 if a pair of adjacent words is out of order. The technique used in this program will be used in Chapter 7 when we study sorting. ***Note:*** The statement in line 5 is a device to get things started. Each word must first be read into the variable *word2$*. In fact, *wordCounter* is incremented only when *word2$* gets a nonsentinel value.

```
REM Count words.  Are they in alphabetical order?
CLS
LET orderFlag = 0
LET wordCounter = 0
LET word1$ = ""
READ word2$
```

```
DO WHILE word2$ <> "EOD"
  LET wordCounter = wordCounter + 1
  IF word1$ > word2$ THEN
      LET orderFlag = 1
  END IF
  LET word1$ = word2$
  READ word2$
LOOP
PRINT "The number of words is"; wordCounter
IF orderFlag = 0 THEN
    PRINT "The words are in alphabetical order."
  ELSE
    PRINT "The words are not in alphabetical order."
END IF
REM --- Data: winning words in U.S. National Spelling Bee
DATA cambist, croissant, deification, hydrophyte, incisor
DATA maculature, macerate, narcolepsy, shalloon, EOD
END

[run]
The number of words is 9
The words are not in alphabetical order.
```

EXAMPLE 7 Write a program to calculate the average of exam grades input by the user and report if any student received a perfect score.

SOLUTION The following program uses the variable *numScores* as a counter, the variable *sum* as an accumulator, *perfectFlag* as a flag, and the trailer value –1.

```
REM Calculate average score
CLS
CALL ShowInstructions
CALL InputScores(numScores, sum, perfectFlag)
CALL DisplayResults(numScores, sum, perfectFlag)
END

SUB DisplayResults (numScores, sum, perfectFlag)
  REM Compute and display average
  REM Announce if there are any perfect scores
  IF numScores >= 1 THEN
      LET average = sum / numScores
      PRINT "The average score is"; average
      IF perfectFlag = 0 THEN
          PRINT "No perfect score."
        ELSE
          PRINT "At least one perfect score."
      END IF
  END IF
END SUB
```

```
SUB InputScores (numScores, sum, perfectFlag)
  REM Input scores from the user
  LET numScores = 0
  LET sum = 0
  LET perfectFlag = 0
  INPUT "Enter a score: ", score
  DO WHILE score <> -1
    LET numScores = numScores + 1
    LET sum = sum + score
    IF score = 100 THEN
        LET perfectFlag = 1
    END IF
    INPUT "Enter a score: ", score
  LOOP
END SUB

SUB ShowInstructions
  REM Display instructions
  PRINT "Enter the scores one at a time. After all of the"
  PRINT "scores have been reported, enter the number -1."
END SUB

[run]
Enter the scores one at a time. After all of the
scores have been reported, enter the number -1.
Enter a score: 80
Enter a score: 90
Enter a score: 82
Enter a score: 88
Enter a score: -1
The average score is 85
No perfect score.
```

The arguments *numScores*, *sum*, and *perfectFlag* were first used to retrieve values from a subprogram and then used to transmit these values to another subprogram. The final values of the counter and accumulator were 4 and 340. After the loop terminated, the average was calculated by dividing 340 by 4.

Comments:

1. In Appendix D, the section "Stepping Through a Program Containing a DO Loop: Chapter 6" uses the QBasic debugging tools to trace the flow through a DO loop.

PRACTICE PROBLEMS 6.2

1. Determine the output of the following program.

```
REM Find the sum of a collection of bowling scores
LET sum = 0
DO WHILE score <> -1
  READ score
  LET sum = sum + score
LOOP
```

```
PRINT sum
REM --- Data: bowling scores
DATA 150, 200, 300, -1
END
```

2. Why didn't the program above produce the intended output?

3. Correct the program above so it has the intended output.

EXERCISES 6.2

In Exercises 1 through 10, determine the output of the program.

1.
```
LET total = 0
READ n
DO WHILE n > 0
  LET total = total + n
  READ n
LOOP
PRINT total
DATA 5, 2, 6, -1
END
```

2.
```
READ name$
DO WHILE name$ <> "EOD"
  PRINT name$
  READ name$
LOOP
DATA Bo, Liz, EOD
END
```

3.
```
REM Display list of desserts
DO
  READ dessert$
  PRINT dessert$
LOOP UNTIL dessert$ = "EOD"
DATA pie, cake, melon, EOD
END
```

4.
```
READ city$, pop
DO WHILE city$ <> "EOD"
  IF pop >= 7 THEN
      PRINT city$, pop
  END IF
  READ city$, pop
LOOP
REM --- Data: city, population (in millions)
DATA San Francisco, 5.6
DATA Boston, 4
DATA Chicago, 8
DATA New York, 17.7
DATA EOD, 0
END
```

5.
```
READ fruit$
DO WHILE fruit$ <> "EOD"
  LET firstLetter$ = LEFT$(fruit$, 1)
  PRINT TAB(3); firstLetter$
  DO WHILE LEFT$(fruit$, 1) = firstLetter$
    PRINT fruit$
    READ fruit$
  LOOP
  PRINT
LOOP
```

```
REM --- Data: fruits
DATA Apple, Apricot, Avocado, Banana
DATA Blueberry, Grape, Lemon, Lime, EOD
END
```

6.
```
REM Display list of numbers
READ num
DO WHILE num <> -1
  READ num
  PRINT num;
LOOP
DATA 2, 3, 8, 5, -1
END
```

7.
```
CALL InputAnimal(animal$)
CALL SearchList(animal$, groupName$)
CALL DisplayResult(animal$, groupName$)
REM --- Data: animal, name of group
DATA lion, pride, duck, brace, bee, swarm, EOD, *
END

SUB DisplayResult (animal$, groupName$)
  IF groupName$ = "*" THEN
      PRINT "Animal not found."
    ELSE
      PRINT "A group of "; animal$; "s is called a "; groupName$
  END IF
END SUB

SUB InputAnimal (animal$)
  REM Request the name of an animal as input
  INPUT "Animal"; animal$
END SUB

SUB SearchList (animal$, groupName$)
  READ creature$, groupName$
  DO WHILE (creature$ <> animal$) AND (creature$ <> "EOD")
    READ creature$, groupName$
  LOOP
END SUB
```

(Assume the response is *duck*.)

8.
```
READ sentence$
CALL Duplicate30(sentence$)
READ sentence$
CALL Duplicate30(sentence$)
REM --- Data: sentence
DATA "I think I can. "
DATA "We're off to see the wizard, the wonderful wizard of OZ."
END

SUB Duplicate30 (sentence$)
  LET flag = 0     'flag tells whether loop has been executed
  DO WHILE LEN(sentence$) < 30
    LET flag = 1
    LET sentence$ = sentence$ + sentence$
  LOOP
```

```
  IF flag = 1 THEN
      PRINT sentence$
    ELSE
      PRINT "Loop not executed."
  END IF
END SUB
```

9.
```
READ word$
DO WHILE word$ <> "EOD"
  IF LEFT$(word$, 1) = "c" THEN
      LET cWord$ = word$
  END IF
  READ word$
LOOP
PRINT cWord$
REM --- Data: saying
DATA time, is, a, child, idly, moving, counters, in, a, game
DATA Heraclitus, EOD
END
```

10.
```
LET max = 0
READ value
DO WHILE value <> -1
   LET rowMax = 0
   DO WHILE value <> -2
     IF value > rowMax THEN
         LET rowMax = value
     END IF
     READ value
   LOOP
   PRINT rowMax
   IF rowMax > max THEN
       LET max = rowMax
   END IF
   READ value
LOOP
PRINT max
REM --- Data: numbers
DATA 5, 7, 3, -2, 10, 12, 6, 4, -2, 1, 9, -2, -1
END
```

In Exercises 11 through 14, identify the errors.

11.
```
READ num
DO WHILE num <> -1
  PRINT num
  READ num
REM --- Data: numbers
DATA 7, 6, 0, -1, 2
END
```

12.
```
LET flag = 0
DO WHILE flag <> 1
  INPUT num
  IF num * num < 0 THEN LET flag = 1
LOOP
END
```

13.
```
REM Display names of some U.S. Presidents
DO
  READ name$
  PRINT name$
LOOP UNTIL name$ = "EOD"
REM --- Data: presidents
DATA Lincoln, Washington, Kennedy, Reagan, EOD
END
```

14.
```
READ num
DO WHILE 1 < num < 5
  PRINT num
  READ num
LOOP
REM --- Data: numbers
DATA 3, 2, 4, 7, 2
END
```

15. Write an interactive program to find the largest of a collection of positive numbers. The user should be prompted to provide numbers until the response –1 is given, at which time, the largest number should be displayed. (Test the program with the collection of numbers 89, 77, 95, and 86.)

16. Write an interactive program that asks the user to INPUT a distance in miles and converts it to kilometers. The process should be repeated until the user signs off by entering –1. **Note:** 1 mile is approximately 1.6 kilometers. Test the program with the values 3 and .625.

17. Table 6.1 shows the different grades of eggs and the minimum weight required for each classification. Write an interactive program in which the user repeatedly inputs the weight of an egg and obtains the appropriate grade. The user should enter a negative number to terminate the process. (**Note:** Eggs weighing less than 1.5 ounces cannot be sold in supermarkets.) Figure 6.6 shows a sample output of the program.

Grade	**Weight (in ounces)**
Jumbo	2.5
Extra Large	2.25
Large	2
Medium	1.75
Small	1.5

Table 6.1 Grades of Eggs

```
Weight of egg in ounces? 2.3
The grade is Extra Large.

Weight of egg in ounces? 1.4
Send it to the bakery.

Weight of egg in ounces? -1
```

Figure 6.6 Output for Exercise 17

18. Table 6.2 contains the meanings of some abbreviations doctors often use for prescriptions. Write a program that requests an abbreviation and gives its meaning. The user should be informed if the meaning is not in the table.

Abbreviation	Meaning
ac	before meals
ad lib	freely as needed
bid	twice daily
gtt	a drop
hs	at bedtime
qid	four times a day

Table 6.2 Physicians' Abbreviations

19. Write a program to request a positive integer as input and carry out the following algorithm. If the number is even, divide it by 2. Otherwise, multiply the number by 3 and add 1. Repeat this process with the resulting number and continue repeating the process until the number 1 is reached. After the number 1 is reached, the program should display how many iterations were required. **Note:** A number is even if INT(*num* / 2) = *num* / 2. (Test the program with the numbers 9, 21, and 27.)

20. Write a program that allows the user 10 tries to answer the question "Which U.S. President was born on July 4?" After three incorrect guesses the program should give the hint: "He once said, 'If you don't say anything, you won't be called upon to repeat it.'" After seven incorrect guesses, the program should give the hint "His nickname was 'Silent Cal.'" **Note:** Calvin Coolidge was born on July 4, 1872.

21. Table 6.3 gives the U.S. Census Bureau projections for the populations (in millions) of the states predicted to be the most populous in the year 2010. Write a program that requests the current population of each of these states as input (one at a time) and then computes the percentage population growth for each state and the average percentage population growth for the five states. The percentage growth is calculated as

100 * (projected pop. – current pop.) / current pop.

(Test the program with the 1996 populations: CA, 31.9; TX, 19.1; NY, 18.2; IL, 11.8; FL, 14.4.)

State	Population in 2010
California	37.6
Texas	22.9
New York	18.5
Illinois	12.5
Florida	17.4

Table 6.3 State Populations in the Year 2010

```
Light bulbs    2.65
Soda           3.45
Soap           1.15
-------------------
Sum            7.25
Tax            0.36
Total          7.61
```

Figure 6.7 Output for Exercise 22

22. Write a program to produce a sales receipt. The items and their prices should be entered one at a time and displayed. After all the entries have been made, the program should display the sum of the prices, the sales tax (5% of total), and the total amount to be paid. Figure 6.7 shows a sample output of the program.

23. Write a program that requests a list of scores and then displays the two highest scores.

24. Extend Example 3 to handle the case in which the name input is already in the list. If so, the program should display the name only once.

25. Write a program to compute a student's grade-point average. A subprogram should request the grade and semester hours credit for each course, and then a function should compute the grade-point average. Another subprogram should display the GPA and then display one of two messages. A student with a GPA of 3 or more should be informed that he has made the honor roll. Otherwise, he should be congratulated on having completed the semester. In either case, he should be wished a merry vacation.

26. Write a program to do the following. (The program should use a flag.)

    (a) Ask the user to input a sentence containing no commas, but possibly one pair of parentheses.

    (b) Display the sentence with the parentheses and their contents removed.

    Test the program with the following sentence as input: BASIC (Beginners All-purpose Symbolic Instruction Code) is the world's most widely known computer language.

27. The salespeople at a health club keep track of the members who have joined in the last month. Their names and types of membership, Bronze, Silver, or Gold, are stored in DATA statements, with the last statement DATA EOD, "". Write a program that displays all the Bronze members, then the Silver members, and finally the Gold members.

28. Table 6.4 gives the prices of various liquids. Write a program that requests an amount of money as input and displays the names of all liquids for which a gallon could be purchased with that amount of money. The information from the table should be contained in DATA statements. A sample output is as follows:

```
[run]
Enter an amount of money: 2.35
You can purchase one gallon of any of the following liquids.
Bleach
Gasoline
Milk
```

Liquid	Price	Liquid	Price
Apple Cider	2.60	Milk	2.30
Beer	6.00	Gatorade	4.20
Bleach	1.40	Perrier	6.85
Coca-Cola	2.55	Pancake Syrup	15.50
Gasoline	1.30	Spring Water	4.10

Table 6.4 Some Comparative Prices per Gallon of Various Liquids

SOLUTIONS TO PRACTICE PROBLEMS 6.2

1. 649.

2. The trailer value was inadvertently added to the scores.

3.
```
REM Find the sum of a collection of bowling scores
LET sum = 0
READ score
DO WHILE score <> -1
  LET sum = sum + score
  READ score
LOOP
PRINT sum
REM --- Data: bowling scores
DATA 150, 200, 300, -1
END
```

6.3 FOR...NEXT LOOPS

When we know exactly how many times a loop should be executed, we can use a special type of loop, called a FOR...NEXT loop. FOR...NEXT loops are easy to read and write, and have features that make them ideal for certain common tasks. The following program uses a FOR...NEXT loop to display a table.

```
REM Display a table of the first 5 numbers and their squares
FOR i = 1 TO 5
  PRINT i; i ^ 2
NEXT i
END

[run]
 1  1
 2  4
 3  9
 4  16
 5  25
```

The equivalent program written with a DO loop is as follows.

```
REM Display a table of the first 5 numbers and their squares
LET i = 1
DO WHILE i <= 5
  PRINT i; i ^ 2
  LET i = i + 1
LOOP
END
```

In general, a portion of a program of the form

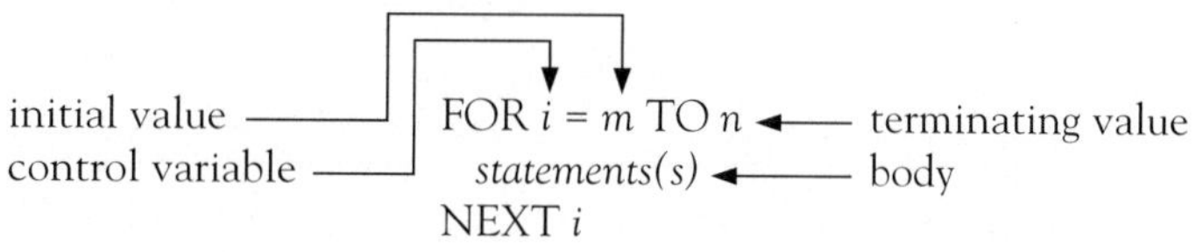

constitutes a FOR...NEXT loop. The pair of statements FOR and NEXT cause the statements between them to be repeated a specified number of times. The FOR statement designates a numeric variable, called the **control variable**, that is initialized and then automatically changes after each execution of the loop. Also, the FOR statement gives the range of values this variable will assume. The NEXT statement increments the control variable. If $m \leq n$, then i is assigned the values m, $m + 1$, . . ., n in order, and the body is executed once for each of these values. If $m > n$, then execution continues with the statement after the FOR loop.

When program execution reaches a FOR...NEXT loop such as the one shown above, the FOR statement assigns to the control variable i the initial value m and checks to see whether i is greater than the terminating value n. If so, then execution jumps to the line following the NEXT statement. If $i \leq n$, the statements inside the loop are executed. Then, the NEXT statement increases the value of i by 1 and checks this new value to see if it exceeds n. If not, the entire process is repeated until the value of i exceeds n. When this happens, the program moves on to the line following the loop. Figure 6.8 contains the pseudocode and flowchart of a FOR...NEXT loop.

```
FOR i = m to n
   Processing step(s)
NEXT i
```

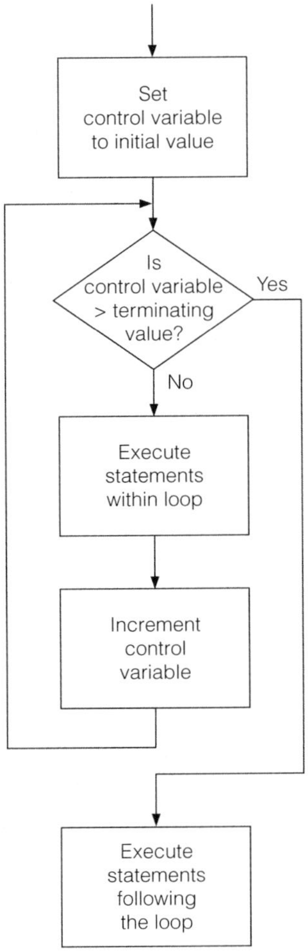

Figure 6.8 Pseudocode and Flowchart of a FOR...NEXT Loop

The control variable can be any numeric variable. The most common single-letter names are *i*, *j*, and *k*; however, if appropriate, the name should suggest the purpose of the control variable.

EXAMPLE 1 Suppose the population of a city is 300,000 in the year 1998 and is growing at the rate of 3% per year. Write a program to display the projected population each year until 2002.

SOLUTION

```
REM Display population from 1998 to 2002
CLS
PRINT "Year", "Population"
LET pop = 300000
FOR year = 1998 TO 2002
  PRINT year,
  PRINT USING "###,###"; pop
  LET pop = pop + .03 * pop
NEXT year
END

[run]
Year          Population
 1998         300,000
 1999         309,000
 2000         318,270
 2001         327,818
 2002         337,653
```

The initial and terminating values can be constants, variables, or expressions. For instance, the FOR statement in the program above can be replaced by

```
LET firstYr = 1998
LET lastYr = 2002
FOR year = firstYr TO lastYr
   .
   .
   .
```

In Example 1, the control variable was increased by 1 after each pass through the loop. A variation of the FOR statement allows any number to be used as the increment. The statement

```
FOR i = m TO n STEP s
```

instructs the NEXT statement to add *s* to the control variable instead of 1. The numbers *m*, *n*, and *s* do not have to be whole numbers. The number *s* is called the **step value** of the loop.

EXAMPLE 2 Write a program to display the multiples of .5 from 0 to a number input by the user.

SOLUTION

```
REM Display multiples of .5
CLS
INPUT "Enter a positive number: ", n
FOR i = 0 TO n STEP .5
  PRINT i;
NEXT i
END

[run]
Enter a positive number: 3.2
 0  .5  1  1.5  2  2.5  3
```

In the examples considered so far, the control variable was successively increased until it reached the terminating value. However, if a negative step value is used and the initial value is greater than the terminating value, then the control value is decreased until reaching the terminating value. In other words, the loop counts backward or downward.

EXAMPLE 3 The following program accepts a word as input and displays it backward.

```
REM Reverse the letters in a word
CLS
INPUT "Enter a word: ", word$
LET n = LEN(word$)
FOR k = n TO 1 STEP -1
  PRINT MID$(word$, k, 1);
NEXT k
END

[run]
Enter a word: SUEZ
ZEUS
```

Note: The initial and terminating values of a FOR...NEXT loop can be expressions. For instance, the third and fourth lines of Example 3 can be consolidated to

```
FOR k = LEN(word$) TO 1 STEP -1
```

The body of a FOR...NEXT loop can contain *any* sequence of QBasic statements. In particular, it can contain another FOR...NEXT loop. However, the second loop must be completely contained inside the first loop and must have a different control variable. Such a configuration is called **nested loops.** Figure 6.9 shows several examples of valid nested loops.

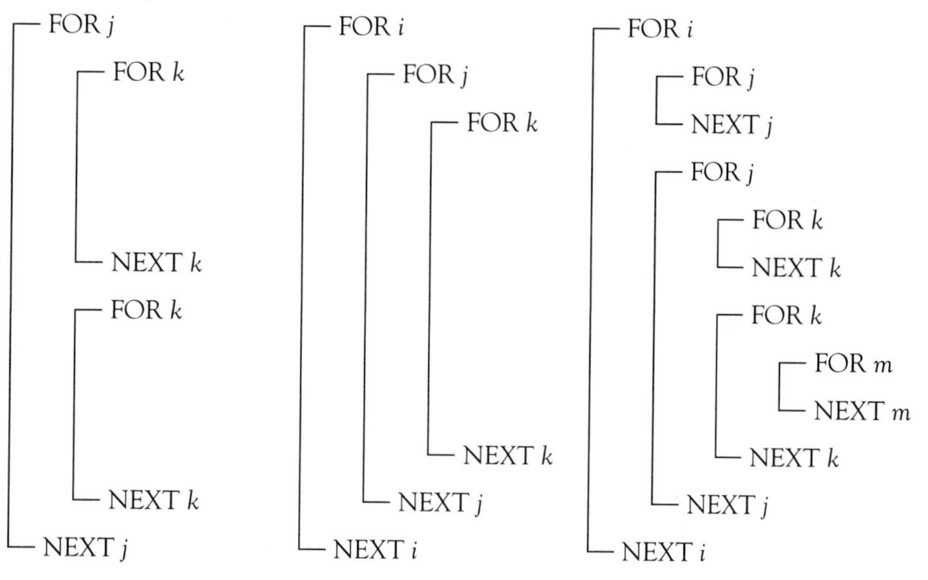

Figure 6.9 Nested Loops

EXAMPLE 4 Write a program to display the products of the integers from 1 to 4.

SOLUTION In the following program, *i* denotes the left factors of the products and *j* denotes the right factors. Each factor takes on values from 1 to 4. The values are assigned to *i* in the outer loop and to *j* in the inner loop. Initially, *i* is assigned the value 1 and then the inner loop is traversed 4 times to produce the first row of products. At the end of these 4 passes, the value of *i* will still be 1 and the value of *j* will have been incremented to 5. The PRINT statement just before NEXT *i* guarantees that no more products will be displayed in that row. The first execution of the outer loop is then complete. Following this, the statement NEXT *i* increments the value of *i* to 2. The statement beginning FOR *j* is then executed. It resets the value of *j* to 1. The second row of products is displayed during the next 4 executions of the inner loop, and so on.

```
REM Display the products of the numbers from 1 through 4
CLS
FOR i = 1 TO 4
  FOR j = 1 TO 4
    PRINT i; "x"; j; "="; i * j,
    NEXT j
  PRINT
NEXT i
END
```

outer loop (FOR i … NEXT i); inner loop (FOR j … NEXT j)

left factor — right factor

```
[run]
 1 x 1 = 1     1 x 2 = 2     1 x 3 = 3     1 x 4 = 4
 2 x 1 = 2     2 x 2 = 4     2 x 3 = 6     2 x 4 = 8
 3 x 1 = 3     3 x 2 = 6     3 x 3 = 9     3 x 4 = 12
 4 x 1 = 4     4 x 2 = 8     4 x 3 = 12    4 x 4 = 16
```

Comments:

1. The body of a FOR...NEXT loop need not be indented. However, since indenting improves the readability of the program, it is good programming style. As soon as you see the word FOR, your eyes can easily scan down the program to find the matching NEXT statement. You then know two facts immediately: the number of statements in the body of the loop and the number of passes that will be made through the loop.
2. FOR and NEXT statements must be paired. If one is missing, the program will generate the error message "FOR without NEXT" or "NEXT without FOR."
3. Consider a loop beginning with FOR $i = m$ TO n STEP s. The loop will be executed once if m equals n. The loop will not be executed at all if m is greater than n and s is positive, or if m is less than n and s is negative.
4. The value of the control variable should not be altered within the body of the loop; doing so might cause the loop to repeat indefinitely or have an unpredictable number of repetitions.
5. Noninteger step values can lead to roundoff errors with the result that the loop is not executed the intended number of times. For instance, a loop beginning with FOR $i = 0$ TO 1 STEP .1 will be executed only 10 times instead of the intended 11 times.

PRACTICE PROBLEMS 6.3

1. Why won't the following program work as intended?

```
FOR i = 15 TO 1
  PRINT i
NEXT i
END
```

2. When is a FOR..NEXT loop more appropriate than a DO loop?

EXERCISES 6.3

In Exercises 1 through 12, determine the output of the program.

1.
```
FOR i = 1 TO 4
  PRINT "Pass #"; i
NEXT i
END
```

2.
```
FOR i = 3 TO 6
  PRINT 2 * i;
NEXT i
END
```

3.
```
FOR j = 2 TO 8 STEP 2
  PRINT j;
NEXT j
PRINT "Who do we appreciate?"
END
```

4.
```
FOR countdown = 10 TO 1 STEP -1
  PRINT countdown;
NEXT countdown
PRINT "blastoff"
END
```

5.
```
LET num = 5
FOR i = num TO 2 * num + 3
  PRINT i;
NEXT i
END
```

6.
```
FOR i = 3 TO 5 STEP .25
  PRINT i;
NEXT i
PRINT i
END
```

7.
```
FOR miler = 1 TO 3
  READ name$, tim$
  PRINT name$, tim$
NEXT miler
REM --- Data: name, time
DATA Steve Cram, "3:46.31"
DATA Steve Scott, "3:51.6"
DATA Mary Slaney, "4:20.5"
END
```

8.
```
LET total = 0
FOR i = 1 TO 4
  READ score
  LET total = total + score
NEXT i
PRINT "Average ="; total / 4
REM --- Data: exam scores
DATA 89, 85, 88, 98
END
```

9.
```
LET a$ = "######"
FOR i = 0 TO 2
  FOR j = 0 TO 3
    PRINT USING a$; i+3*j+1;
  NEXT j
  PRINT
NEXT i
END
```

10.
```
FOR i = 1 TO 5
  FOR j = 1 TO i
    PRINT "*";
  NEXT j
  PRINT
NEXT i
END
```

11.
```
INPUT "Type a word: ", word$
LET num = INT((80 - LEN(word$)) / 2)
CALL Asterisks(num)
PRINT word$;
CALL Asterisks(num)
END

SUB Asterisks (num)
  REM Display num asterisks
  FOR i = 1 TO num
    PRINT "*";
  NEXT i
END SUB
```

(Assume the response is *Hooray*.)

12.
```
REM Display an array of letters
FOR i = 1 TO 4
  READ letter$
  CALL DisplayFive(letter$)
  PRINT        'Move to next line
NEXT i
REM --- Data: letters
DATA D, A, T, A
END

SUB DisplayFive (letter$)
  REM Display letter five times
  FOR i = 1 TO 5
    PRINT letter$;
  NEXT i
END SUB
```

In Exercises 13 through 16, identify the errors.

13.
```
FOR j = 1 TO 25.5 STEP -1
  PRINT j
NEXT j
END
```

14.
```
FOR i = 1 TO 3
READ num
PRINT num
REM --- Data: numbers
DATA 9, 7, 5
END
```

15.
```
FOR i = 1 TO 3
  READ num
NEXT i
REM --- Data: numbers
DATA 9, 7
END
```

16.
```
FOR i = 1 TO 6
  FOR j = 1 TO 3
    PRINT i / j;
  NEXT i
NEXT j
END
```

In Exercises 17 and 18, rewrite the program using a FOR...NEXT loop.

17.
```
LET num = 1
DO WHILE num <= 10
  PRINT num
  LET num = num + 2
LOOP
END
```

18.
```
PRINT "hello"
PRINT "hello"
PRINT "hello"
PRINT "hello"
END
```

In Exercises 19 through 37, write a program to complete the stated task.

19. Display a row of 10 stars (asterisks).

20. Request a number from 1 to 80 with an INPUT statement and display a row of that many stars (asterisks).

21. Display a 10-by-10 square of stars.

22. Request a number with an INPUT statement and call a subprogram to display a square having that number of stars on each side.

23. Find the sum $1 + \frac{1}{2} + \frac{1}{3} + \frac{1}{4} + \ldots + \frac{1}{100}$.

24. Find the sum of the odd numbers from 1 through 99.

25. Suppose you are offered two salary options for ten days of work. Option 1: \$100 per day. Option 2: \$1 the first day, \$2 the second day, \$4 the third day, and so on, with the amount doubling each day. Write a program to determine which option pays better.

26. When \$1000 is deposited at 5% simple interest, the amount grows by \$50 each year. When money is invested at 5% compound interest, the amount at the end of each year is 1.05 times the amount at the beginning of that year. Write a program to display the amounts for ten years for a \$1000 deposit at 5% simple and compound interest. The first few lines of the output should appear as in Figure 6.10.

Year	Amount Simple Interest	Amount Compound Interest
1	1,050.00	1,050.00
2	1,100.00	1,102.50
3	1,150.00	1,157.63

Figure 6.10 Growth of $1000 at Simple and Compound Interest

27. According to researchers at Stanford Medical School (as cited in *Medical Self Care*), the ideal weight for a woman is found by multiplying her height in inches by 3.5 and subtracting 108. The ideal weight for a man is found by multiplying his height in inches by 4 and subtracting 128. Request a lower and upper bound for heights and then produce a table giving the ideal weights for women and men in that height range. One possible outcome of the program is shown in Figure 6.11.

```
Enter lower bound: 62
Enter upper bound: 65

Height        Wt - Women    Wt - Men

 62            109           120
 63            112.5         124
 64            116           128
 65            119.5         132
```

Figure 6.11 Output for Exercise 27

28. Table 6.5 contains statistics on professional quarterbacks. Read this information from DATA statements and generate an extended table with two additional columns, Pct Comp (Percent Completions) and Avg Gain (Average Gain per Completed Pass).

Name	Att	Comp	Yards
Elway	466	287	3328
Favre	543	325	3899
Johnson	311	195	2258
Young	316	214	2410

Table 6.5 1996 Passing Statistics (Attempts, Completions, Yards Gained)

29. Request a sentence and display the number of sibilants (that is, letters S or Z) in the sentence. The counting should be carried out in a FUNCTION, and the total number should be displayed by the main body of the program.

30. Request a number, n, from 1 to 30 and one of the letters *S* or *P*. Then calculate the sum or product of the numbers from 1 to *n* depending upon whether *S* or *P* was selected. The calculations should be carried out with functions.

31. Suppose $800 is deposited into a savings account earning 4% interest compounded annually, and $100 is added to the account at the end of each year. Calculate the amount of money in the account at the end of 10 years. (Determine a formula for computing the balance at the end of one year based on the balance at the beginning of the year. Then write a program that starts with a balance of $800 and makes 10 passes through a loop containing the formula to produce the final answer.)

32. A TV set is purchased with a loan of $563 to be paid off with 5 monthly payments of $116. The interest rate is 1% per month. Display a table giving the balance on the loan at the end of each month.

33. *Radioactive Decay.* Cobalt 60, a radioactive form of cobalt used in cancer therapy, decays or dissipates over a period of time. Each year, 12% of the amount present at the beginning of the year will have decayed. If a container of cobalt 60 initially contains 10 grams, determine the amount remaining after 5 years.

34. *Supply and Demand.* This year's level of production and price for most agricultural products greatly affects the level of production and price next year. Suppose the current crop of soybeans in a certain country is 80 million bushels and experience has shown that for each year,

[price this year] = 20 – .1 * [quantity this year]
[quantity next year] = 5 * [price this year] –10

where quantity is measured in units of millions of bushels. Generate a table to show the quantity and price for each of the next 12 years.

35. Request a number greater than 3 with an INPUT statement and display a hollow rectangle of stars (asterisks) with each outer row and column having that many stars. Do not use the LOCATE statement. (See Figure 6.12(a).)

```
******                  ***********
*    *                  *********
*    *                  *******
*    *                  *****
*    *                  ***
******                  *
  (a)                      (b)
```

Figure 6.12 Outputs for Exercises 35 and 36.

36. Request an odd number with an INPUT statement and display a triangle similar to the one in Figure 6.12(b) with the input number of stars in the top row.

37. Allow any two integers, *m* and *n*, between 2 and 12 to be specified by an INPUT statement and then generate an *m*-by-*n* multiplication table. Figure 6.13 shows the output when *m* is 5 and *n* is 7.

```
1   2   3   4   5   6   7
2   4   6   8  10  12  14
3   6   9  12  15  18  21
4   8  12  16  20  24  28
5  10  15  20  25  30  35
```

Figure 6.13 Output for Exercise 37

38. Write a program to create the histogram in Figure 6.14. A DATA statement should hold the years and values.

```
1994 ******************** 20
1995 ************************* 25
1996 ******************* 19
1997 **************** 16
1998 *************** 15

Percentage Growth (by number of units) in Worldwide
Retail Sales of Personal Computers
```

Figure 6.14 Histogram for Exercise 38

39. A man pays $1 to get into a gambling casino. He loses half of his money there and then has to pay $1 to leave. He goes to a second casino, pays another $1 to get in, loses half of his money again and then pays another $1 to leave. Then he goes to a third casino, pays another $1 to get in, loses half of his money again, and pays another $1 to get out. After this, he's broke. Write a program to determine the amount of money he began with by testing $5, then $6, and so on.

40. In a certain city, police officers receive extra pay for weekend duties. Their hourly rate is increased by 50% for Saturday work and doubled for Sunday. Write a program that requests the name of an officer, the hourly wage, and the number of hours worked each day of the week as input from the keyboard, and returns the wages for the week and the number of hours worked as output. A FOR...NEXT loop should be used to request the hours worked each day. A sample run is as follows:

```
[run]
Enter the officer's name: Richard Tracy
Enter the hourly wage: 23.45
```

```
Enter the number of hours worked each day from Sunday to Saturday.
Sunday: 6
Monday: 5
Tuesday: 8
Wednesday: 0
Thursday: 0
Friday: 6
Saturday: 8
Wages for week: Richard Tracy    $1008.35
Number of Hours Worked: 33
```

41. Write a program to estimate how much a young worker will make before retiring at age 65. Request the worker's name, age, and starting salary as input. Assume the worker receives a 5% raise each year. A sample run is as follows.

```
[run]
Enter the person's name: Helen
Enter the person's age: 25
Enter the person's starting salary: 20000
Helen will earn about $2,415,995
```

SOLUTIONS TO PRACTICE PROBLEMS 6.3

1. The loop will never be entered, since 15 is greater than 1. The intended first line might have been

```
FOR i = 15 TO 1 STEP -1
```

or

```
FOR i = 1 TO 15
```

2. If the exact number of times the loop will be executed is known before entering the loop, then a FOR...NEXT loop should be used. Otherwise, a DO loop is more appropriate.

6.4 A CASE STUDY: ANALYZE A LOAN

This case study develops a menu-driven program to analyze a loan. Assume the loan is repaid in equal monthly payments and interest is compounded monthly. The program should request the amount (principal) of the loan, the annual rate of interest, and the number of years over which the loan is to be repaid. The four options in the menu are as follows.

1. Calculate the monthly payment. The formula for the monthly payment is

$$\text{payment} = p * r / (1 - (1 + r) \wedge (-n))$$

where p is the principal of the loan, r is the monthly interest rate (annual rate divided by 12) given as a number between 0 (for 0%) and 1 (for 100%), and n is the number of months over which the loan is to be repaid.

2. Display an amortization schedule—that is, a table showing the balance on the loan at the end of each month for the duration of the loan. Also show how much of each monthly payment goes toward interest and how much is used to repay the principal. Finally, display the total interest paid over the duration of the loan. The balances for successive months are calculated with the formula

$$\text{balance} = (1 + r) * b - m$$

where r is the monthly interest rate (annual rate / 12, a fraction between 0 and 1), b is the balance for the preceding month (amount of loan left to be paid), and m is the monthly payment.

3. Show the effect of changes in the interest rate. Display a table giving the monthly payment for each interest rate from 1% below to 1% above the specified annual rate in steps of one-eighth of a percent.

4. Quit.

Designing the Analyze-a-Loan Program

In addition to the tasks described in options 1 to 3 above, the basic tasks of this program include inputting the particulars of the loan to be analyzed and presenting a menu to the user. Thus, the first division of the problem is into the following tasks:

1. Input principal, interest, duration.
2. Present menu and get choice.
3. Calculate monthly payment.
4. Calculate amortization schedule.
5. Display the effects of interest rate changes.
6. Quit.

Tasks 1 and 2 are basic input operations and task 3 involves applying the formula given in step 1; therefore, these tasks need not be broken down any further. The demanding work of the program is done in tasks 4 and 5, which can be divided into smaller subtasks.

4. *Calculate amortization schedule*. This task involves simulating the loan month by month. First, the monthly payment must be computed. Then, for each month, the new balance must be computed together with a decomposition of the monthly payment into the amount paid for interest and the amount going toward repaying the principal. That is, task 4 is divided into the following subtasks:

   4.1 Calculate monthly payment.
   4.2 Calculate new balance.
   4.3 Calculate amount of monthly payment for interest.
   4.4 Calculate amount of monthly payment for principal.

5. *Display the effects of interest-rate changes.* A table is needed to show the effects of changes in the interest rate on the size of the monthly payment. First the interest rate is reduced by one percentage point and the new monthly payment is computed. Then the interest rate is increased by regular increments until it reaches one percentage point above the original rate, with new monthly payment amounts computed for each intermediate interest rate. The subtasks for this task are then:

   5.1 Reduce interest rate by 1%.
   5.2 Calculate monthly payment.
   5.3 Increase interest rate by 1/8%.

   The top-down chart in Figure 6.15 shows the stepwise refinement of the problem.

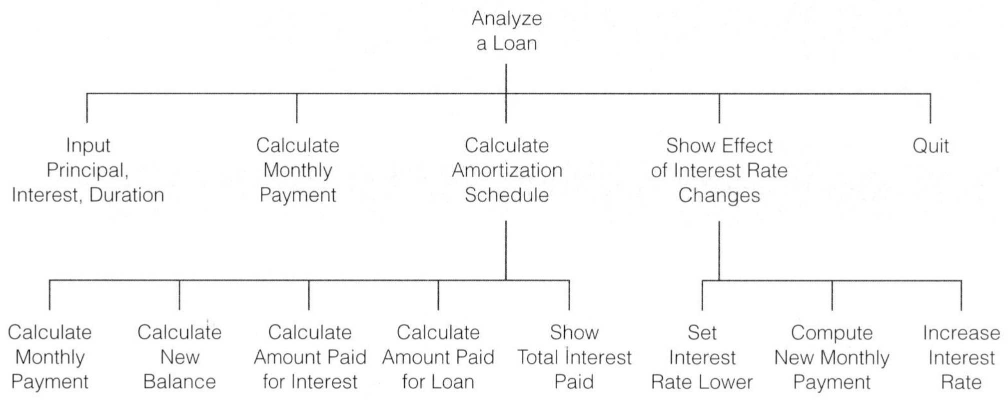

Figure 6.15 Top-Down Chart for the Analyze-a-Loan Program

Pseudocode for the Analyze-a-Loan Program

```
INPUT LOAN DATA (Subprogram InputData)
DO
  PRESENT MENU AND GET CHOICE (Subprogram ShowMenu)
  CASE choice = Calculate monthly payment
    COMPUTE MONTHLY PAYMENT (Function Payment)
    DISPLAY MONTHLY PAYMENT (Subprogram ShowPayment)
  CASE choice = Display amortization schedule
    DISPLAY AMORTIZATION SCHEDULE (Subprogram ShowAmortSched)
    Compute monthly interest rate
    COMPUTE MONTHLY PAYMENT (Function Payment)
    Display amortization table
    Display total interest paid
  CASE choice = Show change-of-interest-rate table
    Decrease annual rate by .01
    DO
      Compute monthly interest rate
      COMPUTE MONTHLY PAYMENT (Function Payment)
      Increase annual rate by .00125
    LOOP UNTIL annual rate > original annual rate + .01
LOOP UNTIL choice = quit
```

Writing the Analyze-a-Loan Program

Table 6.6 shows each task discussed above and the procedure that carries out the task.

Task	Procedure
1. Input principal, interest, duration.	InputData
2. Present menu and get choice.	ShowMenu
3. Calculate monthly payment.	ShowPayment
4. Calculate amortization schedule.	ShowAmortSched
4.1 Calculate monthly payment.	Payment
4.2 Calculate new balance.	Balance
4.3 Calculate amount paid for loan.	ShowAmortSched
4.4 Calculate amount paid for interest.	ShowAmortSched
5. Show effect of interest-rate changes.	ShowInterestChanges
5.1 Reduce interest rate.	ShowInterestChanges
5.2 Compute new monthly payment.	Payment
5.3 Increase interest rate.	ShowInterestChanges

Table 6.6 Tasks and Their Procedures

```
REM Analyze a loan REM
REM ****************************************************
REM *                                                  *
REM *        Variable Table                            *
REM *                                                  *
REM *                                                  *
REM * choice          User's main menu choice (1 to 4) *
REM * numMonths       Number of months to pay loan     *
REM * principal       Amount of loan                   *
REM * yearlyRate      Yearly interest rate             *
REM *                                                  *
REM ****************************************************
REM
CLS
CALL InputData(principal, yearlyRate, numMonths)
DO
  CALL ShowMenu
  INPUT "Choice"; choice
  CLS
  SELECT CASE choice
    CASE 1
      CALL ShowPayment(principal, yearlyRate, numMonths)
    CASE 2
      CALL ShowAmortSched(principal, yearlyRate, numMonths)
    CASE 3
      CALL ShowInterestChanges(principal, yearlyRate, numMonths)
    CASE ELSE
  END SELECT
LOOP UNTIL choice = 4
END
```

```
FUNCTION Balance (monthlyPayment, principal, monthlyRate)
  REM Compute balance at end of month
  Balance = (1 + monthlyRate) * principal - monthlyPayment
END FUNCTION

SUB InputData (principal, yearlyRate, numMonths)
  REM Input the loan amount, yearly rate of interest, and duration
  INPUT "Amount of the loan"; principal
  INPUT "Annual percentage rate of interest"; percentageRate
  LET yearlyRate = percentageRate / 100
  INPUT "Number of years of the loan"; numYears
  LET numMonths = numYears * 12
END SUB

SUB PauseIfNecessary (lineCount)
  REM Pause if screen is full
  REM lineCount records the number of lines of display on the screen
  LET lineCount = lineCount + 1
  IF lineCount >= 22 THEN
      CALL WaitForUser
      LET lineCount = 0
  END IF
END SUB

FUNCTION Payment (principal, monthlyRate, numMonths)
  REM Calculate monthly payment
  Payment = principal * monthlyRate / (1 - (1 + monthlyRate) ^ (-numMonths))
END FUNCTION

SUB ShowAmortSched (principal, yearlyRate, numMonths)
  REM Display amortization schedule
  REM lineCount records the number of lines of display on the screen
  PRINT "           Amount Paid       Amount Paid       Balance at"
  PRINT "Month     for Principal      for Interest     End of Month"
  LET a$ = "####        $$###.##          $$###.##     $$###,###.##"
  LET lineCount = 2
  LET monthlyRate = yearlyRate / 12
  LET monthlyPayment = Payment(principal, monthlyRate, numMonths)
  LET totalInterest = 0
  LET oldBalance = principal
  FOR monthNum = 1 TO numMonths
    LET newBalance = Balance(monthlyPayment, oldBalance, monthlyRate)
    LET principalPaid = oldBalance - newBalance
    LET interestPaid = monthlyPayment - principalPaid
    LET totalInterest = totalInterest + interestPaid
    PRINT USING a$; monthNum; principalPaid; interestPaid; newBalance
    CALL PauseIfNecessary(lineCount)
    LET oldBalance = newBalance
  NEXT monthNum
  PRINT
  PRINT USING "Total interest paid is $$##,###.##"; totalInterest
  IF lineCount <> 0 THEN
      CALL WaitForUser
  END IF
END SUB
```

```
SUB ShowInterestChanges (principal, yearlyRate, numMonths)
  REM Display effect of interest changes
  PRINT "    Annual"
  PRINT "Interest rate            Monthly Payment"
  LET a$ = "##.###%                    $$###.##"
  LET newRate = yearlyRate - .01
  DO
    LET monthlyRate = newRate / 12
    PRINT USING a$; newRate * 100; Payment(principal, monthlyRate, numMonths)
    LET newRate = newRate + .00125
  LOOP UNTIL newRate > yearlyRate + .01
  PRINT
  CALL WaitForUser
END SUB

SUB ShowMenu
  REM Display options
  CLS
  PRINT "1. Calculate monthly payment"
  PRINT "2. Display amortization schedule"
  PRINT "3. Display interest-rate-change table"
  PRINT "4. Quit"   PRINT
END SUB

SUB ShowPayment (principal, yearlyRate, numMonths)
  REM Display monthly payment amount
  LET monthlyRate = yearlyRate / 12
  PRINT USING "The monthly payment for a $$##,###.## loan at"; principal
  PRINT USING "##.##% annual rate of interest for"; yearlyRate * 100
  PRINT USING "## years is"; numMonths / 12;
  PRINT USING "$$#,###.##"; Payment(principal, monthlyRate, numMonths)
  CALL WaitForUser
END SUB

SUB WaitForUser
  REM Pause until user hits Enter key
  PRINT
  INPUT "Press Enter key to continue..."; dummy$
END SUB
```

Comments:

1. In the main body, the subprogram ShowMenu is called repeatedly until a valid menu option is chosen by the user. Once an acceptable choice has been made, SELECT CASE is used to transfer control to the appropriate subprogram.

2. Tasks 4.1 and 4.2 are performed by functions. Using functions to compute these quantities simplifies the computations in ShowAmortSched.

3. If the number of years over which the loan is to be repaid is more than one, then the amortization table produced by ShowAmortSched might fill more than one screen. Two subroutines are used to produce a pause, once the screen is filled. PauseIfNecessary keeps track of the amount of the screen that has been used and calls WaitForUser to produce a pause if the screen is full.

Chapter 6 Summary

1. A DO loop repeatedly executes a block of statements either as long as or until a certain condition is true. The condition can be checked either at the top of the loop or at the bottom.
2. Lists of data are often followed by *trailer values* or *sentinels*, which can be used by DO loops to terminate repetitions after all the data have been read.
3. As various items of data are processed by a loop, a *counter* can be used to keep track of the number of items and an *accumulator* can be used to sum numerical values.
4. A *flag* is a variable used to indicate whether or not a certain event has occurred.
5. A FOR...NEXT loop repeats a block of statements a fixed number of times. The *control variable* assumes an initial value and increments by one after each pass through the loop until it reaches the terminating value. Alternate increment values can be specified with the STEP keyword.

Chapter 6 Programming Projects

1. Write a program to print a company's payroll report on a printer. The program should request each employees' name, hourly rate, and hours worked as input and produce a report in the form of the sample run below. Employees should be paid time-and-a-half for hours in excess of 40.

```
[run]
Enter date of last day of week (month/day/yr): 9/25/98
Enter name, hourly rate, hours worked: Al Adams,  6.50, 38
Enter name, hourly rate, hours worked: Bob Brown, 5.70, 50
Enter name, hourly rate, hours worked: Carol Coe, 7.00, 40
Enter name, hourly rate, hours worked: "", 0, 0

Payroll Report for Week ending 9/25/98

Employee       Hourly Rate    Hours Worked   Gross Pay

Al Adams       $ 6.50          38            $ 247.00
Bob Brown      $ 5.70          50            $ 313.50
Carol Coe      $ 7.00          40            $ 280.00

Final Total  $840.50
```

printed on printer

2. *Checking Account.* Write a program to process a month's transactions for a checking account. The program should request the beginning balance and

each transaction, Check or Deposit. (The response to the transaction request should be checked for validity.) After all items have been entered, the program should display the closing balance, the total amounts of checks written and deposits made, and the service charge. The service charge of 25 cents per check is assessed only if the closing balance is less than $300. (***Note:*** Your program must be able to handle any number of transactions, allow for invalid data entry, and give a warning when the balance is less than zero.) A sample run is as follows:

```
[run]
Enter balance at beginning of month: 1234.50

Enter a transaction (C, D, Q): S
Invalid response.
Enter C, D, or Q for Check, Deposit, or Quit.

Enter a transaction (C, D, Q): C
Enter an amount: 35.00

Enter a transaction (C, D, Q): D
Enter an amount: 45.00

Enter a transaction (C, D, Q): C
Enter an amount: 1000.00

Enter a transaction (C, D, Q): Q

Beginning balance:           1234.50
Total amount of checks:      1035.00
Total amount of deposits:      45.00
Service charge:                 0.50
Closing balance:              244.00
```

3. Table 6.7 shows the standard prices for items in a department store. Suppose prices will be reduced for the annual George Washington's Birthday Sale. The new price will be computed by reducing the old price by 10%, rounding up to the nearest dollar, and subtracting one cent. If the new price is greater than the old price, the old price is used as the sale price. Write a program to produce the output shown in Figure 6.16.

Item	Original Price
GumShoes	39.00
SnugFoot Sandals	21.00
T-Shirt	7.75
Maine Handbag	33.00
Maple Syrup	6.75
Flaked Vest	24.00
Nightshirt	26.00

Table 6.7 Washington's Birthday Sale

```
                    Sale
Item                Price

GumShoes            35.99
SnugFoot Sandals    18.99
T-Shirt              6.99
Maine Handbag       29.99
Maple Syrup          6.75
Flaked Vest         21.99
Nightshirt          23.99
```

Figure 6.16 Output of Project 3

4. An airline flight has 150 seats available—20 First class and 130 Coach class. Passengers have a choice of Regular or Vegetarian meals. Write a menu-driven program to allow the ticket agent to keep track of the number of passengers in each class and the number of each type of meal requested. An attempt to book a passenger into a filled class should result in the message "Class is full." The message "Flight is full." should be displayed when there are no more seats available. The program should terminate when the flight is full or when so requested by the ticket agent. Some sample displays that might occur during the execution of the program are shown below.

```
1. Add an additional passenger.
2. Receive a passenger and meal report.
3. Quit.

Enter a selection (1, 2, 3): 1

Select a class (First or Coach): C
Select the type of meal (R or V): V

1. Add an additional passenger.
2. Receive a passenger and meal report.
3. Quit.

Enter a selection (1, 2, 3): 2

First class: 12
Coach class: 98
Regular meals: 60
Vegetarian meals: 50
```

5. The Rule of 72 is used to make a quick estimate of the time required for prices to double due to inflation. If the inflation rate is r percent, then the Rule of 72 estimates that prices will double in $72/r$ years. For instance, at an inflation rate of 6%, prices double in about 72/6 or 12 years. Write a program to test the accuracy of this rule. The program should display a table showing, for each value of r from 1 to 20, the rounded value of $72/r$ and the actual number of years required for prices to double at an r% inflation rate. (Assume prices increase at the end of each year.) Figure 6.17 shows the first few rows of the output.

Interest Rate (%)	Rule of 72	Actual
1	72	70
2	36	36
3	24	24

Figure 6.17 Rule of 72

6. Table 6.8 shows the number of bachelor degrees conferred in 1980 and 1989 in certain fields of study. Tables 6.9 and 6.10 show the percentage change and a histogram of 1994 levels, respectively. Write a menu-driven program that allows the user to display any one of these tables as an option and quit as a fourth option.

Field of Study	1980	1994
Business and management	185,361	246,654
Computer and info. science	11,154	24,260
Education	118,169	167,600
Engineering	68,893	62,220
Social sciences	103,519	133,680

Table 6.8 Bachelor Degrees Conferred in Certain Fields
Source: U.S. National Center of Educational Statistics

Field of Study	% Change (1980–1994)
Business and management	33.1
Computer and info. science	117.0
Education	–41.8
Engineering	–9.7
Social sciences	29.1

Table 6.9 Percentage Change in Bachelor Degrees Conferred

Business and management	************************* 246,654
Computer and info. science	** 24,200
Education	***************** 167,600
Engineering	****** 62,220
Social sciences	************* 133,680

Table 6.10 Bachelor Degrees Conferred in 1994 in Certain Fields

7. *Least-Squares Approximation.* Table 6.11 shows the 1988 price of a gallon of fuel and the consumption of motor fuel for several countries. Figure 6.18 displays the data as points in the *xy*-plane. For instance, the point with coordinates (1, 1400) corresponds to the U.S.A. Figure 6.18 also shows the straight line that best fits this data in the least-squares sense. (The sum of the squares of the distances of the eleven points from this line is as small as possible.) In general, if $(x_1, y_1), (x_2, y_2), \ldots, (x_n, y_n)$ are n points in the *xy*-coordinate system, then the least-squares approximation to these points is the line $y = mx + b$, where

$$m = \frac{n*(\text{sumof } x_i*y_i) - (\text{sum of } x_i)*(\text{sum of } y_i)}{n*(\text{sum of } x_i*x_i) - (\text{sum of } x_i)\text{^}2}$$

and

$$b = ((\text{sum of } y_i) - m*(\text{sum of } x_i)) \;/\; n$$

Write a program (containing the numeric data from the table in DATA statements) that calculates and displays the equation of the least-squares line, requests a fuel price, and uses the equation of the line to predict the corresponding consumption of motor fuel. A sample outcome is as follows:

```
[run]
The equation of the least-squares line is y = (-291.4) x + 1471.1

Enter a price per gallon: 4.00
The corresponding use is 305.5 tons of oil per 1000 people
```

Country	Price per gallon in U.S. dollars	Tons of oil per 1000 persons	Country	Price per gallon in U.S. dollars	Tons of oil per 1000 persons
U.S.A.	$1.00	1400	France	$3.10	580
W. Ger.	$2.20	620	Norway	$3.15	600
England	$2.60	550	Japan	$3.60	410
Austria	$2.75	580	Denmark	$3.70	570
Sweden	$2.80	700	Italy	$3.85	430
Holland	$3.00	490			

Table 6.11 A Comparison of 1988 Fuel Prices and Per Capita Motor Fuel Use
Source: World Resources Institute

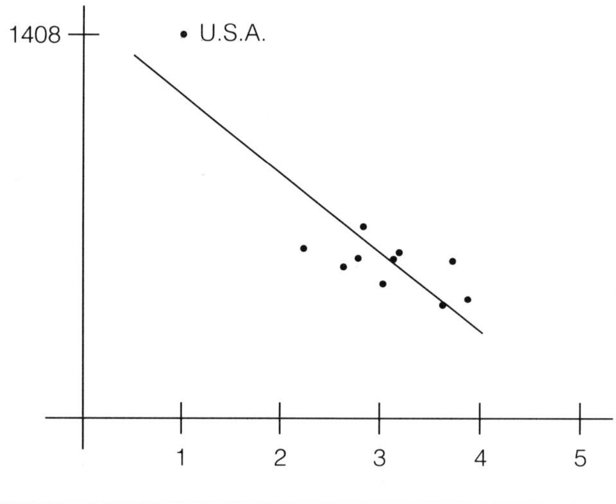

Figure 6.18 Least-Squares Fit to Data from Table 6.11

8. Write a menu-driven program to provide information on the height of a ball thrown straight up into the air. The program should request the initial height, h feet, and the initial velocity, v feet per second, as input. The four options are

(a) Determine the maximum height of the ball. **Note:** The ball will reach its maximum height after $v/32$ seconds.

(b) Determine approximately when the ball will hit the ground. ***Hint:*** Calculate the height after every .1 second and observe when the height is no longer a positive number.

(c) Display a table showing the height of the ball every quarter second for 5 seconds, or until it hits the ground.

(d) Quit.

The formula for the height of the ball after t seconds, $h + v*t - 16*t*t$, should be specified in a user-defined function. (Test the program with $v = 148$ and $h = 0$. This velocity is approximately the top speed clocked for a ball thrown by a professional baseball pitcher.)

9. *Depreciation to a Salvage Value of 0.* For tax purposes an item may be depreciated over a period of several years, *n*. With the *straight-line* method of depreciation, each year the item depreciates by 1 *n*th of its original value. With the *double-declining-balance* method of depreciation, each year the item depreciates by 2 *n*ths of its value at the *beginning* of that year. (In the last year it is depreciated by its value at the beginning of the year.) Write a program that

(a) Requests a description of the item, the year of purchase, the cost of the item, the number of years to be depreciated (estimated life), and the method of depreciation. The method of depreciation should be chosen from a menu.

(b) Displays a depreciation schedule for the item similar to the schedule shown in Figure 6.19.

```
Description: Computer
Year of purchase: 1998
Cost: $2000.00
Estimated life: 5
Method of depreciation: double-declining-balance

           Value at      Amount Deprec.     Total Depreciation
Year       Beg. of Yr.   During Year        to End of Year

1998        2,000.00        800.00              800.00
1999        1,200.00        480.00            1,280.00
2000          720.00        288.00            1,568.00
2001          432.00        172.80            1,740.80
2002          259.20        259.20            2,000.00
```

Figure 6.19 Depreciation Schedule

10. *The Twelve Days of Christmas*. Each year, Provident National Bank of Philadelphia publishes a Christmas price list. See Table 6.12. Write a program that requests an integer from 1 through 12 and then lists the gifts for that day along with that day's cost. On the *n*th day, the *n* gifts are 1 partridge in a pear tree, 2 turtle doves, . . . , *n* of the *n*th item. The program also should give the total cost of all twelve days. A sample output is as follows:

```
[run]
Enter a day from 1 through 12: 3
The gifts for day 3 are
 1 partridge in a pear tree
 2 turtle doves
 3 French hens
Cost:     $92.50

Total cost for the twelve days: $71,613.50
```

Item	Cost	Item	Cost
partridge in a pear tree	27.50	swan-a-swimming	1000.00
turtle dove	25.00	maid-a-milking	4.25
French hen	5.00	lady dancing	289.50
calling bird	70.00	lord-a-leaping	292.50
gold ring	60.00	piper piping	95.75
geese-a-laying	25.00	drummer drumming	95.00

Table 6.12 Christmas Price Index

7

Arrays

7.1 CREATING AND ACCESSING ARRAYS

A **variable** (or simple variable) is a name to which the computer can assign a single value. An **array variable** is a collection of simple variables of the same type to which the computer can efficiently assign a list of values.

Consider the following situation. Suppose you want to evaluate the exam grades for 30 students. Not only do you want to compute the average score, but you also want to display the names of the students whose scores are above average. You might place the 30 pairs of student names and scores in a DATA statement and run the program outlined below.

```
REM Analyze exam grades
READ student1$, score1
READ student2$, score2
READ student3$, score3
 .
 .
READ student30$, score30
REM Compute the average grade
 .
 .
REM Display names of above average students
 .
 .
```

This program is going to be uncomfortably long. What's most frustrating is that the thirty READ statements are very similar and look as if they should be condensed into a short loop. A shorthand notation for the many related variables would be welcome. It would be nice if we could just write

```
FOR i = 1 TO 30
  READ studenti$, scorei
NEXT i
```

Of course, this will not work. The computer will treat *studenti$* and *scorei* as two variables and keep reassigning new values to them. At the end of the loop they will have the values of the thirtieth data item.

QBasic provides a data structure called an **array** that lets us do what we tried to accomplish in the loop. The variable names will be similar to those in the READ statement. They will be

```
student$(1), student$(2), student$(3), ..., student$(30)
```

and

```
score(1), score(2), score(3), ... , score(30).
```

We refer to these collections of variables as the array variables student$() and score(). The numbers inside the parentheses of the individual variables are called **subscripts**, and each individual variable is called a **subscripted variable** or **element**. For instance, student$(3) is the third subscripted variable of the array student$(), and score(20) is the 20th subscripted variable of the array score(). The elements of an array are assigned successive memory locations. Figure 7.1 shows the memory locations for the array score().

	score(1)	score(2)	score(3)	. . .	score(30)
score()				. . .	

Figure 7.1 The Array score()

Array variables have the same kinds of names as simple variables. If *arrayName* is the name of an array variable and *n* is an integer, then the statement

```
DIM arrayName(1 TO n)
```

reserves space in memory to hold the values of the subscripted variables *arrayName*(1), *arrayName*(2), *arrayName*(3), . . . , *arrayName*(*n*). The spread of the subscripts specified by the DIM statement is called the **range** of the array, and the DIM statement is said to **dimension** the array. In particular, the statements DIM student$(1 TO 30) and DIM score(1 TO 30) dimension the arrays needed for the program above. An array holds either all string values or all numeric values, depending on whether or not its name is followed by a dollar sign.

Values can be assigned to subscripted variables with LET statements and displayed with PRINT statements. The statement

```
DIM score(1 TO 30)
```

sets aside a portion of memory for the numeric array score() and places the default value 0 in each element.

	score(1)	score(2)	score(3)	. . .	score(30)
score()	0	0	0	. . .	0

The statements

```
LET score(1) = 87
LET score(3) = 92
```

assign values to the first and third elements.

	score(1)	score(2)	score(3)	. . .	score(30)
score()	87	0	92	. . .	0

The statements

```
FOR i = 1 TO 4
  PRINT score(i);
NEXT i
```

then produce the output 87 0 92 0.

EXAMPLE 1 The following program creates a string array consisting of the names of the first five World Series winners. Figure 7.2 shows the array created by the program.

```
REM Create and access array of five strings
CLS
DIM ws$(1 TO 5)
LET ws$(1) = "Red Sox"
LET ws$(2) = "Giants"
LET ws$(3) = "White Sox"
LET ws$(4) = "Cubs"
LET ws$(5) = ws$(4)
INPUT "Enter a number from 1 to 5: ", n
PRINT "The "; ws$(n); " won World Series number"; n
END

[run]
Enter a number from 1 to 5: 2
The Giants won World Series number 2
```

	ws$(1)	ws$(2)	ws$(3)	ws$(4)	ws$(5)
ws$()	Red Sox	Giants	White Sox	Cubs	Cubs

Figure 7.2 The Array ws$() of Example 1

EXAMPLE 2 Assume the array of Figure 7.2 has been created. The following program segment requests the name of a baseball team as input and searches the array to determine whether or not the team name appears in the array.

```
INPUT "Enter the name of a baseball team: ", team$
LET foundFlag = 0
LET n = 0
DO
  LET n = n + 1
  IF ws$(n) = team$ THEN
     LET foundFlag = 1
  END IF
LOOP UNTIL (foundFlag = 1) OR (n = 5)
IF foundFlag = 0 THEN
    PRINT "The "; team$; " did not win any";
    PRINT " of the first five World Series."
  ELSE
    PRINT "The "; ws$(n); " won World Series number"; n
END IF

[run]
Enter the name of a baseball team: White Sox
The White Sox won World Series number 3
```

```
[run]
Enter the name of a baseball team: Pirates
The Pirates did not win any of the first five World Series.
```

We could have written the program in Example 2 with a FOR...NEXT loop beginning FOR n = 1 TO 5. However, such a loop would unnecessarily search the entire list even if the sought-after item were found early. The wasted time could be significant for a large array.

In Example 1, values were assigned to the elements of the array with LET statements. However, READ and INPUT statements also can assign values to elements.

EXAMPLE 3 Table 7.1 gives names and test scores from a mathematics contest given in 1953. Write a program to display the names of the students scoring above the average for these eight students.

Richard Dolen	135	Paul H. Monsky	150
Geraldine Ferraro	114	Max A. Plager	114
James B. Fraser	92	Robert A. Schade	91
John H. Maltby	91	Barbara M. White	124

Table 7.1 The Top Scores on the Fourth Annual Mathematics Contest Sponsored by the Metropolitan NY Section of the MAA
Source: The Mathematics Teacher, February 1953

SOLUTION The following program creates a string array to hold the names of the contestants and a numeric array to hold the scores. The first element of each array holds data for the first contestant, the second element of each array holds data for the second contestant, and so on. See Figure 7.3.

```
REM Analyze exam scores
CLS
DIM name$(1 TO 8)
DIM score(1 TO 8)
REM Read the names and scores into two arrays and total the scores
LET total = 0                    'Total of exam scores
FOR student = 1 TO 8
  READ name$(student), score(student)
  LET total = total + score(student)
NEXT student
LET average = total / 8
REM Display all names with above average grades
FOR student = 1 TO 8
  IF score(student) > average THEN
      PRINT name$(student)
  END IF
NEXT student
REM --- Data: names, scores
DATA Richard Dolen, 135, Geraldine Ferraro, 114
DATA James B. Fraser, 92, John H. Maltby, 91
DATA Paul H. Monsky, 150, Max A. Plager, 114
DATA Robert A. Schade, 91, Barbara M. White, 124
END
```

```
[run]
Richard Dolen
Geraldine Ferraro
Paul H. Monsky
Max A. Plager
Barbara M. White
```

	name$(1)	name$(2)	. . .	name$(8)
name$()	Richard Dolen	Geraldine Ferraro	. . .	Barbara M. White

	score(1)	score(2)	. . .	score(8)
score()	135	114	. . .	124

Figure 7.3 Arrays Created by Example 3

EXAMPLE 4 The following program segment, which replaces the first ten lines of Example 3, demonstrates an alternate way to place data into arrays.

```
REM Analyze exam scores
CLS
INPUT "Enter number of contestants: ", num
DIM name$(1 TO num)
DIM score(1 TO num)
REM Read the names and scores into two arrays and total the scores
LET total = 0                   'Total of exam scores
FOR student = 1 TO num
  INPUT "Enter name of contestant: ", name$(student)
  INPUT "Enter contestant's score: ", score(student)
  LET total = total + score(student)
NEXT student
```

The range of an array need not just begin with 1. A statement of the form

```
DIM arrayName(m TO n)
```

where *m* is less than or equal to *n*, creates an array with elements *arrayName*(*m*), *arrayName*(*m* + 1), *arrayName*(*m* + 2), . . ., *arrayName*(*n*).

EXAMPLE 5 The following program segment stores the names of the 40th, 41st, and 42nd presidents in the array pictured in Figure 7.4.

```
REM Place names of last three presidents in an array
DIM pres$(40 TO 42)
LET pres$(40) = "Ronald Reagan"
LET pres$(41) = "George Bush"
LET pres$(42) = "Bill Clinton"
```

	pres$(40)	pres$(41)	pres$(42)
pres$()	Ronald Reagan	George Bush	Bill Clinton

Figure 7.4 The Array Created by Example 5

An array can be used as either a checklist or frequency table, as in the next example. The function ASC associates each character with its position in the ASCII table.

EXAMPLE 6 The following program requests a sentence as input and records the number of occurrences of each letter of the alphabet. (We assume the user responds without using commas.) The array count() has range ASC("A") TO ASC("Z"); that is, 65 TO 90. The number of occurrences of each letter is stored in the element whose subscript is the ASCII value of the uppercase letter.

```
REM Count occurrences of different letters in a sentence
CLS
DIM count(ASC("A") TO ASC("Z"))      'occurrences of letters
REM Input sentence
INPUT "Sentence"; sentence$
LET sentence$ = UCASE$(sentence$)
REM Consider and tally each letter of sentence
FOR i = ASC("A") TO ASC("Z")
  LET count(i) = 0
NEXT i
FOR letterNum = 1 TO LEN(sentence$)
  LET letter$ = MID$(sentence$, letterNum, 1)
  IF (letter$ >= "A") AND (letter$ <= "Z") THEN
      LET i = ASC(letter$)
      LET count(i) = count(i) + 1
  END IF
NEXT letterNum
REM List the tally for each letter of alphabet
LET lettersShown = 0    'Number of letters shown in line
FOR letterNum = ASC("A") TO ASC("Z")
  LET letter$ = CHR$(letterNum)
  PRINT USING "\\##      "; letter$; count(letterNum);
  LET lettersShown = lettersShown + 1
  IF lettersShown = 7 THEN
      PRINT
      LET lettersShown = 0
  END IF
NEXT letterNum
END
```

```
[run]
Sentence? Oh Auntie Em; there's no place like home.
A 2      B 0      C 1      D 0      E 7      F 0      G 0
H 3      I 2      J 0      K 1      L 2      M 2      N 2
O 3      P 1      Q 0      R 1      S 1      T 2      U 1
V 0      W 0      X 0      Y 0      Z 0
```

Comments:

1. Arrays must be dimensioned before they are used. This is normally done with a DIM statement. In the absence of a DIM statement, arrays are automatically dimensioned with a range of 0 to 10 the first time one of their subscripted variables is used in a program. For instance, executing a statement such as LET a(6) = 3 dimensions the array a() with range 0 to 10 and assigns the value 3 to a(6). **Note:** Good programming practice dictates that all arrays be dimensioned with DIM statements and that the DIM statements appear near the beginning of the program. A person maintaining the program can then conveniently determine the existing arrays and their ranges.

2. Subscripts can be numeric expressions. Subscripts whose values are not whole numbers are rounded to the nearest whole number. Subscripts outside the range of the array produce an error message as shown below.

```
DIM a(1 TO 5)
LET a(3) = 7
LET t = 4
PRINT a(2 * t - 5)
PRINT a(2.6)
LET a(6) = 100
END

[run]
 7
 7
{Subscript out of range}
```

3. The two arrays in Example 3 are referred to as **parallel arrays** because subscripted variables having the same subscript are related.

4. An array dimensioned with a variable in its range can be removed from memory with the statement ERASE *arrayName*. After the ERASE statement is executed, the array can then be redimensioned with a different range. Arrays not explicitly dimensioned, or arrays dimensioned with specific numbers, cannot be removed from memory or redimensioned. The ERASE statement just resets the elements of such arrays to their default values.

5. The integers *m* and *n* in the statement DIM *arrayName*(*m* TO *n*) can be positive, negative, or zero. The only restriction is that *m* cannot be greater than *n*.

6. Until a value is assigned to an element of an array, the element has its default value. Numeric variables have a default value of 0, and string variables have the default value "", the empty string.

7. The statement DIM *arrayName*(0 TO *n*) can be replaced by the statement DIM *arrayName*(*n*).

8. One DIM statement can be used to dimension several arrays by using commas to separate the different arrays. For instance, the third and fourth lines of Example 3 can be replaced by DIM name$(1 TO 8), score(1 TO 8).

PRACTICE PROBLEMS 7.1

1. When should arrays be used to hold data?

2. (a) Give an appropriate DIM statement to declare a string array to hold the names of the *Time Magazine* "Man of the Year" awards for the years 1980 through 1989.
   (b) Write a statement to assign to the array element for 1982 the name of that year's winner, "The Computer."

EXERCISES 7.1

In Exercises 1 through 6, determine the output of the program.

1.
```
DIM a(1 TO 20)
LET a(5) = 1
LET a(10) = 2
LET a(15) = 7
PRINT a(5) + a(10);
PRINT a(5 + 10);
PRINT a(20)
END
```

2.
```
DIM sq(1 TO 5)
FOR i = 1 TO 5
  LET sq(i) = i * i
NEXT i
PRINT sq(3)
LET t = 3
PRINT sq(5 - t)
END
```

3.
```
DIM fh$(1 TO 4)
FOR i = 1 TO 4
  READ fh$(i)
NEXT i
PRINT fh$(4)
LET n = 1
PRINT fh$(2 * n + 1)
REM --- Data: Four Horsemen
DATA Miller, Layden
DATA Crowley, Stuhldreher
END
```

4.
```
DIM s(1 TO 4)
LET t = 0
FOR k = 1 TO 4
  READ s(k)
  LET t = t + s(k)
NEXT k
PRINT t
REM --- Data: numbers
DATA 3, 5, 2, 1
END
```

5.
```
DIM p(1 TO 6)
FOR k = 1 TO 6
  READ p(k)
NEXT k
FOR k = 6 TO 1 STEP -1
  PRINT p(k);
NEXT k
REM --- Data: numbers
DATA 4, 3, 11, 9, 2, 6
END
```

6.
```
DIM a(1 TO 4), b(1 TO 4), c(1 TO 4)
FOR i = 1 TO 4
  READ a(i), b(i)
NEXT i
FOR i = 1 TO 4
  LET c(i) = a(i) * b(i)
  PRINT c(i);
NEXT i
REM --- Data: numbers
DATA 2, 5, 3, 4, 1, 3, 7, 2
END
```

In Exercises 7 through 12, identify the errors.

7.
```
LET film$(5) = "Hud"
DIM film$(3 TO 7)
LET film$(3) = "Wings"
PRINT film$(5)
END
```

8.
```
DIM p(1 TO 100)
FOR i = 1 TO 200
  LET p(i) = i / 2
NEXT i
END
```

9.
```
DIM a(1 TO 10)
FOR i = 1 TO 9
  READ a(i)
NEXT i
FOR k = 1 TO 9
  LET a(k) = a(5 - k)
NEXT k
REM --- Data: numbers
DATA 1, 2, 3, 4, 5, 6, 7, 8, 9
END
```

10.
```
DIM a(1 TO 5)
READ a(1), a(2), a(3)
PRINT a(3), a(2), a(1)
DIM a(1 TO 3)
READ a(1), a(2)
PRINT a(2), a(1)
REM --- Data: numbers
DATA 5, 4, 3, 2, 1
END
```

11.
```
DIM b(2 TO 8 STEP 2)
FOR t = 2 TO 8 STEP 2
  READ b(t)
NEXT t
REM --- Data: numbers
DATA 1, 4, 8, 19
END
```

12.
```
LET n = 5
DIM yankee(1 TO 2 * n - 7)
FOR i = 1 TO 3
  READ yankee(i)
NEXT i
REM --- Data: baseball players
DATA Ruth, Gehrig, DiMaggio
END
```

13. Assuming the array river$() is as shown below, fill in the empty rectangles to show the progressing status of river$() after the execution of each program segment.

	river$(1)	river$(2)	river$(3)	river$(4)	river$(5)
river$()	Nile	Ohio	Amazon	Volga	Thames

```
LET temp$ = river$(1)
LET river$(1) = river$(5)
LET river$(5) = temp$
```

	river$(1)	river$(2)	river$(3)	river$(4)	river$(5)
river$()					

```
LET temp$ = river$(1)
FOR i = 1 TO 4
  LET river$(i) = river$(i + 1)
NEXT i
LET river$(5) = temp$
```

	river$(1)	river$(2)	river$(3)	river$(4)	river$(5)
river$()					

14. Assuming the array cat$() is as shown below, fill in the empty rectangles to show the final status of cat$() after executing the nested loops.

	cat$(1)	cat$(2)	cat$(3)	cat$(4)
cat$()	Morris	Garfield	Socks	Felix

```
FOR i = 1 TO 3
  FOR j = 1 TO 4 - i
    IF cat$(j) > cat$(j + 1) THEN
        LET temp$ = cat$(j)
        LET cat$(j) = cat$(j + 1)
        LET cat$(j + 1) = temp$
    END IF
  NEXT j
NEXT i
```

	cat$(1)	cat$(2)	cat$(3)	cat$(4)
cat$()				

15. The subscripted variables of the array a() have the following values: a(1) = 6, a(2) = 3, a(3) = 1, a(4) = 2, a(5) = 5, a(6) = 8, a(7) = 7. Suppose i = 2, j = 4, and k = 5. What values are assigned to *n* when the following LET statements are executed?

(a) `LET n = a(k) - a(i)`

(b) `LET n = a(k - i) + a(k - j)`

(c) `LET n = a(k) * a(i + 2)`

(d) `LET n = a(j - i) * a(i)`

16. The array month$() holds the following three-character strings.

```
month$(1)="Jan", month$(2)="Feb", ..., month$(12)="Dec"
```

(a) What is displayed by the following statement?

```
PRINT month$(4), month$(9)
```

(b) What value is assigned to winter$ by the following statement?

```
LET winter$ = month$(12) + "," + month$(1) + "," + month$(2)
```

17. Modify the program in Example 3 to display each student's name and the number of points by which his or her score differs from the average.

18. Modify the program in Example 3 to display only the name(s) of the student(s) with the highest score.

In Exercises 19 through 26, write a program segment to complete the stated task.

19. The arrays a() and b() have been dimensioned to have range 1 to 4, and values have been assigned to a(1) through a(4). Reverse the order of these values and store them in b().

20. Given two arrays, p() and q(), each with range 1 to 20, compute the sum of the products of the corresponding array elements; that is,

```
p(1)*q(1) + p(2)*q(2) + ... + p(20)*q(20)
```

21. Display the values of the array a() of range 1 to 30 in five columns as shown below.

```
a(1)   a(2)   a(3)   a(4)   a(5)
 .      .      .      .      .
 .      .      .      .      .
 .      .      .      .      .
a(26)  a(27)  a(28)  a(29)  a(30)
```

22. A list of 20 integers, all between 1 and 10, is contained in a DATA statement. Determine how many times each integer appears and have the program display the frequency of each integer.

23. Compare two arrays a$() and b$() of range 1 to 10 to see if they hold identical values—that is, if a$(*j*) = b$(*j*) for all *j*.

24. Calculate the sum of the entries with odd subscripts in an array a() of range 1 to 9.

25. Twelve exam grades are stored in the array grades(). Curve the grades by adding 7 points to each grade.

26. Read 10 numbers contained in a DATA statement into an array and then display three columns as follows: Column 1 should contain the original 10 numbers, column 2 should contain these numbers in reverse order, and column 3 should contain the averages of the corresponding numbers in columns 1 and 2.

27. Thirty scores, each lying between 0 and 49, are given in a DATA statement. These scores are used to create an array frequency() as follows:

frequency(1) = # of scores < 10
frequency(2) = # of scores such that 10 <= score < 20
frequency(3) = # of scores such that 20 <= score < 30
frequency(4) = # of scores such that 30 <= score < 40
frequency(5) = # of scores such that 40 <= score < 50.

Write a program to display the results in tabular form as follows:

Interval	**Frequency**
0 to 10	frequency(1)
10 to 20	frequency(2)
20 to 30	frequency(3)
30 to 40	frequency(4)
40 to 50	frequency(5)

28. Given the following flight schedule,

Flight #	**Origin**	**Destination**	**Departure Time**
117	Tucson	Dallas	8:45 a.m.
239	LA	Boston	10:15 a.m.
298	Albany	Reno	1:35 p.m.
326	Houston	New York	2:40 p.m.
445	New York	Tampa	4:20 p.m.

write a program to load this information into four arrays of range 1 to 5, flightNum(), orig$(), dest$(), and deptTime$(), and ask the user to request a flight number. Have the computer find the flight number and display the information corresponding to that flight. Account for the case where the user requests a nonexistent flight.

29. Table 7.2 contains the names and number of units of the top 10 pizza chains in 1995. Write a program to place these data into a pair of parallel arrays, compute the total number of units for these 10 chains, and display a table giving the name and percentage of total units for each of the companies.

Name	Units	Name	Units
1. Pizza Hut	12,140	6. Chuck E. Cheese	319
2. Domino's	5,257	7. Godfather's	520
3. Little Caesar's	4,720	8. Shakey's	310
4. Papa John's	878	9. Pizza Inn	477
5. Round Table	558	10. California Pizza Kitchen	77

Table 7.2 Top 10 Pizza Chains for 1995 (and numbers of units)
Source: Restaurants & Institutions, July 1996

30. A retail store has 5 bins, numbered 1 to 5, each containing a different commodity. At the beginning of a particular day, each bin contains 45 items. Table 7.3 below shows the cost per item for each of the bins and the quantity sold during that day.

Bin	Cost per Item	Quantity Sold
1	3.00	10
2	12.25	30
3	37.45	9
4	7.49	42
5	24.95	17

Table 7.3 Costs of Items and Quantities Sold for Exercise 30

Write a program to

(a) place the cost per item and the quantity sold from each bin into parallel arrays.
(b) display a table giving the inventory at the end of the day and the amount of revenue obtained from each bin.
(c) compute the total revenue for the day.
(d) list the number of each bin that contains fewer than 20 items at the end of the day.

31. Write a program that asks the user for a month by number, and then displays the name of that month. For instance, if the user inputs 2, the program should display February. ***Hint:*** Create an array of 12 strings, one for each month of the year.

SOLUTIONS TO PRACTICE PROBLEMS 7.1

1. Arrays should be used when
   (a) data are entered by INPUT statements and the number of items will be specified by the user
   (b) a large number of pieces of data of the same type will be entered by INPUT statements
   (c) computations must be made on the items of a DATA statement *after* all of the items have been read
   (d) lists of corresponding data are being analyzed.
2. (a) `DIM manOfTheYear$(1980 TO 1989)`

   (b) `LET manOfTheYear$(1982) = "The Computer"`

7.2 USING ARRAYS

This section considers three aspects of the use of arrays: processing ordered arrays, reading part of an array, and passing arrays to procedures.

Ordered Arrays

An array is said to be **ordered** if its values are in either ascending or descending order. The arrays below illustrate the different types of ordered and unordered arrays. In an ascending ordered array, the value of each element is less than or equal to the value of the next element. That is,

[each element] ≤ [next element].

For string arrays, the ASCII table is used to evaluate the "less than or equal to" condition.

Ordered Ascending Numeric Array

dates()	1492	1776	1812	1929	1969

Ordered Descending Numeric Array

discov()	1610	1541	1513	1513	1492

Ordered Ascending String Array

king$()	Edward	Henry	James	John	Kong

Ordered Descending String Array

lake$()	Superior	Ontario	Michigan	Huron	Erie

Unordered Numeric Array

rates()	8.25	5.00	7.85	8.00	6.50

Unordered String Array

char$()	G	R	E	A	T

Ordered arrays can be searched more efficiently than unordered arrays. In this section we use their order to shorten the search. The technique used here is applied to searching sequential files in Chapter 8.

EXAMPLE 1 The following program places an ordered list of names into an array, requests a name as input, and informs the user if the name is in the list. Since the list is ordered, the search of the array ends when an element is reached whose value is greater than or equal to the input name. On average, only half the ordered array will be searched. Figure 7.5 shows the flowchart for this search.

```
REM Sequential search for a name in an ordered list
CLS
DIM name$(1 TO 10)
REM Place the names into the array
FOR i = 1 TO 10
  READ name$(i)
NEXT i
INPUT "Enter a name: ", searchName$
REM Search for searchName$ in list
LET n = 0        'n is the subscript of the array
DO
  LET n = n + 1
LOOP UNTIL (name$(n) >= searchName$) OR (n = 10)
REM Interpret result of search
IF name$(n) = searchName$ THEN
    PRINT "Found."
  ELSE
    PRINT "Not found."
END IF
REM --- Data: name
DATA Al, Bob, Carl, Don, Eric, Fred, Greg, Herb, Ira, Judy
END
```

```
[run]
Enter a name: George
Not found.
```

```
[run]
Enter a name: Don
Found.
```

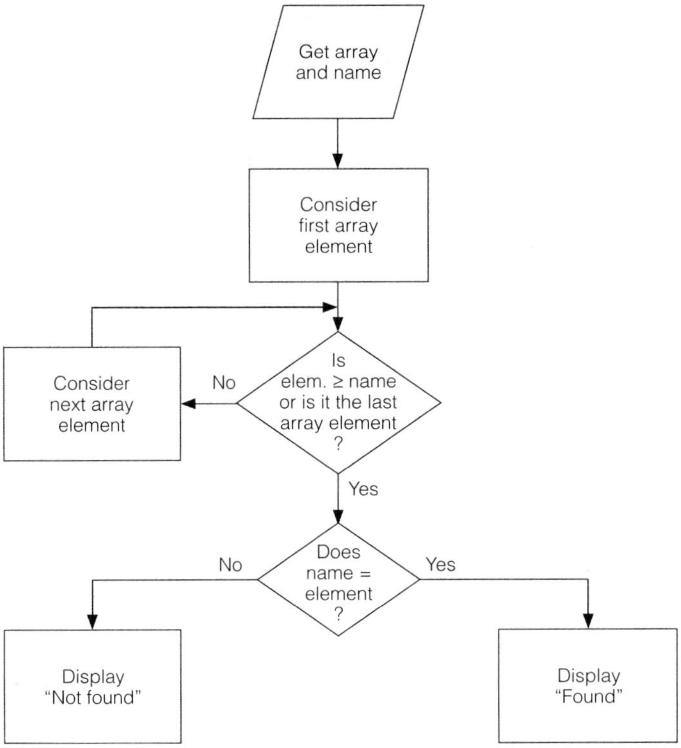

Figure 7.5 Flowchart for a Search of an Ordered Array

Reading Part of an Array

In some programs, we must dimension an array before knowing how many pieces of data are to be placed into it. In these cases we dimension the array large enough to handle all reasonable contingencies. For instance, if the array is to hold exam grades, and classes vary from 5 to 100 students, we use a statement such as DIM grades(1 TO 100). In such situations we must employ a **counter variable** to keep track of the number of values actually stored in the array.

EXAMPLE 2 The following program requests a list of companies and then displays them along with a count.

```
REM Demonstrate reading part of an array
CLS
LET maxNum = 100
PRINT "Enter up to"; maxNum; "companies whose stock you own."
PRINT "Enter EOD when you are finished."
PRINT
DIM stock$(1 TO maxNum)
LET counter = 0
INPUT "Enter a company: ", company$
DO WHILE (company$ <> "EOD") AND (counter < maxNum)
  LET counter = counter + 1
  LET stock$(counter) = company$
  INPUT "Enter a company: ", company$
LOOP
```

```
PRINT
PRINT "You own the following"; counter; "stocks."
FOR i = 1 TO counter
  PRINT stock$(i) + "  ";
NEXT i
END

[run]
Enter up to 100 companies whose stock you own.
Enter EOD when you are finished.

Enter a company: IBM
Enter a company: Texaco
Enter a company: Exxon
Enter a company: EOD

You own the following 3 stocks.
IBM  Texaco  Exxon
```

Suppose you have two ordered lists of customers (possibly with some customers on both lists) and you want to consolidate them into a single ordered list. The technique for creating the third list, called the **merge algorithm**, is as follows.

1. Compare the two names at the top of the first and second lists.
   (a) If one name alphabetically precedes the other, copy it onto the third list and cross it off its original list.
   (b) If the names are the same, copy the name onto the third list and cross out the name from the first and second lists.
2. Repeat step 1 with the current top names until you reach the end of either list.
3. Copy the names from the remaining list onto the third list.

EXAMPLE 3 The following program stores two lists of names in arrays and merges them into a third list. Although at most 10 names will be placed into the third array, duplications will reduce this number. Since the variable r identifies the next position to insert a name in the third array, $r - 1$ is the number of names in the array.

```
REM Merge two lists of names
CLS
DIM first$(1 TO 5)
DIM second$(1 TO 5)
DIM third$(1 TO 10)
FOR i = 1 TO 5  'Read names into the first array
  READ first$(i)
NEXT i
FOR i = 1 TO 5  'Read names into the second array
  READ second$(i)
NEXT i
LET m = 1   'Subscript for first array
```

```
LET n = 1   'Subscript for second array
LET r = 1   'Subscript and counter for third array
DO WHILE (m <= 5) AND (n <= 5)
  SELECT CASE first$(m)
    CASE IS < second$(n)
      LET third$(r) = first$(m)
      LET m = m + 1
    CASE IS > second$(n)
      LET third$(r) = second$(n)
      LET n = n + 1
    CASE second$(n)
      LET third$(r) = first$(m)
      LET m = m + 1
      LET n = n + 1
  END SELECT
  LET r = r + 1
LOOP
REM At most one of the following two loops will be executed
DO WHILE m <= 5        'Copy rest of first array into third
  LET third$(r) = first$(m)
  LET r = r + 1
  LET m = m + 1
LOOP
DO WHILE n <= 5       'Copy rest of second array into third
  LET third$(r) = second$(n)
  LET r = r + 1
  LET n = n + 1
LOOP
REM Display names in third array
LET numNames = r - 1
FOR i = 1 TO numNames
  PRINT third$(i) + "  ";
NEXT i
REM --- Data: name
DATA Al, Carl, Don, Greg, Judy
DATA Bob, Carl, Eric, Greg, Herb
END

[run]
Al  Bob  Carl  Don  Eric  Greg  Herb  Judy
```

Passing Arrays to Procedures

An entire array can be passed to a procedure. The name of the array, followed by an empty set of parentheses, must appear as an argument in the calling statement, and an array variable name of the same type must appear as a corresponding parameter in the procedure definition. The array is DIMensioned in the main body of the program, not in the procedure.

EXAMPLE 4 The following program illustrates passing an array to both a subprogram and a function.

```
REM Read 10 scores and report the average
DIM score (1 TO 10)
CLS
CALL FillArray(score())
PRINT "The average score is"; Sum(score()) / 10
REM --- Data: score
DATA 85, 92, 75, 68, 84, 86, 94, 74, 79, 88
END

SUB FillArray (score())
  FOR i = 1 TO 10
    READ score(i)
  NEXT i
END SUB

FUNCTION Sum (score())
  LET total = 0
  FOR i = 1 TO 10
    LET total = total + score(i)
  NEXT i
  Sum = total
END FUNCTION

[run]
The average score is 82.5
```

EXAMPLE 5 The following program incorporates all three topics discussed in this section. It reads an ordered list of computer languages into an array, requests a computer language as input, and inserts the language into its proper array position (avoiding duplication). The array lang$() is dimensioned to hold up to 20 names; the variable *numLangs* records the actual number of languages in the ordered array.

```
REM Insert an item into an ordered array
CLS
DIM lang$(1 TO 20)
CALL FillArray(lang$(), numLangs)
CALL AddALang(lang$(), numLangs)
CALL DisplayArray(lang$(), numLangs)
REM --- Data: language
DATA ADA, C, COBOL, FORTRAN, PASCAL, QBASIC, EOD
END

SUB AddALang (lang$(), numLangs)
  REM Insert a language into an ordered array of languages
  INPUT "Enter a computer language: ", language$
  LET n = 0
  DO
    LET n = n + 1
  LOOP UNTIL (lang$(n) >= language$) OR (n = numLangs)
  IF lang$(n) < language$ THEN     'Insert new language at end
      LET lang$(numLangs + 1) = language$
      LET numLangs = numLangs + 1
    ELSEIF lang$(n) > language$ THEN    'Insert before item n
```

```
      FOR i = numLangs TO n STEP -1
        LET lang$(i + 1) = lang$(i)
      NEXT i
      LET lang$(n) = language$
      LET numLangs = numLangs + 1
  END IF
END SUB

SUB DisplayArray (lang$(), numLangs)
  REM Display the languages in the array
  FOR i = 1 TO numLangs
    PRINT lang$(i) + "  ";
  NEXT i
END SUB

SUB FillArray (lang$(), n)
  REM Fill the array with the languages in the DATA statement
  LET n = 0
  READ name$
  DO WHILE name$ <> "EOD"
    LET n = n + 1
    LET lang$(n) = name$
    READ name$
  LOOP
END SUB

[run]
Enter a computer language: LOGO
ADA  C  COBOL  FORTRAN  LOGO  PASCAL  QBASIC

[run]
Enter a computer language: FORTRAN
ADA  C  COBOL  FORTRAN  PASCAL  QBASIC
```

Comments

1. In Examples 1 and 5 we searched successive elements of an ordered list beginning with the first element. This is called a **sequential search**. An efficient alternative to the sequential search is the **binary search** considered in the next section.

2. A single element of an array can be passed to a procedure just like any ordinary numeric or string variable.

```
DIM num(1 TO 20)
LET num(5) = 10
PRINT Triple(num(5))
END

FUNCTION Triple (x)
  Triple = 3 * x
END FUNCTION

[run]
 30
```

3. DATA statements are often used to assign values to the elements of an array. However, the DATA statements must be in the main body of the program. They cannot be inside a procedure, even if the assignment statements are inside a procedure.

4. QBasic provides two functions that simplify working with arrays that have been passed to a procedure. If an array has been dimensioned with the range *m* TO *n*, then the values of the functions LBOUND(*arrayName*) and UBOUND(*arrayName*) are *m* and *n*.

```
DIM pres$(40 TO 42)
LET pres$(40) = "Reagan"
LET pres$(41) = "Bush"
LET pres$(42) = "Clinton"
CALL Display(pres$())
END

SUB Display (a$())
  FOR i = LBOUND(a$) TO UBOUND(a$)
    PRINT a$(i) + "  ";
  NEXT i
END SUB

[run]
Reagan  Bush  Clinton
```

PRACTICE PROBLEMS 7.2

1. Can an array be in both ascending and descending order at the same time?

2. How can the SELECT CASE block in Example 3 be changed so all entries of both arrays (including duplicates) are merged into the third array?

EXERCISES 7.2

In Exercises 1 and 2, decide if the array is ordered.

1. month$()

January	February	March	April	May

2. pres$()

Adams	Adams	Bush	Johnson	Johnson

In Exercises 3 through 8, determine the output of the program.

3.
```
DIM lake$(1 TO 5)
LET lake$(3) = "Michigan"
CALL DisplayThird(lake$())
END

SUB DisplayThird (lake$())
  REM Display the third element of an array
  PRINT lake$(3)
END SUB
```

4.
```
DIM square(1 TO 20)
INPUT "Enter a number from 1 to 20: ", num
FOR i = 1 TO num
  LET square(i) = i ^ 2
NEXT i
CALL Total(square(), num)
END

SUB Total (array(), n)
  LET sum = 0
  FOR i = 1 TO n
     LET sum = sum + array(i)
  NEXT i
  PRINT "The sum of the first"; n; "elements is"; sum
END SUB
```

(Assume the response is 4.)

5.
```
DIM value(1 TO 5)
CALL FillArray(value())
FOR i = 1 TO 4
  SELECT CASE value(i)
    CASE IS < value(i + 1)
      PRINT "less than"
    CASE IS > value(i + 1)
      PRINT "greater than"
    CASE ELSE
      PRINT "equals"
  END SELECT
NEXT i
REM --- Data: number
DATA 3, 7, 1, 1, 17
END

SUB FillArray (value())
  REM Place values into an array of five elements
  FOR i = 1 TO 5
    READ value(i)
  NEXT i
END SUB
```

6.
```
DIM ocean$(1 TO 5)
LET ocean$(1) = "Pacific"
CALL Musical(ocean$(1))
END

SUB Musical (sea$)
  PRINT "South "; sea$
END SUB
```

7.
```
DIM rainfall(1 TO 12)
LET rainfall(1) = 2.4
LET rainfall(2) = 3.6
LET rainfall(3) = 4.0
PRINT "The total rainfall for the first quarter is"; Total(rainfall(),3)
END
```

```
FUNCTION Total (rainfall(), n)
  LET sum = 0
  FOR i = 1 TO n
    LET sum = sum + rainfall(i)
  NEXT i
  Total = sum
END FUNCTION
```

8.
```
DIM num(1 TO 8)
FOR i = 1 TO 8
  READ num(i)
NEXT i
PRINT "The array has"; Nonzero(num()); "nonzero entries."
DATA 5, 0, 2, 1, 0, 0, 7, 7
END

FUNCTION Nonzero (digit())
  LET count = 0
  FOR i = 1 TO 8
    IF digit(i) <> 0 THEN
        LET count = count + 1
    END IF
  NEXT i
  Nonzero = count
END FUNCTION
```

In Exercises 9 through 12, identify the error.

9.
```
DIM city$(1 TO 3)
CALL Assign(city$())
PRINT city$(1)
END

SUB Assign (town$())
  DIM town$(1 TO 3)
  LET town$(1) = "Chicago"
END SUB
```

10.
```
DIM planet$(1 TO 9)
CALL Assign(planet$)
PRINT planet$(1)
END

SUB Assign (planet$)
  LET planet$(1) = "Venus"
END SUB
```

11.
```
REM Multiply several numbers together
DIM num(1 TO 5)
PRINT "Enter from one to five positive numbers."
PRINT "Enter -1 after all numbers have been entered."
LET n = 0
DO
  LET n = n + 1
  INPUT "Enter a number: ", number
  IF number <> -1 THEN
      LET num(n) = number
  END IF
LOOP UNTIL number = -1
LET product = 1
FOR i = 1 TO n
  LET product = product * num(i)
NEXT i
PRINT product
END
```

12.
```
DIM hue$(0 TO 15)
LET hue$(1) = "Blue"
CALL Favorite(hue$())
END

SUB Favorite (tone$())
  LET tone$(1) = hue$(1)
  PRINT tone$
END SUB
```

In Exercises 13 and 14, find the error in the program and rewrite the program to correctly perform the intended task.

13.
```
DIM a(1 TO 10)
DIM b(1 TO 10)
FOR i = 1 TO 10
  LET a(i) = i ^ 2
NEXT i
CALL CopyArray(a(), b())
PRINT b(10)
END

SUB CopyArray (a(), b())
  REM Place a's values in b
  LET b() = a()
END SUB
```

14.
```
DIM a(1 TO 3)
LET a(1) = 42
LET a(2) = 7
LET a(3) = 11
CALL FlipFirstTwo(a())
PRINT a(1); a(2); a(3)
END

SUB FlipFirstTwo (a())
  REM Swap first two elements
  LET a(2) = a(1)
  LET a(1) = a(2)
END SUB
```

Suppose an array has been dimensioned with the statement DIM *scores*(1 TO 50) and numbers assigned to each element. In Exercises 15 through 18, write a portion of a program or a procedure to perform the stated task.

15. Determine if the array is in ascending order.

16. Determine if the array is in descending order.

17. With a single loop, determine if the array is in ascending order, descending order, both, or neither.

18. Assuming the array is in ascending order, count the numbers that appear more than once in the array.

In Exercises 19 and 20, suppose arrays a() and b() each contain 20 numbers in ascending order, where each array could contain duplications. For instance, array a() might hold the numbers 1, 3, 3, 3, 9, 9, ...

19. Write a portion of a program or a procedure to place all the 40 numbers from arrays a() and b() into a third ordered array. The third array could contain duplications.

20. Write a portion of a program or a procedure to place the numbers from a() and b() into a third ordered array, where the third array contains no duplications.

21. Write a program to dimension an array with the statement DIM state$(1 TO 50) and maintain a list of certain states. The list of states should always be in alphabetical order and occupy consecutive elements of the array. The options for this menu-driven program should be as follows:

    (a) Request a state as input and insert it into its proper position in the array. (If the state is already in the array, so report.)
    (b) Request a state as input and delete it from the array. (If the state is not in the array, so report.)
    (c) Display the states in the array.
    (d) Quit.

22. Write a program that requests a sentence one word at a time from the user and then checks whether the sentence is a *word palindrome*. A word palindrome sentence reads the same, word by word, backward and forward (ignoring punctuation and capitalization). An example is "You can cage a swallow, can't you, but you can't swallow a cage, can you?" The program should hold the words of the sentence in an array and use procedures to obtain the input, analyze the sentence, and declare whether the sentence is a word palindrome. (Test the program with the sentences, "Monkey see, monkey do." and "I am; therefore, am I?")

23. Write a program to find the number of students with above-average scores on an exam, where the grades are input one at a time with the grade of –1 as trailer value. (Assume the class contains at most 100 students.) Use a procedure to input the grades and a function to calculate the number. ***Note:*** The procedure must have two parameters, an array parameter for the grades and a numeric parameter for the number of elements of the array that have been assigned values.

24. Suppose an array of 1000 names is in ascending order. Write a procedure or portion of a program to search for a name input by the user. If the first letter of the name is N through Z, then the search should begin with the 1000th element of the array and proceed backward.

SOLUTIONS TO PRACTICE PROBLEMS 7.2

1. Yes, provided each element of the array has the same value.

2. The third CASE tests for duplicates and assigns only one array element to the third matrix if duplicates are found in the two arrays. Thus, we remove the third CASE and change the first CASE so it will process any duplicates. A situation where you would want to merge two lists while retaining duplications is the task of merging two ordered arrays of test scores.

```
SELECT CASE first$(m)
  CASE IS <= second$(n)
    LET third$(r) = first$(m)
    LET m = m + 1
  CASE IS > second$(n)
    LET third$(r) = second$(n)
    LET n = n + 1
END SELECT
```

7.3 SORTING AND SEARCHING

A **sort** is an algorithm for ordering an array. Of the many different techniques for sorting an array we discuss two, the **bubble sort** and the **Shell sort**. Both use the QBasic statement SWAP. If *var1* and *var2* are variables of the same type (that is, both numeric or both string), then the statement

```
SWAP var1, var2
```

assigns *var1*'s value to *var2*, and *var2*'s value to *var1*.

EXAMPLE 1 Write a program to alphabetize two words supplied by INPUT statements.

SOLUTION

```
REM Alphabetize two words
CLS
INPUT "First word"; first$
INPUT "Second word"; second$
IF first$ > second$ THEN
    SWAP first$, second$
END IF
PRINT first$; " before "; second$
END

[run]
First word? beauty
Second word? age
age before beauty
```

Bubble Sort

The bubble sort is an algorithm that compares adjacent items and swaps those that are out of order. If this process is repeated enough times, the list will be ordered. Let's carry out this process on the list Pebbles, Barney, Wilma, Fred, Dino. The steps for each pass through the list are as follows:

1. Compare the first and second items. If they are out of order, swap them.
2. Compare the second and third items. If they are out of order, swap them.
3. Repeat this pattern for all remaining pairs. The final comparison and possible swap is between the second-to-last and last elements.

The first time through the list, this process is repeated to the end of the list. This is called the first **pass**. After the first pass, the last item (Wilma) will be in its proper position. Therefore, the second pass does not have to consider it and so requires one less comparison. At the end of the second pass, the last two items will be in their proper position. (The items that must have reached their proper position have been underlined.) Each successive pass requires one less comparison. After four passes, the last four items will be in their proper positions and, hence, the first will be also.

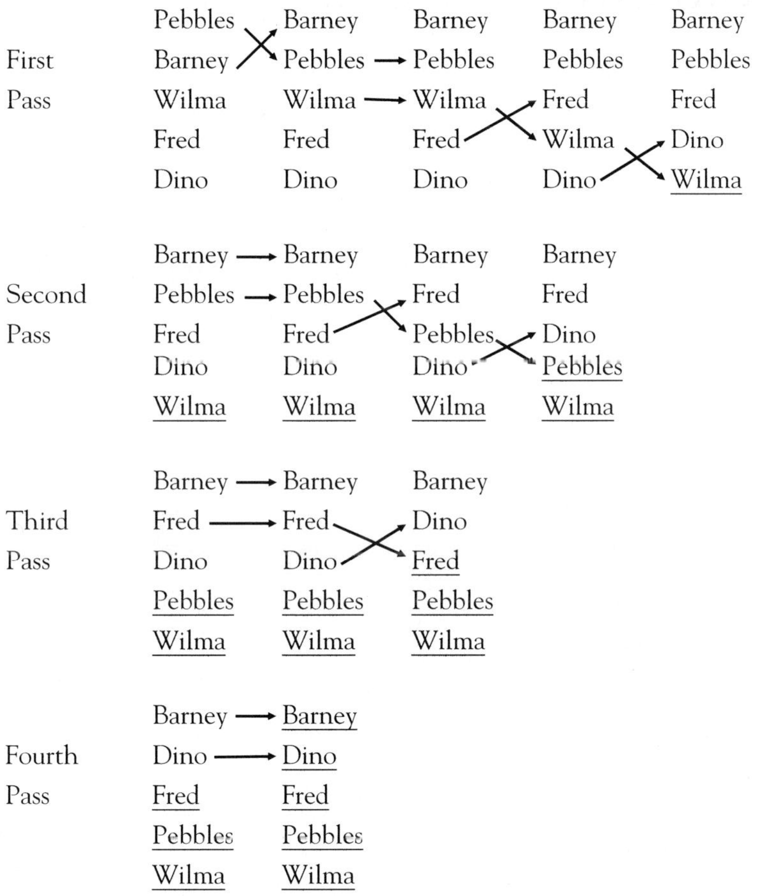

EXAMPLE 2 Write a program to alphabetize the names Pebbles, Barney, Wilma, Fred, Dino.

SOLUTION Sorting the list requires a pair of nested loops. The inner loop performs a single pass and the outer loop controls the number of passes.

```
REM Alphabetize a list of five names
CLS
DIM name$(1 TO 5)
REM Read names
FOR i = 1 TO 5
  READ name$(i)
NEXT i
REM Bubble sort names
FOR passNum = 1 TO 4    'Number of passes is 1 less than number of items
  FOR i = 1 TO 5 - passNum            'Each pass needs 1 less comparison
    IF name$(i) > name$(i + 1) THEN
        SWAP name$(i), name$(i + 1)
    END IF
  NEXT i
NEXT passNum
REM Display alphabetized list
FOR i = 1 TO 5
  PRINT name$(i),
NEXT i
REM --- Data: name
DATA Pebbles, Barney, Wilma, Fred, Dino
END

[run]
Barney        Dino          Fred          Pebbles       Wilma
```

EXAMPLE 3 Table 7.4 contains facts about the ten most populous metropolitan areas with listings in ascending order by city name. Sort the table in descending order by population.

Metro Area	Population in Millions	Median Income per Household	% Native to State	% Advanced Degree
Boston	4.2	$40,666	73	12
Chicago	8.1	$35,918	73	8
Dallas	3.9	$32,825	64	8
Detroit	4.7	$34,729	76	7
Houston	3.7	$31,488	67	8
Los Angeles	14.5	$36,711	59	8
New York	18.1	$38,445	73	11
Philadelphia	5.9	$35,797	70	8
San Francisco	6.3	$41,459	60	11
Washington	3.9	$47,254	32	17

Note: Column 4 gives the percentage of residents who were born in their current state of residence. Column 5 gives the percentage of residents age 25 or older with a graduate or professional degree.

Table 7.4 The Ten Most Populous Metropolitan Areas
Source: The 1990 Census

SOLUTION After the data are written into parallel arrays, the collection of parallel arrays is sorted based on the array pop(). Each time two items are SWAPed in the array pop(), the corresponding items are SWAPed in each of the other arrays. This way, for each city, the items of information remain linked by a common subscript.

```
REM Sort table of metropolitan areas by population
CLS
DIM city$(1 TO 10), pop(1 TO 10), income(1 TO 10)
DIM natives(1 TO 10), advDeg(1 TO 10)
CALL ReadData(city$(), pop(), income(), natives(), advDeg())
CALL SortData(city$(), pop(), income(), natives(), advDeg())
CALL ShowData(city$(), pop(), income(), natives(), advDeg())
REM --- Data: city, pop., med. income, % native, % advanced degree
DATA Boston, 4.2, 40666, 73, 12
DATA Chicago, 8.1, 35918, 73, 8
DATA Dallas, 3.9, 32825, 64, 8
DATA Detroit, 4.7, 34729, 76, 7
DATA Houston, 3.7, 31488, 67, 8
DATA Los Angeles, 14.5, 36711, 59, 8
DATA New York, 18.1, 38445, 73, 11
DATA Philadelphia, 5.9, 35797, 70, 8
DATA San Francisco, 6.3, 41459, 60, 11
DATA Washington, 3.9, 47254, 32, 17
END

SUB ReadData (city$(), pop(), income(), natives(), advDeg())
  REM Read city, pop., med. income, % native, % advanced degree
  FOR i = 1 TO 10
    READ city$(i), pop(i), income(i), natives(i), advDeg(i)
  NEXT i
END SUB

SUB ShowData (city$(), pop(), income(), natives(), advDeg())
  REM Display ordered table
  PRINT , "Pop. in", "Med. income", "% Native", "% Advanced"
  PRINT "Metro Area", "millions", "per hsd", "to State", "Degree"
  PRINT
  FOR i = 1 TO 10
    PRINT city$(i), pop(i), income(i), natives(i), advDeg(i)
  NEXT i
END SUB

SUB SortData (city$(), pop(), income(), natives(), advDeg())
  REM Bubble sort table in descending order by population
  FOR passNum = 1 TO 9
    FOR index = 1 TO 10 - passNum
      IF pop(index) < pop(index + 1) THEN
        CALL SwapData(city$(),pop(),income(),natives(),advDeg(),index)
      END IF
    NEXT index
  NEXT passNum
END SUB
```

```
SUB SwapData (city$(), pop(), income(), natives(), advDeg(), index)
  REM Swap entries
  SWAP city$(index), city$(index + 1)
  SWAP pop(index), pop(index + 1)
  SWAP income(index), income(index + 1)
  SWAP natives(index), natives(index + 1)
  SWAP advDeg(index), advDeg(index + 1)
END SUB

[run]
              Pop. in       Med. income   % Native      % Advanced
Metro Area    millions      per hsd       to State      Degree

New York       18.1          38445         73            11
Los Angeles    14.5          36711         59            8
Chicago        8.1           35918         73            8
San Francisco  6.3           41459         60            11
Philadelphia   5.9           35797         70            8
Detroit        4.7           34729         76            7
Boston         4.2           40666         73            12
Dallas         3.9           32825         64            8
Washington     3.9           47254         32            17
Houston        3.7           31488         67            8
```

Shell Sort

The bubble sort is easy to understand and program. However, it is too slow for really long lists. The Shell sort, named for its inventor, Donald L. Shell, is much more efficient in such cases. It compares distant items first and works its way down to nearby items. The interval separating the compared items is called the **gap**. The gap begins at one-half the length of the list and is successively halved until eventually each item is compared with its neighbor as in the bubble sort. The algorithm for a list of n items is as follows.

1. Begin with a gap of g = INT(n / 2).
2. Compare items 1 and 1 + g, 2 and 2 + g, . . . , $n - g$ and n. Swap any pairs that are out of order.
3. Repeat step 2 until no swaps are made for gap g.
4. Halve the value of g.
5. Repeat steps 2, 3, and 4 until the value of g is 0.

The Shell sort is illustrated below. Crossing arrows indicate that a swap occurred.

Initial Gap = INT([Number of Items] / 2) = INT(5 / 2) = 2

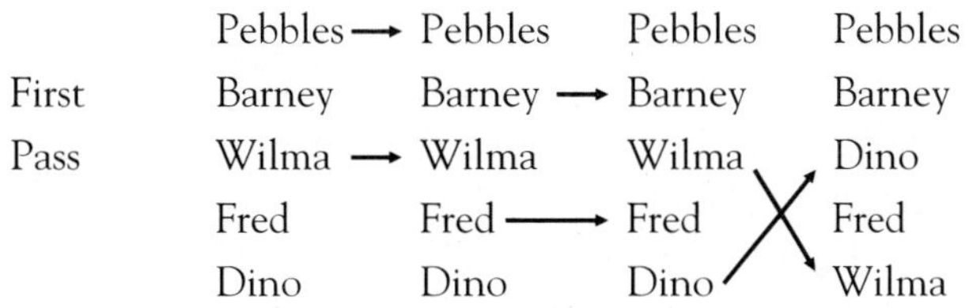

Since there was a swap, use the same gap for the second pass.

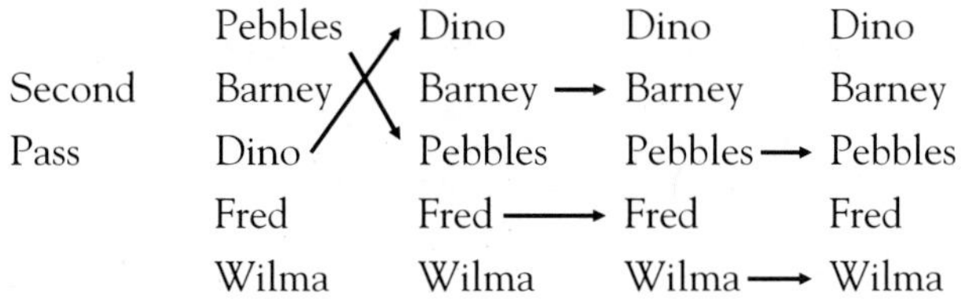

Again, there was a swap, so keep the current gap.

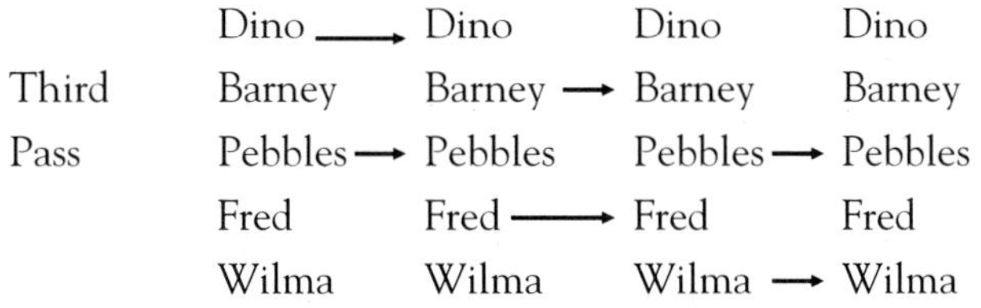

There were no swaps for the current gap of 2, so

Next Gap = INT([Previous Gap] / 2) = INT(2 / 2) = 1

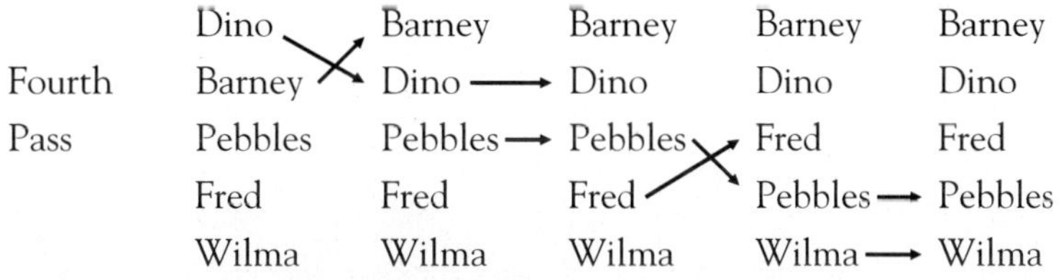

Since there was a swap (actually two swaps), keep the same gap.

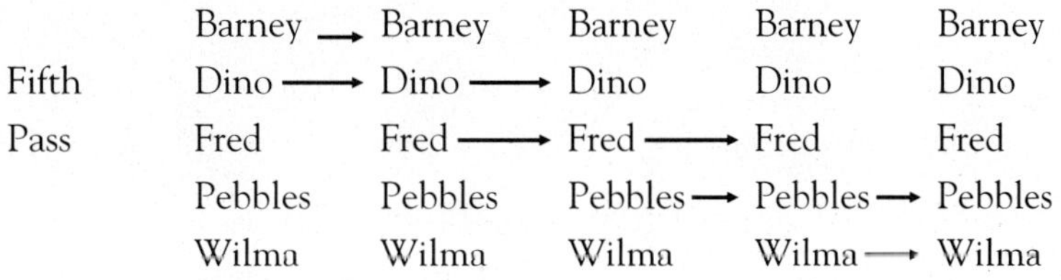

Since there were no swaps for the current gap, then

Next Gap = INT([Previous Gap] / 2) = INT(1 / 2) = 0

and the Shell sort is complete.

Notice that the Shell sort required 14 comparisons to sort the list whereas the bubble sort required only 10 comparisons for the same list. This illustrates the fact that for very short lists, the bubble sort is preferable; however, for lists of 30 items or more, the Shell sort will consistently outperform the bubble sort. Table 7.5 shows the average number of comparisons required to sort arrays of varying sizes.

Array Elements	Bubble Sort Comparisons	Shell Sort Comparisons
5	10	15
10	45	57
15	105	115
20	190	192
25	300	302
30	435	364
50	1225	926
100	4950	2638
500	124,750	22,517
1000	499,500	58,460

Table 7.5 Efficiency of Bubble and Shell Sorts

EXAMPLE 4 Use the Shell sort to alphabetize the parts of a running shoe (see Figure 7.6).

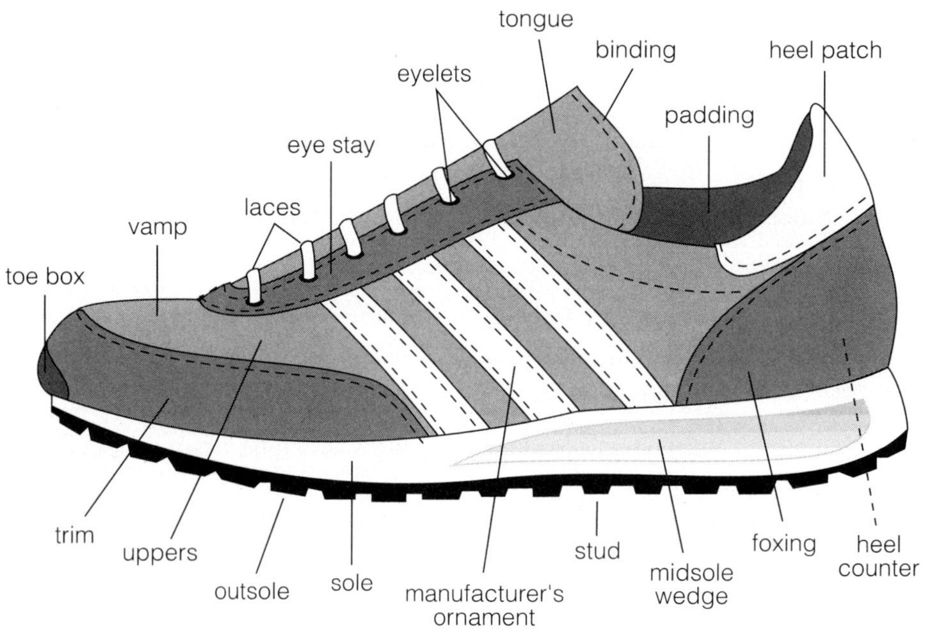

Figure 7.6 Running Shoe

SOLUTION In the following program, the data are read into part of an array. In the subprogram ReadData, the variable *numParts* both provides the subscripts for the array and serves as a counter. The final value of *numParts* is passed to the other subprograms. The subprogram SortData uses a flag to indicate if a swap has been made during a pass.

```
REM Sort and display parts of running shoe
CLS
DIM part$(1 TO 50)
CALL ReadData(part$(), numParts)
CALL SortData(part$(), numParts)
CALL ShowData(part$(), numParts)
REM --- Data: part of running shoe
DATA toe box, vamp, laces, eye stay, eyelets, tongue
DATA binding, padding, heel patch, heel counter, foxing
DATA midsle wdge, mfg's ornmt, sole
DATA uppers, trim, stud, outsole, EOD
END

SUB ReadData (part$(), numParts)
  REM Read part names
  LET numParts = 0     'Number of parts
  READ item$
  DO WHILE item$ <> "EOD"
    LET numParts = numParts + 1
    LET part$(numParts) = item$
    READ item$
  LOOP
END SUB

SUB ShowData (part$(), numParts)
  REM Display sorted list of parts
  FOR i = 1 TO numParts
    PRINT part$(i),
  NEXT i
END SUB

SUB SortData (part$(), numParts)
  REM Shell sort shoe parts
  LET gap = INT(numParts / 2)
  DO WHILE gap >= 1
    DO
      LET doneFlag = 1
      FOR index = 1 TO numParts - gap
        IF part$(index) > part$(index + gap) THEN
            SWAP part$(index), part$(index + gap)
            LET doneFlag = 0
        END IF
      NEXT index
    LOOP UNTIL doneFlag = 1
    LET gap = INT(gap / 2)        'Halve the length of the gap
  LOOP
END SUB
```

```
[run]
binding       eye stay      eyelets       foxing        heel counter
heel patch    laces         mfg's ornmt   midsle wdge   outsole
padding       sole          stud          toe box       tongue
trim          uppers        vamp
```

Searching

Suppose we had an array of 1000 names in alphabetical order and wanted to locate a specific person in the list. One approach would be to start with the first name and consider each name until a match was found. This process is called a **sequential search**. We would find a person whose name begins with "A" rather quickly, but 1000 comparisons might be necessary to find a person whose name begins with "Z." For much longer lists, searching could be a time-consuming matter. However, when the list has already been sorted into either ascending or descending order, there is a method, called a **binary search**, that shortens the task considerably.

Let us refer to the sought item as *quarry*. The binary search looks for *quarry* by determining in which half of the list it lies. The other half is then discarded and the retained half is temporarily regarded as the entire list. The process is repeated until the item is found.

The algorithm for a binary search of an ascending list is as follows (Figure 7.7 shows the flowchart for a binary search):

1. At each stage, denote the subscript of the first item in the retained list by *first* and the subscript of the last item in the retained list by *last*. Initially, the value of *first* is 1 and the value of *last* is the number of items in the list.

2. Look at the middle item of the current list, the item having the subscript *middle* = INT((*first* + *last*) / 2).

3. If the middle item is *quarry*, then the search is over.

4. If the middle item is greater than *quarry*, then *quarry* should be in the first half of the list. So the subscript of *quarry* must lie between *first* and *middle* – 1. That is, the new value of *last* is *middle* – 1.

5. If the middle item is less than *quarry*, then *quarry* should be in the second half of the list of possible items. So the subscript of *quarry* must lie between *middle* + 1 and *last*. That is, the new value of *first* is *middle* + 1.

6. Repeat steps 2 through 5 until *quarry* is found or until the halving process uses up the entire list. (When the entire list has been used up, *first* > *last*.) In the second case, *quarry* was not in the original list.

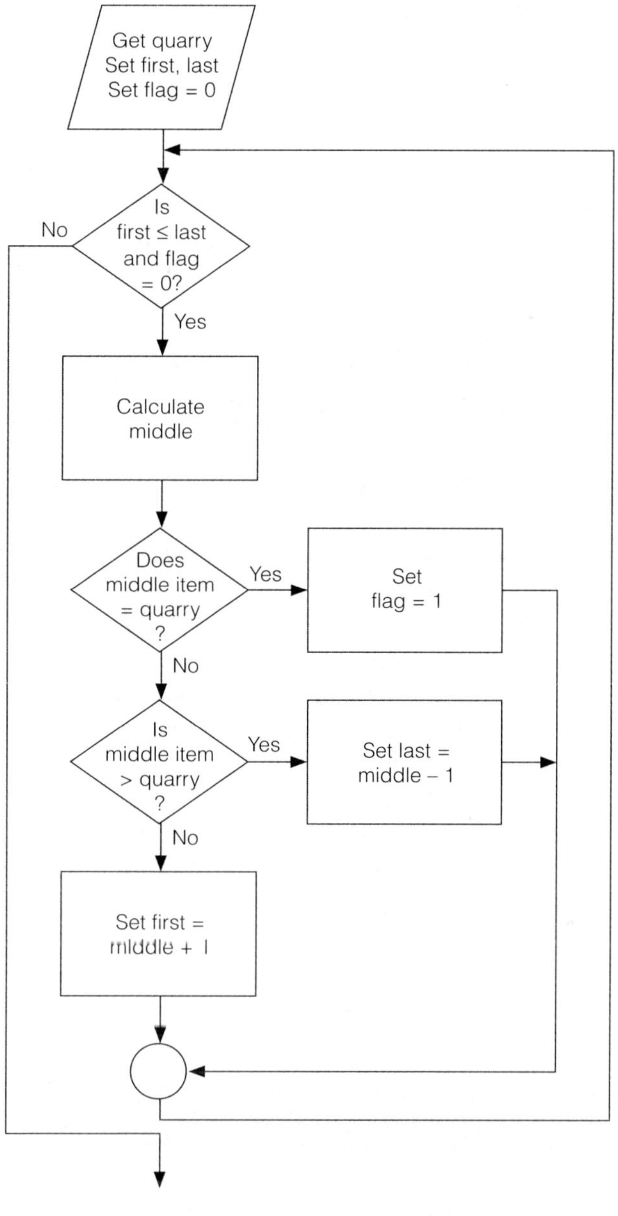

Figure 7.7 Flowchart for a Binary Search

EXAMPLE 5 Assume the array firm$() contains the alphabetized names of 100 corporations. Write a program that requests the name of a corporation as input and uses a binary search to determine whether or not the corporation is in the array.

SOLUTION

```
REM array firm$() already ordered alphabetically
CLS
INPUT "Enter the name of a corporation: ", corp$
REM Binary search of firm$() for corp$
LET foundFlag = 0                       '1 indicates corp$ found
LET first = 1
LET last = 100
```

```
DO WHILE (first <= last) AND (foundFlag = 0)
  LET middle = INT((first + last) / 2)
  SELECT CASE firm$(middle)
    CASE corp$
      LET foundFlag = 1
    CASE IS > corp$
      LET last = middle - 1
    CASE IS < corp$
      LET first = middle + 1
  END SELECT
LOOP
IF foundFlag = 1 THEN
    PRINT corp$; " found."
  ELSE
    PRINT corp$; " not found."
END IF
END
```

Suppose the corporation input in Example 5 is in the second half of the array. On the first pass, *middle* would be assigned INT((1 + 100)/2) = INT(50.5) = 50 and then *first* would be altered to 50 + 1 = 51. On the second pass, *middle* would be assigned INT((51 + 100))/2 = INT(75.5) = 75. If the corporation is not the array element with subscript 75, then either *last* would be assigned 74 or *first* would be assigned 76, depending upon whether the corporation appears before or after the 75th element. Each pass through the loop halves the range of subscripts containing the corporation until the corporation is located.

In Example 5, the binary search merely reported whether or not an array contained a certain item. After finding the item, its array subscript was not needed. However, if related data are stored in parallel arrays (as in Table 7.4), the subscript of the found item can be used to retrieve the related information in the other arrays. This process, called a **table lookup**, is used in the following example.

EXAMPLE 6 Suppose the cities in Example 3 have been ordered alphabetically. Use a binary search procedure to locate the data for a city requested by an INPUT statement.

SOLUTION In the following program, the DATA statements have been ordered by the name of the city.

```
REM Search for city in the metropolitan areas table
CLS
DIM city$(1 TO 10), pop(1 TO 10), income(1 TO 10)
DIM natives(1 TO 10), advDeg(1 TO 10)
CALL ReadData(city$(), pop(), income(), natives(), advDeg())
CALL GetCityName(searchCity$)
CALL FindCity(city$(),pop(),income(),natives(),advDeg(),searchCity$)
REM --- Data: city, pop., med. income, % native, % advanced degree
DATA Boston, 4.2, 40666, 73, 12
DATA Chicago, 8.1, 35918, 73, 8
DATA Dallas, 3.9, 32825, 64, 8
DATA Detroit, 4.7, 34729, 76, 7
DATA Houston, 3.7, 31488, 67, 8
```

```
DATA Los Angeles, 14.5, 36711, 59, 8
DATA New York, 18.1, 38445, 73, 11
DATA Philadelphia, 5.9, 35797, 70, 8
DATA San Francisco, 6.3, 41459, 60, 11
DATA Washington, 3.9, 47254, 32, 17
END

SUB FindCity (city$(),pop(),income(),natives(),advDeg(),searchCity$)
  REM Binary search table for city name
  LET foundFlag = 0                   '1 = city found
  LET first = 1
  LET last = 10
  DO WHILE (first <= last) AND (foundFlag = 0)
    LET middle = INT((first + last) / 2)
    SELECT CASE city$(middle)
      CASE searchCity$
        CALL ShowData(city$(),pop(),income(),natives(),advDeg(),middle)
        LET foundFlag = 1
      CASE IS > searchCity$
        LET last = middle - 1
      CASE IS < searchCity$
        LET first = middle + 1
    END SELECT
  LOOP
  IF foundFlag = 0 THEN
      PRINT "City not in file"
  END IF
END SUB

SUB GetCityName (searchCity$)
  REM Request name of city as input
  INPUT "City"; searchCity$
END SUB

SUB ReadData (city$(), pop(), income(), natives(), advDeg())
  REM Read city, pop., med. income, % native, % advanced degree
  FOR i = 1 TO 10
    READ city$(i), pop(i), income(i), natives(i), advDeg(i)
  NEXT i
END SUB

SUB ShowData (city$(), pop(), income(), natives(), advDeg(), index)
  REM Display city and associated information
  PRINT , "Pop. in", "Med. income", "% Native", "% Advanced"
  PRINT "Metro Area", "millions", "per hsd", "to State", "Degree"
  PRINT
  PRINT city$(index), pop(index), income(index),
  PRINT natives(index), advDeg(index)
END SUB

[run]
City? Baltimore
City not in file
```

Comments:

1. Suppose our bubble sort algorithm is applied to an ordered list. The algorithm will still make $n - 1$ passes through the list. The process could be shortened for some lists by flagging the presence of out-of-order items as in the Shell sort. It may be preferable not to use a flag, since for greatly disordered lists the flag would slow down an already sluggish algorithm.

2. In Example 3, parallel arrays already ordered by one field were sorted by another field. Usually, parallel arrays are sorted by the field to be searched when accessing the file. This field is called the **key field**.

3. Suppose an array of 2000 items is searched sequentially—that is, one item after another—in order to locate a specific item. The number of comparisons would vary from 1 to 2000, with an average of 1000. With a binary search, the number of comparisons would be at most 11, since $2^{11} > 2000$.

4. The built-in function UCASE$ converts all the characters in a string to uppercase. UCASE$ is useful in sorting and searching arrays when the alphabetic case (upper or lower) is unimportant. For instance, in Example 5, if UCASE$ were included in the SELECT CASE comparisons, then the binary search would locate "Mobil" in the array even if the user entered "MOBIL".

5. The SWAP statement cannot be used to switch all the values of two arrays at once. For instance, if a() and b() are arrays, then the statement SWAP a, b or SWAP a(), b() will not do the job. Instead, a loop must be set up to interchange each of the corresponding elements separately.

6. The QBasic function TIMER can be used to determine the speed of a sort. Precede the sort with the statement LET t = TIMER. After the sort has executed, the statement PRINT TIMER – t will display the duration of the sort in seconds.

PRACTICE PROBLEMS 7.3

1. The pseudocode for a bubble sort of an array of n items is given below. Why is the terminating value of the outer loop $n - 1$ and the terminating value of the inner loop $n - j$?

```
FOR j = 1 TO n - 1
  FOR k = 1 TO n - j
    IF [kth and (k+1)st items are out of order] THEN SWAP [them]
  NEXT k
NEXT j
```

2. Complete the table by filling in the values of each variable after successive passes of a binary search of a list of 20 items, where the sought item is in the 13th position.

First	Last	Middle
1	20	10
11	20	

EXERCISES 7.3

In Exercises 1 through 4, determine the output of the program.

1.
```
LET p = 100
LET q = 200
SWAP p, q
PRINT p; q
END
```

2.
```
DIM gag$(1 TO 2)
READ gag$(1), gag$(2)
IF gag$(2) < gag$(1) THEN
    SWAP gag$(2), gag$(1)
END IF
PRINT gag$(1), gag$(2)
REM --- Data: comedians
DATA Stan, Oliver
END
```

3.
```
INPUT x, y
LET swappedFlag = 0
IF y > x THEN
     SWAP x, y
     LET swappedFlag = 1
END IF
PRINT x; y;
IF swappedFlag = 1 THEN
    PRINT "Numbers interchanged."
END IF
END
```

(Use *7* and *11* as input.)

4.
```
DIM a(1 TO 3)
FOR j = 1 TO 3
  READ a(j)
NEXT j
FOR j = 1 TO 2
  FOR k = 1 TO 3 - j
    IF a(k) > a(k + 1) THEN
        SWAP a(k), a(k + 1)
    END IF
  NEXT k
NEXT j
FOR j = 1 TO 3
  PRINT a(j);
NEXT j
REM --- Data: numbers
DATA 7, 4, 3
END
```

In Exercises 5 and 6, identify the errors.

5.
```
DIM c(1 TO 4), d$(1 TO 4)
FOR i = 1 TO 4
  READ c(i), d$(i)
NEXT i
SWAP c(4), d$(4)
REM --- Data: numbers
DATA 1, 2, 3, 4, 5, 6, 7, 8
END
```

6.
```
DIM a(1 TO 3), b(1 TO 3)
FOR i = 1 TO 3
  READ a(i), b(i)
NEXT i
SWAP a(i), b(i)
REM --- Data: numbers
DATA 1, 3, 5, 7, 9, 11
END
```

7. Which type of search would be best for the array shown below?

1	2	3	4	5
Paul	Ringo	John	George	Pete

8. Which type of search would be best for the array shown below?

1	2	3	4	5
Beloit	Green Bay	Madison	Milwaukee	Oshkosh

9. Consider the items Tin Man, Dorothy, Scarecrow, and Lion, in that order. After how many swaps in a bubble sort will the list be in alphabetical order?

10. How many comparisons will be made in a bubble sort of 6 items?

11. How many comparisons will be made in a bubble sort of *n* items?

12. Modify the program in Example 2 so that it will keep track of the number of swaps and comparisons and display these numbers before ending.

13. Rework Exercise 9 using the Shell sort.

14. How many comparisons would be made in a Shell sort of 6 items if the items were originally in descending order and were sorted in ascending order?

15. If a list of 6 items is already in the proper order, how many comparisons will be made by a Shell sort?

16. The following subprogram fills an array of 200 integers with values between 0 and 63 that are badly in need of sorting. Write a program that uses the subprogram FillArray and sorts the array nums() with a bubble sort. Run the program and time the execution. Do the same for the Shell sort.

```
SUB FillArray (nums())
  REM Generate numbers from 0 to 63 and place in array
  LET nums(1) = 5
  FOR i = 2 TO 200
    LET nums(i) = (9 * nums(i - 1) + 7) MOD 64
  NEXT i
END SUB
```

17. Suppose a list of 5000 numbers is to be sorted, but the numbers consist of only 1, 2, 3, and 4. Describe a method of sorting the list that would be much faster than either the bubble or Shell sort.

18. The bubble sort gets its name from the fact that in an ascending sort successive passes cause “lighter” items to rise to the top like bubbles in water. How did the Shell sort get its name?

19. What is the maximum number of comparisons required to find an item in a sequential search of 16 items? What is the average number of comparisons? What is the maximum number of comparisons required to find an item in a binary search of 16 items?

20. Redo Exercise 19 with 2^n items, where n is any positive integer.

In Exercises 21 through 32, write a short program (or partial program) to complete the stated task.

21. Without using the SWAP statement, interchange the values of the variables x and y.

22. Display the names of the seven dwarfs in alphabetical order. As the DATA statement use:

```
DATA Doc, Grumpy, Sleepy, Happy, Bashful, Sneezy, Dopey
```

23. The nation's capital has long been a popular staging area for political, religious, and other large public rallies, protest marches, and demonstrations. The following events have drawn the largest crowds, according to estimates from D.C., U.S. Park, or Capitol police. Read the data into a pair of parallel arrays and display a similar table with the event names in alphabetical order.

Event	Crowd Estimate
LBJ inauguration (8/23/65)	1,200,000
Bicentennial fireworks (7/4/76)	1,000,000
Desert Storm rally (6/8/91)	800,000
Bill Clinton inauguration (1/20/93)	800,000
Beach Boys concert (7/4/85)	625,000
Washington Redskins victory parade (2/3/88)	600,000
Vietnam moratorium rally (11/15/69)	600,000
Ronald Reagan inauguration (1/20/81)	500,000
U.S. Iran hostage motorcade (1/28/81)	500,000

Table 7.6 Largest Public Displays of Emotion in Washington, D.C.

24. Table 7.7 presents statistics on the five leading athletic footware brands. Read the data into three parallel arrays and display a similar table with sales in descending order.

Brand	Pairs of Shoes Sold (in millions)	Percentage Share of U.S. Market
Adidas USA	21.0	6.0
Fila	23.1	6.6
New Balance	9.45	2.7
Nike	146.7	41.9
Reebok	52.9	15.1

Table 7.7 1997 U.S. Market Share in Athletic Footware
Source: Morgan Stanley Dean Whitter research

25. Accept 10 words to be input in alphabetical order and store them in an array. Then accept an 11th word as input and store it in the array in its correct alphabetical position.

26. An airline has a list of 200 flight numbers in an ascending ordered array. Accept a number as input and do a binary search of the list to determine if the flight number is valid.

27. Modify the program in Exercise 16 to compute and display the number of times each of the numbers from 0 through 63 appears.

28. Allow a number n to be input by the user. Then accept as input a list of n numbers. Place the numbers into an array and apply a bubble sort.

29. Write a program that accepts a word as input and converts it into Morse code. The dots and dashes corresponding to each letter of the alphabet are as follows:

A ._	H	O ___	V ..._
B _...	I ..	P .__.	W .__
C _._.	J .___	Q __._	X _.._
D _..	K _._	R ._.	Y _.__
E .	L ._..	S ...	Z __..
F .._.	M __	T _	
G __.	N _.	U .._	

30. Write a program that accepts an American word as input and performs a binary search to translate it into its British equivalent. Use the following list of words for data, and account for the case when the word requested is not in the list.

American	**British**	**American**	**British**
attic	loft	ice cream	ice
business suit	lounge suit	megaphone	loud hailer
elevator	lift	radio	wireless
flashlight	torch	sneakers	plimsolls
french fries	chips	truck	lorry
gasoline	petrol	zero	nought

31. Write a program that accepts a student's name and seven test scores as input and calculates the average score after dropping the two lowest grades.

32. Suppose letter grades are assigned as follows:

97 and above	A+	74–76	C
94–96	A	70–73	C–
90–93	A–	67–69	D+
87–89	B+	64–66	D
84–86	B	60–63	D–
80–83	B–	0–59	F
77–79	C+		

Write a program that accepts a grade as input and displays the corresponding letter. ***Hint:*** This problem shows that when you search an array, you don't always look for equality. Set up an array range() containing the values 97, 94, 90, 87, 84, . . . , 59 and the parallel array letter$() containing A, A–, B+, . . . , F. Next, perform a sequential search to find the first *i* such that range(*i*) is less than or equal to the input grade.

33. The *median* of a set of *n* measurements is a number such that half the *n* measurements fall below the median and half fall above. If the number of measurements *n* is odd, the median is the middle number when the measurements are arranged in ascending or descending order. If the number of measurements *n* is even, the median is the average of the two middle measurements when the measurements are arranged in ascending or descending order. Write a program that requests a number *n* and a set of *n* measurements as input and then displays the median.

SOLUTIONS TO PRACTICE PROBLEMS 7.3

1. The outer loop controls the number of passes, one less than the number of items in the list. The inner loop performs a single pass, and the jth pass consists of $n - j$ comparisons.

2.

First	Last	Middle
1	20	10
11	20	15
11	14	12
13	14	13

7.4 TWO-DIMENSIONAL ARRAYS

Each array discussed so far held a single list of items. Such array variables are called **single-subscripted variables**. An array can also hold the contents of a table with several rows and columns. Such arrays are called **two-dimensional arrays** or **double-subscripted variables**. Two tables are shown below. Table 7.8 gives the road mileage between certain cities. It has four rows and four columns. Table 7.9 shows the leading universities in three disciplines. It has three rows and five columns.

	Chicago	Los Angeles	New York	Philadelphia
Chicago	0	2054	802	738
Los Angeles	2054	0	2786	2706
New York	802	2786	0	100
Philadelphia	738	2706	100	0

Table 7.8 Road Mileage Between Selected U.S. Cities

	1	2	3	4	5
Business	U of PA	U of IN	U of MI	UC Berk	U of VA
Comp Sci.	MIT	Cng-Mellon	UC Berk	Cornell	U of IL
Engr/Gen.	U of IL	U of OK	U of MD	Cng-Mellon	CO Sch. of Mines

Table 7.9 University Rankings
Source: A Rating of Undergraduate Programs in American and International Universities, Dr. Jack Gourman, 1996

Two-dimensional array variables store the contents of tables. They have the same types of names as other array variables. The only difference is that they have two subscripts, each with its own range. The range of the first subscript is determined by the number of rows in the table, and the range of the second subscript is determined by the number of columns. The statement

```
DIM arrayName(m1 TO n1, m2 TO n2)
```

first row (m1), last row (n1), first column (m2), last column (n2) dimensions an array corresponding to a table with rows labeled from *m1* TO *n1* and columns labeled from *m2* TO *n2*. The entry in the *j*th row, *k*th column is *arrayName*(*j*,*k*). For instance, the data in Table 7.8 can be stored in an array named rm(). The statement

```
DIM rm(1 TO 4, 1 TO 4)
```

will dimension the array. Each element of the array has the form rm(row, column). The entries of the array are

rm(1,1) = 0	rm(1,2) = 2054	rm(1,3) = 802	rm(1,4) = 738
rm(2,1) = 2054	rm(2,2) = 0	rm(2,3) = 2786	rm(2,4) = 2706
rm(3,1) = 802	rm(3,2) = 2786	rm(3,3) = 0	rm(3,4) = 100
rm(4,1) = 738	rm(4,2) = 2706	rm(4,3) = 100	rm(4,4) = 0

The data in Table 7.9 can be stored in a two-dimensional string array named univ$(). The statement

```
DIM univ$(1 TO 3, 1 TO 5)
```

will dimension the array. Some of the entries of the array are

univ$(1,1) = "U of PA"
univ$(2,3) = "UC Berk"
univ$(3,5) = "Stevens I.T."

EXAMPLE 1 Write a program to store and access the data from Table 7.8.

SOLUTION Data are read into a two-dimensional array using a pair of nested loops. The outer loop controls the rows and the inner loop controls the columns.

```
REM Determine road mileage between cities
CLS
DIM rm(1 TO 4, 1 TO 4)
CALL ReadMileages(rm())
CALL ShowCities
CALL InputCities(row, col)
CALL ShowMileage(rm(), row, col)
REM --- Data: distances
DATA 0, 2054, 802, 738
DATA 2054, 0, 2786, 2706
DATA 802, 2786, 0, 100
DATA 738, 2706, 100, 0
END

SUB InputCities (row, col)
  REM Input origin and destination cities
  INPUT "Origin"; row
  INPUT "Destination"; col
END SUB
```

```
SUB ReadMileages (rm())
  REM Read mileages into a two-dimensional array
  FOR row = 1 TO 4
    FOR col = 1 TO 4
      READ rm(row, col)
    NEXT col
  NEXT row
END SUB

SUB ShowCities
  REM Show possible cities
  PRINT "1. Chicago"
  PRINT "2. Los Angeles"
  PRINT "3. New York"
  PRINT "4. Philadelphia"
  PRINT
END SUB

SUB ShowMileage (rm(), row, col)
  REM Display mileage between cities
  PRINT "The road mileage is"; rm(row, col)
END SUB

[run]
1. Chicago
2. Los Angeles
3. New York
4. Philadelphia

Origin? 3
Destination? 1
The road mileage is 802
```

So far, two-dimensional arrays have been used only to store data for convenient lookup. In the next example, an array is used to make a valuable computation.

EXAMPLE 2 The Center for Science in the Public Interest publishes *The Nutrition Scorebook*, a highly respected rating of foods. The top two foods in each of five categories are shown in Table 7.10 along with some information on their composition. Write a program to compute the nutritional content of a meal. The table should be read into an array and then the program should request the quantities of each food item that is part of the meal. The program should then compute the amounts of each nutritional component consumed by summing each column with each entry weighted by the quantity of the food item.

	Calories	Protein (grams)	Fat (grams)	Vit A (IU)	Calcium (mg)
spinach (1 cup)	23	3	0.3	8100	93
sweet potato (1 med.)	160	2	1	9230	46
yogurt (8 oz.)	230	10	3	120	343
skim milk (1 cup)	85	8	0	500	302
wh. wheat bread (1 slice)	65	3	1	0	24
brown rice (1 cup)	178	3.8	0.9	0	18
watermelon (1 wedge)	110	2	1	2510	30
papaya (1 lg.)	156	2.4	0.4	7000	80
tuna in water (1 lb.)	575	126.8	3.6	0	73
lobster (1 med.)	405	28.8	26.6	984	190

Table 7.10 Composition of Ten Top-Rated Foods

SOLUTION

```
REM Determine the nutritional content of a meal
CLS
DIM comp(1 TO 10, 1 TO 5)          'Composition table
DIM quantity(1 TO 10)
CALL ReadData(comp())
CALL InputAmounts(quantity())
CALL ShowData(comp(), quantity())
REM --- Data: component data
DATA 23, 3, .3, 8100, 93
DATA 160, 2, 1, 9230, 46
DATA 230, 10, 3, 120, 343
DATA 85, 8, 0, 500, 302
DATA 65, 3, 1, 0, 24
DATA 178, 3.8, .9, 0, 18
DATA 110, 2, 1, 2510, 30
DATA 156, 2.4, .4, 7000, 80
DATA 575, 126.8, 3.6, 0, 73
DATA 405, 28.8, 26.6, 984, 190
REM --- Data: top-rated foods
DATA spinach (1 cup), sweet potato (1 med), yogurt (8 oz)
DATA skim milk (1 cup), wh. wheat bread (1 slice)
DATA brown rice (1 cup), watermelon (1 wedge), papaya (1 lg)
DATA tuna in water (1 lb), lobster (1 med)
REM --- Data: component names
DATA calories, protein (grams), fat (grams)
DATA vitamin A (IU), calcium (mg)
END

SUB InputAmounts (quantity())
  REM Request quantities of foods consumed
  FOR i = 1 TO 10
    READ food$
    PRINT food$;
    INPUT ": ", quantity(i)
  NEXT i
END SUB
```

```
SUB ReadData (comp())
  REM Record composition of foods in array
  FOR row = 1 TO 10
    FOR col = 1 TO 5
      READ comp(row, col)
    NEXT col
  NEXT row
END SUB

SUB ShowData (comp(), quantity())
  REM Display amount of each component
  PRINT
  PRINT "This meal contains the following quantities"
  PRINT "of these nutritional components: "
  FOR col = 1 TO 5
    LET amount = 0
    READ compName$
    FOR row = 1 TO 10
      LET amount = amount + quantity(row) * comp(row, col)
    NEXT row
    PRINT compName$ + ": "; amount
  NEXT col
END SUB

[run]
spinach (1 cup): 1
sweet potato (1 med): 1
yogurt (8 oz): 1
skim milk (1 cup): 2
wh. wheat bread (1 slice): 3
brown rice (1 cup): 0
watermelon (1 wedge): 1
papaya (1 lg): 0
tuna in water (1 lb): .5
lobster (1 med): 0

This meal contains the following quantities
of these nutritional components:
calories:  1175.5
protein (grams):  105.4
fat (grams): 10.1
vitamin A (IU):  20960
calcium (mg):  1224.5
```

Comments:

1. A two-dimensional array variable can hold either numeric data or string data, but not both.
2. We can define three- (or higher-) dimensional arrays much as we do two-dimensional arrays. For instance, a three-dimensional array uses three subscripts, and the assignment of values requires a triple-nested loop. As an example, a meteorologist might use a three-dimensional array to record temperatures for various dates, times, and elevations.

PRACTICE PROBLEMS 7.4

1. Consider the road-mileage program in Example 1. How can the program be modified so the actual names of the cities can be supplied by the user?

2. In what types of problems are two-dimensional arrays superior to parallel arrays?

EXERCISES 7.4

In Exercises 1 through 8, determine the output of the program.

1.
```
DIM a(1 TO 20, 1 TO 30)
LET a(3, 5) = 6
LET a(5, 3) = 2 * a(3, 5)
PRINT a(5, 3)
END
```

2.
```
DIM year(1 TO 100, 1 TO 50)
LET x = 7
LET y = 8
LET year(x, y) = 1937
PRINT year(7, 8) + 50
END
```

3.
```
DIM w$(1 TO 10, 1 TO 15)
LET d$ = "Dorothy"
LET w$(1, 1) = d$
LET n = 1
PRINT w$(n, n)
END
```

4.
```
DIM actor$(1 TO 5, 1 TO 5)
LET b$ = "Bogart"
SWAP actor$(2, 3), b$
PRINT actor$(2, 3)
PRINT actor$(3, 2)
END
```

5.
```
READ p, q
DIM a(1 TO p, 1 TO q)
FOR j = 1 TO p
  FOR k = 1 TO q
    READ a(j, k)
    PRINT a(j, k);
  NEXT k
  PRINT
NEXT j
REM --- Data: numbers
DATA 2, 3, 4, 1, 6, 5, 8, 2
END
```

6.
```
DIM a(1 TO 4, 1 TO 5)
FOR j = 1 TO 4
  FOR k = 1 TO 5
    LET a(j, k) = (j - k) * j
    PRINT a(j, k);
  NEXT k
  PRINT
NEXT j
END
```

7.
```
DIM s(1 TO 3, 1 TO 3)
FOR j = 1 TO 3
  FOR k = 1 TO 3
    READ s(j, k)
  NEXT k
NEXT j
FOR j = 1 TO 3
  PRINT s(j, j);
NEXT j
REM --- Data: numbers
DATA 1, 2, 3, 4, 3, 2, 3, 4, 5
END
```

8.
```
READ x, y
DIM m(1 TO x, 1 TO y)
FOR j = 1 TO x
  FOR k = 1 TO y - j
    READ m(j, k)
    PRINT m(j, k) - k;
  NEXT k
  PRINT
NEXT j
REM --- Data: numbers
DATA 2, 3, 6, 3, 2, 1, 3, 4, 9, 8
END
```

In Exercises 9 and 10, identify the errors.

9.
```
REM Fill an array
DIM a(1 TO 3, 1 TO 4)
FOR j = 1 TO 4
  FOR k = 1 TO 3
    READ a(j, k)
  NEXT k
NEXT j
REM --- Data: numbers
DATA 1,2,3,4,5,6,7,8,9,0,1,2
END
```

10.
```
REM Report individual scores
DIM score(1 TO 3, 1 TO 3)
FOR j = 1 TO 3
  READ student
  FOR k = 1 TO 3
    READ score(k, j)
  NEXT k
NEXT j
INPUT "Student (1, 2, 3)"; student
INPUT "Exam (1, 2, 3): "; exam
PRINT score(student, exam)
REM --- Data: st. no., 3 scores
DATA 1, 80, 85, 90
DATA 2, 72, 80, 88
DATA 3, 87, 93, 90
END
```

In Exercises 11 through 14, write a procedure to perform the stated task.

11. Given an array dimensioned with the statement DIM a(1 TO 10, 1 TO 10), set the entries in the jth column to j (for $j = 1, \ldots, 10$).

12. Given an array dimensioned with the statement DIM a(1 TO 10, 1 TO 10), and values assigned to each entry, compute the sum of the values in the 10th row.

13. Given an array dimensioned with the statement DIM a(1 TO 10, 1 TO 10), and values assigned to each entry, interchange the values in the second and third rows.

14. Given an array dimensioned with the statement DIM a(1 TO 3, 1 TO 45), and values assigned to each entry, find the greatest value and the locations (possibly more than one) at which it occurs.

In Exercises 15 through 24, write a program to perform the stated task.

15. A company has two stores (1 and 2), and each store sells three items (1, 2, and 3). The tables below give the inventory at the beginning of the day and the amount of each item sold during that day.

		Item		
		1	2	3
Store	1	25	64	23
	2	12	82	19

Beginning Inventory

		Item		
		1	2	3
Store	1	7	45	11
	2	4	24	8

Sales for Day

(a) Record the values of each table in an array.
(b) Adjust the values in the first array to hold the inventories at the end of the day and display these new inventories.
(c) Calculate and display the total number of items in the store at the end of the day.

16. Table 7.11 gives the results of a survey on the uses of computers in the workplace. Each entry shows the percentage of respondents from the educational attainment category that use the computer for the indicated purpose.

(a) Place the data from the table in an array.
(b) Determine the average of the percentages in the Inventory Control column.

Educational Attainment	Word Processing	Spreadsheets	Databases	Communi–cations	Desktop Publishing
Not a high school graduate	54.4	22.2	9.9	20.4	20.6
High school graduate	52.5	25.8	13.3	29.4	17.6
Some college	49.5	33.9	20.6	38.5	18.0
Four years of college	40.0	41.5	28.8	45.1	17.0
More than 4 years of college	29.3	41.9	35.3	48.5	10.4

Table 7.11 Computer Use on the Job by Educational Attainment
Source: U.S. Center of Educational Statistics, *Digest of Educational Statistics*, 1994

17. A university offers 10 courses at each of three campuses. The number of students enrolled in each is presented in Table 7.12.

		Course									
		1	2	3	4	5	6	7	8	9	10
	1	5	15	22	21	12	25	16	11	17	23
Campus	2	11	23	51	25	32	35	32	52	25	21
	3	2	12	32	32	25	26	29	12	15	11

Table 7.12 Number of Students Enrolled in Courses

(a) Find the total number of course enrollments on each campus.
(b) Find the total number of students taking each course.

18. Table 7.13 gives the sales volume in dollars for the top five apparel chains.

(a) Place the data into an array.
(b) Calculate the total change in sales volume for these five chains.

	1995 Volume (in billions)	1996 Volume (in billions)
1. Limited	7.88	8.64
2. TJX	3.89	6.69
3. Gap	4.40	5.28
4. Woolworth	3.60	3.75
5. Intimate Brands	2.52	3.00

Table 7.13 Top Apparel Chains
Source: Stores, July 1997

19. The scores for the top three golfers at the 1997 Masters tournament are shown in Table 7.14.

(a) Place the data into an array.
(b) Compute the total score for each player.
(c) Compute the average score for each round.

	Round			
	1	2	3	4
Tiger Woods	70	66	65	69
Tom Kite	77	69	66	70
Tommy Tolles	72	72	72	67

Table 7.14 1997 Masters Leaders

20. Table 7.15 contains part of the pay schedule for federal employees in Washington, DC. Table 7.16 gives the number of employees of each classification in a certain division. Place the data from each table into an array and compute the amount of money this division pays for salaries during the year.

	Step			
	1	2	3	4
GS–1	13,902	14,366	14,828	15,288
GS–2	15,630	16,003	16,521	16,958
GS–3	17,055	17,623	18,192	18,760
GS–4	19,146	19,784	20,422	21,060
GS–5	21,421	22,135	22,850	23,564
GS–6	23,876	24,672	25,468	26,264
GS–7	26,532	27,416	28,300	29,184

Table 7.15 1998 Washington, DC, Locality Pay Schedule

	1	2	3	4
GS–1	0	0	2	1
GS–2	2	3	0	1
GS–3	4	2	5	7
GS–4	12	13	8	3
GS–5	4	5	0	1
GS–6	6	2	4	3
GS–7	8	1	9	2

Table 7.16 Number of Employees in Each Category

21. Consider Table 7.9, the rankings of three university departments. Write a program that places the data into an array, allows the name of a college to be input, and gives the categories in which it appears. Of course, a college might appear more than once or not at all.

22. Table 7.17 gives the monthly precipitation for a typical Nebraska city during a five-year period. Write a program that reads the table from DATA statements into an array and then produces the output shown below.

```
[run]
Total precipitation for each year
 1986  36.53
 1987  31.59
 1988  28.56
 1989  31.96
 1990  22.81

Average precipitation for each month
 Jan   Feb   Mar   Apr   May   Jun   Jul   Aug   Sep   Oct   Nov   Dec
 0.77  0.91  1.91  2.94  4.33  4.08  3.62  4.10  3.50  2.09  1.32  0.77
```

	Jan.	Feb.	Mar.	Apr.	May	June	July	Aug.	Sept.	Oct.	Nov.	Dec.
1986	0.88	1.11	2.01	3.64	6.44	5.58	4.23	4.34	4.00	2.05	1.48	0.77
1987	0.76	0.94	2.09	3.29	4.68	3.52	3.52	4.82	3.72	2.21	1.24	0.80
1988	0.67	0.80	1.75	2.70	4.01	3.88	3.72	3.78	3.55	1.88	1.21	0.61
1989	0.82	0.80	1.99	3.05	4.19	4.44	3.98	4.57	3.43	2.32	1.61	0.75
1990	0.72	0.90	1.71	2.02	2.33	2.98	2.65	2.99	2.55	1.99	1.05	0.92

Table 7.17 Monthly Precipitation (in inches) for a Typical Nebraska City

23. Suppose a course has 15 students enrolled and five exams were given during the semester. Write a program that accepts each student's name and grades as input and places the names in a one-dimensional array and the grades in a two-dimensional array. The program should then display each student's name and semester average. Also, the program should display the median for each exam. (For an odd number of grades the median is the middle grade. For an even number of grades it is the average of the two middle grades.)

24. An n-by-n array is called a **magic square** if the sums of each row, each column, and each diagonal are equal. Write a program to determine if an array is a magic square and use it to determine if either of the arrays below is a magic square. ***Hint:*** If at any time one of the sums is not equal to the others, the search is complete.

(a)

1	15	15	4
12	6	7	9
8	10	11	5
13	3	2	16

(b)

11	10	4	23	17
18	12	6	5	24
25	19	13	7	1
2	21	20	14	8
9	3	22	16	15

25. A company has three stores (1, 2, and 3), and each store sells five items (1, 2, 3, 4, and 5). The tables below give the number of items sold by each store and category on a particular day, and the cost of each item.

(a) Place the data from the left-hand table in a two-dimensional array and the data from the right-hand table in a one-dimensional array.
(b) Compute and display the total dollar amount of sales for each store and for the entire company.

		Item				
		1	2	3	4	5
	1	25	64	23	45	14
Store	2	12	82	19	34	63
	3	54	22	17	43	35

Number of Items Sold During Day

Item	Cost
1	$12.00
2	$17.95
3	$95.00
4	$86.50
5	$78.00

Cost per Item

SOLUTIONS TO PRACTICE PROBLEMS 7.4

1. The subprogram FindCityNum can be used to determine the subscript associated with each city. This subprogram and the modified subprogram InputCities are as follows:

```
SUB FindCityNum (city$, num)
  SELECT CASE UCASE$(city$)
    CASE "CHICAGO"
      LET num = 1
    CASE "LOS ANGELES"
      LET num = 2
    CASE "NEW YORK"
      LET num = 3
    CASE "PHILADELPHIA"
      LET num = 4
  END SELECT
END SUB

SUB InputCities (row, col)
  REM Input origin and destination cities
  INPUT "Origin"; city$
  CALL FindCityNum(city$, row)
  INPUT "Destination"; city$
  CALL FindCityNum(city$, col)
END SUB
```

2. Both parallel arrays and two-dimensional arrays are used to hold related data. If some of the data are numeric and some are string, then parallel arrays must be used, since all entries of an array must be of the same type. Parallel arrays should also be used if the data will be sorted. Two-dimensional arrays are best suited to tabular data.

7.5 A CASE STUDY: CALCULATING WITH A SPREADSHEET

Spreadsheets are the most popular type of software used on personal computers. A spreadsheet is a financial planning tool in which data are analyzed in a table of rows and columns. Some of the items are entered by the user. Other items, often totals and balances, are calculated using the entered data. The outstanding feature of electronic spreadsheets is their ability to recalculate an entire table after changes are made in some of the entered data, thereby allowing the user to determine the financial implications of various alternatives. This is called "What if?" analysis.

Figure 7.8 contains an example of a spreadsheet used to analyze a student's financial projections for the four quarters of a year. Column 5 holds the sum of the entries in the other four columns, rows 4 and 10 hold sums of the entries in rows 1 through 3 and 5 through 9, respectively, and row 11 holds the differences of the entries in rows 4 and 10. Since the total balance is negative, some of the amounts in the spreadsheet must be changed and the totals and balances recalculated.

This case study develops a menu-driven program to produce a spreadsheet with the five columns of numbers shown in Figure 7.8, three user-specified categories of income, and five user-specified categories of expenses. The following three tasks are to be selected from a menu:

1. *Enter data*. The user is prompted for three income categories and five expense categories and for the amounts in each category for each quarter of the year. Then the program should calculate the amounts for totals and balances, display the complete spreadsheet, and display the menu below it horizontally.

2. *Alter data*. The user specifies each entry to be altered by giving its row, column, and new amount. After each change is entered, the amounts for the totals and balances should be recalculated and the total spreadsheet and menu displayed. The user is then prompted for further changes until he responds to the request for row, column, and new amount with 0, 0, 0.

3. *Quit*.

	1 Fall	**2 Winter**	**3 Spring**	**4 Summer**	**5 Total**
Income					
1 Job	1000	1300	1000	2000	5300
2 Parents	200	200	200	0	600
3 Scholarship	150	150	150	0	450
4 Total	1350	1650	1350	2000	6350
Expenses					
5 Tuition	400	0	400	0	800
6 Food	650	650	650	650	2600
7 Rent	600	600	600	400	2200
8 Books	110	0	120	0	230
9 Misc	230	210	300	120	860
10 Total	1990	1460	2070	1170	6690
11 Balance	–640	190	–720	830	–340

Figure 7.8 Spreadsheet for Student's Financial Projections

The 55 locations in the spreadsheet that hold amounts are called **cells**. Each cell is identified by its row and column numbers. For instance, the cell 10, 2 contains the amount 1460.

Designing the Spreadsheet Program

In keeping with the top-down approach to problem solving, we break the problem into a small number of basic tasks, each of which will then be broken down further. The first task is the setting up of the fixed labels. After that, a menu is presented with the following three options.

1. Create spreadsheet
2. Revise spreadsheet
3. Quit

The first two menu items are broken down into specific subtasks.

1. *Create spreadsheet.* To form the spreadsheet, we must request the income and expense categories and amounts from the user, calculate the totals and balances, and then display the resulting spreadsheet; that is, task 1 is divided into the following subtasks.

   1.1 Input income and expense categories
   1.2 Input income and expense amounts
   1.3 Calculate totals and balances
   1.4 Display spreadsheet

2. *Revise spreadsheet.* The user may request a change in just one of the cells by providing its row and column and the new amount. Then the program will recalculate all the totals and balances and display the revised spreadsheet. That is, task 2 is divided into the following subtasks.

   2.1 Input cell (row, column) and new amount
   2.2 Calculate totals and balances
   2.3 Display spreadsheet

   Notice that tasks 2.2 and 2.3 are the same as tasks 1.3 and 1.4. Since the subprogram that performs tasks 1.3 and 1.4 can also be used for tasks 2.2 and 2.3, respectively, considerable work is saved. Whenever possible, general-purpose subprograms such as these should be incorporated in the design of a program.

The next step in designing the program is to examine each of the subtasks identified above and decide which, if any, should be divided further into smaller tasks. The input tasks, 1.1, 1.2, and 2.1, are basic, so we won't divide them any further; but the calculate and display tasks, 1.3 and 1.4, are more involved. These subtasks can be broken down as follows.

1.3 *Calculate totals and balances.* This subtask requires computing income and expense totals for each of the time periods, computing balances for the time periods, and a "row total" corresponding to each income and expense category of the spreadsheet.

   1.3.1 Calculate income totals
   1.3.2 Calculate expense totals
   1.3.3 Calculate balance
   1.3.4 Calculate row totals

1.4 *Display spreadsheet.* To display the spreadsheet, we need to produce the table in Figure 7.8 that contains labels for the income and expense categories and time periods and has its data arranged in rows and columns.

1.4.1 Display labels
1.4.2 Display data

The top-down chart in Figure 7.9 shows the stepwise refinement of the problem. The items in the main part of the chart that are contained in rectangles have continuations below.

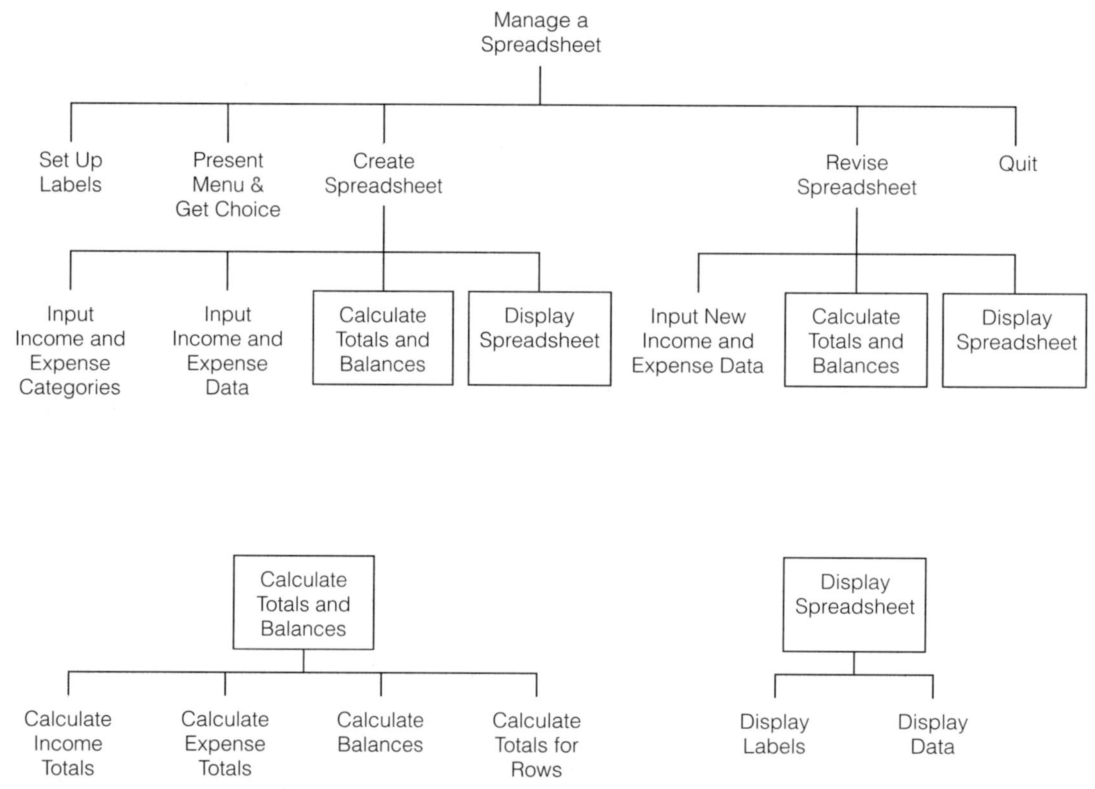

Figure 7.9 Top-Down Chart for Spreadsheet Case Study

Pseudocode for the Spreadsheet Program

The workhorse of the top-down chart is the third row. The following pseudocode shows how these tasks are carried out.

```
INPUT INCOME AND EXPENSE CATEGORIES (Subprogram InputCategories)
Clear the screen
FOR row counter from 1 to 3
   Prompt user for income label corresponding to row counter
NEXT
Display one blank line
FOR row counter from 5 to 9
   Prompt user for expense label corresponding to row counter
NEXT
```

```
INPUT INCOME AND EXPENSE DATA (Subprogram InputData)
Display two blank lines
FOR row counter from 1 to 3
   Prompt user for income data corresponding to row counter
NEXT
Display one blank line
FOR row counter from 5 to 9
   Prompt user for expense data corresponding to row counter
NEXT

CALCULATE TOTALS (Subprogram CalculateSpreadsheet)
Calculate income totals
Calculate expense totals
Calculate balances
Calculate row totals

DISPLAY SPREADSHEET (Subprogram DisplaySpreadsheet)
Display column labels
FOR row counter from 1 to 11
   IF row counter is 1 THEN
      Display income label
   END IF
   IF row counter is 5 THEN
      Display expenses label
   END IF
   IF row counter is 11 THEN
      Display blank line
   END IF
   Display row data
NEXT

INPUT NEW DATA (Subprogram InputNewData)
DO
   Input new data for spreadsheet
LOOP UNTIL data okay
```

Writing the Spreadsheet Program

Three arrays suffice to hold the spreadsheet. (See Table 7.18.) Three of the elements of the array rowLabel—the fourth (Total), 10th (Total), and 11th (Balance)—are fixed. The other elements of that array are the categories to be determined by the user. The column labels are all fixed. The data for all rows except 4, 10, and 11 must be entered by the user.

Arrays	Range	Information Held
rowLabel$()	1 TO 11	Job, Parents, . . . , Balance
colLabel$()	1 TO 5	Fall, Winter, . . . , Total
userData()	1 TO 11, 1 TO 5	Amounts in the 55 cells

Table 7.18 The Arrays That Hold the Spreadsheet

When values have been assigned to the three arrays, the totals are easily calculated with loops containing accumulators. Then the balances are calculated by performing subtractions.

After the user has entered the spreadsheet, he or she is presented with a menu of three options. The user can enter a completely new spreadsheet (with possibly different categories), revise selected data in the current spreadsheet, or quit. The first task is identical to the formation of the original spreadsheet and the last task is trivial.

After selecting the update option, the user is asked for a data entry to alter. The entry is specified by giving the location of the entry, namely its row and column, and the value of the entry. After the three responses are obtained, the program recalculates all the totals and balances. The user can continue to revise the spreadsheet to his heart's content. The user indicates that he or she is finished with the update by responding with 0, 0, 0.

Table 7.19 shows each task discussed above and the subprogram that carries out the task. The program follows.

1. InputSpreadsheet	InputSpreadsheet
1.1 Input income and expense categories	InputCategories
1.2 Input income and expense data	InputData
1.3 Calculate totals and balances	Calculate
1.3.1 Calculate income totals	CalculateIncomeTotals
1.3.2 Calculate expense totals	CalculateExpenseTotals
1.3.3 Calculate balances	CalculateBalances
1.3.4 Calculate row totals	CalculateRowTotals
1.4 Display spreadsheet	DisplaySpreadsheet
1.4.1 Display labels	
1.4.2 Display data	
2. Revise spreadsheet	ReviseSpreadsheet
2.1 Input new data	InputNewData
2.2 Calculate totals and balances	Calculate
2.3 Display spreadsheet	DisplaySpreadsheet
3. Quit	

Table 7.19 Tasks and Their Procedures

```
REM Spreadsheet Program
REM
REM ***********************************************************
REM *                                                         *
REM *        Variable Table                                   *
REM *                                                         *
REM *  choice          User's main menu choice (1, 2, or 3)   *
REM *  colLabel$()     Column labels (seasons and TOTAL)      *
REM *  entries()       Numeric data entered by user, totals   *
REM *  rowLabel$()     Row categories entered by user         *
REM *                                                         *
REM ***********************************************************
CLS
```

```
DIM colLabel$(1 TO 5), rowLabel$(1 TO 11), entries(1 TO 11, 1 TO 5)
CALL SetUpLabels(rowLabel$(), colLabel$())
DO
  CALL GetChoice(choice)
  SELECT CASE choice
    CASE 1
      CALL InputSpreadsheet(rowLabel$(), colLabel$(), entries())
    CASE 2
      CALL ReviseSpreadsheet(rowLabel$(), colLabel$(), entries())
    CASE 3
      PRINT "Have a nice day."
  END SELECT
LOOP UNTIL choice = 3
REM --- Data: column labels
DATA 1 Fall, 2 Winter, 3 Spring, 4 Summer, 5 Total
END

SUB Calculate (entries())
  REM Calculate totals and balances for spreadsheet
  CALL CalculateIncomeTotals(entries())
  CALL CalculateExpenseTotals(entries())
  CALL CalculateBalances(entries())
  CALL CalculateRowTotals(entries())
END SUB

SUB CalculateBalances (entries())
  REM Calculate balances
  FOR col = 1 TO 4
    LET entries(11, col) = entries(4, col) - entries(10, col)
  NEXT col
END SUB

SUB CalculateExpenseTotals (entries())
  REM Calculate total expenses
  FOR col = 1 TO 4
    LET total = 0
    FOR row = 5 TO 9
      LET total = total + entries(row, col)
    NEXT row
    LET entries(10, col) = total
  NEXT col
END SUB

SUB CalculateIncomeTotals (entries())
  REM Calculate total income
  FOR col = 1 TO 4
    LET total = 0
    FOR row = 1 TO 3
      LET total = total + entries(row, col)
    NEXT row
    LET entries(4, col) = total
  NEXT col
END SUB
```

```
SUB CalculateRowTotals (entries())
  REM Calculate totals for all rows
  FOR row = 1 TO 11
    LET total = 0
    FOR col = 1 TO 4
      LET total = total + entries(row, col)
    NEXT col
    LET entries(row, 5) = total
  NEXT row
END SUB

SUB DisplaySpreadsheet (rowLabel$(), colLabel$(), entries())
  REM Display all spreadsheet information
  CLS
  LET a$ = "              \      \  \      \  \      \  \      \  \       \"
  PRINT USING a$; colLabel$(1); colLabel$(2); colLabel$(3); colLabel$(4); colLabel$(5)
  LET a$ = "## \        \ ######    ######    ######    ######  #######"
  FOR row = 1 TO 11
    SELECT CASE row
      CASE 1
        PRINT "  Income"
      CASE 5
        PRINT
        PRINT "  Expenses"
      CASE 11
        PRINT
      CASE ELSE
    END SELECT
    REM The following two lines should be joined and entered as one line.
    PRINT USING a$; row; rowLabel$(row); entries(row, 1); entries(row, 2);
    entries(row, 3); entries(row, 4); entries(row, 5)
  NEXT row
END SUB

SUB EraseLines
  REM Erase two lines near bottom of screen
  LOCATE 21, 1
  PRINT TAB(79);
  LOCATE 22, 1
  PRINT TAB(79);
  LOCATE 21, 1
END SUB

SUB GetChoice (choice)
  REM Input user option for main menu
  LOCATE 21, 1
  PRINT "1. Enter data      2. Update data      3. Quit"
  DO
    LOCATE 22, 1
    INPUT "Number of choice: ", choice
  LOOP UNTIL (choice = 1) OR (choice = 2) OR (choice = 3)
END SUB
```

```
SUB InputCategories (rowLabel$(), colLabel$())
  REM Input category labels
  CLS
  PRINT "Income category"
  FOR row = 1 TO 3
    INPUT "Label"; rowLabel$(row)
  NEXT row
  LET rowLabel$(4) = "Total"
  PRINT
  PRINT "Expense category"
  FOR row = 5 TO 9
    INPUT "Label"; rowLabel$(row)
  NEXT row
  LET rowLabel$(10) = "Total"
  LET rowLabel$(11) = "Balance"
END SUB

SUB InputCategoryData (colLabel$(), entries(), row)
  REM Input amounts for one category
  FOR col = 1 TO 4
    PRINT USING "  \      \: "; colLabel$(col);
    INPUT "", entries(row, col)
  NEXT col
END SUB

SUB InputData (rowLabel$(), colLabel$(), entries())
  REM Input numeric data for entire spreadsheet
  PRINT
  PRINT
  FOR row = 1 TO 3
    PRINT "Enter each season's income from "; rowLabel$(row)
    CALL InputCategoryData(colLabel$(), entries(), row)
  NEXT row
  PRINT
  FOR row = 5 TO 9
    PRINT "Enter each season's expenses for "; rowLabel$(row)
    CALL InputCategoryData(colLabel$(), entries(), row)
  NEXT row
END SUB

SUB InputNewData (row, col, newData)
  REM Input row, column, and new amounts for spreadsheet update
  DO
    CALL EraseLines
    PRINT "Enter 0, 0, 0 to terminate"
    INPUT "Row, Column, New data: ", row, col, newData
  LOOP UNTIL (row >= 0) AND (row <= 10) AND (col >= 0) AND (col <= 4)
  CALL EraseLines
END SUB
```

```
SUB InputSpreadsheet (rowLabel$(), colLabel$(), entries())
  REM Input spreadsheet categories and amounts, and display totals
  CALL InputCategories(rowLabel$(), colLabel$())
  CALL InputData(rowLabel$(), colLabel$(), entries())
  CALL Calculate(entries())
  CALL DisplaySpreadsheet(rowLabel$(), colLabel$(), entries())
END SUB

SUB ReviseSpreadsheet (rowLabel$(), colLabel$(), entries())
  REM Input and change a single spreadsheet entry
  CALL InputNewData(row, col, newData)
  DO WHILE row <> 0
    LET entries(row, col) = newData
    CALL Calculate(entries())
    CALL DisplaySpreadsheet(rowLabel$(), colLabel$(), entries())
    CALL InputNewData(row, col, newData)
  LOOP
END SUB

SUB SetUpLabels (rowLabel$(), colLabel$())
  REM Initialize all pre-set labels
  FOR label = 1 TO 5
    READ colLabel$(label)
  NEXT label
END SUB
```

Chapter 7 Summary

1. For programming purposes, tabular data are most efficiently processed if stored in an *array*. The *ranges* of arrays are specified by DIM statements.
2. Two of the best known methods for ordering (or *sorting*) arrays are the *bubble sort* and the *Shell sort.*
3. Any array can be searched *sequentially* to find the subscript associated with a sought-after value. Ordered arrays can be searched most efficiently by a *binary search.*
4. A table can be effectively stored in a *two-dimensional array*.

Chapter 7 Programming Projects

1. Table 7.20 contains some lengths in terms of feet. Write a program that displays the nine different units of measure, requests the unit to convert

from, the unit to convert to, and the quantity to be converted, and then displays the converted quantity. A typical outcome is shown in Figure 7.10.

1 inch = .0833 feet	1 rod = 16.5 feet
1 yard = 3 feet	1 furlong = 660 feet
1 meter = 3.2815 feet	1 kilometer = 3281.5 feet
1 fathom = 6 feet	1 mile = 5280 feet

Table 7.20 Equivalent Lengths

```
1. inch       2. fathom    3. foot
4. furlong    5. kilometer 6. meter
7. mile       8. rod       9. yard

Convert from: 4
Convert to: 6
Length to be converted: 10
Converted length: 2011.275
```

Figure 7.10 Possible Outcome of Project 1

2. Statisticians use the concepts of **mean** and **standard deviation** to describe a collection of data. The mean is the average value of the items, and the standard deviation measures the spread or dispersal of the numbers about the mean. Formally, if $x_1, x_2, x_3, \ldots, x_n$ is a collection of data, then

$$m = \text{mean} = \frac{x_1 + x_2 + x_3 + \ldots + x_n}{n}$$

$$s = \text{standard deviation} = \sqrt{\frac{(x_1 - m)^2 + (x_2 - m)^2 + (x_3 - m)^2 + \ldots + (x_n - m)^2}{n - 1}}$$

Write a computer program to

(a) Place the exam scores 59, 60, 65, 75, 56, 56, 66, 62, 98, 72, 95, 71, 63, 77, 65, 77, 65, 59, 85, and 62 into an array.
(b) Calculate the mean and standard deviation of the exam scores.
(c) Assign letter grades to each exam score, ES, as follows:

$ES \geq m + 1.5s$	A
$m + .5s \leq ES < m + 1.5s$	B
$m - .5s \leq ES < m + .5s$	C
$m - 1.5s \leq ES < m - .5s$	D
$ES < m - 1.5s$	F

For instance, if m were 70 and s were 12, then grades of 88 or above would receive A's, grades between 76 and 87 would receive B's, and so on. A process of this type is referred to as *curving grades*.
(d) Display a list of the exam scores along with their corresponding grades.

3. *Rudimentary Translator.* Table 7.21 gives English words and their French and German equivalents. Store these words in DATA statements and read them into three parallel arrays, one for each language. Write a program that sorts all three arrays according to the array of English words. The program should then request an English sentence as input from the keyboard and translate it into French and German.

```
[sample run]
Enter an English sentence: MY PENCIL IS ON THE TABLE.
French translation: MON CRAYON EST SUR LA TABLE.
German translation: MEIN BLEISTIFT IST AUF DEM TISCH.
```

YES	OUI	JA	LARGE	GROS	GROSS
TABLE	TABLE	TISCH	NO	NON	NEIN
THE	LA	DEM	HAT	CHAPEAU	HUT
IS	EST	IST	PENCIL	CRAYON	BLEISTIFT
YELLOW	JAUNE	GELB	RED	ROUGE	ROT
FRIEND	AMI	FREUND	ON	SUR	AUF
SICK	MALADE	KRANK	AUTO	AUTO	AUTO
MY	MON	MEIN	OFTEN	SOUVENT	OFT

Table 7.21 English Words and Their French and German Equivalents

4. Write a program that allows a list of no more than 50 soft drinks and their percent growth during the last 5 years to be input and displays the information in two lists titled *gainers* and *losers*. Each list should be sorted by the *magnitude* of the percent change. Try your program on the 1996 data for the top 10 U.S. vendors in Table 7.22. ***Note:*** You will need to store the data initially in an array to determine the number of gainers and losers.

Brand	**% Growth**	**Brand**	**%Growth**
Coca-Cola Classic	20.8	Dr. Pepper	39.3
Caffeine Free Diet Coke	–9.0	Mountain Dew	65.3
Caffeine Free Diet Pepsi	–7.6	Pepsi-Cola	8.6
Diet Coke	9.6	7 Up	5.7
Diet Pepsie	1.3	Sprite	72.8

Table 7.22 Growth During the Last 5 Years of the Top 10 Soft Drinks of 1996
Source: Beverage World, March 1997

5. Each team in a six-team soccer league played each other team once. Table 7.23 shows the winners. Write a program to

(a) Place the team names in a one-dimensional array.
(b) Place the data from Table 7.23 in a two-dimensional array.
(c) Place the number of games won by each team in a one-dimensional array.
(d) Display a listing of the teams giving each team's name and number of games won. The list should be in decreasing order by the number of wins.

	Jazz	**Jets**	**Owls**	**Rams**	**Cubs**	**Zips**
Jazz	—	Jazz	Jazz	Rams	Cubs	Jazz
Jets	Jazz	—	Jets	Jets	Cubs	Zips
Owls	Jazz	Jets	—	Rams	Owls	Owls
Rams	Rams	Jets	Rams	—	Rams	Rams
Cubs	Cubs	Cubs	Owls	Rams	—	Cubs
Zips	Jazz	Zips	Owls	Rams	Cubs	—

Table 7.23 Soccer League Winners

6. A poker hand can be stored in a two-dimensional array. The statement

```
DIM hand(1 TO 4, 1 TO 13)
```

declares a 52-element array where the first dimension ranges over the four suits and the second dimension ranges over the thirteen denominations. A poker hand is specified by placing ones in the elements corresponding to the cards in the hand. See Figure 7.11.

Write a program that requests the five cards as input from the user, creates the related array, and passes the array to subprograms to determine the type of the hand: flush (all cards have the same suit), straight (cards have consecutive denominations—Ace can come either before 2 or after King), straight flush, four-of-a-kind, full house (3 cards of one denomination, 2 cards of another denomination), three-of-a-kind, two pairs, one pair, or none of the above.

	A	2	3	4	5	6	7	8	9	10	J	Q	K
Club	0	0	0	0	0	0	0	0	1	0	0	0	0
Diamond	1	0	0	0	0	0	0	0	0	0	0	0	0
Heart	1	0	0	0	0	0	0	0	0	0	0	1	0
Spade	0	0	0	0	1	0	0	0	0	0	0	0	0

Figure 7.11 Array for the Poker Hand A♥ A♦ 5♠ 9♣ Q♥

7. *Tic-Tac-Toe*. Write a program that "officiates" a game of tic-tac-toe. That is, the program should allow two players to alternate entering X's and O's into a tic-tac-toe board until either someone wins or a draw is reached. If one of the players wins, the program should announce the winner immediately; in case of a draw, the program should display "Cat's game." The players should enter their plays by row and column and the program should check that each play is valid. After a play, the screen should be cleared and the tic-tac-toe board redisplayed in its current state. ***Optional Enhancement:*** Allow the players to enter a number *n*. The program should officiate a best-of-*n* tournament, keeping track of the number of games won by each player until one of them wins more than half of the games. Ignore draws.

8. *Airline Reservations*. Write a reservation system for an airline flight. Assume the airplane has 10 rows with 4 seats in each row. Use a 2-dimensional array of strings to maintain a seating chart. In addition, create an array to be used as a waiting list in case the plane is full. The waiting list should be "first come, first served"—that is, people who are added early to the list get priority over those added later. Display a three-option menu.

(1) Add a passenger to the flight or waiting list.
  (a) Request the passenger's name.
  (b) Display a chart of the seats in the airplane in tabular form.
  (c) If seats are available, let the passenger choose a seat. Add the passenger to the seating chart.
  (d) If no seats are available, place the passenger in the waiting list.
(2) Remove a passenger from the flight
  (a) Request the passenger's name.
  (b) Search the seating chart for the passenger's name and delete it.
  (c) If the waiting list is empty, update the array so the seat is available.
  (d) If the waiting list is not empty, remove the first person from the list, and give him or her the newly vacated seat.
(3) Quit.

9. The Game of Life was invented by John H. Conway to model some genetic laws for birth, death, and survival. Consider a checkerboard consisting of an *n*-by-*n* array of squares. Each square can contain one individual (denoted by 1) or be empty (denoted by –). Figure 7.12(a) shows a 6-by-6 board with four of the squares occupied. The future of each individual depends on the number of his neighbors. After each period of time, called a *generation*, certain individuals will survive, others will die due to either loneliness or overcrowding, and new individuals will be born. Each nonborder square has eight neighboring squares. After each generation, the status of the squares changes as follows:

(a) An individual *survives* if there are two or three individuals in neighboring squares.
(b) An individual *dies* if he has more than three individuals or less than two in neighboring squares.
(c) A new individual is *born* into each empty square with exactly three individuals as neighbors.

Figure 7.12(b) shows the status after one generation. Write a program to do the following:

(a) Dimension an *n*-by-*n* array, where *n* is input by the user, to hold the status of each square in the current generation. To specify the initial configuration, have the user input each row as a string of length *n*, and break the row into 1s or dashes with MID$.
(b) Dimension an *n*-by-*n* array to hold the status of each square in the next generation. Compute the status for each square and produce the display in Figure 7.12(b). **Note:** The generation changes all at once. Only

current cells are used to determine which cells will contain individuals in the next generation.

(c) Assign the next-generation values to the current generation and repeat as often as desired.

(d) Display the number of individuals in each generation.

Hint: The hardest part of the program is determining the number of neighbors a cell has. In general, you must check a 3-by-3 square around the cell in question. Exceptions must be made when the cell is on the edge of the array. Don't forget that a cell is not a neighbor of itself.

(Test the program with the initial configuration shown in Figure 7.13. It is known as the figure-eight configuration and repeats after 8 generations.)

```
- - - - - -     - - - - - -
- - - - - -     - - 1 1 - -
- 1 1 1 1 -     - - 1 1 - -
- - - - - -     - - 1 1 - -
- - - - - -     - - - - - -
- - - - - -     - - - - - -
    (a)             (b)
```

Figure 7.12 Two Generations

```
- - - - - - - - - -
- - - - - - - - - -
- - 1 1 1 - - - - -
- - 1 1 1 - - - - -
- - 1 1 1 - - - - -
- - - - - 1 1 1 - -
- - - - - 1 1 1 - -
- - - - - 1 1 1 - -
- - - - - - - - - -
- - - - - - - - - -
```

Figure 7.13 The Figure Eight

8

Sequential Files

8.1 SEQUENTIAL FILES

In previous chapters, data processed by a program were either assigned to variables by LET statements, stored in DATA statements, or supplied by the user in response to INPUT statements. These methods are fine for small quantities of data that are to be used in only one program; however, large amounts of data, such as data that will be accessed by many different programs or data that will be updated (such as stock prices and class enrollments), must be kept on a disk. One means of storing data is a **sequential file**. In this section we create and use sequential files. The creation process physically records data onto a disk. These data can then be read from the disk and assigned to variables in much the same way as data are read from the keyboard in response to INPUT statements.

The extensions of file names are often used to indicate the type of file. For instance, files consisting of QBasic programs commonly have ".BAS" as their extension. The extension ".DAT" is customary for files consisting of data.

Figure 8.1 shows what a typical sequential file looks like on a disk. This particular file holds some people's names and their years of birth. The file has the name YOB.DAT. The two characters ♪ and ◙ stand for carriage return and line feed. The combination "carriage return, line feed" is a standard way of denoting the end of a line. For instance, we press the Enter key to end a line in a QBasic program. This sends carriage return and line feed characters to the screen, which cause the cursor to move to the beginning of the next row of the screen.

```
"Barbra",1942♪◙Ringo",1940♪◙"Sylvester",1946♪◙
```

Figure 8.1 Contents of the File YOB.DAT

Creating a Sequential File

There are many ways to organize data in a sequential file. The technique presented here is easy to implement. Other techniques are discussed in the comments.

1. Choose a DOS **file name**. A DOS file name is a string consisting of a base name of at most eight characters followed by an optional extension consisting of a period and at most three characters. Letters, digits, and a few other assorted characters (see Comment 1) can be used in either the name or the extension. Blank spaces are not allowed. Some examples of file names are INCOME.86, CUSTOMER.DAT, and FORT500.
2. Choose a number from 1 through 255 to be the **reference number** of the file. While the file is in use, it will be identified by this number.
3. Execute the statement

   `OPEN "`*`filespec`*`" FOR OUTPUT AS #`*`n`*

   where *n* is the reference number. This process is referred to as **opening a file for output**. It establishes a communications line between the computer and the disk drive for storing data *onto* the disk. It allows data to be output from the computer and recorded in the specified file.

4. Place data into the file with the WRITE# statement. If *a$* is a string, then the statement

```
WRITE #n, a$
```

writes the string *a$* surrounded by quotation marks into the file. If *c* is a number, then the statement

```
WRITE #n, c
```

writes the number *c*, without any leading or trailing spaces, into file number *n*. The statement

```
WRITE #n, a$, c
```

writes *a$* and *c* as before, but with a comma separating them. Similarly, if the statement WRITE #*n* is followed by a list of several strings and/or numbers separated by commas, then all the strings and numbers appear as before, separated by commas. After each WRITE# statement is executed, the characters ♪ and ◙ are placed into the file.

5. After all the data have been recorded in the file, execute

```
CLOSE #n
```

where *n* is the reference number. This statement breaks the communications line with the file and dissociates the number *n* from the file. This procedure is referred to as **closing a file**.

EXAMPLE 1 The WRITE statement, without the sharp sign (#), displays information on the screen in much the same way the WRITE# statement records information in a file. The following program illustrates the different aspects of the WRITE statement. Notice the absence of leading and trailing spaces for numbers and the presence of quotation marks surrounding strings.

```
REM Demonstrate use of WRITE statement
CLS
WRITE "ENIAC"
WRITE 1946
WRITE "ENIAC", 1946
LET a$ = "Eckert"
LET b$ = "Mauchly"
WRITE 14 * 139, "J.P. " + a$, b$, "John"
END

[run]
"ENIAC"
1946
"ENIAC",1946
1946,"J.P. Eckert","Mauchly","John"
```

EXAMPLE 2 Write a program to create the file of Figure 8.1. Use EOD as a sentinel to indicate that all the data have been read.

SOLUTION

```
REM Create the file YOB.DAT and record some data into it
OPEN "YOB.DAT" FOR OUTPUT AS #1     'Name file and assign a number
READ name$, year                    'Name, year of birth
DO WHILE name$ <> "EOD"             'Loop while data is left
  WRITE #1, name$, year
  READ name$, year                  'Read next collection of data
LOOP
CLOSE #1
REM --- Data: name, year of birth
DATA Barbra, 1942
DATA Ringo, 1940
DATA Sylvester, 1946
DATA EOD, 0
END
```

Adding Items to a Sequential File

Data can be added to the end of an existing sequential file with the following steps.

1. Choose a number from 1 through 255 to be the reference number for the file. It need not be the number that was used when the file was created.
2. Execute the statement

   OPEN "*filespec*" FOR APPEND AS #*n*

   where *n* is the reference number. This procedure is called **opening a file for append**. It allows data to be output from the computer and recorded at the end of the specified file.
3. Place data into the file with the WRITE# statement.
4. After all the data have been recorded into the file, close the file with the statement CLOSE #*n*.

EXAMPLE 3 The following program adds some data to the end of the file YOB.DAT. Figure 8.2 shows the contents of the file YOB.DAT after the program has been executed.

```
REM Record an additional item into the file YOB.DAT
CLS
OPEN "YOB.DAT" FOR APPEND AS #1
INPUT "Name, Year of Birth"; name$, year
WRITE #1, name$, year
CLOSE #1
END

[run]
Name, Year of Birth? Johnny, 1926
```

```
"Barbra",1942♪◙Ringo",1940♪◙"Sylvester",1946♪◙"Johnny",1926♪◙
```

Figure 8.2 Contents of the Appended File YOB.DAT

Reading Information from a Sequential File

Data stored in a sequential file can be read in order (that is, sequentially) and assigned to variables with the following steps.

1. Choose a number from 1 to 255 to be the reference number for the file. This need not be the number that was used when the file was recorded.
2. Execute the statement

   `OPEN "`*`filespec`*`" FOR INPUT AS #`*`n`*

   where *n* is the reference number. This procedure is referred to as **opening a file for input**. It establishes a communications line between the computer and the disk drive for reading data *from* the disk. Data can then be input from the specified file and assigned to variables in the program.
3. Read data from the file with the INPUT# statement. The INPUT# statement assigns data from a file to variables in much the same way that INPUT assigns data from the keyboard. Correct use of the INPUT# statement requires a knowledge of the WRITE# statement that recorded the data on the disk. The statement

   `INPUT #`*`n`*`, `*`var1`*`, `*`var2`*`, ...`

   assigns to each of the variables *var1*, *var2*, . . . one of the items of the file. (In the file, the items are separated by commas or the pair of characters "carriage return, line feed.") The variables in the INPUT# statement should be the same number and type (that is, string versus numeric) as the variables in the WRITE# statement that created the file.
4. After the desired items have been found or all the data have been read from the file, close the file with the statement CLOSE #*n*.

QBasic has a useful function, EOF, that tells us if we have reached the end of a file from which we are reading. At any time, the condition

`EOF(`*`n`*`)`

will be true if the end of file *n* has been reached, and false otherwise.

EXAMPLE 4 Write a program to display a table showing the ages in 1999 of the people in the sequential file YOB.DAT.

SOLUTION

```
REM Process data from YOB.DAT file to find ages in 1999
CLS
OPEN "YOB.DAT" FOR INPUT AS #1
PRINT "Name", "Age in 1994"
DO WHILE NOT EOF(1)              'Process the entire file
  INPUT #1, name$, year
  PRINT name$, 1994 - year       'Display name and age in 1994
LOOP
CLOSE #1
END

[run]
Name          Age in 1999
Barbra         57
Ringo          59
Sylvester      53
Johnny         73
```

The program in Example 4 illustrates the proper way to process a list of data contained in a file. The DO loop should be tested at the top with an end-of-file condition. (If the file is empty, no attempt is made to input data from the file.) The first set of data should be input *after* the DO statement and then the data should be processed. Figure 8.3 contains the pseudocode and flowchart for this technique.

DO WHILE there are still data in the file
  Get an item of data
  Process the item
LOOP

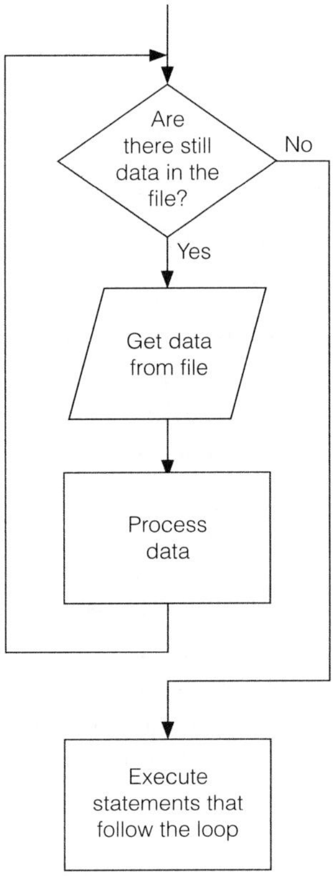

Figure 8.3 Pseudocode and Flowchart for Processing Data from a File

Sequential files can be quite large. Rather than list the entire contents, we typically search the file for a specific piece of information.

EXAMPLE 5 Write a program to search the file YOB.DAT for the year of birth of a specific person.

SOLUTION

```
REM Process data from YOB.DAT file for individual years of birth.
CLS
INPUT "Person (Capitalize first letter only)"; person$
OPEN "YOB.DAT" FOR INPUT AS #1
LET name$ = ""
DO WHILE (name$ <> person$) AND (NOT EOF(1))
  INPUT #1, name$, year
LOOP
IF name$ = person$ THEN
    PRINT person$; " was born in"; year
 ELSE
   PRINT person$; " is not in the file YOB.DAT"
END IF
CLOSE #1
END

[run]
Person (Capitalize first letter only)? Ringo
Ringo was born in 1940

[run]
Person (Capitalize first letter only)? Clint
Clint is not in the file YOB.DAT
```

Comments:

1. DOS file names can consist of digits, letters of the alphabet, and the characters & ! _ @ ' ' ~ ( ) { } – # % $.
2. A string variable can be used for the DOS file name in an OPEN statement. This is advantageous for programs that process data from several different data files. In response to an INPUT statement, the user can identify the data file to be processed.
3. Sequential files make efficient use of disk space and are easy to create and use. Their disadvantages are
   (a) often a large portion of the file must be read in order to find one specific item, and
   (b) an individual item of the file cannot be changed or deleted easily. A new file must be created by reading each item from the original file and recording it, with the single item changed or deleted, into the new file.

   Another type of file, known as a **random-access file**, has neither of the disadvantages of sequential files; however, random-access files typically use more disk space, require greater effort to program, and are not flexible in the variety and format of the stored data. Random-access files are discussed in Chapter 9.

4. The EOF function serves the same role for a file that a trailer value (such as EOD or –1) does for a set of DATA statements. However, there are some important differences. You must first READ a data item before you can check for the trailer value, but you can (and should) use the EOF function before inputting any items from a file. The condition EOF is true if the file is empty or after the last item of the file is input, whereas the trailer value *is* the last item of the file.

5. The following program illustrates a common error in reading a sequential file. The last item in the file will not be processed. Also, if the file has no data in it, then the fourth line will produce the error message "Input past end of file."

```
REM Display names of people born in 1946
CLS
OPEN "YOB.DAT" FOR INPUT AS #1
INPUT #1, name$, year
DO WHILE NOT EOF(1)
  IF year = 1946 THEN
      PRINT name$
  END IF
  INPUT #1, name$, year
LOOP
CLOSE #1
END
```

6. Consider the sequential file of Figure 8.1. This file is said to consist of three records of two fields each. A **record** holds all the data about a single individual. Each item of data is called a **field**. The three records are

```
Barbra, 1942
Ringo, 1940
Sylvester, 1946
```

and the two fields are

```
name field, year of birth field
```

7. The statement CLOSE, without any reference numbers, closes all open files.

8. The APPEND option for OPENing a file is intended to add data to an already existing file. However, it also can be used to create a new file.

9. Normally, at most four files can be open at any one time. (If the program contains no LPRINT statement, then five files can be open.) This limit can be raised with DOS.

10. ***Caution:*** If an existing sequential file is opened for output, the computer will erase the existing data and create a new empty file.

11. The program in the appendix to this chapter displays the contents of a file on the screen *exactly* as it appears on the disk. (Even the carriage return and line feed characters are displayed.) The output of this program resembles Figures 8.1 and 8.2. Another way to view the contents of a sequential file is to exit to DOS and then execute TYPE *filespec* from DOS. (In this case, *filespec* should not be enclosed in quotation marks.) The contents will appear on the screen, but the carriage return and line feed characters will not be displayed. Instead, the "carriage return, line feed" pair will move the cursor to the next line.

12. The screen and printer can be opened as sequential files. The following program allows the user to select the device to receive the output.

```
CLS
INPUT "Enter device to receive output (CON or PRN): "; device$
OPEN device$ FOR OUTPUT AS #1
IF device$ = "CON" THEN
    WRITE #1, "Hi, screen."
  ELSE
    WRITE #1, "Hi, printer."
END IF
CLOSE #1
END
```

This feature is also useful for debugging programs that send output to the printer. Initially respond with "CON". Then the OPEN statement will send output to the screen. After the program has been debugged, respond with "PRN" and the output will be sent to the printer.

PRACTICE PROBLEMS 8.1

1. Compose a program to delete the record for Ringo from the file YOB.DAT.
2. Compose a program to add data to the end of the file YOB.DAT in response to user input. Use a trailer value to terminate the addition of data.

EXERCISES 8.1

In Exercises 1 through 4, determine the screen output of the program.

1.
```
OPEN "GREETING" FOR OUTPUT AS #1
WRITE #1, "Hello"
WRITE #1, "Aloha"
CLOSE #1
OPEN "GREETING" FOR INPUT AS #1
INPUT #1, g$
PRINT g$
CLOSE #1
END
```

2.
```
OPEN "GREETING" FOR OUTPUT AS #2
WRITE #2, "Hello", "Aloha"
CLOSE #2
OPEN "GREETING" FOR INPUT AS #1
INPUT #1, g$, h$
PRINT h$
CLOSE #1
END
```

3.
```
OPEN "GREETING" FOR OUTPUT AS #2
WRITE #2, "Hello"
WRITE #2, "Aloha"
WRITE #2, "Bon Jour"
CLOSE #2
OPEN "GREETING" FOR INPUT AS #1
DO WHILE NOT EOF(1)
  INPUT #1, g$
  PRINT g$
LOOP
CLOSE #1
END
```

4. Assume the file GREETING has been created by the program in Exercise 3. The contents of the file are shown in Figure 8.4.

```
LET file$ = "GREETING"
OPEN file$ FOR APPEND AS #3
WRITE #3, "Buenos Dias"
CLOSE #3
OPEN file$ FOR INPUT AS #3
FOR salutation = 1 TO 4
  INPUT #3, g$
  PRINT g$
NEXT salutation
CLOSE #3
END
```

```
"Hello"♪◙"Aloha"♪◙"Bon Jour"♪◙
```

Figure 8.4 Contents of the File "GREETING" after Exercise 3.

5. Assume the file GREETING has been created by the program in Exercise 3. What is the effect of the following program?

```
OPEN "GREETING" FOR INPUT AS #1
OPEN "WELCOME" FOR OUTPUT AS #2
DO WHILE NOT EOF(1)
  INPUT #1, g$
  IF g$ <> "Aloha" THEN
      WRITE #2, g$
  END IF
LOOP
CLOSE
END
```

6. Assume the file YOB.DAT has been created by the program in Example 2. What is the effect of the following program?

```
OPEN "YOB.DAT" FOR INPUT AS #1
OPEN "YOB2.DAT" FOR OUTPUT AS #2
LET flag = 0
LET name$ = ""
DO WHILE (name$ < "Clint") AND (NOT EOF(1))
  INPUT #1, name$, year
  IF name$ >= "Clint" THEN
      WRITE #2, "Clint", 1930
      LET flag = 1
  END IF
  WRITE #2, name$, year
LOOP
DO WHILE NOT EOF(1)
  INPUT #1, name$, year
  WRITE #2, name$, year
LOOP
```

```
IF flag = 0 THEN
    WRITE #2, "Clint", 1930
END IF
CLOSE
END
```

In Exercises 7 through 12, identify the errors. Assume the files GREETING and YOB.DAT have been created by Exercise 3 and Example 2, respectively. (See Figures 8.4 and 8.1.)

7.
```
OPEN YOB.DAT FOR APPEND AS #1
WRITE #1, "Michael"
CLOSE #1
END
```

8.
```
OPEN "YOB.DAT" FOR OUTPUT AS #2
INPUT #2, name$, year
PRINT year
CLOSE #2
END
```

9.
```
OPEN "GREETING" FOR INPUT AS #1
FOR i = 1 TO EOF(1)
  INPUT #1, g$
  PRINT g$
NEXT i
CLOSE #1
END
```

10.
```
OPEN "GREETING" FOR INPUT AS #1
DO WHILE NOT EOF
  INPUT #1, g$
  PRINT g$
LOOP
CLOSE #1
END
```

11.
```
OPEN "GREETING" FOR INPUT AS #1
READ name$
OPEN name$ FOR OUTPUT AS #2
DO WHILE NOT EOF(1)
  INPUT #1, g$
  WRITE #2, g$
LOOP
CLOSE
REM --- Data: file name
DATA NEW.GREET.DAT
END
```

12.
```
OPEN "GREETING" FOR INPUT AS #1
CLOSE "GREETING"
END
```

13. Which of the following are valid file names or filespecs?

(a) ACCOUNTS.REC
(b) B:SALES.87
(c) QUESTION.???
(d) 123.DAT
(e) INVENTORY.DAT
(f) A:PRINT

14. Correct the program in Comment 5.

Exercises 15 through 22 are related and use the data in Table 8.1. The file created in Exercise 15 should be used in Exercises 16 through 22.

15. Create the sequential file COWBOY containing the information in Table 8.1. The file should appear on disk as shown in Figure 8.5.

Colt Peacemaker	$12.20
Holster	2.00
Levi Strauss Jeans	1.35
Saddle	40.00
Stetson	10.00

Table 8.1 Prices Paid by Cowboys for Certain Items in Mid-1800s

```
"Colt Peacemaker",12.2♪◙"Holster",2♪◙"Levi Strauss Jeans",1.35...
```

Figure 8.5 COWBOY File

16. Write a program to display all items in the file COWBOY that cost more than $10.

17. Write a program to add the data *Winchester rifle, 20.50* to the end of the file COWBOY.

18. Suppose an order is placed for 3 Colt Peacemakers, 2 Holsters, 10 pairs of Levi Strauss Jeans, 1 Saddle, and 4 Stetsons. Write a program to

(a) Create the sequential file ORDER to hold the numbers 3, 2, 10, 1, 4.
(b) Use the files COWBOY and ORDER to display a sales receipt with three columns, giving the name of each item, the quantity ordered, and the cost for that quantity.
(c) Compute the total cost of the items and display it at the end of the sales receipt.

19. Write a program to request an additional item and price from the user. Then create a sequential file called COWBOY.2 containing all the information in the file COWBOY with the additional item (and price) inserted in its proper alphabetical sequence. Run the program for both of the following data items: *Boots, 20* and *Horse, 35.*

20. Suppose the price of saddles is reduced by 20%. Use the file COWBOY to create a sequential file, COWBOY.3, containing the new price list.

21. Write a program to create a sequential file called COWBOY.4, containing all the information in the file COWBOY except for the data *Holster, 2.*

22. Write a program to allow additional items and prices to be input by the user and added to the end of the file COWBOY. Include a method to terminate the process.

23. Suppose the file YOB.DAT contains many names and years and that the names are in alphabetical order. Write a program that requests a name as input and either gives the person's age or reports that the person is not in the file. ***Note:*** Since the names are in alphabetical order, usually there is no need to search to the end of the file.

24. Suppose the file YOB.DAT contains many names and years. Write a program that creates two files, called SENIORS and JUNIORS, and copies all the data on people born before 1940 into the file SENIORS and the data on the others into the file JUNIORS.

25. A publisher maintains two sequential files, HARDBACK.INV and PAPERBCK.INV. Each record consists of the name of a book and the quantity in stock. Write a program to access these files. (The program should allow for the case where the book is not in the file.) A sample output of the program should be

```
[run]
Title of book? Gone with the Wind
Hardback or Paperback (H or P)? P
Number of copies in inventory is 6789
```

SOLUTIONS TO PRACTICE PROBLEMS 8.1

1. An individual item of data cannot be erased from a sequential file. Our only recourse is to create a second file that is identical to the first but with the record for Ringo missing. The following program will accomplish this task.

```
REM Remove Ringo's record from file YOB.DAT
OPEN "YOB.DAT" FOR INPUT AS #1
OPEN "YOB2.DAT" FOR OUTPUT AS #2
DO WHILE NOT EOF(1)
  INPUT #1, name$, year
  IF name$ <> "Ringo" THEN
      WRITE #2, name$, year
  END IF
LOOP
CLOSE #1
CLOSE #2
END
```

   We have accomplished the spirit of the request, if not the exact request. We can do a little better by adding the following two lines before the END statement. (The commands KILL and NAME were discussed in Chapter 1.)

```
KILL "YOB.DAT"
NAME "YOB2.DAT" AS "YOB.DAT"
```

2.
```
REM Record additional items into the file YOB.DAT
CLS
PRINT "Enter *, 0 when finished adding names."
OPEN "YOB.DAT" FOR APPEND AS #1
INPUT "Name, Year of Birth"; name$, year
DO WHILE name$ <> "*"
  WRITE #1, name$, year
  INPUT "Name, Year of Birth"; name$, year
LOOP
CLOSE #1
END
```

8.2 USING SEQUENTIAL FILES

In addition to being accessed for information, sequential files are regularly updated by modifying certain pieces of data, removing some records, and adding new records. These tasks can be performed most efficiently if the files are first sorted.

Sorting Sequential Files

The records of a sequential file can be sorted on any field by first reading the data into parallel arrays and then sorting on a specific array.

EXAMPLE 1 Compose a program to sort the sequential file YOB.DAT of the previous section by year of birth.

SOLUTION

```
REM Sort data from YOB.DAT file by year of birth
CLS
LET numPeople = 4              'Number of people in file
DIM name$(1 TO numPeople), year(1 TO numPeople)
CALL ReadData(name$(), year(), numPeople)
CALL SortData(name$(), year(), numPeople)
CALL WriteData(name$(), year(), numPeople)
END

SUB ReadData (name$(), year(), numPeople)
  REM Read data from file into arrays
  OPEN "YOB.DAT" FOR INPUT AS #1
  FOR index = 1 TO numPeople
    INPUT #1, name$(index), year(index)
  NEXT index
  CLOSE #1
END SUB

SUB SortData (name$(), year(), numPeople)
  REM Bubble sort arrays by year of birth
  FOR passNum = 1 TO numPeople - 1
    FOR index = 1 TO numPeople - passNum
      IF year(index) > year(index + 1) THEN
          CALL SwapData(name$(), year(), index)
      END IF
    NEXT index
  NEXT passNum
END SUB

SUB SwapData (name$(), year(), index)
  REM Swap names and years
  SWAP name$(index), name$(index + 1)
  SWAP year(index), year(index + 1)
END SUB

SUB WriteData (name$(), year(), numPeople)
  REM Write data back into file
  OPEN "YOB.DAT" FOR OUTPUT AS #1
  FOR i = 1 TO numPeople
    WRITE #1, name$(i), year(i)
  NEXT i
  CLOSE #1
END SUB
```

If the program from Example 4 of Section 8.1 is executed after running the program in Example 1, the output will be

```
Name         Age in 1999
Johnny        73
Ringo         59
Barbra        57
Sylvester     53
```

Merging Sequential Files

In Section 7.2 we considered an algorithm for merging two arrays. This same algorithm can be applied to merging two ordered files, provided each file ends with a trailer value. (Relying on the EOF function instead of trailer values requires contorted code.) Trailer values are easily added after opening the files FOR APPEND.

Suppose you have two ordered files (possibly with certain items appearing in both files) ending with the same trailer value, and you want to merge them into a third ordered file (without duplications). The technique for creating the third file is as follows.

1. Add a trailer value to the end of each file.
2. Open the two ordered files FOR INPUT and open a third file FOR OUTPUT.
3. Get the first item from each file.
4. Repeat steps (a) and (b) below until one of the items retrieved is a trailer value.
   (a) If one item precedes the other, write it into the third file and get the next item from its file.
   (b) If the two items are identical, write one into the third file and get the next item from each of the two ordered files.
5. At this point, the item most recently retrieved from one file may not be the trailer value. In this case, write that item and all remaining items preceding the trailer value to the third file.
6. Close the three files.

EXAMPLE 2 The following program merges two ordered files of numbers into a third file.

```
REM Merge two ordered files
CLS
INPUT "Name of first file"; file1$
INPUT "Name of second file"; file2$
INPUT "Name of merged file"; file3$
LET trailer = -1
OPEN file1$ FOR APPEND AS #1
OPEN file2$ FOR APPEND AS #2
WRITE #1, trailer
WRITE #2, trailer
CLOSE #1, #2
```

```
OPEN file1$ FOR INPUT AS #1
OPEN file2$ FOR INPUT AS #2
OPEN file3$ FOR OUTPUT AS #3
INPUT #1, num1
INPUT #2, num2
DO WHILE num1 <> trailer AND num2 <> trailer
  SELECT CASE num1
    CASE IS < num2
      WRITE #3, num1
      INPUT #1, num1
    CASE IS > num2
      WRITE #3, num2
      INPUT #2, num2
    CASE num2
      WRITE #3, num1
      INPUT #1, num1
      INPUT #2, num2
  END SELECT
LOOP
DO WHILE num1 <> trailer
  WRITE #3, num1
  INPUT #1, num1
LOOP
DO WHILE num2 <> trailer
  WRITE #3, num2
  INPUT #2, num2
LOOP
CLOSE #1, #2, #3
END
```

Control-Break Processing

Suppose a small real estate company stores its sales data for a year in a sequential file in which each record contains four fields: month of sale (1 through 12), day of sale (1 through 31), address, price. Typical data for the sales of the first quarter of a year are shown in Figure 8.6. The records are ordered by date of sale.

Month	Day	Address	Price
January	9	102 Elm Street	$203,000
January	20	1 Main Street	$315,200
January	25	5 Maple Street	$123,450
February	15	1 Center Street	$100,000
February	23	2 Vista Drive	$145,320
March	15	205 Rodeo Circle	$389,100

Figure 8.6 Real Estate Sales for First Quarter of Year

Figure 8.7 shows the output of a program that displays the total sales for the quarter year, with a subtotal for each month.

```
[run]
January   9      102 Elm Street       $203,000
January  20      1 Main Street        $315,200
January  25      5 Maple Street       $123,450

           Subtotal for January:      $641,650

February 15      1 Center Street      $100,000
February 23      2 Vista Drive        $145,320

           Subtotal for February:     $245,320

March    15      205 Rodeo Circle     $389,100

           Subtotal for March:        $389,100

Total for First Quarter: $1,276,070
```

Figure 8.7 Output of Example 3

A program to produce the output of Figure 8.7 must calculate a subtotal at the end of each month. The variable holding the month triggers a subtotal whenever its value changes. Such a variable is called a **control variable** and each change of its value is called a **break**.

EXAMPLE 3 Write a program to produce the output of Figure 8.7. Assume the data of Figure 8.6 are stored in the sequential file HOMESALE.DAT.

SOLUTION The following program allows for months with no sales. Since monthly subtotals will be printed, the month-of-sale field is an appropriate control variable.

```
REM Display home sales by month
CLS
OPEN "HOMESALE.DAT" FOR INPUT AS #1
LET format$ = "\       \ ##       \                \ $###,###"
LET format2$ = "           Subtotal for \       \    $###,###"
LET month = 0
LET month$ = ""
LET done = 0                   'Flag to indicate end of list
DO WHILE done = 0
  IF NOT EOF(1) THEN
      INPUT #1, newMonth$, day, addr$, price
    ELSE
      LET done = 1             'End of list
  END IF
```

```
    IF (newMonth$ <> month$) OR (done = 1) THEN  'Control break processing
        IF month >= 1 THEN                       'Don't print on first month
            PRINT
            PRINT USING format2$; month$ + ":"; monthTotal
            PRINT
        END IF
        LET month$ = newMonth$
        LET month = month + 1
        LET monthTotal = 0
    END IF
    IF done = 0 THEN
        PRINT USING format$; newMonth$; day; addr$; price
        LET yearTotal = yearTotal + price
    END IF
    LET monthTotal = monthTotal + price
LOOP
CLOSE #1
PRINT USING "Total for First Quarter: $#,###,###"; yearTotal
END
```

Comments:

1. DOS has a command called SORT that orders the records of a sequential file. The command

   `SORT <filename1 >filename2`

   sorts the records of the first file in ascending order by the first field and places them into a new file called *filename2*. The DOS command

   `SORT <filename1 >filename2  /R`

   produces a descending sort.

PRACTICE PROBLEMS 8.2

1. The program in Example 2 contains three DO loops. Explain why at most one of the last two loops will be executed. Under what circumstances will neither of the last two loops be executed?
2. Modify the program in Example 2 so that duplicate items will be repeated in the merged file.

EXERCISES 8.2

Exercises 1 through 4 are related. They create and maintain the sequential file AVERAGE.DAT to hold batting averages of baseball players.

1. Suppose the season is about to begin. Compose a program to create the sequential file containing the name of each player, his times at bat, and his number of hits. The names should be entered by input statements, and the times at bat and number of hits initially should be set to 0.

2. Each day, the statistics from the previous day's games should be used to update the file. Write a program to read the records one at a time and allow the user to enter the number of times at bat and the number of hits in yesterday's game for each player in response to INPUT statements. The program should update the file by adding these numbers to the previous figures.

3. Several players are added to the league. Compose a program to update the file.

4. Compose a program to sort the file AVERAGE.DAT with respect to batting averages and display the players with the top ten batting averages. ***Hint:*** The file must be read once to determine the number of players and again to load the players into an array.

Exercises 5 and 6 refer to the ordered file BLOCK.DAT containing the names of people on your block and the ordered file TIMES.DAT containing the names of all people who subscribe to the *New York Times***.**

5. Write a program that creates a file consisting of the names of all people on your block who subscribe to the *New York Times*.

6. Write a program that creates a file consisting of the names of all *New York Times* subscribers who do not live on your block.

7. Suppose a file of positive integers is in ascending order. Write a program to determine the maximum number of times any integer is repeated in the file. (For instance, if the entries in the file are 5, 5, 6, 6, 6, and 10, then the output is 3.)

8. Suppose each record of the file SALES.DAT contains a salesperson's name and the dollar amount of a sale, and the records are ordered by the names. Write a program to display the name, number of sales, and average sale amount for each salesperson. For instance, if the first four records of the file are

```
"Adams",123.45
"Adams",432.15
"Brown",89.95
"Cook",500.00
```

then the first two entries of the output would be

```
Salesperson     Number of Sales     Average Sale Amount
Adams           2                   $ 277.80
Brown           1                   $  89.95
```

9. An elementary school holds a raffle to raise funds. Suppose each record of the file RAFFLE.DAT contains a student's grade (1 through 6), name, and the number of raffle tickets sold, and that the records are ordered by grade. Write a program using a control break to display the number of tickets sold by each grade and the total number of tickets sold.

10. *Multiple Control Breaks.* Suppose the sorted sequential file CENSUS.DAT contains names of all residents of a state, where each record has the form

"lastName","firstName". Write a program to determine, in one pass through the file, the most common last name and most common full name. (***Note:*** In the unlikely event of a tie, the program should display the first-occurring name.) For instance, the output might be as follows.

```
[run]
The most common last name is Brown
The most common full name is John Smith
```

In Exercises 11 and 12, suppose the file MASTER contains the names and phone numbers of all members of an organization, where the records are ordered by name.

11. Suppose the ordered file MOVED contains the names and new phone numbers of all members who have changed their phone numbers. Write a program to update the file MASTER.

12. Suppose the ordered file QUIT contains the names of all members who have left the organization. Write a program to update the file MASTER.

13. Suppose a file must be sorted by QBasic but is too large to fit into an array. How can this be accomplished?

14. What are some advantages of files over arrays?

15. Do the following steps at the computer.

(a) Create a sequential file HOMES containing the five records Huron, Ontario, Michigan, Erie, and Superior in the given order.
(b) Execute the command Exit from the Files menu. You will now be in DOS. (If you are in Windows, invoke DOS.)
(c) Enter the command TYPE HOMES to see the Great Lakes displayed in the given order. Their first letters should spell HOMES.
(d) Enter the command SORT <HOMES >HOMES2 to order the great lakes.
(e) Enter TYPE HOMES2 to see the Great Lakes displayed in alphabetical order.

SOLUTIONS TO PRACTICE PROBLEMS 8.2

1. Execution proceeds beyond the first DO loop only after a trailer value is read from one of the input files. Since each of the following DO loops executes only if the trailer value of the associated file was *not* read, at most one loop can execute.

Neither of the loops will be executed if each input file contains only the trailer value or if the last entries of the files are the same.

2. Change the SELECT CASE block to the following:

```
SELECT CASE num1
  CASE IS <= num2
    WRITE #3, num1
    INPUT #1, num1
  CASE IS > num2
    WRITE #3, num2
    INPUT #2, num2
END SELECT
```

8.3 A CASE STUDY: CREATING A RECEIPT

Most supermarkets have automated check-out counters. Scanners read coded information on each item and send the information to a computer that produces an itemized receipt after all the items have been scanned. This case study develops a program to produce an itemized check-out receipt after all the coded information has been entered.

The standard code is the Universal Product Code (UPC), which consists of a sequence of 10 digits appearing below a rectangle of bars. (See Figure 8.8.) The bars have these digits encoded in a form that can be read by an optical scanner. The first five digits encode the manufacturer and the second five specify the product and the size of the package. The digits 37000 00430 appear on a jar of peanut butter. The string 37000 is the code for Procter & Gamble and 00430 is Procter & Gamble's code for a 22-ounce jar of creamy Jif peanut butter. Of course, the string 00430 will have an entirely different meaning for another manufacturer.

37000 00430

Figure 8.8 Universal Product Code

Suppose a supermarket carries four thousand items and a sequential file called MASTER.DAT holds a record for each item consisting of the following information: the UPC, the name of the item, the price. Let us also assume the file has been sorted by the UPC for each record and that the file ends with a sentinel record whose fictitious UPC is greater than any actual UPC. (***Note***: The use of a sentinel is a common practice when an entire file will be read sequentially. The advantage of using a sentinel, as opposed to relying solely on EOF, will become apparent when the program is written.) For instance, the file might contain the following data for three food items.

```
"3700000430","22-oz Jif Peanut Butter",1.76
"4119601012","19-oz Prog Minn Soup",1.19
"7073405307","2.5 oz CS Cinn Rose Tea",1.65
"9999999999","Sentinel",0
```

We wish to write a program that will accept as input UPC codes entered from the keyboard and produce as output a printed itemized receipt. One way to proceed would be to take each UPC as it is input into the computer and then search for it in the master file to find the item description and price. We then would have to search sequentially through a long file many times. A better way to proceed is to first store the input UPCs in an array and then sort the array in increasing order, the same order as the master file. Then the information can be located in just one sequential pass through the master file.

The program must be able to handle the special case in which a UPC code entered is not in the master file. Suppose the first array item, after the array of UPCs has been sorted, is not in the master file. Then its UPC will never equal one of the UPCs in the master file. At some point during the sequential pass through the master file the array UPC will be less than the most recently read UPC from the master file. This indicates that the UPC is not in the master file and that the user must be informed of this fact. After the array of UPCs has been sorted, the search algorithm is as follows.

1. Begin with the first (lowest) array item. (It is most likely higher than the first UPC in the master file.)
2. Read records from the master file until the record is found whose UPC matches or exceeds the array UPC.
3. If the master file UPC matches the array UPC, then print the corresponding description and price of the item from the master file and add the price to the running total. Otherwise, print a message stating that the item is not in the master file.
4. Repeat steps 2 and 3 for each element of the array.

Designing the Supermarket Check-Out Program

The major tasks of the program are as follows:

1. *Input UPC codes from the keyboard* (and count number of items). Task 1 uses a loop that requests the UPCs of the items purchased. A counter should keep track of the number of items purchased and a sentinel should indicate when all the UPCs have been entered.
2. *Sort the array of UPC codes into ascending order.* Task 2 can be accomplished with a bubble sort, since the array is small.
3. *Create an itemized receipt.* Task 3 can be divided into smaller subtasks. After the master file is opened, the file is searched sequentially for the triplet holding the first array UPC. If this record is found, the item name and price are printed and the price is added to the total. Then the second item is looked for in the same manner. This process continues until all possible items and prices have been printed. Of course, any unlocatable item must be reported. Finally, the total price is printed and the master file is closed. That is, task 3 is divided into the following subtasks:

   3.1 Open the master file.
   3.2 Search for array UPCs in the master file.
   3.3 Print an itemized receipt.
   3.4 Close the master file.

   Figure 8.9 shows the top-down chart for the program.

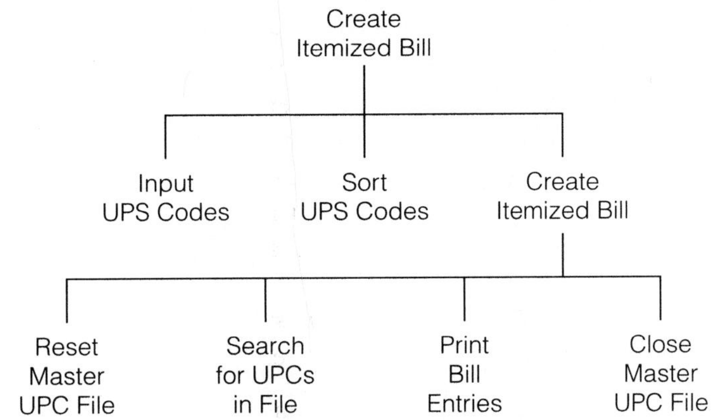

Figure 8.9 Top-Down Chart for the Supermarket Check-Out Program

Pseudocode for the Supermarket Check-Out Program

```
INPUT UPC CODES (Subprogram InputCodes)
Initialize numItems counter to 0
Prompt user for input
DO WHILE there are more items to be entered
   Read the UPC into the current array element
   Increment numItems
   Prompt user for more input
LOOP

SORT UPC CODES (Subprogram SortCodes)
FOR passNum = 1 TO numItems – 1
   FOR i = 1 TO numItems – passNum
      IF the ith array UPC is greater than the (i+1)th THEN
         Switch the ith and (i+1)th array elements
      END IF
   NEXT i
NEXT passNum

CREATE ITEMIZED RECEIPT (Subprogram MakeReceipt)
Open the master file
Initialize total to 0
Read first triplet from the master file
FOR i = 1 TO numItems
   DO WHILE item i's UPC > the current file UPC
      Read the next record from the master file
   LOOP
   IF item i's UPC = the file UPC THEN
         Print the corresponding item description and price
         Increase total by price
      ELSE
         Print that the UPC is not in the master file
   END IF
NEXT i
Print total
Close the master file
```

Writing the Supermarket Check-Out Program

Table 8.2 shows each of the tasks discussed above and the procedure used to perform the task.

	Task	Procedure
1.	Input UPCs and count number of items	InputCodes
2.	Sort the array of UPCs into ascending order	SortCodes
3.	Create itemized receipt	MakeReceipt

Table 8.2 Tasks and Their Procedures

The following program loads the purchased items into an array, sorts the array, and then carries out the search algorithm. A sample run is presented.

```
REM Print out an itemized grocery bill
REM
REM ***********************************************************
REM *                                                         *
REM * itemUPC$()  Array of UPC's for the items purchased      *
REM * numItems    Counts the number of items purchased        *
REM *                                                         *
REM ***********************************************************
REM
DIM itemUPC$(1 TO 100)
CLS
CALL InputCodes(itemUPC$(), numItems)
CALL SortCodes(itemUPC$(), numItems)
CALL MakeReceipt(itemUPC$(), numItems)
END

SUB InputCodes (itemUPC$(), numItems)
  REM Fill the array with UPC codes for items purchased
  LET numItems = 0
  PRINT "Enter * when all items have been entered."
  PRINT
  INPUT "Enter UPC code of item: ", code$
  DO WHILE code$ <> "*"
    LET numItems = numItems + 1
    LET itemUPC$(numItems) = code$
    INPUT "Enter UPC code of item: ", code$
  LOOP
END SUB

SUB MakeReceipt (itemUPC$(), numItems)
  REM Output store receipt
  REM total      Total cost of all purchases
  REM code$      UPC at the current file position
  REM descr$     Description of item at current position
  REM price      Price of current item
  OPEN "MASTER.DAT" FOR INPUT AS #1
  LET total = 0
  INPUT #1, code$, descr$, price    'Read first record from master file
```

```
  FOR i = 1 TO numItems
    DO WHILE itemUPC$(i) > code$
      INPUT #1, code$, descr$, price
    LOOP
    IF itemUPC$(i) = code$ THEN
        LPRINT descr$; TAB(37); price
        LET total = total + price
      ELSE
        LPRINT "** UPC "; itemUPC$(i); " not listed **"
    END IF
  NEXT i
  LPRINT USING "Total ========================>  $$###.##"; total
  CLOSE #1
END SUB

SUB SortCodes (itemUPC$(), numItems)
  REM Perform bubble sort on the array
  FOR passNum = 1 TO numItems - 1
    FOR i = 1 TO numItems - passNum
      IF itemUPC$(i) > itemUPC$(i + 1) THEN
          SWAP itemUPC$(i), itemUPC$(i + 1)
      END IF
    NEXT i
  NEXT passNum
END SUB

[run]
Enter * when all items have been entered.

Enter UPC code of item: 7073405307
Enter UPC code of item: 3700000430
Enter UPC code of item: 3700000430
Enter UPC code of item: 4100034200
Enter UPC code of item: *

22-oz Jif Peanut Butter             1.76
22-oz Jif Peanut Butter             1.76
** UPC 4100034200 not listed **
2.5 oz CS Cinn Rose Tea             1.65
Total ========================>     $5.17
```

Printed on printer

Chapter 8
Appendix: Displaying the Contents of a File

The following program reads the first 2000 characters of a file requested by the user and displays them on a graphics monitor. (To run the program with a monochrome display monitor, change the fourth line to DEF SEG = &HB000.) Carriage returns appear as single musical notes and line feeds appear as reverse-image circles. Press any key to clear the screen. (This program uses some statements not covered in the text.)

```
REM Display every character in a file
CLS
INPUT "FILE TO READ"; file$
DEF SEG = &HB800     'Change to &HB000 for monochrome display
SCREEN 0, 0, 0
OPEN file$ FOR INPUT AS #1
CLS
LET i = 0
DO WHILE (i <> 2000) AND (NOT EOF(1))
  LET char$ = INPUT$(1, #1)  'Read next character from file 1
  POKE 2 * i, ASC(char$)
  LET i = i + 1
LOOP
CLOSE #1
LET a$ = INPUT$(1)              'Pause until a key is pressed
END
```

Chapter 8 Summary

1. Each file has a *filespec* that gives the disk drive holding the file and the *file name*. QBasic programs associate a *reference number* with any file used in a program and refer to the file by that number.

2. When sequential files are *opened*, we must specify whether they will be created and written to, added to, or read from by use of the terms OUTPUT, APPEND, or INPUT. The file must be *closed* before the operation is changed. Data are written to the file with WRITE# statements and retrieved with INPUT# statements. The EOF function tells if we have read to the end of the file.

3. A sequential file can be ordered by placing its data in arrays, sorting the arrays, and then writing the ordered data into a file. This process should precede adding, deleting, or altering items in a master file.

Chapter 8 Programming Projects

1. Table 8.3 gives the leading eight soft drinks and their percentage share of the market. Write and execute a program to place these data into a sequential file. Then write a second program to use the file to

   (a) display the eight brands and their gross sales in billions. (The entire soft-drink industry grosses about $40 billion.)
   (b) calculate the total percentage market share of the leading eight soft drinks.

Coke Classic	20.2	Dr. Pepper	5.7
Pepsi	15.3	Sprite	5.6
Diet Coke	9.4	Diet Pepsi	5.3
Mountain Dew	5.7	7 Up	2.3

Table 8.3 Leading Soft Drinks and Percentages of Market Share
Source: Beverage World, March 1997

2. Suppose the sequential file "ALE" contains the information shown in Table 8.4. Write a program to use the file to produce Table 8.5, in which the baseball teams are in descending order by the percentage of games won.

Team	Won	Lost
Baltimore	98	64
Boston	78	84
Detroit	79	83
New York	96	66
Toronto	76	86

Table 8.4 American League East Games Won and Lost in 1997

American League East			
	W	L	Pct
Baltimore	98	64	.605
New York	96	66	.593
Detroit	79	83	.488
Boston	78	84	.481
Toronto	76	86	.469

Table 8.5 Final 1997 American League East standings

3. Write a rudimentary word processing program. The program should
   (a) Request the name of the sequential file to hold the document as input from the keyboard.
   (b) Clear the screen and display the symbol > as a prompt at the upper left corner of the screen.
   (c) Request the first line of the file as input from the keyboard and write this line to the file when the Enter key is pressed. **Note:** Blank lines are acceptable input, but lines exceeding 60 characters in length should not be accepted (the user should be prompted to reenter the line).
   (d) Display a second prompt at the leftmost position of the next line of the screen and carry out (c) for this line.
   (e) Continue as in (d) with subsequent lines until the user responds with EOD. (EOD should not be written to the file.)

(f) Clear the screen and display the complete text file on the screen.

```
[sample run]
Enter the name of the file to create: MYFILE
[Screen cleared]
>The most important feature of a computer program is that it performs
!!LINE TOO LONG!!
>The most important feature of a computer program is that it
>performs correctly. This is most likely to occur when the
>solution to the problem is systematically planned.
>EOD
The most important feature of a computer program is that it
performs correctly. This is most likely to occur when the
solution to the problem is systematically planned.
```

4. Write a program that counts the number of times a word occurs in the sequential file created in Programming Project 3. The file name and word should be input from the keyboard. For instance, opening MYFILE and searching for "is" would produce the output: "is" occurs 3 times.

5. *Create and Maintain Telephone Directories.* Write a menu-driven program to create and maintain telephone directories. The following menu options should be available:

   (a) create a sequential file consisting of the names and phone numbers of at most 200 people. The information should be supplied in response to INPUT statements.
   (b) print out the names and phone numbers in any of the sequential files that have been created.
   (c) sort the names in any of the sequential files that have been created.
   (d) delete a name from any of the sequential files.
   (e) add a name to the end of any of the sequential files.
   (f) terminate the program.

6. Table 8.6 contains the statistics for a stock portfolio. (The current prices are given for April 1, 1998).

Stock	Number of Shares	Date Purchased	Purchase Price/Share	Current Price/Share
Amgen	200	8/19/97	50 3/4	60 7/8
Delta Airlines	100	12/3/97	111 3/4	118 1/4
Novell	500	8/27/97	10 7/16	10 3/4
PPG	100	12/18/97	56 3/4	67 15/16
Timken	300	3/13/98	34 5/8	33 13/16

Table 8.6 Stock Portfolio

   (a) Compose a program to create the sequential file STOCKS containing the information in Table 8.6.
   (b) Compose a menu-driven program to perform the following tasks.
      (1) Display the information in the file STOCKS as in Table 8.6.
      (2) Add additional stocks onto the end of the file STOCKS.

(3) Update the entries for the Current Price/Share in the file STOCKS. The new entries should be provided in response to INPUT statements.
(4) Process the data in the file STOCKS and produce the display shown in Figure 8.10.
(5) Quit.

```
Company     Cost          Current Value    Profit (or Loss)
-------     ----------    -------------    ----------------
Amgen       10,150.00     12,175.00        2,025.00
...         ...           ...              ...
```

Figure 8.10 Output of Project 6

7. A department store has a file containing all sales transacted for a year. Each record contains a customer's name, zip code, and amount of the sale. The file is ordered first by zip code and then by name. Write a program to display the total sales for each customer, the total sales for each zip code, and the total sales for the store. For instance, if the first seven records of the file are

```
"Adams, John",10023,34.50
"Adams, John",10023,60.00
"Jones, Bob",10023,62.45
"Green, Mary",12345,54.00
"Howard, Sue",12345,79.25
"Smith, George",20001,25.10
```

then the output will begin with

```
Customer       Total Sales
Adams, John     94.50
Jones, Bob      62.45
   Total sales of zip code 10023: 156.95
Green, Mary     54.00
```

8. *Savings Account.* FILE1 is a sequential file containing the name, account number, and beginning-of-month balance for each depositor. FILE2 is a sequential file containing all the transactions (deposits and withdrawals) for the month. Use FILE2 to upgrade FILE1. For each customer, print a statement similar to the one received from banks that shows all transactions and the end-of-month balance. Also, record all overdrawn accounts in a file. (As an optional embellishment, deduct a penalty if the balance fell below a certain level any time during the month. The penalty could include a fixed fee of $10 plus a charge of $1 for each check and deposit.) ***Hint:*** Assume no more than 500 transactions have occurred.

9. A fuel-economy study was carried out for five models of cars. Each car was driven for 100 miles of city driving, then the model of the car and the number of gallons used were placed in the sequential file MILEAGE with the statement

```
WRITE #1, model$, gallons
```

Table 8.7 shows the first entries of the file. Write a program to display the models and their average miles per gallon in decreasing order with respect to mileage. The program should utilize three parallel arrays of range 1 TO 5. The first array should record the name of each model of car. This array is initially empty; each car model name is added when first encountered in reading the file. The second array should record the number of test vehicles for each model. The third array should record the total number of gallons used by that model. ***Note:*** The first array must be searched each time a record is read to determine the appropriate index to use with the other two arrays.

Model	Gal	Model	Gal	Model	Gal
LeBaron	4.9	Cutlass	4.5	Cutlass	4.6
Escort	4.1	Escort	3.8	LeBaron	5.1
Beretta	4.3	Escort	3.9	Escort	3.8
Skylark	4.5	Skylark	4.6	Cutlass	4.4

Table 8.7 Gallons of Gasoline Used in 100 Miles of City Driving

9

Random-Access Files

9.1 DATA TYPES

We can group related variables of different types in packages called *records*. In order to understand records, we must first discuss the use of the DIM statement to declare the type of a variable and then explore another new category of variable, the **fixed-length string**.

Declaring the Type of a Variable with DIM

Normally, the data type of a string variable is declared by adding a dollar sign to the variable name. The absence of a dollar sign, or the use of an exclamation mark as a suffix, declares the variable as numeric. While QBasic has four different types of numeric variables (see Comment 7), in this text we restrict ourselves to the numeric type formally known as **single-precision**.

The statements

```
DIM var AS STRING
```

or

```
DIM var AS SINGLE
```

where the name of the variable is written without any type-declaration suffix, declare the specified variable as a string variable or a numeric variable, respectively.

EXAMPLE 1 The following program uses the DIM statement to declare variables and then assigns values to the variables. Although the program still would be correct without the statement DIM pop AS SINGLE, we will soon see a situation where an analogous declaration is necessary.

```
REM Demonstrate the declaration of variable types with DIM
CLS
DIM city AS STRING
LET city = "New York"
DIM pop AS SINGLE
LET pop = 8586000
PRINT city; pop
END

[run]
New York 8586000
```

Fixed-Length Strings

Fixed-length string variables have the same sorts of names as numeric variables; that is, they do not have a trailing dollar sign. They are declared by statements of the form

```
DIM var AS STRING * n
```

where *n* is a positive integer. After such a declaration, the value of *var* will always be a string of length *n*. Suppose *a$* is an ordinary string and a statement of the form

```
LET var = a$
```

is executed. If *a$* has more than *n* characters, then only the first *n* characters will be assigned to *var*. If *a$* has less than *n* characters, then spaces will be added to the end of the string to guarantee that *var* has length *n*.

EXAMPLE 2 The following program uses fixed-length strings. In the output, San Francisco is truncated to a string of length 9 and Detroit is padded on the right with two blank spaces.

```
REM Illustrate fixed-length strings
CLS
PRINT "123456789"
DIM city AS STRING * 9
LET city = "San Francisco"
PRINT city
LET city = "Detroit"
PRINT city; "MI"
PRINT LEN(city)
END

[run]
123456789
San Franc
Detroit  MI
 9
```

Care must be taken when comparing an ordinary (variable-length) string with a fixed-length string or comparing two fixed-length strings of different lengths.

EXAMPLE 3 In the following program, the strings assigned to *city*, *town$*, and *municipality* have lengths 9, 7, and 12, respectively, and therefore are all different.

```
REM Illustrate fixed-length strings
CLS
DIM city AS STRING * 9
DIM municipality AS STRING * 12
LET town$ = "Chicago"
LET city = "Chicago"
LET municipality = "Chicago"
IF (city = town$) OR (city = municipality) THEN
    PRINT "same"
  ELSE
    PRINT "different"
END IF
```

```
PRINT "123456789012345"
PRINT city + "***"
PRINT town$ + "***"
PRINT municipality + "***"
END

[run]
different
123456789012345
Chicago   ***
Chicago***
Chicago       ***
```

There are times when we want to consider the values assigned to variables of different types as being the same, such as *city* and *town$* in Example 3. In this situation, the function RTRIM$ comes to the rescue. If *a$* is an ordinary string or a fixed-length string, then the value of

```
RTRIM$(a$)
```

is the (variable-length) string consisting of *a$* with all right-hand spaces removed. For instance, the value of RTRIM$("hello ") is the string "hello". In Example 3, if the IF block is changed to

```
IF (RTRIM$(city) = town$) AND (RTRIM$(city) = RTRIM$(municipality)) THEN
    PRINT "same"
  ELSE
    PRINT "different"
END IF
```

then the first line of the output will be "same".

Records

We have worked with four different data types in this text: numbers, strings, arrays, and fixed-length strings. Strings and numbers are built-in data types that can be used without being declared. On the other hand, arrays and fixed-length strings are user-defined data types that must be declared with a DIM statement before being used. A **record** is a user-defined data type that groups related variables of different types.

Figure 9.1 shows an index card that can be used to hold data about colleges. The three pieces of data—name, state, and year founded—are called **fields**. Each field functions like a variable in which information can be stored and retrieved. The **length** of a field is the number of spaces allocated to it. In the case of the index card we see that there are three fields, having lengths 30, 2, and 4, respectively. The layout of the index card can be identified by a name, such as collegeData, called a **record type**.

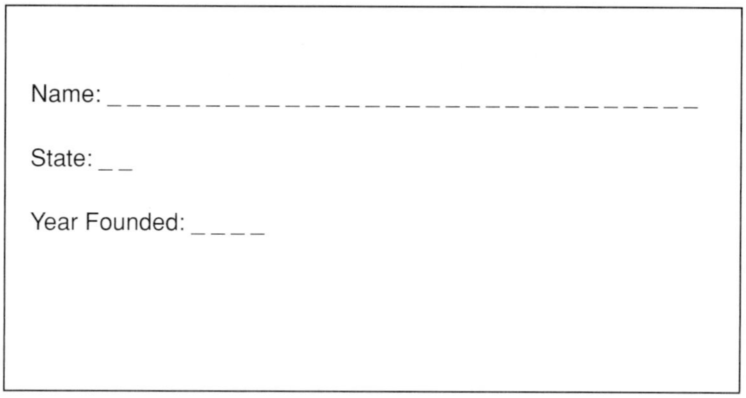

Figure 9.1 An Index Card Having Three Fields

For programming purposes, the layout of the record is declared by the block of statements

```
TYPE collegeData
  nom AS STRING * 30
  state AS STRING * 2
  yearFounded AS SINGLE
END TYPE
```

Each character of a string is stored in a piece of memory known as a byte. Therefore, a field of type STRING * n requires n bytes of memory. However, numbers (that is, the single-precision numbers we use in this text) are stored in a different manner than strings and *always* use four bytes of memory.

A **record** variable capable of holding the data for a specific college is declared by a statement such as

```
DIM college AS collegeData
```

Each field is accessed by giving the name of the record variable and the field, separated by a period. For instance, the three fields of the record variable college are accessed as college.nom, college.state, and college.yearFounded. Figure 9.2 shows a representation of the way the record variable is organized.

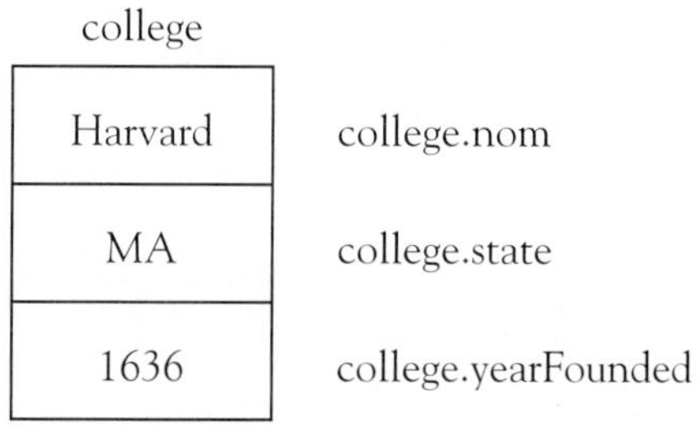

Figure 9.2 Record Variable with Values Assigned to the Fields

In general, a record type is created by a TYPE block of the form

```
TYPE recordType
   fieldName1 AS fieldType1
   fieldname2 AS fieldType2
   :
END TYPE
```

where *recordType* is the name of the user-defined data type, *fieldName1*, *fieldName2*, . . . are the names of the fields of the record variable, and *fieldType1*, *fieldType2*, . . . are the corresponding field types, either STRING * *n*, for some *n*, or SINGLE. A record variable *recordVar* is declared to be of the user-defined type by a statement of the form

```
DIM recordVar AS recordType
```

EXAMPLE 4 The following program processes records.

```
REM Demonstrate use of records
CLS
TYPE collegeData
  nom AS STRING * 30
  state AS STRING * 2
  yearFounded AS SINGLE
END TYPE
DIM college AS collegeData
INPUT "Name"; college.nom
INPUT "State"; college.state
INPUT "Year Founded"; college.yearFounded
LET century = 1 + INT(college.yearFounded / 100)
PRINT RTRIM$(college.nom); " was founded in the"; century;
PRINT "th century in "; college.state
DIM university AS collegeData
LET university.nom = "M.I.T."
LET university.state = "MA"
LET university.yearFounded = 1878
IF college.yearFounded < university.yearFounded THEN
    LET when$ = "before "
  ELSE
    LET when$ = "after "
END IF
PRINT RTRIM$(college.nom); " was founded ";
PRINT when$; RTRIM$(university.nom)
END

[run]
Name? Oberlin College
State? OH
Year Founded? 1837
Oberlin College was founded in the 19 th century in OH
Oberlin College was founded before M.I.T.
```

TYPE statements can appear only in the main body of a program, never in procedures. However, DIM statements can be used in procedures to declare a local record variable. When records are passed to and from procedures, the parameter in the SUB or FUNCTION statement must have the form

parameter AS *recordType*

EXAMPLE 5 The following program uses procedures to perform the same tasks as the program in Example 4.

```
REM Demonstrate use of records with procedures
CLS
TYPE collegeData
  nom AS STRING * 30
  state AS STRING * 2
  yearFounded AS SINGLE
END TYPE
DIM college AS collegeData
CALL GetData(college)
CALL DisplayStatement(college)
END

SUB GetData (school AS collegeData)
  REM Request the name, state, and year founded
  INPUT "Name"; school.nom
  INPUT "State"; school.state
  INPUT "Year Founded"; school.yearFounded
END SUB

SUB DisplayStatement (school AS collegeData)
  REM Display the name, century founded, and state of a school
  LET century = 1 + INT(school.yearFounded/100)
  PRINT RTRIM$(school.nom); " was founded in the"; century;
  PRINT "th century in "; school.state
  DIM university AS collegeData
  LET university.nom = "M.I.T."
  LET university.state = "MA"
  LET university.yearFounded = 1878
  IF school.yearFounded < university.yearFounded THEN
      LET when$ = "before "
    ELSE
      LET when$ = "after "
  END IF
  PRINT RTRIM$(school.nom); " was founded ";
  PRINT when$; RTRIM$(university.nom)
END SUB
```

Comments:

1. Record variables are similar to arrays in that they both store and access data items using a common name. However, the elements in an array must be of the same data types, whereas the fields in a record variable can be a mixture

of different data types. Also, the different elements of an array are identified by their indices, whereas the fields of a record are identified by a name following a period.

2. If the record variables *recVar1* and *recVar2* have the same type, then all the field values of *recVar2* can be assigned simultaneously to *recVar1* by the statement

```
LET recVar1 = recVar2
```

3. Statements of the form

```
PRINT recVar
```

and

```
INPUT recVar
```

are invalid, where *recVar* is a record variable. Each field of a record must appear separately in PRINT, INPUT, and READ statements. Also, comparisons involving records using the relational operators <, >, =, <>, <=, and >= are valid only with the record fields, and not with the records themselves.

4. In addition to being declared as numeric or fixed-length string data types, the elements of a user-defined variable type can also be declared as other types of records. However, we do not use such structures in this text.

5. An array of fixed-length strings is declared by a statement of the form DIM *arrayName (a* TO *b)* AS STRING * *n*

6. When fixed-length strings are passed to and from procedures, the corresponding parameter in the SUB or FUNCTION statement must be a variable-length string.

7. The four different types of numeric variables available in QBasic are shown in Table 9.1. Variables can be specified as one of these types by trailing the name with the proper type-declaration tag or using a DIM statement with the appropriate type identifier.

Numeric Type	Type-Declaration Suffix	Identifier Used in DIM Statement	Bytes of Storage
Integer	%	INTEGER	2
Long integer	&	LONG	4
Single-precision	none or !	SINGLE	4
Double-precision	#	DOUBLE	8

Table 9.1 The Four Types of Numeric Variables

PRACTICE PROBLEMS 9.1

1. In Example 4, why was *nom* used instead of the more common *name* for the variable to hold the name of the college?

EXERCISES 9.1

In Exercises 1 through 4, determine the output of the program.

1.
```
DIM ocean AS STRING * 10
DIM river AS STRING * 10
LET ocean = "Pacific"
LET river = "Mississippi"
PRINT ocean; river
END
```

2.
```
DIM colour as STRING * 6
LET colour = "Blue"
LET color$ = "Red"
PRINT colour; color$; colour
END
```

3.
```
TYPE appearance
  height AS SINGLE
  weight AS SINGLE
  eyeColor AS STRING * 5
END TYPE
DIM person1 AS appearance
DIM person2 AS appearance
LET person1.height = 72
LET person1.weight = 170
LET person1.eyeColor = "brown"
LET person2.height = 12 * 6
LET person2.weight = person1.weight
LET person2.eyeColor = "brownish green"
IF person1.height = person2.height THEN
    PRINT "heights are same"
END IF
PRINT person2.weight
IF person1.eyeColor = person2.eyeColor THEN
    PRINT "eye colors are same"
END IF
END
```

4.
```
TYPE testData
  nom AS STRING * 5
  score AS SINGLE
END TYPE
DIM student AS testData
FOR i = 1 to 3
  CALL GetScore(student)
  CALL PrintScore(student)
NEXT i
REM --- Data: names, scores
DATA Joe, 18, Moe, 20, Albert, 25
END

SUB GetScore (student AS testData)
  READ student.nom, student.score
END SUB

SUB PrintScore (student AS testData)
  PRINT student.nom; student.score
END SUB
```

In Exercises 5 through 10, determine the errors.

5.
```
TYPE zodiac
  nom AS STRING * 15
  sign AS STRING * 11
END TYPE
DIM astrology AS zodiac
LET nom = "Michael"
LET sign = "Sagittarius"
END
```

6.
```
DIM state$ AS STRING * 15
LET state$ = "Maryland"
PRINT state$
END
```

7.
```
TYPE address
  name AS STRING * 15
  streetAddress AS STRING * 15
  cityState AS STRING * 15
  zip AS SINGLE
DIM friend AS address
```

8.
```
TYPE print
  firstWord AS STRING * 5
  secondWord AS STRING * 5
END TYPE
```

9.
```
TYPE values
  label AS STRING * 5
  var2 AS NUMBER
END TYPE
```

10.
```
TYPE vitamins
  a AS SINGLE
  b AS SINGLE
END TYPE
DIM minimum AS vitamins
LET minimum.b = 200
LET minimum.a = 500
PRINT minimum
END
```

In Exercises 11 through 14, write a TYPE block to declare a user-defined data type of the given name and types of elements.

11. Name: planet; Elements: planetName, distanceFromSun

12. Name: taxData; Elements: SSN, grossIncome, taxableIncome

13. Name: car; Elements: make, model, year, mileage

14. Name: party; Elements: numberOfGuests, address

15. Write a program that requests three words as input from the user and then displays them on the screen in the first three zones without using any commas in the PRINT statement. Do this by declaring the variables used to hold the words as fixed-length strings of the appropriate length.

16. Write a program to look up data on notable tall buildings. The program should declare a user-defined data type named "building" with the elements "nom", "city", "height", and "stories". This interactive program should allow the user to input the name of a building and should search through DATA statements to determine the city, height, and number of stories of the building. If the building is not in the DATA statements, then the program should so report. Use the information in Table 9.2 for the DATA statements.

Building	City	Height (ft)	Stories
Empire State	New York	1250	102
Sears Tower	Chicago	1454	110
Texas Commerce Tower	Houston	1002	75
Transamerica Pyramid	San Francisco	853	48

Table 9.2 Tall Buildings

SOLUTIONS TO PRACTICE PROBLEMS 9.1

1. Reserved words may not be used as names of variables. Although *name$* can be used in a LET statement, statements such as DIM *name* AS STRING or DIM *name* AS STRING * 30 are not valid since "name" is a reserved word.

9.2 RANDOM-ACCESS FILES

A random-access file is like an array of records stored on a disk. The records are numbered 1, 2, 3, and so on and can be referred to by their numbers. Therefore, a random-access file resembles a box of index cards, each having a numbered tab. Any card can be selected from the box without first reading every index card preceding it; similarly, any record of a random-access file can be read without having to read every record preceding it.

One statement suffices to open a random-access file for all purposes: creating, appending, writing, and reading. Suppose a record type has been defined with a TYPE block and a record variable, called *recVar*, has been declared with a DIM statement. Then after the statement

```
OPEN "filespec" FOR RANDOM AS #n LEN = LEN(recVar)
```

is executed, records may be written, read, added, and changed. The file is referred to by the number *n*. Each record will have as many characters as allotted to each value of *recVar*.

Suppose appropriate TYPE, DIM, and OPEN statements have been executed. The two-step procedure for entering a record into the file is as follows.

1. Assign a value to each field of a record variable.
2. Place the data into record *r* of file #*n* with the statement

   ```
   PUT #n, r, recVar
   ```

   where *recVar* is the record variable from step 1.

EXAMPLE 1 The following program writes three records to the random-access file COLLEGES.DAT.

```
REM Create the random-access file COLLEGES.DAT
CLS
TYPE collegeData
  nom AS STRING * 25          'Name of college
  state AS STRING * 2         'State where college is located
  yrFounded AS SINGLE         'Year college was founded
END TYPE
CALL CreateFile
END

SUB CreateFile
  REM Create and write three records into the file COLLEGES.DAT
  DIM college AS collegeData
  OPEN "COLLEGES.DAT" FOR RANDOM AS #1 LEN = LEN(college)
  FOR recordNum = 1 TO 3
    INPUT "Name of college"; college.nom
    INPUT "State located"; college.state
    INPUT "Year founded"; college.yrFounded
    PUT #1, recordNum, college
  NEXT recordNum
  CLOSE #1
END SUB

[run]
Name of college? Houston Comm. College
State located? TX
Year founded? 1971
Name of college? Milwaukee Area Tech. Col.
State located? WI
Year founded? 1912
Name of college? Virginia Tech
State located? VA
Year founded? 1872
```

The two-step procedure for reading data from a record is as follows:

1. Execute the statement

   GET #*n*, *r*, *recVar*

   to assign record *r* of file #*n* to the record variable *recVar*.

2. Use the field variables of the record variable either to display values with PRINT or to transfer values to other variables with LET.

EXAMPLE 2 Write a program to display the entire contents of the random-access file COLLEGES.DAT.

SOLUTION

```
REM Access the random-access file COLLEGES.DAT
CLS
TYPE collegeData
  nom AS STRING * 25          'Name of college
  state AS STRING * 2         'State where college is located
  yrFounded AS SINGLE         'Year college was founded
END TYPE
```

```
CALL DisplayFile
END

SUB DisplayFile
  DIM college AS collegeData
  OPEN "COLLEGES.DAT" FOR RANDOM AS #1 LEN = LEN(college)
  PRINT "College", , "State", "Year founded"
  FOR recordNum = 1 TO 3
    GET #1, recordNum, college
    PRINT college.nom, college.state, college.yrFounded
  NEXT recordNum
  CLOSE #1
END SUB

[run]
College                    State          Year founded
Houston Comm. College      TX              1971
Milwaukee Area Tech. Col.  WI              1912
Virginia Tech              VA              1872
```

The total number of characters in the file with reference number *n* is given by the value of the function

```
LOF(n)
```

The number of the last record in the file can be calculated by dividing this value by the record length. The LOF function, rather than the EOF function, should be used to determine when the end of the file has been reached. For instance, in Example 2 the FOR statement in the subprogram DisplayFile can be written as

```
FOR i = 1 TO LOF(1) / LEN(college)
```

Also, the pair of statements

```
LET lastRecord = LOF(1) / LEN(college)
PUT #1, lastRecord + 1, college
```

can be used to add a record to the end of the file.

Comments:

1. Random-access files are also known as **direct-access** or **relative** files. Since each record has the same number of characters, the computer can calculate where to find a specified record and, therefore, does not have to search for it sequentially.
2. Unlike sequential files, random-access files needn't be closed between placing information into them and reading from them.
3. Random-access files do not have to be filled in order. For instance, a file can be opened and the first PUT statement can be PUT #*n*, 9, *recVar*. In this case, space is allocated for the preceding eight records.

4. If the record number *r* is omitted from a PUT or GET statement, then the record number used will be the one following the number most recently used in a PUT or GET statement. For instance, if the line

```
PUT #1, , college
```

is added to the program in Example 2 just before the CLOSE statement, then the information on Virginia Tech will be duplicated in record 4 of the file COLLEGES.DAT.

5. Users often enter records into a random-access file without keeping track of the record numbers. If file #*n* is open, then the value of the function

```
LOC(n)
```

is the number of the record most recently written to or read from file *n* with a PUT or GET statement.

6. Each record in a random-access file has the same length. This length can be any number from 1 to 32767.

7. When the statement OPEN "COLLEGES.DAT" FOR RANDOM AS #1 LEN = LEN(college) is typed, the words "FOR RANDOM" can be omitted. The smart editor will insert them automatically.

8. The decision of whether to store data in a sequential file or in a random-access file depends on how the data are to be processed. If processing requires a pass through all the data in the file, then sequential files are probably desirable. If processing involves seeking out one item of data, however, then random-access files are the better choice.

PRACTICE PROBLEM 9.2

1. In Example 2, the first PRINT statement clearly displays "State" in the third print zone. Why will the second PRINT statement also display the value of college.state in the third print zone?

EXERCISES 9.2

In Exercises 1 through 8, determine the output of the program. For each of the programs, assume the file COLLEGES.DAT was just created by Example 1, record type collegeData has been declared with a TYPE block, and the first two lines of each of these programs are

```
DIM college AS collegeData
OPEN "COLLEGES.DAT" FOR RANDOM AS #1 LEN = LEN(college)
```

1.
```
GET #1, 3, college
PRINT college.state
CLOSE #1
END
```

2.
```
GET #1, 3, college
PRINT LOF(1); LOC(1)
CLOSE #1
END
```

3.
```
FOR i = 1 TO LOF(1) / LEN(college)
  GET #1, i, college
  PRINT college.state
NEXT i
PRINT LOC(1)
CLOSE #1
END
```

4.
```
LET college.yrFounded = 1876
PUT #1, 2, college
GET #1, 2, college
PRINT college.nom; college.yrFounded
CLOSE #1
END
```

5.
```
LET college.nom = "Harvard"
LET college.state = "MA"
LET college.yrFounded = 1636
PUT #1, 4, college
FOR i = 3 TO 4
  GET #1, i, college
  PRINT college.nom, college.state, college.yrFounded
NEXT i
CLOSE #1
END
```

6.
```
LET college.nom = "Michigan State"
LET college.state = "MI"
LET college.yrFounded = 1855
PUT #1, 1, college
FOR i = 1 TO 3
  GET #1, i, college
  PRINT college.nom
NEXT i
CLOSE #1
END
```

7.
```
GET #1, 1, college
GET #1, , college
PRINT college.nom, college.state, college.yrFounded
CLOSE #1
END
```

8.
```
LET lastRec = LOF(1) / LEN(college)
GET #1, lastRec, college
PRINT college.nom, college.state, college.yrFounded
CLOSE #1
END
```

In Exercises 9 through 12, identify the errors. Assume the given code has been preceded with the statements

```
TYPE filmCredits
  nom AS STRING * 25      'Name of actor or actress
  film AS STRING * 35     'Name of film
END TYPE
DIM actor AS filmCredits
```

9.
```
OPEN "ACTORS.DAT" FOR RANDOM AS #2 LEN = LEN(filmCredits)
LET actor.nom = "Bogart"
LET actor.film = "Casablanca"
PUT #2, 3, actor
CLOSE #2
END
```

10.
```
OPEN ACTRESS.DAT FOR RANDOM AS #3 LEN = LEN(actor)
LET actor.nom = "Garland"
LET actor.film = "Wizard of Oz"
LET lastRec = LOF(3) / LEN(actor)
PUT #3, lastRec + 1, actor
CLOSE #3
END
```

11.
```
OPEN "ACTORS.DAT" FOR RANDOM AS #1 LEN = LEN(actor)
LET actor.nom = "Stallone"
LET actor.film = "Rocky"
PUT #1, 1, actor
GET #1, 1, actor
CLOSE #1
PRINT actor
END
```

12.
```
OPEN "ACTRESS.DAT" FOR RANDOM AS #3 LEN = LEN(actor)
PUT #1, 1, actor
CLOSE #1
END
```

13. Give an OPEN statement and TYPE block for a random-access file named NUMBERS.DAT in which each record consists of three numbers.

14. Give an OPEN statement and TYPE block for a random-access file named ACCOUNTS.DAT in which each record consists of a person's name (up to 25 characters) and the balance in their savings account.

15. Consider the sequential file YOB.DAT discussed in Section 8.1 and assume the file contains many names. Write a program to place all the information into a random-access file.

16. Write a program that uses the random-access file created in Exercise 15 and displays the names of all people born before 1970.

17. Write a program that uses the random-access file created in Exercise 15 to determine a person's year of birth. The program should request the name with an INPUT statement, search for the proper record, and either give the year of birth or report that the person is not in the file.

18. Write a program that uses the random-access file created in Exercise 15 and adds the data Joan, 1934 to the end of the file.

Exercises 19 through 22 refer to the file COLLEGES.DAT. Assume many colleges have been added to the file in no particular order.

19. Write a program to allow additional colleges to be added to the end of the file using data entered by INPUT statements.

20. Modify the program in Exercise 19 to insure that the name of the college input has no more than 25 characters.

21. Write a program to find the two oldest colleges.

22. Write a program to display the data on any college requested in response to an INPUT statement. The college should be identified by name and located by a sequential search of the records. ***Note:*** Remember to take into account the fact that each college name retrieved from the file will contain 25 characters.

23. Extend the program in Exercise 22 in the following way: after the information on a college is displayed, exchange its record with the previous record; unless, of course, the displayed record is the first record. (A familiar rule of thumb for office filing is: 80% of the action involves 20% of the records. After the program has been used many times, the most frequently requested records will tend to be near the top of the file and the average time required for searches should decrease.)

SOLUTION TO PRACTICE PROBLEM 9.2

1. The value of *college.nom* will have length 25 for each college. Therefore, it will extend into the second print zone and force the value of *college.state* into the third print zone.

Chapter 9 Summary

1. A *fixed-length string* is a variable declared with a statement of the form DIM *var* AS STRING * *n*. The value of *var* is always a string of *n* characters.

2. A *record* is a composite user-defined data type with a fixed number of fields that are of either fixed-length string or numeric type. TYPE statements define record types, and DIM statements are used to declare a variable to be of that type.

3. After a record type has been specified, the associated *random-access file* is an ordered collection of record values numbered 1, 2, 3, and so on. Record values are placed into the file with PUT statements and read from the file with GET statements. At any time, the value of LOF(*n*) / LEN(*recordVar*) is the number of the highest record value in the file and the value of LOC is the number of the record value most recently accessed by a PUT or GET statement.

Chapter 9 Programming Projects

1. *Balance a Checkbook.* Write an interactive program to request information (payee, check number, amount, and whether or not the check has cleared) for each check written during a month and store this information in a random file. The program should then request the balance at the beginning of the month and display the current balance and the payee and amount for every check still outstanding.

2. A teacher maintains a random-access file containing the following information for each student: name, Social Security number, grades on each of two hourly exams, and the final exam grade. Assume the random-access file GRADES has been created with string fields of lengths 25 and 11 and three numeric fields, and all the names and Social Security numbers have been entered. The numeric fields have been initialized with zeros. Write a menu-driven program to allow the teacher to do the following.

   (a) Enter all the grades for a specific exam.
   (b) Change a grade of a specific student with data entered using INPUT statements.
   (c) Print a list of final grades that can be posted. The list should show the last four digits of the Social Security number, the grade on the final exam, and the semester average of each student. The semester average is determined by the formula (exam1 + exam2 + 2 * finalExam) / 4.

10

The Graphical Display of Data

10.1 INTRODUCTION TO GRAPHICS

QBasic has impressive graphics capabilities. Figure 10.1 shows four types of charts that can be displayed on the screen and printed by the printer.

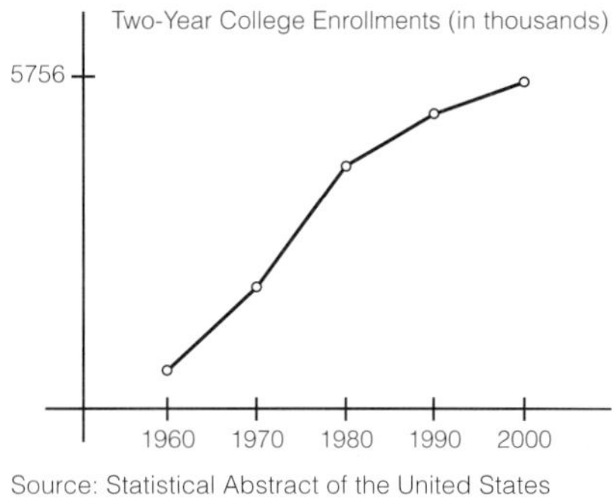

Line Chart

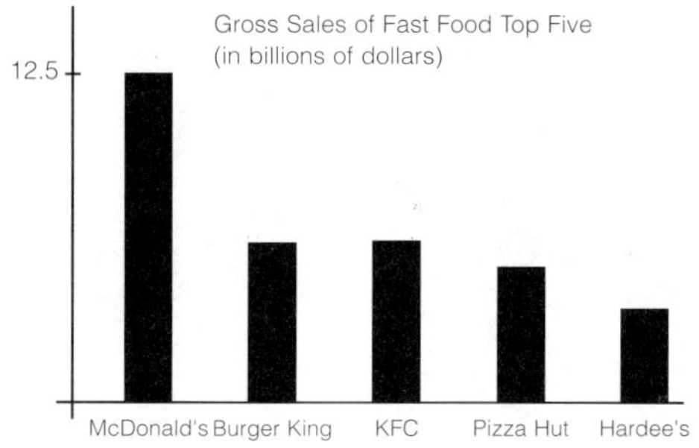

Bar Chart

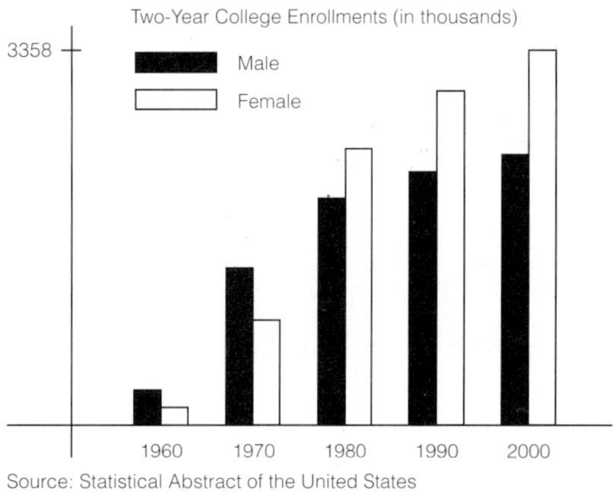

Clustered Bar Chart

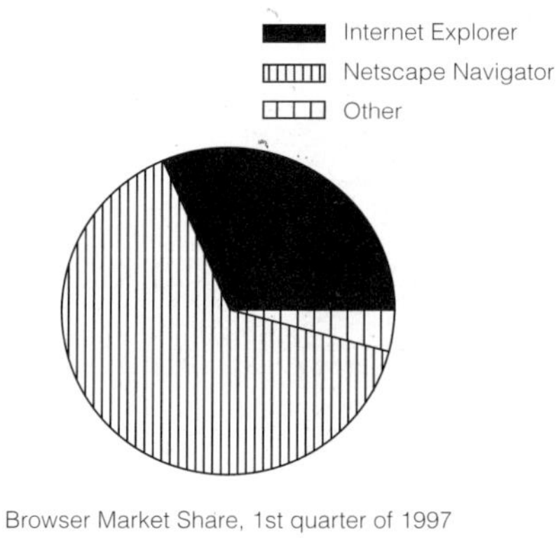

Pie Chart

Figure 10.1 Four Types of Charts

In addition to text, computer monitors can display graphics—that is, points, lines, rectangles, and circles. Nearly all computer monitors sold since 1990 are VGA monitors. Although this section is written for VGA monitors, comments at the end address the modifications needed for older monitors.

VGA monitors have several different display modes. Until now we have been using text mode. In this section we use graphics mode (formally known as "very high resolution graphics mode"), which is invoked with the statement SCREEN 12. In graphics mode, text is displayed in 30 eighty-character rows, and text and graphics can be displayed in 16 colors.

An exact printout of the contents of a graphics screen is called a **screen dump**. The method for obtaining a screen dump depends on the computer's operating system. If your computer has Windows 95 (or a later version of Windows) installed, you must use the first method below. If your computer does not have Windows installed, you must use the second method below. With Windows 3.1 installed, you can use either method.

First Method for Printing the Graphics Screen
(Requires Windows)

Note: This method assumes that you have invoked DOS from the Windows environment; that is, Windows is running.

1. Press the Print Screen key.
2. Return to Windows and invoke Paint (or Paintbrush) from the Accessories program group.
3. Press Ctrl+V to place a copy of the graphics screen in the window.
4. Press Ctrl+I to invert the colors on the screen. (Otherwise, your printout will appear as white-on-black.)
5. Make sure your printer is turned on and ready to print.
6. Press Ctrl+P to print the contents of the Paint (or Paintbrush) window.

Second Method for Printing the Graphics Screen
(Requires DOS only or Windows 3.1)

1. The DOS directory contains a program called GRAPHICS.COM. This program must be executed before QBASIC is invoked in order for printing to be enabled. However, the command used to execute GRAPHICS.COM varies with the type of printer. Some variations are

Printer	Command
Dot-matrix or inkjet	GRAPHICS
HP LaserJet compatible	GRAPHICS LASERJET
HP DeskJet	GRAPHICS DESKJET

(See the DOS manual for other variations.)

2. Make sure your printer is turned on and ready to print.
3. From QBASIC, press Shift+Print Screen to print the contents of a graphics screen.

Comments:

1. Computers purchased during the 1980s usually came with a CGA monitor. If you are using a CGA monitor, replace SCREEN 12 with SCREEN 2 in the programs for this chapter. The main difference will be that the screen will allow only 25 rows of text instead of 30. Therefore, LOCATE statements appearing in programs will have to be modified.
2. Some monitors purchased during the 1980s were called monochrome monitors. These monitors can display graphics only if they are attached to a Hercules card. We refer to such a configuration as a Hercules monitor. In order to display graphics with a Hercules monitor, you must execute the program MSHERC.COM before invoking QBASIC. Also, you must replace SCREEN 12 with SCREEN 3 in the programs for this chapter. The main difference will be that the screen will allow only 25 rows of text instead of 30. Therefore, LOCATE statements appearing in programs will have to be modified. Also, Hercules monitors cannot display colors.

10.2 SPECIFYING A COORDINATE SYSTEM

Suppose we have a piece of paper, a pencil, and a ruler and we want to graph a line extending from (2, 40) to (5, 60). We will most likely use the following three-step procedure:

1. Use the ruler to draw an x-axis and a y-axis. Focus on the first quadrant, since both points are in that quadrant.

2. Select scales for the two axes. For instance, we might decide that the numbers on the x-axis range from –1 to 6 and that the numbers on the y-axis range from –10 to 80.

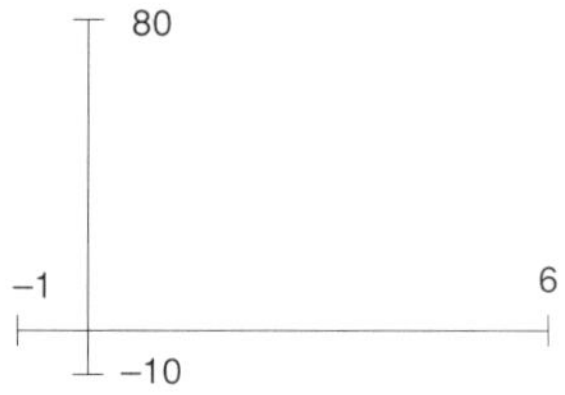

3. Plot the two points and use the ruler to draw the straight-line segment joining them.

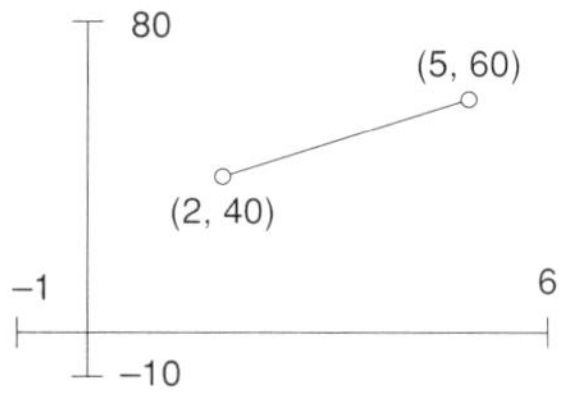

EXAMPLE 1 (a) Draw a coordinate system with the numbers on the x-axis ranging from –2 to 10, and the numbers on the y-axis ranging from –3 to 18.
(b) Draw the straight line from (1, 15) to (8, 6).
(c) Draw the straight line from (–2, 0) to (10, 0).

SOLUTION (a)

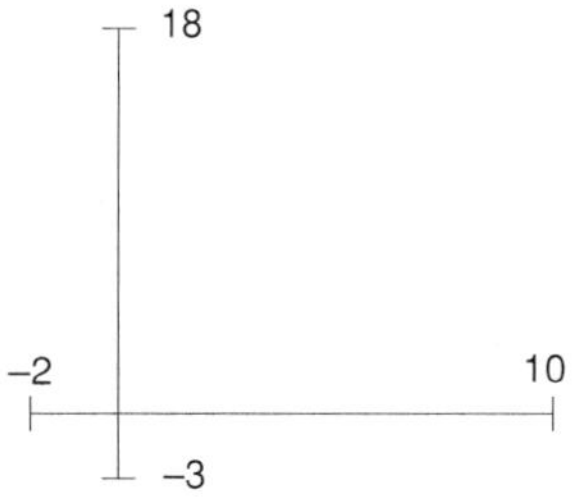

(b)

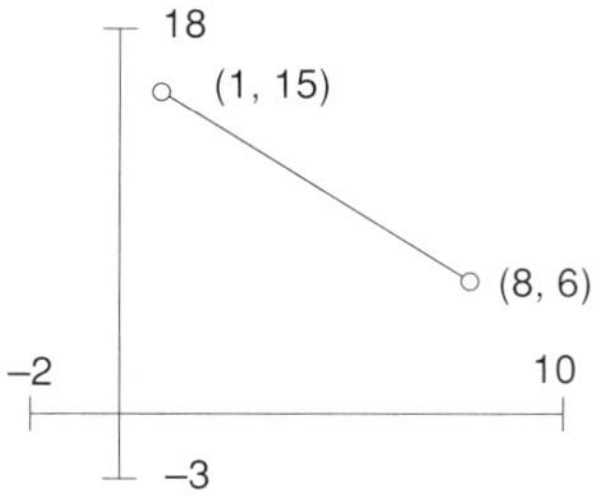

(c) The point (–2, 0) is the left-hand endpoint of the x-axis and the point (10, 0) is the right-hand endpoint; therefore, the line joining them is just the portion of the x-axis we have pictured.

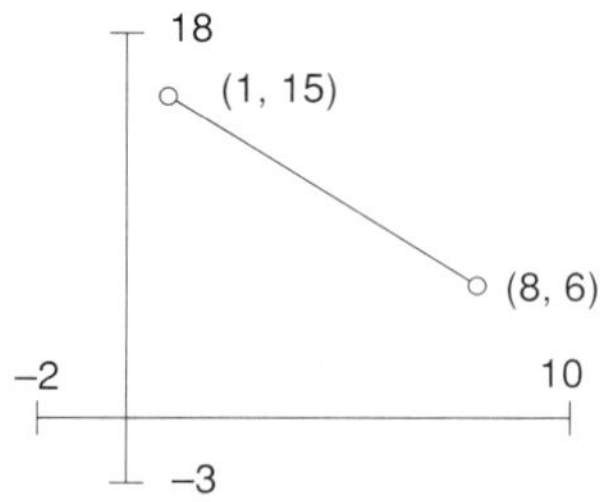

We draw these graphs on the screen with the same three steps we use with paper, pencil, and ruler. The only difference is that we first do step 2, and then steps 1 and 3. The QBasic statement WINDOW is used to specify the range of values for the axes, and the statement LINE serves as the ruler.

The statement

```
WINDOW (a, c)-(b, d)
```

specifies that numbers on the *x*-axis range from *a* to *b* and that numbers on the *y*-axis range from *c* to *d*. (See Figure 10.2.) The ordered pair (*a*, *c*) contains the lowest numbers on the two axes, and the ordered pair (*b*, *d*) contains the highest numbers.

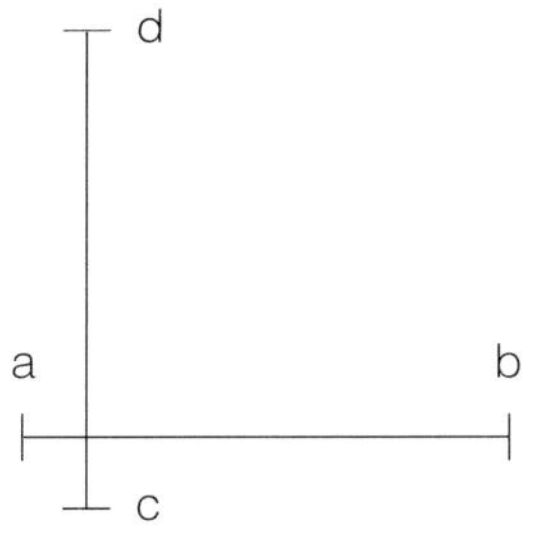

Figure 10.2 Result of WINDOW Statement

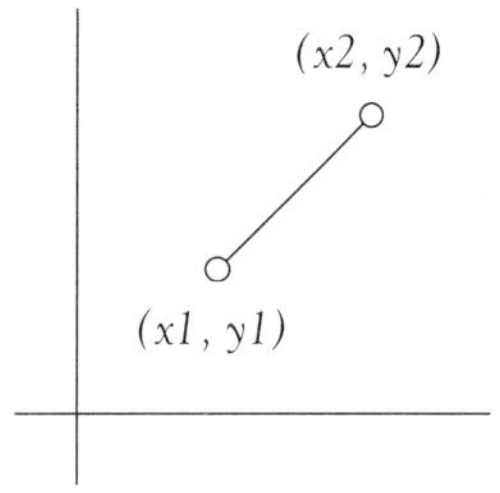

Figure 10.3 Result of LINE Statement

The statement

```
LINE (x1, y1)-(x2, y2)
```

draws the line segment from the point with coordinates (*x1*, *y1*) to the point with coordinates (*x2*, *y2*) (see Figure 10.3). In particular, the statement LINE (a, 0)–(b, 0) draws the *x*-axis, and the statement LINE (0, *c*)–(0, *d*) draws the *y*-axis.

The following program produces the graph of Example 1, part (b):

```
SCREEN 12                    'Go into graphics mode, clear screen
WINDOW (-2, -3)-(10, 18)     'Specify coordinate system
LINE (-2, 0)-(10, 0)         'Draw x-axis
LINE (0, -3)-(0, 18)         'Draw y-axis
LINE (1, 15)-(8, 6)          'Draw the straight line
END
```

EXAMPLE 2 Consider Figure 10.4.

(a) Give the WINDOW statement that specifies the range for the numbers on the axes.
(b) Give the statements that will draw the axes.
(c) Give the statement that will draw the line.

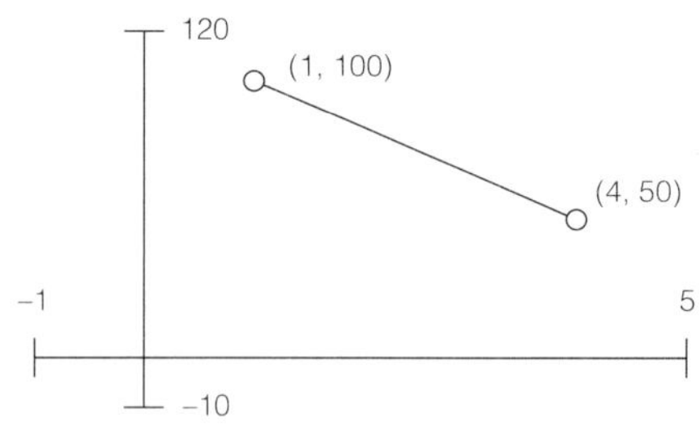

Figure 10.4 Graph for Example 2

SOLUTION (a) `WINDOW (-1, -10)-(5, 120)`

lowest *x*-value, lowest *y*-value, highest *x*-value, highest *y*-value (arrows pointing to -1, -10, 5 and 120 respectively)

(b) *x*-axis: `LINE (-1, 0)-(5, 0)` — *a* (pointing to -1), *b* (pointing to 5)

y-axis: `LINE (0, -10)-(0, 120)` — *c* (pointing to -10), *d* (pointing to 120)

(c) `LINE (1, 100)-(4, 50)`

There are two other graphics statements that are just as useful as the LINE statement. The statement

```
PSET (x, y)
```

plots the point with coordinates (x, y). The statement

```
CIRCLE (x, y), r
```

draws the circle with center (x, y) and radius r.

EXAMPLE 3 Write a program to plot the point (7, 6) and draw a circle of radius 3 about the point.

SOLUTION The rightmost point to be drawn will have *x*-coordinate 10; therefore the numbers on the *x*-axis must range beyond 10. In the following program we allow the numbers to range from –2 to 12. (See Figure 10.5.)

```
REM Draw circle with center (7, 6) and radius 3
SCREEN 12                       'Initialize screen
WINDOW (-2, -2)-(12, 12)        'Specify coordinate system
LINE (-2, 0)-(12, 0)            'Draw x-axis
LINE (0, -2)-(0, 12)            'Draw y-axis
PSET (7, 6)                     'Draw center of circle
CIRCLE (7, 6), 3                'Draw the circle
END
```

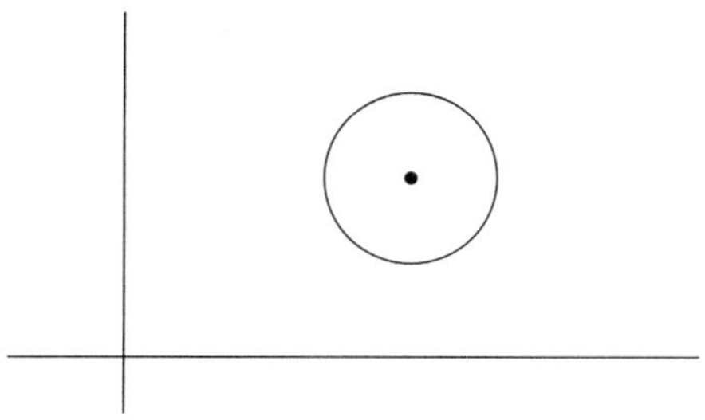

Figure 10.5 Graph for Example 3

The numbers appearing in WINDOW, LINE, PSET, and CIRCLE statements can be replaced by variables or expressions. The following example demonstrates this feature.

EXAMPLE 4 Write a program to draw a graph of the square-root function.

SOLUTION We will graph the function for values of *x* from 0 to 100. (See Figure 10.6.)

```
REM Graph the square-root Function
SCREEN 12                       'Initialize screen
LET r = 100                     'Largest x-value used
LET h = 10                      'Largest y-value used
WINDOW (-20, -2)-(120, 12)      'Specify coordinate system
LINE (-5, 0)-(r, 0)             'Draw x-axis
LINE (0, -1)-(0, h)             'Draw y-axis
FOR x = 0 TO r STEP .2          'Plot about 500 points
  PSET (x, SQR(x))              'Plot point on graph
NEXT x
END
```

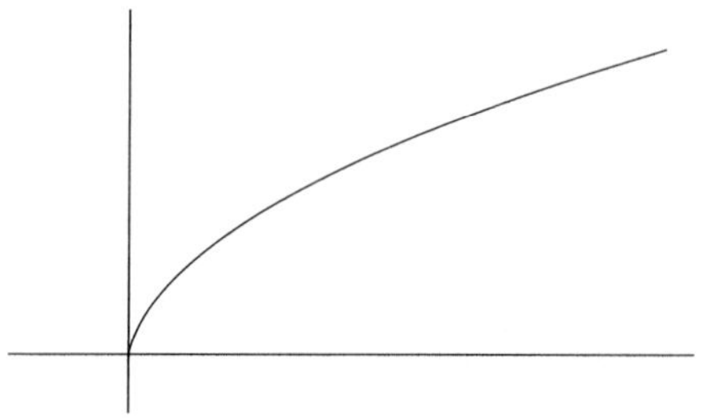

Figure 10.6 Graph of the Square-Root Function

There are times when lines are placed on the screen in conjunction with text. This would be the case if a phrase were to be underlined. Since the graphics screens consist of 80 columns and 30 rows, the statement

```
WINDOW (0, 0)-(80, 30)
```

specifies an advantageous coordinate system for these situations.

EXAMPLE 5 Write a program to display the phrase "Th-that's all Folks!" in the center of the screen and underline it.

SOLUTION For purposes of displaying text, the center of the screen is approximately at row 15, column 40. Since the phrase has 20 characters, it should begin at row 15, column 31. The point at the bottom left of this location has coordinates (30, 15) and is the left endpoint of the underline. In the following program, the PRINT statement displays the phrase in the middle of the screen and the LINE statement underlines it.

```
REM Underline a phrase
SCREEN 12
LET p$ = "Th-that's all Folks!"
LOCATE 15, 31
PRINT p$
WINDOW (0, 0)-(80, 30)
LINE (30, 15)-(30 + LEN(p$), 15)
END
```

Comments:

1. In Examples 1 through 4, the examples that produce graphs, the range of numbers on the axes extends from a negative number to a positive number. Actually, any values of *a*, *b*, *c*, and *d* can be used in a WINDOW statement. In certain cases, however, you will not be able to display one or both of the axes on the screen. (For instance, after WINDOW (1, –1)–(10, 10) has been executed, the *y*-axis cannot be displayed.)

2. The following method can be used to determine a good scale for a WINDOW statement when graphs with only positive values are to be drawn.

   (a) Let *r* be the *x*-coordinate of the rightmost point that will be drawn by any LINE, PSET, or CIRCLE statement.
   (b) Let *h* be the *y*-coordinate of the highest point that will be drawn by any LINE, PSET, or CIRCLE statement.
   (c) Let the numbers on the *x*-axis range from about –(20% of *r*) to about *r* + (20% of *r*). Let the numbers on the *y*-axis range from about –(20% of *h*) to about *h* + (20% of *h*). That is, use

   ```
   WINDOW (-.2 * r, -.2 * h)-(1.2 * r, 1.2 * h)
   ```

3. LOCATE statements are used to place text and therefore are not affected by WINDOW statements.

4. The radius of a circle uses the scale specified for the *x*-axis.

5. If one or both of the points used in the LINE statement are off the screen, the computer draws only the portion of the line that is on the screen. This behavior is referred to as **line clipping** and is used for the CIRCLE statement also.

6. A program can contain two WINDOW statements. Executing the second statement has no effect on the graphics figures that were already drawn; however, future graphics statements will use the new coordinate system. This technique is very useful for drawing charts. The graphs are drawn using a WINDOW statement of the type discussed in Comment 2, and then a WINDOW statement such as the one in Example 5 is used to position lines and text.

7. You can modify the above programs to produce colorful displays in graphics mode. The numbers 0 through 15 identify colors as shown in Table 10.1.

0 Black	4 Red	8 Gray	12 Light red
1 Blue	5 Magenta	9 Light blue	13 Light magenta
2 Green	6 Yellow	10 Light green	14 Light yellow
3 Cyan	7 White	11 Light cyan	15 High-intensity white

Table 10.1 Values for Colors

Lines, points, and circles can be drawn in colors. To use color *c*, place ", *c*" at the end of the corresponding graphics statement. For instance, the statement

```
LINE (x1, y1)-(x2, y2), 4
```

draws a red line.

8. With a CGA or Hercules monitor, replace all occurrences of SCREEN 12 with SCREEN 2 or SCREEN 3, respectively. In Example 5, change the fourth through seventh lines to

```
LOCATE 12, 31
PRINT p$
WINDOW (0, 0)-(80, 25)
LINE (30, 13)-(30 + LEN(p$), 13)
```

In general, numbers that relate to a line of text should be multiplied by 5/6 and then rounded.

PRACTICE PROBLEMS 10.2

Suppose you want to write a program to draw a line from (3, 45) to (5, 80).

1. Use the method of Comment 2 to select an appropriate WINDOW statement.

2. Write a program to draw the axes, the line, and a small circle around each endpoint of the line.

3. Write the statements that draw a tick mark on the *y*-axis at height 80 and label it with the number 80.

EXERCISES 10.2

1. Determine the WINDOW statement corresponding to the coordinate system of Figure 10.7.

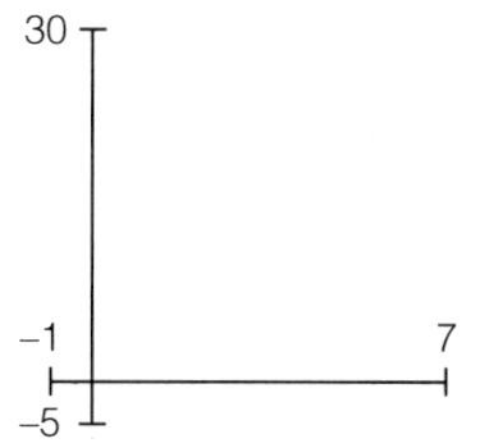

Figure 10.7 Coordinate System for Exercise 1

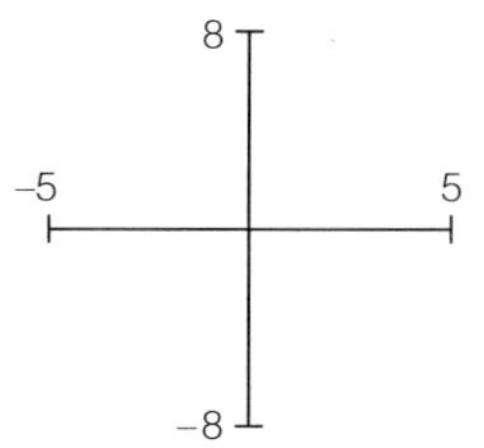

Figure 10.8 Coordinate System for Exercise 2

2. Determine the WINDOW statement corresponding to the coordinate system of Figure 10.8.

3. Suppose the statement WINDOW (–1, –8)–(4, 40) has been executed. Write down the statements that draw the *x*-axis and the *y*-axis.

4. Suppose the statement WINDOW (–3, –.2)–(18, 1) has been executed. Write down the statements that draw the *x*-axis and the *y*-axis.

In Exercises 5 through 8, write a program to draw a line between the given points. Select an appropriate WINDOW statement, draw the axes, and draw a small circle around each endpoint of the line.

5. (3, 200), (10, 150)

6. (4, 4), (9, 9)

7. (2, .5), (4, .3)

8. (5, 30), (6, 30)

In Exercises 9 through 20, write a program to draw the given figures. Draw the axes only when necessary.

9. Draw a circle whose center is located at the center of the screen.

10. Draw a tick mark on the *x*-axis at a distance of 5 from the origin.

11. Draw a tick mark on the *y*-axis at a distance of 70 from the origin.

12. Draw a circle whose leftmost point is at the center of the screen.

13. Draw four points, one in each corner of the screen.

14. Draw a triangle with two sides of the same length.

15. Draw a rectangle.

16. Draw a square.

17. Draw five concentric circles—that is, five circles with the same center.

18. Draw a point in the center of the screen.

19. Draw a circle and a line that is tangent to the circle.

20. Draw two circles that touch at a single point.

In Exercises 21 through 24, consider the following program. What would be the effect on the circle if the WINDOW statement were replaced by the given WINDOW statement?

```
SCREEN 12
WINDOW (-5, -5)-(5, 5)     'Specify coordinate system
CIRCLE (0, 0), 3           'Draw circle centered at origin
END
```

21. `WINDOW (-8, -8)-(8,8)`

22. `WINDOW (-5, -8)-(5, 8)`

23. `WINDOW (-8, -5)-(8, 5)`

24. `WINDOW (-4, -4)-(4, 4)`

In Exercises 25 through 27, write a program to perform the given task.

25. Draw a graph of the function $y = x^2$ for x between 0 and 10.

26. Draw a graph of the function $200 / (x + 5)^2$ for x between 0 and 20.

27. Write a program to produce displays such as the one in Figure 10.9. Let the user enter the maximum number (in this display, 8).

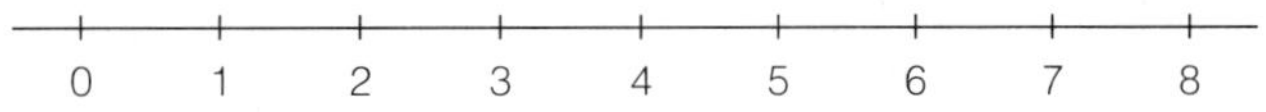

Figure 10.9 Display for Exercise 27

In Exercise 28 through 30, use the statement WINDOW (0, 0)–(80, 25).

28. Write a program to produce Figure 10.10. Let the maximum line number (in this display, 3) be INPUT by the user.

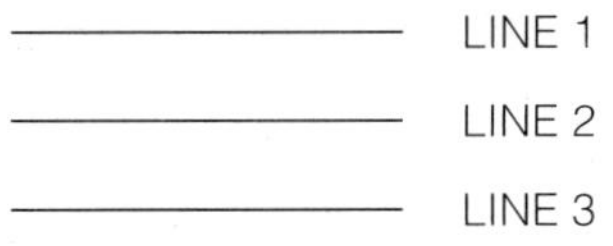

Figure 10.10 Display for Exercise 28

29. Write a program to produce a sheet of graph paper.

30. Write a program to produce a form for a course schedule. (See Figure 10.11.)

COURSE SCHEDULE						
Time	Mon.	Tues.	Wed.	Thurs.	Fri.	Sat./Sun.

Figure 10.11 Course Schedule

SOLUTIONS TO PRACTICE PROBLEMS 10.2

1. The largest value of any *x*-coordinate is 5. Since 20% of 5 is 1, the numbers on the *x*-axis should range from –1 to 6 (= 5 + 1). Similarly, the numbers on the *y*-axis should range from –16 to 96 (= 80 + 16). Therefore, an appropriate WINDOW statement is

```
WINDOW (-1, -16)-(6, 96)
```

2.
```
SCREEN 12
WINDOW (-1, -16)-(6, 96)     'Specify coordinate system
LINE (-1, 0)-(6, 0)          'Draw x-axis
LINE (0, -16)-(0, 96)        'Draw y-axis
LINE (3, 45)-(5, 80)         'Draw the line
CIRCLE (3, 45), .05          'Draw small circle about left endpoint
CIRCLE (5, 80), .05          'Draw small circle about right endpoint
END
```

The radius for the small circles about the endpoints was determined by trial and error. As a rule of thumb, it should be about 1% of the length of the *x*-axis.

3. Add the following lines before the END statement of the preceding program. The length of the tick mark was taken to be the diameter of the circle. The row and column for the LOCATE statement were determined by trial and error. See Figure 10.12 for the output of the entire program.

```
LINE (-.05, 80)-(.05, 80)
LOCATE 5, 7
PRINT 80
```

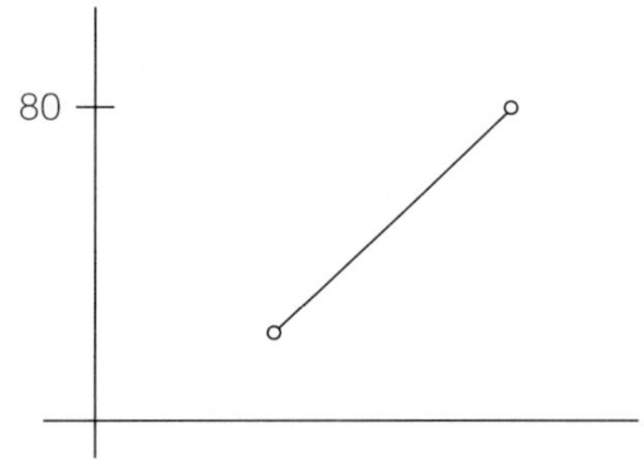

Figure 10.12 Output of Program in Practice Problem 3

10.3 LINE CHARTS

A line chart displays the change in a certain quantity in relation to another quantity (often time). The following steps produce a line chart.

1. Look over the data to be displayed. A typical line chart displays between 5 and 20 items of data corresponding to evenly spaced units of time: years, months, or days. The positions on the *x*-axis will contain labels such as "Jan Feb Mar Apr . . ." or "1995 1996 1997 1998." These labels can be placed at the locations 1, 2, 3, . . . on the *x*-axis.
2. Choose a coordinate system based on the number of data items and the size of the quantities. A convenient scale for the *x*-axis is from –1 to one more than the number of data items. The scale for the *y*-axis is determined by the largest quantity to be displayed.
3. Draw the line segments. It is a good idea to draw a small circle around the endpoints of the line segments.
4. Draw and label tick marks on the coordinate axes. The *x*-axis should have a tick mark for each time period. The *y*-axis should have at least one tick mark to indicate the magnitude of the quantities displayed.
5. Title the chart and give the source of the data.

EXAMPLE 1 Table 10.3 gives enrollment data for two-year colleges taken from the *Statistical Abstract of the United States*. (The data for 2000 are a projection.) Write a program to display the total enrollments for the given years in a line chart.

Year	**1960**	**1970**	**1980**	**1990**	**2000**
Male	283	1375	2047	2233	2398
Female	170	945	2479	3007	3358
Total	453	2320	4526	5240	5756

Table 10.3 Two-Year College Enrollments (in thousands)

SOLUTION Figure 10.13 contains the results of executing the following program. (Explanatory remarks follow the program.) Press Ctrl+Break to terminate the program.

```
REM Line Chart of Total Two-Year College Enrollments
CALL Initialize(numYears)
DIM label$(1 TO numYears), total(1 TO numYears)
CALL ReadData(label$(), total(), numYears, maxEnrollment)
CALL ShowTitle
CALL DrawAxes(numYears, maxEnrollment)
CALL ShowLabels(label$(), numYears, maxEnrollment)
CALL DrawData(total(), numYears)
DO: LOOP          'Suppress "Press any key to continue"
REM --- Data: year, total enrollment
DATA 1960, 453
DATA 1970, 2320
DATA 1980, 4526
DATA 1990, 5240
DATA 2000, 5756
END

SUB DrawAxes (numYears, maxEnrollment)
  REM Draw axes
  WINDOW (-1, -.2 * maxEnrollment)-(numYears + 1, 1.2 * maxEnrollment)
  LINE (-1, 0)-(numYears + 1, 0)
  LINE (0, -.1 * maxEnrollment)-(0, 1.1 * maxEnrollment)
END SUB

SUB DrawData (total(), numYears)
  REM Draw lines connecting data and circle data points
  FOR i = 1 TO numYears - 1
    LINE (i, total(i))-(i + 1, total(i + 1))
    CIRCLE (i, total(i)), .008 * numYears
  NEXT i
  CIRCLE (numYears, total(numYears)), .008 * numYears
END SUB

SUB Initialize (numYears)
  REM Prepare screen and set number of data entries
  SCREEN 12
  LET numYears = 5
END SUB

SUB ReadData (label$(), total(), numYears, maxEnrollment)
  REM Read data into arrays, find highest total enrollment
  LET maxEnrollment = 0
  FOR i = 1 TO numYears
    READ label$(i), total(i)
    IF total(i) > maxEnrollment THEN
        LET maxEnrollment = total(i)
    END IF
  NEXT i
END SUB
```

```
SUB ShowLabels (label$(), numYears, maxEnrollment)
  REM Draw axes' labels and tick marks
  LET tickDist = 80 / (numYears + 2)
  FOR i = 1 TO numYears
    LINE (i, -.02 * maxEnrollment)-(i, .02 * maxEnrollment)
    LOCATE 27, (1 + i) * tickDist - 1
    PRINT label$(i)
  NEXT i
  LINE (-.01 * numYears, maxEnrollment)-(.01 * numYears, maxEnrollment)
  LOCATE 5, 5
  PRINT maxEnrollment
END SUB

SUB ShowTitle
  REM Display source and title
  LOCATE 30, 1
  PRINT "Source: Statistical Abstract of the United States";
  LOCATE 1, 24
  PRINT "Two-Year College Enrollments (in thousands)"
END SUB
```

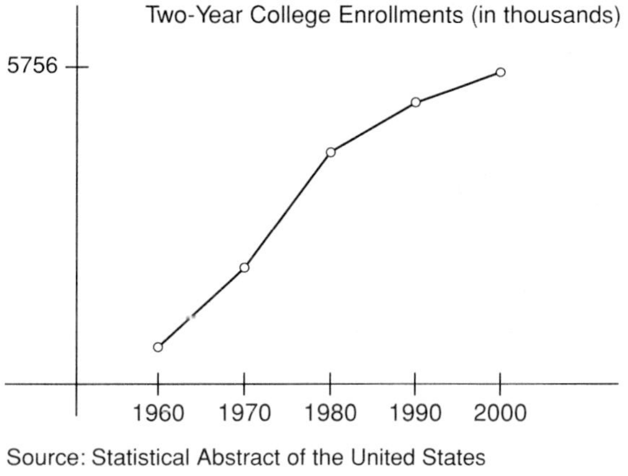

Figure 10.13 Chart for Example 1

Remarks on the program in Example 1:

1. The value of *tickDist* in the subprogram ShowLabels was determined by subdividing the 80-character row into about *numYears* + 2 equal zones. The *y*-axis appears at the end of the first zone, and the labels begin at the end of the second zone. Each zone has length 80/7.

2. In the subprogram ShowLabels, the lengths of the tick marks and the locations of the text were determined by trial and error.

3. The number 5 was specified as a parameter in the subprogram Initialize. This feature makes it easy to add additional data to the line chart. For instance, if we decide to include the data for one additional year, we will only have to change the value of *numYears* and add one more DATA statement.

Line Styling: Patterned or "styled" lines can be drawn between two points. Some examples are shown in Figure 10.14. Each line has an associated number identifying its style. If *s* is one of the numbers in Figure 10.14, then the statement

```
LINE (a, b)-(c, d), , , s
```

draws the line from (*a*, *b*) to (*c*, *d*) in the style corresponding to the number *s*. The relationship between style numbers and style lines is discussed in the appendix to this chapter.

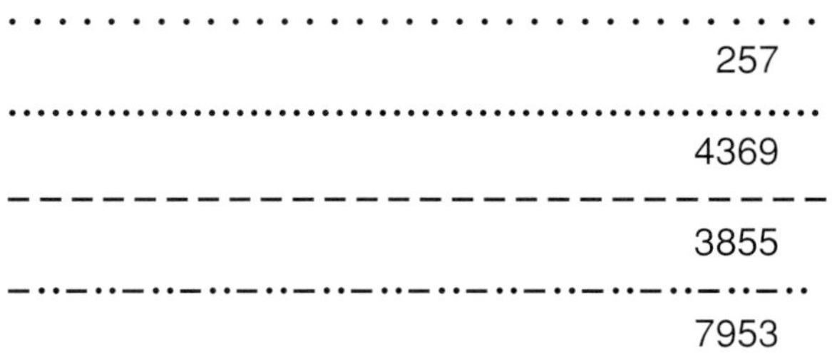

Figure 10.14 Line Patterns

Styling is useful when displaying several line charts on the same coordinate system.

EXAMPLE 2 Alter the program in Example 1 so that it will draw line charts displaying the male, female, and total enrollments of two-year colleges.

SOLUTION The DATA statements must be changed to contain the enrollment figures for males and females, and arrays must be created to hold this information. The totals can be computed from the other numbers. The styled lines for male and female enrollments must be drawn. Finally, legends must be given to identify the different line charts. Figure 10.15 contains the outcome of the modified program.

```
REM Line Charts of Two-Year College Enrollments
CALL Initialize(numYears)
DIM male(1 TO numYears), female(1 TO numYears), total(1 TO numYears)
DIM label$(1 TO numYears)
CALL ReadData(label$(), male(), female(), total(), numYears, maxEnrollment)
CALL ShowTitle
CALL DrawAxes(numYears, maxEnrollment)
CALL ShowLabels(label$(), numYears, maxEnrollment)
CALL DrawData(male(), female(), total(), numYears)
CALL ShowLegend
DO: LOOP          'Suppress "Press any key to continue"
REM --- Data: year, male enrollment, female enrollment
DATA 1960, 283, 170
DATA 1970, 1375, 945
DATA 1980, 2047, 2479
DATA 1990, 2233, 3007
DATA 2000, 2398, 3358
END
```

```
SUB DrawAxes (numYears, maxEnrollment)
  REM Draw axes
  WINDOW (-1, -.2 * maxEnrollment)-(numYears + 1, 1.2 * maxEnrollment)
  LINE (-1, 0)-(numYears + 1, 0)
  LINE (0, -.1 * maxEnrollment)-(0, 1.1 * maxEnrollment)
END SUB

SUB DrawData (male(), female(), total(), numYears)
  REM Draw lines connecting data and circle data points
  FOR i = 1 TO numYears - 1
    LINE (i, male(i))-(i + 1, male(i + 1)), , , 257
    LINE (i, female(i))-(i + 1, female(i + 1)), , , 4369
    LINE (i, total(i))-(i + 1, total(i + 1))
    CIRCLE (i, male(i)), .008 * numYears
    CIRCLE (i, female(i)), .008 * numYears
    CIRCLE (i, total(i)), .008 * numYears
  NEXT i
  CIRCLE (numYears, male(numYears)), .008 * numYears
  CIRCLE (numYears, female(numYears)), .008 * numYears
  CIRCLE (numYears, total(numYears)), .008 * numYears
END SUB

SUB Initialize (numYears)
  REM Prepare screen and set number of data entries
  SCREEN 12
  LET numYears = 5
END SUB

SUB ReadData (label$(), male(), female(), total(), numYears, maxEnrollment)
  REM Read data into arrays, find highest enrollment
  LET maxEnrollment = 0
  FOR i = 1 TO numYears
    READ label$(i), male(i), female(i)
    LET total(i) = male(i) + female(i)
    IF total(i) > maxEnrollment THEN
        LET maxEnrollment = total(i)
    END IF
  NEXT i
END SUB

SUB ShowLabels (label$(), numYears, maxEnrollment)
  REM Draw axes' labels and tick marks
  LET tickDist = 80 / (numYears + 2)
  FOR i = 1 TO numYears
    LINE (i, -.02 * maxEnrollment)-(i, .02 * maxEnrollment)
    LOCATE 28, (1 + i) * tickDist
    PRINT label$(i)
  NEXT i
  LINE (-.01 * numYears, maxEnrollment)-(.01 * numYears, maxEnrollment)
  LOCATE 5, 5
  PRINT maxEnrollment
END SUB
```

```
SUB ShowLegend
  REM Show legend
  WINDOW (0, 0)-(80, 30)      'Coordinate system to mix graphics & text
  LINE (13, 26.6)-(25, 26.6), , , 257       'Draw line in row 4
  LOCATE 4, 27
  PRINT "Male"
  LINE (13, 24.6)-(25, 24.6), , , 4369     'Draw line in row 6
  LOCATE 6, 27
  PRINT "Female"
  LINE (13, 22.6)-(25, 22.6)               'Draw line in row 8
  LOCATE 8, 27
  PRINT "Total"
END SUB

SUB ShowTitle
  REM Display source and title
  LOCATE 30, 1
  PRINT "Source: Statistical Abstract of the United States";
  LOCATE 1, 20
  PRINT "Two-Year College Enrollments (in thousands)"
END SUB
```

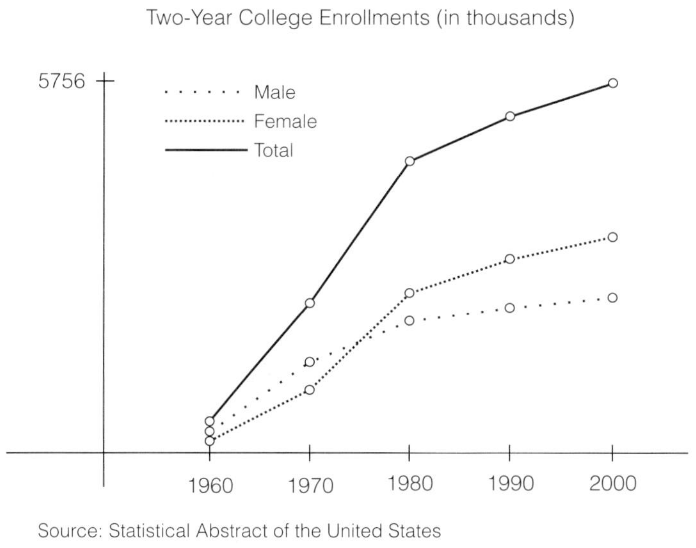

Figure 10.15 Chart for Example 2

PRACTICE PROBLEMS 10.3

Consider the programs of Examples 1 and 2 that draw the three-line chart of two-year college enrollments.

1. The enrollments (in thousands) for 1950 were Males–140, Females–78, Total–218. Change the program to include these data.
2. Suppose the enrollment data were given in units of millions instead of thousands. How would this affect the appearance of the three-line chart?

3. Why wasn't 2000 used in the WINDOW statement to determine the scale for the *x*-axis? It is the largest value of *x*.

EXERCISES 10.3

In Exercises 1 and 2, determine a possible WINDOW statement that could have been used to obtain the chart.

1.

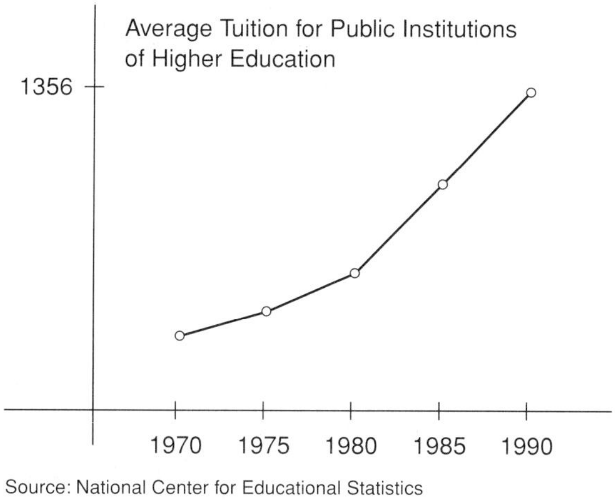

2.

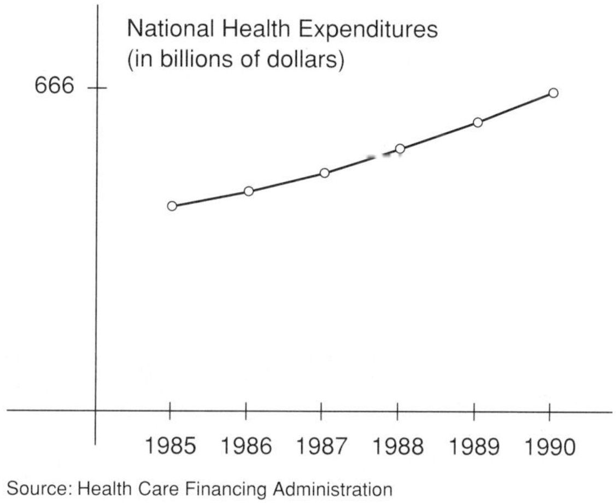

In Exercises 3 through 7, write a program to display the given information in a line chart.

3. The Consumer Price Index is a measure of living costs based on changes in retail prices. The following table uses 1968 as the base year and gives the value of the index in January for several years

Year	1968	1973	1978	1983	1988	1993	1998
CPI	100.0	124.9	183.3	286.6	339.3	418.2	473.9

Source: Bureau of Labor Statistics

4. Percentage of College Freshmen Who Smoke

Year	1987	1989	1991	1993	1995	1997
Percent	8.9	10.3	11.4	11.7	14.6	16.1

Source: Higher Education Research Institute

5. Freshman Life Goals (% of students committed to goal)

	1968	1976	1984	1992
Be very well off financially	45	57	70	73
Develop a meaningful philosophy of life	80	57	45	46

Source: Higher Education Research Institute

6. Normal Monthly Precipitation (in inches)

	Jan	Apr	July	Oct
Mobile, AL	4.6	5.35	7.7	2.6
Phoenix, AZ	.7	.3	.7	.6
Portland, OR	6.2	2.3	.5	3.0
Washington, DC	2.8	2.9	3.9	2.9

Source: Statistical Abstract of the United States

7. Age Distribution (%) of the Labor Force

	16–24	25–34	35–54	Over 54
1975	24	24	36	15
1990	17	29	42	12
2005	16	21	48	15

Source: The 1994 Information Please Business Almanac

SOLUTIONS TO PRACTICE PROBLEMS 10.3

1. Change numYears to 6 in the Initialize procedure and add the DATA line

```
DATA 1950, 140, 78
```

2. Not at all. The value of *maxEnrollment*, 5756, would change to 5.756, but the WINDOW statement would scale the *y*-axis with respect to this new value of maxEnrollment and the line charts would look exactly the same as before.

3. If 2000 had been used, the line charts would have been unreadable. Line charts are used to illustrate from about 3 to 15 pieces of data. These are best placed at the numbers 1, 2, 3, . . . on the *x*-axis. In many cases the classifications given below the tick marks will be words (such as Jan, Feb, . . .) instead of numbers.

10.4 BAR CHARTS

Drawing bar charts requires a variation of the line statement. If (*x1*, *y1*) and (*x2*, *y2*) are two points on the screen, then the statement

```
LINE (x1, y1) - (x2, y2), , B
```

draws a rectangle with the two points as opposite corners. If B is replaced by BF, then a solid rectangle will be drawn (see Figure 10.16).

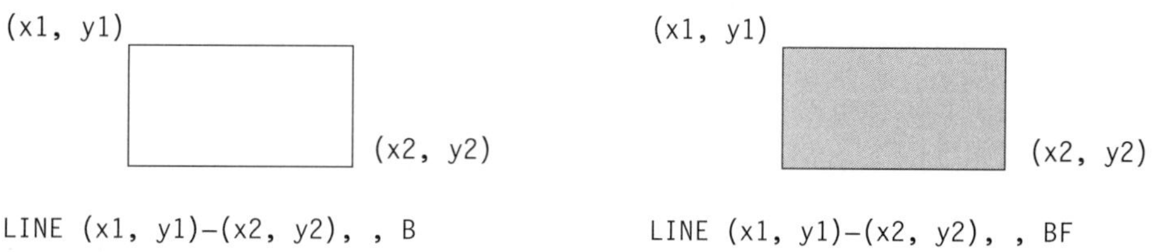

Figure 10.16 LINE Statement with B and BF Options

EXAMPLE 1 The populations of California and New York are 32 and 18 million, respectively. Draw a bar chart to compare the populations.

SOLUTION The following program produces the output shown in Figure 10.17. The first five lines are the same as those of a line chart with two pieces of data. The base of the rectangle for California is centered above the point (1, 0) on the *x*-axis and extends .3 unit to the left and right. (The number .3 was chosen arbitrarily; it had to be less than .5 so that the rectangles would not touch.) Therefore, the upper left corner of the rectangle has coordinates (.7, 32) and the lower right corner has coordinates (1.3, 0). Figure 10.18 shows the coordinates of the principal points of the rectangles.

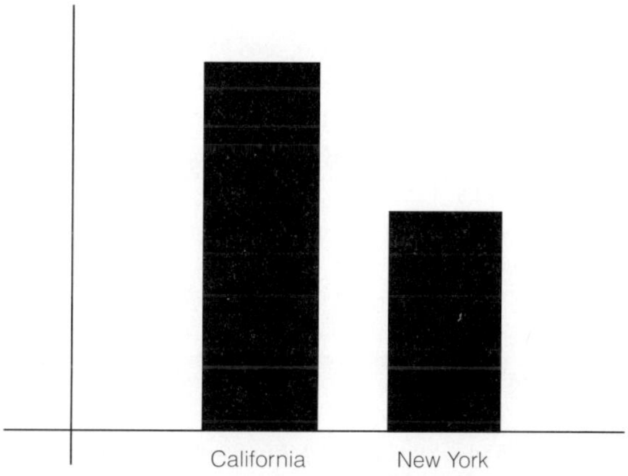

Figure 10.17 Bar Chart for Example 1

```
REM Populations of California and New York
SCREEN 12
WINDOW (-1, -5) - (3, 40)              'Specify coordinates
LINE (-1, 0) - (3, 0)                  'Draw x-axis
LINE (0, -5) - (0, 40)                 'Draw y-axis
LINE (.7, 32) - (1.3, 0), , BF         'Draw solid rectangle for CA
LINE (1.7, 18) - (2.3, 0), , BF        'Draw solid rectangle for NY
LOCATE 29, 36                          'Specify location of labels
PRINT "California          New York"
END
```

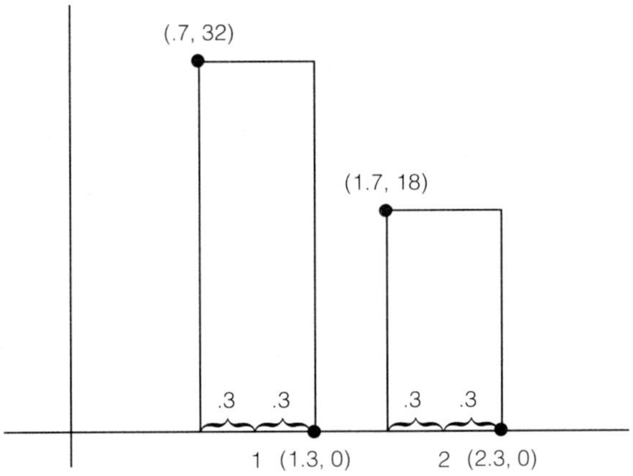

Figure 10.18 Coordinates of Principal Points of Example 1

Any program that draws a line chart can be easily modified to produce a bar chart. Multiple line charts are converted into so-called **clustered bar charts**.

EXAMPLE 2 Display the two-year college enrollments for males and females in a clustered bar chart. Use the data in Table 10.3 of Section 10.3.

SOLUTION The output of the following program appears in Figure 10.19. This program is very similar to the one that produced Figure 10.15 of Section 10.3.

```
REM Bar chart of two-year college enrollments
CALL Initialize(numYears)
DIM male(1 TO numYears), female(1 TO numYears)
DIM label$(1 TO numYears)
CALL ReadData(label$(), male(), female(), numYears, maxEnrollment)
CALL ShowTitle
CALL DrawAxes(numYears, maxEnrollment)
CALL ShowLabels(label$(), numYears, maxEnrollment)
CALL DrawData(male(), female(), numYears)
CALL ShowLegend
DO: LOOP
REM --- Data: year, male enrollment, female enrollment
DATA 1960, 283, 170
DATA 1970, 1375, 945
DATA 1980, 2047, 2479
DATA 1990, 2233, 3007
DATA 2000, 2398, 3358
END

SUB DrawAxes (numYears, maxEnrollment)
  REM Draw axes
  WINDOW (-1, -.2 * maxEnrollment)-(numYears + 1, 1.2 * maxEnrollment)
  LINE (-1, 0)-(numYears + 1, 0)
  LINE (0, -.1 * maxEnrollment)-(0, 1.1 * maxEnrollment)
END SUB

SUB DrawData (male(), female(), numYears)
  REM Draw rectangles
```

```
  FOR i = 1 TO numYears
    LINE (i - .3, male(i))-(i, 0), , BF
    LINE (i, female(i))-(i + .3, 0), , B
  NEXT i
END SUB

SUB Initialize (numYears)
  REM Initialize screen and number of years
  SCREEN 12
  LET numYears = 5
END SUB

SUB ReadData (label$(), male(), female(), numYears, maxEnrollment)
  REM Read data into arrays
  LET maxEnrollment = 0
  FOR i = 1 TO numYears
    READ label$(i), male(i), female(i)
    IF male(i) > maxEnrollment THEN
        LET maxEnrollment = male(i)
    END IF
    IF female(i) > maxEnrollment THEN
        LET maxEnrollment = female(i)
    END IF
  NEXT i
END SUB

SUB ShowLabels (label$(), numYears, maxEnrollment)
  REM Draw axes' labels and tick marks
  LET tickDist = 80 / (numYears + 2)
  FOR k = 1 TO numYears
    LOCATE 28, (k + 1) * tickDist - 1
    PRINT label$(k)
  NEXT k
  LINE (-.01 * numYears, maxEnrollment)-(.01 * numYears, maxEnrollment)
  LOCATE 5, 5
  PRINT maxEnrollment
END SUB

SUB ShowLegend
  REM Place identifying legends
  WINDOW (0, 0)-(80, 25)
  LINE (22, 21)-(32, 20), , BF
  LOCATE 6, 35
  PRINT "Male"
  LINE (22, 19)-(32, 18), , B
  LOCATE 8, 35
  PRINT "Female"
END SUB

SUB ShowTitle
  REM Display source of data and title
  LOCATE 30, 1
  PRINT "Source: Statistical Abstract of the United States";
  LOCATE 1, 20
  PRINT "Two-Year College Enrollments (in thousands)"
END SUB
```

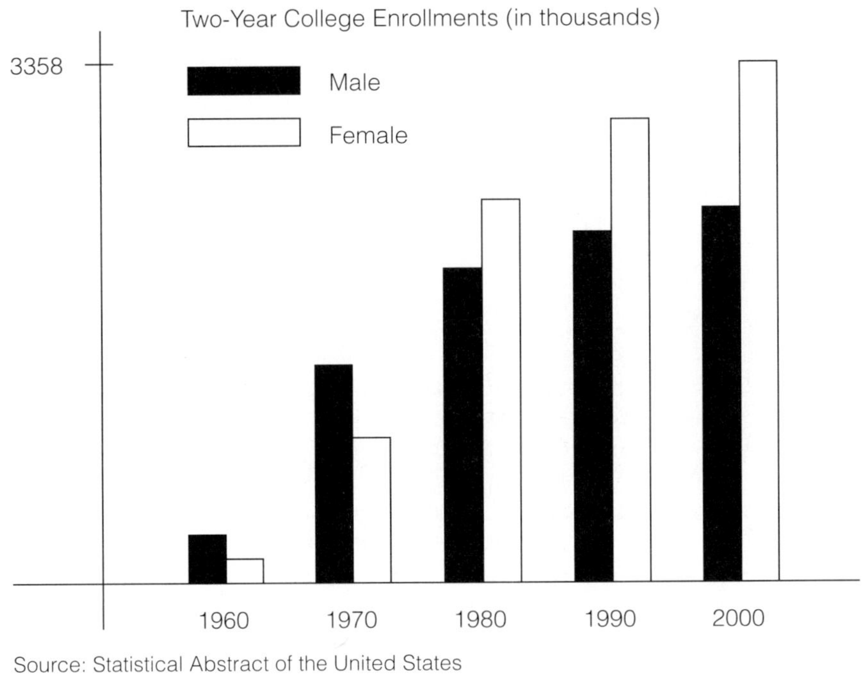

Figure 10.19 Chart for Example 2

Comments:

1. Any line chart can be converted to a bar chart and vice versa. Line charts are best suited for displaying quantities that vary with time. The slopes of the individual line segments clearly portray the rates at which the quantity is changing. Bar charts excel in contrasting the magnitudes of different entities.

2. The LINE statement can produce colored rectangles with a monitor capable of displaying color. The statement LINE (*x1*, *y1*)–(*x2*, *y2*), c, B draws a rectangle in color c. A solid rectangle of color *c* will be produced if B is replaced by BF. The use of color permits clustered bar charts with three bars per cluster.

3. In Section 10.5, we discuss a method to fill in rectangles using various patterns, such as horizontal lines and crosshatches. Using this technique, we can create clustered bar charts having three or more bars per cluster.

PRACTICE PROBLEMS 10.4

Consider the bar chart in Figure 10.20.

1. How does this bar chart differ from the other charts that have been considered so far?

2. Outline methods to achieve the effects referred to in the solution to Practice Problem 1.

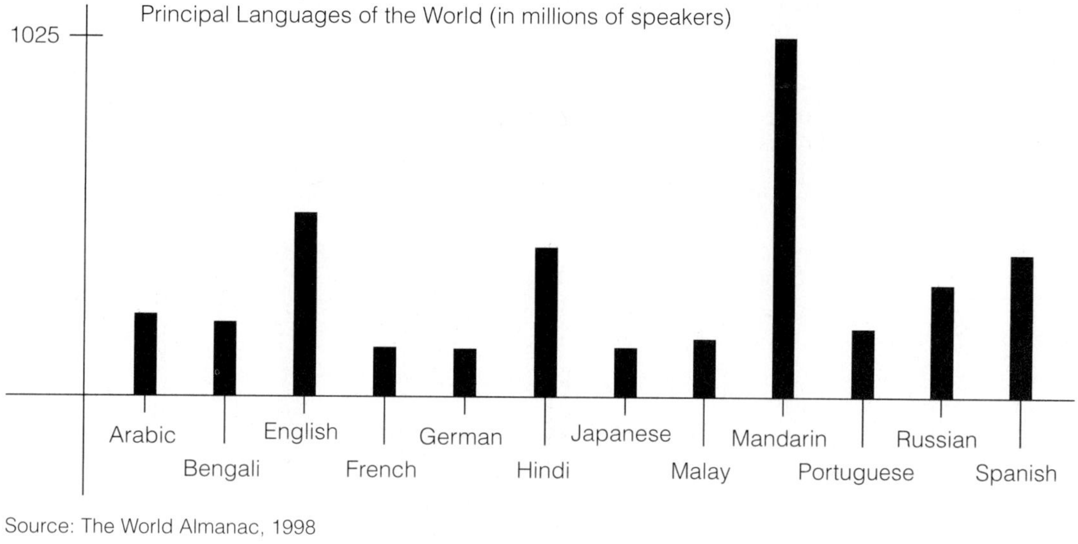

Figure 10.20 Bar Chart for Practice Problems

EXERCISES 10.4

1. Suppose data for a few more years are added to the data of Example 2. What changes will have to be made in the program?

In Exercises 2 through 9, write a program to display the given information in a bar chart.

2. United States Minimum Wage

1958	1.00
1968	1.15
1978	2.65
1988	3.35
1998	5.15

3. Number of Computers in U.S. Public Schools, K-12 (in millions)

1985	.8
1987	1.4
1989	1.7
1991	2.2
1993	4.1

Source: Statistical Abstract of the United States, 1995

4. Most Popular Majors for College Freshmen in Fall 1997

Field	**Percent**
Elementary Education	5.1
Business Administration	4.5
Predent, Premed, Prevet	3.9
Psychology	3.8
Therapy (occup, phys, speech)	3.6

Source: "The American Freshman: National Norms for Fall 1997," Higher Education Research Institute

5. Average Tuition and Required Fees at Four-Year Colleges

	1975	1980	1985	1990	1995
Public	599	840	1388	2035	2977
Private	2614	3811	6843	10348	14527

Source: Statistical Abstract of the United States, 1997

6. Educational Attainment of Persons 25 years Old and Older (in %)

	1975	1985	1995
High School Graduate	62.5	73.9	81.7
College Graduate	13.9	19.4	23.0

Source: U.S. Bureau of the Census

7. Motor Vehicles in Use (in millions)

	1980	1985	1990	1995
Cars	104.6	114.7	123.3	123.2
Trucks	35.2	42.4	56.0	70.2

Source: Statistical Abstract of the United States, 1997

8. Principal Languages of the World (in millions of speakers)

Arabic	235	Japanese	126
Bengali	207	Malay	170
English	497	Mandarin	1025
French	127	Portuguese	187
German	126	Russian	279
Hindi	476	Spanish	409

Source: The World Almanac, 1998

9. 1996 Federal Funding for Research and Development to Universities and Colleges (in millions of dollars)

Johns Hopkins Univ.	710	Univ. of Michigan	281
Univ. of Washington	313	MIT	272
UC, San Diego	292	UC, Los Angeles	237
Stanford Univ.	282	Univ. of Wisconsin	233

Source: National Science Foundation

The program that follows draws a circle in the center of the screen. In Exercises 10 through 12, rewrite the WINDOW statement in order to achieve the stated result.

```
SCREEN 12
WINDOW (-5, -5)-(5, 5)
CIRCLE (0, 0), 2
END
```

10. Draw the circle in the left half of the screen.

11. Draw the circle in the right half of the screen.

12. Draw the circle in the upper left-hand corner of the screen.

13. Cluster bar charts are sometimes drawn with overlapping rectangles. (See Figure 10.21.) What changes would have to be made to do this in the program of Example 2?

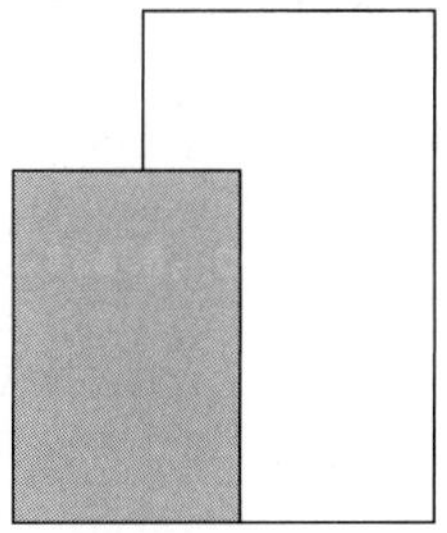

Figure 10.21 Cluster Bar Chart

SOLUTIONS TO PRACTICE PROBLEMS 10.4

1. (a) The number of characters in the labels is so large the labels must be placed in two rows.
   (b) Every other label has to be lowered.
   (c) Short vertical lines extend from the bars to the legends.
2. (a) A slight change in the WINDOW statement will produce extra room at the bottom of the screen. The negative number that specifies the lower range of the y-axis should be increased in magnitude.
   (b) The FOR...NEXT loop that places the label should be replaced by two loops that increment by 2 and place the labels on two rows.
   (c) The FOR...NEXT loops in step (b) should each draw vertical lines at the same spots where tick marks usually appear. The lines should extend from the x-axis to the appropriate label. The length of these lines can be determined by experimentation.

10.5 PIE CHARTS

Drawing pie charts requires two statements, CIRCLE and PAINT. The CIRCLE statement draws not only circles, but also arcs and radius lines of circles. The PAINT statement fills in a closed region with a pattern.

Figure 10.22 shows a circle with several radius lines drawn. The radius line extending to the right from the center of the circle is called the **horizontal radius line**. Every other radius line is assigned a number between 0 and 1 according to the percentage of the circle that must be swept out in the counterclockwise direction in order to reach that radius line. For instance, beginning at the horizontal radius line and rotating 1/4 of the way around the circle counterclockwise, we reach the radius line labeled .25.

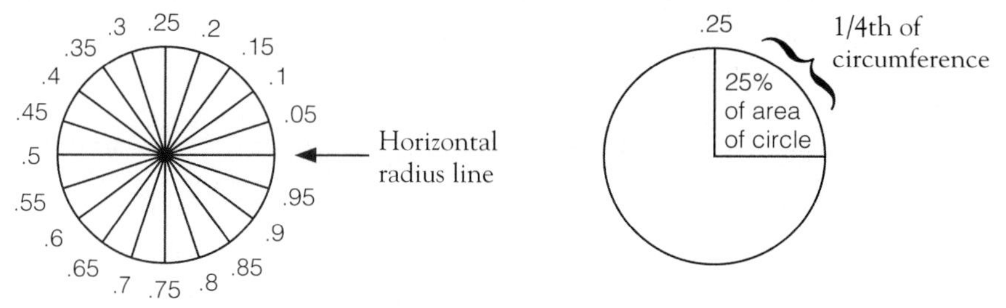

Figure 10.22 Numbers Assigned to Radius Lines

EXAMPLE 1 In Figure 10.23, what percentage of the circle's area lies in the shaded sector?

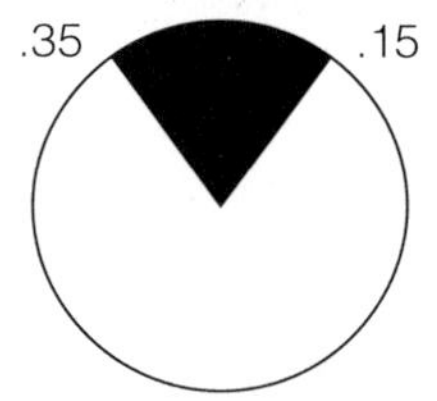

Figure 10.23 Circle for Example 1

SOLUTION The percentage of the circle contained between the radius lines labeled .15 and .35 is 35% – 15% or 20%.

The statement

```
CIRCLE (x, y), r
```

draws the circle with center (*x*, *y*) and radius *r*. More precisely, the length of the horizontal radius line will be *r* units in the scale for the *x*-axis determined by the WINDOW statement. If *a* is a number between 0 and 1, then the statement

```
CIRCLE (x, y), r, , 0, -a * c
```

(where *c* is 2 * π) draws the radius line associated with *a* and the arc from the tip of that line to the rightmost point of the circle.

The circle drawn by the statement CIRCLE (*x*, *y*), *r* has a horizontal radius line of length *r*. The vertical radius line will physically appear on the screen with the same length. However, the length in terms of the *y*-scale set by the WINDOW statement will most likely be different than *r*. For the applications of circles considered in this chapter, these two lengths must agree. This will occur if the WINDOW statement specifies the lengths of the *x*- and *y*-axes in a 4-to-3 ratio. (The reason is that the lengths of the two sides of the screen are in a 4-to-3 ratio.) Some suitable WINDOW statements are WINDOW (–4, –3)–(4, 3), WINDOW (–8, –6)–(8, 6), and WINDOW (–6, –8)–(14, 7).

EXAMPLE 2 Write a program to draw a circle, a horizontal radius line, and the radius line that is 40% of the way around the circle.

SOLUTION The following program draws a circle with its center at the center of the screen. The radius was arbitrarily chosen to be 2, and the scale for the WINDOW statement was chosen so that the circle would be fairly large. (See Figure 10.24.)

```
SCREEN 12
WINDOW (-4, -3)-(4, 3)            'Specify coordinate system
CIRCLE (0, 0), 2                  'Draw circle
LINE (0, 0)-(2, 0)                'Draw horizontal radius line
LET c = 2 * 3.14159
CIRCLE (0, 0), 2, , 0, -.4 * c    'Draw radius line corresponding to 40%
END
```

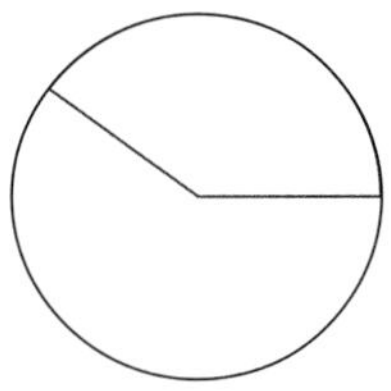

Figure 10.24 Display from Example 2

Any region on the screen that is completely contained within a boundary can be painted. If (x, y) is an interior point of such a region, then the statement

```
PAINT (x, y)
```

fills in the region. ***Note:*** The point (x, y) must be unlit (that is, not turned on) and strictly inside the region; it cannot be on the boundary.

In order to fill in sectors of pie charts, we must be able to obtain the coordinates of some point (other than the center of the circle) on a given radius line. QBasic has two functions that can be used to determine these coordinates when the center of the circle is the origin, (0, 0). Let c denote the constant 6.283185. (c has the value $2 * \pi$, the circumference of the circle of radius 1.) If a is a number between 0 and 1, then the point (COS($a * c$), SIN($a * c$)) lies on the radius line designated by a. The point will be of distance 1 from the center of the circle. (See Figure 10.25.)

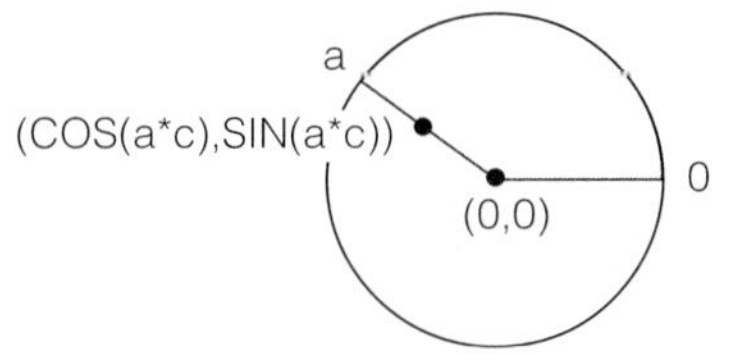

Figure 10.25 Display a Point on a Radius Line

EXAMPLE 3 Consider the circle shown on the right.

(a) Find the values of x and y.

(b) Find the coordinates of a point in the sector between .5 and .6.

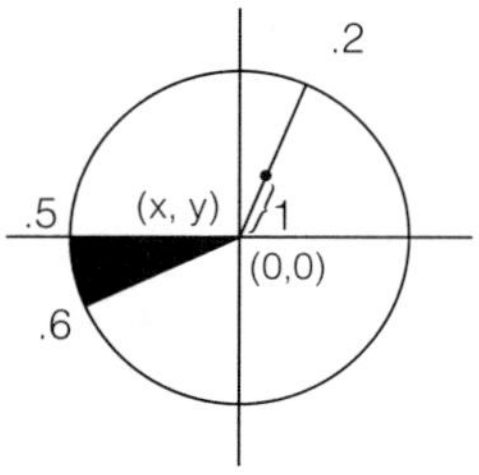

SOLUTION (a) x = COS(.2 * 6.283185) = .3090171

y = SIN(.2 * 6.283185) = .9510566

(b) The technique of part (a) can be used to find the coordinates of a point on the radius line labeled .55. Since .55 is between .5 and .6, the point will lie in the shaded sector. Therefore, the point has coordinates

(COS(.55 * 6.283185), SIN(.55 * 6.283185))

or (–.9510568, –.3090164). In general, if the circle has radius greater than 1, a and b are between 0 and 1, and p = ((a + b) / 2) * 6.283185, then the point (COS(p), SIN(p)) will be in the sector between a and b.

EXAMPLE 4 Write a program to subdivide a circle into four quadrants and fill in the second quadrant—that is, the quadrant extending from radius line .25 to radius line .5.

SOLUTION See Figure 10.26 for the output of the following program.

```
SCREEN 12
WINDOW (-4, -3)-(4, 3)                 'Specify coordinate system
CIRCLE (0, 0), 2                       'Draw circle
LINE (0, 0)-(2, 0)                     'Draw horizontal radius line
LET c = 2 * 3.14159
FOR i = 1 TO 3
  CIRCLE (0, 0), 2, , 0, -.25 * i * c  'Draw a radius line
NEXT i
LET p = ((.25 + .5) / 2) * c           'Obtain point between lines
PAINT (COS(p), SIN(p))                 'Fill in the second quadrant
END
```

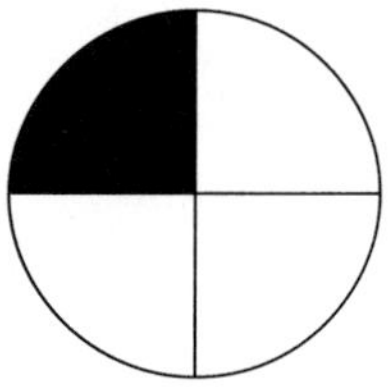

Figure 10.26 Display from Example 4

Figure 10.27 shows several patterns that can be used to fill sectors of a pie chart. Each pattern is specified by a string. [**Note:** In Figure 10.27, STRING$(16, CHR$(n)) is the string consisting of 16 charaters of ASCII value n.] If (x, y) is a point in the interior of a sector (or any closed region), then the statement

```
PAINT (x, y), t$
```

will fill the sector with the pattern specified by the string *t$*. (The appendix of this chapter explains how to design a pattern and determine its specifying string.)

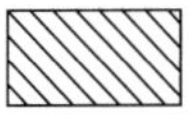

```
CHR$(0)+CHR$(128)+CHR$(128)+CHR$(0)+CHR$(0)+CHR$(64)+CHR$(64)+CHR$(0)+
CHR$(0)+CHR$(32)+CHR$(32)+CHR$(0)+CHR$(0)+CHR$(16)+CHR$(16)+CHR$(0)+
CHR$(0)+CHR$(8)+CHR$(8)+CHR$(0)+CHR$(0)+CHR$(4)+CHR$(4)+CHR$(0)+
CHR$(0)+CHR$(2)+CHR$(2)+CHR$(0)+CHR$(0)+CHR$(1)+CHR$(1)
```

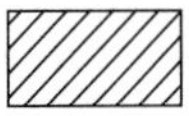

```
CHR$(0)+CHR$(1)+CHR$(0)+CHR$(0)+CHR$(0)+CHR$(2)+CHR$(0)+CHR$(0)+
CHR$(0)+CHR$(4)+CHR$(0)+CHR$(0)+CHR$(0)+CHR$(8)+CHR$(0)+CHR$(0)+
CHR$(0)+CHR$(16)+CHR$(0)+CHR$(0)+CHR$(0)+CHR$(32)+CHR$(0)+CHR$(0)+
CHR$(0)+CHR$(64)+CHR$(0)+CHR$(0)+CHR$(0)+CHR$(128)
```

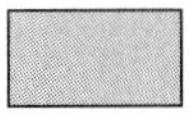

```
CHR$(1)+CHR$(0)+CHR$(1)+CHR$(0)+CHR$(0)+CHR$(0)+CHR$(0)+CHR$(0)+
CHR$(16)+CHR$(0)+CHR$(16)+CHR$(0)+CHR$(0)
```

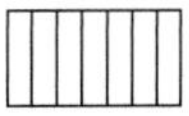

```
STRING$(16,CHR$(128))
```

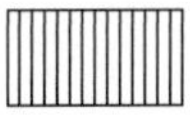

```
STRING$(16,CHR$(136))
```

```
STRING$(16,CHR$(255))
```

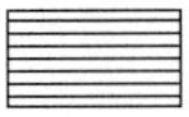

```
CHR$(0)+CHR$(0)+CHR$(255)+CHR$(0)+CHR$(0)+CHR$(0)+CHR$(0)+CHR$(0)+
CHR$(0)+CHR$(0)+CHR$(0)+CHR$(0)+CHR$(0)
```

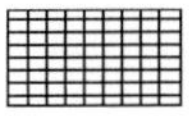

```
CHR$(0)+CHR$(0)+CHR$(0)+CHR$(24)+CHR$(0)+CHR$(0)+CHR$(0)+CHR$(24)+
CHR$(0)+CHR$(0)+CHR$(0)+CHR$(24)+CHR$(0)+CHR$(0)+CHR$(0)+CHR$(255)
```

Figure 10.27 Fill Patterns for SCREEN 12

EXAMPLE 5 Modify Example 4 so the second quadrant is filled with vertical lines.

SOLUTION The wide vertical line pattern in Figure 10.27 is specified by the string CHR$(1). Therefore, delete the current PAINT statement and replace it with the following two lines.

```
LET t$ = STRING$(16,CHR$(128))     'Specify fill pattern
PAINT (COS(p), SIN(p)), t$         'Fill in the second quadrant
```

The procedure for drawing a pie chart is as follows:

1. Read the categories and the quantities into arrays, such as category$() and quantity().
2. Draw the circle and the radius lines. The number associated with the *i*th radius line is cumPercent(*i*). This number is a total of quantity(*i*) and the preceding percentages.
3. Fill in each of the sectors of the circle with a pattern.
4. Draw rectangular legends to associate each sector with its category.

EXAMPLE 6 Table 10.4 gives the market share of Internet browsers for the first quarter of 1997. Construct a pie chart that displays the market share.

	Percent of Total Market
Internet Explorer	31
Netscape Navigator	65
Other	4

Table 10.4 Browser Market Share, 1st quarter of 1997

SOLUTION See Figure 10.28 for the output of the following program.

```
REM Draw pie chart of browser market share
CALL Initialize(numItems)
DIM category$(1 TO numItems), quantity(1 TO numItems)
DIM cumPercent(0 TO numItems), fillPattern$(1 TO numItems)
CALL ReadData(category$(), quantity(), numItems)
CALL ShowTitle
CALL MakeFillPattern(fillPattern$())
CALL DrawData(quantity(), cumPercent(), fillPattern$(), numItems)
CALL ShowLegend(category$(), fillPattern$(), numItems)
DO: LOOP
REM --- Data: category, percentage of market
DATA Internet Explorer, .31
DATA Netscape Navigator, .65
DATA Other, .04
END

SUB DrawData (quantity(), cumPercent(), fillPattern$(), numItems)
  REM Draw circle and radius lines, and fill sectors with patterns
  LET circumf = 2 * 3.14159
  CIRCLE (0, 0), 5
  LINE (0, 0)-(5, 0)
  LET cumPercent(0) = 0
  FOR i = 1 TO numItems
    LET cumPercent(i) = cumPercent(i - 1) + quantity(i)
    IF i < numItems THEN
        CIRCLE (0, 0), 5, , 0, -cumPercent(i) * circumf
    END IF
    LET pt = circumf * (cumPercent(i) + cumPercent(i - 1)) / 2
    PAINT (COS(pt), SIN(pt)), fillPattern$(i)
  NEXT i
END SUB

SUB Initialize (numItems)
  REM Initialize screen and number of items
  SCREEN 12
  WINDOW (-6, -8)-(14, 7)
  LET numItems = 3
END SUB

SUB MakeFillPattern (fillPattern$())
  REM Create fill patterns for pie chart
  LET fillPattern$(1) = (STRING$(16,CHR$(255)))
  LET fillPattern$(2) = (STRING$(16,CHR$(136)))
  LET fillPattern$(3) = (STRING$(16,CHR$(128)))
END SUB

SUB ReadData (category$(), quantity(), numItems)
  REM Read categories and quantities
  FOR i = 1 TO numItems
    READ category$(i), quantity(i)
  NEXT i
END SUB
```

```
SUB ShowLegend (category$(), fillPattern$(), numItems)
  REM Place legend
  WINDOW (0, 0)-(80, 30)
  FOR i = 0 TO numItems - 1
    LINE (46, 25 - 2 * i)-(53, 24 - 2 * i), , B
    PAINT (50, 24.4 - 2 * i), fillPattern$(i + 1)
    LOCATE 2 * i + 6, 55
    PRINT category$(i + 1)
  NEXT i
END SUB

SUB ShowTitle
  REM Display title
  LET title$ = "Browser Market Share, 1st quarter of 1997"
  LOCATE 26, 40 - LEN(title$) / 2       'Center title on 26th line
  PRINT title$
END SUB
```

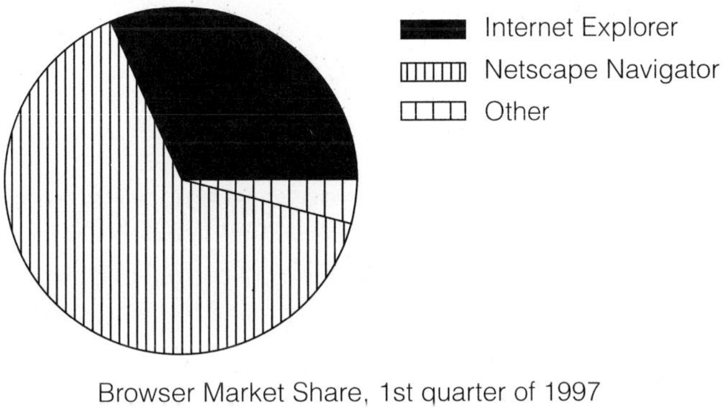

Figure 10.28 Display from Example 6

Comments:

1. If $0 < a < b < 1$ and c (= 2*π) is the circumference of the unit circle, then the statement

   ```
   CIRCLE (x, y), r, ,a * c, b * c
   ```

   draws an arc from the end of radius line a to the end of radius line b [see Figure 10.29(a)]. The statement

   ```
   CIRCLE (x, y), r, , -a * c, -b * c
   ```

   draws the sector corresponding to that arc [see Figure 10.29(b)]. We did not use this variation of the CIRCLE statement in Example 5, since it does not give the desired result when $a = 0$ [see Figure 10.29(c)]. The computer cannot distinguish between 0 and –0.

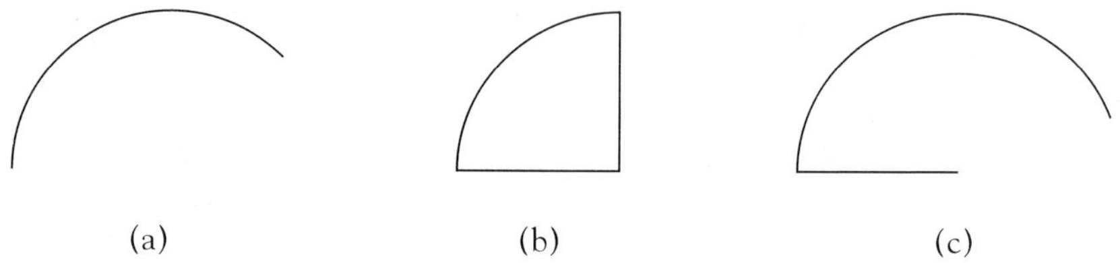

Figure 10.29 Sectors of a Circle

2. The statement

```
CIRCLE (x, y), r, c
```

draws a circle in color *c*. If a closed region has a boundary with the color *b* of the current palette, then the statement

```
PAINT (x, y), c, b
```

fills in this region with color *c*. The method for specifying multicolored fill patterns is complicated.

3. Figure 10.30 gives the fill patterns for a CGA or Hercules monitor.

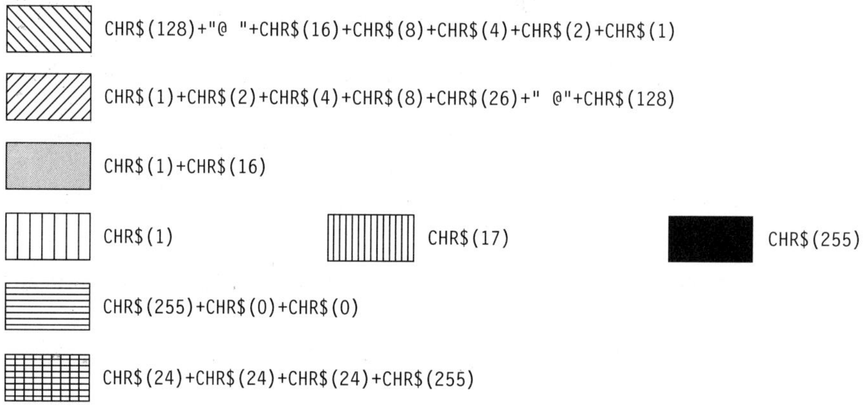

Figure 10.30 Fill Paterns for SCREEN 2 or SCREEN 3

PRACTICE PROBLEMS 10.5

1. Label each of the radius lines in Figure 10.31 with a number from 0 to 1.

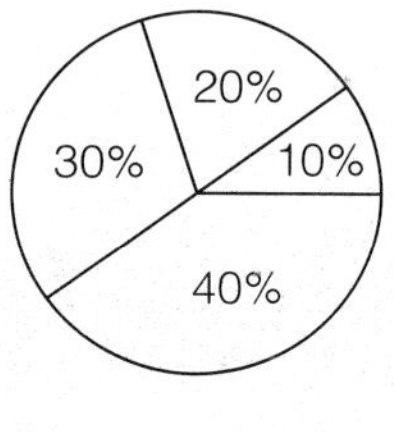

Figure 10.31 Circle for Practice Problem 1

2. Write a program to draw the circle and radius lines in Problem 1 and to fill in the sector consisting of 30% of the area of the circle.

3. The following program attempts to draw a straight line and place small solid circles about its endpoints. Why will the program fail?

```
REM Draw line with circles as endpoints
SCREEN 12
WINDOW (-2, -1)-(6, 5)        'Specify coordinate system
LINE (1, 1)-(3, 3)            'Draw a line from (1,1) to (3,3)
CIRCLE (1, 1), .05            'Draw a small circle at (1,1)
PAINT (1, 1)                  'Fill in the small circle
CIRCLE (3, 3), .05            'Draw a small circle at (3,3)
PAINT (3, 3)                  'Fill in the small circle
END
```

EXERCISES 10.5

1. Label each of the radius lines in Figure 10.32(a) with a number from 0 to 1.

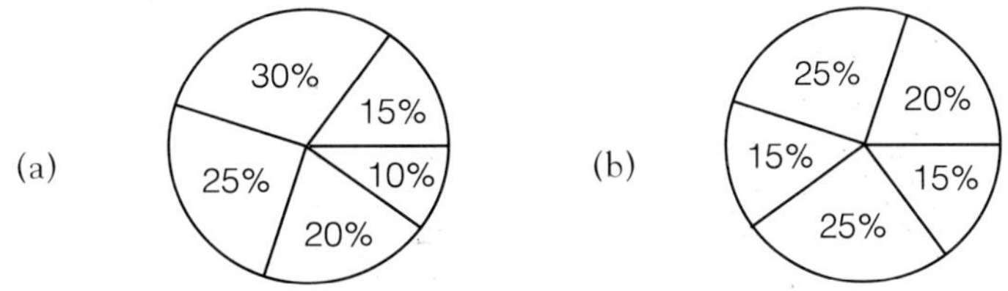

Figure 10.32 Circles for Exercises 1 and 2

2. Label each of the radius lines in Figure 10.32(b) with a number from 0 to 1.

3. Write a program to draw the circle and radius lines of Figure 10.32(a) and to fill in the sector consisting of 10% of the circle.

4. Write a program to draw the circle and radius lines of Figure 10.32(b) and to fill in the sector consisting of 25% of the circle.

In Exercises 5 and 6, draw a pie chart to display the given data.

5. United States Recreational Beverage Consumption (1995)

Soft Drinks	52.9%
Beer	14.7%
Bottled Water	11.1%
Other	21.3%

Source: International Bottled Water Association

6. Average Number of Miles from College to Home for College Freshmen

5 or less	10%	51 to 100	15%
6 to 10	8%	101 to 500	28%
11 to 50	30%	more than 500	9%

Source: Higher Education Research Institute

7. Construct a general pie-chart program that prompts the user for the title, the number of sectors (2 through 8), and legends. Try the program with the following data.

Share of Bagel Market, 1996

Supermarkets	47%
Bagel Stores	20%
Bakeries	20%
Other	6%

Source: Bakery Production and Marketing magazine, Food Marketing Institute

8. Modify the program in Exercise 7 to accept raw data and convert them to percentages. Try the program with the following data.

Fiscal Year 1998 Operating Budget for Montgomery County, Maryland (in millions of dollars)

Education	1052	Health and Human Services	102
Public Safety	220	Reserves	69
Public Works and Transportation	136	Other	118
Capital Investment	102		

Source: Montgomery County Government Department of Finance

9. Write a program that produces the drawing in Figure 10.33.

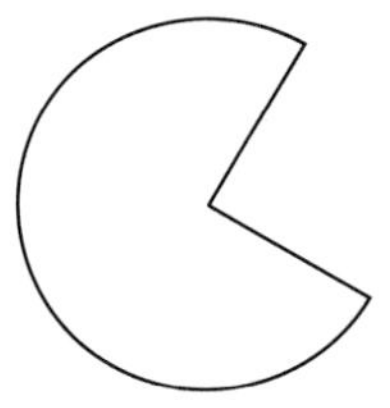

Figure 10.33 Drawing for Exercise 9

10. Write a program that draws a smiling face. See Figure 10.34.

Figure 10.34 Drawing for Exercise 10

SOLUTIONS TO PRACTICE PROBLEMS 10.5

1. Each number was obtained by summing the percentages for each of the sectors from the horizontal radius line to the radius line under consideration.

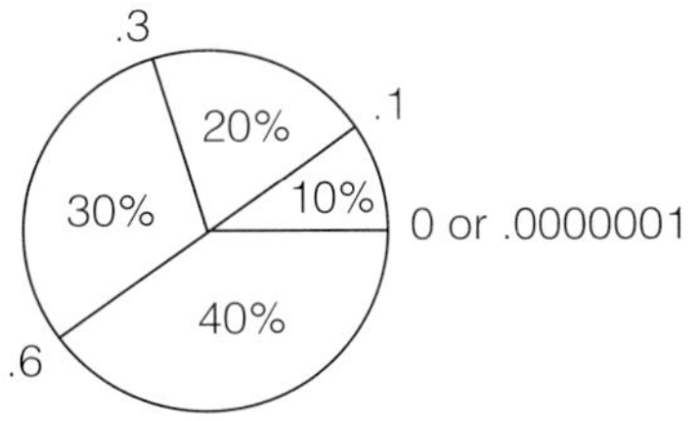

2. The 30% sector extends from radius line .3 to radius line .6. Therefore, the radius line (.3 + .6) / 2 or .45 bisects it. Provided the circle is centered at the origin and has radius greater than 1, the point (COS(.45 * 6.283185), SIN(.45 * 6.283185)) will lie in the sector.

```
SCREEN 12
WINDOW (-4, -3)-(4, 3)              'Specify coordinate system
CIRCLE (0, 0), 2                    'Draw circle
LINE (0, 0)-(2, 0)                  'Draw horizontal radius line
LET c = 2 * 3.14159
FOR i = 1 TO 3
  READ a
  CIRCLE (0, 0), 2, , 0, -a * c     'Draw radius line
NEXT i
PAINT (COS(.45 * c), SIN(.45 * c))    'Fill in the 30% sector
REM --- Data: numbers assigned to nonhorizontal radius lines
DATA .1, .3, .6
END
```

3. The first PAINT command does not produce the intended result, since the point (1, 1) will have previously been lit (that is, turned on) by the LINE statement. The PAINT statement requires that the specified point be unlit. No error message will appear, but the small circle will not be filled in. The program can be corrected by drawing the circles first and then the line.

Chapter 10
Appendix: Specifying Line Style and Fill Patterns

Line Style

A line is just a collection of dots on the screen. A style number specifies a pattern for 16 consecutive dots. This pattern is repeated as many times as necessary to draw the line. To obtain the style number for a 16-dot pattern, write down a sequence of 16 0s and 1s (beginning with a 0) to describe the pattern. The 0s correspond to black (unlit) dots and the 1s to white (lit) dots. Convert this binary representation to the corresponding number in decimal form to obtain *s*. For instance, the sequence 0001000100010001 describes the pattern of the second line of Figure 10.15 of Section 10.3. The binary number 0001000100010001 corresponds to the decimal number 4369. The following program determines the style number for a pattern. The function VAL in the FOR...NEXT loop converts a digit character to its numeric value.

```
REM Determine style numbers for lines
INPUT "Sequence of 16 zeros and ones"; b$
LET d = 0
FOR i = 0 TO 15
  LET d = d + VAL(MID$(b$, 16 - i, 1)) * 2 ^ i
NEXT i
PRINT "The style number for this bit pattern is"; d
END
```

Specifying Fill Patterns—SCREEN 12

The PAINT statement can be thought of as tiling a closed region with copies of a tile. The basic tile is a rectangle of 8 points across and from 1 to 16 points vertically. We specify the tile by giving the color (0 through 15) of each point. The following program translates the colors into the numbers needed for the tiling string.

```
SCREEN 12
DIM h$(0 TO 15)
LET h$(0) = "0000": LET h$(1) = "0001": LET h$(2) = "0010": LET h$(3) = "0011"
LET h$(4) = "0100": LET h$(5) = "0101": LET h$(6) = "0110": LET h$(7) = "0111"
LET h$(8) = "1000": LET h$(9) = "1001": LET h$(10) = "1010": LET h$(11) = "1011"
LET h$(12) = "1100": LET h$(13) = "1101": LET h$(14) = "1110": LET h$(15) = "1111"
REM Create tiling string
LET t$ = ""
DO
  FOR i = 1 TO 8
    READ a(i)
  NEXT i
  IF a(1) = -1 THEN EXIT DO
  FOR i = 4 TO 1 STEP -1
    LET x = 0
    FOR k = 1 TO 8
      LET x = x + VAL(MID$(h$(a(k)), i, 1)) * 2 ^ (8 - k)
    NEXT k
    LET t$ = t$ + CHR$(x)
  NEXT i
LOOP
FOR i = 1 TO LEN(t$)
  PRINT ASC(MID$(t$, i, 1));
NEXT i
REM Eight colors for the first row of the tile
DATA color 1, color 2, ..., color 8
REM Eight colors for the second row of the tile
DATA color 1, color 2, ..., color 8
 .
 .
 .
DATA -1, -1, -1, -1, -1, -1, -1, -1
```

Assume the DATA statements are

```
DATA 0, 0, 0, 2, 0, 0, 0, 2
DATA 0, 0, 2, 0, 0, 0, 2, 0
DATA 0, 2, 0, 0, 0, 2, 0, 0
DATA 2, 0, 0, 0, 2, 0, 0, 0
DATA -1, -1, -1, -1, -1, -1, -1, -1
```

where color 2 (green) is being used to created a diagonal tiling. The output from the program will be

```
0  17  0  0  0  34  0  0  0  68  0  0  0  136  0  0
```

and the corresponding tiling string is

```
CHR$(0) + CHR$(17) + CHR$(0) + CHR$(0) + CHR$(0) + CHR$(34) +
CHR$(0) + CHR$(0) + CHR$(0) + CHR$(68) + CHR$(0) + CHR$(0) +
CHR$(0) + CHR$(136) + CHR$(0) + CHR$(0)
```

Specifying Fill Patterns—SCREEN 2 or SCREEN 3

The PAINT statement can be thought of as tiling a closed region with copies of a tile. The basic tile is a rectangle of 8 points horizontally and from 1 to 64 points vertically. We specify the rectangle by identifying each point as on or off. Each row of the rectangle can be associated with an 8-tuple of 0s and 1s, where the 1s correspond to the points to be on and the 0s to the points to be off. Each 8-tuple is the binary representation of a decimal integer from 0 to 255. Figure 10.35 shows the pattern used in the first rectangle of Figure 10.27A of Section 10.5. The fill string is obtained by concatenating the ASCII characters for each of the decimal numbers.

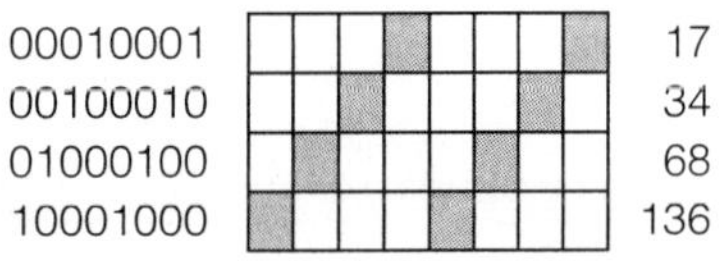

Figure 10.35 Fill Pattern

Chapter 10 Summary

1. Data can be vividly displayed in *line*, *bar*, *clustered bar*, and *pie charts*. Screen dumps of these charts produce printed copy.
2. The programmer can select his or her own coordinate system with the WINDOW statement.

3. The LINE statement draws lines, rectangles, solid rectangles, and styled lines.

4. The CIRCLE statement is used to draw circles and radius lines. Each radius line is specified by a number between 0 and 1. The number 2 * π (or 6.283185) is used by the CIRCLE statement when drawing radii.

5. The PSET statement turns on a single point on the screen and is useful in graphing functions.

6. The PAINT statement fills in closed regions with fill patterns specified as strings. The COS and SIN functions locate interior points of sectors.

Chapter 10 Programming Projects

1. Look in magazines and newspapers for four sets of data: one suited to each type of chart discussed in this chapter. Write programs to display the data in chart form.

2. Figure 10.36 is called a *surface line chart*. Write a program to produce this chart. (Use the data in Section 10.3.)

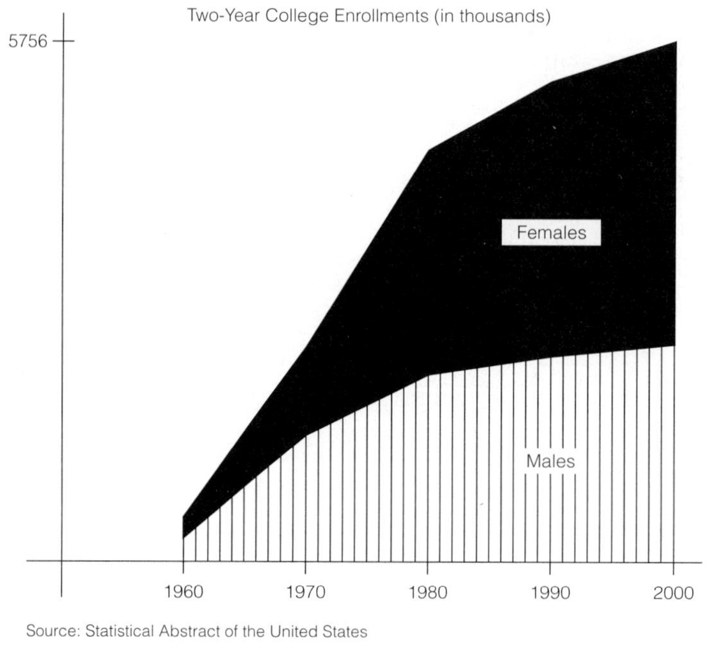

Figure 10.36 Surface Line Chart
Source: Statistical Abstract of the United States

3. Figure 10.37 is called a *horizontal bar chart*. Write a program to produce this chart. **Note:** If the WINDOW statement sets the range on the y-axis from 0 to 25, then the locations for text will be easy to determine.

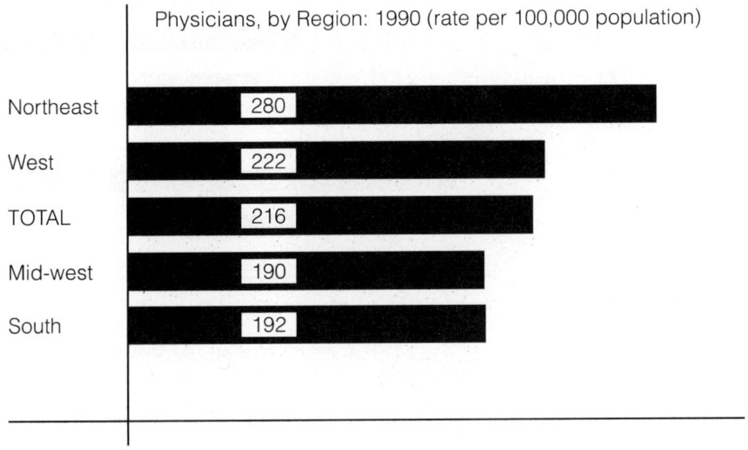

Figure 10.37 Horizontal Bar Chart
Source: Statistical Abstract of the United States

4. Figure 10.38 is called a *segmented bar chart*. Write a program to construct this chart.

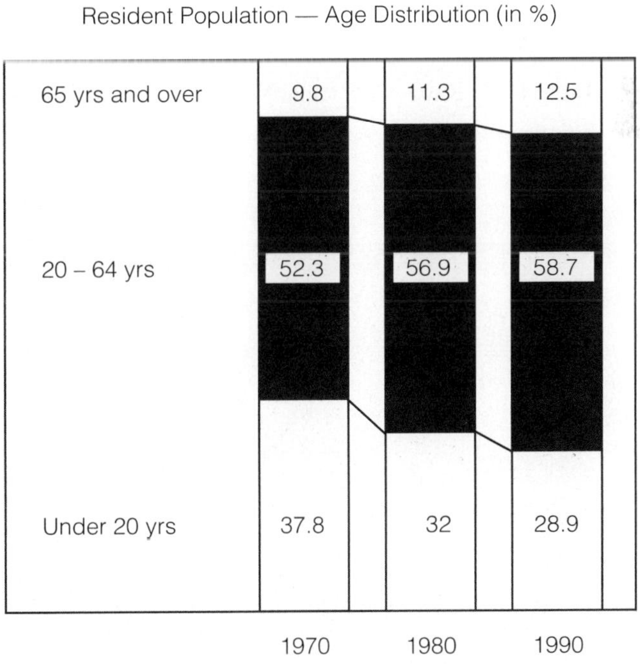

Figure 10.38 Segmented Bar Chart
Source: Statistical Abstract of the United States

5. Figure 10.39 is called a *range chart*. Using the data in Table 10.5, write a program to produce this chart.

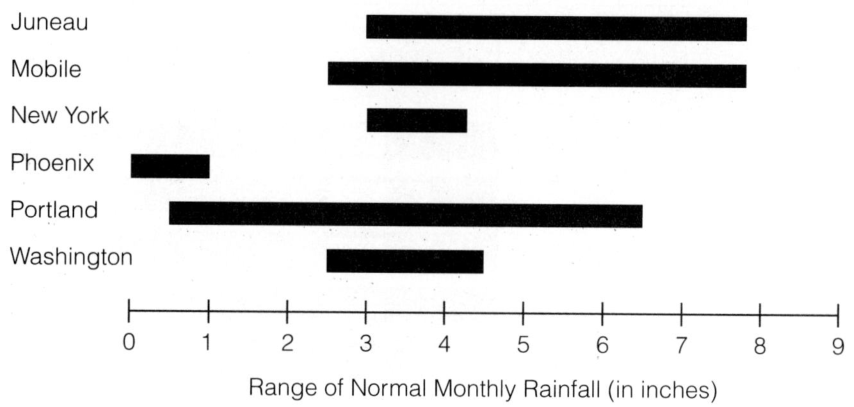

Figure 10.39 Range Chart
Source: Statistical Abstract of the United States

	Lowest NMR	Highest NMR
Mobile	2.6	7.7
Portland	.5	6.4
Phoenix	.1	1.0
Washington	2.6	4.4
Juneau	2.9	7.7
New York	3.1	4.2

Table 10.5 Range of Normal Monthly Rainfall for Selected Cities (in inches)

11

Random Numbers

11.1 GENERATING RANDOM NUMBERS

Consider a specific collection of numbers. We say that a process selects a number at **random** from this collection if any number in the collection is just as likely to be selected as any other and the number cannot be predicted in advance. Some examples are

Collection	**Process**
1, 2, 3, 4, 5, 6	toss a balanced die
0 or 1	toss a coin: 0 = tails, 1 = heads
−1, 0, 1, ..., 36	spin a roulette wheel (interpret −1 as 00)
1, 2, ..., n	write numbers on slips of paper, pull one from hat
numbers from 0 to 1	flip the spinner in Figure 11.1

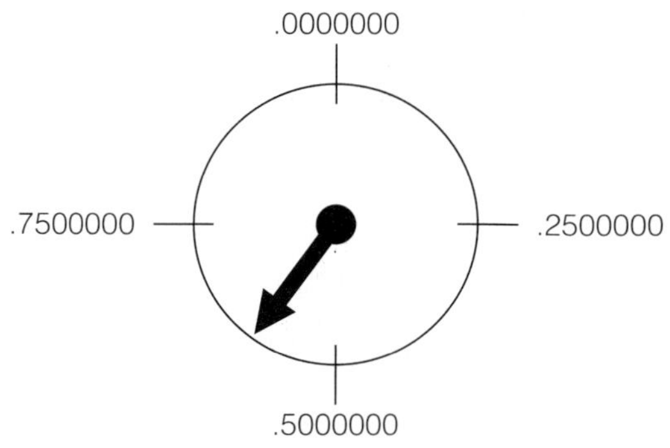

Figure 11.1 Spinner to Randomly Select a Number between 0 and 1

The function RND, which acts like the spinner in Figure 11.1, returns a random number. The statement

```
PRINT RND
```

randomly displays a number from 0 up to (but not including) 1. The statement

```
LET var = RND
```

randomly assigns a number between 0 and 1 to the variable *var*. A different number will be assigned each time RND is called in the program, and any number greater than or equal to 0 and less than 1 is just as likely to be generated as any other. Therefore, although RND looks like a numeric variable, it does not act at all like a variable.

EXAMPLE 1 The following program generates five numbers between 0 and 1. **Note:** The particular sequence of numbers produced by this program will most likely differ on your computer.

```
REM Generate five numbers between 0 and 1
CLS
FOR i = 1 TO 5
  PRINT RND;
NEXT i
END

[run]
 .7151002  .683111  .4821425  .9992938  .6465093
```

EXAMPLE 2 With appropriate scaling, the RND function can generate random numbers from other collections. The following program generates five numbers from the set 1, 2, 3, 4, 5, 6. Since RND always has a value from 0 to 1, excluding 1, 6 * RND has a value from 0 to 6 (excluding 6), and INT(6 * RND) has one of the values 0, 1, 2, 3, 4, 5. Adding 1 shifts the resulting number into the desired range.

```
REM Generate five integers between 1 and 6
CLS
FOR i = 1 TO 5
  PRINT INT(6 * RND) + 1;
NEXT i
END

[run]
 5  5  3  6  4
```

Suppose the upper limit value 5 in the FOR loop of Example 2 is changed to a large number. The integers generated by the program should exhibit no apparent pattern. They should look very much like a sequence of integers obtained from successively rolling a die. For instance, each of the six integers should appear about one-sixth of the time and be reasonably spread out in the sequence. The longer the sequence, the more likely this is to occur.

RND normally generates the same sequence of numbers each time a program is run. However, QBasic has another function, RANDOMIZE, that changes the sequence of numbers generated by RND. When the statement

```
RANDOMIZE
```

is executed, the program stops and asks the user to enter a number between –32768 and 32767. The response changes the sequence of numbers generated by RND. This process is known as **seeding** the random-number generator. Calling RANDOMIZE at the start of a program will ensure that RND generates different values each time the program is executed.

EXAMPLE 3 The following program uses RANDOMIZE to seed the random-number generator.

```
REM Generate five integers between 1 and 6
CLS
RANDOMIZE
FOR i = 1 TO 5
  PRINT INT(6 * RND) + 1;
NEXT i
END

[run]
Random-number seed (-32768 to 32767)? 9876
 2  4  5  3  1

[run]
Random-number seed (-32768 to 32767)? -345
 2  6  3  1  4
```

There is a variation of RANDOMIZE that is available if your computer has a built-in clock, as most computers do. The statement

```
RANDOMIZE TIMER
```

uses the computer's built-in clock to seed the random-number generator automatically. This statement will be used from now on in all programs in this text.

EXAMPLE 4 The DC Lottery number is obtained by selecting a ping-pong ball from each of three separate bowls. Each ball is numbered with an integer from 0 through 9. Write a computer program to produce a lottery number.

SOLUTION The value of INT(10 * RND) will be an integer from 0 through 9, and each of these integers has the same likelihood of occurring. Repeating the process three times produces the requested digits.

```
REM Display a lottery number
CLS
RANDOMIZE TIMER
FOR i = 1 TO 3
  PRINT INT(10 * RND);
NEXT i
END

[run]
 8  3  9
```

The program in Example 4 is said to **simulate** the selection of ping-pong balls.

EXAMPLE 5 Write a program to simulate the tossing of a coin. The outcome should tell whether heads or tails was selected.

SOLUTION The fact that the value of RND has a 50% chance of being between 0 and .5 is used to select the outcome.

```
REM Toss a coin
CLS
RANDOMIZE TIMER
PRINT "The coin came up ";
IF RND < .5 THEN
    PRINT "Heads"
  ELSE
    PRINT "Tails"
END IF
END

[run]
The coin came up Heads
```

EXAMPLE 6 The following program uses the RND function to shuffle a deck of cards and deal 5 cards from the top of the deck. The 52 cards are initially placed into a "fresh deck" array with the twos coming first, then the threes, . . ., and finally the aces. Therefore, cards 1 to 4 will be twos, cards 5 to 8 will be threes, . . ., and cards 49 to 52 will be aces. A string consisting of the denomination and the suit identifies each card. The symbols for heart, diamond, club, and spade have ASCII values 3, 4, 5, and 6, respectively, and can therefore be generated by CHR$(3), CHR$(4), CHR$(5), and CHR$(6). The cards are shuffled by successively interchanging the card at each position in the deck with a randomly selected card.

```
REM Shuffle a deck of cards
CLS
DIM card$(1 TO 52)
CALL SetUpDeck(card$())
CALL ShuffleDeck(card$())
CALL ShowCards(card$())
REM --- Data: denominations
DATA 2, 3, 4, 5, 6, 7, 8, 9, 10, J, Q, K, A
END

SUB SetUpDeck (card$())
  REM Set up fresh deck
  FOR denom = 1 TO 49 STEP 4          'Thirteen denominations
    READ denomination$
    FOR suit = 0 TO 3                 'Four suits
      LET suitChar$ = CHR$(3 + suit)  'Character for suit
      LET card$(denom + suit) = denomination$ + suitChar$
    NEXT suit
  NEXT denom
END SUB
```

```
SUB ShowCards (card$())
  REM Display first five cards
  FOR cardNum = 1 TO 5
    PRINT card$(cardNum) + "  ";
  NEXT cardNum
END SUB

SUB ShuffleDeck (card$())
  REM Shuffle cards
  RANDOMIZE TIMER
  FOR cardNum = 1 TO 52
    SWAP card$(cardNum), card$(INT(52 * RND) + 1)
  NEXT cardNum
END SUB

[run]
7♦   K♥   3♠   A♦   4♣
```

Comments:

1. Each time the function RND appears in a program, it will be reassigned a value. For instance, the task attempted (but not accomplished) by the first program below is achieved by the second program.

```
REM Generate the square of a randomly chosen number
RANDOMIZE TIMER
PRINT "The square of"; RND; "is"; RND * RND
END

REM Generate the square of a randomly chosen number
RANDOMIZE TIMER
LET a = RND
PRINT "The square of"; a; "is"; a * a
END
```

Since each of the RND's in the third line of the first program will assume a different value, it is highly unlikely that the square of the first one will equal the product of the last two.

2. We have seen the uses of the RND function in *sampling* (selecting five cards from a deck) and *simulation* (modeling the drawing of a lottery number). Other uses are

   (a) *Testing programs for correctness and efficiency*. Selecting randomly chosen data avoids any bias of the tester.
   (b) *Numerical analysis*. In Section 11.3 we use randomly selected points to find the area under a curve.
   (c) *Recreation*. Programs can be written to play games such as blackjack.
   (d) *Decision making*. In game theory, a branch of mathematics applied to economics, strategies involve using RND to make decisions. Programming Project 2 in this chapter discusses game theory.

3. RND's alleged flaw is not really a flaw. The fact that in the absence of a RANDOMIZE statement the sequence of values produced by successive RND's will always be the same was intentionally designed into RND. This

aspect is useful in debugging simulations in which many random numbers are generated.

4. The sequence of numbers generated by RND is not truly random, since, in practice, each number actually determines the next number; however, the sequence has the appearance of a randomly generated sequence. For any subinterval of the interval [0,1), the likelihood of generating a number in that subinterval is the same as for any other subinterval of the same length. The sequence of numbers generated by QBasic is said to be **pseudorandom**.

PRACTICE PROBLEMS 11.1

1. Randomly generate 10,000 integers from 1 through 6 and report the number of times the integer 3 occurs in the first thousand numbers, the second thousand, and so on.

2. Modify the program in Example 5 for the case of a biased coin that lands "Heads" three-fourths of the time.

EXERCISES 11.1

In Exercises 1 and 2, determine the output of the program.

1.
```
RANDOMIZE TIMER
PRINT INT(RND * 5) + 1
END
```

2.
```
FOR i = 1 TO RND + 3
  PRINT i;
NEXT i
END
```

In Exercises 3 and 4, find the error.

3.
```
DO WHILE n <> 5
  LET n = INT(RND * 5)
  PRINT n
LOOP
END
```

4.
```
LET RND = .5
PRINT RND
END
```

In Exercises 5 through 10, determine the range of values that can be generated by the given expression.

5. `INT(2 * RND)`

6. `2 * INT(10 * RND)`

7. `INT(38 * RND) - 1`

8. `(RND + 1) * (RND + 2)`

9. `2 * INT(5 * RND) + 1`

10. `INT(10 * RND) + 10`

In Exercises 11 through 14, write the expression(s) that will randomly select a number from the given range.

11. An integer from 5 through 10

12. A number from 2 through 4 (excluding 4)

13. An even integer from 2 through 100

14. A perfect square from 1 through 100

15. Write a program that selects a word at random from among 20 words in DATA statements.

16. Write a program to simulate the tossing of a coin 100 times and keep track of the numbers of "heads" and "tails" that occur.

17. Modify the program in Example 6 so that instead of displaying the first five cards, it determines whether the five cards are all the same suit. Then expand the program to repeat the process 1000 times and count the number of times the first five cards are all the same suit. The program may take quite a while to run.

18. A company has a sequential file containing the names of people who have qualified for a drawing to win an IBM Personal Computer. Write a program to select a name at random from the file. Assume the file contains at most 1000 names. Test your program on a file consisting of 5 names.

19. A club has 20 members. Write a program to select two different people at random to serve as president and treasurer. (The names of the members should be contained in DATA statements.)

20. A true-false exam has 10 questions. Write a program to randomly answer the questions in which each answer is equally likely to be "true" or "false."

21. A multiple-choice exam has 10 questions with five possible choices each. Write a program to randomly answer the questions. Each of the five possible choices should have the same likelihood of being selected.

22. Write a program to simulate the tossing of a pair of dice 120 times and record the number of times that the sum of the two numbers is 7.

23. Write a program to select a letter at random from the alphabet.

24. Although tickets for a popular concert will not be sold until nine o'clock, fans start lining up at the box office at eight o'clock. Suppose that during each minute, either one or two fans arrive and that the likelihood of just one arriving is four times the likelihood of two arriving. Write a program to simulate the arrival of fans at the box office. For each minute, it should report the total number of fans in line.

25. Write a program to simulate 1000 rolls of a die and report the number of times each integer occurs.

26. Write a program to randomly select 50 different people from a group of 100 whose names are contained in data statements. ***Hint:*** Use an array of 100 elements to keep track of whether or not a person has been selected.

27. Example 6 presented a method for selecting a set of 5 cards from a deck of 52. This is a special case of the problem of selecting m objects from a set of n objects; or equivalently, of selecting m integers from the integers 1 to n. A brilliant algorithm for accomplishing this task is shown below. (For details see D. E. Knuth, *The Art of Computer Programming*, Volume 2, p. 121, Addison-Wesley Publishing Company, 1969.) This algorithm has the additional feature that the set of m numbers will be ordered. Do a few pencil-

and-paper walkthroughs with small values of m and n to convince yourself that the algorithm does indeed produce the proper output.

```
REM Select m numbers between 1 and n
INPUT m, n
RANDOMIZE TIMER
LET selct = m
LET remaining = n
FOR i = 1 TO n
  IF RND < selct / remaining THEN
      PRINT i;
      LET selct = selct - 1
  END IF
  LET remaining = remaining - 1
NEXT i
END
```

28. Use the program in Exercise 27 to select 5 cards from a deck of 52 cards.

29. *The Birthday Problem*. Given a random group of 23 people, how likely is it that two people have the same birthday? To answer this question, write a program that creates an array of range 1 TO 23, randomly assigns to each subscripted variable one of the integers from 1 through 365, and checks to see if any of the subscripted variables have the same value. (Make the simplifying assumption that no birthdays occur on February 29.) Now expand the program to repeat the process 100 times and determine the percentage of the time that there is a match. ***Note:*** This program may take a few minutes to run.

SOLUTIONS TO PRACTICE PROBLEMS 11.1

1. In the following program, occurrences(1) records the number of occurrences of 3 in the first 1000 terms, occurrences(2) records the number of occurrences in the second 1000 terms, and so on.

```
REM Report frequency of integer 3 in each tenth part of a list
CLS
DIM occurrences(1 TO 10)
RANDOMIZE TIMER
FOR i = 1 TO 10
  FOR k = 1 TO 1000
    LET n = INT(6 * RND) + 1
    IF n = 3 THEN
        LET occurrences(i) = occurrences(i) + 1
    END IF
  NEXT k
NEXT i
FOR i = 1 TO 10
  PRINT occurrences(i);
NEXT i
END

[run]
168  174  168  183  175  164  152  161  161  164
```

We see that the occurrences of the integer 3 are spread out. In each block of 1000 integers it appeared an average of 167 times, and 167 is close to 1000/6. We expect that in each block of m integers it will occur about $m/6$ times.

2. The IF block of the program should be changed to

```
IF RND < .75 THEN
    PRINT "Heads"
  ELSE
    PRINT "Tails"
END IF
```

Since the interval from 0 to .75 constitutes three-fourths of the interval from 0 to 1, the value of RND is expected to be in this interval about three-fourths of the time. In general, the likelihood that the value of RND is in a particular subinterval is equal to the length of the subinterval. For instance, the likelihood that the value of RND lies between .4 and .7 is .3. That is, about 30% of the time the value of RND can be expected to lie between .4 and .7.

11.2 GAMES OF CHANCE

The computer can be used to simulate games of chance and analyze various strategies.

Roulette

A roulette wheel contains 38 slots labeled 1 through 36, 0, and 00. (See Figure 11.2). When the wheel is spun, a tiny ball bounces around and comes to rest in one of the slots. Players wager various types of bets by placing a chip on a mat. If a player bets $1 on a number and the ball lands on that number, he receives $36 (in addition to the dollar bet).

Figure 11.2 Roulette Wheel

EXAMPLE 1 Write a program to simulate a spin of a roulette wheel.

SOLUTION The expression INT(38 * RND) – 1 evaluates to an integer from –1 through 36. If we associate –1 with 00, then the possible outcomes correspond to the positions on the wheel.

```
REM Simulate spin of a roulette wheel
CLS
RANDOMIZE TIMER
PRINT "The winning number is";
LET n = INT(38 * RND) - 1
IF n <> -1 THEN
    PRINT n
  ELSE
    PRINT " 00"
END IF
END

[run]
The winning number is 7
```

EXAMPLE 2 A gambler arrives at the roulette table with $100. He decides to bet $1 on the number 7 and continue placing this bet until he either doubles his money or goes broke. Write a program to simulate his experience. After each spin of the wheel, record his current bankroll and the number of times he has played.

SOLUTION The program is straightforward. After each play, the gambler's bankroll will either increase by $35 (if he wins) or decrease by $1. The numbers following "Bankroll:" and "Number of games played:" will change steadily until the session is over.

```
REM Simulate double-or-nothing strategy
CLS
CALL Initialize(bankroll, numPlays)
DO WHILE (bankroll > 0) AND (bankroll < 200)
  CALL AdjustBankroll(bankroll, numPlays)
  CALL ShowData(bankroll, numPlays)
LOOP
END

SUB AdjustBankroll (bankroll, numPlays)
  REM Adjust bankroll, increment number of plays
  IF INT(38 * RND) - 1 = 7 THEN
      LET bankroll = bankroll + 35
    ELSE
      LET bankroll = bankroll - 1
  END IF
  LET numPlays = numPlays + 1
END SUB
```

```
SUB Initialize (bankroll, numPlays)
  REM Randomize, initialize bankroll and number of plays
  RANDOMIZE TIMER
  LET bankroll = 100          'Bankroll
  LET numPlays = 0            'number of Plays
END SUB

SUB ShowData (bankroll, numPlays)
  LOCATE 12, 1
  PRINT "Bankroll:"; bankroll
  PRINT "Number of games played:"; numPlays
END SUB

[run]
Bankroll: 0
Number of games played: 217
```

The output of the program of Example 2 shows that the gambler lost during that session; however, at other gambling sessions he might win. We can estimate how likely he is to end a session as a winner by simulating the play of many sessions and recording the number of wins.

EXAMPLE 3 Simulate the play of 100 sessions of roulette using the strategy of Example 2. Display a running count of the number of wins and losses.

SOLUTION The following program calls a subroutine to find the outcome of each individual session. To speed up execution, the program does not report the changes in the bankroll during each session, but only the total number of wins and losses.

```
REM Simulate 100 sessions of "double-or-nothing" roulette
CLS
CALL Initialize(gamesWon, gamesLost)
FOR tries = 1 TO 100
  CALL PlaySession(gamesWon, gamesLost)
  CALL ShowData(gamesWon, gamesLost)
NEXT tries
END

SUB Initialize (gamesWon, gamesLost)
  REM Randomize, set games won and lost to 0
  RANDOMIZE TIMER
  LET gamesWon = 0
  LET gamesLost = 0
END SUB
```

```
SUB PlaySession (gamesWon, gamesLost)
  REM Play a session and remember outcome
  LET bankroll = 100
  DO WHILE (bankroll > 0) AND (bankroll < 200)
    IF INT(38 * RND) - 1 = 7 THEN
        LET bankroll = bankroll + 35
      ELSE
        LET bankroll = bankroll - 1
    END IF
  LOOP
  IF bankroll = 0 THEN
      LET gamesLost = gamesLost + 1
    ELSE
      LET gamesWon = gamesWon + 1
  END IF
END SUB

SUB ShowData (gamesWon, gamesLost)
  LOCATE 12, 1
  PRINT "Sessions Won:"; gamesWon
  PRINT "Sessions Lost:"; gamesLost
END SUB

[run]
Sessions Won: 39
Sessions Lost: 61
```

We expect the gambler to go home a winner about 39% of the time and a loser about 61% of the time. The gambler might try to increase the likelihood of winning by changing the amount of the individual bet or the size of the bankroll. For instance, two possibilities are

1. Bet $2 on each spin and leave the original bankroll at $100.
2. Start with a bankroll of $200 and bet $1 on each spin.

A computer simulation would show that the likelihoods of winning are about 40% and 33%, respectively. Therefore, doubling the bet is a good idea, but doubling the bankroll is not.

Slot Machines

A slot machine, or "one-arm bandit," is operated by inserting a coin in a slot and pulling a lever. (See Figure 11.3.) This causes three wheels containing pictures of cherries, oranges, plums, melons, bars, and bells to spin around and finally come to rest with one picture showing on each wheel. Certain combinations of pictures, such as three of a kind, produce a payoff to the player.

Figure 11.3 Slot Machine

EXAMPLE 4 Suppose each slot machine wheel contains 5 cherries, 5 oranges, 5 plums, 3 melons, 1 bell, and 1 bar. Simulate the outcome of the spin of a single wheel so that each item has the appropriate likelihood of occurring.

SOLUTION Since 5 of the 20 pictures are cherries, we expect cherries to occur 25% of the time. (***Note:*** 5/20 is 25%.) The same is true for oranges and plums. Similarly, we expect melons, bells, and bars to occur 15%, 5%, and 5% of the time, respectively. In Figure 11.4, the interval from 0 to 1 is divided into six subintervals, one for each of the six items. The length of each subinterval is the likelihood that its item will occur. Since this number is also the likelihood that the value of RND will be in the subinterval, these subintervals can be used to simulate the outcome of the wheel.

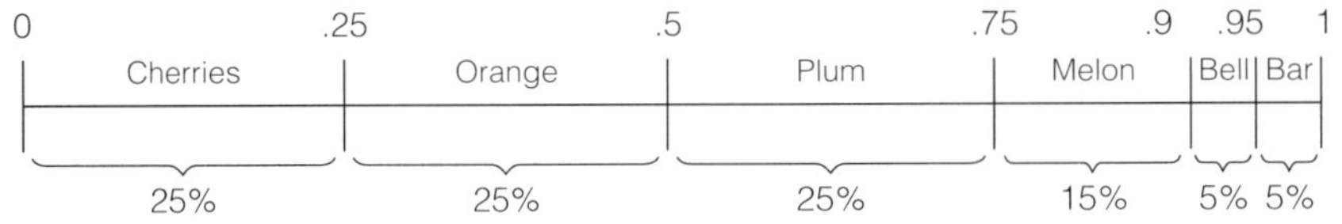

Figure 11.4 Subdivision of [0,1] Used to Simulate Slot-Machine Wheel

```
REM Simulate spin of one slot-machine wheel
CLS
RANDOMIZE TIMER
CALL SpinWheel(pict$)
CALL ShowPicture(pict$)
END

SUB ShowPicture (pict$)
  REM Display picture name
  PRINT pict$
END SUB

SUB SpinWheel (pict$)
  REM Choose from cherries, orange, plum, melon, bell, or bar
  LET n = RND
  SELECT CASE n
    CASE 0 TO .25
      LET pict$ = "Cherries"
    CASE .25 TO .5
      LET pict$ = "Orange"
    CASE .5 TO .75
      LET pict$ = "Plum"
    CASE .75 TO .9
      LET pict$ = "Melon"
    CASE .9 TO .95
      LET pict$ = "Bell"
    CASE ELSE
      LET pict$ = "Bar"
  END SELECT
END SUB

[run]
Plum
```

EXAMPLE 5 Suppose each wheel of a slot machine has the same distribution of pictures as in Example 4 and the payoff is 10 coins for three-of-a-kind and 3 coins if any of the pictures is a bar. Simulate 1000 plays and display a running total of the number of games played and the number of coins won.

SOLUTION The array wheelPict$() holds the pictures for each of the 3 wheels. The program in Example 4 is placed in a subprogram to obtain the outcome for each wheel. The payoff is computed in another subprogram.

```
REM Simulate 1000 plays of a slot machine
CLS
DIM wheelPict$(1 TO 3)
CALL Initialize(numPlays, coinsWon)
FOR tries = 1 TO 1000
  CALL SpinWheels(wheelPict$(), numPlays)
  CALL ComputePayoff(wheelPict$(), coinsWon)
  CALL ShowData(numPlays, coinsWon)
NEXT tries
END
```

```
SUB ComputePayoff (wheelPict$(), coinsWon)
  REM Compute payoff from wheel spins
  LET newCoins = 0
  IF (wheelPict$(1) = wheelPict$(2)) AND (wheelPict$(2) = wheelPict$(3)) THEN
      LET newCoins = 10
    ELSEIF (wheelPict$(1) = "Bar") OR (wheelPict$(2) = "Bar") OR wheelPict$(3) = "Bar") THEN
      LET newCoins = 3
  END IF
  LET coinsWon = coinsWon + newCoins
END SUB

SUB Initialize (numPlays, coinsWon)
  REM Randomize, set number of plays and coins won to 0
  RANDOMIZE TIMER
  LET numPlays = 0
  LET coinsWon = 0
END SUB

SUB ShowData (numPlays, coinsWon)
  REM Show number of plays, coins won
  LOCATE 12, 1
  PRINT "Number of plays:"; numPlays
  PRINT "Total number of coins won:"; coinsWon
END SUB

SUB SpinOneWheel (pict$)
  REM Choose from cherries, orange, plum, melon, bell, or bar
  LET n = RND
  SELECT CASE n
    CASE 0 TO .25
      LET pict$ = "Cherries"
    CASE .25 TO .5
      LET pict$ = "Orange"
    CASE .5 TO .75
      LET pict$ = "Plum"
    CASE .75 TO .9
      LET pict$ = "Melon"
    CASE .9 TO .95
      LET pict$ = "Bell"
    CASE ELSE
      LET pict$ = "Bar"
  END SELECT
END SUB

SUB SpinWheels (wheelPict$(), numPlays)
  REM Spin each of three wheels
  FOR wheel = 1 TO 3
    CALL SpinOneWheel(wheelPict$(wheel))
  NEXT wheel
  LET numPlays = numPlays + 1
END SUB

[run]
Number of plays: 1000
Total number of coins won: 928
```

The simulation shows this slot machine keeps about 7% of the amount of money played. The machines vary from casino to casino in the allocation of the pictures and the payoffs. If the specifications of the machine are known, however, then a simulation can be used to determine how profitable the machine is for the casino.

PRACTICE PROBLEMS 11.2

Suppose a game of chance has four possible outcomes called I, II, III, and IV, which are expected to occur 5/12, 1/4, 1/6, and 1/6 of the time, respectively.

1. Subdivide the interval [0,1), as in Figure 11.4, to correspond to these outcomes.
2. Write a program to simulate the outcome of the game of chance.

EXERCISES 11.2

In Exercises 1 and 2, determine the percentage of the time that the program will produce the output "Red".

1.
```
RANDOMIZE TIMER
LET n = RND
SELECT CASE n
  CASE IS < .3
    LET col$ = "White"
  CASE IS < .7
    LET col$ = "Red"
  CASE ELSE
    LET col$ = "Blue"
END SELECT
PRINT col$
END
```

2.
```
RANDOMIZE TIMER
LET n = RND
IF n < .4 THEN
    LET col$ = "White"
  ELSE
    LET col$ = "Red"
END IF
PRINT col$
END
```

In Exercises 3 and 4, determine why the program does not achieve its objective.

3.
```
REM Simulate toss of a coin
RANDOMIZE TIMER
IF RND < .5 THEN
    LET result$ = "Heads"
END IF
IF RND >= .5 THEN
    LET result$ = "Tails"
END IF
PRINT result$
END
```

4.
```
REM Simulate 1000 coin tosses
RANDOMIZE TIMER
LET n = RND
FOR i = 1 TO 1000
  IF n < .5 THEN
      LET heads = heads + 1
  END IF
NEXT i
PRINT "Number of heads:"; heads
END
```

In Exercises 5 and 6, subdivide the interval [0,1) to correspond to the given outcomes.

5.

Outcome	**Likelihood**
Yes	1/6
No	1/3
Maybe	1/2

6.

Outcome	**Likelihood**
Go	1/7
Stop	2/7
Caution	4/7

Exercises 7 and 8 simulate the "Big Six" wheel. The payoff is the number of chips you receive, in addition to the one you bet, if your number comes up.

Outcome	Appearances	Payoff
1	23	1
2	15	2
5	8	5
10	4	10
20	2	20
Joker	1	45
Casino	1	45

Figure 11.5 Big Six Wheel

7. Write a program to simulate the outcome of the spin of a Big Six wheel so that each item has the appropriate likelihood of occurring.
8. Simulate 10,000 plays of the "5" bet and display the total profit (most likely a negative number).
9. In roulette, a $1 "ODD" bet pays off $1 (in addition to the dollar bet) if the ball comes to rest on an odd number. Simulate 1000 plays of the "ODD" bet and display a running total of the number of games played and the profit. (A loss will correspond to a negative profit.) This type of bet is typical of most roulette bets. That is, approximately the same amount of money should be lost after 1000 plays. The only exception is the "Five Numbers" bet discussed in Exercise 10.
10. In roulette, a $1 "Five Numbers" bet pays off $6 (in addition to the dollar bet) if the ball comes to rest on 0, 00, 1, 2, or 3. Simulate 1000 plays of the "Five Numbers" bet and display a running total of the number of games played and the profit. ***Note:*** This is the worst bet in roulette.

11. In Monte Carlo and most other European casinos, roulette wheels do not have 00. Also, if you place an ODD bet and the ball rests on 0, then your bet is imprisoned; that is, it stays on ODD for another spin of the wheel. If that spin produces an odd number, you get your dollar back, and if it produces a 0, you get 50¢ back. Simulate 1000 plays of the "ODD" bet and display a running total of the number of games played and the profit.

12. Consider the program in Example 3. In each session in which the gambler goes broke, he loses exactly $100. However, each time he comes out ahead during a session, he earns anywhere from $100 to $134. Modify the program so that it keeps track of his actual earnings and losses. By running the program you can determine his expected average loss per session.

13. A candy company puts a baseball card in each pack of bubble gum. If each baseball player is as likely to appear as any other, write a program to request the number of different players and simulate the collection of a complete set of baseball cards. The program should display the number of pictures of each player and the number of packs of bubble gum purchased. (***Note:*** Create an array cards(), where cards(*i*) is the number of cards collected with a picture of the *i*th player.) A possible outcome is as follows:

```
[run]
How many different players are there? 5
 4 pictures of player 1
 6 pictures of player 2
 4 pictures of player 3
 1 pictures of player 4
 3 pictures of player 5
 18 packages of bubble gum were purchased
```

14. Expand the program of Exercise 13 to repeat the process of collecting a set of cards 100 times and report the average number of purchases made in order to obtain a complete set.

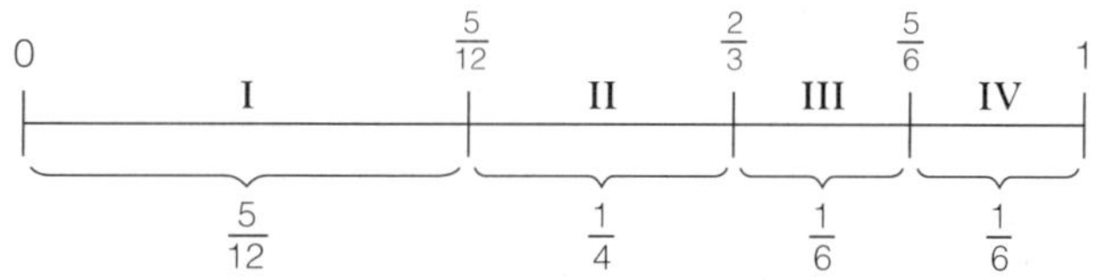

Figure 11.6 Subdivision of [0,1) Used to Simulate Game in Practice Problem 1

SOLUTIONS TO PRACTICE PROBLEMS 11.2

1. The subdivisions are determined by the points 5/12, 5/12 + 1/4 or 2/3, and 2/3 + 1/6 or 5/6. (See Figure 11.6.) In general, the right-hand endpoints of the subintervals are obtained by starting with the first likelihood and successively adding one more likelihood.

2. REM Simulate the game in Practice Problem 1

```
CLS
RANDOMIZE TIMER
LET n = RND
SELECT CASE n
  CASE IS < 5 / 12
   LET result$ = "I"
  CASE IS < 2 / 3
   LET result$ = "II"
  CASE IS < 5 / 6
   LET result$ = "III"
  CASE ELSE
   LET result$ = "IV"
END SELECT
PRINT result$
END
```

11.3 MONTE CARLO METHODS

When we solve a problem by repeatedly generating random numbers, we are said to employ **Monte Carlo methods**. In this section we use Monte Carlo methods to determine the appropriate number of tellers for a bank, evaluate a test-taking strategy, and find the area of a region under a curve.

Bank Tellers

The number of tellers a bank should use depends on several factors: the rate at which customers arrive for service during the time period under consideration, the expected amount of time required to serve each customer, and how much the manager values a short line. Let's first consider the case of a single teller and then expand to the case of any number of tellers.

EXAMPLE 1 Suppose that, on the average, bank customers arrive at the rate of 36 customers per hour and the amount of time required to serve each customer ranges uniformly from 1 to 6 minutes. Assuming that there is only 1 teller, write a program to simulate the operation of the bank for a 2-hour period. The program should display a running count of the number of people in line. At the end of the 2-hour period, the percentage of time the line had more than 3 people should be displayed.

SOLUTION Break the 2-hour period into 1-second slices and monitor the status of the line and the teller every second. Thirty-six customers per hour (3600 seconds) amounts to 1 customer every 100 seconds. During any 1-second period, therefore, the likelihood is 1% that a new customer will arrive. The variable *lineSize* holds the length of the line at any time, and the variable *secsLong* is increased by one during any second at which there are more than 3 people in line. When a customer reaches the teller, the RND function determines a number from 60 through 360, call it *secsLeft*, the number of seconds needed to serve the customer. While a customer is being served, the value of *secsLeft* decreases by 1 each second. When the value of *secsLeft* reaches 0, either a new customer steps forward (if *lineSize* > 0) or the teller is idle until another customer arrives. Although the outcome of this program will vary each time it is run, clearly a single teller can't handle the traffic in this bank.

```
REM Simulate teller serving a bank line
CLS
CALL Initialize(secs, lineSize, secsLeft, secsLong)
FOR seconds = 1 TO secs
  CALL UpdateLine(lineSize, secsLong)     'Check for and record new arrivals
  CALL UpdateTeller(lineSize, secsLeft)  'Update and record status of teller
NEXT seconds
CALL ShowData(secsLong, secs)
END

SUB Initialize (secs, lineSize, secsLeft, secsLong)
  REM Randomize, initialize variables
  RANDOMIZE TIMER
  LET minutes = 120         'Minutes for simulation
  LET secs = 60 * minutes   'Seconds for simulation
  LET lineSize = 0          'Length of line
  LET secsLeft = 0          'Seconds remaining to serve current customer
  LET secsLong = 0          'Seconds line has four or more customers
END SUB

SUB ShowData (secsLong, secs)
  REM Show percentage of time line has four or more people
  PRINT "Line has more than three people ";
  PRINT USING "##.#% of the time."; 100 * secsLong / secs
END SUB

SUB UpdateLine (lineSize, secsLong)
  REM Check for and record new arrivals
  IF RND < .01 THEN                       '1% chance of arrival
      LET lineSize = lineSize + 1
  END IF
  LOCATE 12, 1
  PRINT "Length of line:"; lineSize
  IF lineSize >= 4 THEN
      LET secsLong = secsLong + 1
  END IF
END SUB

SUB UpdateTeller (lineSize, secsLeft)
  REM Update and record status of teller
  IF secsLeft > 0 THEN
      LET secsLeft = secsLeft - 1
  END IF
```

```
  IF (secsLeft <= 0) AND (lineSize > 0) THEN
      LET lineSize = lineSize - 1
      LET secsLeft = RND * 300 + 60
  END IF
END SUB

[run]
Length of line: 41
Line has more than three people 85.8% of the time.
```

EXAMPLE 2 Expand the program in Example 1 to support several tellers. The number of tellers should be input by the user.

SOLUTION The variable *secsLeft*, seconds remaining to serve current customer, must be replaced by an array secsLeft() having one subscripted variable for each teller. The subprogram UpdateTellers must update and record the status of all the tellers.

```
REM Simulate several tellers
CLS
CALL InputTellers(numTellers)
DIM secsLeft(1 TO numTellers)
CALL Initialize(secs, lineSize, secsLong, secsLeft(), numTellers)
FOR seconds = 1 TO secs
  CALL UpdateLine(lineSize, secsLong)
  CALL UpdateTellers(lineSize, secsLeft(), numTellers)
NEXT seconds
CALL ShowData(secsLong, secs)
END

SUB Initialize (secs, lineSize, secsLong, secsLeft(), numTellers)
  REM Randomize, clear array, initialize variables
  RANDOMIZE TIMER
  FOR teller = 1 TO numTellers
    LET secsLeft(teller) = 0
  NEXT teller
  LET minutes = 120         'Minutes for simulation
  LET secs = 60 * minutes   'Seconds for simulation
  LET lineSize = 0          'Length of line
  LET secsLong = 0          'Seconds line has four or more customers
END SUB

SUB InputTellers (numTellers)
  REM Input number of tellers
  INPUT "Number of tellers"; numTellers
END SUB

SUB ShowData (secsLong, secs)
  REM Show percentage of time line has four or more people
  PRINT "Line has more than three people ";
  PRINT USING "##.#% of the time."; 100 * secsLong / secs
END SUB
```

```
SUB UpdateLine (lineSize, secsLong)
  REM Check for and record new arrivals
  IF RND < .01 THEN                         '1% chance of arrival
      LET lineSize = lineSize + 1
  END IF
  LOCATE 12, 1
  PRINT "Length of line:"; lineSize
  IF lineSize >= 4 THEN
      LET secsLong = secsLong + 1
  END IF
END SUB

SUB UpdateTellers (lineSize, secsLeft(), numTellers)
  REM Update and record status of tellers
  FOR teller = 1 TO numTellers
    IF (secsLeft(teller) > 0) THEN
        LET secsLeft(teller) = secsLeft(teller) - 1
    END IF
    IF (secsLeft(teller) <= 0) AND (lineSize > 0) THEN
        LET lineSize = lineSize - 1
        LET secsLeft(teller) = RND * 300 + 60
    END IF
  NEXT teller
END SUB

[run]
Number of tellers? 3
Length of line: 2
Line has more than 3 people 1.5% of the time.
```

By running this program many times and taking the averages of the numbers generated, we can determine the number of tellers that are necessary to achieve an acceptable output.

Test-Taking Strategies

Suppose a true-false exam has ten questions and you answer each one by guessing. It's easy to write a program to produce a sequence of ten trues and falses. Just use RND and guess "true" if its value is less than .5. In the long run, this method should produce an average grade of 50%. Now, suppose you are given the additional information that 60% of the answers are true. How would you proceed to take the exam? You might use a random process that selects "true" 60% of the time.

EXAMPLE 3 Analyze the strategy of randomly selecting "true" 60% of the time and "false" 40% of the time. Suppose the first 6 correct answers to the exam are true and the rest are false. Simulate taking the test 1000 times and compute the average of the grades.

SOLUTION Each question is answered by selecting "true" if the value of RND is less than .6 and "false" otherwise. Hence, 10 points are earned whenever one of the first 6 values of RND is less than .6 or whenever one of the last 4 values of RND is greater than or equal to .6.

```
REM Analyze test-taking strategy
CLS
CALL Initialize(total)
CALL TryMethod(total)
CALL ShowResults(total)
END

SUB Initialize (total)
  REM Randomize and set total points earned to 0
  RANDOMIZE TIMER
  LET total = 0
END SUB

SUB ShowResults (total)
  REM Show average score of 1000 tries
  PRINT "Average score is"; total / 1000
END SUB

SUB TakeTest (score)
  REM Take exam and report score (from 0 to 100)
  LET score = 0
  FOR question = 1 TO 6
    IF RND < .6 THEN
        LET score = score + 10
    END IF
  NEXT question
  FOR question = 7 TO 10
    IF RND >= .6 THEN
        LET score = score + 10
    END IF
  NEXT question
END SUB

SUB TryMethod (total)
  FOR tries = 1 TO 1000
    CALL TakeTest(score)
    LET total = total + score
  NEXT tries
END SUB

[run]
Average score is 52.26
```

Although the strategy used here is the most obvious one, it's not too good. A better strategy is to answer all questions "true." This strategy guarantees a grade of 60%.

Area under a Curve

The areas of regions under certain curves have important interpretations. For instance, the area under the bell-shaped curve in Figure 11.7 gives the percentage of adult males whose height is between 5 and 5.75 feet. The area under the velocity curve in Figure 11.8 gives the total distance traveled by a rocket. One method for determining the area under a curve consists of surrounding the region under consideration by a rectangle, selecting points at random from the rectangle, and counting the percentage that falls under the curve. The area is then estimated to be this percentage of the area of the rectangle.

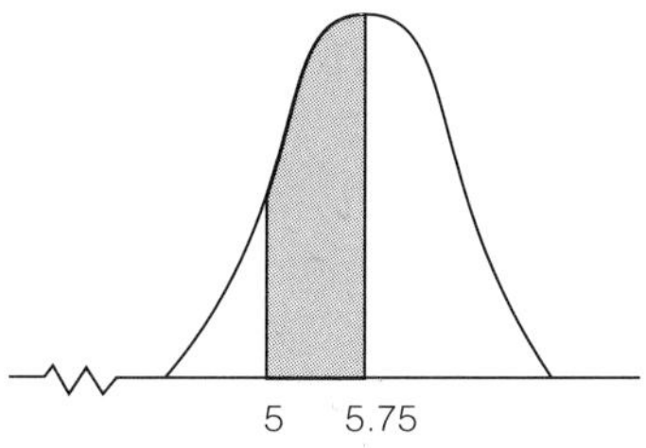

Figure 11.7 Normal Curve

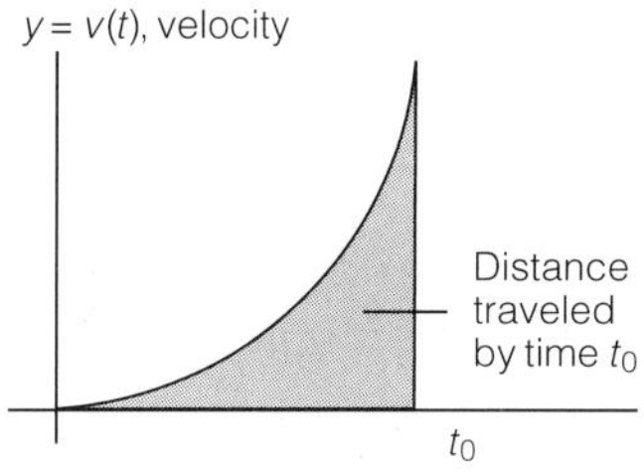

Figure 11.8 Velocity of a Rocket

EXAMPLE 4 Figure 11.9 shows a portion of the graph of the curve $x^2 + y^2 = 1$. Use a Monte Carlo method to estimate the area of this region.

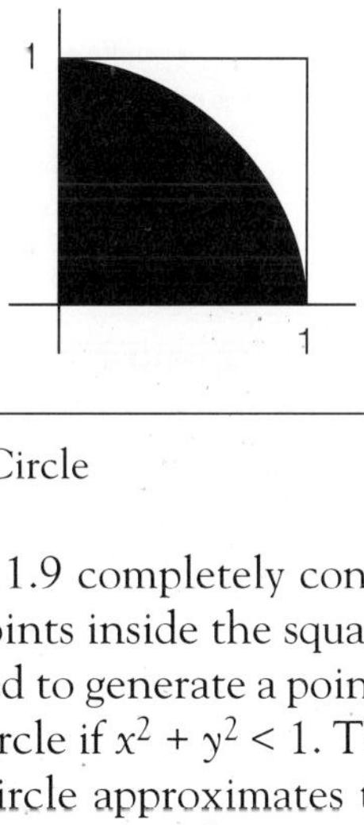

Figure 11.9 Area of a Quarter-Circle

SOLUTION The square drawn in Figure 11.9 completely contains the quarter-circle. Both the x- and y-coordinates of points inside the square have values ranging from 0 to 1. The RND function is used to generate a point inside the square. The point (x, y) will also be inside the circle if $x^2 + y^2 < 1$. The area of the square is 1. The percentage of points in the circle approximates the area of the quarter-circle. ***Note:*** Since the area of the circle is $\pi * 1^2$ or π, the area of the quarter-circle is 3.141593/4 or .7853983.

```
REM Area of one quadrant of unit circle
CLS
RANDOMIZE TIMER
LET total = 0
```

```
FOR tries = 1 TO 1000
  LET x = RND
  LET y = RND
  IF x ^ 2 + y ^ 2 < 1 THEN
      LET total = total + 1
  END IF
NEXT tries
PRINT "Approximate area is"; total / 1000
END

[run]
Approximate area is .782
```

PRACTICE PROBLEMS 11.3

Figure 11.10 shows a shaded region under the graph of the curve $y = x^2$, and a rectangle containing the region.

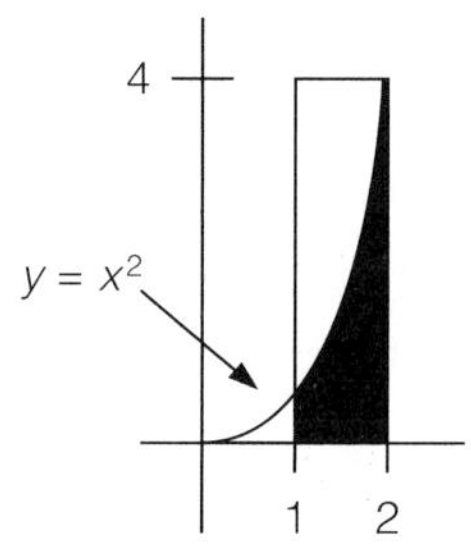

Figure 11.10 Shaded Region

1. Give a pair of formulas using RND to randomly generate the *x*- and *y*-coordinates of a point in this rectangle.
2. What relationship must *x* and *y* satisfy in order for the point (*x*, *y*) to be in the shaded region?
3. Suppose 1000 random points in the rectangle are generated and 58% lie in the shaded region. Estimate the area of the shaded region.

EXERCISES 11.3

Exercises 1 through 4 refer to the bank-teller program of Example 1.

1. Suppose whenever the line has 7 customers in it, any new customers will leave in disgust. Modify the program in this case and also display the number of customers who give up.

2. Modify the program to compute the total number of minutes that the teller is idle during the 2-hour period.

3. Modify the program to compute the average amount of time spent in line by a customer. ***Hint:*** The program should keep track of the total number of customers who enter the bank.

4. Suppose that, owing to greater use of computers in the bank, the amount of time required to serve a customer varies from 30 seconds to 5 minutes. Modify the program to reflect this change.

5. Use Monte Carlo methods to estimate the area of the quarter-ellipse shown in Figure 11.11(a).

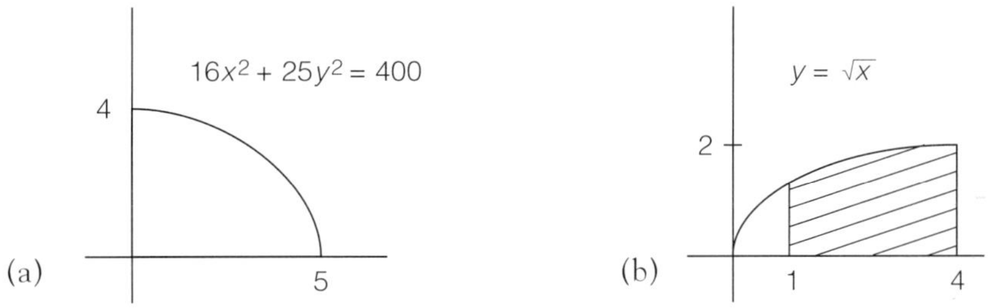

Figure 11.11 Regions under Curves

6. Use Monte Carlo methods to estimate the area of the shaded region under the graph of the parabola shown in Figure 11.11(b).

7. Suppose 5% of the diskettes manufactured by a certain company are defective, and diskettes are packaged 10 to a box. Simulate the manufacturing of 1000 boxes of diskettes and display the number of boxes containing 1 defective diskette, 2 defective diskettes, . . . , 10 defective diskettes.

8. Airlines overbook flights by between 10% and 30% of the capacity of the airplane. Suppose for a certain flight with a capacity of 99 passengers, the likelihood of a person with a reservation not showing up for the flight is 25%. If less than 99 people show up, the airline loses $150 for each unfilled seat. However, if more than 99 people show up, the airline must "bump" the excess people at a cost of $400 per person. (Hotel fees, meals, and monetary compensation make up the bumping cost.) Do a computer simulation to compute the average estimated loss to the airline when 120 seats are booked. (Use 100 trials to make the estimate.) Repeat the simulation for the case where the airline does not overbook at all.

9. Table 11.1 gives the percentages of the different colors of M&M's in each of the two types, plain and peanut. Write a program that requests the type of M&M's as input and then simulates the makeup of a box of 100 M&M's. The program should list the number of M&M's of each color.

Color	Percent in Plain M&M's	Percent in Peanut M&M's
Brown	30	30
Yellow	20	20
Red	20	20
Orange	10	10
Green	10	20
Tan	10	0

Table 11.1 Percentages of Each Color of M&Ms

10. A phone-order software company receives an average of 1 call per minute, with each call taking between 2 and 9 minutes to process. The company employs 6 people to answer phones. If all of them are busy, callers are asked to hold until the next available operator is free. If more than 5 people are on hold, each additional caller is given the option of leaving their name so they can be called back later. About 60% of these people accept that option. These people will be called back as soon as an operator is free and no other callers are waiting. Write a program to simulate the processing of the phone calls for a 4-hour period. At any time, the program should display the number of people on hold and the number of people waiting to have their calls returned.

SOLUTIONS TO PRACTICE PROBLEMS 11.3

1. The *x*-coordinates range from 1 to 2 and the *y*-coordinates from 1 to 4. Therefore, appropriate formulas for generating points are

```
LET x = RND + 1
LET y = 3 * RND + 1
```

2. If $y < x * x$, then the point (x, y) will lie below the point $(x, x * x)$, which is on the graph.

3. Since the area of the rectangle is 4, the estimate for the area of the shaded region is .58 * 4 or 2.32.

Chapter 11 Summary

1. The RND function is used to generate a sequence of numbers between 0 and 1 (including 0, but excluding 1) that have the appearance of being chosen at random.

2. Prior to using the RND function, the statement RANDOMIZE or RANDOMIZE TIMER should be executed to vary the sequence.

3. The ability to select numbers at random can be applied to sampling, simulation, program testing, numerical analysis, recreation, and decision making.

Chapter 11
Programming Projects

1. *Hangman*. Write a program to play Hangman. A list of 20 words should be placed in data statements and one selected at random to be discovered by the user before making 10 incorrect guesses. The program should

   (a) use an array to keep track of the letters already guessed.
   (b) display the appropriate number of dashes.
   (c) prompt the user for a letter. If the letter has already been guessed, inform the user and do not count the guess. Otherwise, if the letter is in the word, display all occurrences above the appropriate dashes. ***Hint:*** Determine the location to display by a statement such as LOCATE 12, 2 + 4 * (*j* – 1) where *j* is the location of the letter in the word, each dash is three characters long, and a single space separates each pair of dashes. If the letter is not in the word, decrease the number of misses remaining by one and display the letter in a table of letters guessed. ***Hint:*** Use the ASCII value of the letter to determine where to display the letter.
   (d) inform the player when either the correct word has been found or the allotment of misses has been used up. ***Hint:*** To determine when the entire word has been guessed, keep track of the number of blanks in the word that have been filled.

2. *Game Theory*. The branch of mathematics called Game Theory is used to maximize gains and minimize losses in business or military problems. As an elementary example of a game theory problem, consider a situation in which you and an opponent each must make choices. Each choice corresponds to a payoff for you as shown in Figure 11.12. For instance, if you make choice *1*, then you gain $2 if your opponent makes choice *1*, and $14 if your opponent makes choice *2*. Each of you will use a random-number generator to make your choice. Suppose your opponent weights his choices so that 75% of the time he chooses *1* and 25% of the time he chooses *2*. How should you weight your choices to maximize your expected earnings? Two possibilities are 33%, 33%, 34%, and 45%, 10%, 45%. Write a program that requests you to input the three percentages, and computes the expected earnings for 1000 encounters. Run the program for each of the two triples of percentages mentioned and determine which one is more advantageous to you.

		Opponent 1	**Opponent** 2
	1	2	14
You	2	6	12
	3	8	6

Figure 11.12 Game-Theory Payoffs

3. *Random Walk.* Figure 11.13 shows a person standing at position 6 on the path to success. Each day he randomly takes one step, either forward or backward. His walk stops when he reaches either end of the path. Write a program that considers each of the nine possible starting positions, simulates the walk 100 times for each starting position, and computes the percentage of walks terminating with success for each starting position. The output should consist of a table displaying the starting positions and the percentages.

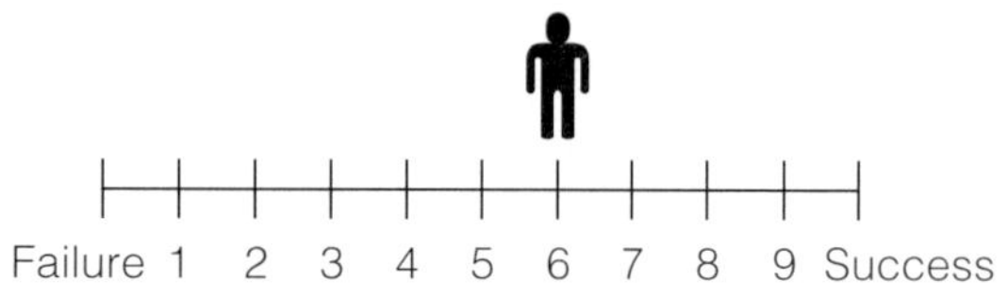

Figure 11.13 Random Walk

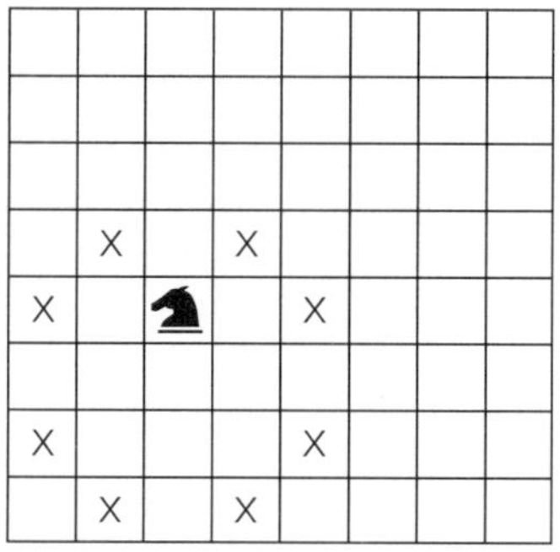

Figure 11.14 Knight's Tour

4. *Knight's Tour.* A knight is randomly placed on a chessboard. On each move the knight takes two steps in a horizontal direction and one step in a vertical direction or two steps in a vertical direction and one step in a horizontal direction. Figure 11.14 shows the eight possibilities. Write a program to do the following.

   (a) Perform the following random tour of the board 100 times and record the number of moves in each tour.
      (1) Randomly place the knight on one of the 64 squares of the chessboard.
      (2) Randomly select one of eight moves for the knight (including possibly a move off the board).
      (3) Repeat step (2) until the knight either moves off the board or occupies a previously occupied position. (First check for the move off the board.)

   (b) A tour can theoretically consist of up to 64 moves (one for each square on the board). Produce a 4-column table showing the 64 possible numbers of moves and the number of tours for each.

5. *Arithmetic Drill.* Write a program that can be used by a child to practice arithmetic skills. The program should contain the following features:

   (a) The child should select a level of difficulty (Easy or Hard) and a category (Addition, Subtraction, Multiplication, or Division).
   (b) The numbers used should be selected randomly. Easy problems should be stated using single-digit numbers, whereas hard problems can include two-digit numbers. To insure that division problems always have whole-number answers, generate the answer first and adjust the range of the

divisor, y, so that answer * y is the appropriate size, and let answer * y be the dividend.

(c) The child should be told if each answer is correct or not and should have three tries before being told the correct answer.

(d) After working ten problems, the child should be able to make another selection as in (a).

(e) After giving four consecutive correct answers, the child should randomly receive one of the responses—"Good Work," "Super," "Nice Job" or "Fantastic."

12

Visual Basic

12.1 AN INTRODUCTION TO VISUAL BASIC

By this point you have learned quite a lot about structured programming in general and QBasic in particular. The purpose of this chapter is to build on what you have already learned by introducing you to Visual Basic—the most exciting development in programming in many years. Visual Basic is the next generation of Basic and is designed to make user-friendly programs easier to develop.

This doesn't sound like much and certainly doesn't seem enough to explain why, for example, Bill Gates, chairman and CEO of Microsoft, described Visual Basic as "awesome." But imagine for a moment how hard it would be to write a program as friendly as QBasic itself. QBasic always knows what you are doing with the mouse, it warns you about actions with message boxes, it lets you choose from menus, and so on.

Prior to the invention of Visual Basic, developing such a friendly user interface usually required teams of programmers using arcane languages like "C" that came in 10-pound boxes with thousands of pages of documentation. Now it can be done by a few people using a language that is a direct descendant of QBasic—the language you now know so well.

Visual Basic comes in two "flavors," one for ordinary DOS programs and the other for Microsoft Windows. Since Microsoft Windows is becoming more and more the dominant environment for PCs, we have chosen to show you the version of Visual Basic developed for Windows programming. Although you don't need to be an expert user of Microsoft Windows, you do need to know the basics before you can master Visual Basic—that is, you need to be comfortable with manipulating a mouse, and you need to know how to manipulate a window and how to use My Computer or Windows Explorer built into Microsoft Windows. All this is covered in Appendix H. However, there is no better way to master Microsoft Windows than to write applications for it—and that is what Visual Basic is all about.

Why Windows and Why Visual Basic?

What people call **Graphical User Interfaces**, or GUIs (pronounced "gooies"), have revolutionized the microcomputer industry. Instead of the cryptic C:\> prompt that DOS users have long seen (and that some have long feared), users are presented with a desktop filled with little pictures called icons. Icons provide a visual guide to what the program can do. See Appendix H for more information on Windows.

Even DOS programs have benefited from the GUI revolution: mouse-aware menu-driven programs like QBasic that warn users of irreversible actions are much easier to use.

Accompanying the revolution in how programs look was a revolution in how they feel. Consider a program that requests information for a database. Figure 12.1 shows how such a QBasic program gets its information. After the program requests six pieces of data, the screen clears and the six inputs are again requested one at a time. Figure 12.2 shows how an equivalent Visual Basic program gets its information. The boxes may be filled in any order. When the user clicks on a box with the mouse, the cursor moves to that box. The user can either type in new information or edit the existing information. When the user is satisfied that all the information is correct, he or she just clicks on the Write to Database button. The boxes will clear, and the data for another person can be entered. After all names have been entered, the user clicks on the Exit button. In Figure 12.1 the program is in control; in Figure 12.2 the user is in control!

```
[run]
Enter Name (Enter EOD to terminate): Mr. President
Enter Address: 1600 Pennsylvania Avenue
Enter City: Washington
Enter State: DC
Enter Zipcode: 20500
Enter Phone Number: 202-395-3000
```

Figure 12.1 Input Screen of a QBasic Program to Create a Database

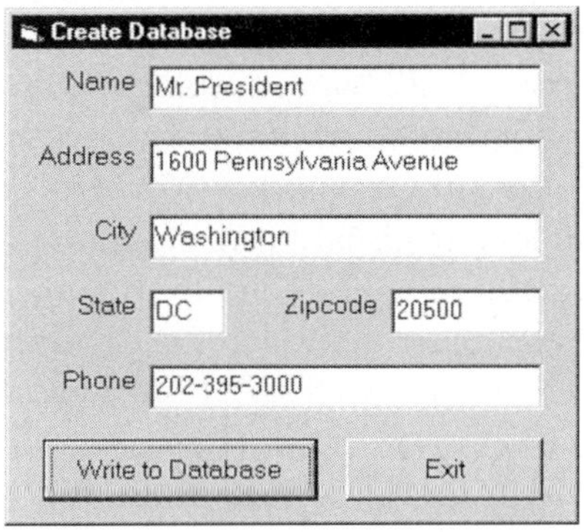

Figure 12.2 Input Screen of a Visual Basic Program to Create a Database

How You Develop a Visual Basic Application

To develop a Visual Basic application, first decide on the data to be processed and how they are to be handled. After the input and output are determined, plan what the user sees—in other words, design the screen. What data will he or she be entering? How large a window should the application use? Where will you place the command buttons—the "buttons" the user clicks on to activate the applications? Will the applications have places to enter text (text boxes) and places to display output? What kind of warning boxes (message boxes) should the application use? In Visual Basic, the responsive controls a program designer places on windows are called *objects*.

Two features make Visual Basic different from almost any other programming tool:

1. You literally draw the user interface, much like using a paint program.

Next, and perhaps more importantly,

2. When you're done drawing the interface, the command buttons, text boxes, and other objects that you have placed in a blank window will automatically recognize user actions such as mouse movements and button clicks. That is, the sequence of procedures executed in your program is controlled by "events" which the user initiates, rather than by a predetermined sequence of procedures in your program.

In any case, only after you design the interface does anything like traditional programming occur. Objects in Visual Basic recognize events like mouse clicks; how the objects respond to them depends on the code you write. You always need to write code in order to make controls respond to events. This makes Visual Basic programming fundamentally different from conventional programming.

Programs in conventional programming languages run from the top, down. For traditional programming languages, execution starts from the first line and moves with the flow of the program to different parts as needed. A Visual Basic program works completely differently. The core of a Visual Basic program is a set of independent pieces of code that are activated by the events they have been told to recognize. This is a fundamental shift. Instead of doing what the programmer thinks should happen, the program gives the user control.

Most of the code that tells your program how to respond to events like mouse clicks occurs in what Visual Basic calls *event procedures*. Essentially, everything executable in a Visual Basic program either is in an event procedure or is used by an event procedure to help the procedure carry out its job. In fact, to stress that Visual Basic is fundamentally different from ordinary programming languages, Microsoft uses the term *project*, rather than *program*, to refer to the combination of programming code and user interface that goes into making a Visual Basic application possible.

Here is a summary of the steps you take to design a Visual Basic application:

1. Decide how the windows that the user sees will look.
2. Determine which events the objects on the window should recognize.
3. Write the event procedures for those events.

Now here is what happens when the application is running:

1. Visual Basic monitors the window and the objects in the window to detect any event that an object can recognize (mouse movements, clicks, keystrokes, and so on).
2. When Visual Basic detects an event, it examines the application to see if you've written an event procedure for that event.
3. If you have written an event procedure, Visual Basic executes the code that makes up that event procedure and goes back to step 1.
4. If you have not written an event procedure, Visual Basic waits for the next event and goes back to step 1.

These steps cycle continuously until the application ends. Usually, an event must happen before Visual Basic will do anything. Event-driven programs are reactive more than active—and that makes them more user friendly.

The Different Versions of Visual Basic

Visual Basic 1.0 first appeared in 1991. It was followed by version 2.0 in 1992, 3.0 in 1993, 4.0 in 1995, and 5.0 in 1997. Having publicly announced that Visual Basic is a key product, Microsoft will continue to add further enhancements to the language. For example, Microsoft has been using versions of Visual Basic to control all its applications. Master Visual Basic and you will be well prepared for almost any office computer environment in the near future!

Visual Basic 5.0 comes in four editions—Control Creation Edition, Learning Edition, Professional Edition, and Enterprise Edition. The Control Creation Edition is contained on the CD packaged with this textbook. All of these editions require Windows 95, Windows NT, or a later version of Windows as the operating system. You can use any edition of Visual Basic 5.0 with this chapter, although some of the opening screens may differ slightly from those shown in this text.

12.2 VISUAL BASIC OBJECTS

Visual Basic programs display a Windows style screen (called a **form**) with boxes into which users type (and edit) information and buttons that they click to initiate actions. The boxes and buttons are referred to as **controls**. Forms and controls are called **objects**. In this section we examine forms and four of the most useful Visual Basic controls.

Note: If Visual Basic has not been installed on your computer, you can install it by following the steps outlined on the first page of Appendix I.

Invoking the Control Creation Edition of Visual Basic 5.0: Appendix I explains how to install the Control Creation Edition and add an icon labeled VB5CCE to the Windows desktop. To invoke VB5.0, double-click the VB5CCE icon.

Invoking the Learning, Professional, or Enterprise Editions of Visual Basic 5.0: To invoke Visual Basic, click the Start button, point to Programs, point to Microsoft Visual Basic 5.0, and click on Visual Basic 5.0.

With all versions of Visual Basic 5.0, the center of the screen will contain the New Project window of Figure 12.3. The main part of the window is a tabbed dialog box with three tabs—New, Existing, and Recent. (If the New tab is not in the foreground, click on it to bring it to the front.) The number of project icons showing is either three (with the Control Creation and Learning Editions) or nine (with the Professional and Enterprise Editions).

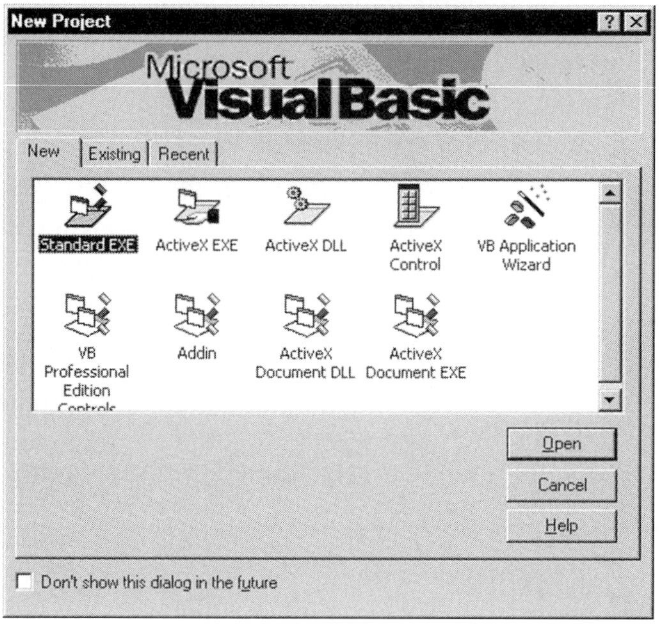

Figure 12.3 New Project Window from Professional Edition of VB 5.0

Double-click the Standard EXE icon to bring up the initial Visual Basic screen in Figure 12.4. The appearance of this screen varies slightly with the different versions of Visual Basic.

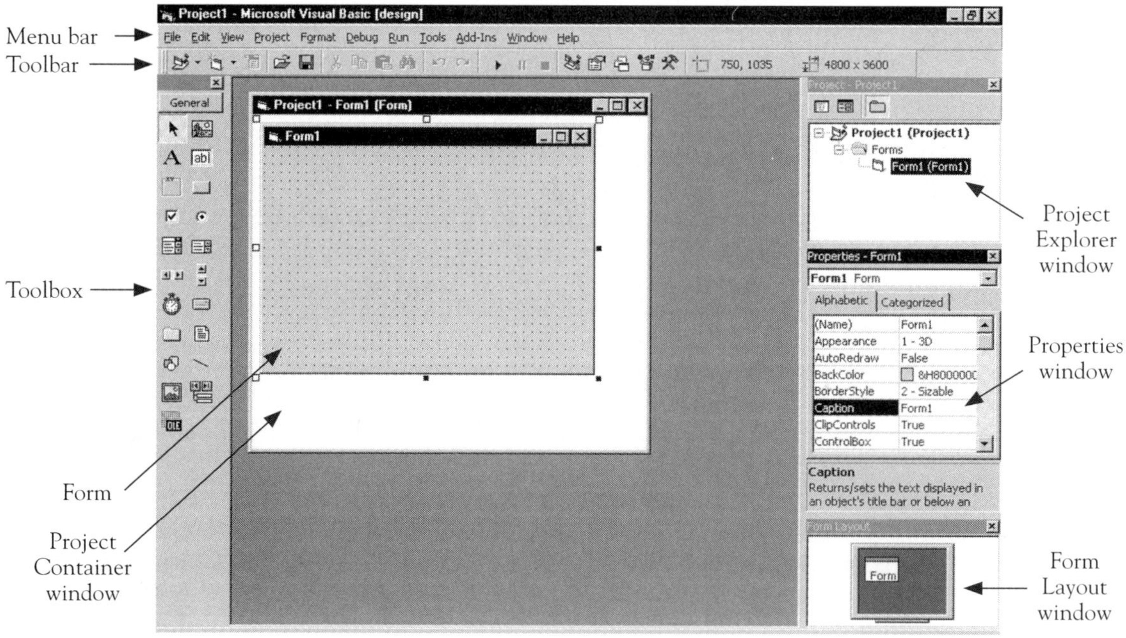

Figure 12.4 The Initial Visual Basic Screen

The menu bar displays the commands you use to work with Visual Basic. Some of the menus, like File, Edit, View, and Window, are common to most Windows applications. Others, such as Project, Format, and Debug, provide commands specific to programming in Visual Basic.

The **Toolbar** is a collection of icons that carry out standard operations when clicked. For example, the fifth icon, which looks like a diskette, can be used to save the current program to a disk. To reveal the function of a Toolbar icon, position the mouse pointer over the icon for a few moments.

The large stippled Form window, or *form* for short, becomes a Windows window when a program is executed. All information displayed by the program appears on the form. The information is displayed either directly on the form or in controls that have been placed on the form. The **Form Layout** window allows you to position the location of the form at run time relative to the entire screen using a small graphical representation of the screen.

The **Project Explorer window** is not needed for our purposes. The **Properties window** is used to change how objects look and react.

The icons in the **Toolbox** represent objects that can be placed on the form. The four objects discussed in this chapter are text boxes, labels, command buttons, and picture boxes.

Text boxes: You use a text box primarily to get information, referred to as **input**, from the user.

Labels: A label is placed next to a text box to tell the user what type of information to enter into the text box.

Command buttons: The user clicks a command button to initiate an action.

Picture boxes: You use a picture box to display text or graphics.

A Text-Box Walkthrough

1. Double-click on the text box icon. (The text-box icon consists of the bold letters **ab** and a vertical bar cursor inside a rectangle and is the fourth icon in the Toolbox.) A rectangle with eight small squares, called **sizing handles**, appears at the center of the screen. See Figure 12.5.

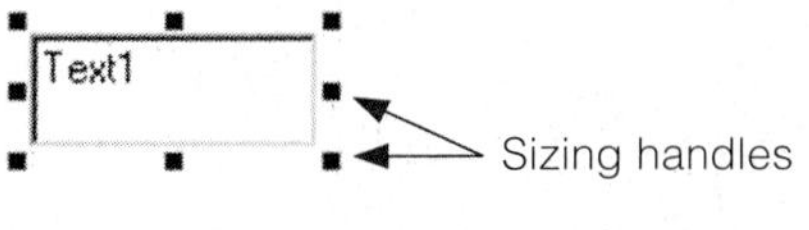

Figure 12.5 A Text Box with Sizing Handles

2. Click anywhere on the form outside the rectangle to remove the handles.

3. Click on the rectangle to restore the handles. An object showing its handles is (said to be) **selected**. A selected object can have its size altered, location changed, and other properties modified.

4. Move the mouse arrow to the handle in the center of the right side of the text box. The arrow should change to a double arrow (↔). Hold down the left mouse button and move the mouse to the right. The text box is stretched to the right. Similarly, grabbing the text box by one of the other handles and moving the mouse stretches the text box in another direction. For instance, you use the handle in the upper left corner to stretch the text box up and to the left. Handles also can be used to make the text box smaller.

5. Move the mouse arrow to any point inside the text box. Hold down the left mouse button and move the mouse. You can now drag the text box to a new location. Using Steps 4 and 5, you can place a text box of any size anywhere on the form.

   Note: The text box should now be selected; that is, its sizing handles should be showing. If not, click anywhere inside the text box to select it.

6. Press the delete key, Del, to remove the text box from the form. Step 7 gives an alternative way to place a text box of any size at any location on the form.

7. Click on the text-box icon in the Toolbox. Then move the mouse pointer to any place on the form. (When over the form, the mouse pointer becomes a pair of crossed thin lines.) Hold down the left mouse button and move the mouse on a diagonal to generate a rectangle. Release the mouse button to obtain a selected text box. You can now alter the size and location as before.

   Note: The text box should now be selected; that is, its sizing handles should be showing. If not, click anywhere inside the text box to select it.

8. Press F4 to activate the Properties window. (You can also activate the properties window by clicking on it or clicking on the Properties window icon in the toolbar.) See Figure 12.6. The first line of the Properties window (called the **object box**) reads "Text1 TextBox". Text1 is the current name of the text box. The two tabs permit you to view the list of properties either alphabetically or grouped into categories. Text boxes have 40 properties which can be grouped into 7 categories. Use the up- and down-arrow keys (or the up- and down-scroll arrows) to glance through the list. The left column gives the property and the right column gives the current setting of the property. We discuss four properties in this walkthrough.

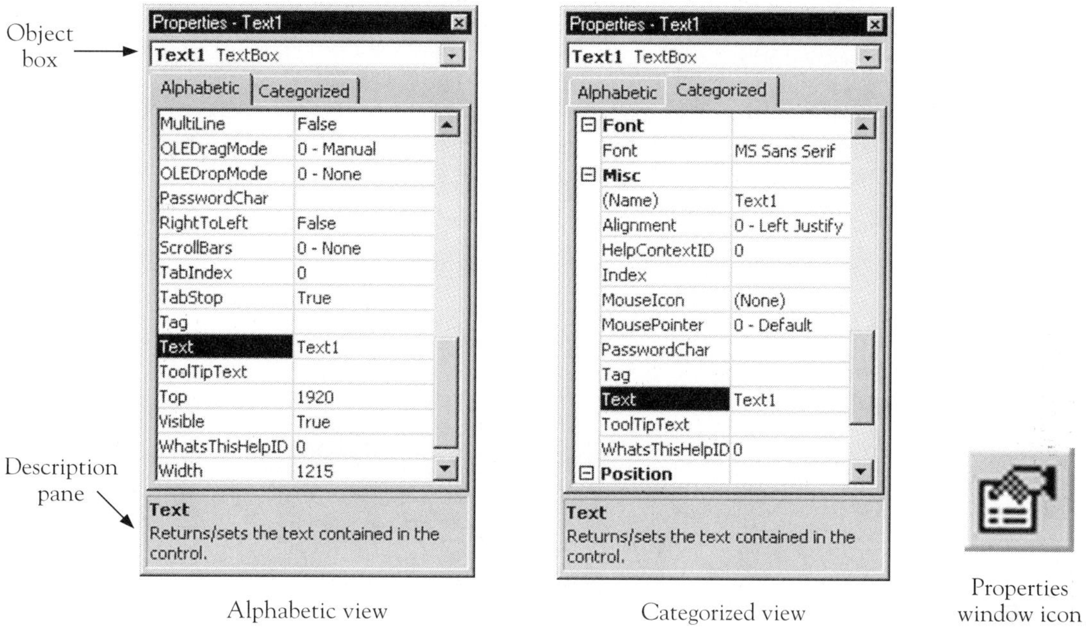

Figure 12.6 Text-Box Properties Window

9. Move to the Text property with the up- and down-arrow keys. (Alternatively, scroll until the property is visible and click on the property.) The Text property is now highlighted. The Text property determines the words in the text box. Currently, the words are set to "Text1" in the **settings box** on the right.

10. Type your first name. As you type, your name replaces "Text1" in both the settings box and the text box. See Figure 12.7. (Alternatively, you could have clicked on the settings box and edited its contents.)

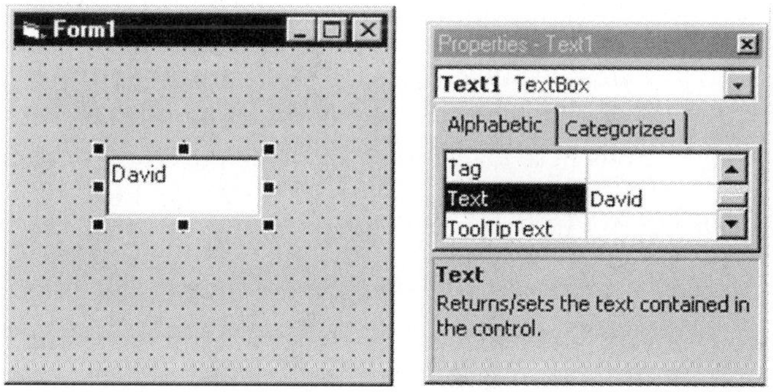

Figure 12.7 Setting the Text Property to David

11. Click at the beginning of your name in the settings box and add your title, such as Mr., Ms., or The Honorable. (If you mistyped your name, you can easily correct it now.)

12. Press Shift+Ctrl+F to move to the first property that begins with the letter F. Now use the down-arrow key or the mouse to highlight the property ForeColor. The foreground color is the color of the text.

13. Click on the down arrow in the right part of the settings box and then click on the Palette tab to display a selection of colors. See Figure 12.8. Click on one of the solid colors, such as blue or red. Notice the change in the color of your name.

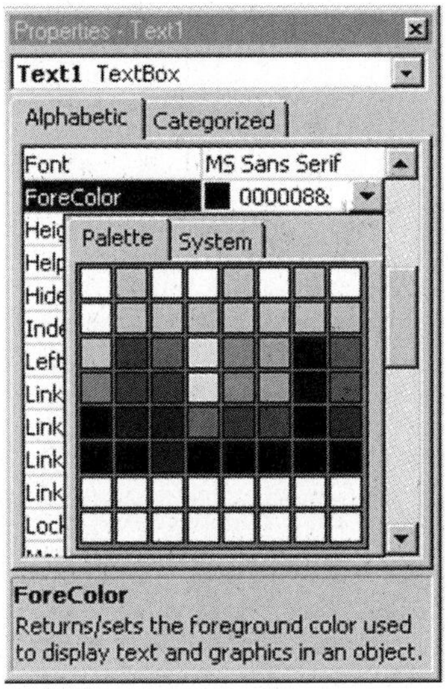

Figure 12.8 Setting the ForeColor Property

14. Highlight the Font property with a single click of the mouse. The current font is named MS Sans Serif.

15. Click on the ellipsis (...) box in the right part of the settings box to display a dialog box. See Figure 12.9. The three lists give the current name (MS Sans Serif), current style (Regular), and current size (8) of the font. You can change any of these attributes by clicking. Click on Bold in the style list and click on 12 in the size list. Now click on the OK button to see your name displayed in a larger bold font.

16. Click on the text box and resize it to be about 3 inches wide and 1 inch high.

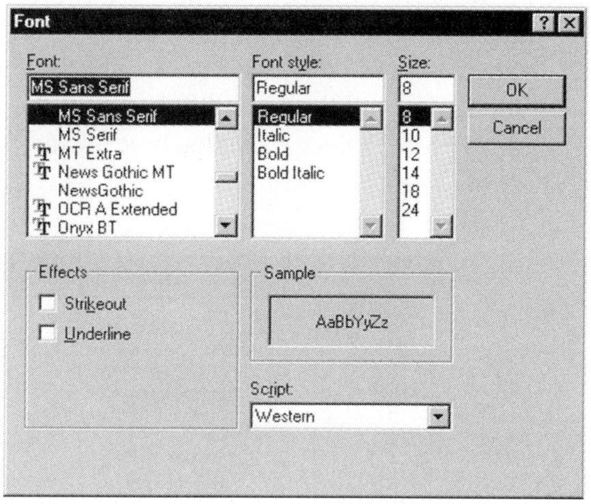

Figure 12.9 The Font Dialog Box

Visual Basic programs consist of three parts—interface, values of properties, and code. Our interface consists of a form with a single object, a text box. We have set a few properties for the text box—the text (namely, your name), the foreground color, the font style, and the font size. In Section 12.2 we see how to place code into a program. Visual Basic endows certain capabilities to programs that are independent of any code. We will now run the existing codeless program and experience these capabilities.

17. Press F5 to run the program. (Alternatively, a program can be run from the menu by pressing Alt/R/S or by clicking on the Start icon ▸, the twelfth icon on the Toolbar.) Notice that the dots have disappeared from the form.

18. The cursor is at the beginning of your name. Press the End key to move the cursor to the end of your name. Now type in your last name, and then keep typing. Eventually, the words will scroll to the left.

19. Press Home to return to the beginning of the text. You have a full-fledged word processor at your disposal. You can place the cursor anywhere you like to add or delete text. You can drag the cursor across text to create a block, place a copy of the block in the clipboard with Ctrl+C, and then duplicate it anywhere with Ctrl+V.

20. To terminate the program, press Alt+F4. Alternatively, you can end a program by clicking on the End icon ▸, the fourteenth icon on the Toolbar, or clicking on the form's close button ☒.

21. Select the text box, activate the Properties window, select the MultiLine property, click on the down-arrow button, and finally click on True. The MultiLine property has been changed from False to True.

22. Run the program and type in the text box. Notice that now words wrap around when the end of a line is reached. Also, text will scroll up when it reaches the bottom of the text box.

23. End the program.

24. Press Alt/F/V or click on the Save Project icon to save the work done so far. A Save File As dialog box appears. See Figure 12.10. Visual Basic creates two disk files to store a program. The first, with the extension .frm, is entered into the Save File As dialog box and the second, with the extension .vbp, into a Save Project As dialog box. Visual Basic refers to programs as **projects**.

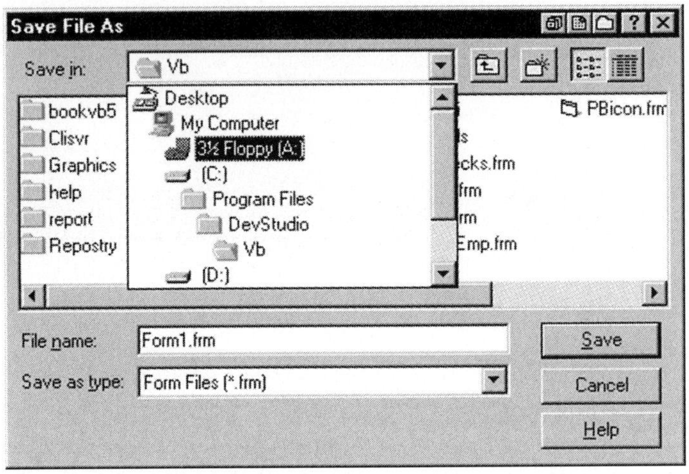

Figure 12.10 The Save File As Dialog Box

25. Type a file name, such as *testprog*, into the "File name" box. The extension .frm automatically will be appended to the name. Do not press the Enter key yet. (Pressing the Enter key has the same effect as clicking Save.) The selection in the large window tells where your program will be saved. Alter these as desired. (***Suggestion:*** If you are using a computer in a campus computer lab, you probably should use a diskette to save your work. If so, place the diskette in a drive, say, the A drive, and select $3^1/_2$ Floppy (A:) in the Drives or "Save in" box.)

26. Click the Save button when you are ready to go on. (Alternatively, press Tab several times until the Save button is highlighted and then press Enter.) The Save Project As dialog box appears.

27. Type a file name into the File Name box. You can use the same name, such as *testprog*, as before. Then proceed as in Steps 25 and 26. (The extension .vbp will be added.)

28. Press Alt/F/N to begin a new program. (As before, select Standard EXE.)

29. Place three text boxes on the form. (Move each text box out of the center of the form before creating the next.) Notice that they have the names Text1, Text2, and Text3.

30. Run the program. Notice that the cursor is in Text1. We say that Text1 has the **focus**. (*Focus* is the ability to receive user input through the mouse or keyboard.) Any text typed will display in that text box.

31. Press Tab once. Now Text2 has the focus. When you type, the characters appear in Text2.

32. Press Tab several times and then press Shift+Tab a few times. With Tab, the focus cycles through the objects on the form in the order the objects were created. With Shift+Tab, the focus cycles in the reverse order.

33. End the program.

34. Press Alt/F/O or click on the Open Project icon to reload your first program. When a dialog box asks if you want to save your changes, click the No button or press N. An Open Project dialog box appears on the screen. Click on the Recent tab to see a list of the programs most recently opened or saved. Your first program and its location should appear at the top of the list. (***Note:*** You can also find any program by clicking on the Existing tab and using the dialog box to search for the program.)

35. Click on the name of your first program and then click on the Open button. Alternatively, double-click on the name. (You also have the option of typing the name into the File Name box and then clicking the Open button.)

A Command-Button Walkthrough

1. Press Alt/F/N and double-click on Standard EXE to start anew. There is no need to save anything.

2. Double-click on the command-button icon to place a command button in the center of the form. (The rectangular-shaped command-button icon is the sixth icon in the Toolbox.)

3. Activate the Properties window, highlight the Caption property, and type "Please Push Me". See Figure 12.11. Notice that the letters appear on the command button as they are typed. The button is too small.

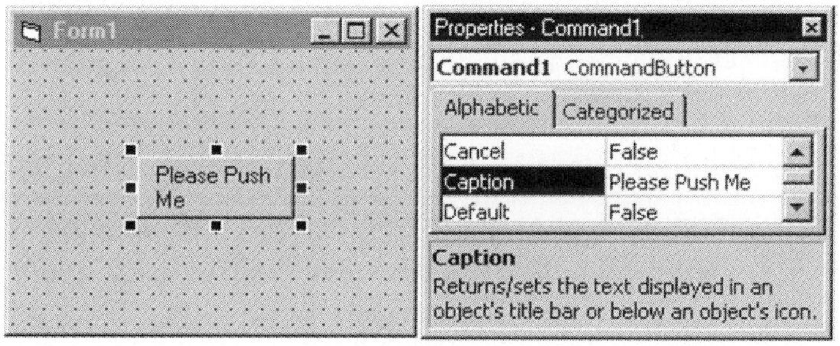

Figure 12.11 Setting the Caption Property

4. Click on the command button to select it and then enlarge it to accommodate the phrase "Please Push Me" on one line.

5. Run the program and click on the command button. The command button appears to move in and then out. In Section 12.2 we write code that is activated when a command button is pushed.

6. End the program and select the command button.

7. From the Properties window, edit the Caption setting by inserting an ampersand (&) before the first letter, P. Notice that the ampersand does not show on the button. However, the letter following the ampersand is now

underlined. See Figure 12.12. Pressing Alt+P while the program is running triggers the same event as clicking the command button. Here, the letter P is referred to as the **access key** for the command button. (The access key is always the key following the ampersand.)

Figure 12.12 Designating P as an Access Key

8. End the program.

A Label Walkthrough 

1. Press Alt/F/N and double-click on Standard EXE to start anew. There is no need to save anything.
2. Double-click on the label icon to place a label in the center of the form. (The label icon, a large letter A, is the third icon in the Toolbox.)
3. Activate the Properties window, highlight the Caption property, and type "Enter Your Phone Number". Such a label would be placed next to a text box into which the user will enter a phone number.
4. Click on the label to select it and then widen it until all words are on the same line.
5. Make the label narrower until the words occupy two lines.
6. Activate the Properties window and double-click on the Alignment property. Double-click two more times. The combination of sizing and alignment permits you to design a label easily.
7. Run the program. Nothing happens, even if you click on the label. Labels just sit there. The user cannot change what a label displays unless you write code to allow the change.
8. End the program.

A Picture Box Walkthrough 

1. Press Alt/F/N and double-click on Standard EXE to start anew. There is no need to save anything.
2. Double-click on the picture box icon to place a picture box in the center of the form. (The picture box icon is the second icon in the Toolbox. It contains a picture of the sun shining over a desert.)

3. Enlarge the picture box.

4. Run the program. Nothing happens and nothing will, no matter what you do. Although picture boxes look like text boxes, you can't type in them. However, you can display text in them with statements discussed later in this chapter, you can draw lines and circles in them, and you can insert pictures into them.

5. End the program and click the picture box to select it.

6. Activate the Properties window and double-click on the Picture property. A Load Picture dialog box appears. See Figure 12.13.

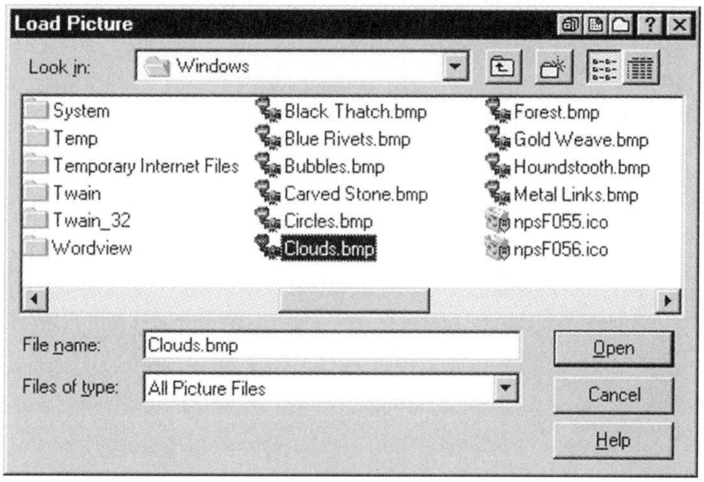

Figure 12.13 The Load Picture Dialog Box

7. Select the Windows folder and then double-click on one of the picture files. (All files with the extension .bmp are picture files.) A good candidate is Clouds.bmp, shown in Figure 12.14. See Comment 17 at the end of this section.

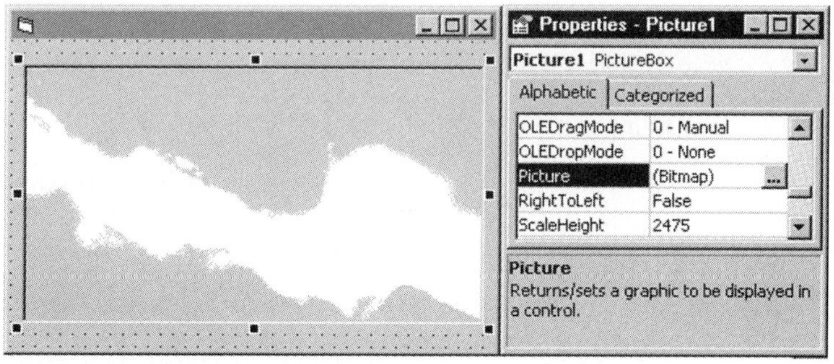

Figure 12.14 A Picture Box Filled with the Clouds.bmp Picture

8. Click on the picture box and press Del to remove the picture box.

Comments

1. When selecting from a list, double-clicking has the same effect as clicking once and pressing Enter.

2. On a form, the Tab key cycles through the objects that can get the focus, and in a dialog box, it cycles through the items.

3. The form itself is also an object and has properties. For instance, you can change the text in the title bar with the Caption property. You can move the form by dragging the title bar of its project container window. Although the project container window does not have sizing handles, you can size it by grabbing it by one of its corners, its bottom edge, or a side and dragging the mouse.

4. The name of an object is used in code to refer to the object. By default, objects are given names like Text1 and Text2. You can use the Properties window to change the Name property of an object to a more suggestive name. (The Name property is always the first property in the list of properties. An object's Name must start with a letter and can be a maximum of 40 characters. It can include numbers and underline (_) characters but can't include punctuation or spaces.) Also, Microsoft recommends that each name begin with a three letter prefix that identifies the type of the control. See the table below. Beginning with Section 12.2, we will use suggestive names and these prefixes whenever possible.

Object	Prefix	Example
command button	cmd	cmdComputeTotal
form	frm	frmPayroll
label	lbl	lblInstructions
picture box	pic	picClouds
text box	txt	txtAddress

5. The Name and Caption properties of a command button are both initially set to something like Command1. However, changing one of these properties does not affect the setting of the other property. Similarly for the Name and Caption properties of forms and labels, and for the Name and Text properties of text boxes.

6. The color settings appear as strings of digits and letters preceded by &H and trailed with &. Don't concern yourself with the notation at this time.

7. Here are some fine points on the use of the Properties window.

   (a) Press Shift+Ctrl+*letterkey* to highlight the first property that begins with that letter. Successive pressings highlight successive properties that begin with that letter.

   (b) To change the selected object from the Properties window, click on the down-arrow icon at the right of the Object box of the Properties window. Then select the new object from the drop-down list.

8. Some useful properties that have not been discussed are the following:

   (a) BorderStyle: Setting the BorderStyle to "0 – None" removes the border from an object.

   (b) Visible: Setting the Visible property to False hides an object when the program is run. The object can be made to reappear with code.

(c) BackColor: Specifies the background color for a text box, label, picture box, or form. Also specifies the background color for a command button that has its Style property set to "1 – Graphical." (Such a command button can display a picture.)

(d) BackStyle: The BackStyle property of a label is opaque by default. The rectangular region associated with the label is filled with the label's background color and caption. Setting the background style of a label to transparent causes whatever is behind the label to remain visible; the background color of the label essentially becomes "see through."

(e) Font: Can be set to any of Windows' fonts, such as Courier and Times Roman. Two unusual fonts are Symbols and Wingdings. For instance, with the Wingdings font, pressing the keys for %, &, ', and J yields a bell, a book, a candle, and a smiling face, respectively. To view the character sets for the different Windows' fonts, click on the Start button, and successively select Programs, Accessories, and Character Map. Then click on Character Map or press the Enter key. After selecting a font, hold down the left mouse button on any character to enlarge the character and obtain the keystroke that produces that character.

9. When you click on a property in the Properties window, a description of the property appears just below the window. Additional information about many of the properties can be found in Appendix C. You can obtain very detailed (and somewhat advanced) information about a property by clicking on the property and pressing F1.

10. Most properties can be set or altered with code as the program is running instead of being preset from the Properties window. For instance, a command button can be made to disappear with a line such as Let Command1.Visible = False. See Section 12.2 for details.

11. The BorderStyle and MultiLine properties of a text box can be set only from the Properties window. You cannot alter them during run time.

12. Of the objects discussed in this section, only command buttons have true access keys.

13. If you inadvertently double-click an object in a form, a window containing two lines of text will appear. (The first line begins Private Sub.) This is a code window and is discussed in the next section. To remove this window, click on its Close button.

14. Objects can be grouped together by attaching them to a picture box. (To attach an object to a picture box, click on the icon in the Toolbox, move the mouse to a point inside the picture box, and drag the mouse until the object has the shape you want. Do not use the double-click method to create the object.)

15. To enlarge (or decrease) the Project Container window, position the mouse cursor anywhere on the right or bottom edge and drag the mouse. To enlarge (or decrease) the form, select the form and drag one of its sizing handles. Alternatively, you can enlarge either the Project Container window or the form by clicking on its Maximize button.

16. We will always be selecting the Standard EXE icon from the New Project window.

17. If the file Clouds.bmp is not in the Windows directory of your computer, you may be able to find it in the directory C:\Program Files\DevStudio\VB\samples\Pguide\PalMode. If not, you can use any picture file in place of Clouds.bmp. The CD accompanying this textbook contains several picture files in the folder Pictures.

PRACTICE PROBLEMS 12.2

1. What is the difference between the Caption and the Name of a command button?
2. Suppose in an earlier session you created an object that looks like an empty rectangle. It might be a picture box, a text box with Text property set to nothing (blanked out by deleting all characters), or a label with a blank caption and BorderStyle property set to Fixed Single. How might you determine which it is?

EXERCISES 12.2

1. Why are command buttons sometimes called "push buttons"?
2. How can you tell if a program is running by looking at the screen?
3. Create a form with two command buttons, run the program, and click on each button. Do you notice anything different about a button after it has been clicked?
4. Design an experiment to convince yourself that picture boxes can get the focus, but labels cannot.
5. Place three command buttons vertically on a form with Command3 above Command2, and Command2 above Command1. Then run the program and successively press Tab. Notice that the command buttons receive the focus from bottom to top. Experiment with various configurations of command buttons and text boxes to convince yourself that objects get the focus in the order in which they were created.
6. While a program is running, an object is said to **lose focus** when the focus moves from that object to another object. In what three ways can the user cause an object to lose focus?

In Exercises 7 through 28, carry out the task. Use a new form for each exercise.

7. Place CHECKING ACCOUNT in the title bar of a form.
8. Create a text box containing the words PLAY IT, SAM in blue letters.
9. Create an empty text box with a yellow background.
10. Create a text box containing the word HELLO in large italic letters.
11. Create a text box containing the sentence "After all is said and done, more is said than done." The sentence should occupy three lines, and each line should be centered in the text box.
12. Create a borderless text box containing the words VISUAL BASIC in bold white letters on a red background.

13. Create a text box containing the words VISUAL BASIC in Courier font.

14. Create a command button containing the word PUSH.

15. Create a command button containing the word PUSH in large italic letters.

16. Create a command button containing the word PUSH in nonbold letters with the letter P underlined.

17. Create a command button containing the word PUSH with the letter H as access key.

18. Create a command button containing the caption TREES, a white background, and the picture file TREES.BMP from the Pictures folder of the CD accompanying this book.

19. Create a label containing the word ALIAS.

20. Create a label containing the word ALIAS in white on a blue background.

21. Create a label with a border containing the centered italicized word ALIAS.

22. Create a label containing VISUAL on the first line and BASIC on the second line. Each word should be right-justified.

23. Create a label containing a picture of a diskette. (***Hint:*** Use the Wingdings character <.) Make the diskette as large as possible.

24. Create a label with a border containing the bold word ALIAS in the Terminal font.

25. Create a picture box with a yellow background.

26. Create a picture box with no border and a red background.

27. Create a picture box containing two command buttons.

28. Create a picture box with a blue background containing a picture box with a white background.

In Exercises 29 through 36, create the interface shown in the figure. (These exercises give you practice creating objects and assigning properties. The interfaces do not necessarily correspond to actual programs.)

29.

30.

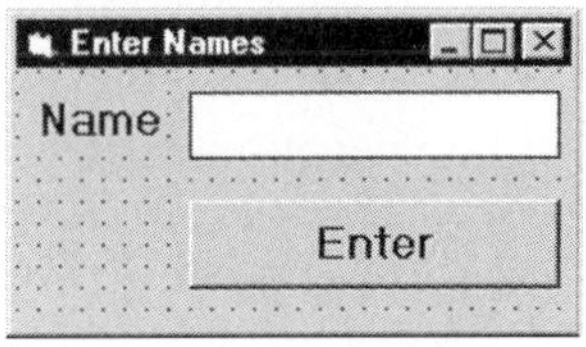

31.

32.

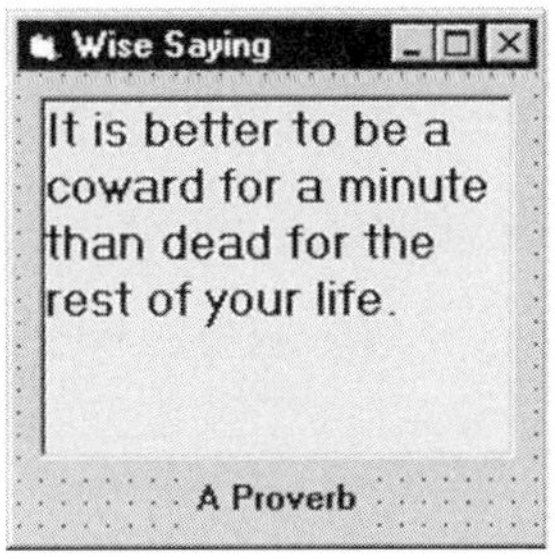

33. 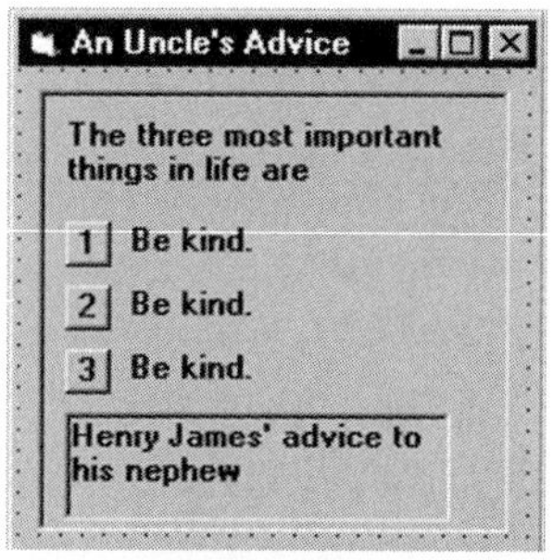

34. 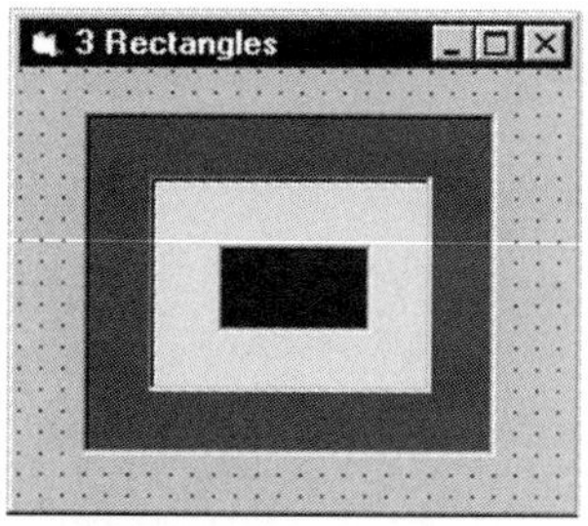

35. 

36. 

37. Create a replica of your bank check on a form. Words common to all checks, such as PAY TO THE ORDER OF, should be contained in labels. Items specific to your checks, such as your name at the top left, should be contained in text boxes. Make the check on the screen resemble your check as much as possible.

38. Create a replica of your campus ID on a form. Words that are on all student IDs, such as the name of the college, should be contained in labels. Information specific to your ID, such as your name and Social Security number, should be contained in text boxes. Simulate your picture with a text box containing a smiling face—a size 24 Wingdings J.

39. If you are familiar with Paintbrush (one of Windows' Accessories), use Paintbrush to make a drawing and then save it as a .bmp file. In Visual Basic, create a picture box containing the picture.

SOLUTIONS TO PRACTICE PROBLEMS 12.2

1. The Caption is the text appearing on the command button, whereas the Name is the designation used to refer to the command button. Initially they have the same value, such as Command1. However, each can be changed independently of the other.

2. Click on the object to select it and then press F4 to activate its Properties window. The Object box gives the Name of the object (in bold letters) and its type, such as Label, TextBox, or PictureBox.

   We have examined only four of the objects from the Toolbox. To determine the type of one of the other objects, hold the mouse pointer over it for a few seconds.

12.3 VISUAL BASIC EVENTS

When a QBasic program runs, usually something happens right away, then other things happen in sequence. Trying to do this with a Visual Basic program defeats the purpose of an event-driven language. Always keep in mind that the point of event-driven programming is that the program sits around waiting for the user to *do something*, such as clicking an object or pressing the Tab key, before it does something.

The three steps to creating a Visual Basic program are as follows:

1. Create the interface; that is, generate, position, and size the objects.
2. Set properties; that is, set relevant properties for the objects.
3. Write the code that executes when the events occur.

This section is devoted to step 3.

QBasic has two types of procedures, subprograms and user-defined functions. Such procedures are also present in Visual Basic and are referred to as **general procedures**. Visual Basic has another kind of procedure, called an **event procedure**. An event procedure is tied to an object and is invoked when a specific event occurs. The programs in this section use three events—Click, GotFocus, and LostFocus.

Although a few QBasic statements (such as READ and DATA) cannot be used in Visual Basic, most statements can be used in Visual Basic exactly as in QBasic. However, a few QBasic statements (such as CLS and PRINT) must be altered slightly. Statements that display text or graphics on the screen must be directed to an object. For instance, text can be PRINTed in the picture box picBox with

```
picBox.Print expression
```

or on the form Form1 with

```
Form1.Print expression
```

Text and graphics (drawn with graphics commands) are erased from picBox with

```
picBox.Cls
```

and from Form1 with

```
Form1.Cls
```

(Notice that in Visual Basic only the first letters of keywords are capitalized. The Visual Basic smart editor automatically does the capitalization.)

During run time, properties are identified by specifying an object and a property in the form

```
objectName.property
```

Some examples are txtInput.Text, lblName.Caption, and picBox.Picture.

The four controls discussed in detail in Section 12.2 are text boxes, picture boxes, labels, and command buttons. You display information in the text box txtBox by assigning a string value to txtBox.Text. For instance,

```
Let txtBox.Text = "Hello"
```

changes the contents of txtBox to Hello. You display text in the picture box picBox with picBox.Print. For instance,

```
picBox.Print "Hello"
```

displays Hello in picBox. Semicolons, commas, and Tab can be used with picBox.Print and have the same effect as in QBasic. Labels don't usually do anything except identify the uses of text boxes and picture boxes. Command buttons just sit around waiting to be pushed.

In this section, we limit ourselves to statements that change properties of objects while a program is running. Properties of an object are changed in code with statements of the form

```
Let objectName.property = setting
```

where *setting* is a valid setting for that object. Here are three such statements.

The statement

```
Let txtBox.Font.Size = 12
```

sets the size of the characters in the text box named txtBox to 12.

The statement

```
Let txtBox.Font.Bold = True
```

converts the characters in the text box to boldface.

The statement

```
Let txtBox.Text = ""
```

clears the contents of the text box; that is, it invokes the blank setting.

Most events are associated with objects. The event *clicking cmdButton* is different from the event *clicking picBox*. These two events are specified cmdButton_Click and picBox_Click. The statements to be executed when an event occurs are written in a block of code called an **event procedure**. The structure of an event procedure is

```
Private Sub objectName_event()
  statements
End Sub
```

The word Sub in the first line signals the beginning of the event procedure, and the first line identifies the object and the event occurring to that object. The last line signals the termination of the event procedure. The statements to be executed appear between these two lines. (***Note:*** The word Private indicates that the event procedure cannot be invoked by an event from another form.) For instance, the event procedure

```
Private Sub cmdButton_Click()
  Let txtBox.Text = ""
End Sub
```

clears the contents of the text box when the command button is clicked.

An Event-Procedure Walkthrough

The form in Figure 12.15, which contains a text box and a command button, will be used to demonstrate what event procedures are and how they are created. Three event procedures will be used to alter the appearance of a phrase that is typed into the text box. The event procedures are txtPhrase_LostFocus, txtPhrase_GotFocus, and cmdBold_Click.

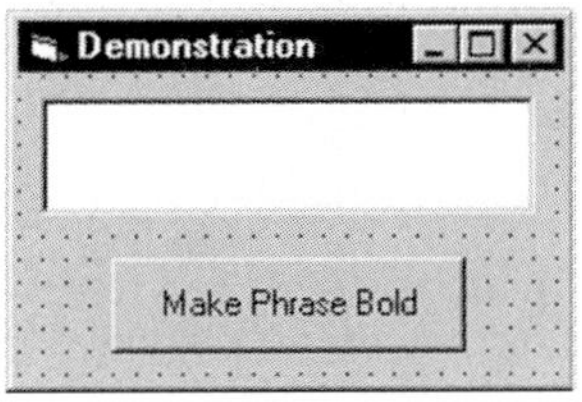

Object	Property	Setting
frmWalkthrough	Caption	Demonstration
txtPhrase	Text	(blank)
cmdBold	Caption	Make Phrase Bold

Figure 12.15 The Interface for the Event-Procedure Walkthrough

1. Create the interface in Figure 12.13. The Name properties of the form, text box, and command button should be set as shown in the Object column. The caption property of the form should be set to Demonstration, the Text property of the text box should be made blank, and the Caption property of the command button should be set to Make Phrase Bold.
2. Double-click on the text box. A window, called the **code window**, appears. See Figure 12.16. Just below the title bar are two drop-down list boxes. The left box is called the Object box, the right box the Procedure box. (When you position the mouse pointer over one of these list boxes, its type appears.)

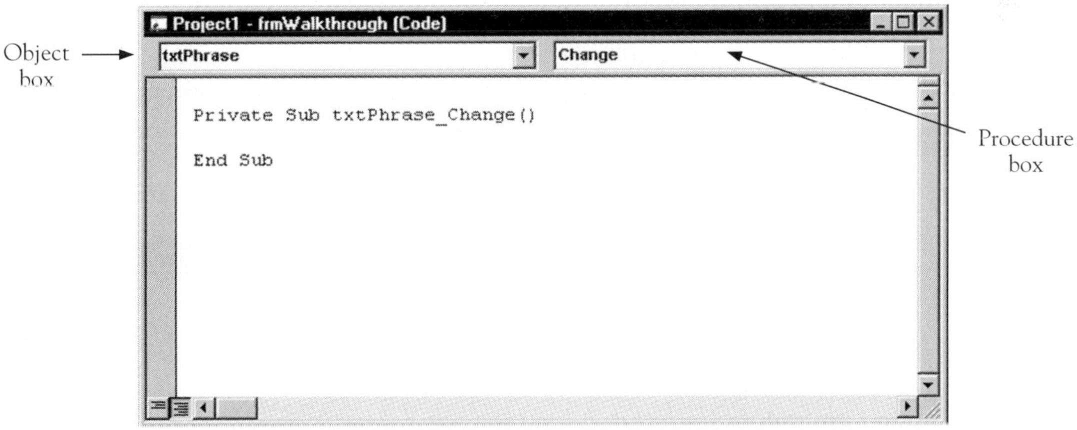

Figure 12.16 A Code Window

3. Click on the down-arrow button to the right of the Procedure box. The drop-down menu that appears contains a list of all possible event procedures associated with text boxes. See Figure 12.17.

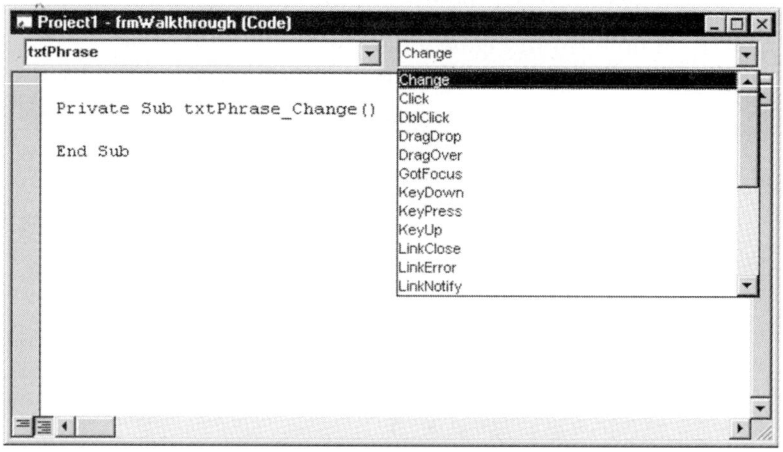

Figure 12.17 Drop-down menu of Event Procedures

4. Scroll down the list of event procedures and click on LostFocus. (LostFocus is the last event procedure.) The lines

   ```
   Private Sub txtPhrase_LostFocus()
   End Sub
   ```

   appear in the code window with a blinking cursor poised at the beginning of the blank line.

5. Type the line

   ```
   Let txtPhrase.Font.Size = 12
   ```

   between the existing two lines. (We usually indent lines inside procedures.) (After you type each period, the editor displays a list containing possible choices of items to follow the period. See Figure 12.18. This new feature, which was added in Visual Basic 5.0, is called "List Properties/Methods." In Figure 12.16, instead of typing the word "Size," you can double-click on "Size" in the displayed list or highlight the word "Size" and press Tab.) The screen appears as in Figure 12.19. We have now created an event procedure that is activated whenever the text box loses the focus.

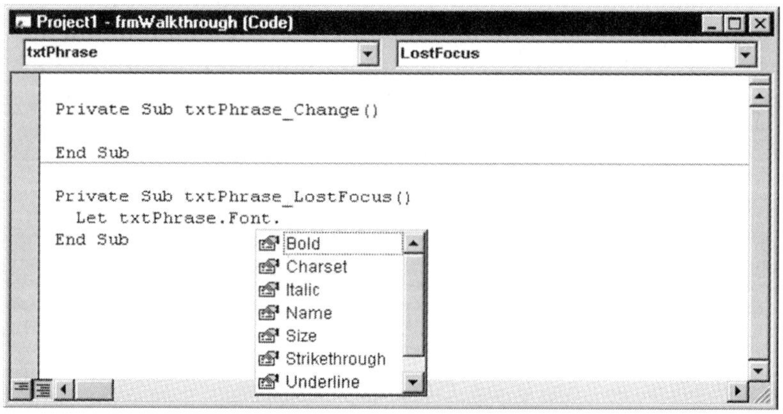

Figure 12.18 A LostFocus Event Procedure

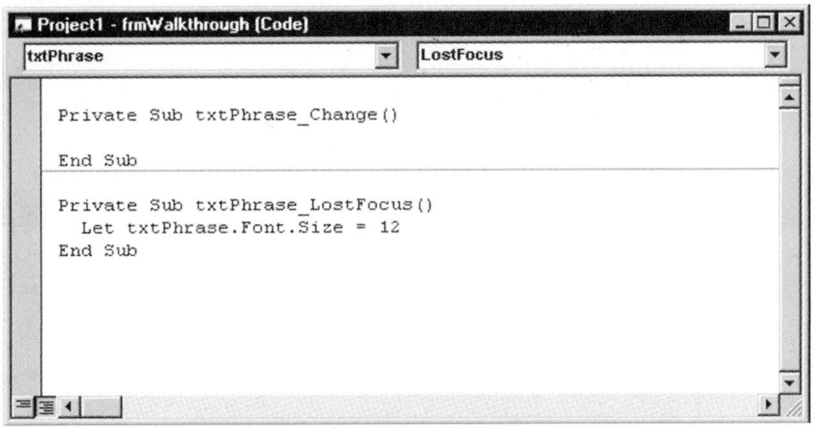

Figure 12.19 A LostFocus Event Procedure

6. Let's create another event procedure for the text box. Click on the down-arrow button to the right of the Procedure box, scroll up the list of event procedures, and click on GotFocus. Then type the lines

```
Let txtPhrase.Font.Size = 8
Let txtPhrase.Font.Bold = False
```

between the existing two lines. See Figure 12.20.

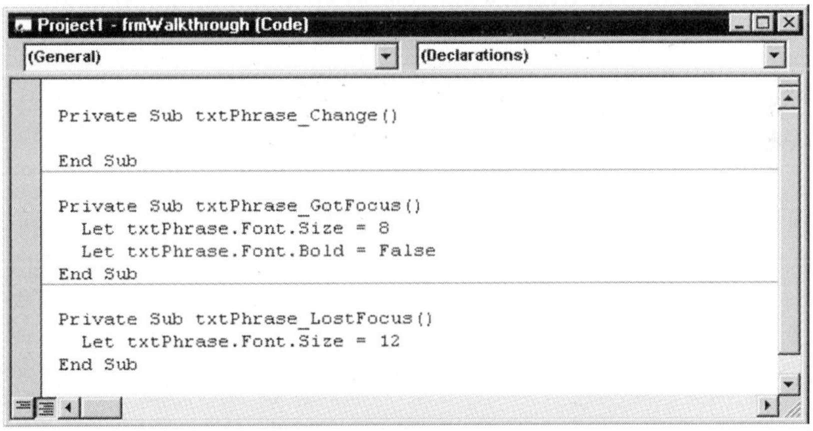

Figure 12.20 A GotFocus Event Procedure

7. The txtPhrase_Change event procedure in Figure 12.20 was not used and can be deleted. To delete the procedure, highlight it by dragging the mouse across the two lines of code, and then press the Del key.

8. Let's now create an event procedure for the command button. Click on the down-arrow button to the right of the Object box. The drop-down menu contains a list of the objects, along with a mysterious object called (General). See Figure 12.21. (We'll discuss (General) later in this chapter.)

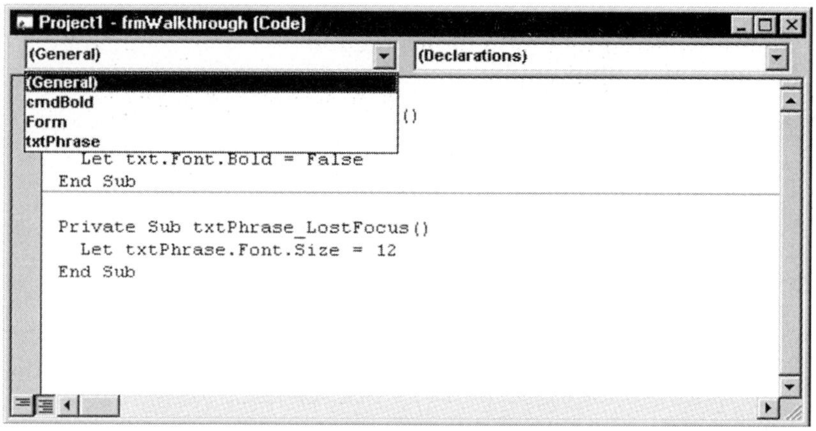

Figure 12.21 List of Objects

9. Click on cmdBold. The event procedure cmdBold_Click is displayed. Type in the line

```
Let txtPhrase.Font.Bold = True
```

The screen appears as in Figure 12.22 and the program is complete.

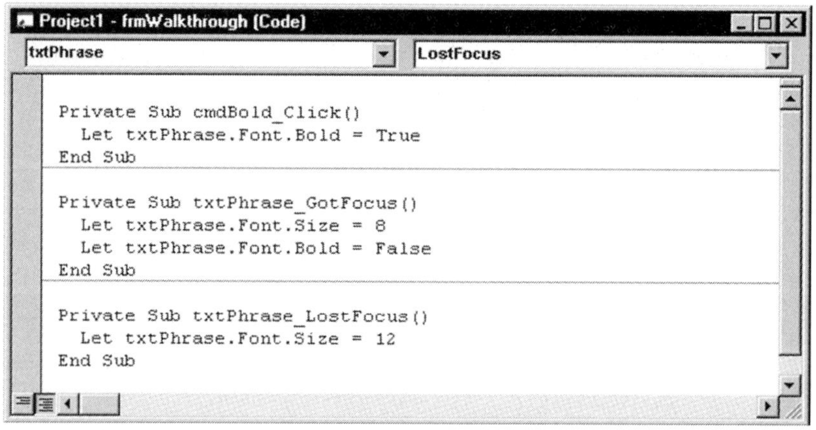

Figure 12.22 The Three Event Procedures

10. Now run the program by pressing F5.

11. Type something into the text box. In Figure 12.23, the words "Hello Friend" have been typed. (A text box has the focus whenever it is ready to accept typing; that is, whenever it contains a blinking cursor.)

Figure 12.23 Text Box Containing Input

12. Press the Tab key. The contents of the text box will be enlarged as in Figure 12.24. When Tab was pressed, the text box lost the focus; that is, the event LostFocus happened to txtPhrase. Thus, the event procedure txtPhrase_LostFocus was called and the code inside the procedure was executed.

Figure 12.24 Text Box after It Has Lost the Focus

13. Click on the command button. This calls the event procedure cmdBold_Click, which converts the text to boldface. See Figure 12.25.

Figure 12.25 Text Box after the Command Button Has Been Clicked

14. Click on the text box or press the Tab key to move the cursor (and therefore the focus) to the text box. This calls the event procedure txtPhrase_GotFocus, which restores the text to its original state.

15. You can repeat Steps 11 through 14 as many times as you like. When you are finished, end the program by pressing Alt+F4, clicking the End icon on the Toolbar, or clicking the Close button (X) on the form.

Comments

1. To hide the code window, press the right mouse button and click on Hide. You can also hide it by clicking on the icon at the left side of the title bar and clicking on Close. To view a hidden code window, press Alt/View/Code. To hide a form, close its container. To view a hidden form, press Alt/View/Object.

2. The form is the default object in Visual Basic code. That is, code such as

   ```
   Let Form1.property = setting
   ```

   can be written as

   ```
   Let property = setting
   ```

   Also, event procedures associated with Form1 appear as

   ```
   Form_event()
   ```

   rather than

   ```
   Form1_event()
   ```

3. Another useful command is SetFocus. The statement

   ```
   object.SetFocus
   ```

   moves the focus to the object.

4. We have ended our programs by clicking the End icon or pressing Alt+F4. A more elegant technique is to create a command button, call it cmdQuit, with caption Quit and the event procedure:

   ```
   Private Sub cmdQuit_Click()
     End
   End Sub
   ```

5. Certain words, such as Sub, End, and Let, have special meanings in Visual Basic and are referred to as **reserved words** or **keywords**. The Visual Basic editor automatically capitalizes the first letter of a reserved word and displays the word in blue.

6. Visual Basic can detect certain types of errors. For instance, consider the line

   ```
   Let txtBox.Font.Size = 12
   ```

   from the walkthrough. Suppose you neglect to type the number 12 to the right of the equals sign before pressing the Enter key. Visual Basic will tell you something is missing by displaying the left message box at the top of page 451. On the other hand, suppose you misspell the keyword Let. You might notice something is wrong when Let doesn't turn blue. If not, you will certainly know about the problem when the program is run, because Visual Basic will display the right message box at the top of page 451 when you click on the command button. After you click on OK, the offending word will be highlighted.

7. Each color can be identified by a sequence of digits and letters beginning with &H. The common colors and their identifying sequences are red (&HFF&), green (&HFF00&), blue (&HFF0000&), yellow (&HFFFF&), black (&H0&), and white (&HFFFFFF&). Whereas these sequences are not required when assigning colors from the Properties window, they are necessary when assigning colors at run time. For instance, the statement

```
Let picBox.BackColor = &HFFFF&
```

gives picBox a yellow background.

8. For statements of the form Let *object.property* = *setting*, with properties Caption, Text, or Font.Name, the setting must be surrounded by quotes. (For instance, Let lblTwo.Caption = "Name", Let txtBox.Text = "45", and Let picBox.Font.Name = "Courier".)

9. Code windows have many features of word processors. For instance, the operations cut, copy, paste, find, undo, and redo can be carried out with the sixth through eleventh icons of the toolbar. These operations, and several others, also can be initiated from the Edit menu.

10. Names of existing event procedures associated with a control are *not* automatically changed when you rename the control. You must change them yourself and also must change any references to the control. Therefore, you should finalize the names of your controls before you put any code into their event procedures.

11. If you find the automatic List Properties/Method feature distracting, you can turn it off by pressing Tools/Options, selecting the Editor page, and clicking on Auto List Members. If you do so, you can still display a list manually at the appropriate time time by pressing Ctrl+J.

12. Earlier versions of Visual Basic used the property FontSize instead of Font.Size. Although Font.Size is preferred, FontSize is allowed for compatibility. Similarly, properties such as FontBold, FontItalic, and FontName have been included for compatibility with earlier versions of Visual Basic.

PRACTICE PROBLEM 12.3

1. You can always locate an existing event procedure by searching through the code window with the Pg Up and Pg Dn keys. Give another way.

EXERCISES 12.3

In Exercises 1 through 6, describe the string displayed in the text box when the command button is clicked.

1.
```
Private Sub cmdButton_Click()
  Let txtBox.Text = "Hello"
End Sub
```

2.
```
Private Sub cmdButton_Click()
  Let txtBox.ForeColor = &HFF&
  Let txtBox.Text = "Hello"
End Sub
```

3.
```
Private Sub cmdButton_Click()
  Let txtBox.Font.Italic = True
  Let txtBox.Text = "Hello"
End Sub
```

4.
```
Private Sub cmdButton_Click()
  Let txtBox.Font.Size = 24
  Let txtBox.Text = "Hello"
End Sub
```

5.
```
Private Sub cmdButton_Click()
  Let txtBox.Text = "Hello"
  Let txtBox.Visible = False
End Sub
```

6.
```
Private Sub cmdButton_Click()
  Let txtBox.Font.Bold = True
  Let txtBox.Text = "Hello"
End Sub
```

In Exercises 7 through 10, assume the three objects on the form were created in the order txtOne, txtTwo, and lblOne. Also assume that txtOne has the focus. Determine the output displayed in lblOne when Tab is pressed.

7.
```
Private Sub txtOne_LostFocus()
  Let lblOne.ForeColor = &HFF00&
  Let lblOne.Caption = "Hello"
End Sub
```

8.
```
Private Sub txtOne_LostFocus()
  Let lblOne.Caption = "Hello"
End Sub
```

9.
```
Private Sub txtTwo_GotFocus()
  Let lblOne.Font.Name = "Courier"
  Let lblOne.Font.Size = 24
  Let lblOne.Caption = "Hello"
End Sub
```

10.
```
Private Sub txtTwo_GotFocus()
  Let lblOne.Font.Italic = True
  Let lblOne.Caption = "Hello"
End Sub
```

In Exercises 11 through 16, determine the errors.

11.
```
Private Sub cmdButton_Click()
  Let frmHi = "Hello"
End Sub
```

12.
```
Private Sub cmdButton_Click()
  Let txtOne.ForeColor = "red"
End Sub
```

13.
```
Private Sub cmdButton_Click()
  Let txtBox.Caption = "Hello"
End Sub
```

14.
```
Private Sub cmdButton_Click()
  Let lblTwo.Text = "Hello"
End Sub
```

15.
```
Private Sub cmdButton_Click()
  Let lblTwo.BorderStyle = 2
End Sub
```

16.
```
Private Sub cmdButton_Click()
  Let txtOne.MultiLine = True
End Sub
```

In Exercises 17 through 33, write a line (or lines) of code to carry out the task.

17. Display "E.T. phone home." in lblTwo.

18. Display "Play it, Sam." in lblTwo.

19. Display "The stuff that dreams are made of." in red letters in txtBox.

20. Display "Life is like a box of chocolates." in Courier font in txtBox.

21. Delete the contents of txtBox.

22. Delete the contents of lblTwo.

23. Make lblTwo disappear.

24. Remove the border from lblTwo.

25. Give picBox a blue background.

26. Place a bold red "Hello" in lblTwo.

27. Place a bold italics "Hello" in txtBox.

28. Make picBox disappear.

29. Give the focus to cmdButton.

30. Remove the border from picBox.

31. Place a border around lblTwo and center its contents.

32. Give the focus to txtBoxTwo.

33. Display "If I had a hi-fi." in picBox.

34. Describe the GotFocus event in your own words.

35. Describe the LostFocus event in your own words.

36. Labels and picture boxes have an event called DblClick that responds to a double-clicking of the left mouse button. Write a simple program to test this event. Determine whether or not you can trigger the DblClick event without also triggering the Click event.

In Exercises 37 through 42, the interface and initial properties are specified. Write the code to carry out the stated task.

37. When one of the three command buttons is pressed, the words on the command button are displayed in the label with the stated alignment.

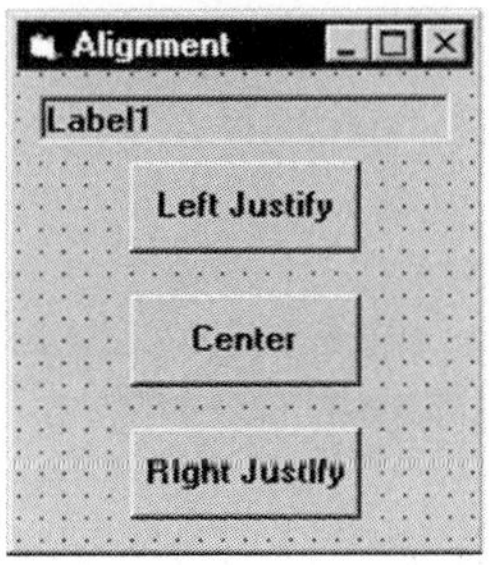

Object	Property	Setting
frmEx37	Caption	Alignment
lblShow	Caption	(blank)
cmdLeft	Caption	Left Justify
cmdCenter	Caption	Center
cmdRight	Caption	Right Justify

38. When one of the command buttons is pressed, the face changes to a smiling face (Wingdings character "J") or a frowning face (Wingdings character "L").

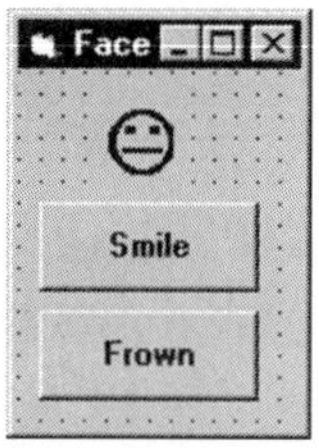

Object	Property	Setting
frmEx38	Caption	Face
lblFace	Font	Wingdings
	Caption	K
	Font Size	24
cmdSmile	Caption	Smile
cmdFrown	Caption	Frown

39. Pressing the command buttons alters the background and foreground colors in the text box.

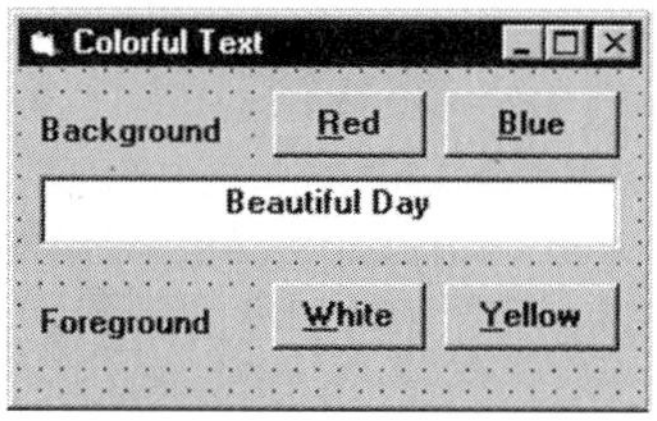

Object	Property	Setting
frmEx39	Caption	Colorful Text
lblBack	Caption	Background
cmdRed	Caption	&Red
cmdBlue	Caption	&Blue
txtShow	Text	Beautiful Day
	MultiLine	True
	Alignment	2 – Center
lblFore	Caption	Foreground
cmdWhite	Caption	&White
cmdYellow	Caption	&Yellow

40. While one of the three text boxes has the focus, its text is bold. When it loses the focus, it ceases to be bold. The command buttons enlarge text (Font.Size = 12) or return text to normal size (Font.Size = 8.25).

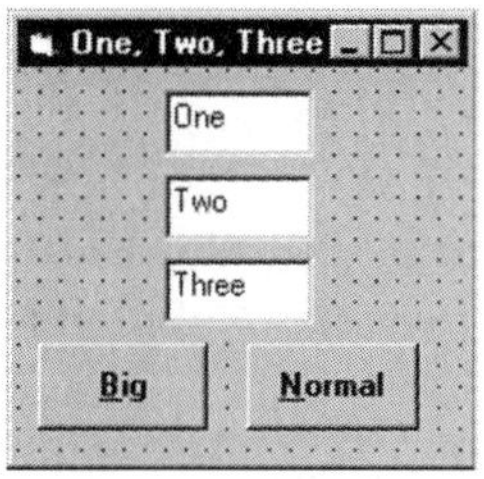

Object	Property	Setting
frmEx40	Caption	One, Two, Three
txtOne	Text	One
txtTwo	Text	Two
txtThree	Text	Three
cmdBig	Caption	&Big
cmdNormal	Caption	&Normal

41. When you click on one of the three small text boxes at the bottom of the form, an appropriate saying is displayed in the large text box. Use the sayings "I like life, it's something to do."; "The future isn't what it used to be."; and "Tell the truth and run."

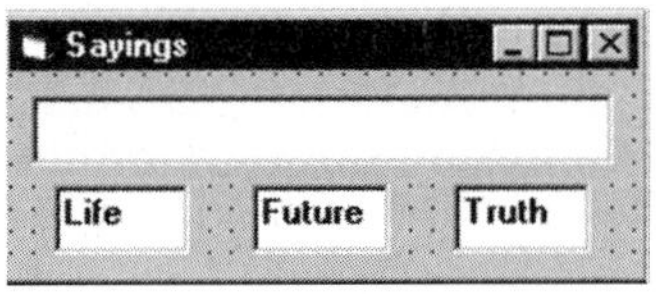

Object	Property	Setting
frmEx41	Caption	Sayings
txtQuote	Text	(blank)
txtLife	Text	Life
txtFuture	Text	Future
txtTruth	Text	Truth

42. After the user types something into the text box, the user can change the font by clicking on one of the command buttons.

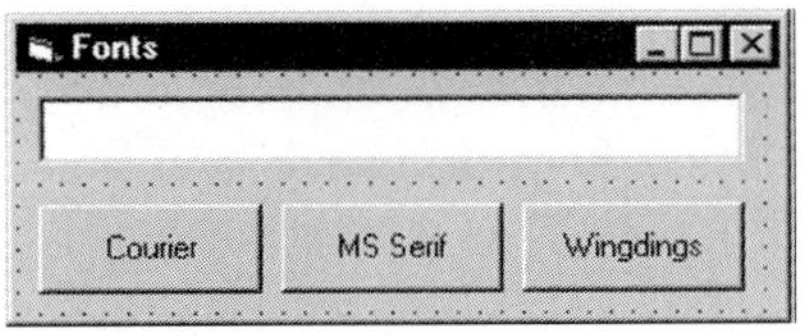

Object	Property	Setting
frmEx42	Caption	Fonts
txtShow	Text	(blank)
cmdCour	Caption	Courier
cmdSerif	Caption	MS Serif
cmdWing	Caption	Wingdings

In Exercises 43 through 48, write a program with a Windows-style interface to carry out the task.

43. Allow the user to click on command buttons to change the size of the text in a text box and alter its appearance between bold and italics.

44. A form contains two text boxes and one large label between them with no caption. When the focus is on the first text box, the label reads "Enter your full name." When the focus is on the second text box, the label reads "Enter your phone number, including area code."

45. Use the same form and properties as in Exercise 38, with the captions for the command buttons replaced with Vanish and Reappear. Clicking a button should produce the stated result.

46. Simulate a traffic light with three small square picture boxes placed vertically on a form. Initially, the bottom picture box is solid green and the other picture boxes are white. When the Tab key is pressed, the middle picture box turns yellow and the bottom picture box turns white. The next time Tab is pressed, the top picture box turns red and the middle picture box turns white. Subsequent pressing of the Tab key cycles through the three colors. ***Hint:*** First, place the bottom picture box on the form, then the middle picture box, and finally the top picture box.

47. The form contains four square buttons arranged in a rectangular array. Each button has the caption "Push Me." When you click on a button, the button disappears and the other three become or remain visible.

48. The form contains two text boxes into which the user types information. When the user clicks on one of the text boxes, it becomes blank and its contents are displayed in the other text box.

SOLUTION TO PRACTICE PROBLEM 12.3

1. With the code window showing, click on the arrow to the right of the Object box and then select the desired object. Then click on the arrow to the right of the Procedure box and select the desired event procedure.

12.4 CONVERTING QBASIC PROGRAMS TO VISUAL BASIC

Although most QBasic statements are supported by Visual Basic, some are not and others must be modified. For instance, Visual Basic does not support the QBasic statements PRINT USING, LOCATE, INPUT, and LPRINT. Visual Basic has alternatives that improve on these statements. In this section we discuss these alternatives, other differences between QBasic and Visual Basic, and ways to compensate for what are perhaps the two most missed QBasic statements—READ and DATA.

Declaring Variables

In the QBasic portion of this book, string-variable names are written with the trailing tag $. Numeric variables are written with no trailing tag or with ! as a trailing tag. In Section 9.1, the DIM statement is used as an alternate way to specify the type of a variable. For instance, the two lines of code

```
LET quantity! = 24
LET item$ = "blackbirds"
```

can be replaced with

```
Dim quantity As Single
Dim item As String
Let quantity = 24
Let item = "blackbirds"
```

In Visual Basic, the use of Dim statements is the preferred way to declare the data types of variables. (In the Visual Basic editor, reserved words, such as Single, String, and Let, appear with only their first letters capitalized.) Actually, since the default data type in Visual Basic is not "single-precision number," the omission of a trailing tag does not produce a numeric variable.

Several Dim statements can be combined into one. For instance, the two Dim statements above can be replaced by

```
Dim quantity As Single, item As String
```

General Procedures

In Section 12.3 we saw that event procedures appear in the Code window, separated by horizontal lines. The following steps insert a general Sub or Function procedure into this window.

1. If the Code window is not open, double-click anywhere on the form or press F7.
2. Press Alt/T/P to select Add Procedure from the Tools menu. (The Add Procedure dialog box will appear.)
3. Type the name of the procedure into the Name text box.
4. Click on Sub or Function in the Type group.

5. Click on Private in the Scope group.
6. Click on OK to obtain a template for the procedure.
7. Type in the additional details as in QBasic.

In the top line of the procedure you should use phrases such as As Single and As String to declare the types of variables and functions. (These declarations are not absolutely necessary, since Visual Basic is very flexible. However, their use can help prevent errors and is considered good programming style.) Some examples are as follows:

The QBasic line

```
Sub ProduceDensity(state$, pop, area)
```

is written in Visual Basic as

```
Private Sub ProduceDensity(state As String,pop As Single,area As Single)
```

The QBasic line

```
Private Function FirstName$(name$)
```

is written in Visual Basic as

```
Private Function FirstName(name As String) As String
```

(The first "As String" declares the variable *name* as a string variable and the second "As String" declares the Function to be a string-valued function.)

The QBasic line

```
Function Hypotenuse(a, b)
```

is written in Visual Basic as

```
Private Function Hypotenuse(a As Single, b As Single) As Single
```

The first item in the list of objects in the drop-down Object box is called (General). When (General) is selected, the drop-down Procedure box will display a list of the general procedures. The first item in the Procedure box is called (Declarations). When you double-click on (Declarations), the cursor moves to the top of the Code window. Nonexecutable statements such as Rem and Dim can be placed in this this section. Variables declared with Dim in the (Declarations) section of (General) have as their scope every procedure (event and general) associated with the form.

String Functions Written without $

In Visual Basic, string functions such as LEFT$ and UCASE$ are normally written as Left and UCase. In order to be compatible with earlier versions of Basic, Visual Basic will not complain if dollar signs are used.

Formatting without PRINT USING

The Visual Basic function Format is used to display numbers, dates, and times in many forms. With Format, you can achieve any result you previously achieved with PRINT USING. However, some results are easier and others are harder to accomplish. We will look at just a few variations of this versatile function. (See the discussion of Format in Appendix J for more nuances.) If *num* is a number, or the string representation of a number, and *fmt* is a format string, then

```
Format(num, fmt)
```

is a formatted version of the number.

Two useful format strings that produce dollars and cents are "$0,0.00" and "Currency." These two format strings are identical except for their effect on negative numbers. With "Currency," negative amounts of money are written in parentheses without a minus sign. This notation is commonly used by accountants. Some examples are:

```
Format(1234, "Currency") is $1,234.00
Format("1234", "$0,0.00") is $1,234.00
Format(1234567890123, "$0,0.00") is $1,234,567,890,123.00
Format(12.348., "Currency") is $12.35
Format(-1234, "$0,0.00") is -$1,234.00
Format(-1234, "Currency) is ($1,234.00)
```

You can format ordinary whole numbers with the format string "#,#" which places commas every three digits. Even though there are only two #'s, large numbers will be accommodated. The format string "#,#.####" rounds to four decimal places. However, it drops ending zeros. (Use "#,#.0000" to retain ending zeros.) Some examples are:

```
Format(1234.111176, "#,#.####") is 1,234.1112
Format(1234.111176, "#,#.###") is 1,234.111
Format("1234.100034", "#,#.####") is 1,234.1
Format("1234.100034", "#,#.0000") is 1,234.1000
```

The string produced by Format never has leading spaces. For instance, the statement

```
picBox.Print "You owe "; Format$(1234.56, "Currency")
```

displays

```
You owe $1,234.56
```

In the picBox.Print statement, the space after owe is essential.

Getting Input without INPUT

In Visual Basic, you can request information from the user with a text box. A label is used as a prompt. The value of the text box's Text property will be the string consisting of the characters typed by the user. If numeric information is requested, you can convert the string to a number with the Val function.

EXAMPLE 1 The following program requests a person's name and annual salary as input, and then approximates the person's hourly wage. The computation is based on a work year of about 2000 hours.

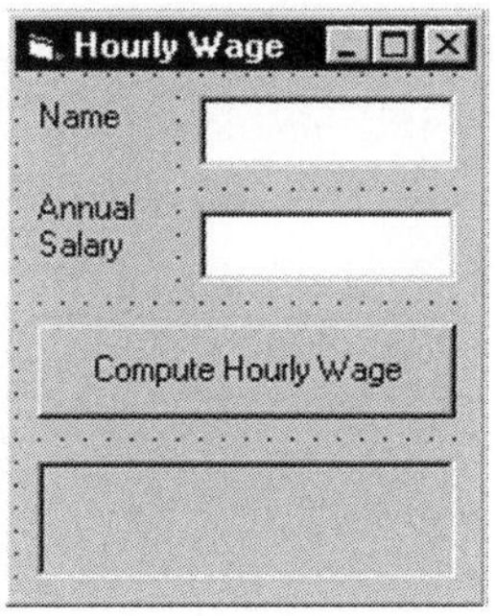

Object	Property	Setting
frm12_4_1	Caption	Hourly Wage
lblName	Caption	Name
txtName	Text	(blank)
lblAnnual	Caption	Annual Salary
txtAnnual	Text	(blank)
cmdCompute	Caption	Compute Annual Wage
picOutput		

Form for Example 1 — Objects and Properties for Example 1

```
Private Sub cmdCompute_Click()
 Dim hourlyWage As Single
 picOutput.Cls     'Clear the picture box
 picOutput.Print txtName.Text + ","
 Let hourlyWage = Val(txtAnnual.Text) / 2000
 picOutput.Print "Your hourly wage is ";
 picOutput.Print Format(hourlyWage, "Currency")
End Sub
```

[Run, type a name into the first text box, type an annual salary into the second text box, and then click on the command button.]

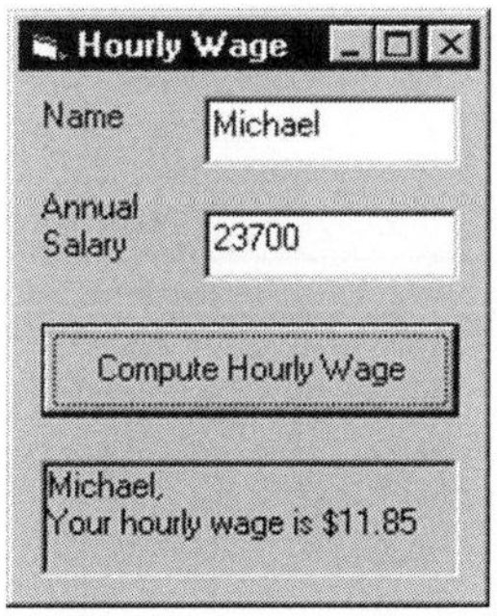

The example above received its input from text boxes, using a label as a prompts. The problem with this approach is that you sometimes want just one piece of input and would rather not have a text box and label stay on the screen forever. The problem can be solved with the InputBox function. When a statement of the form

```
Let stringVar = InputBox(prompt, title)
```

is executed, an **input box** such as the one shown in Figure 12.26 pops up on the screen. (In Figure 12.26, the *prompt* is "Enter the name of the file containing the information." And the *title* is "Name of File.") After the user types a response into the rectangle at the bottom of the screen and presses Enter (or clicks OK), the response is assigned to the string variable. The message to be displayed for the prompt can consist of any string, and the title parameter can be omitted.

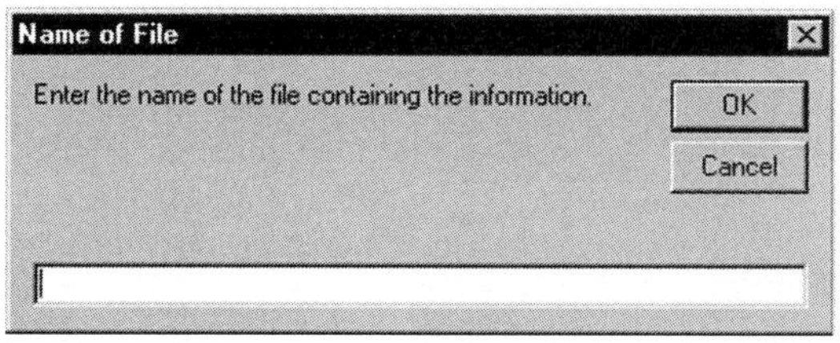

Figure 12.26 Sample Input Box

When you type the parenthesis following the word InputBox, the editor displays a line containing the general form of the InputBox statement. See Figure 12.27. This feature, which was added in Visual Basic 5.0, is called **Quick Info**. The parameters *prompt* and *title* are strings that specify the message to be displayed and the caption in the title bar. Optional parameters are surrounded by brackets. All the parameters in the general form of the InputBox statement are optional except for *prompt*.

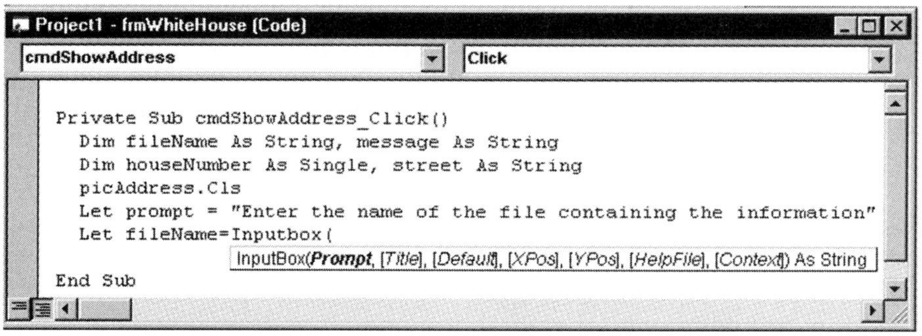

Figure 12.27 Quick Info Feature

Sometimes you want to respond to input with a brief message such as "Correct" or "Nice try, but no cigar." You want this message to appear on the screen only until the user has read it. This mission is easily accomplished with a **message box** such as the one shown in Figure 12.28. When a statement of the form

```
MsgBox prompt, , title
```

is executed, where *prompt* and *title* are strings, a message box with *prompt* displayed appears, and it stays on the screen until the user presses Enter or clicks OK. For instance, the statement MsgBox "Nice try, but no cigar.",,"Consolation" produces Figure 12.28. If you use double quotation marks ("") for *title*, the title bar will be blank.

Figure 12.28 Sample Message Box

Screen Placement without LOCATE

In QBasic, the statement

```
LOCATE r, c
```

moves the cursor to the *r*th row and *c*th column of the screen. If we think of the screen as filled with characters, then counting from the upper left of the screen, the cursor would be moved down to the *r*th character and right to the *c*th character. For the picture box picBox, the same result can be achieved with

```
Let picBox.CurrentY = r - 1
Let picBox.CurrentX = c - 1
```

Actually, CurrentY and CurrentX are capable of using many different units of measurement other than characters. They also can use units such as inches, twips (1/1440th of an inch), and points (1/72nd of an inch). The units character, inch, twip, and point are denoted by the numbers 4, 5, 1, and 2, respectively. The unit is determined by the ScaleMode property. Therefore, to set character units in order to emulate the LOCATE, the statement

```
picBox.ScaleMode = 4
```

should precede the two lines above. (Of course, the ScaleMode property can be set to *character* from the Properties window before the program is run.)

Since most of Visual Basic's fonts use proportional spacing, the precise placing of characters on the screen with CurrentX, CurrentY, and Tab is not completely reliable. To ensure dependable spacing, use a uniform-spaced font like Courier. Fonts are specified with the Font.Name property.

Using the Printer without LPRINT

Visual Basic treats the printer as an object named Printer. If *expr* is a string or numeric expression, then the statement

```
Printer.Print expr
```

sends *expr* to the printer. You can use semicolons, commas for print zones, and Tab just as with LPRINT. You can accurately position the text anywhere you like with Printer.CurrentY and Printer.CurrentX after you have executed Printer.Scale. (See the discussion of graphics for details.) Font properties can be set with statements like

```
Let Printer.Font.Name = "Script"
Let Printer.Font.Bold = True
Let Printer.Font.Size = 12
```

Another useful printer command is

```
Printer.NewPage
```

which starts a new page.

The Windows Print Manager usually waits until an entire page has been completed before starting to print. To avoid losing information, execute the statement

```
Printer.EndDoc
```

when you are finished printing.

With QBasic, a screen dump can be obtained with Shift+Print Screen. In Visual Basic, the statement

```
PrintForm
```

performs a screen dump. (If graphics are to be printed, the AutoRedraw property of the picture box must be set to True.)

Miscellaneous Matters

SWAP *Not Supported by Visual Basic*: The following code can be used to swap the values of *var1* and *var2*. (**Note:** *var1*, *var2*, and *temp* have the same type.)

```
Let temp = var1
Let var1 = var2
Let var2 = temp
```

***Dim Statements*:** Dim statements are used to dimension arrays and declare **variable** types. (See Section 9.1 for a discussion of declaring variable types with DIM.) When a statement such as

```
Dim arrayName(1 To 100) As Single

Dim var As String
```

or

```
Dim var As Single
```

is in the top part of the code window—that is, in the (Declarations) part of (General)—the array or variable is visible to *every* procedure. That is, when it is assigned a value by a procedure, it retains that value when the procedure is exited. Such a variable or array is called **form level**. In QBasic, when one of the above Dim statements appears in a procedure, the array or variable is visible only to that procedure. The same is true in Visual Basic.

When one or both subscripts of an array are specified with a variable or an expression, the word ReDim should be used in place of Dim. For instance, a statement of the form

```
Dim arrayName (1 to n) As varType
```

should be replaced with

```
ReDim arrayName (1 to n) As varType
```

No Main Body in Visual Basic: In QBasic, the main body of the program contains both nonexecutable statements (like REM and DIM) as well as executable statements (like LET and PRINT). Visual Basic programs have no main body. Nonexecutable statements can be placed in the declarations part of the (general) object. Executable statements must be inside procedures.

If you want some code to be executed as soon as your program is run, without waiting for a user-caused event to occur, put the code in the event procedure Form_Load. If the code uses Print or graphics statements to display text or graphics in an object, set the AutoRedraw property of the object to True.

End Statement: Whereas all QBasic programs in this textbook contain an END statement, care must be taken when including an End statement in a Visual Basic program. When End is reached, all output placed on the screen during execution is lost.

ASCII Characters: Most of the fonts available in Visual Basic use the ANSI character set, rather than the ASCII character set of QBasic. The two character sets agree for ASCII characters 32 through 127, but usually disagree elsewhere. Therefore, the value of Chr(*n*) for *n* outside this range can produce different results in the two languages. The only Visual Basic font with the complete ASCII set of characters is Terminal. Therefore, for instance, if you set the Font.Name property to Terminal, the statement Picturel.Print Chr(227) displays the Greek letter pi.

Since Visual Basic has access to all of Windows' fonts, a rich variety of characters are available to display on the screen or printer. Two unusual fonts are Symbol and Wingdings.

To view the characters in the different Windows fonts, click on the Start button, point to Programs, point to Accessories, and click Character Map. After you select a font, hold down the left mouse button on any character to enlarge the character and obtain the keystroke that produces that character.

Reserved Words: Visual Basic has many reserved words. Visual Basic will inform you if you use a reserved word as a variable or procedure name. The following Visual Basic reserved words are especially tempting: Currency, Date, False, Global, Local, Me, Nothing, Set, True.

Assigning Values without READ and DATA

In Visual Basic, information cannot be read from DATA statements with the READ statement. One alternative is to place the information in a sequential file and read it with Input# statements.

Windows provides an easy way to create small sequential files with the use of the Notepad.

1. To open Notepad, click on the Start button, point to Programs, point to Accessories, and click Notepad.
2. Type in the information as it would appear in a sequential file created with WRITE# statements. Press the Enter key whenever a "carriage return, line feed" pair is called for. For instance, the sequential file YOB.DAT of Section 8.1 would be typed into the Notepad as

```
"Barbra",1942
"Ringo",1940
"Sylvester",1946
```

3. Press Alt/File/Save to open the Save As dialog box. Then select a directory for the "Save in" box, type a filename in the "File name" text box, and click on the Save button. If you do not specify an extension for the filename, the extension ".txt" is automatically added.

We suggest that you create a special directory to hold your Visual Basic programs and that you save your sequential files into this directory. If so, a statement of the form

```
Open App.Path + "\YOB.TXT" For Input As #1
```

will look for the file YOB.TXT in the same directory in which the program was saved.

Command Buttons Instead of Sentinel Values

QBasic programs use sentinel values to indicate that all items of data have been entered as input by the user. For instance, the user might be told to enter –1 when all items have been entered. In Visual Basic, a command button is used instead.

EXAMPLE 2 The following program creates a telephone directory file. The names and phone numbers should be entered one at a time. After entering all names and numbers, the user should have the option of printing the directory.

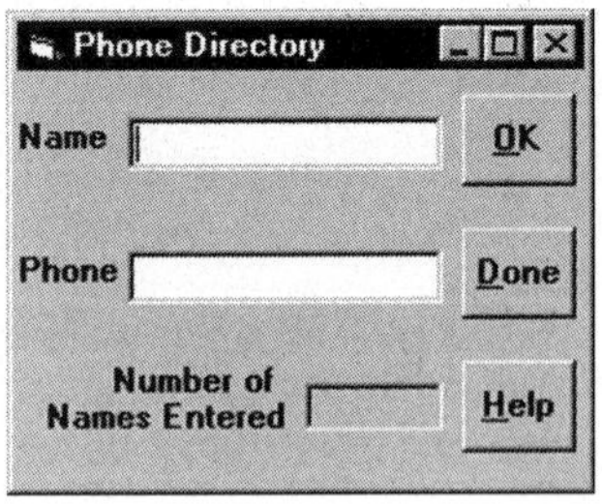

Object	Property	Setting
frm12_4_2	Caption	Phone Directory
lblName	Caption	Name
txtName	Text	(blank)
lblPhone	Caption	Phone
txtPhone	Text	(blank)
lblNumber	Caption	Number of Names Entered
picNumber		
cmdOK	Caption	&OK
cmdDone	Caption	&Done
cmdHelp	Caption	&Help

The boxes labeled Name and Phone are text boxes and the box labeled Number of Names Entered is a picture box.

```
Dim n As Single  'Make n a form level variable

Private Sub cmdOK_Click()
 Write #1, txtName.Text, txtPhone.Text
 Let n = n + 1   'Number of names written to file
 picNumber.Cls
 picNumber.Print n
 Let txtName.Text = ""
 Let txtPhone.Text = ""
 txtName.SetFocus   'Return focus to the Name text box
End Sub

Private Sub cmdDone_Click()
 Dim ans As String, nom As String, phone As String
 Close #1
 Let ans = InputBox("Would you like to print the file?  Y/N")
 If UCase(ans) = "Y" Then
   MsgBox "Check that your printer is turned on.", , "Caution"
   Open App.Path + "\PHONE.TXT" For Input As #1
   Do Until EOF(1)
     Input #1, nom, phone
     Printer.Print nom; Tab(25); phone
   Loop
   Printer.EndDoc
 End If
 End
End Sub

Private Sub cmdHelp_Click()
 Dim msg As String
 Let msg = "After you type in each name and phone number, press OK."
 Let msg = msg + " After all names have been entered, press Done."
 MsgBox msg, , "Help"
End Sub

Private Sub Form_Load()
 Open App.Path + "\PHONE.TXT" For Output As #1
 Let n = 0
End Sub
```

Graphics

In Visual Basic, lines, points, and circles can be drawn on a picture box or form in much the same way as in QBasic. Let's assume we are drawing on picBox. There is no need for a SCREEN statement. In Visual Basic, everything is done on a graphics screen.

The statement

```
WINDOW (a, c)-(b, d)
```

is replaced by

```
picBox.Scale (a, d)-(b, c)
```

Notice that *c* and *d* have been interchanged.

Lines, rectangles, points, circles, and sectors are drawn with the statements

```
picBox.Line (x1, y1)-(x2, y2)
picBox.Line (x1, y1)-(x2, y2),, B
picBox.PSet (x, y)
picBox.Circle (x, y), r
```

Lines can be styled with the DrawStyle property. (See the Property window for a list of the possibilities.) For instance, the statement

```
Let picBox.DrawStyle = 2
```

causes future lines to be drawn dotted.

Color can be added to graphics in several ways. BackColor and ForeColor properties can be set from the properties window or during run time. Text, points, lines, and circles appear in ForeColor on a BackColor background. Colors can also be incorporated into PSet, Line, and Circle statements with the QBColor function. For $n = 0$ to 15, the value of QBColor(n) is the color denoted by n in Table 10.1 of Section 10.2. The following statements draw lines, rectangles, points, circles, and sectors in color n.

```
picBox.Line (x1, y1)-(x2, y2), QBColor (n)
picBox.Line (x1, y1)-(x2, y2), QBColor (n), B
picBox.PSet (x, y), QBColor (n)
picBox.Circle (x, y), r, QBColor (n)
```

Visual Basic does not support PAINT. However, the FillStyle and FillColor properties allow for rectangles, circles, and sectors to be filled with various patterns (such as solid, horizontal lines, vertical lines, upward diagonal lines, and so on) and colors. The patterns and colors can either be specified from the Properties window or specified by code. See the settings boxes in the Properties window for the numerical values to be used in code.

EXAMPLE 3 The following program displays graphics and text. The axis, the word "Origin," and the dotted line are black. The rectangle is filled with red, and the horizontal lines inside the circle are blue.

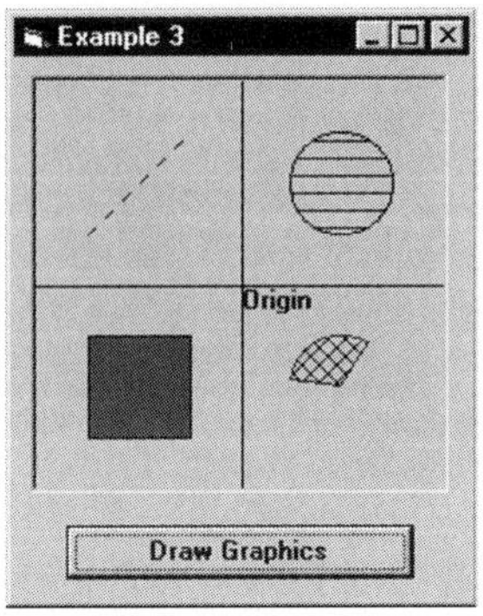

Object	Property	Setting
frm12_4_3	Caption	Example 3
picBox		
cmdDraw	Caption	Draw Graphics

Output of Example 2 after Button Is Pushed

```
Private Sub cmdDraw_Click()
 picBox.Cls
 picBox.Scale (-4, 4)-(4, -4)
 picBox.Line (-4, 0)-(4, 0)  'Draw x-axis
 picBox.Line (0, -4)-(0, 4)  'Draw y-axis
 picBox.CurrentX = 0
 picBox.CurrentY = 0
 picBox.Print "Origin"       'Label the origin
 picBox.DrawStyle = 2        'Dot
 picBox.Line (-3, 1)-(-1, 3)
 picBox.DrawStyle = 0        'Solid
 picBox.Line (-3, -1)-(-1, -3), QBColor(1), B
 picBox.FillColor = &HFF0000 'Blue
 picBox.FillStyle = 2        'Horizontal lines
 picBox.Circle (2, 2), 1
 picBox.FillStyle = 7        'Diagonal crosshatch
 picBox.Circle (2, -2), 1, QBColor(4), -1, -3
End Sub
```

Comments:

1. DEF FN statements are not supported by Visual Basic and should be replaced by Function procedures.

2. This textbook begins nearly every QBasic program with CLS to clear the screen. Cls is not needed in Visual Basic.

3. We recommend always setting the AutoRedraw property of a picture box to True. Otherwise, covering the picture box with an input or message box might permanently obliterate the contents of the picture box.

4. The following steps transport all or part of a QBasic program to Visual Basic.
   (a) Save the QBasic program in text format, as say A:MYPROG.BAS.
   (b) Open the Notepad. (That is, click on the Start button, point to Programs, point to Accessories, and click Notepad.)
   (c) Press Alt/F/O and enter the file name as A:MYPROG.BAS (**Note:** If you use the menu bar, make sure you are using the Notepad menu bar, not the Visual Basic menu bar.)
   (d) Select (as a block) all text you want to transport.
   (e) Press Ctrl+Ins to place the block in the clipboard.
   (f) Return to Visual Basic, open the Code window, and move the cursor to a line preceding any existing event procedures.
   (g) Press Shift+Ins to insert the contents of the clipboard. Of course, all executable statements that are not inside a procedure must be moved.

5. The role of QBasic's graphics concept last point referenced is taken in Visual Basic by CurrentY and CurrentX. For instance, after a statement of the form

   ```
   Picture1.Line (x1, y1)-(x2, y2)
   ```

   CurrentX has value *x2* and CurrentY has the value *y2*.

6. CurrentX and CurrentY allow you to place text with greater precision than is possible with LOCATE. This precision becomes available when you set the ScaleMode property to a value such as twips, points, or inches. When

the ScaleMode is twips (the default mode) and a Scale statement has been executed to specify a coordinate system, the values of CurrentX and CurrentY are interpreted in terms of the coordinate system.

7. The DrawWidth property can be used to specify the thickness of lines and circles.

8. Printouts of programs are initiated with Alt/F/P. A dialog box pops up and allows you to specify what to print. Select Form for a picture of the objects on the form, select Form Text for a list of the properties that have been changed, and select Code for a printout of the declarations and procedures. For our purposes, there is no difference between choosing Current or All.

9. An on-line reference manual can be invoked from the Help menu. This manual refers to commands that affect objects, such as Print and Cls, as **methods**.

10. When you write a procedure without parameters, Visual Basic automatically adds a pair of empty parentheses at the end of the procedure name. However, Call statements should not use the empty parentheses.

11. Visual Basic code windows automatically capitalize the first letter of a reserved word and display the word in blue. Rem statements are colored green.

12. A useful event that has not been discussed is KeyPress. The event

```
Private Sub objectName_KeyPress(KeyAscii As Integer)
```

responds to the user pressing a key (while the object has the focus) by assigning the ASCII value of the key to the variable KeyAscii. Here is an example.

```
Private Sub txtBox_KeyPress(KeyAscii As Integer)
  Rem Suppose user was asked to type a single digit into txtBox
  Rem The digits 0 - 9 have ASCII values from 48 through 57
  If (KeyAscii < 48) Or (KeyAscii > 57) Then
      Let KeyAscii = 0           'Ignore key that is not a digit
  End If
End Sub
```

13. In QBasic, each line of the screen accommodates 80 characters. After a line is filled, subsequent characters automatically wrap around to the next line. In Visual Basic, there is no restriction on the number of characters in each line of a picture box and there is no automatic wraparound. Also, picture boxes do not scroll.

PRACTICE PROBLEM 12.4

1. Give two ways to make a value available to every procedure attached to the form.

EXERCISES 12.4

In Exercises 1 through 6, determine the string displayed in the text boxes when the command button is clicked.

1.
```
Private Sub cmdButton_Click()
  Dim word As String
  Let word = "Goodbye"
  Call Greetings(word)
End Sub

Private Sub Greetings(a As String)
  Let txtBox.Text = a
End Sub
```

2.
```
Private Sub cmdButton_Click()
  Dim word1 As String, word2 As String
  Let word1 = "Hello"
  Let word2 = "Goodbye"
  Call Greetings(word2)
End Sub

Private Sub Greetings(word1 As String)
  Let txtBox.Text = word1
End Sub
```

3.
```
Private Sub cmdButton_Click()
  Dim word(1 To 2) As String
  Let word(1) = "Good"
  Let word(2) = "bye"
  Let txtBox.Text = word(1) + word(2)
End Sub
```

4.
```
Private Sub cmdButton_Click()
  Dim temp As String
  Let txtBox.Text = "Visual"
  Let txtBox2.Text = "Basic"
  Let temp = txtBox2.Text
  Let txtBox2.Text = txtBox.Text
  Let txtBox.Text = temp
End Sub
```

5.
```
Dim num As Single  'In (Declaration) part of (General)

Private Sub Form_Load()
  Let num = 1234.567
End Sub

Private Sub cmdButton_Click()
  Let txtBox.Text = Format(num, "Currency")
End Sub
```

6.
```
Private Sub Form_Load()
  Dim n As Single
  Let n = 100
End Sub

 Sub cmdButton_Click()
  Dim n As Single
  Let n = n + 1
  Let txtBox.Text = Str(n)
End Sub
```

In Exercises 7 through 10, determine the output displayed in the picture box by the code when the command button is clicked.

7.
```
Private Sub cmdButton_Click()
  Dim n As Single
  Let picBox.ScaleMode = 4 'Character
  Let picBox.Font.Name = "Courier"
  picBox.Print "123456789012345"
  For n = 1 To 3
    picBox.Print n;
    Let picBox.CurrentX = picBox.CurrentX + 2
  Next n
End Sub
```

8.
```
Sub cmdButton_Click()
  picBox.Scale (-4, 4)-(4, -4)
  picBox.Circle (0, 0), 2, QBColor(1)  'Color 1 is blue
  Let picBox.CurrentY = 0
  Let picBox.CurrentX = 0
  picBox.Print "Circle"
End Sub
```

9.
```
Private Sub cmdButton_Click()
  picBox.Scale (-4, 4)-(4, -4)
  picBox.Line (0, -4)-(0, 3)
  Let picBox.Font.Name = "Wingdings"
  Let picBox.Font.Size = 24 'Big
  Let picBox.ScaleMode = 2 'Point
  Rem Shift cursor left slightly
  Let picBox.CurrentX = picBox.CurrentX - 3
  picBox.Print "O"      'Flag
End Sub
```

10.
```
Private Sub cmdButton_Click()
  picBox.Scale (-4, 4)-(4, -4)
  picBox.FillStyle = 6      'Cross
  picBox.Line (-4, -4)-(4, 4), , B
End Sub
```

In Exercises 11 through 36, write a line (or lines) of code to carry out the task. Unless otherwise specified, all output should be placed in a picture box.

11. Display the 1997 national debt, $5.376 trillion, in standard dollars-and-cents form.

12. Display the square root of 2 to five decimal places.

13. Display 2^{10} written with commas every three digits.

14. Display the product 1.05 * 23.56 in standard dollars-and-cents form.

15. Display the words "Visual Basic" beginning in the third position of the second row.

16. Display the word "Hello" 2 inches down and 1 inch to the right of the upper left corner of the picture box.

17. Display x^4. (**Note:** 4 is an exponent.)

18. Display H_2O (**Note:** 2 is a small subscript.)

19. Pop up an input box with the question "What is your zodiac sign?" and assign the response to the string variable *sign*.

20. Pop up a message box stating "The future isn't what it used to be."

21. Pop up a message box with "Taking Risks Proverb" in the title bar and the message "You can't steal second base and keep one foot on first."

22. Pop up an input box with the question "What is your age?" and assign the response to the numeric variable *age*.

23. Print the boldface word "Hello" with the printer.

24. Print the word "Hello" with the printer. The word should appear about 3 inches from the left margin and about 4 inches from the top of the page.

25. Interchange the contents of the text property of two text boxes.

26. Interchange the contents of a text box and a caption of a label.

27. Inside a general procedure, dimension the numeric array *sales* to have subscripts ranging from 1975 to 1998.

28. In the declarations part of (general), dimension the array b$ to have subscripts ranging from 10 to 100.

29. Use the Dim statement to declare the variable *nom* as a string variable visible to all parts of the program.

30. Use the Dim statement to declare the variable *nom* as a string variable visible only to the Form_Click event.

31. Dimension the string array *marx*() with subscripts ranging from 1 to 4. Assign the four values Chico, Harpo, Groucho, and Zeppo so that the array is visible to all parts of the program and the values are assigned as soon as the program is run.

32. Dimension the string array *stooges*() with subscripts ranging from 1 to 3. Assign the three values Moe, Larry, and Curly so that the array is visible only to the event procedure cmdButton_Click and the values are assigned as soon as the command button is clicked.

33. Display the Greek letter sigma.

34. Create Figure 12.29 (a).

35. Create Figure 12.29 (b).

36. Create Figure 12.29 (c).

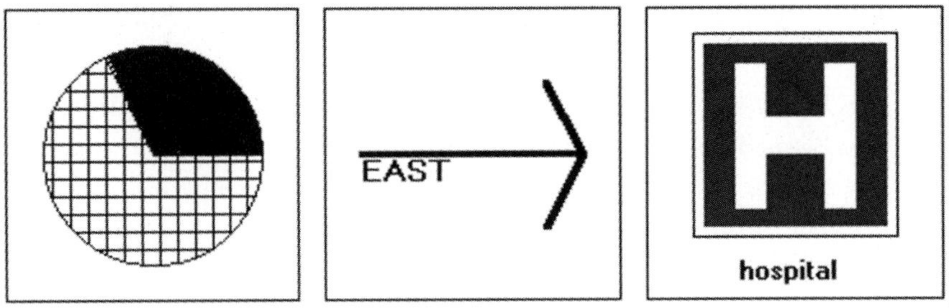

(a) (b) (c)

Figure 12.29 Pictures for Exercises 34–36

In Exercises 37 through 54, write a program with a Windows-style interface to carry out the task.

37. Refer to the Postage Stamp algorithm at the beginning of Section 2.2. Given the number of sheets of paper, calculate the number of stamps required for a letter.

38. Calculate the amount of a waiter's tip, given the amount of the bill and the percentage tip. (Test the program with $20 and 15%.)

39. Given the last name of one of the four most recent U.S. presidents, display his state and a colorful fact about him. (***Notes:*** Carter: Georgia, The only soft drink served in the Carter White House was Coca-Cola; Reagan: California, His Secret Service code name was Rawhide; Bush: Texas, He was the third left-handed president; Clinton: Arkansas, In college he did a good imitation of Elvis Presley.)

40. Allow the user to enter any number of positive numbers. As each number is entered, display the sum of the numbers and the number of numbers entered. The user should be able to start anew at any time.

41. After a number of quarters is entered, the value in dollars and cents is displayed nicely formatted.

42. After payment for a bill of $45 is entered, one of the following messages is displayed as appropriate: "Bill paid in full.", "You owe *formatted amount*.", or "You have a credit of *formatted amount*."

43. Illustrate the growth of money in a savings account. When the user presses the command button, the values in the Amount and Interest Rate text boxes are used to calculate the numbers of years until the money doubles and until it reaches a million dollars. The numbers of years should be obtained with calls to general procedures. ***Notes:*** The balance at the end of each year is (1 + *r*) times the previous balance, where *r* is the annual rate of interest in decimal form. Use Do loops to determine the numbers of years.

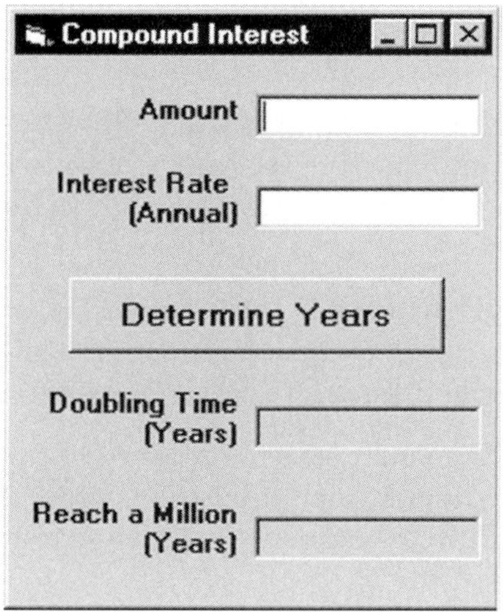

Form for Exercise 43

Object	Property	Setting
frmInterest	Caption	Compound Interest
lblAmount	Caption	Amount
txtAmount	Text	(blank)
lblRate	Alignment	1 – Right Justify
	Caption	Interest Rate (Annual)
txtRate	Text	(blank)
cmdDetermine	Caption	Determine Years
lblDbl	Alignment	1 – Right Justify
	Caption	Doubling Time (Years)
picDbl		
lblMillion	Alignment	1 – Right Justify
	Caption	Reach a Million (Years)
picMillion		

Objects and Properties for Exercise 43

44. The user enters a number into the text box and then clicks on the appropriate command button to have one of three pieces of humor or else one of three insults displayed in the large label below the buttons. Place the humor and insults in general procedures. Also, if the number entered is not between 1 and 3, the text box should be cleared. (***Note:*** Some possible bits of humor are "I can resist everything except temptation.", "I just heard from Bill Bailey. He's not coming home.", and "I have enough money to last the rest of my life, unless I buy something." Some possible insults are "How much would you charge to haunt a house?", "I bet you have no more friends than an alarm clock.", and "When your IQ rises to 30, sell.")

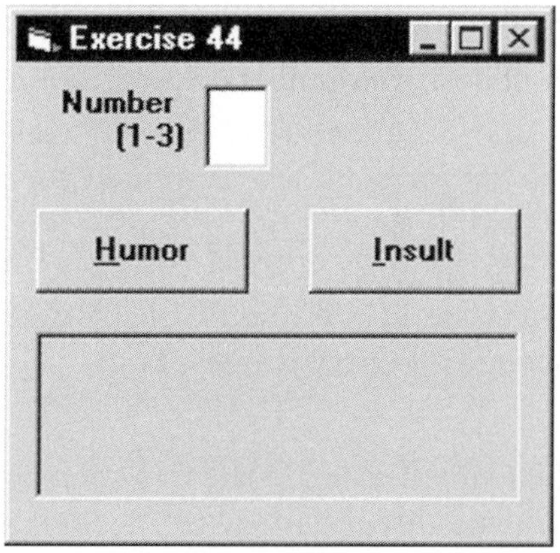

Form for Exercise 44

Object	Property	Setting
frm 12_4_44	Caption	Exercise 44
lblNumber	Alignment	1 – Right Justify
	Caption	Number (1–3)
txtNumber	Text	(blank)
cmdHumor	Caption	&Humor
cmdInsult	Caption	&Insult
lblQuip	BorderStyle	Fixed Single
	Caption	(blank)

Objects and Properties for Exercise 44

45. After a letter and a number are entered, the number is displayed as a subscript of the letter. For instance, the display might be C_7.

46. After a letter, a row, and a column are entered, the letter is displayed in the given row and column.

47. After a person's name, address, and city/state/zip code are entered, the information is printed on the printer as a letterhead.

48. After four strings are entered, use the printer to print a horizontal line and a vertical line that divide the sheet of paper into four quarters, where each quarter has one of the strings as a heading. (***Note:*** Test the program with the strings To Call, To See, To Write, To Do.)

49. A form has a picture box and a command button. The first time the button is clicked, a small circle is drawn in the center of the picture box. Each time the button is clicked, a slightly larger circle is drawn.

50. In a form with a picture box and two command buttons captioned Happy and Sad, an appropriate face should be drawn when a button is pressed. (***Hint:*** The face can either be drawn with circles and lines or displayed from the Wingdings font.)

51. Access the sequential file of names and phone numbers created by Example 2. The form should have two picture boxes (for name and phone number) and a command button (caption: Look up a Name). When the command button is pressed, an input box should request the name, and then the name and phone number should be displayed in the picture boxes. If the name is not in the file, the user should be so informed with a message box.

52. In a form with two command buttons labeled Ascending Order and Descending Order, the eight vegetables in V8 can be displayed in either ascending or descending alphabetic order. The vegetables (tomato, carrot, celery, beet, parsley, lettuce, watercress, and spinach) should be stored in an array.

53. After two numbers are entered, the numbers are added, subtracted, multiplied, or divided by pressing an appropriate button.

54. Phone numbers of the form xxx-xxx-xxxx are entered into a text box and then written into a file when a command button is pressed. However, if the string entered for the phone number does not have 12 characters, a message box tells the user to edit the phone number.

55. Create a form with a picture box and two command buttons captioned Bogart and Raines. When Bogart is first pressed, the sentence "I came to Casablanca for the waters." is displayed in the picture box. The next time Bogart is pressed, the sentence "I was misinformed." is displayed. When Raines is pressed, the sentence "But we're in the middle of the desert." is displayed. Run the program and then press Bogart, Raines, Bogart to obtain a dialogue.

56. Use Windows' Notepad to create the sequential file in the table below. Then write a program to access and possibly modify the file with the form shown below. The form has two picture boxes. Use an input box to obtain the name of a country. (***Note:*** Format(*num*, "#,#") formats the numbers properly.) When you run the program, add Russia with population 147,000,000.

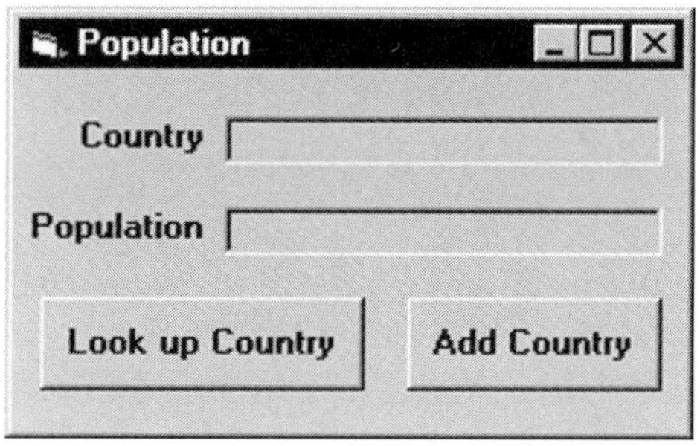

Form for Exercise 56

```
"China",1220000000
"India",968000000
"United States",267000000
"Indonesia",209000000
"Brazil",165000000
```

Table for Exercise 56—Populations of the Five Most Populous Countries

57. According to some Washington, DC, area university officials, the outcome of the 1992 election helped boost their enrollments. The table below gives the full-time freshmen enrollments at the largest DC area universities for 1992 and 1993. Write a program with the form shown that stores the information in parallel arrays. The Info command button should tell the user to type a college into the college text box and then press Tab to obtain the other information. If the user requests information for a college not in the array, the user should be told that the information is not available. (***Note:*** Format$(*num*, "0%" formats the percentages properly.)

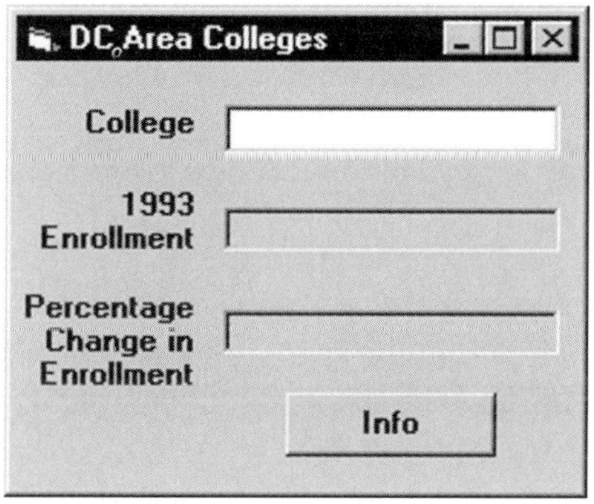

Form for Exercise 57

University	1992	1993
American	1129	1152
George Mason	1615	1700
George Washington	1230	1500
Georgetown	1382	1395
Howard	1321	1400
U. of Maryland	3284	3383

Table for Exercise 57—Freshmen Enrollments

In Exercises 58 through 89, rework the given example in Visual Basic with a Windows-style interface.

58. Section 5.2, Example 4

59. Section 5.2, Example 6

60. Section 6.1, Example 2

61. Section 6.2, Example 1

62. Section 6.2, Example 2

63. Section 6.2, Example 3

64. Section 6.2, Example 4

65. Section 6.2, Example 5

66. Section 6.2, Example 6

67. Section 6.2, Example 7

68. Section 6.3, Example 1

69. Section 7.1, Example 1

70. Section 7.1, Example 2
71. Section 7.1, Example 3
72. Section 7.1, Example 6
73. Section 7.2, Example 1
74. Section 7.2, Example 2
75. Section 7.2, Example 4
76. Section 7.3, Example 1
77. Section 7.3, Example 3
78. Section 7.3, Example 5
79. Section 7.3, Example 1
80. Section 10.2, Example 3
81. Section 10.2, Example 4
82. Section 10.3, Example 1
83. Section 10.3, Example 2
84. Section 10.4, Example 1
85. Section 10.4, Example 2
86. Section 10.5, Example 2
87. Section 10.5, Example 4
88. Section 10.5, Example 5
89. Section 10.5, Example 6

SOLUTION TO PRACTICE PROBLEM 12.4

1. (i) Declare a variable in the General Declarations section with a statement such as Dim var As String and assign the value to the variable in the Form_Load event.

   (ii) Set the Caption property of a label or the Text property of a text box to the value.

12.5 A CASE STUDY: RECORDING CHECKS AND DEPOSITS

This section takes you through the design and implementation of a quality program for personal checkbook management. Nothing in this chapter shows off the power of Visual Basic better than the program in this section. That a user-friendly checkbook management program can be written in only four pages of code clearly shows Visual Basic's ability to improve the productivity of programmers. It is easy to imagine an entire finance program, similar to programs that have generated millions of dollars of sales, being written in only a few weeks by using Visual Basic!

The Design of the Program

Though many commercial programs are available for personal financial management, they include so many bells and whistles that their original purposes—keeping track of transactions and reporting balances—have become obscured. The program in this section was designed specifically as a checkbook program. It keeps track of expenditures and deposits and produces a printed report. Adding a reconciliation feature would be easy enough, although we did not include one.

The program is supposed to be user friendly. Therefore, it showcases many of the techniques and tools available in Visual Basic.

The general design goals for the program included the abilities to

- Automatically enter the user's name on each check and deposit slip.
- Automatically provide the next consecutive check or deposit slip number. (The user can override this feature if necessary.)
- Automatically provide the date. (Again, this feature can be overridden.)
- For each check, record the payee, the amount, and optionally a memo.
- For each deposit slip, record the source, the amount, and optionally a memo.
- Display the current balance at all times.
- Produce a printout detailing all transactions.

The User Interface

With Visual Basic we can place a replica of a check or deposit slip on the screen and let the user supply the information as if actually filling out a check or deposit slip. Figure 12.30 shows the form in its check mode. A picture box forms the boundary of the check. Below the picture box are two labels for the current balance and four command buttons.

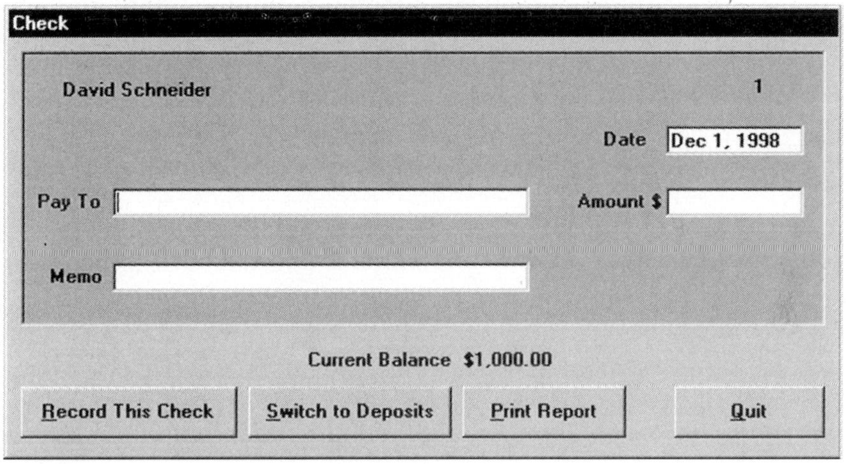

Figure 12.30 Template for Entering a Check

The first time the program is run, the user is asked for his or her name, the starting balance, and the numbers of the first check and deposit slip. Suppose the user's name is David Schneider, the first check has number 1, the starting balance is $1000, and the first deposit slip is also number 1. Figure 12.30 shows the form after the three pieces of input. The upper part of the form looks like a check. The check has a color of light turquoise blue (or cyan). The Date box is automatically set to today's date but can be altered by the user. The user fills in the payee, amount, and optionally a memo. When the user pushes the Record This Check button, the information is written to a file, the balance is updated, and check number 2 appears.

To record a deposit, the user pushes the Switch to Deposits button. The form then appears as in Figure 12.31. The form's title bar now reads Deposit Slip, the words Pay To change to Source, and the color of the slip changes to light yellow. Also, in the buttons at the bottom of the form, the words Check and Deposit are interchanged. A deposit is recorded in much the same way as a check. When the Print Report button is pushed, a printout similar to the one in Figure 12.32 is printed on the printer.

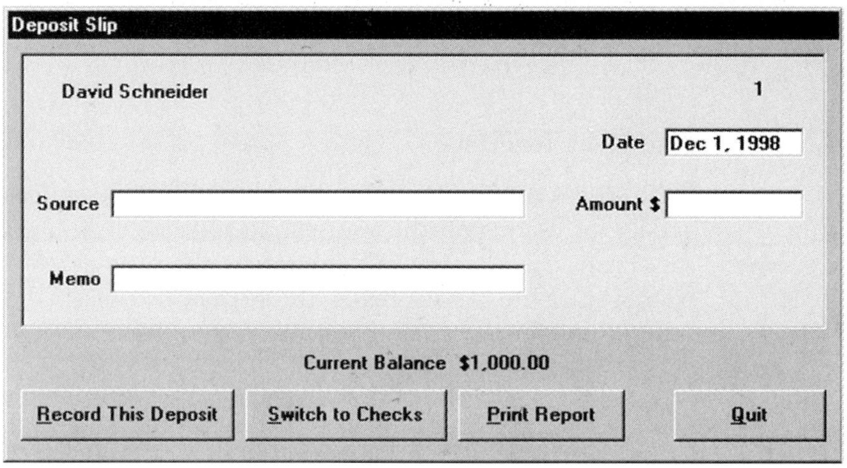

Figure 12.31 Template for Entering a Deposit Slip

Dec. 1, 1998

Name: David Schneider   Starting balance: $1,000.00

Date	Transaction	Amount	Balance
Dec 1, 1998	Check #: 1 Paid to: Land's End Memo: shirts	$75.95	$924.05
Dec 2, 1998	Check #: 2 Paid to: Bethesda Coop Memo: groceries	$125.00	$799.05
Dec 2, 1998	Deposit #: 1 Source: Prentice Hall Memo: typing expenses	$245.00	$1,044.05

Ending Balance: $1,044.05

Figure 12.32 Sample Printout of Transactions

The common design for the check and deposit slip allows one set of controls to be used for both items. Figure 12.33 shows the controls and their suggestive names. The caption of the label lblToFrom will change back and forth between Pay To and Source.

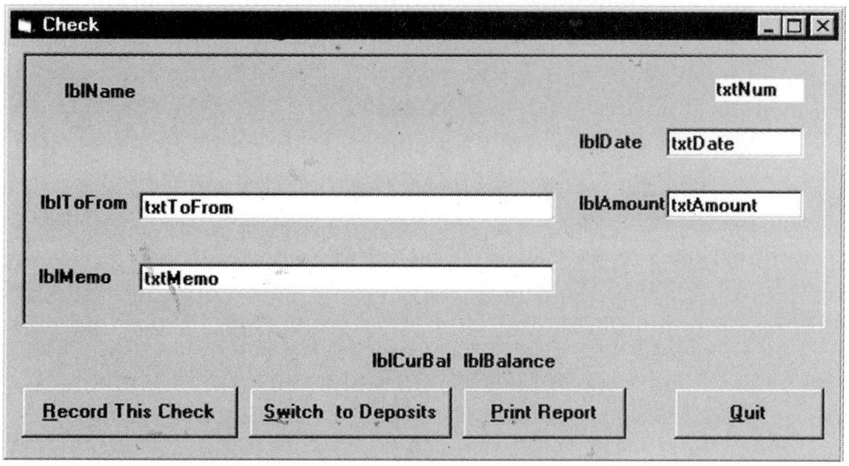

Figure 12.33 Control Names for Checkbook Management Program

Table 12.1 lists the objects and their initial properties. Because the program will always begin by displaying the next check, the various captions and the Background property of the picture box could have been set at design time. We chose instead to leave these assignments to the SetupCheck subprogram, which is normally used to switch from deposit entry to check entry, but also can be called by the Form_Load event procedure to prepare the initial mode (check or deposit) for the form. However, in order to write the setup subprograms, we do note the values that Visual Basic displays for the Background property if we select the light blue or yellow colors from the third row of the color palette. These values are &H00FFFF00& and &H0000FFFF&, respectively.

Object	Property	Setting
frmCheckbook		
picBox		
lblName	BackStyle	0 – Transparent
txtNum	BorderStyle	0 – None
lblDate	BackStyle	0 – Transparent
	Caption	Date
txtDate		
lblToFrom	BackStyle	0 – Transparent
txtToFrom		
lblAmount	BackStyle	0 – Transparent
	Caption	Amount $
txtAmount		
lblMemo	BackStyle	0 – Transparent
	Caption	Memo
txtMemo		
lblCurBal	Caption	Current Balance
lblBalance		
cmdRecord		
cmdMode		
cmdPrint	Caption	&Print Report
cmdQuit	Caption	&Quit

Table 12.1 Objects and Initial Properties for the Checkbook Management Program

The transactions are stored in a data file named CHKBOOK.TXT. The first four entries of the file are the name to appear on the check or deposit slip, the starting balance, the number of the first check, and the number of the first deposit slip. After that, each transaction is recorded as a sequence of eight items—the type of transaction, the contents of txtToFrom, the current balance, the number of the last check, the number of the last deposit slip, the amount of money, the memo, and the date.

Coding the Program

The top row of Figure 12.34 shows the different events to which the program must respond. Table 12.2 identifies the corresponding event procedures and the general procedures they call.

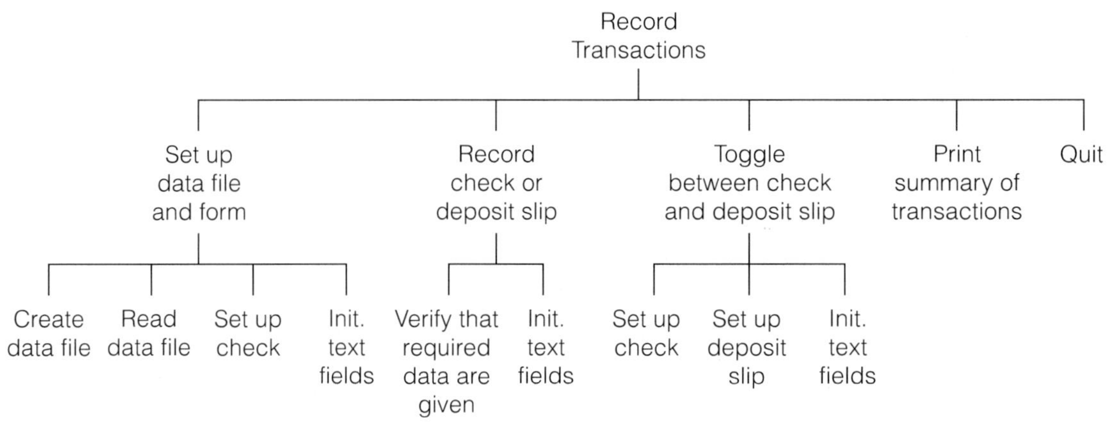

Figure 12.34 Hierarchy Chart for Checkbook Management Program

Task	Procedure
1. Set up data file and form	Form_Load
1.1 Create data file	CreateDataFile
1.2 Read data file	ReadDataFile
1.3 Set up check	SetupCheck
1.4 Initialize text fields	InitializeFields
2. Record check or deposit slip	cmdRecord_Click
2.1 Verify that required data are given	AllDataGiven
2.2 Initialize text fields	InitializeFields
3. Toggle between check & deposit slip	cmdMode_Click
3.1 Set up check	SetupCheck
3.2 Set up deposit slip	SetupDeposit
3.3 Initialize text fields	InitializeFields
4. Print summary of transaction	cmdPrint_Click
5. Quit	cmdQuit_Click

Table 12.2 Tasks and Their Procedures

Let's examine each event procedure.

1. **Form_Load** first looks to see if the file CHKBOOK.TXT has been created. The function Dir returns "CHKBOOK.TXT" if the file exists and otherwise returns the empty string. If CHKBOOK.TXT does not exist, the routine CreateDataFile is called. CreateDataFile prompts the user for the name to appear on the checks and deposit slips, the starting balance, and the numbers of the first check and deposit slip, and then writes these items to the data file. If CHKBOOK.TXT does exist, the routine ReadDataFile is called to read through the entire file to determine all information needed to proceed. The event procedure calls SetupCheck to set the transaction type to Check and set the appropriate captions and background colors for a check. The event procedure then calls InitializeFields, which initializes all the text boxes.

   In the first Let statement of the procedure, the drive is specified as the A drive. Therefore, the data file will be written to and read from a diskette on the A drive. Feel free to change the letter A to whatever drive you prefer. You may even want to specify an entire path.

2. **cmdRecord_Click** first confirms that the required fields contain entries. This is accomplished by calling the function AllDataGiven. If the value returned is "YES", then cmdRecord_Click opens the data file for output as Append, sends eight pieces of data to the file, and closes the file. When AllDataGiven returns "NO", the function itself pops up a message box to tell the user where information is needed. The user must type in the information and then press the Record button again.

3. **cmdMode_Click** toggles back and forth from a check to a deposit slip. It calls SetupCheck, or its analog SetupDeposit, and then calls InitializeFields.

4. **cmdPrint_Click** prints out a complete history of all transactions, as shown in Figure 12.32.

5. **cmdQuit_Click** ends the program.

```
Rem Record Checks and Deposits
Rem
Rem ***********************************************************************
Rem *                                                                     *
Rem *  fileName    Name of the file containing previous data, if any      *
Rem *  nameOnChk   Name to appear on checks                               *
Rem *  lastCkNum   Number of last check written                           *
Rem *  lastDpNum   Number of last deposit slip processed                  *
Rem *  curBal      Current balance in account                             *
Rem *  transType   Type of transaction, check or deposit                  *
Rem *                                                                     *
Rem ***********************************************************************

Dim fileName As String, nameOnChk As String
Dim lastCkNum As Integer, lastDpNum As Integer
Dim curBal As Single, transType As String
```

```
Private Function AllDataGiven() As String
  Dim message As String
  Rem If one of the four required pieces of information
  Rem is missing, assign its name to message
  Let message = ""
  If txtDate.Text = "" Then
      Let message = "Date"
      txtDate.SetFocus
    ElseIf txtToFrom.Text = "" Then
      If transType = "Check" Then
          Let message = "Pay To"
        Else
          Let message = "Source"
      End If
      txtToFrom.SetFocus
    ElseIf txtAmount.Text = "" Then
      Let message = "Amount"
      txtAmount.SetFocus
    ElseIf txtNum.Text = "" Then
      If transType = "Check" Then
          Let message = "Check Number"
        Else
          Let message = "Deposit Number"
      End If
      txtNum.SetFocus
  End If
  If message = "" Then
      Rem All required data fields have been filled; recording can proceed
      AllDataGiven = "YES"
    Else
      Rem Advise user of required data that are missing
      MsgBox "The '" + message + "' field must be filled", , "Error"
      AllDataGiven = "NO"
  End If
End Function

Private Sub cmdMode_Click()
  Rem Toggle from Check to/from Deposit Slip
  If transType = "Check" Then
      Call SetupDeposit
    Else   'transType = "Deposit"
      Call SetupCheck
  End If
  Call InitializeFields
  txtToFrom.SetFocus
End Sub

Private Sub cmdPrint_Click()
  Dim temp As String, lineNo As Integer
  Dim nameOnChk As String, balance As Single, ck As Integer, dp As Integer
  Dim toFrom As String, amount As String, memo As String, theDate As String
  Rem Print out a detailed list of all transactions.
  Let temp = frmCheckbook.Caption             'Save the current form caption
```

```
  Let frmCheckbook.Caption = "Printing..."    'Set form caption to indicate printing
  Let lineNo = 1                              'Line number being printed
  Open fileName For Input As #1               'Open the file
  Input #1, nameOnChk, balance, ck, dp        'Read in the file header
  Rem Print the details of the individual transactions.
  Do Until EOF(1)
    If lineNo >= 57 Then
        Rem 57 or more lines have been printed; start a new page
        Printer.NewPage
        Let lineNo = 1
    End If
    If lineNo = 1 Then
        Rem Print the report header
        Printer.Print
        Printer.Print "Name: ";nameOnChk;Tab(65);Format(Date, "mmm d, yyyy")
        Printer.Print
        Printer.Print , "Starting balance: "; Format(balance, "Currency")
        Printer.Print
        Printer.Print "Date", "Transaction"; Tab(50); "Amount";
        Printer.Print Tab(65); "Balance"
        Printer.Print "____", "___________"; Tab(50); "______";
        Printer.Print Tab(65); "_______"
        Printer.Print
        Printer.Print
        Let lineNo = 10
    End If
    Input #1, transType, toFrom, balance, ck, dp, amount, memo, theDate
    If transType = "Check" Then
        Printer.Print theDate, "Check #: "; ck; Tab(50); amount;
        Printer.Print Tab(65); Format(balance, "Currency")
        Printer.Print , "Paid to: "; toFrom
      Else              'Transaction was a deposit
        Printer.Print theDate, "Deposit #: "; dp; Tab(50); amount;
        Printer.Print Tab(65); Format(balance, "Currency")
        Printer.Print , "Source: "; toFrom
    End If
    Let lineNo = lineNo + 2
    Rem If there was a memo, then print it.
    If memo <> "" Then
        Printer.Print , "Memo: "; memo
        Let lineNo = lineNo + 1
    End If
    Printer.Print
    Let lineNo = lineNo + 1
  Loop
  Close #1                      'Close the file
  Rem Print the ending balance
  Printer.Print
  Printer.Print , "Ending Balance: "; Format(balance, "Currency")
  Printer.EndDoc                       'Send the output to the Printer
  Let frmCheckbook.Caption = temp      'Restore the form caption
  txtToFrom.SetFocus                   'Set focus for the next entry
End Sub
```

```
Private Sub cmdQuit_Click()
  Rem  Exit the program
  End
End Sub

Private Sub cmdRecord_Click()
  Dim amt As String, amount As Single, itemNum As Integer
  Rem Check to ensure all required fields are filled
  If AllDataGiven() = "YES" Then
      Let amt = txtAmount.Text 'Amount of transaction as string
      Let amount = Val(amt)    'Amount of transaction as number
      Let amt = Format(amt, "Currency")
      Let itemNum = Val(txtNum.Text)
      If transType = "Check" Then
          Let curBal = curBal - amount
          Let lastCkNum = itemNum
        Else           'transType = "Deposit"
          Let curBal = curBal + amount
          Let lastDpNum = itemNum
      End If
      Let lblBalance.Caption = Format(curBal, "Currency")
      Open fileName For Append As #1
      Rem The following two lines must be joined and entered as one line
      Write #1, transType, txtToFrom.Text, curBal, lastCkNum, lastDpNum, amt,
                txtMemo.Text, txtDate.Text
      Close #1
      Call InitializeFields
      txtToFrom.SetFocus
  End If
End Sub

Private Sub CreateDataFile()
  Dim startBal As Single, ckNum As integer
  Rem The first time the program is run, create a data file
  Open fileName For Output As #1
  Let nameOnChk = InputBox("Name to appear on checks:")
  Let startBal = Val(InputBox("Starting balance:"))
  Let ckNum = Val(InputBox("Number of the first check:"))
  Let lastCkNum = ckNum - 1   'Number of "last" check written
  Let ckNum = Val(InputBox("Number of the first deposit slip:"))
  Let lastDpNum = ckNum - 1   'Number of "last" deposit slip processed
  Let curBal = startBal       'Set current balance
  Rem First record in data file records name to appear on checks
  Rem plus initial data for account
  Write #1, nameOnChk, startBal, lastCkNum, lastDpNum
  Close #1
End Sub

Private Sub Form_Load()
  Dim drive As String
  Rem If no data file exists, create one. Otherwise, open the
  Rem data file and get the user's name, last used check and
  Rem deposit slip numbers, and current balance.
  Let fileName = App.Path + "\CHKBOOK.TXT"  'Program uses one data file
```

```
  If Dir(fileName) = "" Then
      Rem Data file does not exist, so create it and obtain initial data
      Call CreateDataFile
    Else
      Call ReadDataFile
  End If
  Rem Set name and balance labels
  Let lblName.Caption = nameOnChk
  Let lblBalance.Caption = Format(curBal, "Currency")
  Rem Set the date field to the current date
  Let txtDate.Text = Format(Date, "mmm d, yyyy")
  Call SetupCheck                    'Always start session with checks
  Call InitializeFields
End Sub

Private Sub InitializeFields()
  Rem Initialize all text entry fields except date
  Let txtToFrom.Text = ""
  Let txtAmount.Text = ""
  Let txtMemo.Text = ""
  If transType = "Check" Then
      Rem Make txtNum text box reflect next check number
      Let txtNum.Text = Format(lastCkNum + 1, "#")
    Else               'transType = "Deposit"
      Rem Make txtNum text box reflect next deposit slip number
      Let txtNum.Text = Format(lastDpNum + 1, "#")
  End If
End Sub

Private Sub ReadDataFile()
  Dim t As String, s As String, n As String, m As String, d As String
  Rem Recover name to appear on checks, current balance,
  Rem number of last check written, and number of last deposit slip processed
  Open fileName For Input As #1
  Input #1, nameOnChk, curBal, lastCkNum, lastDpNum
  Do Until EOF(1)
    Rem Read to the end of the file to recover the current balance and the
    Rem last values recorded for ckNum and dpNum.
    Rem t, s, n, m and d are dummy variables and are not used at this point
    Input #1, t, s, curBal, lastCkNum, lastDpNum, n, m, d
  Loop
  Close #1
End Sub

Private Sub SetupCheck()
  Rem Prepare form for the entry of a check
  Let transType = "Check"
  Let frmCheckbook.Caption = "Check"
  Let lblToFrom.Caption = "Pay To"
  Let cmdRecord.Caption = "&Record This Check"
  Let cmdMode.Caption = "&Switch to Deposits"
  Let picBox.BackColor = QBColor(11) ' color of check is light blue
  Let txtNum.BackColor = QBColor(11)
End Sub
```

```
Private Sub SetupDeposit()
  Rem Prepare form for the entry of a deposit
  Let transType = "Deposit"
  Let frmCheckbook.Caption = "Deposit Slip"
  Let lblToFrom.Caption = "Source"
  Let cmdRecord.Caption = "&Record This Deposit"
  Let cmdMode.Caption = "&Switch to Checks"
  Let picBox.BackColor = QBColor(14) ' color of deposit slip is light yellow
  Let txtNum.BackColor = QBColor(14)
End Sub
```

Chapter 12 Summary

1. The Visual Basic screen consists of a collection of objects for which various properties can be set. Some examples of objects are text boxes, labels, command buttons, picture boxes, and the form itself. Some useful properties are Text (set the text displayed by a text box), Caption (set the title of a form, the contents of a label, or the words on a command button), Font.Size (set the size of the characters displayed), Alignment (set the placement of the contents of a label), MultiLine (text box to display text on several lines), Picture (display drawing in picture box), ForeColor (set foreground color), BackColor (set background color), Visible (show or hide object), BorderStyle (alter and possibly remove border), Font.Bold (display boldface text), and Font.Italic (displays italic text).

2. An event procedure is called when a specific event occurs to a specified object. Some event procedures are *object*_Click (*object* is clicked), *object*_Lostfocus (*object* loses the focus), *object*_Gotfocus (*object* receives the focus), and *object*_KeyPress (key is pressed while *object* has the focus).

3. QBasic statements such as PRINT and CLS are applied to objects and are coded as *object*.Print and *object*.Cls.

4. Numbers are formatted with Format.

5. CurrentX and CurrentY are used to position text and graphics in picture boxes and on the form.

6. InputBox invokes an input box and MsgBox invokes a message box.

7. You control the printer with the Printer object and write to it with statements of the form Printer.Print *expression*. You set properties with statements of the form Let Printer.*property* = *setting*. Printer.NewPage starts a new page and PrintForm does a screen dump. A series of commands to the Printer object must end with EndDoc which actually produces the final printed page.

8. Ordinary variables and array variables declared with Dim statements in the (Declarations) part of (General) are visible to every procedure. Array variables are dimensioned inside a procedure with Dim or ReDim.

9. Graphics are displayed in picture boxes and on the form with statements such as *object*.Line, *object*.PSet and *object*.Circle. A coordinate system is specified with *object*.Scale. Color is controlled with the ForeColor and BackColor properties, and with the QBColor function. The DrawWidth property controls the thickness of points, lines, and circles.

Chapter 12 Programming Projects

1. *Multiple-Choice Quiz*. Write a program to ask multiple-choice questions with four possible answers. The figure below shows a typical question. The user selects an answer by clicking a button and is informed as to the correctness of the answer by a message box. After an incorrect answer, the user should be given another guess. After a correct answer, the user should be given the opportunity to have another question or quit. Questions and answers should be held in a sequential file. (***Notes:*** The figure uses five picture boxes with BorderStyle property set to 0 - None. If you use the Form_Load to pose the first question, be sure to set the AutoRedraw property of the picture boxes to True.)

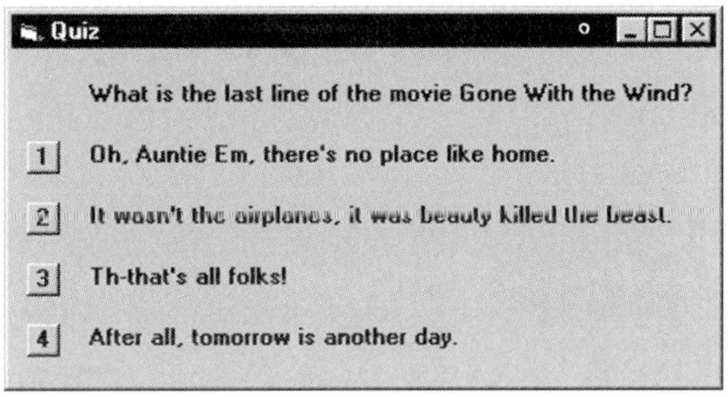

Figure for Programming Project 1—A Typical Question

2. Write a program to analyze a mortgage. The user should enter the amount of the loan, the annual rate of interest, and the duration of the loan in months. After the information is entered, the monthly payment and the total amount of interest paid should be displayed. The formula for the monthly payment is

```
payment = p * r / (1 - (1 + r) ^ (-n))
```

where p is the amount of the loan, r is the monthly interest rate (annual rate divided by 12) given as a number between 0 (for 0%) and 1 (for 100%), and n is the duration of the loan. The formula for the total interest paid is

```
total interest = n * payment - p
```

In Projects 3 through 9, rework the given programming project in Visual Basic with a Windows-style interface.

3. Chapter 5, Programming Project 5 (You Know What They Say): In addition, have the program display the proverbs that were answered incorrectly, along with their truth value.
4. Chapter 6, Programming Project 4 (Airline Reservations)
5. Chapter 6, Programming Project 10 (The Twelve Days of Christmas)
6. Chapter 7, Programming Project 3 (Language Translator): The words should be stored in a sequential file.
7. Chapter 7, Programming Project 7 (Tic-Tac-Toe): The tic-tac-toe grid should consist of nine picture boxes. At each move, a player should click on a picture box to have an O or an X displayed there with Circle or Line.
8. Chapter 7, Programming Project 8 (Airline Reservations with Waiting List)
9. Chapter 9, Programming Project 2 (Teacher's Grade Book)

Appendix A

ASCII Values

ASCII Value	Character	ASCII Value	Character	ASCII Value	Character
000	(null)	038	&	076	L
001	☺	039	'	077	M
002	☻	040	(	078	N
003	♥	041	)	079	O
004	♦	042	*	080	P
005	♣	043	+	081	Q
006	♠	044	,	082	R
007	(beep)	045	-	083	S
008	◘	046	.	084	T
009	(tab)	047	/	085	U
010	(line feed)	048	0	086	V
011	(home)	049	1	087	W
012	(form feed)	050	2	088	X
013	(carriage return)	051	3	089	Y
014	♫	052	4	090	Z
015	☼	053	5	091	[
016	►	054	6	092	\
017	◄	055	7	093	]
018	↕	056	8	094	^
019	!!	057	9	095	_
020	¶	058	:	096	`
021	§	059	;	097	a
022	▬	060	<	098	b
023	↨	061	=	099	c
024	↑	062	>	100	d
025	↓	063	?	101	e
026	→	064	@	102	f
027	←	065	A	103	g
028	(cursor right)	066	B	104	h
029	(cursor left)	067	C	105	i
030	(cursor up)	068	D	106	j
031	(cursor down)	069	E	107	k
032	(space)	070	F	108	l
033	!	071	G	109	m
034	''	072	H	110	n
035	#	073	I	111	o
036	$	074	J	112	p
037	%	075	K	113	q

ASCII Value	Character
114	r
115	s
116	t
117	u
118	v
119	w
120	x
121	y
122	z
123	{
124	¦
125	}
126	~
127	⌂
128	Ç
129	ü
130	é
131	â
132	ä
133	à
134	å
135	ç
136	ê
137	ë
138	è
139	ï
140	î
141	ì
142	Ä
143	Å
144	É
145	æ
146	Æ
147	ô
148	ö
149	ò
150	û
151	ù
152	ÿ
153	Ö
154	Ü
155	¢
156	£
157	¥
158	Pt
159	ƒ
160	á
161	í

ASCII Value	Character
162	ó
163	ú
164	ñ
165	Ñ
166	ª
167	º
168	¿
169	⌐
170	¬
171	½
172	¼
173	¡
174	«
175	»
176	░
177	▒
178	▓
179	│
180	┤
181	╡
182	╢
183	╖
184	╕
185	╣
186	║
187	╗
188	╝
189	╜
190	╛
191	┐
192	└
193	┴
194	┬
195	├
196	─
197	┼
198	╞
199	╟
200	╚
201	╔
202	╩
203	╦
204	╠
205	═
206	╬
207	╧
208	╨
209	╤

ASCII Value	Character
210	╥
211	╙
212	╘
213	╒
214	╓
215	╫
216	╪
217	┘
218	┌
219	█
220	▄
221	▌
222	▐
223	▀
224	α
225	β
226	Γ
227	π
228	Σ
229	σ
230	µ
231	τ
232	Φ
233	θ
234	Ω
235	δ
236	∞
237	Ø
238	ϵ
239	∩
240	≡
241	±
242	≥
243	≤
244	⌠
245	⌡
246	÷
247	≈
248	°
249	•
250	·
251	√
252	^{n}
253	^{2}
254	■
255	(blank 'FF')

Appendix B

Using a Mouse

Preliminaries

Although most mice have two buttons, only the left button is used in the following discussion.

If a mouse has been installed in your computer, a small rectangle or arrow should appear on the screen. This is the *mouse cursor*. As you move the mouse across your desk, the mouse cursor moves across the screen in sync with your movements. The mouse cursor is usually referred to simply as *the mouse*. No confusion should result, since the actual mouse and the mouse cursor on the screen move together.

Move the mouse to a menu name (such as File or Help) and press and release the left button. Moving the mouse to an item and pressing the button in this way is called *clicking on the item*. The menu should drop down and its options should appear. These options in turn can be selected by clicking on the desired option; that is, by moving the mouse to the desired option and pressing and releasing the left button. To remove a drop-down menu, move the mouse cursor to a blank area of the screen and click on nothing.

If the mouse is not visible when QBasic is first invoked, then it possibly is the same color as the screen background. Try moving the mouse around the screen. If the mouse becomes visible in nonbackground regions of the screen, move the mouse to the Options menu, click the (left) button to get a drop-down menu, and then click the (left) button on Display. Press the Tab key and then select a background region that makes the mouse visible by pressing the down-cursor and up-cursor keys to change the color selection until the mouse becomes visible in the background region.

Another way to use the mouse is called *dragging*. Dragging refers to holding down the mouse button while moving the mouse. Dragging can be used to select an option from a menu by moving the cursor to the menu name, dragging the mouse until the desired option is highlighted, and then releasing the button.

Tip: You can pick the mouse up off your desk and replace it without moving the mouse pointer. This is useful, for example, when the mouse pointer is in the center of the screen but the mouse is about to fall off your desk!

Using the Mouse in QBasic (Refer to Figure B.1)

Select a Menu Item

Click on the menu name, and then click on the desired item in the drop-down menu that appears.

or

Move to the menu name and drag downward until the selection bar reaches the item of choice. Then release the button to select the item.

Cancel a Selected Menu

Click anywhere outside the menu.

Open an Existing File

Click on File and then on Open in the drop-down menu. In the resulting dialog box, click once on the desired file name and once on OK.

or

Click on File and then on Open in the drop-down menu. Click twice in rapid succession on the desired file name.

Mark a Section of Text as a Block

Move the mouse to one end of the text and then drag to the other end of the text.

Scroll Vertically

Move the mouse to the vertical elevator, and then drag the mouse in the appropriate direction.

or

Move the mouse to the appropriate arrow at the end of the scroll bar at the right of the screen, and then hold down the left button.

Scroll Horizontally (Pan)

Move the mouse to the horizontal elevator and then drag the mouse in the appropriate direction.

or

Move the mouse to the appropriate arrow at the end of the scroll bar at the bottom of the screen, and then hold down the left button.

Move Text Cursor in View Window

Move the mouse to the desired location and click.

Change Active Windows

Move the mouse to any part of the window to be activated and click.

Fill Screen with Current Window

Click once on the maximize button shown near the upper right corner of Figure B-1.

or

Click twice in rapid succession anywhere in the title bar.

Return Current Window to Normal Size

Click once on the restore (double-arrow) button.

or

Click twice in rapid succession anywhere in the title bar.

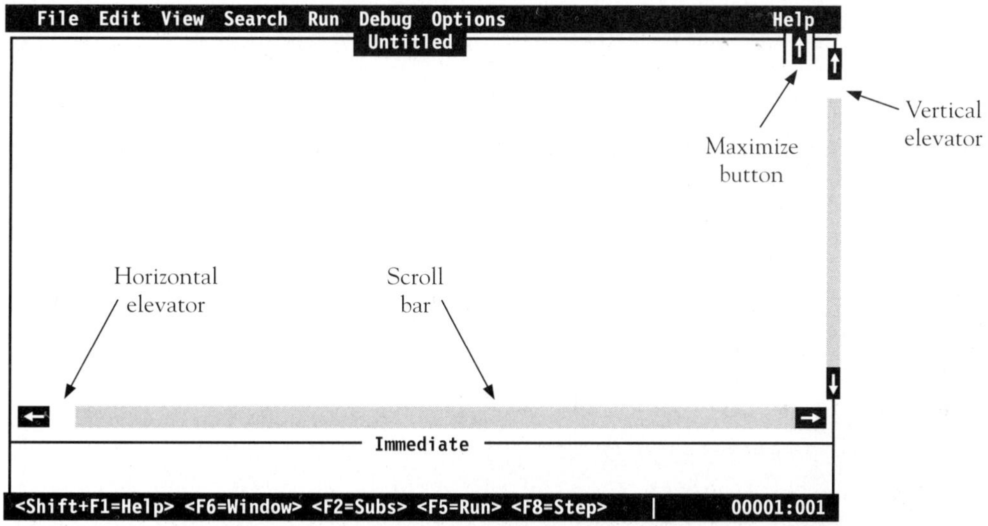

Figure B.1 Items Used by a Mouse

Appendix C

QBasic Statements, Functions, Operators, and Metacommands

Numbers in brackets follow some of the discussions. These numbers refer to supporting topics presented at the end of this appendix.

ABS The function ABS strips the minus signs from negative numbers while leaving other numbers unchanged. If *x* is any number, then the value of ABS(*x*) is the absolute value of *x*.

AND (Logical Operator) The logical expression *condition1* AND *condition2* is true only if both *condition1* and *condition2* are true. For example, (3<7) AND ("abc">"a") is true since 3<7 is true as is "abc">"a", while ("apple">"ape") AND ("earth">"moon") is false since "earth">"moon" is false.

AND (Bitwise Operator) The expression *byte1* AND *byte2* is evaluated by expressing each byte as an 8-tuple binary number and then ANDing together corresponding digits, where 1 AND 1 equals 1, while 1 AND 0, 0 AND 1, and 0 AND 0 all equal 0. For example, the expression 37 AND 157 translated to binary 8-tuples becomes 00100101 AND 10011101. ANDing together corresponding digits gives the binary 8-tuple 00000101 or decimal 5. Thus 37 AND 157 is 5.

ASC The extended ASCII table associates a number (from 0 to 255) with each of the characters available to the computer. The value of ASC(*a$*) is the ASCII value of the first character of the string *a$*.

ATN The trigonometric function ATN, or *arctangent*, is the inverse of the tangent function. For any number *x*, ATN(*x*) is an angle in radians between –pi/2 and pi/2 whose tangent is *x*. [2]

BEEP The statement BEEP produces a sound of frequency 800 Hz that lasts a fraction of a second.

BLOAD The statement BLOAD "*filespec*, *m*" places the bytes contained in the file *filespec* into successive memory locations beginning at offset *m* in the current segment of memory. If the contents of successive memory locations are saved in a file with the BSAVE statement, then they can later be restored with the statement BLOAD "*filespec*". (This process is commonly used to save and later restore the contents of the screen.) [9], [4]

BSAVE The statement BSAVE "*filespec*", *n*, *m* stores in the file *filespec* the contents of the *m* consecutive memory locations beginning at offset *n* in the current segment or memory. [9], [4]

CALL A statement of the form CALL *SubprogramName*(*argList*) is used to execute the named subprogram, passing to it the variables and values in the list of arguments. Arrays appearing in the list of arguments should be specified by the array name followed by empty parentheses. The value of a variable argument may be altered by the subprogram unless the variable is surrounded by parentheses. After the statements in the subprogram have been executed, program execution continues with the statement following CALL. ***Note:*** The keyword CALL may be omitted. In this case, the parentheses are omitted and the statement is written *SubprogramName argList*.

CALL ABSOLUTE The CALL ABSOLUTE statement passes control to a machine-language subprogram in much the same way that CALL passes control to a procedure. The statement CALL ABSOLUTE (*argList*, *offvar*) passes control to the machine-language program beginning at the memory location whose offset in the current segment of memory is the value of the numeric variable *offvar*. The arguments are used by the machine-language subprogram. The statement CALLS ABSOLUTE works like CALL ABSOLUTE except that both segment and offset are passed for each of the arguments. [9]

CDBL The function CDBL converts integer, long integer, and single-precision numbers to double-precision numbers. If *x* is any number, then the value of CDBL(*x*) is the double-precision number determined by *x*.

CHAIN The CHAIN statement passes control from the current program to another program contained on disk. The CHAIN "*filespec*" statement will load and execute the source-code program contained in *filespec* (appending the .BAS extension if none was specified). Placing COMMON statements in the two programs allows the first program to pass the values of the variables appearing in its COMMON statement to corresponding variables in the second program's COMMON statement.

CHDIR The statement CHDIR *path* changes the current directory on the specified disk drive to the subdirectory specified by *path*. For example, CHDIR "C:\" specifies the root directory of the C drive as the current directory. Omitting a drive letter in *path* causes the default drive to be used. [3]

CHR$ If *n* is a number from 0 to 255, then CHR$(*n*) is the character in the ASCII table associated with *n*.

CINT The function CINT converts long integer, single-precision, and double-precision numbers to integer numbers. If *x* is any number from –32768 to 32767, then the value of CINT(*x*) is the (possibly rounded) integer constant that *x* determines.

CIRCLE The statement CIRCLE (*x*,*y*),*r*,*c*,*r1*,*r2*,*a* draws a portion, or all, of an ellipse. The center of the ellipse is the point (*x*,*y*) and the longer radius is *r*. The color of the ellipse is determined by *c*. If *r1* and *r2* are present, then the computer draws only the portion of the ellipse that extends from the radius line at an angle of ABS(*r1*) radians with the horizontal radius to the radius line at an angle of ABS(*r2*) radians with the horizontal radius line in a counterclockwise direction. If either *r1* or *r2* is negative, then the computer also draws its radius line. The ratio of the length of the vertical diameter to the length of the horizontal diameter will be *a*. (If *a* is missing, the figure drawn will be a circle.) [2], [5], [6]

CLEAR The statement CLEAR resets all variables and elements of static arrays to their default values, closes all files, deletes all dynamic arrays from memory, and reinitializes the stack. Also, if ,,*s* is added after the CLEAR statement, the stack size is set to *s*. [17], [1]

CLNG The function CLNG converts integer, single-precision, and double-precision numbers to long integer numbers. If *x* is any number from –2,147,483,648 to 2,147,483,647, then the value of CLNG(*x*) is the (possibly rounded) long integer constant that *x* determines.

CLOSE The statement CLOSE #*n* closes the file that has been opened with reference number *n*. By itself, CLOSE closes all open files.

CLS The statement CLS clears the screen and positions the cursor at the upper-left of the screen. If a graphics viewport is active (see VIEW), then the statement CLS clears the viewport. The statement CLS 0 clears the entire screen. The statement CLS 1 clears the active graphics viewport if one exists; otherwise, it clears the entire screen. The statement CLS 2 clears only the text viewport (see VIEW PRINT).

COLOR In text-only mode (SCREEN 0), the COLOR statement produces either special effects (such as underlined text) or colors, depending on the type of monitor. The statement COLOR *f*, *b*, *bd* sets the foreground color to *f*, the background color to *b*, and the border color to *bd*, where *f* ranges from 0 to 15 and *b* from 0 to 7. The statement COLOR *f*+*16*, *b*, *bd* selects the same colors as the statement just given, but with a blinking foreground.

In screen mode 1, two palettes of four colors each are available. The statement COLOR *b*, *p* specifies *b* as the background color and *p* as the palette. Text will appear in color 3 of the selected palette, and graphics may be displayed in any color of that palette.

In EGA and VGA modes 7, 8, and 9, a palette of 16 colors is available for text and graphics. The statement COLOR *f*, *b* sets the foreground color to the color assigned to palette entry *f* and the background color to the color assigned to palette entry *b*, where *f* and *b* range from 0 to 15.

In the VGA and MCGA modes 12 and 13, the statement COLOR *f* sets the foreground color to the color assigned to palette entry *f*. (The background is set to color *c* with the statement PALETTE 0, *c*.) [5], [6]

COM(n) The statement COM(*n*) enables, disables, or defers trapping of the *n*th communications port depending on whether it is followed by ON, OFF, or STOP, respectively. [15], [10]

COMMON If a statement of the form COMMON *fromVar1*, *fromVar2*, . . . , *fromVarN* precedes a CHAIN statement, and a statement of the form COMMON *toVar1*, *toVar2*, . . . , *toVarN* appears in the chained-to program, then the value of *fromVar1* is assigned to *toVar1*, the value of *fromVar2* is assigned to *toVar2*, and so on. Although the names of corresponding COMMON variables need not be the same, corresponding variables must be of the same type: string, integer, long integer, single-precision, double-precision, or user-defined record type. The type of each variable is determined either by a type-declaration tag or by inserting words of the form AS *type*. When the statement COMMON SHARED *var1*, *var2*, . . . , appears in a program, then the specified variables will be shared with all procedures in the program. COMMON statements must appear before any executable statements in a program. COMMON statements may not appear inside a procedure.

CONST The statement CONST *constantName* = *expression* causes QBasic to replace every occurrence of *constantName* with the value of the expression. This replacement takes place before any lines of the program are executed. Unlike LET, CONST does not set up a location in the program's memory for a variable. A *constantName* may appear in only one CONST statement and may not appear on the left side of a LET statement. We call *constantName* a "symbolic constant" or "named constant."

COS The value of the trigonometric function COS(x) is the cosine of an angle of x radians. [2]

CSNG The function CSNG converts integer, long integer, and double-precision numbers to single-precision numbers. If x is any number, then the value of CSNG(x) is the single-precision number that x determines.

CSRLIN At any time, the value of the function CSRLIN is the number (1, 2, 3, . . .) of the line of the screen on which the cursor is located. [8]

CVI, CVL, CVS, CVD With the buffer method of working with random-access files, numbers to be recorded in files by QBasic's LSET and PUT statements must first be transformed into strings. They are transformed back by these four functions. If an integer was transformed into the string *a$* of length 2, then the value of CVI(*a$*) will be the original number. Similarly, CVL(*a$*), CVS(*a$*), or CVD(*a$*) will be the long integer, single-precision or double-precision numbers that were transformed by QBasic into *a$*, a string of length 4, 4, or 8. [11]

CVSMBF, CVDMBF Random-access files created in Microsoft BASIC, GW-BASIC, BASICA, or early versions of QuickBasic use a method different from QBasic's for storing numbers as strings. Single- and double-precision numbers that have been converted to strings by one of these earlier versions of BASIC and entered into random-access files can be converted to QBasic's numeric format by these two functions. [11]

DATA The statement DATA *const1*, *const2*, . . . holds constants. READ statements read these constants and assign them to variables.

**DATE$** The value of the function DATE$ is the current date returned as a string of the form mm-dd-yyyy. If *d$* is a string of this form, then the statement DATE$ = *d$* resets the date as specified by *d$*.

DECLARE The optional statement DECLARE SUB *SubprogramName* (*par1*, *par2*, . . .) or the statement DECLARE FUNCTION *FunctionName* (*par1*, *par2*, . . .) indicates that the specified procedure is called by the program. The type of each parameter is determined by either a type-declaration tag or words of the form AS *type*. The parameters must match the types of the corresponding parameters in the procedure definition. A parameterless procedure should appear in a DECLARE statement with an empty pair of parentheses. QBasic uses the DECLARE statements to check that subprogram calls use the proper number and types of arguments. DECLARE statements for each procedure are automatically inserted at the top of the program when it is saved. DECLARE statements may not appear inside procedures.

DEF FN/END DEF DEF FN user-defined functions are created in one of two ways: by a single-line definition of the form DEF FN*name*(*parList*) = *expression*; or by a multiline block that begins with a statement of the form DEF FN*name*(*parList*), which is followed by one or more statements that calculate the value of the function, and ends with the statement END DEF. The items appearing in the list of variables *parList* constitute the input for the function. If one of the statements in the block has the form FN*name* = *expression*, then the output of the function is *expression*.

FN functions must be defined before they may be used. That is, they must be physically positioned earlier in the source text. Variables inside a multiline block are global (that is, shared throughout the program) unless they are declared early in the block to be static by a statement of the form STATIC var1, var2, . . . Static variables are not accessible outside of the block; however, they retain their values between subsequent calls to the function. This method of creating user-defined functions is perhaps obsolete with the introduction of the FUNCTION statement, which supports recursion and may take arrays and records as arguments.

DEFINT, DEFLNG, DEFSNG, DEFDBL, DEFSTR A variable can be assigned a type by either a type-declaration tag or an AS clause. A statement of the form DEFINT *letter* specifies that any "untyped" variable whose name begins with the specified letter will have integer type. A statement of the form DEFINT *letter1-letter2* specifies that all "untyped" variables whose names begin with a letter in the range *letter1* through *letter2* will have integer type. The statements DEFLNG, DEFSNG, DEFDBL, and DEFSTR specify the corresponding types for long integer, single-precision, double-precision, and string variables, respectively. A DEFtype statement is automatically displayed above procedures created after the DEFtype statement is placed in the main body of the program.

DEF SEG The statement DEF SEG = *n* specifies that the *current segment of memory* consist of memory locations 16**n* through 16**n* + 65535. Subsequently, all statements that access memory directly—like PEEK, POKE, BLOAD, and BSAVE—will refer to memory locations in this range. [9]

DIM The statement DIM *arrayName*(*m* TO *n*) declares an array with subscripts ranging from *m* to *n*, inclusive, where *m* and *n* are in the normal integer range of –32768 to 32767. A statement of the form DIM *arrayName*(*m* TO *n*,*p* TO *q*) declares a doubly subscripted, or two-dimensional, array. Three- and higher-dimensional arrays are declared similarly. If *m* and *p* are zero, the DIM statements above may be changed to DIM *arrayName*(*n*) and DIM *arrayName*(*n*,*q*). The statement DIM *variableName* AS *variableType*, where *variableType* is INTEGER, LONG, SINGLE, DOUBLE, STRING, STRING*n, or a user-defined type, specifies the type of the variable. Inserting SHARED after the word DIM in the main body of a program allows all procedures to access the array or variable. [17]

DO/LOOP A statement of the form DO, DO WHILE *cond*, or DO UNTIL *cond* is used to mark the beginning of a block of statements that will be repeated. A statement of the form LOOP, LOOP WHILE *cond*, or LOOP UNTIL *cond* is used to mark the end of the block. Each time a statement containing WHILE or UNTIL followed by a condition is encountered, the truth value of the condition determines whether the block should be repeated or the program should jump to the statement immediately following the block. A DO loop may also be exited at any point with an EXIT DO statement.

DOUBLE A variable of type DOUBLE requires 8 bytes of memory and can hold 0, the numbers from 4.94065×10^{-324} to $1.797693134862316 \times 10^{308}$ with at most 17 significant digits, and the negative of these numbers. DOUBLE values and variables are indicated by the type tag #: 2.718281828459045#, Pi#.

DRAW The graphics statement DRAW *a$*, where *a$* is a string of directions and arguments, is used to draw figures on the screen in much the same way figures are drawn with pencil and paper. The rich and varied command strings constitute a miniature graphics language. The DRAW statement can be used to produce straight lines beginning at the last point referenced and extending in several directions. After each line is drawn, the endpoint of that line becomes the "last point referenced" for the next DRAW statement. The possible directions are: U (up), D (down), L (left), R (right), E (northeast), F (southeast), G (southwest), H (northwest). If Y is one of these directions and *n* is a number, then the statement DRAW "Y*n*" draws a line of *n* units in the specified direction. If a direction is preceded by N, the last point referenced will not change after the line is drawn. If a direction is preceded by B, an invisible line will be drawn and the last point referenced will change to the endpoint of that line. Several such statements may be combined into a statement of the form DRAW "Y*n* Z*m* . . .". Some other variations of the DRAW statement are:

DRAW "A*n*"	draw subsequent lines rotated by *n**90 degrees
DRAW "C*n*"	draw subsequent lines in color *n* of the current palette
DRAW "M*x*,*y*"	draw a line from the last point referenced to (*x*,*y*) [Preceding *x* or *y* with a plus sign or minus sign causes relative coordinates to be used.]
DRAW "P*c*,*b*"	fill in the closed region of boundary color *b* containing the last point referenced with the color *c* of the current palette
DRAW "S*n*"	change the unit scale to *n*/4 of the original scale
DRAW "TA*n*"	draw subsequent lines rotated by *n* degrees

DRAW statements can use numeric variables to provide the numeric arguments of commands by employing the STR$ function. For instance, the statement DRAW "M 100,25" may be written as *x*=100: *y*=25: DRAW "M" + STR$(*x*) + "," + STR$(*y*). [7], [8], [6]

$DYNAMIC The metacommand REM $DYNAMIC specifies that any array dimensioned after this point in the program should have its memory allocated dynamically at run time. Dynamic arrays have the advantage that you may ERASE them to free up memory or REDIMension them to change their size. Array memory allocation is automatically dynamic if the array is local to a non-STATIC procedure, the array is DIMensioned using a variable, or the array is declared in a COMMON or REDIM statement. [16], [17]

END The statement END terminates the execution of the program and closes all files. Also, the statements END DEF, END FUNCTION, END IF, END SELECT, END SUB, and END TYPE are used to denote the conclusion of multiline function definitions, function blocks, IF blocks, SELECT CASE blocks, subprograms, and user-defined record type declarations.

ENVIRON QBasic has an environment table consisting of equations of the form "*name=value*" that is inherited from DOS when QBasic is invoked. The

ENVIRON statement is used to alter this table. The statement ENVIRON "*name*=;" removes any equation whose left side is *name*. The statement ENVIRON "*name*=*value*" places the equation in quotes in the table.

ENVIRON$ If *name* is the left side of an equation in QBasic's environment table, then the value of the function ENVIRON$("*name*") will be the string consisting of the right side of the equation. The value of ENVIRON$(*n*) is the *n*th equation in QBasic's environment table.

EOF Suppose a file has been opened for input with reference number *n*. The value of the function EOF(*n*) will be –1 (true) if the end of the file has been reached and 0 (false) otherwise. (***Note:*** The logical condition NOT EOF(*n*) is true until the end of the file is reached.) When used with a communications file, EOF(*n*) will be true if the communications buffer is empty and false if the buffer contains data.

EQV The logical expression *condition1* EQV *condition2* is true (–1) if *condition1* and *condition2* are both true or both false. For example, (1>2) EQV ("xyz"<"a") is true since both 1>2 and "xyz"<"a" are false, whereas ("apple">"ape") EQV ("earth">"moon") is false (0) since "apple">"ape" is true but "earth">"moon" is false.

ERASE For static arrays, the statement ERASE *arrayName* resets each array element to its default value. For dynamic arrays, the statement ERASE *arrayName* deletes the array from memory. **Note:** After a dynamic array has been ERASEd, it may be dimensioned again. However, the number of dimensions must be the same as before. [17], [1]

**ERDEV and ERDEV$** After a device error occurs, the value of ERDEV provides information about the type of error and gives certain attributes of the device. The value of ERDEV$ is the name of the device. These functions are used in error-handling routines. [15], [10]

ERR and ERL After an error occurs during the execution of a program, the value of the function ERR will be a number identifying the type of error, and the value of the function ERL will be the line number of the program statement in which the error occurred. (If the statement containing the error has no line number, then the nearest line number preceding it is returned. If no line number precedes it, a value of 0 is returned.) These functions are used in error-trapping routines. [15]

ERROR The statement ERROR *n* simulates the occurrence of the run-time error identified by the number *n*, where *n* may range from 0 to 255. It is a useful debugging tool.

EXIT The EXIT statement may be used in any of the five forms EXIT FOR, EXIT SUB, EXIT FUNCTION, EXIT DEF, and EXIT DO. The EXIT statement causes program execution to jump out of the specified structure prematurely: EXIT FOR jumps out of a FOR/NEXT loop to the statement following NEXT, EXIT SUB jumps out of a subprogram to the statement following the CALL statement, and so on.

EXP The value of the function EXP(x) is e^x, where e (about 2.71828) is the base of the natural logarithm function.

FIELD With the buffer method of handling random-access files, a statement of the form FIELD #n, *w1* AS *strvar1*, *w2* AS *strvar2*, . . . partitions each record of the file with reference number *n* into fields of widths *w1*, *w2*, . . . and names *strvar1*, *strvar2*, ... The sum *w1* + *w2* + . . . usually equals (but must not exceed) the record length specified when the file was opened. The GET statement assigns values directly to the string variables *strvar1*, *strvar2*, ...

FILEATTR After a file has been opened with reference number *n*, the value of the function FILEATTR (*n*,1) is 1, 2, 4, 8, or 32, depending upon whether the file was opened for INPUT, OUTPUT, APPEND, RANDOM, or BINARY, respectively. The value of the function FILEATTR (*n*,2) is the file's DOS file handle, a number that uniquely identifies the file and is used in assembly-language programming.

FILES The statement FILES *path* produces a listing of the files in the directory specified by *path*. Variations of the statement produce selected sublistings. If *path* is not included, FILES produces a listing of all the files in the current directory of the default drive. [3]

FIX The value of the function FIX(*x*) is the whole number obtained by discarding the decimal part of the number *x*.

FOR/NEXT The statement FOR *index* = *a* TO *b* STEP *s* sets the value of the variable *index* to *a* and repeatedly executes the statements between itself and the statement NEXT *index*. Each time the NEXT statement is reached, *s* is added to the value of *index*. This process continues until the value of *index* passes *b*. Although the numbers *a*, *b*, and *s* may have any numeric type, the lower the precision of the type, the faster the loop executes. The statement FOR *index* = *a* TO *b* is equivalent to the statement FOR *index* = *a* TO *b* STEP 1. The index following the word NEXT is optional.

FRE At any time, the value of the function FRE("") or FRE(0) is the amount of memory available for storing new string data. The value of the function FRE(– 1) is the number of memory locations available for new numeric arrays. This function is useful in determining whether or not sufficient memory remains to declare a new numeric array. The value of FRE(–2) is the smallest amount of space on the stack that has existed at any time during the execution of the program. For *n* different than –1 or –2, the value of FRE(*n*) is the same as the value of FRE(0).

FREEFILE When files are opened, they are assigned a reference number from 1 to 255. At any time, the value of the function FREEFILE is the next available reference number.

FUNCTION A function is a multistatement block beginning with a statement of the form FUNCTION *FunctionName*(*parList*), followed on subsequent lines by one or more statements for carrying out the task of the function, and ending with the statement END FUNCTION. The parameter list, *parList*, is a list of variables through which values will be passed to the function when the function is called. Parameter types may be numeric, (variable-length) string, user-defined record type, or array. The types of the parameters may be specified with type-declaration tags, DEFtype statements, or AS clauses. Array names appearing in the parameter list should be followed by an empty pair of parentheses. Functions are named with the same conventions as variables, except that the name may not begin with FN. The value of a variable argument used in calling a function may be altered by the function unless the variable is surrounded by parentheses. Variables are local to the function unless declared as STATIC or SHARED. A statement of the form FUNCTION *FunctionName*(*parList*) STATIC specifies that all variables local to the function be treated as static by default; that is, they are invisible outside of the function but retain their values between function calls. Functions may invoke themselves (called *recursion*) or other procedures. However, no procedure may be defined inside of a function.

GET (Files) User-defined record types provide an efficient means of working with random-access files. After a user-defined record type is defined and a variable of that type, call it *recVar*, is declared, the file is opened with a length equal to LEN (*recVar*). The *r*th record of the random-access file is retrieved and assigned to *recVar* with the statement GET #*n*,*r*,*recVar*.

The GET statement is also used to retrieve data from a binary file and assign it to any type of variable. Suppose *var* is a variable that holds a value consisting of *b* bytes. (For instance, if *var* is an integer variable, then *b* is 2. If *var* is an ordinary string variable, then *b* will equal the length of the string currently assigned to it.) The statement GET #*n*,*p*,*var* assigns to the variable *var* the *b* consecutive bytes beginning with the byte in position *p* of the binary file having reference number *n*. (**Note:** The positions are numbered 1, 2, 3, ...) If *p* is omitted, then the current file position is used as the beginning position.

With the buffer method of working with random-access files, the statement GET #*n*,*r* retrieves record number *r* from the random-access file having reference number *n* and assigns the record's values to the variables appearing in FIELD statements. (If *r* is omitted, the record after the one most recently accessed by a GET or PUT statement is retrieved.) [11], [12]

GET (Graphics) A graphics statement of the form GET (*x1*,*y1*)–(*x2*,*y2*), *arrayName* stores a description of the rectangular portion of the screen having upper left-hand corner (*x1*,*y1*) and lower right-hand corner (*x2*,*y2*) in the array *arrayName*. The rectangular region can then be duplicated at another location of the screen with a PUT statement. GET and PUT statements are the key tools for animation. [8]

GOSUB A statement of the form GOSUB *label* causes a jump to the statement beginning at *label*. When the statement RETURN is reached, the program jumps back to the statement following the GOSUB statement. **Note:** Both the GOSUB statement and its target must be in the same part of the program, either both in the main body or both in a single procedure. [13], [14]

GOTO The statement GOTO *label* causes an unconditional jump to the first statement after the specified label. **Note:** The GOTO statement and its target must be in the same part of the program. [13]

HEX$ If *n* is a whole number from 0 to 2,147,483,647, then the value of the function HEX$(*n*) is the string consisting of the hexadecimal representation of *n*.

IF (single line) A statement of the form IF *condition* THEN *action* causes the program to take the specified action if *condition* is true. Otherwise, execution continues at the next line. A statement of the form IF *condition* THEN *action1* ELSE *action2* causes the program to take *action1* if *condition* is true and *action2* if *condition* is false.

IF (block) A block of statements beginning with a statement of the form IF *condition* THEN and ending with the statement END IF, indicates that the group of statements between IF and END IF are to be executed only when *condition* is true. If the group of statements is separated into two parts by an ELSE statement, then the first part will be executed when *condition* is true and the second part when *condition* is false. Statements of the form ELSEIF *condition* may also appear and define groups of statements to be executed when alternate conditions are true.

IMP The logical expression *condition1* IMP *condition2* is true except when *condition1* is true and *condition2* is false. For example, (3<7) IMP ("abc">"a") is true since both 3<7 and "abc">"a" are true, while ("apple">"ape") IMP ("earth">"moon") is false since "apple">"ape" is true but "earth">"moon" is false.

**INKEY$** The statement *a$* = INKEY$ assigns to the variable *a$* the one- or two-character string that identifies the next keystroke waiting in the keyboard buffer. Number, letters, and symbols are identified by a single character. Keys such as F1, Home, and Ins are identified by two characters, CHR$(0) followed by CHR$(*n*), where *n* is the "scan code" for the key. If no keystroke is waiting, the null string, "", is assigned to *a$*.

INP The value of the function INP(*n*) is the value of the byte read from port *n*. [10]

INPUT A statement of the form INPUT *var* causes the computer to display a question mark and to pause until the user enters a response. This response is then assigned to the variable *var*. Statements of the form INPUT "*prompt*"; *var* insert a prompting message before the question mark, statements of the form INPUT "*prompt*", *var* display the prompt without the question mark, and statements of the form INPUT; *var* suppress a carriage return following the entering of the response. In each of these statements *var* may be replaced by a number of variables separated by commas. After the user responds with the proper number of values (separated by commas) and presses Enter, each of the values is assigned to the corresponding variable.

INPUT# The statement INPUT #*n*, *var* reads the next item of data from a sequential file that has been opened for INPUT with reference number *n* and assigns the item to the variable *var*. The statement INPUT #*n*, *var1*, *var2*, . . . reads a sequence of values and assigns them to the variables.

**INPUT$** A statement of the form *a$* = INPUT$(*n*) causes the program to pause until the user types *n* characters. The string consisting of these *n* characters is then assigned to *a$*. The statement *a$* = INPUT$(*n*,*m*) assigns the next *n* characters from the file with reference number *m* to *a$*.

INSTR The value of the function INSTR(*a$*,*b$*) is the position of the string *b$* in the string *a$*. The value of INSTR(*n*,*a$*,*b$*) is the first position at or after the *n*th character of *a$* at which the string *b$* occurs. If *b$* does not appear as a substring of *a$*, then the value is 0.

INT The value of the function INT(*x*) is the greatest whole number that is less than or equal to *x*.

INTEGER A variable of type INTEGER requires 2 bytes of memory and can hold the whole numbers from –32,768 to 32,767. INTEGER values and variables are indicated by the type tag %: 345%, Count%.

IOCTL and IOCTL$ After a device has been opened with reference number *n*, the value of the function IOCTL$(*n*) is a control string read from the device driver, and a statement of the form IOCTL #*n*, *a$* sends the string *a$* to the driver. [10]

KEY The statement KEY *n*, *a$* assigns the string *a$* to function key F*n*. The string *a$* must have length 15 or less, and *n* may be any number from 1 to 10 (and also 30 and 31 for function keys F11 and F12 on the 101-key keyboards). After KEY *n*, *a$* is executed, pressing the key F*n* has the same effect as typing the characters in *a$*. The statement KEY ON may be used to display the first six characters of the assigned strings on the last row of the Output window. The statement KEY OFF turns this display off. The statement KEY LIST displays all the assigned strings in their entirety.

KEY(*n*) The statement ON KEY(*n*) GOSUB *label* sets up the trapping of function key *n*. After KEY(*n*) ON is executed, pressing F*n* at any time causes program control to transfer to the subroutine beginning at *label*. Trapping is disabled with KEY(*n*) OFF and deferred with KEY(*n*) STOP. The subroutine at *label* must be in the main body of the program (or after its END statement). [15], [13], [14]

KILL The statement KILL "*filespec*" erases the specified disk file. [4]

LBOUND For a one-dimensional array *arrayName*, the value of the function LBOUND(*arrayName*) is the smallest subscript value that may be used. For any array *arrayName*, the value of the function LBOUND(*arrayName*, *n*) is the smallest subscript value that may be used for the *n*th subscript of the array. For example, after the statement DIM example(1 TO 31,1 TO 12,1990 TO 1999) is executed, the value of LBOUND(example, 3) is the smallest value allowed for the third subscript of example(), which is 1990.

**LCASE$** The value of the string function LCASE$(*a$*) is a string identical to *a$* except that all uppercase letters are changed to lowercase.

**LEFT$** The value of the function LEFT$(*a$*,*n*) is the string consisting of the leftmost *n* characters of *a$*. If *n* is greater than the number of characters in *a$*, then the value of the function is a$.

LEN The value of LEN(*a$*) is the number of characters in the string *a$*. If *var* is not a variable-length string variable, then the value of LEN(*var*) is the number of bytes needed to hold the value of the variable in memory. That is, LEN(*var*) is 2, 4, 4, or 8 for integer, long integer, single-precision, and double-precision variables. LEN(*var*), when *var* is a variable with a user-defined record type, is the number of bytes of memory needed to store the value of the variable.

LET The statement LET *var* = *expr* assigns the value of the expression to the variable. If *var* is a fixed-length string variable with length *n* and LEN(*expr*) is greater than *n*, then just the first *n* characters of *expr* are assigned to *var*. If LEN(*expr*) < n, then *expr* is padded on the right with spaces and assigned to *var*. If *var* has a user-defined type, then *expr* must be of the same type. The statement *var* = *expr* is equivalent to LET *var* = *expr*.

LINE The graphics statement LINE (*x1*,*y1*)–(*x2*,*y2*) draws a line connecting the two points. (If the first point is omitted, then the line is drawn from the last point referenced to the specified point.) The line is in color *c* of the current palette if LINE (*x1*,*y1*)–(*x2*,*y2*),*c* is executed. The statement LINE (*x1*,*y1*)–

(*x2*,*y2*),,*B* draws a rectangle with the two points as opposite vertices. (If B is replaced by BF, a solid rectangle is drawn.) If *s* is a number in hexadecimal notation from 0 to &HFFFF, then LINE (*x1*,*y1*)–(*x2*,*y2*),,,*s* draws a styled line (with the pattern determined by *s*) connecting the two points. [7], [8], [6]

LINE INPUT The statements LINE INPUT *a$*, LINE INPUT "*prompt*"; *a$*, and LINE INPUT "*prompt*", *a$* are similar to the corresponding INPUT statements. However, the user may respond with *any* string, even one containing commas, leading spaces, and quotation marks. The entire string is assigned to the string variable *a$*.

LINE INPUT# After a file has been opened as a sequential file for INPUT with reference number *n*, the statement LINE INPUT #*n*, *a$* assigns to the string variable *a$* the string of characters from the current location in the file up to the next pair of carriage-return/line-feed characters.

LOC This function gives the current location in a sequential, random-access, or binary file. For a sequential file with reference number *n*, LOC(*n*) is the number of blocks of 128 characters read from or written to the file since it was opened. For a random-access file, LOC(*n*) is the current record (either the last record read or written, or the record identified in a SEEK statement). For a binary file, LOC(*n*) is the number of bytes from the beginning of the file to the last byte read or written. For communications, the value of LOC(*n*) is the number of bytes waiting in the communications buffer with reference number *n*. [12]

LOCATE The statement LOCATE *r*,*c* positions the cursor at row *r*, column *c* of the screen. The statement LOCATE,,0 turns the display of the cursor off, while the statement LOCATE,,1 turns the display back on. If *m* and *n* are whole numbers between 0 and 31, then the statement LOCATE,,,*m*,*n* will change the size of the cursor.

LOCK The LOCK command is intended for use in programs that operate on a network. The DOS command SHARE enables file sharing and should be executed from DOS prior to using the LOCK statement. After a file has been opened with reference number *n*, the statement LOCK #*n* denies access to the file by any other process. For a random-access file, the statement LOCK #*n*, *r1* TO *r2* denies access to records *r1* through *r2* by any other process. For a binary file, this statement denies access to bytes *r1* through *r2*. The statement LOCK #*n*, *r1* locks only record (or byte) *r1*. For a sequential file, all forms of the LOCK statement have the same effect as LOCK #*n*. The UNLOCK statement is used to remove locks from files. All locks should be removed before a file is closed or the program is terminated. [11], [12]

LOF After a file has been opened with reference number *n*, the number of characters in the file (that is, the length of the file) is given by LOF(*n*). For communications, the value of LOF(*n*) equals the number of bytes waiting in the communications buffer with reference number *n*.

LOG If *x* is a positive number, then the value of LOG(*x*) is the natural logarithm (base *e*) of *x*.

LONG A variable of type LONG requires 4 bytes of memory and can hold the whole numbers from –2,147,483,648 to 2,147,483,647. LONG values and variables are indicated by the type tag &: 12345678&, Population&.

LPOS Printers have buffers that hold characters until they are ready to be printed. The value of LPOS(1) is the current position in the buffer of the first printer (LPT1), and LPOS(2) is the current position for the second printer (LPT2).

LPRINT and LPRINT USING These statements print data on the printer in the same way PRINT and PRINT USING display data on the screen. In addition, LPRINT may be used to set various print modes, such as the width of the characters and the vertical spacing.

LSET If *af$* is a field variable of a random-access file, then the statement LSET *af$* = *b$* assigns the string *b$*, possibly truncated or padded on the right with spaces, to *af$*. If *a$* is an ordinary variable, then the statement LSET *a$* = *b$* replaces the value of *a$* with a string of the same length consisting of *b$* truncated or padded on the right with spaces. LSET also can be used to assign a record of one user-defined type to a record of a different user-defined type. [11]

**LTRIM$** The value of the function LTRIM$(*a$*) is the string obtained by removing all the spaces from the beginning of the string *a$*. The string *a$* may be of either fixed or variable length.

**MID$** The value of the function MID$(*a$*,*m*,*n*) is the substring of *a$* beginning with the *m*th character of *a$* and containing up to *n* characters. If the parameter *n* is omitted, MID$(*a$*,*m*) is all the characters of *a$* from the *m*th character on. The statement MID$(*a$*,*m*,*n*) = *b$* replaces the characters of *a$*, beginning with the *m*th character, by the first *n* characters of the string *b$*.

MKDIR The statement MKDIR *path\dirName* creates a subdirectory named *dirName* in the directory specified by *path*. [3]

MKI$, MKL$, MKS$, MKD$ These functions convert integer, long integer, single-precision, and double-precision numbers into strings of lengths 2, 4, 4, and 8, respectively. This conversion is needed with the buffer method of working with random-access files. [11]

MKSMBF$, MKDMBF$ With the buffer method of working with random-access files, these functions convert single-precision and double-precision numbers into strings of lengths 4 and 8, respectively, in the Microsoft Binary Format. This conversion is necessary before placing these numbers into random-access files that will be read with Microsoft BASIC, GW-BASIC, BASICA, or early versions of QuickBasic. [11]

MOD The value of the expression *num1* MOD *num2* is the whole-number remainder when *num1* is divided by *num2*. If either *num1* or *num2* is not a whole number, then it is rounded to a whole number before the MOD operation is performed. If one or both of *num1* and *num2* are negative, the result of the MOD operation will have the same sign as *num1*. For example, 25 MOD 7 is 4, 18.7 MOD 3.2 is 1, –35 MOD –4 is –3, and 27 MOD –6 is 3.

NAME The statement NAME "*filespec1*" AS "*filespec2*" is used to change the name and/or the directory of *filespec1* to the name and/or directory specified by *filespec2*. The two filespecs must refer to the same drive. [4]

NOT (Logical Operator) The logical expression NOT *condition1* is true if *condition1* is false and false if *condition1* is true. For example, NOT (3<7) is false since 3<7 is true, while NOT ("earth">"moon") is true since "earth">"moon" is false.

NOT (Bitwise Operator) The expression NOT *byte1* is evaluated by expressing the byte as an 8-tuple binary number and then NOTting each individual digit, where NOT 1 is equal to 0, while NOT 0 is equal to 1. For example, the expression NOT 37 translated to binary 8-tuples becomes NOT 00100101. NOTting each digit gives the binary 8-tuple 11011010 or decimal 218, thus NOT 37 is 218.

OCT$ If *n* is a whole number between 0 and 2,147,483,647, then OCT$(*n*) is the octal (that is, base 8) representation of *n*.

ON COM(n) If *n* is the number 1 or 2, then the statement ON COM(*n*) GOSUB *label* sets up the trapping of the *n*th communications port. After COM(*n*) ON is executed, information coming into the port causes a GOSUB to *label*. The subroutine at *label* must be in the main body of the program (or after its END statement). [15], [10], [13], [14]

ON ERROR The statement ON ERROR GOTO *label* sets up error trapping. An error then causes a jump to an error-handling routine beginning at *label*. The label must be in the main body of the program. See the discussion of RESUME for further details. [15], [13]

ON. . .GOSUB and ON. . .GOTO The statement ON *expression* GOSUB *label1*, *label2*, . . . causes a GOSUB to *label1*, *label2*, . . . depending upon whether the value of the expression is 1, 2, ... Similarly, the GOTO variation causes an unconditional jump to the appropriate label. The GOSUB or GOTO statement and its target must be in the same part of the program, either both in the main body or both in the same procedure. [13]

ON KEY(*n*) The statement ON KEY(*n*) GOSUB *label* sets up trapping of the function key F*n*. After KEY(*n*) ON is executed, pressing F*n* causes a GOSUB to *label*. The subroutine at *label* must be in the main body of the program (or after its END statement). [15], [13], [14]

ON PEN The statement ON PEN GOSUB *label* sets up trapping of a light pen. After PEN ON is executed, pressing the metal clip on the light pen or pressing the light pen to the screen, as appropriate, causes a GOSUB to *label*. The subroutine at *label* must be in the main body of the program (or after its END statement). [15], [13], [14]

ON PLAY(*n*) The music background buffer holds notes that have been specified by PLAY statements and are waiting to be played. If *n* is a whole number, then the statement ON PLAY(*n*) GOSUB *label* sets up trapping of the music buffer. After PLAY ON is executed, as soon as the number of notes in the buffer falls below *n*, the program GOSUBs to *label*. The capacity of the music background buffer is 32 notes, counting pauses between notes as notes. The subroutine at *label* must be in the main body of the program (or after its END statement). [15], [13], [14]

ON STRIG(*n*) If *n* is 0, 2, 4, or 6, the statement ON STRIG(*n*) GOSUB *label* sets up trapping of one of the joystick buttons. The numbers 0 and 4 are associated with the lower and upper buttons of the first joystick and the numbers 2 and 6 are associated with the lower and upper buttons of the second joystick.

After STRIG(*n*) ON is executed, pressing the button associated with *n* causes a GOSUB to *label*. The subroutine at *label* must be in the main body of the program (or after its END statement). [15], [13], [14]

ON TIMER If *n* is an integer from 1 to 86400 (1 second to 24 hours), the statement ON TIMER(*n*) GOSUB *label* sets up trapping of the computer's internal clock. After TIMER ON is executed, every *n* seconds the program GOSUBs to the subroutine beginning at *label*. The subroutine at *label* must be in the main body of the program (or after its END statement). [15], [13], [14]

OPEN The statement OPEN "*filespec*" FOR *mode* AS #*n* allows access to the file *filespec* in one of the following modes: INPUT (information can be read sequentially from the file), OUTPUT (a new file is created and information can be written sequentially to it), APPEND (information can be added sequentially to the end of a file), or BINARY (information can be read or written in an arbitrary fashion). The statement OPEN "*filespec*" FOR RANDOM AS #*n* LEN = *g* allows random access to the file *filespec* in which each record has length *g*. Throughout the program, the file is referred to by the reference number *n* (from 1 through 255). Some other variations of the OPEN statement are OPEN "SCRN" FOR OUTPUT AS #*n*, OPEN "LPT1" FOR OUTPUT AS #*n*, and OPEN "KYBD" FOR INPUT AS #*n*, which allow access to the screen, printer, and keyboard as if they were sequential files. [4], [12]

DOS 3.0 and later versions support networking and make possible two enhancements to the OPEN statement. (The DOS command SHARE enables file sharing and should be executed from DOS prior to the use of the enhanced variations of the OPEN statement.) QBasic accesses data files in two ways; it reads from them or writes to them. When several processes may utilize a file at the same time, accurate file handling requires that certain types of access be denied to anyone but the person who has opened the file. The statement OPEN *filespec* FOR *mode* LOCK READ AS #*n* or OPEN "*filespec*" FOR RANDOM LOCK READ AS #*n* LEN = *g* opens the specified file and forbids any other process from reading the file as long as the file is open. LOCK WRITE forbids any other process from writing to the file as long as the file is open. LOCK READ WRITE forbids any other process from reading or writing to the file as long as the file is open. LOCK SHARED grants full access to any other process. Except with LOCK SHARED, if a file is currently opened and locked by a process for a certain access mode, then another process attempting to open the file for the same mode will receive the message "Permission denied" and be denied access.

OPEN "COM... If *n* is 1 through 4, then the statement OPEN "COM*n*:*b*,*p*,*d*,*s*,*L*" AS #*m* LEN=*g* provides access to the *n*th serial port using reference number *m* and specifies the block size (*g*), the speed of transmission (*b*), the parity (*p*), the number of data bits to be used in transmitting each character (*d*), the number of stop bits (*s*), and the line parameters (*L*).

OPTION BASE After the statement OPTION BASE *m* is executed, where *m* is 0 or 1, a statement of the form DIM *arrayName*(*n*) defines an array with subscripts ranging from *m* to *n*. QBasic's extended DIM statement, which permits both lower and upper subscript bounds to be specified for each array, achieves a wider range of results, making its use preferable to OPTION BASE.

OR (Logical Operator) The logical expression *condition1* OR *condition2* is true except when both *condition1* and *condition2* are false. For example, ("apple">

"ape") OR ("earth">"moon") is true since "apple">"ape" is true, while (1>2) OR ("moon"<"earth") is false since both (1>2) and ("moon"<"earth") are false.

OR (Bitwise Operator) The expression *byte1* OR *byte2* is evaluated by expressing each byte as an 8-tuple binary number and then ORing together corresponding digits, where 1 OR 1, 1 OR 0, and 0 OR 1 are all equal to 1, while 0 AND 0 is equal to 0. For example, the expression 37 OR 157 translated to binary 8-tuples becomes 00100101 OR 10011101. ORing together corresponding digits gives the binary 8-tuple 10111101 or decimal 189. Thus 37 OR 157 is 189.

OUT The statement OUT *n*,*m* sends the byte *m* to port *n*. [10]

PAINT If (*x*,*y*) is an unlit interior point of a region of the screen, then the statement PAINT (*x*,*y*) fills the region. In medium resolution graphics mode, if the boundary has color *b* of the current palette and *c* is one of the colors of the current palette, then the statement PAINT (*x*,*y*),*c*,*b* fills the bounded region with the color *c*. If *t$* is a string of length at most 64 characters, then the statement PAINT (*x*,*y*), *t$* fills the region with a repeating pattern based on a tile determined by *t$*. [8], [6]

PALETTE and PALETTE USING When a graphics monitor is attached to an EGA, VGA, or MCGA display card, the PALETTE statement loads colors into the palette "jars" whose numbers range from 0 to 3, 0 to 15, 0 to 63, or 0 to 255. The statement PALETTE *m*, *n* assigns the *n*th color to the *m*th palette jar. The statement PALETTE USING *array*(0) specifies that each palette jar be filled with the corresponding color number stored in the array element: *array*(0) in jar 0, *array*(1) in jar 1, and so on. [5], [6]

PCOPY Depending upon the screen mode in use, the video adapter card may have extra memory locations that give it the capability of working with several screens, called *pages*. (See the discussion of the SCREEN statement for details.) For instance, with an 80-characters-per-line text mode screen, the Color Graphics Adapter has four pages. The statement PCOPY *m*,*n* copies the contents of page *m* onto page *n*.

PEEK Each memory location contains a number from 0 to 255. If *n* is a number from 0 to 65535, then the value of PEEK(*n*) is the number stored at offset *n* in the current segment of memory. [9]

PEN The statements PEN ON, PEN OFF, and PEN STOP respectively enable, disable, and defer the reading of the status of the light pen. For each *n* from 0 to 9, the value of the function PEN(*n*) gives information about the status of the light pen.

PLAY (function) The music background buffer holds notes that have been specified by PLAY statements and are waiting to be played. The value of the function PLAY(0) is the number of notes currently in the music background buffer waiting to be played.

PLAY (statement) The statement PLAY *a$*, where *a$* is a string of notes and parameters, produces musical notes with most of the embellishments indicated by sheet music. The rich and varied strings constitute a miniature music language. A note can be identified by one of the letters A through G, possibly followed by a plus or minus sign to indicate a sharp or a flat. A 1/*n*th note pause is specified by P *n*. The parameters O, L, T, MF, MB, ML, MS, and MN specify attributes of subsequent notes and are sometimes combined with a number giving a magnitude for the attribute. The parameter O *n*, where *n* ranges from 0 through 6, specifies the octave of subsequent notes. The parameter L *n*, where *n* ranges from 1 to 64, causes subsequent notes to be 1/*n*th notes. (For instance, *n* = 4 produces quarter notes.) The parameter T *n*, where *n* ranges from 32 to 255, sets the tempo of subsequent notes to *n* quarter notes per minute. The default values for the parameters O, L, and T are 4, 4, and 120, respectively. The parameter MF (music foreground) causes all notes to be played before the computer executes additional statements, while MB (music background) places up to 32 notes in a buffer that plays the notes while the program continues to execute. The parameters ML (music legato) and MS (music staccato) decrease and increase, respectively, the durations of notes; MN returns the durations to normal articulation. PLAY statements can give the numeric argument of a command as the value of a numeric variable by using the STR$ function. For instance, the statement PLAY "D8" may be written as *n* = 8: PLAY "D" + STR$(*n*).

PMAP The graphics function PMAP converts the natural coordinates of a point to the physical coordinates and vice versa, as shown in Table C.1. [8]

n	c	value of PMAP(c,n)
0	natural *x*-coordinate	physical *x*-coordinate
1	natural *y*-coordinate	physical *y*-coordinate
2	physical *x*-coordinate	natural *x*-coordinate
3	physical *y*-coordinate	natural *y*-coordinate

Table C.1 The PMAP Function

POINT In graphics mode, the value of the function POINT(*x*,*y*) is the number of the color of the point with coordinates (*x*,*y*). (With an EGA or VGA graphics card, POINT(*x*,*y*) gives the palette number assigned to the point.) The values of the functions POINT(0) and POINT(1) are the first and second physical coordinates of the last point referenced, and the values of POINT(2) and POINT(3) are the first and second natural coordinates of the last point referenced. [7], [5], [8], [6]

POKE Each memory location contains a number from 0 to 255. If *n* is a number from 0 to 65535, then the statement POKE *n*,*m* stores the number *m* at offset *n* in the current segment of memory. [9]

POS The value of the function POS(0) is the column number of the current position of the cursor.

PRESET (See PSET.)

PRINT The PRINT statement is used to display data on the screen. The statement PRINT *expression* displays the value of the expression at the current position of the cursor and moves the cursor to the beginning of the next row of the screen. (Numbers are displayed with a trailing space and positive numbers with a leading space.) If the statement is followed by a semicolon or comma, then the cursor will not move to the next row after the display, but rather will move to the next position or print zone, respectively. Several expressions may be placed in the same PRINT statement if separated by semicolons (to display them adjacent to one another) or by commas (to display them in successive zones).

PRINT USING The statement PRINT USING *a$*; *list of expressions* displays the values of the expressions (possibly interspersed with text from *a$*) in formats specified by *a$*. The statement can be used to align and display financial quantities with dollar signs, commas, asterisks, two decimal places, and preceding or trailing signs (+ or –). Numbers are formatted with the symbols #, +, $, $$, *, **, ^^^^, comma, and period. Strings are formatted with the symbols &, !, and \ \. See Tables C.2 and C.3. ***Note:*** If you wish to use one of the above special symbols for text in a format string, you must precede it with an underscore (_).

Symbol	Meaning	*n*	*a$*	Result
#	Each sharp symbol stands for one digit in a numeric field	1234.6	"########"	1235
		123	"########"	123
		123.4	"########"	123
		12345	"####"	%12345
.	Denotes the placement of the decimal point	123.4	"######.#"	123.4
,	Causes commas to be displayed to the left of every third digit to the left of the decimal point, as appropriate	12345	"#######,"	12,345
$	Displays a $ sign as the first character of the field	23.45	"$####.##"	$ 23.45
$$	Displays a $ sign immediately before the first digit displayed	23.45	"$$###.##"	$23.45
**	Inserts asterisks in place of leading blanks	23.45	"**######"	******23
*	Displays an asterisk as the first character of the field	23.45	"*#######"	* 23
^^^^	(at end) Displays the number in exponential notation	12345	"##.#^^^^"	1.2E+04
		–12	"#.##^^^^"	–.12E+01
^^^^^	(at end) Displays the number in expanded exponential notation	12345	"#.#^^^^^"	1.2E+004
+	Reserves a space for the sign of the variable	12	"+#######"	+12
		–12	"######+"	12–

Table C.2 Results Obtained from Executing PRINT USING *a$*; *n*

a$	Meaning	*x$*	Result
&	Display entire string	"Nebraska"	Nebraska
!	Display first letter of string	"Nebraska"	N
\ \	Display first *n* letters of string (where there are *n*–2 spaces between the slashes)	"Nebraska"	Nebr

Table C.3 Results Obtained by Executing PRINT USING *a$*; *x$*

PRINT# and PRINT# USING After a file has been opened as a sequential file for output or append with reference number *n*, the statements PRINT #*n*,*expression* and PRINT #*n*,USING *a$*;*expression* place the value of the expression into the file in the same way PRINT and PRINT USING display it on the screen.

PSET and **PRESET** In graphics modes, the statement PSET (*x*,*y*) displays the point with coordinates (*x*,*y*) in the foreground color and the statement PRESET (*x*,*y*) displays it in the background color. The statement PSET (*x*,*y*),*c* or the statement PRESET(*x*,*y*),*c* causes the point (*x*,*y*) to be displayed in color *c* of the current palette. [7], [5], [8], [6]

PUT (Files) With the buffer method of working with random-access files, after the file has been opened with reference number *n* and values have been assigned to the field variables, the statement PUT #*n*,*r* places these values in the *r*th record of the file. (If *r* is omitted, the record after the one most recently accessed by a GET or PUT statement will be filled.)

Suppose *recVar* is a variable of a user-defined record type and that a file has been opened with a statement of the form OPEN "*filespec*" FOR RANDOM AS #*n* LEN = LEN(*recVar*). The statement PUT #*n*,*r*,*recVar* places the value of *recVar* in the *r*th record of the file.

The PUT statement is also used to place data into a file opened as a binary file. Suppose *var* is a variable that holds a value consisting of *b* bytes. (For instance, if *var* is an integer variable, then *b* is 2. If *var* is an ordinary string variable, then *b* will equal the length of the string currently assigned to it.) The statement PUT #*n*,*p*,*var* writes the successive bytes of *var* into the *b* consecutive locations beginning with position *p* in the binary file with reference number *n*. (**Note:** The positions are numbered 1, 2, 3, ...) If *p* is omitted, then the current file position is used as the beginning position. [11], [12]

PUT (Graphics) After a rectangular region of the screen has been stored in the array *arrayName* by a GET statement, the statement PUT (*x*,*y*),*arrayName*,PSET places an exact image of the rectangular region on the screen positioned with its upper left-hand corner at the point (*x*,*y*). The following list shows the possible alternatives to PSET in the statement and the conditions in which points on the high-resolution graphics screen will be white after PUT is executed for each alternative. [7], [8]

The point in the resulting graphic image will be white when using:

XOR	if the corresponding point is white in either the stored image or the original screen image, but not both (default).
AND	if the corresponding point is white in the stored image and also in the original screen image.
OR	if the corresponding point is white in either the stored image or the original screen image or both.
PRESET	if the corresponding point is black in the stored image.

RANDOMIZE The statement RANDOMIZE TIMER automatically uses the computer's clock to seed the random-number generator. RANDOMIZE by itself requests a seed, and RANDOMIZE *n* seeds the generator with a number determined by *n*. If the random-number generator is not seeded, the same list of numbers will be generated by RND each time a program is executed.

READ The statement READ *var1*, *var2*, . . . assigns to *var1* the first unused constant stored in a DATA statement, to *var2* the next unused constant, and so on.

REDIM The statement REDIM *arrayName*(. . .) erases the array from memory and recreates it. The information inside the parentheses has the same form and produces the same result as that in a DIM statement. After the REDIMensioning, all elements have their default values. Although the ranges of the subscripts may be changed, the number of dimensions must be the same as in the original DIMensioning of the array. Inserting SHARED right after REDIM in a REDIM statement in the main body of a program allows all procedures in the program to share the array. Only dynamic arrays may be redimensioned. [17], [1]

REM The statement REM allows documentation to be placed in a program. A line of the form REM *comment* is ignored during execution. The REM statement is also used to place metacommands into the program. The REM statement may be abbreviated as an apostrophe.

RESET The statement RESET closes all open files. Using RESET is equivalent to using CLOSE with no file reference numbers.

RESTORE The statement RESTORE *label* causes the next request to READ an item of data to take the first item in the DATA statement following the indicated label. If the *label* parameter is omitted, the first DATA statement in the program will be accessed. Subsequent READ statements will continue selecting data from that point on. [13]

RESUME When the statement RESUME is encountered at the end of an error-handling routine, the program branches back to the statement in which the error was encountered. The variations RESUME *label* and RESUME NEXT cause the program to branch to the statement at the indicated label or to the statement following the statement in which the error occurred, respectively. (The combination of ON ERROR and RESUME NEXT is similar to the combination GOSUB and RETURN.) [13]

RETURN When the statement RETURN is encountered at the end of a subroutine, the program branches back to the statement following the one containing the most recently executed GOSUB. The variation RETURN *label* causes the program to branch back to the statement following the indicated label. [13], [14]

**RIGHT$** The value of the function RIGHT$(*a$*,*n*) is the string consisting of the rightmost *n* characters of *a$*. If *n* is greater than the number of characters of *a$*, then the value of the function is *a$*.

RMDIR If *path* specifies a directory containing no files or subdirectories, then the statement RMDIR *path* removes the directory. [3]

RND The value of the function RND is a randomly selected number from 0 to 1, not including 1. The value of INT(*n**RND)+1 is a random whole number from 1 to *n*.

RSET If *af$* is a field variable of a random-access file, then the statement RSET *af$* = *b$* assigns the string *b$* to *af$*, possibly truncated or padded on the left with spaces. If *a$* is an ordinary variable, then the statement RSET *a$* = *b$* replaces the value of *a$* with a string of the same length consisting of *b$* truncated or padded on the left with spaces. [11]

**RTRIM$** The value of the function RTRIM$(*a$*) is the string obtained by removing all the spaces from the end of the string *a$*. The string *a$* may be of either fixed or variable length.

RUN The statement RUN restarts the currently executing program. All values previously assigned to variables are deleted. The variation RUN "*filespec*" loads the specified program from a disk and executes it. The specified program must be a QBasic program. The statement RUN *label* restarts the current program at the point referenced. [4], [13]

SADD The value of the function SADD(a$) is the offset of the variable-length string *a$* in DGROUP, the default data segment. [9]

SCREEN (Function) The value of the function SCREEN(*r*,*c*) is the ASCII value of the character in the *r*th row, *c*th column of the screen. The value of SCREEN(*r*,*c*,1) is the number of the palette jar used to color the character. [6]

SCREEN (Statement) A monitor can be placed in the desired screen mode by one of the statements in Table C.4.

SCREEN 0	text mode
SCREEN 1	320×200 medium-resolution graphics mode, four colors
SCREEN 2	640×200 high-resolution graphics mode, two colors
SCREEN 3	720×348 Hercules graphics mode, two colors
SCREEN 7	320×200 16-color EGA, VGA adapters
SCREEN 8	640×200 16-color EGA, VGA adapters
SCREEN 9	640×350 4- to 16-color EGA, VGA adapters
SCREEN 10	640×350 monochrome EGA adapters
SCREEN 11	640×480 2-color MCGA, VGA adapters
SCREEN 12	640×480 16-color VGA only
SCREEN 13	320×200 256-color MCGA, VGA adapters

Table C.4 The SCREEN Statement

When a graphics adapter is used in text mode, the computer can store the contents of several different screens, called *pages*. The number of pages allowed, call it *n*, depends on the graphics adapter and selected mode. At any time, the page currently displayed is called the *visual* page and the page currently being written to is called the *active* page. If *a* and *v* are numbers from 0 to (*n*–*1*), then the statement SCREEN ,,*a*,*v* designates page *a* as the active page and page *v* as the visual page. [5]

SEEK The statement SEEK #*n*,*p* sets the current file position in the binary or random-access file referenced by *n* to the *p*th byte or record of the file, respectively. After the statement is executed, the next GET or PUT statement will read or write bytes, respectively, beginning with the *p*th byte or record. The value of the function SEEK(*n*) is the current file position either in bytes or by record number. After a PUT or GET statement is executed, the value of SEEK(*n*) is the number of the next byte or record. [12]

SELECT CASE The SELECT CASE statement provides a compact method of selecting for execution one of several blocks of statements based on the value of an expression. The SELECT CASE block begins with a line of the form SELECT CASE *expression* and ends with the statement END SELECT. In between are statements of the form CASE *valueList* and perhaps the statement CASE ELSE. The items in the *valueList* may be individual values or ranges of values, such as "*a* TO *b*" or "IS < *a*". Each of these CASE statements is followed by a block of one or more statements. The block of statements following the first CASE *valueList* statement for which *valueList* includes the value of *expression* is the only block of statements executed. If none of the value lists include the value of *expression* and a CASE ELSE statement is present, then the block of statements following the CASE ELSE statement is executed.

SETMEM The far heap is the area of memory where variables outside the default data segment are stored. The SETMEM function both alters and returns the size of the far heap. The numeric expression *n* specifies the number of bytes by which to increase or decrease the far heap; the heap size is increased if *n* is positive or decreased if *n* is negative. The value of the function SETMEM(*n*) is the amount of memory in the far heap after the change.

SGN The value of the function SGN(*x*) is 1, 0, or –1, depending upon whether *x* is positive, zero, or negative, respectively.

SHARED A statement of the form SHARED *var1*,*var2*, . . . can be used at the beginning of a procedure to specify that variables *var1*, *var2*, . . . , are shared with the main body. The type of each variable is determined by either a type-declaration tag, a DEFtype statement, or an AS clause. If an AS clause is used in the SHARED statement, then an AS clause must be used to declare the type of the variable in the main body of the program. Any change made to a shared variable by the procedure will change the variable of the same name in the main body, and vice versa. Declaring a variable as SHARED in a procedure allows the variable to be used by both the main body and the procedure without passing it as an argument. Arrays dimensioned in the main body of the program may be shared with procedures by listing their names followed by empty parentheses in a SHARED statement.

SHELL If *c$* is a DOS command, then the statement SHELL *c$* suspends execution of the QBasic program, executes the DOS command specified by *c$*, and then resumes execution of the QBasic program. The statement SHELL by itself suspends program execution and invokes a copy of DOS. Entering the command EXIT resumes execution of the QBasic program after the SHELL statement.

SINGLE A variable of type SINGLE requires 4 bytes of memory and can hold 0, the numbers from 1.40129×10^{-45} to 3.40283×10^{38} with at most seven significant digits, and the negative of these numbers. SINGLE value and variables are indicated by the type tag !: 32.156!, Meters!.

SIN For any number *x*, the value of the trigonometric function SIN(*x*) is the sine of the angle of *x* radians. [2]

SOUND The statement SOUND *f*,*d* generates a sound of pitch *f* Hz for a duration of *d**.055 seconds. The value of *f* must be at least 37. ***Note:*** The keys of the piano have frequencies ranging from 55 to 8372 Hz.

SPACE$ If n is an integer from 0 to 32767, then the value of the function SPACE$($n$) is the string consisting of n spaces.

SPC The function SPC is used in PRINT, LPRINT, and PRINT# statements to generate spaces. For instance, the statement PRINT *a$*; SPC($n$); *b$* skips n spaces between the displays of the two strings.

SQR For any nonnegative number x, the value of the square-root function SQR(x) is the nonnegative number whose square is x.

STATIC A statement of the form STATIC *var1*,*var2*,. . . can be used at the beginning of the definition of a procedure to specify that the variables *var1*, *var2*, . . . are static local variables in the procedure. Memory for static variables is permanently set aside by QBasic, allowing static variables to retain their values between successive calls of the procedure. The type of each variable is determined by either a DEF*type* statement, a type-declaration tag, or an AS clause. Static variables have no connection to variables of the same name outside the procedure, and so may be named without regard to "outside" variables. Arrays may be declared static by listing their names followed by empty parentheses in a STATIC statement and then dimensioning them in a subsequent DIM statement.

$STATIC The metacommand REM $STATIC tells QBasic to use a static, or permanent, allocation of memory for arrays appearing in subsequent DIM statements, if possible. Effectively, the $STATIC metacommand reverses the effect of any previous $DYNAMIC metacommand by allowing arrays that are normally static by default to be allocated as static. An array is static by default if it is DIMensioned with constant upper and lower bounds, implicitly dimensioned by appearing in a statement without first being declared in a DIM statement, or DIMensioned within a STATIC procedure. [16], [17]

STICK For n = 0 or 1, the value of the function STICK(n) is the x- or y-coordinate, respectively, of the first joystick lever. For n = 2 or 3, the function gives the corresponding information for the second joystick.

STOP The statement STOP suspends the execution of a program. Execution can be resumed beginning with the first statement after the STOP statement by pressing F5.

**STR$** The STR$ function converts numbers to strings. The value of the function STR$($n$) is the string consisting of the number n in the form normally displayed by a print statement.

STRIG The statements STRIG ON and STRIG OFF, respectively, enable and disable the reading of the status of the joystick buttons. For each n from 0 to 7, the value of the function STRIG(n) gives information about the status of the joystick button.

STRIG(n) The statement ON STRIG(n) GOSUB *label* sets up the trapping of one of the joystick buttons. The numbers n = 0 and n = 4 are associated with the lower and upper buttons of the first joystick, respectively, and the numbers n = 2 and n = 6 are associated with the lower and upper buttons of the second joystick. The pressing of the corresponding button anytime after STRIG(n) ON is executed causes a GOSUB to the subroutine at *label*. [15], [13], [14]

STRING A variable of type STRING can hold a string of up to 32,767 characters. STRING values are enclosed in quotes: "January 1, 2001". STRING variables are indicated by the type tag $: *FirstName$*. A variable of type STRING**n* holds a string of *n* characters, where *n* is a whole number from 1 to 32,767. Variables of this type have no type tag and must be declared in a COMMON, DIM, SHARED, or STATIC statement. Until assigned a value, these variables contain a string of *n* CHR$(0)'s.

STRING$ If *n* is a whole number from 0 to 32767, then the value of STRING$(*n*,*a$*) is the string consisting of the first character of *a$* repeated *n* times. If *m* is a whole number from 0 to 255, then the value of the function STRING$(*n*,*m*) is the string consisting of the character with ASCII value *m* repeated *n* times.

SUB/END SUB A subprogram is a multistatement block beginning with a statement of the form SUB *SubprogramName*(*parList*), followed on subsequent lines by one or more statements for carrying out the task of the subprogram, and ending with the statement END SUB. The parameter list *parList* is a list of variables through which values will be passed to the subprogram whenever the function is called. (See the discussion of CALL.) Parameters may be numeric or (variable-length) string variables as well as arrays.

SWAP If *var1* and *var2* are two variables of the same type, then the statement SWAP *var1*, *var2* exchanges the values of the two variables.

SYSTEM The statement SYSTEM terminates program execution, closes all files, and returns control to the QBasic environment.

TAB The function TAB(*n*) is used in PRINT, LPRINT, and PRINT# statements to move the cursor to position *n* and place spaces in all skipped-over positions. If *n* is less than the cursor position, then the cursor is moved to the *n*th position of the next line.

TAN For any number *x* (except for *x* = π/2, –π/2, 3*π/2, –3*π/2, and so on), the value of the trigonometric function TAN(*x*) is the tangent of the angle of *x* radians. [2]

**TIME$** The value of the function TIME$ is the current time expressed as a string of the form hh:mm:ss. (The hours range from 0 to 23, as in military time.) If *t$* is such a string, then the statement TIME$ = *t$* sets the computer's internal clock to the corresponding time.

TIMER The value of the function TIMER is the number of seconds from midnight to the time currently stored in the computer's internal clock.

TRON and TROFF These statements, which are abbreviations of "trace on" and "trace off," are used to debug programs. The statement TRON causes the program to execute slower than normal and each statement to be highlighted on the screen as it executes. The statement TROFF terminates this tracing.

TYPE/END TYPE A multistatement block beginning with TYPE *typeName* and ending with END TYPE creates a user-defined record type. Each statement inside the block has the form *elt* AS *type*, where *elt* is a variable (without a type-declaration tag) and *type* is either INTEGER, LONG, SINGLE, DOUBLE, STRING**n* (that is, fixed-length string), or another user-defined record type. After a statement of the form DIM *var* AS *typeName* appears, the element corresponding to the statement *elt* AS *type* is referred to as *var.elt*. TYPE statements may not appear inside procedures.

UBOUND For a one-dimensional array *arrayName*, the value of the function UBOUND(*arrayName*) is the largest subscript value that may be used. For any array *arrayName*, the value of the function UBOUND(*arrayName*, *n*) is the largest subscript value that may be used for the *n*th subscript of the array. For example, after the statement DIM example(1 TO 31,1 TO 12,1990 TO 1999) is executed, the value of UBOUND(example, 3) is the largest value allowed for the third subscript of example(), which is 1999.

**UCASE$** The value of the string function UCASE$(*a$*) is a string identical to *a$* except that all lowercase letters are changed to uppercase.

UNLOCK The UNLOCK command is intended for use in programs that operate on a network. The DOS command SHARE enables file sharing and should be executed from DOS prior to using the LOCK and UNLOCK statements. After a LOCK statement has been used to deny access to all or part of a file (see the discussion of LOCK for details), a corresponding UNLOCK statement can be used to restore access. Suppose a data file has been opened as reference number *n*. The locks established by the statements LOCK #n; LOCK #*n*, *r1*; and LOCK #*n*, *r1* TO *r2* are undone by the statements UNLOCK #*n*; UNLOCK #*n*, *r1*; and UNLOCK #*n*, *r1* TO *r2*, respectively. There must be an exact correspondence between the locking and the unlocking statements used in a program; that is, each set of paired statements must refer to the same range of record numbers or bytes.

VAL The VAL function is used to convert strings to numbers. If the leading characters of the string *a$* correspond to a number, then VAL(*a$*) will be the number represented by these characters. For any number *n*, VAL(STR$(*n*)) is *n*.

VARPTR and VARSEG The values of the functions VARSEG(*var*) and VARPTR(*var*) are the segment of memory and the offset in that segment where the value of *var* (if it is a numeric or fixed-length string) or of the descriptor of *var* (if it is a variable-length string or an array variable) is located. [9]

**VARPTR$** The value of the function VARPTR$(*var*) is a five-character string whose first character identifies the type of the variable and whose last four characters specify the location of the variable in memory. This function can be used in conjunction with DRAW and PLAY.

VIEW The graphics statement VIEW establishes a rectangular portion of the screen as a *graphics viewport* which will contain all subsequent figures drawn by graphics statements. There are three variations of the VIEW statement.

In medium-resolution graphics mode, the pair of statements WINDOW SCREEN (0,0)–(319,199): VIEW (*x1*,*y1*)–(*x2*,*y2*),*c*,*b* establish a viewport with upper left corner at physical coordinates (*x1*,*y1*) and lower right corner at physical coordinates (*x2*,*y2*). The rectangle will have background color *c* and a boundary of color *b*, where *b* and *c* are two colors of the current palette. Subsequent graphics statements will scale their displays and place them into the viewport as if it were the entire screen. For the other graphics modes, the numbers 319 and 199 should be replaced by the physical *x*- and *y*-coordinates of the point in the lower right corner of the screen.

If no WINDOW statement is active, the statement VIEW ($x1$,$y1$)–($x2$,$y2$),c,b establishes a viewport at the same location and with the same colors as above. However, instead of forcing a future drawing to fit inside the viewport, subsequent graphics statements do no scaling, but simply translate the drawing $x1$ points to the right and $y1$ points down and clip the drawing at the edge of the view port; only that portion of the translated drawing which falls inside the viewport is displayed.

If no WINDOW statement is active, the statement VIEW SCREEN ($x1$,$y1$)–($x2$,$y2$),c,b establishes a viewport at the same location and with the same colors as in the first discussion. However, instead of scaling down or translating a future drawing, subsequent graphics statements simply clip the drawing at the edge of the viewport; only that portion of the drawing which falls within the viewport is displayed. [5], [8], [6]

VIEW PRINT Normally, the screen holds 25 lines of text numbered 1 through 25. However, only lines 1 through 24 scroll. These lines are called the "text viewport." The statement VIEW PRINT *lineA* TO *lineB* causes the text viewport to consist of lines *lineA* through *lineB*. After its execution, all text displayed with PRINT statements will appear in the viewport and only the lines in the viewport will scroll. The LOCATE statement is valid only if the line number specified is within the current text viewport, and the CLS statement affects only the viewport. Text lying outside of the text viewport stays fixed. The statement VIEW PRINT by itself causes the entire screen to scroll. It has the same effect as VIEW PRINT 1 TO h, where h is the number of text lines on the screen.

WAIT If p is a port number, q is the value of a byte to be received at port p, and n and m are integers from 0 to 255, then the statement WAIT p, n, m suspends the execution of the program until the condition ((q XOR m) AND n) <> 0 is true for the byte with value q received at port p. [10]

WHILE/WEND A WHILE . . . WEND loop is a sequence of statements beginning with a statement of the form WHILE *condition* and ending with the statement WEND. After the WHILE statement is executed, the computer repeatedly executes the entire sequence of statements inside the loop as long as the condition is true.

WIDTH When used with a monitor other than a monochrome display, the statement WIDTH 40 causes text to be displayed in wide characters with 40 characters per line. (The first PRINT zone contains 14 positions and the second 26 positions.) The standard 80-character-per-line format is restored with the statement WIDTH 80. (The first four PRINT zones consist of 14 positions and the fifth of 24 positions.) In graphics modes, the WIDTH statement either has no effect or alters the mode to one that features the indicated number of characters per line.

The EGA, VGA, and MCGA video adapter cards can display 25, 30, 43, 50, or 60 lines of text, depending on the type of adapter, the type of monitor, and the screen mode. When t is a valid length for the video adapter, the statement WIDTH ,t sets the number of lines of text to t.

If s is an integer less than 255, the statement WIDTH "LPT1",s causes QBasic to permit at most s characters to be printed on a single line by LPRINT statements. QBasic will send a carriage-return/line-feed pair to the printer after s characters have been printed on a line, even if LPRINT would not otherwise start a new line at that point. The statement WIDTH "LPT1",255 specifies infinite width; that is, a carriage-return/line-feed pair will be sent to the printer only when requested by LPRINT. The same effects can be obtained with the statement WIDTH LPRINT *s*.

WINDOW The graphics statement WINDOW (*x1*,*y1*)–(*x2*,*y2*) imposes a standard (right-hand) coordinate system on the screen with the *x*-coordinates of points ranging from *x1* to *x2* and y-coordinates ranging from *y1* to *y2*. Subsequent graphics statements place figures on the screen scaled in accordance with this coordinate system. If the statement WINDOW is replaced by WINDOW SCREEN, then a left-hand coordinate system is imposed. That is, the *y*-coordinates of points are lower in the higher areas on the screen. [8]

WRITE The statement WRITE *exp1*,*exp2*,. . . displays the values of the expressions one after the other on the screen. Strings appear surrounded by quotation marks, and numbers do not have leading or trailing spaces. All commas are displayed and do not induce jumps to successive print zones. After all the values are displayed, the cursor moves to the beginning of the next line.

WRITE# After a sequential file is opened for output or append with reference number *n*, the statement WRITE #*n*, *exp1*,*exp2*,. . . records the values of the expressions one after the other into the file. Strings appear surrounded by quotation marks, numbers do not have leading or trailing spaces, all commas in the expressions are recorded, and the characters for carriage return and line feed are placed following the data.

XOR (Logical Operator) The logical expression *condition1* XOR *condition2* is true if *condition1* is true or *condition2* is true but not if both are true. For example, (3<7) XOR ("abc">"a") is false, since both 3<7 and "abc">"a" are true, while ("apple">"ape") XOR ("earth">"moon") is true, since "apple">"ape" is true and "earth">"moon" is false.

XOR (Bitwise Operator) The expression *byte1* XOR *byte2* is evaluated by expressing each byte as an 8-tuple binary number and then XORing together corresponding digits, where 1 XOR 0 and 0 XOR 1 both equal 1, while 1 XOR 1 and 0 XOR 0 both equal 0. For example, the expression 37 XOR 157 translated to binary 8-tuples becomes 00100101 XOR 10011101. XORing together corresponding digits gives the binary 8-tuple 10111000 or decimal 184. Thus 37 XOR 157 is 184.

Supporting Topics

[1] ***Default values.*** Before a numeric, variable-length string or a fixed-length string variable of length *n* has been assigned a value by the program, its value is 0, the null string (""), or a string of *n* CHR$(0) characters, respectively.

[2] ***Radian measure.*** The radian system of measurement measures angles in terms of a distance around the circumference of the circle of radius 1. If the vertex of an angle between 0 and 360 degrees is placed at the center of the circle, then the length of the arc of the circle contained between the two sides of the angle is the radian measure of the angle. An angle of *d* degrees has a radian measure of $(\pi/180)*d$ radians.

[3] ***Directories.*** Think of a disk as a master folder holding other folders, each of which might hold yet other folders. Each folder, other than the master folder, has a name. Each folder is identified by a *path:* a string beginning with a drive

letter, a colon, and a backslash character, ending with the name of the folder to be identified, and listing the names of the intermediate folders (in order) separated by backslashes. For instance the path "C:\DAVID\GAMES" identifies the folder GAMES which is contained in the folder DAVID, which in turn is contained in the master folder of drive C.

Each folder is called a *directory*, and the master folder is called the *root directory*. When a folder is opened, the revealed folders are referred to as its *subdirectories*. Think of a file as a piece of paper inside one of the folders. Thus, each directory contains files and subdirectories.

At any time, one of the directories is said to be the *current directory*. Initially the root directory is the current directory. The current directory can be changed from DOS with the CD command or from QBasic with the CHDIR command. DOS and QBasic statements that access files, such as DIR and FILES, act on the files in the current directory unless otherwise directed.

The *default drive* is the drive whose letter appeared in the DOS prompt when QBasic was invoked. If a drive is missing from a path, then the drive is assumed to be the default drive.

[4] ***Filespec.*** The filespec of a file on disk is a string consisting of the letter of the drive, a colon, and the name of the file. If directories are being used, then the file name is preceded by the identifying path.

[5] ***Colors.*** Sixteen predefined colors, identified by the numbers 0 through 15, are available on color monitors:

0 Black	4 Red	8 Gray	12 Light Red
1 Blue	5 Magenta	9 Light Blue	13 Light Magenta
2 Green	6 Brown	10 Light Green	14 Yellow
3 Cyan	7 White	11 Light Cyan	15 Intense White

In text mode, which is invoked with the statement SCREEN 0, any of the colors are available as foreground colors and the first eight are also available as background colors. In medium-resolution graphics mode, which is invoked with the statement SCREEN 1, two palettes of four colors each are available.

Palette 0:	0. Background color	1. Green	2. Red	3. Brown
Palette 1:	0. Background color	1. Cyan	2. Magenta	3. White

In high-resolution graphics mode, invoked with the statement SCREEN 2, only two colors, black (0) and white (1), are available. See the discussion of SCREEN for the ranges of colors available in the higher graphics modes.

[6] ***Palettes.*** A palette can be thought of as a collection of numbered jars that can hold paint. The number of jars available varies with the screen mode. Although the jars hold specified default colors, EGA, MCGA, and VGA adapters allow the colors to be changed with the PALETTE statement. Statements of the form PSET (*x*,*y*),*c* and CIRCLE (*x*,*y*),*r*,*c* use the color in the *c*th paint jar. In the absence of a COLOR statement, the PRINT statement displays characters with the color in jar 0 as the background color and the color in the highest-numbered jar as the foreground color.

[7] ***Last point referenced.*** At any time, one point on the screen is designated as the "last point referenced." Initially it is the point in the center of the graphics

screen. After a graphics statement is executed, the point changes to one of the points used in the statement. For instance, after a circle is drawn, the center of the circle becomes the last point referenced. After a line is drawn, the right point named in the LINE statement becomes the last point referenced.

[8] ***Graphics coordinate systems.*** The standard graphics coordinate system is called the *physical* coordinate system. For the high-resolution screen mode (SCREEN 2), the *y*-coordinates range from 0 to 199, moving from the top to the bottom of the screen, and the *x*-coordinates range from 0 to 639, moving from the left to the right side of the screen. See the discussion of SCREEN for the ranges in the higher graphics screen modes. The WINDOW statement can be used to specify a different coordinate system, called a *natural* or *logical* coordinate system. Points can also be specified in terms of *relative coordinates*. The phrase STEP (*x*,*y*) refers to the point obtained by starting at the last point referenced and moving *x* units in the horizontal direction and *y* units in the vertical direction. Relative coordinates can be used in all statements that produce graphics.

[9] ***Memory.*** Each memory location holds an integer from 0 to 255. This unit of data or memory is called a *byte*. The computer's memory is divided into blocks of memory locations called *segments*. Each segment is 65,536 bytes in size. Within a segment, a particular memory location can be specified by giving its *offset* (a number from 0 to 65,535) from the beginning of the segment. Thus, to locate an item in memory, both its segment and offset within that segment must be known, although in many cases just the offset is sufficient. Segments overlap, that is, the same portion of memory may be considered to be within different segments. Segment 0 extends from location 0 to location 65535. Segment 1 extends from location 16 to location 65551. Segment 2 extends from location 32 to 65567, and so on. For instance, the 34th memory location can be identified as segment 0: offset 34, segment 1: offset 18, or segment 2: offset 2. QBasic reserves a special segment, called the *Default Data Segment* or DGROUP, where it stores variables, special values such as the current row and column of the cursor, and the value of the random seed. The *current segment of memory* is used in conjunction with the offsets given in BLOAD, BSAVE, PEEK, and POKE statements. At the start of program execution, the current segment of memory is the Default Data Segment. It can be changed at any time by the DEF SEG statement.

[10] ***Device.*** Some examples of devices are the video screen, keyboard, printer, modem, and diskette drives. The computer's microprocessor receives data from and sends data to the various devices of the computer through what are called *ports*. Each port is identified by a number from 0 to 65535. A *byte* of data consists of a number from 0 to 255.

[11] ***Random-access files.*** The two methods for writing records to and reading records from random-access files are the "record variable method" and the "buffer method." The record variable method is discussed in Chapter 9. With the buffer method, a portion of memory referred to as a buffer is set aside for the file. A FIELD statement specifies fixed-length-string field variables whose values are held in the buffer. LSET and RSET statements assign values to the field variables, and PUT and GET statements move the contents of the buffer into a record of the file, and vice versa, respectively. The functions MKI$, MKL$, MKS$, and MKD$ are used to convert numbers to fixed-length strings prior to being placed

into the buffer by LSET and RSET statements. After a GET statement places a record in the buffer, the functions CVI, CVL, CVS, and CVD are used to convert the these strings back into numbers of the appropriate type.

[12] ***Binary file.*** A file that has been opened with a statement of the form OPEN "*filespec*" FOR BINARY AS #*n* is regarded simply as a sequence of characters occupying positions 1, 2, 3, ... At any time, a specific location in the file is designated as the "current position." The SEEK statement is used to set the current position. Collections of consecutive characters are written to and read from the file beginning at the current position with PUT and GET statements, respectively. After a PUT or GET statement is executed, the position following the last position accessed becomes the new current position.

[13] ***Label.*** QBasic supports two mechanisms for identifying program lines that are the destinations of statements such as GOTO and GOSUB: line numbers and descriptive labels. Descriptive labels are named using the same rules as variables and are followed by a colon. When a label appears in a GOTO or GOSUB statement, execution jumps to the statement following the line containing the label. We use the word *label* to refer to either a descriptive label or a line number.

[14] ***Subroutines.*** A subroutine is a sequence of statements beginning with a label and ending with a RETURN statement. A subroutine is meant to be branched to by a GOSUB statement and is usually placed so that it cannot be entered inadvertently. For instance, in the main body of a program, subroutines might appear after an END statement.

[15] ***Event trapping.*** Special events, such as the pressing of a function key or the occurrence of an error, can be set to trigger a jump to a subroutine. These events are specified by statements of the general form *Event* ON and ON *Event* GOSUB *label* that cause the computer to check for the event after the execution of each statement. If the event has occurred, the computer then performs a GOSUB to the subroutine at *label*. Trapping is disabled with *Event* OFF and deferred with *Event* STOP.

[16] ***Metacommand.*** The statements $STATIC and $DYNAMIC are called metacommands. Metacommands instruct the interpreter to insert certain code into the program or to treat certain QBasic statements in a particular way. Because metacommands are not executed, they are preceded by the reserved word REM (or an apostrophe). For instance, the statement REM $STATIC or '$STATIC tells the interpreter to store arrays in a special way.

[17] ***Static vs. dynamic.*** QBasic uses two methods of storing arrays, dynamic and static. The memory locations for a static array are set aside at compile time, and this portion of memory may not be freed for any other purpose. The memory locations for a dynamic array are assigned at run time and *can* be freed for other purposes. Although dynamic arrays are more flexible, static arrays can be accessed faster. QBasic uses the dynamic allocation of arrays if either the range in a DIM statement is specified by a variable or the programmer insists on dynamic allocation with a $DYNAMIC metacommand.

Appendix D

QBasic Debugging Tools

Errors in programs are called *bugs* and the process of finding and correcting them is called *debugging*. Since the QBasic interpreter does not discover errors due to faulty logic, they present the most difficulties in debugging. One method of discovering a logical error is by **desk checking**, that is, tracing the values of variables on paper by writing down their expected value after "mentally executing" each line in the program. Desk checking is rudimentary and highly impractical except for small programs.

Another method of debugging involves placing PRINT statements at strategic points in the program and displaying the values of selected variables or expressions until the error is detected. After correcting the error, the PRINT statements are removed. For many programming environments, desk checking and PRINT statements are the only debugging methods available to the programmer.

The QBasic debugger, used in conjunction with the Immediate window, offers an alternative to desk checking and PRINT statements. The debugging tools are invoked from the Debug menu.

Using the Immediate Window

The F6 key moves the cursor back and forth between the Immediate window and the View window. The Immediate window can hold several lines of QBasic statements. When the cursor is placed on one of these lines and the Enter key is pressed, the line is executed immediately. The following walkthrough uses the Immediate window to display and alter the values of variables.

1. Notice that the title bar, centered above the View window, is highlighted.
2. Press the function key F6 to activate the Immediate window. Notice that the bar containing the word "Immediate" is highlighted and the cursor is located in the Immediate window.
3. Press F6 to reactivate the View window. The title bar is now highlighted and the cursor is in the View window.
4. Press Alt/F/N to clear any previous program from memory and then type the following program into the View window. Do not run this program yet.

```
CLS
LET x = 1
LET y = 2
PRINT x + y
END
```

5. Activate the Immediate window and type the line

```
PRINT "x="; x, "y="; y, x > y
```

into the Immediate window.

6. With the cursor on the line, press the Enter key. The values of the variables *x* and *y* and the condition *x* > *y*, all zero, will be displayed in the output window. The value of a condition is displayed as –1 if the condition is true and 0 if the condition is false.

7. Press any key to return to the Immediate window.

8. Activate the View window and run the program.

9. Activate the Immediate window, move the cursor to the line typed in 5, and press the Enter key. The new values of the variables and the value of the condition will be displayed on the Output screen.

10. Press any key to return to the Immediate window.

11. On a new line in the Immediate window, type the statement

```
LET x = 100
```

12. Press the Enter key with the cursor on this new line. The Output screen reappears but is unchanged, since no new items have been displayed.

13. Press any key to return to the Immediate window, move the cursor to the PRINT statement, and press the Enter key. The values of *x*, *y*, and the condition *x* > *y* are displayed, with new values for *x* and the condition. Since *x* > *y* is now true, its value appears as –1.

Using the QBasic Debugger

The two main features of the QBasic debugger are stepping and breakpoints.

The program can be executed one statement at a time, with each press of an appropriate function key executing a statement. This process is called **stepping**. After each step, values of variables, expressions, and conditions can be displayed from the Immediate window, and the values of variables can be changed.

When a procedure is called, the lines of the procedure can be executed one at a time, referred to as "stepping through the procedure," or the entire procedure can be executed at once, referred to as "stepping over a procedure." A step over a procedure is called a **procedure step**.

Normally, stepping begins with the first statement of the program and proceeds to execute the statements in order. However, at any time the programmer can specify the next statement to be executed.

As another debugging tool, QBasic allows the programmer to specify certain lines as **breakpoints**. Then, when the program is run, execution will stop at the first breakpoint reached. The programmer can then either step through the program or continue execution to the next breakpoint.

The tasks discussed above are summarized below, along with a means to carry out each task. The tasks invoked with function keys can also be produced from the menu bar.

Step (ordinary): Press F8

Procedure step: Press F10

Set a breakpoint: Move cursor to line, press F9

Remove a breakpoint: Move cursor to line containing breakpoint, press F9

Clear all breakpoints: Press Alt/D/C

Set next statement: Press Alt/D/N

Execute program to the line containing the cursor: Press F7

Continue execution to next breakpoint or the end of the program: Press F5

Toggle between View window and Output screen: Press F4

Six Walkthroughs

The following walkthroughs use the debugging tools with the programming structures covered in Chapters 3, 4, 5, and 6.

Stepping Through an Elementary Program: Chapter 3

The following walkthrough demonstrates several capabilities of the debugger.

1. Type the following program into the View window.

```
CLS
INPUT "Enter a number: ", num
LET num = num + 1
LET num = num + 2
PRINT num
END
```

2. Press F8. The CLS statement is highlighted to indicate that it is the next statement to be executed.

3. Press F8. The CLS statement is executed and the INPUT statement is highlighted to indicate that it is the next statement to be executed. To confirm that CLS really was executed, press F4 to see the blank Output screen. (Press F4 again to return to the View window.)

4. Press F8 to execute the INPUT statement and respond to the request by entering 5.

5. Press F8 four more times to execute the rest of the program.

6. Move the cursor to the line LET *num* = *num* + 2. Press F9 to highlight the line and set it as a breakpoint. (Pressing F9 has the same consequence as invoking the "Toggle Breakpoint" option from the Debug menu by pressing Alt/D/B.)

7. Press Shift+F5. The program executes the first three lines and stops at the breakpoint. The breakpoint line is not executed. (Again, respond to the INPUT statement with 5.)

8. Type the statement

```
PRINT "num ="; num
```

into the Immediate window and then press Enter to execute the statement. The appearance of *num* = 6 in the Output window confirms that the breakpoint line was not executed.

9. Press any key and then F6 to return to the View window.

10. Move the cursor to the line LET *num* = *num* + 1 and then press Alt/D/N to specify that line as the next line to be executed.

11. Press F8 to execute the selected line.

12. Use the Immediate window to confirm that the value of *num* is now 7, and then return to the View window.

13. Move the cursor to the breakpoint line and press F9 to deselect the line as a breakpoint.

14. Press F5 to execute the remaining lines of the program. The value displayed is 9.

Stepping Through a Program Containing a Procedure: Chapter 4

The following walkthrough uses the single-stepping feature of the debugger to trace the flow through a program and a subprogram CALL.

1. Type the following program into the View window.

```
CLS
LET p = 1000 'Principal
CALL GetBalance(p, b)
PRINT "The balance is"; b
END

SUB GetBalance (prin, bal)
  REM Calculate the balance at 5% interest rate
  LET interest = .05 * prin
  LET bal = prin + interest
END SUB
```

2. Press F8. The CLS statement is highlighted to indicate that it is the next statement to be executed.

3. Press F8 two more times. The CALL statement is highlighted.

4. Press F8 once and observe that the subprogram GetBalance is now displayed on the screen with its first executable statement highlighted. (The subprogram heading and REM statement have been skipped.)

5. Press F8 twice to execute the LET statements and to highlight the END SUB statement.

6. Press F8 and notice that the main body is again displayed in the View window with the highlight on the statement immediately following the CALL statement.

7. Press F8 twice to execute the PRINT statement and the END statement.

Communication Between Arguments and Parameters

The following walkthrough uses the Immediate window to monitor the values of arguments and parameters during the execution of a program.

1. If you have not already done so, type the preceding program into the View window.

2. Press F6 to activate the Immediate window. Type in, but do not execute, the following two lines. (Use the Home key and cursor-down key to move to the beginning of a new line instead of pressing the Enter key.)

```
PRINT "p ="; p, "b ="; b
PRINT "prin ="; prin, "bal ="; bal
```

3. Press F8 three times to highlight the CALL statement.

4. Activate the Immediate window, place the cursor on the first PRINT statement created in step 2, and press the Enter key to display the values of *p* and *b*.

5. Press any key, and then Press F8 to call the subprogram.

6. Activate the Immediate window, place the cursor on the second PRINT statement created in step 2, and press the Enter key to display the values of *prin* and *bal*. The variables *prin* and *bal* have inherited the values of *p* and *b*.

7. Press any key, and then press F8 twice to execute the subprogram.

8. Activate the Immediate window and display the values of *prin* and *bal*.

9. Press any key, and then press F8 to return to the main body of the program.

10. Activate the Immediate window and display the values of *p* and *b*. The variable *b* now has the same value as the variable *bal*.

11. Press F8 twice to complete execution of the program.

12. Activate the Immediate window and display the values of *prin* and *bal*. These variables both have value 0, since they are not recognized by the main body of the program.

Stepping Through Programs Containing Selection Structures: Chapter 5

IF Blocks

The following walkthrough demonstrates how an IF statement evaluates a condition to determine whether to take an action.

1. Type the following program into the View window.

```
CLS
INPUT wage
IF wage < 5.15 THEN
    PRINT "Below minimum wage."
  ELSE
    PRINT "Wage Ok."
END IF
END
```

2. Press F8 twice. The CLS statement will be highlighted and executed, and then the INPUT statement will be highlighted.

3. Press F8 once to execute the INPUT statement. Type a wage of 3.25 and press the Enter key. The IF statement is highlighted but has not been executed.

4. Press F8 once and notice that the highlight for the current statement has jumped to the statement PRINT "Below minimum wage." Since the condition "wage < 5.15" is true, the action associated with THEN was selected.

5. Press F8 to execute the PRINT statement. Notice that ELSE, the statement immediately following the PRINT statement, is highlighted.

6. Press F8 again. Since the ELSE action is bypassed, we are through with the IF block, and the statement following the IF block, END, is highlighted.

7. Press F8 once more to complete execution of the program.

8. If desired, try stepping through the program again with 5.75 entered as the wage. Since the condition "wage < 5.15" will be false, the ELSE action will be executed instead of the THEN action.

SELECT CASE Blocks

The following walkthrough illustrates how a SELECT CASE block uses the selector to choose from among several actions.

1. Type the following program into the View window.

```
CLS
INPUT age
SELECT CASE age
  CASE IS < 12
    LET price = 0
  CASE IS < 18
    LET price = 3.5
  CASE IS >= 65
    LET price = 4
  CASE ELSE
    LET price = 5.5
END SELECT
PRINT USING "Your ticket price is $#.##"; price
END
```

2. Press F8 twice. The CLS statement will be highlighted and executed, and then the INPUT statement will be highlighted.

3. Press F8 once to execute the INPUT statement. Type an age of 8 and press the Enter key. The SELECT CASE statement is highlighted but has not been executed.

4. Press F8 once and observe that the action associated with CASE IS < 12 is highlighted.

5. Press F8 once to execute the LET statement. Notice that the clause following the LET statement, "CASE IS < 18," is highlighted.

6. Press F8 once. Observe that although the selector, age, is less than 18, the action associated with that CASE clause was ignored and the highlight jumped outside the SELECT CASE block to the PRINT USING statement. This demonstrates that when more than one CASE clause is true, only the first is acted upon.

7. Press F8 twice to complete execution of the program.

8. If desired, step through the program again, entering a different age and predicting which CASE clause will be acted upon.

Stepping Through a Program Containing a DO Loop: Chapter 6

DO Loops

The following walkthrough demonstrates use of the Immediate window to monitor the value of a condition in a DO loop that searches for a name.

1. Enter the following program into the View window.

```
REM Look for a specific name
CLS
INPUT "Name"; searchName$ 'Name to search for in list
READ name$
DO WHILE (searchName$ <> name$) AND (name$ <> "EOD")
  READ name$
LOOP
PRINT name$ 'Print found name or EOD
REM --- Data: name
DATA Bert, Ernie, Grover, Oscar, EOD
END
```

2. Press F6 to activate the Immediate window.

3. Type, but do not Enter,

```
PRINT searchName$, name$, (searchName$ <> name$) AND (name$ <> "EOD")
```

4. Press F8 three times to execute CLS and the INPUT statement. Enter the name "Grover" at the prompt.

5. Press F8 once to execute the READ statement.

6. Press F6 to activate the Immediate window, move the cursor to the PRINT statement, and press the Enter key. The variable *name$* has been assigned the first item in the DATA statement, "Bert", and the value of the WHILE condition is displayed as –1. (True conditions are displayed as –1; false conditions are displayed as 0.) Since the two conditions (searchName$ <> *name$*) and (searchName$ <> "EOD") are both true, the compound condition is true. (Press any key to continue.)
7. Press F8 once. Since the WHILE condition is true, the DO loop is entered.
8. Press F8 once to READ the next DATA item.
9. Execute the statement in the Immediate window. The value of *name$* is now "Ernie." (Press any key to continue.) Although the highlight is on the word LOOP, QBasic is really preparing to evaluate the WHILE condition to see if the loop should be executed again.
10. Press F8. Since the WHILE condition is true, the statement inside the loop is highlighted.
11. Press F8 to READ the next item from the DATA statement.
12. Execute the statement in the Immediate window. Since searchName$ and *name$* have the value "Grover", the condition (searchName$ <> *name$*) is false. Hence the entire WHILE condition is false, and is displayed with the value 0.
13. Press F8 once. Since the WHILE condition has become false, the highlight will move from the LOOP statement to the statement immediately following the DO loop, that is, PRINT *name$*.
14. Press F8. The value displayed on the screen by PRINT is the same as the value of *name$* most recently displayed from the Immediate window. (Press F4 to view the Output screen.)
15. Press F8 once to complete execution of the program.

Appendix E

A Summary of QBasic Editing Commands

The charts below summarize the editing commands presented in Chapter 1. These charts are followed by some advanced editing commands that use QBasic's Clipboard.

Commands to Move Cursor	
Left one character	Left Arrow
Right one character	Right Arrow
Left to start of word	Ctrl+Left Arrow
Right to start of word	Ctrl+Right Arrow
Left to start of line	Home
Right to end of line	End
Up one line	Up Arrow
Down one line	Down Arrow
Up to first line in program	Ctrl+Home
Down to last line in program	Ctrl+End
Commands to Scroll	
Up to a new page	PgUp
Down to a new page	PgDn
Scroll view up one line in program	Ctrl+Up Arrow
Scroll view down one line in program	Ctrl+Down Arrow
Commands to Delete Text	
Delete character left of cursor	Backspace
Delete character at cursor	Del
Delete from cursor to end of word	Ctrl+T
Delete from cursor to end of line	Shift+End/Del
Delete entire line	Ctrl+Y

Using the Clipboard

QBasic sets aside a part of memory, called the *Clipboard*, to assist in moving and copying selected portions of text. Whenever text is deleted with one of the commands Ctrl+T (erase word) or Ctrl+Y (erase current line), the text is placed in the Clipboard. At any time, pressing Shift+Ins inserts the contents of the Clipboard at the cursor position.

The following steps can be used to move a line of code to a new location.

1. Place the cursor on the line.
2. Press Ctrl+Y to erase the line and place it into the Clipboard.

3. Move the cursor to the desired new location for the line.

4. Press Shift+Ins to duplicate the line at the cursor position.

Note: After the contents of the Clipboard are copied at the cursor position, the text remains in the Clipboard and therefore can be duplicated in several locations.

Larger portions of contiguous text, called *blocks*, also can be stored in the Clipboard. To select a segment of text as a block, move the cursor to the beginning of the segment, hold down the shift key, move the cursor to the end of the segment of text, and then release the shift key. The selected block will be highlighted. (Moving the cursor deselects the portion of text as a block.) After highlighting a block, the following commands can be applied to the selected block.

Shift+Del	Erases the selected block and places it in the Clipboard
Ctrl+Ins	Places a copy of the selected block in the Clipboard while leaving the block intact
Del	Erases the selected block without placing it in the Clipboard

After placing a block of text into the Clipboard, the following steps can be used to copy the contents of the Clipboard anywhere in a program.

1. Move the cursor to the location where the block stored in the Clipboard should be inserted.

2. Press Shift+Ins to insert the block at the cursor position.

Appendix F

The QBasic Environment

This appendix discusses the eight Menu bar selections and their drop-down menus.

The File Menu Commands

Pressing F from the Menu bar (or Alt/F from the View or Immediate window) drops down the File menu, presenting the following six command options.

New

The New command clears any current program from the editor's memory, allowing a new program to be written. The new program is given the default name of Untitled.BAS. If the New command is given when a recently edited program is in memory, QBasic provides an opportunity to save this edited program before the editor's memory is loaded with the new program.

Open

The Open command copies a program from a disk into the View window so that the program can be edited or run. If the Open command is given when a recently edited program is in memory, QBasic provides an opportunity to save this edited program before the editor's memory is loaded with the new program.

The Open command exhibits a box with the cursor in a rectangle entitled "File Name." To load a file, type the file name (including the drive and path if warranted) into the rectangle and press the Enter key. If the file name has the standard extension of BAS, you need not include the extension. (To specify a file whose name has no extension, include the period at the end of the file name.) If the file you request is not present, QBasic assumes you want to start working on a new program that will later be saved in a file with this new name.

An alternate way of loading a file is provided by the Files rectangle, which displays the names of all the files with extension BAS in the current directory of the current drive. A program can be loaded by pressing the Tab key, moving to the desired name with the cursor-moving keys, and pressing the Enter key. The drive can be changed by making a selection from the Dir/Drives rectangle.

The drive and/or directory of the programs displayed in the Files rectangle can be changed by typing and entering the identifying path in the File Name rectangle. *Wild-card characters*, the asterisk and question mark, can be used to request a class of file names from the directory. A question mark in a file name indicates that any character can occupy that position. An asterisk in either part of the file name, the first eight positions or the extension, indicates that any character can occupy that position and all the remaining positions in the part. For instance, typing and entering A:\TOM\?R*.BAS displays all files on the

A drive in the directory TOM having R as the second letter and having the extension BAS.

Save

The Save command copies the program currently in memory onto a disk. If the program has not been named (that is, if its current name appears as Untitled in the Title bar), QBasic exhibits an input box titled File Name that provides the opportunity to give the file a meaningful name. If the file name ends with a period, then it will be saved with no extension. Otherwise, if the file name has no extension, the extension BAS will automatically be added. The file is saved in the current directory of the current drive unless its name is preceded with a drive and/or path. The drive also can be selected from the Dir/Files rectangle.

Save As

The Save As command copies the program currently in memory onto a disk after providing an opportunity to save the program under a name other than the current name. The dialog box is identical to the one for Save.

Print

The Print command prints a hard copy of the part of the program that has been selected as a block, the current window (that is, the View window, the Immediate window, or a procedure), or the entire program, depending on which option is selected.

Exit

The Exit command abandons QBasic and returns to DOS. If the Exit command is given when the program in the View window has not been saved in its current form, the user is given the opportunity to save before QBasic is abandoned.

The Edit Menu Commands

Pressing E from the Menu bar (or Alt/E from the View or Immediate windows) pulls down the Edit menu, presenting the following six command options.

Cut

The Cut command removes the selected block of text from the View window and places it in the clipboard.

Copy

The Copy command places a copy of the selected block of text into the clipboard. The copied text will still be in the View window.

Paste

The paste command inserts, at the cursor, a copy of the contents of the clipboard.

Clear

The Clear command removes the selected text without saving it in the clipboard. (Clipboard contents remain unaltered.)

New SUB

The New SUB command opens a dialog box in which the programmer enters the name of a new subprogram. After pressing the Enter key, the new subprogram will be created and the cursor will appear below the heading.

New FUNCTION

The New FUNCTION command opens a dialog box in which the programmer enters the name of a new function. After pressing the Enter key, the new function will be created and the cursor will appear below the heading.

The View Menu Commands

Pressing V from the Menu bar (or Alt/V from the View or Immediate window) pulls down the View menu, presenting the following three command options.

SUBs

The SUBs command displays a dialog box used to select a procedure to view or delete.

Split

The Split command divides the View window horizontally so two parts of a program can be accessed at the same time. The F6 and Shift+F6 keys move between the windows. The size of the active window can be expanded one line at a time with Alt+Plus and shrunk with Alt+Minus. Ctrl+F10 toggles between an expanded View window and its regular size.

Output Screen

The Output Screen command toggles to and from the display of the output screen. The same function is performed by the F4 key.

The Search Menu Commands

Pressing S from the Menu bar (or Alt/S from the View or Immediate window) pulls down the Search menu, presenting the following three command options.

Find

The Find command begins at the cursor and searches for the first occurrence of a specified symbol, word, or phrase.

Repeat Last Find

The Repeat Last Find command looks for the next occurrence of the text most recently searched for by the Find command.

Change

The Change command begins at the cursor, finds the first occurrence of specified text, and replaces it with new text.

The Run Menu Commands

Pressing R from the Menu bar (or Alt/R from the View or Immediate windows) pulls down the Run menu, presenting the following three command options.

Start

The Start command executes the program currently in memory, beginning with the first line. Pressing Shift+F5 performs the same function.

Restart

When a program has been suspended before completion, the Restart command specifies that the next call for execution of the program should restart the program from the beginning.

Continue

When a program has been suspended before completion, the Continue command resumes execution at the suspension point. The same function is performed by the F5 key.

The Debug Menu Commands

Pressing D from the Menu bar (or Alt/D from the View or Immediate windows) pulls down the Debug menu, presenting the following six command options.

Step

The Step command executes the program one statement at a time. Each invocation of the command executes the next statement.

Procedure Step

The Procedure Step command executes the program one statement at a time without stepping through the statements inside procedures one at a time. An entire procedure is executed as if it were a single statement.

Trace On

The Trace On line shows the current status of the Trace toggle. When Trace On is preceded by a dot, each statement will be highlighted as it is executed. This feature lets you observe the general flow of the program.

Toggle Breakpoint

A breakpoint is a line of the program at which program execution is automatically suspended by QBasic. The Toggle Breakpoint command toggles (that is, sets or clears) the line containing the cursor as a breakpoint.

Clear All Breakpoints

The Clear All Breakpoints commands removes all breakpoints that have been set with the toggle breakpoint command.

Set Next Statement

The Set Next Statement specifies that the line containing the cursor be the next line executed when program execution continues.

The Options Menu Commands

Pressing O from the Main Menu (or Alt/O from the View or Immediate windows) pulls down the Options command menu, presenting the following three command options.

Display

The Display command generates a dialog box that can be used to custom-color the foreground and background of text typed into the View windows and statements highlighted during debugging, to select or deselect the scroll bars used by a mouse, and to specify the number of spaces tabbed by the Tab key.

Help Path

The Help Path command is used to tell QBasic where to look for the file QBasic.HLP, the file containing the Help information. Normally, the file is in the same directory as QBasic.EXE. If not, the path specifying the directory containing QBasic.HLP should be entered in the rectangle invoked by the Help Path command. A complete path consists of a disk drive followed by a sequence of subdirectories.

Syntax Checking

Normally, when a line of text is Entered, QBasic's smart editor automatically checks the correctness of the line, capitalizes keywords, and adds extra spaces to improve readability. This feature is enabled when Syntax Checking is preceded with a dot. The Syntax Checking command toggles this state.

The Help Menu Commands

Pressing H from the Menu bar (or Alt/H from the View or Immediate windows) pulls down the File menu, presenting the following five command options.

Index

The Index command displays an alphabetical list of keywords. Information on a keyword can be obtained by placing the cursor on the keyword and pressing the Enter key or F1. Pressing a letter key moves the cursor to the first keyword beginning with that letter.

Contents

The Contents command displays a menu of topics on which information is available. After the Tab or direction keys are used to move the cursor to a topic, pressing Enter or F1 displays the information.

Topic

When the cursor is located at a keyword in the View window, you can invoke the Topic command to obtain information about that word.

Using Help

The Using Help command displays information about how to obtain online help.

About

The About command displays the version number and copyright dates of the QBasic currently in use.

Appendix G

How To (QBasic)

HOW TO: Invoke and Exit QBasic

(We assume that the computer has a hard disk with DOS 5.0 or a later version of DOS installed.)

A. Invoke QBasic.

1. Turn on the computer and monitor.
2. At the DOS prompt, type QBASIC and press the Enter key.
3. When the screen querying about the Survival Guide appears, press the Esc key.

Note: If step 2 does not work, enter DIR \QBASIC.EXE /S at the DOS prompt to determine the directory in which QBASIC resides. (Normally, this will be the directory C:\DOS.) Then enter CD *nameOfDirectory* and repeat step 2. (For example, in the most common case, enter CD \DOS and then enter QBASIC.)

B. Allow graphics when the monitor is a Monochrome display that is attached to a Hercules card.

1. Before invoking QBasic, enter MSHERC at the DOS prompt.

Note 1: If this does not work, enter DIR \MSHERC.COM /S at the DOS prompt to determine the directory in which MSHERC resides. (Normally, this will be the directory C:\DOS.) Then enter CD *nameOfDirectory* and repeat step 1. (For example, in the most common case, enter CD \DOS and then enter MSHERC.)

Note 2: The statement SCREEN 3 must appear in any program prior to the use of graphics statements.

C. Exit QBasic.

1. Press the Esc key.
2. Press Alt/F/X.
3. If the program in the View window has not been saved, QBasic will prompt you about saving it.

Note: In many situations, step 1 is not needed.

HOW TO: Manage Programs

A. Run a program from QBasic.

1. Press Alt/R/S.

Or,

1. Press Shift+F5. (Normally, F5 alone will run the program. However, if the program has been stopped before its end, F5 continues execution from the stopping point, whereas Shift+F5 executes the program from the beginning.)

B. Save the current program on a disk.

1. Press Alt/F/S or Alt/F/A.
2. Type the name of the program, if requested, and press the Enter key.

Note: After a program has been saved once, updated versions can be saved under the same name by pressing Alt/F/S. Alt/F/A is used to save the program under a new name.

C. Begin a new program in the View window.

1. Press Alt/F/N.
2. If an unsaved program is in the View window, QBasic will prompt you about saving it.

D. Open a program stored on a disk.

1. Press Alt/F/O.
2. Type a filespec into the top rectangle of the dialog box and press the Enter key. Alternately, press the Tab key to penetrate the region containing the names of the files on the disk, and then use the cursor-moving keys and the Enter key to select one of the listed files.
3. If the program in the View window has not been saved, QBasic will prompt you about saving it.

E. Name a program.

1. Save it with Alt/F/A.

HOW TO: Use the Editor

A. Determine the row and column position of the cursor.

1. Look at the pair of numbers at the bottom right of the screen separated by a colon on the status bar.
2. The first number gives the row, and the second number gives the column.

B. Mark a section of text as a block.

1. Move the cursor to the beginning or end of the block.
2. Hold down a Shift key and use the direction keys to highlight a block of text.
3. To unblock text, release the Shift key and press a cursor key.

C. Delete a line of a program.

1. Move the cursor to the line.
2. Press Ctrl+Y.

Or,

1. Mark the line as a block. (See item B of this section.)
2. Press Shift+Del.

Note: In the maneuvers above, the line is placed in the clipboard and can be retrieved by pressing Shift+Ins. To delete the line without placing it in the clipboard, mark it as a block and press Del.

D. Move a line within the View window.

1. Move the cursor to the line and press Ctrl+Y.
2. Move the cursor to the target location.
3. Press Shift+Ins.

E. Use the clipboard to move or duplicate statements.

1. Place the cursor on the first character of the statement (or group of statements).
2. Hold down a Shift key and move the cursor to the right (and/or down) to highlight the selected block of text.
3. Press Shift+Del to delete the block and place it into the clipboard. Or, press Ctrl+Del to place a copy of the block into the clipboard.
4. Move the cursor to the location where you desire to place the block.
5. Press Shift+Ins to place a copy of the text in the clipboard at the cursor.

F. Search for specific text in program.

1. Press Alt/S/F.
2. Type sought-after text into rectangle.
3. Select desired options if different from the defaults.
4. Press the Enter key.
5. To repeat the search, press F3.

G. Search and change.

1. Press Alt/S/C.
2. Type sought-after text into first rectangle.
3. Press Tab.
4. Type replacement text into second rectangle.
5. Select desired options if different from the defaults.
6. Press the Enter key.

H. Change from "Syntax Checking On" to "Syntax Checking Off" or vice versa.

1. Press Alt/O.
2. "Syntax checking" is preceded by a dot if the feature is active. Press S if you want to change the selection, or press the Esc key to exit.

I. Check the syntax of a line. (Assuming "Syntax checking" is enabled.)

1. Move the cursor to the line.
2. Edit the line in some way. For example, type = and then press Backspace.
3. Press the Down Arrow key.

Note: The syntax of a line is automatically checked, whenever the cursor is moved off an edited line, by pressing either the Enter key or a cursor-moving key.

J. Cancel changes made to a line.

1. Do not move the cursor from the line.
2. Press Ctrl+Q/L to restore the line to the form it had when the cursor was last moved from the line.

HOW TO: Get Help

A. View the syntax and purpose of a QBasic keyword.

1. Type the word into the View window.
2. Place the cursor on, or just following, the keyword.
3. Press F1.

Or,

1. Press Alt/H/I/[first letter of keyword].
2. Use the direction keys to highlight the keyword.
3. Press the Enter key.

B. Display an ASCII table.

1. Press Alt/H/C.
2. Press the letter A to move the cursor to "ASCII Character Codes" and press the Enter key.
3. Use PgDn and PgUp to move between the extended and standard ASCII character sets.

C. Obtain a list of common editing and debugging commands.

1. Press Alt/H/C/S/Enter.

D. Obtain other useful reference information.

1. Press Alt/H/C.
2. Use Tab and Shift+Tab to highlight a topic.
3. Press the Enter key.

E. Obtain general information about using the help menu.

1. Press Shift+F1.

F. Obtain information about the selections in a drop-down menu.

1. See item D in HOW TO: Manage Menus.

G. Obtain a list of QBasic's reserved words.

1. Press Alt/H/I and use the Down Arrow key to scroll through the list.

Note: To obtain information about a word, move the cursor to the word and press the Enter key.

HOW TO: Manipulate a Dialog Box

A. Use a dialog box.

A dialog box contains three types of items: rectangles, option lists, and command buttons. An option list is a sequence of option buttons of the form ( ) *option* or [ ] *option*, and a command button has the form < *command* >.

1. Move from item to item with the Tab key. (The movement is from left to right and top to bottom. Use Shift+Tab instead of Tab to reverse the direction.)
2. Inside a rectangle, either type in the requested information or use the direction keys to make a selection.
3. In an option list, an option button of the form ( ) *option* can be activated with the direction keys. A dot inside the parentheses indicates that the option has been activated.
4. In an option list, an option button of the form [ ] *option* can be activated or deactivated by pressing the space bar. An X inside the brackets indicates that the option has been activated.
5. A highlighted command button is invoked by pressing the Enter key.

B. Cancel a dialog box.

1. Press the Esc key.

Or,

1. Press the Tab key until the command button < Cancel > is highlighted and then press the Enter key.

HOW TO: Manage Menus

A. Close a drop-down menu.

1. Press the Esc key.

B. Open a drop-down menu.

1. Press Alt.
2. Press the first letter of the name of the menu. Alternately, press the Down Arrow key, use the direction keys to move the highlighted cursor bar to the menu name, and press the Enter key.

C. Make a selection from a drop-down menu.

1. Open the drop-down menu. One letter in each item that is eligible to be used will be emphasized by being highlighted or having a different color than the other letters.
2. Press the emphasized letter. Alternately, use the Down Arrow key to move the cursor bar to the desired item and then press the Enter key.

D. Obtain information about the selections in a drop-down menu.

1. Open the drop-down menu.
2. Use the Down Arrow key to move the highlighted cursor bar to the desired item.
3. The status bar at the bottom of the screen will give a brief description of the item.
4. Pressing F1 gives additional information.

E. Look at all the menus in the menu bar.

1. Press Alt/F.
2. Press the Right Arrow key each time you want to see a new menu.

HOW TO: Manage Procedures

A. Look at an existing procedure.

1. Press Shift+F2 repeatedly to cycle through all the procedures.

Or,

1. Press F2. The top entry is the main body of the program and the remaining entries are procedures.
2. Use the direction keys and the Enter key to select the desired procedure.

B. Create a procedure.

1. Move to a blank line.
2. Type SUB (for a subprogram) or FUNCTION (for a function) followed by the name of the procedure and any parameters.
3. Press the Enter key. (A new window will appear containing the procedure heading and an END statement.)
4. Type the procedure into the new window.

Or,

1. Press Alt/E/S (for a subprogram) or Alt/E/F (for a function). (A dialog box will appear.)
2. Type the name of the procedure and any parameters into the *Name* rectangle.
3. Press the Enter key. (A new window will appear containing the procedure heading and an END statement.)
4. Type the procedure into the new window.

Note: To return to the main body of the program, press F2/Enter.

C. Alter a procedure.

1. Press Shift+F2 until the desired procedure is displayed.
2. Make changes as needed.

Or,

1. Press F2.
2. Move the cursor bar to the desired procedure.
3. Press the Enter key.

D. Remove a procedure.

1. Press F2.
2. Move the cursor bar to the desired procedure.
3. Press Tab/D/Enter.

E. Insert an existing procedure into a program.

1. Open the program containing the procedure and press Shift+F2 until the procedure appears on the screen.
2. Mark the procedure as a block. That is, move the cursor to the first statement of the procedure, hold down a Shift key, and move the cursor to the last statement of the procedure.
3. Press Ctrl+Ins to place the procedure into the clipboard.
4. Open the program in which the procedure is to be inserted.

5. Move the cursor to a blank line.
6. Press Shift+Ins to place the contents of the clipboard into the program.

HOW TO: Manage Windows

A. Change the active window, that is, the window which contains the cursor and has its title highlighted.

1. Press F6 until desired window becomes active.

B. Split a screen to obtain multiple View windows.

Option I: Both parts will contain same text.

1. Press Alt/V/P.

Option II: Second part will contain any procedure.

1. Press Alt/V/P.
2. Press F6.
3. Press F2.
4. Move cursor bar to desired procedure.
5. Press Enter.

C. Unsplit a screen.

1. Use F6 to select window to be retained.
2. Press Alt/V/P.

D. Zoom the active window to fill the entire screen.

1. Press Ctrl+F10.
2. To return window to original size, press Ctrl+F10 again.

E. Make a small change in the size of the active window.

1. Press Alt+Plus to enlarge by one line.
2. Press Alt+Minus to contract by one line.

HOW TO: Alter the Appearance of the View Window

A. Remove the scroll bars from or add them to the View window. (The scroll bars are needed when a mouse is used.)

1. Press Alt/O/D/Tab/Tab/Tab.
2. The space bar can be pressed to alternate between having and not having an X at the cursor. The presence of an X produces scroll bars.
3. Press the Enter key.

B. Change certain colors used by QBasic.

1. Press Alt/O/D.
2. Press Tab or Shift+Tab to move around the dialog box.
3. Use the direction keys to make a selection within each region of the dialog box.
4. To change a toggled selection, such as "Scroll bars," press the Space bar.
5. When all selections have been made, press the Enter key.

Note: When QBasic is exited, these selections will be saved in a file named QB.INI. If this file is present on the same disk and directory as QBASIC.EXE when QBasic is next invoked, it will determine QBasic's display settings.

C. Invoke QBasic in black & white.

1. Type QBASIC /B and press the Enter key when invoking QBasic from DOS.

D. Invoke QBasic with the maximum number of lines supported by the adapter.

1. Type QBASIC /H and press the Enter key when invoking QBasic from DOS.

HOW TO: Use the Printer

A. Obtain a printout of a program.

1. Press Alt/F/P.
2. Press the Enter key.

Note: To print just the text selected as a block or the active (current) window, use the direction keys to select the desired option.

B. Obtain a printout of a text Output window.

1. Press F4 to switch to the Output window if necessary.
2. Press Shift+Print Screen. ***Tip:*** After the program terminates, the phrase "Press any key to continue" can be removed by pressing F4 twice.

C. Obtain a printout of a graphics Output window when not using Windows 95.

The command needed to ready the printer for graphics depends on the type of printer.

1. (Dot matrix or ink-jet printer) Before invoking QBasic, enter GRAPHICS at the DOS prompt.

Or,

1. (Laser printer) Before invoking QBasic, enter GRAPHICS HPDEFAULT at the DOS prompt.
2. Press Shift+Print Screen. ***Tip:*** After the program terminates, the phrase "Press any key to continue" can be removed by pressing F4 twice.

Note: The above steps will produce an improper printout with certain types of printers. See the discussion of the GRAPHICS graphics command in the DOS reference manual for details.

HOW TO: Use the Debugger

A. Stop a program at a specified line.

1. Place the cursor at the beginning of the desired line.
2. Press F9. (This highlighted line is called a *breakpoint*. When the program is run, it will stop at the breakpoint before executing the statement.)

Note: To remove this breakpoint, repeat steps 1 and 2.

B. Remove all breakpoints.

1. Press Alt/D/C.

C. Run a program with each statement highlighted as it is executed.

1. Press Alt/D.
2. If the "Trace On" selection is preceded by a mark, press F5. Otherwise, Press T/F5.

Note: To turn off tracing, press Alt/D/T.

D. Run a program one statement at a time.

1. Press F8. The first executable statement will be highlighted.
2. Press F8 each time you want to execute the currently highlighted statement.

Note: At any time you can view the Output screen by pressing F4.

E. Run the program one statement at a time, but execute each procedure call without stepping through the statements in the procedure one at a time.

1. Press F10. The first executable statement will be highlighted.
2. Press F10 each time you want to execute the currently highlighted statement.

Note: At any time you can view the Output screen by pressing F4.

F. Continue execution of a program that has been suspended.

1. Press F5.

Note: Each time a change is made in a suspended program that prevents the program from continuing, QBasic displays a dialog box with two options to choose from: continue without the change, or restart the program from the beginning.

G. Execute a program up to the line containing the cursor.

1. Press F7.

H. Have further stepping begin from the top of the program with all variables cleared.

1. Press Alt/R/R.

I. Have further stepping begin at the line containing the cursor (no variables are cleared).

1. Press Alt/D/N.

J. Execute a statement from the Immediate window.

1. Press F6 to move the cursor to the Immediate window.
2. Type the statement into the Immediate window.
3. Press the Enter key with the cursor on the statement.

Appendix H

An Introduction to Windows

Programs such as the latest versions of Visual Basic, which are designed for Windows 95 and Windows 98, are supposed to be easy to use—and they are, once you learn a little jargon and a few basic techniques. This section explains the jargon, giving you enough of an understanding of Windows to get you started in Visual Basic. Although Windows may seem intimidating if you've never used it before, you only need to learn a few basic techniques, which are covered right here.

Mouse Pointers

When you use Windows, think of yourself as the conductor and Windows as the orchestra. The conductor in an orchestra points to various members, does something with his or her baton, and then the orchestra members respond in certain ways. For a Windows user, the baton is called the **pointing device**; most often it is a **mouse**. The idea is that as you move the mouse across your desk, a pointer moves along the screen in sync with your movements. Two basic types of mouse pointers you will see in Windows are an arrow and an hourglass.

The **arrow** is the ordinary mouse pointer you use to point at various Windows objects before activating them. You will usually be instructed to "Move the pointer to . . . ." This really means "Move the mouse around your desk until the mouse pointer is at . . . ."

The **hourglass** mouse pointer pops up whenever Windows is saying: "Wait a minute; I'm thinking." This pointer still moves around when you move the mouse, but you can't tell Windows to do anything until it finishes what it's doing and the mouse pointer no longer resembles an hourglass. (Sometimes you can press the Esc key to tell Windows to stop what it is doing.)

Note: The mouse pointer can take on many other shapes, depending on which document you are using and what task you are performing. For instance, when entering text in a word processor or Visual Basic, the mouse pointer appears as a thin, large, uppercase I (referred to as an I-beam).

Mouse Actions

After you move the (arrow) pointer to a place where you want something to happen, you need to do something with the mouse. There are four basic things you can do—point, click, double-click, and drag.

Tip: You can pick the mouse up off your desk and replace it without moving the mouse pointer. This is useful, for example, when the mouse pointer is in the center of the screen but the mouse is about to fall off your desk!

Pointing means moving your mouse across your desk until the mouse pointer is over the desired object on the screen.

Clicking (sometimes people say single-clicking) means pressing and releasing the left mouse button once. Whenever a sentence begins "Click on . . . ," you need to

1. Move the mouse pointer until it is at the object you are supposed to click on.
2. Press and release the left mouse button.

An example of a sentence using this jargon might be "Click on the button marked Yes." You also will see sentences that begin "Click inside the. . . ." This means to move the mouse pointer until it is inside the boundaries of the object, and then click.

Double-clicking means clicking the left mouse button twice in quick succession (that is, pressing it, releasing it, pressing it, and releasing it again *quickly* so that Windows doesn't think you single-clicked twice). Whenever a sentence begins "Double-click on . . . ", you need to

1. Move the mouse pointer until it is at the object you are supposed to double-click on.
2. Press and release the left mouse button twice in quick succession.

For example, you might be instructed to "Double-click on the little box at the far left side of your screen."

Note: An important Windows convention is that clicking selects an object so you can give Windows or the document further directions about it, but double-clicking tells Windows (or the document) to do something. Double-clicking on the icon that represents a program starts the program.

Dragging usually moves a Windows object. If you see a sentence that begins "Drag the . . . ", you need to

1. Move the mouse pointer until it is at the object.
2. Press the left mouse button and hold it down.
3. Now move the mouse pointer until the object moves to where you want it to be.
4. Finally, release the mouse button.

Sometimes this whole activity is called *drag and drop*.

Starting Windows

Windows 95 and Windows 98 start automatically when you turn on your computer. After a little delay, you will first see the Windows logo and finally a screen looking something like Figure H.1. The four little pictures (with labels) are called **icons**. You double-click on the My Computer icon to see your computer's contents and manage your files. The Network Neighborhood icon is used to see available resources on the network, and the Recycle Bin is a temporary storage place for deleted files. You click on the **Start button** (at the bottom left corner of the screen) to run programs such as Visual Basic, end Windows, and carry out several other tasks. (The Start menu also can be accessed with Ctrl+Esc.)

Figure H.1 Windows Desktop

Windows and Its Little Windows

Windows gets its name from the way it organizes your screen into rectangular regions. When you run a program, the program runs inside a bordered rectangular box. Unfortunately Windows jargon calls all of these windows, so there's only a lowercase "w" to distinguish them from the program called Windows.

When Windows' attentions are focused on a specific window, the bar at the top of the window is highlighted and the window is said to be **active**. The active window is the only one that can be affected by your actions. An example of a sentence you might see is "Make the window active." This means that if the title bar of the window is not already highlighted, click inside the window. At this point, the (new) window will be responsive to your actions.

Using the Notepad

We will explore the Windows application Notepad to illustrate the Windows environment. The Notepad can be used to create data files for documents. Most of the concepts learned here carry over to Visual Basic and other Windows applications.

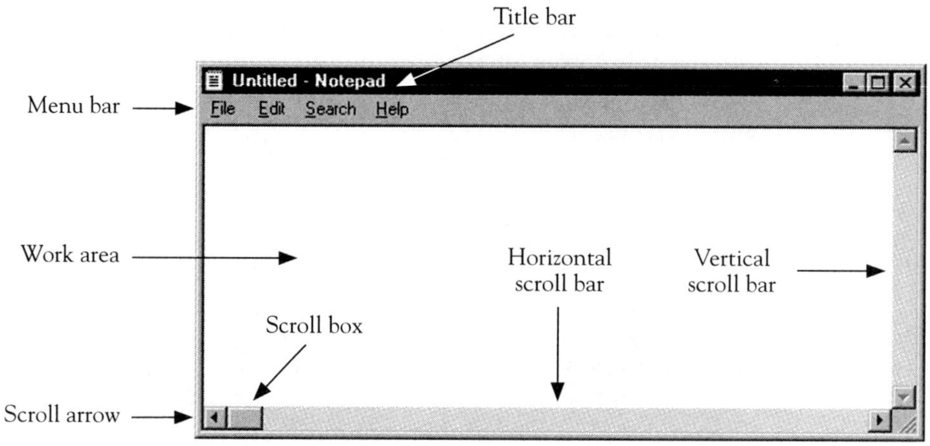

Figure H.2 The Notepad Window

To invoke Notepad from Windows, click the Start button, point to Programs, point to Accessories, and click Notepad. As its name suggests, Notepad is an elementary word processor. You can type text into the Notepad window, edit the text, print the text on the printer, and save the text for later recall.

The Notepad window is divided into four parts (Figure H.2). The part containing the cursor is called the **Work area**. It is the largest and most important part of the window, because documents are typed into it.

The **Title bar** at the top of the screen holds the name of the document currently being written. Until the document is given a name, the document is called "Untitled."

The title bar of the Notepad window, or of any window, contains buttons that can be used to maximize, minimize, or close the window. See Figure H.3.

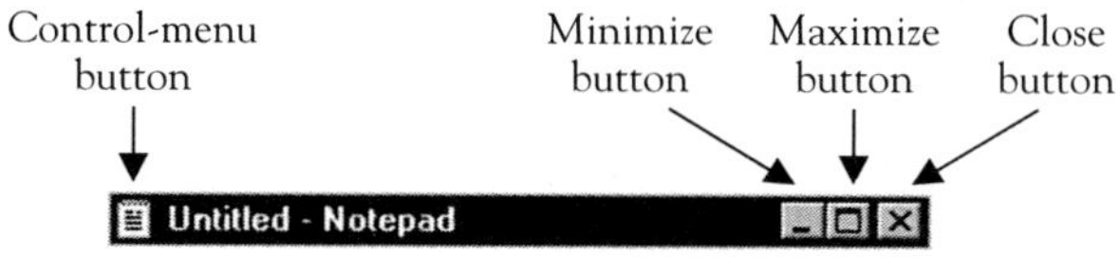

Figure H.3 Title Bar of the Notepad Window

You can click on the Maximize button to make the Notepad window fill the entire screen, click on the Minimize button to change the Notepad window into a button on the taskbar, or click on the Close button to exit Notepad. As long as a window isn't maximized, you can usually move it around the screen by dragging its title bar. (Recall that this means to move the mouse pointer until it is in the title bar, hold down the left mouse button, move the mouse until the window is where you want it to be, and then release the mouse button.) ***Note 1:*** If you have maximized a window, the Maximize button changes to a pair of rectangles called the **Restore button**. Click on this button to return the window to its previous size. ***Note 2:*** If the Notepad window has been minimized, it can be restored to its previous size by clicking on the button that was created when the Minimize button was clicked.

You can change the window to exactly suit your needs. To adjust the size:

1. Move the mouse pointer until it is at the place on the boundary you want to adjust. The mouse pointer changes to a double-headed arrow.
2. Drag the border to the left or right or up or down to make it smaller or larger.
3. When you are satisfied with the new size of the window, release the left mouse button.

If the Work area contains more information than can fit on the screen, you need a way to move through this information so you can see it all. For example, you will certainly be writing instructions in Visual Basic that are longer than one screen. You can use the mouse to march through your instructions with small steps or giant steps. A **Vertical scroll bar** lets you move from the top to the bottom of the window; a **Horizontal scroll bar** lets you move within the left and right margins of the window. Use this Scroll bar when the contents of the window are too wide to fit on the screen. Figure H.2 shows both Vertical and Horizontal scroll bars.

A scroll bar has two arrows at the end of a channel and sometimes contains a box (usually called the **Scroll box**). The Scroll box is the key to moving rapidly; the arrows are the key to moving in smaller increments. Dragging the Scroll box enables you to quickly move long distances to an approximate location in your document. For example, if you drag the Scroll box to the middle of the channel, you'll scroll to approximately the middle of your document.

The **Menu bar** just below the Title bar is used to call up menus, or lists of tasks. Several of these tasks are described in this section.

Documents are created from the keyboard in much the same way they would be written with a typewriter. In computerese, writing a document is referred to as editing the document; therefore, the Notepad is called a **text editor**.

To store the document as a file on a disk, press Alt/File/Save, which opens the Save As dialog box in Figure H.4. The cursor is in a narrow rectangular box labeled "File Name:". Type a drive letter, a colon, and a name, and then press the Enter key or click on Save. For instance, you might type A:PERSONAL. Notepad automatically adds a period and the extension TXT to the name. Therefore, the complete file name is PERSONAL.TXT on the disk. ***Note:*** If you want to save the document in a specific directory of the disk, also type the directory name. For instance, you might type A:\MYFILES\ PERSONAL. (***Note:*** You can also select the drive and directory by clicking on the down-arrow at the right of the Save In box, searching for the desired location, and double-clicking on the directory.)

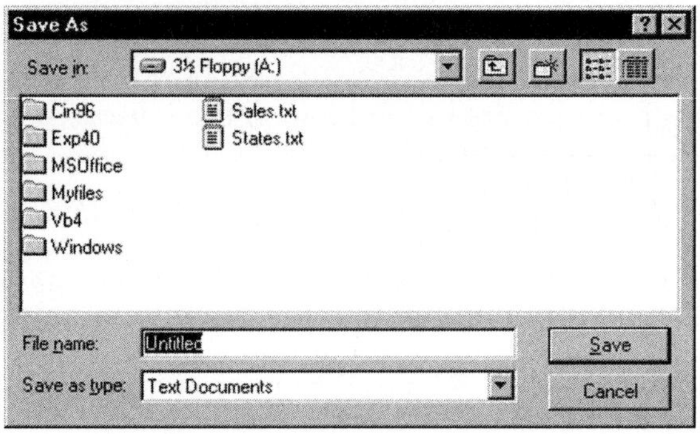

Figure H.4 Save As Dialog Box

Ending Windows

To close Windows, click the Start button and then click Shut Down. You are presented with a message box that looks like the right window in Figure H.5. Click Yes. (If you forgot to save changes to documents, Windows will prompt you to save changes.) A screen message will appear to let you know when you can safely turn off your computer.

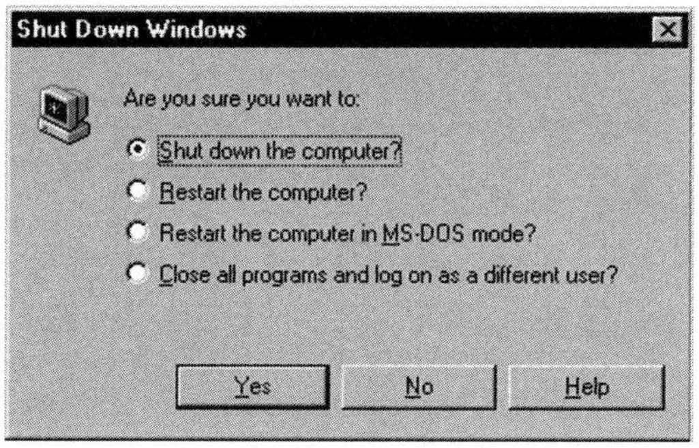

Figure H.5 Dialog Box for Ending Windows

Appendix I

How To (Visual Basic)

HOW TO: Install, Invoke, and Exit Visual Basic

A. Install the Control Creation Edition of Visual Basic.

1. Place the CD accompanying this book into your CD drive.
2. From the Windows Desktop, double-click on My Computer.
3. (A window showing the different disk drives will appear.) Double-click on the icon containing a picture of a CD (along with a drive) and labeled "Cce" (followed by a drive letter).
4. (A new window appears.) Double-click on the icon labeled Vb5ccein.exe in the new window.
5. (The following message appears. "Would you like to install Visual Basic 5.0 Control Creation Edition? You will be prompted for an install directory. This application requires Microsoft Windows 95 or greater, or else Microsoft Windows NT 4.0 or greater.") Click on the Yes button.
6. (A license agreement appears.) Click on the Yes button to signify that you accept the terms of the agreement.
7. (You will be shown a list of the folders and files on your hard drive, and you will be asked "Where you would like to copy the Visual Basic 5.0 CCE files?") We recommend that you use the default location C:\Program Files\VB5CCE.
8. (The following statement will appear. "The folder C:\Program Files\VB5CCE does not exist. Do you want to create it?") Click on the Yes button.
9. (After little wait, the following message will appear. "VB5.0 Control Creation installation complete.") Click on the OK button.
10. Return to My Computer and double-click on the file Ccehelp.exe in the Help folder of the CD to install the Visual Basic help files.
11. (Optional) The DOCS folder on the CD contains six programs which install extensive (32 MB) documentation about Visual Basic. Most of the material is not relevant to the topics covered in this textbook. To install some of the documentation, return to My Computer and double-click on one of the files.
12. Close the My Computer window and any other related windows that are open by clicking on the X buttons in their upper right corners.
13. We recommend that you create a shortcut icon to invoke Visual Basic. This can be accomplished with the following steps.
    a. From the Windows desktop, position the mouse pointer over a blank spot and press the right mouse button.
    b. (A pop-up menu will appear.) Point to New and then click on Shortcut in the second pop-up menu that appears.
    c. (A dialog box will appear.) Type in the location and name "C:\Program Files\VB5CCE\VB5CCE.EXE."

   d. Click on the Next button.
   e. (A dialog box requesting a name will appear.) Type in your choice of name, such as VB5CCE.
   f. Click on the Finish button.

B. Install the Learning, Professional, or Enterprise Editions of Visual Basic.

1. Place the CD containing the software into your CD drive.
2. From the Windows Desktop, double-click on My Computer.
3. (A window showing the different disk drives will appear.) Double-click on the icon containing a picture of a CD and having a label beginning "VB50."
4. Double-click on the Setup folder.
5. Double-click on Setup.
6. Follow the directions given by the setup process.

C. Invoke Visual Basic after installation.

1. Click the Start button.
2. Point to Programs.
3. Point to Microsoft Visual Basic 5.0.
4. Point to Visual Basic 5.0.
5. Click on Visual Basic Control Creation Edition or similar name.

D. Exit Visual Basic.

1. Press the Esc key.
2. Press Alt/F/X.
3. If an unsaved program is present, Visual Basic will prompt you about saving it.

Note: In many situations, Step 1 is not needed.

HOW TO: Manage Programs

A. Run a program from Visual Basic.

1. Click on the Start icon (right arrowhead).

   or

1. Press F5.

   or

1. Press Alt/R and make a selection from the Run menu.

B. Save the current program on a disk.

1. Press Alt/F/V [or click the Save Project icon (shows a diskette) on the Toolbar].
2. Fill in the requested information. Do not give an extension as part of the project name or the file name. Two files will be created—one with extension .VBP and the other with extension .FRM. The .VBP file holds a list of files related to the project. The .FRM file actually holds the program.

Note: After a program has been saved once, updated versions can be saved with the same filenames by pressing Alt/F/V. Alt/F/E is used to save the program with new filenames.

C. Begin a new program.

1. Press Alt/F/N.
2. If an unsaved program is present, Visual Basic will prompt you about saving it.

D. Open a program stored on a disk.

1. Press Alt/F/O [or click the Open Project icon (shows an open folder) on the Toolbar].
2. Click on one of the two tabs, Existing or Recent.
3. If you selected Existing, choose a folder for the "Look in:" box, type a filename into the "File name:" box, and press the Enter key. Alternatively, double-click on one of the filenames displayed in the large box in the middle of the dialog box.
4. If you selected Recent, double-click on one or the files in the list.

Note 1: (In Steps 3 and 4, if an unsaved program is present, Visual Basic will prompt you about saving it.)

Note 2: The form for the project may not appear, but it can be accessed through the Project Explorer window.

E. Use the Project Explorer.

Note: Just below the Project Explorer title bar are three icons (View Code, View Object, and Toggle Folders), and below them is the List window. At any time, one item in the List window is selected.

1. Click on View Code to see the code associated with the selected item.
2. Click on View Object to see the Object (usually the form) associated with the selected item.

F. Display the form associated with a program.

1. Press Alt/V/B.

or

1. Press Shift+F7.

or

1. Press Alt/V/P to activate the Project Explorer window.
2. Click on the View Object button.

HOW TO: Use the Editor

A. Mark a section of text as a block.

1. Move the cursor to the beginning or end of the block.
2. Hold down a Shift key and use the direction keys to highlight a block of text.
3. Release the Shift key.

or

1. Move the mouse to the beginning or end of the block.
2. Hold down the left mouse button and move the mouse to the other end of the block.
3. Release the left mouse button.

Note 1: To unblock text, press a direction key or click outside the block.

Note 2: To select a word, double-click on it. To select a line, move the mouse pointer just far enough into the left margin so that the pointer changes, and then single-click there.

B. Delete a line of a program.

1. Move the cursor to the line.
2. Press Ctrl+Y.

   or

1. Mark the line as a block. (See item A of this section.)
2. Press Alt/E/T or press Ctrl+X.

Note: In the preceding maneuvers, the line is placed in the clipboard and can be retrieved by pressing Ctrl+V. To delete the line without placing it in the clipboard, mark it as a block and press Del.

C. Move a line within the Code window.

1. Move the cursor to the line and press Ctrl+Y.
2. Move the cursor to the target location.
3. Press Ctrl+V.

D. Use the clipboard to move or duplicate statements.

1. Mark the statements as a block.
2. Press Ctrl+X to delete the block and place it into the clipboard. Or, press Ctrl+C to place a copy of the block into the clipboard.
3. Move the cursor to the location where you desire to place the block.
4. Press Ctrl+V to place a copy of the text from the clipboard at the cursor.

E. Search for specific text in the program.

1. Press Alt/E/F or Ctrl+F.
2. Type sought-after text into the rectangle.
3. Select desired options if different from the defaults.
4. Press the Enter key.
5. To repeat the search, press Find Next or press Cancel and then F3.

F. Search and change.

1. Press Alt/E/E or Ctrl+H.
2. Type sought-after text into first rectangle.
3. Press Tab.
4. Type replacement text into second rectangle.
5. Select desired options if different from the defaults.
6. Press the Enter key.
7. Press Replace to make the change or press Replace All to make all such changes.

G. Cancel a change.

1. Press Alt/E/U to undo the last change made to a line.

HOW TO: Get Help

A. Obtain information about a Visual Basic topic.

1. Press Alt/H/M.
2. Click on the Index tab and follow the instructions.
3. To display a topic, double-click on it.
4. If a second list pops up, double-click on it.

B. View the syntax and purpose of a Visual Basic keyword.

1. Type the word into a Code window.
2. Place the cursor on, or just following, the keyword.
3. Press F1.

C. Display an ANSI table.

1. Press Alt/H/M and click on the Index tab.
2. Type ANSI and press the Enter key.
3. To move between the displays for ANSI characters 0-127 and 128-255, click on "See Also," and then click on the Display button.

D. Obtain a list of Visual Basic's reserved words.

1. Press Alt/H/M.
2. Type "keywords," press the down-arrow key, and double-click on a category of keywords from the list below the blue bar.

E. Obtain a list of shortcut keys.

1. Press Alt/H/M and click on the Contents tab.
2. Double-click on the Additional Information book.
3. Double-click on the Keyboard Guide book.
4. Double-click on one of the collections of shortcut keys.

F. Obtain information about a control.

1. Click on the control at design time.
2. Press F1.

G. Exit Help.

1. Press Esc.

HOW TO: Manipulate a Dialog Box

A. Use a dialog box.

A dialog box contains three types of items: rectangles (text boxes), option lists, and command buttons. An option list is a sequence of option buttons of the form ◯ *option* or ☐ *option*.

1. Move from item to item with the Tab key. (The movement is from left to right and top to bottom. Use Shift+Tab to reverse the direction.)
2. Inside a rectangle, either type in the requested information or use the direction keys to make a selection.
3. In an option list, an option button of the form ◯ *option* can be activated with the direction keys. A dot inside the circle indicates that the option has been activated.

4. In an option list, an option button of the form ☐ *option* can be activated or deactivated by pressing the space bar. An X or ✓ inside the square indicates that the option has been activated.
5. A highlighted command button is invoked by pressing the Enter key.

B. Cancel a dialog box.

1. Press the Esc key.

   or

1. Press the Tab key until the command button captioned "Cancel" is highlighted and then press the Enter key.

HOW TO: Manage Menus

A. Open a drop-down menu.

1. Click on the menu name.

   or

1. Press Alt.
2. Press the first letter of the name of the menu. Alternatively, use the Right Arrow key to move the highlighted cursor bar to the menu name, and then press the down-arrow key.

B. Make a selection from a drop-down menu.

1. Open the drop-down menu.
2. Click on the desired item.

   or

1. Open the drop-down menu. One letter in each item that is eligible to be used will be underlined.
2. Press the underlined letter. Alternatively, use the down-arrow key to move the cursor bar to the desired item and then press the Enter key.

C. Obtain information about the selections in a drop-down menu.

1. Press Alt/H/M and click on the Contents tab.
2. Double-click on the Interface Reference book.
3. Double-click on the Menu book.
4. Double-click on the name of the menu of interest.
5. Double-click on the selection of interest.

D. Look at all the menus in the menu bar.

1. Press Alt/F.
2. Press the Right Arrow key each time you want to see a new menu.

E. Close a drop-down menu.

1. Press the Esc key or click anywhere outside the menu.

HOW TO: Utilize the Windows Environment

A. Place a section of code in the Windows clipboard.

1. Mark the section of code as a block as described in the "How to Use the Editor" section.

2. Press Ctrl+C.

B. Access the Windows Notepad.

1. Click the Start button.
2. Point to Programs.
3. Point to Accessories.
4. Click Notepad.

C. Display all characters in a font.

1. Click the Start button.
2. Point to Programs.
3. Point to Accessories.
4. Click Character Map.
5. Click on the underlined down arrow at the right end of the Font box.
6. Highlight the desired font and press the Enter key or click on the desired font.

D. Display an ANSI or ASCII code for a character with a code above 128.

1. Proceed as described in item C above to display the font containing the character of interest.
2. Click on the character of interest. Displayed at the right end of the bottom line of the font table is Alt+0xxx, where xxx is the code for the character.

HOW TO: Design a Form

A. Display the ToolBox.

1. Press Alt/V/X.

B. Place a new control on the form.

Option I: (new control with default size and position)

1. Double-click on the control's icon in the ToolBox. The new control appears at the center of the form.
2. Size and position the control as described in item H, which follows.

Option II: (a single new control sized and positioned as it is created)

1. Click on the control's icon in the ToolBox.
2. Move the mouse to the approximate position on the form desired for the upper left corner of the control.
3. Press and hold the left mouse button.
4. Move the mouse to the position on the form desired for the lower right corner of the control. A dashed box will indicate the overall shape of the new control.
5. Release the left mouse button.
6. The control can be resized and repositioned as described in what follows.

Option III: (multiple instances of the same control)

1. Click on the control's icon in the ToolBox while holding down the Ctrl key.

2. Repeatedly use steps 2 through 5 of Option II to create instances of the control.
3. When finished creating instances of this control, click on the arrow icon in the ToolBox.

C. Create a related group of controls.

1. To hold the related group of controls, place a PictureBox or Frame control on the form.
2. Use Option II or III in item B of this section to place controls on the PictureBox or Frame.

D. Set the focus to a particular control.

1. Click on the control.

or

1. Press the Tab key until the control receives the focus.

E. Delete a control.

1. Set the focus to the control to be deleted.
2. Press the Del key.

F. Delete a related group of controls.

1. Set the focus to the PictureBox or Frame holding the related group of controls.
2. Press the Del key.

G. Move a control, related group of controls, or form to a new location.

1. Move the mouse onto the control, the PictureBox or Frame containing the related group of controls, or the title of the form.
2. Drag the object to the new location.

H. Change the size of a control.

1. Set the focus to the desired control.
2. Move the mouse to one of the eight sizing handles located around the edge of the control. The mouse pointer will change to a double arrow pointing in the direction in which resizing can occur.
3. Drag to the desired size.

I. Change the size of a Project Container window.

1. Move the mouse to the edge or corner of the window that is to be stretched or shrunk. The mouse pointer will change to a double arrow pointing in the direction in which resizing can occur.
2. Drag to the desired size.

J. Use the color palette to set foreground and background colors.

1. Set the focus to the desired control or the form.
2. Press Alt/V/L to activate the Color Palette.
3. If the Color Palette obscures the object you are working with, you may wish to use the mouse to grab the Color Palette by its title bar and move it so that at least some of the object shows.

4. To set the foreground color, click on the square within a square at the far left in the Color Palette and click on the desired color from the palette.
5. To set the background color, click on the region within the outer square but outside the inner square and click on the desired color from the palette.

or

1. Set the focus to the desired control or the form.
2. Press Alt/V/W to activate the Properties window.
3. To set the foreground color, click on the down arrow to the right of the ForeColor settings box, click on the Palette tab, and click on the desired color.
4. To set the background color, click on the down arrow to the right of the BackColor settings box, click on the Palette tab, and click on the desired color.

HOW TO: Work with the Properties of an Object

A. Activate the Properties window.

1. Press Alt/V/W.

or

1. Press F4.

or

1. Click on an object on the form with the right mouse button.
2. In the shortcut menu, click on Properties.

B. Highlight a property in the Properties window.

1. Activate the Properties window and press the Enter key.
2. Use the Up or Down Arrow keys to move the highlight bar to the desired property.

or

1. Activate the Properties window.
2. Click on the up or down arrow located at the ends of the vertical scroll bar at the right side of the Properties window until the desired property is visible.
3. Click on the desired property.

C. Select or specify a setting for a property.

1. Highlight the property whose setting is to be changed.
2. Click on the settings box or press Tab to place the cursor in the settings box.
   a. If a black down arrow appears at the right end of the settings box, click on the down arrow to display a list of all allowed settings, and then click on the desired setting.
   b. If an ellipsis (three periods: . . .) appears at the right end of the settings box, press F4 or click on the ellipsis to display a dialog box. Answer the questions in the dialog box and click on OK.
   c. If the cursor moves to the settings box, type in the new setting for the property.

D. Change a property setting of an object.

1. Set the focus to the desired object.
2. Activate the Properties window.
3. Highlight the property whose setting is to be changed.
4. Select or specify the new setting for the property.

E. Let a label change size to accommodate its caption.

1. Set the label's AutoSize property to True. (The label will shrink to the smallest size needed to hold the current caption. If the caption is changed, the label will automatically grow or shrink horizontally to accommodate the new caption. If the WordWrap property is set to True as well, the label will grow and shrink vertically, keeping the same width.)

F. Let a label caption use more than one line.

1. Set the label's WordWrap property to True. [If the label is not wide enough to accommodate the entire caption on one line, part of the caption will wrap to additional lines. If the label height is too small, then part or all of these wrapped lines will not be visible (unless the AutoSize property is set to True).]

G. Let a text box display more than one line.

1. Set the text box's MultiLine property to True. (If the text box is not wide enough to accommodate the text entered by the user, the text will scroll down to new lines. If the text box is not tall enough, lines will scroll up out of view, but can be redisplayed by moving the cursor up.)

H. Assign a hot key to a label or command button.

1. When assigning a value to the Caption property, precede the desired hot key character with an ampersand (&).

I. Allow a particular command button to be activated by a press of the Enter key.

1. Set the command button's Default property to True.

Note: Setting the Default property to True for one command button automatically sets the property to False for all the other command buttons on the form.

J. Adjust the order in which the Tab key moves the focus.

1. Set the focus to the first object in the tabbing sequence.
2. Change the setting of the TabIndex property for this object to 0.
3. Set the focus to the next object in the tabbing sequence.
4. Change the setting of the TabIndex property for this object to 1.
5. Repeat Steps 3 and 4 (adding 1 to the Tab Index property) until all objects on the form have been assigned a new TabIndex setting.

Note: In Steps 2 and 4, if an object is moved to another position in the sequence, then the TabIndex property for the other objects will be renumbered accordingly.

K. Allow the pressing of Esc to activate a particular command button.

1. Set the command button's Cancel property to True. (Setting the Cancel property to True for one command button automatically sets it False for all other command buttons.)

L. Keep the contents of a picture box from being erased.

1. Set the picture box's AutoRedraw property to True. (The default is False. Unless the property is set to True, the contents will be erased when the picture box is obscured by another window.)

HOW TO: Manage Procedures

A. Access the Code Window.

1. Press the Esc key followed by F7. (It is not always necessary to press the Esc key.)

   or

1. Press Alt/V/C.

   or

1. Press Alt/V/P to activate the Project Explorer window.
2. Click on the "View Code" button.

B. Look at an existing procedure.

1. Access the Code Window.
2. Press Ctrl+Down Arrow or Ctrl+Up Arrow to see all the procedures.

   or

1. Access the Code Window.
2. Click on the Down Arrow at the right of the Object box and then select an object. [For general procedures select (General) as the Object.]
3. Click on the Down Arrow at the right of the Procedure box and then select a procedure.

C. Create a procedure.

1. Access the Code Window.
2. Move to a blank line that is not inside a procedure.
3. Type Private Sub (for a subprogram) or Private Function (for a function) followed by the name of the procedure and any parameters.
4. Press the Enter key. (The Code Window will now display the new procedure heading and an End Sub or End Function statement.)
5. Type the procedure into the Code Window.

   or

1. Access the Code Window.
2. Press Alt/T/P. (A dialog box will appear.)
3. Type the name of the procedure into the Name rectangle.
4. Select the type of procedure.
5. Select the Scope by clicking on Public or Private. (In this book we primarily use Private.)

6. Press the Enter key. (The Code window will now display the new procedure heading and an End Sub or End Function statement.)
7. Type the procedure into the Code Window.

D. Alter a procedure.

1. View the procedure in the Code Window as described in item B of this section.
2. Make changes as needed.

E. Remove a procedure.

1. Bring the procedure into the Code Window as described in item B of this section.
2. Mark the entire procedure as a block. That is,
   a. Press Ctrl+PgUp to move the cursor to the beginning of the procedure.
   b. Hold down the Shift key and press Ctrl+PgDown to move the cursor to the start of the next procedure.
   c. Press the up-arrow key until just after the end of the procedure to be deleted.
3. Press the Del key.

F. Insert an existing procedure into a program.

1. Open the program containing the procedure.
2. View the procedure in the Code Window as described in item B of this section.
3. Mark the entire procedure as a block, as described in item E of this section.
4. Press Ctrl+C to place the procedure into the clipboard.
5. Open the program in which the procedure is to be inserted and access the Code Window.
6. Move the cursor to a blank line.
7. Press Ctrl+V to place the contents of the clipboard into the program.

HOW TO: Manage Windows

A. Zoom the active window to fill the entire screen.

1. Click on the maximize button (page icon—second icon from the right) on the title bar of the window.
2. To return the window to its original size, click on the restore (double-page) button that has replaced the maximize button.

B. Move a window.

1. Move the mouse to the title bar of the window.
2. Drag the window to the desired location.

C. Change the size of a window.

1. Move the mouse to the edge of the window which is to be adjusted or to the corner joining the two edges to be adjusted.
2. When the mouse becomes a double arrow, drag the edge or corner until the window has the desired size.

D. Close a window.

1. Click on the X button on the far right corner of the title bar.

HOW TO: Use the Printer

A. Obtain a printout of a program.

1. Press Alt/F/P.
2. Press the Enter key.

Note: To print just the text selected as a block or the active (current) window, use the direction keys to select the desired option.

B. Obtain a printout of the form during run time.

1. Place the statement PrintForm in the Form_Click( ) or other appropriate procedure of the program which will be executed at the point when the desired output will be on the form.

HOW TO: Use the Debugger

A. Stop a program at a specified line.

1. Place the cursor on the desired line.
2. Press F9 or Alt/D/T to highlight the line in red. (This highlighted line is called a *breakpoint*. When the program is run, it will stop at the breakpoint before executing the statement.)

Note: To remove this breakpoint, repeat steps 1 and 2.

B. Remove all breakpoints.

1. Press Alt/D/C or Ctrl+Shift+F9.

C. Run a program one statement at a time.

1. Press F8. The first executable statement will be highlighted. (An event must first occur for which an event procedure has been written.)
2. Press F8 each time you want to execute the currently highlighted statement.

Note: You will probably need to press Alt+Tab to switch back and forth between the form and the VB environment. Also, to guarantee that output is retained while stepping through the program, the AutoRedraw property of the form and any picture boxes may need to be set to True.

D. Run the program one statement at a time, but execute each procedure call without stepping through the statements in the procedure one at a time.

1. Press Shift+F8. The first executable statement will be highlighted.
2. Press Shift+F8 each time you want to execute the currently highlighted statement.

E. Continue execution of a program that has been suspended.

1. Press F5.

Note: Each time an attempt is made to change a suspended program in a way that would prevent the program from continuing, Visual Basic displays a dialog box, warning that the program will have to be restarted from the beginning, and gives the option to cancel the attempted change.

F. Have further stepping begin at the line containing the cursor (no variables are cleared).

1. Press Alt/D/R or Ctrl+F8.

G. Set the next statement to be run in the current procedure.

1. Place the cursor anywhere in the desired statement.
2. Press Alt/D/N or Ctrl+F9.

H. Determine the value of an expression during run time.

1. Press Alt/D/A (Add Watch)
2. Type the expression into the Expression text box, adjust other entries in dialog box (if necessary), and click on OK.

Note: The value of the expression will appear in the Watches window during break mode.

Appendix J

Visual Basic Statements, Functions, Methods, Properties, Data Types, and Operators

This appendix applies to the following objects: form, printer, text box, command button, label, and picture box. The last four are also called *controls*. Terms in brackets follow some of the discussions. These terms refer to supporting topics presented at the end of this appendix.

Abs See Appendix C.

Alignment The Alignment property of a text box or label affects how the text assigned to the Text property is displayed. If the Alignment property is set to 0 (the default), then text is displayed left-justified, if set to 1, then text is right-justified, and if set to 2, then text is centered.

And (Logical Operator) See Appendix C.

And (Bitwise Operator) See Appendix C.

Asc Characters are stored as numbers from 0 to 255. If *str* is a string of characters, then Asc(*str*) is the number corresponding to the first character of *str*. For any *n* from 0 to 255, Asc(Chr(*n*)) is *n*.

Atn See Appendix C.

AutoRedraw The AutoRedraw property determines what happens to graphics and Printed material on a form or picture box after another object (for example, another picture box) temporarily obscures part of the form or picture box. If AutoRedraw is True, then Visual Basic will restore the graphics and Printed material from a copy that it has saved in memory. If AutoRedraw is False, then Visual Basic does not keep track of what graphics and Printed material have been obscured, but it does invoke the Paint event of the form or picture box when the obstruction is removed. Thus only graphics and Printed material generated by the Paint event will be restored when AutoRedraw is False.

AutoSize If the AutoSize property of a label is True, then Visual Basic automatically sets the width and height of the label so that the entire caption can be accommodated. If the AutoSize property is False, then the size of the label is not adjusted by Visual Basic, and captions are clipped if they do not fit.

BackColor The BackColor property determines the background color of an object. For a command button, the background color is used only when the Style property is set to "1 – Graphical." (Such a command button can display a picture.) If the BackColor of a form or picture box is changed while a program is running, all graphics and Printed text directly on the form or picture box are erased.

BackStyle The BackStyle property of a label is opaque (1) by default. The rectangular region associated with the label is filled with the label's background color and caption. If the BackStyle is set to transparent (0), then whatever is behind the label remains visible; the background color of the label essentially becomes "see through."

Beep See Appendix C.

BorderStyle The BorderStyle property determines the type of border on a form, label, picture box, or text box. A BorderStyle of 0 results in no border. This is the default for labels. A BorderStyle of 1 produces a single-line border. This is the default for a picture box or text box. For forms, a BorderStyle of 1 also means that the size of the form cannot be changed by the user when the program is running. For forms, the default BorderStyle is 2, which produces a single-line border and allows the user to change the size of the form when the program is running. Finally, for forms, a BorderStyle of 3 produces a double-line border which cannot be resized by the user.

Call See Appendix C.

Cancel The Cancel property provides a means of responding when the user presses the Esc key. At most one command button on a form may have its Cancel property set to True. If the Esc key is pressed while the program is running, then Visual Basic will execute the click event procedure of the command button whose Cancel property is True.

Caption The Caption property holds the text which is to appear as the caption for a form, command button, or label. If an ampersand (&) is placed in the caption of a command button or label, then the ampersand will not be displayed, but the character following the ampersand will become an underlined hot key. Hot keys provide a quick way to access a command button or the control (usually a text box) following (in tab index order) a label. Hot keys are activated by holding down the Alt key and pressing the hot-key character.

CCur The function CCur converts integer, long integer, single-precision, and double-precision numbers to currency numbers. If x is any number, then the value of CCur(x) is the currency number determined by x.

CDbl See Appendix C.

ChDir See Appendix C.

ChDrive The statement ChDrive *drive* changes the default drive to the drive specified by *drive*. For example, ChDrive "A" specifies the A drive as the new default drive.

Chr See CHR$ in Appendix C.

CInt See Appendix C.

Circle The graphics method *objectName*.Circle $(x,y),r,c,r1,r2,a$ draws on *objectName* a portion, or all, of an ellipse as described for the Circle statement in Appendix C. If k is a number corresponding to one of the 16 standard colors listed in footnote [5] of Appendix C, then using QBColor(*k*) for *c* will produce an ellipse in color *k*. In general, *c* may be any valid RGB color. [color]

Clear The method ClipBoard.Clear clears the clipboard, setting its contents to the null string.

CLng See Appendix C.

Close See Appendix C.

Cls The method *formName*.Cls clears the form *formName* of all text and graphics which have been placed directly on the form with methods like *formName*.Print, *formName*.Circle, etc. The method *pictureBox*.Cls clears the named picture box. The Cls method resets the CurrentX and CurrentY properties of the cleared object to the coordinates of the upper left corner (usually (0,0)).

Const See Appendix C.

Control The Control data type may be used in the parameter lists of Sub and Function definitions to allow the passing of control names to the procedure.

ControlBox The ControlBox property determines whether or not a form has a Control-menu box button in the upper left corner. If the ControlBox property is set to True (the default), then the Control-menu box button is displayed. Among the operations available from the Control-menu box menu is the ability to close the form and thereby end the program. If the ControlBox property of a form is set to false, then the ControlBox button is not displayed. Since, in this case, the user cannot end the program by using the ControlBox or by pressing Alt+F4, it is important to provide a command button for this purpose.

Cos See Appendix C.

CSng See Appendix C.

CStr The function CStr converts integer, long integer, single-precision, double-precision, currency, and variant numbers to strings. If *x* is any number, then the value of CStr(*x*) is the string determined by *x*. Unlike the Str function, CStr does not place a space in front of positive numbers. [variant]

CurDir The value of the function CurDir(*drive*) is a string specifying the current directory on the drive specified by *drive*. The value of CurDir("") or CurDir is a string specifying the current directory on the default drive.

Currency The currency data type is extremely useful for calculations involving money. A variable of type Currency requires 8 bytes of memory and can hold any number from –922,337,203,685,477.5808 to 922,337,203,685,477.5807 with at most four decimal places. Currency values and variables are indicated by the type tag @: 21436587.01@, Balance@.

CurrentX, CurrentY The properties CurrentX and CurrentY give the horizontal and vertical coordinates of the point on a form, picture box, or printer at which the next Print or graphics method will begin. Initially, CurrentX and CurrentY are the coordinates of the upper left corner of the object. The default coordinate system defines the upper left corner of the object as (0,0), with *x* increasing from left to right and *y* increasing from top to bottom in twips. After a graphics method, (CurrentX, CurrentY) are the coordinates of the last point referenced.

CVDate The function CVDate converts a numeric or string expression to an equivalent serial date. If *x* is any expression representing a valid date, then the value of CVDate(*x*) is the serial date determined by *x*. Valid numeric values are –657434 (January 1, 100) to 2958465 (December 31, 9999). Valid string expressions look like one of these valid numeric values (e.g. ,"19497" corresponding to May 18, 1953) or else like a date (e.g., "10 Feb 1955", "August 13, 1958", etc.). [date]

CVar The function CVar converts strings and integer, long integer, single-precision, double-precision, and currency numbers to variants. If *x* is any string or number, then the value of CVar(*x*) is the variant determined by *x*. [variant]

Date See DATE$ in Appendix C.

DateSerial The value of the function DateSerial(*year*,*month*,*day*) is the serial date corresponding to the given year, month, and day. Values from 0 to 9999 are acceptable for *year*, with 0 to 99 interpreted as 1900 to 1999. Values of 1 to 12 for *month* and 1 to 31 for *day* are normal, but any Integer value is acceptable. Often, numeric expressions are used for *month* or *day* which evaluate to numbers outside these ranges. For example, DateSerial(1993, 2, 10 + 90) is the date 90 days after Feb. 10, 1993. [date]

DateValue The value of the function DateValue(*str*) is the serial date corresponding to the date given in *str*. DateValue recognizes the following date formats: "2-10-1955","2/10/1955", "February 10, 1955", "Feb 10, 1955", "10-Feb-1955", and "10 February 1955". For the years 1900 through 1999, the initial "19" is optional. [date]

Day The function Day extracts the day of the month from a serial date. If *d* is any valid serial date, then the value of Day(*d*) is an integer from 1 to 31 giving the day of the month recorded as part of the date and time stored in *d*. [date]

Default When the Default property of a command button is set to True and the focus is on an object that is not another command button, then pressing the Enter key has the same effect as clicking on the button. At most one command button on a form can have True as the value of its Default property.

DefInt, DefLng, DefSng, DefDbl, DefStr, DefCur, DefVar See Appendix C for a general discussion of DefType statements. The statements DefCur and DefVar specify which starting letters for the names of variables are to identify the default variable types currency and variant, respectively. DefType statements are placed in the declarations section of (general). [variant]

Dim See Appendix C for a general discussion of Dim. Visual Basic also permits currency and variant variables. Variables and arrays Dimmed in the (Declarations) section of (General) are available to all procedures. [variant]

Dir If *fileTemplate* specifies a file (or a collection of files by including ? or *), then the value of the function Dir(*fileTemplate*) is the filespec of the first file matching the pattern specified by *fileTemplate*. If this value is not the null string, then the value of the function Dir is the next file that matches the previously specified pattern. For example, the value of Dir("*.VBP") will be a string specifying the first file in the current directory of the default drive whose name has the .VBP extension.

Do/Loop See Appendix C.

DoEvents Executing the statement DoEvents permits Visual Basic to act upon any events which may have occurred while the current event procedure has been executing.

Double See Appendix C.

DrawMode The property DrawMode determines whether graphics are drawn in black, white, foreground color, or some interaction of these colors with the current contents of the form or picture box. The following table lists the allowed values for the DrawMode property and the rules for what RGB color number will be assigned at a given point when the RGB color number for the color currently displayed at that point is *display* and the RGB color number for the draw color is *draw*. [color]

DrawMode	Color produced	
1	&H00000000& (Black)	
2	Not *draw* And Not *display*	(inverse of #15)
3	*display* And Not *draw*	(inverse of #14)
4	Not *draw*	(inverse of #13)
5	*draw* And Not *display*	(inverse of #12)
6	Not *display*	(inverse of #11)
7	*draw* Xor *display*	
8	Not *draw* Or Not *display*	(inverse of #9)
9	*draw* And *display*	
10	Not (*draw* Xor *display*)	(inverse of #7)
11	*display*	(transparent)
12	*display* Or Not *draw*	
13	*draw*	(draw color)
14	*draw* Or Not *display*	
15	*draw* Or *display*	
16	&H00FFFFFF& (White)	

DrawStyle When DrawWidth is 1 for a form or picture box (the default), the property DrawStyle determines whether graphics are drawn using a solid line or some combinations of dots and dashes. Use a DrawStyle of 0 (the default) for solid lines, 1 for dashed lines, 2 for dotted lines, 3 for dash-dot lines, or 4 for dash-dot-dot lines. A DrawStyle of 5 produces "invisible" graphics.

When thick lines are drawn as a result of setting DrawWidth to values greater than 1, graphics are always drawn using solid lines. In this case, DrawStyle can be used either to center the thick line over where a line with a DrawWidth of 1 would be drawn or, when drawing closed figures like ellipses and rectangles, to place the thick line just inside where the line with a DrawWidth of 1 would be drawn. To draw thick graphics inside the normal closed figure, use a DrawStyle of 6. DrawStyles 1 through 4 will center thick graphics over the normal location.

DrawWidth The property DrawWidth determines the width in pixels of the lines which are drawn by graphics methods. The default is 1 pixel. Values from 1 to 32,767 are permitted.

Enabled The property Enabled determines whether or not a form or control responds to events. If the Enabled property of a form or control is set to True (the default), then, if an event occurs for which an event procedure has been written, the event procedure will be executed. When the Enabled property of a form or control is set to False, all events relating to that control are ignored; no event procedures are executed.

End See Appendix C.

EndDoc The method Printer.EndDoc is used to indicate that the document currently being printed is complete and should be released to the printer.

Environ See ENVIRON$ in Appendix C.

Eof See Appendix C.

Eqv See Appendix C.

Erase See Appendix C.

Err and Erl (Functions) See Appendix C.

Err (Statement) See Appendix C.

Error See Appendix C.

Error The value of the function Error is the error message corresponding to the run-time error which has most recently occurred. The value of the function Error(*errNum*) is the error message corresponding to the run-time error designated by *errNum*.

Exit See Appendix C.

Exp See Appendix C.

False A predefined constant whose value is 0. False is used when setting the value of properties that are either True or False. For example, Picture1.FontItalic = False.

FileAttr See Appendix C.

FileCopy The statement FileCopy *source*, *destination* creates the file specified by *destination* by making a copy of the file specified by *source*. Both *source* and *destination* may specify drive and path information. If the file specified by *destination* already exists, it will be overwritten without a warning being issued.

FileDateTime The value of the function FileDateTime(*filename*) is a string giving the date and time that the file specified by *filename* was created or last modified.

FileLen The value of the function FileLen(*filename*) is the length in characters (bytes) of the file specified by *filename*.

FillColor When the FillStyle property of a form or picture box is set to a value other than the default of 1, the property FillColor determines what color is used to paint the interior of ellipses and rectangles drawn with the Circle and Line graphics methods. The FillColor property may be set using the QBColor function or any valid RGB color. The default value for FillColor is black (0). [color]

FillStyle The property FillStyle determines what pattern is used to paint the interior of ellipses and rectangles drawn on forms or picture boxes with the Circle and Line methods. The default value for FillStyle is transparent (1), which means that interiors are not painted. Other values available for FillStyle are solid (0), horizontal lines (2), vertical lines (3), diagonals running upward to the right (4), diagonals running downward to the right, (5) vertical and horizontal lines [crosshatched] (6), and diagonal crosshatched (7). ***Note:*** Using BF in a Line method has the same effect as setting the FillStyle to 0 and the FillColor to the color of the bordering line.

Fix See Appendix C.

Font.Bold The property Font.Bold (or FontBold) determines whether or not the characters Printed on a form, picture box, or printer or assigned to a text box, command button, or label appear in bold or normal type. If the Font.Bold property is set to True (the default), then for a form, picture box, or printer subsequent Printed characters appear bold. For a text box, command button, or label the text or caption is immediately changed to bold. If the Font.Bold property is set to False, then subsequent characters are Printed in normal type, while characters assigned to the text or caption property change immediately to normal type.

FontCount The value of the property Screen.FontCount is the number of fonts available for use on the screen. Similarly, the value of the property Printer.FontCount is the number of fonts available on the printer. The FontCount property is set according to your Windows environment and generally is used to determine the limit on the index for the Fonts property.

Font.Italic The property Font.Italic (or FontItalic) determines whether or not the characters Printed on a form, picture box, or printer or assigned to a text box, command button, or label appear in italic or upright type. If the Font.Italic property is set to True, then for a form, picture box, or printer, subsequent characters appear in italic. For a text box, command button, or label the text or caption is immediately changed to italic. If the FontItalic property is set to False (the default), then subsequent characters are Printed in upright type, while characters assigned to the text or caption property change immediately to upright type.

Font.Name The property Font.Name (or FontName) determines what type face is used when characters are Printed on a form, picture box, or printer or assigned to a text box, command button, or label. If the Font.Name property of a form, picture box, or printer is set to a font obtained from the Fonts property, then all subsequently Printed characters will appear in the new type face. When the Font.Name property of a text box, command button, or label is set to a new font, characters assigned to the text or caption property change immediately to the new type face.

Fonts The value of the property Screen.Fonts(*fontNum*) is the name of a screen font available in the current Windows environment. The index *fontNum* can range from 0 to Screen.FontCount–1. Similarly, the value of the property Printer.Fonts(*fontNum*) is the name of an available printer font. The values in the Fonts property are set by your Windows environment and are generally used to determine which fonts are available for setting the Font.Name property.

Font.Size The property Font.Size (or FontSize) determines the size, in points, of characters Printed on forms, picture boxes, and the printer or displayed in text boxes and on command buttons and labels. Available font sizes depend on your Windows environment but will always be between 1 and 2048. Default font sizes are usually between 8 and 12 point. ***Note:*** One point equals 1/72nd of an inch.

Font.StrikeThru The property Font.StrikeThru (or FontStrikeThru) determines whether or not the characters Printed on a form, picture box, or printer or assigned to a text box, command button, or label appear in a strikethru or standard font. If the Font.StrikeThru property is set to True, then for a form, picture box, or printer, subsequent Printed characters appear with a horizontal line through the middle of each character. For a text box, command button, or label the text or caption is immediately changed so that a horizontal line goes through the middle of each character. If the Font.StrikeThru property is set to False (the default), then subsequent characters are Printed in standard type, while characters assigned to text or caption property change immediately to standard type.

FontTransparent The property FontTransparent determines the degree to which characters Printed to forms and picture boxes obscure existing text and graphics. If the FontTransparent property is set to True (the default), the existing text and graphics is only obscured by the dots (pixels) needed to actually form the new character. If the FontTransparent property is set to False, then all text and graphics are obscured within the character box (small rectangle surrounding a character) associated with the new character. Those dots (pixels) not needed to form the character are changed to the background color.

Font.Underline The property Font.Underline (or FontUnderline) determines whether or not the characters printed on a form, picture box, or printer or assigned to a text box, command button, or label appear with an underline. If the FontUnderline property is set to True, then for a form, picture box, or printer subsequent characters Printed appear underlined. For a text box, command button, or label the text or caption is immediately changed to underlined. If the FontUnderline property is set to False (the default), then subsequent characters are Printed without underlines, while characters assigned to the text or caption property change immediately to nonunderlined.

For/Next See Appendix C.

ForeColor The property ForeColor determines the color used to display text, captions, graphics, and Printed characters. If the ForeColor property of a form or picture box is changed, then subsequent characters will appear in the new color. For a text box, command button, or label the text or caption is immediately changed to the new color. [color]

Format The value of the function Format(*expression*, *str*) is a string representing *expression* (a number, date, time, or string) formatted according to the rules given by *str*. Format is useful when assigning values to the Text property and when Printing to a form, picture box, or the printer.

Numeric output can be formatted with commas, leading and trailing zeros, preceding or trailing signs (+ or –), and exponential notation. This is accomplished either by using for *str* the name of one of several predefined numeric formats or by combining in *str* one or more of the following special numeric formatting characters: #, 0, decimal point (period), comma, %, E–, and E+. The expression to be formatted can evaluate to one of the numeric types or a string representing a number.

Predefined numeric formats include "General Number," which displays a number as is; "Currency," which displays a number with a leading dollar sign and with commas every three digits to the left of the decimal, displays two decimal places, and encloses negative numbers in parentheses; "Fixed," which displays two digits to the right and at least one digit to the left of the decimal point; "Standard," which displays a number with commas and two decimal places but does not use parentheses for negative numbers; "Percent," which multiplies the value by 100 and displays a percent sign after two decimal places; and "Scientific," which displays numbers in standard scientific notation. For example, Format(–5432.352, "Currency") gives the string "($5,432.35)".

The symbol # designates a place for a digit. If the number being formatted does not need all the places provided by the #'s given in *str*, then the extra #'s are ignored. The symbol 0, like #, designates a place for a digit. However, if the number being formatted does not need all the places provided by the 0's given in *str*, then the character 0 is displayed in the extra places. If the number being converted has more whole-part digits than there is space reserved by #'s and 0's, then additional space is used as if the format string had more #'s at its beginning. For example, Format(56, "####") yields "56", Format(56, "#") yields "56", Format(0, "#") yields "", Format(56, "0000") yields "0056", Format(56, "0") yields "56", and Format(0, "0") yields "0".

The decimal-point symbol (.) marks the location of the decimal place. It separates the format rules into two sections, one applying to the whole part of the number and the other to the decimal part. When included in the format string, a decimal point will always appear in the resulting string. For example, Format(56.246, "#.##") yields "56.25", Format(.246, "#.##") yields ".25", Format(.246, "0.##") yields "0.25", and Format(56.2, "0.00") yields "52.20".

The comma symbol (,) placed to the left of the decimal point between #'s and/or 0's causes commas to be displayed to the left of every third digit to the left of the decimal point, as appropriate. If commas are placed to the immediate left of the decimal point (or to the right of all #'s and 0's when the decimal-point symbol is not used), then before the number is formatted, it is divided by 1000 for each comma, but commas will not appear in the result. In order to divide by 1000's and display commas in the result, use format strings like "#,#,.00", which displays the number with commas in units of thousands, and "#,#,,.00", which displays the number with commas in units of millions. For example, Format(1234000, "#,#") yields "1,234,000", Format(1234000, "#,") yields "1234", Format(1234000, "#,.") yields "1234.", Format(1234000, "#,,.0") yields "1.2", and Format(1234000, "#,0,.0") yields "1,234.0".

The percent symbol (%) placed to the right of all #'s, 0's, and any decimal point causes the number to be converted to a percentage (multiplied by 100) before formatting and the symbol % to be displayed. For example, Format(.05624, "#.##%") yields "5.62%", and Format(1.23, "#%") yields "123%".

The symbols E+ and E– placed to the right of all #'s, 0's, and any decimal point cause the number to be displayed in scientific notation. Places for the digits in the exponent must be reserved to the right of E+ or E– with #'s or 0's. When E+ is used and the exponent is positive, a plus sign appears in front of the exponent in the result. When E– is used and the exponent is positive, no sign or space precedes the exponent. When scientific notation is used, each position reserved by #'s to the left of the decimal point is used whenever possible. For example, Format(1234.56, "#.##E+##") yields "1.23E+3", Format(1234.56, "##.##E–##") yields "12.34E2", Format(1234, "###.00E+##") yields "123.40E+1", and Format(123, "###E+00") yields "123E+00".

Date & time output can be formatted using numbers or names for months, putting the day, month, and year in any order desired, using 12-hour or 24-hour notation, etc. This is accomplished either by letting *str* be the name of one of several predefined date/time formats or by combining in *str* one or more special date/time formatting characters. The expression to be formatted can evaluate to a number which falls within the range of valid serial dates or to a string representing a date/time.

Predefined date/time formats include "General Date," which displays a date in mm/dd/yyyy format and, if appropriate, a time in hh:mm:ss PM format; "Long Date," which displays the day of week, the full name of month, the day, and a four-digit year; "Medium Date," which displays the day, abbreviated month name, and two-digit year; "Short Date," which displays mm/dd/yy"; "Long Time," which displays the time in hh:mm:ss PM format; "Medium Time," which displays time in hh:mm PM format; and "Short Time," which displays time in 24-hour format as hh:mm. For example, let dt = DateSerial(55,2,10) + TimeSerial (21,45,30). Then Format(dt, "General Date") yields "2/10/55 9:45:30 PM", Format(dt, "Medium Date") yields "10-Feb-55", and Format(dt, "Short Time") yields "21:45".

Format symbols for the day, month, and year include d (day as number but no leading zero), dd (day as number with leading zero), ddd (day as three-letter name), dddd (day as full name), m (month as number but no leading zero), mm (month as number with leading zero), mmm (month as three-letter name), mmmm (month as full name), yy (year as two-digit number), and yyyy (year as four-digit number). Separators such as slash, dash, and period may be used as desired to connect day, month, and year symbols into a final format. For example, Format("August 13, 1958", "dddd, d.mmm.yy") yields "Wednesday, 13.Aug.58" and Format("July 4, 1776", "ddd: mmmm dd, yyyy") yields "Thu: July 04, 1776". Additional format symbols for dates include w (day-of-week as number 1–7), ww (week-of-year as number 1–53), q (quarter-of-year as number 1–4), y (day-of-year as number 1–366), ddddd (same as short date), and dddddd (same as long date).

Format symbols for the second, minute, and hour include s (seconds with no leading zero), ss (seconds as two-digit number), n (minutes with no leading zero), nn (minutes as two-digit number), h (hours with no leading zero), hh (hours as two-digit number), AM/PM (use 12-hour clock and uppercase), am/pm (use 12 hour clock and lowercase), A/P (use 12-hour clock and single uppercase letter), a/p (use 12-hour clock and single lowercase letter), and ttttt (same as general date). Separators such as colons and periods may be used as desired to connect hour, minute, and second symbols into a final format. For example, Format ("14:04:01", "h:nn AM/PM") yields "2:04 PM", Format("14:04:01", "h.n.s") yields "14.4.1", and Format(0.75, "h:nna/p") yields "6:00p".

String output can be formatted as all uppercase, all lowercase, left-justified or right-justified. Symbols used to format strings are @ (define a field for at least as many characters as there are @ symbols; if less characters than @ symbols, fill remainder of field with spaces; if more characters than @ symbols, display the extra characters—don't clip), & (reserve space for entire output string), < (convert all characters to lowercase before displaying), > (convert all characters to uppercase before displaying), ! (left-justify within field defined by @ symbols; default is to right-justify). For example, Format("Red", "@") yields "Red", Format("Red", "@@@@@@") yields "   Red" (3 leading spaces), Format("Red", "!>@@@@@@") yields "RED   " (3 trailing spaces), and Format("Red", "<&") yields "red".

FreeFile See Appendix C.

Function See Appendix C.

Get (Files) See Appendix C. ***Note:*** The buffer method of working with random-access files is not available in Visual Basic.

GetAttr The value of the function GetAttr(*filename*) is a number indicating the file attributes associated with the file specified by *filename*. Let *attrib* be a variable holding the value returned by GetAttr. Then the file specified by *filename* is a read-only file if *attrib* And 1 = 1, is a hidden file if *attrib* And 2 = 2, is a system file if *attrib* And 4 = 4, is a volume label if *attrib* And 8 = 8, is a directory name if *attrib* And 16 = 16, or has been modified since the last back-up if *attrib* And 32 = 32.

GetText The value of the method ClipBoard.GetText is a string containing a copy of the data currently stored in the clipboard.

GoSub See Appendix C. ***Note:*** Both the GoSub statement and its target must be in the same procedure.

GoTo See Appendix C. ***Note:*** The GoTo statement and its target must be in the same procedure.

Height The property Height determines the vertical size of an object. Height is measured in units of twips. For the Printer object, Height may be read (ph = Printer.Height is OK) but not assigned (Printer.Height = 100 causes an error).

Hex See HEX$ in Appendix C.

Hour The function Hour extracts the hours from a serial date. If *d* is any valid serial date, then the value of Hour(*d*) is a whole number from 0 to 23 indicating the hours recorded as part of the date and time store in *d*. [date]

If (single line) See Appendix C.

If (block) See Appendix C.

If TypeOf To test for the type of a control when the control name is passed to a procedure, use If TypeOf *controlName* Is *controlType* Then *action*1 Else *action*2 in either the single-line or block form of the If statement. ElseIf TypeOf is also permitted. For *controlType*, use one of the control names which appear in the Form Design ToolBox (CommandButton, Label, TextBox, etc.)—for example, If TypeOf objectPassed Is Label Then . . . .

Imp See Appendix C.

Input# See Appendix C.

Input The statement *strVar* = Input(*n*,*m*) assigns the next *n* characters from the file with reference number *m* to *strVar*.

InputBox The value of the function InputBox(*prompt*) is the string entered by the user in response to the prompt given by *prompt*. The InputBox$ function automatically displays the prompt, a text box for user input, an OK button, and a Cancel button in a dialog box in the center of the screen. If the user selects Cancel, the value of the function is the null string (""). For greater control, use the function InputBox(*prompt, title, default, xpos, ypos*), which places the caption *title* in the title bar of the dialog box, displays *default* as the default value in the text box, and positions the upper left corner of the dialog box at coordinates (*xpos, ypos*) on the screen.

Instr See Appendix C.

Int See Appendix C.

Integer See Appendix C.

IsDate The value of the function IsDate(*str*) is True (–1) if the string *str* represents a date between January 1, 100 and December 31, 9999. Otherwise, the value is False (0). [date]

IsEmpty The value of the function IsEmpty(*v*) is True (–1) if *v* is a variable of unspecified type (i.e., is a variant) which has not yet been assigned a value. In all other cases the value of IsEmpty is False (0). [variant]

IsNull The value of the function IsNull(*v*) is True (–1) if *v* is a variant variable which has been assigned the special value Null. In all other cases the value of IsNull is False (0). [variant]

IsNumeric The value of the function IsNumeric(*v*) is True (–1) if *v* is a number, numeric variable, or a variant variable which has been assigned a number or a string which could be obtained by Formatting a number. In all other cases the value of IsNumeric is False (0). [variant]

Kill See Appendix C.

LBound See Appendix C.

LCase See LCASE$ in Appendix C.

Left The property Left determines the position of the left edge of a form or control. The units of measure are twips for forms. The units of measure for a control are determined by the ScaleMode property of the container (form, picture box, etc.) upon which the control has been placed, with the position of the control measured from the edge of its container using the coordinate system established by the various Scale. . . properties for the container. By default, the unit of measure for a container is twips, with a value of 0 for the Left property placing the control against the left edge of the container.

Left See LEFT$ in Appendix C.

Len See Appendix C. If *var* is a variant variable, then Len(*var*) is the number of bytes needed to store *var* as a string. [variant]

Let See Appendix C.

Line The graphics method *objectName*.Line (*x1*,*y1*)–(*x2*,*y2*),c,*rect*,s draws a line or rectangle on *objectName* as describe for the Line statement in Appendix C. If *k* is a number corresponding to one of the 16 standard colors listed in footnote

[5] of Appendix C, then using QBColor(*k*) for *c* will produce a line or rectangle in color *k*. In general, *c* may be any valid RGB color. [color]

Line Input# See Appendix C.

LoadPicture The statement *objectName*.Picture = LoadPicture(*pictureFile*), where *objectName* is a form or picture box, places the picture defined in the file specified by *pictureFile* on *objectName*

Loc See Appendix C.

Lock See Appendix C.

Lof See Appendix C.

Log See Appendix C.

Long See Appendix C.

LSet If *strVar* is a string variable, then the statement LSet *strVar* = *str* replaces the value of *strVar* with a string of the same length consisting of *str* truncated or padded on the right with spaces. LSet also can be used to assign a record of one user-defined type to a record of a different user-defined type.

LTrim See LTRIM$ in Appendix C.

MaxButton The MaxButton property determines whether or not a form has a Maximize button in the upper right corner. If the value of the MaxButton property is set to True (the default), a Maximize button is displayed when the program is run. The user then has the option to click on the Maximize button to cause the form to enlarge and fill the entire screen. If the value of the MaxButton property is set to False, then the Maximize button is not displayed when the program is run, and the user is thus unable to "maximize" the form.

MaxLength The property MaxLength determines the maximum number of characters that a text box will accept. If the MaxLength property for a text box is set to 0 (the default), then an unlimited number of characters may be entered in the text box.

Mid See MID$ in Appendix C.

MinButton The MinButton property determines whether or not a form has a Minimize button in the upper right corner. If the value of the MinButton property is set to True (the default), a Minimize button is displayed when the program is run. The user then has the option to click on the Minimize button to cause the form to be replaced by a small icon in the Taskbar at the bottom of the screen. If the value of the MinButton property is set to False, then the Minimize button is not displayed when the program is run, and the user is thus unable to "minimize" the form.

Minute The function Minute extracts the minutes from a serial date. If *d* is any valid serial date, then the value of Minute(*d*) is a whole number from 0 to 59 giving the minutes recorded as part of the date and time stored in *d*. [date]

MkDir See Appendix C.

Mod See Appendix C.

Month The function Month extracts the month from a serial date. If *d* is any valid serial date, then the value of Month(*d*) is a whole number from 1 to 12 giving the month recorded as part of the date and time stored in *d*. [date]

MousePointer The property MousePointer determines what shape the mouse pointer takes when the mouse is over a particular form or control. Valid values for the MousePointer property are whole numbers from 0 to 12. A value of 0 (the default) indicates that the mouse pointer should take on the normal shape for the control it is over. (The normal shape over text boxes is an I-beam, while for a form, picture box, label, or command button it is an arrow.) Use a MousePointer value of 1 for an arrow, 2 for cross hairs, 3 for an I-beam, 4 for a small square within a square, 5 for a four-pointed arrow, 6 for a double arrow pointing up to the right and down to the left, 7 for a double arrow pointing up and down, 8 for a double arrow pointing up to the left and down to the right, 9 for a double arrow pointing left and right, 10 for an up arrow, 11 for an hourglass, and 12 for a "do not" symbol (circle with diagonal line).

Move The method *objectName*.Move *xpos*, *ypos* moves the named form or control so that its upper left corner has coordinates (*xpos*, *ypos*). For forms, positioning is relative to the upper left corner of the screen. For controls, positioning is relative to the upper left corner of the form, frame, or picture box to which the control is attached. The method *objectName*.Move *xpos*, *ypos*, *width*, *height* also resizes the named form or control to be *width* units wide and *height* units high. The Move method may be used whether or not a form or control is visible. If you wish to specify just a new width for an object, you CANNOT use *objectName*.Move ,,*width*. Instead, use *objectName*.Move *objectName*.Left, *objectName*.Top, *width*. Similar considerations apply for changing just *ypos*, *height*, *width* and *height*, etc.

MsgBox (Statement and Function) The statement MsgBox(*message$*) displays *message$* in a dialog box with an OK button. The more general statement MsgBox *message*, *buttons*, *title* displays *message* in a dialog box with *title* in the title bar and containing from one to three buttons as determined by the value of *buttons*. The value of *buttons* also determines which button is the default (has the focus) and which if any of 4 icons is displayed. The value to use for *buttons* can be computed as follows:

buttons = set number + default number + icon number

where set number, default number and icon number are determined from the following tables:

Buttons Set	**Set Number**
OK	0
OK, Cancel	1
Abort, Retry, Ignore	2
Yes, No, Cancel	3
Yes, No	4
Retry, Cancel	5

Focus Default	**Default Number**
First Button	0
Second Button	256
Third Button	512

Icon	Icon Number
Stop sign	16
Question mark	32
Exclamation mark	48
Information	64

The value of the function MsgBox(*message$*, *buttons*, *title*) indicates which of the displayed buttons the user pushed; in all other aspects the MsgBox statement and function act in the same manner. The values returned for each of the possible buttons pressed are 1 for OK, 2 for Cancel (or Esc), 3 for Abort, 4 for Retry, 5 for Ignore, 6 for Yes, and 7 for No.

MultiLine The property MultiLine determines whether or not a text box can accept and display multiple lines. If the MultiLine property of a text box is set to True, then text entered in the text box will wrap to a new line when the right side of the text box is reached. Pressing the Enter key will also start a new line. If the MultiLine property of a text box is set to False (the default), then input is restricted to a single line, which scrolls if more input is entered than can be displayed within the width of the text box.

Name (Property) The property Name is used at design time to give a meaningful name to a form or control. This new name will then be used by Visual Basic in naming all event procedures for the form or control.

Name (Statement) See Appendix C.

NewPage The method Printer.NewPage indicates that the current page of output is complete and should be sent to the printer. A form feed (Chr(12)) will also be sent to the printer to cause the paper to advance to the top of a new page.

Not (Logical Operator) See Appendix C.

Not (Bitwise Operator) See Appendix C.

Now The value of the function Now() is the serial date for the current date and time as recorded on the computer's internal clock. [date]

Oct See OCT$ in Appendix C.

On Error See Appendix C. ***Note:*** The On Error statement and its target must be in the same procedure.

On. . .GoSub and On. . .GoTo See Appendix C. ***Note:*** The On. . .GoSub or On. . .GoTo statement and its target must be in the same procedure.

Open See Appendix C.

Option Base See Appendix C.

Option Compare The statement Option Compare Text, placed in the (Declarations) section of (General), causes string comparisons to be case insensitive. Thus, if Option Compare Text is in effect, the comparison "make" = "MaKe" will be true. The statement Option Compare Binary placed in the Declarations section produces the default comparison rules which are case sensitive and use the character order given in the ANSI/ASCII character tables.

Option Explicit If the statement Option Explicit appears in the Declarations section of (General), then each variable must be declared before it is used. A variable is declared by appearing in a Const, Dim, Global, ReDim, or Static statement or by appearing as a parameter in a Sub or Function definition.

Or (Logical Operator) See Appendix C.

Or (Bitwise Operator) See Appendix C.

Picture The property Picture allows a form or picture box to be assigned a picture or icon for display. If *iconOrPicture* is a file defining an icon or bitmapped picture, then *objectName*.Picture = LoadPicture(*iconOrPicture*) places the icon or picture on the form or picture box identified by *objectName*.

Point The value of the method *objectName*.Point(*x*,*y*) is the RGB number of the color of the point with coordinates (*x*,*y*) on the form or picture box identified by *objectName*. Thus if the point with coordinates (*x*,*y*) has been painted using color RGB(*r*,*g*,*b*), then the value of Point(*x*,*y*) will be *r*+256**g*+65536**b*. If the coordinates (*x*,*y*) identify a point which is not on *objectName*, then the value of Point(*x*,*y*) will be –1. [color]

Print The method *objectName*.Print displays information on the form, printer, or picture box identified by *objectName* in much the same manner as described for the Print statement in Appendix C. In Visual Basic, there is no limit to the number of characters or the number of print zones on a line.

Printer The Printer object provides access to the printer. Methods available are Print to send text to the printer, NewPage to execute a form feed to begin a new page, EndDoc to terminate the printing process, and the graphics methods. Many properties available for forms and picture boxes, such as fonts and scaling, are also available for the printer.

PrintForm The method *formName*.PrintForm prints on the printer an image of the named form and all its contents.

PSet The graphics method *objectName*.PSet(*x*,*y*) displays the point with coordinates (*x*,*y*) in the foreground color. The method *objectName*.PSet(*x*,*y*),*c* causes the point (*x*,*y*) to be displayed in the RGB color specified by *c*. The size of the point is determined by the value of the DrawWidth property. The actual color(s) displayed depend on the values of the DrawMode and DrawStyle properties. [color]

Put (Files) See Appendix C. **Note**: The buffer method of working with random-access files is not available in Visual Basic.

QBColor The value of the function QBColor(*colorAttrib*) is the RGB color number associated with the QBasic color attribute *colorAttrib*. Valid values for *colorAttrib* are whole numbers from 0 to 15. This function is included in Visual Basic for easy access to QBasic's 16 standard colors. [color]

Randomize See Appendix C.

ReDim See Appendix C. ReDim may only be used within procedures; it may not be used in the (Declarations) section of (General). To establish a global array which may be resized, Dim it with empty parentheses in the (Declarations) section of (General) and then ReDim it as needed within appropriate procedures.

Refresh The method *objectName*.Refresh causes the named form or control to be refreshed, that is, redrawn reflecting any changes made to its properties.

Generally, refreshing occurs automatically, but if not, it may be forced with the Refresh method.

Rem See Appendix C.

Reset See Appendix C.

Resume See Appendix C.

Return See Appendix C.

RGB The value of the function RGB(*red, green, blue*) is the color number corresponding to a mixture of *red* red, *green* green, and *blue* blue. This color number is assigned to color properties or used in graphics methods to produce text or graphics in a particular color. Each of the three color components may have a value from 0 to 255. The color produced using RGB(0,0,0) is black, RGB(255,255,255) is white, RGB(255,0,0) is bright red, RGB(10,0,0) is a dark red, etc. (The value of the function RGB(*r,g,b*) is the long integer *r*+256**g*+ 65536**b*.) [color]

Right See RIGHT$ in Appendix C.

RmDir See Appendix C.

Rnd See Appendix C.

RSet If *strVar* is a string variable, then the statement RSet *strVar* = *str* replaces the value of *strVar* with a string of the same length consisting of *str* truncated or padded on the left with spaces.

RTrim See RTRIM$ in Appendix C.

Scale The method *objectName*.Scale (*x1*, *y1*) – (*x2*, *y2*) defines a coordinate system for the form or picture box identified by *objectName*. This coordinate system has horizontal values ranging from *x1* at the left edge of *objectName* to *x2* at the right edge and vertical values ranging from *y1* at the top edge of *objectName* to *y2* at the bottom edge. Subsequent graphics methods and control positioning place figures and controls in accordance with this new coordinate system. As a result of using the Scale method, the ScaleMode property of *objectName* is set to 0, the ScaleLeft property to *x1*, the ScaleTop property to *y1*, the ScaleHeight property to *y2–y1*, and the ScaleWidth property to *x2–x1*. The method *objectName*.Scale without arguments resets the coordinate system of *objectName* to the standard coordinate system where the unit of measure is twips and the upper left corner of *objectName* has coordinates (0,0).

ScaleHeight The property ScaleHeight determines the vertical scale on a form or picture box. After the statement *objectName*.ScaleHeight = *hght* is executed, the vertical coordinates range from *objectName*.ScaleTop at the top edge of *objectName* to *objectName*.ScaleTop + *hght* at the bottom edge. The default value of the ScaleHeight property is the height of *objectName* when measured in the units specified by *objectName's* ScaleMode property.

ScaleLeft The property ScaleLeft determines the horizontal coordinate of the left edge of a form or picture box. After the statement *objectName*.ScaleLeft = *left* is executed, the horizontal coordinates will range from *left* at the left edge of *objectName* to *left* + *objectName*.ScaleWidth at the right edge. The default value of the ScaleLeft property is 0.

ScaleMode The property ScaleMode determines the horizontal and vertical unit of measure for the coordinate system on a form or picture box. If the ScaleMode property of a form or picture box is set to 1 (the default), then the unit of measure become twips. Other possible values for ScaleMode are 2 for points (72 points = 1 inch), 3 for pixels, 4 for characters (1 horizontal unit = 120 twips; 1 vertical unit = 240 twips), 5 for inches, 6 for millimeters, and 7 for centimeters. A value of 0 for the ScaleMode property indicates that units of measure are to be determined from the current settings of the ScaleHeight and ScaleWidth properties. Visual Basic automatically sets the ScaleMode property of an object to 0 when any of the object's Scale. . . properties are assigned values.

ScaleTop The property ScaleTop determines the vertical coordinate of the top edge of a form or picture box. After the statement *objectName*.ScaleTop = *top* is executed, the vertical coordinates range from *top* at the top edge of *objectName* to *top* + *objectName*.ScaleHeight at the bottom edge. The default value for the ScaleTop property is 0.

ScaleWidth The property ScaleWidth determines the horizontal scale on a form or picture box. After the statement *objectName*.ScaleWidth = *wdth* is executed, the horizontal coordinates range from *objectName*.ScaleLeft at the left edge of *objectName* to *objectName*.ScaleLeft + *wdth* at the right edge. The default value of the ScaleWidth property is the width of *objectName* when measured in the units specified by *objectName's* ScaleMode property.

Second The function Second extracts the seconds from a serial date. If *d* is any valid serial date, then the value of Second(*d*) is a whole number from 0 to 59 giving the seconds recorded as part of the date and time stored in *d*. [date]

Seek See Appendix C.

Select Case See Appendix C.

SendKeys The statement SendKeys *str* places in the keyboard buffer the characters and keystrokes specified by *str*. The effect is exactly the same as if the user had typed the series of characters/keystrokes at the keyboard. The statement SendKeys *str*, True places keystrokes in the keyboard buffer and waits until these keystrokes are processed (used) before allowing program execution to continue with the next statement in the procedure containing the SendKeys statement. Keystrokes can be specified which do not have a displayable character or which result from using the Shift, Ctrl, or Alt keys. See the Visual Basic Help Topics for further details.

Set The statement Set *objectVar* = *objectExpression* associates the name *objectVar* with the object identified by *objectExpression*. For example, if the statements

```
Dim Scenery AS PictureBox
Set Scenery = Picture1
```

are executed, then Scenery becomes another name for Picture1, and references like Scenery.Print *message* are equivalent to Picture1.Print *message*.

SetAttr The statement SetAttr *filename*, *attribute* sets the file attribute of the file specified by *filename*. A file's attribute can be 0 for "Normal" or a combination of 1, 2, or 4 for "Read-only", "Hidden", and "System." In addition, a file can be marked as "changed since last backup" by adding 32 to its attribute. Thus, for example, if a file's attribute is set to 35, (1+2+32) the file is classified as a Read-only Hidden file which has been changed since the last backup.

SetFocus The method *objectName*.SetFocus moves the focus to the named form or control. Only the object with the focus can receive user input from the keyboard or the mouse. If *objectName* is a form, the form's default control, if any, receives the focus. Disabled and invisible objects cannot receive the focus. If an attempt is made to set focus to a control which cannot receive the focus, the next control in tab order receives the focus.

SetText The method ClipBoard.SetText *info* replaces the contents of the clipboard with the string *info*.

Sgn See Appendix C.

Shell See Appendix C.

Sin See Appendix C.

Single See Appendix C. While QBasic's default variable type is Single, Visual Basic's default variable type is Variant. [variant]

Space See SPACE$ in Appendix C.

Spc See Appendix C.

Sqr See Appendix C.

Static See Appendix C. In a procedure, arrays created by Dim or ReDim are lost when the procedure is exited. Arrays which are local to a procedure yet retained from one invocation of the procedure to the next can be created by dimensioning the array in the procedure with a Static statement rather than a Dim or ReDim statement. Dimensions for static arrays must be numeric constants.

Stop See Appendix C.

Str See STR$ in Appendix C.

StrComp The value of the function StrComp(*str1*, *str2*, *compMode*) is –1, 0, 1, or Null, depending on whether *str1* < *str2*, *str1* = *str2*, *str1* > *str2*, or either of *str1* and *str2* is Null. The comparison will be case sensitive if *compMode* is 0 and case insensitive if *compMode* is 1.

String See Appendix C.

String See STRING$ in Appendix C.

Sub/End Sub See Appendix C.

Tab See Appendix C.

TabIndex The property TabIndex determines the order in which the tab key moves the focus about the objects on a form. Visual Basic automatically assigns successive tab indexes as new controls are created at design time. Visual Basic also automatically prevents two controls on the same form from having the same tab index by renumbering controls with higher tab indexes when the designer or program directly assigns a new tab index to a control.

Tan See Appendix C.

Text The property Text holds the information assigned to a text box. A statement of the form *textBoxName*.Text = *str* changes the contents of *textBoxName* to the string specified by *str*. A statement of the form *str* = *textBoxName*.Text assigns the contents of *textBoxName* to *str*.

TextHeight The value of the method *objectName*.TextHeight(*str*) is the amount of vertical space required to display the contents of *str* using the font currently assigned for *objectName*. These contents may include multiple lines of text resulting from the use of carriage-return/line-feed pairs (Chr(13) + Chr(10)) in *str*. The units of height are those specified by the ScaleMode and ScaleHeight properties of *objectName* (the default is twips).

TextWidth The value of the method *objectName*.TextWidth(*str*) is the amount of horizontal space required to display the contents of *str* using the font currently assigned for *objectName*. When carriage-return/line-feed pairs (Chr(13) + Chr(10)) create multiple lines in *str*, this will be the space required for the longest line.

Time See TIME$ in Appendix C.

Timer See Appendix C.

TimeSerial The value of the function TimeSerial(*hour,minute,second*) is the serial date corresponding to the given hour, minute, and second. Values from 0 (midnight) to 23 (11 p.m.) for *hour*, and 0 to 59 for both *minute* and *second* are normal, but any Integer value may be used. Often, numeric expressions are used for *hour*, *minute*, or *second* which evaluate to numbers outside these ranges. For example, TimeSerial(15–5, 20–30, 0) is the serial time 5 hours and 30 minutes before 3:20 p.m.

TimeValue The value of the function TimeValue(*str*) is the serial date corresponding to the time given in *str*. TimeValue recognizes both the 24-hour and 12-hour time formats: "13:45:24" or "1:45:24PM".

Top The property Top determines the position of the top edge of a form or control. The units of measure are twips for forms. The units of measure for a control are determined by the ScaleMode property of the container (form, picture box, etc.) upon which the control has been placed, with the position of the control measure from the edge of its container using the coordinate system established by the various Scale. . . properties for the container. By default, the unit of measure for a container is twips, with a value of 0 for the Top property placing the control against the top edge of the container.

True A predefined constant whose value is –1. True is used when setting the value of properties that are either True or False. For example, Picture1.FontItalic = True.

Type/End Type See Appendix C. User-defined types may also include Currency or Variant elements. [variant]

UBound See Appendix C.

UCase See UCASE$ in Appendix C.

Unlock See Appendix C.

Val See Appendix C.

Variant A variable of type Variant can be assigned numbers, strings, and several other types of data. Variant variables are written without type declaration tags. [variant]

VarType The value of the function VarType(*var*) is a number indicating the type of value stored in *var*. This function is primarily used to check the type of data stored in a variant variable. The values returned by VarType are 0 for "Empty," 1 for "Null," 2 for Integer, 3 for Long Integer, 4 for Single Precision, 5 for Double Precision, 6 for Currency, 7 for Date, and 8 for String. [variant]

Visible The property Visible determines whether or not a form or control is displayed. If the Visible property of an object is True, then the object will be displayed (if not covered by other objects) and respond to events if its Enabled property is True. If the Visible property of an object is set to False, then the object will not be displayed and cannot respond to events.

WeekDay The value of the function WeekDay(*d*) is a number giving the day of the week for the date store in *d*. These values will range from 1 for Sunday to 7 for Saturday.

While/Wend See Appendix C.

Width (Property) The property Width determines the horizontal size of an object. Width is measured in units of twips. For the Printer object, Width may be read (pw = Printer.Width is ok) but not assigned (Printer.Width = 100 causes an error).

Width (Statement) If *s* is an integer less than 255 and *n* is the reference number of a file opened in sequential mode, then the statement Width #*n*,*s* causes Visual Basic to permit at most *s* characters to be printed on a single line in the file. Visual Basic will send a carriage-return/line-feed pair to the file after *s* characters have been printed on a line, even if the Print# or Write# statement would not otherwise start a new line at that point. The statement Width #*n*,0 specifies infinite width; that is, a carriage-return/line-feed pair will be sent to the printer only when requested by Print# or Write#.

WordWrap The WordWrap property of a label with AutoSize property set to True determines whether or not long captions will wrap. (When a label's AutoSize property is False, word wrap always occurs, but the additional lines will not be visible if the label is not tall enough.) Assume a label's AutoSize property is True. If its WordWrap property is set to True, then long captions will wrap to multiple lines, while if its WordWrap property is False (the default), then the caption will always occupy a single line. If a label has its WordWrap and AutoSize property set to True, then the label's horizontal length is determined by its Width property, with long captions being accommodated by having the label expand vertically so that word wrap can spread the caption over several lines. If a label's WordWrap property is set to False while its AutoSize property is True, then the label will be one line high and will expand or shrink horizontally to exactly accommodate its caption.

Write# See Appendix C.

Xor (Logical Operator) See Appendix C.

Xor (Bitwise Operator) See Appendix C.

Year The function Year extracts the year from a serial date. If *d* is any valid serial date, then the value of Year(*d*) is a whole number from 100 to 9999 giving the year recorded as part of the date and time stored in *d*. [date]

Supporting Topics

[color]: Numbers written in base 16 are referred to as hexadecimal numbers. They are written with the digits 0, 1, 2, 3, 4, 5, 6, 7, 8, 9, A (= 10), B (= 11), C (= 12), D (= 13), E (= 14), and F (= 15). A hexadecimal number such as *rst* corresponds to the decimal integer $t + 16^*s + 16^2{}^*r$. Each color in Visual Basic is identified by a long integer (usually expressed as a hexadecimal number of the form &H. . .&) and referred to as an RGB color number. This number specifies the amounts of red, green, and blue combined to produce the color. The amount of any color is a relative quantity, with 0 representing none of the color and 255 representing the maximum available. Thus black corresponds to 0 units each of red, green, and blue, while white corresponds to 255 units each of red, green, and blue. The RGB color number corresponding to *r* units of red, *g* units of green, and *b* units of blue is *r*+256**g*+65536*b, which is the value returned by the function RGB(*r*,*g*,*b*). Hexadecimal notation provides a fairly easy means of specifying RGB color numbers. If the amount of red desired is expressed as a two-digit hexadecimal number, *rr*, the amount of green in hexadecimal as *gg*, and the amount of blue in hexadecimal as *bb*, then the RGB color number for this color is &H00*bbggrr*&. For example, the RGB color number for a bright green would come from 255 (FF in hexadecimal) units of green, so the RGB color number in hexadecimal is &H0000FF00&.

[date]: Functions dealing with dates and times use the type 7 variant data type. Dates and times are stored as serial dates, double-precision numbers, with the whole part recording the date and the decimal part recording the time. Valid whole parts range from –657434 to 2958465, which correspond to all days from January 1, 100 to December, 31, 9999. A whole part of 0 corresponds to December 30, 1899. All decimal parts are valid, with .0 corresponding to midnight, .25 corresponding to 6 a.m., .5 corresponding to noon, and so on. In general, the decimal equivalent of *sec*/86400 corresponds to *sec* seconds past midnight. If a given date corresponds to a negative whole part, then times on that day are obtained by adding a negative decimal part to the negative whole part. For example, October, 24, 1898, corresponds to a whole part of –432. A time of 6 p.m. corresponds to .75, so a time of 6 p.m. on 10/24/1898 corresponds to –432 + –.75 = –432.75.

[variant]: Variant is a new variable type that is not present in QBasic. Any variable which is used without a type declaration tag ($, %, &, !, #, @) or without being declared as a specific type using an As clause or a DefType statement is treated as a variant variable. A variable of type Variant can hold any type of data. When values are assigned to a variant variable, Visual Basic keeps track of the "type" of data which has been stored. Visual Basic recognizes 8 types of data: type 0 for "Empty" (nothing yet has been stored in the variable; the default), type 1 for "Null" (the special value Null has been assigned to the variable), type 2 for Integer, type 3 for Long integer, type 4 for Single precision, type 5 for Double precision, type 6 for Currency, type 7 for Date/time, and type 8 for String. A single variant variable may be assigned different data types at different points in a program, although this is usually not a good programming technique. The data assigned to a variant array need not all be of the same type. As a result, a variant array can be used in much the same way as a user-defined type to store related data.

Answers

To Selected Odd-Numbered Exercises

CHAPTER 1

Exercises 1.2

1. View window
3. Disk Operating System
5. Untitled
7. A toggle key changes back and forth between two states.
9. Ctrl+Y
11. Backspace
13. Del
15. Home
17. Shift+F5
19. Cursor down
21. Alt/F/X
23. Ctrl+End
25. Esc
27. Tab
29. Alt/F/N
31. Enter
33. F1
35. PgUp
37. Alt/H/I or Alt/H/C

Exercises 1.3

1. COPY
3. RENAME
5. DIR
7. MD
9. RD
11. NAME

CHAPTER 3

Exercises 3.1

1. 12
3. .03125
5. 8
7. 3E+09
9. 4E–08
11. Valid
13. Valid
15. Not valid
17. 10
19. 16
21. 9
23.
```
CLS
PRINT 7 * 8 + 5
END
```
25.
```
CLS
PRINT .055 * 20
END
```
27.
```
CLS
PRINT 17 * (3 + 162)
END
```
29.

x	*y*
2	0
2	6
11	6
11	6
11	7
11	7

31. 6
33.
```
 1    2    3    4
 11
```
35.
```
 0
 64
```
37. 27 12
39. The third line should read LET c = a + b
41. The first line should not contain a comma. The second line should not contain a dollar sign.
43.
```
PRINT 1; 2; 1 + 2
END
```

45.
```
CLS
LET revenue = 98456
LET costs = 45000
LET profit = revenue - costs
PRINT profit
END
```

47.
```
CLS
LET price = 19.95
LET discountPercent = 30
LET markDown = (discountPercent / 100) * price
LET price = price - markDown
PRINT price
END
```

49.
```
CLS
LET balance = 100
LET balance = balance + balance * .05
LET balance = balance + balance * .05
LET balance = balance + balance * .05
PRINT balance
END
```

51.
```
CLS
LET balance = 100
LET balance = balance * (1.05 ^ 10)
PRINT balance
END
```

53.
```
CLS
LET acres = 30
LET yieldPerAcre = 18
LET corn = yieldPerAcre * acres
PRINT corn
END
```

55.
```
CLS
LET distance = 233
LET time = 7 - 2
LET averageSpeed = distance / time
PRINT averageSpeed
END
```

57.
```
CLS
LET waterPerPersonPerDay = 1600
LET people = 260000000
LET days = 365
LET waterUsed = waterPerPersonPerDay * people * days
PRINT waterUsed
END
```

Exercises 3.2

1. Hello
   1234

3. 12 12 TWELVE

5. A ROSE IS A ROSE IS A ROSE

7. 1234 Main Street

9. "We're all in this alone." Lily Tomlin

11. phone should be phone$.

13. The sentence in the first line must be enclosed by quotation marks.

15. mid$ is a keyword and cannot be used as a variable name.

17.
```
CHR$(52)+CHR$(116)+CHR$(104)+CHR$(58)+CHR$(32)+CHR$(34)+CHR$(66)+
CHR$(97)+CHR$(98)+CHR$(101)+CHR$(34)+CHR$(32)+CHR$(82)+CHR$(117)+
CHR$(116)+CHR$(104)
```

19.
```
CLS
LET item$ = "ketchup"
LET regularPrice = 1.8
LET discount = .27
PRINT regularPrice - discount; "is the sale price of "; item$
END
```

21.
```
CLS
LET prefix$ = "Fore"
PRINT prefix$; "warned is "; prefix$; "armed."
END
```

23.
```
CLS
LET totalPrice = 68
LET numberOfOunces = 17
LET pricePerOunce = totalPrice / numberOfOunces
PRINT "The price per ounce is"; pricePerOunce; "cents."
END
```

25.
```
CLS
LET radius = 6170
LET volume = (4 / 3) * 3.14159 * (radius ^ 3)
PRINT "The volume of the earth is"; volume; "cubic kilometers."
END
```

27.
```
CLS
PRINT CHR$(218); CHR$(196); CHR$(196); CHR$(196); CHR$(191)
PRINT CHR$(192); CHR$(196); CHR$(196); CHR$(196); CHR$(217)
END
```

Exercises 3.3

1. 16

3. unspeakable

5. The White House has 132 rooms.

7. What is the current year? 1998
   Harvard University is 360 years old.

9. Enter your favorite color: red
How many red sweaters do you have? 2
You have 2 red sweaters.

11. Illegal to READ a + 2 to a numeric variable.

13. DATA and READ variables do not match.

15.

t	c$	*p*
0	“”	0
0	“phone”	35.25
35.25	“phone”	35.25
35.25	“postage”	14.75
50	“postage”	14.75
50	“postage”	14.75
50	“postage”	14.75
50	“postage”	14.75
50	“postage”	14.75

17.
```
REM Compute change in majors
CLS
READ major$ percent1990, percent1997
PRINT "The percentage change for "; major$; " was"; percent1997 - percent1990
READ major$, percent1990, percent1997
PRINT "The percentage change for "; major$; " was"; percent1997 - percent1990
DATA "Biological sciences", 4, 7
DATA "Computer Science", 2, 3
END
```

19.
```
REM Report percent price increase for a basket of goods
CLS
LET begOfYearPrice = 200
INPUT "Enter price at the end of the year: ", endOfYearPrice
LET percentIncrease = 100 * (endOfYearPrice - begOfYearPrice) / begOfYearPrice
PRINT "The percent increase for the year is"; percentIncrease
END
```

21.
```
REM Report checking account activity
CLS
REM 1st account
READ account$, beginningBalance, deposits, withdrawals
LET endOfMonth = beginningBalance + deposits - withdrawals
LET total = endOfMonth
PRINT "Monthly balance for account "; account$; " is"; endOfMonth
REM 2nd account
READ account$, beginningBalance, deposits, withdrawals
LET endOfMonth = beginningBalance + deposits - withdrawals
LET total = total + endOfMonth
PRINT "Monthly balance for account "; account$; " is"; endOfMonth
REM 3rd account
READ account$, beginningBalance, deposits, withdrawals
LET endOfMonth = beginningBalance + deposits - withdrawals
LET total = total + endOfMonth
PRINT "Monthly balance for account "; account$; " is"; endOfMonth
PRINT "Total for all accounts ="; total
REM --- Data: account number, beginning balance, deposits, withdrawals
DATA AB4057, 1234.56, 345.67, 100.00
DATA XY4321,  789.00, 120.00, 350.00
DATA GH2222,  321.45, 143.65,   0.00
END
```

23.
```
REM Compute semester averages
CLS
REM 1st student
READ socNmb$, exam1, exam2, exam3, final
LET average = (exam1 + exam2 + exam3 + final * 2) / 5
LET total = average
PRINT "Semester average for "; socNmb$; " is"; average
REM 2nd student
READ socNmb$, exam1, exam2, exam3, final
LET average = (exam1 + exam2 + exam3 + final * 2) / 5
LET total = total + average
PRINT "Semester average for "; socNmb$; " is"; average
REM 3rd student
READ socNmb$, exam1, exam2, exam3, final
LET average = (exam1 + exam2 + exam3 + final * 2) / 5
LET total = total + average
PRINT "Semester average for "; socNmb$; " is"; average
PRINT "Class average is"; total / 3
REM --- Data: soc. sec. #, exam 1, exam 2, exam 3, final
DATA 123-45-6789, 67, 85, 90, 88
DATA 111-11-1111, 93, 76, 82, 80
DATA 123-32-1234, 85, 82, 89, 84
END
```

25.
```
REM Predict storm distance
CLS
INPUT "Enter seconds between lightning and thunder: ",
seconds
PRINT "Storm is"; seconds / 5; "miles away."
END
```

27.
```
REM Calculate number of pounds lost from various activities
CLS
INPUT "Enter number of hours bicycling: ", bicycling
INPUT "Enter number of hours jogging: ", jogging
INPUT "Enter number of hours swimming: ", swimming
LET pounds = (bicycling * 200 + jogging * 475 + swimming * 275) / 3500
PRINT "Number of pounds worked off ="; pounds
END
```

29.
```
REM Add 5 points to a grade
CLS
INPUT "Enter the grade: ", grade
LET grade = grade + 5
PRINT "The new grade is"; grade
END
```

Exercises 3.4

1. MCD'S
3. 10
5. 6
7. AB
9. e
11. 4
13. 0
15. now
17. 17
19. 2
21. 3
23. −3
25. 0
27. Lul
29. ullaby
31. LULLABY
33. 0
35. by
37. 5
39. kylab
41. Today is Thu
43. o
45. I guess your answer is yes
47. Bill, your house number is 1600
49. In the second line, k should be "k".
51. DATA statements cannot contain an expression.
53. The variable numString is numeric, but VAL can only be applied to a string variable.

55.
```
REM Display the units digit of a number
CLS
INPUT "Enter a positive integer with at most 7 digits: ", num
PRINT "The units digit is "; RIGHT$(STR$(num), 1)
END
```

57.
```
REM Calculate speed of a car given distance skidded
CLS
INPUT "Enter the distance skidded: ", d
LET speed = SQR(24 * d)
PRINT "Estimated speed ="; speed; "miles per hour."
END
```

59.
```
REM Display number of trick-or-treaters you can treat
CLS
INPUT "Enter number of pieces of Halloween candy: ", candy
LET children = INT(candy / 3)
PRINT "The number of children you can treat is"; children
END
```

61.
```
REM Convert inches to feet and inches
CLS
INPUT "Length in inches"; length
LET feet = INT(length / 12)
LET remainder = length - feet * 12
PRINT feet; "feet,"; remainder; "inches"
END
```

63.
```
REM Position of letter in sentence
CLS
LET s$ = "THE QUICK BROWN FOX JUMPS OVER A LAZY DOG"
INPUT "Letter"; letter$
LET position = INSTR(s$, UCASE$(letter$))
PRINT letter$; " first occurs in position"; position
END
```

65.
```
REM Day of the week
CLS
LET week$ = "SUMOTUWETHFRSA"
INPUT "Day of week"; day$
LET d2$ = UCASE$(LEFT$(day$, 2))
LET position = (INSTR(week$, d2$) + 1) / 2
PRINT day$; " is day number"; position
END
```

67.
```
REM Modify a sentence
CLS
INPUT "Sentence"; s$
INPUT "Word to find"; f$
INPUT "Replace with"; r$
LET n = INSTR(s$, f$)
PRINT LEFT$(s$, n - 1); r$; MID$(s$, n + LEN(f$), LEN(s$))
END
```

Exercises 3.5

1. 1 one   won

3.
```
1234567890
    5
```

5. hello (on line 20 of the screen)

7. hello (begins at third row, second column)

9.
```
1234567890
ABC abc
```

11. 1234567890
%123456

13. No 26th row

15. Comma in first line should be a semicolon.

17. 300.00

19. $ 98.76

21. The median age in the U.S. is 31.3

23. LET a$ = "$######.##"

25.
```
LET r = 2
LET c = 0
```

27.
```
REM Produce table for 1990-96 earnings of athletes
CLS
PRINT TAB(31); "Salary or"
PRINT "Athlete"; TAB(17); "Sport"; TAB(31); "Winnings";
PRINT TAB(42); "Endorsements"; TAB(57); "Total"
LET a$ = "\            \ \        \    ###.#        ###.#       ###.#"
READ athlete$, sport$, salary, income
LET total = salary + income
PRINT USING a$; athlete$; sport$; salary; income; total
READ athlete$, sport$, salary, income
LET total = salary + income
PRINT USING a$; athlete$; sport$; salary; income; total
READ athlete$, sport$, salary, income
LET total = salary + income
PRINT USING a$; athlete$; sport$; salary; income; total
READ athlete$, sport$, salary, income
LET total = salary + income
PRINT USING a$; athlete$; sport$; salary; income; total

REM --- Data: athlete, sport, salary, other income
DATA M. Jordan, basketball, 29.3, 193.2
DATA E. Holyfield, boxing, 110.3, 7.5
DATA A. Agassi, tennis, 11.3, 63.5
DATA W. Gretsky, hockey, 36.8, 31.5
END
```

29.
```
REM Center a string
CLS
INPUT "String"; a$
LET position = (82 - LEN(a$)) / 2
PRINT TAB(position); a$
END
```

31.
```
REM Compute balance
CLS
INPUT "Principal"; principal
INPUT "Interest rate (percent)"; interest
LET earnings = .01 * interest * principal
PRINT "                Earned            New"
PRINT " Principal    Interest        Balance"
PRINT
LET a$ = "$##,###.##       ###.##    $$##,###.##"
PRINT USING a$; principal; earnings; principal + earnings
END
```

33.
```
REM Display number flush left
CLS
INPUT "Number to display: ", num
INPUT "Screen Row: ", row
CLS
LOCATE row, 1
LET num$ = STR$(num)
PRINT RIGHT$(num$, LEN(num$) - 1)
END
```

CHAPTER 4

Exercises 4.1

1. It isn't easy being green.
   Kermit the frog

3. Why do clocks run clockwise?
   Because they were invented in the northern hemisphere where sundials move clockwise.

5. Divorced, beheaded, died;
   Divorced, beheaded, survived.

7. Keep cool, but don't freeze.
   Source: A jar of mayonnaise.

9. 88 keys on a piano

11. It was the best of times.
    It was the worst of times.

13. Your name has 7 letters.
    The first letter is G

15. abcde

17. 144 items in a gross

19. 30% of M&M's Plain Chocolate Candies are brown.

21. 1440 minutes in a day

23. t is the 6 th letter of the word.

25. According to a poll in the May 31, 1988 issue of PC Magazine,
    75% of the people polled write programs for their companies.
    The four most popular languages used are as follows.
     22 percent of the respondents use BASIC
     16 percent of the respondents use Assembler
     15 percent of the respondents use C
     13 percent of the respondents use Pascal

27. President Bush is a graduate of Yale University
    President Clinton is a graduate of Georgetown University

29. The first 2 letters are QB

31. The negative of worldly is unworldly

33. 24 blackbirds baked in a pie.

35. There is a parameter in the subprogram, but no argument in the statement calling the subprogram.

37. Since Print is a keyword, it cannot be used as the name of a subprogram.

39.
```
REM Display a lucky number
CLS
LET num = 7
CALL Lucky(num)
END

SUB Lucky (num)
  REM Display message
  PRINT num; "is a lucky number."
END SUB
```

41.
```
REM Give information about trees
CLS
READ tree$, height
CALL Tallest(tree$, height)
READ tree$, height
CALL Tallest(tree$, height)
DATA redwood, 362, pine, 223
END

SUB Tallest (tree$, height)
  REM Display information about tree
  PRINT "The tallest ";tree$;" in the U.S. is";height;"feet."
END SUB
```

43.
```
REM Given a number, display its triple
CLS
INPUT "Enter a number: ", num
CALL Triple(num)
END

SUB Triple (num)
  REM Multiply the value of the number by 3
  PRINT "The number's triple is"; 3 * num
END SUB
```

45.
```
REM Enter a word and column number to display
CLS
INPUT "Enter a word: ", word$
INPUT "Enter a column number between 1 and 10: ", col
CALL PlaceNShow(word$, col)
END

SUB PlaceNShow (word$, col)
  REM Display the word at the given column number
  PRINT TAB(col); word$
END SUB
```

47.
```
REM Intended college majors
CLS
CALL DisplaySource
READ students, field$
CALL Majors(students, field$)
READ students, field$
CALL Majors(students, field$)
DATA 16, business, 3, computer science
END

SUB DisplaySource
  REM Display the source of the information
  PRINT "According to a 1997 survey of college freshmen"
  PRINT "taken by the Higher Educational Research Institute:"
  PRINT
END SUB

SUB Majors (students, field$)
  REM Display the information about major
  PRINT students; "percent said they intend to major in"; field$
END SUB
```

49.
```
REM Favorite number
CLS
INPUT "What is your favorite number"; num
CALL Sum (num)
CALL Product(num)
END

SUB Product (num)
  PRINT "The product of your favorite number with itself is"; num * num
END SUB

SUB Sum (num)
  PRINT "The sum of your favorite number with itself is"; num + num
END SUB
```

51.
```
REM Old McDonald Had a Farm
CLS
READ animal$, sound$
CALL ShowVerse(animal$, sound$)
PRINT
READ animal$, sound$
CALL ShowVerse(animal$, sound$)
PRINT
READ animal$, sound$
CALL ShowVerse(animal$, sound$)
PRINT
READ animal$, sound$
CALL ShowVerse(animal$, sound$)
REM --- Data: animal, sound
DATA lamb, baa, firefly, blink, chainsaw, brraap, computer, beep
END

SUB ShowVerse (animal$, sound$)
  REM Display a verse from Old McDonald Had a Farm
  PRINT "Old McDonald had a farm. Eyi eyi oh."
```

```
    PRINT "And on his farm he had a "; animal$; ".  Eyi eyi oh."
    PRINT "With a "; sound$; " "; sound$; " here,";
    PRINT "and a "; sound$;" "; sound$; " there."
    PRINT "Here a "; sound$; ", there a "; sound$;
    PRINT ", everywhere a "; sound$; " "; sound$; "."
    PRINT "Old McDonald had a farm. Eyi eyi oh."
  END SUB
```

53.
```
REM Display a table of occupations experiencing fastest job growth 1994-2005
CLS
PRINT TAB(57); "Percent"
PRINT "Occupation"; TAB(35); "1994"; TAB(46); "2005"; TAB(57); "Change"
PRINT
CALL ComputeChange
CALL ComputeChange
CALL ComputeChange
CALL ComputeChange
REM --- Data: field, 1994 jobs, 2005 jobs
DATA "Personal home care aids", 179, 391
DATA "Home health aides", 420, 848
DATA "Systems analysts", 483, 928
DATA "Computer engineers", 195, 372
END

SUB ComputeChange
  REM Read data and compute change, display all data
  READ job$, jobs94, jobs05
  LET change = 100 * (jobs05 - jobs94) / jobs94
  PRINT job$;
  PRINT USING "####"; TAB(34); jobs94; TAB(45); jobs05;
  PRINT USING "###%"; TAB(57); change
END SUB
```

Exercises 4.2

1. 9
3. Can Can
5. 25
7. Less is more
9. Gabriel was born in the year 1980
11. Buckeyes
13. 0
15. 1 1
17. discovered Florida
19. The variable *c* should be a parameter in the subprogram. That is, the SUB statement should be SUB Sum (x, y, c).

21.
```
REM Calculate sales tax
CLS
CALL InputPrice(price)
CALL Compute(price, tax, cost)
CALL ShowData(price, tax, cost)
END

SUB Compute (price, tax, cost)
  REM Calculate the cost
  LET tax = .05 * price
  LET cost = price + tax
END SUB

SUB InputPrice (price)
  REM Get the price of the item
  INPUT "Enter the price of the item: ", price
END SUB

SUB ShowData (price, tax, cost)
  REM Display bill
  PRINT "Price: "; price
  PRINT "Tax: "; tax
  PRINT "-----------"
  PRINT "Cost: "; cost
END SUB
```

23.
```
REM Compute area of rectangle
CLS
CALL InputSize(length, wdth)
CALL ComputeArea(length, wdth, area)
CALL ShowArea(area)
REM --- Data: length, width
DATA 4, 5
END

SUB ComputeArea (length, wdth, area)
  REM Calculate the area
  LET area = length * wdth
END SUB

SUB InputSize (length, wdth)
  REM Get the dimensions of the rectangle
  READ length
  READ wdth
END SUB

SUB ShowArea (area)
  REM Display the area of the rectangle
  PRINT "The area of the rectangle is"; area
END SUB
```

25.
```
REM Display initials
CLS
CALL InputNames (first$, last$)
CALL ExtractInitials(first$, last$, fInit$, lInit$)
CALL DisplayInitials(fInit$, lInit$)
END

SUB DisplayInitials (fInit$, lInit$)
  REM Display the initials
  PRINT "The initials are "; fInit$;". "; lInit$; "."
END SUB

SUB ExtractInitials (first$, last$, fInit$, lInit$)
  REM Determine the initials of the first and last names
  LET fInit$ = LEFT$(first$,1)
  LET lInit$ = LEFT$(last$,1)
END SUB

SUB InputNames (first$, last$)
  REM Get the persons first and last name
  INPUT "Enter your first name: ", first$
  INPUT "Enter your last name: ", last$
END SUB
```

27.
```
REM Calculate percentage markup
CLS
CALL InputAmounts(cost, price)
CALL ComputeMarkup(cost, price, markup)
CALL DisplayMarkup(markup)
END

SUB ComputeMarkup (cost, price, markup)
  LET markup = 100 * ((price - cost) / cost)
END SUB

SUB DisplayMarkup (markup)
  PRINT "The markup is"; markup; "percent."
END SUB

SUB InputAmounts (cost, price)
  INPUT "Enter the cost: ", cost
  INPUT "Enter the selling price: ", price
END SUB
```

29.
```
REM Calculate batting average
CLS
CALL ReadStats(name$, atBats, hits)
CALL ComputeAverage(atBats, hits, ave)
CALL DisplayInfo(name$, ave)
DATA Sheffield, 557, 184
END

SUB ComputeAverage (atBats, hits, ave)
  LET ave = hits / atBats
END SUB

SUB DisplayInfo (name$, ave)
  PRINT "Name", "Batting Average"
  PRINT name$,
  PRINT USING ".###"; ave
END SUB

SUB ReadStats (name$, atBats, hits)
  READ name$, atBats, hits
END SUB
```

31.
```
REM Display Hat Rack mall comparison table
CLS
PRINT "Mall Name    Rent per Square Foot    ";
PRINT "Total Feet    Monthly Rent"
PRINT
LET a$ = "\        \        $$##.##               ####        $#,###.##"
CALL DisplayInfo(a$)
CALL DisplayInfo(a$)
CALL DisplayInfo(a$)
REM --- Data: mall, rent per square foot, number of square feet
DATA Green Mall, 6.50, 583, Red Mall, 7.25, 426, Blue Mall, 5.00, 823
END
```

```
SUB ComputeRent (rent, feet, total)
  REM Compute monthly rent given rent/foot and number of feet
  LET total = rent * feet
END SUB

SUB DisplayInfo (a$)
  REM Display the information for a single mall
  READ mall$, rentPerFoot, squareFeet
  CALL ComputeRent(rentPerFoot, squareFeet, rent)
  PRINT USING a$; mall$; rentPerFoot; squareFeet; rent
END SUB
```

Exercises 4.3

1. 35

3. The population will double in 24 years.

5. Volume of cylinder having base area 3.14159 and height 2 is 6.28318
   Volume of cylinder having base area 28.27431 and height 4 is 113.0972

7. train

9. moral has the negative amoral
   political has the negative apolitical

11. A dollar sign is missing from the end of the function name.

13.
```
REM Convert Celsius to Fahrenheit
CLS
CALL InputTemp(t)
CALL ShowNewTemp(t)
END

FUNCTION CtoF (t)
  REM Calculate Fahrenheit temperature from Celsius
  CtoF = (9 / 5) * t + 32
END FUNCTION

SUB InputTemp (t)
  INPUT "Enter a temperature in Celsius: ", t
END SUB

SUB ShowNewTemp (t)
  PRINT t; "degrees Celsius is"; CtoF(t); "degrees Fahrenheit"
END SUB
```

15.
```
REM Round a number m to n decimal places
CLS
CALL InputData(m, n)
CALL RoundIt(m, n)
END

SUB InputData (m, n)
  INPUT "Enter a number to round: ", m
  INPUT "Round it to how many decimal places"; n
END SUB
FUNCTION Rounded (m, n)
  REM Round a number to a given number of decimal places
  Rounded = INT (m * 10 ^ n  + .5) / (10 ^ n)
END FUNCTION

SUB RoundIt (m, n)
  PRINT m; "rounded to"; n; "places is"; Rounded(m, n)
END SUB
```

17.
```
REM Popcorn Profits
CLS
CALL InputAmounts(popCost, butterCost, bucketCost, price)
CALL ShowProfit(popCost, butterCost, bucketCost, price)
END

SUB InputAmounts (popCost, butterCost, bucketCost, price)
  INPUT "What is the cost of the popcorn kernels"; popCost
  INPUT "What is the cost of the butter"; butterCost
  INPUT "What is the cost of the bucket"; bucketCost
  INPUT "What is the sale price"; price
END SUB

FUNCTION Profit (popCost, butterCost, bucketCost, price)
  REM Calculate the profit on a bucket of popcorn
  Profit = price - (popCost + butterCost + bucketCost)
END FUNCTION

SUB ShowProfit (popCost, butterCost, bucketCost, price)
  PRINT "The profit is";
  PRINT Profit(popCost, butterCost, bucketCost, price)
END SUB
```

19.
```
REM Cost of airmail
CLS
CALL InputWeight(weight)
CALL ShowCost(weight)
END

FUNCTION Ceil (x)
  Ceil = -INT(-x)
END FUNCTION

FUNCTION Cost (weight)
  REM Calculate the cost of an airmail letter
  Cost = .05 + .10 * Ceil(weight - 1)
END FUNCTION

SUB InputWeight (weight)
  INPUT "Enter the weight of the letter in ounces: ", weight
END SUB

SUB ShowCost (weight)
  PRINT "The cost of mailing the letter is"; Cost(weight)
END SUB
```

21.
```
REM Display a greeting for a senator
CLS
INPUT "Enter the senator's name: ", name$
PRINT
PRINT "The Honorable "; name$
PRINT "United States Senate"
PRINT "Washington, DC 20001"
PRINT
PRINT "Dear Senator "; LastName$(name$); ","
END

FUNCTION LastName$ (name$)
  REM Determine the last name of a two part name
  LET spaceNmb = INSTR(name$, " ")
  LastName$ = MID$(name$, spaceNmb + 1, LEN(name$) - spaceNmb)
END FUNCTION
```

CHAPTER 5

Exercises 5.1

1. TRUE
3. TRUE
5. TRUE
7. TRUE
9. FALSE
11. FALSE
13. TRUE
15. TRUE
17. FALSE
19. FALSE
21. FALSE
23. TRUE
25. Equivalent
27. Not Equivalent
29. Equivalent
31. Not Equivalent
33. Equivalent
35. a <= b
37. (a >= b) OR (c = d)
39. (a$ = “”) OR (a$ >= b$) OR (LEN(a$) >= 5)

Exercises 5.2

1. Less than ten
3. Tomorrow is another day.
5. 10
7. The cost of the call is $11.26
9. The number of vowels is 2
11. positive
13. Incorrect conditional. Should be IF (1 < num) AND (num < 3) THEN
15. no THEN
17. Comparing numeric and string data
19. Incorrect conditional. Should be IF (j = 4) OR (k = 4) THEN
21. LET a = 5
23.
```
IF j = 7 THEN
    LET b = 1
  ELSE
    LET b = 2
END IF
```
25.
```
INPUT "Is Alaska bigger than Texas and California combined"; answer$
IF UCASE$(LEFT$(answer$, 1)) = "Y" THEN
    PRINT "Correct"
  ELSE
    PRINT "Wrong"
END IF
END
```

27.
```
REM Give waiter a tip
CLS
INPUT "Enter cost of meal: ", cost
LET tip = cost * .15
IF tip < 1 THEN
    LET tip = 1
END IF
PRINT USING "Leave $$#.## for the tip."; tip
END
```

29.
```
REM Order diskettes
CLS
INPUT "Number of diskettes"; num
IF num < 25 THEN
    LET cost = num
  ELSE
    LET cost = .7 * num
END IF
PRINT USING "The cost is $$##.##"; cost
END
```

31.
```
REM Savings account withdrawal
CLS
INPUT "Current balance"; balance
INPUT "Amount of withdrawal"; amount
IF balance >= amount THEN
    LET balance = balance - amount
    PRINT "New balance is"; balance
    IF balance < 150 THEN
        PRINT "Balance below $150"
    END IF
  ELSE
    PRINT "Withdrawal denied."
END IF
END
```

33.
```
REM Lottery
CLS
INPUT "Enter three digits (d,d,d): ", d1, d2, d3
LET lucky$ = "Lucky seven"
IF d1 = 7 THEN
    IF (d2 = 7) OR (d3 = 7) THEN
        PRINT lucky$
    END IF
  ELSE
    IF (d2 = 7) AND (d3 = 7) THEN
        PRINT lucky$
    END IF
END IF
END
```

35.
```
REM Convert to Pig Latin
CLS
INPUT "Enter a word: ", word$
LET f$ = LEFT$(word$, 1)
IF INSTR("aeiou", f$) <> 0 THEN
    LET word$ = word$ + "way"
  ELSE
    LET word$ = MID$(word$, 2, LEN(word$) - 1) + f$ + "ay"
END IF
PRINT "The word in pig latin is"; word$
END
```

37.
```
REM Calculate New Jersey state income tax
CLS
INPUT "Taxable income"; income
IF income <= 20000 THEN
    LET tax = .02 * income
  ELSE
    IF income <= 50000 THEN
        LET tax = 400 + .025 * (income - 20000)
      ELSE
        LET tax = 1150 + .035 * (income - 50000)
    END IF
END IF
PRINT USING "Tax is $$##,###.##"; tax
END
```

Exercises 5.3

1. 3.75
3.75

3. Mesozoic Era
Paleozoic Era
?

5. Nope.
He worked with the developer, von Neumann, on the ENIAC.
Correct

7. The less things change, the more they remain the same.
Less is more.
Time keeps everything from happening at once.

9. Should have a CASE.

11. Comparing numeric (0 TO 9) and string data (a$).

13. Error in second CASE.

15. Selector is a condition.

17. Valid

19. Invalid

21. Valid

23.
```
SELECT CASE a
  CASE 1
    PRINT "one"
  CASE IS > 5
    PRINT "two"
END SELECT
```

25.
```
SELECT CASE a
  CASE 2
    PRINT "yes"
  CASE IS < 5
    PRINT "no"
END SELECT
```

27.
```
REM Determine degree of cloudiness
CLS
INPUT "Percentage of cloud cover"; percent
SELECT CASE percent
  CASE 0 TO 30
    PRINT "Clear"
  CASE 31 TO 70
    PRINT "Partly cloudy"
  CASE 71 TO 99
    PRINT "Cloudy"
  CASE 100
    PRINT "Overcast"
  CASE ELSE
    PRINT "Percentage must be between 0 AND 100."
END SELECT
END
```

29.
```
REM Give number of days in month
CLS
CALL InputMonth(month$)
CALL GetDays(month$, days)
CALL ShowDays(days, month$)END
END

SUB GetDays (month$, days)
  REM Compute number of days in the month
  SELECT CASE UCASE$(month$)
    CASE "FEBRUARY"
      INPUT "Is it a leap year"; ans$
      IF UCASE$(LEFT$(ans$, 1)) = "Y" THEN
          LET days = 29
        ELSE
          LET days = 28
      END IF
    CASE "APRIL", "JUNE", "SEPTEMBER", "NOVEMBER"
      LET days = 30
    CASE "JANUARY", "MARCH", "MAY", "JULY", "AUGUST", "OCTOBER", "DECEMBER"
      LET days = 31
  END SELECT
END SUB

SUB InputMonth (month$)
  REM Input a month of the year
  INPUT "Enter a month (do not abbreviate): ", month$
END SUB

SUB ShowDays (days, month$)
  REM Report number of days in month
  PRINT month$; " has"; days; "days."
END SUB
```

31.
```
REM Give letter grade for number score
CLS
CALL InputScore(score)
CALL ShowGrade(score)
END

FUNCTION Grade$ (score)
  REM Return letter grade for score
  SELECT CASE score
    CASE 90 TO 100
      Grade$ = "A"
    CASE 80 TO 89
      Grade$ = "B"
    CASE 70 TO 79
      Grade$ = "C"
    CASE 60 TO 69
      Grade$ = "D"
    CASE 0 TO 59
      Grade$ = "F"
    CASE ELSE
      Grade$ = "Invalid"
  END SELECT
END FUNCTION

SUB InputScore (score)
  REM Input a number score
  INPUT "What is the score"; score
END SUB

SUB ShowGrade (score)
  REM Show letter grade for score
  PRINT "The letter grade is "; Grade$(score)
END SUB
```

33.
```
REM Determine cash award
CLS
INPUT "How much was recovered"; amount
SELECT CASE amount
  CASE IS <= 75000
    LET amount = .1 * amount
  CASE IS <= 100000
    LET amount = 7500 + .05 * (amount - 75000)
  CASE IS > 100000
    LET amount = 8750 + .01 * (amount - 100000)
    IF amount > 50000 THEN
        LET amount = 50000
    END IF
END SELECT
PRINT "The amount given as reward is $"; amount
END
```

CHAPTER 6

Exercises 6.1

1. 17
3. You are a super programmer!
5. 2
7. Program never stops
9. DO and LOOP interchanged
11. WHILE num >= 7
13. UNTIL response$ <> "Y"
15. UNTIL name$ = ""
17. UNTIL (a <= 1) OR (a >= 3)
19. WHILE n = 0
21.
```
REM Request and display three numbers
CLS
LET count = 0
DO WHILE count < 3
  INPUT "Enter a number: ", num
  PRINT num
  LET count = count + 1
LOOP
END
```

23.
```
REM Convert Celsius to Fahrenheit
CLS
CALL InputTemp(celsius)
CALL ShowFahrenheit(celsius)
END

FUNCTION Fahrenheit (celsius)
  REM Convert Celsius to Fahrenheit
  Fahrenheit = (9 / 5) * celsius + 32
END FUNCTION

SUB InputTemp (celsius)
  REM Input a Celsius temperature
  DO
    INPUT "Enter a Celsius temperature: ", celsius
  LOOP UNTIL (celsius >= 0) AND (celsius <= 100)
END SUB

SUB ShowFahrenheit (celsius)
  REM Give Fahrenheit equivalent
  PRINT "The Fahrenheit temperature is"; Fahrenheit(celsius)
END SUB
```

25.
```
REM Forecast weather in Oregon
CLS
DO
  INPUT "Can you see the mountains (Y/N)"; ans$
  LET ltr$ = UCASE$(LEFT$(ans$, 1))
  IF ltr$ = "Y" THEN
      PRINT "It is going to rain."
    ELSEIF ltr$ = "N" THEN
      PRINT "It is raining."
  END IF
LOOP UNTIL (ltr$ = "Y") OR (ltr$ = "N")
END
```

27.
```
REM Ask for number until product exceeds 400
CLS
LET highest = 0
LET product = 1
CALL Description
DO
  CALL InputNumber(num)
  CALL Calculate(num, product, highest)
LOOP UNTIL product > 400
CALL ShowHighest(highest)
END

SUB Calculate (num, product, highest)
  REM Calculate product and highest number
  LET product = product * num
  IF num > highest THEN
      LET highest = num
  END IF
END SUB

SUB Description
  REM Give directions of program
  PRINT "Continue entering numbers until their product exceeds 400."
  PRINT "The computer will tell you which number is highest."
  PRINT
END SUB

SUB InputNumber (num)
  REM Input a number
  INPUT "Enter a positive number: ", num
END SUB

SUB ShowHighest (highest)
  REM Show highest number entered
  PRINT "The highest number was"; highest
END SUB
```

29.
```
REM Determine the year when the population
REM of Mexico City reaches 20 million
CLS
LET pop = 14
LET yr = 0
DO WHILE pop < 20
  LET pop = pop + pop * .03
  LET yr = yr + 1
LOOP
PRINT "The population will reach 20 million in"; yr; "years."
END
```

31.
```
REM Tell which letter, r or n, appears first
CLS
DO
  CALL InputWord(word$)
  CALL FindLetters(word$, rPlace, nPlace)
LOOP UNTIL (rPlace >= 1) AND (nPlace >= 1)
CALL ShowFirst(rPlace, nPlace)
END

SUB FindLetters (word$, rPlace, nPlace)
  REM Find position of letters in word
  LET rPlace = INSTR(word$, "r")
  LET nPlace = INSTR(word$, "n")
END SUB

SUB InputWord (word$)
  REM Input a word
  INPUT "Enter a word: ", word$
END SUB

SUB ShowFirst (rPlace, nPlace)
  REM Tell which letter, r or n, comes first
  IF nPlace > rPlace THEN
      PRINT "r is first"
    ELSE
      PRINT "n is first"
  END IF
END SUB
```

33.
```
REM Years to deplete savings account
CLS
LET amt = 15000
LET yrs = 0
DO
  LET amt = amt * 1.05 - 1000
  LET yrs = yrs + 1
LOOP UNTIL amt <= 0
PRINT "It takes"; yrs; "years to deplete the account."
END
```

35.
```
REM Years to get a million dollars
CLS
LET amt = 1000
LET yrs = 0
DO
  LET amt = amt * 1.05 + 1000
  LET yrs = yrs + 1
LOOP UNTIL amt >= 1000000
PRINT yrs; "years are required to reach one million dollars."
END
```

37.
```
REM Prime factorization
CLS
INPUT "Enter an integer: ", n
LET f = 2
DO WHILE n > 1
  IF n / f <> INT(n / f) THEN
      LET f = f + 1
    ELSE
      PRINT f
      LET n = n / f
  END IF
LOOP
END
```

Exercises 6.2

1. 13

3. pie
cake
melon
EOD

5.
```
  A
Apple
Apricot
Avocado

  B
Banana
Blueberry

  G
Grape

  L
Lemon
Lime
```

7. A group of ducks is called a brace

9. counters

11. LOOP missing

13. EOD will be printed.

15.
```
REM Find largest of a collection of numbers
CLS
PRINT "Enter -1 when finished."
LET largest = 0
DO
  INPUT "Enter a number: ", num
  IF num > largest THEN
      LET largest = num
  END IF
LOOP UNTIL num = -1
PRINT "The largest number is"; largest
END
```

17.
```
REM Report grades of eggs
CLS
PRINT "Enter negative number when finished."
PRINT
CALL InputWeight(ounces)
DO WHILE ounces >= 0
  CALL ShowGrade(ounces)
  CALL InputWeight(ounces)
LOOP
END

SUB InputWeight (ounces)
  REM Input weight in ounces
  INPUT "Weight of egg in ounces"; ounces
END SUB

SUB ShowGrade (ounces)
  IF ounces < 1.5 THEN
      PRINT "Send it to the bakery."
    ELSE
      PRINT "The grade is";
      SELECT CASE ounces
        CASE IS < 1.75
          PRINT "Small"
        CASE IS < 2
          PRINT "Medium"
        CASE IS < 2.25
          PRINT "Large"
        CASE IS < 2.5
          PRINT "Extra Large"
        CASE ELSE
          PRINT "Jumbo"
      END SELECT
  END IF
  PRINT
END SUB
```

19.
```
REM Half problem
CLS
INPUT "Enter a positive integer: ", n
LET count = 0
DO WHILE n <> 1
  LET count = count + 1
  IF (n / 2) = INT(n / 2) THEN
      LET n = n / 2
      PRINT n;
    ELSE
      LET n = 3 * n + 1
      PRINT n;
  END IF
LOOP
PRINT
PRINT "It took"; count; "steps to reach 1."
END
```

21.
```
REM Population growth
CLS
LET counter = 0
LET totGrowth = 0
LET growth = 0
READ state$, pop2010
DO WHILE state$ <> "EOD"
  LET counter = counter + 1
  CALL InputPop(state$, popNow)
  CALL Compute(pop2010, popNow, growth, totGrowth)
  CALL ShowGrowth(growth)
  READ state$, pop2010
LOOP
CALL ShowAveGrowth(totGrowth, counter)
REM --- Data: state, population in millions
DATA California, 37.6
DATA Texas, 22.9
DATA New York, 18.5
DATA Illinois, 12.5
DATA Florida, 17.4
DATA EOD, 0
END

SUB Compute (pop2010, popNow, growth, totGrowth)
  REM Compute growth and total growth
  LET growth = 100 * (pop2010 - popNow) / popNow
  LET totGrowth = totGrowth + growth
END SUB

SUB InputPop (state$, popNow)
  REM Input current population of state
  PRINT "What is the current population (in millions) of "; state$;
  INPUT popNow
END SUB

SUB ShowAveGrowth (totGrowth, counter)
  REM Compute and display the average growth
  LET aveGrowth = totGrowth / counter
  PRINT "The average growth for these states is"; aveGrowth; "percent."
END SUB

SUB ShowGrowth (growth)
  REM Report the population growth, in percent
  PRINT "The population grew by"; growth; "percent."
  PRINT
END SUB
```

23.
```
REM Report two highest scores
CLS
LET highest = 0
LET nextHighest = 0
CALL InputScore(score)
DO WHILE score >= 0
  CALL CheckForHighScore(score, highest, nextHighest)
  CALL InputScore(score)
LOOP
CALL ShowHighScores(highest, nextHighest)
END

SUB CheckForHighScore (score, highest, nextHighest)
  REM Check if score is highest or next to highest
  IF score > highest THEN
      LET nextHighest = highest
      LET highest = score
    ELSE
      IF score > nextHighest THEN
          LET nextHighest = score
      END IF
  END IF
END SUB

SUB InputScore (score)
  REM Input a score
  INPUT "Enter a score (-1 to stop): ", score
END SUB

SUB ShowHighScores (highest, nextHighest)
  REM Show highest and next highest scores
  PRINT "The highest score is"; highest
  PRINT "The next to highest score is"; nextHighest
END SUB
```

25.
```
REM Compute grade-point average and give message
CLS
LET totalCredHrs = 0
LET totalQualityPts = 0
CALL InputCourseInfo(totalQualityPts, totalCredHrs)
CALL ShowGPA(totalQualityPts, totalCredHrs)
END

SUB InputCourseInfo (totalQualityPts, totalCredHrs)
  REM Input a letter grade and the number of credit hours
  PRINT "Enter *, 0 after all grades have been reported."
  PRINT "Letter grade and number of credit hours for a
course";
  INPUT grade$, credits
  DO WHILE grade$ <> "*"
    SELECT CASE UCASE$(grade$)
      CASE "A"
        LET grade = 4
      CASE "B"
        LET grade = 3
      CASE "C"
        LET grade = 2
      CASE "D"
        LET grade = 1
      CASE ELSE
        LET grade = 0
    END SELECT
    LET totalQualityPts = totalQualityPts + grade * credits
    LET totalCredHrs = totalCredHrs + credits
    PRINT "Grade and number of credit hours for a course";
    INPUT grade$, credits
  LOOP
END SUB

SUB ShowGPA (totalQualityPts, totalCredHrs)
  REM Display the grade-point average and a message
  LET average = GPA (totalQualityPts, totalCredHrs)
  PRINT "The GPA is ";
  PRINT USING "#.##"; average
  IF average >= 3 THEN
      PRINT "Congratulations! You made the honor roll."
    ELSE
      PRINT "Congratulations on your completed semester."
  END IF
  PRINT "Have a merry vacation."
END SUB

FUNCTION GPA (totalQualityPts, totalCredHrs)
  REM Calculate grade-point average
  IF totalCredHrs = 0 THEN
      GPA = 0
    ELSE
      GPA = totalQualityPts / totalCredHrs
  END IF
END FUNCTION
```

27.
```
REM Display health club members by type
CLS
CALL DisplayMembers("Bronze")
CALL DisplayMembers("Silver")
CALL DisplayMembers("Gold")
DATA Bill Clark, Silver
DATA John Smith, Bronze
DATA Hillary Johnson, Gold
DATA James Turner, Bronze
DATA Theresa Brown, Silver
DATA EOD, ""
END

SUB DisplayMembers (memberType$)
  PRINT memberType$
  RESTORE
  READ name$, class$
  DO WHILE name$ <> "EOD"
    IF memberType$ = class$ THEN
        PRINT name$
    END IF
    READ name$, class$
  LOOP
  PRINT
END SUB
```

Exercises 6.3

1. Pass # 1
   Pass # 2
   Pass # 3
   Pass # 4

3. 2 4 6 8 Who do we appreciate?

5. 5 6 7 8 9 10 11 12 13

7.

Steve Cram	3:46.31
Steve Scott	3:51.6
Mary Slaney	4:20.5

9.

1	4	7	10
2	5	8	11
3	6	9	12

11. ***...****Hooray***...****

13. Loop is never executed, since 1 is less than 25.5 and the step is negative.

15. Not enough data.

17.
```
FOR num = 1 TO 10 STEP 2
  PRINT num
NEXT num
```

19.
```
REM Display a row of ten stars
CLS
FOR i = 1 TO 10
  PRINT "*";
NEXT i
END
```

21.
```
REM Display 10 x 10 array of stars
CLS
FOR i = 1 TO 10
  FOR j = 1 TO 10
    PRINT "*";
  NEXT j
  PRINT
NEXT i
END
```

23.
```
REM Compute the sum 1 + 1/2 + 1/3 + 1/4 + ... + 1/100
CLS
LET sum = 0
FOR denominator = 1 TO 100
  LET sum = sum + 1 / denominator
NEXT denominator
PRINT "The sum is"; sum
END
```

25.
```
REM Compare salaries
CLS
CALL Option1(result1)
CALL Option2(result2)
IF result1 > result2 THEN
    PRINT "Option 1";
  ELSE
    PRINT "Option 2";
END IF
PRINT " pays better"
END

SUB Option1 (result1)
  REM Compute $100 per day
  LET result1 = 0
  FOR i = 1 TO 10
    LET result1 = result1 + 100
  NEXT i
  PRINT USING "Option 1 = $$####"; result1
END SUB

SUB Option2 (result2)
  REM Compute $1 then $2 ...
  LET result2 = 0
  LET daySalary = 1
  FOR i = 1 TO 10
    LET result2 = result2 + daySalary
    LET daySalary = daySalary * 2
  NEXT i
  PRINT USING "Option 2 = $$####"; result2
END SUB
```

27.
```
REM Ideal weights for men and women
CLS
CALL InputBounds(lower, upper)
CALL ShowWeights(lower, upper)
END

FUNCTION IdealMan (height)
  REM Compute the ideal weight of a man given the height
  IdealMan = 4 * height - 128
END FUNCTION

FUNCTION IdealWoman (height)
  REM Compute the ideal weight of a woman given the height
  IdealWoman = 3.5 * height - 108
END FUNCTION

SUB InputBounds (lower, upper)
  REM Input the lower and upper bounds on height
  INPUT "Enter lower bound: ", lower
  INPUT "Enter upper bound: ", upper
END SUB

SUB ShowWeights (lower, upper)
  REM Display table of weights
  PRINT
  PRINT "Height", "Wt - Women", "Wt - Men"
  PRINT
  FOR height = lower TO upper
    PRINT height, IdealWoman(height), IdealMan(height)
  NEXT height
END SUB
```

29.
```
REM Number of sibilants in sentence
CLS
INPUT "Enter a sentence: ", sent$
PRINT "There are"; Sibilants(sent$); "sibilants."
END

FUNCTION Sibilants (sent$)
  REM Count number of sibilants
  LET count = 0
  FOR i = 1 TO LEN(sent$)
    LET letter$ = UCASE$(MID$(sent$, i, 1))
    IF (letter$ = "S") OR (letter$ = "Z") THEN
        LET count = count + 1
    END IF
  NEXT i
  Sibilants = count
END FUNCTION
```

31.
```
REM Bank interest for ten years
CLS
LET amt = 800
FOR year = 1 TO 10
  LET amt = amt * 1.04 + 100
NEXT year
PRINT "The final amount is";
PRINT USING "$$#,###.##"; amt
END
```

33.
```
REM Radioactive decay
CLS
LET grams = 10
FOR year = 1 TO 5
  LET grams = .88 * grams
NEXT year
PRINT USING "#.## grams remain"; grams
END
```

35.
```
REM Draw a hollow box
CLS
INPUT "Number of stars"; stars
CALL DrawSide(stars)
FOR i = 1 TO stars - 2
  CALL DrawRow(stars)
NEXT i
CALL DrawSide(stars)
END

SUB DrawRow (stars)
  REM Draw a row (put spaces between the two stars)
  PRINT "*";
  FOR i = 1 TO stars - 2
    PRINT " ";
  NEXT i
  PRINT "*"
END SUB

SUB DrawSide (stars)
  REM Draw a solid side of stars
  FOR i = 1 TO stars
    PRINT "*";
  NEXT i
  PRINT
END SUB
```

37.
```
REM Create a multiplication table
CLS
INPUT "Enter m (rows) and n (columns): ", m, n
FOR row = 1 TO m
  FOR col = 1 TO n
    PRINT USING "###    "; row * col;
  NEXT col
  PRINT
NEXT row
END
```

39.
```
REM Gambling casino problem
CLS
LET testValue = 4
DO
  LET testValue = testValue + 1     'Start test with $5
  LET amount = testValue
  FOR i = 1 TO 3        'One iteration for each casino
    LET amount = amount - 1     'Entrance fee
    LET amount = amount / 2     'Funds lost
    LET amount = amount - 1     'Exit fee
  NEXT i
LOOP UNTIL amount = 0
PRINT USING "Starting amount = $$###"; testValue
END
```

41.
```
REM Compute total earnings at retirement
CLS
LET earnings = 0
INPUT "Enter the person's name: ", name$
INPUT "Enter the person's age: ", age
INPUT "Enter the person's starting salary: ", salary
FOR i = age TO 64
  LET earnings = earnings + salary
  LET salary = salary + .05 * salary
NEXT i
PRINT USING "& will earn about $$####,###"; name$; earnings
END
```

CHAPTER 7

Exercises 7.1

1. 3 7 0

3. Stuhldreher
Crowley

5. 6 2 9 11 3 4

7. First statement automatically dimensions film$() with subscripts from 0 to 10. Therefore, the second statement produces the error message "Array already dimensioned."

9. Array subscript out of range (when $k > 4$).

11. Improper syntax in DIM statement.

13.

river$(1)	river$(2)	river$(3)	river$(4)	river$(5)
Thames	Ohio	Amazon	Volga	Nile

river$(1)	river$(2)	river$(3)	river$(4)	river$(5)
Ohio	Amazon	Volga	Nile	Thames

15. a) 2 b) 7 c) 10 d) 9

17. Replace lines 12 through 17 with:
```
REM Display all names and difference from average
FOR i = 1 TO 8
  PRINT name$(i), score(i) - average
NEXT i
```

19.
```
REM Reverse array a() and store in b()
FOR i = 1 TO 4
  LET b(i) = a(5 - i)
NEXT i
```

21.
```
REM Display the elements of the array a()
FOR i = 1 TO 26 STEP 5
  FOR k = 0 TO 4
    PRINT USING "######  "; a(i + k);
  NEXT k
  PRINT
NEXT i
```

23.
```
REM Compare arrays a$() and b$() for same values
LET differFlag = 0
FOR i = 1 TO 10
  IF a$(i) <> b$(i) THEN
      LET differFlag = 1
  END IF
NEXT i
IF differFlag = 1 THEN
    PRINT "The arrays are not identical."
  ELSE
    PRINT "The arrays have identical values."
END IF
```

25.
```
REM Curve grades by adding 7
FOR i = 1 TO 12
  LET grades(i) = grades(i) + 7
NEXT i
```

27.
```
REM Create and display the frequency of scores
CLS
DIM frequency(1 TO 5)
REM Set array elements to 0
FOR range = 1 TO 5
  LET frequency(range) = 0
NEXT range
REM Read scores, count scores in each of five intervals
FOR dataElement = 1 TO 30
  READ score
  LET range = INT(score / 10) + 1    'Number in the range of 1 - 5
  LET frequency(range) = frequency(range) + 1
NEXT dataElement
REM Display frequency in each interval
PRINT "Interval Frequency"
PRINT
LET a$ = "## to ##      ##"
FOR interval = 1 TO 5
   PRINT USING a$; 10 * (interval - 1), 10 * interval, frequency(interval)
NEXT interval
REM --- Data: arbitrary list of scores
DATA 10, 5, 25, 23, 45, 46, 49, 47, 2, 44
DATA 3, 4, 11, 12, 30, 31, 40, 45, 20, 21
DATA 19, 18, 17, 16, 15, 14, 13, 12, 11, 10
END
```

29.
```
REM Display names, percentage of units of top ten pizza chains
CLS
DIM name$(1 TO 10), units(1 TO 10)
REM Read and record names and number of units
REM Compute total units
LET total = 0                       'Total units
FOR i = 1 TO 10
  READ name$(i), units(i)
  LET total = total + units(i)
NEXT i
REM Display names and percentage of total units
PRINT"  Name                    Percentage of total units"
LET a$ = "\                       \           ##"
FOR i = 1 TO 10
  PRINT USING a$; name$(i); 100 * units(i) / total
NEXT i
REM --- Data: company names, number of units
DATA Picca Hut, 12140, Domino's, 5257
DATA Little Ceasar's, 4720, Papa John's, 878
DATA Round Table, 558, Chuck E. Cheese, 319
DATA Pizza Inn, 477, California Pizza Kitchen, 77
END
```

31.
```
REM Display month name
DIM month$(1 TO 12)
CLS
FOR i = 1 TO 12
  READ month$(i)
NEXT i
INPUT "Enter month number: ", monthNmb
PRINT "Month name is "; month$(monthNmb)
REM --- Data: months
DATA January, February, March, April, May, June
DATA July, August, September, October, November, December
END
```

Exercises 7.2

1. No.

3. Michigan

5. less than
greater than
equals
less than

7. The total rainfall for the first quarter is 10

9. Duplicate DIM statement in subprogram.

11. n is set 1 too high.

13.
```
SUB CopyArray (a(), b())
  REM Place a's values in b
  FOR i = 1 to 10
    LET b(i) = a(i)
  NEXT i
END SUB
```

15.
```
REM Determine if array is ascending
LET order = 1
FOR i = 1 TO 49
  IF scores(i) > scores(i + 1) THEN
    LET order = 0
  END IF
NEXT i
IF order = 1 THEN
  PRINT "Array is ascending."
ELSE
  PRINT "Array is not ascending."
END IF
```

17.
```
REM Determine if order is ascending, descending, both, or neither
LET ascend = 1
LET descend = 1
FOR i = 1 TO 49
  IF scores(i) > scores(i + 1) THEN
    LET ascend = 0
  ELSEIF scores(i) < scores(i + 1) THEN
    LET descend = 0
  END IF
NEXT i
IF (ascend = 1) AND (descend = 1) THEN
    PRINT "Array is both"
  ELSEIF (ascend = 0) AND (descend = 0) THEN
    PRINT "Array is neither ascending nor descending."
  ELSEIF (ascend = 1) THEN
    PRINT "Array is ascending."
  ELSE
    PRINT "Array is descending."
END IF
```

19.
```
REM Merge ascending arrays, with duplications
DIM c(1 TO 40)
LET indexA = 1
LET indexB = 1
LET doneA = 0
LET doneB = 0
FOR i = 1 TO 40
  IF ((a(indexA) <= b(indexB)) AND doneA = 0) OR doneB = 1
THEN
      LET c(i) = a(indexA)
      IF indexA < 20 THEN
          LET indexA = indexA + 1
        ELSE
          LET doneA = 1
      END IF
    ELSE
      LET c(i) = b(indexB)
      IF indexB < 20 THEN
          LET indexB = indexB + 1
        ELSE
          LET doneB = 1
      END IF
  END IF
NEXT i
```

21.
```
REM Maintain a list of states
DIM state$(1 TO 50)
LET ans = 0
LET count = 0
DO WHILE ans <> 4
  CLS
```

```
  PRINT "1) Enter a State"
  PRINT "2) Delete a State"
  PRINT "3) Display the States"
  PRINT "4) Quit"
  PRINT
  INPUT "Please enter 1-4: ", ans
  SELECT CASE ans
    CASE 1
      CALL Enter(state$(), count)
    CASE 2
      CALL Del(state$(), count)
    CASE 3
      CALL Display(state$(), count)
  END SELECT
LOOP
END

SUB Del (state$(), count)
  REM Delete a state from the list
  INPUT "Enter a State to Delete: ", name$
  LET i = 1
  DO WHILE (i <= count) AND (name$ > state$(i))
    LET i = i + 1
  LOOP
  IF (i > count) OR (name$ < state$(i)) THEN
      PRINT "State does not exist"
    ELSE  ' Shuffle rest of array down by 1
      LET count = count - 1
      FOR i = i TO count - 1
        LET state$(i) = state$(i + 1)
      NEXT i
  END IF
END SUB

SUB Display (state$(), count)
  REM Display the states in the list
  FOR i = 1 TO count
    PRINT state$(i)
  NEXT i
  PRINT
  INPUT "Press ENTER to Continue.", ent
END SUB

SUB Enter (state$(), count)
  REM Enter a new state in the correct position
  INPUT "Enter a State: ", name$
  LET i = 1
  DO WHILE (i <= count) AND (name$ > state$(i))
    LET i = i + 1
  LOOP
  IF name$ = state$(i) THEN
      PRINT "State already exists"
    ELSEIF i > count THEN
      LET state$(i) = name$
      LET count = count + 1
    ELSE   ' Shuffle array, insert state
      FOR j = count TO i STEP -1
        LET state$(j + 1) = state$(j)
      NEXT j
      LET state$(i) = name$
      LET count = count + 1
  END IF
END SUB
```

23.
```
REM Report the number of students scoring above the class average
DIM grades(1 TO 100)
CALL InputGrades(grades(), num)
PRINT
PRINT Ave(grades(), num); "students scored above the average"
END

FUNCTION Ave (grades(), num)
  REM Compute the average and number of students above it
  LET sum = 0
  LET tot = 0
  FOR i = 1 TO num
    LET sum = sum + grades(i)
  NEXT i
  IF num <> 0 THEN
      LET classAve = sum / num
    ELSE
      LET classAve = 0
  END IF
  FOR i = 1 TO num
    IF grades(i) > classAve THEN
        LET tot = tot + 1
    END IF
  NEXT i
  Ave = tot
END FUNCTION

SUB InputGrades (grades(), num)
  REM Input up to 100 grades
  CLS
  PRINT "Enter the grades, one at a time. Finish with -1."
  PRINT
  LET num = 0
  LET grd = 0
  DO WHILE (grd <> -1) AND (num <= 100)
    INPUT grd
    IF grd <> -1 THEN
        LET num = num + 1
        LET grades(num) = grd
    END IF
  LOOP
END SUB
```

Exercises 7.3

1. 200 100
3. 11 7 Numbers interchanged.
5. Variables being swapped are not of the same type.
7. Sequential
9. 4 swaps
11. $(n - 1) + (n - 2) + \dots + 1$
13. 5 swaps
15. 12 comparisons.
17. Determine the number of times that each of the four integers occurs and then list the determined number of 1s, followed by the determined number of 2s, etc.
19. 16; $8\frac{1}{2}$; 5
21.
```
REM Interchange the values of x and y
LET temp = x
LET x = y
LET y = temp
```

23.
```
REM Display public events in DC and crowd estimates
REM in alphabetical order
CLS
DIM event$(1 TO 9), crowd(1 TO 9)
CALL ReadData(event$(), crowd())
CALL SortData(event$(), crowd())
CALL ShowData(event$(), crowd())
REM --- Data: event, crowd (in thousands)
DATA LBJ inauguration, 1200, Bicentennial fireworks, 1000
DATA Desert Storm rally, 800, Bill Clinton inauguration, 800
DATA Beach Boys concert, 625, Washington Redskins victory parade, 600
DATA Vietnam moratorium rally, 600, Ronald Reagan inauguration, 500
DATA U.S. Iran hostage motorcade, 500
END

SUB ReadData (event$(), crowd())
  REM Read event names, crowd
  FOR i = 1 TO 9
    READ event$(i), crowd(i)
  NEXT i
END SUB

SUB ShowData (event$(), crowd())
  REM Display event names and crowd
  LET title$ = "Event                         Crowd estimate (thousands)"
  LET a$ = "\                          \           ####"
  PRINT title$
  PRINT
  FOR i = 1 TO 9
    PRINT USING a$; event$(i); crowd(i)
  NEXT i
END SUB

SUB SortData (event$(), crowd())
  REM Shell sort data by event names
  LET elements = 9
  LET gap = INT(elements / 2)
  DO WHILE gap >= 1
    DO
      LET doneFlag = 1
      FOR index = 1 TO elements - gap
        IF event$(index) > event$(index + gap) THEN
            SWAP event$(index), event$(index + gap)
            SWAP crowd(index), crowd(index + gap)
            LET doneFlag = 0
        END IF
      NEXT index
    LOOP UNTIL doneFlag = 1
    LET gap = INT(gap / 2)
  LOOP
END SUB
```

25.
```
REM Input list of words, insert additional element
CLS
DIM wordList$(1 TO 11)
CALL InputWords(wordList$())
CALL InsertWord(wordList$())
CALL ShowWords(wordList$())
END

SUB InputWords (wordList$())
  REM Input first ten words
  PRINT "Input ten words, in alphabetical order"
  PRINT
  FOR i = 1 TO 10
    PRINT "Word number"; i;
    INPUT wordList$(i)
  NEXT i
END SUB

SUB InsertWord (wordList$())
  REM Insert eleventh word in alphabetical order
  PRINT
  INPUT "Word to add"; word$
  LET wordList$(11) = word$
  FOR i = 10 TO 1 STEP -1
    IF wordList$(i) > wordList$(i + 1) THEN
      SWAP wordList$(i), wordList$(i + 1)
    END IF
  NEXT i
END SUB

SUB ShowWords (wordList$())
  REM Show list of eleven words
  PRINT
  FOR i = 1 TO 11
    PRINT wordList$(i); " ";
  NEXT i
END SUB
```

27.
```
REM Sort array of 200 numbers
CLS
DIM nums(1 TO 200)
DIM dist(0 TO 63)
CALL FillArray(nums())
CALL GetOccurrences(nums(), dist())
CALL ShowDistribution(dist())
END

SUB FillArray (nums())
  REM Generate numbers from 0 to 63 and place in array
  LET nums(1) = 5
  FOR i = 2 TO 200
    LET nums(i) = (9 * nums(i - 1) + 7) MOD 64
  NEXT i
END SUB
```

29.
```
REM Encode word in Morse Code
CLS
DIM codes$(ASC("A") TO ASC("Z"))
CALL ReadCodes(codes$())
CALL InputWord(word$)
CALL ShowCode(codes$(), word$)
REM --- Data: morse codes
DATA ._, _..., _._., _.., ., .._., __., ...., ..
DATA .___, _._, ._.., __, _., ___, .__., __._, ._.
DATA ..., _, .._, ..._, .__,_.._,_.__, __..
END

SUB InputWord (word$)
  REM Input word to encode
  INPUT "Word to encode"; word$
  LET word$ = UCASE$(word$)      ' capitalize word
END SUB
```

```
SUB GetOccurrences (nums(), dist())
  REM Record occurrences for each number
  FOR i = 1 TO 200
    LET dist(nums(i)) = dist(nums(i)) + 1
  NEXT i
END SUB

SUB ShowDistribution (dist())
  REM Display distribution array
  FOR i = 1 TO 63
    PRINT USING "## ##            "; i; dist(i);
  NEXT i
END SUB
```

31.

```
REM Compute average of five highest test scores
CLS
DIM score(1 TO 7)
CALL InputData(name$, score())
CALL SortData(score())
CALL ShowData(score(), name$)
END

SUB InputData (name$, score())
  REM Input student's name and seven test scores
  INPUT "Student's name"; name$
  FOR i = 1 TO 7
    INPUT "Test score"; score(i)
  NEXT i
END SUB

SUB ShowData (score(), name$)
  LET sum = 0
  FOR passNum = 1 TO 5
    LET sum = sum + score(passNum)
  NEXT passNum
  PRINT name$, sum / 5
END SUB

SUB SortData (score())
  REM Bubble sort scores in descending order
  FOR passNum = 1 TO 6
    FOR index = 1 TO 7 - passNum
      IF score(index) < score(index + 1) THEN
          SWAP score(index), score(index + 1)
      END IF
    NEXT index
  NEXT passNum
END SUB
```

```
SUB ReadCodes (codes$())
  REM Read code for each letter
  FOR letter = ASC("A") TO ASC("Z")
    READ codes$(letter)
  NEXT letter
END SUB

SUB ShowCode (codes$(), word$)
  REM Show code for each index in word
  FOR index = 1 TO LEN(word$)
    LET letter$ = MID$(word$, index, 1)
    PRINT codes$(ASC(letter$)), letter$
  NEXT index
END SUB
```

33.

```
REM Input array of measurements and determine their median
CLS
CALL InputNumberOfMeasurements(n)
DIM nums(1 TO n)
CALL InputNums(nums())
CALL DisplayMedian(nums())
END

SUB DisplayMedian (nums())
  REM Display the median of the n measurements
  PRINT "The median is"; Median(nums())
END SUB

SUB InputNumberOfMeasurements (n)
  REM Input number of measurements
  INPUT "Number of measurements"; n
END SUB

SUB InputNums (nums())
  REM Input list of measurements
  FOR i = 1 TO UBOUND(nums)
    INPUT "Enter number: ", nums(i)
  NEXT i
END SUB

FUNCTION Median (nums())
  CALL SortNums(nums())
  LET n = UBOUND(nums)
  IF INT(n / 2) = n / 2 THEN     'n is even
      LET m = n / 2
      LET med = (nums(m) + nums(m + 1)) / 2
    ELSE                         'n is odd
      LET med = nums((n + 1) / 2)
  END IF
  Median = med
END FUNCTION

SUB SortNums (nums())
  REM Bubble sort list of numbers
  LET n = UBOUND(nums)
  FOR i = 1 TO n - 1
    FOR j = 1 TO n - i
      IF nums(j) > nums(j + 1) THEN
          SWAP nums(j), nums(j + 1)
      END IF
    NEXT j
  NEXT i
END SUB
```

Exercises 7.4

1. 12

3. Dorothy

5. 4 1 6
   5 8 2

7. 1 3 5

9. The dimension statement should read DIM(1 TO 4, 1 TO 3) (currently the error is Subscript Out of Range.)

11.
```
SUB FillArray (a())
  REM Fill an array
  FOR row = 1 TO 10
    FOR col = 1 TO 10
      LET a(row, col) = col
    NEXT col
  NEXT row
END SUB
```

13.
```
SUB Exchange (a())
  REM Interchange values of 2nd and 3rd row
  FOR col = 1 TO 10
    SWAP a(2, col), a(3, col)
  NEXT col
END SUB
```

15.
```
REM Program to calculate inventory
CLS
DIM inv(1 TO 2, 1 TO 3), sales(1 TO 2, 1 TO 3)
CALL ReadArrays(inv(), sales())
CALL ShowInventory(inv(), sales())
REM --- Data: beginning inventories, sales
DATA 25,7,64,45,23,11
DATA 12,4,82,24,19,8
END

SUB ReadArrays (inv(), sales())
  REM Read beginning inventory and sales for day
  FOR store = 1 TO 2
    FOR item = 1 TO 3
      READ inv(store, item), sales(store, item)
    NEXT item
  NEXT store
END SUB

SUB ShowInventory (inv(), sales())
  REM Calculate and show inventory at end of the day
  LET total = 0
  PRINT, "Item1", "Item2", "Item3"
  FOR store = 1 TO 2
    PRINT "store"; store,
    FOR item = 1 TO 3
      LET inv(store, item) - inv(store, item) - sales(store, item)
      PRINT inv(store, item),
      LET total = total + inv(store, item)
    NEXT item
    PRINT
  NEXT store
  PRINT
  PRINT "Total inventory is now"; total
END SUB
```

17.
```
REM Compute course enrollments by campus, no. of students by course
CLS
DIM enrollment(1 TO 3, 1 TO 10)
CALL ReadData(enrollment())
CALL ShowCampusTotals(enrollment())
CALL ShowCourseTotals(enrollment())
REM --- Data: course enrollments
DATA 5, 15, 22, 21, 12, 25, 16, 11, 17, 23
DATA 11, 23, 51, 25, 32, 35, 32, 52, 25, 21
DATA 2, 12, 32, 32, 25, 26, 29, 12, 15, 11
END
```

```
SUB ReadData (enrollment())
  REM Read enrollment data
  FOR campus = 1 TO 3
    FOR course = 1 TO 10
      READ enrollment(campus, course)
    NEXT course
  NEXT campus
END SUB

SUB ShowCampusTotals (enrollment())
  REM Compute and show total enrollments for each campus
  FOR campus = 1 TO 3
    LET total = 0
    FOR course = 1 TO 10
      LET total = total + enrollment(campus, course)
    NEXT course
    PRINT "The total course enrollments on campus"; campus; "is"; total
  NEXT campus
END SUB

SUB ShowCourseTotals (enrollment())
  REM Compute total enrollment for each course
  FOR course = 1 TO 10
    LET total = 0
    FOR campus = 1 TO 3
      LET total = total + enrollment(campus, course)
    NEXT campus
    PRINT "The total enrollment in course"; course; "is"; total
  NEXT course
END SUB
```

19.

```
REM Compute golf statistics
CLS
DIM name$(1 TO 3), score(1 TO 3, 1 TO 4)
CALL ReadData(name$(), score())
CALL ComputeTotalScore(name$(), score())
CALL ComputeAveScore(name$(), score())
REM --- Data: name, golf scores
DATA Tiger Woods, 70, 66, 65, 69
DATA Tom Kite, 77, 69, 66,70
DATA Tommy Tolles, 72, 72, 72, 67
END

SUB ComputeAveScore (name$(), score())
  REM Compute average score for each round
  FOR round = 1 TO 4
    LET total = 0
    FOR player = 1 TO 3
      LET total = total + score(player, round)
    NEXT player
    PRINT "The average for round"; round; "was"; total / 3
  NEXT round
END SUB

SUB ComputeTotalScore (name$(), score())
  REM Compute total score for each player
  FOR player = 1 TO 3
    LET total = 0
    FOR round = 1 TO 4
      LET total = total + score(player, round)
    NEXT round
    PRINT "The total score for "; name$(player); "was"; total
  NEXT player
  PRINT
END SUB
```

21.

```
REM Access information from University Rankings Table
CLS
DIM prog$(1 TO 3), univ$(1 TO 3, 1 TO 5)
CALL ReadData(prog$(), univ$())
CALL InputUniv(university$)
CALL ShowRankings(prog$(), univ$(), university$)
REM --- Data: departments, universities
DATA Business, U of PA, MIT, U of IN, U of MI, UC Berk
DATA Comp Sc., MIT, Cng-Mellon, UC Berk, Cornell, U of IL
DATA Engr/Gen., UCLA, U of IL, U of MD, U of OK, Stevens I.T.
END

SUB InputUniv (university$)
  REM Input university name to search for
  INPUT "Name of university"; university$
END SUB

SUB ReadData (prog$(), univ$())
  REM Read university rankings in three departments
  FOR dept = 1 TO 3
    READ prog$(dept)
    FOR ranking = 1 TO 5
      READ univ$(dept, ranking)
    NEXT ranking
  NEXT dept
END SUB
```

```
SUB ReadData (name$(), score())
  REM Read names and scores
  FOR player = 1 TO 3
    READ name$(player)
    FOR round = 1 TO 4
      READ score(player, round)
    NEXT round
  NEXT player
END SUB
```

```
SUB ShowRankings (prog$(), univ$(), university$)
  REM Show rankings of university
  LET foundFlag = 0
  FOR dept = 1 TO 3
    FOR ranking = 1 TO 5
      IF univ$(dept, ranking) = university$ THEN
          PRINT prog$(dept), ranking
          LET foundFlag = 1
      END IF
    NEXT ranking
  NEXT dept
  IF foundFlag = 0 THEN
      PRINT "Sorry! No information listed."
  END IF
END SUB
```

23.

```
REM Analyze exam scores
CLS
DIM name$(1 TO 15), score(1 TO 15, 1 TO 5)
CALL ReadData(name$(), score())
CALL ShowAverages(name$(), score())
CALL SortScores(score())
CALL ShowMedians(score())
END

SUB ReadData (name$(), score())
  REM Read names and scores
  FOR student = 1 TO 15
    INPUT "Student"; name$(student)
    FOR exam = 1 TO 5
      INPUT "Exam score"; score(student, exam)
    NEXT exam
    PRINT
  NEXT student
END SUB

SUB ShowAverages (name$(), score())
  REM Compute and show semester score averages
  CLS
  PRINT "Name            Semester average"
  FOR student = 1 TO 15
    LET sum = 0
    FOR exam = 1 TO 5
      LET sum = sum + score(student, exam)
    NEXT exam
    PRINT USING "\              \  ###"; name$(student); sum / 5
  NEXT student
END SUB

SUB ShowMedians (score())
  REM Show medians for each exam
  FOR exam = 1 TO 5
    PRINT "The median on exam"; exam; "was"; score(8, exam)
  NEXT exam
END SUB
```

```
SUB SortScores (score())
  REM Bubble sort scores
  FOR exam = 1 TO 5
    FOR passNum = 1 TO 14
      FOR index = 1 TO 15 - passNum
        IF score(index, exam) > score(index + 1, exam) THEN
            SWAP score(index, exam), score(index + 1, exam)
        END IF
      NEXT index
    NEXT passNum
  NEXT exam
END SUB
```

25.
```
REM Compute total sales for each storeRevenue and for entire company
CLS
DIM sales(1 TO 3, 1 TO 5), cost(1 TO 5)
CALL ReadData(sales(), cost())
CALL ShowRevenues(sales(), cost())
REM --- Data: number of items sold
DATA 25, 64, 23, 45, 14
DATA 12, 82, 19, 34, 63
DATA 54, 22, 17, 43, 35
REM --- Data: costs of items
DATA 12, 17.95, 95, 86.5, 78
END

SUB ReadData (sales(), cost())
  REM Read sales and cost
  FOR store = 1 TO 3
    FOR item = 1 TO 5
      READ sales(store, item)
    NEXT item
  NEXT store
  FOR item = 1 TO 5
    READ cost(item)
  NEXT item
END SUB

SUB ShowRevenues (sales(), cost())
  REM Compute and show revenues
  PRINT "Store Total"
  LET totalRevenue = 0
  FOR store = 1 TO 3
    LET storeRevenue = 0
    FOR item = 1 TO 5
      LET storeRevenue = storeRevenue + sales(store, item) * cost(item)
    NEXT item
    LET totalRevenue = totalRevenue + storeRevenue
    PRINT USING "  #    $$#,###.##"; store; storeRevenue
  NEXT store
  PRINT USING "Total revenue for the company was $$#,###.##"; totalRevenue
END SUB
```

CHAPTER 8

Exercises 8.1

1. Hello

3. Hello
   Aloha
   Bon Jour

5. Copies Hello and Bon Jour into the file "WELCOME"

7. No quotes surrounding filename

9. Using EOF(1) as the terminating value in a FOR loop.

11. Illegal file name NEW.GREET.DAT

13. a, b, d, f.

15.
```
REM Create file of names and prices of items bought by cowboys
CLS
OPEN "COWBOY" FOR OUTPUT AS #1
READ item$, price
DO WHILE item$ <> "EOD"
  WRITE #1, item$, price
  READ item$, price
LOOP
CLOSE #1
REM --- Data: item, price
DATA Colt Peacemaker, 12.20
DATA Holster, 2
DATA Levi Strauss Jeans, 1.35
DATA Saddle, 40
DATA Stetson, 10
DATA EOD, 0
END
```

17.
```
REM Add Winchester rifle to end of file COWBOY
CLS
OPEN "COWBOY" FOR APPEND AS #1
WRITE #1, "Winchester rifle", 20.5
CLOSE #1
END
```

19.
```
REM Insert an item into COWBOY file in proper sequence
CLS
CALL InputItemData(newItem$, newPrice)
CALL AddItemData(newItem$, newPrice)
END

SUB AddItemData (newItem$, newPrice)
  REM Create second COWBOY file with new inserted item
  OPEN "COWBOY" FOR INPUT AS #1
  OPEN "COWBOY.2" FOR OUTPUT AS #2
  LET insertedFlag = 0     'Tells if item has been inserted
  LET item$ = ""
  DO WHILE (item$ < newItem$) AND (NOT EOF(1))
    INPUT #1, item$, price
    IF item$ >= newItem$ THEN
        WRITE #2, newItem$, newPrice
        LET insertedFlag = 1
    END IF
    WRITE #2, item$, price
  LOOP
  DO WHILE NOT EOF(1)
    INPUT #1, item$, price
    WRITE #2, item$, price
  LOOP
  IF insertedFlag = 0 THEN
      WRITE #2, newItem$, newPrice
  END IF
  CLOSE #1
  CLOSE #2
END SUB

SUB InputItemData (newItem$, newPrice)
  REM Input new item name and price
  INPUT "Item to be inserted, price"; newItem$, newPrice
END SUB
```

21.
```
REM Produce COWBOY.4 with Holster removed
CLS
OPEN "COWBOY" FOR INPUT AS #1
OPEN "COWBOY.4" FOR OUTPUT AS #2
DO WHILE NOT EOF(1)
  INPUT #1, item$, price
  IF item$ <> "Holster" THEN
      WRITE #2, item$, price
  END IF
LOOP
CLOSE #1
CLOSE #2
END
```

23.
```
REM Search for a name in YOB.DAT
CLS
INPUT "Enter name to search for: ", search$
OPEN "YOB.DAT" FOR INPUT AS #1
LET name$ = ""
DO WHILE (search$ > name$) AND (NOT EOF(1))
  INPUT #1, name$, year
LOOP
IF name$ = search$ THEN
    PRINT name$; "'s age is"; 1999 - year
  ELSE
    PRINT search$; " is not in YOB.DAT"
END IF
CLOSE #1
END
```

25.
```
REM Access publisher's inventory files
CLS
CALL InputData(searchTitle$, filename$)
OPEN filename$ FOR INPUT AS #1
LET title$ = ""
DO WHILE (title$ <> searchTitle$) AND (NOT EOF(1))
  INPUT #1, title$, copies
LOOP
IF title$ = searchTitle$ THEN
    PRINT "Number of copies in inventory is"; copies
  ELSE
    PRINT "Book is not listed."
END IF
CLOSE #1
END
```

```
SUB InputData (searchTitle$, filename$)
  REM Input book name and determine file name
  INPUT "Title of book"; searchTitle$
  INPUT "Hardback or Paperback (H or P)"; bookType$
  IF UCASE$(bookType$) = "H" THEN
      LET filename$ = "HARDBACK.INV"
    ELSE
      LET filename$ = "PAPERBCK.INV"
  END IF
END SUB
```

Exercises 8.2

1.
```
REM Create AVERAGE.DAT to hold batting averages
CLS
OPEN "AVERAGE.DAT" FOR OUTPUT AS #1
PRINT "Enter EOD to end input"
INPUT "Player"; name$
DO WHILE name$ <> "EOD"
  WRITE #1, name$, 0, 0       'Initialize counters
  INPUT "Player"; name$
LOOP
CLOSE #1
END
```

3.
```
REM Add players to the end of the file AVERAGE.DAT
CLS
OPEN "AVERAGE.DAT" FOR APPEND AS #1
PRINT "Enter EOD to end update"
INPUT "Player"; name$
DO WHILE name$ <> "EOD"
  WRITE #1, name$, 0, 0
  INPUT "Player"; name$
LOOP
CLOSE #1
END
```

5.
```
REM NY Times subscribers on the block
CLS
OPEN "BLOCK.DAT" FOR INPUT AS #1
OPEN "TIMES.DAT" FOR INPUT AS #2
OPEN "NAMES.DAT" FOR OUTPUT AS #3
INPUT #2, subscriber$
DO WHILE NOT EOF(1)
  INPUT #1, name$
  DO WHILE (name$ > subscriber$) AND NOT EOF(2)
    INPUT #2, subscriber$
  LOOP
  IF name$ = subscriber$ THEN
      WRITE #3, name$
  END IF
LOOP
CLOSE #1
CLOSE #2
CLOSE #3
END
```

7.
```
REM Count maximum number of repeated integers
CLS
OPEN "NUMBERS.DAT" FOR INPUT AS #1
LET max = 0
LET lastNum = 0
LET count = 0
DO WHILE NOT EOF(1)
  INPUT #1, number
  IF number <> lastNum THEN
      IF count > max THEN
          LET max = count
      END IF
      LET lastNum = number
      LET count = 1
    ELSE
      LET count = count + 1
  END IF
LOOP
PRINT "The maximum number of repeats is"; max
CLOSE #1
END
```

9.
```
REM Display student raffle ticket totals
CLS
OPEN "RAFFLE.DAT" FOR INPUT AS #1
LET cntrlVar = 0
LET gradeTotal = 0
LET total = 0
DO WHILE NOT EOF(1)
  INPUT #1, grade, name$, nmbTix
  IF cntrlVar = 0 THEN        'Reset cntrlVar after first grade is read
     LET cntrlVar = grade
  END IF
  IF (grade <> cntrlVar) THEN   'Display gradeTotal if new grade found
     PRINT "Grade"; cntrlVar; "sold"; gradeTotal; "tickets"
     LET total = total + gradeTotal
     LET gradeTotal = 0
     LET cntrlVar = grade
  END IF
```

```
  LET gradeTotal = gradeTotal + nmbTix
  IF EOF(1) THEN              'At end-of-file, print last grade's total
      PRINT "Grade"; cntrlVar; "sold"; gradeTotal; "tickets"
      LET total = total + gradeTotal
  END IF
LOOP
PRINT
PRINT "Total = "; total
CLOSE #1
END
```

11.
```
REM Update phone number master file
CLS
OPEN "MASTER" FOR INPUT AS #1
OPEN "MOVED" FOR INPUT AS #2
OPEN "TEMP" FOR OUTPUT AS #3
INPUT #1, mstName$, mstNmb$
DO WHILE NOT EOF(2)
  INPUT #2, name$, nmb$
  DO WHILE name$ <> mstName$
    WRITE #3, mstName$, mstNmb$
    INPUT #1, mstName$, mstNmb$
  LOOP
  WRITE #3, name$, nmb$
  IF NOT EOF(1) THEN
      INPUT #1, mstName$, mstNmb$
  END IF
LOOP
DO WHILE NOT EOF(1)
  WRITE #3, mstName$, mstNmb$
  INPUT #1, mstName$, mstNmb$
LOOP
CLOSE #1
CLOSE #2
CLOSE #3
OPEN "MASTER" FOR OUTPUT AS #1
OPEN "TEMP" FOR INPUT AS #2
DO WHILE NOT EOF(2)
  INPUT #2, name$, nmb$
  WRITE #1, name$, nmb$
LOOP
CLOSE #1
CLOSE #2
END
```

13. Split the file into two or more files which can be stored in arrays, sort these files using arrays, and then merge them.

CHAPTER 9

Exercises 9.1

1. Pacific Mississipp

3. heights are same
   170
   eye colors are same

5. The variables used in the LET statements are invalid. They should be astrology.nom and astrology.sign.

7. Reserved word "name" used as field name and no END TYPE statement.

9. NUMBER is an invalid data type.

11.
```
TYPE planet
  planetName AS STRING * 20
  distanceFromSun AS SINGLE
END TYPE
```

13.
```
TYPE car
  make AS STRING * 20
  model AS STRING * 20
  year AS SINGLE
  mileage AS SINGLE
END TYPE
```

15.
```
REM Input three words and display them in first three zones
CLS
DIM name1 AS STRING * 14
DIM name2 AS STRING * 14
DIM name3 AS STRING * 14
INPUT "Input name 1: ", name1
INPUT "Input name 2: ", name2
INPUT "Input name 3: ", name3
PRINT name1; name2; name3
END
```

Exercises 9.2

1. VA

3. TX
WI
VA
3

5. Virginia Tech VA 1872
Harvard MA 1636

7. Milwaukee Area Tech. Col. WI 1912

9. Cannot take length of a variable type. Should be LEN(actor).

11. Cannot PRINT record variable.

13.
```
TYPE typeNums
  num1 AS SINGLE
  num2 AS SINGLE
  num3 AS SINGLE
END TYPE
DIM numbers AS typeNums
OPEN "NUMBERS.DAT" FOR RANDOM AS #1 LEN = LEN(numbers)
```

15.
```
REM Make random file YOB2.DAT from sequential file YOB.DAT
CLS
TYPE typePerson
  nom AS STRING * 15
  yr AS SINGLE
END TYPE
DIM person AS typePerson
OPEN "YOB.DAT" FOR INPUT AS #1
OPEN "YOB2.DAT" FOR RANDOM AS #2 LEN = LEN(person)
LET recNum = 1
DO WHILE NOT EOF(1)
  INPUT #1, name$, year
  LET person.nom = name$
  LET person.yr = year
  PUT #2, recNum, person
  LET recNum = recNum + 1
LOOP
CLOSE #1
CLOSE #2
END
```

CHAPTER 10

Exercises 10.2

1.
```
WINDOW (-1, -5)-(7, 30)
```

3.
```
LINE (-1, 0)-(4, 0)       'x-axis
LINE (0, -8)-(0, 40)      'y-axis
```

5.
```
REM Draw axes and line
SCREEN 12
WINDOW (-2, -40)-(12, 240)
LINE (-2, 0)-(12, 0)        'Draw x-axis
LINE (0, -40)-(0, 240)      'Draw y-axis
LINE (3, 200)-(10, 150)     'Draw line
CIRCLE (3, 200), .05
CIRCLE (10, 150), .05
END
```

7.
```
REM Draw axes and line
SCREEN 12
WINDOW (-.2 * 4, -.2 * .5)-(1.2 * 4, 1.2 * .5)
LINE (-.2 * 4, 0)-(1.2 * 4, 0)     'Draw x-axis
LINE (0, -.2 * .5)-(0, 1.2 * .5)   'Draw y-axis
LINE (2, .5)-(4, .3)               'Draw line
CIRCLE (2, .5), .03
CIRCLE (4, .3), .03
END
```

9.
```
REM Draw a circle in the center of the screen
SCREEN 12
WINDOW (-10, -10)-(10, 10)
CIRCLE (0, 0), 4
END
```

11.
```
REM Draw a tick mark at 70 on the y-axis
SCREEN 12
WINDOW (-10, -10)-(100, 100)
LINE (0, -10)-(0, 100)          'y-axis
LINE (-1, 70)-(1, 70)           'tick mark
END
```

13.
```
REM Draw points in the 4 corners of the screen
SCREEN 12
WINDOW (0, 0)-(10, 10)
PSET (0, 0)
PSET (0, 10)
PSET (10, 0)
PSET (10, 10)
DO: LOOP    'Pause until Ctrl+Break is pressed
END
```

15.
```
REM Draw a rectangle
SCREEN 2  'For VGA use SCREEN 12
WINDOW (0, 0)-(10, 10)
LINE (1, 1)-(1, 6)
LINE (1, 6)-(6, 6)
LINE (6, 6)-(6, 1)
LINE (6, 1)-(1, 1)
END
```

17.
```
REM Draw five concentric circles
SCREEN 12
WINDOW (0, 0)-(10, 10)
FOR r = .5 TO 2.5 STEP .5
  CIRCLE (5, 5), r
NEXT r
END
```

19.
```
REM Draw a circle and tangent line
SCREEN 2    'For VGA use SCREEN 12
WINDOW (0, 0)-(10, 10)
CIRCLE (5, 5), 1
LINE (6, 0)-(6, 10)
END
```

21. The circle will be smaller.

23. The circle will be the same size as in Exercise 21.

25.
```
REM Graph the Square Function
SCREEN 12
LET maxX = 10
LET maxY = maxX * maxX
WINDOW (-.2 * maxX, -.2 * maxY)-(1.2 * maxX, 1.2 * maxY)
LINE (-.2 * maxX, 0)-(1.2 * maxX, 0)  'Draw x-axis
LINE (0, -.2 * maxY)-(0, 1.2 * maxY)  'Draw y-axis
FOR x = 0 TO maxX STEP .01
  PSET (x, x * x)
NEXT x
END
```

27.
```
REM Draw a number line
SCREEN 12
INPUT "Maximum number to be displayed"; maxNum
CLS
WINDOW (0, 0)-(80, 30)
LINE (0, 15)-(80, 15)                'Draw x-axis
LET interval = 80 / (maxNum + 2)
FOR i = 1 TO maxNum + 1
  LINE (interval * i, 14.5)-(interval * i, 15.5)
  LOCATE 20, interval * i
  PRINT i
NEXT i
END
```

29.
```
REM Draw a sheet of graph paper
SCREEN 12
WINDOW (0, 0)-(10, 7)
FOR x = 0 TO 10 STEP .5
  LINE (x, 0)-(x,  8)
NEXT x
FOR y = 0 TO 8 STEP .5
  LINE (0, y)-(10, y)
NEXT y
END
```

Exercises 10.3

1. `WINDOW (-1, -250)-(6, 1600)`

Exercises 10.4

1. The variable *numYears* will have to be increased and the new data added.

11. `WINDOW (-7, -5)-(2, 5)`

13. Only procedure DrawData needs to be changed

```
SUB DrawData (male(), female(), numYears)
  REM Draw rectangles
  FOR i = 1 TO numYears
    LINE (i - .4, male(i))-(i, 0), , BF
    LINE (i - .2, female(i))-(i + .2, 0), , B
  NEXT i
END SUB
```

Exercises 10.5

1. Counterclockwise the numbers are 0, .15, .45, .70, .90.

3.
```
REM Draw circle and radius lines and fill one sector
SCREEN 12
WINDOW (-14, -8)-(14, 8)
CIRCLE (0, 0), 5
LINE (0, 0)-(5, 0)
DIM percent(1 TO 5), cumPercent(0 TO 5)
LET cumPercent(0) = 0
LET circumf = 2 * 3.141593
FOR i = 1 TO 5
  READ percent(i)
  LET cumPercent(i) = cumPercent(i - 1) + percent(i)
  IF i < 5 THEN
      CIRCLE (0, 0), 5, , 0, -cumPercent(i) * circumf
  END IF
NEXT i
LET midAngle = circumf * .95
PAINT (COS(midAngle), SIN(midAngle)), STRING$(16, CHR$(255))
REM --- Data: sector percentages
DATA .15, .30, .25, .20, .10
END
```

9.
```
REM Draw Pacman
SCREEN 12
WINDOW (-4, -3)-(4, 3)
CIRCLE (0, 0), 2, , -.8, -5.5
END
```

CHAPTER 11

Exercises 11.1

1. An integer from 1 to 5.

3. Infinite loop

5. 0, 1

7. Integers from –1 through 36

9. Odd integers from 1 through 9

11. `INT(6 * RND) + 5`

13. `2 * INT(RND * 50) + 2`

15.
```
REM Select a word at random
CLS
RANDOMIZE TIMER
LET wordNumber = INT(20 * RND) + 1
FOR i = 1 TO wordNumber
  READ word$
NEXT i
PRINT word$
REM --- Data: (Your own selection of words)
DATA (words)
END
```

19.
```
REM Select President and Treasurer
CLS
DIM member$(1 TO 20)
CALL ReadNames(member$())
CALL ChooseNames(pres, treas)
CALL ShowNames(member$(), pres, treas)
REM --- Data: club members
DATA (Names of members)
END

SUB ChooseNames (pres, treas)
  REM Choose president and treasurer
  RANDOMIZE TIMER
  CALL ChoosePerson(pres)
  DO
    CALL ChoosePerson(treas)
  LOOP UNTIL treas <> pres
END SUB
```

```
SUB ChoosePerson (personNum)
  REM Choose one person from twenty
  LET personNum = INT(RND * 20) + 1
END SUB

SUB ReadNames (member$())
  REM Read names into an array
  FOR i = 1 TO 20
    READ member$(i)
  NEXT i
END SUB

SUB ShowNames (member$(), pres, treas)
  PRINT "The new president is "; member$(pres)
  PRINT "and the new treasurer is "; member$(treas)
END SUB
```

21.

```
REM Select answers to a multiple-choice exam
CLS
RANDOMIZE TIMER
FOR i = 1 TO 10
  LET ans = INT(RND * 5) + ASC("A")
  PRINT CHR$(ans)
NEXT i
END
```

23.

```
REM Select a letter from the alphabet
CLS
RANDOMIZE TIMER
LET num = INT(RND * 26) + ASC("A")
PRINT CHR$(num)
END
```

27. Sample walkthrough: Suppose n = 5 and m = 2

i	RND	selct	remaining	selct/remaining	PRINT
1	.5	2	5	2/5 = .4	
2	.625	2	4	2/4 = .5	
3	.334	2	3	2/3 = .666	3
4	.899	1	2	1/2 = .5	
5	.2	1	1	1/1 = 1	5

29. (a)

```
REM The Birthday Problem
CLS
RANDOMIZE TIMER
DIM day(1 TO 23)
CALL CreateBirthdays(day())
CALL CheckForMatch(day(), matchFlag)
IF matchFlag = 1 THEN
    PRINT "At least two people had the same birthday."
  ELSE
    PRINT "No two people had the same birthday."
END IF
END

SUB CheckForMatch (day(), matchFlag)
  REM Check for match
  LET matchFlag = 0
  FOR j = 1 TO 22
    FOR k - j + 1 TO 23
      IF day(j) = day(k) THEN
          LET matchFlag = 1
      END IF
    NEXT k
  NEXT j
END SUB

SUB CreateBirthdays (day())
  REM Determine birthdays
  FOR j = 1 TO 23
    LET day(j) = INT(RND * 365) + 1
  NEXT j
END SUB
```

Exercises 11.2

1. 40%
3. The values of RND in each line will differ.
5. [0, 1/6), [1/6, 1/2), [1/2, 1)

7.
```
REM Simulate the Big Six wheel
CLS
RANDOMIZE TIMER
LET total = 54
LET num = total * RND
SELECT CASE num
  CASE IS < 23
    LET outcome$ = "1"
  CASE IS < 38
    LET outcome$ = "2"
  CASE IS < 46
    LET outcome$ = "5"
  CASE IS < 50
    LET outcome$ = "10"
  CASE IS < 52
    LET outcome$ = "20"
  CASE IS < 53
    LET outcome$ = "Joker"
  CASE ELSE
    LET outcome$ = "Casino"
END SELECT
PRINT "The outcome is "; outcome$
END
```

9.
```
REM Simulate ODD bet for 1000 spins of a roulette wheel
CLS
RANDOMIZE TIMER
LET profit = 0
FOR games = 1 TO 1000
  LET num = INT(38 * RND) - 1
  IF (INT(num / 2) <> num / 2) AND (num > 0) THEN
      LET profit = profit + 1
    ELSE
      LET profit = profit - 1
  END IF
  LOCATE 15, 1
  PRINT "games: "; games; "profit: "; profit
NEXT games
END
```

Exercises 11.3

5.
```
REM Find the area under a quarter-ellipse
CLS
RANDOMIZE TIMER
LET total = 0
FOR i = 1 TO 1000
  LET x = RND * 5
  LET y = RND * 4
  IF 16 * x * x + 25 * y * y < 400 THEN
      LET total = total + 1
  END IF
NEXT i
PRINT "Approximate area is"; 20 * total / 1000
END
```

CHAPTER 12

Exercises 12.2

1. Command buttons appear to be pushed down and then let up when they are clicked.

3. After a command button is clicked, its border becomes boldfaced and a rounded rectangle of small dots surrounds the caption.

(In Exercises 7 through 27, begin by pressing Alt/F/N to create a new form.)

7. Click on the Properties window or Press F4 to activate the Properties window.

   Press Shift+Ctrl+C to highlight the Caption property.

   Type in "CHECKING ACCOUNT".

9. Double-click the text-box icon in the toolbox.

   Activate the Properties window and highlight the BackColor property.

   Click on the ". . ." icon to the right of the Settings box.

   Click on the Palette tab.

   Click on the desired yellow in the palette.

   Press Shift+Ctrl+T followed by three down arrows to highlight the Text property.

   Click on the settings box and delete "Text1".

   Click on the form to see the empty, yellow text box.

11. Double-click on the text box icon in the toolbox.
Activate the Properties window and highlight the Text property.
Type the requested sentence.
Highlight the MultiLine property.
Double-click on the highlighted MultiLine property to change its value to True.
Highlight the Alignment property.
Double-click twice on the highlighted Alignment property to change its value to 2-Center.
Click on the form.
Use the mouse to resize the text box so that the sentence occupies three lines.

13. Double-click on the text box icon in the toolbox.
Activate the Properties window and highlight the Text property.
Type "VISUAL BASIC".
Highlight the Font property.
Click on the ellipsis to the right of the Settings box.
Click on "Courier" in the Font box and click OK.
Click on the form to see the resulting text box.

15. Double-click on the command button icon in the toolbox.
Activate the Properties window and highlight the Caption property.
Type "PUSH".
Highlight the Font property and click on the ellipsis.
Click on Italic in the Font Style box.
Click on 24 in the Size box.
Click OK.
Click on the form to see the resulting command button.
Resize the command button to properly accommodate its caption.

17. Double-click on the command button icon in the toolbox.
Activate the Properties window and highlight the Caption property.
Type "PUS&H".
Click on the form to see the resulting command button.

19. Double-click on the label icon in the toolbox.
Activate the Properties window and highlight the Caption property.
Type "ALIAS".
Click on the form to see the resulting label.

21. Double-click on the label icon in the toolbox.
Activate the Properties window and highlight the Alignment property.
Double-click twice on the highlighted Alignment property to change its value to "2-Center".
Highlight the Caption property.
Type "ALIAS".
Double-click on the BorderStyle property to change its value to "1–Fixed Single".
Highlight the Font property and click on the ellipsis.
Click on Italic in the Font Style box and click OK.
Click on the form to see the resulting label.

23. Double-click on the label icon in the toolbox.
Activate the Properties window and highlight the Font property.
Click on the ellipsis to the right of the Settings box.
Click on Wingdings in the Font box.
Click on the largest size available (72) in the Size box.
Click OK.
As one means of determining which keystroke in the Wingdings font corresponds to a diskette, follow steps (a)–(g).
(a) Click the Start button.
(b) Point to Programs and then point to Accessories.
(c) Click the Character Map.
(d) Click on the down arrow in the font box and click on Wingdings.
(e) Click on the diskette character (fourth from the right end of the first row).
(f) Note at the bottom of the font-map window that the keystroke for the diskette character is a less-than sign.
(g) Close the Character Map and Accessories windows and return to Visual Basic.
Highlight the Caption property.
Change the caption setting to a less-than sign by pressing <.
Click on the label and enlarge it.

25. Double-click on the picture box icon in the toolbox.
Activate the Properties window and highlight the BackColor property.
Click on the ". . ." icon to the right of the Settings box.
Click on the Palette tab.
Click on the desired yellow in the palette.
Click on the form to see the yellow picture box.

27. Double-click on the picture box icon in the toolbox.
Increase the size of the picture box so that it can easily hold two standard size command buttons.
Click (do NOT double-click) on the command button icon in the toolbox.
Move the mouse to the desired location in the picture box of the upper left corner of the first command button.
Press and hold the left mouse button and drag the mouse down and to the right until the rectangle attains the size desired for the first command button
Release the left mouse button.
Repeat the preceding four steps (starting with clicking on the command button icon in the toolbox) to place the second command button on the picture box.

29. Create a new project. Change the form's caption to "Dynamic Duo". Place two command buttons on the form. Enter as the caption of the first "&Batman" and of the second "&Robin". Increase the font size for both command buttons to 13.5.

31. Create a new project. Change the form's caption to "Fill in the Blank". Place a label, a text box, and another label on the form at appropriate locations. Change the caption of the first label to "Toto, I don't think we're in" and of the second label to "A Quote from the Wizard of Oz". Delete "Text1" from the text property of the text box. Resize and position the labels as needed.

33. Create a new project. Change its caption to "An Uncle's Advice". Place a picture box on the form and increase its size to provide plenty of space. Place on the picture box five labels and three command buttons. Change the captions of each label to the appropriate text. Change the BorderStyle property of the last label to "1–Fixed Single". Change the captions of the command buttons to "1", "2", and "3". Resize and position the labels and command buttons as is appropriate. Finally, the size of the picture box can be adjusted down as appropriate.

35. Create a new project. Change the form's caption to "Picture Box Icon." Place a picture box and a label on the form. Change the label's caption property to the sentence shown. Change the label's Background property to white and its Font Size property to 18. Access the picture box's picture property and select the picture file picbox.bmp from the Pictures folder on the CD accompanying this textbook.

Exercises 12.3

1. The word Hello.
3. The word Hello in italic letters.
5. The text box vanishes; nothing is visible.
7. The word Hello in green letters.
9. The word Hello in big, fixed-width letters.
11. The name of the control has been given but not the property being assigned. Let frmHi ="Hello" needs to be changed to Let frmHi.Caption = "Hello".
13. Text boxes do not have a Caption property. Information to be displayed in a text box must be assigned to the Text property.
15. Only 0 and 1 are valid values for the BorderStyle property of a label.

17.
```
Let lblTwo.Caption = "E.T. phone home."
```

19.
```
Let txtBox.ForeColor = &HFF&
Let txtBox.Text = "The stuff that dreams are made of."
```

21.
```
Let txtBox.Text = ""
```

23.
```
Let lblTwo.Visible = False
```

25.
```
Let picBox.BackColor = &HFF0000&
```

27.
```
Let txtBox.Font.Bold = True
Let txtBox.Font.Italic = True
Let txtBox.Text = "Hello"
```

29.
```
cmdButton.SetFocus
```

31.
```
Let lblTwo.BorderStyle = 1
Let lblTwo.Alignment = 2
```

33.
```
picBox.Print "If I had a hi-fi."
```

37.
```
Private Sub cmdLeft_Click()
  Let lblShow.Alignment = 0
  Let lblShow.Caption = "Left Justify"
End Sub

Private Sub cmdCenter_Click()
  Let lblShow.Alignment = 2
  Let lblShow.Caption = "Center"
End Sub

Private Sub cmdRight_Click()
  Let lblShow.Alignment = 1
  Let lblShow.Caption = "Right Justify"
End Sub
```

39.
```
Private Sub cmdRed_Click()
  Let txtShow.BackColor = &HFF&
End Sub

Private Sub cmdBlue_Click()
  Let txtShow.BackColor = &HFF0000&
End Sub

Private Sub cmdWhite_Click()
  Let txtShow.ForeColor = &HFFFFFF&
End Sub

Private Sub cmdYellow_Click()
  Let txtShow.ForeColor = &HFFFF&
End Sub
```

41.
```
Private Sub txtLife.GotFocus()
  Let txtQuote.Text = "I like life, it's something to do."
End Sub

Private Sub txtFuture.GotFocus()
  Let txtQuote.Text = "The future isn't what it used to be."
End Sub

Private Sub txtTruth.GotFocus()
  Let txtQuote.Text = "Tell the truth and run."
End Sub
```

43.

Object	Property	Setting
cmdLarge	Caption	Large
cmdSmall	Caption	Small
cmdBold	Caption	Bold
cmdItalics	Caption	Italic
txtShow	Text	(blank)

```
Private Sub cmdLarge_Click()
  Let txtShow.Font.Size = 18
End Sub

Private Sub cmdSmall_Click()
  Let txtShow.Font.Size = 8.25
End Sub

Private Sub cmdBold_Click()
  Let txtShow.Font.Bold = True
  Let txtShow.Font.Italic = False
End Sub

Private Sub cmdItalics_Click()
  Let txtShow.Font.Italic = True
  Let txtShow.Font.Bold = False
End Sub
```

45.

Object	Property	Setting
frmEx45	Caption	Face
lblFace	Font.Name	Wingdings
	Caption	K
	Font.Size	24
cmdVanish	Caption	Vanish
cmdReappear	Caption	Reappear

```
Private Sub cmdVanish_Click()
  Let lblFace.Visible = False
End Sub

Private Sub cmdReappear_Click()
  Let lblFace.Visible = True
End Sub
```

47.

Object	Property	Setting
cmdPush1	Caption	Push Me
cmdPush2	Caption	Push Me
cmdPush3	Caption	Push Me
cmdPush4	Caption	Push Me

```
Private Sub cmdPush1_Click()
  Let cmdPush1.Visible = False
  Let cmdPush2.Visible = True
  Let cmdPush3.Visible = True
  Let cmdPush4.Visible = True
End Sub

Private Sub cmdPush2_Click()
  Let cmdPush1.Visible = True
  Let cmdPush2.Visible = False
  Let cmdPush3.Visible = True
  Let cmdPush4.Visible = True
End Sub

Private Sub cmdPush3_Click()
  Let cmdPush1.Visible = True
  Let cmdPush2.Visible = True
  Let cmdPush3.Visible = False
  Let cmdPush4.Visible = True
End Sub

Private Sub cmdPush4_Click()
  Let cmdPush1.Visible = True
  Let cmdPush2.Visible = True
  Let cmdPush3.Visible = True
  Let cmdPush4.Visible = False
End Sub
```

Exercises 12.4

1. Goodbye

3. Goodbye

5. $1,234.57

7.
```
1234567890123456789
 1    2    3
```

9. A flag at the top of a flagpole.

11. `PicBox.Print Format(5.376*1000000000000, "Currency")`

13. `picBox.Print Format(2^10, "#,#")`

15.
```
Let picBox.ScaleMode = 4    'Position using units of characters
Let picBox.CurrentX = 2   'Third column (first column is 0)
Let picBox.CurrentY = 1   'Second row (first row is 0)
picBox.Print "Visual Basic"
```

17.
```
Let picBox.ScaleMode = 4  'Position using units of characters
Let picBox.CurrentY = 1   'Display on second row
picBox.Print "x";
Let picBox.CurrentY = .5  'Display halfway between 1st & 2nd row
picBox.Print "4"
```

19.
```
Dim sign As String
Let sign = InputBox("What is your zodiac sign?")
```

21.
```
Dim phrase As String
Let phrase = "You can't steal second base and keep one foot on first."
MsgBox phrase, , "Taking Risks Proverb"
```

23.
```
Let Printer.Font.Bold = True
Printer.Print "Hello"
```

25.
```
Dim Temp As String
Let Temp = txtBox1.Text
Let txtBox1.Text = txtBox2.Text
Let txtBox2.Text = Temp
```

27. `Dim sales(1975 To 1998) As Single`

29. In the (Declarations) section of (General) place the statement Dim nom As String

31.
```
Dim marx(1 To 4) As String   'in (Declarations) section of (General)
Sub Form_Load( )
  Let marx(1) = "Chico"
  Let marx(2) = "Harpo"
  Let marx(3) = "Groucho"
  Let marx(4) = "Zeppo"
End Sub
```

33.
```
picBox.Font.Name = "Symbol"
PicBox.Print "S"
```

35.
```
picBox.DrawWidth = 3
picBox.Scale (0, 4)-(10, -4)
picBox.Line (1, 0)-(9, 0)
picBox.Line (9, 0)-(8. 2)
picBox.Line (9, 0)-(8, -2)
picBox.CurrentX = 1
picBox.CurrentY = -.1
picBox.Print "EAST"
```

37.

Object	Property	Setting
frmStamps	Caption	Stamps
lblNumSheets	Caption	Number of Sheets of Paper
txtNumSheets	Text	(blank)
cmdDetermine	Caption	Determine Stamps Required
lblNumStamps	Caption	Number of Stamps
picNumStamps		

```
Private Sub cmdDetermine_Click()
  Dim stamps As Single
  Let stamps = Val(txtNumSheets.Text) / 5
  If stamps > Int(stamps) Then
      Let stamps = Int(stamps) + 1
  End If
  picNumStamps.Cls
  picNumStamps.Print stamps
End Sub
```

39.

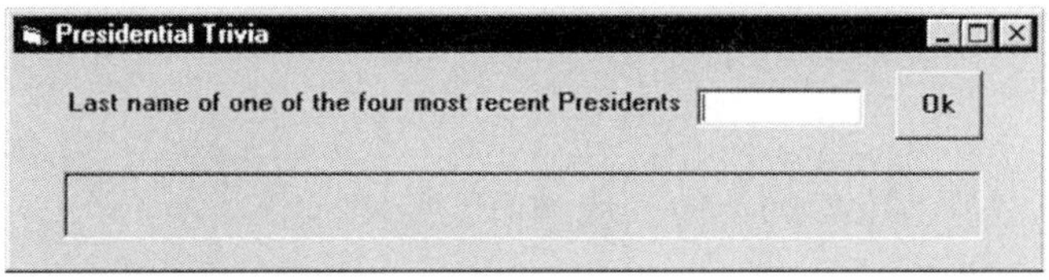

Object	Property	Setting
frmPres	Caption	Presidential Trivia
lblPres	Caption	Last name of one of the four most recent Presidents
txtPres	Text	(blank)
cmdOk	Caption	Ok
picFact		

```
Private Sub cmdOk_Click()
  Dim pres As String
  Let pres = Trim(txtpres.Text)
  Select Case UCase(pres)
    Case Is = "CARTER"
      Let state = "Georgia"
      Let trivia = "The only soft drink served in the Carter White House was Coca-Cola."
    Case Is = "REAGAN"
      Let state = "California"
      Let trivia = "His Secret Service code name was Rawhide."
    Case Is = "BUSH"
      Let state = "Texas"
      Let trivia = "He was the third left-handed president."
    Case Is = "CLINTON"
      Let state = "Arkansas"
      Let trivia = "In college he did a good imitation of Elvis Presley."
  End Select
  picFact.Cls
  picFact.Print "President " + pres + "'s ";
  picFact.Print "home state was " + state + "."
  picFact.Print trivia
  Let txtpres.Text = ""
  txtpres.SetFocus
End Sub
```

41. 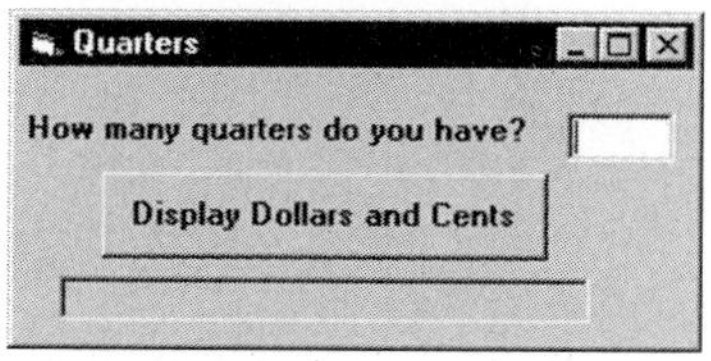

Object	Property	Setting
frmQuarters	Caption	Quarters
lblQuarters	Caption	How many quarters do you have?
txtQuarters	Text	(blank)
cmdDisplay	Caption	Display Dollars and Cents
picOutput		

```
Private Sub cmdDisplay_Click()
  picOutput.Cls
  picOutput.Print txtQuarters.Text + " quarters is ";
  picOutput.Print Format(0.25 * Val(txtQuarters.Text), "Currency")
End Sub
```

43.

```
Private Sub cmdDetermine_Click()
   Dim amount As Single, rate As Single
   Let amount = Val(txtAmount.Text)
   Let rate = Val(txtRate.Text)
   If amount > 0 And rate > 0 Then
       picDbl.Cls
       picDbl.Print DoubleYears(amount, rate)
       picMillion.Cls
       picMillion.Print MillionYears(amount, rate)
   End If
End Sub

Private Function DoubleYears(amount As Single, rate As Single) As Single
  Dim bal As Single, years As Single
  Let bal = amount
  Let years = 0
  Do While bal < 2 * amount
    Let bal = (1 + rate) * bal
    Let years = years + 1
  Loop
  DoubleYears = years
End Function

Private Function MillionYears(amount As Single, rate As Single) As Single
  Dim bal As Single, years As Single
  Let bal = amount
  Let years = 0
  Do While bal < 1000000
    Let bal = (1 + rate) * bal
    Let years = years + 1
  Loop
  MillionYears = years
End Function
```

45. 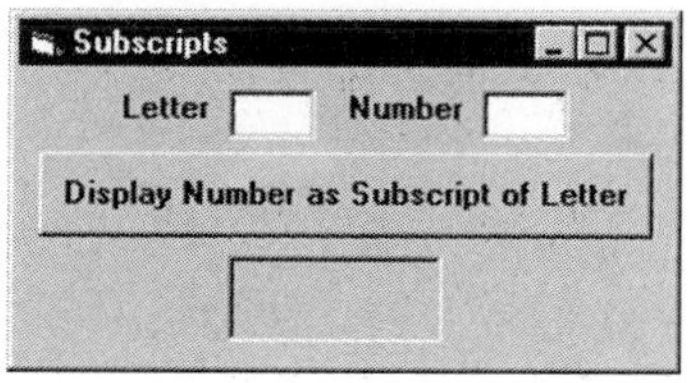

Object	Property	Setting
frmSubscripts	Caption	Subscripts
lblLetter	Caption	Letters
txtLetter	Text	(blank)
lblNumber	Caption	Number
txtNumber	Text	(blank)
cmdDisplay	Caption	Display Number as Subscript of Letter
picOutput		

```
Private Sub cmdDisplay_Click()
  picOutput.ScaleMode = 4  'character units
  picOutput.Cls
  picOutput.Print Trim(txtLetter.Text);
  picOutput.CurrentY = picOutput.CurrentY + 0.3
  picOutput.Print txtNumber.Text
End Sub
```

47. 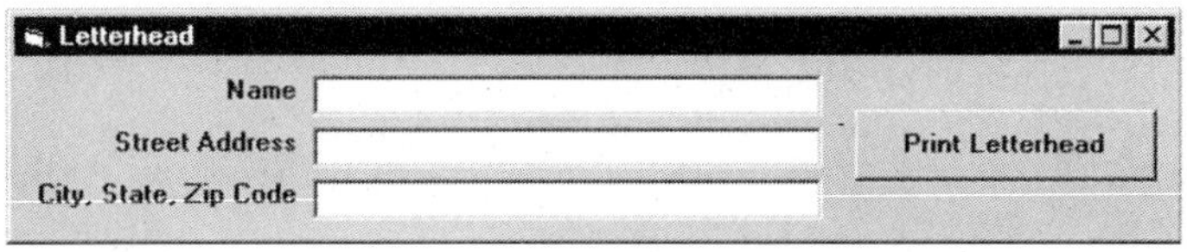

Object	Property	Setting
frmLetterhead	Caption	Letterhead
lblName	Caption	Name
txtName	Text	(blank)
lblAddress	Caption	Street Address
txtAddress	Text	(blank)
txtCity	Text	City, State, Zip Code
cmdPrint	Caption	Print Letterhead

```
Private Sub cmdPrint_Click()
  Rem The number 93 was chosen by trial & error
  Printer.ScaleMode = 4            'characters
  Printer.CurrentX = (93 - Len(txtName.Text)) / 2
  Printer.Print txtName.Text
  Printer.CurrentX = (93 - Len(txtAddress.Text)) / 2
  Printer.Print txtAddress.Text
  Printer.CurrentX = (93 - Len(txtCity.Text)) / 2
  Printer.Print txtCity.Text
  Printer.EndDoc
End Sub
```

53. 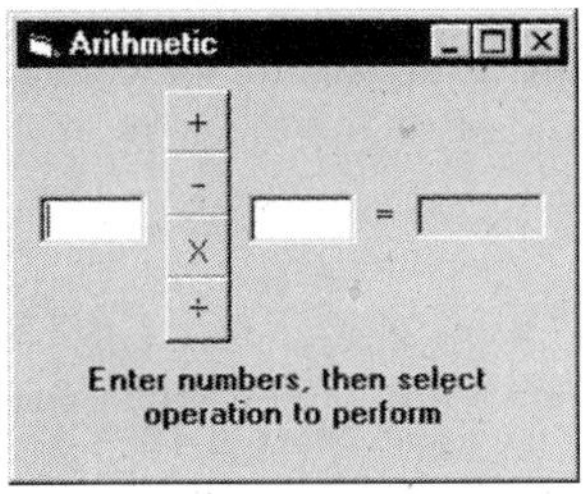

Object	Property	Setting
frmArithmetic	Caption	Arithmetic
txtFirstNum	Text	(blank)
cmdAdd	Caption	+
	Font.Size	12
cmdSubtract	Caption	–
	Font.Size	12
cmdMultiply	Caption	×
	Font.Size	12
cmdDivide	Font.Name	Symbol
	Font.Size	12
	Caption	÷
txtSecondNum	Text	(blank)
picResult		
lblEnter	Caption	Enter numbers, then select operation to perform.

```
Private Sub cmdAdd_Click()
  picResult.Cls
  picResult.Print Val(txtFirstNum.Text) + Val(txtSecondNum.Text)
End Sub

Private Sub cmdSubtract_Click()
  picResult.Cls
  picResult.Print Val(txtFirstNum.Text) - Val(txtSecondNum.Text)
End Sub

Private Sub cmdMultiply_Click()
  picResult.Cls
  picResult.Print Val(txtFirstNum.Text) * Val(txtSecondNum.Text)
End Sub

Private Sub cmdDivide_Click()
  Dim denom As String
  picResult.Cls
  Let denom = Val(txtSecondNum.Text)
  If denom = 0 Then
      MsgBox "Division by zero is not possible"
    Else
      picResult.Print Val(txtFirstNum.Text) / denom
  End If
End Sub
```

Index

Accompanying CD

The CD in this book contains a subdirectory called EXAMPLES, along with an EXE file and several other subdirectories. (This EXE file and other subdirectories are used to install the Control Creation Edition of Visual Basic 5.0. See the first part of Appendix I for installation directions.)

Examples

The subdirectory EXAMPLES contains all the programs from the examples and case studies of this textbook. The QBasic case studies programs have the suggestive names LOAN.BAS, PAYROLL.BAS, SPRSHEET.BAS, and CHECKOUT.BAS. The other QBasic programs have names of the form *chapter-section-number*.BAS. For instance, the program in Chapter 3, Section 2, Example 4 has the name 3-2-4.BAS. Visual Basic examples have the same type base names, but end in VBP. We recommend that you copy the entire subdirectory EXAMPLES onto a diskette. The following steps open these programs from QBasic. (Assume that the diskette is in the A drive.)

1. Press Alt/F/O
2. Enter A:\EXAMPLES
3. Press Tab
4. Cursor to the desired program (**Note:** To move quickly to the beginning of the programs from Chapter 3, press 3.)
5. Press Enter key.

MICROSOFT SOFTWARE LICENSE

READ THIS FIRST. Your use of the Microsoft software (the "SOFTWARE") is governed by the legal agreement below.

BY OPENING THE SEALED CD PACKAGE YOU ARE AGREEING TO BE BOUND BY THE TERMS AND CONDITIONS SET BELOW. IF YOU DO NOT AGREE WITH SUCH TERMS AND CONDITIONS, YOU SHOULD RETURN THE UNOPENED CD PACKAGE TOGETHER WITH THE BOOK TO THE PLACE YOU OBTAINED THEM FOR A REFUND.

1. GRANT OF LICENSE. Microsoft grants to you the right to use the enclosed SOFTWARE. You may make additional copies for demonstration purposes.

2. COPYRIGHT. The SOFTWARE is owned by Microsoft or its suppliers and is protected by United States copyright laws and international treaty provisions.

3. OTHER RESTRICTIONS. You may not rent, sell, or lease the SOFTWARE. You may not reverse engineer, decompile or disassemble the SOFTWARE.

DISCLAIMER OF WARRANTY AND LIMITED WARRANTY

THE SOFTWARE AND ACCOMPANYING WRITTEN MATERIALS (INCLUDING INSTRUCTIONS FOR USE) ARE PROVIDED "AS IS" WITHOUT WARRANTY OF ANY KIND. FURTHER, MICROSOFT DOES NOT WARRANT, GUARANTEE, OR MAKE ANY REPRESENTATIONS REGARDING THE USE, OR THE RESULTS OF THE USE, OF THE SOFTWARE OR WRITTEN MATERIALS IN TERMS OF CORRECTNESS, ACCURACY, RELIABILITY, CURRENTNESS, OR OTHERWISE. THE ENTIRE RISK AS TO THE RESULTS AND PERFORMANCE OF THE SOFTWARE IS ASSUMED BY YOU. IF THE SOFTWARE OR WRITTEN MATERIALS ARE DEFECTIVE YOU, AND NOT MICROSOFT OR ITS DEALERS, DISTRIBUTORS, AGENTS, OR EMPLOYEES, ASSUME THE ENTIRE COST OF ALL NECESSARY SERVICING, REPAIR, OR CORRECTION.

The CD in this book was reproduced by Prentice Hall, Inc. under a special arrangement with Microsoft Corporation. For this reason, Prentice Hall, Inc., is responsible for the product warranty and for support. If your CD is defective, please return it to Prentice Hall, Inc., which will arrange for its replacement. In no event shall Microsoft's liability and your exclusive remedy as to defective software, written materials, and disks be other than either (a) return of the purchase price or (b) replacement of the disk, which is returned to Microsoft with a copy of the receipt. If failure of the disk has resulted from accident, abuse, or misapplication, Microsoft shall have no responsibility to replace the disk or refund the purchase price. Any replacement disk will be warranted for thirty (30) days.

NO OTHER WARRANTIES. MICROSOFT DISCLAIMS ALL OTHER WARRANTIES, EITHER EXPRESS OR IMPLIED, INCLUDING BUT NOT LIMITED TO IMPLIED WARRANTIES OF MERCHANTABILITY AND FITNESS FOR A PARTICULAR PURPOSE, WITH RESPECT TO THE SOFTWARE AND ANY ACCOMPANYING HARDWARE. THIS LIMITED WARRANTY GIVES YOU SPECIFIC LEGAL RIGHTS. YOU MAY HAVE OTHERS, WHICH VARY FROM STATE TO STATE.

NO LIABILITY FOR CONSEQUENTIAL DAMAGES. IN NO EVENT SHALL MICROSOFT OR ITS SUPPLIERS BE LIABLE FOR ANY DAMAGES WHATSOEVER (INCLUDING WITHOUT LIMITATION DAMAGES FOR LOSS OF BUSINESS PROFITS, BUSINESS INTERRUPTION, LOSS OF BUSINESS INFORMATION, OR OTHER PECUNIARY LOSS) ARISING OUT OF THE USE OR INABILITY TO USE THIS MICROSOFT PRODUCT EVEN IF MICROSOFT HAS BEEN ADVISED OF THE POSSIBILITY OF SUCH DAMAGES. BECAUSE SOME STATES DO NOT ALLOW THE EXCLUSION OR LIMITATION OF LIABILITY FOR CONSEQUENTIAL OR INCIDENTAL DAMAGES, THE ABOVE LIMITATION MAY NOT APPLY TO YOU.

U.S. GOVERNMENT RESTRICTED RIGHTS

The SOFTWARE and documentation are provided with RESTRICTED RIGHTS. Use, duplication, or disclosure by the Government is subject to restrictions as set forth in subparagraph (c)(1)(ii) of the Rights in Technical Data and Computer software clause at DFARS 252.227-7013 or subparagraphs (c)(1) and (2) of the Commercial Computer Software—Restricted Rights at 48 CFR 52.227-19, as applicable. Manufacturer is Microsoft Corporation/One Microsoft Way/Redmond, WA 98052-6399.

If you acquired this product in the United States, this Agreement is governed by the laws of the State of Washington.